MULTICULTURAL
HANDBOOK
OF SCHOOL PSYCHOLOGY

An Interdisciplinary Perspective

D1468867

MULTICULTURAL HANDBOOK OF SCHOOL PSYCHOLOGY

An Interdisciplinary Perspective

Edited by

Giselle B. Esquivel
Fordham University

Emilia C. Lopez
Queens College, City University of New York

Sara G. Nahari
Queens College, City University of New York

LEA
2007

LAWRENCE ERLBAUM ASSOCIATES, PUBLISHERS
Mahwah, New Jersey   **London**

Editorial Director: Lane Akers
Editorial Assistant: Anthony Messina
Cover Design: Tomai Maridou

Lawrence Erlbaum Associates, Inc., Publishers
10 Industrial Avenue
Mahwah, New Jersey 07430
www.erlbaum.com

**CIP information for this volume may be obtained by contact-
ing the Library of Congress**

ISBN 978–0–8058–4561–7 — 0–8058–4561–5 (case)
ISBN 978–0–8058–4562–4 — 0–8058–4562–3 (paper)
ISBN 978–1–4106–1414–8 — 1–4106–1414–X (e-book)

Books published by Lawrence Erlbaum Associates are printed
on acid-free paper, and their bindings are chosen for strength
and durability.

Printed in the United States of America

10 9 8 7 6 5 4 3 2 1

DEDICATIONS

To Nivia Zavala, Gila Rivera, Nancy Villarreal de Adler, Angela Carrasquillo, Pedro J. Ruiz, Emilia Lopez, and to all the educators, colleagues and friends with whom I shared and labored towards a common dream of seeing immigrant children and their families become part of a society where their cultural and linguistic diversity is accepted. To my mentor Giselle Esquivel, and to Paul, Samantha, Emma and David, my beloved grandchildren, who are growing up in an environment of multiculturalism and bilingualism.

Sara Nahari

To my *familia*. You are what keep me centered and remind me every day of what is most important. But most of all to my *Mom*, who I miss every single day. She contributed generously to this task as a supportive *Mamá* and as a loving *Abuelita*.

Emilia C. Lopez

In memory of my mother Aurora, whose own memories were erased as a result of her illness, but whose gifts of faith, compassion, and service to those in need remain ever present in my memories and in the lives of those she touched. In honor of my older brother Ruben, who protected me when we immigrated from Cuba, while he was yet an adolescent and I was a child. In memory of Armando, my younger brother who died at a young age, but whose short life taught me the meaning of perennial life. In honor of my husband, Rene, who as a young adolescent arrived at the airport from Cuba without a cent in his pocket or plans for where he would be sleeping that night. In honor of my mentor and role model, Judith Kaufman, who represents for me the understanding mind, the open heart, and the hands of so many who have reached out to the immigrant child in all of us. With love to my children Daniel and Kristen who are the promise for a future when all can live together in peace as children of God.

Giselle B. Esquivel

CONTENTS

I
A MULTICULTURAL FRAMEWORK

II
MULTICULTURAL CONSULTATION

III
INSTRUCTIONAL AND CLASSROOM
INTERVENTIONS

IV
MULTICULTURAL AND BILINGUAL ASSESSMENT

V
MULTICULTURAL THERAPEUTIC INTERVENTIONS

VI
SPECIAL POPULATIONS

VII
FUTURE PERSPECTIVES

FOREWORD

Sylvia Rosenfield

University of Maryland

School psychology straddles two different world views, the scientific culture that seeks the clarity of experimental design in research, the psychometric indicators of individual assessment, and the monitoring of implementation of evidence based practice. On the other hand, we acknowledge the importance of context and of the interaction of individuals with their environments, or, to cite Bronfenbrenner (1979), the "progressive, mutual accommodation between an active growing human being and the changing properties of the immediate settings in which the developing person lives, as this process is affected by relations between these settings, and by the larger contexts in which the settings are embedded" (p. 21). Integrating these two different cultures has been one of the greatest challenges for school psychology and school psychologists as we moved into the multicultural context of American society and the increasing globalization of the 21st century.

How much more demanding integrating this dualism becomes when we examine our work with students and families from culturally and linguistically diverse cultures. Whether serving in research or practice roles, we are aware that students "of color are complex individuals, living in dynamic environments, with multiple interacting social networks that influence their schooling experiences in a variety of ways" (Wong & Rowley, 2001, p. 64). Moreover, we bring ourselves to our work, with all the biases, assumptions and stereotypes, as well as the questions, methods and hypotheses that guide our own views of the world (Wong & Rowley, 2001).

The challenge of negotiating this double world view was one with which I became involved in the 1970s, as a faculty member in Fordham University's Urban School Psychology Program. Because the school psychology program was located at the Lincoln Center campus of Fordham University, which was built on an urban renewal site, our program was labeled "Urban School Psychology." Applicants to the program would ask, as one might expect, what differentiated the Fordham school psychology program from other school psychology programs. It seemed to me not enough to say that we were housed in an urban development site in a city and that we were required to acknowledge that serendipitous heritage. One of the answers to that challenge was our development of a bilingual school psychology program (Rosenfield & Esquivel, 1985). I have always been extraordinarily proud of that program, but even more so of the professionals who collaborated in the development of the program, including Dr. Esquivel, and those who are alumni, including Dr. Lopez and Dr. Nahari.

But one of the lessons I learned from my involvement in the bilingual school psychology program was a result of the total integration of the bilingual faculty and students with the other faculty and students in the program. It made a difference in every class and every program meeting that diverse voices were present. Multicultural competence is a way of thinking and a way of framing the world, not just to be pulled out periodically by the ethnic diverse psychologists among us or reserved for one course in multicultural issues. Isn't that the subtext of this volume—it is not just for or about "them," but for the whole school psychology community. This book provides a new opportunity within school psychology to see where we are in integrating our scientific tradition with the multicultural context of society and our practice.

This book provides an important landmark in school psychology, bringing together the fragmented and still emerging knowledge base on multicultural issues for research and practice, beginning with the development of a multicultural framework to guide the rest of the book. Further, the editors have conceptualized the order of the remaining chapters in a way congruent with current thinking in school psychology, beginning with consultation and school-based interventions, before the more traditional assessment and therapeutic interventions. It is also noteworthy that the authors in this book are from a number of different disciplines. Their voices make important contributions as they apply the multicultural knowledge base from their individual disciplines to school psychology practice, research and training. The editors close the dialogue about multiculturalism in school psychology with a series of commentaries from diverse interdisciplinary perspectives. The content of this book enables us to see where we are and where we need to go forward in the development of a strong and sound focus on the multicultural perspective in school psychology.

The need for such a volume could not be more essential at this point in time. At the Futures of School Psychology Conference in 2002, Curtis, Grier and Hunley (2004) reminded the participants that at the Olympia Conference in the early 1980's, it was predicted that there would be increasing percentages of minorities and handicapped children in public education over the next several decades, a prediction that has certainly proven true. However, Curtis et al. (2004) also described the limited success since then in enticing a more diverse pool of school psychologists into the field, citing data on the lag in minority membership in school psychology. Although the need for diversity in practitioners of school psychology was stressed at the Futures Conference and has been a consistent source of concern, understanding multicultural issues in practice and research is, of course, equally critical. Strein, Cramer, and Lawser (2003) reflect how far school psychology, as a field, needs to move in integrating diversity into practice and research. They found that 2.6% of journal articles in school psychology journals published between 1994 and 1998 focused on multicultural issues as their primary content, with only about 6% including both a primary or secondary focus on multicultural issues. Further, in responding to questions about the need for research in school psychology, multicultural issues were ranked 12th by journal authors and 15th by practitioners out of 18 topical categories.

While writing this Foreword, I saw again the 1998 movie, *Pleasantville*. In the movie, the people in the village of Pleasantville go from seeing the world in black and white, to beginning to see the world in color. Although the introduction of color brings confusion and chaos at first for some and a sense of wonder for others, viewing the world in color opened up the lives of the villagers in ways they had never imagined. As America moves increasingly toward a population of diverse color and culture, some of us will see diversity as a wonderful opportunity and some will have difficulty with the change. Perhaps we will look back on the practice of school psychology in the 20th century with all its limitations in a similar way and move forward to agree with a conclusion of the Futures Conference, that "**understanding diversity and its impact on children, families and schools is vitally important to effective school psychology in the 21st century**" [bold in original] (Dawson et al., 2004, p. 118).

REFERENCES

Bronfenbrenner, U. (1979). *The ecology of human development: Experiments by nature and design.* Cambridge, MA: Harvard University Press.

Curtis, M. J., Grier, J. E. C., & Hunley, S. A. (2004). The changing face of school psychology: Trends in data and projections for the future. *School Psychology Review, 33,* 49–66.

Dawson, M., Cummings, J. A., Harrison, P. L., Short, R. J., Gorin, S., & Palomares, R. (2004). The 2002 multisite conference on the future of school psychology: Next steps. *School Psychology Review, 33,* 115–125.

Rosenfield, S., & Esquivel, G. (1985). Educating school psychologists to work with bilingual/bicultural populations. *Professional Psychology, 16,* 199–208.

Strein, W., Cramer, K., & Lawser, M. (2003). School psychology research and scholarship. *School Psychology International, 24,* 421–436.

Wong, C. A., & Rowley, S. J. (2001). The schooling of ethnic minority children: Commentary. *Educational Psychologist, 36,* 57–66.

PREFACE

The *Handbook of Multicultural School Psychology: An Interdisciplinary Perspective* represents the fruition of a life-long developmental process for the editors, who are committed to addressing the needs of children and families from diverse cultural backgrounds. The authors in this handbook have each dedicated the scope of their professional lives on behalf of children of all colors and cultural backgrounds, and have contributed in unique ways to the unfolding of a multicultural perspective in school psychology. The handbook is a timely contribution in its attempt to stimulate renewed awareness and understanding of the current multicultural issues and interdisciplinary contributions that are integral to school psychology as a profession. It is also the culmination of a "timeless" endeavor that seeks to provide historical continuity and professional meaning to that process. The ideas and actions that help to advance our human understanding are good markers of what is lasting and impels us towards future change and growth. We hope that this handbook will be an enduring gift for the enhancement of multicultural understanding in school psychology and for the future generations of culturally and linguistically diverse children and families.

ORGANIZATION OF CHAPTERS

The 30 chapters in this handbook are organized to reflect, from an interdisciplinary perspective, the critical issues that impact culturally diverse and immigrant children and youth. The handbook is divided into multiple sections that mostly reflect the major functions and roles of school psychologists as they work with special populations from diverse cultural backgrounds. The chapters also integrate a scientist-practitioner approach that is reflected in discussions of theory and research, as well as training and practice.

Section I, A Multicultural Framework provides a historical overview of the development of a multicultural perspective in school psychology and addresses critical professional, ethical, and training issues. Multicultural consultation is the subject of Section II, which examines issues related to instructional, consultee-centered, and systemic (organizational) consultation. The chapters in that section address consultation as related to teachers, parents, and schools. The goal of Section III, Instructional and Classroom Interventions, is to provide the readers with an overview of a

---

Editors' Note: The editors have made a joint and comparable editorial contribution in the development of the handbook.

number of instructional and classroom interventions appropriate for CLD children and youth. Programs such as multicultural and bilingual education are described from research as well as practical perspectives. Assessment has traditional been an important component of the roles and functions of school psychologists, a topic that is addressed in Section IV, Multicultural and Bilingual Assessment. The chapters within that section cover a wide spectrum of assessment practices in the areas of language proficiency, cognitive, personality, neuropsychological, vocational, acculturation, and academic assessment. The Multicultural Therapeutic Interventions section, Section V, discusses theoretical, research, and practice issues relevant to the development and implementation of therapeutic interventions for CLD children and youth in school settings. The chapters specifically focus on providing counseling and vocational interventions within a multicultural framework. The needs of special populations are explored in Section VI, Special Populations. Various topics are discussed in relationship to gifted and talented, preschool, and college age students. Other chapters in that section will help school psychologists and other school professionals to identify and provide services to CLD children and youth with low incidence and learning disabilities. Working with migrant families and conducting parent conferences are also topics covered in that section. The last section in the handbook, Section VII, is entitled Future Perspectives. One chapter is devoted to exploring directions for future research. Given the diverse topics covered and the wide range of expertise of the contributors within this book, we felt that a section was needed that would summarize and integrate the important contributions of various disciplines to multicultural school psychology. The last chapter has a unique structure because it provides readers with various commentaries written by leaders in the fields of bilingual special education, multicultural counseling, clinical psychology, social psychology, and organizational psychology. The authors of those commentaries provide interesting perspectives and challenges as school psychologists continue to address the needs of CLD students and their families.

ACKNOWLEDGMENTS

We wish to thank those individuals who have contributed to the completion of this arduous task in so many different ways. We offer acknowledgment to our student assistants who labored over computer screens, printers, photocopy machines, and even at post offices: Lisa Dieker, Mitchelle Johnson, and Jennifer Kong. Special thanks are given to Geraldine Oades-Sese, our research assistant, for her many substantive contributions. We are grateful to colleagues who offered their invaluable views and insights on specific sections or various issues addressed in the Handbook: Vincent Alfonso, Fredda Brown, Marian Fish, Tom Fagan, Antoinette Miranda, and Lea Theodore. Lane Akers' guidance was steady and we are thankful for his helpful suggestions. Recognition is given to Sylvia Rosenfield for the inspiring foreword and for her pioneering role in the development of a bilingual school psychology training model. She along with many others (e.g., Laura Hines, Tom Oakland, Abbie Salny) have helped to promote a multicultural and international perspective to our field. We are indebted to all the authors who contributed of their dedication and expertise to the content of the chapters. Last but not least, we could not have completed this handbook without the support of our family and friends. They listened and provided love, advise, cheers, computer expertise and much patience.

ABOUT THE EDITORS

Giselle B. Esquivel is Professor in the School Psychology Program, Division of Psychological and Educational Services, Graduate School of Education at Fordham University. She is past Division Chair, the current Director of the PHD, PD and Bilingual PD School Psychology Programs, and Coordinator of the Psychology of Bilingual Students and Therapeutic Interventions Master's Degree Specialization Programs. Dr. Esquivel is a diplomate of the American Board of Professional Psychology, Fellow of the American Academy of School Psychology, Fellow of the American Psychological Association, and current President of the American Board of School Psychology. She is a Nationally Certified School Psychologist, and a NY and NJ Licensed Psychologist. Dr. Esquivel's research and publications are in the areas of resilience, spirituality, culturally-sensitive narrative methods, and creativity among culturally diverse students. She has held a number of leadership positions in national professional organizations and has led the development of a nationally recognized model of multicultural training at Fordham since 1981.

Emilia C. Lopez was born in Cuba and immigrated to the United States at the age of 12. Her own experiences in schools as a limited English proficient child motivated her to seek out a career working with culturally and linguistically diverse students. She became a certified school psychologist in 1984 after graduating from Fordham University with a specialization in bilingual school psychology. She completed her doctoral work in school psychology at Fordham University in 1989. While completing her doctoral studies she worked as a school psychologist in preschool, elementary and high school settings. She has been a full time faculty member in the Queens College, City University of New York, Graduate Program in School Psychology Program since 1989. She was instrumental in creating the Bilingual and Multicultural School Psychology Specializations in the school psychology program at Queens College. She is currently the editor of the *Journal of Educational and Psychological Consultation*. Her teaching and scholarly interests are in the areas of multicultural issues in school psychology and consultation.

Sara G. Nahari is an Associate Adjunct Professor of School Psychology at Queens College, City University of New York. She received her doctorate from Fordham University, where she also received a Professional Diploma in bilingual school psychology. She was also the Assistant Director of the Bilingual Psychological and Academic Assessment Support Center, and her entire career as teacher, guidance counselor and psychologist in the New York City Public Schools was devoted to multicultural and bilingual issues. In 1992, she received the Bilingual Support Personnel of the Year Award of the New York State Association for Bilingual Education and in 2004, she received the Fordham School of Education Alumni Achievement Award. Her teaching and scholarly interests are multicultural assessment and parental involvement.

LIST OF CONTRIBUTORS

Howard Adelman, PhD; University of California, Los Angeles; Professor of Psychology and Co-director of the School Mental Health Project/Center for Mental Health in Schools; Department of Psychology.

Vincent C. Alfonso, PhD, Professor and Associate Dean; Fordham University; Graduate School of Education; Division of Psychological and Educational Services; Doctorate Program in School Psychology.

Cecilia Añon, PD; Graduate Student; Fordham University; Graduate School of Education; Division of Psychological and Educational Services Department; Doctorate Program in School Psychology.

Carmen G. Armengol, PhD, ABPP/ABCN; Associate Professor; Northeastern University; College of Health Sciences; Department of Counseling and Applied Psychology; School Psychology Program.

Leonard Baca, EdD; Professor; University of Colorado at Boulder; School of Education; Bueno Center for Multicultural Education; Bilingual Special Education Program.

Ernesto M. Bernal, PhD; Independent Educational Consultant, San Antonio, Texas.

Alejandro E. Brice, PhD, CCC-SLP; Associate Professor; University of Central Florida; College of Health and Public Affairs; Communication Sciences and Disorders.

Alberto M. Bursztyn, PhD; Professor; Brooklyn College of the City University of New York; School of Education; Graduate Programs in School Psychology and Special Education.

Mary M. Clare, PhD; Professor and Director of the Oregon Center for Inquiry and Social Innovation; Lewis & Clark College; Graduate School of Education and Counseling Psychology; Department of Counseling Psychology.

Nancy Cloud, EdD ; Professor; Rhode Island College; Feinstein School of Education and Human Development; Department of Educational Studies.

Catherine Collier, PhD; Director; Cross-Cultural Developmental Education Services, Ferndale, Washington.

Agnieszka M. Dynda, MS; Graduate Student; St. John's University; Department of Psychology; School Psychology Program.

Graciela Elizalde-Utnick, PhD; Assistant Professor and Coordinator of the Bilingual Specializations in School Psychology and School Counseling; Brooklyn College of the City University of New York; School of Education; Graduate Programs in School Psychology and School Counseling.

Michael R. Emmons, MSEd, PD.; School Psychologist; Cooke Center for Learning and Development, New York, New York.

Giselle B. Esquivel, PsyD, ABPP; Professor; Fordham University; Graduate School of Education; Division of Psychological and Educational Services; School Psychology Program.

Sandra Fradd, PhD; Researcher and Author in the areas of second language acquisition and teaching English as a second language (TESOL).

Jairo N. Fuertes, PhD, ABPP; Magis Associate Professor; Fordham University; Graduate School of Education; Division of Psychological and Educational Services; Masters Program in Counseling and Personnel Services and Doctoral Program in Counseling Psychology.

Georgina García, MS; School Psychologist; Beaverton School District, Beaverton, Oregon.

Barbara S. C. Goldstein, PhD; School Psychologist; California Department of Education, Diagnostic Center Southern California, Los Angeles, California.

Margo Gottlieb, PhD; Director, Assessment and Evaluation of Illinois Resource Center, Des Plaines, Illinois.

Patricia M. Greenfield, PhD; Distinguished Professor of Psychology and Director of UCLA-FPR Center for Culture, Brain, and Development; University of California, Los Angeles; Department of Psychology; Developmental Psychology program.

Tresmaine R. Grimes, PhD; Associate Professor; Iona College; School of Arts and Science; Department of Psychology.

Else Hamayan, PhD; Director; Illinois Resource Center, Des Plaines, Illinois.

Abigail M. Harris, PhD; Associate Professor; Fordham University; Graduate School of Education; Division of Psychological and Educational Services; School Psychology Program.

Kathleen C. Harris, PhD; Assistant Professor; Cal Poly San Luis Obispo; College of Education; Department of Graduate Studies in Education; Special Education Program.

Colette L. Ingraham, PhD, NCSP, NCC; Professor; San Diego State University; College of Education; Department of Counseling and School Psychology; School Psychology and School Counseling Graduate Programs

Margo A. Jackson, PhD; Associate Professor and Director; Fordham University; Graduate School of Education; Division of Psychological and Educational Services; Counseling and Counseling Psychology Programs.

Jaclyn Mendelson Kacanski, MSEd; Graduate Student; Fordham University; School of Education; Division of Psychological and Educational Service; Counseling Psychology Program.

Judith Kaufman, PhD; Professor; Director of Freshman Year Experience; Fairleigh Dickinson University; Division School of Psychology; School Psychology Program.

Shannon M. Kelly, MS; Graduate Student; Indiana University; Department of Counseling and Educational Psychology; Counseling Program.

Laura B. Kestemberg, PhD; Clinical Associate Professor and Director of School Consultation and Early Childhood Centers; Fordham University; Graduate School of Education; Division of Psychological and Educational Services; School Psychology Program.

Samantha W. Kohn, PhD; School Psychologist; Orange County, New York.

Chieh Li, EdD, NCSP; Associate Professor; Northeastern University; Divison of Educational Psychology; Department of Counseling and Applied Educational Psychology; School Psychology Program.

Emilia C. Lopez, PhD; Associate Professor and Director of Bilingual and Multicultural Specializations in School Psychology; Queens College of the City University of New York; Division of Education; Department of Educational and Community Programs; Graduate Program in School Psychology.

Gelasia Marquez, PhD; School Psychologist/Bilingual School Psychologist; Union City Board of Education; George Washington Elementary School, Union City, New Jersey.

Danielle Martines, PhD; Associate Professor and Director of the School Psychology Program; Montclair State University; Department of Psychology; School Psychology Program.

Craig A. Michaels, PhD; Professor and Program Coordinator; Queens College of the City University of New York; Division of Education; Department of Educational and Community Programs; Graduate Programs in Special Education.

Sara G. Nahari, PhD; Adjunct Associate Professor and Coordinator of the Practica and Internship Placements; Queens College of the City University of New York; Division of Education; Educational and Community Programs; Graduate Program in School Psychology.

Geraldine V. Oades-Sese, MSEd, Graduate Student; Fordham University; Graduate School of Education; Division of Psychological and Educational Services; Doctorate Program in School Psychology.

Sarah Littman Olitzky, Graduate Student; Fordham University; Graduate School of Education; Division of Psychological and Educational Services; Doctorate Program in School Psychology.

Samuel O. Ortiz, PhD; Associate Professor; St. John's University; Department of Psychology; School Psychology Program.

Kristin Phoenix, MS; Graduate Student; Northeastern University; Department of Applied Educational and School Psychology; Combined School and Counseling PhD Program

Blanca Quiroz, EdD; Assistant Professor; Texas A & M University, College Station; School of Education and Human Development; Teaching Learning and Culture; Curriculum and Culture.

Angela Reyes-Carrasquillo, PhD; Distinguished Professor; Fordham University; Graduate School of Education; Division of Curriculum and Teaching; Teaching English to Speakers of Other Languages (TESOL) Program.

Charles R. Ridley, PhD; Professor; Indiana University; School of Education; Department of Counseling and Educational Psychology; Counseling Psychology Program.

Ofelia Rodriguez-Srednicki, PhD; Associate Professor; Montclair State University; College of Humanities and Social Sciences; Department of Psychology; Graduate Psychology Program.

Margaret R. Rogers, PhD, Associate Professor; University of Rhode Island; College of Arts and Sciences; Psychology Department; School Psychology Program.

Sylvia Rosenfield, PhD; Professor; University of Maryland; College of Education; Department of Counseling and Personnel Services; School Psychology.

Mariana Rotenberg, MS; School Psychologist; Long Beach Public Schools, Long Beach, New York.

Carrie Rothstein-Fisch, PhD; Associate Professor and Co-coordinator, Early Childhood Education; California State University, Northridge; Michael D. Eisner College of Education; Educational Psychology and Counseling.

Jonathan P. Rust, MSEd; Graduate Student; Fordham University; Graduate School of Education; Psychological and Educational Services; Counseling Psychology Doctorate Program.

Jonell Sanchez, MA; Higher Education Assessment Manager; The College Board, New York, New York.

Jonathan H. Sandoval, PhD, ABPP; Professor; University of California, Davis; School of Education; Educational Psychology.

Natasha DeFio Santiago, MSEd; School Based Mental Health Clinician; Neighborhood Center Child Guidance Clinic; Utica City School District, Utica, New York.

Janet T. Schultz, MSEd, PD; School Psychologist; Montclair Public Schools, Montclair, New Jersey.

Denise Scorcia, MS; Consulting School Psychologist; All About Kids, Plainview, New York.

Melissa Tarnofsky Silverman, PhD; School Psychologist; Dumont Public Schools, Dumont, New Jersey.

Joan Silverstein, PhD, NCSP; School Psychologist; Clark County School District, Las Vegas, Nevada.

Stanley Sue, PhD, Distinguished Professor, University of California, Davis; Division of Social Sciences; Psychology and Asian American Studies.

Harold Takooshian, PhD; Professor of Psychology and Director of Organizational Leadership; Past President of APA Division of International Psychology; Fordham University; Department of Psychology; Psychology Program.

Linda Taylor, PhD; Clinical Psychologist and Co-director, School Mental Health Project/Center for Mental Health in Schools; University of California, Los Angeles; Department of Psychology.

LeeAnn Truesdell, PhD; Associate Professor; Queens College of the City University of New York; Division of Education; Educational and Community Programs; Special Education.

Elise Trumbull, EdD; Lecturer; California State University, Northridge; Michael D. Eisner College of Education; Department of Educational Psychology and Counseling; Early Childhood Education.

Ena Vazquez-Nuttall, EdD; Professor and Assistant Dean for Multicultural Education; Northeastern University; Department of Counseling and Applied Educational Psychology; School and Counseling Psychology Program.

Joan Wiley Walton, EdD; School Psychologist (Retired), Tuanton Public Schools, Tuanton, Massachusetts.

Tanya M. Warren, MSEd; Graduate Student; Fordham University; Graduate School of Education; Psychological and Educational Services; Doctorate Program in School Psychology.

Chun Zhang, PhD; Associate Professor; Fordham University; Graduate School of Education; Division of Curriculum and Teaching; Early Childhood Special Education Program.

I

A MULTICULTURAL FRAMEWORK

1

A HISTORICAL REVIEW OF THE DEVELOPMENT OF MULTICULTURAL SCHOOL PSYCHOLOGY

Giselle B. Esquivel, Tanya M. Warren,
and Sarah Littman Olitzky
Fordham University

This chapter aims to provide a historical review of the development of a multicultural perspective within the field of school psychology. The emergence of multiculturalism in school psychology as a discipline began slowly, but it is gradually becoming a vital component of academic preparation, research, and practice. Multiculturalism in school psychology emerged in its earliest sense, as a need to assimilate an increasing number of immigrant children in school systems. Over the century, this movement has evolved into a more integrated interdisciplinary approach within the field of school psychology, aimed at maximizing psychological and educational experiences for diverse school populations. In essence, multiculturalism is becoming a critical aspect of the identity of school psychology as a profession.

This chapter may be considered a meta-review of the literature relevant to the development of multiculturalism in school psychology. A developmental perspective has been chosen to provide a historical overview of multicultural school psychology in the context of important demographic changes, sociopolitical thought, legal precedents, interdisciplinary contributions, professional academic growth, and research developments. This historical progression is organized around three major thematic eras: The Formative Era, 1900s–1940s; The Legislative Era, 1950s–1970s; and The Era of Research and Professional Standards, 1980s–2000s. A disclaimer is made, that the organization of the events and trends in this chapter

3

does not necessarily reflect their actual sequential development, but serves to add conceptual clarity to the historical review. Breaking the historical development of multicultural school psychology into these categories also provides an evolutionary perspective, one that parallels Fagan's (1986) description of the three major developmental phases (i.e., initial, growing, maturing) of school psychology as a profession.

THE FORMATIVE ERA, IMPLICATIONS OF DEMOGRAPHIC CHANGE IN THE 1900s–1940s

A comprehensive discussion of multiculturalism in the schools, must first begin with an understanding of the changes occurring in the American educational system at the beginning of the last century. This will be followed by a closer look at how increased immigration and changing demographics played an influential role as a catalyst for further change in that system, leading to the initial formative stages of multiculturalism in school psychology.

Throughout most of the 19th century, education was a pragmatic tool embedded in the context of the home, and intended primarily to teach children the skills and trades that would sustain the livelihood and resources of family life. The statistic that fewer than 7% of the 14–17 year-old children were in school in 1890, demonstrates that a large majority of children had already begun to work (primarily at home or in the father's occupation) by the time they reached their teens (Braden, DiMarino-Linnen, & Good, 2001). Only children from privileged families had access to a lengthier education.

During the turn of the century, however, a sociological shift occurred changing the status of children from economic assets for the family to respect for the wholeness of children as individual persons and as future adult members of society (Zelizer, 1985 as cited in Fagan, 2000). Such a change in values and attitudes toward children prompted the creation of compulsory schooling laws, increasingly enforced from the 1900s to the 1930s (Braden et al., 2001). Because so many previously uneducated children were required to attend school for the first time, schools were faced with an influx of children from differing economic, cultural, and academic backgrounds. Important to the development of school psychology, these children also varied with respect to their educational and mental health needs. "Compulsory school and increased variability in the student population led to the creation of special classes for the needs of 'atypical' students" (Braden et al., 2001, p. 3). As reflected by the initial developmental phase described by Fagan (1986), school psychology partly emerged in response to the special needs of these students. As the physical make up of the population changed, along with the percentage of children attending school, this new profession negotiated its identity and role and functions within the school environment.

Demographics (1900s–1940s)

The diversity that came to characterize the American population in the first part of the 1900s has since permeated nearly every facet of American life. Its pervasive influence extends from governmental policy and laws to increasingly pluralistic cultural trends and customs. The change in demographics at this time also played a significant role in the development of multicultural school psychology. Had the United States remained an insular nation with a rather homogeneous population, a focus on the unique needs and educational and psychological services required for diverse students would not have been necessary. Instead, the profile has been one of increased diversity and multiculturalism.

A look at statistical figures from the U.S. Census during this time period provides some revealing information. In the early decades (1900–1930s), approximately 13% of the U.S. population was foreign born (U.S. Bureau of the Census, 1998). As a result, classrooms began to fill with children noticeably different from the largely white, Anglo-Saxon. Children of immigrants from Southern and Eastern Europe, as well as African-Americans who had migrated from the south, were among those newcomers most numerous in northern classrooms (Braden et al., 2001). It became increasingly clear, as this diversity was confronted, that much of school psychology's identity challenge was to focus on how to best tailor services to accommodate these differing cultures, languages, and socio-economic levels.

Sociopolitical Development, 1900s–1940s

In the early 1900s, the U.S. dealt with the wave of new immigrants by adopting an approach of rapid assimilation. The primary vehicle for this type of acculturation was the public school, as the school environment was a convenient place for young immigrants to gain exposure to important components of American culture. Mirel (2002) explains that America dealt with the increasingly diverse population through education focused on civic allegiance and immersion in the host culture as a means of preserving the American way of life. In his article *Civic Education and Changing Definitions of American Identity, 1900–1950*, Mirel (2002) asserts:

> The process of civic education was simple and straightforward. Immigrants had to learn English; learn to think of themselves as Americans rather than as members of distinct ethnic groups; had to proclaim that individualism was one of America's greatest character traits; espouse American political values; and learn patriotism through an interpretation of history that stressed America's triumphs and ignored its faults. (p. 145)

Perhaps no concept embodies the attitude of the era better than that of the "melting pot," in which cultural diversity became immersed into predominantly mainstream values and culture. This popular interpretation of the phrase is somewhat ironic, as it was first coined by Jewish immigrant Israel Zangwill, to indicate a fusion of "old stock Americans and the immigrants to form a new and stronger national alloy" (Mirel, 2002, p. 145).

The constant stream of new immigrants, so strong at the turn of the century, was unable to maintain its momentum. An increase in ethnic nationalism following World War I led the United States to curtail immigration through acts of Congress in both 1921 and 1924 (Thomas, 1986). Not long thereafter, the Great Depression of the 1930s brought immigration to a virtually complete halt (Mirel, 2002). While the number of new immigrants decreased during and after the Great Depression, American-born children of earlier immigrants began to play a more significant role in the everyday life of the United States. This generation gained visibility through representatives of the new face of the American population, such as sports stars Joe DiMaggio, Hank Greenberg, and Jackie Robinson.

The movie *Bataan* provides an excellent example of how the Hollywood media also brought multiculturalism into the spotlight. Released in 1943, this movie told the story of a group of American soldiers from many different ethnic and religious backgrounds. "The film quickly became a Hollywood archetype that highlighted the importance of diversity but also depicted a shared commitment to common American ideals" (Mirel, 2002, p. 149). As one might imagine, these trends had a profound effect on the popular conceptualization of diversity, and helped usher a wider embrace of cultural pluralism in the U.S. educational system.

Legal Development, 1900s–1940s

The most salient laws and legal actions to emerge from this era generally focused on attempts to regulate the growing public education system and, in a larger sense, regulate the number of immigrants allowed into the country. All states had enacted compulsory attendance laws by 1920, and the number of students enrolled in the school system increased significantly. Snyder, Hoffman, and Geddes (1997), detail the outcome of such laws, where public school enrollment increased from 12.7 to 25.7 million students. In the secondary schools alone, attendance jumped from 203,000 to 4.4 million in the 1920s.

Caps on the number of immigrants permitted entry into the United States were a focal point in the national government. Immigration acts of Congress in 1921 and 1924 "designed to curtail immigration from non-northern-European countries by establishing quotas, showed all too clearly the pervasive hysteria over certain foreigners coming into the United States" (Thomas, 1986, p. 26). As mentioned previously, this cap on immigration did not curtail the need for multicultural services within the emerging field of school psychology, as the children of previous immigrants entered the expanding school system.

It is evident, that the first half of the 20th century had a tremendous sociopolitical impact, as the United States tackled the challenge of accommodating masses of ethnically diverse newcomers through sociological and legal means. In an interesting and important parallel, the early 1900s also saw rapid growth in the field of psychological assessment.

Assessment Development and Trends, 1900s–1940s

Cognitive theories developed in the first decade of the 20th century by Binet and Thorndike led to the creation and use of the Stanford-Binet scale in the U.S. in 1916. Intelligence testing, along with other historical and sociopolitical dynamics, paved the way for several advancements in assessment. Interestingly, early concern and motivation for the development of mental ability tests focused on the non-biased nature of such instruments. In Thorndike's (1997) discussion on the early history of cognitive assessment, he asserts that part of Binet's purpose was to develop a scale that would assess a child's ability in an unbiased way, independent of the bias inherent in teachers' opinions of their students. Thorndike (1997) also cites the proceedings of an 1899 committee meeting of the American Psychology Association (APA), where committee member Kirkpatrick "called for tests 'of such a nature that they can be taken by children as well as adults, that they shall be such that all persons tested will have had about an equal opportunity for the exercise of the power tested'..." (p. 6). This deliberate focus on reducing bias and ensuring equality across assessments will be reflected to a much greater degree in assessment competencies in the second half of the 20th century.

Decades later, in response to the demand World War I placed on the assessment of soldiers for placement purposes, the Army Alpha and Army Beta (for persons who were illiterate and non-English speakers) Tests of Intelligence were developed and widely used (Laosa, 1977). The success of this military testing caught on in American education. Frank Graves, Commissioner of Education in New York at that time, urged teachers in the state to use these tests, predicting them to be "destined to be the greatest asset of modern education" (Graves, 1921, as cited in Thomas, 1986, p. 15).

As testing became increasingly popular within the field of education, questions of what and who should be assessed inevitably surfaced. Thomas (1986) explains that in the 1920s, tests in American education were utilized primarily to assist in the social adjustment of a so-called "underclass" of recent immigrants (mostly Italian and Polish) and African-American children from the South. Mental tests were used to "identify and isolate socially maladjusted children, who teachers feared were headed for a life of crime" (p.14). Thomas argues that, "although these teachers of the 1920s were obliged to teach a diverse pupil population, they overlooked the invidious effects of their pupils' status upon their mental test scores" (p.10). Thus, although assessment of America's culturally and linguistically diverse children occurred early on in the development of school psychology, there was limited sensitivity to the legal, sociopolitical, and professional implications and the unique challenges that assessing diverse students presented to the validity of testing.

Although a better understanding of the issues involved in the assessment process with culturally and linguistically diverse (CLD) students did not become prominent until the latter half of the 20th century, it has been noted that some educators and parental groups were cautious about the outcomes of grouping children erroneously using test scores. Thomas (1986) cites the observations of a 1926 "psychological clinician" from her work with immigrant children, quoting a warning that education professionals should " 'exercise great care in estimating children from non-English speaking homes,' reminding them that mistakes in judging foreigners on a simple test were not uncommon" (Webb, 1926, as cited in Thomas, 1986, p. 23).

Multiculturalism in School Research and Professional Development (1900s–1940s)

During these early formative decades, research on multiculturalism within the field of education and training, focused primarily on supposed differences in ability between races and revealed a lack of scientific rigor and sensitivity in accounting for disparities and differences in environmental, cultural, and linguistic conditions. For example, Garth (1923, as cited in Olmedo,1981) discusses different levels of intelligence among five 'blood groups' of different mixes of Mexican Indian and Caucasian (p. 1080). This work is representative of the general thought and practice regarding the assessment of intelligence among culturally and linguistically diverse individuals of the time period, focusing on the supposed superiority of some ethnicities over others. Olmedo refers to Padilla and Ruiz's (1973, as cited in Olmedo, 1981) summary of this early study, citing Garth's "attempts to use group mean differences in IQ scores as corroborative evidence for the superiority of certain races, even while admitting that groups differ on such key variables as educational attainment and socioeconomic factors" (p. 1080).

The before-his-time research of George Sanchez, "the father of Chicano psychology" (Olmedo, 1981, p. 1080) in the 1930s challenged the heredity argument in the definition of intelligence. Sanchez questioned the interpretations of test administrators who did not acknowledge the environmental and educational differences between English and Spanish-speaking children, and the apparent failure of the school system to provide these different groups with comparable educations. "That many of these criticisms are relevant and valid even today, almost a half-century later, is telling not only of Sanchez's depth and perceptiveness, but also of the extent to which many of our institutions are impervious to change" (Olmedo, 1981, p. 1080).

Another voice in the multicultural wilderness of this time period belonged to George Counts. Counts (1941, as cited in Mirel, 2002) espoused the urgent need for educators to commit to democratic ideals, which were deemed especially pertinent during this era due to the threat of communism in Europe. He stressed that these ideals should be displayed particularly through embracing diversity, arguing that in schools (and throughout American society) "racial, cultural, and political minorities should be tolerated, respected, and valued" (Mirel, 2002, p. 149). This notion of a non-discriminatory system in the public schools, where the differences in ancestry, background, and aptitude should "enrich the common good" (p. 149), contrasts sharply with the idea of the melting pot, which permeated sociological thought in the 1920s and 1930s. This consideration of the benefits of diversity in the American educational system foreshadows the rise of multiculturalism in the second half of the century.

THE LEGISLATIVE ERA, THE RISE OF MULTICULTURALISM 1950s–1970s

In contrast to the beginning of the 20th century, the 1950s, 1960s and 1970s saw fewer foreign-born members of the U.S. population. As a result, the focus shifted from recent immigrants to the children of those already arrived. Questions to be addressed included how these young citizens fit into the U.S. educational system and their access to equal rights protection under the law with regards to which schools they could attend, classroom placement, assessment, and how school psychology professional organizations would incorporate such issues into their standards of professional practice. Given that there were only 20 state associations by 1970, much of the efforts in adopting multicultural standards came at a later time.

Sociopolitical Developments 1950s–1970s

Throughout this time period, children of ethnic minority and low socioeconomic backgrounds consistently demonstrated poorer outcomes on academic assessments.

Literature attests to the reality of lower performance of CLD children on standardized tests and an over-representation of minority students in special education classrooms (Esquivel, 1996a). In the 1960s, these discrepancies were often addressed through a "deficit hypothesis," which linked poorer success of ethnic minorities to their frequently lower socioeconomic level. This popular hypothesis posited that a majority of minority children "live in conditions which result in various forms of deficits...such as symbolic, linguistic, and affective aspects necessary for a child to develop fully to his or her intellectual potential" (Laosa, 1977, p. 13). The widespread acceptance of this hypothesis led directly to the development of many early intervention programs aimed at minimizing detrimental effects of impoverished environments upon development. Head Start is a well-known example of a program created to meet the early learning needs of children considered to be "culturally disadvantaged," a popular categorical term that emerged during the 1960s.

During this time period, the shift away from the concept of the "melting pot" was of social significance. In its place, cultural pluralism, "a movement which reflects a positive recognition of cultural and linguistic differences and which views subcultural variability as a societal asset" (Laosa, 1977, p. 12) emerged in the late 1960s and early 1970s. Following this line of thought, the extreme views of complete separation and assimilation were largely disputed, giving way to an appreciation of differences in the diverse citizenry of the United States.

Legal Precedents 1950s–1970s

On the legislative level, the proliferation of relevant court cases and the precedents set during this era played their own significant role in setting the stage for more mainstreamed multicultural acceptance. A brief summary of some of the most influential cases gives a sense of the critical link between law and evolving practices in school psychology.

Arguably the most groundbreaking court decision for all of public education was that of *Brown v. Board of Education* (1954). It has been identified as "the single most important step in opening the door such that all children could enjoy access to equal educational opportunity" (Reynolds, Gutkin, Elliot, & Witt, 1984, p. 231). The ruling against "separate but equal" schools recognized the necessity for equality in education, regardless of race. This support of equal rights in education on the part of the courts, even if largely symbolic and theoretical in nature, led the way for future rulings and legislative changes. The interested reader is referred to Benjamin and Crouse (2002) and Schofield and Hausmann (2004) for further information on school desegregation.

In the case of *Stell v. Savannah-Chatham County Bd. of Education* (1963), the California Achievement Test and California Test of Mental Maturity were used to allege that African-American students' cognitive abilities were so inferior to Caucasian students' cognitive abilities, that these children should not be educated together. The court's decision stated that integrated education "would seriously impair the educational opportunities of both white and Negro and cause them grave psychological harm" (Reynolds et al., 1984, p. 249). The case also references the prominent thought of the time that these standardized tests measure genetic intelligence, and can be understood as an example of how school systems attempted to bypass the previous ruling of *Brown v. Board of Education*.

In the decades that followed, other court rulings demonstrated a growing sensitivity toward children of diverse backgrounds by recognizing biases built into school practices and legislating system changes necessary to make educational policies more equitable. *Hobson v. Hanson* (1967) critiqued educational tracking, a practice by which children were grouped in classrooms according to ability. The court ruled that such grouping, and the tests that determined a child's placement, were unfair to the poor and the African-American children of Washington, D.C. under the 14th Amendment. More specifically, the ruling of Judge Skelly Wright in this case "established a nearly impossible criterion for the acceptance of tests as part of a placement process where disproportionality resulted" (Reschly, Kicklighter, & McGee, 1988a, p. 11). This set a precedent of judicial recognition that tests had the potential to be racially biased due to their standardization on primarily white, middle class populations. They also promoted the logical conclusion that tests used to track students must test innate ability—and that no tests exist (or conceivably ever could exist) that measure such a construct (Reschly et al., 1988b; Reynolds et al., 1984).

During the following year, the case of *Arreola v. Santa Ana Board of Education* (1968) argued on behalf of 11 Mexican-American children in California that reforms in the process of putting children in special education classrooms were necessary. This ruling led to more comprehensive examinations of children before placement in special education classrooms, including seeking out and encouraging parental involvement, taking cultural backgrounds into consideration, and improving the special education curriculum (Oakland & Laosa, 1977). School psychologists were, therefore, required to expand their job roles to include more than the cut-and-dry testing and placement of these CLD children.

Diana v. California State Board of Education (1970), "perhaps the most influential court case concerning assessment practices for this [LEP and bilingual] population of children" (Lopez, 1997, p. 504), also advocated for the educational rights of Mexican-American children in California. This case brought to light the disproportionate placement of Mexican-American students in "educable mentally retarded" (EMR) classrooms. Its rulings had a significant impact upon the area of bilingual assessment, prompting several important outcomes. Children from non-English speaking homes were now required to be tested in both their native language and

English, and interpreters were required if such a bilingual examiner were unavailable. Additionally, examiners were now required to minimize their reliance on verbally oriented and general information tests, as they were considered unfair to these children (Figueroa, 1989).

One outcome of this ruling included the re-testing of all Mexican-American and Chinese-American children placed special education classrooms at the time of the court case (Oakland & Laosa, 1977). Once re-tested, several thousand students went back to the regular classroom. Reschly (1979) reported, "The fact that many students, previously classified as educable mentally retarded were successful in regular classroom programs, illustrates the need for periodic and thorough review of placement decisions, and perhaps, demonstrates the wisdom of routinely returning special class students to regular classrooms on a trial basis" (p. 219).

Several other important outcomes sprung from the *Diana* ruling. Most notable, is the echo of *Diana*'s ruling on native-language use in communicating and testing in Public Law 94–142, the Education for All Handicapped Children Act of 1975 (Figueroa, 1989). PL 94–142 was created to provide all children with disabilities the right to a free and appropriate education, including limited English proficient (LEP) and bilingual children (Lopez, 1997). These public laws brought nondiscriminatory assessment methods and practice to the forefront of the American political and educational fields and helped to define much of the research, legislative actions, and trends in multiculturalism in education and school psychology. Another federal outcome from the *Diana* ruling is reflected in a memo issued from the Office for Civil Rights, specifying procedures for minority assessment. "This memorandum was particularly concerned with the possible relationship of over-representation of minority students in special education to the broader issue of segregation in public schools" (Reschly, 1979, p. 219). Due in part to this increasing federal and judicial involvement in the area of assessment of minority children in the 1960s and 1970s, consideration of multicultural issues inevitably became more prominent in the field of school psychology.

Following the ruling on *Diana v. California Board of Education*, several other court cases focusing on the challenges of linguistic diversity came to the forefront. *Guadelupe v. Tempe Elementary School District* (1972), for example, addressed issues pertaining to the testing and placement of Hispanic and Native American children in special education classrooms. This case specifically targeted the use of tests that emphasized verbal skills as well as practices that alienated parents and children from the testing process—seen partly as the consequence of not communicating to caregivers in their native language (Reynolds et al., 1984). *Guadalupe* took assessment practices instituted by *Diana* a step further, requiring "a multifaceted evaluation that included assessment of adaptive behavior and an interview with the parents in the child's home" (Jacob-Timm & Hartshorne, 1998, p. 188).

An additional precedent relevant to multiculturalism within school psychology came from *Lau v. Nichols* (1974). In this case, the Supreme Court decided that the rights of non-English speaking Chinese students were violated when they were denied special language instruction in their California schools. Although the court did not provide a particular method to alleviate the situation, a task force of what was then the U.S. Department of Health was created to deal with the assessment of bilingual and non-English speaking children. This task force developed what are known as the "Lau remedies," which involve recommendations for the assessment and diagnosis of, as well as prescriptive programs for, students of limited English proficiency (Olmedo, 1981).

The court did not advocate for any one particular method of assessing, diagnosing, and teaching these students, perhaps due in part to the lack of research-based assessment practices available at the time. A detailed discussion of actual instruments and the myriad processes involved in assessing a limited English proficient (second language learner) student are beyond the scope of this introductory chapter. Suffice it to say, that the lack of empirical support for any one assessment method, as well as the lack of focused and substantial training in bilingual assessment during the 1970s (see Ochoa, Rivera, & Ford, 1997), left a gap in the field of school psychology to be filled in future decades.

In a final example of legal precedence during this time period, the case of *Debra P. v Turlington* (1979) focused on a population of African-American students in Florida who were denied high school diplomas after failing a minimum competency examination. The judge ruled that although the tests did have adequate construct validity, the testing program was unconstitutional "because it perpetuated the effects of past discrimination and had been implemented without a phase-in period" (Haney, 1981, pp. 1026–1027). The controversy surrounding minimum competency testing has ebbed and flowed in subsequent years, and many states have gone on to initiate and utilize competency exams (which reach far beyond testing basic skills), despite this previous ruling (Beard, 1986).

Assessment Competencies 1950s–1970s

As social and legislative trends demonstrated increasing sensitivity toward student diversity, intense debate and research characterized the field of assessment. Influenced by society's increased attention to individual differences among students, much of the debate centered upon whether such differences could be accounted for by heredity or environment. A good deal of the renewed interest in the nature vs. nurture controversy was sparked by Jensen's (1969) article on the issue. His conclusion that genetic influences are primarily responsible for differences in IQ scores was contrary to generally accepted notions of the era (Laosa, 1977). "A bitter controversy both in professional journals and the public press immediately ensued upon the publication of Jensen's article" (Laosa, 1977, p. 10). The controversy surrounding Jensen's conclusions sparked much academic discourse about these issues, opening the door to further multicultural research. Jensen's (1969) article and conclusion are still controversial to this day. Flynn's (1999) discussion of IQ gains and race provides a thought-provoking perspective on the ongoing debate regarding disparities in IQ scores among individuals from different ethnicities.

This heated controversy spawned another related debate over the use of standardized tests with minority group children. The matters of test bias and the relevancy and use of test results have engendered a slew of criticisms against standardized assessment practices. In Haney's (1981) historical review of social concerns with standardized testing, he reports that in the 1970s "standardized tests were viewed variously as indicators of social ills; as solutions to some of those same ills; and, at least by some, as causes of both educational and social problems" (p. 1026). While the issue of bias in tests with CLD children was tossed around in research, literature, and the media, the notion of fairness and cultural sensitivity in assessment grew. In response to the criticisms of culturally loaded psychological tests, several new trends in assessment began, and test developers began to update norms to include more diverse samples. The inclusion of minorities in test norms became profitable to psycho-educational testing publishers, a business which often follows as well as sets the trends in assessment.

Also important to the growth of the multicultural focus within school psychology is the discussion of the assessment of bilingual children in the 1970s. While bias in the assessment of native English speakers has yet to be empirically proven, it is dangerous to assume the same for those individuals from non-English speaking homes and backgrounds. Cummins' (1979) discussion of the distinction between basic interpersonal communication skills (BICS) and cognitive/academic language proficiency (CALP), from a psycholinguistic perspective, was a significant leap forward in the recognition of a research-based approach needed in assessing limited English proficient (LEP) children. In Cummins' (1980) article on the assessment of immigrant children, he makes the point that native-like conversational skills in a child do not necessarily reflect native-like academic language proficiency. He posits that interpretation of such a child's low scores on a cognitive test can lead to "incorrect placement decisions" which "can have serious consequences for minority students' academic progress" (p. 103). He concludes "the labeling of minority language children as 'low ability' or even 'mentally deficient' on the basis of tests administered in their weaker language will remain a very real possibility so long as issues relating to the educational development of minority language children continue to be neglected in the training of teachers and clinical psychologists" (p. 108).

The issue of how and what to assess in minority populations fairly and validly was not ignored throughout the decade of the 1970s, as had been the case prior to that time. A special issue of the *Journal of School Psychology* dedicated to the assessment of minority children was released in 1973. This issue dealt with the challenges faced when assessing these children, alternative models to interpret tests, and the consequences of labels and decisions made based on unfair tests. Instruments specific to certain populations of children were concurrently being developed, and these tests were unique in their increasingly marked attention to cultural and linguistic variability with student populations. Two of these culture-specific tests include The Enchilada test (Ortiz & Ball, 1972) and The Black Intelligence Test of Cultural Homogeneity (Williams, 1972). These instruments dealt exclusively with the experiences of Mexican American and Black children, respectively.

Whereas the above tests were specifically designed for children of one culture, another body of tests represented a pluralistic approach in which the socio-cultural characteristics of an individual's background were considered when evaluating scores of intellectual abilities (Laosa, 1977). Criterion-referenced (as opposed to norm-referenced testing) was also seen as potentially valuable for minority students in the 1970s. Drew (1973) contends that while criterion-referenced tests may not have been criticized as strongly as norm-referenced tests with regards to CLD children, the potential for bias in this framework still exists. He states that the implicit link between evaluation and instruction is a desirable aspect of criterion-referenced measurements, but the question of the selected criterion, and who specifies this criterion, can still be tainted by "a lack of multicultural awareness" (p. 327). Drew concludes with the recommendation that diverse approaches, measures, and formats be utilized in assessing this population rather than any one framework—an approach developed and recommended still today.

Growing concerns with test bias and over-representation of minority children (e.g., California ethnic surveys of over-representation) gave impetus to the development of the System of Multicultural Pluralistic Assessment (SOMPA; Mercer & Lewis, 1978). Within this comprehensive system, children are assessed through a medical model, a social systems model, and a pluralistic model. The SOMPA is " an attempt to develop a comprehensive assessment package to assess not only children's current skills and behavior, but also those aspects of their socio-cultural environment that influence these skills" (Brown, 1979, p. 37). SOMPA was initially heralded with much fanfare and became quite popular. Figueroa (1979) unequivocally supports that "this innovative approach 'SOMPA' meets all the testing specifications in 94–142. There are really no other materials that comply so fully with the law on questions of non- discriminatory testing" (p. 29). However, controversy surrounding separate means and standard deviations for three ethnic groups (African American, Hispanic, and White), the use of parents rather than teachers for a measure of adaptive behavior (the ABIC), and the ABIC's poor correlation with the measure of intelligence (the WISC-R) were among the criticisms that led to a decline in the use of the SOMPA in the 1980s (Coulter, 1996). The test never really gained much appeal or widespread usage after the novelty effects of its original publication.

With regard to decisions made based on school assessment outcomes, bodies such as the Office of Civil Rights (OCR) recommended the creation of a board of parents and teachers in every school, "representative of the ethnic makeup of the student body" (Laosa, 1977, p. 17) to review all placement decisions. However, it is questionable whether such boards ever gained appeal or widespread usage (T. Fagan, personal communication, March 9, 2005). Interested readers may want to refer to Laosa's (1977) chapter in *Psychological and Educational Assessment of Minority Children* for further discussion on this topic during this era.

Multiculturalism in School Research and Professional Development (1950s–1970s)

The decades between 1950 and 1980 were also marked by the increased participation of professional associations, research institutions, and scholarly researchers on issues pertaining to multiculturalism in schools and education, as well as in other related fields (e.g., bilingual education, special education) and other sub-disciplines in psychology (e.g., counseling, clinical, cross-cultural psychology). In 1964, Division 9 of APA, the Society for the Study of Social Issues, published a paper on the need to use "tests with minority group children in ways that will enable these children to attain the full promise that America owes to all of its children" (Deutsch, Fishman, Kogan, North, & Whiteman, 1964, as cited in Oakland & Laosa,

1977, p. 22). This was an early foray of professional organizations into the debate on fair assessments for minority children. At the annual APA convention in 1968, the Association of Black Psychologists presented a manifesto for a moratorium on all psychological tests for disadvantaged children (Oakland & Laosa, 1977). Four years later, in 1972, the National Education Association (NEA) followed suit in the drive to abolish standardized tests in 1972.

The National Association of School Psychologists (NASP) was formed in 1969 for professional and political reasons. These included the need to make better connections with state groups, attain greater representation of non-doctoral level school psychologists, gain greater state representation at the national level, promote political agendas, and increase the commitment to provide effective services to children (Cobb & Dawson, 1989; Fagan, 2005). In its first decade of existence, "services to states were unclear, fragmented, and informal" (Fagan, Block, Dwyer, Petty, St. Cyr, & Telzrow, 1989, p. 152). However, it is notable that discussions regarding testing minority students, understanding issues relevant to these children, and the recruitment of minority school psychologists all occurred early on in the formation of this professional association (EB Minutes, 1971; DA Minutes, 1972, as cited in Cobb & Dawson, 1989, p. 204).

The growing multicultural sensitivity at the professional and practice levels, was yet to be generalized to research and publications. Only 7.5% of all articles published between 1975–1979 in the major school psychology journals (i.e., *Journal of School Psychology, Psychology in the Schools,* and *School Psychology Review*) focused on minority issues. Although this number does grow in the decades that follow, the increase is relatively small and does not extend beyond the narrow scope of assessment issues. Nonetheless, research developments in related fields of bilingual education, bilingual special education, and multicultural counseling psychology provided an interdisciplinary basis and impetus for school psychology's incipient development of its own multicultural research agenda. The interested reader should see Rogers's (1992) article on the prevalence of minority research.

The demographics of the professionals themselves also reveal a striking lack of multicultural representation among psychologists. Less than 1% of the members of Division 16 of APA identified themselves as Hispanic at the end of the 1970s (Oakland & Mowder, 1980, as quoted in Rosenfield & Esquivel, 1985). Literature is scarce about the ethnic make-up of students and faculty in school psychology programs of the era. Zins and Halsell (1986) quote an unpublished survey study by Novick (1978), which found that 11.7% of students enrolled in respondent programs were of minority and/or bilingual backgrounds. However, it is noted that "since he included both groups in his survey, it is not clear how many of these persons were ethnic minorities" (Zins & Halsell, 1986, p. 77).

Multiculturalism in Academia and Training Programs (1950s–70s)

Besides a dearth in minority representation within school psychology training programs, the curricula of these programs in the 1950s–70s also demonstrated a marked absence of reference to multiculturalism. Ochoa, Rivera, and Ford's (1997) study of NASP members' training in bilingual assessment practices following the case of *Diana v. California Board of Education* (1970) reveals that on measures of competency in knowledge of second language acquisition factors, knowledge of methods to conduct bilingual assessment, and knowledge of how to interpret results of bilingual assessment, most respondents reported "very little" training. "The results of this study clearly indicate that since the case of *Diana v. California*, the profession of school psychology had not made sufficient progress in addressing and improving training pertaining to assessment practices with students from linguistically diverse backgrounds" (Ochoa, Rivera, & Ford, 1997, p. 341).

Studies on the representation of culturally and linguistically diverse individuals enrolled in training programs, courses offered on minority and nonbiased assessment topics, and the prevalence of related topics in the literature all appear later in the timeline, as will be illustrated in the next era of focus. (See Table 1–1.)

THE ERA OF RESEARCH AND PROFESSIONAL STANDARDS IN MULTICULTURAL SCHOOL PSYCHOLOGY, 1980s–2000s

The final era to be covered in this historical review of the development of multiculturalism within the field of school psychology is marked by significant growth. The decades from 1980 to the present may be characterized by a continued focus on issues specific to minority children and practitioners, and may therefore be set apart from earlier eras by the emphasis on research and regulation of multicultural competencies and standards in all spheres of the discipline. Compared to previous years, distinguished by challenges which are consistent with Fagan's (1986) incipient stages of growth, this current era has given rise to increased research, theoretical models, best practices, minority recruitment efforts, and greater recognition of multiculturalism within professional organizations. In regard to professional organizations, although it was late in the 1970s that NASP standards and the accreditation policies of NCATE and APA addressed multicultural issues, there has been a continued strengthening and expansion of professional standards in broader diversity issues.

An illustrative example of the more detailed attention and focus paid to multicultural issues may be seen in *Best Practices in School Psychology* (2002), where several sections are devoted to cultural considerations in the field of school psychology. Ortiz and Flanagan's (2002) chapter on work with culturally diverse children and families, discusses the need to expand on the content of multicultural best practices, since "school psychology training programs do not appear to provide sufficient direct supervision or instructional opportunities necessary to promote development of such competency" (p. 338). Nonetheless, multicultural competence development within the field is viewed as progressing, although it is still far from complete.

Rogers et al.'s (1999) conceptual article on culturally competent service delivery for school psychologists illustrates several of the realms deemed necessary for multicultural professional development. Six domains are highlighted to define competence in this area, including (a) legal and ethical issues; (b) school culture, educational policy, and institutional advocacy; (c) psychoeducational assessment;

TABLE 1–1
Timeline

	Formative Era: 1900s–40s	Legislative Era: 1950s–70s	Era of Research and Professional Standards: 1980s–2000s
Demographics	• Significant increase in foreign-born population. • Migration of African Americans out of the South.	• Fewer foreign-born citizens.	• Large increase in culturally diverse school-age population. • Disparity between number of CLD students and CLD practitioners.
Sociopolitical	• Concept of the "melting pot." • Assimilation adopted as primary acculturation strategy.	• Deficit hypothesis. • Shift from "melting pot" to "cultural pluralism."	• Greater acceptance and promotion of diversity.
Legal	• Compulsory school attendance laws. • Quotas regulate immigration.	• Proliferation of multiculturally relevant court cases. • Landmark cases set precedents. • Authorization of PL 94–142.	• Reauthorization of IDEA. • No Child Left Behind
Assessment	• Intelligence tests used to identify maladjusted CLD students. • Few recognized potential test biases.	• Nature/nurture controversy. • Recognition of test biases. • Initial development of culturally sensitive tests.	• Continued debate on best practices for CLD assessment. • Potential biases identified and researched.
Research and professional development	• Focus on inherent differences between races/ethnicities. • Heredity intelligence argument surfaces.	• Professional organizations adopt multicultural focus. • Limited research on minority issues.	• Expansion of diversity literature base and use of interdisciplinary research. • APA minority recruitment resolution.
Academia and training programs	• No formalized multicultural emphasis in academia.	• Low minority representation in training programs. • Limited multicultural emphasis in academia.	• Mandates to incorporate multicultural curricula. • Emergence of model bilingual school psychology programs.

(d) academic, therapeutic, and consultative interventions; (e) working with interpreters; and (f) research. These competencies will be touched upon in the review of this final era.

Demographics (1980s–2000s)

As in the beginning of the century, changing demographics again play a major role in school psychology in the most recent decades. Between 1980 and 1990, the United States experienced an increase in minority representation among its population. During this decade, the white population grew by 7.7%, while the African American population grew by 15.8% and the Hispanic population grew by 34.5% (Rogers, Close Conoley, Ponterotto, & Wiese, 1992). In 1996, 1 in every 10 U.S. residents was foreign born (24.6 million people). Also important was the census finding that in 1996, the Hispanic population was considerably younger than the non-Hispanic white population (U.S. Bureau of the Census, 1998). Projected population profiles anticipate growth of minority-group populations cultures to consistently continue. By 2050, less than 53% of the U.S. population will be non-Hispanic Caucasian, 15% will be African American, greater than 24% will be Hispanic, and 9% will be Asian/Pacific Islander (U.S. Bureau of the Census, 1998).

A specific look at the demographics of school children compared with school psychologists reveals a consistent disparity. A large number of culturally and linguistically diverse children in the school systems are to be serviced by a limited number of practitioners from bilingual and culturally diverse backgrounds. In the 2000–2001 school year, 61.2% of students were Caucasian, 17.2% of students were Black, 16.3% Hispanic, 4.1% Asian/Pacific Islander, and 1.2% American Indian (Young, 2002). Miranda and Gutter (2002) report that one out of every three school age children is from a minority group. In stark contrast, the demographics of school psychology practitioners have remained relatively constant. In the beginning of the 1980s APA membership included only 3.1% ethnic minorities (Russo, Olmedo, Strapp, & Fulcher, 1981, as quoted in Zins & Halsell, 1986). In their 1984 article on educating school psychologists to work with CLD populations, Rosenfield and Esquivel reported less than 1% of APA members identified themselves as Hispanic. Minority membership in NASP in 1991 was similarly low, consisting of 1.9% African American, 1.5% Hispanic, 1.1% Native American, and 1.7% others (Graden & Curtis, 1991). Finally, in Texas, a state with one of the largest populations of LEP children and families, Palmer, Hughes, and Juarez (1991) report results from the Texas Psychological Association, finding only 4 licensed Hispanic school psychologists in 1989.

In an attempt to increase minority representation among psychologists, APA (1987) passed a resolution (1987) to increase minority recruitment of students and faculty in school psychology programs (Rogers, Hoffman, & Wade, 1998). A similar commitment was echoed in NASP, which Curtis and Zins (1989) identified as "a priority issue by both the Association and the profession at large" (p. 188). The Social Issues Committee of NASP formed in the 1970s, became the Multicultural Affairs Committee "to specifically support ethnic and racial minority issues involving children and families within the field of school psychology" (NASP's Multicultural Affairs Committee, n.d.). Efforts to increase the number of minority practitioners include a special task force for recruitment and retention in the field, minority scholarships, and the development of training programs in pertinent geographic regions. Some researchers, however, maintain, "it appears unlikely that the field will attract a greater minority population in the next decade" and while the need for skills and knowledge to work with these populations has been recognized, "that need historically has not been reflected in school psychology literature" (Miranda & Gutter, 2002, p. 597). More on this concern will be discussed in the section on research and training. However, it must be noted that minority representation in school psychology is no worse (and probably better) than in other areas of professional psychology.

Sociopolitical and Legal Developments (1980s–2000s)

In spite of attempts to revert to traditional assimilation approaches, the recent movement of tougher regulation and accountability in educational policy and practice has, in effect, provided a rationale for legislative advances that protect the rights of children from cultural and linguistically diverse backgrounds. An illustrative example comes from a California law passed in 1981, requiring the education credentialing authorities to "develop rules, regulations, standards, and training programs for a certificate of bilingual, cross-cultural competence" in all certified school personnel (Figueroa, Sandoval, & Merino, 1984, p. 133). This approach to the regulation of educational practice would be echoed in other state and national laws throughout the next two decades.

Perhaps most salient in the areas of sociopolitical and legal developments in the recent era, may be the reauthorization of PL 94–142 in 1990 and again in 1997, which modified and renamed the Education of All Handicapped Children Act of 1975 into the Individuals with Disabilities Act (IDEA). Portions of IDEA most relevant to this discussion of multiculturalism are the focus on nondiscriminatory testing (prompted in part by the misclassification of minority children into "educable mentally retarded" classes in the past) and equal protection, or equal educational opportunity, as provided by the 14th amendment. Jacob-Timm and Hartshorne (2003) identify that the 1997 amendments to equal protection in the act require states to investigate and discern whether race is a significantly disproportionate variable in the identification and placement of children classified as disabled. This act requires state and federal agencies to keep structured records on the number of minority children entering the school, and also obliges schools to review and revise policies and practices if disproportionality exists.

The case of Parents in Action in Special Education (*PASE) v. Hannon* (1980) presents the question of whether the intelligence tests employed by the Chicago Board of Education were culturally biased against Black children. The case questions what an IQ test precisely measures. After listening to expert testimony and making a personal examination of test materials, the presiding Judge Grady ruled that "the plaintiffs have failed to prove their contention that [the tests used] are culturally unfair to black children, resulting in discriminatory placement of black children in classes for the educable mentally handicapped" (PASE, 1980, p. 15), ruling in favor of the school system. This case is notable for the judge's singularly personal attempts to determine bias in the questions of the Wechsler and Binet scales (Jacob-Timm & Hartshorne, 2003).

In contrast, the *Larry P. v. Riles* (1975) and *Larry P.* (1984, 1986) court cases argued a similar issue in the San Francisco school system with much different outcomes. The original case contended the use of IQ tests in special education placement, as it resulted in a disproportionate number of black students in educable mentally retarded (EMR) classrooms in the school system. The case was decided and appealed several times, resulting in an injunction by the court forbidding the use of IQ test with black students being considered for placement in EMR classrooms. (Reschly, Kicklighter, & McKee, 1988b).

Finally, the *No Child Left Behind Act of 2001* (NCLB) is a landmark in educational reform that places among its major premises an increase in accountability of measurable achievement outcomes, evidence-based instructional methods, and expansion of parental involvement and options. In *No Child Left Behind: Now What Do We Need to Do to be Culturally Responsive*, Day-Vines and Patton (2003) specify the evidence-based strategies for making NCLB culturally responsive. These strategies include recognition of the need for cultural competency training, implementation of culturally appropriate instructional practices, and links with parents and community-based cultural informants.

Assessment Competencies and Interventions (1980s–2000s)

Despite the formal rulings and regulations of this era, Lopez (1997) states "the bottom line is that practitioners are left to implement those guidelines and mandates at a time when the fields of education and psychology are confronted with many questions regarding testing bias, a lack of assessment resources…and a questionable knowledge base as to how to assess children from LEP and bilingual backgrounds" (pp. 505–506). Thus, many of the issues at the forefront of assessment philosophy and literature of the past several decades are still pertinent in the present, especially as they relate to bilingual and limited English proficient children.

The question on how to best assess this population of children has been openly addressed from the outset of the 1980s. In October of 1981, *The American Psychologist* published an issue devoted entirely to the social responsibility of psychological testing. However, as Lopez (1997) asserts, this commitment to addressing the challenges of cognitive assessment of bilingual and LEP children needs to be followed by more empirically validated testing instruments and methods. While intelligence tests may not be biased for native or proficient English speakers, research into the level of bias for bilingual or less proficient students has been generally overlooked (Lopez, 1997). Similarly, the training of interpreters as adjuncts to the assessment process, and other aspects of bilingual assessment need to be subject to empirical validation.

Best practices also call for the initial assessment of a child's language proficiency level prior to the cognitive measure—such measures have been developed for Spanish speakers, but "formal measures of language proficiency are generally not available in other languages" (Lopez, 1997, p. 507).

In the latest edition of *Best Practices in School Psychology*, Ortiz (2002) presents a 10-step comprehensive framework for nondiscriminatory assessment. This approach is far from rigid, in the sense of more formal testing procedures. Instead, Ortiz's model is "a more practical approach" which emphasizes the recognition of possible bias and the use of instruments and procedures that reduce bias (p. 1333). The challenge for the assessment of multicultural students rests on the notion that such evaluations are "best carried out within the provisions of an overarching framework that brings bias reduction procedures together in a cohesive and logical manner and which assists not only in interpreting data fairly but also the collection of data in ways that are similarly less biased" (p.1333).

Multiculturalism in School Research and Professional Development (1980s–2000s)

The last two decades have seen greater proliferation of multicultural advocacy leadership roles, professional, and research activities among school psychologists. In the 1980s, for example, NASP appointed a Multicultural Affairs Committee, which focused upon diversity during the 1991 national convention (Rogers, 1992). Similarly, the APA created a task force on the delivery of Services to Ethnic Minorities in 1988 "in response to the increased awareness about psychological service needs associated with ethnic and cultural diversity" (American Psychological Association, 1993).

Other multicultural activities of the APA include the passing of a resolution (1987) to increase minority recruitment of students/faculty in school psychology programs, as mentioned previously, as well as the publication of APA Guidelines for Providers of Psychological Services to Ethnic Cultural, and Linguistically Diverse Populations (1991). These guidelines were expanded in 1999 (Rogers et al., 1999).

Rogers (1992) reports a growing trend in school psychology articles on minority issues published in the three major journals, from 7.5% between 1975–79 to 8.8% from 1980–84, and 9.2% from 1985–1990. Miranda and Gutter's (2002) continuation study found that 10.6% of those published from 1990–99 focused on diversity issues—a slight increase from the previous decades. The inclusion of multicultural school psychology issues in best practices handbooks, historical encyclopedia, and other major book resources has also expanded (e.g., Esquivel, 1996b; Esquivel & Houtz, 2000; Fagan & Warden, 1996; Rhodes, Ochoa, & Ortis, 2005). However, one area of diversity research that has declined during the past two decades is that of the effects of school desegregation, "once quite common in psychology and related fields" (Schofield & Hausmann, 2004, p. 538). In general, research on a significant number of diversity issues still lacks representation in the professional literature. Miranda and Gutter (2002) remark, "Without a diversity literature base, the field of school psychology will continue to be limited in our understanding of the relevance of diversity issues" (p. 602). This could be related, in part, to the fact that there are few minorities in the field to conduct such research, as well as a relatively small number of diverse readers of this research (Fagan, 2005).

The need has also been argued for research studies that extend beyond assessment issues and are more inclusive of specific instructional strategies (Gersten & Baker, 2000), educational equity (Barona & Garcia, 1990), and counseling interventions (Esquivel, 1998) with diverse populations. Ingraham's (2000) introduction to the *School Psychology Review* mini-series dedicated to cross-cultural consultation also acknowledges the need for more research on multicultural consultation in the schools. A step forward in that direction is offered by a column of Erlbaum's *Journal of Educational and Psychological Consultation* edited by E. Lopez that is devoted to "Diversity in Consultation" issues. While growing in the dissemination of multicultural issues and benefiting from the research base of other disciplines (e.g., bilingual education, psycholinguistics, cross-cultural psychology, multicultural counseling psychology), it is important that school psychology develop its own research agenda and methodologies pertinent to CLD children within specific educational and psychological contexts.

Multiculturalism in Academia and Training Programs (1980s–2000s)

As would be expected, training programs for school psychologists have embraced the trend toward multicultural sensitivity and have begun to incorporate specific multicultural training as part of their curricula. Martinez (1985) describes a new theoretical model for a bilingual school psychology program: "The academic and professional fields of bilingual school psychology should integrate scientifically based research and training concerning school psychology and specialized training and familiarity with research on linguistic, cultural, socioeconomic factors, and assessment procedures appropriate in dealing with language minority and culturally different children" (p. 148).

A few universities broke ground in the development and creation of such a training program, slightly preceding the publication of Martinez's (1985) article. One prominent example is Texas A&M's 1980 introduction of an emphasis within its doctoral-level school psychology program on Handicapped Hispanic Children and Youth (HHCY). Additionally, Fordham University set a precedent with the development of its bilingual school psychology specialization in 1981. Rosenfield and Esquivel (1985) detail the specific competencies, curriculum, faculty, and students essential to this exemplary program which evolved from a Spanish and Chinese bilingual specialization to a multicultural specialization at both advanced certificate and doctoral levels. The Ph.D. Program was invited to present as a national multicultural training model in school psychology at the Annual Convention of the APA in 1996. San Diego State University followed as another pioneer in the development of a well-recognized multicultural school psychology program, which also encompasses issues of low socioeconomic status and cultural diversity. Other programs dedicating noteworthy attention to diversity include Temple University and Arizona State University, which focuses on Native Americans.

Multiculturally oriented training programs have continued to develop and grow at a national level and the link between multiculturalism and state certification in school psychology has become better recognized at state levels. For example, New York State has led the way by making a provision for a bilingual extension to certification in school psychology. A number of universities in the New York area now have school psychology programs that lead to bilingual certification. Additionally, international efforts are exemplified by the affiliation initiated by Thomas Oakland between Florida State University in Gainsville and the Universidad Ibero-americana in Costa Rica. Students from school psychology programs in the United States are involved in a full Spanish language and cultural immersion program working with children in very economically disadvantaged areas in Costa Rica, while reciprocally gaining multicultural experiences and competencies that can be applied in their work as school psychologists in the United States.

In spite of the growth on multicultural programs, an academic profile of limited coverage of cultural diversity in the general coursework of school psychology training programs has persisted. Rogers, Close Conoley, Ponterotto, and Wiese (1992) report that only 6% of training programs required a foreign language and 60% of programs offered at least one multicultural course. APA accredited doctoral level programs were more likely to emphasize multicultural issues than non-accredited programs. However, in a study of 10 "exemplary" multicultural-focused, APA accredited training programs by Rogers, Hoffman, and Wade (1998), the authors found that such programs reported a relatively high percentage of ethnic minority faculty and students (22%), and all incorporated multicultural perspectives within the curriculum—not just in the offering of one particular course on diversity issues.

Although the above data needs to be updated, the profile reflects concerns with academic training and real problems with recruiting ethnic minority students due to a low pool of these students at the undergraduate level. Even when recruitment is a possibility, it is important to provide these students with financial incentives and on-going social and academic support. Programs are often not self-sufficient in providing these resources and need to rely on other sources of funding, such as grants, scholarships, and paid internships. It is hoped that the emphasis by NASP and APA on student diversity and multicultural competencies may serve as an impetus for institutional support of students and to the enhancement of multicultural school psychology training models. Future directions in this area are exemplified by the *School Psychology: Blueprint for Training and Practice* (Ysseldyke et. al., 1997) report on the professional mandate for programs to integrate multicultural issues into their training curriculum and the 2002 Futures Conference goals that emphasize providing comprehensive services to children in the context of gender, language, ethnicity, family, and socio-economic background (Harrison et. al., 2002).

CONCLUSION

In sum, an overview of the development of a multicultural perspective in school psychology reflects that the field has become, over the years, increasingly more responsive to the needs of immigrant and CLD children, in terms of legislative mandates, advocacy activities, professional standards, academic preparation programs, research, and practices. Growth has been seen, for example, in the identification of critical issues impacting immigrant and culturally diverse children and families, greater efforts in providing culturally appropriate services, and proactive involvement from school psychology professional organizations. Overall, given the formative trends and growing efforts of the past three decades, much has been accomplished. Yet, the path to maturity is a life-long process, with obstacles to overcome and new directions to be sought. The development of a multicultural research agenda, setting long-term strategies for recruiting and retaining minority students, continued emphasis on preparing school psychologists with multicultural competencies, the implementation and evaluation of culturally effective practices, and interdisciplinary affiliations are among the major goals to pursue in the future. The purpose of this handbook is to serve as a resource that gives direction to this on-going professional process and ultimately leads to the complex task of formulating an overarching conceptual model to guide research, training, and practice in multicultural school psychology. Geared specifically toward that end, the chapters that follow will provide an interdisciplinary perspective on research, training, and best practices in multicultural competencies in school psychology. These contributions are intended to improve the preparation of future school psychologists, enhance the type and quality of professional services provided to CLD students, and serve to further the development of a multicultural identity in school psychology.

REFERENCES

American Psychological Association. (1993). Guidelines for providers of psychological services to ethnic, linguistic, and culturally diverse populations. *American Psychologist, 48,* 45–48.

Arreola v. Santa Ana Board of Education, 476 U.S. 267 (1968).

Barona, A., & Garcia, E. (Eds.). (1990). *Children at risk: Poverty, minority status, and other issues in education equality.* Washington, DC: National Association of School Psychologists.

Beard, J. G. (1986). *Minimum competency testing. Update.* Princeton, NJ: ERIC Clearinghouse on Tests Measurement and Evaluation. (ERIC Document Reproduction Service No. ED284910)

Benjamin, L. T., & Crouse, E. M. (2002). The American Psychological Association's response to Brown v. Board of Education: The case of Kenneth B. Clark. *The American Psychologist. 57.* 38–50.

Braden, J. S., DiMarino-Linnen, E., & Good, T. L. (2001). Schools, society, and school psychologists: History and future directions. *Journal of School Psychology, 39,* 203–219.

Brown v. Board of Education of Topeka, 347 U.S. 483 (1954).

Brown, F. (1979). The SOMPA: A system of measuring potential abilities? *School Psychology Digest, 8,* 37–46.

Cobb, C. T., & Dawson, M. M. (1989). The evolution of children's services: Approaching maturity. *School Psychology Review, 18,* 203–208.

Coulter, W. A. (1996). System of multicultural pluralistic assessment. In T. K. Fagan & P. G. Warden (Eds.), *Historical encyclopedia of school psychology* (pp. 382–383). Westport, CT: Greenwood Press.

Cummins, J. (1979). Linguistic interdependence and the educational development of bilingual children. *Review of Educational Research, 49,* 222–251.

Cummins, J. (1980). Psychological assessment of immigrant children: Logic or intuition? *Journal of Multilingual and Multicultural Development, 1,* 97–111.

Curtis, M. J., & Zins, J. E. (1989). Trends in training and accreditation. *School Psychology Review, 18,* 182–192.

Day-Vines, N. L., & Patton, J. M. (2003). No Child Left Behind: Now what do we need to do to be culturally responsive? Retrieved August 18, 2004, from http://www.wm.edu/ttac/articles/legal/nowwhat.htm

Diana v. California State Board of Education, C–70–37 RFP (1970).

Drew, C. J. (1973). Criterion-referenced and norm-referenced assessment of minority group children. *Journal of School Psychology, 11,* 323–329.

Esquivel, G. B. (1996a). Bilingual assessment. In T. K. Fagan & P. G. Warden (Eds.), *Historical encyclopedia of school psychology* (pp. 41–42). Westport, CT: Greenwood Press.

Esquivel, G. B. (1996b). Multicultural understanding. In T. Fagan & P. Warden (Eds.). *Historical encyclopedia of school psychology.* Westport, Conn.: Greenwood Press.

Esquivel, G. B. (1998). Group interventions with culturally diverse children. In K. Stoiver & T. Katrochwill (Eds.), *Group interventions in school and community* (pp. 252–267). Needham Heights, MA: Allyn & Bacon.

Esquivel, G. B., & Houtz, J. C. (Eds.). (2000).*Creativity and giftedness in culturally diverse students.* Cresskill, NJ: Hampton Press.

Fagan, T. K. (1986). School psychology's dilemma: Reappraising solutions and directing attention to the future. *American Psychologist, 41,* 851–861.

Fagan, T. K. (2000). Practicing school psychology: A turn-of-the-century perspective. *American Psychologist, 55,* 754–757.

Fagan, T. K. (2005). The 50th anniversary of the Thayer conference: Historical perspectives and accomplishments. *School Psychology Quarterly, 20,* 224–251.

Fagan, T. K., Block, N., Dwyer, K., Petty, S., St. Cyr, M., & Telzrow, C. (1989). Historical summary and analysis of the first 20 years of the National Association of School Psychologists. *School Psychology Review, 2,* 151–164.

Fagan, T. K., & Warden, P. G. (Eds.). (1996). *Historical encyclopedia of school psychology* (pp. 41–42). Westport, CT: Greenwood Press.

Figueroa, R. A. (1979). The system of multicultural pluralistic assessment. *School Psychology Digest, 8,* 28–36.

Figueroa, R. A. (1989). Psychological testing of linguistic-minority students: Knowledge gaps and regulations. *Exceptional Children, 56,* 142–152.

Figueroa, R. A., Sandoval, J., & Merino, B. (1984). School psychology and limited-English-proficient (LEP) children: New competencies. *Journal of School Psychology, 22,* 131–143.

Flynn, J. R. (1999). Searching for justice: The discovery of IQ gains over time. *American Psychologist, 54,* 5–20.

Gersten, R., & Baker, S. (2000). The professional knowledge base of instructional practices that support cognitive growth for English-language learners. In R. Gersten, E. Schiller, &

S. Vaughan (Eds.), *Contemporary special education research: Synthesis of the knowledge base on critical instructional issues* (pp. 31–79). Mahwah, NJ: Erlbaum.

Graden, J. L., & Curtis, M. J. (1991). *A demographic profile of school of psychology: Report to the NASP Delegate Assembly.* Silver Spring, MD: National Association of School Psychologists.

Guadalupe v. Tempe Elementary School District, CIV 71–435 U.S. (1971).

Haney, W. (1981). Validity, vaudeville, and values: A short history of social concerns over standardized testing. *American Psychologist, 36*, 1021–1034.

Harrison, P. L., Cummings, J.A., Dawson, M., Short, R. J., Gorin, S., & Palomares, R. (2002). Responding to the needs of children, family, and schools: The 2002 multisite conference on the future of school psychology. *School Psychology Review, 3*, 12–33.

Hobson v. Hansen, 269 F. Supp. 401 (1967).

Ingraham, C. L. (2000). Consultation through a multicultural lens: Multicultural and cross-cultural consultation in schools. *School Psychology Review, 29*, 320–343.

Jacob-Timm, S., & Hartshorne, T. S. (1998). *Ethics and law for school psychologists* (3rd ed.). Hoboken, NJ: Wiley.

Jacob-Timm, S., & Hartshorne, T. S. (2003). *Ethics and law for school psychologists* (4th ed.). Hoboken, NJ: Wiley.

Jensen, A. R. (1969). How much can we boost IQ and scholastic achievement? *Harvard Educational Review, 39*, 1–123.

Laosa, L. M. (1977). Nonbiased assessment of children's abilities: Historical antecedents and current issues. In T. Oakland (Ed.), *Psychological and educational assessment of minority children* (pp. 1–20). New York: Brunner/Mazel.

Larry P. v. Riles, 495 F. Supp. 926 N.D. Cal (1979).

Larry P. v. Riles, 793 F. 2d 969 9th. Cir. (1984).

Larry P. v. Riles, C–71–2270 RFP N.D. Cal. (1986).

Lau v. Nichols, 414 U.S. 563 (1974).

Lopez, E. C. (1997). The cognitive assessment of limited English proficient and bilingual children. In D. P. Flanagan, J. L. Genshaft, & P. L. Harrison (Eds.), *Contemporary intellectual assessment: Theories, tests, and issues* (pp. 503–516). New York: Guilford.

Martinez, M. A. (1985). Toward a bilingual school psychology model. *Educational Psychologist, 20*, 143–152.

Mercer, J. R., & Lewis, J. F. (1978). *System of multicultural pluralistic assessment.* New York: The Psychological Corporation.

Miranda, A. H., & Gutter, P. B. (2002). Diversity research literature in school psychology: 1990–1999. *Psychology in the Schools, 39*, 597–604.

Mirel, J. (2002). Civic education and changing definitions of American identity, 1900–1950. *Educational Review, 54*, 143–152.

Mowder, B. A. (1980). A strategy for the assessment of bilingual handicapped children. *Psychology in the Schools, 17*, 7–11.

NASP's Multicultural Affairs Committee. (n.d.). Retrieved March 24, 2004, from http://www.nasponline.org/culturalcompetence/committees.html

Novick, J. I. (1978). *Survey of minority and bilingual participation in school psychology training.* Unpublished paper, Southern Connecticut State College, New Haven, CT.

Oakland, T., & Laosa, L. M. (1977) Professional, legislative, and judicial influences on psychoeducational assessment practices in schools. In T. Oakland (Ed.), *Psychological and educational assessment of minority children* (pp. 21–51). New York: Brunner/Mazel.

Ochoa, S. H., Rivera, B., & Ford, L. (1997). An investigation of school psychology training pertaining to bilingual psycho-educational assessment of primarily Hispanic students: Twenty-five years after Diana v. California. *Journal of School Psychology, 35,* 329–349.

Olmedo, E. L. (1981). Testing linguistic minorities. *American Psychologist, 36,* 1078–1085.

Ortiz, C. C., & Ball, G. (1972). The Enchilada Test: Institute for Personal Effectiveness in Children. Unpublished manuscript.

Ortiz, S. O. (2002). Best practices in nondiscriminatory assessment. In A. Thomas & J. Grimes (Eds.), *Best practices in school psychology IV: Vol. 2.* (pp. 1321–1336). Bethesda, MD: National Association School Psychologists.

Ortiz, S. O., & Flanagan, D. P. (2002). Best practices in working with culturally diverse children and family. In A. Thomas & J. Grimes (Eds.), *Best practices in school psychology IV: Vol. 1* (pp. 337–352). Bethesda, MD: NASP.

Palmer, D. J., Hughes, J. N., & Juarez, L. (1991). School psychology training and the education of minority at-risk youth: The Texas A&M University program emphasis on handicapped Hispanic children and youth. *School Psychology Review, 20,* 472–484.

PASE (Parents in Action in Special Education) v. Hannon, 506 F. Supp. 831 (N.D. Ill. 1980).

Reschly, D. J. (1979). Nonbiased assessment. In G. D. Phye & D. J. Reschly (Eds.) *School psychology perspectives and issues* (pp. 215–253). New York: Academic Press.

Reschly, D. J., Kicklighter, R., & McKee, P. (1988a). Recent placement litigation, part I, regular education grouping: Comparison of *Marshall* (1984, 1985) and *Hobson* (1967, 1969). *School Psychology Review, 17,* 9–21.

Reschly, D. J., Kicklighter, R., & McKee, P. (1988b). Recent placement litigation part II, minority EMR overrepresentation: Comparison of *Larry P.* (1979, 1984, 1986) with *Marshall* (1984, 1985) and *S–1* (1986). *School Psychology Review, 17,* 22–38.

Reynolds, C. R., Gutkin, T. B., Elliott, S. N., & Witt, J. C. (1984). *School psychology essentials of theory and practice.* New York: Wiley & Sons.

Rhodes, R. I., Ochoa, S. H., & Ortiz, S. O. (2005). *Assessing culturally and linguistically diverse students: A practical guide.* New York, NY: Guilford

Rogers, M. R., Close Conoley, J., Ponterotto, J. G., & Wiese, M. J. (1992). Multicultural training in school psychology: A national survey. *School Psychology Review, 21,* 603–616.

Rogers, M. R., Hoffman, M. A., & Wade, J. (1998). Notable multicultural training in APA-approved counseling psychology and school psychology programs. *Cultural Diversity and Mental Health, 4,* 212–226.

Rogers, M. R., Ingraham, C. L., Bursztyn, A., Cajigas-Segredo, N., Esquivel, G. B., Hess, R., Nahari, S. G., & Lopez, E. C. (1999). Providing psychological services to racially, ethnically, culturally, and linguistically diverse individuals in the schools: Recommendations for practice. *School Psychology International, 20,* 243–264.

Rogers Wiese, M. R. (1992). Racial/ethnic minority research in school psychology. *Psychology in the Schools, 29,* 267–272.

Rosenfield, S., & Esquivel, G. B. (1985). Educating school psychologists to work with bilingual/bicultural populations. *Professional Psychology: Research and Practice, 16,* 199–208.

Schofield, J. W., & Hausmann, L. R. M. (2004). School desegregation and social science research. *American Psychologist, 59,* 538–546.

Snyder, T. D., Hoffman, C. M., & Geddes, C. M. (1997). *Digest of educational statistics 1997.* Washington, DC: U.S. Department of Education, Office of Educational Research and Improvement.

Stell v. Savannah Chatham Board of Education, 220 F. Supp. 667 (1963).

Thomas, W. B. (1986). Mental testing and tracking for the social adjustment of an urban underclass, 1920–1930. *Journal of Education, 168*, 9–30.

Thorndike, R. M. (1997). The early history of intelligence testing. In D. P. Flanagan, J. L. Genshaft, & P. L. Harrison (Eds.), *Contemporary intellectual assessment: Theories, tests, and issues* (pp. 3–16). New York: Guilford.

U.S. Bureau of the Census. (1998). *Population profile of the United States: 1997* (Current Population Reports, Series P23–194). Washington, DC: U.S. Government Printing Office.

Williams, R. (1972, September). *The BITCH–100: A culture specific test.* Paper presented at the 80th annual convention of the American Psychological Association, Honolulu, HI.

Young, B. A. (2002). *Public school student, staff, and graduate counts by state: School year 2000–01.* Washington, DC: National Center for Education Statistics.

Ysseldyke, J., Dawson, P., Lehr, C., Reschly, D., Reyolds, M., & Telzrow, C. (1997). *School psychology: A blueprint for training and practice II.* Bethesda, MD: National Association of School Psychologists.

Zins, J. E., & Halsell, A. (1986). Status of ethnic minority group members in school psychology training programs. *School Psychology Review, 15*, 76–83.

2

PROFESSIONAL STANDARDS, GUIDELINES, AND ETHICAL ISSUES WITHIN A MULTICULTURAL CONTEXT

Jonathan H. Sandoval

University of California, Davis

In many areas of psychology skilled professionals have endeavored to inform peers, novices, and the public about best practices in providing service to clients in general or to clients sharing a feature in common. These best practices are established by research and the accumulated wisdom of skilled professionals. An example is the recently approved the *Guidelines for Psychotherapy with Lesbian, Gay, and Bisexual Clients* (American Psychological Association [APA], 2000). Professional organizations also create statements about particular areas of practice such as educational and psychological testing. For example, the *Standards for Educational and Psychological Testing,* developed by the American Educational Research Association (AERA), American Psychological Association (APA), and the National Council on Measurement in Education (NCME), have been revised over the years and have shaped the practice of assessment in school psychology. In addition, most professional associations of psychologists take the time to develop codes of ethics for their members. In school psychology, national organizations such as APA, the National Association of School Psychologists (NASP), and many State Associations (e.g. California Association of School Psychologists) have developed both statements about ethics, and about best practices.

Most statements generated by professional organizations in psychology have concerns about working in a multicultural context, and the APA has produced sets of guidelines explicitly directed at working with individuals cross-culturally (APA, 1990, 2003). Professional associations in other countries are also concerned about ethics and best practices with different cultural groups within their populations, e.g. Sociedad Mexicana de Psicologia (2002).

This chapter will examine the standards, guidelines and issues identified so far with respect to school psychology within a multicultural context. The first section will look at general issues that arise in our work as school psychologists. The following sections will examine issues related to assessment, counseling and intervention, consultation, and research. The first task, however, is to clarify the terms *standards* and *guidelines*.

The terms "standards" and "guidelines" are often used interchangeably or inconsistently in statements about ethical behavior, best practices with clients or the content of education and training. The National Center for Education Statistics (2001), has defined a "standard" as *something established for use as a rule or basis of comparison in measuring or judging capacity, quantity, content, extent, value, quality, etc.* (p. 3). Standards in psychology are summary descriptions regarding what it is that practitioners should know and/or be able to do (Kendall, 2001). Standards may be concrete, or they may reference a quality or set of qualities expected of psychologists and thus be abstract. When issued by regulatory organizations, the term "standard" is typically interpreted to describe a minimal or threshold requirement. Standards are typically seen as mandatory and may be accompanied by guidelines that provide interpretive clarification about how they might be met or about how their achievement is to be assessed. Standards often have enforcement mechanisms, either through the courts, accrediting bodies, or the ethics committees of professional associations. For example, documents such as the *Standards for Educational and Psychological Testing* (AERA, APA, NCME, 1999) have been used in deciding court cases and may be used to establish malpractice. The intent of standards is to facilitate the continued systematic development of the profession and to help assure a high level of professional practice in order to protect the public.

In contrast, guidelines are often viewed as suggestions or recommendations, which are advisory or aspirational. The APA defines guidelines as pronouncements, statements, or declarations that suggest or recommend specific professional behavior, endeavors, or conduct for psychologists (APA, 2001). Guidelines are not intended to be exhaustive or mandatory and are not intended to take precedence over professional judgment.

The distinction between standards and guidelines is not clear-cut. Many principles identified as standards may be aspirational, and many guidelines may be viewed as mandatory. In this chapter there will be an attempt to maintain a distinction, however, by using the strict definition of terms, i.e. standards as mandatory.

In addition, groups and individuals also publish documents outlining what are termed *best practices*. The NASP has published several volumes with this title, for example (Miranda, 2002; Ortiz, 2002; Paredes, 2002). The contents of chapter or articles on best practice are typically considered to be advisory and the opinion of the authors. Ideally they are research-based reviews of empirically validated professional practices, but the advice offered in such works often is based on the authors' judgments and observations, particularly in areas that have not been widely researched. Statements of best practices do not have the status of guidelines or standards, but can be helpful in molding practice.

GENERAL ETHICAL ISSUES

The APA (2002a) has recently adopted a set of ethical principles of psychologists and code of ethics. It begins with a set of five guidelines it terms general principles. The five principles are (a) Beneficence and Nonmaleficence, (b) Fidelity and responsibility, (c) Integrity, (d) Justice, and (e) Respect for People's Rights and Dignity. These principles all articulate ideals with strong implications for work with multicultural populations. However, the last two are particularly relevant.

General Principle of Justice

APA's principle of Justice states

"Psychologists recognize that fairness and justice entitle all persons to access to and benefit from the contributions of psychology and to equal quality in the processes, procedures, and services being conducted by psychologists. Psychologists exercise reasonable judgment and take precautions to ensure that their potential biases, the boundaries of their competence, and the limitations of their expertise do not lead to or condone unjust practice." (APA, 2002a, p. 1062–1063)

This principle implies that school psychologist must recognize that they must work to serve all of the children and families in the schools they serve, but also recognize their own limitations. If a psychologist is hampered by biases, or is not competent to work with a population, he or she must strive to find ways that members of this population receive appropriate services. In essence it is recommending that psychologist increase their level of competence to include serving multicultural populations, or at least increasing awareness of one's own limitations of knowledge and skill. This guideline or principle is aspirational in recognition of the difficulty of avoiding bias in human decision-making.

General Principle of Respect for People's Rights and Dignity

This principle states

"Psychologists respect the dignity and worth of all people, and the rights of individuals to privacy, confidentiality, and self-determination. Psychologists are aware that special safeguards may be necessary to protect the rights and welfare of persons or communities whose vulnerabilities impair autonomous decision making. Psychologists are aware of and respect cultural, individual, and role differences, including those based on age, gender, gender identity, race, ethnicity, culture, national origin, religion, sexual orientation, disability, language, and socioeconomic status and consider these factors when working with members of such groups. Psychologists try to eliminate the effect on their work of biases based on those factors, and they do not knowingly participate in or condone activities of others based upon such prejudices" (APA, 2002a, p. 1063).

In addition to charging psychologist to be aware of and to respect cultural, individual and role differences, this principle suggests that psychologists become advocates for individuals from historically discriminated against groups, and work to protect their rights and welfare. School psychologists should not practice discrimination, nor should they tolerate it in others with whom they work (see also NASP, 2000a, p. 21).

Members of NASP (2000a) are subject to ethical principles. Two underlying assumptions serve as the foundation for this code of conduct, that "school psychologists will act as advocates for their students/clients" and "at the very least, school psychologists will do no harm" (NASP, p. 12). An earlier version of the NASP statement of professional ethics (1985) spoke specifically of "the uncertainties associated with delivery of psychological services in a situation where rights of the student, the parent, the school and society may conflict" (NASP, 1985, p. 2). The 2000 document referred to the necessity of school psychologists to 'speak up' for the needs and rights of their students/clients even at times when it may be difficult to do so ... Given one's employment situation and the array of recommendations, events may develop in which the ethical course of action is unclear" (NASP, 2000a, p. 12). In contrast to the APA's Ethics Code, the most recent NASP document, although not as explicit as its predecessor document, is sensitive to the fact that school psychologists most frequently function within an organizational setting, where the primary mission is not that of providing psychological services. This status means that school psychologists must be aware of institutionalized practices as well as individual practices based on a different mission that may be discriminatory.

The NASP *Professional Conduct Manual for School Psychology* similarly identifies respect as a central value: "School psychologists respect all persons and are sensitive to physical, mental, emotional, political, economic, social, cultural, ethnic and racial characteristics, gender sexual orientation and religion" (Sec. III A 2, NASP, 2000a, p. 17).

Ethics codes are not without their critics, who view them as originating from a dominant cultural perspective, and oversimplifying complex issues (Ridley, Liddle, Hill, & Li, 2001). In an excellent article on ethical decision-making, Ridley and his colleagues argue that responsible ethical decision making requires practitioners to consider a client's cultural context as part of the problem space. Ridley et al. posit a more complex model and list eight steps in ethical decision making in the face of a cultural conflict:

1. Practice flexible representation of ethical concerns in multicultural situations.
2. Discern whether an ethical problem exists.
3. Make ethical perspectives explicit.

4. Solicit suggestions from others about what to do.
5. Explicate implicit assumptions about culture.
6. Brainstorm with the client and associated professionals about how concerns about the ethical problem arose.
7. Once the genesis of the cultural conflict has been explored, brainstorm about possible solutions.
8. Analyze the goodness-of-fit of each potential solution based on whether it is ethically valid, pragmatically feasible, and commensurate with treatment goals.

The implementation of ethical and professional standards requires sensitivity, complex thinking, and broad background knowledge. The eight step model implies that practitioners must reflect on their experiences in multicultural contexts, must be open and willing to consult with others before acting, and must balance many factors in making decisions to help clients.

ISSUES RELATED TO ASSESSMENT

The APA and the NASP, the two largest national associations with members who assess children, have each developed ethical standards for professional conduct that are binding on their members and contain sections relative to assessment goals and activities (APA, 2002a; NASP, 2000a). In addition, *Standards for Educational and Psychological Testing* have been developed jointly by three national professional organizations to speak to issues around assessment (AERA, APA, & NCME, 1999). Each of these documents has undergone revision in recent years, and future revisions are anticipated as knowledge and professional practice values change.

The APA Office of Ethnic Minority Affairs published an early set of guidelines with specific direction for persons involved in the psychological assessment of children in 1991. These guidelines for providers of psychological services to ethnic, linguistic, and culturally diverse populations include advice on assessment. Other guideline documents include *Specialty Guidelines for the Delivery of Services by School Psychologists* (APA, 1981) and *Standards for the Provision of School Psychological Services* (NASP, 1985), documents setting forth guidelines for the provision of school psychological services, including assessment activities. *Guidelines for Computer Based Tests and Interpretations* (APA, 1987) also were developed to give specific direction in response to the increasing usage of technology in various aspects of the assessment process. In addition, APA also has adopted a set of *Guidelines for Test User Qualifications* (Turner, DeMers, Fox, & Reed, 2001). Although there are some differences in the specificity contained within the multiple guidelines, there is much commonality with the respect to the need to attend to multicultural issues.

The Standards for Educational and Psychological Testing perhaps provide the greatest degree of specificity regarding the comprehensive nature of the assessment effort in a multicultural context and contains ideas, that overlap with the other documents. Although the focus is on "tests," they are defined broadly enough to encompass a variety of assessment techniques and methodologies. As standards, they are more likely to be used to define proper practice when disputes arise.

Test Selection and Usage

A basic principle articulated by the *Standards for Educational and Psychological Testing* and elsewhere is that the selection of assessment techniques and rationale for interpretation for any given evaluation should reflect appropriate understanding of differences in age, gender, socioeconomic status, sexual orientation, and cultural and ethnic backgrounds (APA, 1992; NASP, 2000a) as well as differences in religion, race, gender identity, national origin, disability, and language (APA, 2002a). Test selection and use should be based on these understandings. These understanding are necessarily quite complex because all of these factors may interact in a particular individual. For example, an immigrant from South-East Asia may be from one of several religious traditions, from various ethnicities, and may have a disability. One approach does not fit all with the same national origin.

The implication here is that school psychologists are obliged to be knowledgeable about assessment techniques and specific tests whose validity, reliability, and measurement equivalence have been studied across culturally diverse populations. It is particularly important to establish that the constructs assessed by instruments they use have the same meaning and function across cultures before using them (Rogler, 1999). School psychologists must avoid tests that have not been adapted for the group to which the child belongs if at all possible. When no adapted or developed tests exist suitable for a child from a particular culture and not acculturated to the dominant culture, the psychologist must proceed with caution and rely on other sources of information.

The new ethics code focuses on psychologists' use of assessment methods in a manner appropriate to an individual's language preference and competence, and cultural background. It is explicit about testing in the language preferred by the client. Section 9.02 states, "Psychologists use assessment methods that are appropriate to an individual's language preference and competence unless the use of an alternative language is relevant to the assessment issues." It is not clear how assessment in English for the purposes of establishing school performance in English is appropriate. Testing a non-fluent English-speaking child in English or their home language depends on the inference being made about the results. If the inference is about current functioning, it is one thing; if the inference is about aptitude, it is another. It must be acknowledged that appropriate tests for some diverse populations may never be developed. In such instances modifications in administration and interpretation procedures may be utilized if these modifications "are appropriate in light of the research on or evidence of the usefulness and proper application of the technique" (APA, 2002a, p. 1071). School psychologists need to be knowledgeable not only about the linguistic equivalence of the instrument (e.g., that it is appropriately translated into the target language), but also the conceptual and functional equivalence of the constructs tested.

Validity for population.   The APA ethics code states "Psychologists use assessment instruments whose validity and reliability have been established for use with members of the population tested. When such validity or reliability has not been established, psychologists describe the strengths and limitations of test results and interpretation (9.02 (b), APA, 2002a, p. 1071). Clearly there are many populations for whom particular tests have not been validated, so caution often is warranted.

Use of interpreters.   The APA ethics code Section 9.03 (c) reads, "Psychologists using the services of an interpreter obtain informed consent from the client/patient to use that interpreter, ensure that confidentiality of test results and test security are maintained, and include in their recommendations, reports, and diagnostic or evaluative statements, including forensic testimony, discussion of any limitations on the data obtained" (APA, 2002a, p. 5). The practice of using interpreters, in some sense, amounts to delegation of work to others. The code goes on to state, "Psychologists who use the services of others, such as interpreters, take reasonable steps to (1) avoid delegating such work to persons who have a multiple relationship with those being serve that would likely lead to exploitation or loss of objectivity; (2) authorize only those responsibilities that such persons can be expected to perform competently on the basis of their education, training, or experience, either independently or with the level of supervision being provide, and (3) see that such persons perform these services competently." This standard implies that school psychologists must select interpreters carefully. When using family members, for example to translate, one is likely to find that the interpreter, because of multiple relationships, is not objective. The practice of using children to translate to parents should be avoided when possible, for this reason. This provision also suggests that interpreters must be trained and carefully supervised, prior to acting on behalf of the school psychologist. Lopez (2002) has commented on best practices for working with interpreters.

Validity and Nonbiased Assessment

The *Standards for Educational and Psychological Testing* (AERA, APA, & NCME, 1999) is most explicit in regard to nonbiased assessment. These standards include not only those related to the assessment of persons from racial/ethnic minority groups and of lower socioeconomic status, but specific attention is also called to the particular needs of persons in linguistic minority groups and persons who have handicapping conditions. Clients are to be tested in their dominant language or an alternative communication system, as required; modifications of the conditions under which the test is administered should be considered for handicapped persons.

Yet there remain many unanswered, even un-researched questions about the effect of such non-standardized accommodations upon the ability to use such test data. Does the test still measure that which was intended by the test developer (i.e., has the validity of the instrument been altered)? Because the ethical standards do not provide case-specific answers to many of the questions that will confront the ethically sensitive psychologist regarding the use of a given instrument in a specific situation, caution is advised when tests are administered to persons whose particular linguistic or handicapping condition is not represented in the standardized sample.

The APA ethics code (9.05; APA, 2002a) explicitly states that test developers have an obligation to use procedures to reduce or eliminate bias in their tests. Although the various standards provide cautions to the practicing psychologist about the need to use instruments in assessment that are culture-fair, Ysseldyke and Algozzine (1982) reviewed the literature and concluded that there is little agreement among the experts as to the definition of a "fair test." They went on to cite Peterson and Novick's belief that some of the models are in themselves internally contradictory. These issues raised over twenty years ago have still not been adequately addressed. Typically test developers have members of ethnic and cultural groups, acting as cultural informants, review test items and formats for sensitivity. They are asked to determine if item content has unanticipated connotations for different groups, or seems otherwise unfair. Following this armchair analysis, using data from pilot tests and the standardization sample, test developers use various statistical procedures for identifying and eliminating items that perform differentially for particular groups. Reynolds (2003) has reviewed methods of identifying bias in psychological tests.

In spite of the ambiguity about the identification of "fair" tests, school psychologists need to be aware of non-biased assessment techniques (Ortiz, 2002). In many cases alternatives to traditional approaches may be appropriate, such as curriculum based measurement and test-teach-test protocols. The problem of non-biased assessment is particularly acute when the child is and English language learner and a recent immigrant. Other chapters in this volume elaborate on the topic of non-biased assessment as well as other issues raised in this chapter.

Competence of Examiner

The Individuals with a Disability Education Act (IDEA) requires that a multidisciplinary team be used in the assessment process when educational decisions are to be made for children entitled to public educational services, but only persons professionally trained are to use assessment techniques (APA, 1981). If the assessment need is outside the scope of the psychologist's training, the psychologist is to refer the client to another professional who is competent to provide the needed service. The various ethical standards also require that the professional psychologist keep current in the use of professional skills, including those involved in assessment. The implication from these sources is that psychologists should continually seek professional development as demographics of clients and developments in assessment evolve.

ISSUES RELATED TO COUNSELING AND INTERVENTION

APA's Guideline #5 of the *Guidelines on Multicultural Education, Training, Research, Practice and Organizational Change for Psychologists* reads: "Psychologists strive to apply culturally-appropriate skills in clinical and other applied psychological-centered practices." The authors go on to state, "… culturally appropriate psychological applications assume awareness and knowledge about one's worldview as a cultural being and as a professional psychologist, and the worldview of others' particularly as influenced by ethnic/racial heritage. …It is not necessary to develop an entirely new repertoire of psychological skills to practice in a culture-centered manner. Rather, it is helpful for psychologists to realize that there will likely be situations where culture-centered adaptations in interventions and practices will be more effective" (APA, 2003, p. 45).

Counseling is generally considered a common intervention practiced by school psychologists. However, standards specifically directed at multicultural counseling have not been developed by the professional organizations. Nevertheless, handbooks exist which discuss the issues involved in counseling across cultures, (Pedersen & Carey, 2003; Ponterotto, Casas, Suzuki, & Alexander, 2001). Typically psychologists counseling children from cultural backgrounds different from their own are advised to develop skills and practices attuned to the unique worldview and cultural perspective of the child. They are encouraged to learn about helping practices used in non-Western cultures. This may result in asking for assistance from community leaders or influential individuals such traditional healers to assist with the process. Traditional counseling approaches, such as cognitive-behavioral or Adlerian counseling may not be appropriate cross-culturally, as they may rely on verbal interaction and may stress individual accountability and de-emphasize collective responsibility. It will also be important to respect the language preferences of the client and the client's parents, to consider acculturation status, and to obtain informed consent for counseling or other interventions in the home language, making sure the parents comprehend what will occur.

APA's Division of Counseling Psychology has had a long interest in developing standards, guidelines and competency statements about preparation for multicultural counseling (Sue et al., 1982). They have proposed a three stage developmental sequence for counselors starting with awareness of self, particularly the attitudes, opinions and values held that might contrast with alternative viewpoints held by counselees and their families. The second stage involves accumulating cultural knowledge. The effective counselor must be able to acquire facts and understandings about other cultures. In the final stage, the counselor needs specific skills in planning, conducting and evaluating multicultural counseling interventions.

The above guidelines and competency statements have been developed generally for work with children, youth and adults, and have not been formulated for the types of counseling and interventions conducted by school psychologists. A set of possibly more relevant recommendations were developed by the Taskforce on Cross-Cultural School Psychology Competencies of the APA Division of School Psychology (Rogers et al., 1999). The taskforce pointed out that the racial, ethnic, cultural and linguistic characteristics of children and families may increase the risk of inadequate interventions, and that school psychologists must determine whether problems presumed to reside within the students, may result from institutional biases in the school.

In addressing counseling, the Division 16 Taskforce also identified the importance of considering, "the involvement of trained bilingual interpreters, community consultants, extended family members and other paraprofessionals as resources in counseling intervention" (p. 254). They identified the need for knowledge about racial and ethnic identify development in children, minority family structures, relocation and migration processes, the acculturation process, the impact of poverty, and differential responses to medical intervention. Although competencies were identified by the Taskforce, these have not been codified as guidelines at this point.

Crisis Intervention

NASP's Practice Guideline 7 states, "School psychologists shall appropriately utilize prevention, health promotion, and crisis intervention methods based on knowledge of child development, psychopathology, diversity, social stressors, change and systems." (p. 48). Crisis intervention is yet another area where school psychologists must consider diversity. A recently published volume, *Best Practices in School Crisis Prevention and Intervention* (Brock, Lazarus, & Jimerson, 2002), contains a chapter on cultural consideration in crisis counseling (Sandoval & Lewis, 2002). Sandoval and Lewis discuss the use of language and verbal communication, nonverbal communication, religious concepts, and other cultural factors in assisting children and families who are culturally different from the mainstream. They suggest five steps in culturally sensitive crisis intervention: (a) examine the fit of the individual and cultural norms, (b) consider culturally relevant external resources, (c) determine the capacity of the student and family to use the resources, (d) focus on communication, and (e) make appropriate referrals. Of these steps, the use of community leaders and the capacity of the family to support resilience are particularly important.

Programmatic Intervention

NASP Practice Guideline 5, 5.1 "School psychologists develop academic and behavioral interventions. They recognize that interventions most likely to succeed are those which are adapted to the individual needs and characteristics of the student(s) for whom they are being designed" (NASP, 2000a, p. 46). The Division 16 Taskforce noted, "Psychologists implement culturally sensitive approaches that are acceptable to and have demonstrated effectiveness with culturally divers children and their families…They avoid using techniques that are inconsistent with the cultural-personal values or preferred styles of the student. They attempt to incorporate cultural customs such as folk methods into intervention design" (Rogers et al., 1999, p. 254). Working in schools does present a problem in that interventions must be both legal and acceptable to the broad school community, and must be economically feasible. As a result, the school psychologist must be aware of the constraints operating in a school, and at the same time be "an advocate for public policy and educational law that best serves the needs of racially, ethnically, culturally and linguistically diverse youth" (Rogers et al., 1999, p. 246–247). In many states, issues around delivering instruction in a language other than English, may have both political and legal ramifications. In California, for example, severe limits have been placed on bilingual education through the initiative process.

ISSUES RELATED TO CONSULTATION

Using a Delphi technique, Lopez and Rogers (2001) identified 89 essential competencies for school psychologists, as judged by expert panelists. In the area of consultation, 4 were highlighted: (a) Skill in working with others (e.g., patience, good judgment); (b) Skill in demonstrating sensitivity toward the culture of school personnel involved in consultation, (c) Skill in responding flexibility with a range of possible solutions that reflect sensitivity to cross-cultural issues, and (d) Knowledge of the culturally related factors that may affect accurate assessment of the "problem" in the problem-solving sequence.

Further, after surveying a *School Psychology Review* special issue on multicultural consultation (NASP, 2000b), Rogers (2000) noted unanimity across the authors of the volume with respect to cross-cultural consultation competencies. Consultants need to understand one's own and other's culture, develop cross-cultural communication and interpersonal skills, examine the cultural embeddedness of consultation, and acquire culture-specific knowledge (e.g. regarding acculturation, immigration, and understanding and skill in work with interpreters). This set of competencies might be translated into a set of guidelines, assuming they are cross-validated by research.

Another phenomenon noted by two of the authors (Ingraham, 2000; Sheridan, 2000) of the special issue on multicultural consultation was that explicit acknowledgement of race and racial issues is important. A "color blind" approach is not effective, at the same time diversity within cultural and racial groups also must be acknowledged, and culture can be over-emphasized. In general, it seems best to match consultation methods to the consultee's style, whether that style is culturally based or not.

ISSUES RELATED TO RESEARCH AND EVALUATION

School psychologists increasingly engage in research and evaluation efforts in the schools. Guideline #4 of the *Guidelines on Multicultural Education, Training, Research, Practice and Organizational Change for Psychologists* declares, "Culturally sensitive psychological researchers are encouraged to recognize the importance of conducting culture-centered and ethical psychological research among persons from ethnic, linguistic, and racial minority backgrounds" (APA, 2003, p. 38). The Division of School psychology Taskforce offered three important notions: (a) consider the social, linguistic and cultural context in which research takes place; (b) insure that informed consent of all research participants is secured and has been elicited in the language the family is most comfortable with; and (c) work to determine the appropriateness and adequacy of instructional programs specifically aimed at racially, ethnically, culturally and linguistically diverse youngsters (Rogers et al., 1999).

One simple strategy in research and evaluation is the dis-aggregation of results by cultural group. In research, one can look for main effects or interactions with ethnicity, and in evaluation one can search for the differential effectiveness of programs for different populations. Too often research results from an atypical group, such as college males, have been generalized as applying universally. Interventions may prove to be of value if they increase the functioning of a particular minority group, but do not disadvantage the majority. If the results for a subgroup are not examined, the larger numbers of the entire group may mask them. With the emphasis on empirically validated interventions in schools, it will be important to ask, "validated for whom?"

ISSUES RELATED TO EDUCATION AND TRAINING

Several of APA's ethical standards and guidelines (2002a) have relevance to the pre-service and continuing education of school psychologists. Section 2.01 (a) reads, "psychologists provide services, teach and conduct research with populations and in areas only within the boundaries of their competence." Next section 2.01(b) states, "Where scientific or professional knowledge in the discipline of psychology established that an understanding of factors associated with age, gender, gender identity, race, ethnicity, culture, national origin, religion, sexual orientation, disability, language, or socioeconomic status is essential for effective implementation of their services or research, psychologists have or obtain the training experience, consultation, or supervision necessary to ensure the competence of their service or they make appropriate referrals...." Acquiring and maintaining competence implies that experience gained in graduate training has created a knowledge and skill base related to multicultural issues that may be built upon throughout a professional lifetime.

Likely as a result of the civil rights movement of the 1960s, the first reference to the need to attend to culture in clinical practice emerged at the Vail conference of 1973 (Korman, 1974). Conference participants urged that training in cultural diversity be included in all psychology preparation programs and provided to practitioners through continuing education. The APA Committee on Accreditation listed cultural diversity as a component of effective training first in 1986 and more recently in the 2002 guidelines (APA, 2002b). In addition, Guideline #3 of the *Guidelines on Multicultural Education, Training, Research, Practice and Organizational Change for Psychologists* states, "As educators psychologists are encouraged to employ the constructs of multiculturalism and diversity in psychological education" (APA, 2003, p. 31).

The National Council of Schools and Programs of Professional Psychology defines a diversity competence in the context of preparing professional psychologists. The following is posted on its website:

> Diversity refers to an affirmation of the richness of human differences, ideas, and beliefs. An inclusive definition of diversity includes but is not limited to age, color, dis-

ability and health, ethnicity, gender, language, national origin, race, religion / spirituality, sexual orientation, and social economic status, as well as the intersection of these multiple identities and multiple statuses. Exploration of power differentials, power dynamics, and privilege is at the core of understanding diversity issues and their impact on social structures and institutionalized forms of discrimination.

Training of psychologists should include opportunities to develop understanding, respect and value for cultural and individual differences. A strong commitment to the development of knowledge, skills, and attitudes that support high regard for human diversity should be integrated throughout the professional psychology training program and its organizational culture.

Competence in diversity issues may be best accomplished with a multifaceted approach, including integration throughout the curriculum, as well as through specific required coursework and experiences. Students and faculty benefit from exposure to the knowledge base, theories, and research findings that serve as a foundation to guide their understanding and skill development, utilizing this knowledge to critically analyze all aspects of practice. Attention to social and cultural values influencing the profession, as well as development of awareness of individual differences and values within the practitioner, are themes to be interwoven across the training of professional psychologists. Students benefit from the opportunity to explore integration and adaptation of models necessary for work with diverse, marginalized or underserved populations.

Students should have varied opportunities for acquiring knowledge and skills as well as understanding the professional values and attitudes that reflect social responsibility, social justice, and respect for human diversity. These experiences may include among others: classroom learning, programmatic activities, practicum experiences, supervision, and internship training. It is expected that this competency is integrated across all aspects of education and training and forms an integral part of each student's professional development and identity.

Increasingly textbooks and other materials have been developed for use in undergraduate courses on multicultural awareness. In addition workshops presented at national and state conventions often are available for continuing education.

Education and training does not cease upon entry into the profession of school psychology. Continuing education is an expectation. The APA code of ethics contains section 2.03 Maintaining Competence: "Psychologists undertake ongoing efforts to develop and maintain their competence" (APA, 2002a p. 1060) Similarly NASP section II A. 1, and NASP section II A 4 speak to the need and expectation for continuing professional education (NASP, 2000a).

IMPLICATIONS FOR FUTURE RESEARCH AND DEVELOPMENT

The fact that there are few guidelines related to intervention, counseling, and consultation in school psychology is a reflection on the fact that multicultural practice in these area (in contrast to assessment) has not been researched thoroughly nor subject to the same level of scrutiny by the courts and others. However, research on multicultural issues is increasing as witnessed by the contents of this volume. As the multicultural research base in intervention and consultation develops, it will become more possible to identify standards and guidelines for practice and training.

One important area for research will be on ethical decision making in school psychologists. What level of awareness is there among practitioners of how ethical issues may arise in cross-cultural work, and how do they seek to resolve those issues that they identify?

Once research has identified issues of importance in working in a multicultural context, these finding will need to be translated into competencies for school psychologists. In turn, the competencies will be operationalized into valid and reliable measurement tools. If multicultural competencies may be measured and assessed, they may be used in accrediting training programs for school psychologists, and in regulating entry into practice. When this process is complete, we would hope to see fewer inappropriate referrals for service, fewer mis-assessments of children's needs, fewer ineffective interventions in multicultural settings, and better education and training of school psychologists to work in all settings.

ANNOTATED BIBLIOGRAPHY

American Educational Research Association, American Psychological Association, National Council on Measurement in Education. (1999). *Standards for educational and psychological testing.* Washington, DC: American Educational Research Association.

These standards, authored by a committee drawn from the three organizations, represent the current consensus about best practice in test development and test use. The standards have been reexamined and up-dated every decade. The chapter on fairness in testing is particularly important.

American Psychological Association (2002a). Ethical principles of psychologists and code of conduct. *American Psychologist, 57,* 1060–1073.

This document represents the best thinking of psychologists on how they should conduct themselves in research and practice. Several important references to multicultural issues are contained throughout.

American Psychological Association (2003). Guidelines on multicultural education, training, research, practice, and organizational change for psychologists. *American Psychologist, 58,* 377–402.

This recent statement from a joint Taskforce of APA's Division 17 (Counseling Psychology) and 45 (Psychological Study of Ethnic Minority Issues) "provides psychologists with (a) the rationale and needs for addressing multiculturalism and diversity in education, training, research, practice and organizational change; (b) basic information, relevant terminology, current empirical research from psychology and related disciplines, and other data to support the proposed guidelines and underscore their importance; (c) references to enhance on-going education, training, research, practice, and organizational change methodologies; and d) paradigms that broaden the purview of psychology as a profession."

National Association of School Psychologists (2000). *Professional conduct manual principles for professional ethics: Guidelines for the provision of school psychological services*. Bethesda, MD: Author.

Explicitly prepared for school psychologists, this set of guidelines addresses issues faced in a variety of roles in multicultural settings and in majority cultural contexts. Attention to multicultural issues is given throughout the document. This document is or should be required reading in the pre-service education of school psychologists.

Ridley, C. R, Liddle, M. C., Hill, C. L., & Li, L. C. (2001). Ethical decision making in multicultural counseling. In J. G. Ponterotto, J. M. Casas, L. A. Suzuki, & C. M. Alexander (Eds.), *Handbook of multicultural counseling*. (2nd ed., pp. 165–188). Thousand Oaks, CA: Sage.

This chapter in an important handbook is a model for translating ethical knowledge into ethically appropriate multicultural counseling practice. The authors discuss a superordinate ethical principle of multicultural counseling. Four ethical standards are highlighted as the basic units of ethical knowledge to be applied to multicultural practice. Finally a set of guidelines is offered to help clinicians conduct reasoned application of the ethical standards to the activities of multicultural counseling. The emphasis is the need to think systematically about ethical dilemmas in multicultural settings.

RESOURCES

American Psychological Association Ethics pages:
http://www.apa.org/ethics/

The website for the American Psychological Association includes the new ethics code adopted by the APA Council of Representatives, effective June 1, 2003. The website provides the following titles: "Ethical Principles of Psychologists and Code of Conduct," "APA Ethics Committee Rules and Procedures," "Statement by the Ethics Committee on Services by Telephone, Teleconferencing, and Internet," "Guidelines for Ethical Conduct in the Care and Use of Animals," and "Research with Animals in Psychology."

The American Psychological Association Pages on Ethnic Minority Affairs Guidelines:
http://www.apa.org/pi/oema/

The website for the American Psychological Association provides requests for grant proposals for ProDIGs, Promoting Psychological Research and Training on Health Disparities Issues at Ethnic Minority Serving Institutions, and the following publications, "APA Guidelines on Multicultural Education," Training, Research, Practice, and Organizational Change Psychologists," and, "Toward an Inclusive Psychology: Infusing the Introductory Psychology Textbook with Diversity Content."

National Association of School Psychologists Position papers:
http://www.nasponline.org/information/position_paper.html

The website for the National Association of School Psychologists provides position papers and fact sheets on a variety of topics of interests to professionals, consumers and advocates.

REFERENCES

American Educational Research Association, American Psychological Association, & National Council on Measurement in Education. (1999). *Standards for educational and psychological testing.* Washington, DC: American Educational Research Association.

American Psychological Association. (1981). *Specialty guidelines for the delivery of services by school psychologists.* Washington, DC: Author.

American Psychological Association. (1987). *General Guidelines for providers of psychological services.* Washington, DC: Author.

American Psychological Association. (1990). *Guidelines for providers of psychological services to ethnic, linguistic, and culturally diverse populations.* Washington, DC: Author.

American Psychological Association. (1992). Ethical principles and code of conduct. *American Psychologist, 48,* 1597–1611.

American Psychological Association. (2000). Professional Practice guidelines for psychotherapy with lesbian, gay and bisexual clients. *American Psychologist, 55,* 1440–1451.

American Psychological Association. (2001). *Criteria for practice guideline development and evaluation.* Washington, DC: Author.

American Psychological Association. (2002a). Ethical principles of psychologists and code of conduct. *American Psychologist, 57,* 1060–1073.

American Psychological Association. (2002b). *Guidelines and principles for accreditation.* Washington, DC: Author.

American Psychological Association. (2003). Guidelines on multicultural education, training, research, practice, and organizational change for psychologists. *American Psychologist, 58,* 377–402.

Brock, S. E., Lazarus, P. J., & Jimerson, S. R. (2002). Best practices in school crisis prevention and intervention. Bethesda, MD: NASP.

Ingraham, C. L. (2000). Consultation through a multicultural lens: Multicultural and cross cultural consultation in schools. *School Psychology Review, 29,* 320–343.

Kendall, J. S. (2001). *A technical guide for revising or developing standards and benchmarks.* Aurora, CO: Mid-Continent Research for Education and Learning (McREL).

Korman, M. (1974). National conference on levels and patterns of professional training in psychology. *American Psychologist, 29,* 441–449.

Lopez, E. C. (2002). Recommended practices in working with school interpreters to deliver psychological services to children and families. In A. Thomas & J. Grimes (Eds.), *Best Practices in School Psychology IV,* (pp. 1419–1432). Washington, DC: NASP.

Lopez, E. C., & Rogers, M. R. (2001). Conceptualizing cross-cultural school psychology competencies. *School Psychology Quarterly, 16,* 270–302.

Miranda, A. H. (2002). Best practices in increasing cross-cultural competence. In A. Thomas & J. Grimes (Eds.), *Best Practices in School Psychology IV,* (pp. 353–362). Washington, DC: NASP.

National Association of School Psychologists. (1985). *Standards for the provision of school psychology services.* Bethesda, MD: Author.

National Association of School Psychologists. (2000a). *Professional conduct manual: principles for professional ethics: Guidelines for the provision of school psychological services.* Bethesda, MD: Author.

National Association of School Psychologists. (2000b). Mini-Series—Multicultural and cross-cultural consultation in schools—Introduction to multicultural and cross-cultural consultation in schools: Cultural diversity issues in school consultation. *School Psychology Review, 29,* 313–428.

National Center for Education Statistics. (2001). *Staff Data Handbook*. Washington, DC: U.S. Department of Education.

Ortiz, S. O. (2002). Best practices in nondiscriminatory assessment. In A. Thomas & J. Grimes (Eds.), *Best practices in school psychology IV* (pp. 1321–1336). Washington, DC: NASP.

Ortiz, S. O., & Flanagan, D. P. (2002). Best Practices in Working With Culturally Diverse Children and Families. In A. Thomas & J. Grimes (Eds.), *Best practices in school psychology IV*, (pp. 337–351). Washington, DC: NASP.

Paredes, A. (2002). Best assessment and intervention practices with second language learners. In A. Thomas & J. Grimes (Eds.), *Best practices in school psychology IV*, (pp. 1485–1499). Washington, DC: NASP.

Ponterotto, J. G., Casas, J. M., Suzuki, L. A., & Alexander, C. M. (Eds.). (2001). *Handbook of multicultural counseling* (2nd ed.). Thousand Oaks, CA: Sage.

Ridley, C. R., Liddle, M. C., Hill, C. L., & Li, L. C. (2001). Ethical decision making in multicultural counseling. In J. G. Ponterotto, J. M. Casas, L. A. Suzuki, & C. M. Alexander (Eds.), *Handbook of multicultural counseling* (2nd ed., pp. 165–188).Thousand Oaks, CA: Sage.

Rogers, M. R. (2000). Examining the cultural context of consultation. *School Psychology Review, 29*, 414–418.

Rogers, M. R., Ingraham, C. L., Bursztyn, A., Cajigas-Segredo, N., Esquivel, G., Hess, R., et al. (1999). Best practices in providing psychological services to racially, ethnically, culturally, and linguistically diverse individuals in the schools. *School Psychology International, 20*, 243–264.

Rogler, L. H. (1999). Methodological sources of cultural insensitivity in mental health research. *American Psychologist, 54*, 424–433.

Sandoval, J., & Lewis, S. (2002). Cultural considerations in crisis intervention. In S. E. Brock, P. J. Lazarus, & S. R. Jimerson, *Best practices in school crisis prevention and intervention* (pp. 293–308). Bethesda, MD: NASP

Sheridan, S. M. (2000). Considerations of multiculturalism and diversity in behavioral consultation with parents and teachers. *School Psychology Review, 29*, 344–353.

Sociedad Mexicana de Psicologia. (2002). *Código Ético del Psicólogo* [Psychologist's ethical code]. Mexico, D. F.: Trillas

Sue, D. W., Bernier, J. E., Durran, A., Feinberg, L., Pedersen, P., Smith, C. J., et al. (1982). Cross-cultural counseling competencies. *The Counseling Psychologist, 19*(2), 45–52.

Turner, S. M., DeMers, S. T., Fox, H. R., & Reed, G. M. (2001). APA's guidelines for test user qualifications: An executive summary. *American Psychologist, 56*, 1099–1113.

Ysseldyke, J. E., & Algozzine, B. (1982) *Critical issues in special and remedial education*. Boston, MA: Houghton, Mifflin.

3

MULTICULTURAL COMPETENCIES AND TRAINING IN SCHOOL PSYCHOLOGY: ISSUES, APPROACHES, AND FUTURE DIRECTIONS

Emilia C. Lopez
Queens College, City University of New York

Margaret R. Rogers
University of Rhode Island

Given the significant demographic changes occurring in the U.S., many practicing school psychologists are delivering services to a clientele diverse in ethnicity, race, language and cultural background, and nationality. Currently, White students make-up 62.1% of public school enrollments, African Americans 17.2%, Hispanic/Latinos 15.6%, Asian Americans 4%, American Indians 1.2% (National Center for Education Statistics, 2002) and youngsters whose native language is not English comprise 16.7% of the school-age population (U.S. Census, 2001). This diverse demographic profile implies that school psychology training programs must prepare their graduates to work with a diverse clientele.

Irrefutable evidence exists that there are differences in important quality of life indices on the basis of one's racial, ethnic, linguistic, cultural, and socioeconomic status in the U.S. Different subgroups of the American population have different histories with and exposure to prejudice, discrimination, institutionalized oppression, environmental risks, and social stigmatization. These experiences, as well as the stress associated with them, likely have a profound influence on psychological development and functioning. A person's race, ethnicity, language, gender, sexual orientation, and socioeconomic status affects identity, health status, and access to health care including mental health services (Bradford, Ryan, & Rothblum, 1994; Clark, Anderson, Clark, & Williams, 1999; Fisher et al., 2002; Garbarino, 1995; Lott, 2002; McLoyd, 1998; Vaughan, 1993; Williams, Yu, Jackson, & Anderson, 1997). In a recent report, the U.S. Surgeon General documented the existence of racial/ethnic disparities in mental health services for adults as well as children and youth, and explored the consequences of the disparities on psychological and physical well being (U.S. Department of Health and Human Services, 2001). There can be little doubt that school psychologists need to be informed about the nature of these disparities, and about how life events and experiences with prejudice and discrimination shape perceptions and daily life. Yet, it is quite likely that many school psychologists are not well informed, or if they are informed, are not clear about how to integrate this information into their professional practices. Empirical evidence in the school psychology literature is often lacking about how to make psychological services more effective, relevant, and contextually congruent on the basis of clients' diverse backgrounds and life experiences (e.g., see Henning-Stout & Brown-Cheatham, 1999; Sheridan, 2000). Contributing to this dilemma is the fact that many pertinent advances and research developments helpful to more fully understanding the complex issues involved in serving clients from diverse cultural and language backgrounds are so recent that they are just now beginning to enter mainstream psychological knowledge and have as yet to trickle down to practicing school psychologists.

Despite these barriers trainers are faced with the press to respond to calls from the American Psychological Association (APA 2002b) and the National Association of School Psychologists (NASP, 2000a) to increase the cross-cultural competencies of school psychology graduates (American Psychological Association [APA], 2002b; National Association of School Psychologists [NASP], 2000a). A call has also been issued by the APA and NASP via their ethical standards for practicing school psychologists to increase their cross-cultural expertise (APA, 2002a; NASP, 2000b). However, those calls for increasing school psychologists' cross-cultural knowledge and skills are not accompanied by a comprehensive discussion of what we know and what we need to accomplish in order to respond. The present chapter is designed to provide a discussion of: (a) the history of multicultural training in school psychology within the context of cross-cultural competencies, (b) the challenges that the profession faces in developing and improving school psychologists' cross-cultural competencies, (c) suggested approaches to meet those challenges, and (d) future implications for research in this area. The term culturally and linguistically diverse (CLD) will be used throughout the chapter when referring to individuals from diverse ethnic, racial, national, cultural and language backgrounds.

THEORETICAL AND RESEARCH BASIS

The early history of school psychology training is documented in a number of surveys conducted in the 1960s and 1970s that gave scant attention to multicultural issues. The surveys are similar in recording the number of school psychology programs and their institutional locations, the degrees offered, the degree requirements, the number of students and faculty, and the types of financial support offered (e.g., Bardon & Walker, 1972; Brown & Lindstrom, 1978; Cardon & French, 1968–1969; French & McCloskey, 1980; Smith, 1964–1965; White, 1963). Several surveys carried out during this time period also examined the training emphasis, content, and curriculum of programs (e.g., Bardon & Wenger, 1976; "Descriptions of Representative Training Programs," 1964–1965; French & McCloskey, 1980; Goh, 1977; Pfeiffer & Marmo, 1981; White, 1963) but none reported any programs offering diversity issues courses nor any type of multicultural training. Bardon and Wenger's survey is the first from this group to have asked about and reported the racial/ethnic breakdown of enrolled students. According to their sample, about 10% of the students attending school psychology programs were identified as CLD graduate students. A handful of case studies of individual training programs were also found (e.g., Bardon & Bennett, 1967; Zach, 1970). Zach's description of the program at Yeshiva University appears to be among the first to describe a training environment actively devoted to training school psychology students to provide services to a low-income urban CLD population. Altogether, with these two exceptions, published studies from the 1960s and 1970s about school psychology training provide little information about the extent to which programs were attending to multicultural training.

It is not until the 1980's that we begin to see evidence in the school psychology literature of a growing attention to the status of culturally diverse group members within the profession, culturally diverse student and faculty recruitment efforts, and coverage of multicultural issues in coursework and applied training. Zins and Halsell's (1986) nationwide survey of school psychology training programs examined students' and faculties' ethnic diversity group membership as well as recruitment strategies employed by programs to recruit students from diverse backgrounds. They found that 11.5% of the students and 17.5% of faculty were from culturally diverse backgrounds and noted an array of recruitment strategies used by the programs. Like Zins and Halsell, Barona and Flores (as cited in Barona, Santos de Barona, Flores, & Gutierrez, 1990) studied the kinds of information APA accredited programs presented to applicants from diverse cultural backgrounds. They found that about 58% indicated the presence of culturally diverse students, 37% employed a culturally diverse faculty member, and 26% offered financial aid.

Other studies looked at the curriculum provided at training programs across different levels of training. Brown and Minke (1986) examined the courses offered at 211 school psychology programs and found that doctoral degree programs could be distinguished from specialist degree programs by being more likely to offer cross-cultural coursework. They noted this distinction while also pointing out that the NASP and APA training guidelines that existed at that time required exposure to cross-cultural content in the curriculum, suggesting that at least some specialist programs were out of compliance with NASP guidelines. These studies, in combination, began to flesh out the demographic composition of students and faculty in school psychology programs, noted the need for increased representation of culturally diverse group members in the field, offered a glimpse at recruitment strategies leading programs already used, and revealed the uneven presence of multicultural coursework across programs.

Two articles published in the mid–1980s took the field a step further by beginning to articulate the content of multicultural training and discussing specific cross-cultural competencies. Figueroa, Sandoval, and Merino (1984) identified six major areas of competencies school psychologists need when delivering assessment services to limited English proficient (LEP) Hispanic children. These assessment-related competencies included proficiency in a second language, knowledge of first and second language development, skills in working with interpreters, knowledge of appropriate assessment techniques used with LEP youngsters, and knowledge of cross-cultural differences. Rosenfield and Esquivel's (1985) article on the competencies school psychologists need when working with bilingual and bicultural populations emphasized three major skill areas: language competencies, cross-cultural knowledge competencies, and assessment competencies. Figueroa et al. and Rosenfield and Esquivel enriched our understanding of the specific cross-cultural competencies needed by professionals when working with bilingual and bicultural clients and provided trainers with a beginning look at cross-cultural competencies to use in designing culturally relevant training experiences.

The 1990s were characterized by even more widespread and sustained attention to multicultural training and diversity issues in the school psychology literature, and provide evidence of significant gaps between the needs of an increasingly diverse clientele and the training that school psychologists receive. The first nationwide survey of multicultural training in school psychology programs (Rogers, Ponterotto, Conoley, & Wiese, 1992) showed that 40% of the programs did not offer diversity issues courses, over 90% of the programs devoted less than 25% of class time in core courses (assessment, interventions, consultation, and roles and function) to diversity issues, 31% provided students with minimal exposure to CLD clients during applied training, and about 13% of the faculty and 15% of the students were identified as culturally diverse group members. Consistent with Brown and Minke (1986), doctoral programs in the Rogers et al. study were more likely to offer diversity coursework than non-doctoral programs. These findings imply that many students were receiving insufficient preparation for work with a diverse clientele in their courses as well as their field placements.

More recent research raises added concerns about students' level of preparedness. Ochoa, Rivera, and Ford (1997) investigated the training experiences and professional assessment competencies of school psychologists working with bilingual and Hispanic clients. Ochoa et al. targeted school psychologists working in the eight states (Arizona, California, Colorado, Florida, New Jersey, New Mexico, New York, and Texas) with the highest concentrations of Hispanic and bilingual group members in the U.S. to find out how prepared they were to perform psychoeducational assessments in their communities. They found that about 80% of the school psychologists had not taken a bilingual assessment course and 87% considered their training in conducting bilingual psychoeducational assessments to be inadequate. The implication of these findings is clear: School psychologists with the greatest likelihood of serving bilingual students are most likely ill-prepared to do so. These results are compounded by the shortage of bilingual school psychologists nationwide. Curtis, Hunley, Walker, and Baker (1999) showed that about 10% of school psychologists speak a language other than English, suggesting that the need for bilingual professionals is outstripped by current availability. The findings raise serious concerns about the degree that training programs have prepared school psychologists for the needs of the bilingual and racially/ethnically diverse students in their care.

At least part of the difficulty trainers may have experienced in integrating multicultural content into their curriculum and training experiences may have been their own lack of knowledge about the specific skills school psychologists need to effectively serve a diverse clientele. Following Figueroa et al. (1984) and Rosenfield and Esquivel's (1985) discussions of cross-cultural assessment competencies, the cross-cultural competencies that school psychologists need received sporadic attention in the school psychology literature. More than 10 years after these early contributions, a number of publications appeared in school psychology venues to help expand and further clarify important cross-cultural school psychology competencies. In 1997, Gopaul-McNicol made recommendations about the competencies needed by monolingual school psychologists who work with CLD students.

Recent studies by Lopez and Rogers (2001) and Rogers and Lopez (2002) empirically identified the cross-cultural school psychology competencies that school psychologists should have within 14 domains: Academic Interventions, Assessment, Consultation, Counseling, Culture, Language, Laws and Regulations, Organizational Skills, Professional Characteristics, Report Writing, Research Methods, Theoretical Paradigms, Working with Interpreters, and Working with Parents. In both studies, a panel of experts in cross-cultural school psychology formulated the final set of competencies. The Lopez and Rogers experts identified 89 competencies and the experts from the Rogers and Lopez study identified 102 competencies, and together these competencies reflect those needed to provide a complete array of psychological services (assessment and intervention, consultation, counseling, report writing, research) as well as work with specific groups (e.g., interpreters, organizations, parents). Now, for the first time, school psychology trainers have a comprehensive picture of cross-cultural competencies most relevant to the practices delivered by school psychologists to guide their curriculum transformation efforts.

Several scholars have described and explored the characteristics of school psychology programs that specialize in multicultural training. For example, Palmer, Juarez, and Hughes (1991) described a training option available at Texas A & M University's school psychology program that prepares bilingual students to specialize in service delivery to Hispanic clients with disabilities. In addition, descriptions of nine school psychology programs (Arizona State University, Brooklyn College—CUNY, Georgia State University, Howard University, San Diego State University, Temple University, University of Nebraska-Lincoln, University of Texas—Pan American, and Utah State University) renowned for their efforts to engage in multicultural training were presented in the Fall and Winter 1995 editions of the Division 16 publication *The School Psychologist*.

More recently, Rogers (2006) studied the features of 17 school psychology programs identified as exemplary models of multicultural training. At the exemplary programs, 94% required a diversity issues course, all exposed their students to

CLD clients during field training, 59% specialize in training students to work with specific CLD populations, and most programs used multiple multicultural curriculum models. In addition, the programs used a wide range of student recruitment and retention techniques to attract CLD students, with all programs offering financial aid and making personal contacts with applicants as recruitment techniques. Twenty-five percent of the program faculty at the exemplary programs were bilingual, and 25% of the program faculty and 31% of the students represented a CLD group member.

Studies carried out within the closely related specialty of counseling psychology provide additional insight about the content of multicultural training. Studies have looked at various methods used to train for cross-cultural competence (e.g., Pedersen, 1988; Ridley, Mendoza, & Kanitz, 1994), examined student's assessments of the multicultural training they received (Mintz, Rideout, & Bartels, 1994; Neville et al., 1996; Phillips & Fischer, 1998), and assessed outcomes of multicultural training for clients as well as trainees (Constantine, 2002; Diaz-Lazaro & Cohen, 2001; Fuertes & Brobst, 2002; Kiselica, Maben, & Locke, 1999). Four models of multicultural training are generally recognized (i.e., separate course, interdisciplinary, area of concentration, integration) (LaFromboise & Foster, 1992). The separate course model involves offering students a single course in multicultural issues. The interdisciplinary model involves students taking core multicultural courses in departments outside of the department that houses the graduate psychology program. The area of concentration model combines didactic coursework in multicultural issues with applied training involving CLD clients. The integration model refers to infusing multicultural content into all graduate courses, including applied training activities. Even though the integration model is generally considered to be superior to the others, virtually all published studies conducted to date have looked at the impact of a separate diversity issues course (e.g., Brown, Parham, & Yonker, 1996; Heppner & O'Brien, 1994; Leonard, 1996; Neville et al., 1996; Phillips & Fischer, 1998; Sevig & Etzkorn, 2001; Steward, Wright, Jackson, & Jo, 1998).

In sum, the profession of school psychology and those who train school psychologists face multiple challenges in developing and improving school psychologists' and future school psychologists' cross-cultural competencies. A shortage of bilingual and multiculturally competent school psychologists, gaps in knowledge about best practices for providing psychological services to CLD clients, and the press to understand and act on inequities affecting the mental health of group members are all realities shaping the present context of multicultural training.

IMPLICATIONS FOR PRACTICE

We propose that there are two major challenges that must be addressed to reach the goal of equipping school psychologists with cross-cultural competencies: (a) continuing efforts to investigate and validate cross-cultural competencies, and (b) meeting training needs. Those challenges are explored below with examples provided to further operationalize those challenges. Readers will note that the examples given may be universal in the sense that they are prevalent nationally across settings and locations, whereas some examples may pertain to specific locations and situations (e.g., urban, rural, or suburban settings, specific parts of the country).

Continuing Efforts to Investigate and Validate Cross-cultural Competencies

Although several researchers have identified competencies for school psychologists working with culturally and linguistically diverse populations, most have relied on reviews of the literature or the authors' own expertise to generate the areas of competency (Gopaul-McNicol, 1997; Figueroa et al., 1984; Rosenfield & Esquivel, 1985). Research based competencies were recently generated by Lopez and Rogers (2001) and Rogers and Lopez (2002). Both investigations asked panels of experts to identify essential cross-cultural competencies. However, those two investigations generated two sets of essential cross-cultural competencies that are not yet integrated nor validated.

Specific competencies must also be investigated and validated for bilingual psychologists working with bilingual students and English language learners. Bilingual language skills (i.e., skills in communicating in two languages) are only some of the competencies that bilingual school psychologists need to provide effective services to linguistically diverse children and their families (Figueroa et al., 1984; Rosenfield & Esquivel, 1985). Bilingual school psychologists must also have knowledge of language development in the languages that they are proficient in to be able to examine children's first and second acquisition skills. Such skills would be helpful to bilingual school psychologists as they examine children's assessment results in two languages (e.g.., assessment of cognitive, academic and/or language skills in Chinese and English). Also relevant is knowledge about how the use of two languages can impact the counseling process as in situations where clients may respond to issues differently depending on the language(s) used during sessions (e.g., speaking to a client in her native language about family relationship issues may evoke themes that did not emerge in previous discussions conducted only in English; Oquendo, 1996).

School psychologists who are bilingual in specific languages (e.g., a Chinese and English speaking school psychologist) are also often called to work with other linguistically diverse clients via interpreters (e.g., clients speaking Spanish, Urdu, Hindi, or Russian). As such, bilingual school psychologists need to have, in addition to special competencies related to the specific language groups they support, skills and knowledge relevant to working with other linguistically diverse clients.

In addition to the challenge of systematically identifying cross-cultural competencies, there is also a need to develop valid and reliable tools to assess the cross-cultural competencies of graduate students in school psychology programs, faculty in training programs, and of practitioners in the field. The counseling field has clearly taken the lead on confronting this challenge. For example, three tools reviewed by Ponterotto, Rieger, Barrett, and Sparks (1994) are available as self-report measures of multicultural counseling competencies. A fourth measure, the Cross-Cultural Counseling Inventory-Revised (LaFromboise, Coleman & Hernandez, 1991) was designed for supervisors to evaluate counselor's multicultural competencies. In school psychology, the only published instrument is the Multicultural School Psychology Counseling Competency Scale (Rogers &

Ponterotto, 1997), a measure specifically designed to assess counseling skills. Other instruments are needed to assess the full array of services that school psychologists deliver.

Meeting Training Needs

The challenges related to meeting training needs are multiple and interrelated. The available research suggests that there is a shortage of practicing school psychologists well prepared to provide psychological services to CLD clients (Ochoa et al, 1997). The shortage of multicultural competent school psychologists leads us to question the consequences of providing services to populations we are not equipped to work with. For example, what are the consequences of (a) Using psychological and educational measures not validated for specific populations of students, (b) translating tests on the spot and using those scores as if they are representative of students' levels of functioning, and (c) developing and implementing interventions that do no take into account the children's and families' cultural backgrounds? These questions and many others must be examined to continue to move the field to further explore cross-cultural competencies in practice and training.

Training programs face the challenges of meeting the training standards set by the NASP (2000a) and the accreditation guidelines established by the APA (2002b) regarding multicultural training. A careful examination of these standards point to areas of overlap as well as points of divergence. Both the NASP and the APA training standards emphasize coverage of multicultural issues in all aspects of the curriculum, and stress the need to provide applied training experiences and placements with diverse clients. In addition, both advise programs to promote the recruitment and retention of CLD students and faculty. APA's standards go one step further by noting that minority recruitment efforts must be "systematic, coherent, and long-term" (p. 12). NASP's standards extend to include the need for training programs to communicate their commitment to diversity in their mission and program philosophy. In addition, NASP's standards also make specific statements about the need for future school psychologists to (a) recognize their own biases and the ways that bias affects "decision-making, instruction, behavior, and long-term outcomes for students" (p. 29), and (b) "develop…interventions that reflect knowledge and understanding of children and families' cultures…" (p. 28). What the standards do not state are specific recommendations for how training programs should engage in these objectives, leaving trainers with little explicit guidance or insight about how to achieve excellence in these areas.

Training programs may not have faculty with cross-cultural expertise to train future school psychologists to work with CLD populations. Questions then arise as to the need to prepare trainers so that they are able to integrate cross-cultural issues into the program curricula and applied training experiences. Do trainers recognize their own need for cross-cultural competencies? How do we go about preparing trainers? What areas do we emphasize when preparing trainers (e.g., specific cross-cultural competencies related to their areas of specialty, overview of issues)? Of concern also is research in psychology and education suggesting that CLD faculty members who are hired for tenure track positions confront a number of personal and institutional barriers that may result in lower retention rates of CLD faculty within university settings (e.g., lack of CLD faculty serving as models and mentors, lack of institutional support, unfamiliarity with the tenure process and demands) (Hendricks, 1997).

Training programs encounter barriers when attempting to recruit CLD graduate students. For example, financial constraints prevent CLD students from attempting graduate school. In addition, the university community may not be ethnically diverse or may not reflect the students' backgrounds (Constantine & Ladany, 1996). Muñoz-Dunbar and Stanton (1999) suggest that CLD students may measure institutional sensitivity to cultural diversity by the presence or absence of faculty members from diverse cultural and linguistic backgrounds.

Bilingual graduate students may be difficult to recruit because although they may have oral language skills in English and/or a language other than English, those bilingual skills may not translate into proficiency in reading and/or writing. This pattern is not unusual because oral skills in a second language typically develop earlier than writing skills (Collier, 1992). Other bilingual applicants may also be able to communicate well orally in their first language but never had the opportunity to receive instruction in reading or writing in the first language and thus lack the corresponding reading and writing skills.

Retention of CLD graduate students is also a challenge for training programs. Studies suggest that relative to White students, minority students tend to experience greater feelings of alienation and isolation in academic environments that lack cultural diversity (Bernal et al., 1999). When culturally diverse faculty are not present in a graduate program or department, CLD students lack role models, mentors, and important sources of support (Constantine & Ladany, 1996). Other CLD students struggle with acculturation conflicts as in situations where women students experience confusion and stress as a result of their culturally traditional families questioning their desire to acquire a higher level of education and a profession. Graduate students from CLD backgrounds who were not educated in American educational systems also experience difficulties in understanding how to succeed in an university system that is new to them, and in figuring out how to function in fieldwork settings (e.g., clinics, schools) that reflect majority values and use unfamiliar instructional or classroom practices.

Trainers also face the often difficult task of identifying practicing school psychologists who are multiculturally competent and/or bilingually proficient to provide supervision to trainees during field-based training. Potential supervisors may not have had adequate training in multicultural and/or bilingual issues during their own formal preparation, may vary in their utilization of best practices in service delivery to bilingual and racial/ethnic diverse students, or may be ill-equipped to address the structural and interpersonal inequities that CLD group members face. Studies have shown that both practicing psychologists and psychologists-in-training frequently report being unprepared for delivering services to Blacks/African Americans, Latinos, Asian Americans, Native Americans, people with disabilities, and gays/lesbians/bisexuals (Allison, Crawford, Echemendia, Robinson, & Knepp, 1994; Mintz, Bartels, & Rideout, 1995; Phillips & Fischer, 1998). Furthermore, Allison et al. (1994) found that even though the clinical and counseling psychologists in their sample did not feel competent to deliver services to some

CLD group members, they continued to provide services. Ochoa, Rivera, and Ford (1997) found that about 80% of the practicing school psychologists they sampled had not been trained to perform bilingual psychoeducational assessments although more than half (57%) had conducted such assessments. The practice of providing highly specialized services to clients in the absence of demonstrated competency raises serious ethical concerns about the practitioner's compliance with both the APA (2002a) and NASP (2000b) ethical codes and the degree that the services provided meet the highest standards for service delivery.

Specific challenges also exist in locating bilingual school psychologists to supervise practica and internship students. Some bilingual school psychologists have the experience that, by virtue of being the only bilingual school psychologist in a specific district, they are assigned to restricted roles such as only conducting assessments because of a backlog of bilingual assessment cases. Practicing supervisors in such situations would provide limited experiences for practica and internship students because they do not deliver consultation, counseling, and intervention/prevention services. Districts with serious shortages of bilingual school psychologists and other bilingual personnel assessment personnel often respond to their immediate needs by contracting with outside agencies to complete bilingual assessment cases instead of planning long-term by hiring a CLD cadre of school psychologists who can meet their communities' ongoing needs.

Other systemic issues also impact training experience. Bilingual school psychologists may be hired to work in urban districts where most community members use a language different than the bilingual school psychologist's second language (e.g., Greek speaking school psychologist is hired to work in a Polish speaking community instead of in a district with a Greek speaking community) because the school system and the union dictate school placements not by need (i.e., what the community needs) but by seniority (i.e., school psychologist X has more seniority and gets to choose what school to work in within the district).

Given the challenges in identifying competencies, meeting training needs, recruiting and retaining CLD students and faculty, and confronting systemic issues, it seems imperative to identify actions to meet those challenges. The next section discusses approaches to meet the identified challenges.

IMPLEMENTATION AND APPROACHES

The approaches discussed in this section identify the steps we need to engage in to address the identified challenges. Part of the process of meeting these challenges is to identify the goals that will help our profession to prepare school psychologists to work with children and families from CLD backgrounds.

Approaches to Investigating and Validating Cross-cultural Competencies

Our first goal must be to continue to conduct research to systematically identify cross-cultural competencies for all school psychologists. Although the work has begun in that area (Lopez & Rogers, 2001; Rogers & Lopez, 2002) more work is needed to validate the competencies in practice. The work must also be extended to identify and validate specific competencies for bilingual school psychologists. Another goal is to develop valid and reliable tools to identify school psychology students' and practitioners' competencies. Such tools will be instrumental in helping university programs to establish training goals and conduct program evaluations (e.g., Are students obtaining cross-cultural competencies in courses and field experiences?). Those tools will also help practitioners as well as school psychology students to self-assess their cross-cultural knowledge and skills.

Approaches to Meet Training Needs for Practitioners

The goal of preparing practicing school psychologists to work with CLD populations entails training programs and school systems working together to develop training experiences for practitioners and students in a variety of forums (e.g., university training program, workshops within the district, internet courses). Training can be provided in specific areas of functioning (e.g., assessment, counseling, consultation), specific topics (e.g., second language acquisition, acculturation), and about specific groups (e.g., working with a variety of Latino/Hispanic populations such as Ecudorians, Hondurians, Puerto Rican). Research suggests that specific courses (Keim, Warring, & Rau, 2001; Neville et al., 1996), workshops (Byington, Fischer & Walker, 1997) and a variety of learning activities such as structured feedback, surveys, and games are effective means to improve cross-cultural awareness, knowledge and skills (Dana, Aguilar-Kitibutr, Diaz-Vivar, & Vetter, 2002; Kim & Lyons, 2003; Roysircar, Webster, & Germer, 2003). Training experiences can include self-exploration, structured activities designed to increase awareness of diverse groups (e.g., trips to ethnically diverse communities led by members of the community or peers from those communities), reading of the literature, and supervised work experiences (LaFromboise & Foster, 1992). Developing communities of peer support via local (e.g., peer supervision provided within a district or across districts) or national mentoring programs (e.g., use of technology and the internet for distance supervision support and distance learning) should also be explored. The training research supports the use of follow-up mentoring, supervision, and coaching to help practitioners apply the knowledge and skills learned in workshops and courses (Showers & Joyce, 1996). In addition, the field needs more training programs for bilingual school psychologists.

One way to meet the many training needs is through the creation of national and regional training centers. Regional centers may be established through APA and NASP or through funding from federal and state sources to address diversity issues such as training, recruitment and retention issues for practitioners, graduate students and faculty. Such centers can provide training opportunities and disseminate information. For example, the Queens College and Brooklyn College, City University of New York campuses obtained a three-year grant (1998–2001) to create the Bilingual Psychological and Educational Assessment Support Center. The Center was supported through New York State Education funding and was created to provide training support to school psychologists and other school professionals working with CLD children and youth. The Center (a) created and received feedback from an Advisory Council composed of trainers, practitioners, and researchers; (b) provided support to various New York State Education programs and offices about training issues; (c) implemented workshops on a variety of topics and in a variety of locations (e.g., national, at the two campuses, at local school districts), (c) provided consultation services (e.g., to local school psychology programs about training issues, to school districts about locating bilingual assessment personnel, to practitioners seeking information about assessment practices); and (d) created a website where a variety of information was disseminated (e.g., syllabi, training materials, newsletter summarizing research as well as practice based information [http://forbin.qc.edu/ECP/bilingualcenter/]).

Greater collaboration is needed between university training programs, state education departments, school districts, unions, and community leaders to draft common goals to increase the number of school psychologists with multicultural competencies and the numbers of CLD school psychologists, including bilingual psychologists, who can respond to the individual needs of each community. For example, the New York State Education Department (NYSED) consulted with school psychology trainers to create a bilingual specialization for school psychologists. Bilingual school psychologists are now credentialed by the NYSED and must take a series of courses on bilingual and multicultural issues. In addition, they must complete a bilingual fieldwork experience and must demonstrate bilingual language skills via a language proficiency exam given by the NYSED. This decision has led to the credentialing of many bilingual school psychologists throughout the State and has provided an incentive for school psychologists with bilingual expertise to seek appropriate training. Incentives must also be provided to encourage school psychologists to acquire multicultural expertise, perhaps through a national certification or specialization in multicultural issues, local incentives (e.g., salary increments), and special recognitions (e.g., credentials awarded through state education departments).

Practitioners, trainers, and professional organizations also need to work together to expand the roles of bilingual school psychologists beyond the roles of assessors to focus on prevention and intervention roles and provide a full compliment of psychological services. Collaboration amongst those sources can also lead to mutually beneficially ventures such as identifying specialized field placements that provide future school psychologists with opportunities to work with CLD groups

Approaches to Meet Training Needs in School Psychology Graduate Programs

Recruitment and retention strategies are also needed targeting school psychology graduate students committed to working with CLD populations. Recruitment strategies found to be effective at increasing enrollments for CLD students include financial support, personal contacts from CLD faculty and students, soliciting recruits from other higher education institutions (particularly historical institutions of color), employing CLD faculty, offering peer support groups, mentorship programs, involvement in special projects and research with mentoring from faculty and/or field supervisors (Maton & Hrabowski, 2004; Rogers, 2006; Rogers & Molina, 2005; Salzman, 2000). Bidell, Turner, and Casas (2002) found that information included in application materials had an impact on enrollment rates for diverse students. Specifically, high enrollments of a diverse student body were found at programs that included financial aid information, an antidiscrimination policy, and a statement communicating a commitment to diversity in training and student recruitment in their application materials. Among other strategies that can be used are developing a strong national campaign through local, state, and national contacts; developing recruitment materials targeting CLD graduate students; working with community leaders to refer promising students; advertising in local newspapers that target particular communities and groups; and conducting presentations with community agencies (Garman & Mortense, 1997; Muñoz-Dunbar & Stanton, 1999; Puente, Blanch, & Candland, 1993).

Outreach activities designed to target young children as well as high school and undergraduate students are other sources of recruitment that can be adopted and evaluated. For example, members of the Education and Science directorate within the APA participated in a program where children of all ages were exposed to activities (e.g., puzzles, hands-on activities) and demonstrations designed to introduce them to psychological concepts ("Encouraging Children to Discover Psychology," 2005). The APA Teachers of Psychology in Secondary Schools and the APA Psychology Teachers at Community Colleges organized activities designed to provide information to high school students about careers in psychology ("Ethnic Minority Recruitment Project," 2005). The creation of a school psychology recruitment day or week with dissemination of specially designed materials developed through the school psychology division of the APA (Division 16) and the NASP can encourage practitioners and trainers across the country to plan and implement recruitment activities for students of all ages with emphases on recruiting a culturally diverse cadre of future school psychologists. School psychology courses on roles and functions can also incorporate recruitment assignments whereby CLD school psychology graduate students can participate in presentations and demonstrations based within schools. Within the APA, the Office of Ethnic Minority Affairs and the Commission on Ethnic Minority Recruitment, Retention, and Training in Psychology have published a number of helpful guides, pamphlets and brochures describing how graduate programs can improve their minority recruitment and retention efforts (see the Resources section at the end of this chapter).

Bilingual and bicultural training experiences can also be provided within training programs and in collaboration with other training programs. For example, reading and writing workshops for bilingual school psychologists who lack literacy skills in languages other than English, and national as well as international exchange programs should be explored (e.g., taking series of courses in another university in the country or outside of the country).

Providing direct contact with CLD clients through local, national as well as international field placements may also provide school psychology students with exposure to a variety of practical experiences with different populations and contexts (e.g., rural, urban). Field experiences should be comprehensive in providing graduate students with the opportunity to engage in assessment, counseling, consultation, research and other activities with CLD children and families. Investigations in counseling psychology have demonstrated that counseling students acquire multicultural knowledge and skills through workshops, coursework, structured experiences with CLD clients (e.g., the percentage of caseloads are of culturally and linguistically diverse clients), contact with CLD staff, training seminars, assignments of supervisors from ethnically diverse backgrounds and with cross-cultural expertise, assessment of the interns' acquisition of cross-cultural knowledge and skills, annual client feedback surveys, case presentations, self assessments of cross-cultural competencies, and participation in multicultural research (Manese, Wu, & Nepomuceno, 2001; Pope-Davis, Reynolds, Dings & Ottavi, 1994).

We need to identify useful strategies and techniques to develop the cross-cultural competence of existing faculty, and recruit and retain CLD faculty. Faculty would benefit from course releases to learn about multicultural curriculum transformation and to incorporate their new competencies into their teaching. Mentorship relationships whereby faculty with cross-cultural expertise provide feedback and support as peers develop syllabi, plan courses, choose readings and activities may also be fruitful. One of the challenges of teaching multicultural issues is that faculty often encounter situations where learners respond to diversity issues with a range of emotions that include anger (e.g., "I have no right to speak up because I am not from a culturally diverse background!"), withdrawal (e.g., "I am afraid to talk about my cultural group because others may not understand"), defensiveness (e.g., "I am not a racist!"), guilt (e.g., "As a member of the majority group I feel responsible for acts of racism"), and confusion (e.g., "How do I integrate this new knowledge given my current perceptions and experiences?") (Jackson, 1999). Support in the form of a workshops, supervision or mentorship is helpful as faculty confront the challenges associated with teaching diversity issues that are often charged by conflicting points of view and emotions.

IMPLICATIONS FOR FUTURE RESEARCH

The challenges are numerous as well as complex. A research agenda focusing on these challenges will likely improve our future practice and training. Although fields such as counseling, social psychology, and education have a substantial body of research focusing on CLD clients and diversity issues, there is a dearth of relevant research in school psychology. Training future school psychologists as scientist practitioners will benefit our profession by enhancing practice based research efforts designed to focus on multicultural issues. A national research center focusing on multicultural and bilingual school psychology with block grants that can be awarded to researchers throughout the country may stimulate research in this direction. Future research investigations exploring issues related to cross-cultural competencies and training should utilize a variety of research methods and procedures. Researchers will also need to engage practitioners, trainers, as well as school professionals from other disciplines (e.g., teachers, administrators) in validating cross-cultural competencies for school psychologist. Validation methods can incorporate surveys as well as qualitative approaches to further identify and clarify relevant competencies.

Pope-Davis et al. (2002) found that cultural competence was identified as important by counseling clients depending on the nature of the counselor-client relationship, the issues recognized by the client, and the level of skill that the counselor exhibited in incorporating diversity within the counseling process. Consequently, it will also be crucial to engage CLD children, youth and families (i.e., our clients) in identifying the knowledge and skills needed by school psychologists and other school professionals to demonstrate cross-cultural competencies in school settings. Methods based on interviews and focus groups will be helpful to investigate clients' perceptions of cross-cultural competencies.

The competencies identified should be useful in the training and practical arenas so that trainers, school psychology students, and practitioners are able to translate those competencies into plans for training and supervision (e.g., establishment of workshops in specific issues, provision of supervisory experiences in specific areas). In the cross-cultural competency counseling research, most studies rely on graduate students' and practitioners' self reports, which means that the outcomes are based on beliefs rather than actual demonstrations of awareness, knowledge and/or skills (Constantine, 2001). Observations of school psychologists' actual behaviors delivering services to CLD clients are needed to supplement self-report assessments.

Research is also needed that updates our understanding of the status of multicultural school psychology training in programs across the country. The last investigation was by Rogers' et al. in 1992 and current research is needed to understand more recent practices. Investigations are also needed examining the effectiveness of services delivered by graduates of programs specializing in multicultural training versus graduates of other programs. Most research currently available on the effectiveness of multicultural training models has focused on the outcomes associated with taking a single diversity issues course and has not looked at the impact of other models of multicultural training (e.g., Phillips & Fischer, 1998; Steward et al., 1998). Consequently, future research efforts should be directed at examining the impact of the integration, interdisciplinary, and area of concentration models of multicultural training. Examining outcomes from a variety of teaching models will be helpful in planning future training programs and restructuring existing programs.

Future research investigating effective recruitment strategies, retention strategies, and fieldwork experiences within training programs will benefit training programs as they plan and implement effective practices. Practice-based and qualitative research that suggests strategies for overcoming challenges and barriers have the potential to benefit clients from diverse CLD backgrounds as well as practitioners and training programs.

CONCLUSION

The issues that trainers confront in attempting to integrate multicultural content and experiences into the curriculum and training environment—dealing with gaps in the knowledge base, translating the NASP and APA training guidelines into high quality training experiences, and providing for the continuing education needs of field-based supervisors—are complex and require considerable energy and expertise to address. Despite the vexing nature of these issues, school psychology trainers must ensure that trainees learn to deliver the highest quality psychological services to all clients.

ANNOTATED BIBLIOGRAPHY

Lynch, E. W. & Hanson, M. J. (Eds.) (2004). *Developing cross-cultural competence: A guide for working with children and their families.*Baltimore: Paul H. Brookes.

This is an excellent resource for practitioners. The first section of the book begins with a conceptual framework for cross-cultural competencies. Cultural perspectives of families from diverse cultural backgrounds are discussed in the second section of the book. The book ends with a discussion of implications for practice. The authors provide practical suggestions for working with families from diverse cultural and linguistic backgrounds.

Lopez, E. C., & Rogers, M. R. (2001). Conceptualizing cross-cultural school psychology competencies. *School Psychology Quarterly, 16*, 270–302.

Rogers, M. R., & Lopez, E. C. (2002). Identifying critical cross-cultural school psychology competencies. *Journal of School Psychology, 40*, 115–141.

The two articles cited above provide readers with the results of investigations designed to systematically identify cross-cultural competencies for school psychologists across 14 domains: Academic Interventions, Assessment, Consultation, Counseling, Culture, Language, Laws and Regulations, Organizational Skills, Professional Characteristics, Report Writing, Research Methods, Theoretical Paradigms, Working with Interpreters, and Working with Parents.

RESOURCES

American Psychological Association:
www.APA.org/pi/online.html

The website for provides the following titles: "Directory of Selected Scholarship, Fellowship, and Other Financial Aid Opportunities for Women and Ethnic Minorities in Psychology and Related Fields, " "Psychology Education and Careers: Guidebook for High School Students of Color," "Psychology Education and Careers: Guidebook for College Students of Color," "Psychology Education and Careers: Guidebook for College Students of Color Applying to Graduate and Professional Programs," "Psychology Education and Careers: Resources for Psychology Training Programs Recruiting Students of Color," and "Surviving and Thriving in Academia: A Guide for Women and Ethnic Minorities."

National Association of School Psychologists pages on Culturally Competent Practice:
http://www.nasponline.org/culturalcompetence/index.html

The website provides the following titles: "Why NASP is Committed to Culturally Competent Practice," "Defining Culture," "Journey to Thinking Multiculturally," "The Provision of Culturally Competent Services in the School Setting," and other resources for cultural competence among professional, advocates and families.

REFERENCES

Allison, K. W., Crawford, I., Echemendia, R., Robinson, L., & Knepp, D. (1994). Human diversity and professional competence: Training in clinical and counseling psychology revisited. *American Psychologist, 49*, 792–796.

American Psychological Association. (2002a). *Ethical principles of psychologists and code of conduct.* Retrieved February 1, 2003, from www.apa.org/ethics/code2002.html

American Psychological Association. (2002b). *Guidelines and principles for accreditation of programs in professional psychology.* Washington, DC: Author.

Bardon, J. I., & Bennett, V. D. C. (1967). Preparation for professional psychology: An example from a school psychology training program. *American Psychologist, 22*, 652–656.

Bardon, J. I., & Walker, N. W. (1972). Characteristics of graduate training programs in school psychology. *American Psychologist, 27*, 652–656.

Bardon, J. I., & Wenger, R. D. (1976). School psychology training trends in the early 1970s. *Professional Psychology, 7*, 31–37.

Barona, A., Santos de Barona, M., Flores, A. A., & Gutierrez, M. H. (1990). Critical issues in training school psychologists to serve minority school children. In A. Barona & E. E. Garcia (Eds.), *Children at risk: Poverty, minority status, and other issues in educational equity* (pp. 187–200). Washington, DC: National Association of School Psychologists.

Bernal, M. E., Sirolli, A. A., Weisser, S. K., Ruiz, J. A., Chamberlain, V. J., & Knight, G. P. (1999). Relevance of multicultural training to students' applications to clinical psychology programs. *Cultural Diversity and Ethnic Minority Psychology, 5*, 43–55.

Bidell, M. P., Turner, J. A., & Casas, J. M. (2002). First impressions count: Ethnic/racial and lesbian/gay/bisexual content of professional psychology application materials. *Professional Psychology: Research and Practice, 33*, 97–103.

Bradford, J., Ryan, C., & Rothblum, E. D. (1994). National Lesbian health care survey: Implications for mental health care. *Journal of Consulting and Clinical Psychology, 62*, 228–242.

Brown, D. T., & Lindstrom, J. P. (1978). The training of school psychologists in the United States: An overview. *Psychology in the Schools, 15*, 37–45.

Brown, D. T., & Minke, K. M. (1986). School psychology graduate training: A comprehensive analysis. *American Psychologist, 41*, 1328–1338.

Brown, S. P., Parham, T. A., & Yonker, R. (1996). Influence of a cross-cultural training course on racial identity attitudes of White women and men: Preliminary perspectives. *Journal of Counseling and Development, 74*, 510–516.

Byington, K., Fischer, J., & Walker, L. (1997). Evaluating the effectiveness of a multicultural counseling ethics and assessment training. *Journal of Applied Rehabilitation Counseling, 28*, 15–19.

Cardon, B. W., & French, J. L. (1968–1969). Organization and content of graduate programs in school psychology. *Journal of School Psychology, 7*, 28–32.

Clark, R., Anderson, N. B., Clark, V. R., & Williams, D. R. (1999). Racism as a stressor for African Americans: A biopsychosocial model. *American Psychologist, 54*, 805–816.

Collier, V. P. (1992). A synthesis of studies examining long-term language minority student data on academic achievement. *Bilingual Research Journal, 16*, 187–212.

Constantine, M. G. (2001). Predictors of observer ratings of multicultural counseling competence in Black, Latino, and White American Trainees. *Journal of Counseling Psychology, 48*, 456–462.

Constantine, M. G. (2002). Predictors of satisfaction with counseling: Racial and ethnic minority clients' attitudes toward counseling and ratings of their counselors' general and multicultural counseling competence. *Journal of Counseling Psychology, 49*, 255–263.

Constantine, M. G., & Ladany, N. (1996). Students' perceptions of multicultural training in counseling psychology programs. *Journal of Multicultural Counseling and Development, 24*, 241–253.

Curtis, M. J., Hunley, S. A., Walker, K. J., & Baker, A. C. (1999). Demographic characteristics and professional practices in school psychology. *School Psychology Review, 28*, 104–116.

Dana, R. H., Aguilar-Kitibutr, A., Diaz-Vivar, N., & Vetter, H. (2002). A teaching method for multicultural assessment: Psychological report contents and cultural competence. *Journal of Personality Assessment, 79*, 207–215.

Descriptions of Representative Training Programs in School Psychology. (1964–1965). *Journal of School Psychology, 3*, 45–57.

Diaz-Lazaro, C. M., & Cohen, B. B. (2001). Cross-cultural contact in counseling training. *Journal of Multicultural Counseling and Development, 29*, 41–56.

Encouraging children to discover psychology. (2005, Spring/Summer). *The Educator: Newsletter of the Education Directorate*, p. 10.

Ethnic minority recruitment project. (2005, Spring/Summer). *The educator: Newsletter of the education directorate*, p. 10.

Figueroa, R. A., Sandoval, J., & Merino, B. (1984). School psychology and limited-English-proficient (LEP) children: New competencies. *Journal of School Psychology, 22*, 131–143.

Fisher, C. B., Hoagwood, K., Boyce, C., Duster, T., Frank, D. A., Grisso, T., et al. (2002). Research ethics for mental health science involving ethnic minority children and youths. *American Psychologist, 57*, 1024–1040.

French, J. L., & McCloskey, G. (1980). Characteristics of doctoral and nondoctoral school psychology programs: Their implications for the entry-level doctorate. *Journal of School Psychology, 18*, 247–255.

Fuertes, J. N., & Brobst, K. (2002). Clients' ratings of counselor multicultural competency. *Cultural Diversity and Ethnic Minority Psychology, 8*, 214–223.

Garbarino, J. (1995). *Raising children in a socially toxic environment*. San Francisco: Jossey Bass.

Garman, A. N., & Mortensen, S. (1997). Using targeted outreach to recruit minority students into competitive service organizations. *College Student Journal, 31*, 174–180.

Goh, D. S. (1977). Graduate training in school psychology. *Journal of School Psychology, 15*, 207–218.

Gopaul-McNicol, S. (1997). A theoretical framework for training monolingual school psychologists to work with multilingual/multicultural children: An exploration of the major competencies. *Psychology in the Schools, 34*, 17–29.

Hendricks, F. M. (1997). Career experiences of Black women faculty at Research 1 universities. *Dissertation Abstracts international, 57*, 12A. (UMI No. 9717161).

Henning-Stout, M., & Brown-Cheatham, M. (1999). School psychology in a diverse world: Considerations for practice, research, and training. In C. R. Reynolds & T. B. Gutkin (Eds.), *Handbook of school psychology* (3rd ed., pp. 1041–1055). New York: Wiley.

Heppner, M. J., & O'Brien, K. M. (1994). Multicultural counselor training: Students' perceptions of helpful and hindering events. *Counselor Education and Supervision, 34*, 4–18.

Jackson, L. C. (1999). Ethnocultural resistance to multicultural training: Students and faculty. *Cultural diversity and Ethnic Minority Psychology, 5*, 27–36.

Keim, J., Warring, D. F., & Rau, R. (2001). Impact of multicultural training on school psychology and education students. *Journal of Instructional Psychology, 28*, 249–252.

Kim, B. K., & Lyons, H. Z. (2003). Experiential activities and multicultural counseling competence training. *Journal of Counseling & Development, 81,* 400–409.

Kiselica, M. S., Maben, P., & Locke, D. C. (1999). Do multicultural education and diversity appreciation training reduce prejudice among counseling trainees? *Journal of Mental Health Counseling, 21,* 240–254.

LaFromboise, T. D., Coleman, H. L. K., & Hernandez, A. (1991). Development and factor structure of the Cross-Cultural Counseling Inventory—Revised. *Professional Psychology: Research and Practice, 22,* 380–388.

LaFromboise, T. D., & Foster, S. L. (1992). Cross-cultural training: Scientist-practitioner model and methods. *The Counseling Psychologist, 20,* 472–489.

Leonard, P. J. (1996). Consciousness-raising groups as a multicultural awareness approach: An experience with counselor trainees. *Cultural Diversity and Mental Health, 2,* 89–98.

Lopez, E. C., & Rogers, M. R. (2001). Conceptualizing cross-cultural school psychology competencies. *School Psychology Quarterly, 16,* 270–302.

Lott, B. (2002). Cognitive and behavioral distancing from the poor. *American Psychologist, 57,* 100–110.

Manese, J. E., Wu, J. T., & Nepomuceno, C. A. (2001). The effect of training on multicultural counseling competencies: An exploratory study over a ten-year period. *Journal of Multicultural Counseling & Development, 29,* 31–41.

Maton, K. I., & Hrabowski, F. A. (2004). Increasing the number of African American PhDs in the sciences and engineering: A strengths-based approach. *American Psychologist, 59,* 547–556.

McLoyd, V. C. (1998). Socioeconomic disadvantage and child development. *American Psychologist, 53,* 185–204.

Mintz, L. B., Bartels, K. B., & Rideout, C. A. (1995). Training in counseling ethnic minorities and race-based availability of graduate school resources. *Professional Psychology: Research and Practice, 26,* 316–321.

Mintz, L. B., Rideout, C. A., & Bartels, K. B. (1994). A national survey of interns' perceptions of their preparation for counseling women and of the atmosphere of their graduate education. *Professional Psychology: Research and Practice, 25,* 221–227.

Muñoz-Dunbar, R., & Stanton, A. L. (1999). Ethnic diversity in clinical psychology: Recruitment and admission practices among doctoral programs. *Teaching of Psychology, 26,* 259–263.

National Association of School Psychologists. (2000a). *Standards for training and field placement programs in school psychology.* Bethesda, MD: Author.

National Association of School Psychologists. (2000b). *Principles for professional ethics guidelines for the provision of school psychological services.* Bethesda, MD: Author.

National Center for Education Statistics. (2002). *Digest of education statistics 2001.* Washington, DC: U.S. Department of Education.

Neville, H. A., Heppner, M. J., Louie, C. E., Thompson, C. E., Brooks, L., & Baker, C. E. (1996). The impact of multicultural training on White racial identity attitudes and therapy competencies. *Professional Psychology: Research and Practice, 27,* 83–89.

Ochoa, S. H., Rivera, B., & Ford, L. (1997). An investigation of school psychology training pertaining to bilingual psycho-educational assessment of primarily Hispanic students: Twenty-five years after Diana v. California. *Journal of School Psychology, 35,* 329–349.

Oquendo, M. A. (1996). Psychiatric evaluation and psychotherapy in the patient's second language. *Psychiatric Services, 17,* 614–618.

Palmer, D. J., Juarez, L., & Hughes, J. N. (1991). School psychology training and the education of minority at-risk youth: The Texas A & M university program emphasis on handicapped Hispanic children and youth. *School Psychology Review, 20,* 472–484.

Pedersen, P. (1988). *A handbook for developing multicultural awareness.* Alexandria, VA: American Association of Counseling and Development.

Pfeiffer, S. I., & Marmo, P. (1981). The status of training in school psychology and trends toward the future. *Journal of School Psychology, 19,* 211–216.

Phillips, J. C., & Fischer, A. R. (1998). Graduate students' training experiences with lesbian, gay, and bisexual issues. *The Counseling Psychologist, 26,* 712–734.

Ponterotto, J. G., Rieger, B. P., Barrett, A., & Sparks, R. (1994). Assessing multicultural counseling competence: A review of instrumentation. *Journal of Counseling and Development, 72,* 316–322.

Pope-Davis, D. B, Toporek, R. L., Ortega-Villalobos, L., Ligiero, D. P., Brittan-Powerll, C. S., Liu, W. M., et al. (2002). Client perspective of multicultural counseling comptence: A qualitative examination. *Counseling Psychologist, 30,* 355–393.

Pope-Davis, D. B., Reynolds, A. L., Dings, J. G., & Ottavi, T. M. (1994). Multicultural competencies of doctoral interns at university counseling centers: An exploratory investigation. *Professional Psychology: Research and Practice, 25,* 466–470.

Puente, A. E., Blanch, E., & Candland, D. K. (1993). Toward a psychology of variance: Increasing the presence and understanding of ethnic minorities in psychology. In T. V. McGovern (Ed.), *Handbook for enhancing undergraduate education in psychology* (pp. 71–92). Washington, DC: American Psychological Association.

Ridley, C. R., Mendoza, D. W., & Kantiz, B. E. (1994). Multicultural training: Reexamination, operationalization, and integration. *The Counseling Psychologist, 22,* 227–289.

Rogers, M. R. (2006). Exemplary multicultural training in school psychology programs. *Cultural Diversity and Ethnic Minority Psychology, 12,* 115–133.

Rogers, M. R., & Lopez, E. C. (2002). Identifying critical cross-cultural school psychology competencies. *Journal of School Psychology, 40,* 115–141.

Rogers, M. R., & Molina, L. E. (2005). Exemplary efforts in psychology to recruit and retain graduate students of color. Manuscript submitted for publication.

Rogers, M. R., & Ponterotto, J. G. (1997). Development of the Multicultural School Psychology Counseling Competency Scale, *Psychology in the Schools, 34,* 211–217.

Rogers, M. R., Ponterotto, J. G., Conoley, J. C., & Wiese, M. J. (1992). Multicultural training in school psychology: A national survey. *School Psychology Review, 21,* 603–616.

Rosenfield, S., & Esquivel, G. B. (1985). Educating school psychologists to work with bilingual/bicultural populations. *Professional Psychology: Research and Practice, 16,* 199–208.

Roysircar, G., Webster, D. R., & Germer, J. (2003). Experiential training in multicultural counseling: Implementation and evaluation of counselor process. In G. Roysircar (Ed.), *Multicultural competencies: A guidebook of practices* (pp. 3–15). Alexandria, VA: Association for multicultural Counseling & Development.

Salzman, M. (2000). Promoting multicultural competence: A cross-cultural mentorship project. *Journal of Multicultural Counseling & Development, 28,* 119–125.

Sevig, T., & Etzkorn, J. (2001). Transformative training: A year-long multicultural counseling seminar for graduate students. *Journal of Multicultural Counseling and Development, 29,* 57–72.

Sheridan, S. M. (2000). Considerations of multiculturalism and diversity in behavioral consultation with parents and teachers. *School Psychology Review, 29,* 344–353.

Showers, B., & Joyce, B. (1996). The evolution of peer coaching. *Educational Leadership, 53,* 12–16.

Smith, D. C. (1964–1965). Institutions offering graduate training in school psychology. *Journal of School Psychology, 3,* 58–66.

Steward, R. J., Wright, D. J., Jackson, J. D., & Jo, H. I. (1998). The relationship between multicultural counseling training and the evaluation of culturally sensitive and culturally insensitive counselors. *Journal of Multicultural Counseling and Development, 26,* 205–217.

U.S. Census. (2001). *Statistical abstract of the United States.* (p. 142). Washington, DC: U.S. Census Bureau.

U.S. Department of Health and Human Services. (2001). *Mental health: Culture, race, and ethnicity—a supplement to mental health: A report of the surgeon general* (DHHS Publication No. SMA 01–3613). Rockville, MD: U.S. Department of Health and Human Services, Public Health Service, Office of the Surgeon General.

Vaughan, E. (1993). Individual and cultural differences in adaptation to environmental risks. *American Psychologist, 48,* 673–680.

White, M. A. (1963). Graduate training in school psychology. *Journal of School Psychology, 2,* 34–42.

Williams, D. R., Yu, Y., Jackson, J., & Anderson, N. (1997). Racial differences in physical and mental health: Socioeconomic status, stress, and discrimination. *Journal of Health Psychology, 2,* 335–351.

Zach, L. (1970). Training psychologists for the urban slum school. *Psychology in the Schools, 7,* 345–350.

Zins, J. E., & Halsell, A. (1986). Status of ethnic minority group members in school psychology training programs. *School Psychology Review, 15,* 76–83.

II

MULTICULTURAL CONSULTATION

4

MULTICULTURAL ISSUES IN INSTRUCTIONAL CONSULTATION FOR ENGLISH LANGUAGE LEARNING STUDENTS

Emilia C. Lopez and LeeAnn Truesdell
Queens College, City University of New York

Consultation is defined as an indirect process that facilitates problem solving between consultants (i.e., school psychologists, counselors) and consultees (i.e., teachers) as they collaborate to address clients' (i.e., students) problems (Brown, Pryzwansky, & Schulte, 2001). Several models of consultation are available in the literature with models varying in terms of theoretical orientations (e.g., mental health, behavioral, organizational). Instructional consultation (IC) approaches address clients' instructional needs in schools. Idol, Nevin, and Paolucci-Whitcomb (1994) and Friend and Cook (2003) conceptualized a consultation model designed for groups of educators working together to address students' learning needs. Idol (1993) as well as Heron and Harris (2001) developed frameworks emphasizing collaboration between general and special educators. Sylvia Rosenfield (1987) conceptualized an IC model designed for school psychologists as consultants and teachers as consultees. Rosenfield's IC model was extended to instructional consultation teams ([ICT]; Rosenfield & Gravois, 1996). ICTs are composed of school personnel from various disciplines working together to examine how instructional environments can be modified to meet students' learning needs.

According to Rosenfield (1987), the essential elements of IC are: (a) the process is driven by stages that each have specific tasks, (b) decisions are made by relying on instructional and behavioral data, (c) the focus of the process is on academic issues, (d) communication is an essential part of the process because it is how consultants and consultees problem solve together, and (e) collaboration is important to accomplish the consultation goals. Models based on IC generally advocate the use of a problem solving approach whereby consultants and consultees collaborate through the following stages: establishment of a contract (i.e., an informal agreement about what students and instructional issues will be the focus of consultation), rapport building, problem identification, problem analysis, intervention planning and implementation, evaluation, and termination (Brown et al., 2001).

RATIONALE FOR USING INSTRUCTIONAL CONSULTATION WITH ENGLISH LANGUAGE LEARNERS

English language learning (ELL) students are in the process of acquiring English as a second language. As such, they demonstrate limitations in their abilities to speak, read, and/or write in English. Demographic data indicate that a significant number of ELL students are part of our school system. The National Clearinghouse for English Language Acquisition and Language Instruction (2001) estimates that about four million limited English language learners speaking over 400 different languages attend public schools in the United States. Other demographic data indicate that the number of ELL students increased by 72% between 1992 and 2002 (U.S. Department of Education, Office of Civil Rights, 2000). Many of those students are newly arrived immigrants while others were born in the U.S. but reside in homes where a language other than English is the primary mode of communication. Their levels of language proficiency range from little to no ability to communicate in English, to mixed proficiency (e.g., better able to communicate orally than in writing), to more advanced levels of English proficiency. The expectation is that the number of students with limited English proficiency will continue to increase.

There are concerns that a significant number of culturally and linguistically diverse students, including ELL students, are not achieving as well as non-minority students. Compared to non-minority students, students from culturally and linguistically diverse backgrounds are often reported to have deficient reading and writing skills in English; high rates of dropping out of school, grade retentions, suspensions, and expulsions; and high incidences of referrals for and placements in special education programs (Meece & Kurtz-Costes, 2001). Many factors are discussed as contributing to these patterns of low achievement, deficiencies, and educational placements including low socioeconomic (SES) backgrounds, a history of a lack of or inconsistent school attendance, cultural discontinuities (i.e., values of home and school conflict), limited proficiency in English, and slow progress in acquiring English as a second language (Gersten & Jimenez, 1998). Other factors discussed in the literature include the use of poorly designed or inappropriate instructional strategies (Gersten & Baker, 2000). There is research suggesting that school professionals are not well trained to provide instructional support to students from English language learning backgrounds (Ovando, Collier & Combs, 2003). A dearth of research in the area of effective instructional practices for ELL students also implies that school professionals are not receiving guidance as to how to implement effective instructional practices for this population (Gersten & Baker, 2000).

IC has the potential to support ELL students by helping teacher consultees to explore (a) language and cultural differences that impact the learning process, (b) teachers' perceptions about ELL students' instructional progress and difficulties; (c) effective instructional adaptations, strategies and interventions to help ELL students to succeed academically; (d) culturally sensitive classroom management strategies to create more supportive learning environments; (e) strategies to collaborate with culturally and linguistically diverse parents regarding learning and instructional issues; and (e) school-wide instructional practices and policies relevant to ELL students.

The focus of IC on prevention also implies that the model has the potential to prevent inappropriate special education referrals and placements of ELL students. In a recent study, Silva and Rosenfield (2004) investigated the use of ICTs to address ELL students' instructional concerns and found that the teams decreased the number of ELL students who were referred for and placed in special education programs. However, the investigators also found that a disproportionate number of ELL students, as compared to non-ELL students, were eventually referred for special education, evaluated, and classified as handicapped in categories such as mental retardation, speech and language impairment, emotional disturbance, and specific learning disabilities. Silva and Rosenfield recommend that further work be conducted to better prepare members of ICTs to address the needs of ELL students.

The consultation literature has begun to address the need to approach the consultation process using a multicultural framework. Proponents of a multicultural framework argue that consultation services must be provided while addressing cultural and language diversity issues that have a direct influence on the process and outcome of consultation (Ingraham, 2000). The purposes of this chapter are to review the primary principles of available multicultural consultation frameworks; discuss the available research related to those principles; consider the implications of applying a multicultural framework to the process of providing IC to ELL students; and explore future practice, training, and research trends in this area.

THEORETICAL AND RESEARCH BASIS

Conceptualizing Consultation Within Multicultural Contexts

In a comprehensive review of the literature, Rosenfield and Silva (in press) discuss the available research supporting the core components of the IC model. A substantial amount of research, both quantitative and qualitative, is available investigating IC processes and outcomes. Although there is no research demonstrating the utility and effectiveness of the IC model with ELL students, literature is available documenting IC services for that student population (e.g., Ingraham, 2003; Lopez, 2000; Goldstein & Harris, 2000). Providing consultation to ELL students implies that consultants must attend to cultural and linguistic factors that impact the IC process and must ask questions such as: What do instructional consultants need to know to address instructional and learning concerns for ELL students? How do cultural differences influence the relationships between instructional consultants and teacher consultees? How can consultants and consultees communicate effectively about cultural and language differences relevant to instruction? How do cultural differences shape the ways in which consultants work with consultees to identify students' instructional problems? What factors should consultants and consultees consider when planning and implementing instructional interventions for ELL students? What does the research suggest are effective interventions to instruct ELL students?

Brief Historical Overview of a Multicultural Perspective in Consultation

Westermeyer and Hausman (1974) state that Caplan, a pioneer in the area of consultation, alluded to the need to incorporate a multicultural approach in the consultation process as early as 1967 in his classic volume *Concepts of Mental Health Consultation: Their Application in Public Health Social Work*. Westermeyer and Hausman quote Caplan as stating 'In order to work well, we must have certain special information of the people with whom we are dealing' (p. 34). They also refer to Caplan's efforts to prepare to consult with the Indian Health Service in Arizona and with Alaskan natives by reading extensively about the ethnic groups he would come in contact with through his consultation work.

Various authors in psychology and education have rendered explicit calls for consultants to incorporate a multicultural framework within their practices. Westermeyer and Hausman (1974) provided an early call based on their own cross-cultural experiences in consultation. In the 1980s two frameworks were presented incorporating multicultural issues. Gibbs (1980) developed an interpersonal model of consultation between African Americans and European Americans. Gibbs argued that cultural difference influence the ways in which we approach establishing a consultation relationship with consultees. Gibbs (1985) proposed training consultants to address multicultural issues in consultation using a variety of approaches that included didactic, laboratory, fieldwork, and supervision experiences. Pinto (1981) addressed multicultural issues within organizational contexts by exploring the interactions between organizational norms (i.e., culture of the organization) and the consultants' own value system.

In the 1990s various authors began to clearly articulate the need for multicultural perspectives in consultation and to conceptualize consultation within the context of cultural diversity (e.g., Brown, 1997; Duncan, 1995; Jackson & Hayes, 1993; Lateer & Curtis, 1991; Ramirez, Lepage, Kratochwill & Duffy, 1998; Miranda, 1993; Soo Hoo, 1998; Steward, 1996; Tarver Bhering & Gelinas; 1996; Warner & Morris, 1997). It was at the end of this decade that Tarver Behring and Ingraham (1998) defined multicultural consultation as "a culturally sensitive, indirect service in which the consultant adjusts the consultation services to address the needs and cultural values of the consultee, the client, or both" (p. 58). A special issue in *School Psychology Review* (Ingraham & Meyers, 2000) devoted to multicultural consultation followed their ardent call for a multicultural framework. In that special issue, Ingraham (2000) presented a comprehensive Multicultural School Consultation (MSC) framework that described five principal components: (a) Domains for consultant learning and development; (b) Domains of consultee learning and development; (c) Cultural variations in the consultation constellation; (d) Contextual and power influences; and (e) Hypothesized methods for supporting consultee and client success.

Underlying Principles in Multicultural Consultation Frameworks

An examination of the available literature indicates that there are common underlying principles across the various multicultural frameworks applicable to consultation. Although there is a lack of research examining multicultural issues in consultation, the available research is discussed to highlight important findings in this area. It is clear that much research is needed to obtain a better understanding of how cultural differences impact the consultation process and how those elements should be addressed within the consultation models, including instructional consultation.

Consultants are sensitive to cultural differences. This principle addresses the need for consultants to (a) be aware of how cultural differences impact behaviors, attitudes, and perceptions of consultants, consultees, and clients; (b) respect and value cultural differences and alternative points of view; and (c) develop an awareness of their own attitudes, beliefs, biases, and perceptions, as well as how their cultural contexts (e.g., ethnicity, race) influence their interactions with consultees (Harris, 1991; Ingraham, 2000; Lateer & Curtis, 1991; Ramirez et al., 1998; Pinto, 1981; Tarver Behring & Ingraham, 1998). The first line of research in this area was a series of studies examining the impact of the consultants' race on intervention acceptability and consultant's credibility, effectiveness, and cultural sensitivity (Duncan & Pryzwansky, 1993; Naumann, Gutkin, & Sandoval, 1996; Rogers, 1998). The results of these analogue investigations indicated that race was not a significant factor in how subjects viewed consultants; however, consultants who addressed cultural issues were viewed as more competent about and sensitive to multicultural issues in consultation (Rogers, 1998). Ingraham (2003) conducted qualitative research using cross-cultural consultation case studies, some of which used the IC model, and found that if novice consultants ignored cultural factors or were unsuccessful in approaching them with experienced consultees, the consultation process was not effective.

Consultants and consultees acquire knowledge about their clients' cultural backgrounds. The multicultural framework calls for consultants to acquire knowledge about cultural differences and their clients' cultural backgrounds (Brown, 1997; Ingraham, 2000; Jackson & Hayes, 1993; Ramirez et al., 1998; Westermeyer & Hausman, 1974). Cultural differences vary across a number of variables that include family structure and composition; child-rearing practices; perceptions about education, disabilities, and mental health; perceptions about help seeking and interventions; and patterns of communication (Lynch, 2004). In a survey investigation conducted by Ramirez and Alghorani (2003) school psychologists indicated recognizing cultural differences between Hispanic and White students and considering those differences as important elements in consultation. However, the school psychologists in the survey also indicated "moderate success in incorporating Hispanic cultural issues in their consultation" (p. 18). Many of the respondents reported receiving little training related to multicultural issues, a finding which may be related to the consultants' moderate success in addressing cultural differences.

Tarver Behring, Cabello, Kushida, and Murguia (2000) documented modifications to school based consultation approaches by interviewing beginning consultants about their practices with consultees and culturally diverse parents and students. All the consultants reported using various modifications, and culturally different consultants reported using more modifications when consulting with culturally diverse parents and students than non-minority consultants. The modifications targeting teacher consultees included helping teachers to (a) develop an awareness of the students' cultural differences in class, (b) develop an openness to discussing culture with students, (c) develop culturally sensitive skills with students, and (d) allow more time for relationship building with students. The consultants also offered support to teachers in coping with students' cultural differences. The modifications with parent consultees were (a) allowing more time with parents for relationship building and developing trust, (b) developing awareness of and respect for parental cultural style, (c) communicating with parents in their native languages and in their dialects, (d) behaving as an ethnic role model, and (e) making home visits. The consultants also reported making modifications for specific cultural groups. For example, when working with Latino parents the consultants helped the parents to gain awareness of differences between home and school expectations and when working with Asian families the consultants reported respecting "their cultural style by using more formalized relations with the family" (p. 360).

Consultants are mindful of cultural differences in communication.   Various consultation authors recommend culturally appropriate communication styles that are sensitive to cross-cultural differences in speech patterns, nonverbal communication, eye contact, facial expressions, proximity, body language, and gestures (Harris, 1991; Miranda, 1993; Ramirez et al., 1998; Tarver Behring & Gelinas, 1996; Jackson & Hayes, 1993; Westermeyer & Hausman, 1974). Lateer and Curtis (1991) refer to possible language barriers as consultants attempt to communicate with consultees who have limited English proficient skills such as parents of ELL students. Lopez (2000) conducted a qualitative investigation involving the use of interpreters to communicate with parents during IC activities. The results indicated that although the interpreters facilitated communication with the parents, situations in which the interpreters did not accurately translate messages negatively influenced the communication process between the consultants, teacher consultees, and the clients' parents. Knotek (2003a, b) conducted two qualitative investigations examining communication within teams designed to address students' learning difficulties. The investigations were conducted in school settings with significant numbers of African American students. In one investigation Knotek (2003a) described teams that focused on the students as the sources of the learning problems (e.g., low socioeconomic status as source of the problems) and approached issues with a lack of objectivity. In a second investigation Knotek found that team members used professional jargon and informal patterns of communication that resulted in disjointed and implicit assumptions about students' skills and deficits (2003b). The consultant bridged the communication between team members and was able to document changes in the team members' communication patterns that reflected a "collaborative negotiation" of the students' learning difficulties and contexts.

Cultural differences influence interpersonal relationships between consultants and consultees. Multicultural approaches call for consultants to approach the consultation relationship and rapport building with cultural sensitivity (Brown, 1997; Ingraham, 2000; Lateer & Curtis, 1991). Westermeyer and Hausman (1974) and Ingraham discuss the possible cross-cultural combinations that may occur in consultation relationships when cultural differences are present within the consultation triad (e.g., consultant is from a culturally different background than consultee and client; consultant and consultee have different background than the client). Gibbs (1980) developed a model of interpersonal orientation to consultation hypothesizing that African Americans approach the consultation relationship with an interpersonal style (i.e., approach consultation from an interpersonal perspective) whereas European Americans approach the relationship with an instrumental style (i.e., approach consultation focused on the goal or task). Duncan and Pryzwansky (1993) conducted an investigation to examine consultees' preferences within the context of racial background (African American and White consultants) and interpersonal orientations (interpersonal vs. instrumental). The results did not support the hypothesis that there was an interaction between race and interpersonal orientations but the consultees indicated a preference for the instrumental orientation.

Other elements emphasized within a multicultural framework include power authority dimensions that influence the working relationship in consultation (i.e., consultant is from majority culture and consultee is from minority culture), resistance to consultation due to differences in frames of reference, and differences in how collaboration is defined and viewed by culturally different individuals (Gibbs, 1985; Jackson & Hayes, 1993; Lateer & Curtis, 1991; Soo-Hoo, 1998; Tarver Behring & Gelinas, 1996; Warner & Morris, 1997). For example, when Ingraham (2003) analyzed the factors that led to unsuccessful consultation cases in her qualitative investigation she found that power influences were present in cases where the novice consultants worked with experienced teacher consultees who may not have viewed the consultants as having sufficient expertise. Ingraham reported that the consultants who were successful in approaching cultural issues with their consultees used strategies such as onedownmanship, expression for empathy for the clients, self-disclosure (i.e., disclosed information regarding their own cultural backgrounds and experiences), reframing cultural perspectives, bridging across differences, creating emotional safety, and co-constructing the problem with the consultees. Ingraham hypothesized that these interpersonal strategies were instrumental in the establishment of positive working relationships that led to conceptual changes in how the consultees viewed the students' problems.

Multicultural issues are addressed throughout every stage of the consultation process. The emphasis of this principle is on entering the consultation process using culturally sensitive communication styles and interpersonal skills while also being aware of how social and cultural variables influence the establishment of a collaborating working relationship (Duncan, 1995; Gibbs, 1985). In an organization consultation project conducted within a multicultural framework, B. Meyers (2002) described a consultation project that focused on contracting with several schools to implement reform efforts around instructional strategies for African American students. B. Meyers attributed unsuccessful consultation outcomes partly to conflicted cultural reference points as consultants and consultees were unable to successfully address and resolve differences in expectations and beliefs about how to instruct students of African American backgrounds.

Approaching the problem identification stage with careful consideration as to how "the problem" is viewed by members of the consultation triad is a key underlying assumption within the multicultural consultation framework (Brown, 1997; Ingraham, 2000; Lateer & Curtis, 1991; Ramirez et al., 1998; Warner & Morris, 1997). B. Meyers' (2002) results addressed this element as she found that a major barrier was that teachers had diverse views of the educational reforms suggested by the consultants (i.e., some teachers felt that the call to change instructional strategies was not needed and was a function of the consultants viewing them as racists and as culturally insensitive, whereas other teacher consultees were open to changing instructional strategies to meet the students' needs). Goldstein and Harris (2000) explored the implications of using a consultation approach in two schools with significant numbers of Spanish speaking students and found that the parents and school staff had very different perceptions of the students' difficulties. In one school, parents wanted their children to be instructed solely in English and blamed bilingual education for their children's learning difficulties. In contrast, the staff perceived bilingual education as a way to transition the students into English and rejected the parents' perceptions. In a second school, the parents and school staff agreed that native language instruction was a resource to help the children to learn and progress. In that second school parents and school staff saw the problem as a lack of bilingual special education personnel; however, there were conflicting views among school personnel since the bilingual and special education staff did not view collaboration between their two programs as a way to educate the linguistically diverse students with special education needs.

Within a multicultural framework, planning and executing interventions is approached with consideration as to how consultees and clients view the intervention and find it acceptable within their cultural contexts (Brown, 1997; Harris, 1991; Ingraham, 2000). In her organizational consultation case study B. Meyer (2002) found that pedagogical dissonance or dissonance in how consultants and consultees viewed curriculum models for African American students (i.e., consultants emphasized direct instruction and the schools they consulted with emphasized whole language approaches) led to consultees rejecting the consultants' instructional methodologies. B. Meyer concluded that consultants must approach the planning and implementation of interventions with flexibility in responding to consultees' belief systems about instruction and curriculum.

Lateer and Curtis (1991) expand the multicultural framework to the evaluation phase of consultation. They argue that the evaluation process must be based on a culturally appropriate definition of the identified problem and on goals for change that are sensitive to cultural differences. For example, Ingraham (2003) examined consultee outcomes and noted that several of the consultees who changed their perceptions about the culturally different children's difficulties were bilingual and had background knowledge about bilingual and cultural issues. She also found that consultees who did not change their perceptions tended to take a color blind approach when examining their students' difficulties and worked with consultants who had difficulties addressing those color blind perceptions. These findings suggest that outcome evaluation within a multicultural consultation framework must take into consideration the level of the consultants' skill in addressing consultees' perceptions and the consultees' characteristics in regards to background knowledge about cultural issues, range of skills in working with culturally diverse students, and attitudes about cultural differences.

Little has been said about multicultural issues related to the stage of termination. Sheridan (2000) suggests finding on-going systems of support to facilitate the termination of behavioral consultation services to culturally diverse parents and students.

Consultants acknowledge how systemic issues impact the cultural context in consultation. A multicultural framework encourages consultants to explore and evaluate organizational policies and practices that might negatively impact consultants, consultees, and clients from diverse cultural backgrounds (Duncan, 1995; Harris, 1991; Ingraham, 2000; Jackson & Hayes, 1993). Pinto (1981) elaborated on this principle by exploring how an organization's norms and the consultants' and consultees' perceptions of those norms, which may be based on their culturally diverse backgrounds, interact with the "the technology of consultation" (p. 60). B. Meyers's (2002) case study in organizational consultation sheds insight into multiple systemic issues that played a part in the consultants' attempts to implement a specific pedagogical approach for African American students. In that investigation systemic factors such as a lack of commitment by consultees to participate in the project; dissatisfaction in procedures, policies, and allocation of resources; and differing cultural perspectives about the instructional needs of African American students (i.e., schools with small numbers of African American students did not view the pedagogical reforms suggested by the consultants as important for their school settings) resulted in unsuccessful reform efforts. The qualitative investigation conducted by Goldstein and Harris (2000) also reported systemic barriers as the bilingual education and special education staff had difficulties in collaborating and integrating their services to support the learning needs of ELL students with learning problems.

IMPLICATIONS FOR THE PRACTICE OF INSTRUCTIONAL CONSULTATION WITH ELL CLIENTS

The common underlying multicultural consultation principles and the corresponding research have multiple implications for consultants providing IC support to ELL students. Instructional consultants must attend to a number of elements that are part of a multicultural framework including (a) the relationship between consultees' and students' cultural backgrounds within the context of classroom expectations, (b) parents' expectations, (c) cross-cultural communication, (d) co-constructed definitions of collaboration, (e) the infusion of culturally responsive strategies throughout all the consultation stages, and (f) the impact of systemic factors on ELL students' needs.

Consultees' and Students' Cultural Backgrounds Within the Context of Classroom Expectations

Because ELL students are from culturally and linguistically diverse backgrounds, instructional consultants must be aware of how cultural differences influence students' classroom behaviors, attitudes toward learning, and perceptions of the classroom environment. For example, classroom structures emphasizing (a) independent work, (b) public attention and rewarding (e.g., frequent public praise for good work), (c) public demonstrations of learning (e.g., raising hand and answering instructional questions), (d) rapid pace of instruction, (e) competitive activities (e.g., groups competing for the best behavior or work), and (f) teacher led instruction with little student interaction or collaboration may be in contrast to values taught to students from diverse cultural backgrounds at home, within their communities, and in educational settings in their native countries (Okagaki, 2001). Students who do not respond to those classroom structures may in turn be viewed by consultants and consultees as too dependent, unresponsive to positive feedback, uninvolved in lessons, and unable to keep up with the instruction.

Tharp (1989) reviewed research in sociolinguistics showing that there are cross-cultural differences in wait time, or the amount of time teachers wait for students to respond to questions, and students' preferences for wait time. Tharp indicates that children from Navajo backgrounds prefer longer wait times than Anglo students, and Hawaiian children prefer negative wait time or overlapping speech. Differences have also been noted in rhythm or the tempo of teaching sequences across different cultures. For example, in Indian cultures the tempo is slow and fluid whereas Alaskan native classrooms have a faster tempo. Participation structures may also vary across cultural groups as in the case of individuals from Navajo cultures preferring longer patterns of speech and patient turn taking and individuals from Hawaiian cultures preferring exchanges characterized by "rapid fire responses, liveliness, mutual participation, interruptions, overlapping volunteered speech, and joint narration" (p. 352).

Knowledge about the consultees' cultural backgrounds will also be helpful to instructional consultants in order to recognize instances where the teachers' and students' styles conflict in classroom situations. For example, the teacher consultees' own patterns related to wait time, rhythms of lessons, and participation structures may be incompatible with the ELL students' behavioral preferences. In such scenarios, consultants will want to use consultation modifications such as the ones described by Tarver Behring et al. (2000) to help teacher consultees to recognize these cultural differences and to explore strategies to work with the students.

Okagaki (2001) also emphasizes an understanding of children's social identities. She argues that children need positive academic identities while also experiencing positive "ethnic identity" (p. 16). For ELL students positive ethnic identity involves healthy bicultural development, characterized by "knowledge of both cultures, positive attitudes toward both cultures, significant social relationships in both cultures, and bicultural efficacy or the belief that one can be true to one's culture and still be able to function in the majority culture" (p. 60).

Parents' Expectations

Understanding culturally different parents' expectations of their children's behaviors is another important component for instructional consultants. It is not unusual for cultural values and behaviors to conflict as in situations where Latino and Asian immigrant parents expect their children to sit quietly in class and only speak when the teacher approves while the classroom teachers expect these students to actively participate, ask questions, and even at times challenge the knowledge presented by the teacher via discussions and further inquiry. Thus, developing specific knowledge relevant to the parents' perceptions and beliefs about education issues facilitates consultants' and consultees' understanding of the students' classroom and instructional functioning.

Cross-Cultural Communication

Cross-cultural differences in communication are relevant in terms of consultant-consultee and consultee-client relationships. When communicating with consultees, consultants must monitor how the culturally different consultee communicates and respond by using culturally responsive communication styles. For example, Cheng (1996) states that "Asian verbal interaction is considered linear" (p. 17) because subjects are approached indirectly. In contrast, the American style is to speak about subjects directly and to ask pointed questions about those subjects. These two communicative styles may be at odds in situations where White American consultants interview Asian American teachers about their instructional styles and strategies. Lynch (2004) proposes that effective cross-cultural communicators respect individuals from diverse cultures, make continued and genuine attempts to understand others' perspectives, welcome new learning experiences, approach others with flexible attitudes, and tolerate ambiguity. Communication issues between consultees and ELL students may also be the focus of the consultation problem. Because ELL students are in the process of acquiring English as a second language they may be struggling with words that have multiple meanings, idiomatic expressions, the emotional meaning of words, humor, metaphors, proverbs, and pragmatics aspects such as greetings and gesturing (Cheng, 1996). Any or all of those variables can negatively impact communication between consultation clients, their peers, and teacher consultees.

Co-Constructed Definitions of Collaboration

Tarver Behring and Gelinas (1996) contrast the collaborative approach recommended by educators whereby teachers and parents generate intervention ideas together with contrasting values about collaboration. For example, the Asian value system of viewing teachers and other school personnel as experts may mean that parents will feel discomfort being asked to generate ideas about interventions with consultants. A definition of collaboration must be re-constructed and co-constructed between consultants, consultees and clients within the context of diverse cultural perspectives. In essence, collaboration must be defined *with*, instead of *for* culturally and linguistically diverse parents and consultees. A multicultural framework has not been applied to investigating preferences for collaborative styles between consultants and consultees. Schulte and Osborne (2003) describe several collaborative styles identified as equal but different, peer facilitator, unique service-delivery model, consultant-structured consultee-participation, shared assent to variable roles, and equal value/equal power. It is possible that preferences for collaborative styles interact with consultants' and consultees' cultural characteristics such as acculturation levels. As such, a less acculturated Asian or Hispanic consultee may prefer a more expert oriented or directive approach (i.e., consultant leads the process by asking questions from the consultee and consultant generates ideas for interventions) whereas a more acculturated consultee may prefer a more egalitarian collaborative relationship.

Infusion of Culturally Responsive Strategies Throughout all the Consultation Stages

Given that IC is driven by problem solving stages, infusing a multicultural framework throughout all the consultation stages enhances its utility with ELL clients. Ingraham (2000) highlights the importance of culturally sensitive approaches in developing and maintaining rapport with consultees. Power authority dimensions may play a part in situations where consultees who have little knowledge and skills about teaching ELL students work with consultants who have expertise in those areas; however, the reverse situation can also apply (i.e., consultee has more expertise than the consultant). Consultants' and consultees' lack of knowledge and skills about instructional issues relevant to ELL students may lead to feelings of inadequacy and fears of being labeled culturally insensitive or racist, as in the case of the teachers described by B. Meyers (2002).

Instructional consultants need knowledge about bilingualism and second language development to guide them through the problem identification stage. Teachers of ELL students are often concerned about these students' progress in acquiring English and frame their consultation referrals within the context of distinguishing if the students' instructional difficulties in reading comprehension, math or other academic areas are due to the second language acquisition process or to serious learning difficulties (Lopez, Liu, Papoutsakis, Rafferty & Valero, 1998). Knowledge about developmental processes underlying language acquisition, general stages of second language acquisition, levels of language proficiency, length of time it takes to acquire proficiency at different levels (e.g., oral language vs. written language, social conversation vs. discussions of academic content), and the relationship between the development of first and second language skills are all pivotal for instructional consultants providing support to teacher consultees educating ELL students (Lopez, 2006).

Equally important is using problem identification strategies and tools that are sensitive to cultural and language differences (Harris, 1991; Warner & Morris, 1997). Among the recommended strategies are classroom observations, interviews, informal academic assessment (e.g., reading inventories, error analysis) and test teach methods to examine ELL students' difficulties with instructional tasks (Bentz & Pavri, 2000; Lopez et al., 1998). Analyzing errors in language samples and work samples (e.g., writing tasks) is helpful to investigate if the errors made by the student are a function of language transference (i.e., a common phenomenon in second language acquisition whereby the learner transfers syntactic and semantic rules from the first language to the second language). Both curriculum based assessment (CBA) and curriculum based measurement (CBM) methodologies are recommended (Baker & Good, 1995; McCloskey & Athanasiou, 2000) and later we elaborate on important points to consider when using these approaches with ELL students. In general, for the CBA tools to be useful they should be (a) connected to the classroom instruction and (b) appropriate in terms of the students' cultural and experiential backgrounds. If a mismatch is suspected between the students' level of language proficiency and the content of the task, consultants and consultees should gather problem identification data about the students' level of language proficiency using activities and materials at varied levels of language proficiency.

Problem analyses must be conducted while taking into consideration factors such as the ELL students' (a) level of proficiency in English and the first language, (b) past educational experiences (e.g., attended school in native country, grades completed in native country), and (c) past history with educational programs (e.g., bilingual education, ESL). These students' skills and educational histories must then be examined within the context of the instructional task. Given these students' cultural differences and low levels of language proficiency, they often have difficulties succeeding in tasks where they need specific background information that they are not familiar with as a result of cultural differences and/or a lack of exposure to concepts. Recent immigrants may also not be familiar with the structure of specific tasks such as multiple choice items. Accomplishing consultee conceptual change is certainly a goal of IC and the problem analysis stage is often the vehicle by which to provide the consultee with alternative ways of examining the students' difficulties with instructional tasks. As such, a consultee who initially viewed an ELL student as unable to learn may start to view the student as learning but not demonstrating his/her knowledge because of a culturally related slower style of responding to instructional questions. In another scenario a consultee who viewed a student as unable to comprehend reading passages may change his/her frame of reference when considering that the ELL student may not have the background knowledge, underlying concepts or cultural experiences to understand the content of the passages.

Issues of treatment acceptability and treatment integrity must be carefully considered as teacher consultees educating ELL students may be asked to adapt or modify instruction in complex and demanding ways. It is thus possible that consultees may experience a conceptual change in how they view the ELL students' difficulties but that they do not change the ways in which they instruct those students because the strategies may be difficult to integrate within the general curriculum. Barriers such as lack of knowledge, skills, time, or resources may overshadow the conceptual change and result in poor treatment acceptability and treatment integrity. Teacher consultees implementing strategies that are new to them or that involve extensive accommodations may need considerable support in the form of background materials or information, observations of other teachers using similar strategies, modeling, coaching, intervention scripts and frequent encouragement. Support from and collaboration with bilingual education and ESL staff to arrange co-teaching experiences and peer collaborative efforts focusing on curriculum planning, organization of activities, and the development of instructional materials are valuable resources for teachers.

Differences in cultural values may also influence intervention acceptability and integrity as in situations where consultees may opt for interventions that match their cultural styles (e.g., consultee from cultural background that values cooperation may reject interventions that emphasize competition; consultees from cultural backgrounds that value written communication styles may reject strategies that emphasize oral communication to demonstrate knowledge) (Brown et al., 2001). Consultees need support in examining those contrasting cultural viewpoints and in finding ways to address them. In general, consultants are encouraged to carefully consider what factors are leading to poor intervention acceptability or integrity without quickly jumping to the conclusion that the consultee is not engaging in behavior change because of cultural insensitivity or biased attitudes.

Although beyond the scope of this chapter, consultants need to have knowledge about the different programs available for ELL students, including transitional bilingual education, maintenance bilingual education, and ESL programs. This background knowledge is important in understanding the structure and goals of the curriculum within those programs (see Ochoa and Rhodes [2005] for a recent discussion of this topic). The consultants' and consultees' attitudes toward these education programs and philosophies should also be the subject of scrutiny in the IC framework. As discussed by Ochoa and Rhodes, there is a wide range of attitudes toward bilingual instruction vs. English only instruction. It is the authors' experience that these attitudes can interfere with the consultants' and consultees' decision-making in IC. Decisions made about instructional programs and strategies should be undertaken with extensive background knowledge about available practices and the research concerning the effectiveness of those practices.

The evaluation stage of IC can also be approached with a multicultural perspective. Process evaluation efforts focused on multicultural issues serve the function of examining how cultural and language differences have been considered throughout every stage of the consultation process. Tools to measure outcomes for ELL clients should be matched to the identified problems and to the interventions that were designed. Outcome evaluation should involve an examination of changes in consultees' attitudes, beliefs and perceptions about ELL students' instructional functioning as well the extent of the effectiveness of the instructional strategies implemented for ELL students.

Finally, culturally responsive interpersonal styles are important as consultants address termination with consultees. For example, individuals from some Middle Eastern cultures tend to disapprove of the provision of excessive amounts of positive feedback. These differences in interactive styles must be considered when following Rosenfield's (1987) suggestion to provide consultees with positive feedback about their contributions to the consultation process. A termination strategy that is useful to teacher consultees is providing them with a summary of the instructional strategies and interventions that were developed targeting ELL students so that they are able to refer to those strategies when instructing other ELL students with similar difficulties in the future.

Impact of Systemic Factors on ELL Students' Needs

An analysis of organizational factors impacting ELL students is also valuable within the IC framework. For example, despite research showing that it takes 7 to 10 years to obtain high levels of language proficiency in a second language, ELL students are often exited from ESL programs after only two or three years of support (Ovando et al., 2003). Although ELL students tend to demonstrate high proficiency when communicating in social situations or in some academic contexts, they tend to continue to struggle with academic tasks that demand higher levels of comprehension and expressive skills (e.g., comprehending technical information in science, using vocabulary related to abstract concepts they are unfamiliar with). Many districts have policies that deny these students further ESL services once they have demonstrated proficiency via language tests. In such situations, the ESL staff is not even available to provide consultation services to those students. Such discontinuities in ESL services are often the result of school or district-wide policies that leave classroom teachers and students with inadequate instructional support.

A lack of collaboration between bilingual staff, ESL teachers, and other educators is another systemic barrier that does not benefit ELL students (Goldstein & Harris, 2000). Attitudes communicating message such as "ELL students belong to ESL and bilingual teachers" foster educational environments where teachers do not perceive ELL students as their collective responsibility. Conflicting views about instructional approaches may also result in systemic barriers as in situations where bilingual education teachers who emphasize whole language approaches and natural communicative intent (i.e., learning language in natural situations) may conflict with the more structured linguistic approaches embraced by ESL teachers (e.g., emphasizing formal structure of language such as syntax), or the structured task analytic approaches used by special education staff (Gersten & Woodward, 1994). Shortages of bilingual or ESL personnel, a lack of instructional materials designed for ELL students, and the absence of administrative support for instructional services can all influence the implementation of interventions in IC. Poorly designed bilingual and ESL programs or inconsistent instructional practices are other contributing factors (Borden, 1998; Gersten & Woodward, 1994). Efforts focused on systemic changes via staff training, program evaluation, integration of services, collaboration across programs, and program redesign are vehicles for instructional consultants to address these systemic problems while working closely with school administrators and other school personnel.

IMPLEMENTATION AND APPROACHES: HIGHLIGHTING PROBLEM IDENTIFICATION AND INSTRUCTION

Language use in the context of the school curriculum is the most significant factor in determining whether children succeed academically (Miller, as cited in Losardo

& Notari-Syverson, 2001). Therefore, the focus for IC for ELL students is primarily on the intersection of language learning and academic learning. Cummins (1980) delineates this intersection as the language that is needed for students to understand and perform competently within an academic milieu where little context is provided for the language used to develop conceptual understanding. He contrasts academic language, Cognitive Academic Language Proficiency (CALP), with the informal language, Basic Interpersonal Communication Skills (BICS), used in day-to-day exchanges where context supports language use and understanding.

The school learning environment is often bereft of visual and concrete referents and provides little experience with the abstract concepts and accompanying language (i.e., CALPS) used to discuss and develop understanding of the curriculum. Within this unsupportive environment, students for whom English is a second language struggle to make sense of the curriculum because they do not have the English language needed to engage in classroom discussion and to read texts with understanding. Unaware of the impact that their teaching and classroom environments have on ELL students, teachers often refer these students to special education assuming that they have a learning disability (Ortiz & Garcia, 1995). IC is a means by which teachers who struggle with ELL students can problem solve with other teachers and professionals such as school psychologists to determine what factors may be affecting classroom performance and to find interventions effective for ELL students.

Assessment of ELL Students Within the IC Framework

When ELL students are the clients for IC, then the process needs to be sensitive to and incorporate knowledge of culture and language. An early phase of IC is to identify the problem as clearly as possible. Through a careful dialogue of questioning and probing, a description of behavior is gradually formed of the student's classroom functioning. In addition, classroom observations are jointly planned to "understand better how teachers, learners, and curriculum are interacting" (Rosenfield & Gravois, 1996, p.106). Systematic observation of ELL students in classroom settings must consider cultural issues in addition to behavioral and academic issues. Observations are jointly planned by the consultant and classroom teacher to focus on both the student's participation in classroom academic activities and the ways in which the teacher provides academic supports. Since the student's culture, as well as English language development affects classroom participation, close attention to behavior as a cultural phenomenon is needed to delineate cultural issues from other factors affecting learning. For example, children from Asian American communities may appear reticent and withdrawn from a lively classroom discussion; Hispanic students may seek ways to work together and share their academic expertise with one another; ELL students in the early stages of learning English, may be silent as they listen and take in this new language (Krashen, 1981).

Observations should also capture the instructional strategies that the teacher uses to engage ELL students in completing academic tasks and promoting understanding and learning. Where is the child in proximity to the teacher? What is the pattern of interaction between the teacher and the ELL student and among class-mates and the ELL student? What does the teacher do to prompt, guide, and scaffold student's engagement in doing the academic tasks? What language and concepts are central to the lesson and how does the teacher present the vocabulary and develop understanding of the concepts? Descriptive evidence of the lesson demands and student's participation are helpful in understanding what the ELL student experiences each day in the classroom's learning environment.

Assessment of the ELL students in the IC process focuses on the student's functioning in the curriculum by examining how he or she engages in academic tasks and makes sense of them. CBA is a way to determine instructional needs of ELL students (Rhodes, Ochoa, & Ortiz, 2005) and to examine how those students respond to the curriculum tasks and understand the concepts and content. CBA was developed to gather information about student skills and knowledge needed in the curriculum of the classroom in order to plan instruction and modifications (Rosenfield, 1987). In CBA, students complete academic tasks that are central to the curriculum and their responses are analyzed to determine the knowledge and skills they have and what they need to be successful. In addition, students may explain how they do tasks, why they approach the task or "think aloud" as they complete tasks. These processes illuminate the students' language, strategies, and understanding. For ELL students, CBA is extended to examine the language and vocabulary they use to participate in lessons and make sense of the curriculum.

Nelson (1994) as well as Jitendra and Rohena-Diaz (1996) combined a curriculum focus with the language elements and vocabulary needed to understand and function in the curriculum for a curriculum-based language assessment process that is used to determine whether children have the language skills and strategies and the vocabulary for processing information within the context of the curriculum. The process includes (a) identifying the objectives and the contextually based language areas critical to mastery of the objectives; (b) reviewing the specific vocabulary and language requirements; (c) identifying the child's language resources and repertoire in relation to these language requirements; and (d) determining ways to teach in order to enhance student language competence and ways to modify the curriculum if needed (Losardo & Notari-Syverson, 2001). These strategies are based on dynamic assessment approaches, derived from Vygotsky's (1962) socio-cultural theory of learning, and focus on engaging teachers and students in an interactive process of instruction to examine learners' responses to teaching. Jitendra and Rohena-Diaz illustrate in a case study a curriculum-based dynamic language assessment of an ELL student within naturalistic situations. The assessment process engaged the student in explaining how to do familiar tasks and revealed the student's lack of vocabulary. The dynamic nature of the assessment illuminated how well the student responded to vocabulary prompts, concrete and familiar materials, multimodal presentations and real contexts.

Instructional Interventions for ELL Students

While research on effective instruction for ELL students is limited, studies converge on a set of practices that promote literacy, conceptual learning, and language development. Instruction is effective when learners are successful in doing academic tasks and understand the concepts inherent in the task. Understanding develops through a process of language mediation, placing language and vocabulary at the center of the learning process. Since language mediation is important for all learners, the interventions that are effective for ELL students are effective for all learners (Gersten & Jimenez, 1998).

Effective instruction for ELL students departs from special education practices that focus on specific skills organized hierarchically, taught with direct instruction and supported with drill and practice. Effective instruction that facilitates and supports language acquisition and learning occurs within a socio-cultural framework. Tharp and Gallimore (1988) draw from Vygotsky's (1962) socio-cultural theory of learning that pairs social interaction and cognitive development. Understanding of the curriculum is constructed jointly between the teacher and learners through discourse with word meaning central to concept development. They contrast conversational instruction with direct instruction, often the hallmark of special education, indicating the importance of dialogue in promoting language learning. However, within instruction that emphasizes discussion and meaning making, it is recognized that vocabulary and phonics may need to be taught directly and connected to students' first language (Gersten & Baker, 2000).

Tharp and Gallimore (1988) place literacy at the center of school learning and argue that literacy and language development are inseparable. Language learning occurs in natural communities where adults do not teach language directly, but rather respond to children at their level, engaging in topic centered pragmatic conversation. Thus, they recommend that language and concept learning in school occur within connected discourse focused on content and concepts. Language, vocabulary and concept learning occur through the development of word meaning, which in everyday situations functions with the support of context and concrete objects and experiences. In schools, curriculum learning and word meaning are decontextualized. Written text, rather than experience, becomes the primary source of concept learning. Tharp and Gallimore, therefore, suggest that in order to support learning for ELL students and all other students, concepts found in the curriculum must be connected to everyday concrete concepts and experiences in order to help students develop meaning.

Many researchers have examined effective teaching for ELL and often found that focusing on vocabulary and concept learning within a socio-cultural perspective promoted students' understanding and language development. An observational study of early childhood teachers of ELLs, revealed that language learning and pre-literacy skills were developed in classrooms where language was used constantly within authentic activities, students interacted in a print rich environment, and understanding of lessons was promoted by connections to family and community experiences (Goldenberg, 1998).

In a review of the research of the cognitive reading processes of students for whom English is a second language, Fitzgerald (1995) found that vocabulary was a critical variable affecting reading. In addition, prior knowledge or the schema that students bring to the text, as well as different text structures, impact understanding of ESL. Furthermore, native reading scores predicted English reading scores in elementary readers, while oral proficiency predicted reading scores in middle school. In general, cognitive reading processes were substantially the same for ESL and native English speakers. However, ESL readers used somewhat fewer metacognitive strategies; performed reading tasks more slowly, recalled subordinate ideas less well, and monitored comprehension more slowly than native English speakers.

The ELL student's native language plays a critical role in the development of the second language. Furthermore, the literacy abilities and concept development in the native language impact the literacy learning and conceptual formation in the second language (Cummins & Swain, 1986). Cummins (1981) determined a developmental interdependence in learning a second language and hypothesized a common underlying proficiency (CUP) in which the first language influences the learning and proficiency of the second language. An important implication of this theory is that children and families should continue to develop literacy skills in the native language as this learning supports and enhances literacy development in the second language. Also, concepts learned in the native language transfer readily to English, once the English vocabulary is introduced and learned.

Several instructional factors important for ELL have been identified by researchers (Anderson & Roit, 1996; Chamot, 1998; De Leon & Medina, 1998; Gersten & Baker, 2000; Gersten, Marks, Keating, & Baker, 1998; Goldenberg, 1998). Among these factors are the integration of language learning with concept learning and deliberate, explicit vocabulary instruction, as well as students' use of their native language within classroom discussion. Research findings also identified classroom discussion or dialogue as an important instructional process for ELL students because interactive discussion rather than "chalk and talk" (i.e., a lecture lesson format) promotes understanding and language learning. Interaction with peers in small cooperative groups also facilitates and promotes understanding and language learning (Gersten & Baker, 2000). Effective teachers of ELL students model, elaborate and paraphrase language, and use consistent vocabulary when teaching new concepts. Research findings further indicate that effective instruction for ELL students utilize structure and scaffolding to guide students in completing academic tasks (Gersten & Baker, 2000). Teachers allow more wait time for ELL students to formulate their ideas in English. In addition, instruction in learning strategies and metacognition help ELL students develop into independent learners.

Literacy development is a critical area for ELLs students. Based on a review of the literature on literacy development for ELL students, Anderson and Roit (1996) recommend ways to support literacy development in ELL students. Balanced literacy with explicit instruction in phonics provides ELL students with early literacy experiences, an opportunity to develop written expression, and experience with a plethora of literature that includes selections from a wide range of cultures. Shared reading, choral reading and rereading enhance fluency and understanding. Reading comprehension is fostered when students explain the text rather than simply retell the story, when they discern important from less important ideas, and when they learn about different text structures. Effective teachers provide ELL students with accessible texts to support concept learning, engage ELL students in using imagery, and connect the text with students' prior knowledge and cultural experience. Anderson and Roit hypothesize that reading promotes learning English because the text is stable and can be revisited while spoken language is fleeting. Based on this hypothesis, engaging ELL students in learning to read in English will enhance language learning. Teachers often believe that learning English is a prerequisite to learning to read in English. Cummins and Swain (1986) explain the level of English language learning needed to read as the threshold hypothesis, which argues that there is a level of English language development needed to begin learning in English. Once the threshold has been reached, the learner has enough English language to make sense of text (written at an initial level). As learning to read in English progresses, reading and writing in English actually facilitate English language learning.

Supportive classroom environments for ELL students are grounded in principles of multicultural education most especially by connecting to students' families and cultural communities. They are created by teachers with high expectations and positive attitudes who develop personal relationships and respect and accept students, their language and culture. In these classrooms, students feel safe to experiment and make mistakes (Chamot, 1998; Gersten, 1996). These classrooms have adult native speakers and provide opportunities for students to connect to their cultural heritage. Effective classrooms for ELL students have challenging curriculum, promote critical thinking, and engage students in active learning and discourse that is intellectually stimulating, clear and explicit. Learning is supported with materials in students' native languages, extended time, and informal assessments that are used to monitor learning and inform instruction.

IMPLICATIONS FOR FUTURE RESEARCH AND TRAINING

Ramirez et al. (1998) recommend examining the impact of cultural variables on consultation. They propose a cultural variable research framework for a series of studies comparing outcomes of consultations that vary by cultural characteristics of consultants, consultees, and clients, cultural information/data available during the consultation process, and/or the uses of cultural information in the process. Using group comparison and time series designs, Ramirez et al. propose studies examining the outcomes of consultation in student achievement and consultee outcomes in terms of knowledge and skills. They pose a number of research questions, among which are: In what ways is information regarding cultural variables helpful in problem-solving consultation? Are theories and models of consultation equally applicable to all cultural groups? What are appropriate, relevant, and effective (culturally responsive) assessment, intervention, and evaluation problem-solving strategies/skills for working with culturally different clients and consultees in consultation?

Ingraham (2000) calls for research that examines the communication style of the consultant, research on actual consultation sessions, as well as the impact of culture on the objectivity, bias, and stereotyping prevalent in cross-cultural situations. Future research should focus on examining the impact of such factors as race, levels of acculturation, and racial identity on consultation processes and outcomes.

A conceptual framework for research of multicultural consultation focusing on ELL students should combine multicultural knowledge and skills, cross cultural communication, and cultural differences with the stages of IC and effective interventions for ELL. Careful examination of multiple cross-cultural consultation processes using qualitative and experimental methodologies would provide valuable insight into the complexities of this work. Some of the questions and issues that may inform this research include: What are the cultural issues that impact the stages of IC? How are problems viewed by different members of IC teams and how does culture play a role in their different perspectives? What are the cultural factors that affect collaboration in IC? To what extent does language and culture affect rapport, relationship building, and communication among members of ICTs? What are the cultural issues inherent in collaboration and developing parity? How do ELL students' language skills and vocabulary knowledge impact learning of school curriculum?

In addition to cultural issues, interventions for ELL students are, for the most part, divergent from many typical classroom and special education practices. A variety of research methodologies can be used to examine the processes used by individual consultants and teams in selecting interventions that are effective for ELL students and are also compatible with current classroom and school practices.

Ingraham (2000) argues that case study research on multicultural consultation investigate "subtle cross-cultural issues such as pressures on consultees for student achievement and multicultural education, power differentials associated with privilege or cultural/professional status, and the intersection of consultant, consultee(s), and client(s) individual and cultural variables" (p. 323). Through participant action research, examination into the processes and choices that instructional consultants make during the consultation process could provide insight into the influence of culture. Additionally, action research may be used to examine the efficacy of the interventions employed in the IC process as well as its impact on consultees' knowledge and skills. The school psychology scientist practitioner paradigm is a useful vehicle by which to engage practicing instructional consultants in examining their practices in multicultural frameworks and with ELL clients (J. Meyers, 2002).

Using single subject design and CBA, research also needs to examine outcomes in the context of ELL students' understanding of the curriculum and their progress in acquiring language and literacy skills. CBM is used to measure the growth systematically of curriculum skills such as reading fluency and comprehension within the regular curriculum. Research is needed to examine the validity of CBM with ELL students who are learning to read while they continue to acquire and learn English, and to compare reading progress with culturally relevant and typical texts.

Finally, Wong and Rowley-Johnson (2001) recognize the importance of the researcher's role and assumptions, bounded by cultural experience, that impact the investigative process and interpretation of outcomes. They recognize the impact that their own culture has on the research process and that the process is not void of cultural influence as objectivity of research often claims.

The preparation of consultants for multicultural consultation, and in particular IC, for ELL students requires specialized knowledge and skills in cross-cultural communication, multicultural education and English language instruction. The essential elements for IC delineated by Rosenfield (1987) provide a blueprint for the preparation of consultants. These elements take on new meaning within a multicultural IC framework. However, Anton-LaHart and Rosenfield's (2004) survey study indicates that little time is being spent in school psychology consultation courses on examining multicultural issues.

Cross-cultural communication influences much of IC from entry and rapport building, through collaboration, intervention and exiting. The very foundation of cross-cultural communicative competence is the knowledge and awareness of one's own culture. Therefore, the preparation of consultants for ELL students should begin with a self-examination of culture and perspective and how these affect consultation (Harris, 1996; Ingraham, 2000; Ramirez et al., 1998). Knowledge of different cultural groups and their values and ways of behaving is central to building the awareness and sensitivity needed to communicate cross-culturally and to work effectively to support ELL students. Thus, training programs need to incorporate both a knowledge base of cultural information and the experiences needed to develop effective skills in cross-cultural communication.

As an essential element of IC, collaboration is impacted by issues of parity and power, which are especially influenced by cultural and social differences. A. B. Meyers (2002) prepares consultants to (a) recognize the expertise of parents, teachers and other professionals, while helping them to recognize their own expertise as they enter into field situations; (b) strike a balance between confidence and deference and to know when to be more or less direct in a cross-cultural situation; and (c) understand the complexity of power differences and how to develop parity within power differences. A. B. Meyers uses four dimensions of Black feminist epistemology articulated by Collins (2000) to inform the training of consultants for multicultural consultation: the contribution of lived experience to expertise; the use of dialogue, or the reciprocal and respectful exchange of views, to develop knowledge; the use of empathy and caring to speak and behave in ways congruent with your own feelings; and a genuineness in wanting to help children. A. B. Meyer uses these dimensions to help students (consultants-in-training) overcome their differences in status, culture, and education, so that they will work effectively with consultees and families.

Knowledge of second language acquisition and effective interventions for ELL students is central to effective multicultural IC (Harris, 1996; Ingraham, 2000; Ramirez, et al., 1998). Training of instructional consultants should include courses in second language and literacy learning as well as effective interventions built on the principle that "language learners are active learners who, when exposed to sufficient language input from others, devise hypotheses about rules, test them out, modify them, and gradually construct their own language" (Willing & Ortiz, as cited in Harris, 1996, p. 291). Cummins (1986) suggested that appropriate curriculum for multicultural society incorporate students' native languages and cultures and that instruction should be interactive and experiential to support language development and higher order thinking.

Issues of appropriate assessment for ELL students are critical factors in the IC process. In addition to the psychometric factors that are examined in measurement courses related to bias, consultants need to learn a number of informal assessment procedures including CBA, CBM, observations, and clinical interviewing whereby the consultant engages "the student in academic tasks that focus on the attainment of concepts and assessing the student's ability to learning these concepts in English and the native language" (Harris, 1996, p. 361).

Programs preparing instructional consultants for working with ELL students should incorporate didactic, laboratory, and field experiences with ELL students (Gibbs, 1985; Westermeyer & Hausman, 1974). Both knowledge and experiences are needed to develop the expertise needed to be effective instructional consultants for ELL students. Field experiences in schools settings would also provide examples of systemic and organizational issues that affect the education of ELL students (e.g., bilingual programs, ESL programs, resource rooms, and special education programs each with different paradigms, criteria, and interventions). Professional preparation of future consultants should also provide knowledge, skills and experience in conducting action and/or participant research. These inquiry processes are important tools for professionals to examine their own practice and the efficacy of their practice on the learning and functioning of students. These qualitative research methods differ from the quantitative and experimental research designs. Thus, programs preparing instructional consultants (e.g., school psychology programs, general and special education training programs) would need to expand their research perspectives to include qualitative methlogies.

CONCLUSION

IC has the potential to provide support to teacher consultees instructing ELL students. Its promise is contingent on instructional consultants who have the knowledge and skills to consult within multicultural frameworks, on training programs that prepare instructional consultants to deliver culturally responsive consultation services, and on research that will continue to expand our understanding of multicultural consultation processes and outcomes.

ANNOTATED BIBLIOGRAPHY

Gersten, R. M., & Baker, S. (2000). The professional knowledge base on instructional practices that support cognitive growth for English-language learners. In R. Gersten, E. P. Schiller, & S. Vaughn (Eds.), *Contemporary special education research: Synthesis of the knowledge base on critical instructional issues* (pp. 31–79). Mahwah, NJ: Erlbaum.

Gersten and colleagues used a multivocal synthesis method to examine the professional knowledge base on instructional practices for English language learners. The researchers used experimental studies, descriptive investigations, and professional work groups as data sources to synthesize the available knowledge in this area.

Ingraham, C. L., & Meyers, J. (2000). Multicultural and cross-cultural consultation in schools [Special Issue]. *School Psychology Review, 29,* 3.

This special issue provides readers with an excellent overview of multicultural issues in consultation. Several conceptual articles articulate multicultural frameworks in consultation. Several qualitative research investigations focus on a number of different topics in multicultural consultation. The special issue ends with several commentaries.

RESOURCES

Culturally Competence Consultation in the Schools: Information for School Psychologists and School Personnel. Web page at the National School Psychologists website. http://www.nasponline.org/culturalcompetence.

This is a practical handout that provides a brief overview of multicultural issues in consultation. It is especially useful in training situations to provide readers with a quick introduction and overview of basic topics in multicultural consultation.

Center for Research on Education, Diversity and Excellence (CREDE). www.crede.org.

The Center engages in research and development for improving the education of students from diverse language and cultural communities. Research teams have synthesized findings into five standards of effective pedagogy. The website provides research reports, practitioner reports, professional development resources and materials to support effective instruction for ELL students.

REFERENCES

Anderson, V., & Roit, M. (1996). Linking reading comprehension instruction to language development for language-minority students. *Elementary School Journal, 96*, 296–309.

Anton-LaHart, J., & Rosenfield, S. (2004). A survey of preservice consultation training in school psychology programs. *Journal of Educational and Psychological Consultation, 15*, 41–62.

Baker, S. K., & Good, R. (1995). Curriculum-based measurement of English reading with bilingual Hispanic students: A validation study with second-grade students. *School Psychology Review, 24*, 561–578.

Bentz, J., & Pavri, S. (2000). Curriculum-based measurement in assessing bilingual students: A promising new direction. *Diagnostique, 25*, 229–248.

Borden, J. F. (1998). The pitfalls and possibilities for organizing quality ESL programs. *Middle School Journal, 29*(3), 25–33.

Brown, D. (1997). Implications of cultural values for cross-cultural consultation with families. *Journal of Counseling & Development, 76*, 29–35.

Brown, D., Pryzwansky, W. B., & Schulte, A. C. (2001). *Psychological consultation: Introduction to theory and practice* (5th ed.). Boston: Allyn & Bacon.

Chamot, A. U. (1998). Effective instruction for high school for English language learners. In R. M. Gersten & R. T. Jimenez (Eds.), *Promoting learning for culturally and linguistically diverse students: Classroom applications from contemporary research* (pp. 187–209). Belmont, CA: Wadsworth Publishing Company.

Cheng, L. L. (1996). Beyond bilingualism: A quest for communicative competence. *Topics in Language Disorder, 16*, 9–21.

Collins, P. H. (2000). *Black feminist thought: Knowledge, consciousness, and the politics of empowerment* (2nd ed.). New York: Routledge.

Cummins, J. (1980). The construct of language proficiency in bilingual education. In J. E. Alatis (Ed.), *Georgetown University roundtable on languages and linguistics* (pp. 73–76). Washington, DC: Georgetown University Press.

Cummins, J. (1981). Four misconceptions about language proficiency in bilingual education. *NABE Journal, 5*(3), 31–45.

Cummins, J. (1986). Empowering minority students: A framework for intervention. *Harvard Educational Review, 56,* 18–36.

Cummins, J., & Swain, M. (1986). *Bilingualism in education: Aspects of theory, research and practice.* London: Longman.

De Leon, J., & Medina, C. (1998). Language and preliteracy development of English as a second language learners in early childhood special education. In R. M. Gersten & R. T. Jimenez (1998). *Promoting learning for culturally and linguistically diverse students: Classroom applications from contemporary research* (pp. 26–41). Belmont, CA: Wadsworth Publishing Company

Duncan, C. F. (1995). Cross-cultural school consultation. In C. Lee (Ed.), *Counseling for diversity* (pp. 129–139). Boston: Allyn & Bacon.

Duncan, C. F., & Pryzwansky, W. B. (1993). Effects of race, racial identity development, and orientation style on perceived consultant effectiveness. *Journal of Multicultural Counseling and Development, 21,* 88–96.

Fitzgerald, J. (1995). English-as-a-second-language learners' cognitive reading processes: A review of research in the United States. *Review of Educational Research, 65,* 145–190.

Friend, M., & Cook, L. (2003). *Interactions: Collaboration skills for school professionals* (2nd ed.). White Plains, NY: Longman.

Gersten, R. M. (1996). Literacy instruction for language-minority students: The transition years. *The Elementary School Journal, 96,* 227–244.

Gersten, R. M., & Baker, S. (2000). The professional knowledge base on instructional practices that support cognitive growth for English-language learners. In R. Gersten, E. P. Schiller, & S. Vaughn (Eds.), *Contemporary special education research: Synthesis of the knowledge base on critical instructional issues* (pp. 31–79). Mahwah, NJ: Erlbaum.

Gersten, R. M., & Jimenez, R. T. (1998). *Promoting learning for culturally and linguistically diverse students: Classroom applications from contemporary research.* Belmont, CA: Wadsworth Publishing Company

Gersten, R. M., Marks, S. U., Keating, S., & Baker, S. (1998). Recent research on effective instructional practices in content area ESOL. In R. M. Gersten & R. T. Jimenez (Eds.), *Promoting learning for culturally and linguistically diverse student* (pp. 57–72). New York: Wadsworth Publishing.

Gersten, R., & Woodward, J. (1994). The language-minority student and special education: Issues, trends, and paradoxes. *Exceptional Children, 60,* 310–322.

Gibbs, J. T. (1980). The interpersonal orientation in mental health consultation: Toward a model of ethnic variations in consultation. *Journal of Community Psychology, 8,* 195–207.

Gibbs, J. T. (1985). Can we continue to be color-blind and class-bound? *The Counseling Psychologist, 13,* 426–435.

Goldenberg, C. (1998). A balanced literacy approach to early Spanish literacy instruction. In R. M. Gersten & R. T. Jimenez (Eds.), *Promoting learning for culturally and linguistically diverse student* (pp. 3–25). New York: Wadsworth Publishing.

Goldstein, B. S. C., & Harris, K. C. (2000). Consultant practices in two heterogeneous Latino schools. *School Psychology Review, 29,* 368–377.

Harris, K. C. (1991). An expanded view on consultation competencies for educators serving culturally and linguistically diverse exceptional students. *Teacher Education and Special Education, 14*(1), 25–29.

Harris, K. C. (1996). Collaboration within a multicultural society: Issues for consideration. *Remedial and Special Education, 17,* 355–362.

Heron, T. E., & Harris, K. C. (2001). *The educational consultant: Helping professionals, parents, and mainstreamed students* (4th ed.). Austin: ProEd.

Idol, L. (1993). *Special educator's consultation handbook* (2nd ed.). Austin: ProEd.

Idol, L., Nevin, A., & Paolucci-Whitcomb, P. (1994). *Collaborative consultation* (2nd ed.). Austin: ProEd.

Ingraham, C. L. (2000). Consultation through a multicultural lens: Multicultural and cross-cultural consultation in schools. *School Psychology Review 29*, 320–343.

Ingraham, C. L. (2003). Multicultural consultee-centered consultation: When novice consultants explore cultural hypotheses with experienced teacher consultees. *Journal of Educational and Psychological Consultation*, 14, 329–362.

Ingraham, C. L., & Meyers, J. (2000). Multicultural and cross-cultural consultation in schools [Special Issue]. *School Psychology Review, 29.*

Jackson, D. N., & Hayes, D. H. (1993, November/December). Multicultural issues in consultation. *Journal of Counseling & Development 72*, 144–147.

Jitendra, A. K., & Rohena-Diaz, E. (1996). Language assessment of students who are linguistically diverse: Why a discrete approach is not the answer. *School Psychology Review, 25*(1), 40–57.

Knotek, S. E. (2003a). Bias in problem solving and the social process of student study teams: A qualitative study. *Journal of Special Education, 27,* 2–14

Knotek, S. E. (2003b). Making sense of jargon during consultation: Understanding consultees' social language to effect change in student study teams. *Journal of Educational and Psychological Consultation, 14,* 181–208.

Krashen, S. (1981). Bilingual education and second language acquisition theory. In California State Department of Education (Ed.). *Schooling and language minority students: A theoretical framework.* Los Angeles: Evaluation, dissemination and Assessment Center, California State University.

Lateer, A., & Curtis, M. J. (1991, March). *Cross-cultural consultation: Responding to diversity.* Paper presented at the meeting of the National Association of School Psychologists, Dallas, TX.

Lopez, E. C. (2000). Conducting instructional consultation through interpreters. *School Psychology Review, 29*, 378–388.

Lopez, E. C. (2006). English language learners. In G. Bear, K. Minke, & A. Thoams (Eds.), *Children's Needs III: Psychological perspectives* (pp. 647–660). Washington DC: National Association of School Psychologists.

Lopez, E. C., Liu, C., Papoutsakis, M., Rafferty, T., & Valero, C. (April, 1998). *An examination of content and process variables in cross-cultural consultation.* Poster session presented at the National Association of School Psychology Conference, Orlando, FL.

Losardo, A., & Notari-Syverson, A. (2001). *Alternative approaches to assessing young children.* Baltimore: Brookes Publishing.

Lynch, E. W. (2004). Developing cross-cultural competence. In E. W. Lynch & M. J. Hanson (Eds.), *Developing cross-cultural competence: A guide for working with children and their families* (3rd ed., pp. 41–77).Baltimore: Paul H. Brookes.

McCloskey, D., & Athanasiou, M. S. (2000). Assessment and intervention practices with second language learners among school psychologists. *Psychology in the Schools, 3*, 209–225.

Meece, J. L., & Kurtz-Costes, B. (2001). Introduction: The schooling of ethnic minority children and youth [Special issue]. *Educational Psychologist, 36*(1), 1–7.

Meyers, A. B. (2002). Developing nonthreatening expertise: Thoughts on consultation training from the perspective of a new faculty member. *Journal of Educational and Psychological Consultation, 13,* 55–67.

Meyers, B. (2002). The contract negotiation stage of a school-based, cross-cultural organizational consultation: A case study. *Journal of Educational and Psychological Consultation, 13,* 151–183.

Meyers, J. (2002). A 30 year perspective on best practices for consultation training. *Journal of Educational and Psychological Consultation 13,* 35–54.

Miranda, A. H. (1993). Consultation with culturally diverse families. *Journal of Educational and Psychological Consultation, 4,* 89–93.

National Clearinghouse for English Language Acquisition and Language Instruction. (2001). *Survey of the states' limited English proficient students and available educational programs and services, 1999–2001 Summary report.* Washington, DC: Author.

Naumann, W. C., Gutkin, T. B., & Sandoval, S. R. (1996). The impact of consultant race and student race on perceptions of consultant effectiveness and intervention acceptability. Journal of Educational and Psychological Consultation, 7, 151–160.

Nelson, N. W. (1994). Curriculum-based language assessment and intervention across the grades. In E. Wallach & K. Butler (Eds.), *Language learning disabilities in school- aged children and adolescents* (pp. 104–131). New York: Macmillan.

Ochoa, S. H., & Rhodes, R. L. (2005). Assisting parents of bilingual students achieve equity in public schools. *Journal of Educational and Psychological Consultation, 16,* 75–94.

Okagaki, L. (2001). Triarchic model of minority children's school achievement [Special issue]. *Educational Psychologist, 36*(1), 9–20.

Ortiz, A., & Garcia, S. B. (1995). Serving Hispanic students with learning disabilities. Recommended policies and practices. *Urban Education, 29,* 471–481.

Ovando, C. J., Collier, V. P., & Combs, M. C. (2003). *Bilingual and ESL classrooms: Teaching in multicultural contexts* (3rd ed.). New York: McGraw Hill.

Pinto, R. F. (1981). Consultant orientation and client system perceptions: Styles of cross-cultural consultation. In R. Lippitt & G. L. Lippitt (Eds.), *Systems thinking: A resource for organizational diagnosis and intervention* (pp. 57–74). Washington, DC: International Consultants.

Ramirez, S. Z., Alghorani, M. A. (2003). School psychologists' consideration of Hispanic cultural issues during consultation. *Journal of Applied School Psychology, 20,* 5–26.

Ramirez, S. Z., Lepage, K. M., Kratochwill, T. R., & Duffy, J. L. (1998). Multicultural issues in school-based consultation: Conceptual and research considerations. *Journal of School Psychology, 36,* 479–509.

Rhodes, R. L. Ochoa, S. H., & Ortiz, S. O. (2005). *Assessing culturally and linguistically diverse students: A practical guide.* New York: Guilford.

Rogers, M. R. (1998). The influence of race and consultant verbal behavior on perceptions of consultant competence and multicultural sensitivity. *School Psychology Quarterly, 13,* 265–280.

Rosenfield, S. A. (1987). *Instructional consultation.* Hillsdale, NJ: Erlbaum.

Rosenfield, S. A., & Gravois, T. A. (1996). *Instructional consultation teams: Collaborating for change.* New York: Guildford.

Rosenfield, S. A., & Silva, A. (in press). The process of instructional consultation: A research perspective. In W. Erchul & S. Sheridan (Eds.). *Handbook of research in school consultation.* Mahwah, NJ: Erlbaum.

Schulte, A. C., & Osborne, S. S. (2003). When assumptive worlds collide: A review of definitions of collaboration in consultation. *Journal of Educational and Psychological Consultation, 14,* 109–138.

Sheridan, S. M. (2000).Considerations of multiculturalism and diversity in behavioral consultation with parents and teachers. *School Psychology Review, 29,* 344–353.

Silva, A. S., & Rosenfield, S. (2004, April). *Documenting English language learners' cases in instructional consultation teams schools*. Poster session presented at the annual meeting of the National Association of School Psychologists conference, Dallas, TX.

Soo-Hoo, T. (1998). Applying frame of reference and reframing techniques to improve school consultation in multicultural settings. *Journal of Educational and Psychological Consultation, 9*, 325–345.

Steward, R. J. (1996). Training consulting psychologists to be sensitive to multicultural issues in organizational consultation. *Consulting Psychology Journal: Practice and Research, 48*, 180–189. students: An exploratory study of six high schools. *Harvard Educational Review, 60*, 315–340.

Tarver Behring, S., Cabello, B., Kushida, D., & Murguia, A. (2000). Cultural modifications to current school-based consultation approaches reported by culturally diverse beginning consultants. *School Psychology Review, 29*, 354–367.

Tarver Behring, S., & Gelinas, R. T. (1996). School consultation with Asian American children and families. *The California School Psychologist, 1*, 13–20.

Tarver Behring, S., & Ingraham, C. L. (1998). Culture as a central component to consultation: A call to the field. *Journal of Educational and Psychological Consultation, 9*, 57–72.

Tharp, R. G. (1989). Psychocultural variables and constants. *American* Psychologist, 44, 349–358.

Tharp, R. G., & Gallimore, R. (1988). *Rousing minds to life: Teaching, learning and schooling in a social context.* New York: Cambridge University Press.

U.S. Department of Education Office of Civil Rights. (2000). OCR Elementary and Secondary School Survey. Retrieved on July 6, 2005, from http:/205.207.175.84/ocr2000r/.

Vygotsky, L. S. (1962). *Thought and language* (E. Hanfmann & G. Vakar, Eds. & Trans.). Cambridge, MA: The MIT Press. (Original work published in 1934)

Warner, C. M., & Morris, J. R. (1997). African Americans and consultation. *Journal of Multicultural Counseling and Development, 25*, 244–255.

Westermeyer, J., & Hausman, W. (1974). Cross cultural consultation for mental health planning. *International Journal of Social Psychiatry, 20*(1–2), 34–38.

Wong, C. A., & Rowley, S. J. (2001). The schooling of ethnic minority children: Commentary. *Educational Psychologist, 36*(1), 57–66.

5

FOCUSING ON CONSULTEES IN MULTICULTURAL CONSULTATION

Colette L. Ingraham
San Diego State University

Within the educational system, teachers hold a powerful role in determining the success of students, including those from culturally and linguistically diverse (CLD) backgrounds. When teachers form positive relationships with their students, learning is enhanced, students are empowered, and self-esteem and perceived competence for both teacher and students expand (Covington, 1992; Ingraham, 2004). When cultural differences or issues are part of the teacher-student relationship, a variety of factors can impede the development of strong, positive teacher-student relationships. Multicultural consultation is a valuable tool for increasing teachers' cultural competence and success in working with their students. A multicultural perspective to consultee-centered consultation gives consultants tools for enhancing teacher-student relationships and developing teacher knowledge, skill, perspective, and confidence for working with their CLD students. The emphasis of this chapter is on consultation with teachers regarding issues that will directly or indirectly support the success of CLD students.

An emerging body of work focuses on multicultural consultation as a means to develop and support teacher competence and student success in diverse schools (see Goldstein & Harris, 2000; Harris, 1991; Ingraham, 2000, 2002, 2003; Ingraham & Tarver Behring, 1998a; Lopez, 2000; Tarver Behring, Cabello, Kushida, & Murguia, 2000; Tarver Behring and Ingraham, 1998). In a special issue of the *School Psychology Review* on multicultural and cross-cultural consultation (Ingraham & Meyers, 2000), this author proposed a framework for consultation through a multicultural lens (Ingraham, 2000) that can be used with a variety of models of consultation. This framework focuses attention on the development of cultural competence in both the consultee and the consultant.

Why focus on teachers? Multicultural consultation can be used on an individual, group, or systems basis for intervening in schools to help develop the positive learning communities in which all students can thrive and succeed (Ingraham, 2000, 2002; Korn & Bursztyn, 2002; Nastasi, Vargas, Berstein, & Jayasena, 2000; Rogers et al., 1999). This chapter emphasizes multicultural consultation with teachers for five reasons:

1. Teachers determine the classroom environment(s) in which students spend a large portion of their waking hours each day. They are responsible for the learning and progress of students in their classes and can have a major influence over how students fare in school.
2. Teachers are often the persons carrying out interventions for students who are experiencing difficulty in school, and the role of the interventionist is critical to the outcomes of the interventions. Wampold, Licktenberg, and Waehler (2002) asserted that 90% of the outcome of interventions is attributable to the interventionist. Interventionists need cultural competence to work with today's diverse children and youth (Lynch & Hanson, 2004).
3. Teachers often have minimal training for working with culturally and linguistically diverse students (U.S. Department of Education [USDE], 2000) and need support in this area (Ingraham, 1999, 2002; Ingraham & Tarver Behring 1998a).
4. School psychologists are in a position to consult with teachers about a wide range of problem situations, often focusing on individuals or groups of students who the teacher feels are not succeeding in school. Through a problem-solving, ecological approach, these consultations can aid in the development of interventions to improve student success in school.
5. Consultants who are trained in multicultural consultation can educate teachers about contextual factors such as home culture, language, learning styles, minority status, racism, communication styles, cross-cultural interactions, power and status within the school and larger community, and how these can influence learning, development and behavior.

When teachers are supported in developing culturally appropriate interventions for students, multiple positive outcomes result. Students learn and develop successfully, teachers expand their capacity to work effectively with a diverse group of students, teachers increase their cultural competence and confidence in teaching diverse students, and systems change is fostered in schools (Ingraham, 2002, 2003; Ingraham & Tarver Behring, 1998a, b; Tarver Behring & Ingraham, 1998).

In Ingraham and Tarver Behring (1998a), we proposed ways to use consultation to develop teacher capacity to work effectively with diverse learners. We noted that teachers face a wide variety of challenges as they work in culturally diverse school settings. Teachers need to be able to draw upon their knowledge and skill in applying theories and methods of instruction to the classroom settings in which they work. While ideally, multicultural education would be infused in all aspects of teacher development, we believe (Ingraham & Tarver Behring, 1998a) that teachers need special support once they are working in the classroom to apply their learned theories and methodologies.

Teachers and support professionals need the knowledge and skills to fully serve the multicultural populations in today's schools. Caplan and Caplan (1993) asserted that teachers are often faced with situations that challenge their knowledge, skill, confidence and professional objectivity in the classroom. Teacher needs in these four areas can increase dramatically when viewed through a multicultural lens (Ingraham, 2000). As the diversity of a teacher's classroom increases, so can the cognitive and affective complexities of effective instruction for a multicultural society. Unfortunately, the current professional development opportunities for teachers and support professionals are inadequate to prepare them to serve the diverse individuals in their schools. While some districts use in-services as a way to expose teachers to strategies for instructing their diverse students, 70% percent of these involved less than a day of training (USDE, 2000). Similarly, practicing school psychologists have identified a need for additional training in developing interventions for at-risk and culturally diverse students (Ingraham, 1999). Ongoing relationships, not just a few hours of workshops, are needed to foster and sustain changes in teacher attitudes, beliefs and behaviors regarding diverse students. Thus, teachers and consultants need preparation in multicultural consultation to provide effective services in multicultural schools.

This chapter is organized into five additional sections. The first section discusses the theoretical and research basis for multicultural consultation with teachers and specifically the use of multicultural consultee-centered consultation with teachers. This is followed by a section titled Implications for Practice that suggests ways that multicultural consultee-centered consultation can be used in school settings, and a section that addresses the Implementation and Approaches for Multicultural Consultation. The chapter concludes with a section on the Implications for Future Research and Practice that highlights possibilities for new research, training and practice.

THEORETICAL AND RESEARCH FOUNDATIONS

Teachers are not adequately prepared to teach culturally and linguistically diverse students. According to a report by the U.S. Department of Education (2000), about two-thirds of US teachers were initially trained over 10 years ago, and only a small portion of today's teachers have received sustained professional development training that focuses on diverse students. Of the nation's full-time teachers who participated in professional development in 1998, less than a third had training addressing the needs of English language learners or students from diverse cultural backgrounds, and the vast majority of these involved less than one day of training. If teachers are not receiving enough pre-service or in-service training in working with CLD students, then who can support their professional growth in these areas?

Consultation is an excellent tool for working with teachers to prevent and resolve problem situations because school-based consultants can work with teachers and others to develop effective interventions for a wide range of problems (e.g., Allen & Graden, 2002; Bergan & Kratochwill, 1990; Brown, Pryzwansky & Schulte,

2006; Conoley & Conoley, 1992; Parsons & Meyers, 1984; Zins, Curtis, Graden, & Ponti, 1988). In schools, the consultation process involves at least three parties: the consultant, a consultee (usually the teacher, sometimes the parent), and client (usually one or more students). The consultant is frequently a member of the support team such as a school psychologist, school counselor, resource teacher, mentor teacher, etc. The consultant works with the adults who are influential in the lives of children. To date, more appears to be written about the process of consultation with culturally diverse parents (e.g., Brown, 1997; Edens, 1997; Miranda, 1993; Tarver Behring & Gelinas, 1996) than with teachers of diverse students.

Seeking a Multicultural Perspective in Consultation With Teachers

While traditional consultation models do not address cultural issues, recent literature is highlighting the importance and efficacy of developing a more multicultural perspective to guide consultation services in schools (Ingraham, 2000, 2003; Ramirez, Lepage, Kratochwill, & Duffy, 1998; Soo-Hoo, 1998; Tarver Behring & Ingraham, 1998). The development of a multicultural perspective for consultation draws on scholarship from multiple disciplines, including multicultural counseling, cross-cultural psychology, intergroup communications, and international school psychology. Scholars have examined how literature in multicultural counseling and cross-cultural psychology informs the theory, research, and practice of multicultural consultation (see Brown, 1997; Gibbs, 1980; Harris, 1991; Ingraham, 2000; Ramirez, et al., 1998; Rogers, 1998; Tarver Behring & Ingraham, 1998). Within the intergroup communication literature, Gudykunst (1991) describes an approach-avoidance dynamic where individuals want to learn more about people different from themselves but then avoid contacts due to the anxiety and uncertainties they experience in cross-cultural interchanges. Maital (2000) referred to a process called "reciprocal distancing" in multicultural consultation in which the consultee and client enter a process of "progressive disengagement resulting in a series of 'interactive failures'" that leads to chronic problems in cross-cultural relations (p. 390). In this process, the consultant and consultee continue moving further apart in their understanding as each fails to meet the others' needs.

Earlier studies of culture and consultation focused on racial factors in consultant-consultee relationships. Gibbs (1980) studied relationship building and consultation between Black consultants and Black and White teacher consultees in an urban school district. She observed in her cases that an interpersonal consultation style was important to build trust and elicit participation with the Black consultees, whereas the White consultees used a more instrumental communication style with the Black consultant. Subsequent analog studies (Duncan & Pryzwansky, 1993; Naumann, Gutkin, & Sandoval, 1996; Rogers, 1998) examined how consultant and/or consultee race influences ratings of consultant competence, multicultural sensitivity, intervention acceptability, and preferences for consultation style. Rogers (1998) specifically examined the influence of the content of videotaped consultation sessions with respect to discussing racial issues. In her study, both African American and Caucasian female pre-service teachers rated the consultants' attention and inclusion of race-sensitive content as positive and important. Her findings indicated that when the consultation video involved race-sensitive vs. race-blind communication, consultants of both races who attended to the racial issues mentioned by the consultees were rated as more competent and more multiculturally sensitive. Regardless of race, consultants who ignored potential racial themes were rated as less competent and less multiculturally sensitive. Analysis of the similarities and differences among these empirical studies of racial factors in consultation suggests that consultant actions, rather than race, seem to influence ratings of consultants. In these analog studies of race and consultation, it appears that it is not the race of the consultant but the attentiveness and responsiveness of the consultant to racial issues brought up in the session that determines ratings of consultant effectiveness and multicultural sensitivity (Ingraham, 2000).

Recently, some have studied multicultural issues in consultation through case studies and qualitative methods. Case studies were used to study and illustrate the process and outcomes of consultation with and without a multicultural approach (Ingraham & Tarver Behring, 1998b; Tarver Behring & Ingraham, 1998). Qualitative research methods with real consultation cases in school settings highlight the complexities and positive outcomes attained through multicultural consultation. For example, Tarver Behring et al. (2000) studied the cultural modifications made by beginning consultants of differing ethnicities, trained in multicultural consultation, who made modifications to traditional consultation approaches to better match the cultures of those in their consultation systems. The African American, Latino American, and Asian American consultants made more culture-specific modifications in the consultation approaches (e.g., consultation in homes, adoption of culturally relevant styles of communication and relationship-building, speaking in the language of parent consultees) than their European American counterparts. Similarly, Ingraham (2003) found that bi/multicultural novice consultants were more successful in educating teachers about the cultures of their students and developing successful interventions compared with a European American consultant, despite her positive commitment to multicultural education and consultation. In addition, qualitative methods were used in studies of instructional consultation through interpreters in New York City schools (Lopez, 2000), consultation on behalf of immigrants in Israeli schools (Maital, 2000), and participatory culture-specific consultation in Sri Lanka (Nastasi et al., 2000). Taken together, these studies show that consultation across cultures and languages is possible when the consultants are highly attuned to the cultural nuances of the students' and schools' cultures and work to educate teachers and others about how to best develop culturally appropriate interventions.

A Framework for Multicultural Consultation in Schools

My colleague, Shari Tarver Behring, and I have advocated for culture to become a core component of consultation theory, research and practice (Tarver Behring & Ingraham, 1998). For the past several years, we have been collaborating about our multicultural approach in our research and teaching of consultation within the fields of school psychology, counseling, and education. Our multicultural consultation approach (Ingraham, 2000, 2002; Ingraham & Tarver Behring, 1998a, b; Tarver Behring & Ingraham, 1998) considers the potential influence of culture on the entire consultation process and the individuals involved in the consultation triad. We refer to multicultural consultation as an approach to consultation where cultural issues are brought to the forefront and adjustments in traditional consultation processes are made (Ingraham, 2000; Tarver Behring & Ingraham, 1998). *Multicultural consultation* is defined as "a culturally sensitive, indirect service in which the consultant adjusts the consultation services to address the needs and cultural values of the consultee, the client, or both" (Tarver Behring & Ingraham, 1998, p. 58). It includes situations where members of the consultation triad share the same culture (Gibbs, 1980; Tarver Behring & Gelinas, 1996), as well as cross-cultural diversity among members of the consultation triad (Duncan, 1995; Ingraham, 2000; Pinto, 1981). The consultation triad is defined flexibly to include different constellations of consultant, consultee(s), and client(s) and the context in which they work. Consultees and clients may consist of individuals, groups, or systems. Culture-specific approaches (i.e., approaches where the communication and relationship patterns are consistent with those of a specific cultural group) to consultation may be used when there is cultural similarity among the members of the consultation system.

We use a broad definition of culture that involves an organized set of thoughts, beliefs, norms for interaction and communication, all of which may influence thoughts, behaviors, and perceptions. It is important for consultants to recognize both the pervasiveness and limits of cultural context, *exploring cultural, as well as individual differences,* but not over generalizing about potential cultural underpinnings at play. Consultants are cautioned to remain cognizant that culture is very complex, far more complex than one's physical appearance, language, or country of origin (Ingraham, 2000, 2003). In this spirit, the consultant must continually examine the potential for his or her own stereotypes and biases and actively work to reduce interpretations or hypotheses developed out of the consultant's own lack of knowledge, perspective, or worldview. The consultant seeks to understand the influences of culture on the thoughts, expectations, and behaviors for each party in the consultation process, including the consultee(s), client(s), school system, larger culture, and of course, oneself, as a means to establish and maintain rapport and appropriateness.

A comprehensive framework for Multicultural School Consultation (MSC; Ingraham, 2000) identified five areas of knowledge and skill as important in successful multicultural consultation: (a) consultant development in multicultural consultation (understanding of own culture, other cultures, cross-cultural consultation skills), (b) understanding of consultee needs for development (knowledge, skill, self-confidence, and professional objectivity), (c) cultural variations in consultation triads and consultation approaches typically successful for each, (d) issues of context and power, and (e) methods to support consultees in increasing their capacity to work with diversity. MSC includes attention to issues such as communication style, power, empowerment, development of cultural competence, and dimensions of diversity, thereby attending to the development of cultural competence of both consultee and consultant. Caplan and Caplan (1993) define consultee-centered consultation as consultation that focuses on the consultee's perceptions and thinking, and recent scholars are showing how consultee-centered consultation can lead to conceptual change for the consultee (Lambert, Hylander, & Sandoval, 2004.) Multicultural consultee-centered consultation (MCCC; Ingraham, 2003, 2004) integrates the multicultural consultation components of MSC with consultee-centered consultation. MCCC is one model of MSC that can involve co-constructing a new conceptualization of the problem situation, thereby offering a non-threatening, supportive approach that is particularly sensitive to the consultee's affect and evolving cultural knowledge. This approach seems well-suited to working with teachers in culturally diverse schools because, in contrast to traditional in-services, it enhances professional growth in a naturally occurring, problem-focused "window of opportunity" when teachers are motivated to succeed.

Eight domains for consultant learning and development were proposed in the MSC framework (Ingraham, 2000): (a) Understanding one's own culture, (b) understanding the impact of one's own culture on others, (c) respecting and valuing other cultures, (d) understanding individual differences within cultural groups, (e) cross-cultural communication and multicultural consultation approaches for rapport development and maintenance, (f) understanding cultural saliency and how to build bridges across salient differences, (g) understanding the cultural context for consultation, and (h) multicultural consultation and interventions appropriate for the consultee(s) and client(s). Numerous references are included in the article to offer readers specific sources of detailed information about each of the eight domains. These references can be used to develop consultant knowledge and skill related to their own and the consultee's development of cultural competence for consultation and interventions.

The first and most crucial component in MSC is the consultant's own cultural learning by understanding one's own culture, other cultures, and learning skills in cross-cultural consultation and intervention. One can't guide others in the development of cultural competence unless one is highly aware of one's own cultural lenses and how these influence one's cognitions, behaviors, and conceptualizations of problem situations. Most approaches for multicultural counseling (e.g., Arredondo et al., 1996; Ponterotto, Casas, Suzuki, & Alexander, 1995; Sue & Sue, 1999) and early intervention (Lynch & Hanson, 2004) place this as a crucial step in developing effective knowledge and skills for work in multicultural contexts. From this beginning, one can learn about other cultures, methods for building communication across cultures, and specific approaches of multicultural consultation.

IMPLICATIONS FOR PRACTICE

Multicultural consultee-centered consultation (MCCC) offers a wide range of implications for practice. When consultants are aware of some of the dynamics that can arise in consultation when cultural issues are involved, they are better equipped to address them in ways that support the goals of problem-solving consultation and the development of cultural competence among teacher consultees. This author reframed Caplan and Caplan's (1993) articulation of consultee needs for knowledge, skill, objectivity and confidence into a more developmental approach that works with multicultural consultee-centered consultation with teacher consultees (Ingraham, 2000, 2003, 2004).

Knowledge, Skill, Perspective, and Confidence

In MCCC, consultants monitor their own and their consultee's potential for developing increased knowledge, skill, perspective, and confidence (Ingraham, 2003, 2004). In consultee-centered consultation, the consultant thinks, "Why is this consultee having difficulty with this problem situation?" As the consultant is learning about the consultee's perception of the problem situation, he or she is also mentally forming and testing hypotheses to identify the areas of consultee development that might benefit from attention through the consultation process. Would the consultee benefit from some type of knowledge or skill to handle this problem situation? Is the consultee viewing the problem with a clear perspective or is there a need for greater objectivity or another perspective to viewing the problem? Is the consultee showing limited confidence in working with this problem situation? Often a teacher is experiencing challenges in several of these four areas. This analysis can guide the consultant in knowing which direction to take the consultation because the consultant can work to develop the teacher in needed areas.

Teacher needs for knowledge, skill, perspective, and confidence are prevalent in many of today's changing schools and consultants can support teachers in developing in each of these four areas (Ingraham, 2000). Frequently when consultees are culturally different from their students, there is a need for knowledge about the culture of the students. With the growing numbers of cultures and backgrounds of students in today's classrooms, it is difficult for teachers to have depth of knowledge in each. Consultants can support teachers in learning more about their students' home cultures, customs, interests, and patterns of communication and behavior. With the number of teachers who were not trained in multicultural teaching approaches, teachers may need to expand their teaching skills to be inclusive of the diversity within their classrooms. Consultants can assist teachers in adjusting assignments to match the reading and language levels of their students, and in using teaching methods that correspond to students' diverse learning styles and interests (e.g., partnered learning, multimodal instructions, cooperative learning, projects, simulations). A need for increased teacher confidence frequently arises when teachers are not feeling a positive connection with their students or are unsure about how to work with them. Through co-constructing the problem definition and collaborating to develop successful interventions, teachers' feelings of confidence, efficacy and empowerment rise (Ingraham, 2003).

The Multicultural School Consultation framework (Ingraham, 2000), describes several threats to objectivity or perception that can arise in multicultural contexts. Some of the processes that can challenge teacher perceptions in multicultural consultation include filtering perceptions through stereotypes, taking a color blind approach, fear of being called a racist, and overemphasizing culture. Because of their affect on the teacher's ability to use problem-solving strategies and develop effective interventions, each is discussed here in more detail.

When situations are ambiguous, as cross-cultural interactions frequently are, one tends to construct meaning out of whatever limited knowledge one has. This can lead to *the use of stereotypes* to guide decision-making when one does not have complete information about the culture of a particular group. When teachers filter their understanding of a student or group of students through stereotypes, they may fail to see the unique characteristics of these students' experiences, making inaccurate assumptions based on stereotypes and not on accurate interpretation of information or events. Thinking that all members of a particular cultural group like math, music, cooperative learning, or other common stereotypes can lead to inaccurate interpretations of the problem situation and ineffective interventions.

Another threat to a clear perspective is a *color blind* approach (Ingraham, 2000). In this dynamic, a teacher may seek to treat all students equally, regardless of their race or ethnicity, potentially neglecting to attend to cultural characteristics that are meaningful to the students. For example, when an adolescent is developing a group ethnic identity as a Latino, a teacher who does not recognize the student's identity may unknowingly act to negate or threaten the cultural identity, thereby making the student feel culturally invisible, unaccepted by the teacher, or of diminished value. Consultants can work to educate teachers that students may *want* to be recognized for their cultural affiliation and this is part of their healthy identity development. Working to reframe a teacher's color blind approach can be very challenging (Ingraham, 2003). In contrast to the color blind approach, valuing the cultural diversity that students bring to the classroom can be shown in ways that affirm cultural identity and support student success in school.

Most teachers, like other members of society, do not want people to think of them as racist. *Fear of being called a racist* can lead to teachers taking extraordinary efforts to appear fair and supportive of students and avoid treating students as cultural beings (Ingraham, 2000). Sometimes, teachers are afraid to take disciplinary action with a student of color using the same methods that they would take with European American or Caucasian students because they are fearful of being called a racist. Teacher defensiveness increases and confidence is often compromised in such situations.

The *overemphasis on culture* appears commonly when teachers are beginning to develop an understanding of multiculturalism and the many ways that the cultures of their students can be different from their own (Ingraham, 2000). In this situation, their emerging knowledge about different cultures leads teachers to develop cultural hypotheses or explanations for everything they see, sometimes neglecting the importance of individual differences, variations, and diversity *within* cultural groups, and other factors that are also important to consider.

In multicultural consultation, consultee confidence is frequently at risk. Teachers are expected to be able to teach all of their students, to know what strategies to use to address the specific needs of students, and to be respectful and inclusive of their diverse students. When teachers experience challenges in finding success with students, they sometimes feel sensitive to any criticism about their teaching, and if they believe that cultural factors may be involved, they may adopt one of two response patterns. First, some people develop *intervention paralysis*, described in Ingraham (2000) as an awareness of cultural differences with an inability to develop any intervention for fear that it might not be culturally appropriate for a child who is culturally different from the teacher. With intervention paralysis, the consultant can support the teacher in identifying and analyzing the relevant elements of the problem situation and developing a corresponding intervention. The consultant can do much to break the paralysis and move the consultee into problem solving.

Another dynamic is *reactive dominance*, where "the consultee reacts to the collision of their own needs with the complexities of cross-cultural interaction by asserting dominance or imposing their patterns of thinking and behavior on the interaction" (Ingraham, 2000, p. 333). Some people are threatened when they find themselves operating outside of their comfort zones. A consultee who has needs for control, predictability, acceptance, success, or structure may assert a particular course of action or belief system, regardless of its appropriateness for the client, as a reaction to the uncertainties of cross-cultural interaction. Soo-Hoo (1998) described a consultee who operated from her own frame of reference rather than understanding the cultural perspective of the client. In this case, the consultee was a psychologist who was working with a mother culturally different from the psychologist. The consultant used reframing to help the consultee understand the mother's cultural frame of reference, including deference to authorities, and developed a way for both mother and psychologist to find a common ground. This case demonstrates how a consultant intervened with consultee reactive dominance by reframing and supporting alternative explanations to achieve a shared understanding.

When the consultant believes a teacher needs to develop a broader or different perspective in viewing the problem, some of the most challenging aspects of multicultural consultee-centered consultation become apparent. There are many ways that a consultee's perspective or professional objectivity can be threatened in multicultural consultation (Ingraham, 2000, 2002, 2003). As Caplan and Caplan (1993) note, professional objectivity can be threatened by theme interference, when the consultee's own issues or biases cloud their judgment and accurate perception of events. Teacher consultees can become over-identified with the student, such as when they are of the same minority cultural background or share a common experience like an alcoholic parent, a disability, or other significant point of similarity. As described previously, teacher consultees can also project stereotypes or cultural biases onto students, overemphasize the influence of culture, or use a color blind approach to neglect the cultural identity of students. Multicultural consultee-centered consultation calls on the consultant to use reframing, self-disclosure, parables, and sharing of cultural information, thereby gently challenging the stereotype through contrary examples in an effort to reconstruct a new understanding of the cultural factors and their relationship with the presenting problem (Ingraham, 2000, 2003). The dynamics between consultants and consultees are complex when consultants seek to expand consultee perceptions regarding culture. Consultants may need coaching and supervision in working to reframe the cultural perspectives of consultees, however, even novice consultants can successfully reframe teachers' cultural conceptualization of the problem and develop successful interventions (Ingraham, 2003).

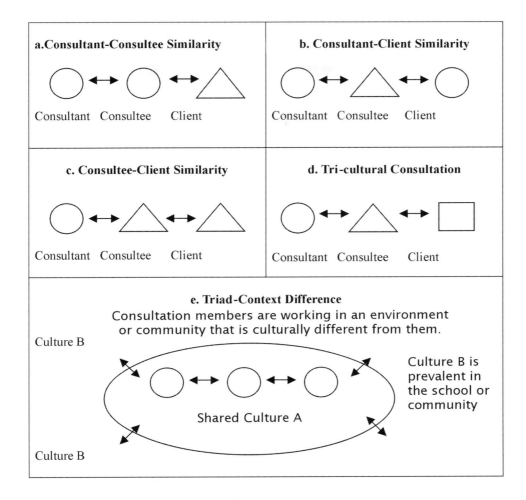

FIGURE 5–1.   Ingraham's (2000) five different consultation constellations in multi-cultural consultation. (*Source:*   From "Consultation through a multicultural lens: Multicultural and cross-cultural consultation in schools," by C. L. Ingraham, 2000, *School Psychology Review, 29*, 320–343. Copyright 2000 by the National Association of School Psychologists. Adapted with permission of the publisher.)

Constellations: Different Ways Culture Is Located Within the Consultation System

The MSC framework includes different constellations of the members of the consultation system that can vary by culture or perspective (see Ingraham, 2000, for a more thorough discussion of the constellations and their impact on consultation dynamics). Figure 5–1 shows five different constellations that can arise in MSC.

When one of more members of the consultation system (consultant, consultee[s], client[s]) differs significantly in culture or perspective from the others, special approaches in MSC are used. MSC details different issues that can arise and available strategies when the cultures or perspectives of consultation members differ. As in all descriptions of cultural influences on people, it is important to recognize that one's culture(s) and perspective are determined by a whole tapestry of factors that shape the paradigm and worldview from which one operates. Two individuals from the same family, ethnicity and linguistic background may have different worldviews or cultural perspectives due, for example, to their different levels of acculturation. Most people have multiple identities (e.g., mother, wife, eldest daughter, sister, teacher, Protestant, White female, humanitarian, generous, dedicated, mid-western, third generation American, middle class) that include their individual, group, and universal identity and affiliations, thus determinations of cultural similarity or difference are not simplistic.

In the consultee-centered form of multicultural consultation, the consultant works to find bridges of understanding, first between the consultant and consultee in order to establish rapport, empathy, and a shared conceptualization of the problem (Ingraham, 2002, 2003, 2004). Once the consultant-consultee relationship is strong, the consultant shifts the emphasis to building the consultee-client relationship. The different diagrams of the constellations are used as symbolic representations of the most salient similarities and differences, and they can help illustrate when various consultant strategies are needed. For example, when the consultant and client are culturally similar and the consultee is culturally different (see constellation b in Figure 5–1), two challenging scenarios are possible. First, the consultee may request that the consultant assume primary responsibility for the intervention with comments such as, "You know much more about working with these kinds of students than I do. Can you do some counseling with him?" Consultants in this constellation will need to work hard to keep the teacher as the primary person responsible for the interventions, thereby using the case to educate the teacher about working with this cultural group. One-downsmanship (Caplan & Caplan, 1993) and similar strategies can accomplish this. One-downsmanship is when the consultant makes a comment that defers to the consultee's knowledge and expertise in an effort to elevate the consultee's position and equalize the perceived balance of power between consultee and consultant. In this case, the consultant might use one-downsmanship in response to the teacher's request for the consultant to counsel the student by saying, "Well, you have this student in your classroom and have probably observed some things that would be very helpful to us in developing a successful intervention. Can you talk a little about what kinds of behaviors you have seen in your class between this student and his peers?"

In the second scenario, the consultee may project onto the consultant stereotypes about the consultant's and client's culture. When this happens, the consultant can use self-monitoring to consider how and when best to respond in a way that the teacher can hear the perspective without getting too defensive. An "I" statement or an example of a case where the stereotype did not bear out may be a good way to counteract consultee stereotyping and projection. In both cases, the consultant uses the emerging consultant-consultee relationship to show support for the consultee in learning about the client's culture and to gradually build the consultee-client relationship.

Another set of dynamics occurs with consultant-consultee similarity (see constellation a in Figure 5–1). Here the consultant and consultee share a common culture or perspective and the consultant can use this similarity to establish rapport and bridge with the consultee's perspective. The consultant can model methods for learning about the culture of the client, use self-disclosure to show their own mistakes or vulnerability as they are learning about a new culture, and provide emotional and motivational supports for the consultee as the consultee is learning about a new culture, trying new strategies, and expanding their capacity to work with students like the client (Ingraham, 2000, 2002). Preliminary findings suggest that consultant self-disclosure about cross-cultural experiences or learning may be a key factor in successful multicultural consultation (Ingraham, 2002, 2003).

IMPLEMENTATION AND APPROACHES

There are some promising approaches for using multicultural consultation to focus on consultee development. Within the past few years, studies have begun to examine the outcomes of using various consultation approaches with real consultation cases in multicultural contexts (e.g., Ingraham, 2003; Ingraham & Tarver Behring, 1998b; Tarver Behring et al., 2000). These studies, along with the models and approaches developed by those working in this area, offer guidance to consultants wishing to develop their competence in multicultural consultation.

Brown (1997), Tarver Behring et al. (2000), and Tarver Behring and Gelinas (1996) described modifications to traditional problem-solving consultation approaches when working with consultees or clients of differing cultures. Tarver Behring et al. (2000) studied the modifications made by beginning consultants when working with students of African American, Latino, and Asian American backgrounds. The consultants who were most knowledgeable about the cultures of the clients were best able to make culturally appropriate modifications such as addressing parents by their formal names, visiting the home, accepting reciprocity from families, and adjusting the conceptualization of the problem to match the values and interests of the parent(s).

This author has been teaching students to use the MSC and MCCC methods for the past few years, both as a means to focus on a range of methods to support consultees and as a way for consultants to conceptualize the support strategies and their potential impact on consultation outcomes. In conceptualizing cases, we consider factors such as: salient similarities and differences among members of the consultation constellation and the structure of the consultation system (i.e., which constellation from Figure 5–1 best represents the system). We examine the consultant's perception of the consultee's (as well as his or her own) developmental needs for knowledge, skill, perspective and confidence following each consultation session and at the end of the entire case. Consultants record quotes and evidence to support their hypotheses, approaches they took to address the identified needs, and consultee responses to these approaches. We use the MSC Framework (Ingraham, 2000) to examine the dimensions of diversity, context and power, how

TABLE 5–1
Methods for Supporting Consultee and Client Success

Framing the Problem and the Consultation Process

1. *Value Multiple Perspectives.* Use cross-cultural communication skills to gain entry into the worldview of the consultee and client by using cross-cultural communication skills (Leong, 1996; Lynch & Hanson, 2004; Sue & Sue, 1999) and knowledge of pluralism (e.g., Ponterotto, et al., 1995) to honor the cultures of each party and to attend to differing frames of reference (Soo-Hoo, 1998).

2. *Create Emotional Safety and Motivational Support.* Remain attentive to the affective risks and vulnerability inherent in cross-cultural work, understanding that these feelings may influence all three members of the cross-cultural consultation relationship. Communicate empathy for both the consultee and client and an experimental attitude with comments such as, "Let's give it a try and see what happens" to enhance feelings of emotional safety.

3. *Balance Affective Support with New Learning.* Monitor the relationship for balance between partnering/empathy versus informing/guiding. Both styles may be needed at various points in the consultation process.

4. *Build on Principles for Adult Learning.* Build on the notion of continuing professional development to open the pathway for learning knowledge and skills. This may involve reframing feelings of vulnerability, limited self-confidence, and clouded objectivity as part of a learning process, not pathology. Encourage and support new learning through cognitive and affective means.

5. *Seek Systems Interventions for Learning and Development among Consultees and Clients.* Seek systemic interventions, such as anti-racism programs (Parks, 1999), when multiple consultees and/or clients can be affected.

Multicultural Consultation Strategies for Working with Consultees

1. *Support Cross-Cultural Learning and Motivation.* Support the consultee's commitment. To working with complex cross-cultural interchanges, concern for the client, willingness to engage in the new area of cross-cultural service delivery, and exploration and self-reflection about one's values in relation to the client's culture. Maintain confidentiality and avoid evaluation of the consultee.

2. *Model Bridging and Processes for Cross-Cultural Learning.* Build cross-cultural bridges and promote inclusive thinking (and avoid "we-they" statements). Co-construct shared understandings by attending to different frames of reference (Soo-Hoo, 1998), encouraging bridging with integrity (Ingraham, 2003), and respecting each perspective, thereby establishing points of commonality and cross-cultural learning.

3. *Use Consultation Methods Matched with the Consultee's Style.* Attend to the consultee's frame of reference and select approaches and communication styles that are matched with the consultee's style (e.g., direct, indirect, storytelling, data-based). Self-disclosure, narrative, anecdotes, information sharing, and/or modeling can be used to support cross-cultural learning and development.

4. *Build Consultee Confidence and Self-Efficacy.* Work to expand the consultee's capacity to take risks before taking on larger challenges and goals. Throughout the consultation process, highlight the consultee's efficacy and role in effecting changes in the targeted problem situation (i.e., credit the consultee with the successes), thereby supporting consultee motivation and ownership.

5. *Increase Knowledge, Skill, and Perspective.* Use specialized multicultural skills to support learning and development of increased knowledge, skill and perspective for consultees and clients.

Continue One's Professional Development and Reflective Thinking

1. *Continue to Learn.* There is much to learn, and the biggest danger is thinking that one knows it all. There are countless ways that one's culture affects members of other cultures (Brislin & Yoshida, 1994).

112

TABLE 5–1 (continued)

2. *Engage in Formal and Informal Continuing Professional Development.* Continue learning about other cultures and cross-cultural work through a variety of methods. (See examples of self-assessment tools in Brislin & Yoshida, 1994; Cushner & Brislin, 1997; Ponterotto & Pedersen, 1993).

3. *Seek Feedback.* Encourage and invite feedback from consultees, colleagues, and others as a means to continually develop one's multicultural consultation approaches, learn about culturally divergent perspective and interpretations, and explore how others perceive one's bridging and consultation approaches.

4. *Seek Cultural Guides and Teachers.* Seek out cultural guides in the school and community to provide critical feedback. When one demonstrates respect and a genuine interest in cultural learning, members of the other culture may be willing to serve as teachers to the consultant. (Also, see Nastasi et al., 2000, for examples of using "cultural brokers.")

Note. From "Consultation through a multicultural lens: Multicultural and cross-cultural consultation in schools," by C. L. Ingraham, 2000, *School Psychology Review, 29,* 320–343. Copyright 2000 by the National Association of School Psychologists. Adapted with permission of the publisher.

these may have emerged within the consultation system, and methods the consultant used to support consultee and client success. Table 5–1 summarizes the methods for supporting consultee and client success proposed in the MSC framework (Ingraham, 2000) that this author teaches developing consultants to utilize. Reflective practice and cross-cultural feedback from others are used to support consultant conceptualizations and learning.

Consultants for the three cases reported in Ingraham (2003) used this method of case analysis to examine their multicultural consultee-centered consultation with a specific teacher consultee. From these case studies, three factors appear to contribute to MCCC success: (a) consultant use of self-disclosure about the consultant's own process of cross-cultural learning, (b) the teacher's understanding that cultural factors can affect classroom, and (c) consultant use of multicultural consultation methods (see Table 5–1). Additionally, it is possible that consultants who combine a focus on the instructional process with mental health consultation may be more successful in creating conceptual change in teachers compared with consultants who only focus on the teacher's attitudes, but additional research is needed to confirm this.

IMPLICATIONS FOR FUTURE RESEARCH AND PRACTICE

There is much to be done to further the research and practice of multicultural consultee-centered consultation with teachers. Ramirez et al. (1998) described several multicultural issues relevant to school-based consultation and proposed a series of research questions and methodologies to empirically investigate the degree to which consideration or inclusion of culture contributes to successful consultation outcomes. Tarver Behring and Ingraham (1998) called for culture to become a central component of consultation theory, research and practice, not just a consideration or variable to include. The MSC framework (Ingraham, 2000) offered ways to conceptualize and integrate a cultural perspective into all aspects of the consultation process, and now studies with real consultation cases using the framework are emerging (e.g., Ingraham, 2003). These advances offer guidance for the training and practice of multicultural consultation (e.g., Ingraham, 2002), but there are needs for additional research in many areas.

Recently several questions for future research to address were outlined (see Ingraham, 2003). These questions involved the role of ethnicity among consultants and consultees, multicultural consultation methods and approaches, and education and training experiences for consultants and consultees. Among these questions were: What is the relationship between the consultant and consultee ethnicity and its influence on consultation processes and outcomes? Do European American versus consultants of ethnically and linguistically diverse backgrounds encounter different reactions from consultees when they raise cultural hypotheses about the problem definition? Is there a difference in willingness to explore cultural hypotheses through consultation among bilingual teachers compared with monolingual English speakers? When consultees have similar cultural and linguistic backgrounds, are there differences in the success of European American versus bi/multicultural consultants? Which features of Ingraham's (2000) framework for consultant approaches to support consultee's cultural learning are most linked with consultant success? What kinds of training and support do European American consultants need to effectively raise cultural hypotheses with their senior European American consultees?

Some scholars are asking that future research more fully include the perceptions of consultees and clients to better understand the outcomes of multicultural consultation. Henning-Stout and Meyers (2000) called for the inclusion of the perspectives of those most marginalized in the school or community systems. They caution researchers and practitioners to consider the limitations of consultation strategies grounded in the dominant culture and to seek ways to include alternative and marginalized perspectives. Similarly, Ingraham (2003) suggested that future research include data regarding the perspectives and conceptualizations of consultees and clients, especially those who may represent diverse or minority worldviews and perspectives. Future research that includes the perspectives of diverse consultees and clients will contribute to a fuller understanding of the effects and outcomes of multicultural consultation.

While it may be easiest to gather data on the outcomes and perceptions of the clients, consultee perceptions may be more challenging to collect. Researchers and practitioners seeking feedback will need to find ways to invite consultee comments that do not sound like an evaluation of the consultant effectiveness, or a measure of how well the consultee adapted to the consultant's style. For example, in this author's own research and teaching, there is a challenge with how to help consultants identify the consultee's ethnic identity when it has not surfaced as part of the natural multicultural consultation discussion. Many consultants find it awkward to ask consultees how they identify ethnically, yet without the consultee's perspectives on this, consultants are left to inferring cultural orientations, which is an ill-advised and imperfect way to understand one's cultural perspectives. Future research and practice will need to develop and validate methods for learning about the consultee's perceptions, values, worldview and cultural identity in order to more deeply study how culture impacts the consultation process.

Another area for future work involves identifying training approaches to support European Americans in making cultural adaptations and raising cultural hypotheses with consultees. Studies by Tarver Behring et al. (2000) and Ingraham (2003) both identified challenges European American novice consultants faced in cross-cultural consultation. While they had the desire to raise cultural issues and modify approaches for cultural appropriateness, they appeared to lack some of the knowledge of specific cultural practices and/or strategies for how to challenge cultural stereotypes among consultees. If one of the goals of multicultural consultation is to support consultees in developing increased cultural competence, then European American consultants may need specialized coaching or practice to fulfill this goal (Ingraham, 2003). Without this, consultants may be susceptible to the same threats to cultural competence (e.g., intervention paralysis, avoidance of sensitive topics, overemphasis of culture, or fear of offending) described as threats to consultee objectivity and confidence (see Ingraham, 2000).

With education in multicultural consultation and practice in the approaches that support consultee and client success, school psychologists have an important role to play in developing effective consultations and interventions. Studies have shown that multicultural consultation can increase student learning and development by supporting consultees in developing culturally informed and effective interventions for students (e.g., Ingraham, 2003; Ingraham & Tarver Behring, 1998b; Lopez, 2000; Nastasi et al., 2000; Tarver Behring et al., 2000; Tarver Behring & Ingraham, 1998). School psychologists can enhance their competence and effectiveness through reflective practice and feedback, as well as future research, on the wonderfully rich and rewarding use of multicultural consultation. When school psychologists build multicultural bridges of understanding and success, they create win-win situations where consultees expand their cultural competence and confidence and students benefit through positive learning and development.

ANNOTATED BIBLIOGRAPHY

Ingraham, C. L. (2003). Multicultural consultee-centered consultation: When novice consultants explore cultural hypotheses with experienced teacher consultees. *Journal of Educational and Psychological Consultation, 14* (3 & 4), 329–362.

    This article uses case study qualitative methodology and naturalistic inquiry to investigate how beginning consultants use multicultural consultee-centered consultation to explore cultural hypotheses with experienced teachers. Through the use of Ingraham's (2000, 2002) multicultural consultation framework, this study focuses on consultation stages, communication processes, factors associated with success and failure, and their relationship with co-constructing problem definitions with consultees. Questions for future research are identified. These case studies are useful in training and learning how consultants use multicultural consultation approaches.

Ingraham, C. L., & Meyers, J. (2000). Multicultural and cross-cultural consultation in schools [Special Issue]. *School Psychology Review, 29,* 3.

This special issue provides readers with an excellent overview of multicultural issues in consultation. Several conceptual articles articulate multicultural frameworks in consultation. Qualitative research investigations focus on a number of topics in multicultural consultation. The special issue ends with commentaries addressing various issues related to multicultural and cross-cultural consultation.

RESOURCES

Culturally Competent Consultation in the Schools: Information for School Psychologists and School Personnel. Web page at the National School Psychologists website: http://www.nasponline.org/culturalcompetence

This is a practical handout that provides a brief overview of multicultural issues in consultation. It is especially useful in training situations to provide readers with a quick introduction and overview of basic topics in multicultural consultation.

Journal of Educational and Psychological Consultation

The journal publishes manuscripts and special issues that expand our knowledge base of practice and research in consultation. The Diversity in Consultation column publishes papers that focus on diversity issues.

REFERENCES

Allen, S. J., & Graden, J. L. (2002). Best practices in collaborative problem solving for intervention design. In A. Thomas & J. Grimes (Eds.), *Best practices in school psychology IV* (pp. 565–582). Bethesda, MD: National Association of School Psychologists.

Arredondo, P., Toporek, R., Brown, S. P., Jones, J., Locke, D. C., Sanchez, J., & Stadler, H. (1996). Operationalization of the multicultural counseling competencies. *Journal of Multicultural Counseling and Development, 24,* 42–78.

Bergan, J. R., & Kratochwill, T. R. (1990). *Behavioral consultation and therapy.* New York: Plenum.

Brislin, R. W., & Yoshida, T. (Eds.). (1994). *Improving intercultural interactions: Modules for cross-cultural training programs.* Thousand Oaks, CA: Sage.

Brown, D. (1997). Implications of cultural values for cross-cultural consultation with families. *Journal of Counseling & Development, 76,* 29–35.

Brown, D., Pryzwansky, W. B., & Schulte, A. C. (2006). *Psychological consultation* (6th ed.). Boston: Pearson.

Caplan, G., & Caplan, R. B. (1993). *Mental health consultation and collaboration.* San Francisco: Jossey-Bass.

Conoley, J. C., & Conoley, C. W. (1992). *School consultation: Practice and training* (2nd ed.). Boston: Allyn & Bacon.

Covington, M. V. (1992). *Making the grade.* New York: Cambridge.

Cushner, K., & Brislin, R. W. (1997). *Improving intercultural interactions: Modules for cross-cultural training programs, Vol. 2.* Thousand Oaks, CA: Sage.

Duncan, C. F. (1995). Cross-cultural school consultation. In C. Lee (Ed.), *Counseling for diversity* (pp. 129–139). Boston: Allyn & Bacon.

Duncan, C., & Pryzwansky, W. B. (1993). Effects of race, racial identity development, and orientation style on perceived consultant effectiveness. *Journal of Multicultural Counseling and Development, 21,* 88–96.

Edens, J. H. (1997). Home visitation programs with ethnic minority families: Cultural issues in parent consultation. *Journal of Educational and Psychological Consultation, 8,* 373–383.

Gibbs, J. T. (1980). The interpersonal orientation in mental health: Toward a mode of ethnicvariations in consultation. *Journal of Community Psychology, 8,* 195–207.

Goldstein, B. S. C., & Harris, K. C. (2000). Consultant practices in two heterogeneous Latino schools . *School Psychology Review, 29,* 368–377.

Gudykunst, W. B. (1991). *Bridging differences: Effective intergroup communication.* Newbury Park, CA: Sage.

Harris, K. C. (1991). An expanded view on consultation competencies for educators serving culturally and linguistically diverse exceptional students. *Teacher Education and Special Education, 14,* 25–29.

Henning-Stout, M., & Meyers, J. (2000). Consultation and human diversity: First things first. *School Psychology Review, 29,* 419–425.

Ingraham, C. L. (1999). Towards systems interventions in multicultural schools: Practitioners' training needs. *The School Psychologist, 53,* 72–76.

Ingraham, C. L. (2000). Consultation through a multicultural lens: Multicultural and cross-cultural consultation in schools. *School Psychology Review, 29,* 320–343.

Ingraham, C. L. (2002, February). *Multicultural consultation in schools to support teacher and student success.* Workshop presented at the annual meeting of the National Association for School Psychologists, Chicago, IL. Audiotapes available (# WS 16) from NASP and Gaylor MultiMedia, Inc., http://www.GaylorOnline.com.

Ingraham, C. L. (2003). Multicultural consultee-centered consultation: When novice consultants explore cultural hypotheses with experienced teacher consultees. *Journal of Educational and Psychological Consultation, 14,* 329–362.

Ingraham, C. L. (2004). Multicultural consultation: A model for supporting consultees in the development of cultural competence. In N. M. Lambert, I. Hylander, & J. Sandoval (Eds.), *Consultee centered consultation: Improving the quality of professional services in schools and community organizations* (pp. 133–148). Mahwah, NJ: Erlbaum.

Ingraham, C. L., & Meyers, J. (Eds.). (2000). Multicultural and cross-cultural consultation in schools: Cultural diversity issues in school consultation. [Special issue]. *School Psychology Review, 29,* 3.

Ingraham, C. L., & Tarver Behring, S. (1998a, April). *Developing teachers' capacity to work effectively with diverse learners.* Paper presented at the annual conference of the American Educational Research Association, San Diego, CA.

Ingraham, C. L., & Tarver Behring, S. (1998b, August). *Multicultural consultation: A model for consultation in culturally diverse schools and communities.* Paper presented at the International Congress of Applied Psychology, San Francisco, CA.

Korn, C. & Bursztyn, A. (Eds.). (2002). *Rethinking multicultural education: Case studies in cultural transition.* Westport, CT: Bergin & Garvey.

Lambert, N. M., Hylander, I., & Sandoval, J. (Eds.). (2004). *Consultee centered consultation: Improving the quality of professional services in schools and community organizations.* Mahwah, NJ: Erlbaum.

Leong, F. T. L. (1996). Toward an integrative model for cross-cultural counseling and psychotherapy. *Applied & Preventive Psychology, 5,* 189–209.

Lopez, E. (2000). Conducting consultation through interpreters. *School Psychology Review, 29,* 378–388.

Lynch, E. W., & Hanson, N. J. (Eds.). (2004). *Developing cross-cultural competence: A guide for working with children and their families* (3rd ed.). Baltimore: Paul H. Brookes.

Maital, S. L. (2000). Reciprocal Distancing: A systems model of interpersonal processes incross-cultural consultation. *School Psychology Review, 29,* 389–400.

Miranda, A. H. (1993). Consultation with culturally diverse families. *Journal of Educational and Psychological Consultation, 4*, 89–93.

Nastasi, B., Vargas, K., Berstein, R., & Jayasena, A. (2000). Conducting participatory culture-specific consultation: A global perspective on multicultural consultation. *School Psychology Review, 29*, 401–413.

Naumann, W. C., Gutkin, T. B., & Sandoval, S. R. (1996). The impact of consultant race and student race on perceptions of consultant effectiveness and intervention acceptability. *Journal of Educational and Psychological Consultation, 7*, 151–160.

Parks, S. (1999). Reducing the effects of racism in schools. *Educational Leadership, 56*, 14–18.

Parsons, R. D., & Meyers, J. (1984). *Developing consultation skills*. San Francisco: Jossey-Bass.

Pinto, R. F. (1981). Consultant orientations and client system perceptions: Styles of cross-cultural consultation. In R. Lippitt & G. L. Lippitt (Eds.), *Systems thinking: A resource for organizational diagnosis and intervention* (pp. 57–74). Washington, DC: International Consultants.

Ponterotto, J. G., Casas, J. M., Suzuki, L. A., & Alexander, C. M. (Eds.). (1995). *Handbook for multicultural counseling*. Thousand Oaks, CA: Sage.

Ponterotto, J. G., & Pedersen, P. B. (1993). *Preventing prejudice*. Newbury Park, CA: Sage.

Ramirez, S. Z., Lepage, K. M., Kratochwill, T. R., & Duffy, J. L. (1998). Multicultural issues in school-based consultation: Conceptual and research considerations. *Journal of School Psychology, 36*, 479–509.

Rogers, M. R. (1998). The influence of race and consultant verbal behavior on perceptions of consultant competence and multicultural sensitivity. *School Psychology Quarterly, 13*, 265–280.

Rogers, M. R., Ingraham, C. L., Bursztyn, A., Cajigas-Segredo, N., Esquivel, G., Hess, R., Lopez, E. C., & Nahari, S. G. (1999). Providing psychological services to racially, ethnically, culturally, and linguistically diverse individuals in the schools: Recommendations for practice. *School Psychology International Journal, 20*, 243–264.

Soo-Hoo, T. (1998). Applying frame of reference and reframing techniques to improve school consultation in multicultural settings. *Journal of Psychological and Educational Consultation, 9*, 325–345.

Sue, D. W., & Sue, D. (1999). *Counseling the culturally different: Theory and practice* (3rd ed.). New York: John Wiley & Sons.

Tarver Behring, S., Cabello, B., Kushida, D., & Murguia, A. (2000). Cultural modifications to current school-based consultation approaches reported by culturally diverse beginning consultants. *School Psychology Review, 29*, 354–367.

Tarver Behring, S., & Gelinas, R. T. (1996). School consultation with Asian American children and families. *The California School Psychologist, 1*, 13–20.

Tarver Behring, S., & Ingraham, C. L. (1998). Culture as a central component of consultation: A call to the field. *Journal of Educational and Psychological Consultation, 9*, 57–72.

U.S. Department of Education. (2000). National Center for Education Statistics. *Monitoring school quality: An indicators report*, NCES 2001–030 by Daniel P. Mayer, John E. Mullens, and Mary T. Moore. John Ralph, Project Officer. Washington DC: Author. Available from: http://nces.ed.gov/pubsearch/pubsinfo.asp?pubid = 2001030

Wampold, B. E., Licktenberg, J. W., & Waehler, C. A. (2002). Principles of empirically supported interventions in counseling psychology. *The Counseling Psychologist, 30*, 197–217.

Zins, J. E., Curtis, M. J., Graden, J. L., & Ponti, C. R. (1988). *Helping students succeed in the regular classroom*. San Francisco: Jossey-Bass.

6

CONSULTING WITH CULTURALLY AND LINGUISTICALLY DIVERSE PARENTS

Sara G. Nahari
Queens College, City University of New York

Danielle Martines
Montclair State University

Gelasia Marquez
Union City Board of Education

As a result of the implementation of PL 94–142 The Education for All Handicapped children Act of 1975, now known as the Individuals with Disabilities Education Act (1997) (IDEA), school districts nationwide are required by State and Federal education agencies to form parental partnerships based on the belief that parental involvement benefits the students, parents, and schools. However, organized efforts by public schools to involve culturally and linguistically diverse (CLD) parents are more recent (Koonce & Harper, in press; Lynch & Hanson, 2004).

Investigations of parent involvement in schools cite amongst the benefits for involved parents the acquisition of (a) better skills to help their children, (b) greater familiarity with educational programs, and (c) increased knowledge of the school's organizational system (Epstein, 1992). In addition, parents involved with schools become increasingly supportive of their children and show improved confidence in ways to help their children (Epstein, 1992). Xitao (2001) conducted an investigation on the effect of parental involvement and found that "the effects, or lack thereof, of parental involvement on students' academic growth were consistent, especially the positive effect of parents' Education Aspiration for their children." Education aspirations were defined in this study as the parents' desire for the educational success of their children. Children of parents who exhibited higher education aspirations were found to demonstrate higher academic achievement. The research also indicates that parental involvement brings about benefits for teachers and schools such as improvements in teachers' morale and student achievement (Epstein, 1992; Henderson & Berla, 1994).

In light of demographic changes occurring in the United States, the implementation of these laws is even more crucial for the CLD population of students and parents. Data from the National Center of Education Statistics (2003) indicate that the number of 5 to 24-year-olds who were reported speaking a language other than English at home increased from 6.3 million in 1979 to 13.7 million in 1999. The Commerce Department's Census Bureau also reported that in the year 2000, 39% of public school students were of a minority background. These sources predict that the number of CLD children and families will continue to increase in the future (Lullock, 2001).

The influx of families who demonstrate diverse backgrounds in terms of culture, race, ethnicity, language, economic conditions, and the expectations that our future school population will continue to diversify (National Center of Education Statistics, 2004) implies that educators and psychologists will continue to be faced with the challenging task of working with members of culturally diverse groups (Ingraham & Meyers, 2000; Jackson & Hayes, 1993; Nastasi, Varjas, Bernstein, & Jayasena, 2000). Culturally diverse families' characteristics, values and behaviors that are different from the mainstream influence interactions between professionals, children and families (Harry, 1992). Demographic changes certainly imply that changes are needed in how school professionals provide consultation services to parents. Recognizing cultural differences and how those differences influence the consultation process requires appreciating the reality that each family is unique in terms of its ethnic heritage, attitudes, values, norms, customs, socioeconomic status, level of acculturation, language practices, belief systems, religious beliefs, life-style orientations, and family structures (Jackson & Hayes, 1993).

In 2002 the American Psychological Association (APA) approved the "Guidelines on Multicultural Education, Training, Research, Practice, and Organizational Change for Psychologists." The guidelines support a call for the integration of multicultural competencies in practice. The work of Rogers et al. (1999) further supports the need for multicultural competencies for school psychologists in a number of areas, including consultation with parents.

This chapter will discuss the delivery of consultation services to parents, and families who are culturally and linguistically diverse (CLD) by: (a) addressing the research and theoretical basis for consultation with parents, (b) exploring the practical implications of the available research, (c) exploring approaches to parent consultation, and (c) identifying future research and practical issues in the area of consulting with CLD parents. Emphasis is placed on consulting with immigrant grants.

THEORETICAL AND RESEARCH BASIS

Multicultural consultation is defined as "a culturally sensitive approach in which the consultant adjusts the consultation services to address the needs and cultural values of the consultees and/or clients from various cultural groups" (Ingraham & Meyers, 2000, p. 316). The process of consulting with families takes place in a multiple settings including schools, mental health centers, rehabilitation settings, and community agencies. School psychologists and other school professionals are faced ever more with the complex task of consulting with members of culturally diverse families (Ingraham & Meyers, 2000; Jackson & Hayes, 1993; Nastasi, Varjas, Bernstein, & Jayasena, 2000). Establishing a relationship during consultation when the participants differ in terms of race, culture, ethnicity, exceptionality, sexuality, socioeconomic status, and/or age requires that consultants possess an understanding of cultural diversity (Sue, Arrendondo, & McDavis, 1992). Furthermore, because beliefs, values, and attitudes of individuals are strongly related to psychological functioning, consultants need to consider the multicultural perspectives of their clients (Takushi & Uomoto, 2001).

The relevance of consultation-based delivery systems is strongly supported in the education and psychology literature. The consultation literature addresses the need for psychologists to work collaboratively with parents and educators to design and implement instructional alternatives and behavioral interventions through a consultation-based service delivery system (Fletcher & Cardona-Morales, 1990; Ponti, Zins, & Graden, 1988; Rosenfield & Gravois, 1996; Sheridan, 2000). The preventative nature of consultation should benefit CLD students by providing parents with consultation support aimed at improving students' behavioral and instructional difficulties.

Harris (1998) elaborates on a triadic model of consultation applicable for work with parents. This model involves collaboration between a consultant and an activate mediator or consultee (i.e., parent, general or special education teacher) that has access to the targeted client (i.e., children, youth). When the consultees and clients are culturally and linguistically diverse, Jackson and Hayes (1993) suggest that it is necessary to integrate multicultural concerns into the consultation process to assure that students' needs are met with cultural sensitivity. Moreover, in order for the schools to meet their goals of educating children, the collaboration of CLD parents is essential.

Sheridan (2000) notes that it is important during the problem identification stage for consultants to explore not only cultural differences but also individual differences as well. As an example, Asian-Americans follow a number of religious practices that differ across groups (e.g., Catholicism, Buddhism, Protestant and Islamism). Thus, individual differences must be acknowledged for consultants to understand religious observances and traditions between different Asian American families.

Cultural differences mean that consultants and consultees may perceive problems differently and may not even agree as to what are the problem(s). In a longitudinal consultation project Maital (2000) found that consultants face the task of reframing a child's "difficult" behaviors within the perspective of the child's culture of origin in order to understand how specific behaviors may be appropriate in the child's native culture.

Culturally mediated variables may also influence the manner in which problems manifest themselves (Sheridan, 2000). As an example, some groups do not perceive independent behavior as a favorable trait in children, therefore consultants' attempts to foster independent behaviors in clients may find resistance from some CLD parents. Parents' ideas, values, strategies, and beliefs should be obtained and incorporated within the problem identification stage of parent consultation to delineate a better picture of the child's functioning and environmental conditions. Once consultants identify and understand which culturally mediated variables are playing a role on specific behaviors, they can encourage a collaborative relationship with the family to identify and implement interventions. Jackson and Hayes (1993) suggest that by engaging in this type of collaborative relationship the consultant is not only modeling cooperation but empowering the parents as well. Collaboration is particularly important for ethnic minorities because historically they have felt disenfranchised by the mental health system (U.S. Department of Mental Health and Human Services Office of the Surgeon General, 2002). A collaborative approach also engages the consultants as change agents to develop new strategies *with* CLD parents that foster desired change (Jackson & Hayes, 1993).

Cultural differences may also arise during the establishment of goals for interventions. Tamura and Lau (1992) contrasted the intervention preferences of Japanese and British parents and concluded that Japanese families prefer interventions that encourage integration and harmony. Conversely, British families favor goals that promote autonomy and the establishment of clear personal boundaries. According to Brown (1997), these differences in values are the foundation of people's beliefs and perceptions of how parenting should be conducted. Sheridan (2000) recommends the examination of childrearing cultural practices and suggests considering their congruency with the school's own goals and expectations of childrearing practices. Since parents' levels of tolerance and expectations for certain behaviors may differ across cultural groups, solutions to problems will likely differ as well. For instance, trying to set goals that require time limits to complete tasks may not be understood by families who perceive dimensions of time differently than the Eurocentric tradition of time. Also, Asians and American Indians often view change in terms of establishing harmony within the family or the community, appreciating one's person, and regaining one's place in nature (Brown, 1997). In these instances, consultants must acknowledge values, beliefs and behaviors that may not be similar to the Western traditions.

Rogers (1998) suggests that consultees, in this case parents, should view consultants as culturally sensitive professionals that are aware of cultural differences. In this respect, culturally sensitive consultants would be perceived by parents as highly skilled when compared to other consultants that have not adopted a multicultural approach to consultation. Sheridan (2000) points out that consultants who do not acknowledge differences and treat all consultees in an identical manner communicate a message that individual differences do not matter. By doing so, the consultants increases the distance between parents and the school, and fail to develop meaningful relationships with parents as consultees.

Focusing on Issues of Migration and Acculturation Within Parent Consultation

Consultation with parents requires attention to the environment within which each family functions. This includes contexts such as the neighborhood, peer groups, church, school, and workplace that touch family members directly, as well as the larger political, governmental, and economic contexts in which the family functions. Every family belongs to a defined cultural community by identifying itself with a common group in terms of such characteristics as race, religion, nationality, or by some mixture of these categories. These categories serve as social-psychological referents and create, through historical circumstances, a sense of peoplehood (Gordon, 1964). Consequently, every family is interwoven in a continuous interchange with its own economic and sociocultural environment to accomplish its universal functions or tasks (Bronfenbrenner, 1986).

Migration certainly changes families' daily experiences of their environments and plays a significant role in how families interact with those various contexts (e.g., church, neighborhood). An understanding of the migration processes is necessary to facilitate the consultation process. Families undergoing the migration experience find themselves between two impinging socio-cultural and economic contexts—the society of origin and the host society. Rogler, Gurak and Cooney (1987) describe the migration process as composed of three fundamental traditions: (a) alterations in the bonding and reconstruction of interpersonal social networks, (b) extraction from one socioeconomic system and insertion into another, and (c) movement from one cultural system to a different one. These processes of adjustment can produce stressors that result in a sense of loss of personal control and in feelings of being overwhelmed (Cervantes, Padilla, & Salgado de Snyder,1991; Padilla, Cervantes, Maldonado, & Garcia, 1988; Plante, Manuel, Menendez, & Marcotte, 1995).

Families respond to the migration experience and diverse ways. For example, some families retain their native ethnic values for many generations after migration (Greeley, 1974). Other families incorporate selected values and attitudes from the majority culture over generations (Gilgaud & Kutzik, Lieberman, Teper, as cited in McGoldrick 1982; Torres-Matrullo, 1980). One of the experiences that immigrant families share is the process of acculturation, which can result in radical transformations in the meanings individuals and families attribute to the social world (Lorenzo-Hernandez, 1998; Padilla, 1980).

Acculturation is defined as the process of psychological change in values, beliefs, and behaviors when adapting to a new culture (Takushi & Umoto, 2001). Acculturation involves (a) becoming knowledgeable of the language, norms, and values of the new culture, (b) readjusting to a new system of values by modifying behaviors and attitudes, and (c) relinquishing some old customs, beliefs, and behaviors. It can be conceptualized as the path that facilitates the movement from one cultural system to another. Although the very act of migration may constitute a brief transition, the more pre-migration traumatic events experienced by immigrants, the greater the experience of acculturative stress later (Cervantes et. al., 1991). Whether immigration is voluntary or involuntary, it constitutes an "uprooting" experience when immigrants need to interrupt their personal histories, sever their social ties, and later begin the formation of new relationships within a strange environment. Thus, the process of acculturation can be very stressful (Cervantes et. al.).

Several complex issues require attention as acculturation changes occur in the immigrant family. The social sciences literature suggest that every family is involved in a continuous interchange with its economic and sociocultural environment to accomplish its universal functions or tasks such as safeguarding health, and providing shelter and adequate nutrition to its members(Bronfenbrenner, 1986). Consequently, the cultural values and ethnicity of the family mediates their interactions with the external world and how they accomplish those basic universal functions. The family's cultural values also define the family structure and internal organization, values, communication patterns, and behaviors.

The processes of migration and acculturation often create conflicts that result in feelings of confusion and disorganization for individual members as well as for the whole family (Ho, 1987). In the process of acculturation, for example, immigrant children may acquire values and attitudes that are different from those of their parents. The differences between the family's child-rearing practices and their children's newly acquired set of values can lead to chronic unresolved conflicts within the family (Santisteban & Szapocznik, 1982). Szapocznik and Hernandex (1988) suggest that when these intergenerational differences arise, the parents experience alienation from their highly acculturated children, and the "children, in turn, experience alienation from their less acculturated parents" (pp. 196–170). In an effort to cope with these acculturation differences, the parents may attempt to restrict or slow down the process of acculturation for their children. However, such attempts can further alienate the youngsters from family interactions and the values of the parents' culture, precipitating a rejection of the parental lifestyle and a fuller adherence to the behavior characteristics of the host culture. The literature suggests that in such situations some immigrant youngsters may become marginalized and develop difficulties identifying with either group (i.e., culture of the family vs. host culture) (Santisteban & Szapocznik, 1982). Cross-generational differences in acculturation can also surface in consulting with extended family structures as in situations where more traditional grandparents wish to consult a health healer and more acculturated parents prefer behavior modification interventions.

In general, consultants need to be familiar with migration, the process of acculturation and the influence they have on their consultees and clients. An understanding of migration and acculturation issues will help consultants to understand the context within which problems are being manifested and addressed by immigrant parents.

IMPLICATIONS FOR PRACTICE

Ingraham (2000) identifies eight multicultural school consultation competence domains. Those competencies are applicable to consultants who work with CLD parents. The competencies entail understanding (a) one's own culture, (b) the impact of one's own culture on others, (c) cultural saliency and how to build bridges across salient differences, (d) the cultural context forconsultation, and (e) individual differences within cultural groups and multiple cultural identities. Ingraham emphasizes respecting and valuing other cultures, and developing multicultural communication and multicultural consultation approaches for rapport development and maintenance.

Lopez and Rogers (2001) and Rogers and Lopez (2002) identified several research-based competencies essential to multicultural consultants that include (a) interpersonal skills to consult with others; (b) knowledge of cultural differences that influence how problems are defined in consultation; (c) knowledge of cultural and linguistic factors that influence the input, process, and outcome of consultation; (d) skills in responding with sensitivity to cross-cultural differences; (e) skills in using a variety of data collection techniques to identify clients' problems; and (f) skills in recognizing how prejudice may influence the consultation process. Skills in how to work with interpreters are also essential for consultants communicating with limited English proficient parents. Rogers (2000) suggests that consultants need culture specific information particular to the families they work with to deliver culturally responsive consultation services.

Brown (1997) argues that cross-cultural miscommunication and misinterpretation can be overcome if consultants identify the values and beliefs of CLD family members. Cross-cultural conflicts can also be overcome if consultants are willing to make modifications in their consultation approaches. When consultants are not knowledgeable about cultural differences that are operating in a particular case, problems may be approached or defined incorrectly or insensitively (Henning-Stout & Meyers, 2000). It is the consultant's role to educate him/herself and others participating in consultation relationships about cultural differences. Consultants that are skilled in cross-cultural communication and possess cultural awareness are able to assume the role of cultural brokers by providing support to parents and students within a consultative model (Harry et al., 1998; Lynch & Hanson, 2004; Tarver Behring & Ingraham, 1998).

Knowledge about and contact with a different culture may not be sufficient to address cross-cultural differences in consultation. Maital (2002) conducted a qualitative study with Ethiopian clients to examine reciprocal distancing, an experience defined as 'mutual distancing' interactions that generate problems in cross-cultural relations (p. 390). Maital found that the consultants' personal commitment was important in addressing challenges during cross-cultural contacts. When consulting with parents, she reported that the development of an active parent support network empowered "parents as a group to find solutions" (p. 398). Maital argues that skills in conducting group consultation were essential when consulting with CLD parents.

With the 1997 reauthorization of IDEA, parental involvement is included in all stages of assessment, identification, and intervention implementation (Bos, Nahmias, & Urban, 1999). Although in the past parents have been included as contributors in their children's multidisciplinary and individualized education program (IEP) teams, IDEA also calls for parents to have input during pre-referral and eligibility meetings, and when planning behavioral interventions. A collaborative approach can benefit students by enabling parents to partake in a consultation process to plan for instructional, behavioral, and mental health services or other interventions. However, establishing a collaborative relationship may be challenging when consulting with CLD parents. Harry's (2002) findings showed that parents' ability to become partners in the process of educating children might be put at risk by parents' culturally different ways of understanding special education and their children's disabilities of their children. For example some Asian cultures view disability as a spiritual phenomenon whereby parents may perceive a child with a disability as either a reward or a retribution for past deeds. In such situations parents may have difficulties accepting special education related or mental health interventions. CLD parents of students in special education are also often reluctant to step into situations that are foreign to them and may hesitate to engage in consultation relationships with school personnel. Schools can distance these parents when: (a) communication styles, conversational rules, and discourse patterns that vary widely across culture are not taken into consideration in planning parental involvement programs; (b) rearing practices of CLD families that are not congruent with the expectations of the educational system are not recognize and addressed; and (c) values, experiences, and beliefs about special education held by members of various culturally and ethnically diverse groups are not understood by school consultants (Nahari, 1999).

The success of establishing a cross-cultural collaborative relationship in consultation partly depends on the consultant's understanding and awareness of the different communication styles of their consultees and clients. For example, different cultural groups are comfortable with differing amounts of conversation and, accordingly, with silence. Hammer and Turner (1996) describe patterns of communication amongst African American families as placing emphasis on affective and interpersonal relations. Mothers tend to communicate with their children through nonverbal means. Intense eye contact is one way mothers impress their points to their children. Verbal communication patterns in the home frequently consist of few words, instructions are broken down, and directions are brief and delivered in small units.

Differences in children's rearing practices can often dictate what interventions are chosen during consultation. For example, for Chinese and other Asians the concepts of strictness and control are not interpreted as attempts to dominate children. On the contrary, strictness and control in those cultural groups are regarded by parents as signs of concern, involvement, and caring. These rearing practices are grounded in their beliefs and values concerning children's behaviors. Parents also hold beliefs and values about how to teach their children and about how others, including schools, should teach their children (Stipek, Milburn, Galluzzo, & Daniels,

1992). These perceptions manifest themselves in behaviors at home and in the parents' relationships with their children, teachers and other school professionals (Goldenberg, Reese, &Gallimore, 1992).

Many CLD parents view school professionals as the experts whose opinions and decisions cannot be questioned and refrain from advocating for their children even though they are expected to do so by the schools. Consultants can help CLD parents to advocate and to question schools in behalf of their children with the purpose of enhancing the children's academic achievement and well being.

In general, when consulting with CLD parents it is important that consultants are aware of differences in values, experiences, and beliefs that may be held by members of various cultural and ethnic groups. Additionally, professionals such as school consultants and teachers who are working and communicating with parents of CLD diverse children with disabilities should be prepared to help the parents to understand their rights and the value of parental involvement as necessary for the success of long-term treatments, consultations or implementation of interventions (Mowder, 1994). All this must be balanced with the CLD parents' perceptions of how they wish to collaborate with school professionals. In essence, "collaboration must be defined *with*, instead of *for*, CLD parents" (Lopez, this volume, p. 000).

IMPLEMENTATION AND APPROACHES

It is likely that among social institutions most affected by the changing demographics experienced during the last three decades are the private and public schools that have received and continue to receive the children of immigrant families. For these families, the school has had to perform an extraordinarily difficult role, that of serving as "an intersection between the home culture and the mainstream American culture" (Provenzo, 1985, p. iii).

Esquivel (1985) recommends that practitioners working with children whose culture they are not familiar with obtain information about the children's and families' cultural backgrounds to carefully plan for intervention implementation. The multicultural approach to parent consultation discussed in this chapter suggests that the possible responses to immigrant families in cultural transitions can include a combination of services such as providing (a) information, (b) education, (c) opportunities for emotional ventilation and support, (d) opportunities for contact with other families who have similar difficulties, (e) professional support during times of crisis, and (f) support in the form of intermediary structures that mediate between the individual family and the new culture (e.g., relationships formed during parent's workshops become supports for newcomers families).

A review of the consultation literature indicates a lack of research focusing on consultation with parents. Several authors have provided culturally responsive frameworks for parent consultation. Sheridan (2000) developed a conjoint behavioral consultation model that provides consultants with the opportunity to consult with CLD parents and the students' teachers. Sheridan indicates that establishing trusting relationships, acknowledging diversity, and achieving clear communication are all important variables for the success of the consultation process with CLD parents and teachers.

Marquez (1989, 2000) implemented several consultation programs with different goals and formats. The programs aimed to (a) help immigrant Hispanic children and their families in their adjustment to the mainstream society, and (b) to foster the development of collaborative partnerships between immigrant parents and their children's schools. The consultation programs were preventive in nature. They included actions and strategies intended for the early identification of expected crises, problems, and difficulties associated with the processes of migration and acculturation in students and their immigrant Hispanic families. Through indirect and direct consultation services, the consultant provided the families with opportunities to participate in parent education workshops and culturally sensitive individual and family counseling. The services were provided with the goals of helping students and their immigrant families to develop new coping mechanisms as they adjusted to a new physical environment, culture, language, and society.

Nahari (1999) targeted parents of severely disabled CLD students. This model used a collaborative format in which the consultant assumed the role of "resource-collaborator" as suggested by Tyler, Pargament, and Gatz (1983). The goals of this program were to empower CLD parents to become active participants in their children's educational and psychological well-being. The parents were asked to respond to a survey to identify positive and negative experiences they encountered during contacts with the school. Five major themes were identified in the data collected that related to the participation of parents in the schools. The themes identified by the parents were: (a) language and cultural differences were often barriers in interacting with school staff; (b) parents felt feelings of helplessness when confronting the provision of specialized services for their children because they lacked information about school services; (c) parents had everyday concerns about their children's autonomy and self-esteem; (d) cultural differences were noted in the intensity of the parents' involvement whereby parents defined involvement in different ways; and (e) communication was often a barrier between school and parents. These findings assisted the school staff in understanding the many issues confronting CLD parents and in addressing the themes and concerns expressed by the parents. The parents' concerns were addressed through monthly workshops conducted by guest speakers. The monthly workshops provided the CLD parents with information about the school system, special education services, and with strategies to cope with their children's difficulties. The workshops were also structured to provide parents with opportunities to voice their concerns and problem-solve solutions with each other. In addition to addressing the themes identified by the parents, resources provided included flyers in several languages and interpreters to translate the content of the training workshops and the discussions. These experiences helped the parents to develop of a sense of community with the school and amongst parents as they expressed feeling less segregated by differences in languages and culture. Parent training and short term group consultation experiences followed by on-going consultation services have the potential to support CLD parents in the process of establishing stronger parent-school ties and in their efforts to negotiate improved school services for their children.

Koonce and Harper (in press) describe a parental involvement consultation model with African American parents that emphasizes the establishment of a positive collaborative relationship with families. The model seeks to support parents faced with the challenge of effectively advocating for their children to gain equity in schools. Consultants from community agencies consulted with the parents as they interacted with school staff to target the children's educational needs. The consultation process strengthened the parents' interpersonal relations, taught parents to use human relation strategies in communicating with school staff, and provided parents with behavioral and instructional strategies.

Although these case studies provide us with a glimpse of a variety of ways to consult with CLD parents, the parent consultation literature is devoid of extensive discussions of such programs. The consultation literature is also devoid of research focusing on consultation efforts with CLD parents.

IMPLICATIONS FOR FUTURE RESEARCH AND PRACTICE

There is a need for parents and teachers to work collaboratively to help CLD students to achieve in schools. Some suggestions for a parent and teacher collaborations directed by the consultant school psychologist include teachers and CLD parents: (a) participating in conducting a culture-specific needs assessment of the school and/or community (e.g., some needs might include establishing prejudice prevention interventions in the classroom and in the community; developing cultural fairs; having training sessions on multicultural education techniques; instituting reach-out programs for CLD parents), (b) collaborating to develop collaborative interventions and the implementation of the assessed school and community-related cultural needs, and (c) collaborating to formulate instructional and behavioral changes at home and in the classroom.

To undertake a multicultural consultation role, consultants need to become informed about cultural differences to provide support to CLD parents. Skills in cross-cultural communication are also essential in working with CLD parents to establish home- school partnerships. Cross-culturally competent consultants need to collaborate with schools to enhance partnerships with families.

Given the current CLD student population and the noted need to increase culturally sensitive consultation practices for CLD children and families, a multicultural consultative approach model is certainly a priority in the present and in the future. The actual application of such an approach is clearly in its infancy stage and much more research is needed in order to establish solid foundations for successful practice.

Future research is needed to examine conjoint behavioral consultation frameworks with CLD parents (Sheridan, 2000). The research should also focus on identifying critical factors in consulting with CLD parents and families to provide consultants that engage in cross-cultural consultation with a systematic model that can also be used to train future school consultants within a multicultural framework (Ingraham, 2003).

There are several research considerations for consulting school-psychologists in the schools. There is a need to conduct research examining multicultural consultation approaches with CLD parents across a variety of consultation models (i.e., behavioral, instructional, mental health, organizational, consultee-centered). One such deliberation involves the utilization of the mental health consultee-centered consultation model as a potential training catalyst for optimizing teachers' cultural sensitivity, knowledge, and skills to work with CLD parents (Caplan & Caplan, 1993; Erchuls & Martens, 2002; Martines, 1999, 2005).The consultee-centered consultation model can be modified with the inclusion of a multicultural framework. Such a modified model would focus on imparting culturally sensitive knowledge and skills to teachers within a consultee-centered consultation framework and in small group consultation situations.

Qualitative and quantitative studies should be designed to explore culturally responsive modifications and their implications for parent consultation. The home-school collaboration and multicultural parent consultation approaches are important for school consultants since so many consultative school-based intervention plans will ultimately require the support of parents. Consequently, research should be oriented toward the study of practical interventions for CLD families within a cross-cultural home-school consultation approach. Schools need to generate ways to retain CLD parents' cooperation and involvement. School consultants such as school psychologists can play a crucial role in the development of such programs in establishing their effectiveness (Dettmer; Thruston, & Dyck, 2002).

Research, as well as documented experiences (e.g., case studies) from consultants conducting cross-cultural consultation will also provide benefits to the fledging field of cross-cultural consultation. Without exploration into these areas, school consultants will be limited in their ability to provide appropriate consultation services for parents and teachers as they address the needs of CLD students.

Along the same theme, more research is necessary on the use of an educational cross-cultural consultation model and on the role of consultant school psychologist in the development of programs and curriculum for culturally and linguistically diverse students via consultation. Since this is a new area for school psychologists, there is a need for descriptive qualitative studies that will explore consultation processes within a multicultural framework. In particular, research should be conducted on the effects of implementing collaborative cross-cultural parent consultation programs designed to prevent and reduce students' failures in schools. Furthermore, we need research focusing on behavioral and instructional consultation methods that are effective in cross-cultural consultation with parents. Research designed to identify the skills that will provide school consultants with the necessary tools and competencies to enhance the consultation process when working with CLD parents will certainly benefit future training efforts.

Marquez's (2000) study with immigrant Hispanic families found that their interactions with intermediate structures like schools and churches are particularly important in the first years after migration. These structures provide CLD families with key support systems as they acculturate into the host culture. Therefore, there is a great need for consultation programs that (a) bridge the communication gap between schools and the homes of CLD parents, (b) minimize the psychosocial and cultural effects associated with migration and acculturation, (c) provide parents with information about strategies for parenting their children in their new environments, and, (d) create a consultative and collaborative unit between the community, school professionals, teachers, students, and their immigrant parents.

Another area that needs examination is resistance. What are the patterns of parental resistance in home-school consultation? In what areas is the resistance most predictable (e.g., privacy, ethnic norms, values, time management, and disciplinary methods). If CLD children and families are to participate in home-school consultation interventions, training for consultant school psychologists should include culturally sensitive training on identifying and addressing resistance.

In conclusion, it is important to note that unless further research in cross-cultural consultation practice and training is implemented, we stand the risk of continuing to practice without a solid understanding of the consultation process. The consultation field will benfit from research that enhances our understanding of multicultural consultation training and practice. What better way than to question and study our current practices.

ANNOTATED BIBLIOGRAPHY

Harry, B., Kalyanpur, M. & Day, M. (1999) *Building cultural reciprocity with families: Case studies in special education.* Baltimore, MD: Paul Brooks.

> The case studies in this book take readers into the lives of eight families and discuss how to utilize cultural reciprocity to help strengthen practitioners' interactions with parents or caregivers.

Lynch, E. W. & Hanson, M. J. E. (Eds.). (2004). *Developing cross-cultural competence: A guide for working with children and their families.* Baltimore, MD: H. Paul Brooks, Co.

> The new edition of this book is an excellent resource for professionals who are working with children and families from diverse cultural and linguistic backgrounds. It includes descriptions of some of the challenges that service providers may encounter such as the influence of culture on people's beliefs, values, behaviors and issues confronting families in the acculturation process. The authors also provide strategies for fostering respectful and effective interactions with children and families.

Ponterotto, J. J., Casas, M., Suzuki L. A. & Alexander, C. M (Eds.). (2002). *Handbook on multicultural counseling.* Thousand Oaks, CA: Sage Publications.

> Drawing on the insight of expert contributors who are members of diverse cultural groups this handbook explores beliefs, customs, and courtesies of peoples from Anglo-European, Native American, African American, Latino, Asian, Philipino, Native

Hawaiian and Pacific Island, and Middle Eastern heritages. The book provides an excellent overview of multicultural counseling and explores strategies that should also be helpful to consultants.

Lott, B. & Rogers, M (Eds.) (in press). Helping non-mainstream families achieve equity in the public schools [Special issue]. *Journal of Educational and Psychological Consultation, 16.*

This special issue focuses on consultation as a service delivery model that can empower consultants to address multicultural issues when working with families with diverse cultural and linguistic backgrounds.

RESOURCES

The Harvard Family Involvement Network of Educators:
http://www.gse.harvard.edu/hfrp/projects/fine.html

Under the leadership of the Harvard Family Research Project, the Family Involvement Network of Educators, or FINE, develops the human resource capacity for effective family-school-community partnerships. Through a rich and diverse offering of research materials and tools, FINE equips teachers to collaborate with families and informs families and communities about leading-edge approaches to full partnership with schools.

Child and Family program supported by The NW Regional Educational Laboratory:
http://www.nwrel.org/index.html

The mission of the Child and Family Program is to help ensure educators, human service providers, and family members have the knowledge, skills, and resources to meet the increasingly complex needs of children and families at all developmental stages of life.

ASPIRA Association, Inc., 1444 I St., NW, Suite 800. Washington, D.C. 20005. Phone: (202) 835–3600 Fax: (202) 835–3613.
http://aspira.org/

A national Hispanic education leadership development organization, ASPIRA administers a national parent involvement demonstration project in Hispanic communities in nine cities and produces booklets to help Hispanic parents with their children's education. Request a catalog of materials in Spanish.

National Network of Partnership Schools, Johns Hopkins University, 3003 N. Charles Street, Suite 200, Baltimore, MD 21218, Phone 410–516–8800.
nnps@csos.jhu.edu

This network provides information, prototypes and materials on teacher practices of parent involvement, students' reactions to parent involvement, research and policy implications of parent involvement, and materials for teachers.

National Coalition for Parent Involvement in Education (NCPIE), Box 39, 1201 16th Street NW, Washington, D.C. 20036.
http://www.ncpie.org/

This organization is comprised of 34 national organizations involved in education, research and advocacy. It is dedicated to the development of family/school partnerships.

REFERENCES

American Psychological Association. (2002*). Guidelines on multicultural Education: Training, research, practice, and organizational change for psychologists*. Washington, DC: American Psychological Association.

Bos, C. S., Nahmias, M. L., & Urban, M. A. (1999). Targeting home-school collaboration for students with ADHD. *Teaching Exceptional Children, 31*(6), 4–11.

Bronfenbrenner, J. (1986). Ecology of the family as context for human development. *Developmental Psychology, 22*, 723–742.

Brown, D. (1997).Implications of cultural values for cross-cultural consultation with families. *Journal of Counseling and Development, 76*, 29–35.

Caplan, G., & Caplan, R. B. (1993). *Mental health consultation and collaboration*. Prospect Heights, IL: Waveland Press, Inc.

Cervantes, R. C., Padilla, A. M., & Salgado-de-Snyder, N. V. (1991). The Hispanic Stress Inventory: A culturally relevant approach to psychosocial assessment. *Psychological Assessment: A Journal of Consulting and Clinical Psychology, 1*, 438–447.

Dettmer, P., Thurston, L.P., & Dyck, N. (2002). *Consultation, collaboration, and teamwork for students with special needs* (4th ed.). Boston, MA: Allyn and Bacon.

Epstein, J. L. (1992). School and family partnerships. In M. Alkin (Ed.), *Iowa Department of Education encyclopedia of educational research* (6th ed, pp. 1139–1151). New York: McMillan.

Erchul, W. P, & Martens, B. K. (2001). School *consultation: Conceptual and empirical bases of practice*. New York: Plenum Press.

Esquivel, G. B. (1985). Best practices in the assessment of limited English proficiency and bilingual children. In A. Thomas & J. Grimes (Eds.), *Best practices in school psychology* (pp. 113–123). Baltimore, MD: National Association of School Psychologists.

Fletcher, T. V., & Cardona-Morales, C. (1990). Implementing effective instructional interventions for minority students. In A. Barona, & E. E. Garcia (Eds.), *Children at risk: Poverty, minority status, and other issues in educational equity* (pp. 151–170). Washington, DC: National Association of School Psychologists.

Goldenberg, C., Reese, L., & Gallimore, R. (1992). Effects of school literacy materials on Latino children's home experiences and early reading achievement. *American Journal of Education 100*, 497–536.

Gordon, M. (1964). *Assimilation in American life: The role of race, religion and national origins*. New York: Oxford University Press.

Hammer, T. J., & Turner, P. H. (1996). *Parenting in contemporary society*. Boston: Allyn & Bacon.

Harry, B. (1992). *Cultural Diversity, Families and the Special Education System*. New York: Teachers College Press.

Harry, B. (2002). Trends and issues in serving culturally diverse families of children with disabilities. *The Journal of Special Education, 36*, 131–138, 147.

Harry, B., Grenot-Scheyer, M., Smith-Lewis, M., Park, H., Xin, F., & Schwartz, I. (1998). Developing culturally inclusive services for individuals with severe disabilities. *The Journal of the Association for Persons with Severe Handicaps, 20,* 99–109.

Harris, K. C. (1998). How educational consultation can enhance instruction for culturally and linguistically diverse exceptional students. In L. Baca, & H. T. Cervantes (Eds.), *The bilingual education interface* (3rd ed., pp.326–349). Upper Saddle River, NJ: Prentice Hall.

Henderson, A. T., & Berla, N. (1994). A new generation of evidence: The family is critical to student achievement. Flint, MI: Mott Foundation.

Henning-Stout, M., & Meyers, J. (2000). Consultation and human diversity: First things first. *School Psychology Review. 29,* 419–425.

Ho, M. K. (1987). *Family therapy with ethnic minorities.* Newbury Park, CA: Sage.

Ingraham, C. L. (2000). Consultation through a multicultural lens: Multicultural and cross-cultural consultation in schools. *School Psychology Review, 29,* 320–343

Ingraham, C. L. (2003). Multicultural consultee-centered consultation: When novice consultants explore cultural hypotheses with experienced teacher consultees. *Journal of Educational and Psychological Consultation, 14,* 329–362.

Ingraham, C. L., & Meyers, J. (2000). Introduction to multicultural and cross-cultural consultation in schools: cultural diversity issues in school consultation. *School Psychology Review, 29,* 315–319.

Jackson, D. N., & Hayes, H. D. (1993). Multicultural issues in consultation. *Journal of Counseling and Development, 72,* 144–147.

Koonce, D. A., & Harper, W. (in press). Engaging African American parents in the schools: A community-based consultation model. *Journal of Educational and Psychological Consultation, 16.*

Lopez, E. C. , & Rogers, M. R. (2001). Conceptualizing cross-cultural school psychology competencies. *School Psychology Quarterly, 16,* 270–302.

Lorenzo-Hernandez, J. (1998). How social categorization may inform the study of Hispanic immigration. *Hispanic Journal of Behavioral Sciences, 20,* 39–59.

Lullock, L. (2001). Foreign-born population nears 30 million, Census Bureau estimates. *US Census Bureau. US Department of Commerce.* Retrieved November 12, 2004, from http://www.census.gov/Press-Release/www/2001/cb01–04.html

Lynch, E. W., Hanson, M. J. (Eds.) (2004). *Developing cross-cultural competence: A guide for working with young children and their families.* Baltimore, MD: Paul H. Brookes.

Maital, S. L. (2000). Reciprocal distancing: A system model of interpersonal processes in cross-cultural consultation. *School Psychology Review, 29,* 389–400.

Marquez, G. (1989). *Helping hands: A counseling program for Hispanic families in cultural transition.* Unpublished manuscript.

Marquez, G. (2000). *Qualitative study of the acculturative process followed by immigrant Hispanic families.* Unpublished doctoral dissertation. Fordham University, New York.

Martines, D. (1999). *Teachers' multicultural awareness within the consultee-centered consultation model.* Dissertation Abstracts International, (UMI No. 9923436).

Martines, D. (March, 2005). Teacher's multicultural perceptions in psychoeducational settings. *The Qualitative Report, 10* (1).

McGoldrick, M. (1982). Ethnicity and family therapy: An overview. In M. McGoldrick, K. J. Pearce, & J. Giordano (Eds.), *Ethnicity and family therapy* (pp. 3–31). New York: Guilford Press.

Mowder, B. A. (1994) Consultation with families of young at- risk, handicapped children. *Journal of Educational and Psychological Consultation, 5,* 309–320.

Nahari, S. (1999, August). Conducting cross-cultural consultation with parents of students with severe disabilities. In E. Vazquez-Nutall (Chair). *Cross-cultural Consultation Themes.* Symposium conducted at the annual meeting of the American Psychological Association, Boston.

Nahari, S., Cheng, S., & Falquez, A. (1999, Summer). Enhancing the school involvement of culturally diverse students with severe disabilities. *The School Psychologist,* Newsletter of the American Psychological Association: Division 16.

Nastasi, B. K., Varjas, K., Bernstein, R., & Jayasena, A. (2000). Conducting participatory culture-specific consultation: A global perspective on multicultural consultation. *School Psychology Review, 29*(3), 401- 413.

Padilla, A. M. (Ed.). (1980). The role of cultural awareness and ethnic loyalty in acculturation. *Acculturation: theory, models and some new findings* (pp. 47–84). Boulder, CO: Westview.

Padilla, A. M., Cervantes, R. C., Maldonado, M., & Garcia, R. E. (1988). Coping responses to psychosocial stressors among Mexican and Central American immigrants. *Journal of Community Psychology,* 18, 418–427.

Plante, T. G., Manuel, G. M., Menendez, A. V., & Marcotte, D. (1995). Coping with stress among Salvadoran immigrants. *Hispanic Journal of Behavioral Sciences,* 17, 471–479.

Ponti, C. R., Zins, J. E., & Graden, J. (1988). Implementing a consultation-based services delivery system to decrease referrals for special education: A case study of organizational considerations. *School Psychology Review,* 17, 89–100.

Provenzo, E. F. (1985). Preface. In H. Silva (Ed.), *The children of Mariel: Cuban refugee children in South Florida schools* (p. iii). Washington DC: The Cuban American National Foundation.

Public Law 101–476, the Individuals with Disabilities Education Act (IDEA 1990)

Public Law 105–17: Reauthorization of the Individual with Disabilities Act (IDEA 1997)

Rogers, M. R. (1998). The influence of race and consultant verbal behavior on perceptions of consultant competency and multicultural sensitivity. *School Psychology Quarterly,* 13, 265–280.

Rogers, M. R. (2000). Examining the cultural context of consultation. *School Psychology Review,* 29, 414–418.

Rogers, M. R., Ingraham, C. L., Bursztyn, A., Cajigas-Segredo, N., Esquivel, G., Hess, R., et al. (1999). *School Psychology International,* 20, 243–264.

Rogers, M. R. & Lopez, E.C. (2002). Identifying critical cross-cultural school psychology competencies. *Journal of School Psychology,* 40, 115–141.

Rogler, L. H., Gurak, D., & Cooney, R. S. (1987). The migration experience and mental health: Formulations relevant to Hispanics and other immigrants. In M. Gaviria & J. D. Arana (Eds.), *Health and behavior: Research agenda for Hispanics* (pp. 72–84). Chicago: University of Illinois at Chicago.

Rosenfield, S., & Gravois, T. (1996). Instructional consultation teams. New York: Guilford Press.

Santisteban, L. H., & Szapocznik, J. (1982). Substance abuse disorders among Hispanics: A focus on prevention. In R. M. Becerra, M. Karno, & J. I. Escobar (Eds.), *Mental health and Hispanic Americans: Clinical perspective* (pp. 83–100). New York: Grune & Stratton.

Sheridan, S. M. (2000). Considerations of multiculturalism and diversity in behavioral consultation with parents and teachers. *School Psychology Review,* 29, 344–353.

Stipek, D., Milburn, S., Galluzzo, D., & Daniels, D. (1992). Parents' beliefs about appropriate education for young children. *Journal of Applied Development Psychology* 13, 293–310.

Sue, D., Arrendondo, P., & McDavis, R. (1992). Multicultural counseling competencies and standards: A call to the profession. *Journal of Multicultural Counseling and Development, 20,* 64–88.

Suzuki, L. A., Ponterotto, J. G., & Meller, P. J. (Eds.). (2001). *Handbook of multicultural assessment: Clinical, psychological, and educational applications* (2nd ed.).San Francisco, CA: Jossey Bass.

Szapocznik, J., & Hernandex, R. (1988). The Cuban American family. In C. H. Mindel, R. W. Habenstein, & R. Wright, Jr., (Eds.). *Ethnic families in America: Patterns and variations* (pp. 160–173). New York: Elsevier.

Takushi, R., & Uomoto, J. M. (2001). The clinical interview from a multicultural perspective. In: L. L. A. Suzuki, J. G. Ponterotto, & P. J. Meller (Eds.). *Handbook of multicultural assessment: clinical, psychological, and educational applications* (2nd ed, pp. 47–66). San Francisco, CA: Jossey-Bass.

Tamura, T., & Lau, A. (1992). Connectedness versus separateness: Applicability of family therapy to Japanese families. *Family Process, 31,* 319–340.

Tarver Behring, S., & Ingraham. C. L. (1998). Culture as a central component of consultation: A call to the field. *Journal of Educational & Psychological Consultation, 9,* 57–73.

The National Center for Education Statistics. (2003). *State of education, 2004.* U.S. Department of Education. Retrieved October 29, 2004, from http://nces.ed.gov//programs/coe/2003/section1/indicator04.asp

The National Center for Education Statistics. (2004). US Department of Education. Retrieved October 29, 2004, from http://nces.ed.gov//prorams/coe/2004/section1/indicator05.asp

Torres-Matrullo, C. J. (1980). Sex-role values and mental health. In A. M. Padilla (Ed.), *Acculturation: Theory, models and some new findings* (pp. 111–137). Boulder, CO: Westview Press.

Tyler, F. B., Pargament, K. I, & Gatz, M. (1983). The resource collaborator role: A model for interactions involving psychologists. *American Psychologist, 38,* 338–339.

U.S. Census Bureau (2002). Retrieved November 12, 2004, from http://www.cenus.gov/prod/2002pubs/p23–206.pdf

U.S. Department of Mental Health and Human Services Office of the Surgeon General:A Report of the Surgeon General. (2002). *Mental health: Culture, race and ethnicity.* Retrieved March 13, 2004, from: http://www.mentalhealth.samhsa.gov/cre/default.asp

Xitao, F. (2001) Parental involvement and students' academic achievement: A growth modeling analysis. *Journal of Experimental Education 70*(1), 27–61.

7

SYSTEMIC CONSULTATION IN A MULTILINGUAL SETTING

Abigail M. Harris
Fordham University

Imagine you are the psychologist in a school district where the demographics mirror those of many American small cities and towns. When you started working in the district, the student population was drawn from a predominantly stable, middle class, monolingual English-speaking community. In recent years the neighborhood has become increasingly diverse with a rich blend of cultures and languages. Although the school district has adapted by adding a few services for limited-English speaking students, it hasn't really embraced the challenges of multilingual education. In fact, you have noticed that a disproportionate percentage of culturally and linguistically diverse (CLD) children are being referred for special education and many others seem to be under-performing and dropping out without graduating. Teachers don't seem sure about how to teach the CLD children—should they use the same curriculum? …the same standards? Are the goals the same?

You're the psychologist. What should you tell them? What can you do to insure that all children receive a high quality education? Perhaps even more basic, you wonder, what is quality education within this context?

Schools today are faced with greater diversity in the student population than ever before and yet few have stepped up to the challenge of how best to educate students for whom Standard English is not the home language. What is pedagogically "best" practice for educating non-English speakers? Does it matter if the home language is a language like Spanish with an established place in America and the global society versus one of the thousands of low incidence languages? The decision is not only pedagogical—deciding what methods are most effective—but it is also value laden. It takes place in a context that is charged with competing political and pedagogical agendas and ever greater competition for shrinking resources.

If you were the psychologist in this scenario, you could advocate for CLD students and families by intervening on a variety of levels. Ethically, you must intervene by insuring that the direct psychological and educational services that you provide are consistent with best practice and not contributing to overrepresentation of CLD students in special education and underperformance of CLD students generally. Ethically you must also make sure that your knowledge base and skills are continually updated to reflect new findings on how best to educate CLD students.

You might also consider broadening your impact by recognizing as a programmatic need the teacher inquiries about how best to teach CLD students. Gerald Caplan (1970) in his seminal work on mental health consultation and subsequently others (Conoley, 1981; Meyers, Parsons, & Martin, 2001) have described the critical contribution psychologists make when they use their experience with consultees to identify and address professional development needs on a programmatic basis. Results might include in-service training for educators and parents on principles and strategies for supporting second language acquisition and the overall learning of CLD students.

Ultimately however, these strategies, while constructive, are unlikely to produce the desired outcome of maximizing the quality of education for all CLD students (Sarason, 1996). They address pieces of the system without taking a holistic look at how the pieces fit together and interrelate. Systemic consultation provides the vehicle for school psychologists to serve as change agents and to play a vital leadership role in insuring quality education for all students, including those who are culturally and linguistically different. This chapter describes systemic consultation including its theoretical and research bases as well as its practical application. The purpose is to illustrate how culturally sensitive systemic consultation is an essential tool for ensuring equity and quality education for all students within a multilingual context.

THEORETICAL AND RESEARCH BASES FOR SYSTEMIC CONSULTATION

Systemic consultation is defined as a collaborative, problem-solving process in which the client is a system (or element of the system) and the consultee(s) are stakeholders in the system (Brown, Pryzansky, & Schulte, 2001; Curtis & Stollar, 1996). The goals include planned change. The consultant uses many of the same skills as in individual consultation. Establishing rapport, sensitivity to cultural influences, effective listening, clarifying, paraphrasing, reflecting back, recapping, summarizing, and so on, are all important skills that the consultant brings to the process (Conoley & Conoley, 1992; Gallessich, 1986; Tarver Behring & Ingraham, 1998). The primary difference is in the complexity of the "client" (system) (Brown et al., 2001). Individually oriented consultation usually involves a single consultee and one or a few clients and their respective environments, whereas systemic consultation usually involves more than one consultee (often those individuals charged with the management of the organization) and a "client system" often composed of dozens of people who have formed into subgroups each with their own norms and cultures. Because of the complexity of the system, consultants need a broader framework for conducting the consultation, a framework that will allow them to conceptualize the ways in which systems function and undergo change (Brown et al., 2001; Connell & Klem, 2000).

Consultants engaging in systemic consultation often base this broader framework on principles drawn from systems theory and organizational development (Gallessich, 1986; Meyers, 2002; Meyers, Parsons, & Martin, 1979). In viewing the school district as a system, the consultant relies on systems theory to provide a structure for analyzing the culture of the school district, its schools and its community. As social systems, schools are characterized by norms, structures, and procedures that explain and predict functioning within the system. Organizational development contributes to the analysis of the system and provides strategies for intervening to improve organizational functioning.

Understanding the norms—both formal and informal—is especially important for the system level consultant. Norms evolve in all human relations and exert powerful controls over behavior. They exist when group members share expectations that certain behaviors will be rewarded, punished, or ignored. Norms provide tacit rules that reduce ambiguity and conflict. They shape and stabilize behavior and are very resistant to change. Although norms are ordinarily implicit rather than explicit, group members are keenly aware of them and typically they can articulate them (Gallessich, 1986).

Recognition of the powerful influence of cultural groups norms is an essential part of the analytic process in systemic consultation (Ramirez, Lepage, Kratochwill, & Duffy, 1998). Frequently, these norms dictate who communicates with whom within the system and research supports that they define such important elements as parental role construction (e.g., how parents construct their role in relation to their child's education and schooling) and expectations for student behavior and performance (Goldstein & Harris, 2000; Grolnick & Slowiaczek, 1994; Hill & Craft, 2003; Weinstein, Madison, & Kuklinski, 1995).

Structures in social systems are both formal and informal. In a workable social system, structures define the networks of interdependencies and sequences of interaction necessary to accomplish the organization's primary tasks (Schmuck, 1990). Formal structures can be diagramed as in organizational charts of roles and reporting relationships. In a public school system, it is typical to think of the school board and district level administrators (e.g., superintendent, director of special services, etc.) as overseeing the school level administrators who oversee the instructional and non-instructional staff. Sometimes psychologists, social workers, and other specialists report to the principal or to a district level manager/administrator, or sometimes they are contracted through an outside agency.

In addition to the formal structures in schools, there are the informal networks of interrelationships involving friendship, conflict, influence, and social support. A consultant analyzing the system makes note of informal alliances as well as the frictions or conflictual relationships within the district and between elements of the district and the community. Alliances often form along lines of educational philosophy, loyalty to administration, gender, ethnicity, age, or political affiliation. Some alliances are stable over time while others are temporary such as when individuals cluster together to support or oppose a new policy.

Frequently, alliances form based on cultural or linguistic background. Although often there is considerable heterogeneity within cultural groups (Goldstein & Harris, 2000), in situations of conflict or stress, cultural norms exert a strong influence to promote within-group cohesion and support (Tarver Behring & Ingraham, 1998). Group differences in language competence can serve to strengthen alliances and isolate outsiders (Goldstein & Harris, 2000).

Related to structure is power. As Sarason (1996) illustrated repeatedly,

> "...power suffuses all relationships in the culture of the school...any nontrivial attempt to change a feature of the school culture immediately brings to the fore the power basis of relationships, i.e., 'someone' decides that something will be changed and 'others' are then *required* appropriately to implement that change. If others have had no say in the decision, if there was no forum or allotted time for others to express their ideas or feelings, if others come to feel they are not respected, they feel their professionalism has been demeaned, the stage is set for the change to fail" (p. 335).

Most obvious in terms of legitimized power are the official hierarchies within the structure of the school system. In addition to the school board and district administrators, there are union leaders as well as state and federal overseers. Of these, the principal is often the focus of discussions about school change (Fullan, 1997; Fullan & Hargreaves, 1996, 1998; Gillette & Kranyik, 1996; Sarason, 1996). Principals are viewed as critical to successful change because they set the tone in the school by creating an atmosphere characterized by collegiality and openness, autocracy or a more participatory decision-making style, suspicion or trust, and so on. Their style of leadership dictates the role of teachers, other staff, and the community in school-level decision-making.

Alongside the official hierarchies, most schools have internal "pecking orders" with some teachers and staff members wielding considerable influence over others. Sometimes this power is supported by seniority or official roles (e.g., department or grade level chairperson) while other times it is based on other criteria such as cultural expectations, professional competency or charisma. Successful systemic consultants are alert to both sources of power in their analysis of the system. Differences and prejudice in status, privilege and power (related to cultural background, gender, economic status, educational level, etc.) persist and are resistant to change. Research on how status influences roles (e.g., who is likely to be selected for leadership, who is afforded opportunities to speak, whose ideas are evaluated positively, etc.) in mixed-status groups affirms the benefits of higher status (Berger, Ridgeway, Fisek, & Norman, 1998; Fisek, Berger, & Moore, 2002). Systemic consultants need to be alert to the impact of power differentials on communications patterns and potential for change. Readers are referred to Ingraham (2000) for a useful discussion of multicultural issues surrounding disruptions in the balance of power.

Procedures in social systems refer to "the organization's formal activities for accomplishing tasks and for maintaining itself" (Schmuck, 1990, p. 901). For example, meetings are called in a particular way and run according to some agreed-on patterns, records are kept in standard forms, memos are routed through prescribed hierarchies, job hiring and evaluations are carried out in certain fashions, and so on.

Procedures are carried out through system structures and often are guided by strong norms. All of these elements make up the culture of the school.

Beyond understanding the school culture, the systemic consultant plays a key role in orchestrating change. Organizational development (OD), defined as "the planned and sustained effort to bring about system-level improvement through self-analytic and problem-solving methods"(Curtis & Stollar, 1996, p. 411), provides a conceptual framework and specific strategies by which consultants can help schools change and meet the challenges of a pluralistic society. It assumes that organizational change occurs through changes in the behavior of the members of the organization. The informal system of personal feelings, attitudes, and social norms and values of groups within the organization are focal dimensions of these change efforts. Two dominant values permeate OD theory. First, people are viewed as self-actualizing within an organizational context, attempting to satisfy not only the goals and needs of the organization but also personal goals and needs. Second, the nature of the organizational context is viewed as fostering conflicting relationships. However, OD theory assumes that people can learn to accomplish goals, exert influence, and interact with co-workers more effectively. Although the dynamics of organizational groups may hinder efforts to solve problems confronting the system, OD theory provides a technology to help schools become self-renewing and self-correcting systems. It enables the school to monitor and respond to its environment, and to find, maintain and use the human resources, ideas, and energy needed to respond to that environment. (Curtis & Stollar, 1996; Jerrell & Jerrell, 1981; Meyers, Parsons, & Martin, 1979; Schmuck, 1990).

Examples of OD strategies that a consultant might employ include (adapted from French & Bell, 1978; Nastasi, Varjas, Berstein, & Jayasena, 2000):

1. Team-building activities to foster greater trust and improved communications;
2. Assessment and feedback activities that involve the collection of diagnostic data regarding attitudes, performance, perceptions, and so on, and the utilization of the data to stimulate and guide specific structured planning and development activities;
3. Education and training activities designed to improve skills, knowledge, and abilities; that can be conducted through didactic or more experiential methods;
4. Coaching, counseling, or consulting activities may be conducted individually, especially with leaders who are experiencing difficulty in developing new behaviors that would facilitate other desired organizational changes;
5. Strategic planning and goal-setting activities are used to increase the frequency of these activities, promote problem solving, and to build consensus for future actions;
6. Forming partnerships between diverse stakeholders to promote a participatory process and enhance consensus building;
7. Process observation and consultation activities are designed to help participants perceive, understand, and act upon process events such as communica-

tion patterns, leader-member roles and interaction patterns, covert norms, and decision-making styles;

8. Structural analysis and redesigning of activities to review current procedures and consider alternative routes to desired outcomes.

These are just a sampling of the many kinds of techniques available to systemic consultants. Which techniques are used depends on the consultant's orientation, the specific circumstances within in the system, and the stage of the change process.

IMPLICATIONS FOR PRACTICE

Systemic consultation can be conceptualized as following similar stages as those associated with other models of school-based consultation. These include entry, problem identification, problem definition/analysis, intervention, and evaluation. Each of these stages will be described from the stand-point of a school district as the system. However, the same stages apply in consultation with other educational systems such as a program or school within a district or the umbrella group that oversees educational programs such as a state department of education.

Entry

Entry refers to the initiation of the consultation process and the agreements or arrangements that begin the process. Although some systemic change is initiated by forces outside of the system (e.g., when change is imposed as a result of federal, state, or legal mandates and the consultant serves as the importer), a more desirable situation occurs when the motivation for change comes from within the system. When members of the system recognize that there is a problem and seek a person or process to help address the concerns, the act of seeking help indicates at least a minimal level of motivation.

Much of the systemic consultation literature assumes that the consultant is someone from outside of the system (e.g., Caplan & Caplan, 1993; Connell & Klem, 2000; Gallessich, 1981, 1986). When the consultant is brought in from outside the district, the entry period is used to negotiate the parameters or rules of the relationship and to begin the process of establishing mutual rapport and trust.

In a richly described case study, Meyers (2002) revealed some of the pitfalls encountered during and following contract negotiation while conducting school-based, cross-cultural organizational consultation with the primary goal to "facilitate the best educational practices for African-American students" (p. 152). In the case study's focal school site, the reform was terminated prematurely despite considerable initial efforts by the outside consultants to secure administrative, teacher and parent "buy-in" to the reform process. Qualitative analyses identified themes related to conflicting expectations and beliefs, dissatisfaction with procedures and policies, lack of empowerment, pedagogical dissonance and feelings of blame, inadequacy, and racism as contributing to the school's withdrawal from the project.

By contrast to reforms orchestrated or guided by outside consultants, consultants who emerge from within the system either assume this role through their legitimate leadership position in the district or through some acknowledgement from within the system giving them the authority or administrative support to assume this role. For example, if we refer back to the original scenario, it might be that the psychologist assembles data to illustrate the concern and approaches administrators within the district to solicit support for intervening. Although an internal consultant still needs to establish the parameters of the consultation relationship (e.g., gain authorization and resources to set up and lead a multidisciplinary task force), presumably the consultant has insights into how the system operates, has established working relationships with some of the key leaders, and has gained the rapport and trust of at least some members of the school community.

Internal consultants should be cognizant of the power structure within their district as they decide how best to move forward an agenda through systemic consultation. It is important to approach supervisors early in the process in order to gauge their interest and solicit their support. No supervisor likes to be surprised to learn of activities going on "behind their back" and even initially non-supportive supervisors can often be brought into the process by a focus on quality and meeting the needs of children.

Important questions for the consultant during entry are: Who within the system recognizes that there is a concern or problem? Who has an interest or investment in addressing the concern? What resources are available? What are possible sources of resistance? How are different cultural lens affecting perceptions of the situation? By thinking through the answers to these questions, the consultant is in a better position to help the district conceptualize a process for addressing the concern and clarify mutual expectations (Ingraham, 2000; Maher & Illback, 1982; Meyers, 2002).

Problem Identification

Central to resolving a concern is understanding it. During the problem identification stage, the consultant seeks to build consensus within the district on the nature of the concern(s) and the possibilities for change (Nastasi, Varjas, Berstein, & Jayasena, 2000; Sarason, 1996). Initial probes focus on analyzing the system and its power structure (both formal and informal) by identifying relevant stakeholders, recognizing the norms and regularities in the system, and identifying factors (patterns of decision-making, motivational incentives and disincentives, etc.) that are likely to affect the success of change efforts. Consultants are gathering data all the time by observing interactions and using the identified concern as a point of entry for exploring the dynamics within the district.

Consultants often start by identifying the relevant stakeholders (people or groups within or outside of the school district that have a stake in what happens) and exploring how the situation is viewed by each of these stakeholders. Referring back to the original scenario, the likely stakeholders include the psychologist(s), principal, teachers, school board, parents, and children. The teacher group would likely subdivide into those teachers seeking support for teaching CLD students, those not interested or resistant, and those who are ambivalent or uncertain. For example, teachers of English as a second language might be ambivalent—wanting more support and resources for teaching CLD students but fearful that change might jeopardize their position. Similarly, parents of CLD children might be ambivalent or uncertain—wanting more resources for their children but not wanting their children derailed from achieving the same high standards as their non-CLD peers.

Identifying the norms and regularities operating in the district and within the various stakeholder groupings is another important part of the problem identification stage (Gallessich, 1981). Within a school setting, norms govern staff attitudes and behaviors related to authority, student behavior, parent involvement, professional identify, and so on. For example, in some schools the principal exhibits an authoritarian leadership style and staff are cautious about challenging the principal's decisions. In other schools the leadership style is more participatory and staff are expected to and rewarded for contributing to decision making. Another example of the impact of norms can be seen in schools where every staff member feels responsibility for the well-being of all children in the school versus schools were teachers feel that their responsibility is to their own students and they shouldn't "interfere" with children from other classrooms (Rosenholtz, 1991). The cooperative nature of participatory leadership and shared responsibility situations versus situations with authoritarian leadership and/or an isolationist orientation likely would lead to very different receptivity to school level change.

Cultural norms affect the attitudes and behavior of school personnel and families in relation to education and schooling. There is wide cultural variability in expectations for parental involvement in education. Similarly, there are differences in perceptions of the goals of education (Grolnick & Slowiaczek, 1994; Hill & Craft, 2003). Since invitations for parents to become involved in their children's schooling are strong predictors of subsequent participation (Hoover-Dempsey & Sandler, 1997; Lupiani, 2004), consultants need to facilitate culturally appropriate opportunities for full involvement of all stakeholders, including parents.

Assessment is a powerful tool for generating ownership in the improvement process and motivating change (Maher & Illback, 1982; Nastasi, Varjas, Berstein, & Jayasena, 2000; Sarason, 1996). Assessment in this case refers to gathering and sharing data within the network of stakeholders. Successful consultation is inclusive rather than solitary. When stakeholders participate in data collection, they participate as the findings emerge, there are discussions along the way and the participants have greater confidence in the findings. Participatory assessment also provides an opportunity for the consultant to identify the norms and regularities likely to impact change efforts. By contrast, when a consultant works in isolation collecting interview or survey data, respondents are likely to feel vulnerable and defensive when ultimately the findings are shared.

Problem Definition and Analysis

This diagnosis and analysis stage often involves a group process that engages stakeholders (or representatives of stakeholders) in reviewing the findings and reflecting on their implications. It is not unusual to identify gaps in understanding and the need to gather additional information—from within the district and sometimes from the literature or from other districts. Conflict can arise when stakeholders disagree about the findings or their interpretation. By addressing the conflict the consultant can help clarify the norms and roles and replace norms for avoiding conflict with norms for collaboration (Schmuck, 1983). Often consultants use reframing techniques to help stakeholders with different frames of reference to better understand one another (Soo-Hoo, 1998). When data collection activities have been inclusive and participatory, there is a natural flow from problem identification activities into problem analysis.

Typically, recommendations emerge during the analysis. Care should be taken to not jump too quickly to adopt emerging ideas. When there is premature closure, the result is likely to be fragmented and lack the ownership that comes from a more deliberate and participatory process. Interventions that are developed and refined as a series of progressive approximations are more likely to reflect multiple inputs and to garner the support of a broader base of stakeholders. (Caplan & Caplan, 1993).

Often it is useful to work toward consensus on some specific goals and guiding principles. For example, in the hypothetical case, the school psychologist working collaboratively with a district task force might recommend adoption by the school board of a vision or policy statement such as the following:

> School District USA views the cultural and linguistic diversity in our community as a strength.
>
> - We expect all children in our district to benefit from the multicultural sharing that this diversity offers. Our district policies and practices actively support enhanced understanding and respect between people of different ethnic, cultural, linguistic, and religious backgrounds.
> - We expect all students to leave our district with competence in English and at least one other language.
> - We affirm the rights of CLD children to a high quality education that reflects "best practice" in terms of bilingual education and supports achievement by CLD students of the same high standards we expect for all of our students.

This vision statement then provides a foundation on which to structure interventions. If the school board and superintendent can't agree on such a statement or, for example, they don't support dual language competence, efforts to establish such programs would likely fail. Lack of support at this point suggests the need for more groundwork including possibly education, individual consultation, and consensus building activities (Meyers, 2002).

Intervention

The intervention stage is when plans are finalized and implemented. It is also the time when it becomes evident as to whether there is sufficient motivation and support to effect change. Effective problem solving and enthusiasm are necessary but not sufficient ingredients to generate successful action. Each action that is considered must be evaluated to determine what resources are needed (time, money, etc.),

TABLE 7–1

Action Plan to Support the School District USA Policy on Cultural and Linguistic Diversity

Priority Concern	Source/Data	Possible Actions	Resources Needed	Responsibility (Primary and Others)	Time Frame
1. Many CLD students start school without pre-literacy skills in Spanish or English.	Low performance on Kindergarten screening; parent and teacher interviews.	(a) Investigate starting pre-K bilingual language enrichment classes.	(a) Teacher release time (number of days); travel (site visit), administrative support to investigate funding options and survey parents.	Primary: Kindergarten teacher. Other: CLD parent, Assistant Superintendent for Curriculum; School Board member.	Update: 1 month Later: Site visit/proposal writing, etc.
2. Disproportionate number of CLD children in special education programs.	Percentage in special education is higher than percentage in regular education even after socio-economic status is considered.	(a) Committee review of psycho-educational evaluation practices for bias; (b) Strengthen pre-referral intervention.	(a) Professional development funds (for training and materials); (b) Teacher in-service days (2×45 teachers); honoraria for guest speaker.	Primary: Psychologist. Other: Director of Special Services; learning specialist; ESL teacher, parent advocate.	(a) Schedule and plan review process: 1 month; (b) Schedule and plan in-service (within 6 months).
3. Bilingual competence under-valued in current curriculum.	Little support for bilingual literacy in grades 1–7; "foreign" language instruction starts in upper grades (too late for dual competence).	(a) Investigate dual-language programs; (b) Seek funding and use current library budget to expand availability of materials in other languages; possibly involve Parent Teacher Organization (PTO).	(a) Teacher release time (number of days), travel (site visit), administrative support to investigate funding options and survey parents; (b) Cost of subscriptions to multilingual resources.	(a) Primary: Foreign language chairperson. Other: CLD parent, ESL teacher, Assistant Superintendent for Curriculum; School Board member. (b) Primary: ESL teacher, Librarian, and PTO representative (CLD parent).	(a) Update in one month; (b) Create "wish list" in 1 month (update as more materials identified and recommended).

Limited programs and resources for CLD children from low incidence language groups.	Staff interviews; classroom and library observations; interpreters not available to conduct parent or student interviews.	(a) Investigate "best practice"; (b) Develop/maintain listings of bilingual specialists; (c) Identify and train interpreters; (d) Actively recruit bilingual staff to fill vacancies.	(a) Professional development time/money; (b) Clerical support; (c) Professional; development support and money for training program; (d) Extra outreach and ads for recruiting.	Primary: Psychologist and Learning specialistOther: Director of Special Services; learning specialist; ESL teacher, parent advocates	Update in 1 month.
4.					
5. Many CLD students are not integrated into school culture (may help explain early dropout).	CLD children rarely participate in after-school activities such as the chess and science clubs or athletic programs; critical period seems to be middle school.	(a) Create task force at middle school (parents, middle and high school age youth, etc.) to develop mentoring program and support pride in educational success of CLD students .	Teacher professional development and release time; funding for weekend retreat to train mentors	Primary: Middle school assistant, Principal. Other: High school and middle school counselors, community social worker, local clergy member, local business leader, coach.	Update in 1 month; "kickoff" program scheduled to occur within 3 months.

Table 7–1 (Continued)

147

TABLE 7–1
(continued)

Priority	Concern	Source/Data	Possible Actions	Resources Needed	Responsibility (Primary and Others)	Time Frame
6. CLD parents are not involved in Parent Teacher Organization (PTO) and participate less in back-to-school night and parent conferences.	Parent, teacher and principal interviews.	(a) Specifically invite CLD parents to participate; (b) Identify CLD parent leaders and encourage them to involve parents; (c) Make sure times of meetings are convenient, provide child care; (d) Provide translation; (e) Sponsor activities that honor different cultures.	Funding for local advertising Funding for translation services, software, and training in use of computer keyboards for Chinese, Greek, and Hebrew letters	Primary: CLD parent and elementary school Principal. Other: PTO Vice President, CLD classroom aide, social worker	First week: Identify possible CLD representatives for inclusion in "kickoff" planning and task forces; update in 1 month.
7. Classroom efforts to honor diversity are scattered and unsystematic.	Teachers express uncertainty about how to avoid stereotypes and simultaneously promote ethnic pride and social integration.	(a) Conduct curriculum revie; (b) Sponsor professional development activities, set up proposal process for teachers seeking support.	(a) Teacher release time for curriculum review; (b) Funding for in-house and out of district professional development activities (20 teachers × 3 days).	Primary: Assistant Superintendent for Curriculum. Others: High school social studies teacher, School Board member, CLD parent(s).	Update 1 month.

what authorization or policies are involved, who might resist the change, and so on (Gallessich, 1986; Maher & Illback, 1982; Schmuck.1983).

Table 7–1 provides an example of the action plan that might emerge from a problem analysis workshop conducted as part of our hypothetical systemic consultation scenario. Note that links are made between identified concerns, data used to evaluate the concerns, and possible actions. All of the actions are consistent with the previously discussed hypothetical vision statement. One subsequent activity might be to prioritize the activities and cast some as short-term goals and others as long-term goals.

Follow-up and Evaluation

The process of change doesn't begin and end with the intervention; it is ongoing. Similarly, effective change builds into the process a system for ongoing assessment, monitoring and feedback about the change process (Comer, Haynes, Joyner, & Ben-Avie, 1996). Often one action uncovers the need for another and adjustments are needed along the way. For example, returning to our hypothetical action plan, a decision to provide more written resources for various language groups (books, translated notes for parents, etc.) would raise the need for people to help translate the notes and committees to help select the materials. It may be necessary to update computers with new keyboards and editing tools, and so on. Similarly, there may be unintended consequences that lead to resistance. The most common hurdle is one created if the resources for other unrelated school programs are reduced or frozen in order to generate resources to fuel the new programs. Frequently, motivation for change wanes as resistance mounts. In his pessimistic but insightful book, *The Predictable Failure of Educational Reform*, Sarason (1990) illustrated many of the challenges of implementing and sustaining change.

External consultants often don't have the opportunity of participating actively in follow-up and evaluation. Hopefully, the consultant has worked with the district to incorporate into the change process interim strategies and benchmarks for monitoring the interventions as they are implemented. Ultimately however, if the reform is deemed successful, the district may feel little need to invest additional resources in engaging a consultant to prove or document the success. If the changes were not successful, the district may not want this outcome recognized or made public.

Internal consultants have the advantage that they remain in the district as activities are planned and implemented. Unlike most external consultants, there are no contractual parameters to the relationship. Because the psychologists are in the schools on a daily basis, they are more likely than external consultants to witness when obstacles arise or problems occur that threaten the sustainability of change efforts.

IMPLEMENTATION AND APPROACHES

Implementation of systemic reform is a co-constructed, participatory process that takes courage and initiative. Effective consultants build consensus as they go, avoiding rigid adherence to a plan in the face of difficulties (Meyers, 2002). They anticipate potential resistance and barriers to success and sustainability of the reform and they are intentional in the use of process skills to overcome hurdles along the way. Examples of common challenges are discussed below.

Hidden Agendas

Consultants should be alert for hidden agendas. It is not unusual for members within a system to withhold their real viewpoints or feelings and instead present a position that is less risky, reduces vulnerability, or shows them in a more favorable light (Pipes, 1981). They may decide to withhold endorsement of a plan until they see whether there is sufficient support for it to be successful. Resistance emerges through indirect or covert actions such as delays or failure to allocate sufficient resources in a timely fashion. In addition, the point of entry for an external consultant may not be the real problem. Finally, there may be superficial but not substantive support for a "politically correct" agenda. A wise consultant anticipates these "hidden agendas" and networks amongst the elements of the system to diffuse resistance (Meyers, 2002).

Turf Issues

When individuals or groups in the system feel threatened by the consultant or the proposed change, the resulting alienation can pose a serious obstruction to successful change. Often people whose roles overlap with the consultant or who feel that they are not sufficiently valued as part of the process resent the consultant. Overtly or covertly they may engage in activities that undermine or sabotage the success of the change process. Consultants can avoid turf skirmishes by being inclusive during the assessment and planning processes and openly valuing the contributions of those who might feel threatened (Nastasi, Varjas, Berstein, & Jayasena, 2000; Sarason, 1996).

Failure to Secure Sufficient Time and Resources

The most common barrier to successful, sustainable change is the failure to secure sufficient resources. It is easy to underestimate the amount of time and energy necessary for successful change. During the weeks preceding an anticipated change and the subsequent weeks of adjustment, all those affected by the change are likely to be distracted and possibly anxious. Prior to instituting a new program or reorganizing an existing one, the disruption caused by preparing for the change coupled with fears of the unknown can result in unpredictable or erratic behavior. Following a change, those affected often experience some confusion or discomfort until norms and routines are reestablished (Hirschowitz, 1977). The consultant should encourage the district to allow sufficient time for planning and follow-up as implementation occurs. Time for staff to plan together and communicate with one another can be crucial to success but coordinating schedules to create this time can be difficult.

IMPLICATIONS FOR FUTURE RESEARCH AND PRACTICE

Ultimately, effective psychologists are change agents. As Jane Conoley pointed out, "The target of change may be as small as a single behavior that a client finds troublesome, or as vast as a shift in the social structure" (1981, p. 1). Many psychologists are most comfortable working on the individual or small group level but for those who have trouble sitting by when they see poor quality or inequality in education, systemic consultation provides a means to constructively channel this discontent.

Available research, while limited, illustrates the challenges and the potential for psychologists to influence educational quality (e.g., Maher & Illback, 1982; Meyers, 2002; Nastasi, Varjas, Berstein, & Jayasena, 2000). Each case study enhances understanding of roadblocks and facilitating strategies. More of such case studies are needed. Drawing from and building on the literature and research from other disciplines—both basic research (e.g., Berger, Ridgeway, Fisek, & Norman, 1998; Fisek, Berger, & Moore, 2002) and applications (e.g., Connell & Klem, 2000; Fullan, 1997)—is also critical if we are to take advantage of lessons learned and move forward the field toward more effective systemic practice.

Unfortunately, many psychologists are ill prepared to assume the role of change agent. School psychology training programs rarely focus on systemic change beyond the classroom level (Sheridan & Gutkin, 2000). Often trainees learn component skills such as the interpersonal and analytic skills needed for individually oriented consultation and the assessment skills needed for non-biased assessment. Also, given professional standards and priorities, it is likely that some coverage is given to multicultural sensitivity (hopefully both awareness of the need for a multicultural lens as well as practice and self reflection to identify personal style and potential biases). Less frequently covered are the knowledge and analytic skills needed for understanding how systems function and how to catalyze constructive organizational change. The dynamics of multi-ethnic, participatory change efforts are exponentially more complex—requiring an understanding of cultural influences on bureaucracies, norms, traditions, vulnerabilities, and so on.

Competencies that need to be integrated into professional training programs include such skills as (a) analyzing systems, including practice identifying stakeholders, power structures, communications patterns, norms; (b) facilitating participatory decision-making; (c) negotiating system entry; (d) practicing identifying potential enhancers and barriers to change; and (e) assessing impact of consultation on all relevant constituents. In all these skills trainees need to be assisted in developing sensitivity to the impact of culture and status.

Change occurs in a dynamic context. Often the psychologist within the school system works gradually on multiple levels to build the networks needed for systemic influence. Attending school board and PTA meetings, navigating between the various subgroups without taking sides and without alienating those on the fringes, serving as a neutral mediator when frictions flare up are all examples of strategies for laying the foundation for systemic consultation. Even the best-laid plans can be undermined or thwarted by failing to analyze and gain access to the powerful formal and informal forces that could make a meaningful difference in efforts to improve the quality of education for all children and their families.3

ANNOTATED BIBLIOGRAPHY

Fullan, M. (2001). *Leading in a culture of change.* San Francisco: Jossey-Bass.
Fullan, M., & Hargreaves, A. (1999). *La escuela que queremos: Los objetivos por los cuales vale la pena luchar*.

Fullan and his colleagues have published a series of books designed for educators (ostensibly for administrators and teachers but with valuable insights for all educators) with the intent to provide an analysis of the school system and practical guidelines for action to promote positive change. In *Leading in a culture of change*, Fullan weaves together theory and research as he discusses five components of effective change: moral purpose, understanding change, relationship building, knowledge creation and sharing, and coherence making.

Meyers, B. (2002). The contracts negotiation stage of a school-based, cross-cultural organizational consultation: A case study. *Journal of Educational and Psychological Consultation, 13,* 151–183.

This article presents an excellent case study of challenges encountered in the contract negotiation phase and subsequent problem definition phase of cross-cultural, organizational consultation. Barbara Meyers provides useful lessons-learned and suggestions for increasing the likelihood of sustainable school-based change.

Nastasi, B. K., Varjas, K., Bernstein, R., & Jayasena, A. (2000). Conducting participatory culture-specific consultation: A global perspective on multicultural consultation. *School Psychology Review, 29,* 401–413.

This article describes the Participatory Culture-Specific Consultation Model and how it was applied to develop mental health promotion programs in Sri Lanka. The model takes a scientist-practitioner approach, using on-going ethnographic and action research and participatory interpersonal processes to guide the development of culture-specific interventions.

RESOURCES

Consulting Psychology Journal: Practice and Research

The journal is published by the Society of Consulting Psychology (Division 13) of the American Psychological Association. The journal publishes articles focusing on consultation.

Journal of Educational and Psychological Consultation (JEPC)

JEPC is published by Lawrence Erlbaum Associates. The journal provides a forum for advancing research and practice in educational and psychological consultation.

REFERENCES

Alpert, J. L., & Meyers, J. (Eds.). (1983). *Training in consultation: Perspectives from mental health, behavioral and organizational consultation.* Springfield, IL: Charles C. Thomas.

Berger, J., Ridgeway, C. L., Fisek, M. H., & Norman, R. Z. (1998). The legitimation and delegitimation of power and prestige orders. *American Sociological Review, 63,* 379–405.

Brown, D., Pryzwansky, W. B., & Schulte, A. C. (2001). *Psychological consultation: Introduction to theory and practice* (5th ed.). Boston: Allyn & Bacon.

Caplan, G. (1970). *The theory and practice of mental health consultation.* New York: Basic.

Caplan, G., & Caplan, R. B. (1993). *Mental health consultation and collaboration.* San Francisco: Jossey-Bass.

Cohen, E. G., & Lotan, R. A. (1995). Producing equal-status interaction in the heterogeneous classroom. *American Educational Research Journal, 32,* 99–120.

Comer, J. P., Haynes, N. M., Joyner, E. T., & Ben-Avie, M. (Eds.). (1996). *Rallying the whole village: The Comer process for reforming education.* New York: Teachers College Press.

Connell, J. P., & Klem, A. M. (2000). You *can* get there from here: Using a theory of change approach to plan urban educational reform. *Journal of Educational and Psychological Consultation, 11,* 193–120.

Conoley, J. C. (1981). The process of change: The agent of change. In J. C. Conoley (Ed.), *Consultation in schools: Theory, research, procedures.* (pp. 11–34). New York: Academic Press.

Conoley, J. C., & Conoley, C. W. (1992). *School consultation: Practice and training* (2nd ed.). Boston: Allyn & Bacon.

Curtis, M. J., & Stollar, S. A. (1996). Applying principles and practices of organizational change to school reform. *School Psychology Review, 25,* 409–417.

Fisek, M. H., Berger, J., & Moore, J. C. (2002). Evaluations, enactment, and expectations. *Social Psychology Quarterly, 65,* 329–345.

French, W. L., & Bell, C. H. (1978). *Organizational development* (2nd ed). Englewood Cliffs, NJ: Prentice-Hall.

Fullan, M. (1997). *What's worth fighting for in the principalship?* New York: Teachers College Press.

Fullan, M., & Hargreaves, A. (1996). *What's worth fighting for in your school?* New York: Teachers College Press.

Fullan, M., & Hargreaves, A. (1998). *What's worth fighting for "out there"?* New York: Teachers College Press.

Fullan, M., & Hargreaves, A. (1999). *La escuela que queremos: Los objetivos por los cuales vale la pena luchar.* Capital Federal, Argentina: Amorrortu Editores.

Gallessich, J. (1981). Organizational factors influencing consultation in schools. In M. J. Curtis & J. E. Zins (Eds.), *The theory and practice of school consultation.* (pp. 149–158). Springfield, IL: Charles C. Thomas.

Gallessich, J. (1986). *The profession and practice of consultation: A handbook for consultants, trainers of consultants, and consumers of consultation services.* San Francisco: Jossey-Bass.

Gillette, J. H., & Kranyik, R. D. (1996). Changing American schools: Insights from the School Development Program. In J. P. Comer, N. M. Haynes, E. T. Joyner, & M.

Ben-Avie (Eds.), *Rallying the whole village: The Comer process for reforming education* (pp. 147–161). New York: Teachers College Press.

Goldstein, B. S., & Harris, K. C. (2000). Consultant practices in two heterogeneous Latino schools. *School Psychology Review, 29,* 368–377.

Grolnick, W. S., & Slowiaczek, M. L. (1994). Parents' involvement in children's schooling: A multidimensional conceptualization and motivational model. *Child Development, 65,* 237–252.

Hill, N. E., & Craft, S. A. (2003). Parent-school involvement and school performance: Mediated pathways among socioeconomic comparable African and Euro-American families. *Journal of Educational Psychology, 95,* 74–83.

Hirschowitz, R. G. (1977). Consultation to complex organizations in transition: The dynamics of change and the principles of applied consultation. In S. C. Plog & P. I. Ahmed (Eds.), *Principles and techniques of mental health consultation* (pp. 169–197). New York: Plenum.

Hoover-Dempsey. K. V., & Sandler, H. M. (1997). Why do parents become involved in their children's education? *Review of Educational Research, 67,* 3–42.

Ingraham, C. L. (2000). Consultation through a multicultural lens: Multicultural and cross-cultural consultation in schools. *School Psychology Review, 29,* 320–343.

Jerrell, J. M., & Jerrell, S. L. (1981). Organizational consultation in school systems. In J. C. Conoley (Ed.), *Consultation in schools* (pp. 133–156). New York: Academic.

Lupiani, J. L. (2004). *Parental role construction, parent sense of efficacy, and perceptions of teacher invitations as factors influencing parent involvement.* Unpublished doctoral dissertation, Fordham University, New York.

Maher, C. A., & Illback, R. J. (1982). Organizational school psychology: Issues and considerations. *Journal of School Psychology, 20,* 244–253.

Meyers, B. (2002). The contracts negotiation stage of a school-based, cross-cultural organizational consultation: A case study. *Journal of Educational and Psychological Consultation, 13,* 151–183.

Meyers, J., Parsons, R. D., & Martin, R. (1979). *Mental health consultation in the schools.* San Francisco: Jossey-Bass.

Nastasi, B. K., Varjas, K., Bernstein, R., & Jayasena, A. (2000). Conducting participatory culture-specific consultation: A global perspective on multicultural consultation. *School Psychology Review, 29,* 401–413.

Pipes, R. B. (1981). Consulting in organizations: The entry problem. In J. C. Conoley (Ed.), *Consultation in schools: Theory, research, procedures* (pp. 11–34). New York: Academic Press.

Ramirez, S. Z., Lepage, K. M., Kratochwill, T. R., & Duffy, J. L. (1998). Multicultural issues in school-based consultation: Conceptual and research considerations. *Journal of School Psychology, 36,* 479–509.

Rosenholtz, S. J. (1991). *Teachers' workplace: The social organization of schools.* New York: Teachers College Press.

Sarason, S. B. (1990). *The predictable failure of educational reform.* San Francisco: Jossey-Bass.

Sarason, S. B. (1996). *Revisiting "The culture of the school and the problem of change."* New York: Teachers College Press.

Schmuck, R. A. (1983). System-process mental health models. In S. Cooper & W. F. Hodges (Eds.), *The mental health consultation field* (pp. 71–88). New York: Human Sciences Press.

Schmuck, R. A. (1990). Organizational development in schools: Contemporary concepts and practices. In T. B. Gutkin & C. R. Reynolds (Eds.), *The handbook of school psychology* (2nd ed). New York: Wiley.

Sheridan, S. M., & Gutkin, T. B. (2000). The ecology of school psychology: Examining and changing our paradigm for the 21st century. *School Psychology Review, 29,* 485–502.

Soo-Hoo, T. (1998). Applying frame of reference and reframing techniques to improve school consultation in multicultural settings. *Journal of Educational and Psychological Consultation, 9*, 325–345.

Tarver Behring, S., & Ingraham, C. L. (1998). Culture as a central component of consultation: A call to the field. *Journal of Educational and Psychological Consultation, 9*, 57–72.

Weinstein, R. S., Madison, S. M., & Kuklinski, M. R. (1995). Raising expectations in schooling: Obstacles and opportunities for change. *American Educational Research Journal, 32*, 121–160.

III

INSTRUCTIONAL AND CLASSROOM INTERVENTIONS

8

IMPLEMENTING CULTURALLY SENSITIVE INTERVENTIONS IN CLASSROOM SETTINGS

Kathleen C. Harris
California Polytechnic State University, San Luis Obispo

Barbara S. C. Goldstein
Azusa Pacific University

Never before has the need for culturally sensitive classroom interventions been more evident than now given the following trends and reports. School communities in rural areas that have traditionally been white/Euroamerican and English speaking are struggling to provide appropriate instruction and procedures to meet the needs of their rapidly changing clientele (U.S. Department of Commerce Bureau of the Census, 1991; U.S. Department of Education Office for Civil Rights, 1992). Latinos are the fastest growing student group in public schools. Many of these are newcomers who are spurred by the proliferation of jobs and relatively little competition for the factory and farm work positions in these geographic areas. The children of the new residents enter school often with limited formal educational experience (Katz, 1996).

The impact of immigration and high birth rates has continued to impact the urban school districts that are struggling to meet the needs of the socioeconomically, ethnically, and linguistically diverse school population (Alonso-Zaldivar, 1999; Obiakor & Utley, 1997; Tobar, 2001). Furthermore, the majority of teachers in both urban and rural school districts tend to be teachers whose backgrounds are markedly different from their students in language, culture, ethnicity, and economic class (Darder, 1991). In districts historically composed of people of color, and/or poor and working class communities, the drop out rates continue to be disproportionately "minority," poor, and male, although there is more evidence to suggest that Black and Latina females are just as likely to drop out of school as their male counterparts (Ginorio & Huston, 2001). Reform efforts have done little to address the real needs of students, their teachers, and the school staff (Howe & Welmer, 2002; Patton & Edgar, 2002; Townsend, 2002).

Interventions will be discussed within the context of the classroom environment as a social-political construct, and from the perspective of education for social justice and democratic schooling. Before we decide to change student "misbehavior" we need to explore the context in which the behavior occurs and the communication implicit in the actions and consequences of such behavior. This means analyzing student behavior in an ecological fashion: probing educational, health, and family history; using observational and interviewing techniques for gathering data across home and school settings; and researching academic achievement through portfolio analysis, document review, and interactive assessment procedures. It also means analyzing student behavior from a critical social constructivist perspective: probing school staff's funds of knowledge regarding the cultural and linguistic interaction style of their students; researching participation and collaboration between and among students, parents, teachers and administrators in the policy and decision-making regarding behavioral expectations; analyzing curriculum and instruction for cultural congruency and relevance to students' lives; and determining the availability of high quality academic programs and materials to all students.

This chapter attempts to cover a small piece of the intervention puzzle that focuses on classroom interventions that are sensitive to the needs and strengths of both students and teachers in what is increasingly a global village. However, readers are encouraged to further examine the complex sociocultural, political, and economic factors that impact the way that culturally and linguistically diverse youngsters are educated in public schools.

THEORETICAL AND RESEARCH BASIS

Resistance theories provide a theoretical framework that is consistent with a critical social constructivist perspective in which to analyze student behavior. Danforth (2000) describes resistance theories as "a group of sociological explanations for the behavior of students who are members of politically marginalized groups" (p. 14). He identifies four forms of resistance that emerge from ethnographic studies of three critical ethnographers. Based on the work of McLaren (1985, 1993), Willis (1977) and Foley (1990), Danforth identifies clowning, ritualized group rebellion, playful making-out games, and aggressive making-out games as forms of resistance that occur in the classroom. "Each mode of resistance ritual demonstrates a unique way of delaying, disrupting, or sidetracking a standard school exercise in order to clear space for the subjectively and culturally salient world of working class student meaning. The students literally work to free themselves from the typical dome of school-required attitudes and behaviors" (Danforth, 2000, p. 19).

In addition, cross-cultural communication competencies provide a standard by which miscommunication and misinterpretation of behavior due to cultural incongruity can be analyzed. The classroom environment can be examined from a democratic and culturally inclusive classroom perspective. Finally, implications for practice and implementation can be examined from an ecosystemic and critical social constructivist point of view.

The embedded theme in resistance theories, cross-cultural communication competencies, democratic and inclusive classrooms, and critical social constructivism is one that not only embraces diversity in all of its forms (culture, language, ethnicity, class, etc.) but also one that encourages a mode of engagement that is critical. By this we mean to acknowledge that cross cultural encounters whether in the classroom or in the world at large will always be fraught with tension between power and culture, or power and language, or power and economics. To embrace this diversity means to embrace this reality and to commit to working across the tension, acknowledging the power differentials, and working together to identify and reshape the structures that sustain and promote "business as usual."

Cultural Sensitivity and Behavioral Expectations

African American and Latino students are consistently overrepresented in special education, particularly as students with emotional disturbances and comorbid conduct disorders (Harry & Anderson, 1995; Patton, 1998; Salend, Duhaney, & Montgomery, 2002; Zhang & Katsiyannis, 2002). Townsend (2002) cites differences in behavioral expectations, misinterpretation of cultural interaction styles, and differences in social and linguistic norms as reasons for the greater referrals and subsequent overidentification of these youngsters. She notes the disparity in treatment between African American male students and their non-Black counterparts for the same school and classroom infractions. More Black males receive suspensions, expulsions or referrals to special education than other students. She cites shortages of teachers of color who can be role models, and also persons who understand the students' sociocultural and class differences and the impact these differences have on student behavior and school attitudes. She also states that different learning and communication styles between students and teachers contribute to teachers' misinterpretation of behavior as willful, defiant or off-task. Partnerships with communities and parents, and activities that promote an exchange of ideas and relationship building can help to offset the misunderstandings and their consequences that arise across cultural gulfs.

Culturally sensitive interventions require an acknowledgement from the consultant, psychologist, or counselor, that culture is a set of explicit and implicit rules for survival and daily living. Frisby and Lorenzo-Luaces (2000) point out that culture and ethnicity or racial group is not synonymous with a homogenous culture that encompasses fixed values. Cultural groups vary in nationality, ethnicity, socioeconomic status, racial group, religion, and language. While culture is not specifically tied to a racial or ethnic group, and is rich in its heterogeneity within and across different characteristics of various self-identified groups, it is important to understand that cultural values and behaviors emerge in response to repeated and institutional mistreatment that may reflect the dominant culture's assumptions and bias against the "ethnic" minority culture. Furthermore, when ethnic minority groups such as Mexican-Americans, Puerto Ricans, or Salvadoran-Americans are lumped together into a statistical label such as "Latinos" and also experience similar kinds of prejudice, social and linguistic discrimination, and economic disparities, what may draw them together in opposition to the dominant culture are those values that they may share across nationality, racial or ethnic group, or linguistic style.

Democratic Classrooms

Classrooms are socially constructed places that exist within a specific time and place. Furthermore, the classroom culture is subject to the social, cultural, political, and economic forces that sustain its existence. If individuals construct meaning from their environment and knowledge is shared meaning that occurs through social interaction with others, then classrooms should reflect the dialogue between students and teachers and the ideas that emerge from that exchange.

Glasser's (1990) work on the quality school, Nelson, Lott, and Glenn's (1997) work on class meetings and positive discipline, Kohl's (1969) seminal work on open schools, and Giroux and McLaren's (1986) analysis of democratic schooling, describe practical and theoretical considerations for this type of classroom. Special educators have also examined the role that democratic classrooms and authentic curriculum and instructional tasks play in meeting the needs of culturally and linguistically diverse students with special needs (Goldstein, 1995; Ruiz & Enguidanos, 1997). This work suggests that authentic communication and literacy activities, behavioral management practices that are viewed as fair and just by students and teachers, and the inclusion of student voices in the decision making processes of the classroom are characteristic of democratic classrooms. Key features of democratic classrooms are: the students' freedom to contribute to the course of study; the method of study; organizational structure of the classroom, and the ability to make relevant choices; the teachers' willingness to share decision-making with students; the ability to facilitate, guide, and provide direct instruction as needed to meet the individual learning needs of students; and flexibility to work collaboratively with students and families.

Social Constructivism and Students with Behavioral Challenges

Habel, Bloom, Ray, and Bacon (1999) use the framework of social constructivist theory and the Native American Navajo philosophy of community building to examine the responses of students who were referred for disciplinary measures and/or behavioral programs for identified or at-risk behavioral disorders. They analyzed the students' responses in light of the "circle of courage": a tradition that embraces the growing individual and guides him toward full participation in the society. The circle of courage looks at four aspects of the development of affiliation within the community: belonging, mastery, independence, and generosity. These four "spirits" identify the social and psychological need for mentors, success, autonomy, and sharing that young people have for developing their role and status within their communities. Thus, we can use the circle to create environments, build relationships, and generate activities that satisfy and promote the mental health and emotional needs of students. Schools that enable students to engage these ways of being within the larger community, respect the student, nurture self-esteem, and thereby decrease student oppositional behavior because students are contributors to the behavioral and social expectations of their community. The circle of courage concept has much potential for looking at noncompliant behaviors and behavioral interventions from a nonwestern, collective identity perspective using ecological assessment that focuses on the classroom and school environment.

Resistance Theories and Critical Social Constructivism

Drawing from the work of Freire (1970), Giroux (1983), Giroux and McLaren (1986), and Ogbu (1982), resistance theories describe how students of color from subordinated cultural groups develop behaviors that are in opposition to what they perceive as mainstream, White, middle class expectations and norms. These oppositional behaviors serve as a flag of their identification with the subordinated cultural group, as a means for self-preservation and identity as a member of the group, and as a way to reject the identified values, subscribed roles, and the dominant group's expectations of how the subordinate group should be socialized within the school life and larger society (Fordham, 1988). An example of an oppositional behavior from a resistance theory perspective might be a student who thinks that academic achievement and positive school behavior is "acting White."

"Resistance theories view the oppositional behaviors of students from oppressed groups as living artifacts of the broader social inequalities that limit the democratic possibilities within society, demonstrating that even the school is a politically contested space…" additionally, these behaviors "may be viewed as often personally and socially meaningful efforts to craft identity, relationship, and freedom within educational institutions that fail to acknowledge and respect the subjectivity, history, and cultural background of these students" (Danforth, 2000, p. 16). A critical social constructivist perspective described by Danforth (2000) is embedded in the work of Freire (1970) and other critical theorists (Apple & Beane, 1995; Giroux, 1983; McLaren, 1993; Shor, 1987). A critical social constructivist perspective asks educators to examine and actively engage how government and educational policies and programs actively serve to undermine the interests of poor and minority students and examine how these policies have resulted in perpetuating an educational class system that mirrors the economic, social, political, and cultural disparity that exists in the nation's economic and political distributions of power and capital. Furthermore, as we examine school and classroom practices for culturally sensitive interventions and suggest ways that these might become more respectful of students who are members of subordinated cultural and ethnic groups, Danforth (2000) states that educators must "understand the political nature of oppositional behavior" (p. 13). That is, teachers need to explore how seemingly innocent or prevalent practices reflect and exacerbate class and racial/ethnic disparities in how students are "managed" and disciplined, and how and why students intuitively rebel against the values that are inherent in school rules and procedures. Student acts of oppositional behavior can be viewed as socially, politically, and culturally meaningful acts and forms of self-preservation.

Beyond Cultural Competencies: The Classroom as a Negotiated Space

Research has identified cultural competencies that facilitate cross cultural communication and collaboration for problem-solving academic and behavioral problems (Harris, 1996; Heron & Harris, 2001; Lynch & Hanson, 1998). Efforts toward expanding the notion of cultural competence to include a critical stance such that educators can also look at the behaviors of poor, working class and minority students from a political perspective holds promise for a genuine dialogue that addresses class as well as cultural, ethnic and linguistic diversity. From this point of view, the classroom can be seen as a cultural space that encompasses the histories of those who live in it; as such it is subject to negotiation among all who dwell there.

The following sections will discuss interventions in classroom settings from the perspective of politics and class as previously described in the hope that educators, including school psychologists, will begin to also analyze behavior from a social-political and social justice perspective. This approach has the potential of addressing the social milieu from which many of these behaviors stem: rather like rebuilding the dam instead of just putting countless fingers in the individual holes in the dike.

IMPLICATIONS FOR PRACTICE

Since many skills are needed to address the variety of language and instructional needs of culturally diverse students, individuals often deliver services as teams. One type of school-wide team identified by Friend and Cook (1997) is the team that focuses on helping teachers deal with the problems experienced by students in schools. Though known by many names (e.g., teacher assistance teams, intervention assistance teams, mainstream assistance teams, prereferral teams, and student support teams), the basic premise of these problem-solving teams is that professionals work cooperatively using a problem-solving approach to address the needs of students and/or the professional concerns of teachers. These problem-solving teams can alleviate or reduce invalid special education referrals and placements (Fuchs, Fuchs, & Bahr, 1990; Graden, Casey, & Christenson, 1985); help classroom teachers solve academic or social problems, short of full-scale referral to special education (Friend & Cook, 1996; Fuchs, Fuchs, & Bahr, 1990; Pugach & Johnson, 1989); and prevent future problems in the classroom (Fuchs & Fuchs, 1989; Graden, Casey & Christenson, 1985; Pugach & Johnson, 1989; Zins, Heron, & Goddard, 1999). The problem-solving team is supported by legislation (e.g., Individuals with Disabilities Education Act of 1997, P.L. 105–17) requiring that teams be used for decision-making.

It is helpful to consider the work of Ortiz (1990) in conducting problem-solving teams that will meet the needs of culturally diverse students. She stressed the importance of including bilingual educators as members of these teams since these individuals often have resources for appropriate assessment and instructional strategies to use with culturally diverse students. It is also important to identify other individuals who might be helpful. For example, extended family members, unrelated significant individuals in the student's life, neighbors, friends, healers, and representatives from institutions such as churches and local self-help groups may be among the appropriate resources needed in a problem-solving team to develop effective culturally sensitive interventions (Delgado, 1994). It is crucial to include someone on the team who not only is representative of the community cultural, linguistic, and ethnic make-up, but also someone who can provide some insight into the impact of the class and economic obstacles that may exist in implementing recommended interventions.

In addition to school-wide problem-solving teams, co-teaching teams may instruct culturally diverse students. Co-teaching usually takes place in the general education environment and is defined as two or more teachers planning and instructing the same group of students at the same time and in the same place. Though much has been written in recent years about co-teaching among general and special educators (e.g., Bauwens & Hourcade, 2003; Boudah, Schumacher, & Deshler, 1997; Cook & Friend, 1995; Dieker, 2001; Fennick & Liddy, 2001; Harris, 1998; Murawski & Swanson, 2001; Salend, Johansen, Mumper, Chase, Pike, & Dorney, 1997; Walther-Thomas, 1997), it can occur among a variety of individuals, including bilingual educators, instructors of English language learners (ELL), general educators, special educators, and speech and language therapists (Salend, Dorney, & Mazo, 1997).

The team approach to offering services requires collaboration among *all* members of the team, including school psychologists, special educators, general educators, English language development educators, speech and language therapists, counselors, and administrators. Based on a review of the educational consultation and bilingual special education literatures, Harris (1991) developed a set of generic and specific collaboration competencies needed by all who serve culturally diverse students. Four general competencies emerged from this literature review: (a) understanding one's perspective; (b) using effective interpersonal, communication, and problem-solving skills; (c) understanding the role(s) of collaborators; and (d) using appropriate assessment and instructional strategies.

Understanding one's own perspective is a necessary prerequisite to any collaborative activity. This understanding is necessary to establish a climate for the collaboration that will foster growth and change. It is important for bicultural collaborators to engage in this activity as well. Bicultural collaborators can't assume that because they share the same ethnicity and/or language, they share the same perspective. Bicultural collaborators must examine their assimilation and acculturation experiences as influences on their perspectives, especially when working with people who share their ethnicity and language (Goldstein, 1998). Collaborators might ask themselves the following questions when striving to understand their culture and its relationship to other cultures: (a) Am I willing to learn from others who serve culturally diverse students as well as share my expertise with them? (b) What are my beliefs regarding the abilities of culturally diverse students? What is the basis for those beliefs, and do I expect all educators serving culturally diverse students to share those beliefs and values? (c) What are the beliefs of my collaborators regarding the abilities of culturally diverse students? What is the basis of those beliefs?

Team members may find themselves working in many different types of cross-cultural collaborative activities (e.g., when gathering information from culturally diverse students and their families, as well as when meeting with professionals from other disciplines who represent a different cultural orientation and/or ethnic or racial background). In order to facilitate effective cross-cultural collaborations, individuals should demonstrate respect for individuals from other cultures, acknowledge cultural differences in communication and relationship building, ascertain if organizational mores tend to privilege or silence different groups of people, and ensure that the problem identification does not conflict with cultural beliefs (Harris, 1996; Roberts, Bell, & Salend, 1991). In addition, team members must learn the culture of the team. As Daniels and DeWine (1991) suggest, team members should work to establish the same interpretation and meaning of issues. In this way, through their interpersonal communicative interactions, collaborators develop a common culture for collaborative activities.

There are many roles that collaborators can assume. Collaboration to meet the needs of culturally diverse students might result in any of the following activities: (a) facilitating problem solving sessions with individuals with different values and problem-solving styles, (b) promoting the use of native language and culture for culturally diverse students, or (c) collaborating with culturally diverse professionals. The roles collaborators assume usually depend upon the purpose of the collaboration. Therefore, it is important to clearly define the purpose of each collaboration and identify the appropriate roles to accomplish that purpose. In her work with bilingual special education teacher assistance teams, Harris (1995) found that collaborators often approached their roles in the school differently, and the roles assumed were not always dictated by ethnic identity. For example, in one elementary bilingual special education team, the principal of the elementary school, a Mexican-American male, identified his role in the school as "instructional leader." Though he stated that he valued bilingual education advocates, he did not consider that to be a role he played in the school. In a junior high school in the same district, the English language development teachers, more than other Hispanic team members, strongly identified with the needs of culturally diverse students. The collaborators often struggled with their roles. For some, their roles were clearly influenced by their ethnic identity; for others, their roles were clearly influenced by their job titles. As Ortiz and Garcia (1995) caution, being bilingual does not ensure one advocates for culturally diverse students or has the knowledge of the student's culture and the skills for appropriate instruction. The next section addresses principles to consider for appropriate instruction.

IMPLEMENTATION AND APPROACHES

Whether or not one is working within the structure of a team, to work successfully with culturally diverse students, every educator needs to develop skills in the following areas: culture, language, families, assessment, curriculum, instructional planning, instruction, materials, and consultation and collaboration (Harris, 2000). Since culture, language, families, assessment, and consultation and collaboration are addressed thoroughly in the other chapters, we will discuss strategies to develop competencies in curriculum development, instructional planning, and instruction. The key principle in all approaches is to incorporate the student's culture, language, and social/political history as it pertains to the experiences of group membership.

Curriculum Development

As suggested by Cummins (1986), students' native language and culture should be incorporated into the curriculum and families and communities should be involved in collaboratively developing the school's mission and activities. The questions related to family dynamics, student behavior, student characteristics and disciplinary style posed by Sileo and Prater (1998) would be useful for teams to consider as they develop culturally appropriate curriculum. For example, team members could answer the following questions about students' families: What are the important family rules? What are the primary disciplinary methods used at home and the students' reactions to those methods? How do class differences among the families in the community impact family rules and disciplinary methods? In order too incorporate the students' culture, team members can ask: What roles do silence, questions, and responses play in the students' cultures? Do students assume a competitive or a cooperative posture in their learning and interactions with other students? Do the political histories of students' families contribute to a student's social orientation as a member of a specific cultural, ethnic, and linguistic group whose members are interdependent as opposed to someone whose socialization values independence and autonomy?

In addition to incorporating aspects of native culture into the curriculum, educators need to consciously address the cultural identity of students. Franklin, James, and Watson (1996) discuss strategies that educators should use at various stages of a student's development of cultural identity. For example, at the beginning stage of cultural identity development, the student tends to reject his or her cultural values and prefer those of the dominant culture. In this case, educators should use multicultural content to help the student develop cultural awareness and appreciation. When a student is confused about the importance of his or her culture in relation to that of other cultures, educators can design instruction that reflects the contributions of the student's culture to society, as well as the contributions of other cultural groups. As educators develop culturally sensitive interventions, it is important that they assess the cultural identity of each student. According to Lynch and Hanson (1998) getting to know the students and their families as individuals can be the basis for this assessment. In this way, team members can ascertain the values of the children and their families and not just assume that they identify with particular values because they belong to a particular ethnic group. However, it is equally important to recognize that cultural integrity and congruity exists within groups that have a collective consciousness of their shared historical, economic and social obstacles, particularly if they are from a group that has experienced subordination and limited power within the dominant cultural institutions and its policies.

Antonia Darder (1991) provides a model of bicultural development that is useful in examining the interplay of culture and power in the consciousness of members of historically subordinated bicultural groups such as African Americans, Chicanos, Asian Americans, and Native Americans. Darder describes how the tension between the dominant and subordinate cultures impacts the development, behavior, and self-identification of individuals from these groups. The resistance to the dominant culture in the effort to protect the primary culture, and the subordination of the primary culture to the dominant culture reflects the often-ambivalent state that bicultural individuals from subordinated cultures experience (Darder, 1991). Belonging to a specific ethnic group does not mean that shared values exist (e.g., all Latinos share the same family values), or that belonging to a specific ethnic group guarantees a particular type of psychological or sociological development and character. However, it is important to acknowledge that being a member of a historically marginalized group that has experienced cultural, linguistic, social, political, and economic disenfranchisement through governmental policies and laws of a nation, has a powerful impact on the individual identities of group members as a whole.

In summary, educators must consider the cultural and social/historical background students bring to the educational setting. Educators should develop curriculum in consideration of the following characteristics of the child: (a) the student's familiarity of the Euroamerican culture, (b) the student's familiarity and identification with his or her own traditional culture, (c) the student's contemporary culture, (d) the student's expectation of the educational environment, (e) the extent to which the student has been successful in becoming part of the education community, (f) where students are in their own bicultural development using Darder's model, (g) what they know about their own individual and family history (e.g., Are they refugees? Do they know from what?), (h) how they identify their own class and ethnic/racial affiliations (e.g., How might a black Nicaraguense working class student deal with contradictory messages about his identity?), and (i) their familiarity with the educational outcomes for group members from their own communities (e.g., Does formal education deliver what it promises to members of their class/ethnic community?).

Instructional Planning

Instructional planning is particularly important for educators working with linguistically diverse students because, given the language needs of these students, many educators will find it necessary to plan instruction collaboratively with bilingual or English Language Development teachers. If educators are using co-teaching to deliver instruction to culturally diverse students, instructional planning should assure that both teachers are actively involved in teaching (Schumm, Vaughn, & Harris, 1997; Walther-Thomas, Bryant, & Land, 1996).

In addressing learner needs and effective instructional delivery, the suggestions offered by Fueyo (1997) should be considered. First, consider the kind of language that will be required of the students. Incorporate language requirements that will enable students to use their conversational fluency, but also develop their language skills. Second, clearly identify the language of classroom instruction and match it to students' needs. Third, if there are many English-language learners, determine the instructional strategies that will maximize students' comprehension. Fourth, make sure the level of teacher language is appropriate for students' levels of proficiency. Furthermore, when addressing the needs of students who are Standard English Learners (SEL), such as speakers of African American Language or Chicano English, it is important to stress the validity, dignity, and importance of the student's primary language. Teachers need to be explicit about the status of English as the language of power, but also insure that students have opportunities to discuss how their home/primary languages are rich in meaning by using literature that incorporates these languages. Students will become aware of the diminished status of their language and so it behooves us to make sure that there are opportunities for them to analyze this issue using examples in literature and other media.

Instruction

Differentiated instruction is not a new concept in education but it is one that has taken own new importance as educators strive to establish culturally sensitive classrooms. We can trace it back to John Dewey (1915, 1916) who described a vision of school as a caring community that actively engaged students. Differentiation is essentially the teacher's response to a learner's needs. Therefore, it is not a particular instructional strategy. Rather, it is a "synthesis of a number of educational theories and practices" (Tomlinson & Allan, 2000, p. 16). Two educational practices for differentiating instruction hold particular promise for the culturally sensitive classroom, i.e., scaffolding instruction and peer-mediated instruction.

Extensive reviews of the literature (Garcia, Pearson, & Jiménez, 1990; Gersten & Woodward, 1992) indicate that it is essential for teachers of language-minority students to scaffold or support students' learning experiences. Scaffolding instruction is based on the work of Vygotsky (1962, 1978). When a learner cannot function independently because of the complexity of a task, the teacher is encouraged to support the learner in moving through complex applications. The area in which a learner cannot function alone but can be successful with teacher support is that child's "zone of proximal development." In this zone, new learning takes place. Research in psychology support Vygotsky's theory (Howard, 1994; Jensen, 1998). Byrnes (1996) states, "The consensus of a broad range of psychologists and brain researchers is that: is Instruction should always 'be in advance' of a child's current level of mastery. That, teacher should teach within a child's zone of proximal development. If material is presented at or below the mastery level, there will be no growth. If presented well above the zone, children will be confused and frustrated" (p. 33).

The challenge for teachers implementing culturally sensitive interventions is to accurately determine each student's zone of proximal development. This requires educators to understand the cultural differences of their students so that each student's strengths and needs can be accurately determined. If students' cultural differences are misunderstood or ignored, it can have a negative effect (Delpit, 1995).

Reviews of the literature indicate that peer-mediated instruction is an effective strategy for differentiating instruction (i.e., Gardner et. al., 1994; Lloyd, Forness, & Kavale, 1998). In peer-mediated approaches, the students themselves, after training, take on the primary tasks of delivering instruction and providing prompts and feedback during each learning experience. Two types of peer-mediated instruction hold particular promise, i.e., tutoring and cooperative learning.

The research data on the beneficial effects of tutoring systems are overwhelming, whether used as a stand-alone intervention or in combination with other procedures (see Heron & Harris, 2001). Tutoring systems have been shown to be effective to teach basic skills (e.g., Arreaga-Mayer, 1998; Ezell, Kohler, & Strain, 1994), English as a second language (e.g., Houghton & Bain, 1993), and a wide variety of other academic and nonacademic behaviors across an even wider range of students with and without special needs in different settings (Miller, Barbetta, & Heron, 1994). According to Schloss, Kobza, & Alper (1997): "tutoring contributes to achievement outcomes in that students achieve a significantly higher rate of academic engagement…[and]…a higher rate of academic engagement has been linked to greater student learning " (p. 191).

Cooperative learning is "small groups of learners working together as a team to solve a problem, complete a task, or accomplish a common goal" (Artz & Newman, 1990, p. 448). Tateyama-Sniezek's (1990) and Slavin's (1990) review of the effects of cooperative learning supports its use as a viable educational practice for meeting the diverse needs of students in inclusive classrooms. Cooperative learning provides students with the opportunity to become critically engaged in learning through participation as members of a group who practice choice making and participate in their own success (Carpenter, Bloom, & Boat, 1999). Cooperative grouping techniques can be appropriately used across all age groups. This requires flexibility in grouping for specific activities and instruction. Using heterogeneous grouping enhances peer-assisted instruction, provides age appropriate models for communication and behavior for students in inclusive settings, and promotes recognition of everyone's strengths and value to the community of learners (such as in a reciprocal teaching lesson). Homogeneous grouping enables the teacher and students to concentrate on specific skills that are tailored to their learning needs. Flexible grouping works best in a classroom that employs differentiated curriculum to address the multiple needs of a diverse classroom.

In general, it is recommended that educators (a) assess and secure resources for providing appropriate language instruction, (b) determine the level of congruence between the teacher's views and expectations of students and the students' educational needs, (c) develop congruence between the culture and language of the home and those of the school, and (d) use differentiated instructional strategies that are effective with culturally and linguistically diverse students (Heron & Harris, 2001). Furthermore, teachers of students who have English as a second language need to reflect on their own biases toward the primary languages of these students. It is important for teachers and support staff to become aware of how they are unconsciously communicating their attitudes about the students' primary languages.

If a teacher does not have mastery of a student's native language or it is no longer using this resource because of changes in bilingual education law, it is essential that the teacher use sheltered instructional techniques that incorporate many modalities in presenting content. Further, if a teacher uses many modes in presenting content, he or she has a better chance of matching the learning style of the student with the mode of presentation. When using sheltered instruction, teachers provide assistance to learners through visuals and modified texts and within the context of each student's proficiency in English. Planning a sheltered lesson involves identifying critical content and presenting it in meaningful units. In a sheltered lesson, there is a high level of student interaction and a student-centered focus to the instruction in addition to high-context clues provided through visuals and other concrete materials. It is important to explicitly make the connection between students' knowledge and experience and the lesson. The teacher must also be aware of her or his speech (e.g., adjusting it to the student's level and rate) as well as body language and gestures that are used to enhance meaning (Echevarria & Graves, 1998).

IMPLICATIONS FOR FUTURE RESEARCH AND PRACTICE

School reform has been with us for decades. As Goodlad reminds us "… reform era after reform era—each politically driven—puts policy and practice out of balance …Whether soft and tender or hard and tough, school reforms fade and die…But their side effects live on as 'eduviruses' that add cost to the system and create roadblocks to the serious redesign and sustained improvement we need" (2002, p. 18). It is imperative that we carefully consider what truly makes an inclusive and culturally sensitive school.

Researchers have been consistent in their recommendations for practical solutions and procedures to address the related educational issues of poor working class and minority students (Edgar, Patton, & Day-Vines, 2002; Salend, Duhaney, & Montgomery, 2002; Sileo & Prater, 1998; Townsend, 2002). These recommendations consist of: (a) recruitment and retention of a diverse staff; (b) culturally and linguistically sensitive and appropriate curriculum and instruction; (c) training in non-biased assessment and multicultural sensitivity, including opportunities for becoming aware of one's own worldview; (d) access to quality programs and services; (e) working collaboratively with the parents and community; and (f) an understanding of bicultural development and communication styles.

The continued overrepresentation of African American and Latino students in special education programs for students with emotional disturbance and specific learning disabilities is partly related to cultural and social differences that have led to misdiagnoses and misplacements (Ortiz & Garcia, 1995). More importantly however, the institutional culture of U.S. schools and the hegemonic structure of education that sustains that culture seem to promote the miseducation of poor working class, minority students and subsequent referrals to remedial and special programs. The tragic consequences of miseducation result in high drop-out rates, low academic achievement, truancy, entrance into the juvenile justice system, mediocre educational opportunities and experiences, and overzealous zero tolerance and punitive disciplinary procedures. Eventually, the results are the completion of school with no diploma or a diploma that will not even open doors to a meaningful, well-paying job. As Danforth (2000) points out, students who take to heart the adage that hard work, respect, following the rules, and staying in school is the ticket to what has belonged to the privileged class, are in for a rude slap when they realize that they've been "playing him for a sucker" (p. 17). It is crucial that those of us who take seriously the phrase that "education is political" and that it should be "transformative" need to create and support classroom dialogues that make explicit the reality of formal education as it is, and as it could be. We need to share with our students, their families, and their communities the research that informs the policies that directly affect them and their educational opportunities. How are disciplinary procedures developed? What is the research base? What is considered a mild, moderate or serious infraction? How are rules agreed upon? What is the procedure for students and their parents to advocate for themselves within the system? Who decides the number of bilingual waivers a school can issue? What policies have informed the limits of primary language use as an additional resource? Have teachers, counselors, and school psychologists undergone cultural sensitivity training? Who conducted it and what was the political perspective with which the training was imbued? The opportunity for students and community folks to voice these questions and have access to the research is a first step to democratic schools and a true school-community partnership and ownership of the schools by the community.

Education and mentorship of educators, including teachers, administrators, counselors, and school psychologists are key elements if this dialogue is to occur. Educational and training programs geared for practice in schools are seriously devoid of political content and critical analysis and instead seem to strive for neutrality in topics and discussion, reducing problems and challenges to one of methodology (Bartolome, 1994; Freire, 1970; Freire & Macedo, 1987, 1995). Critical educators who are not afraid of tackling potentially divisive issues are encouraged to: (a) examine the social/political roots of the methodologies we are teaching or espousing and the contexts in which they are applied; (b) speak to the ethics of teaching and using procedures, assessments, and interventions that have had grave consequences for poor and working class students of color; and (c) become examples of how principles of educational justice can be reflected in our teaching, research, and relationships with colleagues, students, and communities.

Because teachers and support staff such as school psychologists and counselors are not familiar or always comfortable within the communities in which they practice, it is important to develop support groups in collaboration with people who are knowledgeable about the history, language, culture, and social, political, and economic obstacles that face the members of the community. These support groups have the potential to become communities of learners that can provide a forum for staff to: explore their own cultural, political and economic heritage; learn about the histories of their students' community; and discover the role of education as it is perceived in the community and how it might change to serve their needs. Finally the support group has the potential to become a true partnership opportunity between staff and community members to develop local policies and practices that utilize and integrate the expertise that each group has to offer.

ANNOTATED BIBLIOGRAPHY

Artiles, A. J., & Ortiz, A. A. (Eds.). (2002). *English language learners with special education needs-Identification, assessment, and instruction.* McHenry, IL: The Center for Applied Linguistics and Delta Systems, Co. Inc.

The chapters in this edited book address the issues that are germane to the effective instruction and intervention that impact English language learners. Chapters address the following: prevention and early intervention; assessment and identification; parent-professional collaboration; instructional planning, teaching, and critical pedagogy; and future directions. The contributing authors and editors present clear guidelines for practice, rationale based on research, and a consistent philosophical stance that gives this book a clear vision of what needs to occur in our schools and classrooms if we are going to meet the needs of English language learners. The suggestions in this book will enhance the school psychologist's understanding of best practices in the teaching/learning process and will provide a window into the daily world of the students and their teachers.

Danforth, S. (2000). Resistance theories: Exploring the politics of oppositional behavior. *Multiple Voices for Ethnically Diverse Learners*, 13–29.

This article explores the need for educators to include a mode of analysis that goes beyond the traditional psychological explanations for behavior, particularly those behaviors that often result in poor, long-term academic and social consequences for poor, working class, and children of color. Danforth proposes that sociological explanations for behavior based on the work of critical theorists and ethnographers can be useful in the development of interventions that account for societal inequities reflected in educational institutions, values, and practices.

Darder, A. (Ed.). (1998). *Cultural studies in education: Schooling as a contested terrain.* Claremont, CA: Institute for Cultural Studies in Education and Claremont Graduate University.

This edited collection of short research papers by teacher-researchers offers school psychologists and other educators and support staff the opportunity to examine the social-political contexts of education from a bicultural perspective and from inside the classroom. Chapters on affirmative action, proposition 187 (The English for the Children Proposition that became law in California and virtually eliminated bilingual education in that state), and the construction of "deviance" and youth of color, add to our comprehension of how these issues continue to impact poor and working class students of color. The chapters on bicultural identity and the development of voice can be used to begin a dialogue with colleagues about the dominant US ideology that informs our practice, research, and educational structures, including how we live our practice in the schools in which we work.

Sirotnik, K. A. (2001). *Renewing schools and teacher education: An odyssey in educational change.* Washington, DC: American Association of Colleges for Teacher Education.

This volume chronicles over fifteen years of work by John I. Goodlad and others through the National Network for Educational Renewal, the Institute for Educational Inquiry, and the Center for Educational Renewal.

RESOURCES

California Consortium of Critical Educators:
   www.ccce.net
Center for Education Renewal:
   http://depts.washington.edu/cedren/CER.htm
Institute for Education Inquiry:
   http://depts.washington.edu/cedren/IEI.htm
Instituto Paulo Freire:
   www.paulofreire.org
James Crawford Language Policy Website:
   www.ourworld.compuserve.com/homepages/jwcrawford/

Pew Hispanic Center:
  www.pewhispanic.org
Tomas Rivera Policy Institute:
  www.trpi.org

REFERENCES

Alonso-Zaldivar, R. (1999, February 19). Big apple takes on a flavor of Mexico. *Los Angeles Times*.

Apple, M. W., & Beane, J. A. (1995). *Democratic schools*. Alexandria, VA: The Association for Supervision and Curriculum Development.

Arreaga-Mayer, C. (1998). Increasing active student responding and improving academic performance through class wide peer tutoring. *Intervention in School and Clinic, 34,* 89–94, 117.

Artz, A. F., & Newman, C. M. (1990). Cooperative learning. *Mathematics Teacher, 83,* 448–449.

Bartolome, L. I. (1994). Beyond the methods fetish: toward a humanizing pedagogy. *Harvard Educational Review, 64,* 173–194.

Bauwens, J., & Hourcade, J. J. (2003). *Cooperative teaching: Rebuilding the schoolhouse for all students* (2nd ed.). Austin, TX: Pro-Ed.

Boudah, D. Schumaker, J., & Deshler, D. (1997). Collaborative instruction: Is it an effective option for inclusion in secondary classrooms? *Learning Disabilities Quarterly, 20,* 293–316.

Byrnes, J. (1996). *Cognitive development and learning in instructional contexts*. Boston: Allyn & Bacon.

Carpenter, C. D., Bloom, L. A., & Boat, M. B. (1999). Guidelines for special educators: Achieving socially valid outcomes. *Intervention in School and Clinic, 34,* 143–149.

Cook, L., & Friend, M. (1995). Co-teaching: Guidelines for creating effective practices. *Focus on Exceptional Children, 28,* 1–16.

Cummins, J. (1986). Empowering minority students: A framework for intervention. *Harvard Educational Review, 56,* 18–36.

Danforth, S. (2000). Resistance theories: Exploring the politics of oppositional behavior. *Multiple Voices for Ethnically Diverse Learners,* 13–29.

Daniels, T. D., & DeWine, S. (1991). Communication process as target and tool for consultancy intervention: Rethinking a hackneyed theme. *Journal of Educational and Psychological Consultation, 2,* 303–322.

Darder, A. (1991). *Culture and power in the classroom*. New York: Bergin & Garvey.

Delgado, M. (1994). Hispanic natural support systems and the AODA field: A developmental framework for collaboration. *Journal of Multicultural Social Work, 3,* 11–37.

Delpit, L. (1995). *Other people's children: Cultural conflict in the classroom*. New York: The New Press.

Dewey, J. (1915). *The school and society*. Chicago: University of Chicago Press.

Dewey, J. (1916). *Democracy and education: An introduction to the philosophy of education*. New York: Macmillan.

Dieker, L. A. (2001). What are the characteristics of "effective" middle and high school co-taught teams for students with disabilities? *Preventing School Failure, 46,* 14–23.

Echevarria, J., & Graves, A. (1998). *Sheltered content instruction: Teaching English-language learners with diverse abilities*. Boston: Allyn & Bacon.

Edgar, E., Patton, J. M., & Day-Vines, N. (2002). Democratic dispositions and cultural competency. *Remedial and Special Education, 23,* 231–241.

Ezell, H. K., Kohler, R. W., & Strain, P. (1994). A program description of evaluation of academic peer tutoring for reading skills of children with special needs. *Education and Treatment of Children, 17,* 52–67.

Fennick, E., & Liddy, D. (2001). Responsibilities and preparation for collaborative teaching: Co-teachers' perspectives. *Teacher Education and Special Education, 24,* 229–240.

Foley, D. E. (1990). *Learning capitalist culture.* Philadelphia: University of Pennsylvania Press.

Fordham, S. (1988). Racelessness as a factor in Black students' school success: Pragmatic strategy or pyrrhic victory? *Harvard Educational Review, 58,* 54–84.

Franklin, M. E., James, J. R., & Watson, A. L. (1996). Utilizing a cultural identity developmental model to plan culturally responsive reading and writing instruction. *Reading and Writing Quarterly: Overcoming Learning Difficulties, 12,* 21–58.

Freire, P. (1970). *Pedagogy of the oppressed.* New York: Seabury Press.

Freire, P., & Macedo, D. (1987). *Literacy: reading the word and the world.* Hadley, MA: Bergin & Garvey.

Freire, P., & Macedo, D. (1995). A dialogue: Culture, language, and race. *Harvard Educational Review, 65,* 377–402.

Friend, M., & Cook, L. (1996). *Interactions: Collaboration for school professionals* (2nd ed.). White Plains, NY: Longman.

Friend, M., & Cook, L. (1997). Student-centered teams in schools: Still in search of an identity. *Journal of Educational and Psychological Consultation, 8,* 3–20.

Frisby, C. L., & Lorenzo-Luaces, L. M. (2000). The structure of cultural difference judgments in a Cuban American sample. *Hispanic Journal of Behavioral Sciences, 22,* 194–222

Fuchs, D., & Fuchs, L. (1989). Mainstream assistance teams to accommodate difficult-to-teach students in general education. In J. L. Graden, J. E. Zins, & M. J. Curtis (eds.), *Alternative educational delivery systems: Enhancing instructional options for all students* (pp. 49–70). Washington, DC: National Association of School Psychologists.

Fuchs, D., Fuchs, L., & Bahr, M. (1990). Mainstream Assistance Teams: A scientific basis for the art of consultation. *Exceptional Children, 57,* 128–139.

Fueyo, V. (1997). Below the tip of the iceberg: Teaching language-minority students. *Teaching Exceptional Children, 30,* 61–65.

Garcia, G., Pearson, P., & Jiménez, R. (1990). *The at risk dilemma: A synthesis of reading research.* Champaign, IL: University of Illinois at Urbana-Champaign, Reading Research and Education Center.

Gardner, R., III, Sainato, D., Cooper, J. P., Heron, T. E., Heward, W. L., Eshleman, J., & Grossi, T. A. (Eds.). (1994). *Behavioral analysis in education: Focus on measurably superior instruction.* Monterey, CA: Brooks-Cole.

Gersten, R., & Woodward, J. (1992). The quest to translate research into classroom practice: Strategies for assisting classroom teachers' work with "at-risk" students and students with disabilities. In D. Carnine & E. Kameenui (Eds.), *Higher cognitive functioning for all students* (pp. 201–218). Austin, TX: Pro-Ed.

Ginorio, A., & Huston, M. (2001). *Si, se puede! Yes, we can—Latinas in school.* Washington, DC: American Association of University Women Educational Foundation.

Giroux, H. (1983). *Theory and resistance in education: A pedagogy for the opposition.* South Hadley, MA: Bergin & Garvey.

Giroux, H., & McLaren, P. (1986). Teacher education and the politics of engagement: The case for democratic schooling. *Harvard Educational Review, 56,* 213–238.

Glasser, W. (1990). *The quality school.* New York: Harper & Row.

Goldstein, B. S. C. (1998). Creating a context for collaborative consultation: Working across bicultural communities. *Journal of Educational and Psychological Consultation, 9,* 367–374.

Goldstein, B. (1995). Critical pedagogy in a bilingual special education classroom. *Journal of Learning Disabilities, 28*, 463–475.

Goodlad, J. I. (2002). Kudzu, rabbits, and school reform. *Phi Delta Kappan, 84*, 16–23.

Graden, J. L., Casey, A., & Christenson, S. (1985). Implementing a prereferral intervention system: Part I. The model. *Exceptional Children, 51*, 377–384.

Habel, J., Bloom, L. A., Ray, M. S., & Bacon, E. (1999). Consumer Reports: What students with behavior disorders say about school. *Remedial and Special Education, 20*, 93–105.

Harris, K. C. (1991). An expanded view on consultation competencies for educators serving culturally and linguistically diverse exceptional students. *Teacher Education and Special Education, 14*, 25–29.

Harris, K. C. (1995). School-based bilingual special education teacher assistance teams. *Remedial and Special Education, 16*, 337–343.

Harris, K. C. (1996). Collaboration within a multicultural society: Issues for consideration. *Remedial and Special Education, 17*, 355–362.

Harris, K. C. (1998). *Collaborative elementary teaching: A casebook for elementary special and general educators.* Austin, TX: PRO-ED.

Harris, K. C. (2000). Professional competencies for working with culturally and linguistically diverse students. In *Encyclopedia of Special Education* (2nd ed., pp. 1436–1438). New York: John Wiley & Sons.

Harry, B., & Anderson, M.G. (1995). The disproportionate placement of African American males in special education programs: A critique of the process. *Journal of Negro Education, 63*, 602–619.

Heron, T. E., & Harris, K. C. (2001). *The educational consultant: Helping professionals, parents, and students in inclusive classrooms* (4th ed.). Austin, TX: PRO-ED.

Houghton, S., & Bain, A. (1993). Peer tutoring with ESL and below-average readers. *Journal of Behavioral Education, 3*, 135–142.

Howard, P. (1994). *An owner's manual for the brain.* Austin, TX: Leornian Press.

Howe, K. R., & Welmer, K. G. (2002). School choice and the pressure to perform: Déjà vu for children with disabilities. *Remedial and Special Education, 23*, 212–221.

Individuals with Disabilities Education Act of 1997, P.L. 105–17.

Jensen, E. (1998). *Teaching with the brain in mind.* Alexandria, VA: Association for Supervision and Curriculum Development.

Katz, J. (1996, November 11). 1000 miles of hope, heartache: aspiring factory workers abandon desperate lives to enter human pipeline from Mexican border to poultry job in middle America. *Los Angeles Times.*

Kohl, H. R. (1969). *The open classroom.* New York: Vintage Books.

Lloyd, J. W., Forness, S. R., & Kavale, K. A. (1998). Some methods are more effective than others. *Intervention in School and Clinic, 33*, 195–200.

Lynch, E. W., & Hanson, M. J. (Eds.). (1998). *Developing cross-cultural competence* (2nd ed.). Baltimore: Paul H. Brookes.

McLaren, P. L. (1985). The ritual dimensions of resistance: Clowning and symbolic inversion. *Journal of Education, 167*, 84–97.

McLaren, P. (1993). *Schooling as a ritual performance.* New York: Routledge.

Miller, A. D., Barbetta, P., & Heron, T. E. (1994). START tutoring: Designing, training, implementing, and adapting tutoring programs for school and home settings. In R. Gardner, J. O. Cooper, T. E. Heron, W. L. Herward, J. Eshleman, & D. Sainato (Eds.), *Behavioral analysis in education: Focus on measurably superior instruction* (pp. 265–282). Monterey, CA: Brooks-Cole.

Murawski, W. W., & Swanson, M. Z. (2001). A meta-analysis of co-teaching research: Where are the data? *Remedial and Special Education, 22,* 258–267.

Nelson, J., Lott, L., & Glenn, H. S. (1997). *Positive discipline in the classroom* (2nd ed.). Rocklin, CA: Prima Pub.

Obiakor, F. E., & Utley, C. A. (1997). Rethinking preservice preparation for teachers in the learning disabilities field: working multicultural strategies. *Learning Disabilities Research and Practice, 12,* 100–106.

Ogbu, J. (1982). Cultural discontinuities and schooling. *Anthropology and Education Quarterly, 13,* 290–301.

Ortiz, A. A. (1990). Using school-based problem-solving teams for prereferral intervention. *Bilingual Special Education newsletter, 10,* 3–5.

Ortiz, A. A., & Garcia, S. B. (1995). Serving Hispanic students with learning disabilities: Recommended policies and practices. *Urban Education, 29,* 471–481.

Patton, J. M. (1998). The disproportionate representation of African-Americans in special education: Looking behind the curtain for understanding and solutions. *Journal of Special Education, 32,* 25–31.

Patton, J. M., & Edgar, E. (2002). Introduction to the special series: Special education and school reform. *Remedial and Special Education, 23,* 194.

Pugach, M. C., & Johnson, L. J. (1989). Prereferral interventions: Progress, problems, and challenges. *Exceptional children, 56,* 217–226.

Roberts, G. W., Bell, L. A., & Salend, S. J. (1991). Negotiating change for multicultural education: A consultation model. *Journal of Educational and Psychological Consultation, 2,* 323–342.

Ruiz, N. T., & Enguidanos, T. (1997). Authenticity and advocacy in assessment of bilingual students in special education. *Primary Voices, 5,* 35–46.

Salend, S. J., Dorney, J. A., & Mazo, M. (1997). The roles of bilingual special educators in creating inclusive classrooms. *Remedial and Special Education, 18,* 54–64.

Salend, S. J., Duhaney, L. M. G., & Montgomery, W. (2002). A comprehensive approach to identifying and addressing issues of disproportionate representation. *Remedial and Special Education, 23,* 289–299.

Salend, S. J., Johansen, M., Mumper, J., Chase, A. S., Pike, K. M., & Dorney, J. A. (1997). Cooperative teaching: The voices of two teachers. *Remedial and Special Education, 18,* 3–11.

Schloss, P. J., Kobza, S. A., & Alper, S. (1997). The use of peer tutoring for the acquisition of functional math skills among students with moderate retardation. *Education and Treatment of Children, 20,* 189–208.

Schumm, J. S., Vaughn, S., & Harris, J. (1997). Pyramid power for collaborative planning. *Teaching Exceptional Children, 29,* 62–66.

Shor, I. (Ed.). (1987). *Freire for the classroom: A sourcebook for liberatory teaching.* Portsmouth, NH: Boynton/Cook.

Sileo, T. W., & Prater, M. A. (1998). Creating classroom environments that address the linguistic and cultural backgrounds of students with disabilities. *Remedial and Special Education, 19,* 323–337.

Slavin, R. E. (1990). *Cooperative learning: Theory, research, and practice.* Englewood Cliffs, NJ: Prentice-Hall.

Tateyama-Sniezek, K. M. (1990). Cooperative learning: Does it improve the academic achievement of students with handicaps? *Exceptional Children, 56,* 426–437.

Tobar, H. (2001, May 16). A lotta cultures goin' on—In Elvis' town—and elsewhere in the South—Latinos and Asian are adding to the cultural mix. *Los Angeles Times.*

Tomlinson, C. A., & Allan, S. D. (2000). *Leadership for differentiating schools & classrooms.* Alexandria, VA: Association for Supervision and Curriculum Development.

Townsend, B. L. (2000). The disproportionate discipline of African American learners: Reducing school suspensions and expulsions. *Exceptional Children, 66,* 381–391.

Townsend, B. L. (2002). "Testing while Black": Standards-based school reform and African American learners. *Remedial and Special Education, 23,* 222–230.

U.S. Department of Commerce, Bureau of the Census. (1991). *Final census population counts.* Washington, DC: Government Printing Office.

U.S. Department of Education, Office for Civil Rights (1992). *1990 elementary and secondary school civil rights survey.* Washington, DC: Government Printing Office.

Vygotsky, L. (1962). *Thought and language.* Cambridge, MA: MIT Press.

Vygotsky, L. (1978). *Mind in society.* Cambridge, MA: Harvard University Press.

Walther-Thomas, C. S. (1997). Co-teaching experiences: The benefits and problems that teachers and principals report over time. *Journal of Learning Disabilities, 30,* 395–407.

Walther-Thomas, C. S., Bryant, M., & Land, S. (1996). Planning for effective co-teaching. *Remedial and Special Education, 17,* 255-Cover 3.

Willis, P. (1977). *Learning to Labour.* Farmborough, England: Saxon House.

Zhang, D., & Katsiyannis, A. (2002). Minority representation in special education—A persistent challenge. *Remedial and Special Education, 23,* 180–187.

Zins, J. E., Heron, T. E., & Goddard, Y. (1999). Secondary prevention: Applications through intervention assistance programs and inclusive education. In C. R. Reynolds & T. B. Gutkin (Eds.), *The handbook of school psychology* (3rd ed., pp. 800–821). New York: Wiley.

9

MULTICULTURAL EDUCATION PRACTICES: PRACTICAL APPLICATIONS

Angela Reyes-Carrasquillo
Fordham University

The field of multicultural education emerged as the result of the social upheavals of the1960s and the concern of many educators that there was a critical need for research-based knowledge of the socio-cultural contexts of education (Banks, 2003; Ladson-Billings, 2001; Lynch & Hanson, 1998a; Sleeter & Grant, 2003). The multicultural educational approach was very popular in the 1970s and 1980s and continued to expand as educators and policy makers began to link race, ethnicity, language, culture, gender, and disability issues toward making schools celebrate human diversity and equal educational opportunity (Nieto, 2001). Socially concerned educators have spread the beliefs that all educators should know, respect and value the cultural heritages of their students and colleagues. Likewise, all students and colleagues should have the right to know and develop pride in their own cultural heritages and be able to appreciate the cultural heritages of others. In the United States, the main rationale for this pluralistic perspective has been that the country is a racially and ethnically diverse nation, and that diversity is reflected in all educational settings, especially in schools. Census and school demographic data confirm that the school population continues to diversify and that both urban and suburban schools show a significant increase in culturally and linguistically diverse students. Presently, there are more immigrant students, more students learning English as a second language, and more students representing a diversity of ethnic backgrounds.

The data from the 2000 United States Census Bureau show the following trends about the United States population's ethnic composition: (a) a decrease of the

White/Anglo population, (b) 14% of the population is Hispanic, (c) 13% of the population is African American, (d) 5% of the population is Asian, and (e) almost 1% of the population is Native/Indian American.

Culturally and linguistically diverse (CLD) students in the United States are predominately Hispanic, Asian, or African-Americans with a significant representation of other ethnic groups (e.g., Urdu, Haitians, Bangladesh, Russians) (Carrasquillo & Rodriguez, 2002). This diversity is directly reflected in all U.S. classrooms, schools, colleges and universities. Although urban areas are the most diverse by far, suburban areas and small cities are experiencing an influx of families from diverse cultural backgrounds (U.S. Census Bureau, 2002). What does this census data and information convey to educators and policy makers? The data imply that: (a) educators at all levels need to be prepared to understand diverse students' linguistic, ethnic and academic needs; and (b) even in schools with small percentages of diverse students, the school staff and the students need to have an understanding of issues of diversity because it is this diverse society that students will encounter once they move outside their small communities. However, researchers (Cuban, 1993; Goodlad, 1984; Soto, 1997) have found that in many schools in the United States, issues related to ethnicity, race, and language are not totally integrated in all the components of the school system (school climate, curriculum, instruction, assessment practices, staffing, parental involvement).

In many instances, schools emphasize one component and ignore the other ones. Goodlad (1984), in an extensive investigation in secondary schools, found that textbooks were often a substitute for pedagogy, teaching methods tended to be mechanistic and un-engaging, memorization and rote learning were favored consistently over creativity and critical thinking. Cuban's study (1993) of teachers' pedagogical approaches over the past century concluded that teacher-centered instruction has persevered as the basic method of teaching in spite of progressive educational movements to promote student-centered approaches. Teachers control what is going on in the classroom and students have little opportunity to add in terms of concepts, skills or new ways of doing the assigned tasks. Many of the teachers in the schools that Cuban studied were not even aware of current school multicultural practices.

Multicultural education has several dimensions and domains, and there is an extensive body of theory on what constitutes its major components. This chapter will provide an overview of multicultural education in terms of the critical theoretical and conceptual issues, the most salient educational practices associated with socio-cultural and ethnic domains, and implications for practice in educational and school settings.

THEORETICAL AND RESEARCH BASIS

Multicultural education is a process of school reform that permeates (a) the climate surrounding the school, curriculum, instruction and other intervention practices; (b) the interactions among teachers, counselors, psychologists, administrators, students and parents; and (c) the way that schools conceptualize the nature of teaching and learning (Diaz, 2001; Nieto, 1999, 2001). The literature on multicultural education is extensive, and prominent authorities in the field (Banks, 1994, 1997, 2001, 2003; Diaz, 2001; Gollnick & Chinn, 1998; Ladson-Billings, 2001; Lynch & Hanson, 1998a; Nieto, 1999, 2001; Sleeter & Grant, 2003) provide educators with a wealth of insightful information on teaching, learning as well as psychological and social intervention strategies. These scholars define multicultural education within the context of various teaching and learning components.

Banks (1994, 1997, 2003), Bennett (1999), Freire (1970, 1973), Lynch and Hanson (1998a), Nieto (2001), and Sleeter and Grant (2003) provided theoretical frameworks comprising key components of multicultural education that have multiple implications for classrooms and schools. Sleeter and Grant (2003) define multicultural education as an umbrella concept that deals with educational practices related to class, culture, language, social class, sexuality and disability. They define it as an approach to describe education policies and practices that recognize, accept, and affirm human differences and similarities related to gender, race, disability, class and sexuality. Banks (1994, 1997), on the other hand, defines multicultural education as an approach to help students to develop cross-cultural competency within the American national culture, within their own subculture, and within and across different sub-societies and cultures.

Nieto (1999, 2001) focuses on ways in which educators, especially teachers, can modify their teaching in order to increase the academic achievement of students from those racial and ethnic groups that are experiencing massive failure in the nation's schools, and consequently in society. Nieto defines multicultural education as a sociopolitical context that permeates all areas of schooling and that is characterized by a commitment to social justice and critical approaches to learning. Nieto's definition comprises race, ethnicity, language, gender, social class, sexual orientation, and ability.

These definitions frame multicultural education from the perspective of individuals and systems (e.g., the school) involved in the process of developing their own unique personal identities, practices and strategies through a conscious quest to embrace people of all cultural heritages. Multicultural practices, especially those implemented in educational settings, provide the framework for group and individual transformation. Freire's (1970, 1973) work with "illiterate" adults in Brazil who were able to achieve high levels of literacy demonstrated that achievement can be attained through appropriate "transformation" and empowerment. Freire proposed the concept of "transformation" or "conscientizao" as a component of a multicultural perspective, meaning that learning is reflected in the ability to work with colleagues in collaborative and mutually supportive ways. It means challenging conventional school policies and practices so that these become more equitable and just, and it means working for changes beyond the confinements of schools.

In general, the essential goals of multicultural education are: (a) recognizing and valuing diversity, (b) developing a greater understanding of other cultural patterns, (c) respecting individuals of all cultures, and (d) developing positive and productive interactions and experiences among people of diverse cultural groups

(Diaz, 2001; Gollnick & Chinn, 1998; Lynch & Hanson, 1998a). These goals provide the framework to implement or increase effective multicultural education practices. The following section addresses key components in the implementation of multicultural practices.

Including and Integrating Cultural Content

Multicultural content provides avenues for participatory tolerance and promotes positive attitudes toward others of differing cultural backgrounds. Within this framework the goal is for students to learn to be accepting, caring, and compassionate individuals. Educators are influential agents in changing the face of the prejudiced view many students bring to schools from their homes and neighborhoods. Banks (2001) discusses several frameworks that schools use to integrate cultural content into the school and university curriculum. These approaches are:

1. *Contributions Approach*: The content about ethnic and cultural groups is limited primarily to holidays and celebrations. Examples of this approach are including Martin Luther King Day, Puerto Rican Heritage Week, and Chinese New Year into the curriculum. Although the approach provides opportunities to learn about other groups' contributions to society, these contributions are included in an isolated way.
2. *Additive Approach*: Cultural content, themes and concepts are added to the curriculum without changing its basic structure. An example of this approach is adding an appendix in a social studies text or adding readings about multicultural issues. Sometimes this new content is in contradiction to what is already in place in the basic curriculum.
3. *Transformation Approach*: This approach enables students to view concepts, issues, themes and problems from different perspectives. An example of this approach is reading two different perspectives about the arrival of Christopher Columbus to the new world.
4. *Decision Making/Social Action Approach*: Students are encouraged to pursue projects and activities that allow them to take personal, social and civic actions related to the concepts, problems, and issues they are exploring in the classroom. An example of this approach is facilitating students' presentation in a community center about racial relations within the community. For example, students are asked to interview a group of residents of a community to identify their opinions about recent immigrants and write recommendations on how to better serve the immigrant community.

Although there is little research on which approach is more prevalent, scholars in the field of multicultural education recognize that the last two approaches, transformative and decision making, are the most effective approaches in providing students with experiences to integrate cultural content and perspectives into their own lives (Gollnick & Chinn, 1998; Nieto, 2001; Sleeter & Grant, 2003). The "contributions" approach is the most simplistic one and is criticized for merely emphasizing contributions as "interesting" additions, possibly resulting in tokenism and disconnected experiences.

Several scholars go beyond this "contribution" approach and propose a "cultural responsible pedagogy" to foster trust and understanding between students and school staff, especially teachers. Erickson (1996) theorizes that this curriculum helps students to be informed and to reflect on and evaluate history, literature, public policy, mathematical content, and ethical issues. Ladson-Billings (2001) describing the findings of a qualitative, ethnographic study affirms that success for all students requires teachers to focus on students' academic achievement, the development of cultural competence and the fostering of students' sense of sociopolitical consciousness. Diaz (2001) proposes that: "A true multicultural content integrates cultural content throughout subjects and grade levels, placing new content when it is pedagogically and contextually appropriate. This infusion approach involves a review of the entire curriculum and affects all the school's faculty" (p. 2).

Students need to understand traditional, geographical, economic and political concepts (mainstream knowledge) in order to analyze global issues. However, despite demographic changes in the past four decades, Anglo-and European centered curricula prevail in most United States schools (Carrasquillo & Rodriguez, 2002). A number of educators argue that when multicultural content is taught, it is frequently presented in an ethnic-additive manner usually in special courses, and offered as an elective in the curriculum (Banks, 1994, 1997, 2003; Erickson, 1996; Nieto, 1999). These authors also add that it is equally important for students to be exposed to perspectives that sometimes challenge mainstream knowledge and the perspectives of other nations. Diaz, Massialas, and Kanthopouolos (1999) provide an example:

In teaching about slavery in the Americas, upper elementary teachers who first introduce the topic to students can point out that a variety of European nations engaged in the trans-Atlantic slave trade. They should mention the need for additional labor (relative to land) in both North and South America. They could also point out the huge profits in the slave trade as well as the economic value of labor slaves provided. (p. 69)

Banks (1994, 1997), Diaz (2001), Garcia (1993), and Nieto (1999) note that despite attempts made in schools to apply multicultural education to the curriculum, many schools and universities have a limited conceptualization of multicultural education, viewing it primarily as curriculum reform that involves changing or restructuring the curriculum to include content about ethnic groups, women, and other cultural groups rather than as an activity to change participants' actions and attitudes.

Diaz (2001) posits that although there is no unique effective teaching method to include and to integrate cultural content in the curriculum, multicultural education literature identifies a list of effective teaching practices. He describes five school curriculum strategies that integrate content and classroom management: (a) establishing teaching environments and friendships between students and teachers; (b) creating genuine partnerships with students so that they are active participants in making decisions about how their learning experiences will occur and will be evaluated; (c) changing the roles and procedures that govern life in the classroom so that they reflect some of the codes of behavior, social etiquette, and participation styles of culturally different students; (d) developing a concept of "family" to provide cohesion and focused meaning to interpersonal relations in the classroom; and (e) routinely incorporating a wide variety of multicultural images, artifacts, icons, and individuals in classroom decorations and instructional materials. Ethnically specific books, music, magazines, posters, and student-created art are valuable tools. Most multicultural education experts recommend that cultural content be present in all components of the educational settings such as the school hall, the assemblies, the staff development efforts, teaching styles, instructional approaches, and even in parents' community activities. In addition to including cultural content, these activities foster cross-cultural awareness (Cuban, 1993, Gay, 2001, Nieto, 1999).

The field of multicultural education has emphasized that there are ways of improving educators and students' cross cultural knowledge and skills. The following section discusses three cross-cultural approaches: fostering cross-cultural awareness, dialogue in multicultural education and moving from knowledge to reflection.

Fostering Cross-cultural Awareness

Cross-cultural awareness is a general understanding of the defining characteristics of world cultures with an emphasis on understanding differences and similarities (Lynch, 1998; Tye & Tye, 1992). Brislin, Cushner, Cherrie, and Yong (1986) indicated that an important component of teaching is the fostering of cross-cultural communication, one that involves the process of exchanging information between individuals from different social groups and cultures. Sending messages and understanding messages that are being received are prerequisites to effective interpersonal interactions (Lynch, 1998). The use of cross-cultural instructional strategies improves cross-cultural understandings. Brislin et al. (1986) observed that strategies that have proven to be most effective on people's knowledge, affect, and behavior, appear to be cognitive approaches that effectively engage students in connecting knowledge to their experiences and emotions. That is, "cross-cultural" training strategies that go beyond mere information and actively engage students in developing empathy or an insider's view of another culture, have a significant effect on students' perceptions and behavior. Brislin et al. argue that students need to be aware of what is appropriate and normative within other social groups, and need to avoid using their own cultural norms as "the standard" for judging behaviors within cross-cultural contexts. Lynch (1998) says that there are several characteristics that seem to be shared by people who are effective cross-cultural communicators. She says that communication effectiveness is improved when the interventionist: (a) respects individuals from other cultures, (b) makes continued and sincere attempts to understand the world from others' point of view, (c) is open to new learning, (d) is flexible, (e) has a sense of humor, (f) tolerates ambiguity well, and (g) approaches others with a desire to learn.

Fostering Dialogue in Multicultural Education

There is a body of literature indicating that learning occurs essentially in community with others (Cuban, 1993; Erickson, 1996; Freire, 1973; Gay, 2001; Goodlad,

1984; Ladson-Billings, 2001; Lynch & Hanson, 1998a; Moll, 1992). Schools are communities and, like communities, some are less or more effective than others. Similarly, each school develops a particular culture, with its own values, rituals and symbols that either welcome or reject messages to students and educators about their roles and responsibilities, talents, limitations and future prospects. A cohesive school community requires the establishment of a dialogue between parents, community representatives and school faculty. This dialogue creates trusting interpersonal relationships among all those involved (parents, teachers, counselors, psychologists, administrators) to work toward shared visions and effective decision-making processes. However, communicating about cross-cultural differences and issues is often difficult and challenging for educators and students. Olsen et al. (1994) studied 73 schools in San Francisco in the process of restructuring. They found that these schools had not acknowledged the students' diverse cultures and identities. When the research team alerted the leadership of these schools, many of them had difficulty in establishing a dialogue to discus cultural differences in their student body.

Cazden (1989) provided an illustration of how educators can make a school more receptive to its cultural community. She cited Richmond Road School in Auckland, New Zeeland. In 1989, this school had 269 students of whom 21% were Samoan, 20% were European New Zealanders, 18% were Maori, 34% were Polynesian, and 4% were Indians. Teachers, administrators and related school staff had on going meetings to change the climate and the curriculum of the school. The principal in the school was the facilitator to transform the school. Teachers worked in teams and collectively with students and staff, interacted in "systems" to promote vertical/family groupings of students, and developed and implemented interactive curriculum activities.

Freire (1973) and Nieto (1999, 2001) argue that engaging in dialogue is an important way for students to become actively engaged in school. Educators have to establish a school environment in which students come to understand their learning process as they accomplish their academic and social goals. The promotion of positive and independent interactions between teachers and students and among students, is an important school objective. Learning is facilitated by extensive interactions among educators and students and among students of different backgrounds and socioeconomic levels. Kerman (1980) found that this interaction such as questioning and debating among students contributed to improvements in students' academic performance. When educators participate in genuine dialogues with students, it facilitates learning and encourages the development of higher-level cognitive skills rather than just factual recall of information (Ladson-Billings, 2001; Lynch, 1998).

From Knowledge to Reflection

The field of education is concerned with how to prepare reflective individuals who have the capability and orientation to make informed and intelligent decisions about the bases for their actions and outcomes. Reflection is recommended for educators as well as students (Gollnick & Chinn, 1998). Reflective decision makers are intrinsically motivated to analyze situations, set goals, plan and monitor actions, and evaluate results as they work closely with others. Educators and students learn to perform new actions not solely because they "now have new information" but because they have become engaged in an active, introspective process through which they are, in some manner, transformed.

Langer and Colton (1994) propose that responsible educators should consider how their attitudes toward race, gender, ethnicity, and class influence their interpretation of the knowledge base that they impart to students. In general, within multicultural frameworks reflective teaching is associated with (a) a dynamic view of subject-matter knowledge informed by the belief that to more fully understand reality, one must develop the habit of reflecting on multiple and contradictory perspectives; (b) an interactive style of teaching that emphasizes class discussion, writing about ideas, and having students revise assignments based on their experiences and viewpoints rather than an imposed culture; and (c) a student-centered pattern of instruction that provides different students in the same class with different assignments and that encourages students' choices of assignments; and foster an environment where students can reflect about what they learned from their assignment.

IMPLICATIONS FOR PRACTICE

Education, teaching and learning involve more than creating curriculum designs and engaging classroom discourse. The physical, social, and interpersonal climate or environments created for learning are important variables in the teaching- learning process (Banks, 1997; Cazden, 1989; Ladson-Billings, 2001; Lynch & Hanson, 1998a; Nieto, 1999). These components are embedded within the goals of multicultural practices, which are: (a) the promotion of equal opportunities for every student and staff member, (b) equity among all types of students, (c) multicultural teaching and learning, (d) the integration of students' comments and input within the teaching/learning process, (e) a sense of "we" among all school individuals, and (f) opportunities for reflection about cultural diversity content and themes in the curriculum and instructional programs. In addition, multicultural practices build on students' learning styles, are adapted to students' skill levels, involve students actively in thinking and analyzing, and use a variety of learning approaches and strategies (Sleeter & Grant, 2003, Tiedt & Tiedt, 1995).

However, multicultural education does not stop with the improvement of attitudes; it seeks to develop skills and a strong knowledge base to support multiculturalism (Lynch, 1998). It seeks to change schooling, services and interventions related to curriculum, instruction, assessment, and home-school-community relationships. The following recommendations are provided as vehicles to meet the goals of multicultural education:

Recommendation 1: Schools need to restructure their curricula to reflect high expectations for all.   Curriculum is the outcome of planned and deliberated instructional decisions designed to impact students' academic and cognitive development (Nieto, 2001). In other words, curriculum is the interrelated set of plans and experiences that students undertake under the guidance of the school staff. All educators (teachers, counselors, psychologists, administrators) are directly involved in making decisions about content, teaching, and learning by constantly monitoring and adjusting the curriculum, and the instructional tasks. The most fundamental aspect in this process is that all members of the school, the school district and the community agree that, although not all students in the educational setting are at the same cognitive, achievement and linguistic level, all students must receive access to quality curricula that emphasize high academic standards (Gay, 2001). Educators must reinforce the belief that all students can achieve by conveying and communicating high expectations. One way of communicating high expectations is by engaging in equitable practices within the contexts of providing time to listen to students' responses, waiting for students' responses, and responding to students' questions. Ladson-Billings (2001) describes a Teach for Diversity program where she found that "A core of teachers are committed to child-centered pedagogy. Their classrooms reflect a more "open" approach to teaching where children make most decisions about learning. Others teach in a more traditional way. Their teaching is more directive" (p. 61). Educators' attitudes and expectations play a significant role in classrooms and all students must be provided with an equal opportunity to learn the same challenging and high-level content that the school reform movement advocates for all students (Breslin et al., 1986; Burbules & Rice, 1991; Kerman, 1980).

Recommendation 2: Schools need to restructure their curricula to reflect multicultural perspectives and practices. A multicultural curriculum should reflect the following multicultural perspectives: (a) provides content geared to develop cross- cultural competence, (b) it is organized around contributions and perspectives of diverse groups, (c) promotes critical thinking, (d) provides analysis of alternative viewpoints, (e) it is relevant to students' experiential backgrounds, (f) encourages the learning of more than one language, (g) includes international perspectives, (h) its content emphasizes similarities and differences of views and perspectives, (i) creates opportunities for students to articulate various points of view, and (j) contributes to the students' ability to think from a multicultural perspective and to interact with individuals from diverse cultural backgrounds (Sleeter & Grant, 2003, Tiedt & Tiedt, 1995). Cross-cultural competent teachers adjust their teaching to meet the demands of both the learners and the subject matter disciplines (Ladson-Billings, 2001). According to Lynch and Hanson (1998b) cross-cultural competence includes: "(a) an awareness of one's own cultural limitations, (b) openness, appreciation, and respect for cultural differences, (c) view of intercultural interactions as learning opportunities, (d) the ability to use cultural resources in interventions,, and (e) an acknowledgment of the integrity and value of all cultures" (p. 493).

A multicultural curriculum helps all students to understand themselves, to define their strengths and their concerns, and to empower themselves to critically encounter their own personal and social realities (Brislin et al., 1986; Burbules & Rice, 1991). This is a task each student must begin to enact in childhood and practice in adolescence in order to empower themselves as they interpret and evaluate their own experiences. The task can be integrated and effectively achieved within the intellectual mission of the school. One way to do this is to encourage students to interpret and critically evaluate the texts that they read and to openly and actively discuss multicultural issues in class (Erickson, 1996; Nelson, 1995). Each student needs to be able to explore the boundaries of his/her intellectual strengths and

weaknesses and to explore the social boundaries they encounter within and outside of schools (e.g., community).

An important function of schooling is to broaden students' individual experiences and to help them develop sustained and deliberate attention to topics and activities that make learning possible (Cazden, 1996; Nelson, 1995). It is important for
the school curriculum and the delivery of instruction to be exciting and challenging. Also valuable are opportunities for students to feel successful and recognized
for their accomplishments. The curriculum must also go beyond examining artifacts and holidays, and fostering a superficial knowledge base of the multicultural
content. A recommended approach is to guide students through learning experiences that increase their cultural awareness, immerse them in a variety of cross-cultural experiences, foster opportunities to examine issues and events from diverse
perspectives, and encourage students to engage in assignments that allow them to
take actions about issues they have learned (e.g., writing a letter to congressman
about community issues).

Instructional programs must insure appropriate applications of general effective principles of teaching and learning for all students (Nelson, 1995, Sleeter &
Grant, 2003). If a school has a significant number of language minority students,
the school and the district need to address their curriculum needs and identify their
strengths. Addressing the needs of CLD students calls for a deeper understanding
of the interactions between students' cultures and languages, and the curriculum.
A deeper understanding of these interactions will help educators to provide curricula and classroom settings appropriate to all students' discourse patterns, non-verbal communication styles, socialization skills, cultural traits, and learning styles
(Garcia, 1993; Ladson-Billings, 2001; Lynch, 1998). Providing a quality curriculum;
delivering instruction to students according to their needs, characteristics, and
strengths; and providing necessary specialized services are all ingredients that
must be available to all students. If college preparatory classes are offered, CLD
students as well as students with disabilities should be encouraged to apply and
participate. It means that curriculum content, activities, resources, and evaluation
procedures should always be offered to all students and across all domains of the
subject areas.

*Recommendation 3: Multicultural instruction should foster cross-cultural com-
munication.*   Cross-cultural communication is enhanced when emphasis is
"placed on understanding one's own culture and heritage, learning culture-specific information about the families in their interventionist's community,
and developing strategies to improve cross cultural communication" (Lynch, 1998,
p. 83). Self-awareness is a beginning point moving toward learning culture-specific
information and practicing new communication strategies. But as Lynch (1998) recommends, people -oriented skills are better learned within a group, and she suggests that "having cross-cultural friends and colleagues who are willing to answer
questions and who are able to provide feedback, and with whom one can practice,
can only improve the learning experience" (p. 83).

One recommended strategy to improve cross-cultural communication *is* the
provision of multicultural curricula and instructional framework classroom settings where students demonstrate and share diverse discourse patterns, non-verbal communication patterns, socialization preferences, cultural traits, and learning

styles (Garcia, 1993). Multicultural instruction fosters cross-cultural communication by: (a) building on students' learning strengths, (b) building on students' learning styles, (c) incorporating students' voices, (d) helping students discover their own particular style of learning, (e) promoting positive classroom dialogue and communication, (f) identifying and working around students' learning preferences and styles of learning, and (g) establishing an ongoing process of reflection, renewal and growth (Lynch, 1998; Nieto, 2001; Tiedt & Tiedt, 1995). Other recommended strategies include working with families through acknowledging and respecting cultural differences rather than minimizing them. When educators do not share the same language of the families, effective interpreters and or translators are recommended (Lynch, 1998). But interpreters and translators need preparation as well as training.

Recommendation 4: Multicultural/cross-cultural competencies should not exist in isolation of subject matter and pedagogical knowledge. The school staff patterns should reflect culturally diverse and nonsexist roles, and multicultural professionals are visible as administrators, teachers, teacher assistants, counselors, psychologists, social workers as well as aides and custodians. They communicate and work together on professional decisions and curricular implementations. They also provide feedback to each other in adapting instruction to students' needs.

Academic and pedagogical knowledge are required foundations for teachers and support personnel as they craft ways to frame and link knowledge to students' experiences, backgrounds, and interests. Educators, especially teachers require personal growth and change (Lynch & Hanson, 1998b). This process of change and growth leads to insights regarding attitudes and behaviors that can help to reframe practice. Teachers and support personnel who are willing to devote time and energy to reflect on their values and beliefs, and acquire new skills, knowledge, and perspectives can increase their multicultural competencies. The process involves self-examination, insight, and developing a plan to reach multicultural knowledge. Increased self-awareness helps educators to discover unknown prejudices that can have subtle but pervasive effects on intercultural interactions (Lynch & Hanson, 1998a). This self-awareness is a key element in the development of cross-cultural competencies. An essential element in the effective implementation of cross-cultural competencies is an appropriate intervention process. Curriculum is training a multicultural staff. The quality of multicultural schools depends on the adults who work daily within the educational setting. Effective schools are characterized by (a) staffing patterns that reflect pluralistic strategies and interventions, (b) high expectations for all students, and (c) school staff that promote respect and cooperation among all members of the school.

All educators need to be cross-culturally competent to be able to work successfully with students from diverse populations and to help students from all groups acquire the skills, knowledge, and attitudes needed to function effectively in a pluralistic society. Educators with multicultural competencies reflect the following behaviors: (a) a clear understanding of how their values and beliefs influence their teaching or professional activities; (b) mastery of an identifiable body of knowledge, and skills that constitute critical attributes of multicultural learning and teaching; (c) model reflective practices based on life experiences as well as multicultural knowledge and skills; (d) welcome opportunities/experiences to work with students and colleagues from diverse populations; and (e) establish an ongoing process of reflection, renewal and growth.

Educators' attitudes are very significant factors in the success or failure of multicultural education. All school staff needs to develop and foster a positive self-concept among students, and need to have high and realistic expectations for all students. Staff members who feel enabled to succeed with students are more committed and thus more effective than those who feel unsupported in their teaching and in their practices (Banks, 2003, Hollins & Spencer, 1990). Those staff members who have access to professional networks, enriched professional roles, and collegial work feel supported in their teaching. They feel more efficacious in gaining the knowledge they need to meet the needs of their students and they are more positive about staying in their professions (Bennett, 1999). Darling-Hammond (1998) suggests that teachers who are provided with opportunities for shared decision making have more rigorous graduation standards, perform instruction based on appropriate assessment practices, place emphasis on in-depth understanding rather than on superficial content coverage and are able to connect classroom practices with students' home experiences.

Teachers and support staff have many factors to consider when planning and delivering instructional interventions. For example, they must consider their own philosophy of education (e.g., child-centered, teacher-centered, constructivist); they have to decide the content to be taught, and how this content will be organized and presented; they have to choose the strategies and the materials needed to present the content. All school staff involved in providing instruction and specialized interventions to students must have background knowledge in how students learn, how to motivate them, and how to promote critical thinking, and cross-cultural understanding. They must be able to reflect on the learning processes occurring in the classroom and the goals and objectives they have identified for their students. Educators must be knowledgeable about multicultural practices and how to integrate everyone into the process of learning. Successful educators, especially teachers, are those with "deep personal commitment" to their subject area; they have clear instructional objectives and goals; they create environments that encourage interactions and mutual exchanges (Carrasquillo & Rodriguez, 2002; Ladson-Billings, 2001; Lynch, 1998). Overall, teaching requires culturally relevant pedagogical knowledge, a deep understanding of the content area, and a fund of instructional interventions.

There is evidence suggesting that students' positive identifications with teachers and other support staff promotes learning. Hollins and Spencer (1990) found that young African American students identified their favorite teachers as those who had positive interactions with them and who acknowledged aspects of their lives outside of the classroom. Such positive interactions and identification patterns may help students define schools as places that can provide them with positive academic and cultural identities. There is a need for teachers, counselors, and psychologists to forge deep and meaningful relationships with their CLD students. In order to develop meaningful relationships with their students, educators need to first transform their own attitudes and beliefs about their students.

Recommendation 5: Multicultural curriculum should bring the community to the school and the school to the community. Multicultural practices provide opportunities for schools to maintain strong relationships with parents and the community. There is evidence suggesting that parents are an important influence on children's academic development, and parents' involvement in educational activities positively affects students' achievement (Bermúdez & Marquez, 1996; Sanders, Allen-Jones, & Abel, 2002). The research supports parental involvement as an important contributor to children's academic achievement (Bermúdez & Marquez, 1996; Epstein, 2001; Sanders, Allen-Jones, & Abel, 2002). Parents' active participation in their children's learning and schooling has long-term benefits such as: (a) children's academic outcomes are much more effective if families are directly involved in those efforts; (b) the more parents know about what is going on in their children's schools, and the more active participants they become, the more effective they will be in helping their children to become successful learners; and (c) in general, children whose parents are involved in their learning do better in school, and they stay in school longer than those children of uninvolved parents.

Parents are natural advocates for their children, and yet, may not know when and how to get involved. Schools need to view CLD parents as concerned individuals who are able to contribute to the improvement of their children's education. Recent education reforms by the U.S. Department of Education, such as the No Child Left Behind Act (2001) stress the important role of parental participation in children's schooling. Family involvement efforts are most successful when educators and schools assume that all parents want to do their best for their children and can make important contributions to their children's education (Carrasquillo & London, 1993; Bermúdez & Marquez, 1996). Taking an approach that identifies and builds on family strengths and resources helps educators to encourage parent participation, especially from those parents who may seem uninvolved. In addition, educators need to understand that there are barriers to parental and community involvement due to poverty, financial and employment constraints. However, it is up to the school to develop a systematic plan for involving parents and the community; schools cannot wait for parents to initiate the collaboration. A multicultural curriculum may be a way to bridge positive interactions with CLD parents by reflecting multicultural diversity, inviting community participation, and encouraging cross-cultural encounters (Lunenburg & Irby, 2002).

Educators, and especially teachers, counselors and psychologists, should make special efforts to open up communication with parents, encouraging them to take an active interest in their children's schoolwork and progress. Federal education programs and policies specify the involvement of families in children's education. For instance, federal law mandates that parents of special education students be involved in developing an Individual Educational Plan (IEP) with teachers and other school and professional personnel. Title I funds aimed at helping low achieving children meet challenging academic standards require schools to develop effective family involvement programs that include agreements of shared responsibility developed collaboratively with parents (No Child Left Behind Act, 2001). These agreements describe school goals for student achievement, outline each stake holder's role in achieving these goals, and require effective communication between the school personnel and parents. Because parents are part of the community, attracting parents is the first step to welcoming other members of the community. Community members should be invited to be part of the school advisory board as presenters of multicultural topics as well as financial advisers and planners.

IMPLEMENTATION AND APPROACHES

As students learn to negotiate a multicultural world they will also face the challenge of actualizing democratic values in a pluralistic society. Students and educators will need to be prepared to respond to these new challenges. Multicultural education prepares educators and students to live in a multicultural society and to better understand their own culture and others' cultures. Lynch and Hanson (1998b) recommend the creation of a culturally appropriate intervention process to foster and develop cross-cultural competence. Their model includes planning, implementation, monitoring and evaluation and can be use by classroom teaches as well as psychologists or counselors. A brief description of the model follows:

Family-Professional Collaboration

It is an exchange if information about the group represented in one's community. It includes the collection and analysis of information regarding each family's cultural community, determination of the degree to which each family operates transculturally, and examination of each family's orientation to issues of child rearing.

Data Gathering and Assessment

The information collected in the fist step of the intervention is organized and analyzed. This analysis ensures that the assessment process is family focused and conducted in a manner desired by families.

Implementation of the Intervention.   The family and other members of the team formulate goals, objective and practices for each child/youth. The outlined program fits into the cultural community that it serves. The implementation relates to all members involved, making adjustments, if necessary.

Monitoring and Evaluation of the Interventions.   It includes the regular assessment of the practices implemented and the evaluation of the services provided to each child/youth and family. The described approach lists steps, activities and skills for educators to reach cross-cultural competence, including awareness, knowledge and skills.

Other researchers (Diaz, 2001; Cushner, McClelland, & Safford, 1992; Nieto, 1999) have identified more specific areas, such as curriculum and instructional materials. In addition, they have identified four stages of instruction that can guide educators as they plan for students' multicultural experiences:

1. Level 1: Provide individuals with knowledge of a new cultural concept or event (e.g., a holiday, cultural celebrations).
2. Level 2: Students are encouraged to compare and contrast the cultural characteristics to that of their own culture.
3. Level 3: Individuals are engaged in explaining the specific cultural elements that they are studying.
4. Level 4: Full cultural immersion provides learners with an opportunity to know the culture from an inside point of view.

These instructional levels imply that educators need to make efforts to provide students with the strategies and experiences they need to learn from the cultural perspectives of other groups so that all students might be better equipped to comprehend alternative and diverse definitions of their social environments (Diaz, Massialas, & Kanthopouolos, 1999; Gollnick & Chinn, 1998, Lynch & Hanson, 1998a). Furthermore, Nieto (1999) and Kerman (1980) propose that cross-cultural competence is accomplished when the school curriculum presents diverse perspectives, experiences, and contributions. Recognition of cultural values is of primary importance in the process of students' self-conceptualizations and in their understanding of the multiple roles they play both in and out of school.

As educators plan and deliver a multicultural curriculum, thought must also be given to curriculum materials. Instructional and assessment materials and all visual displays need to be free of stereotypes and biases, especially those associated with race, gender and disability issues and should include members of all groups in a positive manner (Gay, 2001, Gollnick & Chinn, 1998). Textbooks play an important role in the development of a basic multicultural curriculum. Gollnick and Chinn (1998) identified six types of bias in educational materials:

1. *Fragmentation:* the separation of information about different groups, which often results in a lack of clarity and disconnected concepts.
2. *Imbalance:* the overrepresentation of members of one cultural group in comparison to other groups.
3. *Invisibility:* the absence of members of various groups.
4. *Language:* the use of stereotyped representations of speech or gender-biased terms.
5. *Stereotyping:* presentation of individuals in accordance with over-generalized attributes or traditional roles.
6. *Unreality:* unrealistic portrayal of history and contemporary life experiences.

Educators are encouraged to carefully evaluate texts and teaching materials to identify tools that are nonbiased and provide diverse multicultural perspectives. Teaching must reflect the experiences, contributions, lifestyles and learning styles of a wide variety of ethnic groups by presenting a realistic portrayal of history. Monroe (2002), for example, discusses Disney's image of Pocahontas as "perpetuating an inaccurate, stereotypical and generic image: a playful, childlike and naive female protagonist whose character development is limited to her relationship to the natural world and her subordination to males' figures. She is portrayed as a provocative and physically attractive young woman who is willing to sacrifice her life for a European male" (p. 103). In contrast to the Disney version, Brandt's (1992) *Grandmothers of a New World* depicts Pocahontas as a strong image of diplomacy, political finesse, literacy and spiritual prowess. Her father sent Pocahontas on varying missions to other Nations. Serving as a spokeswoman for the Algonquian Confederacy, she arranged new trade arrangements, cemented old friendships, and built new ones. Pocahontas was a skilled orator and a politician. In a multicultural education program, the portrayal of Pocahontas by Disney and Brandt can be part of the school instruction by allowing students to read and discuss both representations and ultimately draw their own conclusions.

IMPLICATIONS FOR FUTURE RESEARCH AND PRACTICE

Multicultural education/cross-cultural practices should permeate all components of the school, and it should be directed toward educators, all students from both the dominant and minority cultures as well as their parents. It is important for students in a multicultural setting as well as those in homogeneous settings to develop a cross-cultural perspective. Multicultural education helps students to affirm their identity, it embraces collective heritages, and it strives for equity and justice. Multicultural education teaches that in embracing diversity, individuals are also embracing humanity. Multicultural education is most effective when delivered by a diverse cadre of educators who are well-trained in multicultural curriculum approaches (Diaz, 2001, Nieto, 2001). Since educators, parents and students are cultural beings, certain behaviors, attitudes and perspectives they exhibit may become barriers in their quest to learn about others. However, knowledge of these potential obstacles and attention to educating ourselves and others about multicultural perspectives and practices will help to eliminate cultural conflicts and to encourage effective intercultural interactions.

For multicultural education to succeed, it must have the support of all educators and needs a continued collegial dialogue through scholarship, reflection and implementation. This collegial spirit is particularly important within a multicultural education framework so that educators from diverse backgrounds can collaborate to create a multicultural curriculum and a school culture that promotes cross-cultural interactions.

For multicultural education to move beyond its current stage in American education, it is imperative that educators understand the strength it brings to the curriculum. However, we must also acknowledge the challenges that lie ahead in implementing multicultural/cross-cultural education frameworks. Educators often expect all students to learn via similar strategies and to demonstrate similarities in their cognitive processes, as well as in their patterns of achievement and behaviors. However, diversity (whether it is cultural, racial, cognitive, ethnic, or linguistic) among learners means that educators cannot consider the entire class as a homogeneous group of learners who need the same educational experiences.

Another challenge we face is providing educators with training opportunities to acquire the knowledge and skills they need to create multicultural education programs. Although single workshops and conferences or in-service meetings are helpful, these strategies are not enough to support sustained multicultural inquiry, reflection and culturally-relevant pedagogy (Cazden, 1989; Gay, 2001; Lynch & Hanson, 1998a). Educators need incentives and rewards to learn; they need to exchange their ideas with innovative colleagues, and to practice and receive coaching on multicultural education approaches. They also need to reflect on the process and implications of changing their practices (Lynch, 1998; Nelson, 1995). Promising approaches for teacher development tend to foster professional networks in study groups or other forms of learning communities. Educators can learn a common language and develop collegial relationships that support ongoing dialogue within learning communities. Sustained dialogue about subject matter, teaching, instructional interventions and learning permits educators to develop new ideas, exchange resources, reflect on problems, and celebrate accomplishments (McDonald & Klein, 2003).

Today's complex, interdependent world demands that individuals, especially educators, are able to work with a diversity of people to solve their own and the world's problems. Because the 21st century is an era of greater communication linkages, we have access to technological resources such as the World Wide Web that can provide numerous experiences and sources of information about multicultural issues. Today, almost every school is electronically connected to the Internet as an informational tool. Educators should take advantage of this technology to become multicultural competent and be able to guide students and parents to become multiculturally proficient too.

Although there is a strong theoretical foundation to build implications and application for learning, teaching, assessment and interventions, there are few studies validating theories on multicultural education. Action research provides a useful research methodology in which researchers can hypothesize on behaviors or actions observed within school contexts. Participatory research paradigms are also useful in exploring multicultural education frameworks in school settings. It is necessary to move from theoretical interpretations to research paradigms that will help us to achieve (a) rigorous multicultural/cross-cultural curricula, (b) collaborative relationships across cross-cultural contexts, (c) effective instructional strategies, (d) CLD students' success in academic areas, and (e) strong home-school-community partnerships.

In writing this chapter, the author found that although the literature on the topic of multicultural education is extensive, most of these publications are mainly theoretical. Therefore, there is a need for research to validate and test all these theories and assumptions on multicultural practices. The following four areas are in need of additional empirical evidence: (a) additional research showing that parental involvement is effective in multicultural settings, (b) research on the cross-cultural competencies of effective teachers, (c) reflective multicultural/cross-cultural teaching, and (d) relationship between cross-cultural teaching and students' academic achievement.

ANNOTATED BIBLIOGRAPHY

Brown, J. E., & Stephen, E. (1998). *United in diversity*. Urbana, ILL: National Council of Teachers of English.

It presents a collection of materials in which writers discuss their work in multicultural education. The book has a resource section and provides practical ideas to use in literature and language arts classes.

Hernandez Sheets, R. (2005). *Diversity pedagogy: Examining the role of culture in the teaching-learning process*. Needham, MA: Allyn & Bacon

This book demonstrates and explains the interconnectedness of culture and cognition to the teaching-learning process. The author introduces a new theory—diversity pedagogy—constructs that provide explicit applications to practice by presenting examples of real-life classroom situations throughout, ultimately unifying schooling, culture, and psychology.

Ladson-Billings, G. (2001). *Crossing over to Canaan: The journey of new teachers in diverse classrooms*. San Francisco, CA: Jossey-Bass.

Throughout the book, Ladson-Billings gives narrative accounts about the eight participants in a teacher education program and how they learn to be aware of different students' cultures, focus on academics in the classroom, and of the influence of the outside world on their students.

Schultz, F. (2004). *Annual editions: Multicultural education*. New York: McGraw-Hill.

Part of a series of over seventy-five volumes, each one designed to provide selected articles from magazines, newspapers and journals providing perspectives on topics of multicultural education.

RESOURCES

Center for Multicultural Education:
http://depts.washington.edu/centerme/home.htm.

The Center's goals are to focus on research and on improving multicultural practices.

Classroom Connect website:
http://www.classroom.net

A Web 1ist for K–12 educators and students with links to schools, teachers, and resources online. It includes a discussion of the issue of technology in the classroom.

Global School Net Foundation website:
http://www.globalschoolnet.org/index.html

This site has multicultural education information. It includes news for teachers, students and parents, links to educational resources and programs.

National Parent Information Network/ERIC website:
http://npin.org

This is a clearinghouse of information in education for parents and for people who work with parents.

National Association of Multicultural Education:
www.nameorg.org.

An organization for individuals from diverse fields and disciplines. Resources includes materials for educators, students, and parents. The organization also hosts various conferences.

REFERENCES

Banks, J. A. (1994). *Multicultural education: Theory and practice*. Boston: Allyn & Bacon.

Banks, J. A. (1997). Multicultural education: Characteristics and goals. In J. A. Banks & C. A. McGee Banks (Eds.), *Multicultural education: Issues and perspectives* (pp. 1–31). Boston: Allyn & Bacon.

Banks, J. A. (2001). Multicultural education: Goals, possibilities, and challenges. In C. F. Diaz (Ed.), *Multicultural education in the 21st century* (pp.11–22). New York: Longman.

Banks, J. A. (2003). *Teaching strategies for ethnic studies*. New York: Allyn & Bacon.

Bennett, C. I. (1999). *Comprehensive multicultural education* (4th ed.). Boston: Allyn & Bacon.

Bermúdez, A., & Marquez, J. (1996). An examination of a four-way collaborative to increase parental involvement in the schools. *Journal of Educational Issues of Minority Students, 16*, 1–16.

Brislin, R., Cushner, K., Cherrie, C., & Yong, M. (1986). *Understanding culture's influence and behavior*. Forth Worth: Harcourt Brace Jovanovich.

Brandt, B. (1992). Grandmothers of a new world. In B. Slapin & D. Searle (Eds.), *Through Indian eyes* (pp. 102–1130). Philadelphia: New Society.

Burbules, N. C., & Rice, S. (1991). Dialogue across differences: Continuing the conversation. *Harvard Educational Review, 61*, 393–416.

Carrasquillo, A., & London, C. (1993). *Parents and schools*. New York: Garland.

Carrasquillo, A. Rodriguez, V. (2002). *Language minority students in the mainstream classroom*. Clevedon, England: Multilingual Matters

Cazden, C. B. (1989). Richmond Road: A multilingual multicultural primary school in Auckland, New Zeeland. *Language Education, 3*, 143–166.

Cuban, L. (1993). *How teachers taught: Constancy and change in American classrooms: 1880–1990* (2nd ed.). New York: Teachers College Press.

Cushner, K., McClelland, K., & Safford, P. (1992). *Human diversity in education*. New York: McGraw-Hill.

Darling-Hammond, L. (1998).The quiet revolution: Rethinking teacher development. In R. Bernhardt, C. N. Hedley, G. Cattaro, & V. Svolopoulos (Eds.), *Curriculum leadership: Rethinking schools for the 21st century* (pp. 9–19). Cresskill, NJ: Hampton Press..

Diaz, C. F. (2001). *Multicultural education in the 21st century*. New York: Longman.

Diaz, C. F., Massialas, B. G., & Kanthopoulos, J. A. (1999). *Global perspectives for educators*. Boston: Allyn & Bacon.

Epstein, J. L. (2001). *School, family, and community partnerships: Preparing educators and involving schools*. Boulder, CO: Westview Press.

Erickson, F. (1996). Transformation and school success: The politics and culture of educational achievement. In E. Jacob & G. C. Jordan, (Eds.), *Minority education: Anthropological perspectives* (pp. 27–52). Norwood, NJ: Ablex.

Freire, P. (1970). *Pedagogy of the oppressed*. New York: Seabury.

Freire, P. (1973). *Education for critical consciousness*. New York: Continuum.

Garcia, E. E. (1993). Language, culture and education. In L. Darling-Hammond (Ed.), *Review of research in education* (pp. 51–98). Washington, DC: American Educational Research Association.

Gay, G. (2001). Effective multicultural practices. In C. F. Diaz (Ed.), *Multicultural education in the 21st century.* (pp. 23–41). New York: Macmillan.

Goodlad, J. I. (1984). *A place called school*. New York: McGraw-Hill.

Gollnick, P. C., & Chinn, D. M. (1998). *Multicultural education in a pluralistic society*. Upper Saddle River, NJ: Merrill-Prentice Hall.

Hollins, E. R., & Spencer, K. (1990). Reconstructing school for cultural inclusion: Changing the school process for African American youngsters. *Journal of Education, 172,* 89–100.

Kerman, S. (1980). *Teacher expectations and student achievement*. Downey, CA: Office of Los Angels County Superintendent of Schools.

Ladson-Billings, G. (2001). *Crossing over to Canaan: The journey of new teachers in diverse classrooms*. San Francisco, CA: Jossey-Bass.

Lunenburg, F. C. & Irby, B. J. (2002, August). *Parent involvement: A key to student achievement.* Paper presented at the annual meting of the National Council of Professors of Educational Administration, Burlington, VT.

Lynch, E. W. (1998). Developing cross-cultural competence. In E. W. Lynch & M.. L. Hanson. *Developing cross-cultural competence* (pp. 47–86). Baltimore, MD: Jossey Bass.

Lynch, E. W. & Hanson, M. L. (Eds.). (1998a). *Developing cross-cultural competence*. Baltimore, MD: Jossey Bass.

Lynch, E. W. & Hanson, M. L. (Eds.). (1998b). Steps in the right direction. In E. W. Lynch & M.. L. Hanson. *Developing cross-cultural competence* (pp. 491–512). Baltimore, MD: Jossey Bass.

Langer, J. A., & Colton, A. B. (1994). Reflective decision making: The cornerstone of school reform. *Journal of Staff Development, 15,* 1–7.

McDonald, J. P. & Klein, E, J. (2003). Networking for Teacher Learning: Toward a Theory of Effective Design. *Teachers College Record, 105*(8), 1606–1621.

Moll, Z. L. D. (1992). Bilingual classroom studies and community analysis: Some recent trends. *Educational Researcher, 2,* 20–24.

Monroe, S. S. (2002). Beyond Pocahontas: Authentic images of Native American females in children's literature. In F. Schultz (Ed.), *Annual editions: Multicultural education* (pp. 102–107). New York: McGraw-Hill.

Nieto, S. (1999). *The light in their eyes: Creating multicultural learning communities*. New York: Teachers College Press.

Nieto, S. (2001). *Affirming diversity* (3rd ed.). New York: Longman.

Nelson, B. S. (1995). *Inquiry and the development of teaching*. Newton, MA: Center for the Development of Teaching.

No Child Left Behind Act (2001). PL 107–110 United States at Large.

Olsen, L., Chang, H., De la Rosa Salazar, D., Leong, C., Perez, Z., McClain, G., & Raffel, L. (1994). *The unfinished journey: Restructuring schools in a diverse society*. San Francisco, CA: California Tomorrow.

Sanders, M. G., Allen-Jones, G. L. & Abel, Y. (2002). Involving families and communities in the education of children and youth placed at risk. In S. Springfield & D. Land, (Eds.), Educating at-risk students (pp. 171–188). Chicago, Il: National Society for the Study of Education.

Sleeter, C. E., & Grant, C. A. (2003). *Making choices for multicultural education: Five approaches of race, class and gender.* Boston: Jossey-Bass.

Soto, L. E. (1997). *Language, culture and power,* New York: State University of New York Press.

Tiedt, P. I., & Tiedt, I. L. (1995). *Multicultural teaching: A handbook of activities, information and resources* (4th ed.). Boston: Allyn & Bacon.

Tye, B., & Tye, K. (1992). *Global education: A study for school change.* Albany, NY: State University of New York.

U.S. Census Bureau. (2002). *Population profiles of the United States.* Washington, DC: United States Government Printing Office.

10

BILINGUAL EDUCATION PRACTICES

Nancy Cloud
Rhode Island College

School psychologists and related service personnel are called upon to determine whether students would benefit from instruction or other services provided in their native languages. In addition, these professionals are expected to be able to provide comprehensive information about bilingual programs and services to those students' parents. In order to communicate effectively with parents, school psychologists and related professionals must develop an understanding of bilingual education programs and practices. This chapter was designed to meet those needs. The chapter considers the factors that enter into instructional decisions and outlines the developmental, linguistic, psychological, and educational rationales for the use and development of the native language in instruction or to support other learner goals.

In thinking about bilingual education practices, it is important to distinguish between the delivery of a full bilingual program and the delivery of individual services. Full programs typically extend over a number of years and are designed to foster language and literacy development, academic subject matter learning and to support the social and emotional development of children in two languages. Individual bilingual services (e.g., speech and language services, parental outreach services) may be offered in conjunction with such a full day bilingual education program or may be offered as stand-alone services. School psychologists and related service personnel will want to consider both the full program and the individual services options in planning for the needs of individual children and their families.

Because personnel availability and other factors may limit bilingual services and programs, school psychologists and other service providers will also want to understand the characteristics of the children who are most in need of native language support. While developing the linguistic abilities and cross-cultural skills of all learners through bilingual programming is a worthwhile educational objective, scarcity of resources may require service providers to consider placement procedures that offer these services first to the children who need them most. Those children would include language minority children with underdeveloped native language skills (e.g., children who do not score at a proficient level in either language); young children in need of native language enrichment (e.g., Head Start candidates); and children with language delays/disorders in their native language. Children, who for psychosocial reasons, would benefit from strengthening their cultural identity and linguistic skills before transitioning to the all-English classroom are also a priority.

This chapter provides the theoretical and research basis for the use of the native language in educational contexts and a summary of the positions of professional associations that endorse native language use. The primary models of bilingual instruction are described in order to frame a discussion of program and service delivery options and highlight implementation issues such as the characteristics of effective bilingual programs, parental concerns about bilingual programming, models of language use within bilingual programs, and research-based practices that promote bilingual competence. The chapter closes with implications for future research and practice, focusing on bilingual education's potential for building the capacity of citizens to respond to the demands of international interdependence and globalization in all spheres of life.

THEORETICAL AND RESEARCH BASIS

Benefits of Bilingualism and of Native Language Support

The benefits of bilingualism have been documented in five areas: (a) personal (i.e., developing identity/self concept); (b) social (i.e., maintaining strong relationships with family and community), (c) intellectual (i.e.,insuring the child's uninterrupted cognitive development), (d) educational (i.e, strengthening and utilizing the native language to insure academic success), and (f) economic (i.e., widening employment opportunities in a worldwide marketplace) (National Clearinghouse for English Language Acquisition and Language Instruction Educational Programs, 1996).

While the development of full bilingualism and biliteracy is not mandated by law, the use of the native language is either required or permitted in many states (e.g., Rhode Island, New York) to ensure instructional effectiveness when students' proficiency in English is limited (New York State Education Department, 2003; Rhode Island Department of Elementary and Secondary Education, 2000). Additionally, in order to ensure nondiscriminatory assessment, the native language of the student is required if assessment in English would not produce valid or reliable results (American Psychological Association, 1999; IDEA, 1997; National Association of School Psychologists, 1994). Thus, the native language is viewed as beneficial to the educational process and the development of proficient bilingualism as a worthwhile educational goal.

Justification for Instructional Use of the Native Language

The importance of the development of bilingual, biliterate individuals can be argued on two levels. On a societal level, the development of a linguistically and cross-culturally competent citizenry is essential in a world characterized by international economic and social interdependence (Genesee & Cloud, 1998). On an individual child level, three major arguments are advanced to justify the use and development of the native language in instruction or to support other learning goals: (a) a developmental and educational rationale, (b) a linguistic rationale, and (c) a psychological rationale.

Developmental and educational rationale. Many proponents of bilingual instruction (e.g., Baker, 2001; Cummins, 1986) argue that it makes sense in strictly developmental terms. For language minority students enrolled in a bilingual program, the program provides an opportunity to continue the development of the first language rather than curtail or restrict it. Students can also make use of knowledge and experience provided by the primary cultural group to enhance learning (e.g., in the culturally and experientially-based examples used to support the learning of new concepts), rather than have their backgrounds be viewed as "deficient" because they have not had the same experiences as the dominant group. When students receive primary academic instruction in their home language while they learn English, they attain greater academic success than when they try to learn challenging academic material in a new language they have not yet mastered (Genesee & Cloud, 1998; Thomas & Collier, 1998). Students do not have to lose precious instructional time, finding "their classroom experiences wholly incomprehensible and in no way meaningful" (Lau v. Nichols, 1974), for they have access to learning through the vehicles provided through the primary cultural transmission process. In short, in additive bilingual programs, language minority children can use their primary language and culture as vehicles to support their learning, rather than having these assets become barriers to learning. The research shows that the more the native language is academically supported in combination with balanced second language development, the higher language minority students are able to achieve academically in the long run and the sooner they acquire the academic language proficiency to do so, as compared to those instructed only in the second language (Collier & Thomas, 1999; National Clearinghouse for English Language Acquisition and Language Instruction Educational Programs [NCELA], 1995; Ramirez, Yuen, & Ramey, 1991; Thomas & Collier, 1998).

For language majority and minority students alike, when there is an opportunity to begin the development of a second language at an early age, the research shows that cognitive development is enhanced (Diaz, 1983; Latham, 1998). The experience of developing two languages is positively related to cognitive development. In an article summarizing research Latham (1998) iscusses the advantages of bilingualism, more specifically the relationship between proficient bilingualism and cognitive development (Cataldi, 1994; Diaz, 1985). Latham concludes that: "Most researchers believe that knowing two languages and perspectives gives bilingual children a more diversified and flexible basis for cognition than their monolingual peers have" (p. 79). Proficient dual language development has been shown to enhance mental flexibility, superiority in concept formation, and a more diversified set of mental abilities (Cataldi, 1994). For example, truly bilingual students outperform their monolingual peers on several verbal and nonverbal tests of intelligence (Bialystok & Hakuta, 1994; Diaz, 1983). While researchers are still working to understand the exact nature and extent of the relationship, it is clear that the development of two languages to proficient levels benefits learners; certainly it does not detract from or interfere with cognitive functioning as was previously thought.

Linguistic rationale.   Because cognitive and linguistic development is so intimately intertwined, a portion of the linguistic rationale has already been made in the previous section. However, there are other linguistic justifications that further strengthen the argument for bilingual instruction. First, students with well developed native languages experience greater success in learning English (Cummins, 1986; Riches & Genesee, 2006; Genesee, Lindholm-Leary, Saunders, & Christian, 2005; Genesee, Paradis, & Crago, 2004). The learning of another language enhances children's understanding of their native language, its structure and other features. This metalinguistic awareness serves as a critical component in the development of intelligence (Diaz, 1983) and contributes positively to learning languages. Through the comparison of their own and the target language, children learn that there are many ways to accomplish similar linguistic functions and they acquire important insights about cultural worldviews and perspectives on events (Cloud, Genesee & Hamayan, 2000; Genesee et al., 2004).

For the reasons cited above, Teachers of English to Speakers of Other Languages (TESOL, 1997) has endorsed the following 2 principles when listing 8 general principles of language acquisition in its *ESL Standards for Pre-K–12 Students*: (a) Native language proficiency contributes to second language acquisition; and (b) bilingualism is an individual and societal asset. Supporting the first principle, they conclude: "The most effective environments for second language teaching and learning are those that promote ESOL students' native language and literacy development as a foundation for English language and academic development" (p. 8). Supporting the second principle, they conclude: "Bilingualism benefits the individual and serves the national interest, and schools need to promote the retention and development of multiple languages" (p. 8).

Psychological rationale.   For language minority students enrolled in a bilingual program, the full development of their primary cultural and linguistic identity enhances their psychological health and contributes positively to all other aspects of functioning. Children with high self esteem work harder, learn better, and achieve more (McGrath, 2003; Reasoner, 2005). Rumberger (1998) observes, "It is narrow minded to believe that immigrants' problems can be solved with English proficiency—that is too simplistic. Ethnic identity does affect success, students need to be taught to have pride in their heritage and culture" (p. 1). Indeed, this is among the most important reasons cited by parents for preserving the native language—their children's development of a strong and positive identity; to have their language valued and respected (Checkley, 1996). Conversely, it has been shown that loss of the first language is disruptive to family functioning and can even alienate children from their primary caregivers (Wong-Fillmore, 1991). Thus, it is a pro-family stance to respect the primary language and culture and provide for continuity between the primary learning environments of home and school through bilingual instruction.

Language majority students enrolled in a dual language program come to know themselves as speakers of a particular world language; one of many. This balanced placement of oneself in the world provides the majority culture child a more realistic vantage point and stance from within which to perceive and interpret their experiences. In a bilingual program, both languages have status and both cultures are portrayed in a positive light. The cross-cultural learning and intercultural experiences enjoyed by both groups of children (language majority and language minority) enhances their understanding of themselves and others in very beneficial ways to their own psychological and emotional development. The children experience the world from two perspectives and, when this unique educational experience results in proficient bilingualism, it offers them maturational advantages in linguistic and metalinguistic abilities, and concept formation (Cataldi, 1994; Diaz, 1983, 1985).

IMPLICATIONS FOR PRACTICE

Position Statements of Professional Associations on the Use of the Native Language

Associations that endorse the instructional use of the native language. The National Association for the Education of Young Children (NAEYC, 1995) position statement *Responding to Linguistic and Culture Diversity—Recommendations for Effective Early Childhood Education* reads:

> For the optimal development and learning of all children, educators must *accept* the legitimacy of children's home language, *respect* (hold in high regard) and *value* (esteem, appreciate) the home culture, and *promote* and *encourage* the active involvement and support of all families, including extended and nontraditional family units. (p. 5)

The statement notes that young children are "cognitively, linguistically, and emotionally connected to the language and culture of their home" (p. 8). For this reason, it urges providers to "encourage and assist all parents in becoming knowledgeable about the cognitive value for children of knowing more than one language, and provide them with the strategies to support, maintain, and preserve home-language learning" (p. 9) and encourages schools to "support and preserve home language usage" (p. 11).

The National Education Association (NEA, 2002) supports the work of the English Plus Information Clearinghouse (EPIC), an organization that affirms the value of cultural and linguistic pluralism. In its *ResolutionB22—Educational Programs for*

English Language Learners, the association affirms the value of equal educational opportunities for all students, specifically stating that it "values bilingual and multicultural competence and supports programs that assist individuals in attaining and maintaining proficiency in their native language before and after they acquire proficiency in English" (p. 292). The resolution endorses bilingual programs as the best programmatic option for students who are limited in English proficiency.

TESOL has published a number of statements about the value of bilingualism for individuals, for society, and for the learning of English. Among its research-based position statements is its 2001 *Statement on Language and Literacy Development for Young English Language Learners*. In this statement, the organization reiterates the principle that oral language and literacy development in English is supported by the development and use of students' native language, noting that successful early childhood programs build upon the knowledge that young learners bring from home, and for young ESOL learners, this knowledge is learned and expressed in their native language. Research in second language development has shown that literacy in a second language is much more easily achieved when literacy is developed in the native language, as literacy skills are more easily transferred from the first language to the second language (Faltis & Hudelson, 1998; Genesee et al. 2005; Riches & Genesee, 2006).

The International Reading Association takes the same position in its 2000 statement *Making a Difference Means Making It Different: Honoring Children's Right to Excellent Reading Instruction*. This statement espouses the principle that "children have a right to reading instruction that makes meaningful use of their first language skills," and states that "initial reading instruction should be provided in a child's native language whenever possible" (p. 10) because research shows that it is beneficial to do so (Faltis & Hudelson, 1998; Genesee et al. 2005; Riches & Genesee, 2006).

The Conference on College Composition and Communication (CCCC) also endorses bilingualism and bilingual education. Its *National Language Policy* (1988) states in part that the organization's members

> support programs that assert the legitimacy of native languages and dialects and ensure that proficiency in one's mother tongue will not be lost; and ... foster the teaching of languages other than English so that native speakers of English can rediscover the language of their heritage or learn a second language. (pp. 1–2)

Associations that endorse the use of the native language in assessment. The reauthorization of the Individuals with Disabilities Education Act (IDEA, 1997) guarantees specific rights and protections to ethnic and linguistic minorities. IDEA requires that tests and other evaluation materials be "provided and administered in the child's native language or other mode of communication" and be "selected and administered to ensure that they measure the extent to which the child has a disability and needs special education, rather than measuring the child's English language skills" (34 C,F.R.§300.532, Evaluation Procedures). In keeping with IDEA, the policy of the National Association of School Psychologists (1994) promotes nondiscriminatory assessment practices with respect to both ethnicity and native language.

In 1999, the American Educational Research Association (AERA), the National Council on Measurement in Education (NCME), and the American Psychological Association (APA) outlined specific "Fairness in Testing" procedures for testing individuals of diverse linguistic backgrounds in its *Standards for Educational and Psychological Testing*. These standards are designed to ensure that psychologists select appropriate assessment procedures, assess in linguistically and culturally non-discriminatory ways, and take affirmative steps to interact in the language understood by the client.

The *Position Statement Concerning High-Stakes Testing in Pre-K–12 Education* (AERA, 2000) argues against the use of tests in English by those still learning that language. It states:

> If a student lacks mastery of the language in which a test is given, then that test becomes, in part, a test of language proficiency. Unless a primary purpose of a test is to evaluate language proficiency, it should not be used with students who cannot understand the instructions or the language of the test itself. (n.p.)

Some school psychologists and linguists argue against single language testing, whether in the native language or in English (Figueroa, 1991; Valdes & Figueroa, 1994). They assert that it may be time to abandon the use of tests with bilingual students completely, because such testing belies the realities of bilingual functioning (where learners always draw upon both languages in performing tasks) and presents seemingly insurmountable technical difficulties in establishing appropriately designed and normed dual language measures for a linguistically heterogeneous group of students (Figueroa; Figueroa & Garcia, 1994; Valdes & Figueroa, 1994). Still, these experts acknowledge that the native language is a significant variable that must be taken into account in designing and conducting assessment with culturally and linguistically diverse students. Thus, the use of the native language has been endorsed by major professional associations to enhance instructional and assessment outcomes for students.

Models of Bilingual Instruction and Their Goals

Bilingual education is a type of school program in which English and a language other than English are used to provide instruction to students.[1] Bilingual education programs are of three major types: (a) Transitional bilingual education (TBE) or early exit bilingual education; (b) developmental bilingual education (DBE), maintenance, or late-exit bilingual education; and (c) two-way bilingual education, two-way immersion (TWI), or dual language immersion (DLI) (Baker, 2001; Genesee, 1999; Rennie, 1993). According to Cloud and her colleagues (2000), in TBE programs language minority students' primary language is used for some instruction for a limited number of years. Such instruction, which takes place for 3 years in most states, is designed to promote students' mastery of academic material while they are learning English and to aid them with the transition to an all-English program. TBE programs, the most common form of bilingual education in the U.S.

---

[1]For a history of bilingual education, see Crawford (1991). For factors to consider in selecting a program model, see Genesee (1999) or Rennie (1993).

(Baker. 2001), do not aim to maintain or develop the students' primary language. Instead, the emphasis is on exiting as quickly as possible to participate in mainstream all-English classrooms.

Developmental bilingual education (DBE) programs (also referred to as maintenance programs), on the other hand, do intend to develop and maintain full proficiency in the students' home language while promoting full proficiency in English. Like TBE, DBE programs are designed for language minority students only. DBE programs offer continuous, well-articulated native and English language instruction across the grades (additive bilingualism), and promote high levels of academic achievement using both instructional languages in highly planned ways.

Two-way bilingual education (TWI or DLI) serves language minority and language majority students in the same classrooms. In this enrichment form of bilingual education, native speakers of English and of another language receive integrated language and academic instruction with the goals of high academic achievement, first and second language proficiency (additive bilingualism) and cross-cultural understanding. Most programs start in kindergarten or first grade and continue through grade 6 or 8. Each class is composed of 50% native English speakers and 50% speakers of the other language. The non-English language is used at least 50% of the time during academic instruction.[2]

In terms of the effectiveness of various models of bilingual education, research shows that students enrolled in bilingual programs benefit from strong cognitive and academic instruction conducted in their first language, and that these benefits are cumulative (Baker, 2001; Collier & Thomas, 1999; Gutierrez-Clellen, 1999; Thomas & Collier, 1998). Students in programs that stress fluent bilingualism do best (Ramirez et al., 1991). The more years in which first-language-based plus English-language-based instruction is present, the greater is students' eventual English-based achievement (Center for Research on Education, Diversity, & Excellence, 1998).

Students in TWI and DBE programs have been shown to outperform those in TBE programs (Collier & Thomas, 1999; Thomas & Collier, 1998). In fact, TBE programs are only slightly more effective than programs in which students receive English-only instruction, presumably because students do not use or develop the native language to the same extent they do in long term developmental programs (TWI and DBE).

Service Delivery Options

In terms of service delivery, in general, full-day programs are more beneficial than time-limited programs (i.e., half-day; single class period) (Baker, 2001; Collier & Thomas, 1999; Thomas & Collier, 1998; Ramirez et al., 1991); however, this can only be determined in relation to the educational needs of a particular student. There could be students for whom limited support is quite sufficient given their proficiency characteristics and educational backgrounds.

At the elementary level, in terms of time-limited support, pullout and push-in service delivery arrangements each have logistical problems. In a pullout program,

---

[2]See http:/www.dualu.org for a visual representation and description of the various programs.

children spend most of their day in an English-only classroom and are "pulled out" for support from a bilingual teacher. In push-in models, the bilingual teacher or paraprofessional goes into the classroom to provide support to the student, following a collaborative teaching model of instruction.

Pull-out models waste valuable instructional time while students are in transit between classrooms, interrupt the flow of the instructional day, and cause students to miss some of the regular classroom instruction while they are "pulled out." Push-in models face challenges in terms of how to provide specialized instruction within the classroom while other instruction is occurring and how to use both instructors effectively (Dettmer, Dyck, & Thurston 1999; Walther-Thomas, Korinek, McLaughlin, & Williams, 2000). Both types of programs rely on careful coordination among members of the teaching staff, and therefore can fail when the administrative planning time needed to make the program succeed is not provided (Dettmer et al., 1999; Walther-Thomas et al., 2000).

In secondary settings, the choice of language of delivery may be governed by subject matter. Subjects such as math, which are viewed as less language dependent, are taught in English, whereas subjects that are viewed as language intensive are selected for delivery in the native language. However, the language dependent/language intensive premise is false; the learning of math concepts depends upon understanding the language of the textbook and the teacher just as in learning science and social studies concepts (Chamot & O'Malley, 1994; Echevarria, Vogt, & Short, 2000). A main obstacle to the success of such arrangements, therefore, is lack of knowledge of students' language support needs in different subjects. A second difficulty is having the full range of courses in a specific content area available in the native language. All too often, basic or general courses are taught in the native language but the more advanced courses are not. This relegates those needing bilingual instruction to lower level courses when they may be capable of much more.

A final service delivery challenge is having bilingual instruction available in all of the languages in which it might be needed. Difficulties include finding qualified bilingual personnel in all of the languages needed, and securing funding for their positions. This situation would improve if districts added linguistic and cultural competence to their standard lists of hiring criteria in order to enhance their ability to deliver services in the major world languages represented in the local school-aged population.

The Role of ESL in Bilingual Programs

English as a Second Language (ESL) instruction is always offered as a part of a bilingual education program. Its goals are cultural adaptation, acquisition of social English and the development of sufficient proficiency in academic English to succeed on grade level (Genesee, 1999; Rennie, 1993; TESOL, 1997). Currently, many districts offer content-based or "sheltered English" content area classes in addition to traditional ESL classes. In these classes, students learn subject-specific academic English while they learn the content associated with particular subject area classes required for their grade level. Thus, for example, a secondary student's day might include an ESL class, a sheltered English content area class in social studies, mathematics, science, or health, and other classes taught in the native language.

Native Language Support Services

Use of the native language has been advocated by many professionals and professional associations for specific purposes, such as in early hearing detection and intervention programs (American Academy of Audiology, 2000), conducting speech and language assessment and intervention (Roseberry-McKibbin, 2002), and the provision of counseling services (Lynch & Hanson, 1998). Parent outreach services must also be available in languages other than English. For example, in order to encourage family literacy, schools can create a home-school library program, including audio/video-recorded books in the native language. In addition, all educational and informational materials must be provided in languages other than English to ensure that family and community outreach efforts are effective (NAEYC, 1995).

IMPLEMENTATION AND APPROACHES

Evaluating Program Adequacy

Effective bilingual education programs have certain characteristics that help to ensure student success. Reviews of the literature in this area indicate various practices that make programs effective (Baker, 2001; Cloud et al., 2000; Faltis & Hudelson, 1998). An effective program has well prepared teachers who are fully proficient in the oral and written forms of the languages of instruction. The program is well articulated across grade levels and its curriculum is well aligned with the mainstream program and with relevant state and national standards. Classroom environments are adequate for learning and high quality, appropriately leveled books and materials are available.

Effective programs construct teaching-learning environments in culturally responsive ways (Cloud, 2002; Zehler, 1994). For example, curriculum and materials acknowledge the life experiences and background knowledge of the students, reflect the values and beliefs of all children, and are free of bias and stereotypes. Classroom interactions and use of time and space are structured in ways that create a comfortable and predictable learning environment for children.

Children in effective bilingual programs have access to technology at the same levels, as students in other programs in the school (Butler-Pascoe & Wiburg, 2003). Each classroom has enough teaching staff to meet students' academic needs, and staff development is ongoing and rigorous (Faltis & Hudelson, 1998). Student progress is measured by a well developed program of ongoing assessment, and the program is fully accountable using appropriate measures and standards of performance (Cloud et al., 2000; Faltis & Hudelson, 1998). Parents are full partners with teaching staff in the education of their children (Faltis & Hudelson, 1998; NAEYC, 1995).

All of these qualities may seem obvious. Often, however, when children in bilingual programs are not successful, responsibility is placed on them rather than on the construction and development of the educational program. Thus, a first task in assessing a child's needs is to determine if the program itself is lacking in any way (e.g., it employs teachers who are bilingual but are not well prepared or certified). Where deficiencies exist, education reform efforts should be designed to strengthen bilingual programs rather than eliminate them.

Observing Students in Bilingual Learning Contexts

In order to understand the effectiveness of students' placements and of the instructional use of each language, school psychologists or other service providers should observe students in their bilingual instructional environments (Genesee et al., 2004; Roseberry-McKibbin, 2002), noting the following:

1. *Student's ability to comprehend instruction delivered in each instructional language.* For example, the observer might note that a student seems to comprehend better in one language than the other or that comprehension appears equivalent irrespective of the language of instruction.
2. *Student's preference for one instructional language over the other, if a preference exists.* For example, the observer may note that, when choosing instructional materials or language used for making inquiry, the student tends to use one language more than the other.
3. *Student's actual use of the two languages.* The observer should note the locations where each language is used (classroom vs. playground vs. library), the purposes accomplished with each language, and the amount of each language used in an instructional day.
4. *Student's choice of peers in instructional interactions.* The observer should note with whom the child tends to pair when given opportunities to work with peers and the instructional language that dominates those interactions.
5. *The amount of code switching (switching from one language to the other at natural junctures while respecting the rules of both languages), word borrowing (the insertion of a word or phrase when the word or phrase is unknown), and mixing (the blending or mixing of the two languages in innovative but inappropriate ways, including word inventions such as "lunche" for lunch/almuerzo).* It is important to note which language exists more independently and which relies on support from the other for communication to be successful.
6. *Student's apparent interest (affective response) when instruction is delivered in each language.* This would include positive behaviors such as animated participation, attentiveness, and enthusiasm, as well as negative behaviors such as active resistance, complaints, and requests to switch to the other language.

7. *Student's level of participation.* All aspects related to instructional engagement of the student should be investigated (e.g., time on task and amount of question asking and class contributions by the student).

8. *Classroom performance in each language.* The observer might note in which language performance is more competent and in which it is more restricted and limited. This could include, for example, the student's fluency or expressiveness in each language.

The proficiency of the teacher and the other students can affect the variables listed above. Thus, these must also be documented in order to accurately interpret the child's behavior.

Responding to Parents' Concerns About Bilingual Programming

Federal law requires that all parents with children in federally funded bilingual education programs be notified why their child was selected for participation, be provided with alternatives to participation, and be given the option of declining to enroll their child in the program. This information must be presented to parents in a language that they can understand (National Association for Bilingual Education, 2001).

However, some parents are not well informed about the research-based educational rationale for bilingual programs, nor do they understand the many benefits of well developed bilingualism (Crawford, 1991; Cummins, 1986; NAEYC, 1995). Thus, one role of the school psychologist is to explain the rationale for and benefits of well developed and executed bilingual programs to parents. It is important for school psychologists to present a well-informed and balanced portrayal of bilingual programs in responding to parents' concerns.

A common parental concern is whether children will develop full proficiency in English if they are placed in a bilingual program. School psychologists can point out that, as TESOL (2001) notes, the full development of the native language enhances second language acquisition. Individuals who develop proficiency in two languages benefit both themselves and society; a fact that must be shared with parents. They can also share with parents the research discussed in this chapter showing that students who are placed in quality bilingual programs do develop proficient skills in both languages and that this is very beneficial to their academic achievement (Baker, 2001; Collier & Thomas, 1999; Genesee et al., 2005; Riches & Genesee, 2006; Gutierrez-Clellen, 1999; NCELA, 1996; Ramirez et al., 1991; Rumberger, 1998; Thomas & Collier, 1998).

Other concerns are more specific. Parents may wonder which program model is best, or for how long their child should participate in a bilingual program. In addition, they may wonder if the program being offered is well designed and delivered by competent professionals. Because model designs, goals, and outcomes differ, school staff must help parents understand the differences among the various models. School psychologists can share the characteristics of effective bilingual programs outlined above so that parents know what aspects define quality programs.

Models of Language Use in Bilingual Classrooms and Bilingual Instruction

Language separation is advocated in bilingual classrooms for sociolinguistic and practical reasons (Baker, 2001). The languages can be separated by subject or topic, person, time, place, activity or function. For example, science may be taught in English and social studies in Spanish. In TWI programs, typically one teacher teaches exclusively in one language and the other teacher in the other. Time is often used to demarcate instructional language; for example, in the morning, subjects are taught in Spanish, and in the afternoon, they are taught in English.

More refined allocation practices are possible, with particular topics, activities, or functions conducted in one language exclusively (Baker, 2001). For example, certain routines like lining up for lunch may be conducted consistently in one language or the other. The status distinctions that might be conveyed by such decisions need to be carefully considered prior to establishing a particular policy (Faltis & Hudelson, 1998). In addition, decision makers may use information about curricular resources or teacher proficiency as the basis for particular allocation practices (Cloud et al., 2000). It is also wise to alternate languages over time, so that neither language is consistently excluded from use for a particular purpose, because such exclusion could undermine the goal of balanced bilingualism (Cloud et al., 2000).

Planned use of each language is urged, and random use of the two languages is to be avoided. Simultaneous translation or concurrent use of the two languages (repeating information first in one language, then immediately in the other) is particularly problematic (Baker, 2001; Ovando, Collier, & Combs, 2002). It is extremely time consuming and it teaches students to tune out the language they have not yet fully mastered because they know the information will be repeated in their proficient language.

In some bilingual classrooms, both languages are used in carefully planned ways during the same lesson using a preview/review model of instruction (Baker, 2001; Ovando et al., 2002). In this approach, one of the two languages is used to introduce the topic of instruction. The lesson is then taught exclusively in the other language, and at the end a review is provided in the original language. These phases of instruction frame the instruction, insuring comprehension and reinforcing new learning

Another decision to be made is the amount of time to be allocated to the use of each language in the curriculum. Some TWI programs use a 90/10-minority/majority language split in the first year, moving to equal use of the two languages over time; others use a 50/50 split from the outset (Cloud et al., 2000). In TBE programs, as much as 90% of instruction may be delivered in the native language in the first year; by the time a student exits the program 3 years later, the language allocation is the exact reverse, with up to 90% of instruction delivered in the second language.

It is important to understand how languages are allocated in a given bilingual program. The program's aims, not teacher proficiency or preferences, should dictate language use. For example, testing TBE students in English in the spring of their first year in the program could cause teachers to abandon use of the native language in order to prepare students for testing, thus undermining the goals and language use design of the program.

In general, careful attention must be given to how both languages will be used in instruction. Planning must consider how the policies being implemented will lead to full, proficient bilingualism and biliteracy for those in TWI and DBE programs while ensuring that instruction is meaningful to the learners involved.

Research-based Instructional Practices That Promote Bilingual Competence

Research has documented the practices that are critical to the development of full bilingual competence. Fuller descriptions of these are provided in Cloud, Genesee, and Hamayan (2000), Echevarria, Vogt and Short (2000), Gersten and Baker (2000), and Herrell (2000).

1. Teachers provide comprehensible input, using language interactions designed with students' language proficiency characteristics in mind to ensure understanding (Cummins, 1986; Krashen & Terrell, 1983). Language experience activities, leveled questions, modeled talk, and multimedia presentations are some examples of strategies that insure comprehensible input to students (Herrell, 2000).

2. Students have opportunities to practice listening, speaking, reading, and writing with feedback on their performance (Echevarria et al., 2000). Active involvement is critical, especially any activity that increases verbal interaction in classroom activities (Fern, Anstrom, & Silcox, 1995; Zehler, 1994). Cooperative learning and other grouping practices such as partner work and peer tutoring, collaborative reading, and interactive writing are ways to ensure that students are actively involved and given opportunities to practice (Cloud et al., 2000; Gibbons, 2002; Herrell, 2000).

3. Instruction is contextualized so that language can be scaffolded onto rich instructional interactions (Echevarria et al., 2000; Gibbons, 2002). Conducting experiments and other discovery-oriented learning is helpful for this purpose, as are methods that use visual learning (e.g., graphic organizers, photographs, film and video, student produced visuals) to support verbal learning (Herrell, 2000; Echevarria et al., 2000).

4. The program plans for the development of social and academic language in both languages (Chamot & O'Malley, 1994). As outlined in the TESOL ESL Standards for Pre-K–12 Students (TESOL, 1997), students need to develop two types of proficiency in a target language: the language needed for social purposes and the language needed for academic purposes. Students must also develop the ability to use the language in socially and culturally appropriate ways. In order to become truly proficient, students must have opportunities to develop all of these competencies. This may mean the provision of after-school or outside-of-school opportunities for language use in addition to in-school language learning.

5. The program plans for the transfer of skills from one language to the other. Teachers must provide opportunities for students to draw from what they have learned in the primary language and to practice applying and extend-

ing their learning in second language contexts (Cloud et al., 2000). This means that teachers must understand the transfer process and how to facilitate it, including how to involve families in the process (Thonis, 1983).

6. The curriculum supports well articulated, integrated development of language, literacy and subject matter. The use of an interdisciplinary, thematic curriculum is highly recommended for accomplishing this goal(Gibbons, 2002; Kucer, Silva, & Delgado-Larocco, 1995; Zehler, 1994). While challenging and complex, this kind of curriculum planning has the added benefit of allowing for the effective integration of local, state and national curriculum standards (Cloud, 2002). In order to do this type of curriculum planning, teachers and other resource specialists need support in the form of release time or paid curriculum development time. They need to work collaboratively with other teachers within and across grades to ensure the kind of vertical and horizontal curriculum coordination that promotes program success.

IMPLICATIONS FOR FUTURE RESEARCH AND PRACTICE

Enrichment Models of Bilingual Education

Because enrichment models of bilingual education are either at early stages in their implementation (i.e., TWI) or not widely available (i.e., DBE), the existing research is not very extensive. There is much to learn about the design and delivery of these programs and ways to maximize their effectiveness. For TWI, a highly complex program involving two groups of students, there are many aspects to be studied, from the ideal models of language use, to ways to encourage equal use of both languages both in and outside of school, to how to design curriculum within and across the grades to support all of the program's goals.

Promoting Linguistic and Cross-cultural Competence in all Learners

The United States has an increasingly diverse population and its economic and social interdependence with other nations is clear. The nation's interests are best served, therefore, when schools promote the linguistic and cross-cultural competence of all students. All bilingual education programs hold promise for accomplishing this important goal, but the enrichment forms of bilingual education—DBE and TWI programs—offer the greatest opportunities for developing the full range of linguistic ability and cross-cultural understanding.

Determining When Native Language Use Is Warranted in Intervention With Bilingual Children With Special Needs

While some information is available to assist service providers in determining the best language(s) of intervention (Brice & Roseberry-McKibbin, 2001; Gutierrez-Clellen, 1999), more research is needed to help providers determine which language will promote the greatest growth for children with specific language or learning delays and disorders. The research in this area must include careful analysis of the child's disability characteristics, age, home language characteristics, and so forth, to provide more finely differentiated guidance to providers charged with making this important programming decision.

ANNOTATED BIBLIOGRAPHY

Baker, C. (2001). *Foundations of bilingual education and bilingualism* (3rd ed.). Clevedon, England: Multilingual Matters.

This book provides the most comprehensive introduction to bilingualism and bilingual education, including the latest research findings on both. It is an excellent introductory text that provides information on the nature of bilingualism, bilingual education policies and practices, and the legal, historical, and political contexts of such programs worldwide.

Becker, H. (2001). *Teaching ESL K–12: Views from the classroom*. Boston: Heinle & Heinle.

This helpful resource addresses how to prepare English language learners for the demands of mainstream classrooms, curricula, and schools. Chapters focus on ESL curriculum, program models for elementary and secondary programs, assessment, special education concerns, parental involvement and effective schoolwide practices.

Christian, D., & Genesee, F. (Eds.). (2001). *Bilingual education*. Alexandria, VA: Teachers of English to Speakers of Other Languages.

A series of case studies of bilingual education programs in diverse environments. The case studies fall into three categories: learning a majority language through bilingual education, maintaining an indigenous language through bilingual education, and learning an international language through bilingual education. Each case study outlines the social and educational context, describes the program, and sets out practical ideas that could be used by others.

Cloud, N., Genesee, F., & Hamayan, E. (2000). *Dual language instruction: A handbook for enriched education*. Boston: Heinle & Heinle.

A practical volume for teachers and administrators, this text is divided into three sections: Foundations, The Instructional Process and Applications and Resources. Section I introduces the critical features of and strategies for the development and implementation of dual language programs. Section II focuses on principles and practices for oral language development, teaching literacy in two languages, teaching content and assessment. Section III provides model lessons and assessment procedures and advocacy strategies for school-based professionals implementing programs.

Lessow-Hurly, J. (2000). *Foundations of dual language instruction* (3rd ed.). Reading, MA: Addison Wesley.

This text provides legal, political, historical foundations as well as international perspectives on dual language education. The author discusses program models, language development, primary and second language instruction, and the relationship of culture to academic success.

Lindholm-Leary, K. J. (2001). *Dual language education*. Clevedon, England: Multilingual Matters.

> This book provides the knowledge and research base for dual language programs in the U.S. and makes recommendations for future practice. Part 1 gives the sociopolitical and theoretical contexts of dual language education. In Part 2, the classroom, administrative and familial contexts in dual language education are explored. In Part 3, research evidence regarding student outcomes in dual language education programs are presented and discussed. The book is an invaluable resource for those implementing dual language programs.

Ovando, C. J., Collier, V. P., Combs, M. C., & Cummins, J. (2002). *Bilingual and ESL classrooms* (3rd ed.). New York: McGraw-Hill.

> Written by renowned experts in the field, this text integrates theory and practice and provides comprehensive coverage of important issues in the delivery of bilingual and ESL programs. It provides examples of effective practices as well as their underlying research knowledge base. Chapters include Policy and Programs, Teaching, Language, Culture, Mathematics and Science, Social Studies, Assessment and Evaluation, School and Community.

RESOURCES

Center for Applied Linguistics (CAL):
> http://www.cal.org/

> This center's mission is to promote and improve the teaching and learning of languages, identify and solve problems related to language and culture, serve as a resource for information about language and culture, and conduct research on issues related to language and culture.

National Association for Bilingual Education (NABE):
> http://www.nabe.org

> NABE's web site offers a section on research that highlights significant developments for educational practitioners and advocates. It publishes *Language Learner*, the NABE news magazine, the Bilingual Research Journal and the NABE Review of Research and Practice.

Center for Research on Education, Diversity and Excellence (CREDE). University of California, Santa Cruz:
> http://crede.berkeley.edu/

> CREDE is a federally funded research and development program focused on improving the education of students whose ability to reach their potential is challenged by language or cultural barriers, race, geographic location, or poverty.

Teaching Diverse Learners (TDL). Northeast and Islands Regional Educational Laboratory at Brown University:
> http://www.alliance.brown.edu/tdl

> This is a resource dedicated to enhancing the capacity of teachers to work effectively and equitably with English language learners (ELLs). The Web site provides ac-

cess to information—publications, educational materials, and the work of experts in the field—that promotes high achievement for ELLs.

REFERENCES

American Academy of Audiology. (2000). *Year 2000 position statement and guidelines: Principles and guidelines for early hearing detection and intervention programs.* McLean, VA: Author.

American Educational Research Association. (2000, July). *AERA position statement concerning high-stakes testing in pre-K–12 education.* Retrieved May 1, 2003, from http://www.aera.net/about/policy/stakes.htm

American Psychological Association. (1999). *Standards for educational and psychological testing.* Washington, DC: Author.

Baker, C. (2001). *Foundations of bilingual education and bilingualism.* Clevedon, England: Multilingual Matters.

Bialystok, E., & Hakuta, K. (1994). *In other words: The science and psychology of second language acquisition.* New York: Basic Books.

Brice, A., & Roseberry-McKibbin, C. (2001). Choice of languages in instruction: One language or two. *Teaching Exceptional Children, 33,* 10–16.

Butler-Pascoe, M. E., & Wiburg, K. M. (2003). *Technology and teaching English Language Learners.* Boston: Allyn and Bacon.

Cataldi, R. J. (1994). Bilingualism and early acquisition-great assets. *NASSP Bulletin, 78,* 62–64.

Center for Research on Education, Diversity & Excellence. (1998, April 8). *Findings on the effectiveness of bilingual education* [press release]. Santa Cruz, CA: Author.

Chamot, A., & O'Malley, J. (1994). *The CALLA handbook: Implementing the cognitive academic language learning approach.* Reading, MA: Addison-Wesley.

Checkley, K. (1996). Keeping native languages alive. *Education Update, 38,* 1, 6, 8.

Cloud, N. (2002). Culturally and linguistically responsive instructional planning. In A. J. Artiles & A. A. Ortiz (Eds.), *English language learners with special education needs: Identification, assessment, and instruction* (pp. 107–132). Washington, DC: ERIC Clearinghouse on Languages and Linguistics, Center for Applied Linguistics.

Cloud, N., Genesee, F., & Hamayan, E. (2000). *Dual language instruction: A handbook for enriched education.* Boston: Heinle & Heinle.

Collier, V. P., & Thomas, W. P. (1999). Making U.S. schools effective for English language learners, Part 2. *TESOL Matters, 9,* 1, 6.

Conference on College Composition and Communication. (1988). *National language policy.* Urbana, IL: National Council of Teachers of English. Retrieved June 25, 2005, from http://www.ncte.org/about/over/positions/category/lang/107643.htm

Crawford, J. (1991). *Bilingual education: History, politics, theory and practice* (2nd ed.). Los Angeles: Bilingual Education Services.

Cummins, J. (1986). Empowering minority students: A framework for interaction. *Harvard Review, 56,* 18–36.

Dettmer, P., Dyck, N., & Thurston, L. P. (1999). *Consultation, collaboration and teamwork for students with special needs. Third edition.* Boston: Allyn and Bacon.

Diaz, R. M. (1983). Thought and two languages: The impact of bilingualism on cognitive development. *Review of Research in Education, 10,* 23–54.

Diaz, R. M. (1985). *The intellectual power of bilingualism.* (ERIC Document Reproduction Service No. ED 283 368).

Echevarria, J., Vogt, M. E., & Short, D. J. (2000). *Making content comprehensible for English language learners: The SIOP model.* Boston: Allyn & Bacon.

Faltis, C. J., & Hudelson, S. J. (1998*). Bilingual education in elementary and secondary school communities.* Boston: Allyn and Bacon.

Fern, V., Anstrom, K., & Silcox, B. (1995). Active learning and the limited English proficient student. *Directions in Language Education, 1,* 1–7.

Figueroa, R. A. (1991). Bilingualism and psychometrics. *Diagnostique, 17,* 70–85.

Figueroa, R. A., & Garcia, E. (1994). Issues in testing students from culturally and linguistically diverse backgrounds. *Multicultural Education, 2,* 10–23.

Genesee, F. (Ed.). (1999). *Program alternatives for linguistically diverse students.* Santa Cruz, CA: Center for Research on Education, Diversity & Excellence.

Genesee, F., & Cloud, N. (1998). Multilingualism is basic. *Educational Leadership, 55,* 62–65.

Genesee, F., Lindholm-Leary, K., Saunders, W., & Christian, D. (2005). English Language Learners in U.S. schools: An overview of research findings. *Journal of Education for Students Placed At Risk, 10,* 363–385.

Genesee, F., Paradis, J., & Crago, M. B. (2004). *Dual language development & disorders: A handbook on bilingualism & second language learning.* Baltimore: Paul H. Brookes Publishing.

Gersten, R., & Baker, S. (2000). What we know about effective instructional practices for English language learners. *Exceptional Children, 66,* 454–470.

Gibbons, P. (2002). *Scaffolding language, scaffolding learning: Teaching second language learners in the mainstream classroom.* Portsmouth, NH: Heinemann.

Gutierrez-Clellen, V. F. (1999). Language choice in intervention with bilingual children. *American Journal of Speech-Language Pathology, 8,* 291–302.

Herrell, A. L. (2000). *Fifty strategies for teaching English language learners.* Upper Saddle River, NJ: Merrill.

Individuals with Disabilities Education Act (IDEA), 20 U.S. C. §§ 1400 (1997). Retrieved May 1, 2003, from http://www/ed.gov/offices/OSERS/Policy/IDEA/the_law.html

International Reading Association. (2000). *Making a difference means making it different: Honoring children's right to excellent reading instruction.* Newark, DE: Author. Retrieved May 7, 2003, from http://newbookstore.reading.org/cgi-bin/OnlineBookstore.storefront/3eb95e3501c2f8b427171868063e064b/Product/View/1042B&2D553

Krashen, S., & Terrell, T. (1983). *The natural approach: Language acquisition in the classroom.* Oxford: Pergamon.

Kucer, S. B., Silva, C., & Delgado-Larocco, E. L. (1995). *Curricular conversations: Themes in multilingual and monolingual classrooms.* York, ME: Stenhouse.

Latham, A. S. (1998). The advantages of bilingualism. *Educational Leadership, 56,* 79–80.

Lau v. Nichols, 414 U.S. 563 (1974). Retrieved March 19, 2003, from http://www.ed.gov/offices/OCR/ELL/lau.html

Lynch, E. W., & Hanson, M. J. (Eds.). (1998). *Developing cross-cultural competence: A guide to working with young children and their families* (2nd ed.). Baltimore: Paul H. Brooks.

McGrath, H. (Winter, 2003). New thinking on self-esteem. *EQ Australia,* Issue Two. Retrieved July, 28, 2005 from <http://www.curriculumedu.au/eq/archive/winter2003/html/article_01.shtml>

National Association for Bilingual Education. (2001). *Frequently asked questions: What does Federal law say regarding services for LEP students?* Washington, DC: Author. Retrieved May 7, 2003, from http://www.nabe.org/faq_detail.asp?ID = 16

National Association for the Education of Young Children. (1995). *Responding to linguistic and culture diversity—Recommendations for effective early childhood education.* Retrieved May 7, 2003, from http://www.naeyc.org/resources/position_statements/psdiv98.htm

National Association of School Psychologists. (1994). *Position statement on school psychologists' involvement in the role of assessment.* Bethesda, MD: Author.

National Clearinghouse for English Language Acquisition and Language Instruction Educational Programs. (1995, April). *How does native language development influence academic achievement in a second language? (AskNCELA No. 4).* Retrieved May 1, 2003, from http://www.ncela.gwu.edu/askncela/04academic.htm

National Clearinghouse for English Language Acquisition and Language Instruction Educational Programs. (1996, October). *Why is it important to maintain the native language?* (Ask NCELA No. 12). Washington, DC: Author. Retrieved May 1, 2003, from http://www.ncela.gwu.edu/askncela/12native.htm

National Education Association. (2002). Resolution B22: Educational programs for English language learners. In *National Education Association Handbook: Making public schools great for every child 2002–2003* (pp. 292). Washington, DC: Author.

New York State Education Department (May, 2003). *Commissioner's Regulations/CR Part 154 (Ammended). Apportionment and Services for Pupils with Limited English Proficiency.* (NYS Education Law Secions 3204 and 3602).

Ovando, C. J., Collier, V. P., & Combs, M. C. (2002). *Bilingual and ESL classrooms: Teaching in multicultural contexts. Third edition.* New York: McGraw-Hill Book Company.

Ramirez, J. D., Yuen, S. D., & Ramey, D. R. (1991). *Final report: Longitudinal study of structured immersion strategy, early-exit, and late-exit transitional bilingual education programs for language-minority children. Executive Summary.* San Mateo, CA: Aguirre International.

Reasoner, R. W. (2005). *Review of self-esteem research.* Retrieved July 28, 2005, from <http://www.self-esteem-nase.org/research.shtml>

Rennie, J. (1993). *ESL and bilingual program models.* Washington, DC: ERIC Clearinghouse on Languages and Linguistics, Center for Applied Linguistics.

Rhode Island Department of Elementary and Secondary Education. (September 14, 2000). *Limited English Proficiency (LEP) Regulations. Chapters 16–54.*

Riches, C., & Genesee, F. (2006). Literacy: Crosslinguistic and crossmodal issues. In F. Genesee, K. Lindholm-Leary, W. M. Saunders, & D. Christian (Eds.). *Educating English Language Learners: A synthesis of research evidence* (pp. 64–108). New York: Cambridge University Press.

Roseberry-McKibbin, C. (2002). *Multicultural students with special language needs: Practical strategies for assessment and intervention* (2nd ed.). Oceanside, CA: Academic Communication Associates.

Rumberger, R. W. (1998). Knowledge of English and Spanish helps Latino children succeed at school. *University of California Linguistic Minority Research Institute, 7,* 1.

Teachers of English to Speakers of Other Languages. (1997). *ESL standards for pre-K–12 students.* Alexandria, VA: Author.

Teachers of English to Speakers of Other Languages. (2001). *TESOL statement on language and literacy development for young English language learners.* Alexandria, VA: Author.

Thomas, W. P., & Collier, V. P. (1998). Two languages are better than one. *Educational Leadership, 55,* 23–27.

Thonis, E. (1983). *The English-Spanish connection.* Northvale, NJ: Santillana.

Valdes, G., & Figueroa, R. A. (1994). *Bilingualism and testing: A special case of bias.* Norwood, NJ: Ablex.

Walther-Thomas, C., Korinek, L., McLaughlin. V. L., & Williams, B. T. (2000). *Collaboration for inclusive education: Developing successful programs.* Boston: Allyn and Bacon.

Wong-Fillmore, L. (1991). When learning a second language means losing the first. *Early Childhood Research Quarterly, 6,* 323–346.

Zehler, A. M. (1994). *Working with English language learners: Strategies for elementary and middle school teachers* (NCBE Program Information Guide Series #19). Washington, DC: National Clearinghouse for Bilingual Education.

11

INTEGRATING ENGLISH LANGUAGE LEARNERS IN GENERAL EDUCATION

Sandra H. Fradd
University of Florida

Intuitively, as they interact with people learning English as a new language, most English-proficient speakers adjust their communication to make it more comprehensible. Such adjustments illustrate the speaker's inherent awareness of the importance of communicating at the listener's language proficiency level. Communication adjustments resulting in "comprehensible input," or language at the listener's level of comprehension, include not only changing the words, but also "contextualization" of the message through the use of gestures, demonstrations, and other ways to actively convey the meaning.

Observing an English-proficient child or adult interact with a beginning English Language Learner (ELL), one intuitively realizes the need for understanding language proficiency and the importance of contextualization in making communication meaningful. Informally, such communication adjustments often occur naturally between speakers and listeners. These natural occurrences suggest the utility of more formal practices for ELLs' classroom instruction. Identifying ELLs' levels of language proficiency and using contextualization in meaning-making can offer these students important learning opportunities in general classroom settings.

Providing comprehensible input in classroom situations through contextualization includes modification in the amount and the type of language used to promote comprehension, participation, and achievement. Because not all ELLs require the same modifications to make the communication comprehensible, teachers must be aware of individual and group learning needs and knowledgeable of specific modifications for meeting them. Teachers might select to use keywords and phrases combined with pictures and gestures for beginning ELL students. For more advanced ELLs, associations of written and verbal information with pictures, graphics, and three-dimensional objects might be more appropriate. School psychologists can assist teachers and other professionals in matters of placement and instruction by informally identifying ELLs' proficiency levels and contextualization needs. Collaboration among school psychologists, teachers, and other instructional support personnel can also facilitate the use of instructional modifications and interventions to promote ELLs' participation and achievement. An understanding of the theoretical frameworks and practical applications can assist both school psychologists and teachers integrate ELLs into mainstream instruction. Applications may be used in a variety of programs, including regular, English to Speakers of Other Languages (ESOL), bilingual, and exceptional student education.

The purpose of this chapter is to provide an overview of two theoretical frameworks, contextualization and instructional assessment, and applications as classroom strategies to promote ELLs' participation in general classroom settings. First, the theoretical and research basis for each of the frameworks is presented. Next, the implications of these frameworks are discussed with respect to classroom instruction. Subsequently, suggestions for instruction and observation of classroom practices are discussed. Finally, the importance of future research and practice in personnel preparation are addressed. In addition to enhancing professional development, the chapter promotes collaboration among school psychologists and classroom teachers in meeting ELLs' learning needs.

THEORETICAL AND RESEARCH BASIS

Contextualization and instructional language assessment, the two theoretical frameworks discussed in this chapter, are described in this section. Relevant terminology is defined and the research supporting the frameworks' development is briefly discussed.

Contextualization

One of the most powerful and instructionally relevant developments in the explanatory theory of ELLs' academic performance in classroom contexts (referred to here as "contextualization") was developed by Jim Cummins. Cummins (1981) initially used the terms Basic Interpersonal Communication Skills (BICS) and Cognitive Academic Language Proficiency (CALP) to differentiate between two types of communication: (a) language comprehended by observing the speakers and environment (context-embedded discourse), and (b) communication requiring knowledge of the language and content for comprehension (context-reduced language). Although use of the terms "BICS" and "CALP" have given way to other labels, such as "social" and "academic" language, recognition of the importance of "contextualization" in meaningful classroom instruction continues to evolve (Echevarria & Graves, 2003; Fradd & Larrinaga-McGee, 1994). The terminology and constructs associated with contextualization are discussed next.

Context-embedded and context-reduced.   With regard to classroom instruction, contextualization encompasses all of the ways information is made available

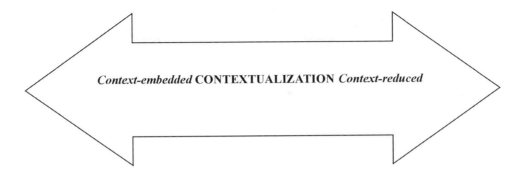

FIGURE 11–1. Contextualization continuum.

to enhance ELLs' comprehension and participation in oral and written communication. Examples of contextualization, or context-embedded language, include: facial expressions, gestures, and physical movements; voice intonation and communication speed; pictures and graphics; instructional realia, such as concrete real-world materials and easily observable activities; and the use of memorized words and phrases in consistent and new patterns. Contextualization also occurs through students' interactions with each other in hands-on, problem-solving tasks. With contextualization ELLs learn to comprehend the meaning of language of the classroom.

The amount of contextualization available within the learning environment can be observed and described along a continuum ranging from context-embedded to context-reduced discourse (see Figure 11–1). An example of a context-embedded activity could include written directions accompanied by pictorial representations ELLs use collaboratively to complete a hands-on task. Contextualization offers students opportunities for meaning-making and provides instruction and support for both social and academic language development. In contrast, a context-reduced activity would require that students bring their own understandings of language and content with little support provided by the environment or the task itself. An example of a context-reduced activity would be an assignment to read a selection and respond to questions in writing (see Figure 11–1).

On the context-embedded side of the continuum, meaning-making for participating in classroom activities occurs through observation and interactions with others. As activities become more context-reduced, students must apply their own knowledge of language and content in order to engage. According to Teachers of English to Speakers of Other Languages (TESOL; 1997), acquisition of both context-embedded social and context-reduced academic language is essential for ELLs' full participation in English-speaking society. Examples of social and academic discourse are presented in Table 11–1. Although this table and the related discussion suggests a dichotomy of language forms (context-embedded social and context-reduced academic language), classroom observations suggest that rather than distinct types of language, there are many gradations between the two proto-

TABLE 11–1
Examples and Characteristics of Context-Embedded and Context-Reduced Language

Context-embedded Social Language	Context-reduced Academic Language
Examples	
Words and phrases associated with specific events, such as greetings and leave-takings	The discourse of lectures and written texts
Ritualized familiar questions	Academic content questions
Conversations with friends about familiar topics	An oral class report
Small group discussion of a hands-on activity	Individual completion of a written academic test
Characteristics	
Group interactions with frequent turn-taking	Lengthy individual discourse
Use of non-specific terms, such as "thing," "stuff," "this," "that"	Use of precise specific terms
Use of general vocabulary	Use of varied, specific, comprehensive vocabulary
Frequent use of non-verbal support, such as gestures, intonation, pauses	Non-verbal support limited to graphics, charts, tables, and other illustrations

types (Chin, 2002). Recognition of these gradations is important in organizing classrooms where ELLs have opportunities to acquire a wide range of discourse.

Cognitively-undemanding and cognitively-demanding. Two additional terms are important with respect to the framework of contextualization: identification of instructional activities as cognitively-undemanding or cognitively-demanding, referring to the level of difficulty, or the knowledge and skill required for participation. Activity demands can also be organized on a continuum, as illustrated in Figure 11–2. For school-age children, examples of cognitive demand include learning to paint a picture, an activity considered relatively cognitively-undemanding because students can paint with little instruction. In contrast, learning to use a telescope to identify stars and planets in the solar system would be considered cognitively-demanding. The intersection of the two continua forms a four-quadrant graphic. Activities characteristic of each quadrant are illustrated Figure 11–3.

There are two important points for consideration when applying the contextualization framework in classroom instruction. First, just as learning to use a new telescope might be cognitively undemanding for a skilled astronomer, language and activities that may be cognitively-demanding for ELLs at one level of language-learning may become cognitively-undemanding as their proficiency and academic knowledge increases. Second, ELLs require opportunities to participate in cognitively-demanding and context-reduced activities as well as those with contextualization and limited cognitive demand. Like the need for a balanced diet,

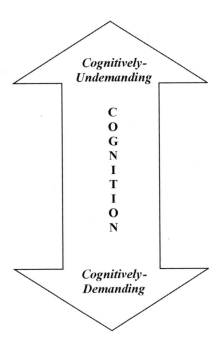

FIGURE 11–2. Cognitive demand continuum.

ELLs require instructional opportunities in all four quadrants on a regular basis. Like their age-peers, ELLs benefit from opportunities to engage in academically challenging material and to achieve. By understanding the process of second language acquisition, school psychologists can assist teachers in modifying input and activity demands without compromising expectations for ELLs' academic achievement.

Instructional Language Assessment

Stephen Krashen's theories of second language acquisition have contributed to greater understanding of the need for comprehensible input, or meaningful instruction, in meeting ELLs' learning needs (Krashen, 1981). In terms of meaning-making, language proficiency is inseparable from academic achievement. As a result, for ELLs, all assessments in English can also be tests of proficiency. Because educators may not be aware of the relationship of language proficiency and achievement, school psychologists can assist teachers in promoting both instruction and appropriate assessment by making this relationship clear. In addition, informal assessment can provide insight into the type of comprehensible input students require when participating and achieving in classrooms. The second theoretical framework, instructional assessment, provides an informal way of looking at the language acquisition process. Assessors can use scales or rubrics, for example, to identify ELLs' progress in acquiring English. Information from this

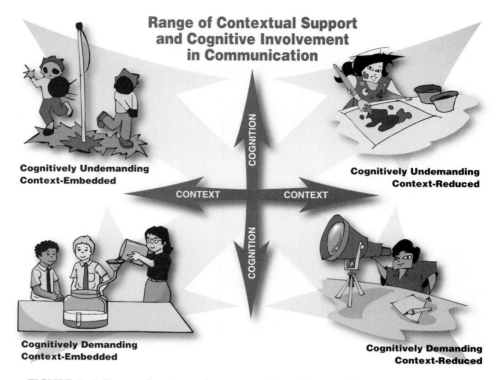

FIGURE 11–3. Range of contextual support and cognitive involvement in communication.

process can be used to modify language input, vary amount of contextualization, and change the activity demands for instruction and assessment.

Instructional language assessment as a process.   Instructional language assessment links instruction and assessment to plan, instruct, and monitor ELLs' learning progress (Fradd & Larrinaga-McGee, 1994; Fradd, 1999). Examples of instructional assessment include the analyses of ELLs' oral and written discourse and the use of this information in providing comprehensible input that enables ELLs to respond to classroom texts, assignments, and informal documents.

Instructional language assessment as a set of icons.   The inverted tripartite (three-component) triangle composed of form, function, and content can be attributed to the American Council of Teachers of Foreign Language (ACTFL; Omaggio, 1986). ACTFL also developed assessment vignettes and rubrics for use in determining the oral language proficiency of adults and teenagers acquiring additional languages, including English. The ACTFL language-acquisition knowledge base, in combination with research on child-language acquisition in first and second languages, provides a foundation for the instructional language assessment framework (Fradd & Larrinaga-McGee, 1994) as illustrated in Figure 11–4 (Fradd, 1999, in press). This graphic illustrates the language-learning process as a whole as well as by the components of form, function, and content. Proficiency development oc-

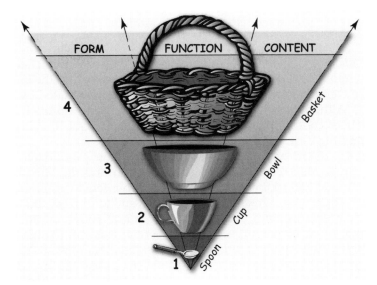

FIGURE 11–4. Language proficiency levels in the instructional language assessment rubric.

curs within and across these components. The containers, from spoon to basket, suggest the amount of language typically produced at each level. These icons also suggest the amount of language ELLs may comprehend at those levels. Although quantity is not the only feature defining proficiency, identification of the quantity provides a starting point for further proficiency considerations.

The descriptors associated with each level suggest the type of input required for comprehension. These level descriptors also suggest specific aspects of proficiency ELLs must acquire to move from one level to the next. They further suggest the type of instruction required at each level for academic and social language proficiency. Extending the graphic analogy, just as each of the smaller containers fits into the subsequent larger ones, the language learned at each of the earlier levels provides the foundation for learning at each of the subsequent higher levels.

Levels. The term "level" refers to specific characteristics of language acquisition that ELLs exhibit at different stages in the language acquisition process. These levels can be viewed as constellations of performance, or communication patterns with subsets of characteristics. Each sublevel is associated with specific features referred to as "entry" represented with a "–" "mid," and "exit" with a "+." ELLs' progress in acquiring new skills and levels of proficiency can be monitored and tracked as movement up the triangle.

Thresholds. The horizontal lines that divide proficiency levels represent thresholds that students must cross in terms of attaining specific skills and language abilities (see Figure 11–4). Students crossing a threshold typically exhibit language development patterns characteristic of two levels, the one they are leaving and the new one they are entering. Educators can plan specific instruction to promote language learning and academic achievement at ELLs' proficiency levels by being aware of the characteristic changes in students' language production and comprehension as they progress through levels and cross the thresholds,.

Form, function, and content.   The triangle graphic (see Figure 11–4) is divided into three components: form, function, and content. Research on the importance of each of these components of language development was initiated by Bloom and Lahey (1978). Although their focus was primarily on English-proficient students, these researchers' contributions are relevant in language acquisition in general and in identifying ELLs' strengths and language-learning needs.

Form refers to the more noticeable aspects of language production, such as the appearance (in written discourse) and the sound (in oral discourse) of the language. In both oral and written language, form also refers to grammar (e.g., subject-verb and article-noun agreement, word order, and tense), vocabulary use, and the overall "correctness" of a communication. In oral communication, form includes pronunciation, accent, prosody, and general fluency; in written language, it includes handwriting, spelling, organization, and general appearance. Although form is the most easily assessed aspect of proficiency, the other two components, function and content, make substantial contributions to academic language achievement.

Function refers to the purposes for which language is used. Building on the work of Halliday (1973) and Tough (1976), this component considers use-language in authentic communication. Examples of language functions include questioning, reasoning, reporting, or imagining. Students acquire different language functions according to their needs and purposes for communicating. Each function requires grammatical structures that support communication for a specific outcome. Some of these structures are unique to particular functions, such as those for asking and answering questions. In using the questioning function, for example, students must differentiate asking from answering questions, as in "John comes" and "Does John come?" When learning their first languages, children acquire the language functions necessary for the culture in which they live. Such is not necessarily the case in acquiring additional languages. Differences in cultures, socioeconomic status, and variations in life experiences influence the ways students learn and use languages (Bennett, 2003). As a result, ELLs may require assistance in learning the functions required in school. The academic language of schools requires that students acquire functions relevant to specific content areas. For example, in language arts instruction focusing on literature students may be required to project and explain the actions and feelings of others, whereas in science inquiry they learn to make predictions, collect and interpret data, and explain findings. Each of these tasks requires a different set of language functions (Fradd & Lee, 1999).

Content refers to knowledge and information about a topic or subject area. Content-learning involves understanding processes, relationships, sequences, categories, and consequences, and other aspects of knowledge. Although vocabulary plays an important role in content knowledge, it is not sufficient to demonstrate knowledge of content. Content is the essence of instruction. Content instruction is not limited to vocabulary development, or the mastery of facts and lists of information. It requires students not only comprehend, but apply their knowledge in a variety of ways. For ELLs, contextualization is particularly important in developing content knowledge.

Integrating language components.   Aspects of language form, such as grammar, spelling, and vocabulary, are more easily taught and assessed than the comprehension of content (Fradd, in press). School psychologists can assist teachers in looking beyond ELLs' acquisition of language forms to consider what students actually understand about a topic (ELLs' content knowledge) and how they use language meaningfully (ELLs' language function use) to communicate their understandings. Psychologists can also share their insights in decision-making procedures concerning ELLs' learning needs and educational placements.

Integrating the Frameworks of Contextualization and Instructional Assessment

Research integrating the frameworks of instructional language assessment and contextualization suggests a powerful impact in meeting ELLs' learning. For example, within the context of science instruction, Fradd, Lee, and their colleagues found that by using these frameworks, teachers were able to promote their ELLs' performance in science and literacy to levels comparable to the English-proficient peers (Fradd, Lee, et al., 1997; Fradd, Lee, Sutman, & Saxton, 2001). Important aspects of this research included teachers' informal assessment of what ELLs' knew and could do and contextualized instruction combining language development with content-learning. In these classrooms, initial performance measures included the use of gestures in oral discourse and drawings in written communication (Lee, Fradd, & Sutman, 1995). This research suggests that by examining ELLs' understandings of content separate from form, and by encouraging ELLs' expressions of knowledge through graphics, demonstrations, and the use of real world materials, school psychologists and teachers can facilitate students' development of language functions and knowledge of context as a process for acquiring English (Fradd & Lee, 2001).

This section presented a brief overview of the research and theoretical underpinnings of two frameworks, contextualization and instructional assessment, which were discussed throughout this chapter. Each of the frameworks provides insights that contribute to ELLs' effective instruction. In combination these frameworks offer an approach for providing the input and informal assessment ELLs require to achieve on par with their age-peers in general education settings. School psychologists can assist teachers in organizing instruction to promote ELLs' success by becoming familiar with the process of contextualization at students' levels of language proficiency.

IMPLICATIONS FOR CLASSROOM USE

Although research establishing the frameworks for contextualization and instructional assessment has been conducted over the past several decades, current demands for standards-based instruction make the relevance of the evolving applications particularly appropriate in today's diverse classrooms. This section describes levels of language proficiency and provides an overview of information on classroom applications in the context of standards-based instruction. An understanding of the relationship of contextualization and proficiency levels is important in selecting or developing instructional activities and monitoring ELLs' progress in acquiring language and subject area content. Typically, the amount of contextualization decreases as their language proficiency increases (Fradd, 1999). Observations of the amount of contextualization required to communicate content knowledge provide insight into ELLs' academic learning needs.

Instructional Assessment Level Descriptors and Proficiency Examples

Most students want to communicate, participate, and achieve. In their desire to succeed, most ELLs are similar to their English-proficient age-peers. School psychologists can use the instructional assessment continuum described here with teachers in informally assessing ELLs and using the information for plan for their movement toward English proficiency and achievement.

Level one: Sounds, words, and phrase. The icon for level one is a teaspoon. Imagine the language that could be contained on a teaspoon—only a small amount. Level one language is a halting collection of sounds, gestures, and approximations of English and words from other languages. At the entry level (1-), ELLs use sounds, gestures, and other non-verbal communication to achieve basic needs or convey ideas and information. At the exit level (1+) ELLs may recite learned material including songs, poems, and vocabulary lists. As these students' begin to connect two and three words or modify memorized phrases to make new expressions, they reduce their dependence on gestures. This progress indicates a transition to level two.

Level two: Phrases, sentences, and the beginnings of paragraphs. The second-level icon is the cup. A cup can contain different amounts of language, such as "just a little at the bottom," a "half-full" or "a full" cup. Similarly within level two, there are multiple stages of language development as ELLs acquire the grammar and structure of English.

At entry-two (2-) ELLs with large repertoires of phrases may appear less proficient then at level one as they shift from memorized to creative language and expand their phrases to sentences. Although the topics of these ELLs communication is generally to personal needs and experiences, with assistance, these students can communicate basic subject area content. Initially, past and future tense are often marked by descriptive words (e.g., "Last night I go movie;" "Tomorrow I come school"), rather than the correct verb forms (i.e., went, will come to). Similarly, questions are differentiated from statements by intonation, rather than word order. At mid-level (2), ELLs begin to become aware of word order and tense. Although ELLs at this level may initiate conversations, they require a more experienced communicator to sustain interactions. Students begin to demonstrate an understanding of relationships, characteristics, and sequences as they classify, organize information. At level two ELLs ask, and respond to what, who, where questions. An example of a 2: "I go out. See friends. Have to do a lot of work, the homework. I like go see friends" illustrates movement toward paragraph development.

Transition to level three (2+) communication includes the beginnings of paragraphs. At this level, ELLs have acquired fairly consistent use of high-frequency past, present, and future tense verbs. On concrete topics grammatical accuracy should be about 80 percent. Although these ELLs can communicate using topic-centered short paragraphs, they frequently pause and collect their thoughts and substitute known words for missing vocabulary. The result is that their oral communication often sounds more as a collection of short sentences strung together, than as a cohesive paragraph. An example of a 2+: "I was in my house and then I saw a garbage can of fire. /den/ the whole street got fire. /den/ I called a fire crier and then they put water on the floor and it went away" illustrates this progress. From this oral communication, although the listener can understand the message, additional information is required to know what happened. Considering the grammatical structures that have been acquired and amount of language produced, there is a great deal to celebrate, especially if the student was able to prevent a serious fire from occurring.

Level three: Paragraphs of concrete to abstract discourse. The bowl is the icon for level-three language: paragraphs and larger segments of language. As the bowl symbolizes the integration of multiple ingredients that form, like dough inside the bowl, new, larger cohesive units, it also represents the movement from concrete to abstract thinking. Like the formation of dough from its constituent components, the development of new ideas and understandings requires ELLs integrate the smaller pieces of language acquired in level two into new, more comprehensive ways of understanding, communicating, and thinking. An example of a 3- ELL: "It was hot, so hot. I /din/ know what to do. I went to the refrigerator, but it was broken. Everything was spoiled. I wish we had gone on vacation. We stayed home and now we are not having any fun."

At –3, ELLs may initially appear less proficient than at earlier stages as they become aware of their limitations and strive toward more comprehensive communication. Level three ELLs show evidence of reasoning and cohesion not seen at level two. Throughout level-three development, ELLs, like their age-peers, move from the concrete language used to describe basic context-embedded experiences to communicating context-reduced understandings. The shift in grammatical structures from coordinating (e.g., and, or) to subordinating conjunctions (e.g., although, however) offers a supporting example of changes in thinking (from parallel to subordinating associations and relationships). Throughout level three, ELLs also learn to differentiate literal and figurative meanings, to reason, explain, predict outcomes, and project others' feelings—all important language functions (Halliday, 1973; Tough, 1976). In the transition to level four, areas of potential difficulties include terms with multiple definitions, cultural differences in organizing and presenting ideas, and other pragmatic aspects of interactions. Because of these requirements, young ELLs would not be expected to attain upper level three and four proficiency.

Level four: Movement toward full English proficiency. The icon of the picnic basket suggests a larger container filled with a variety of smaller containers and implements for a complete meal and suggests language proficiency on a broad range of social and academic topics. At level four, ELLs are similar, in many ways, to their age-peers. They can use language for many purposes from persuading and arguing to hypothesizing and developing abstract meanings. ELLs, however, continue to retain some specific language learning needs, such as accent reduction, differentiation of literal and figurative meanings, and the development of pragmatic appropriateness for social participation.

Learning to Use Instructional Assessment and Contextualization

There are a number of ways in which professionals can develop the skills for using instructional assessment and contextualization. Rubrics and level descriptors provide a structure for shared learning and development of the skills required for instructional assessment. Pre-rated video clips of ELLs' communication provide opportunities for becoming familiar with the oral and written analysis. Rating video samples with and without accompanying transcripts of the students' language samples provide practice in observing the ways ELLs engage in meaning-making and convey their understandings to others. In addition to providing valuable information about students' ability to communicate in real-world contexts, such observations can assist school psychologists in separating language differences from disabilities. For example, in considering the learning needs of ELLs with limited literacy experiences, students who appear to have learning disabilities or developmental delays may, in fact, have adequate abilities, but lack the background knowledge and literacy experiences to express themselves in context-reduced settings. Observations of ELLs' engagement in follow-up activities where they must reason, explain, or even draw their understandings after participating in meaningful learning experiences can illustrate strengths sometimes not demonstrated on more formal tasks.

Gestures and facial expressions provide insights into students' understandings. For example, in explaining how hurricanes are formed, Spanish-speaking ELLs were observed to move their index fingers around in an upward spiraling motion to illustrate the hurricane movement, even though they did not communicate the scientific terms for hurricane formation. Similarly, Haitian students used their hands as if they were a set of scales to indicate the notion of equal, even though they did not communicate the term. Initially, these students' science knowledge was discounted until observers recognized the accuracy of the information conveyed (Lee et al., 1995).

In assessing students' content knowledge, initially gestures and drawings (context-embedded communication) may be more useful than oral and written communication in determining their understandings. As ELLs' communication begins to assume the qualities expected at school oral and written discourse begin to convey students' understandings. School psychologists can assist teachers in determining ELLs strengths and accomplishments as they plan and provide appropriate amount of contextualization by observing the quantity (spoon to bowl) and quality (context-embedded to context-reduced) of students' discourse.

Materials are available to facilitate individual and group preparation in learning these new skills (see, for example, a review of the contents of the *Instructional Assessment* CD-ROM by Culturally and Linguistically Appropriate Services, 2001). Other resources include texts from Teachers of English to Speakers of Other Languages (TESOL), such as *ESL Standards for Pre-K–12 Students* (TESOL, 1997) and *Scenarios for ESL Standard-Based Assessment* (TESOL, 2001). Both texts provide guidelines for observing ELLs' performance at different proficiency levels and grade ranges. TESOL has a variety of resources for personnel preparation and classroom instruction, including the development of thematic units that promote standards-based instruction (see the annotated bibliography, the chapter references, and the TESOL website http://www.tesol.org/pubs/catalog/index.html for additional information). In addition, *Authentic Assessment for English Language Learners: Practical Approaches for Teachers* (O'Malley & Valdez Pierce, 1996) offers models for creating rubrics and observing students in content areas.

IMPLEMENTATION AND APPROACHES

The utility of an effective educational theory is its application in classroom contexts. Both instructional assessment and contextualization have important classroom applications. This section addresses the need for standards-based instruction and provides examples and suggestions for observing classroom applications for instructional assessment and contextualization.

Standards-Based Instruction

At a national level, the *ESL Standards for Pre-K–12 Students* (TESOL, 1997) provide a bridge between performance expectations, as embodied in national content area standards, and ELLs' knowledge, skills, and language development as described and exemplified in the national English as a Second Language (ESL) standards. In addition to national content area and ESL standards, most states have subject area standards which serve as guides for standards-based instruction. School psychologists and teachers should already be familiar with national and state standards and other instructional requirements. Most recognize the importance of these with English-proficient students. Although not every state has standards for ELLs, an example illustrates the utility of using state or national standards to ensure ELLs receive comparable instruction.

Keeping in mind the dangers of applying national and state standards that were developed for English-proficient learners with students just acquiring English, the following examples illustrate how standards may be adapted for ELLs. Language arts is an essential content area for all students. Many states have standards that require students recognize types of literature, such as fiction and nonfiction. This particular example addresses the learning needs of middle-school ELLs in dealing with different literature genre. Multimedia presentations, such as VCR or DVD, can supplement traditional literature instruction. After viewing a brief segment of a DVD containing action scenes from fictional literature selection (no more than a few minutes of video, not the entire story), middle school 1+ ELLs use sets of terms on word cards to describe the main characters of the story. Using similar cards, 2-ELLs construct brief statements describing the characters and then organize the descriptive words in a table as a character grid. Similarly, 2+ ELLs use word cards and phrase strips to develop oral descriptions of the main characters. After sharing their ideas with each other, ELLs write and compare their descriptions. Working with the level 1 and 2 ELLs, or collaborating among themselves, 3-ELLs discuss and then write brief summaries of the video segment providing who, what, when, and why information. During a subsequent time period, ELLs repeat these or similar tasks using a comparable non-fictional literature selection or DVD presentation. A follow-up activity would compare the characters and story-lines in the two selections using written texts. Finally, after multiple experiences with literature genre, ELLs would create a chart indicating similarities and differences in the two types of literature.

Knowledge of state and national standards, the process of contextualization, and the use of instructional assessment, can enable educators to assist ELLs in moving toward the level of academic achievement specified in the standards and required of all students. Maps, realia, graphics, and interactions with more knowledgeable peers can assist ELLs in bridging the gap between their understandings and the language and content required for context-reduced, academic performance. Although the process of using contextualizing resources can be time-consuming, ELLs must receive comprehensible input to achieve in general classroom instruction (Irujo, 2000).

Making Observations in Order to Develop Instructional Interventions

In addition to using proficiency level descriptors as a guide for moving ELLs from one level to another, descriptors can also be used to observe the opportunities available to ELLs for attaining comprehensible input for language proficiency and content-knowledge learning. School psychologists, in collaboration with teachers and speech-language pathologists, can use the descriptors to observe classroom interactions to determine ELLs' learning needs and instructional opportunities. Such observations can be used for collaborative brain-storming to develop interventions and monitor ELLs' progress. The following suggestions offer a starting point for conducting such observations. School psychologists may also use this information in discussions with teachers about their ELLs' learning needs and in learning more about teachers' classroom instructional practices as they impact ELLs' opportunities to learn.

Level one.   At level one, ELLs are encouraged to participate in instruction through movement, music, drawings, and the use of keywords and phrases to comprehend and demonstrate meaning. Collaborative small group activities encourage ELLs to interact without the penalty of embarrassment of making mistakes. Although level-one-ELLs are not required to participate verbally in whole classroom discourse, they are encouraged to join others in sharing content knowledge. Considerations:

1.   How do level-one-ELLs provided receive meaningful input?
2.   How is subject-area content contextualized for level-one-ELLs?
3.   How are others involved in promoting ELLs' participation and success?

Level two.   At level two, ELLs are developing their English-language grammar system and overall awareness of communication in English. Although these ELLs typically communicate in phrases and sentences, they require positive corrective feedback in learning to correctly link words in creating their own ideas and intents. Considerations:

1. How are patterned language and simple texts used to build meaning that enables ELLs to effectively communicate orally and in writing?
2. How is content contextualized to enable level-two-ELLs to comprehend and participate?
3. How is assessment used to promote achievement and monitor ELLs' learning progress?
4. What opportunities do level-two-ELLs have to collaborate in completing tasks and refining their oral and written discourse?

Level three. As level-three-ELLs learn to organize their ideas and understandings in increasingly complex paragraphs and larger units of discourse, the initial focus is on concrete, personal experiences in cohesive passages. The focus shifts from the concrete to more abstract discourse with increasing proficiency. Considerations:

1. How is instruction organized to enable level-three-ELLs to comprehend and communicate in paragraphs and larger units of discourse?
2. How is assessment used to provide feedback that promotes ELLs' achievement?
3. What classroom-learning opportunities are available to enable ELLs to shift from context-embedded to context-reduced communication?
4. What opportunities do level-three-ELLs have to collaborate in participating and achieving?

Collaboration in observing ELLs' participation in general classrooms can provide insight into available learning opportunities. School psychologists and teachers' reflections of such observations can also promote opportunities for research and enhanced instructional practices.

IMPLICATIONS FOR FUTURE RESEARCH AND PRACTICE

Watching an English-proficient child or an adult interact with an ELL illustrates the importance of contextualization and instructional assessment. As listeners become aware of ELLs' proficiency, they tend to make contextual and linguistic adjustments that promote the new language learners' comprehension and communication. Although contextual and linguistic adjustments can enhance comprehension in informal interactions, they are not sufficient to ensure ELLs' effective instruction in general education classrooms. This chapter has presented two frameworks to assist educators in meeting ELLs' learning needs in these settings.

In an era of increasing accountability where standards-based instruction leads to evaluation of professional abilities as well as students' knowledge (Eisner, 2001; Falk, 2002), skill in identifying and responding to ELLs' learning needs is particularly important. Although suggestions for instructional interventions to meet ELLs' learning needs are available in the growing literature on standards-based classroom instruction (TESOL, 2001) and teacher preparation (Snow, 2000), research is still required to determine the most effective and appropriate ways to apply such interventions. Research is also required on how best to prepare professionals to provide standards-based instruction with ELLs. How do teachers modify instruction to meet the learning needs of ELLs with different proficiency levels and background experiences (Chin, 2002)? How do school psychologists provide useful assistance to classroom teachers who must meet the challenges of academic instruction with diverse ELLs?

For many educators, the links between assessment and instruction and between proficiency levels and the contextualization of instruction have not yet been made apparent. Frequently, professional preparation programs treat assessment and instruction as two separate, unrelated activities, rather than one unified process with multiple components (Darling-Hammond, Ancess, & Falk, 1995; Díaz-Rico & Weed, 2002). This chapter offers examples for enhancing the preparation of school psychologists in addressing ELLs' learning needs and for collaborating with teachers of ELLs in general classroom settings.

Collaboration across professional groups is essential in developing comprehensive interventions that meet the needs of large groups of ELLs as well as the specific requirements of individual students with unique learning needs. Collaboration is also important in sharing information on ELLs' learning needs as larger cohorts and individual learners. Research to enhance collaboration could impact processes for collecting and sharing such student information. School psychologists and classroom teachers require generalizeable and specialized opportunities to use informal assessments and to share performance information. Classroom-based and large-scale research could provide a dual approach for promoting collaboration among support personnel and teachers in identifying and addressing ELLs' learning needs (Rosa-Lugo & Fradd, 2000).

In considering the use of informal assessment to determine students' strengths and learning needs, this chapter has exemplified ELLs' culturally-based communication patterns. Although culturally-based ways of communicating and performing influence ELLs' engagement in classroom learning, these patterns are often not considered in assessment or instruction (Bennett, 2003; Fradd & Lee, 1999). Research is needed to assist school psychologists in recognizing the role of culture in learning and assisting teachers in identifying specific culturally-based communication patterns that can be used to promote academic achievement.

School psychologists can play an important role in promoting ELLs' effective instruction in general classrooms. They can assist teachers in identifying and meeting ELLs' learning requirements by understanding how to combine contextualization and instructional assessment to promote standards-based instruction. Inherent within these expectations is the need for instruction on par with the English-proficient students. Research is required to address the challenges of providing comprehensible input while ensuring all students' access to high academic standards (Echevarria & Graves, 2003). Although strides have been made over the past several decades, much remains to be learned and to be accomplished. The challenge to school psychologists is to actively accept this role. School psychologists can ensure that ELLs are effectively and successfully integrated into the mainstream of general education by encouraging high standards and assisting teachers in providing meaningful assessments and relevant instruction practices.

ANNOTATED BIBLIOGRAPHY

Bennett, C. I. (2003). *Comprehensive multicultural education: Theory and practice* (5th ed.). Boston: Allyn & Bacon.

> Terms and issues of multicultural education are frequently overlapping and sometimes so confusing that educators may withdraw from considering them in classroom instruction. This text provides clear insights into these issues in practical, relevant approaches that can influence the ways educators think about as well as address cultural diversity. The text organizes discussion of the issues in four dimensions, each with three related areas for exploration and consideration. Emphasizing both theoretical and practical approaches, case studies highlight many of the major issues, as lesson plans exemplify important content.

Díaz-Rico, L. T., & Weed, K. Z. (2002). *The crosscultural, language, and academic development handbook: A complete K–12 reference guide* (2nd ed.). Boston: Allyn & Bacon.

> As the title suggests, this text provides a comprehensive overview of the terms and approaches to meeting ELLs' learning needs. Of particular interest are the sections on cultural diversity and language planning for special populations. A major limitation of this text is its focus on issues particular to California, rather than providing a national focus. Nevertheless, the content provided here is clear, relevant, and useful.

Echevarria, J., & Graves, A. (2003). *Sheltered content instruction: Teaching English-language learners with diverse abilities.* Boston: Allyn & Bacon.

> This text provides a theoretical framework and comprehensive practical suggestions for making content area instruction relevant and appropriate for ELLs. The text considers the overlap between regular and special education in addressing learning needs. Unfortunately, the target audience for this text also appears to be California, rather than the nation as a whole. Useful aspects of the text include the many examples, case studies, and scenarios depicting classroom interactions.

Irujo, S. (Ed.). (2000). *Integrating the ESL standards into classroom practice, grades 6–8.* Alexandria, VA: Teachers of English to Speakers of Other Languages.

> This text is in one of four available from the professional organization, Teachers of English to Speakers of Other Languages (TESOL) that offer explanations and practical suggestions for implementing the national *ESL Standards for Pre-K–12.* These texts are organized by grade level, K–2, 3–5, 6–8, 9–12. Each of the texts contains six instructional units, some addressing specific populations, grade levels, or language proficiencies, others with a more open and general focus. Each unit focuses on what students need to know and be able to do to achieve the expectations established in national and many state language arts standards.

Teachers of English to Speakers of Other Languages. (2001). *Scenarios for ESL standards-based assessment.* Alexandria, VA: Author.

The national *ESL Standards for Pre-K–12* (Teachers of English to Speakers of Other Languages, 1997) is a text that presents goals and standards for providing ELLs with instruction to develop social and academic language proficiency and an understanding of culture to successfully participate in school and society at large. Whereas the original 1997 text presented vignettes, or snapshots, illustrating standards-based instruction for ELLs, the focus of this text is on expanding the vignettes to scenarios, or figurative videos, illustrating assessment as a part of the instructional process. This text provides many suggestions and practical applications for promoting a variety of classroom assessments for students learning English as a new language.

REFERENCES

Bennett, C. I. (2003). *Comprehensive multicultural education: Theory and practice* (5th ed.). Boston: Allyn & Bacon.

Bloom, L., & Lahey, M. (1978). *Language development and language disorders.* New York: Wiley.

Chin, J. (2002). *What secondary English to speakers of other languages (ESOL) teachers know about social and academic language and instructional strategies for limited English proficient students.* Unpublished doctoral dissertation, Florida International University, Miami, Florida.

Culturally and Linguistically Appropriate Services. (2001). *Instructional language assessment CD-ROM* [electronic version]. Champaign, IL: Early Childhood Research Institute, University of Chicago at Urbana-Champaign. Available from http://128.174.128.220/cgibin/clasSearch/viewitem.cgi?id = 2893

Cummins, J. (1981). Age on arrival and immigrant second language learning in Canada. A reassessment. *Applied Linguistics, 2,* 132-149.

Darling-Hammond, L., Ancess, J., & Falk, B. (1995). *Authentic assessment in action.* New York: Teachers College Press.

Díaz-Rico, L. T., & Weed, K. Z. (2002). *The crosscultural, language, and academic development handbook: A complete K–12 reference guide* (2nd ed.). Boston: Allyn & Bacon.

Echevarria, J., & Graves, A. (2003). *Sheltered content instruction: Teaching English-language learners with diverse abilities.* Boston: Allyn & Bacon.

Eisner, E. (2001). What does it mean to say a school is doing well? *Phi Delta Kappan, 82,* 367–372.

Falk, B. (2002). Standards-based reforms: Problems and possibilities. *Phi Delta Kappan, 83,* 612–620.

Fradd, S. H. (1999). *Instructional language assessment* (a multi-platform CD-ROM). Tallahassee, FL: Florida Department of Education.

Fradd, S. H. (in press). *Language arts through ESOL* (5 multimedia modules for preparing classroom teachers and support personnel to effectively assess and instruct students learning English as a new language). Tallahassee, FL: Florida Department of Education.

Fradd, S. H., & Klingner, J. K. (Eds.). (1995). *Classroom inclusion strategies for students learning English.* San Antonio, TX: Psychological Corporation.

Fradd, S. H., & Larrinaga-McGee, P. (1994). *Instructional assessment.* New York: Addison-Wesley.

Fradd, S. H., & Lee, O. (1999). Teachers' roles in promoting science inquiry with students from diverse language backgrounds. *Educational Researcher, 28,* 14–20, 42.

Fradd, S. H., & Lee, O. (2001). Needed: A framework for integrating standardized and informal assessment for students developing science language proficiency. In J. V. Tinajero & S. Hurley (Eds.), *Literacy assessment of bilingual learners* (pp.132–148). Boston: Allyn & Bacon.

Fradd, S. H., Lee, O., Cabrera, P., del Rio, V., Leth, A., Morin, R., Ceballos, M., Santalla, M., Cross, L., & Mathieu, T. (1997). School-university partnerships to promote science with students learning English. *TESOL Journal, 7,* 35–40.

Fradd, S. H., Lee, O., Sutman, F. X., & Saxton, M. K. (2001). Promoting science literacy with diverse learners. *Bilingual Research Journal, 25,* 479–501.

Halliday, M. (1973). *Explorations in the functions of language.* New York: Elsevier North Holland.

Irujo, S. (Ed.). (2000). *Integrating the ESL standards into classroom practice, grades 6–8.* Alexandria, VA: Teachers of English to Speakers of Other Languages.

Krashen, S. D. (1981). *Principles and practice in second language acquisition.* London: Prentice-Hall International.

Lee, O., Fradd, S. H., & Sutman, F. X. (1995). Science knowledge and cognitive strategy use among culturally and linguistically diverse students. *Journal of Research in Science Teaching, 32,* 797–816.

Omaggio, A. C. (1986). *Teaching language in context.* Boston: Heinle & Heinle.

O'Malley, J. M., &Valdez Pierce, L. (1996). *Authentic assessment for English language learners: Practical approaches for teachers.* Reading, MA: Addison-Wesley.

Rosa-Lugo, L. I., & Fradd, S. H. (2000). Preparing professionals to serve communicatively disordered English language learners. *Communication Quarterly Journal, 22,* 29–42.

Snow, M. A. (Ed.). (2000). *Implementing the ESL standards for Pre-K–12 students through teacher education.* Alexandria, VA: Teachers of English to Speakers of Other Languages.

Teachers of English to Speakers of Other Languages. (1997). *ESL standards for Pre-K–12 students.* Alexandria, VA: Author.

Teachers of English to Speakers of Other Languages. (2001). *Scenarios for ESL standards-based assessment.* Alexandria, VA: Author.

Tough, J. (1976). *Listening to children talking: A guide to the appraisal of children's use of languages.* Portsmouth, NH: Heinemann.

IV

MULTICULTURAL AND BILINGUAL ASSESSMENT

12

ASSESSING ORAL AND WRITTEN LANGUAGE PROFICIENCY: A GUIDE FOR PSYCHOLOGISTS AND TEACHERS

Margo Gottlieb and Else Hamayan
Illinois Resource Center

Language assessment is often part of the centerpiece of psychological evaluations in K–12 school settings for all students; it is the key component, however, for English Language Learners (ELLs) who may have possible special education needs. ELLs are a heterogeneous group of students who are exposed to languages and cultures outside of English and the mainstream on a daily basis and, due to their linguistic and cultural differences, have not yet reached academic parity with their native English speaking peers. In United States schools today, we have surpassed a total enrollment of 4.6 million ELLs, or approximately 9.6% of the total student population (Kindler, 2002). These demographics represent a sizeable and continuous increase in the numbers of linguistically and culturally diverse students that teachers face each day.

Figures from the Office for Civil Rights for 1997 estimate that 5.5 %of ELLs enrolled in language support services are also categorized with a disability (U.S. Department of Education, 2001). The vast majority of these students (approximately 75%) are Latino, from Spanish speaking backgrounds, followed by Vietnamese (4%), and Hmong, Cantonese, Cambodian, and Korean (each reported at 2%). The socioeconomic status of this group is depressed, with 77% of ELLs eligible for free or reduced lunch, which is twice as great as the 38% of the general school population.

The assessment of ELLs with potential disabilities is one of the most puzzling issues facing the field of special education today. There are several factors that contribute to this perplexity. First, a shortage of qualified personnel (including teachers, psychologists, and social workers) exacerbates attempts to instruct and assess these students with sound educational practices. Second, the instruments available to assess ELL students are woefully inadequate and inaccurate. Third, the professional development afforded teachers does not substantially address how to differentiate the academic difficulties of ELLs attributed to language and culture differences and those that are endemic to special education diagnoses. Fourth, parents of ELLs are often disenfranchised themselves and are unaware of their rights within the U.S. school system. These factors seem to lead to over-identification of ELLs as students with learning disabilities and thus, a disproportionate representation of this population receiving special education services (Burnette, 2000).

These demographics and dilemmas serve as the backdrop for our chapter on language assessment. In it, we address major topics that pertain to psychologists, teachers, and administrators who work with ELLs with potential disabilities. Since language assessment is an ongoing process for any ELL and not only to be used for students who are suspected of having a special education need, the topics discussed in this chapter also pertain to mainstream classroom, English as a Second Language (ESL), and bilingual teachers. Included is an examination of the theoretical underpinnings of the construct of language proficiency and language proficiency assessment. Moving from research to practice, we identify the stakeholders and purposes for language proficiency assessment in a special education setting. In particular, we explore approaches for formative and summative assessment within their respective contexts, the influence of recent legislation on assessment, and finally, the use of language proficiency information in a special education setting.

THEORETICAL AND RESEARCH BASIS

Defining Bilingual Language Proficiency

Language proficiency has been defined as the ability to use language accurately and appropriately in its oral and written forms in a variety of settings (Cloud, Genesee, & Hamayan, 2000). This definition incorporates the four domains of language: listening, speaking (oral language), reading and writing (literacy). Although the four domains of language are highly interrelated, they can develop independently of one another, especially when the language is not native to the learner (Bialystock & Hakuta, 1994). Thus, it is possible that a child develop oral proficiency in English outside of school without having had any exposure to written English. Similarly, it is possible to have learned English as a foreign language in the home country primarily through literacy, without having had interaction with spoken English. This makes bilingual language proficiency a highly complex phenomenon (Hamers & Blanc, 2000).

While listening and reading represent receptive skills (i.e., the person receives information), speaking and writing represent expressive skills (i.e., the person gives information). Receptive skills typically develop ahead of expressive skills because receiving information is easier than giving it; therefore, most learners understand more language than they can express (Spolsky, 1989).

Proficiency in all these aspects of language is rarely equal in both languages for a bilingual person (Bialystock & Hakuta, 1994). The person who is equally proficient in all aspects of both native and second languages—that is, the balanced bilingual—is the exception rather than the rule. Most bilinguals have more proficiency in some domains of one language than the other, and it is not always the native language that is the more proficient one (Bialystock & Hakuta, 1994). Bilingual proficiency can best be represented by a series of constantly changing continua (Hornberger, 2003).

Not only is there an array of factors that influence language learning, there are also a myriad of conditions that affect bilingualism (Spolsky, 1989). For one thing, proficiency varies as a function of the context of communication. The extent to which language is contextualized makes a difference in how easy it is to process. Language that is highly contextualized (e.g., an illustrated story) is easier to use and is learned more quickly than language that occurs in a reduced, or low, context (e.g., a conversation over the phone).

Proficiency also varies as a function of the purpose and content of communication (Gottlieb, 2003). The language needed in informal social settings and particularly about concrete topics (e.g., describing the physical attributes of a person or object) may be easier to master than language that is needed in more formal settings, especially when the content is abstract and cognitively demanding (e.g., explaining the concept of democracy or justice).

To add to the complexity of this picture, we also know that bilingual proficiency develops in different ways. The length of time it takes to become proficient in a second language varies significantly among learners. Estimates have been given that range from three to five years for social everyday language and five to ten years for more cognitively demanding academic language (Cummins, 1980; Thomas & Collier, 2002). Several factors contribute to these differences. Individual learner characteristics, such as attitudes, motivation and personality traits, predict ease of learning a second language, as do characteristics of the learning environment (Cloud, Genesee, & Hamayan, 2000). Adding to this variety is the fact that many ELLs experience attrition of their native language in the process of learning a second one (Hamers & Blanc, 2000).

All these variables that define bilingual language proficiency make the assessment process quite complex. It is important that all students who interact in two languages, no matter in which aspects of language proficiency, be assessed for their oral language development and literacy in both languages and in a variety of contexts (Damico, 1991). To summarize, the variables that need to be taken into account in the assessment of students who have been exposed to two languages include: (a) the overall use of L1 (first or native language) in relation to L2 (second language, or in this case, English), (b) the learner's history of language learning, (c) the extent of contextualization present, (d) the degree of formality or register required, and (e) the intent of the communication.

Psychologists, administrators, and teachers must keep this complexity in mind when making educational and programmatic decisions regarding ELLs.

Why Is it Important to Assess Oral and Written Language?

Language forms the heart of communication and through language we witness conceptual development and cognitive growth. The interaction between language and cognition is multi-faceted and for ELLs who, by their very nature, face language obstacles, the two constructs are often intertwined and difficult to differentiate. One of the most effective ways of solving this puzzle is through assessment of the students' oral and written language proficiency.

The English language proficiency of ELLs, by definition, cannot be on par with their native English-speaking peers. This lack of proficiency obviously interferes with learning academic content in English and with demonstrating academic achievement especially when the instruction and assessment are not conducted through ESL strategies (LaCelle-Peterson & Rivera, 1994). However, it must be very clear that this lack of English proficiency does not in and of itself constitute a predisposition to a language disability as defined by the special education community. There is a substantial body of research on second language acquisition that documents the developmental process of language learning for students across age spectrums, cultures, and educational experiences (Bialystock & Hakuta, 1994). We, as advocates of students, must bring this knowledge to the table when a special education label is being contemplated for ELLs.

Therefore, we must ascertain the contribution of language to a student's total development, especially for linguistically and culturally diverse students who have been exposed to a language other than English, even if incidentally. To obtain this information, it is critical that we assess the four major domains of language, listening, speaking, reading, and writing, in the students' L1 and L2. Only then, can we determine the full extent language plays in a student's academic performance.

IMPLICATIONS FOR PRACTICE

Identifying Components, Audiences, and Purposes of Language Proficiency Assessment

The most extensive assessment of language proficiency provides information about all the different domains of language, in a variety of contexts, for a variety of topics—both informal and formal, as well as concrete and abstract—and in both native and second languages. Table 12–1 illustrates the range of language proficiency components that would give the most complete picture of a student's bilingual performance.

The most striking feature of the figure is the symmetry in language proficiency assessment when conducted in the native language (L1) and the second language (L2), English. Language proficiency assessment entails examining a series of components across the language domains- listening, speaking, reading, and writing. The first component, the context, refers to the amount of linguistic or visual support (either high or low) afforded the student during assessment. The second component, the register, takes the delivery of the message into account, that is, whether it is under formal or informal conditions. The last component addresses the nature of the message; generally, it may be classified as abstract/ implicit or concrete/ explicit. However, not all assessments of language proficiency need to encompass the entire gamut of components illustrated in Table 12–1. We assess whatever we need information on and for specific purposes in order to make specific decisions. How-

TABLE 12–1
The Range of Language Proficiency Components of Bilingual Students

	Context	Register	Nature of Message	Listening	Speaking	Reading	Writing
L1	High Context	Formal	Abstract				
			Concrete				
		Informal	Abstract				
			Concrete				
	Low Context	Formal	Abstract				
			Concrete				
		Informal	Abstract				
			Concrete				
L2	High Context	Formal	Abstract				
			Concrete				
		Informal	Abstract				
			Concrete				
	Low Context	Formal	Abstract				
			Concrete				
		Informal	Abstract				
			Concrete				

ever, unless the student has zero (or close to zero) proficiency in one of the two languages, it is recommended that proficiency in both languages be assessed.

In the framework proposed in this chapter, the different aspects of the education of ELLs must determine the information that we obtain regarding a student's language proficiency. For example, in order to make the decision regarding the language(s) of instruction, we must obtain information on how well the student processes academic language required to succeed in school at grade level in all four domains. In order to make a decision as to whether a student has special reading difficulties in English, we must obtain information about the students' ability and history with native language literacy.

What is assessed and how the results are used depend largely on the purposes and the audiences for assessment (Gottlieb, 2006). The purposes and audiences for assessing language proficiency are wide-ranging. Table 12–2 lists various purposes that different groups of people may have for language proficiency assessment.

Once the determination is made as to the purpose of the assessment, the audience, the languages of assessment, and how the results are going to be used, we can then select the most appropriate assessment approaches for ELLs. Systematic planning is key to the data gathering process. The next section addresses issues revolving around this phase of assessment.

TABLE 12–2
**The Purposes and Audiences for Language Proficiency Assessment
of English Language Learners**

Audience	*Purposes for Assessment*
Teachers	Monitor student progress Inform and plan instruction
Psychologists	Obtain diagnostic information on students Make decisions based on reliable and valid data
Administrators	Document student performance (for accountability) Use information to improve services
Parents	Monitor growth of child in language proficiency Understand how services support child's learning
Students	Engage in self-assessment Use data as evidence of language acquisition

IMPLEMENTATION AND APPROACHES

Several approaches are possible to obtain information regarding language proficiency. Some approaches entail the use of standardized norm-referenced measures, while others are more qualitative, and rely on formative, authentic, direct and descriptive measures (O'Malley & Pierce, 1996). As is the case with the choice of what is assessed, it is important to choose the assessment approach that yields the information that is needed for a specific purpose. Table 12–3 provides some examples of how classroom-based, language proficiency data can be gathered for each of the language domains (Gottlieb, 2002).Among these alternative measures are language use surveys, anecdotal information collected by teachers, interviews, conferences, language samples (oral or written), and observations (Farr & Trumbull, 1997). Language proficiency information can be kept in portfolios, and it can be recorded by using checklists, rating scales, inventories or narrative form (Gottlieb, 1995; Hamayan, 1995).

Regardless of the approaches to be used, it is essential that assessment be planned carefully. The following questions can guide the planning process (Genesee & Hamayan, 1994):

1. Who will use the results of assessment and for what purpose?
2. What will I assess?
3. When will I assess, and has this information already been gathered?
4. How will I assess?
5. How will I record the results of my assessment?

Assessment for Specific Purposes

Assessment is most effective when it is systematically employed for each of its specified purposes and contexts (Damico, 1991). In this section, three contexts

TABLE 12–3
Strategies or Tasks Useful for Gathering Language Proficiency Data

Listening	Speaking	Reading	Writing

• Illustrations
• Observation
• Picture/word sorts
• Dramatizations/
  reenactments
	• Interviews
	• Two-way tasks
	• Student-led
	  conferences
	• Oral language
	  samples
	• Speeches
	• Demonstrations
	• Book talks
	• Debates
	• Story (re)tellings
	• Task analyses
		• Informal reading
		  inventories
		• Oral or written
		  responses
		• Word/phrase sorts
			• Dialog journals
			• Written language
			  samples, including
			  essays
			• Reports
			• Exhibits
			• Brochures,
			  newsletters
			• Lists
			• Memos
			• Letters
			• Note taking
			• Outlining

TABLE 12–4
Planning Sheet for Assessing Oral and Written Language Proficiency
of English Language Learners in First (L1) and Second (L2) Languages
Within Special Education Contexts

	Listening/Speaking		Reading		Writing	
Language of assessment	L1	L2	L1	L2	L1	L2
(Pre)referral	_____	_____	_____	_____	_____	_____
Instruction	_____	_____	_____	_____	_____	_____
Accountability	_____	_____	_____	_____	_____	_____

within a special education setting, (pre)referral, instruction, and accountability, are examined in terms of the stakeholders involved and the types of oral and written language proficiency measures that are appropriate. Later in this chapter, these same contexts are explored in regard to the potential uses of the assessment information. Table 12–4 provides a planning sheet for assessing oral and written language proficiency in first and second languages within special education contexts. Teachers and assessment personnel, such a school psychologists, can use the planning sheet to map the types of language proficiency assessments that are used in each context.

Given the three major contexts for special education assessment, we must now determine who are the primary persons responsible for planning, collecting, analyzing, and reporting the information (the stakeholders) and what types of language proficiency information are needed. Table 12–5 lists broad categories of applicable tools for (pre)referral, instruction, and accountability by aligning oral and written assessments of ELLs with special education contexts and stakeholders

(Pre)referral.

Teachers must be astutely aware of the students' oral and written language proficiency at the pre-referral stage. That is, before a teacher embarks on the formal referral process, extensive language proficiency data need to be gathered. This infor-

TABLE 12–5
**Aligning Oral and Written Assessments of English Language Learners
With Special Education Contexts and Stakeholders**

Context for Assessment	Stakeholders	Oral Assessment	Written Assessment
(Pre)referral	Multi-disciplinary Team	• Language Use Survey • Standardized language proficiency tool • Standards-based measures • Anecdotal information	• Standardized language proficiency tool • Standards-based measures
Instruction	Teachers	• Interviews/conferences • Performance tasks • Observation of students	• Informal Reading Inventories • Writing samples
Accountability	Teachers, Administrators, and the State	• Alternate assessment portfolio • Standardized language proficiency tool • Standards-based measures	• Alternate assessment portfolio

mation, collected in the student's L1 and L2, assists teachers and other school staff involved in prereferral activities in making the preliminary decision as to whether the student should be brought before a multi-disciplinary team for further evaluation. In addition, if the process does move forward, the language proficiency data are invaluable for psychologists who make the determination of the language in which the psychological testing is to be conducted. The choice of language for psychological testing is key to a student's educational future; therefore, it is incumbent upon teachers to have accurate language proficiency evidence so that ultimately, psychologists, in turn, can obtain reliable and valid information.

Within the context of referral, there are three main purposes for language proficiency assessment of ELLs. First, information on a student's oral and written language proficiency serves as criteria in the determination of a student's eligibility for special education services. Second, language proficiency information helps define the necessary amount of L1 and L2 instructional support and therefore, is important for placing students in appropriate educational environments. Third, the information can be applied to creating the language-related goals and objectives of a student's Individual Educational Plan (IEP) if one becomes necessary.

Several types of oral and written assessment tools are tied to (pre)referral. To gain an overall understanding of ELLs' language preference inside and outside of school and to inspect the students' interaction patterns with various language models and in varied settings, a language use survey is suggested (see Appendix A for a sample survey). Although, for example, ELLs may interact only in English (L2) at school, it is important to ascertain their exposure and use of their first language. The sample survey is intended to be read to the student, however, it may be translated and adapted for parents as well.

Standardized language proficiency tests are another data source for (pre)referral information; results must be current for both ELLs' oral language proficiency and literacy. States now must comply with the federal mandate that standards-based, language proficiency testing be conducted on an annual basis for ELLs in grade levels K–12 across the four language domains (No Child Left Behind Act, 2001). Therefore, these data should be readily available in English. For Latino students, there is also a choice of several instruments in Spanish. Minimally, older ELLs whose native language is other than Spanish, should produce a writing sample in L1.

The definitions of language proficiency and, axiomatically, language proficiency assessment have changed substantially since the passage of the No Child Left Behind Act of 2001. With the impetus on increased accountability, states must develop English language proficiency standards that are anchored in their academic content standards, minimally in language arts/reading, mathematics, and science. A new generation of language proficiency instruments have become available that measures ELLs' social and academic language. These tools provide a more comprehensive profile of student performance linked to school success.

In addition, information from standards-based measures that are part of a school district's repertoire of either norm-referenced or criterion-referenced tests is helpful as a means of comparison between ELLs and their peers, ideally other ELLs with a similar profile. And lastly, anecdotal information on the students that has been logged by teachers on an ongoing basis lends valuable insight into the students' overall performance (Hamayan,M arler, Sanchez Lopez, & Damico, forthcoming). In conclusion, for (pre)referral, current information on students' oral and written language proficiency in L1 and L2 that is based on multiple sources provides a well-rounded picture of ELLs' total language development.

Instruction.

Once a determination has been made that a student is indeed in need of special education services and that the student has been placed within a special education setting, it is important to assess ELLs' oral and written language proficiency in order to establish a student's baseline performance levels. In this way, appropriate and effective instructional services can be provided. The intensity and duration of L1 and/or L2 support should be clearly stipulated in every IEP to maximize the potential for academic success for each ELL with special needs. In addition, specific instructional accommodations for individual ELLs with identified disabilities, such as reading content area material to students or having students dictate their responses, need to be clearly delineated in their IEPs as a means of ensuring the same accommodations during state assessment.

Knowledge of ELLs' language proficiencies is important in being able to design a coordinated instructional plan. Provision of an integrated set of support services including special education, ESL, bilingual education, and Title I are necessary in order to facilitate continuity of instruction for students throughout the school day (Hamayan & Freeman Field, 2006). To accomplish this goal, teachers serving ELLs need to collaborate regularly with open and clear lines of communication (Boals, 2001).

Through instruction, teachers constantly monitor students' language development and through assessment, teachers are apprised of the students' movement along the language proficiency continuum as well as their acquisition of academic concepts. The primary purposes of instructional assessment are two-fold;

to document student progress and to inform instruction. In a special education setting, teachers need to customize classroom measures to take into account the ELLs' language proficiency and specific disabilities.

As in (pre) referral, teachers' reliance on multiple measures is required for on-going language proficiency assessment. Oral language data on the students can be readily obtained through teacher/student interviews or conferences that focus on objectives in the students' IEP; this means of assessment also allows for periodic student feedback and student self-evaluation (Hamayan et al., in press). Another way of assessing oral language is through observations of students' interactions (Fradd & McGee, 1994). If conducted systematically, observing students as part of instruction provides ample opportunities for teachers to log their students' use of language. For example, for documentation purposes, teachers might create an oral language checklist similar to the survey in Appendix A. In the checklist, however, the left-hand column is devoted to specific language functions, that is, how students use language to communicate. Such functions might include that the students respond to commands, ask questions, converse with one another, hypothesize, discuss school-related topics, and /or explain a process.

Within the context of instruction, performance tasks, when coupled with rubrics or scoring guides, can also serve as assessments (Gottlieb, 2002). These tasks are hands-on activities where students manipulate, construct, or work with concrete objects or other forms of representation, such as graphs, charts, and tables. They are often bound to subject area concepts and specified learning standards. To accompany performance tasks, many rubrics have been developed for ELLs that address language proficiency and academic achievement. Three such resources are *The Language Proficiency Handbook: A Practitioner's Guide to Instructional Assessment* (Illinois State Board of Education, 1999), *Authentic Assessment for English Language Learners: Practical Approaches for Teachers* (O'Malley & Pierce, 1996), and *Assessing English Language Learners: Bridges from Language Proficiency to Academic Achievement* (Gottlieb, 2006).

In performance tasks students demonstrate academic language proficiency, as language is taught through content. All four domains of language may be incorporated into a task, which may be as lengthy as a thematic unit, so both oral and written language proficiency are assessed. In sum, teachers and other assessment personnel ought to collect various forms of assessment information within the context of instruction that chronicle ELLs' language development.

Examining Accountability in Light of the No Child Left Behind Act

The passage of the No Child Left Behind Act (U.S. Congress, 2001) has had, and will continue to have, profound effects on students, parents, teachers, and administrators throughout the United States. For ELLs, and ELLs with disabilities, the legislation is clear that accountability does indeed reach all students. Although there is some flexibility in the design and implementation of large-scale alternate academic assessments, the one unwavering tenet is that the measures are to be of comparable rigor and technical quality as other state assessments. Equally important, each state's academic content standards in the areas of language arts, mathematics, and science are not to be compromised for these students; that is, the identical yardstick is to be used in the measurement of academic progress, except for those with severe cognitive disabilities..

It is incumbent upon the bilingual education community to verify that the measures that are created are indeed reliable and valid for our student populations. Scrutiny is to be given throughout the development process to ensure that every consideration unique to ELLs, and ELLs with disabilities, has been taken into account, incorporated into the blueprint, analyzed, and reported with accuracy. It is only then that we can have confidence in the results and can use the information appropriately to improve services and instructional practices.

Considering Alternate Assessment and Summative Language Proficiency Tools

Language proficiency assessment for ELLs is embedded into Title III of the No Child Left Behind Act of 2001. Every state that receives Title III funding is required to develop English language proficiency standards and Annual Measurable Achievement Objectives. Beginning the 2002–03 school year, language proficiency assessment of listening, speaking reading, and writing is to be administered to ELLs, including ELLs with disabilities, on an annual basis. The data generated from these measures are carefully monitored and reported to the federal government with evidence that the benchmarks that have been set are being met.

Just as language proficiency assessment is a critical component of (pre)referral and instruction, so too does its importance extend to the context of accountability. In special education settings, accountability for student learning occurs at different levels. The first level is the classroom, where teachers design and deliver instruction. It is here where the students' IEPs become the binding contract and legal document; teachers must produce defensible data that justify the extent to which an individual student's objectives and goals have been met. As part of the teachers' commitment to student learning, with each annual review, ELLs' oral and written language proficiency information must be updated.

Ultimately, according to the U.S. constitution, the responsibility for educating our students resides with the state. Accountability measures for all students in special education, including ELLs, are summative, based on cumulative performance, and anchored in a state's academic content standards. The thrust of state accountability lies in measuring student progress in language arts/ reading and mathematics. For ELLs, the emphasis on literacy assessment at the state level has to be offset by oral language assessment at the classroom level in order to create a balanced and comprehensive picture of the students' language proficiency (Gottlieb & Nguyen, forthcoming). In measuring oral and written language of ELLs, the use of both standardized and classroom tools are not only important, it is invaluable in determining what students know and are able to do.

Using Language Proficiency Information in Special Education Contexts

Now that we have defined bilingual language proficiency, discussed the importance of assessment of oral and written language, and described appropriate language proficiency data sources and measures, we now turn to how language profi-

TABLE 12–6
The Uses of Assessment Information on Language Proficiency in Special
Education Contexts

Context for Assessment	*Uses of Assessment Information on Language Proficiency*
(Pre)referral	• Determine relative language proficiency • Determine the relationship between oral and written language • Compare individual student performance over time and with that of other ELLs
Instruction	• Diagnose strengths and weaknesses • Detect trends or patterns of language use • Plan and modify instruction • Review IEP goals and objectives • Share with students and parents
Accountability	• Report to stakeholders • Determine student gains from year to year • Document movement toward IEP goals and learning standards

ciency information can be effectively used in special education settings. Parallel to the discussion on the necessity for language proficiency assessment for ELLs, in this section, the uses of assessment data are described for (pre)referral, instruction, and accountability. A summary of how assessment information applies to special education contexts is presented in Table 12–6. Irrespective of the context, however, the overriding use of reliable and valid assessment information is to promote sound educational decision-making.

(Pre)referral. For pre-referral, teachers gather both standardized and class-room information on ELLs' oral and written language proficiency in the students' L1, to the extent feasible, and L2, English. Using comparable measures, teachers can compare student performance in L1 with L2 for a given language domain (listening, speaking, reading, and writing) to ascertain the student's preferred or stronger language. Table 12–7 is a matrix that teachers, psychologists and other professionals may complete to assist them in determining relative language proficiency across language areas based on specified data sources.

Staff may approach this task in several ways. One suggestion is that the L1 and L2 columns be color-coded according to preferred/non-preferred language and, based on the information from language proficiency assessment, the assessor fills in the appropriate cell for each language area with the data source(s) and date(s) noted in the last column. Another option is that assessors enter test scores directly in the listening, speaking, reading, and writing cells for L1 and L2 while identifying the instrument(s) and date(s) in the right-hand column. In either case, staff will have a summary of an ELL's language proficiency information that can be used in deciding whether a special education referral is warranted.

Within the context of referral, the information from Table 12–7 can be reanalyzed to establish the relationship between the student's oral (listening and speaking) and written (reading and writing) language proficiency or between the student's

TABLE 12–7
Determining Relative Language Proficiency of Ells Across Language Domains
Based on Specified Data Sources

	First Language L1	English L2	Data Source(s), Instrument(s) and Date(s)
Listening	_____	_____	_____
Speaking	_____	_____	_____
Reading	_____	_____	_____
Writing	_____	_____	_____

receptive (listening and reading) and productive (speaking and writing) language proficiency. For ELLs, discrepancies among the language areas may be attributed to the developmental nature of the language acquisition process or the discontinuity of exposure to a particular language. Disabilities usually manifest themselves across languages for ELLs; therefore, the only means to capture all the pertinent language proficiency information is through bilingual assessment (Cummins, 1984).

Once language proficiency information is made available on a linguistically and culturally diverse student to a multidisciplinary team during referral, current student performance can be compared with prior performance to mark individual gains over time. Additionally, the oral and written language proficiency of an individual ELL, when compared with other ELLs of similar backgrounds and profiles, yields information about the average expectations for the group. Language proficiency data of ELLs must be carefully combed and evaluated in L1 and L2 during pre-referral and referral before assigning any language-related, special education label.

Instruction. Teachers who work with ELLs with disabilities are attuned to the their individual strengths and weaknesses in L1 and L2. Assessment based on classroom activities and tasks provides the day-to-day diagnostic information teachers constantly use in introducing, reinforcing, and reviewing strategies and skills. In addition, the information on students' oral and written language directs teachers to reflect upon how effectively they teach the language objectives identified in each lesson and adjust their instruction to better meet the linguistic needs of their students.

Information from assessment is to be shared with students and parents (or family members) alike. Assessment is not a clandestine activity, it is a vital component of schooling, and reliable results that have been accrued over time produce a quite accurate portrayal of a student's performance. Students have a right to know what is expected of them (the criteria) and how they are expected to achieve those expectations (through exemplars or models). Equally important, students should receive specific feedback on what they do (again, based on set criteria) and shown ways to improve.

Parents or family members are to be part of the instructional assessment cycle as well (Hamayan & Freeman, 2006). Every attempt should be made to have ongoing assessment information about their child in the language best understood by the parents. In addition, states often require that the contents of the alternate assessment portfolio, if used in lieu of state assessment, be validated by parents or guardians each data collection period.

Accountability.   Per No Child Left Behind legislation, states have an obligation to report assessment information to stakeholders for ELLs in special education in one of two ways. First, if the students participate in state assessment, data are disaggregated for those with IEPs and, as with other ELLs, if the numbers are warranted (the number of students required per cell varies from state to state), are reported at the state, school district, school, and student levels. Second, for those ELLs involved in the alternate assessment, state, district, school and student level data are reported as well. Thus, information on students' oral and written language assessment as well as academic achievement can be tracked more reliably.

Lastly, teachers working with ELLs with disabilities are to remind themselves of each student's IEP goals and objectives when planning instruction and collecting language proficiency data. Representative samples of student work provide the evidence of each student's language-related accomplishments. For ELLs with severe disabilities, information on the students' oral and written language gathered within a specified time frame, such as in conjunction with that of the alternate assessment, can serve for both formative, classroom, and summative, state level, purposes.

FUTURE RESEARCH AND PRACTICE

There are two major topics that fall under the assessment umbrella of language proficiency that warrant empirical exploration. First, as the notion of what constitutes language proficiency has come to assume a more academic stance, we must explore its affect not only across language and cultural groups, but on those ELLs with disabilities as well. That is, to what extent are English language proficiency standards that have been designed for ELLs reflective of the performance of those with disabilities? What are reasonable expectations of annual growth in the areas of oral language and literacy development and do the patterns of those with disabilities deviate from those of other ELLs? Finally, what are the implications of implementing more rigorous standards for ELLs with disabilities who are acquiring two languages simultaneously?

The second area of research entails the examination of language proficiency measures and tests of academic achievement that are currently used as part of statewide accountability. To what extent are these assessments fair and valid for ELLs with disabilities? We already suggested that construct validity may be an issue, but have these measures been constructed, piloted, field tested, and normed on this subpopulation of students? Are accommodations that are written into the students' IEPs being honored in assessment, and, if so, do they change the nature of what is being tested? What other supports may ELLs with disabilities need that could be incorporated into a test's universal design?

The passage of the No Child Left Behind Act of 2001 has ushered in a new set of regulations regarding the assessment of ELLs. Titles I and III specify the nature of language proficiency assessment that has been the impetus for changing the educational measurement landscape. We are still in flux between the old and new generations of English language proficiency tests.

The new measures must be anchored in English language proficiency standards that are aligned with state academic content standards, minimally in language arts, math, and science. Never before have English language proficiency tests rested on academic proficiency that is standards-based. Therefore, those tests in existence prior to this most current legislation, in large part, have become obsolete.

The language proficiency tests currently under development not only will meet compliance with the federal mandate, but, in addition, will be more reflective of a field that has come to embrace content-based instruction. While some test publishers are revising their language proficiency instruments, there are also consortia of states that are designing their own measures. Hopefully, the new generation of language proficiency tools will be more reliable and valid indicators of the performance of ELLs with disabilities.

CONCLUSION

We admit that language assessment of ELLs, in general, and those with disabilities, in particular, is a complex undertaking. Recognition of the linguistic and cultural diversity of our students and acknowledgement of the importance of assessing two languages is the first step. It is our sincere wish that in this era of accountability, appropriate and accurate assessment of oral and written language proficiency will produce information that will lead to improved education for all ELLs (Gottlieb, 1999, 2001).

ANNOTATED BIBLIOGRAPHY

Gottlieb, M. (2003). *Large-scale assessment of English language learners: Addressing accountability in K–12 settings: TESOL Professional Papers #6*. Alexandria, VA: Teachers of English to Speakers of Other Languages.

This monograph responds to the pressing need to develop assessments for English language learners that reflect effective educational theory and practice while meeting the requirements of the No Child Left Behind Act. The roles of language and content are integrated in a series of useful models that help define and measure academic language proficiency.

Brice, A. E. (2002). The Hispanic child: Speech, language, culture and education. Needham Heights, MA: Allyn & Bacon.

This book provides school-based speech-language pathologists and special educators with information as to how to provide suitable services to CLD population. It helps practitioners to understand their bilingual caseloads and to approach their interactions in an informed and considerate manner.

Roseberry-McKibbin, C. (2002). *Serving multicultural students with special language needs: Practical strategies for assessment and intervention* (2nd ed). Oceanside, CA: Academic Communication Associates.

This book includes a wealth of information about cultural groups, their customs, and the variables that are important to consider in assessment and program planning for multicultural students with language disorders and other special learning needs.

RESOURCES

Bilingual Verbal Ability Tests-Normative Update (BVAT-NU) (2005).

A. F. Munoz-Sandoval, J. Cummins, C. G Alvarado, M. Ruef, and F. Schrank are the authors of this latest edition of the BVAT. Available in Arabic, Polish, French, German, Haitian Creole, Russian, Hindi, Italian, Korean, Japanese, Portuguese, Turkish, Vietnamese, Chinese, Spanish, Hmong, Navajo and English. Itasca, IL: Riverside Publishing Company.

Woodcock-Munoz Language Survey —Revised WMLS-R (2005).

The latest edition was created by R. Woodcock, A. F. Munoz-Sandoval, M. Ruef, and C. G Alvarado. The WMLS-R is available in English and Spanish. Itasca, IL: Riverside Publishing Company.

National Clearinghouse for English Language Acquisition & Language Instruction Educational Programs (NCELA):
http://www.ncela.gwu.edu

This site collects, analyzes, synthesizes, and disseminates information about language instruction and educational programs for limited English proficient children, and related programs. Priority is given to information on academic content and English proficiency assessments and accountability.

American Speech—Language-Hearing Association(ASHA):
http://www.asha.org/

The organization seeks to identify and promote research and education relevant to the communication needs, differences, delays, and disorders of persons within the multicultural communities and facilitate the ability of all ASHA members to provide appropriate services to diverse populations.

REFERENCES

Bialystock, E., & Hakuta, K. (1994). *In other words: The science and psychology of second language acquisition*. New York: Basic Books.

Boals, T. (2001). Ensuring academic success: The real issue in educating English language learners. *Midwestern Educational Researcher, 14,* 3.

Burnette, J. (2000). *Assessment of culturally and linguistically diverse students for special education eligibility*. (ERIC Document Reproduction Service No. E604).

Cloud, N., Genesee, F., & Hamayan, E. (2000). *Dual language instruction: A handbook for enriched education*. Boston: Heinle & Heinle.

Cummins, J. (1984). *Bilingualism and special education: Issues in assessment and pedagogy*. Clevedon, England: Multilingual Matters.

Cummins, J. (1980). The cross-lingual dimensions of language proficiency: Implications for bilingual education and the optimal age issue. *TESOL Quarterly, 14,* 175–185.

Damico, J. (1991). Descriptive assessment of communicative ability in limited English proficient students. In E. Hamayan & J. Damico (Eds.), *Limiting bias in the assessment of bilingual students* (pp.157–218). Austin, TX: Pro-Ed.

Farr, B. P., & Trumbull, E. (1997). *Assessment alternatives for diverse classrooms*. Norwood, MA: Christopher-Gordon.

Fradd, S. H. & McGee, P. L. (1994). *Instructional assessment: An integrative approach to evaluating student performance*. Reading, MA: Addison-Wesley.

Genesee, F., & Hamayan, E. (1994). Classroom-based assessment. In F. Genesee (Ed.), *Educating second language children*. Cambridge: Cambridge University Press.

Gottlieb, M. (1995). *Nurturing student learning through portfolios. TESOL Journal, 5*, 12–14.

Gottlieb, M. (1999). Assessing ESOL adolescents: Balancing accessibility to learn with accountability for learning. In C. J. Faltis & P. M. Wolfe (Eds.), *So much to say: Adolescents, bilingualism, and ESL in the secondary school* (pp. 176–201). New York: Teachers College.

Gottlieb, M. (2001). Four 'A's needed for successful standards-based assessment and accountability. *NABE News, 24*, 8–12.

Gottlieb, M. (2002). *Wisconsin alternate assessment for students with limited English proficiency: Teacher's guide*. Madison: Wisconsin Department of Public Instruction.

Gottlieb, M. (2003). *Large-scale assessment of English language learners: Addressing accountability in K–12 settings: TESOL Professional Papers #6*. Alexandria, VA: Teachers of English to Speakers of Other Languages.

Gottlieb, M. (2006). *Assessing English language learners: Bridges from language proficiency to academic achievement*. Thousand Oaks, CA: Corwin Press.

Gottlieb, M., & Nguyen, D. (Forthcoming). *Authentic assessment and accountability systems for language education programs: A guide for administrators and teachers*. Philadelphia: Caslon.

Hamayan, E. (1995). Approaches to alternative assessment. *Annual Review of Applied Linguistics, 15*, 212–226.

Hamayan, E. & Freeman, R. (Eds.). (2006). *English language learners at school: A guide for administrators*. Philadelphia, PA: Caslon.

Hamayan, E., Marler, B., Sanchez Lopez, C., & Damico, J. (in press). *Special education considerations for English language learners: A handbook for intervention teams*. Philadelphia, PA: Caslon.

Hamers, J. F., & Blanc, M. H. (2000). *Bilinguality and Bilingualism*. New York: Cambridge University Press.

Hornberger, N. (Ed.). (2003). *Continua of biliteracy: An ecological framework for educational policy, research, and practice in multilingual settings*. Clevedon, England: Multilingual Matters.

Illinois State Board of Education. (1999). *The language proficiency handbook: A practitioner's guide to instructional assessment*. Springfield, IL: Author.

Kindler, A. L. (2002). *Survey of the states' limited English proficient students and available educational programs and services: 2000–2001 summary report*. Washington, DC: National Clearinghouse for English Language Acquisition and Language Instruction Educational Programs.

LaCelle-Peterson, M., & Rivera, C. (1994). Is it real for all kids? A framework for equitable assessment policies for English language learners. *Harvard Educational Review, 64(1)*, 55–75.

O'Malley, J. M., & Pierce, L. V. (1996). *Authentic assessment for English language learners: Practical approaches for teachers*. New York: Addison-Wesley.

Spolsky, B. (1989). *Conditions for second language learning*. New York: Oxford University Press.

Thomas, W., & Collier, V. (2002). *A national study of school effectiveness for language minority students' long term academic achievement*. Santa Cruz, CA: Center for Research on Education, Diversity & Excellence.

No Child Left Behind Act (2001). PL 107–110 United States at Large.

U.S. Department of Education, Office of Special Education Programs. (2001). *23rd annual report to Congress on the implementation of the Individuals with Disabilities Education Act.* Available from http://www.ed.gov/offices/OSERS/OSEP/Products/OSEP2001AnlRpt/Section_II.pdf

APPENDIX A
Sample Language Use Survey

Which language or languages do you use around home, your neighborhood, and school? Tell me if you use your first language, _____, English, or both languages with the people and places that I name.

(As the student responds, mark the appropriate box.)

	First Language (L1)	Second Language (L2), English	Both Languages	Not Applicable
Around home				
1. With your parents or guardians	_____	_____	_____	_____
2. With your grandparents	_____	_____	_____	_____
3. With your brothers and sisters	_____	_____	_____	_____
4. With relatives who live with you	_____	_____	_____	_____
5. With your caregivers	_____	_____	_____	_____
6. With your neighbors	_____	_____	_____	_____
7. With your friends	_____	_____	_____	_____
Around your neighborhood				
8. At the store	_____	_____	_____	_____
9. At the clinic	_____	_____	_____	_____
10. At church	_____	_____	_____	_____
11. In the park	_____	_____	_____	_____
12. At a restaurant	_____	_____	_____	_____
Around school				
13. On the playground	_____	_____	_____	_____
14. In the lunchroom	_____	_____	_____	_____
15. In the halls	_____	_____	_____	_____
16. During free time	_____	_____	_____	_____
17. On the bus	_____	_____	_____	_____
18. In the library	_____	_____	_____	_____

13

COGNITIVE ASSESSMENT OF CULTURALLY AND LINGUISTICALLY DIVERSE STUDENTS

Ena Vazquez-Nuttall and Chieh Li
Northeastern University

Agnieszka M. Dynda and Samuel O. Ortiz
St. John's University

Carmen G. Armengol, Joan Wiley Walton, and Kristin Phoenix
Northeastern University

Cognitive assessment has comprised a significant part of a school psychologist's activities since the very inception of the profession. Much of the focus with respect to assessment has been on the diagnosis of disabilities (e.g., mental retardation, learning disability, and other exceptionalities) and school psychologists continue to spend a significant amount of time performing cognitive evaluations and writing reports (Ochoa, Riccio, Jimenez, Garcia de Alba, & Sines, 2004). Perhaps the most dramatic change in the assessment practices of school psychologists has to do with the nature of the population being served. Diversity within the school-aged population in the U.S. has expanded at a rapid rate within the past two decades and shows little sign of slowing down (U.S. Bureau of the Census, 2001). The implications of this fact are reflected in an increased interest in issues related to the assessment of culturally and linguistically diverse (CLD) students (Rhodes, Ochoa & Ortiz, 2005). More than ever, the need to develop competency in the evaluation of children from diverse cultures is becoming an indispensable skill in the assessment repertoire of all school psychologists.

There are many facets of diversity that influence the evaluation process. Discussion of all of them is well beyond the scope of this chapter. There are two major aspects of diversity that, when attended to properly by school psychologists, will allow evaluations to be conducted in a manner that is consistent with the nondiscriminatory intent of both legislative mandates (e.g., IDEA 2004) and ethical standards (e.g., Standards for Educational and Psychological Testing; AERA, APA & NCME, 1999). These factors are English language proficiency and acculturation.

THEORETICAL AND RESEARCH BASIS

Language Proficiency and Acculturation Issues

Evaluation of individuals from other cultures and who speak other languages is problematic from the outset for the very reason that the constructs, procedures, tools, and standards used in the process were conceived, developed, and designed from the vantage point of a particular culture. That is, tests are reflections of the values, attitudes, and beliefs of the culture that gave rise to them and those developed in the U.S. are bound by its culture as much as anything else that might emanate from it including novels, automobiles, cuisine, and so forth (Sattler, 1992; Scarr, 1978). When tests developed in one culture are used with individuals raised in another, questions of fairness rise to the forefront and permeate all aspects of the evaluation process.

LANGUAGE PROFICIENCY AND ACCULTURATION ISSUES

Understanding the impact of diversity in assessment can be distilled into an examination of validity. With respect to culture, the question revolves around how "different" the individual to be evaluated is from the cultural demands and expectations embedded in the procedures or tools to be employed. The question can be turned around, however, and viewed in terms of level of acculturation. The more acculturated an individual is to the culture of the test, the less "difference" there exists and the more likely that the evaluation will yield results that are fairer and more accurate estimates of actual ability, behavior, or whatever is being measured. In such cases, the constructs will have been measured validly. Conversely, the less acculturated an individual is to the culture of the tests, the more a "difference" exists that will affect the evaluation and lead to results that are more discriminatory and inaccurate because the intended constructs (e.g., ability, behavior, trait, etc.) were not in fact measured validly. In this second example, not only is the intended construct not valid, but what was actually measured is an entirely different and unintended construct—level of acculturation.

The effect of diversity with respect to language is much the same, albeit more readily apparent. Once again, the question revolves around the degree of difference between the language of the test and the language of the individual being tested. It is not difficult to imagine that a test developed and administered in English to an individual who does not speak English would yield results that in no way reflect the individual's actual ability or behavior, but rather reflect the individual's proficiency in that language. As before, when the language proficiency of the examinee approaches that of native speakers of the language of the test, the more likely that results will be valid estimates of the constructs being measured. But when the language development and proficiency of the examinee is not at the level demanded by the test's expectations, the test degenerates into a test of language proficiency (Figueroa, 1990; Valdés & Figueroa, 1996).

Differences in culture and language, as exemplified in level of acculturation and English language development and proficiency, are woven intricately throughout all aspects of the assessment process. However, the manner in which they influence practice varies slightly depending on the specific issue in evaluation, particularly those issues related to professional competency, assessment orientation, psychometric approaches, and alternative approaches. The reader will notice that this chapter is organized largely around these issues. By attending to the manner in which cultural and linguistic issues operate within the context of each of these issues in assessment, practitioners will have at their disposal a comprehensive framework for conducting evaluations that are as fair and equitable as possible and in keeping with current research and best practices.

Professional Competency

One of the least discussed issues in the assessment of CLD individuals relates to professional competency. The tendency to overlook concerns about competency may have resulted from several factors, particularly the lack of nondiscriminatory assessment training in graduate education programs, limited opportunities for working with diverse populations, and the mistaken notion that any examiner from a diverse background or with bilingual ability is competent to conduct unbiased assessment (Ortiz, 2002; Rhodes et al., 2005).

There are many areas of skill and competency that form the repertoire of a competent and qualified assessor. Clearly, possession of culture-specific knowledge gained from personal or professional experience is an important skill for practitioners. Likewise, the ability to communicate in an examinee's native language or primary mode of communication (e.g., sign language) imbues examiners with the opportunity to engage in forms of communication that are not available to non-bilingual examiners. However, as noted by Ortiz and Flanagan, "mere possession of the capacity to communicate in an individual's native language does not ensure appropriate, nondiscriminatory assessment of that individual. Traditional assessment practices and all their inherent biases can be quite easily replicated in any number of languages" (1998, p. 426). Thus, practitioners, bilingual and otherwise, should receive direct training and instruction in nondiscriminatory assessment that includes the ability to recognize when culture may be affecting behavior or test performance and specific, defensible methods for reducing the many sources of potential bias in assessment (Ortiz, 2002; Ortiz, 2006; Flanagan & Ortiz, 2001).

As with its original incarnations, the recent reauthorization of the Individuals with Disabilities Education Act (IDEA 2004) continues to require the use of culturally appropriate and nondiscriminatory assessment methods. Professional associations, such as the American Psychological Association (APA; 2002) (and the National Association of School Psychologists (NASP; 2000), have developed specific ethics and practice guidelines to address these concerns. In general, they require psychologists to: (a) use assessment instruments with well-established validity and reliability for use with members of the population tested; (b) acknowledge the impact of second language learning and cultural differences on the cognitive and socio-emotional development of individuals; and (c) recognize the limitations of standardized tests and the ramifications of using such tests in the assessment of CLD children. Compliance with these requirements is anything but straightforward, especially in light of the lack of empirically supported practices and validated assessment instruments for use with CLD children. Guidance on these matters is provided, however, in the sections that follow later in this chapter.

Cultural competence in assessment is largely a function of the examiner's personal cultural awareness and understanding because this will determine the manner and nature regarding how the evaluation is conceptualized, the data collected, and interpreted. If examiners are not aware of their own biases, assuming that their views of intelligence are universal, and using their views as "the" standard to evaluate a person from a different culture, there is a danger of conducting a biased evaluation. Thus, it is recommended that examiners explore their own values and views of intelligence and intelligence tests and how their values impact their choices of cognitive procedures as well as their interpretations. Seeking supervision from peers who have multicultural expertise may be helpful in this regard as well as discussions with fellow professionals who may have appropriate experiences or expertise in the area.

Use of Interpreters and Translators

Faced with the need to evaluate CLD children, some examiners have resorted to directly translating tests into the dominant languages of the children they assess. This practice is fraught with multiple problems, and has been criticized on several grounds. One problem with using interpreters is the lack of training and expertise of the interpreters, which leads to, for instance, answering for the child, or misinterpreting the meaning of certain items (Li, Walton, & Vazquez-Nuttall, 1999). Second, there are no commonly accepted standards for the manner in which interpreters should be used and thus there can be significant variability from one administration to another (Lopez, 2002). Third, languages are rarely monolithic and variations can be significant to the extent that speakers of ostensibly the same language cannot in fact communicate. Whereas Spanish spoken in Mexico may be understood by Spanish speakers from Cuba, there is enough difference between the languages such that communication may not be optimal and at times limited in ways that affect the examinee's performance. And last, there are no tests that have been standardized with the use of an interpreter. Indeed, the very use of an interpreter for the purpose of assessment violates the standardization of the test and renders the results automatically invalid. In short, there is no way to make the process of using an interpreter a valid procedure (Ortiz, 2002; Ortiz & Ochoa, 2005b; Rhodes et al., 2005).

Combine these problems with the lack of education or training in the part of examiners in the advantages and disadvantages of using interpreters and it is clear that professional competency deserves far more attention than it has garnered. As such, practitioners should remain well aware of their limits of competency and recognize what they are capable of doing as well as what they are not.

Assessment Orientation

Traditional psychological assessment practices are rooted largely in a deficit or medical model that carries various assumptions regarding the nature, etiology, and amelioration of a suspected disability. These assumptions contribute significantly to sources of potential bias and discrimination in the evaluation of CLD individuals. Fair and equitable assessment of diverse populations, and perhaps nondiscriminatory evaluation for *any* individual, must adopt an alternative orientation. The perspective that has garnered the most attention and favor in this endeavor is based primarily on ecological and systems theory, and provides a particularly useful framework for equitable evaluation.

Ecological and systems (or ecosystems) approaches evolved primarily from the work of Bronfenbrenner's (1977, 1979) who recognized the importance of viewing an individual within the context of their unique ecology and its attendant elemental systems. Bronfenbrenner referred to the smallest element in an ecology as the microsystem, which "is the complex relations between the developing person and the environment in an immediate setting containing that person (e.g., home, school, work place, etc)" (1979, p.514). A setting is further defined as:

> [a] place with particular physical features in which participants engage in particular roles (e.g., daughter, parent, teacher, employee, etc.) for particular periods of time. The factors of place, time, physical features, activity, participant, and role constitute the elements of setting (p. 514).

The microsystem is contained within the mesosystems, which are the interrelations among the major settings containing a person at any given point in time. The latter are in turn contained within a broader setting known as the exosystem, which includes the formal and informal specific social structures that impinge on the target person. Beyond the exosystems are the macrosystems, or overarching institutional patterns of the culture or subculture that generally carry information and endow meaning and motivation to institutions and activities. When a child's cognitive development is viewed within Bronfenbrenner's ecological framework, the contexts of the entire ecological system are considered, including all the factors of the micro, meso, exo, and macrosystem. This means, of course, that to properly understand the cognitive behavior and performance of diverse individuals (as may be measured by standardized tests) requires that attention be paid to the significant influence of the individual's entire cultural ecology.

Several researchers have formalized ecological and systems theory into specific orientations that can guide assessment efforts with diverse individuals. The more popular frameworks include the Ecomap of Child and Family Functioning system developed by Vazquez-Nuttall, Nuttall-Vazquez and Hampel (1999) and the four-tiered bio-ecological assessment system (Gopaul-McNicol & Presswood, 1998).

In their assessment system, Gopaul-McNicol and Presswood (1998) applied the ecological framework to educational and cognitive assessment. In generally, they advocate for a more flexible and ecologically sensitive assessment system that allows for greater heterogeneity in the expression of intelligence. In this system, the first tier is psychometric assessment, where traditional testing is used. The second tier is psychometric potential assessment, which involves using approaches such as suspending time, contextualizing vocabulary, allowing the use of paper and pencil for arithmetic subtests, and using test-teach-test strategies. The third tier is ecological assessment, which consists of four components: (a) observing the students' functioning in schools (classroom, cafeteria, gym and playground), homes, and communities (church, playground and or other recreational sites); (b) assessing the family and community supports; (c) determining if the CLD students can perform the skills typical of their native land (comparable to the test items) via item equivalency assessment; and (d) examining the tasks that the children were able to perform in various settings, and those that they were unable to do in the IQ testing. The fourth tier consists of the assessment of other intelligences such as musical, bodily kinesthetic, interpersonal and intrapersonal intelligence, which are based directly on alternative conceptualizations of intelligence espoused by Gardner (1983).

One of the main benefits of the ecological approach developed by Gopaul-McNichol and Presswood (1998) is that it broadens the focus of cognitive assessment to include an evaluation of the intellectual strengths and weaknesses of children at the home, school, and community. It views formal intelligence testing as only one piece of the evaluation. It is also very inclusive by allowing a variety of tools and procedures.

Another formal ecosystems orientation developed by Vazquez-Nuttall, Nuttall-Vazquez, and Hampel (1999) is known as the Ecomap of Child and Family Functioning. This orientation is based primarily on Bronfenbrenner's theory (1977, 1979) as well as later adaptations made by Knoff (1986). The system is illustrated in Figure 13–1.

As is evident in Figure 13–1, the cognitive/educational capacity of CLD children is the major focus of analysis and problem solving. The child and family as well as the school are the two central concepts placed in parallel in the Microsystem Level. Within this level, assessment efforts are geared toward collection of information regarding variables relative to the child and family that may include number of children in the home, extent of the nuclear and extended family, level of education of the parents, immigration and acculturation history, religious affiliations or identification, and native language and culture. Similarly, the variables of interest in assessing school factors include, but are not limited to the school principal and personnel, the school board, special education staffing, and availability and quality of teachers and bilingual professionals.

Unlike the formal school resources that comprise the focus of assessment at the Microsystem level, the focus of assessment efforts at the Exosystem level would include broader factors and educational resources such as the availability of organizational facilities, professional and advocacy organizations, university and private educational facilities, community health and welfare services, social and mental health agencies, the religious community, and neighbors. The Exosystem level re-

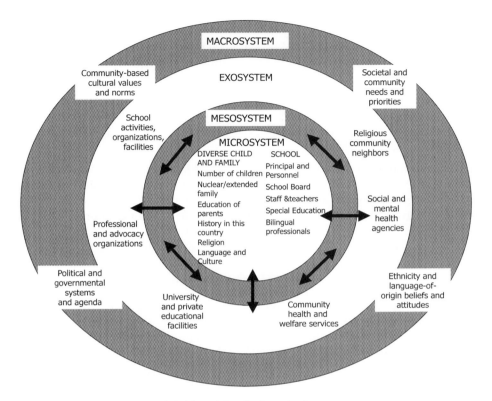

FIGURE 13–1.   Ecomap of child and family functioning.

lates primarily to organizational structures that may affect the course of children's educational outcomes, particularly in the long run.

Figure 13–1 also contains a representation of the Macro-system. Bronfenbrenner (1992) refers to this level as "the cultural repertoire of belief systems" (p.228). When assessing CLD children, the focus of analysis at the Macro-system level should include political and governmental systems and agendas, community—based cultural values and norms, and societal and economic priorities. Because it is at this level that societies make decisions about how to solve their major problems, it is necessary to evaluate factors at this level in order to determine what the possibilities for broad-based educational interventions might be.

It is important to note that ecosystems models are more broad conceptual frameworks regarding targets for assessment and the manner in which collected data should be interpreted, as opposed to being specific protocols for evaluation. The legitimacy of these models is not based on research that seeks to demonstrate proven outcomes but is tied more simply to the change in perspective from the traditional medical or deficit model. Human behavior, cognitive performance included, is not understood validly when the cross-cultural implications are ignored (Ortiz, 2006). The failure to use a broad, ecologically based framework within which to guide and frame assessment would likely lead to far more discriminatory evaluations because it would effectively discount perhaps the two most important influences on development and cognitive performance—culture and language.

PSYCHOMETRIC APPROACHES

General Issues of Bias

There are fundamental theoretical and psychometric problems that arise when traditional psychometric procedures and tools are used with CLD children. Indeed, the very concept of intelligence is largely culturally defined and its definition varies across cultures (Neisser et al., 1996). Different cultures value different behaviors as intelligent. For example, speed of thinking and action is valued in the mainstream culture of the United States, but not valued to the same extent in other cultures (Yang & Sternberg, 1997; Armengol, in press). In the home and community, children's intelligence may be judged by those groups' own standards, rather than by standards held by the school or the mainstream culture. Thus, it cannot be assumed that people from other cultures and contexts share the same definition of intelligence with the examiners and test developers.

It follows logically then, that all tests of intelligence must be anchored in some originating culture (Lonner, 1985; Sternberg, 2004). Although the degree to which they are culturally loaded differs on a process-dominant and product-dominant continuum (Newland, 1971) there is no question that tests are direct reflections of the culture that gave rise to them (Flanagan & Ortiz, 2001; Ortiz, 2002; Sanchez, 1934; Sattler, 1992; Scarr, 1978). Intelligence tests developed in the U.S. reflect middle class Euro-American cultural values and experiences (Cernovsky, 1997; Kaufman, 1994). Not surprisingly, verbally-oriented tests tend to contain more of the influence of North American culture than the nonverbal subtests (Flanagan, McGrew & Ortiz, 2000; Flanagan & Ortiz, 2001; Ortiz & Flanagan, 1998). Likewise, process-dominant tests tend to contain less country-specific content or questions about social values than product dominant tests (Elliott, 1990) but they are never culture-free (Figueroa, 1990; Ortiz, 2002; Sattler, 1992; Valdés & Figueroa, 1996).

Recognition that verbal tests were very likely to lead to discriminatory results in the evaluation of non-native English speakers (Jensen, 1974) gave rise to the popularity of so-called "nonverbal" tests of intelligence. The most popular procedure in this regard has been administration of the performance subtests from one of the various Wechsler Scales (Wechsler, 2004a). Such a method is far too simplistic, however, and given the fact that many of the subtests require significant levels of receptive language ability, they have at times been more discriminatory than verbal subtests (Figueroa, 1990). Nonverbal scales of intelligence are not in fact completely nonverbal (McCallum, Bracken, & Wasserman, 2001; Ortiz, 2002). All tests, nonverbal and otherwise, require some degree of communication to occur between the examiner and examinee. That communication need not be verbal, but it remains a function of linguistic competence and processes that suggest such tests should more rightly be viewed as language-reduced, not language free instruments (Ortiz 2002; Rhodes et al., 2005). In addition, nonverbal does not imply culture-free. Some tests designed to be nonverbal actually contain content that is highly culturally bound (Braden & Athanasiou, 2005; Flanagan & Ortiz, 2001; Ortiz & Dynda, 2005). And despite having eliminated verbal directions, other types of bias may occur, for example, if examinees are not familiar with the nature and process of individualized testing. Moreover, nonverbal tests do not address practical intelligence and other aspects of intellectual functioning germane to specific cultural experiences; thus, we cannot assume that they fairly measure aspects of intelligence valued by many other cultures (Sternberg, 1999).

Psychometric Bias Issues

Beyond problems with item content or conceptual definitions of intelligence, traditional definitions of bias have been rooted primarily around concepts related to indices of reliability (e.g., prediction, factor structure, sequence, difficulty, etc.). When viewed in this manner, research has rarely uncovered evidence of systematic bias and has even suggested at times that bias operates in favor of diverse populations (Figueroa, 1990; Jensen, 1974, 1980; Sandoval, Frisby, Geisinger, Scheuneman, & Grenier, 1998). Indeed, when defined from strict psychometric conceptualizations related to reliability and related concepts, bias is rarely found (Figueroa, 1990; Valdés & Figueroa, 1996). When used with CLD children, traditional tests of intelligence and cognitive ability exhibit bias related more to issues of validity than reliability that affect the process of evaluation in other important ways, particularly in interpretation.

The basis of structural problems inherent to tests that compromise validity is multifaceted. One principal problem has to do with the common practice of equating culture with race or ethnicity in the construction of normative samples (Flanagan & Ortiz, 2001; Ortiz & Dynda, 2005; Ortiz & Ochoa, 2005b). Such practice is problematic because culture and race are not the same thing and although they are often related, they can not be treated as interchangeable variables. The particular cultural experiences and acculturation levels of diverse individuals simply cannot be captured by the vague categories of race and ethnicity used to form norm samples. A similar problem exists with differences in language proficiency. Non-native English-speaking school children in the U.S. are not adequately represented or systematically included in any normative sample of any currently available test (Lopez, 1997; Ortiz & Dynda, 2005). Even tests that purport to include bilinguals (e.g., the Spanish version of the WISC-IV) do not do so in a manner that attends to differences in the various stages of English language acquisition. The assumption of comparability that underlies tests and the construction of norm samples is predicated upon a shared similarity between the background and experiences of the individuals who make up the norm sample and those to whom the test is administered (Salvia & Ysseldyke, 1991). Yet, this assumption, precisely because of cultural and linguistic differences, is rarely and perhaps never actually met with respect to diverse children (Ortiz & Ochoa, 2005a, 2005b, 2005c; Rhodes et al., 2005). As such, inferences and interpretations based upon data collected with standardized tests is likely to result in varying levels of discriminatory outcomes for CLD individuals.

Acculturation and language proficiency.   For about a century now, research on the testing of diverse individuals has consistently pointed two to major factors that influence performance—level of acculturation and English language proficiency (Cummins, 1984; Figueroa, 1990; Goddard, 1917; Jensen, 1974; Sanchez, 1934; Valdés & Figueroa, 1996; Vukovich & Figueroa, 1982; Yerkes, 1921). The effect of these factors is to attenuate scores for individuals who are either less acculturated to the mainstream or who possess lower levels of language development and proficiency than that expected for a given task. Of course, these variables are often significantly correlated and it is generally the combination of both that creates the observed decrease in test performance.

In order to elevate the evaluation process and collect data to a less discriminatory level, practitioners will need to assess the degree of acculturation and English language proficiency of individual's whose abilities they seek to measure. Acculturation is important to the extent that it is the difference between what an individual raised in the country and culture of the test is expected to have at a given age and what the examinee actually possesses (Ortiz & Dynda, 2005; Ortiz & Ochoa, 2005b; Rhodes et al., 2005). By definition, culturally different individuals do not have the same degree of exposure to the mainstream culture (Li, 1998; Liu & Li, 1998). How much they differ is a function of several factors including age at immigration to the U.S., desire for assimilation, adherence to native values and traditions, and so forth. In general, the more acculturated an individual is, the more test results reflect actual ability than degree of acculturation. Conversely, the less acculturated an individual is, the less that test results reflect ability than they do level of acculturation (Ortiz & Ochoa, 2005c; Rhodes et al., 2005; Valdés & Figueroa, 1996;).

The need to assess an individual's level of English language proficiency is an obvious issue but one that is poorly understood. There is often a mistaken notion that once an individual becomes English-dominant (i.e., their English language ability has surpassed development of their native language ability) that the administration of a test is considered valid. This idea, often espoused by test publishers, fails to recognize that simply because an individual becomes dominant in one language or another does not mean they suddenly cease to be bilingual or become comparable to monolinguals (Ortiz, 2002; Ortiz & Dynda, 2005; Ortiz & Ochoa, 2005a; Rhodes et al., 2005). What is important is the degree to which an individual's English language proficiency differs from the age-based developmental expectations of the test. Once again, the more age-appropriate the language proficiency of an individual, the more likely that tests given in that language will better reflect ability as opposed to proficiency. In contrast, the less age-appropriate the individual is in the language of the test, the more likely that results will be a measure of proficiency than ability. This premise holds even when the language of the test matches the native language of the individual, particularly for children who are not native English speakers and begin school in the U.S. with no or very little formal instruction in their native language. The effect is to disrupt the native language development and place the child on a trajectory that is at best several years behind that of their monolingual peers—a disadvantage that they can not overcome through any form of English language instruction and that remains evident in the pattern of results from standardized testing in English throughout their educational careers (Cummins, 1984; Ramirez, Yuen, & Ramey, 1991; Thomas & Collier, 1997, 2002).

Addressing bias in tests. Standardized instruments often form an important part of assessments aimed at evaluating the abilities of individuals from diverse countries and ethnic groups. This need has given birth to a host of techniques and strategies for increasing the utility and validity of tests with diverse populations. One common example involves adaptation of the language of the test by translating it into another language and then perhaps validating it on a group of individuals who speak the language. Unfortunately, this process is fraught with significant difficulties, including difficulties in making the test truly equivalent across languages, changes to the meaning or nature of constructs that are being measured, and as discussed previously, norm sample composition that utilizes monolingual speakers of the native language, rather than bilinguals with attendant variations in proficiency and acculturation even to the native culture (Hambleton, 2002). To reiterate—bilinguals cannot be evaluated as if they were monolinguals. They are inherently different groups and such adaptations are likely to lead to results that are as discriminatory as those obtained from tests given in English.

Test publishers do make efforts to address issues of potential bias in other ways. With the ever increasing proportion of diverse children in the U.S. population, developers of various psychometric instruments have explored ways to improve their tests. For example, the Kaufman Assessment Battery for Children—Second Edition (K-ABC-II; Kaufman & Kaufman, 2004), much like its predecessor and other tests, was put through a careful and extensive process of bias review with the intention of reducing the cultural loading of test items and language requirements. The KABC-II is also unique in the sense that it allows examiners to use whatever wording may be necessary to mediate the concept and nature of the task during administration of the sample items to an examinee before proceeding with administration of the actual items. The manual for the KABC-II also contains wording for administration of the subtest instructions and sample items in Spanish, albeit the actual items must be given in English.

Many tests are beginning to include "nonverbal" composites that are comprised of tests that are language reduced and thus fairer estimates of ability (e.g., KABC-II; Kaufman, & Kaufman, 2004; SB-V; Roid, 2003; WJ-III DS; Woodcock, McGrew, Mather, & Schrank, 2003). Some tests include information specific to particular ethnic groups (e.g., KABC-II) although as noted previously, the impact on testing comes from differences in acculturation and ethnic group identification is only an indirect correlate of that difference. Several tests, including the K-ABC-II and the Woodcock-Johnson-III: Tests of Cognitive Abilities (WJ-III; Woodcock, McGrew, & Mather, 2001) allow examiners to accept subjects' responses in languages other than English (e.g., students who are asked to provide the name of a object in a picture may do so in whatever language they are able to do so). To be sure, these techniques and strategies are helpful when the goal for examiners is to assess cognitive abilities, but they are not sufficient enough to adequately address the many areas where bias exists.

One test that is pioneering a new avenue in terms of development is the Bilingual Verbal Ability Test (BVAT, Muñoz-Sandoval, Cummins, Alvarado, & Ruef, 1998; Muñoz-Sandoval, Woodcock, McGrew, & Mather, 2005). The BVAT has been translated and normed into 17 different languages, giving it a wider range of potential application than any other instrument. It measures the verbal abilities that individuals possess in both English and the native language. The BVAT is first administered in English and then any items that were incorrectly answered are repeated in the examinee's native language. The attempt to address the language repertoire of bilingual individuals is a new direction in standardized assessment. Unfortunately, measuring proficiency in one language and then another, as opposed to simultaneously, is still a sequential process that does not truly capture the nature of the language ability of bilinguals. Moreover, the norms of the BVAT are problematic for the same reasons already discussed. Nevertheless, the BVAT may well usher in an important new trend in the manner in which tests are conceived and designed for CLD individuals.

PRACTICE AND IMPLEMENTATION ISSUES

The preceding sections have discussed a wide range of issues related to the cognitive assessment of CLD students. Practitioners may well feel overwhelmed by the numerous implications and the complexity of the dynamic interplay of the variables at play. Practical guidance and methods regarding how to carry out nondiscriminatory evaluations are scarce and often require a level of knowledge and expertise that greatly exceeds that which may have been provided in professional training programs.

DECISION-MAKING AND INTERPRETIVE FRAMEWORKS

In recognition of the need to distill the process of assessment into a more manageable activity, researchers have begun to examine the process of decision-making in the approach to assessment. An example of this type of guiding framework is the Ochoa and Ortiz Multidimensional Assessment Model for Bilingual Individuals (MAMBI; Ortiz & Ochoa, 2005c). The primary intention of the MAMBI is to provide a simplified integration matrix of the major variables relevant to assessment that assist in determining the modality (native language, English, nonverbal, or bilingual) of assessment that would likely yield the most valid results. The MAMBI integrates three important variables relative to assessment: (a) current degree of language proficiency in both English and the native language; (b) current and previous types of educational programs; and (c) current grade level. Depending on the manner in which these characteristics describe the individual, the examiner is provided with recommendations regarding the most appropriate choice of modality for conducting the assessment—the one most likely to yield fairer and more accurate estimates of actual ability. The modalities, however, are not mutually exclusive and may be used in combination with each other depending on the needs of the examiner and purpose of the assessment. Overall, the MAMBI offers practitioners the ability to manage a complex range of variables in a relatively simple manner and may serve to guide assessment in directions that are less discriminatory than what might otherwise be accomplished.

Another framework to guide the assessment process, particularly interpretation, evolved initially as the cultural and linguistic extensions of the CHC Cross-Battery approach (Flanagan & Ortiz, 2001; Flanagan et al., 2000; Ortiz, 2001; Ortiz & Flanagan, 1998). These extensions were originally conceived simply as a table of cognitive ability tests classified according to degree of cultural loading (the extent to which a subtest contains or requires knowledge of culturally-bound content) and degree of linguistic demand (the amount of receptive or expressive language ability necessary to respond to or complete a task). The purpose was to provide practitioners with a compendium of tests that could be selected, in conjunction with CHC Cross-Battery principles, with respect to the lowest degree of cultural loading and linguistic demand—thereby resulting in the fairest possible assessment of particular cognitive abilities. They are now known as the Culture-Language Test Classifications (C-LTC; Ortiz & Dynda, 2005; Ortiz & Ochoa, 2005c).

Although the classifications remain valuable in selecting tests that are less discriminatory, Flanagan and Ortiz (2001) noted that only certain abilities could be measured with tests low in both cultural loading and linguistic demand (e.g., visual processing, fluid intelligence). Other important abilities (e.g., crystallized intelligence, auditory processing) could not be measured with tests low on both dimensions because the very abilities being tested were culturally or linguistically bound. Flanagan and Ortiz recognized, however, that when test results were placed within a matrix that corresponded to the classifications (basically a 3 x 3 arrangement with levels of cultural loading and linguistic demand [low, moderate, high] along each dimension) a pattern of results could be deduced. This pattern consists of a systematic decline in performance as a function of the level of cultural loading and linguistic demands required by tests. Such an attenuating pattern is consistent with the decades of research on CLD individuals that demonstrate lower performance on tests that are more verbally or culturally oriented than those that are not (Cummins, 1984; Figueroa, 1990; Goddard, 1917; Jensen, 1974; Sanchez, 1934; Valdés & Figueroa, 1996; Vukovich & Figueroa, 1982; Yerkes, 1921).

By comparing an individual's performance on tests that share the same characteristics regarding cultural loading and linguistic demand (as opposed and prior to comparing performance on tests that are measures of the same construct), Flanagan and Ortiz (2001) provided a systematic method for evaluating the effect of cultural and linguistic differences on the validity of test performance, now known as the Culture-Language Interpretive Matrix (C-LIM; Ortiz & Dynda, 2005; Ortiz & Ochoa, 2005a, 2005c). According to Flanagan and Ortiz (2001), the C-LIM is an interpretive, not diagnostic, framework that assists practitioners in addressing the fundamental and most difficult question in the assessment of diverse individuals—that is, to what extent is performance due more to difference than disorder? The answer to this question bears directly upon the validity of the obtained results. If the effect of cultural loading and linguistic demand is present and identifiable in the pattern of test results, then the attempt to measure the individual's abilities has failed and instead unintended constructs have been measured (i.e., level of acculturation and English language proficiency). When validity is thus compromised, there can be no further meaning ascribed to tests results. Thus, when tests are used in assessment, the C-LIM may help practitioners determine whether or not any valid inferences may be drawn from the collected data. Although, further research is needed to validate the utility of the framework with respect to its ability to aid in distinguishing normal individuals from those with possible disabilities in diverse populations, the C-LIM represents a promising approach that places sophisticated strategies for data analysis that are well within the professional reach of all practitioners (Flanagan & Ortiz, 2001; Ortiz, 2002; Ortiz & Dynda, 2005; Ortiz & Ochoa, 2005a, 2005c).

ALTERNATIVE APPROACHES

Perhaps due to the many complex issues involved in the use of traditional psychometric instruments, a host of alternative approaches have sprung up in response. Driven by the very same goal that underlies all multicultural assessment practices, to reduce potential bias and increase the fairness and equity in measurement of intelligence and cognitive abilities, these approaches offer alternatives to typical methods of evaluation. Such approaches generally involve the use of qualitative and dynamic procedures, including administration of standardized tests in non-standard ways; evaluation of the processes used by the examinee in completing tasks; or the use of completely different tools based on entirely different conceptualizations of mental processing and intellectual functioning.

Qualitative Analyses

School-based practitioners involved in the assessment of CLD children must often wrestle with the inherent limitations of standardized instruments. Moreover, standard administrations and use of test scores as summaries of performance are not extremely informative about the specific processes in which children engage in completing tasks. Tests also offer little insight regarding particular areas of dysfunction or dysfunctional processes. For example, determining whether a low score on the Coding subtest is due to slow processing, poor visual scanning ability, poor graph-motor skills, and so forth, is rather complicated. Qualitative analyses seek to expand assessors' analyses and interpretations beyond simple score patterns and indices by providing useful information about how children approach the process of solving problems. Such data may be particularly helpful in the conceptualization and design of intervention strategies.

Two qualitative approaches designed for these goals are the process-approach and variations on testing-of-limits. The testing-of-limits approach has been defined as "an assessment technique in which the examiner changes standardized assessment conditions in some way" (Gonzalez, Castellano, Bauerle, & Durán, 1996). Sattler (2001) specifies five procedures that may be undertaken after a standard administration is completed in order to obtain further information regarding performance. He recommends providing additional clues, re-administering failed items, changing the modality of stimuli, eliminating time limits, and asking children to correct their errors by providing them with additional information. The testing-of-limits approach can be used in combination with other test modification methods for CLD children such as administering tests in both English and the child's native language and accepting alternative responses (e.g., culture-specific, non-verbal gestures) (Ortiz, 2002: Ortiz & Ochoa, 2005a, 2005b).

Another method that incorporates a testing-of-limits procedure is known as the "process approach" (Armengol, Moes, & Kaplan, 2003; Kaplan, 1988; Kaplan, Fein,

Morris, & Delis, 1991). This approach has gained recognition in the past 20 years primarily within the field of neuropsychology. Current versions of some popular cognitive assessment tools (e.g. the WISC-IV Integrated and the WISC-III as a Process Instrument; Wechsler, 2004a, 2004b) reflect the level of influence this approach has had. Unfortunately, there is little research regarding whether this approach has any utility when used with CLD children. Examinees from diverse backgrounds may well make the same mistakes and utilize the same inefficient strategies and processes as children with disabilities simply as a function of cultural and linguistic differences (Ortiz, 2002; Ortiz & Dynda, 2005; Ortiz & Ochoa, 2005a).

Dynamic Assessment

For more than three decades now, school-based practitioners have been using dynamic assessment methods with CLD students to obtain a more equitable evaluation of their intellectual potential and provide a clearer assessment-intervention link (Budoff, 1968, Campione & Brown, 1987; Feuerstein, Rand, & Hoffman, 1979; Lidz, 2003; Swanson, 1996; Vygotsky, 1978). Sternberg and Grigorenko (2002) conceptualize dynamic testing as "testing plus an instructional intervention" (p. 29) and described it as taking two formats: (a) the instruction may be given between a pre-test and a post-test, or (b) individuals are given instructions and guidance item by item until they solve the problem. Dynamic assessment avoids defining a child's abilities only as what he or she can do presently and independently and instead attempts to measure, in a quantitative or qualitative manner, the amount of learning and intervention needed for learning to occur.

Feuerstein and colleagues (1979) proposed a theory and evaluation system using a model based on Vygotsky's (1978) work, in particular the "zone of proximal development." Feuerstein and colleagues operationalized the theory into a collection of instruments that permitted application of the process they termed "dynamic assessment" known as the Learning Potential Assessment Device (LPAD). Confusion surrounding the term "potential" led to later adoption of the term "propensity," which emphasized assessment of the rate and nature of an individual's learning pattern. Research with the LPAD has been accomplished on a variety of children including those with disabilities and from diverse cultural and linguistic backgrounds (Lidz, 2003). The available research on the LPAD continues to evolve, and although used frequently in Israel and other parts of the world, it has yet to gain significant acceptance in the U.S. The reasons for the failure of dynamic assessment to catch on in school psychology practice are multifaceted, however, the most significant reason tends to be the lack of evidence regarding reliability, validity, and generalizability (Lidz, 2003; Sternberg & Grigorenko, 2002).

Various dynamic assessment approaches have evolved from the work of pioneering work of Feuerstein. For example, Budoff's (1968) model includes specific interventions or clues to enhance the growth of a learner's cognitive abilities. Working with children with disabilities, Budoff attempted to obtain more robust psychometric measurements of pre-scores, post-scores, and difference scores. Budoff's approach makes dynamic assessment more amenable to research, and is effective in distinguishing low functioning students who profit from academic instruction from those who do not (Lidz, 2003). The model developed by Campione and Brown (1987) further refines methods for teaching by use of graduated prompts that provide students a supportive framework for success in solving tasks. One of the more recently developed approaches has been proposed by Lidz and is known as Curriculum Based Dynamic Assessment. Lidz noted that some older children, conditioned to failure at schoolwork, respond better to novel tasks than to tests modeled after traditional academic work. Hoping to strengthen the connection between assessment and treatment, she tied dynamic testing procedures directly to instruction. She proposed to carefully build a test-teach-retest framework with planned teaching by using a small part of the current curriculum of a referred child (Lidz, 2003).

The various approaches to dynamic assessment described here are viewed by Sternberg and Grigorenko (2002) as two ends of an assessment continuum, with standardized instruments on one side and dynamic, process-oriented ones on the other. They note that even in static testing situations some learning does take place and conversely, many dynamic assessment tasks are drawn from activities embedded in static tests. Sternberg and Grigorenko suggest that future assessment endeavors might look toward a synthesis of the two methods that builds on the strengths of each. Although they acknowledge that research is needed in this area, they do believe that there is much promise in such approaches and that modern psychometrics will actually help push the field of dynamic assessment forward (Sternberg & Grigorenko).

What has not been clearly elucidated is the manner in which dynamic and process-oriented approaches are inherently, or through modification, helpful in the evaluation of CLD individuals. Practitioners who work with CLD children, particularly those who can speak the native language of their examinees and who are well versed in the manner in which cultural difference affects test performance, may find some utility in these dynamic approaches as they put them into practice in school settings. But what advantages such approaches might hold are not entirely clear and yet to be demonstrated. Lopez (1997) also affirms that "dynamic assessments remain promising because they may provide examiners with more flexible ecologically oriented testing formats" (pp. 513). Future research will reveal ultimately if indeed such approaches offer a viable method for assessing the cognitive abilities and processes of diverse individuals.

IMPLICATIONS FOR RESEARCH, TRAINING, AND PRACTICE

The challenge to develop valid measures and processes for the effective assessment of CLD children grows exponentially as our schools become more diverse and the variety of ethnic and linguistic backgrounds these students exhibit continues to grow. Adding to this, national and state pressures to increase the academic achievement of all children in our schools places a greater premium on the need to appropriately assess and educate CLD students in order to meet those standards.

In some states, failure to meet these academic standards results in children being denied a graduation diploma, thus curtailing their ability to pursue higher education (La Roche & Shriberg, 2004). Such policies have the serious consequences of limiting children's ability to become professionals or access to jobs that provide better benefits and greater renumeration. With the U.S. economy depending more and more on a well educated workforce, high stakes testing puts the future of CLD children in serious jeopardy. School psychology as a profession needs to respond to these critical conditions by developing innovative assessment and intervention approaches based on comprehensive, ecosystemic-based models that take into account children's languages, cultures, acculturation status, families, schools, and community contexts. The processes and outcomes of all approaches employed in the evaluation of CLD individuals needs to be thoroughly researched . Professional training programs also need to dedicate more time and effort in training graduate students in the different components of nondiscriminatory evaluation and provide well-supervised and meaningful practice in appropriate settings with appropriate populations. In this section, we describe the research, training and practice implications regarding the implementation of such models of assessment.

Research Implications

The implementation of a comprehensive, nondiscriminatory model of assessment would benefit significantly from the availability of appropriate measures normed with sufficient numbers of CLD children on the basis of cultural differences and stages of language proficiency (Ortiz & Dynda, 2005). Despite efforts on the part of academic researchers and testing companies to produce fairer and better normed instruments, there are still problems with current tests that continue to make them inadequately representative of CLD individuals (Ortiz, 2002; Ortiz & Dynda, 2005; Ortiz & Ochoa, 2005c).

Measures of intelligence and cognitive ability in current publication do sometimes include diverse individuals in proportion to the percentages contained in the national population. However, such individuals are identified primarily by racial category and, for measures to be administered in English, by fluency in English. That is, as long as the individual demonstrates enough proficiency to be able to understand the questions being asked, they are included despite the fact that they are not necessarily equivalent in their language development to same-age monolingual English-speaking peers. In addition, other critical information such as country of origin, acculturation, migration history, years in the U.S., and so forth are routinely omitted and ignored. For example, children who are identified as Hispanic or Latino may well be from different countries of Latin America, Central America, Europe, or the Caribbean. As such, racial identification explains very little in terms of the differences that actually exist between peoples who ostensibly share the same culture or speak the same language. Moreover, the perception of what intelligence is differs by country and will affect how well children do in different tests (Neisser et al., 1996; Rhodes et al., 2005).

Translations and adaptations continue to present unique challenges. Native language versions of tests tend to lag well behind the publication dates of their English predecessors and still fail to address potential regional and dialectical differences that may affect the performance of respondents (e.g., Mexican vs. Puerto Rican Spanish). Although Spanish is reasonably comprehensible among the countries where it is the dominant language, the effect that differences in vocabulary, pronunciation, and pragmatics might create in terms of performance have not been adequately studied.

The increase in nonverbal measures in the last ten years and the renewed interest in dynamic assessment are significant advances in addressing the needs of CLD children as they fill the demand for assessment approaches that are more flexible and less reliant on verbal responses. These tools provide an important alternatives to traditional approaches. Despite their popularity in the evaluation of diverse learners, practitioners should remain well aware that such nonverbal tests continue to require some type of communication between the examiner and examinee. That is, they are language-reduced but not completely language free. In some cases, receptive language requirements may not be reduced by much at all. In addition, such tests remain culturally loaded and are normed on individuals who are not bilingual or where there is no control for bilingualism or level of acculturation. The potential biases that exist as a function of these characteristics cannot be ignored, and should form the focus of future research on the performance of diverse individuals on such instruments, as well as any others, that are promoted for use with this population.

Training Implications

Training students in the implementation of a comprehensive, ecologically-based, nondiscriminatory assessment model requires foundations in intelligence and cognitive theory as well as knowledge of important developmental variables including first and second language acquisition processes, bilingual and ESL pedagogy, acculturation patterns, and language proficiency, among others. The training curriculum should contain courses in traditional and contextual assessment with emphasis on how the nature of evaluation changes when conducted with diverse individuals. It should also include training in forms of assessment that are often downplayed in terms of importance, including observations of children in their homes, schools, and communities. Students should also be trained how to interview diverse children and parents, as well as their teachers and community members to obtain the relevant information required for assessment and evaluation (Ortiz, 2002). Effective use of interpreters or direct administration of translated instruments will be necessary competencies.

For students who are bilingual, training programs should facilitate the learning of the languages most frequently spoken in the schools of the CLD children they seek to serve. Field experiences in relevant countries or in the United States in various contexts or placements (e.g., schools, mental health clinics, community agencies, etc.) where diverse populations are served would be ideal training experiences for all students. For students from both diverse and mainstream backgrounds, training in nondiscriminatory methods will remain crucial. Given the critical shortage of qualified bilingual evaluators, training programs should not view instruction in nondiscriminatory assessment as specialized curriculum intended only for a special few. Although a competent, qualified bilingual evaluator is always the best choice in the evaluation of CLD students (Figueroa, 1990; Lopez, 1997; Ortiz, 2002; Valdés & Figueroa, 1996), there will be many instances where for a variety of reasons such an evaluator may not be available and the assessment will be conducted by a monolingual English evaluator (Rhodes et al., 2005). In such cases, training in the use and application of nondiscriminatory methods (e.g., the C-LTC and C-LIM; Flanagan & Ortiz, 2001) may assist non-bilingual evaluators in conducting assessments that are less discriminatory than what might otherwise be accomplished with typical assessment procedures.

Practice Implications

In short, nondiscriminatory assessment practices must improve. Educational and governmental groups still play a large role in influencing this process. They continue to mandate procedures such as high stakes testing and establish regulations that require fairer and more valid assessment approaches for diverse individuals. These agencies have specified the use of culturally appropriate instruments that are validated for use with diverse individuals and require additional informal measures to obtain information on variables that affect the educational achievement of children who are culturally and linguistically different, or economically or environmentally disadvantaged. Yet, many of these decision-makers are not fully aware of what helps children do well in school, especially diverse children. Often, they do not take into account the important role that developmental differences have on the academic attainment of diverse children. Even factors that should be well understood in terms of their relation to school achievement are often overlooked including the physical condition of school buildings, qualifications of teachers, quality and availability of resources, and appropriateness of the curriculum.

School psychologists and other school professionals can play an important role in developing awareness of these issues among students, parents, teachers, administrators, political leaders, and mobilizing efforts toward change. Determining the cognitive and intellectual abilities of a student from a diverse cultural and linguistic background and constructing appropriate interventions on the basis of that information involves more than administering tests, regardless of how well constructed they may be or how much collateral information was collected. Embedded in a comprehensive, nondiscriminatory approach is activism and advocacy in school psychology practice where school professionals seek to raise the consciousness of both the stakeholders and decision-makers so as to reach the least biased and most equitable solutions possible. Clearly, nondiscriminatory assessment is a transdisciplinary endeavor where collaboration in practice among the many individuals, groups, and agencies is necessary in order to truly understand the intelligence and cognitive abilities of students from diverse backgrounds.

ACNOWLEDGMENTS

The authors want to thank graduate students Daniel Nelson and Christine Hanley for their invaluable help in reviewing the literature and for their editorial assistance.

ANNOTATED BIBLIOGRAPHY

Rhodes, R.L., Ochoa S.H., & Ortiz, S.O. (2005). *Assessing cultural and linguistically diverse students: A practical guide.* New York: Guilford.

This book is a "must read" for pre- or postservice psychologists looking for an integrated approach to assessing culturally and linguistically different children. All relevant areas involved in conducting these assessments are discussed, including legal and ethical requirements, use of interpreters, acculturation, tests of language proficiency, academic achievement, and bilingual education. The book is very practical as it includes aspects of the assessment process such as English and Spanish forms, educational and psychological process and outcomes forms to use with children, parents and teachers. This book is not only a first class textbook to prepare psychologists but also for allied health professionals and bilingual, special and general education teachers who work with diverse children. The three authors are experts in their respective areas.

Paniagua, F.A. (2001). *Diagnosis in a multicultural context: A casebook for mental health professionals.* Thousand Oaks, CA: Sage.

This casebook illustrates the applicability of cultural variables to the assessment and treatment of psychiatric disorders. It emphasizes applying cultural differences to the Diagnostic and Statistical Manual-IV guidelines. The book is composed of eight chapters. The first chapter presents an overview of the four ethnic groups emphasized: African Americans, American Indians, Asians and Hispanics. Two cultural variables affecting all groups: "familismo" and acculturation as well as some affecting only specific groups such as "personalismo" (Hispanics) are described. Three chapters present clinical cases with extensive discussion of the applicability of cultural differences to the four different groups for both psychiatric diagnosis involving children and adults, and to other conditions often originating from conflicts and stresses produced by cultural norms. General characteristics of a psychiatric condition are first introduced (e.g., ADHD), and then a case is presented by a clinician. An interpretation by the author follows this clinical discussion, so that all cases follow a similar culture-centered framework. General guidelines for practitioners are presented in the last chapter.

RESOURCES

NASP website on *Culturally Competent Practice:*
http://www.nasponline.org/culturalcompetence/index.html

The NASP website covers a wide range of resources, including Providing Culturally Competent Services, NASP Cultural Competence Resources, NASP Committees, Task Forces, & Listservs, Spotlight on NASP Practitioners, Directory of Bilingual School Psychologists Powerpoint Presentations & Handouts, References, Web Links and Resources for Families.

National Association of School Psychologists (2003). *Portraits of the children: Culturally competent assessment.* Bethesda, MD: NASP.

NASP produced a multi-media package that includes a video as well as other useful materials in a CD-ROM. The video depicts children from diverse cultural backgrounds and discusses multicultural assessment practices. The CD-ROM also provides useful handouts for parents and school professionals as well as websites and other helpful resources for practitioners and school psychology trainers.

REFERENCES

American Educational Research Association, American Psychological Association, & National Council on Measurement in Education. (1999). *Standards for Educational and Psychological Testing*. Washington, DC: American Psychological Association.

American Psychological Association. (2002). Ethical principles of psychologists and code of conduct, *American Psychologist, 57,* 1060–1073.

Armengol, C. G. (2007). Executive functions in Hispanics: Towards an ecological neuropsychology. In B. Uzzell, M. Pontón, & A. Ardila (Eds.), *Handbook of cross-cultural neuropsychology*. Mahwah, NJ: Erlbaum.

Armengol, C. G., Moes, E. J., & Kaplan, E. (2003). Neuropsychological assessment. In R. Fernández-Ballesteros (Ed.), *International encyclopedia of assessment.* (pp. 497–506). London, England: Sage.

Braden, J. P., & Athanasiou, M. S. (2005). A comparative review of nonverbal measures of intelligence. In D. P. Flanagan and P. L. Harrison (Eds.), *Contemporary intellectual assessment: Theories, tests, and issues* (pp. 557–577). New York: Guilford.

Bronfenbrenner, U. (1977). Toward an experimental ecology of human development. *American Psychologist, 32,* 513–531.

Bronfenbrenner, U. (1979). *The ecology of human development*. Cambridge, MA: Harvard University Press.

Bronfenbrenner, U. (1992). Ecological systems theory. In R. Vasta (Ed.), *Annals of child development: Six theories of child development: Revised formulations and current issues* (pp. 187–249), London: Jessica Kingsley.

Budoff, M. (1968). Learning potential as a supplementary testing procedure. In J. Hellmuth (Ed.), *Learning disorders: Vol.3* (pp. 295–343). Seattle, WA: Special Child.

Campione, J., & Brown, A. (1987). Linking dynamic testing with school achievement. In C.S. Lidz (Ed.), *Dynamic assessment: An interactional approach to evaluating learning potential* (pp. 82–115). New York: Guilford Press.

Cernovsky, Z. Z. (1997). A critical look at intelligence research. In Fox, D., & Prilleltensky (Eds.), *Critical psychology: An introduction* (pp. 121–133). London: Sage.

Cummins, J. (1984). *Bilingualism and special education: Issues in assessment and pedagogy*. San Diego: College-Hill.

Elliott, C. D. (1990). *Differential ability scales: Introductory and technical handbook*. San Antonio, TX: Psychological Corporation.

Feuerstein, R., Rand, Y., & Hoffman, M. (1979). *The dynamic assessment of retarded performers: The learning potential assessment device theory, instruments and techniques*. Baltimore, MD: University Park.

Figueroa, R. A. (1990). Best practices in the assessment of bilingual children. In A. Thomas & J. Grimes (Eds.), *Best practices in school psychology* (pp. 93–106). Washington, DC: National Association of School Psychologists.

Flanagan, D. P., & Ortiz, S. O. (2001). *Essentials of cross-battery assessment*. New York: *Wiley.*

Flanagan, D. P., McGrew, K. S., & Ortiz, S. O. (2000). *The Wechsler Intelligence Scales and Gf-Gc theory: A contemporary interpretive approach*. Boston, MA: Allyn & Bacon.

Gardner, H. (1983). *Frames of mind: The theory of multiple intelligences*. New York: Basic Books.

Goddard, H. H. (1917). Mental tests and the immigrant. *Journal of Delinquency, 2*, 243–277.

Gonzalez, V., Castellano, J. A., Bauerle, P., & Durán, R. (1996). Attitudes and behaviors toward testing-the-limits when assessing LEP students: Results of a NABE-sponsored national survey. *The Bilingual Research Journal, 20*, 433–463.

Gopaul-McNicol, S. A., & Thomas-Presswood, T. (1998). *Best Practices in intellectual/educational assessment: A bio-ecological approach to intellectual assessment.* Needham, MA: Allyn & Bacon.

Hambleton, R. K. (2002). Adapting achievement tests into multiple languages for international assessment. In Porter, A. C. & Gamoran, A. (Eds.), *Methodological advances in cross-national surveys of educational achievement* (pp. 58–69). Washington, D.C.: National Academy Press.

Individuals with Disabilities Education Improvement Act. PL No. 108–446, 20 U.S.C. (2004).

Jensen, A. R. (1974). How biased are culture-loaded tests? *Genetic Psychology Monographs, 90*, 185–244.

Jensen, A. R. (1980). *Bias in mental testing.* New York: Free Press.

Kaplan, E. (1988). A process approach to neuropsychological assessment. In T. Boll & B. K. Bryant (Eds.), *Clinical neuropsychology and brain function: Research, measurement, and practice.* (pp.125–168). Washington, D.C.: American Psychological Association.

Kaplan, E., Fein, D., Morris, R., & Delis, D. (1991). *WAIS-R NI manual.* San Antonio, TX:

Kaufman, A. S. (1994). *Intelligence testing with the WISC-R.* New York: Wiley

Kaufman, A. S., & Kaufman, N. L. (2004). *KABC-II Kaufman assessment battery for children* (2nd ed.). Circle Pines, MN: AGS Publishing.

Knoff, H. (1986). *The assessment of child and adolescent personality.* New York: Guilford Press.

La Roche, M. S., & Shriberg, D. (2004). High stakes exams and Latino students: Toward a culturally sensitive education for Latino children in the United States. *Journal of Educational and Psychological Consultation,* 15 (2), 206–223.

Li, C. (1998). Impact of acculturation on Chinese-Americans' life and its implications for helping professionals. *International Journal of Reality Therapy, 17*(2), 7–11.

Li, C., Walton, J., & Vazquez-Nuttall, E. V. (1999). Preschool evaluation of culturally and linguistically diverse children. In E. Vazquez-Nuttall, I. Romero, & J. Kalesnik (Eds.), *Assessing and screening preschoolers: Psychological and educational dimensions* (pp. 296–317). Needham, MA: Allyn & Bacon.

Lidz, C. (2003). *Early childhood assessment.* Hoboken, NJ: Wiley.

Liu, T., & Li, C. (1998). Psychoeducational interventions with Southeast Asian students: An ecological approach. *Special Services in the Schools, 13*(1/2), 129–148.

Lonner, W. J. (1985). Issues in testing and assessment in cross-cultural counseling. *The Counseling Psychologist, 13*, 599–614.

Lopez, E. C. (2002). Best practices in working with school interpreters to deliver psychological services to children and families. In A. Thomas & J. Grimes (Eds.), *Best practices in school psychology IV: Volume 2* (pp. 1419–1432). Washington, DC: National Association of School Psychologists.

Lopez, E. C. (1997). The cognitive assessment of limited proficiency bilingual children. In D. P. Flanagan, J. L. Genshaft & P. L. Harrison (Eds.), *Contemporary intellectual assessment: Theories, tests, and issues* (pp. 503–516). New York: Guilford Press.

McCallum, S., Bracken, B., & Wasserman, J. (2001). *Essentials of nonverbal assessment.* New York: Wiley.

Muñoz-Sandoval, A. F., Cummins, J., Alvarado, C. G., & Ruef, M. L. (1998). *Bilingual verbal ability tests: Comprehensive manual.* Itasca, IL: Riverside.

Muñoz-Sandoval, A. F., Woodcock, R., McGrew, K., & Mather, N. (2005). *Batería III Woodcock-Muñoz: Pruebas de habilidades cognitivas and Batería III Woodcock-Muñoz: Pruebas de aprovechamiento.* Itasca, IL: Riverside.

National Association of School Psychologists. (2000). *Professional conduct manual: Principles for professional ethics.* Bethesda, MD: Author.

Neisser, U., Boodoo, G., Bouchard, T. J., Boykin, A. W., Brody, N., Ceci, S. J., et al. (1996). Intelligence: Knowns and unknowns. *American Psychologist, 51*, 77–101.

Newland, T. E. (1971). Psychological assessment of exceptional children and youth. In W. Cruickshank (Ed.), *Psychology of exceptional children and youth* (pp. 115–172). Englewood Cliffs, NJ: Prentice-Hall.

Ochoa, S. H., Riccio, C. A., Jimenez, S., Garcia de Alba, R., & Sines, M. (2004). Psychological assessment of limited English proficient and/or bilingual students: An investigation of school psychologists' current practices. *Journal of Psychoeducational Assessment, 22*, 93–105.

Ortiz, S. O. (2001). Assessment of cognitive abilities in Hispanic children. *Seminars in Speech and Language, 22*(1), 17–37.

Ortiz, S. O. (2002). Best practices in nondiscriminatory assessment. In A. Thomas & J. Grimes (Eds.), *Best practices in school psychology IV* (pp. 1321–1336). Washington, DC: National Association of School Psychologists.

Ortiz, S. O. (2006). Multicultural issues in working with children and families: Responsive intervention in the educational setting. In R. B. Menutti, A. Freeman, & R. W. Christner, (Eds.), *Cognitive Behavioral Interventions in Educational Settings: A handbook for practice* (pp. 21–36). New York: Brunner-Rutledge Publishing.

Ortiz, S. O., & Dynda, A. M. (2005). Use of intelligence test with culturally and linguistically *diverse* populations. In D. P. Flanagan, & P. L. Harrison (Eds.), *Contemporary intellectual assessment* (pp. 545–556). New York: The Guilford Press.

Ortiz, S. O., & Flanagan, D. P. (1998). Gf-Gc cross-battery interpretation and selective cross-battery assessment: Referral concerns and the needs of culturally and linguistically diverse populations. In K. S. McGrew & D. P. Flanagan (Eds.), *The Intelligence Test Desk Reference (ITDR): Gf-Gc Cross-Battery Assessment* (pp.401–444). Boston: Allyn & Bacon.

Ortiz, S. O., & Ochoa, S. H. (2005a). Advances in cognitive assessment of culturally and linguistically diverse individuals: A nondiscriminatory interpretive approach. In D. P. Flanagan, & P. L. Harrison (Eds.), *Contemporary intellectual assessment* (pp. 545–556). New York, NY: The Guilford Press.

Ortiz, S. O., & Ochoa, S. H. (2005b). Cognitive assessment of culturally and linguistically diverse individuals: An integrated approach. In R. Rhodes, S. H. Ochoa, & S. O. Ortiz (Eds.), *Assessing culturally and linguistically diverse students: A practical guide* (pp. 168–201). New York: Guilford Press.

Ortiz, S. O. ,& Ochoa, S. H. (2005c). Conceptual measurement and methodological issues in cognitive assessment of culturally and linguistically diverse individuals. In R. Rhodes, S. H. Ochoa, & S. O. Ortiz (Eds.), *Assessing culturally and linguistically diverse students: A practical guide* (pp. 153–167). New York: Guilford Press.

Ramirez, J. D., Yuen, S. D., & Ramey, D. R. (1991). *Final report: Longitudinal study of study of* structured *English immersion strategy, early-exit, and late-exit transitional bilingual education programs for language-minority students: Executive summary.* San Mateo, CA: Aguirre International.

Rhodes, R. L., Ochoa, S. H., & Ortiz, S. O. (2005). *Assessing culturally and linguistically diverse students.* New Cork: Guilford Press.

Roid, G. H. (2003). *Stanford-Binet Intelligence Scales* (5th ed.). Itasca, IL: Riverside Publishing.

Salvia, J., & Ysseldyke, J. E. (1991). *Assessment* (5th ed.) New York: Houghton Mifflin.

Sanchez, G. (1934). Bilingualism and mental measures: A word of caution. *Journal of Applied Psychology, 18,* 765–772.

Sandoval, J., Frisby, C. L., Geisinger, K. F., Scheuneman, J. D., & Grenier, J. R. (Eds.). (1998). *Test interpretation and diversity: Achieving equity in assessment.* Washington, DC: American Psychological Association.

Sattler, J. M. (1992). *Assessment of children* (Rev. 3rd ed.). San Diego, CA: Jerome M. Sattler.

Sattler, J. M. (2001). *Assessment of children* (4th ed.). San Diego, CA: Jerome M. Sattler.

Scarr, S. (1978). From evolution to Larry P., or what shall we do about IQ tests? *Intelligence, 2,* 325–342.

Sternberg, R. J. (1999). A triarchic approach to the understanding and assessment of intelligence in multicultural populations. *Journal of School Psychology, 37,* 145–159.

Sternberg, R. J. (2004). Culture and intelligence in multicultural populations. *American Psychologist, 5,* 325–338.

Sternberg, R. J., & Grigorenko, E. (2002). *Dynamic testing, the nature and measurement of learning potential.* Cambridge, U.K.: Cambridge University Press.

Swanson, H. (1996). *Swanson cognitive processing test.* Austin, TX: Pro-Ed.

Thomas, W. P., & Collier, V. P. (1997). *School effectiveness for language minority students.* Washington, DC: National Clearinghouse for Bilingual Education.

Thomas, W. P., & Collier, V. P. (2002). *A national study of school effectiveness for language minority students' long-term academic achievement*: Retrieved September 4, 2002, from html <http://www.crede.uscu.edu/research/llaa1.html>.

U.S. Bureau of the Census. (2001). *Percent of persons who are foreign born: 2000.* Washington, DC: Author.

Valdés, G., & Figueroa, R.. A. (1996). *Bilingualism and testing: A special case of bias.* Norwood, NJ: Ablex.

Vazquez-Nuttall, E. V., Nuttall-Vazquez, K., & Hampel, A. (1999). Introduction. In Nuttall, E. V., Romero, I., & Kalesnik, J. (Eds.), *Assessing and screening preschoolers: Psychological and educational dimensions* (2nd ed., pp. 1–8). Boston, MA: Allyn and Bacon.

Vukovich, D., & Figueroa, R. A. (1982). *The validation of the system of multicultural pluralistic assessment: 1980–1982.* Unpublished manuscript, University of California at Davis, Department of Education.

Vygotsky, L. (1978). *Mind in society: The development of higher psychological processes.* Cambridge, MA: Harvard University Press.

Wechsler, D. (2004a). *Wechsler intelligence scale for children–Fourth edition–Integrated.* San Antonio, TX: The Psychological Corporation.

Wechsler, D. (2004b). *Wechsler intelligence scale for children–Fourth edition–Spanish.* San Antonio, TX: The Psychological Corporation.

Woodcock, R., McCrew, K., & Mather, N. (2001). *Woodcock-Johnson-III test of cognitive abilities.* Itasca, IL: Riverside Publishing.

Woodcock, R. W., McGrew, K. S., Mather, N., & Schrank, F. A. (2003). *Diagnostic Supplement to the Woodcock-Johnson III Tests of Cognitive Abilities.* Itasca, IL: Riverside Publishing.

Yang, S., & Sternberg, R. J. (1997). Taiwanese Chinese people's conceptions of intelligence. *Intelligence, 25(1),* 21–36.

Yerkes, R. M. (Ed.). (1921). Psychological examining in the United States Army. *Memoirs of the National Academy of Sciences, 15,* 1–890.

14

PERSONALITY AND BEHAVIORAL ASSESSMENT: CONSIDERATIONS FOR CULTURALLY AND LINGUISTICALLY DIVERSE INDIVIDUALS

Samantha W. Kohn and Denise Scorcia
Crossroads School for Child Development, New York

Giselle B. Esquivel
Fordham University

The demographics of the United States, much like the field of psychological assessment itself, are in a constant state of transition. Census data indicate that each year the number of culturally and linguistically diverse (CLD) individuals increases, and as such, many of our nation's school children are members of various diverse groups. In the U.S., the main culturally and linguistically diverse groups are African Americans, Asians, Hispanics, and Native Americans, all of which include individuals in need of psychological assessment and intervention (Dana, 1993). A major concern, however, is whether or not the instruments psychologists use are culturally sensitive and/or provide a fair and adequate assessment of personality functioning. Another concern is whether psychologists who utilize these instruments do so in a nonbiased manner.

Recently, many psychologists have demonstrated an interest in cultural diversity and the effects on assessment. However, much of the literature base discusses cognitive and achievement assessment tools with regard to CLD individuals (Dana, 1993). Empirical investigations of personality and behavioral assessment measures appear to have lagged behind. As diversified cultural practices and traditions are becoming more prevalent in many aspects of society, school psychologists working with CLD individuals must consider these differences in order to make informed decisions in routine personality assessment and intervention practices (American Psychological Association, 1993). Psychologists have a responsibility to recognize cultural diversity when selecting instruments for personality assessment. Moreover, psychologists must be sensitive to the role differing cultural beliefs play in personality development. They must recognize their own cultural biases and limitations in the understanding of different cultural practices, consider level of acculturation, assist clients in resolving difficulties, and design therapeutic interventions that are culturally appropriate. School psychologists often find themselves in less than ideal situations, where an apparent shortage of bilingual practitioners (particularly in urban schools) coupled with increasing numbers of CLD individuals creates a great dilemma with regard to culturally competent personality assessment. Models have been developed in order to improve personality assessment practices when working with CLD individuals (e.g., Dana, 2000). Some of the ways to improve assessment and intervention practices have included conducting personality assessments in the client's native language, increasing psychologists' cultural competence, using interdisciplinary consultation when developing intervention strategies, and becoming familiar with the strengths and weaknesses of individual assessment tools (Dana, 1993).

This chapter provides an overview of cultural and linguistic issues in personality/behavioral assessment and practical approaches when working with CLD individuals. The first section includes a general discussion of psychometric and clinical considerations in the use of personality/behavioral assessment tools for a CLD population. The second section describes the specific strengths and weaknesses of commonly used personality and behavior assessment tools in an attempt to assist psychologists working in school and mental health settings to make culturally competent decisions with regard to test selection. This section is followed by practical suggestions in order to help psychologists increase the validity and clinical utility of personality and behavioral assessments when working with CLD individuals. Finally, suggestions for future research and practice are discussed.

PSYCHOMETRIC AND CLINICAL CONSIDERATIONS IN ASSESSING INDIVIDUALS FROM CULTURALLY AND LINGUISTICALLY DIVERSE BACKGROUNDS

There are many factors to consider in the personality and behavioral assessment of CLD individuals. Ethical guidelines dictate that psychologists are responsible for selecting nonbiased assessment instruments and administering and interpreting them in a way that is culturally appropriate (Jacob-Timm & Hartshorne, 1998). The psychometric properties of many measures of personality and behavior have resulted in concerns regarding their usefulness, not just with CLD populations, but with non-minority groups as well. However, they continue to be widely used and therefore, necessitate discussion on their utility in assessing CLD populations.

Dana (2000) proposed a model that assumes differences in personality and behavior functioning on the basis of cultural identification. According to this model, the initial phase of any assessment should be to evaluate the extent of cultural differences determining whether there is a need for culture-specific modifications on standard instruments or the need for culture-specific instruments. Dana's model distinguishes between *etic* instruments (i.e., those that are considered universal or culture-general) and *emic* instruments (i.e., those that are culture-specific). Information regarding the degree to which the individual being assessed has assimilated to the dominant culture is used to help determine which instruments, with or without cultural modifications, should be used. Embedded in his model are many psychometric and clinical considerations regarding test use and appropriateness. This section discusses the psychometric and clinical properties of assessment procedures that need to be considered when evaluating CLD individuals.

Psychometric Considerations

An important aspect of evaluating CLD individuals is being knowledgeable about the psychometric characteristics of assessment procedures (Rogers, 1998). However, the psychometric difficulties with which personality assessment, especially projective techniques, have been criticized (e.g., deficiency of norms, poor reliability and validity), makes the investigation of how appropriate these measures are with CLD individuals that much more complicated. In addition, many psychometric techniques, such as test-score distributions, reliability and validity estimates, factor analyses, and other statistical procedures used to investigate test bias are problematic when applied to measures of personality (Moran, 1990). Two major psychometric problems with regard to assessing CLD populations are the issues of standardization and validity.

Standardization sample.   One major concern when selecting an appropriate instrument to use with CLD children is whether the test norms adequately represent the racial/ethnic or linguistic background of the child being assessed (Lopez, 1995; Rogers, 1998). According to Rogers, a norm-referenced instrument designed to represent the current demographics of children in the U.S. should include samples of minority and majority group members in proportion to the latest census data with regard to age, sex, race, and socioeconomic status (SES), to name a few. However, some instruments under-represent or do not include many minority groups in the standardization process. This limits the applicability of the test norms to the majority group on which it was normed. Rogers also states that even when minority groups are represented in adequate numbers, they are not evenly sampled with regard to characteristics such as SES, thereby limiting the accuracy and usefulness of the test norms.

Validity.   Test bias refers to a "systematic error in the estimation of some 'true' value for a group of individuals" (Reynolds, Lowe, & Saenz, 1999, p. 563). Test bias may affect the content, construct, and predictive validity of an instrument. For example, the content of a personality or behavioral measure (i.e., specific items) can be problematic when different ethnic groups perform differently on items when other variables, such as level of a specific psychological construct are held constant. Specific items may be biased because: (a) the items may ask for information that individuals from a specific ethnic group have not had an equal opportunity to learn; (b) a response may be considered correct based on mainstream culture and scored as such; however, CLD individuals may provide answers that are correct based on their culture; (c) the language of the question may be difficult for CLD individuals to understand and contribute to their not choosing the correct response (Reynolds et al., 1999). In general, test content for a personality/behavioral assessment instrument is considered biased if the items yield a systematic difference in scores on a specific trait being measured for individuals from CLD groups than for individuals from the mainstream culture, provided that the construct being measured for each group is held constant and there is no other reasonable explanation for the differences in responses (Moran, 1990; Reynolds et al., 1999).

According to Reynolds, Lowe, and Saenz (1999), "Bias exists in regard to measuring different hypothetical traits (psychological constructs) for different groups..." (p. 573). Moran (1990) reasoned, however, that with regard to cross-cultural theory, it might be likely that real differences between the cultural groups are assessed by personality/behavioral measures. Thus, it is important that if instruments are to be used with various groups and scores are to be interpreted comparably across groups, then that instrument must be measuring the equivalent construct for those groups. If differences in the identified constructs of the instrument occur among various cultural groups and are found to be based upon some real difference between the groups or upon test error, then use of that instrument for the group in question would be unethical without alteration in scoring, norm use, or interpretation for each group. Two very important questions need to be answered with regard to bias in construct validity. The first is whether the constructs are being measured in the same way for each group. The second is whether the constructs are being measured with equal accuracy for each group (Moran, 1990).

In addition, Dana (1993) stated that most personality constructs that are measured using objective personality techniques are of European and American origin. Different languages and cultures will not necessarily recognize the same constructs. If the culture does have a similar construct, but uses a different vocabulary to describe it, one must ensure that the construct carries the same meaning in each culture. Dana cautioned that when the individual being assessed does not share a Eurocentric world view, a cultural context of the interpretation of the constructs is necessary.

Bias in predictive validity occurs when the relationship between a test score and some external criterion differ across groups. With regard to personality/behavioral assessment, the factor being predicted by the test (e.g., indictor of pathology or personality trait) should be equally predicted across different groups (Moran, 1990; Reynolds et al., 1999). For example, an instrument designed to measure suicidal tendencies has adequate predictive validity if it predicts well those individuals who may attempt suicide. If an instrument differs in predicting equally well for one group, then one must question whether this is due to real differences between the groups with regard to the construct being measured or bias within the instrument. In each case, revisions to the instrument with regard to psychometric properties must take place.

Clinical Considerations

In addition to the psychometric considerations that must be understood when conducting cross-cultural assessments, there is a need for an increased awareness about the clinical and underlying factors that influence the personality and behavioral assessment of CLD individuals. Undue emphasis on the psychometric and empirical basis of personality assessment may lead to limited consideration of the value of qualitative methods in yielding clinical information. In this regard, objective approaches have been critiqued as having a narrow focus on surface behavior and failing to capture the underlying subjective meaning of the individual child's experience in the context of culture. The use of quantifiable or behavioral data alone may lead to inaccurate inferences, particularly for children whose cultural and linguistic experience and values have an impact on the manner they behave outwardly or the way they are perceived by teachers, whose observations may be misguided by possible limited cultural understanding (Flanagan & Esquivel, in press). Moreover, components of assessment such as level of acculturation, translation, and service delivery style need to be taken into account when providing cross-cultural personality evaluations (Dana, 1993, 1996).

Level of acculturation. The assessment of CLD populations can be carried out competently only with an understanding of how the contribution of the client's culture influences the presenting problem (Dana, 1993). Cultural orientation provides a way of describing the range of differences within each racial or ethnic group that results from different degrees of acculturation. The different categories of cultural orientation, such as traditional, marginal, bicultural, and assimilated should be identified prior to conducting any evaluation so as to know whether or not the assessment instruments and service delivery style developed within the mainstream culture are applicable to a particular CLD population (Dana, 1996). Measures of acculturation can be used as moderator variables to adjust for cultural differences during the assessment process. (Refer to the chapter on acculturation for a description of these measures).

Dana (1993) described the purpose of a moderator variable as "to obtain a reliable estimate of the potential contribution of cultural variance to an assessment procedure" (p. 113). The use of *etic* assessment procedures, in which the instrument was developed and normed within the dominant society, necessitates a way to adjust for the influence of acculturation. Otherwise, the assessment may magnify the differences among groups. With regard to personality/behavioral assessment, information from these moderator variables can be useful to use for interpretation of objective or projective assessment data. The information may be used to understand the contribution of culture and thus, minimize the over identification of pathology that can result when using techniques developed and normed using the mainstream population.

Translation. In addition to the effects that different levels of acculturation have on the assessment process of CLD populations, another factor is translation of normed instruments. Translating normed instruments is a popular option for psychologists because of the lack of instruments to assess individuals in languages other than English. However, Lopez (1995) cautions against using this approach because of the inherent problems in the translation of test items. For instance, many concepts (especially with regard to social/emotional functioning and pathology) cannot be directly translated from one language to another. This is in part due to the difference in vocabulary, but also may be based on different cultural beliefs. Concepts may have a different meaning once translated into another language. Thus, both linguistic and construct equivalence are significant concerns when translating an instrument (Dana, 1993, 1996). If translations are necessary, a trained and qualified translator may serve as an adjunct and the report on the process and findings should be qualified by the examiner as deviating from formal standardized assessment procedures. Interpretations in this situation should be made with caution and in consultation with a professional peer with multicultural competencies.

Service delivery.   Those conducting assessments in the United States have been influenced by a medical model style of service delivery that carries with it the expectation that those we are assessing will be compliant and attend to the task in a relatively impersonal manner (Dana, 1996). This, by no means discounts the importance the Anglo-American culture places on establishing rapport. However, it should be realized when working with children and parents who maintain traditional levels of acculturation, that this style of service delivery may not be comfortable to them and may even be considered intrusive. This has important implications for the validity of the evaluation results. The information that the student and/or parent is willing to provide (e.g., responses to a Rorschach or omissions on a questionnaire) is dependent on their feeling comfortable with the assessment process. The psychologist needs to be aware of how her or his style of service affects the assessment process so as to avoid misinterpretation of assessment data (Dana, 1998b).

In sum, there are many psychometric and clinical factors to consider in the personality and behavioral assessment of CLD individuals. Knowledge and awareness of these factors need to be an initial part of providing a culturally competent assessment. This knowledge can then be applied in regard to test selection and method of assessment.

Implications for Test Selection: Specific Assessment Tools

In the advent of research regarding culturally competent personality/behavioral assessment and *emic-etic* approaches, school psychologists face a great challenge as they take on the complex task of selecting personality assessment tools that will provide psychometrically sound and clinically valid measures of CLD children. Until recently, empirical evidence for appropriate assessment tools was scarce and a review of the current literature suggests much more research is essential with regard to investigating the clinical utility of commonly used measures of personality/behavioral assessment when working with CLD children. This section describes the strengths and weaknesses of several commonly used objective and projective personality/behavioral assessment tools in an attempt to assist school psychologists in making culturally competent decisions in selecting the most appropriate combination of instruments and methods to use when working with CLD children.

Behavior Assessment System for Children, 2nd ed. (BASC–2; Reynolds & Kamphaus, 2004).   Overall, a review of the literature on the original edition of the Behavior Assessment System for Children (BASC; Reynolds & Kamphaus, 1998) suggested this to be a promising instrument with regard to culturally competent assessment. The general norms consisted of a relatively large sample size, which included a high number of minority children. The sample was weighted, and potential confounding variables such as race, ethnicity, age, and gender were taken into account when selecting participants for the normative sample. The BASC–2 overcomes a number of limitations over its predecessor, including significant improvement in the updating of norms to be more representative of the current U.S. population and inclusive of minority representation. The BASC and BASC–2 are notable for the development of a Spanish version of the Parent Rating Scale. This scale was created by translating test items as universally as possible so that the scale would be psychometrically sound for use with members of varying Spanish cultural backgrounds, while carefully maintaining item content (Reynolds & Kamphaus, 2004). The Structured Developmental History that is part of the BASC–2 also provides questions in various domains, including language spoken at home, and may be interpreted within a cultural background context.

The Achenbach Empirically Based System of Assessment (AESBA; Achenbach & Rescorla, 2001).   The AESBA represents a comprehensive behavioral assessment tool with an updated normative sample, a strong empirical base, wide culturally diverse representation; and which yields information from multiple informants, multiple settings, and both quantitative data and qualitative individual responses. The test offers cross-cultural applications, translations in 69 languages, and Spanish pre-school through late adolescence forms.

Conners' Rating Scales—Revised.   The Conners' Scales (Conners, 1997) have become synonymous with the assessment of Attention Deficit Hyperactivity Disorder (ADHD) and is a frequently utilized behavior assessment tool. Normative samples for each scale (i.e., Parent, Teacher, and Adolescent Self Report) were based on predominantly Caucasian/White subjects, accounting for up to 84 percent of the sample size (Conners). The manual provides comparability of ratings across different ethnic groups particularly between African Americans and Caucasians. However, little is mentioned in the literature as to use of this instrument in assessing CLD children. Norms are available for African Americans in the appendix of the manual and additional normative samples are currently being collected for Hispanics, Asians, and Native Americans (Conners). Moreover, the scale has been translated into Spanish and additional translations into several other languages are currently underway (Conners).

Projective Techniques

Rorschach Comprehensive System.   As compared to objective methods of assessment described earlier, the use of the Rorschach Comprehensive System (Exner, 1993) with CLD individuals has been the subject of greater attention in the literature. Normative data are available for scoring and interpretation. However, serious criticisms of the norms have been reported. One major problem is that there are no norms available for use with specific cultural groups. Perhaps of greater importance is the fact that the Rorschach has been criticized for its questionable reliability and validity with non-CLD populations (i.e., Lilienfeld, Wood, & Garb, 2000).

Despite inherent psychometric difficulties, the Rorschach has been described as a "culture-free method" (e.g., Ritzler, 2001; p. 237). According to Ritzler, the Rorschach stimuli have a high level of ambiguity and are not likely to resemble any culturally specific objects. In addition, all subjects undergo uniform assessment procedures, which in turn limits potential examiner bias (Ritzler, 2001). The Rorschach does not largely rely on language and can be administered in the absence of extensive translation procedures limiting changing the inherent meaning of test items (Viglione, 1999). While much of the discussion on the clinical utility of the Rorschach with CLD individuals has been promising, there are some caveats.

A major issue is the manner in which the Rorschach is interpreted, particularly when responses of individuals from various ethnic groups are interpreted similarly without consideration for cultural differences (Dana, 1993; Garb, Wood, Nezworski, Grove, & Stejskal, 2001). When the examiner is unfamiliar with differing cultural practices, possible over-identification of pathology may result (Garb et al., 2001), suggesting that cultural competence is essential in administration and interpretation processes. For example, misinterpretations of responses are likely to occur, without an understanding of cultural differences in symbolism, metaphors, associations, psychological import of colors, and values. Preliminary investigations have also revealed differing responses that emerge when the Rorschach is administered in a subject's native and second language (Ritzler, 2001). Therefore, Ritzler suggests if a subject's level of acculturation is low, the Rorschach should be administered in the individual's native language and interpreted in cultural context.

Holtzman Inkblot Test (HIT).   The Holtzman Inkblot Test (HIT) has been compared to the Rorschach in the literature. However, unlike the Rorschach, the HIT has promising psychometric properties (Holtzman, 2000). The ambiguity of task stimuli coupled with ease of administration (i.e., simplistic instructions) has made the HIT an appealing option when testing CLD individuals (Dana, 1993). In addition, the HIT requires only a single response for each card, thereby decreasing bias/misinterpretation due to linguistic factors (Holtzman, 2000). The HIT has been examined through many empirical investigations, particularly with regard to its clinical utility in assessing members of Hispanic cultures (Dana, 1993). According to Dana, the HIT is the preferred inkblot technique for assessing personality in Hispanic subjects as well as individuals from different cultural groups.

Thematic Apperception Test (TAT).   Despite several attempts at creating a scoring system and interpretation guidelines for the Thematic Apperception Test (TAT), variability in administration, absence of a consistent scoring system, and differing stimulus sets has resulted in inadequate norms (Lilienfield, Wood, & Garb, 2000). Therefore, information on psychometric properties (i.e., reliability and validity) is scarce (Kamphaus & Frick, 1996). Consequently, there are some significant questions with regard to bias in the assessment of CLD individuals. With no standard psychometric properties on which to base interpretation, clinicians are most likely going to interpret TAT stories according to their inherent cultural beliefs and practices, which may lead to greater identification of psychological difficulties when assessing subjects from differing cultural backgrounds (Dana, 1993). In addition, the TAT has been criticized for containing pictures that are not recognizable or applicable to members of varying cultural groups (Dana, 1993). Research suggests that CLD children provide shorter stories and incorporate fewer emotional themes into TAT stories (Costantino & Malgady, 1983; Costantino, Malgady, & Vazquez, 1981). Given the psychometric limitations of the TAT, it has been viewed as an inappropriate assessment tool for use with CLD individuals (Costantino, Flanagan, & Malgady, 2000).

An early attempt to modify the TAT picture stimuli to be relevant to children of color and to develop standardized procedures (e.g., Thompson Modification of the TAT [T-TAT]; Thompson, 1949) proved unsuccessful. However, more recent systems of interpretation applied to the Thematic Apperception Techniques using "narrative" approaches are promising for use with CLD children since these emphasize the importance of personal, interpersonal, and cultural experiences in constructing meaning as reflected through stories. (Cramer, 1996; McAdams, 2001; Teglasi, 2002). While these approaches have empirical validation, more research needs to be conducted in their application with CLD children. The development of culturally-sensitive alternatives is also important.

Tell-Me-A-Story (TEMAS). The Tell-Me-A-Story (TEMAS; Costantino, Malgady, & Rogler, 1988) has been identified as a "milestone in personality assessment" (Ritzler, 1993, p. 381). Dana (1993) commends the TEMAS because it is a culturally appropriate assessment tool and one of the first projective measures to incorporate a scoring system with adequate norms and promising psychometric properties. The TEMAS is normed on a sample from urban New York City, which included Whites, Blacks, and members of various Hispanic groups (Costantino, Malgady, & Rogler, 1988). The norms are unique in the fact that they are separated into categories: Combined Minorities, Combined Hispanics, and Total. The TEMAS consists of a minority (e.g., Hispanic) and non-minority version of stimuli. It should be noted that TEMAS stimuli also exist for Asian-American children and are undergoing empirical validation (Costantino & Malgady, 2000). The TEMAS demonstrates good inter-rater reliability; however, lower levels of internal consistency and test-retest reliability have been reported (Costantino et al., 1988; Ritzler, 1993). In addition, the manual provides information on studies that investigated content, construct, and criterion-related validity (Costantino et al., 1988). The TEMAS contains separate administration forms for minorities and non-minorities and the stimuli are in color and depict culturally appropriate characters and situations (Costantino et al., 1981).

Early research on the TEMAS suggested that in contrast to other measures (i.e., TAT and Rorschach), Hispanic and Black subjects are more verbally fluent in response to TEMAS stimuli and are more likely to respond to TEMAS stimuli in their native languages (Costantino, Malgady & Vazquez, 1981). Other research conducted with native Puerto Rican and Argentinean children raised some questions regarding the clinical utility of this test in assessing members of these cultural groups (Costantino, Malgady, Casullo, & Castillo, 1991). For instance, pictures depicting urban themes may not be suitable for members of varying Hispanic cultures. As such, the TEMAS has been criticized for not including minority subjects residing outside of urban areas (i.e., New York City) in the normative sample (Flanagan & DiGiuseppe, 1999). Overall, Flanagan and DiGiuseppe suggested that the TEMAS is a promising alternative for use with Black and Hispanic subjects within the context of a comprehensive assessment.

Drawing techniques.   The use of drawings in the personality assessment of CLD children is also constrained by similar psychometric and norm issues detailed in the discussion of other projective instruments. On the positive side, drawings may have descriptive as well as therapeutic value (e.g., Del Valle, McEachern, & Sabina, 1999) when interpreted with cultural sensitivity and understanding; as these reflect children's underlying processes (e.g., cognitive, perceptual, affective) that are influenced by cultural experiences. Human figure drawings (e.g., Harris, 1963; Koppitz, 1968; Naglieri, Mc Neish, & Bardos, 1991) have been traditionally used as supplemental estimates of cognitive maturity with preschool and elementary school age children, particularly those with limited verbal ability. Cross-cultural research studies throughout the years have indicated both universal commonalities in the developmental stages of drawings (e.g., scribbles, lines, circles, tadpole figures) and differences in style, content, emphasis, elaborations, use of space, size and other elements, based on cultural experiences, and gender roles (Cox, Koyasu, Hiranuma, & Perara, 2001; Dana, 1998a; Dennis, 1957; De La Serna, 1979; Levinson, 1959). There is evidence also that adults, art education, environmental contingencies, and religious values may influence both the sequence of developmental attainments in figure reproduction and the expression of mood and anxiety (e.g., Dennis, 1957; Jolley, Zhi, & Thomas, 1998).

When using human figure drawings and other techniques such as The Kinetic Family Drawings (Burns & Kaufman, 1970) or the House-Tree-Person (Buck, 1970), particular attention needs to be given to differences in family dynamics and patterns based on cultural group membership (Handler & Habenicht, 1994). There is evidence for the clinical utility of drawings when interpreted to generate hypotheses within a holistic context that includes behavioral and cultural data, such as acculturation level and ethnic identity (Reithmiller & Handler, 1997).

Overall, there are many factors to consider in the selection of personality/behavioral assessment instruments for use with CLD children. A thorough review of test manuals and current research can lead to informed decisions when selecting assessment tools. Recent advances in test construction (i.e., administration and psychometric properties) for projective instruments such as the TEMAS provide an alternative option to personality assessment with CLD children. Likewise, the use of projective techniques and narrative methods can be valuable in providing an understanding of ideographic and covert aspects of personality functioning when interpreted with cultural knowledge and competence.

A great deal of research must be conducted regarding the empirical and/or clinical utility of both objective and projective measures. When assessing CLD populations, psychologists in school and clinical settings are often faced with few options, but to utilize instruments that are not considered culturally sensitive. Suggestions to improve assessment practices are discussed in the next section.

ASSESSMENT APPROACHES FOR SCHOOL PSYCHOLOGISTS

There are some guiding principles that school psychologists should follow to conduct a culturally competent personality or behavioral assessment. They should have the knowledge and skills in nonbiased assessment (Lopez, 1995), taking into consideration the level of acculturation of the student and his/her family and being sensitive to culture-specific styles of service delivery (Dana, 1993, 1996, 1998b).

Before an assessment is even considered, the school psychologist should carefully consider the reasons for which the child was referred. Consultation with the individual, who referred the child, whether it is the teacher or other school personnel, is recommended to rule out misperceptions as a result of differing cultural backgrounds. In addition, a multidisciplinary team meeting should be held to review the referral information and decide if a comprehensive assessment is warranted (Rogers, 1998).

Once it is established the child is in need of a formal evaluation, an interview with the child and his/her parents provides a good opportunity to learn about the child's cultural background and language exposure and preferences (Rogers, 1998). The assessment may not progress in a culturally competent manner if it is conducted without awareness of the family's level of acculturation. Moderator variables should be used as part of the assessment process whenever you have a child whose family does not have an Anglo-American cultural background. Even if the child and his/her parents speak English, it should not be assumed that the family identifies with an Anglo-American way of life. In contrast, it should not be assumed that the family of an African American child or Asian American child necessarily follows their traditional culture (Dana, 1993). In addition, the psychologist should recognize the differences that are inherent between the child's and the family's cultural experiences. Due to the influence of peer and school experiences, the child may be acculturating at a faster pace than their parents. For that reason, it is very important to determine both the child's as well as the family's level of cultural orientation.

Observations of the child and interviews with the teacher and parents may also result in knowledge of differences in discipline techniques and parental attitude toward school. Behavior that may be considered appropriate in the home may not be considered suitable for the classroom. Rogers (1998) recommended noting cultural similarities as well as differences between the settings so that the child's behavior can be interpreted within an appropriate cultural framework. Observations can also include comparisons with peers of the same age and cultural orientation in order to gain information regarding how the child to be assessed compares to others of similar cultural/linguistic backgrounds (Rogers, 1998).

The psychologist needs to determine and subsequently evaluate the child in his or her dominant language. Information needs to be gathered such as how many years the child has been exposed to the English language, the age of the child at the time English was first introduced, and his or her current level of English language acquisition. These factors should be considered upon interpretation of assessment data. Studies with bilingual children suggest that responses to projective instruments may vary depending on the language the child is using (Lopez, 1995). Lopez concluded that "projective techniques developed and normed with non-minority subjects fail to capture the influence of language and culture on bilingual children's belief systems; fear, guilt, and anger" (p. 1115).

Selection of instruments needs to be carefully considered with regard to appropriateness of *emic* or *etic* measures to be used. Dana (1993) recommends that *emic* measures should be used for individuals who have "non-European origins and demonstrate cultural intactness in their world views, self-concepts, and behaviors" (p. 107). Therefore, if standardized versions of instruments exist and apply to what needs to be measured (e.g., Spanish version of BASC2 —PRS), then they should be used. When *etic* measures are adapted for use with CLD populations, it is important to take into consideration the clinical issues as well as psychometric issues that will arise. Issues regarding translation, cultural bias, and response styles will arise and affect interpretation. For instance, children from certain cultures may be more reluctant to elaborate on their answers when their responses are questioned or may give shorter and less detailed stories on instruments such as the TAT (Knauss, 2001).

Lopez (1995) cautioned against using normed instruments in the assessment of bilingual children. Some of her reasons include: (a) test norms tend to be limited to small samples of CLD children; (b) norming procedures routinely leave out students with limited English proficiency; and (c) possible bias in item content. School psychologists have an ethical responsibility to review manuals of norm-referenced instruments to ensure that they contain a representative sample of the characteristics of the child being assessed, ascertain whether the instrument has adequate reliability and validity (Rogers, 1998), and to examine the research on that instrument regarding test bias in order to determine whether the instrument is appropriate for use with the culturally diverse individual to be assessed.

An "integrative" personality assessment paradigm is suggested by Flanagan and Esquivel (in press) that calls for the use of both clinical and empirical methods (e.g., objective and projective) based on an understanding of personality in children as multidimensional, including surface-level behaviors, traits, formative processes, underlying subjective experiences, and socio-cultural contexts. These authors propose that assessment be comprehensive and that findings be organized as a descriptive profile that integrates multiple level data including cultural dimensions.

Styles of service delivery need to be considered in order to obtain a valid representation of the child's personality/behavioral functioning. Dana (1996) discussed how individuals with different levels of acculturation might have different needs with regard to how the assessor (i.e., school psychologist) approaches the assessment. For instance, a person from a traditional cultural background may be uncomfortable if the assessment is conducted in a way that is perceived as intrusive, frustrating, or alienating. Conducting an assessment in an individual's second language may result in less self-disclosure and poor communication of feelings. Individuals with a bicultural orientation may respond to both the social etiquette of their original culture as well as the dominant society (Dana, 1996).

Once the assessment is complete, a report should be written that includes information regarding the race/ethnicity of the child and his or her family, the languages the child is exposed to at home, the language used for the assessment, and any adaptations in standardization of instruments (Rogers, 1998). If interpreter was used, describe in what capacity. In addition, indication of how cultural orientation, including the use of moderator variables, and service delivery and response style affected interpretation of results should be discussed.

Communication of findings in a culturally sensitive manner is an important aspect of the assessment process not to be overlooked. The assessor should discuss the validity of the findings and provide results in qualitative and descriptive formats if scores are not appropriate.

Dana (1996) recommends first addressing information regarding cultural orientation so as to encourage rapport and show understanding of possible cultural influences. He also pointed out that in an Anglo-American culture, the individual being assessed (e.g., student or student's parents) takes ownership of the information from the assessment and responsibility for intervention decisions. Other cultures differ in the amount of power the individual being assessed (especially children) has and their beliefs in external sources of control. Finally, communication of assessment results should be sensitive to how specific cultural-specific beliefs about health and illness may influence the decisions regarding intervention (Dana, 1996).

SUMMARY AND IMPLICATIONS FOR FUTURE RESEARCH AND PRACTICE IN ASSESSING CLD POPULATIONS

The purpose of this chapter was to provide a brief overview of some of the issues psychologists must consider in the personality and behavior assessment of CLD populations. Issues of bias, including different types of validity and the need for adequate standardization are important to the psychometric integrity of the assessment; however, questionable psychometric properties of many personality measures (i.e., projective instruments) make it difficult to assess for bias. Clinical considerations, such as cultural orientation, the need for moderator variables, and issues in translation are all important aspects of the assessment process with CLD children. Measures of personality and behavior functioning were reviewed with regard to their utility with a culturally diverse population. Results of this review indicated that further research is needed for both objective and projective personality/behavioral instruments. Some progress in this area has been made, as there has been the development of instruments that are more specific to language and culture, such as the Spanish version of the BASC–2: PRS and the TEMAS. Research on emic instruments, such as the HIT is promising and is encouraged. However, as Suzuki, Ponterotto, and Meller (2001) pointed out, "little has been done to shake up the assessment community" (p. 569). Finally, a walk through of the assessment process from pre-referral to communication of findings provided some practical considerations for the school psychologist.

With regard to the future practice of personality and behavioral assessment with CLD populations, Gray-Little (1995) indicated that the most important factor that needs to be addressed is assessor bias and misuse of assessment information. After all, the person conducting the evaluation is a product of family experiences, beliefs, social-group membership as well as formal training. There is also a need for continued formal education addressing the nonbiased assessment of CLD populations.

Rogers (1998) called for an upgrading of professional skills. Less formal education, such as workshops and in-services can serve to raise awareness of the psychological issues that confront CLD members of the school community and cultural and social characteristics of the groups of CLD students that attend the school.

Graduate education addressing culturally competent psychological assessment needs to combine standard and multicultural assessment training with currently used tests or provide a course dedicated exclusively to multicultural assessment (Dana, Aguilar-Kitibutr, Diaz-Vivar, & Vetter, 2002). These authors recommended several considerations to be incorporated in a multicultural assessment course including: (a) providing a background in cultural issues in psychopathology and personality theory; (b) familiarizing the students with research guidelines for minority populations, including sources of bias in assessment research; (c) training to reduce possible negative feelings and reactions to cultural content (Jackson, as cited in Dana et al., 2002); (d) providing early exposure to a variety of clinical frameworks for addressing cultural identity (Ponterotto, Gretchen, & Chauhan, as cited in Dana et al., 2002); and (e) providing experience to students of non-Euro-American origin on what it is like to be assessed with standard tests that have not been appropriately designed or normed for CLD individuals.

An understanding of psychopathology and diagnosis in various ethnic groups is vital to enhancing clinical judgment. Assessors need to be aware of the ways different ethnic groups manifest feelings of distress so that they can distinguish between culturally appropriate coping skills and symptoms of psychopathology (Gray-Little, 1995). There is also the need to be cognizant of the diversity and heterogeneity within ethnic groups. For instance, Velasquez (1995) reasoned, "the experiences of a third-generation Chicano born and raised in an urban barrio are quite different from those of a Cuban or Central American refugee" (p. 128).

Flanagan and Esquivel (in press) propose preparing school psychologists in an *integrative paradigm* of personality assessment that includes grounding in theories of personality in children and adolescents (including multicultural perspectives); knowledge of and skills in the use of multiple methods; the development of multicultural competencies in assessment, interpretation, communication of results; and the ability to link descriptive and diagnostic profiles to culturally-sensitive interventions.

Schools and clinical settings can form committees that address cultural and linguistic diversity. These committees can plan and develop in-services, promote parental involvement, and raise awareness in the school community. Various disciplines (i.e., education, psychology, speech/language) should participate in the committee to bring different areas of expertise and discussion of how the assessment of CLD children affects each area of assessment.

In addition to changes that should take place with regard to the training and practice of personality assessment with CLD populations, the research community needs to define and develop a research agenda in this area. The questionable psychometric properties of many personality and behavior measures make it imperative that the scientific community continues to conduct research on the validity of these instruments with both CLD and non-CLD populations. There is an abundance of research with regard to cultural bias in cognitive and achievement measures; however, "research on bias in personality assessment instruments is at an earlier point in its development" (Knauss, 2001, p. 235). Personality assessment measures, particularly projective instruments, have been criticized for their lack of adequate reliability and validity (Lilienfeld et al., 2000). In turn, the strict use of standardized tests limits the clinical utility of the personality assessment process. As mentioned previously, this results in greater difficulty when assessing bias with regard to CLD individuals.

Emic measures, which are designed for use with specific cultures, have received limited research attention in the assessment literature. They have not been emphasized in assessment training programs and few practitioners are experienced in using them (Dana, 1993). Development of *emic* measures (whether objective or projective) would provide significant contributions to culturally competent assessment and have important impact on intervention planning and implementation. For instance, Dana (1996) stated, "These new emics can provide specification of problems-in-living, culture-specific syndromes, and *DSM* group-specific base rates for traditional and marginal persons" (p. 483). Most practitioners rely on adapting *etic* measures, which can result in a decrease in validity and subsequent misclassifications or inappropriate utility of the instrument. Related to this is the need for research examining the cross-cultural construct validity of standard psychological instruments (Dana, 1996) or the clinical utility of qualitative approaches when applied to CLD children and adolescents.

The present state of personality and behavioral assessment with culturally and linguistically diverse children leaves many challenges to be addressed. Research on the validity of standard *etic* measurements as well as the development of *emic* measures and clinical approaches is still at a young stage. Psychologists working in schools and clinical settings have an important responsibility in the selection and utilization of personality and behavior instruments in the assessment of CLD populations and in the methods or techniques employed. It is imperative that psychologists place greater emphasis on training that is comprehensive in nature and continued professional development of culturally competent personality assessment. As Weiner (1988) put it so eloquently, "What does a poor, black, or Hispanic boy experience when asked to tell a story about a well-scrubbed, nicely dressed white boy looking at a violin?" (p. xi).

ANNOTATED BIBLIOGRAPHY

American Psychological Association (2003). Guidelines on multicultural education, training, research, practice, and organizational change for psychologists. *American Psychologist, 58*, 377–402.

   Provides guidelines on how multicultural issues should be considered across various areas within the field of psychology.

Dana, R. H. (2000). *Handbook of cross-cultural and multicultural personality assessment.* Mahwah, NJ: Erlbaum.

   Provides a theoretical framework for cross-cultural and multicultural personality assessment and an overview of the research on the use of objective and projective personality techniques with culturally diverse populations.

Rogers, M. R. (1998). Psychoeducational assessment of culturally and linguistically diverse children and youth. In H. B. Vance (Ed.), *Psychological assessment of children* (2nd ed.). New York: Wiley.

Provides practical information for school psychologists on the issues involved in the assessment of culturally and linguistically diverse children.

Suzuki, L. A., Ponterotto, J. G., & Meller, P. J. (2001). *Handbook of multicultural assessment: Clinical, psychological, and educational applications* (2nd ed.). San Francisco, CA: Wiley.

Provides an overview of issues related to multicultural assessment, including cognitive and personality assessment. The use of specific objective and projective personality assessment instruments are discussed.

RESOURCES

Thorough list of references provided by the National Association of School Psychologists on different aspects of cross-cultural competence:
   http://www.nasponline.org/culturalcompetence/references.html

REFERENCES

Achenbach, T. M., & Rescorla, L. A. (2001). *Manual for the AESBA School Age Forms and Profiles.* Burlington, VT.: University of Vermont, Research Center for Children, Youth, & Families.

American Psychological Association. (1993). Guidelines for providers of psychological services to ethnic, linguistic, and culturally diverse populations. *American Psychologist, 48,* 45–48.

Buck, J. N. (1970). *The House-Tree-Person Technique: Revised Manual.* Los Angeles: Western Psychological Services.

Burns, R. C., & Kaufman, S. H. (1970). *Kinetic Family Drawings (K-F-D): An introduction to understanding children through kinetic drawings.* New York: Brunner-Mazel.

Conners, C. K. (1997). *Conners Rating Scales—Revised technical manual.* Toronto, Canada: Multi-Health Systems.

Costantino, G., Flanagan, R., & Malgady, R. G. (2000). Narrative assessments TAT, CAT and TEMAS. In L. A. Suzuki, J. G. Ponterotto, & P. J. Meller (Eds.), *Handbook of multicultural assessment: Clinical, psychological, and educational applications* (2nd ed., pp. 217–236). San Francisco: Wiley.

Costantino, G., & Malgady, R. G. (1983). Verbal fluency of Hispanic, Black, and White children on TAT and TEMAS: A new thematic apperception test. *Hispanic Journal of Behavioral Sciences, 5,* 199–206.

Costantino, G., & Malgady, R. G. (2000). Multicultural and cross-cultural utility of the TEMAS (Tell-Me-A-Story) test. In R. H. Dana (Ed.), *Handbook of cross-cultural and multicultural personality assessment* (pp. 481–513). Mahwah, NJ: Erlbaum.

Costantino, G., Malgady, R. G., Casullo, M. M., & Castillo, A. (1991). Cross-cultural standardization of TEMAS in three Hispanic subcultures. *Hispanic Journal of Behavioral Sciences, 13,* 48–62.

Costantino, G., Malgady, R. G., & Rogler, L. H. (1988). *TEMAS (Tell-Me-A-Story) manual.* Los Angeles: Western Psychological Services.

PERSONALITY AND BEHAVIOR ASSESSMENT

305

Costantino, G., Malgady, R. G., & Vazquez, C. (1981). A comparison of the Murray TAT and a new thematic apperception test for urban Hispanic children. *Hispanic Journal of Behavioral Sciences, 3,* 291–300.

Cox, M. V., Koyasu, M., Hiranuma, H., & Perara, J. (2001). Children's human figure drawings in the UK and Japan: The effects of age, sex, and culture. *British Journal of Developmental Psychology, 19,* 275–292.

Cramer, P. (1996). *Storytelling, narrative, and the thematic apperception test.* NY: Guilford Press.

Dana, R. H. (1993). *Multicultural assessment perspectives for professional psychology.* Boston: Allyn & Bacon.

Dana, R. H. (1996). Culturally competent assessment practice in the United States. *Journal of Personality Assessment, 66,* 472–487.

Dana, R. H. (1998a). Assessment of Latinos in the United States: Current realities, problems, and prospects. *Cultural Diversity and Ethnic Minority Psychology, 4,* 165–184.

Dana, R. H. (1998b). Cultural identity assessment of culturally diverse groups: 1997. *Journal of Personality Assessment, 70,* 1–16.

Dana, R. H. (2000). An assessment-intervention model for research and practice with multicultural populations. In R. H. Dana (Ed.), *Handbook of cross-cultural and multicultural personality assessment* (pp. 5–16). Mahwah, NJ: Erlbaum.

Dana, R. H., Aguilar-Kitibutr, A., Diaz-Vivar, N., & Vetter, H. (2002). A teaching method for multicultural assessment: Psychological report contents and cultural competence. *Journal of Personality Assessment, 79,* 207–215.

De La Serna, M., Helwig, L., & Richmond, B. O. (1979). Cultural impact on human figure drawings. *Social Behavior and Personality, 7,* 29–32.

Del Valle, P., McEachern, A. G., & Sabina, M. Q (1999). Using drawings and writings in a group counseling experience with Cuban rafter children, 'Los Balseritos'. *Guidance and Counseling.* 20–29.

Dennis, W. (1957). Performance of Near Eastern children on the Draw-A-Man Test. *Child Development, 28,* 427–430.

Exner, J. E. (1993). *The Rorschach: A comprehensive system. Volume 1: Basic foundations* (3rd ed.). New York: Wiley.

Flanagan, R., & DiGiuseppe, R. (1999). Critical review of the TEMAS: A step within the development of thematic apperception instruments. *Psychology in the Schools, 36,* 21–30.

Flanagan, R., & Esquivel, G. B. (in press). Empirical and clinical methods in the assessment of personality and psychopathology: An integrative training approach. *Psychology in the Schools.*

Garb, H. N., Wood, J. M., Nezworski, M. T., Grove, W. M., & Stejskal, W. J. (2001). Toward a resolution of the Rorschach controversy. *Psychological Assessment, 13,* 433–448.

Gray-Little, B. (1995). The assessment of psychopathology in racial and ethnic minorities. In J. N. Butcher (Ed.), *Clinical personality assessment: Practical approaches* (pp. 140–157). New York: Oxford University Press.

Handler, L., & Habenicht, D. (1994). The kinetic family drawing technique: A review of the literature. *Journal of Personality Personality Assessment, 62,* 440–464.

Harris, D. B. (1963). *Children's drawings as measures of intellectual maturity.* NY: Harcourt, Brace and World.

Holtzman, W. H. (2000). Application of the Holtzman inkblot technique in different cultures. In R. H. Dana (Ed.), *Handbook of cross-cultural and multicultural personality assessment.* (pp. 393–417). Mahwah, NJ: Erlbaum.

Jacob-Timm, S., & Hartshorne, T. S. (1998). *Ethics and law for school psychologists* (3rd ed.). New York: Wiley.

Jolley, R. P., Zhi, Z., & Thomas, G. V. (1998). How focus of interest in pictures changes with age: A cross-cultural comparison. *International Journal of Behavioral Development, 22,* 127–149.

Kamphaus, R. W., & Frick, P. J. (1996). *Clinical assessment of child and adolescent personality and behavior.* Needham Heights, MA: Allyn & Bacon.

Knauss, L. K. (2001). Ethical issues in psychological assessment in school settings. *Journal of Personality Assessment, 77,* 231–241.

Koppitz, E. M. (1968). *Psychological evaluation of children's human figure drawings.* NY: Grune and Stratton.

Levinson, B. M. (1959). A comparison of the performance of bilingual and monolingual native born preschool children of traditional parentage on four intelligence tests. *Journal of Clinical Psychology, 15,* 74–76.

Lilienfeld, S. O., Wood, J. M., & Garb, H. N. (2000). The scientific status of projective techniques. *Psychological Science in the Public Interest, 1,* 27–66.

Lopez, E. C. (1995). Best practices in working with bilingual children. In A. Thomas & J. Grimes (Eds.), *Best practices in school psychology-III* (pp. 1111–1121). Washington, DC: National Association of School Psychologists.

McAdams, D.P. (2001). *The person: An integrated introduction to personality psychology.* CITY, FL: Harcourt.

Moran, M. P. (1990). The problem of cultural bias in personality assessment. In C. R.Reynolds & R. W. Kamphaus (Eds.), *Handbook of psychological and educational assessment of children: Personality, behavior, and context* (pp. 524–545). New York: Guilford.

Naglieri, J.A., McNeish, R.J., & Bardos, A.N. (1991). *Draw-A-Person: Screening Procedure for Emotional Disturbance.* Austin, TX: ProEd.

Reithmiller, R. J., & Handler, L. (1997). Problematic methods and unwarranted conclusions in DAP research: Suggestions for improved research procedures. *Journal of Personality Assessment, 69,* 459–475.

Reynolds, C. R., & Kamphaus, R. W. (1998). *Behavior Assessment System for Children (BASC) manual.* Circle Pines, MN: American Guidance Service.

Reynolds, C. R., & Kamphaus, R. W., (2004). *Behavior Assessment System for Children* (2nd ed.). Circle Pines, MN: American Guidance Service.

Reynolds, C. R., Lowe, P. A., & Saenz, A. L. (1999). The problem of bias in psychological assessment. In C. R. Reynolds & T. B. Gutkin (Eds.), *The handbook of school psychology* (3rd ed., pp. 549–595). New York: Wiley.

Ritzler, B. A. (1993). Test review: TEMAS. *Journal of Psychoeducational Assessment, 11,* 381–389.

Ritzler, B. A. (2001). Multicultural usage of the Rorschach. In L. A. Suzuki, J. G. Ponterotto, & P. J. Meller (Eds.), *Handbook of multicultural assessment: Clinical, psychological, and educational applications* (2nd ed., pp. 237–252). San Francisco: Wiley.

Rogers, M. R. (1998). Psychoeducational assessment of culturally and linguistically diverse children and youth. In H. B. Vance (Ed.), *Psychological assessment of children* (2nd ed.). New York: Wiley.

Suzuki, L. A., Ponterotto, J. G., & Meller, P. J. (2001). Multicultural assessment: Trends and directions revisited. In L. A. Suzuki, J. G. Ponterotto, & P. J. Meller (Eds.), *Handbook of multicultural assessment: Clinical, psychological, and educational applications* (2nd ed., pp. 237–252). San Francisco: Wiley.

Teglasi, H., (2002). *Essentials of TAT and other storytelling techniques assessment.* New York, NY: Wiley.

Thompson, C. E. (1949). The Thompson modification of the Thematic Apperception Test. *Rorschach Research Exchange and Journal of Projective Techniques, 15,* 394–400.

Velasquez, R. J. (1995). Personality assessment of Hispanic clients. In J. N. Butcher (Ed.), *Clinical personality assessment: Practical approaches* (pp. 120–139). New York: Oxford University Press.

Viglione, D. J. (1999). A review of recent research addressing the utility of the Rorschach. *Psychological Assessment, 11,* 251–265.

Weiner, I. B. (1988). *TEMAS (Tell-Me-A-Story) manual.* Los Angeles: Western Psychological Services.

15

NEUROPSYCHOLOGICAL ASSESSMENT OF CULTURALLY AND LINGUISTICALLY DIVERSE CHILDREN: A REVIEW OF RELEVANT ISSUES AND APPROPRIATE METHODS

Laura B. Kestemberg, Melissa Tarnofsky Silverman, and Michael R. Emmons

Fordham University

Drawing from the fields of anatomy, biology, biophysics, ethology, pharmacology, physiology, physiological psychology, and philosophy, neuropsychology is the study of the relationship between human brain function and behavior (Kolb & Whishaw, 2003). According to Lezak (1995), the field of neuropsychology has grown to encompass the diagnosis of individuals, patient care and planning, rehabilitation and treatment evaluation, and research with regard to neuropsychological functioning. Assessment continues to be emphasized as a component of neuropsychology, and it typically involves an evaluation of the following domains: intellectual status, language and academic abilities, executive processes, attention, concentration, learning and memory, visuoconstructive abilities, motor functioning, sensory functioning, and emotional functioning, including mood, behavior, and personality (Groth-Marnat, 2000; Lezak, 1995; Spreen & Strauss, 1998).

The neuropsychological assessment of children has historically involved a downward extension of adult neuropsychological assessment practices (Marlowe, 2000). However, the application of adult inferences and hypotheses to children's development fails to address known differences in the functional organization and development of the infant-child brain (Riccio & Wolfe, 2003). Assessment of neuropsychological functioning in children requires a thorough understanding of the relationship between the development of the human central nervous system and the cognitive functions that emerge between birth and adulthood (Batchelor, 1996). There are several concerns that arise when assessing the neuropsychological development of children. These concerns include the dynamic, continuous, and rapid development of children that may affect the accurate establishment of baseline performance; poorly documented prenatal and perinatal histories; environmental effects such as poverty; and, the failure of caretakers to provide accurate developmental histories for their children (Batchelor). Furthermore, differences exist in course and outcome of disorders in children and adults, which is an important factor in recognizing the relevance of child neuropsychology as a distinct specialty (Riccio & Wolfe).

The neuropsychological assessment of children and adults can be further refined to address the needs of individuals who are culturally and linguistically diverse (CLD). According to Nell (2000), the assumption that the neuropsychological functioning of individuals can be approached from a universalist perspective, as is physiological functioning, can lead to a number of concerns. The neuropsychological functioning of individuals is not free from the effects of variables such as language, culture, age, and education; however, the specific effect of each is poorly understood especially when children and youth are involved (Ardila, Rosselli, & Puente, 1994; Puente, Mora, & Munoz-Cespedes, 1997). Current standardized neuropsychological instruments typically do not identify the effects of these variables. While difficult, the work of developing and standardizing new neuropsychological instruments for use with CLD populations is essential if individuals representing a variety of cultures and languages are to be effectively assessed (Lamberty, 2002). As most neuropsychological tests designed for adults fail to address the needs of CLD populations, and as much of the research relating to the neuropsychological functioning of CLD individuals has been conducted with adults rather than children, the applicability of results gathered from such testing for CLD children is often questionable (Marlowe, 2000).

It is commonly understood that there is little agreement on the definitions of culture and ethnicity (Organista, Chun, & Marin, 1998). Sue and Sue (1990) noted that culture "consists of all those things that people have learned to do, believe, value, and enjoy in their history. It is the totality of ideals, beliefs, skills, tools, customs, and institutions into which each member of a society is born" (p. 35). The concept of ethnicity "often refers to group-shared patterns of social interaction, values, social customs, behavioral roles, perceptions, and language usage" (Canino & Spurlock, 2000). For the purpose of this chapter, the concept of cultural and linguistic diversity refers to the range of different cultural and linguistic identities that may be applied to children. Ethical guidelines recommend that psychologists assess children with techniques that address their specific cultural and linguistic backgrounds.

Traditional cultural classifications may not provide the specificity that is necessary for an adequate assessment. One should not assume, for example, that grouping all Hispanic or Latino children in the same category is acceptable, as the specific subgroup that the child belongs to (i.e., Mexican or Puerto Rican) may be more useful. It would be beyond the scope of this chapter to discuss neuropsychological functioning in children with respect to their specific cultures and languages. In response to these limitations, this chapter will use the term CLD when referring to any child who is not of the perceived mainstream American culture and/or dominant in the English language. The practices defined in this chapter are therefore generalized to a broad range of cultures and languages, and must be further refined by the practitioner. The terms child and children in this chapter, will refer to individuals at developmental stages from birth to late adolescence.

This chapter will review relevant issues and provide a basic framework of effective techniques that will assist school psychologists confronted with the need to perform a neuropsychological assessment on CLD children and adolescents. After a discussion of relevant terms, this chapter will review several theoretical approaches with respect to current assessments of CLD children. A description of each domain of neuropsychological functioning will be presented and adapted to address the unique challenges posed by the assessment of CLD children. Recommendations for such adaptations and their effective application will be offered for each domain of functioning. Specific examples of best practice and clinical issues, implications for research, and a brief bibliography of relevant literature will be provided.

THEORETICAL AND RESEARCH BASES

The application of neuropsychological theory, techniques, and methods when evaluating children, who may or may not be suffering from a neurological disorder, is a recent development in the field, since clinical neuropsychology and neuropsychological theory progressed as a discipline for the purpose of evaluating the results of adult brain injury (Holmes-Bernstein & Waber, 1990). In current neuropsychological practice, there exists a change of emphasis from the localization of brain lesions to the assessment of change in cognitive functioning, representing a shift of focus from the study of group differences to the study of intraindividual change (Baron, 2004). Similar to the field of adult neuropsychology, there is little agreement in the field of child neuropsychology as to how to perform a neuropsychological assessment on a child, what the best measures or techniques are, or how to interpret particular findings (Holmes-Bernstein & Waber). Nevertheless, there does appear to be agreement that all child neuropsychology evaluations need to take a child's developing nervous system into account. Child neuropsychologists have strongly noted that children's test performance is quantitatively and qualitatively different than that of adults (Fletcher & Taylor, 1984; Hale & Fiorello, 2004). Children and adults will also manifest brain pathology in different ways, leading to distinct behavioral problems (Riccio & Wolfe, 2003). Additionally, a child's brain is considered to be more neurologically plastic than an adult's, resulting in a higher potential for recovery or reorganization of affected areas (Riccio & Wolfe).

Although there is no single agreed upon method to assess a child's neuropsychological functioning, practitioners have historically espoused either a fixed (a set of predetermined tests) or flexible (a set of tests specifically chosen for a particular child) test battery approach to assessment. Theoretical issues, research studies, and practical restraints may underlie an examiner's decision to use either approach (Bornstein, 1990). Because flexible batteries are more time and cost efficient, they have become more popular, whereas the fixed battery approach predominated in the early history of neuropsychological assessment (Hale & Fiorello, 2004). The fixed battery approach recommends the use of a "predetermined set of measures that samples behavior in areas of interest. In this approach, it is intended that that all patients be given the complete set of tests, regardless of the patient's presenting problems, suspected etiology, or reason for referral"(Bornstein, p. 283). The advantages of the fixed battery approach are the ability to amass a great deal of data for research purposes using a wide variety of measures and the potential to compare different diagnostic groups across particular deficit profiles (Bornstein).

The flexible battery approach is less useful for research purposes but is more client-centered and clinical in nature. The examiner uses the information initially revealed by the client to determine the tests to be administered, and the goal in this approach is to determine the reason for and nature of the client's deficits (Bornstein, 1990). The choice in the selection of tests is therefore not predetermined, but rather develops as the examiner learns more about specific issues confronting the client. Current approaches to neuropsychological testing seem to adopt a combination of both the fixed and flexible battery approaches, whereby "tests batteries are designed to respond to specific questions that arise within particular diagnostic populations" (Bornstein, p. 285).

A major principle of neuropsychological theory is that the observation of behavior can assist in making inferences regarding the brain's functioning. Due to neurodevelopmental differences and the functional organization of the brain as children mature, this theory does not accurately portray the young. Neurodevelopment occurs over a predictable course, with only the primary cortical areas being developed by birth and other areas continuing to develop into adolescence (Riccio &Wolfe, 2003). The cortical areas that develop later in childhood and adolescence include those areas of the brain involved in higher order processing, such as learning, memory, attention, cognition, emotion, and language. Despite advances in neuropsychological theory, Riccio and Wolfe state that researchers have only recently begun to understand the complicated nature of the changing organization of brain function in children throughout the lifespan. The nervous system matures according to a predetermined pattern, commencing as a neural tube and gradually gaining characteristics of the adult brain. There are four major phases in the development of the nervous system: neurogenesis or the birth of neurons; neuronal migration to the appropriate location; differentiation and maturation of neurons; and, cell death and synaptic pruning (Kolb & Fantie, 1997). For a detailed description of the development of the child's brain and associated behavior, please refer to the Bibliography of relevant literature for suggested readings.

IMPLICATIONS FOR PRACTICE

According to Reynolds and Fletcher-Janzen (1997), child neuropsychology is no longer confined to the clinical setting, but is present in the schools. In the school setting, "personnel actively assess soft neurological signs (that may or may not affect learning) and they communicate directly with child neurologists and neuropsychologists who evaluate the hard neuropsychological signs" (p. xi). As neuropsychological issues become more prominent in school systems, school psychologists may be called upon to evaluate neuropsychological functioning. School psychologists are commonly exposed to children with various neurological syndromes such as epilepsy and autism, as well as those children recovering from traumatic brain injury, brain tumors, and pediatric stroke.

The neuropsychological assessment and treatment of children represents a distinct challenge requiring specific training that may or may not be included in the repertoire of a traditional school psychologist. According to the American Psychological Association's (APA) Division of Clinical Neuropsychology, a proficient neuropsychologist must demonstrate evidence of successful training in neuropsychology and neuroscience at an accredited university, two or more years of supervised training of the application of neuropsychological services, formal licensing and certification, and peer review of competency (APA, 1989). When appropriately trained, the school psychologist can serve as a case manager, consultant, evaluator, and counselor to children with needs stemming from neurological conditions (Walker, Boling, & Cobb, 1999). A developing focus on neuropsychological issues is reflected in the National Association of School Psychologists' (NASP) standards for training and field placement programs in school psychology (NASP, 2000). According to Walker et al., "the broadening of the role of the school psychologist into the areas of neuropsychology and brain injury seems to be a natural progression of their training" (p. 138).

School psychologists who have received training in providing neuropsychological services to children should be cognizant of the specific factors that impact upon the assessment of CLD children. For example, when reviewing the use of neuropsychological tests for CLD populations, several issues arise. Such issues include the use of too few individuals from diverse cultures in the standardization of instruments (Horton, Carrington, & Lewis-Jack, 2001); specific problems related to translation of tests (Ardila, Rosselli, & Puente, 1994; Cohen & Spenciner, 1998; Sattler, 1988); as well as the paucity of information pertaining to the behavioral and social-emotional assessment of CLD individuals (Merrell, 2003). When conducting neuropsychological assessments of CLD children, concerns are even more pronounced. The combination of the fields of child neuropsychology and multicultural neuropsychology into the interdisciplinary field of neuropsychological assessment of CLD children and adolescents represents an initial effort to establish a clinical and research base for an underserved population. It is a challenge, therefore, to utilize a scientist-practitioner model to ascertain best practice for comprehensive neuropsychological assessments of

CLD children and adolescents that result in valid findings and guide appropriate treatment. However, given that school psychologists are increasingly involved in the neuropsychological assessment of CLD children, it is important that they have guidelines that provide a framework for these assessments. The next section suggests domains of functioning to assess and special considerations for the assessment of CLD children.

IMPLEMENTATION AND APPROACHES

There is a wide range of domains of functioning investigated by neuropsychologists in a general child neuropsychological evaluation. For example, clinical and family history, behavioral observations, attention and concentration, language ability, verbal and nonverbal memory, intelligence, executive functioning, visual-spatial skills, processing speed, emotion, and behavior are among the domains that may be included in a comprehensive neuropsychological assessment. The following sections will discuss components of a comprehensive neuropsychological assessment with an emphasis on the areas that should be highlighted in the assessment of CLD children: level of acculturation, language proficiency, and language development.

Acculturation level.   The effect of acculturation on an individual's performance on cognitive tests has been well documented (Gopaul-McNicol & Armour-Thomas, 2002). However, there remains a "notable absence of a body of established and cohesive research directly relating multicultural concerns to neuropsychological assessment" (Friedman & Clayton, 1996, p. 292). The assessment of neuropsychological functioning is not free of the cultural and racial biases that are commonly found in other psychological assessments (Horton, Carrington, & Lewis-Jack, 2001). Most psychological research defines the concept of acculturation as the learning of culture that occurs due to contacts between members of two or more groups (Berry, 1980). Acculturation is a complicated process that can occur at both the societal and the individual level (Szapocznik, Scopetta, Kurtines, & de los Angeles-Aranalde, 1978). Earlier definitions of acculturation proposed that individuals lost or discarded their native culture and language, however, it has been more recently defined as a fluid process that includes an ongoing interchange involving adaptation and adjustment in the beliefs, values, and behaviors of people who have migrated to a new culture (Guarnaccia & Rodriguez, 1996; Marin, 1992), without the intentional or unintentional loss of beliefs, values, and behaviors of their native country. Of great importance to the understanding of acculturation is that it is conceived as a fluid and unending process (Berry, Trimble, & Olmeda, 1986).

Echemendía and Julian (2002) have described the measurement of the acculturation of children as potentially more complex than the measurement of adult acculturation. When evaluating the acculturation of children, it is important to consider family contexts and sociocultural factors within the home and neighborhood environments. The evaluation of acculturation level for adolescents is further confounded by struggles with ethnic/racial identity and "issues regarding adulthood vs. childhood" (Echemendía & Julian, p. 186).

Berry (1980) has suggested that there are six areas of psychological functioning where acculturation has a direct effect: language, cognitive styles, personality, identity, attitudes, and acculturative stress. Berry argued that, as an individual undergoes the process of acculturation, changes occur in each of these six areas. As many of these areas strongly relate to the process of a neuropsychological assessment, it is essential that a CLD child's acculturation level be assessed prior to the evaluation of functioning in other domains. According to Gopaul-McNicol and Armour-Thomas (2002), this information is typically identified through the administration of a checklist, rating scale or questionnaire. These tools enable an examiner to "seek information about an examinee's value orientations, language dominance and proficiency, prior knowledge, culture-specific attitudes, food practices, level of participation in ethnic organizations, and traditional holiday celebrations" (Gopaul-McNicol & Armour-Thomas, p. 56). It is also important to gather information regarding immigration circumstances, community and school factors affecting acculturation, familiarity with and attitude toward formal testing practices, home language, financial stability, SES in the host country and country of origin, and other factors in a thorough clinical interview (Echemendía & Julian, 2002).

Language proficiency and development.   An essential component of a neuropsychological evaluation of a CLD child is the assessment of language proficiency (Harris, Echemendía, Ardila, & Rosselli, 2001; Puente & Ardila, 2000; Rogers, 1998). Language proficiency impacts upon many facets of the CLD child's functioning, such as learning, socialization, and acculturation. According to Gopaul-McNicol and Armour-Thomas (2002), acculturation level and language proficiency are interdependent, despite their theoretical distinctions. A CLD child is likely to be bilingual or multilingual and alternating intermittently between each language (Centeno & Obler, 2001). A valid neuropsychological assessment, therefore, should consider a child's language proficiency in native and second languages.

Several factors may influence CLD children's linguistic abilities and expertise such as age, cognitive ability, sequence in which languages were acquired, dominant academic language, language context, attitudes toward each language, verbal ability, as well as neuropsychological and organic factors (Puente & Ardila, 2000). For example, Cummins (1984) suggested that younger children more quickly acquire a second language than older children. It has been suggested that monolingual children be assessed in their dominant language and bilingual children be assessed in their first and second languages (Rogers, 1998). It is also important that a thorough history of the development and use of each language be assessed as this may influence the choice of language for the assessment. For example, evaluating a child in her or his native language because the child speaks that language at home may be inappropriate if the child is more proficient and comfortable communicating in her or his second language. Additionally, throughout the process of acculturation, language dominance may shift between native and second languages.

When assessing language proficiency, it is also important to consider the differential development of basic communication second language skills and the ability to use a second language on academic and cognitively demanding tasks (Cummins, 1984). Cummins suggests that the ability to converse at a basic level develops within the first two years of exposure to a language, while the ability to effectively utilize a second language in an academic setting requires five to seven years of exposure. Therefore, the evaluator must keep the differential rate of second language skill development in mind when evaluating and interpreting the child's linguistic skills. Furthermore, as children gain second language fluency, their first language skills may regress (Fradd, Barona, & Santos de Barona, 1989). It is important, therefore, to obtain current language proficiency results prior to conducting the neuropsychological evaluation of a CLD child.

The examiner conducting the neuropsychological evaluation must be familiar with the language development of CLD children so that disorders are not inaccurately diagnosed or overlooked. For example, the mixing of words and phrases between languages is a common behavior exhibited by many CLD children that does not necessarily reflect a neuropsychological deficit (Puente & Ardila, 2000). In addition to formal testing, informal conversation with a CLD child in both languages may provide additional insight into her or his higher reasoning skills, language organization ability, attention, as well as other domains of functioning.

Although a common practice when working with CLD individuals is the use of interpreters and translators to assist in the neuropsychological assessment, this practice is highly discouraged (Ardila, Roselli, & Puente, 1994; Harris et al., 2001; Puente & Ardila, 2000; Rogers, 1998). Interpreters and translators may not be familiar with the purpose, concepts and terminology of psychological tests and may create translations that although are literally correct do not make sense to the examinee (Puente & Ardila). Subtleties of the examinee's behaviors may also be overlooked. Additionally, administering a translated version of a test, standardized and normed in English, may alter the psychometric properties of the test (Puente & Ardila; Rogers). Therefore, it is important that examiners be proficient in the child's dominant language and personally administer all tests in the neuropsychological battery.

When collecting information regarding language functioning, the examiner should be aware that neuropsychological delays in language can be evident in both the native and second language as seen in the "characteristics of acquired aphasia, dysarthria, apraxia, and traumatic brain injury" (Rhodes, Kayser, & Hess, 2000, p. 326). Once acculturation level, language proficiency, and language development have been adequately assessed, the examiner can be more confident in assessing other, more traditional domains of neuropsychological functioning.

Clinical interview and behavioral observations.   Gathering specific information pertaining to the child's background is one of the initial stages of any comprehensive neuropsychological assessment. A detailed summary of historical information improves the examiner's ability to establish rapport, identify cultural variables, conduct valid assessments, provide accurate diagnoses, and design effective interventions (Sattler, 2001). Clinical interview and behavioral observation data provide the examiner with information that is important to the interpretation of the examinee's performance on other measures in the neuropsychological battery (Strub & Black, 1993).

While acquiring the necessary background history, the examiner gathers information from behavior observations, family or caretaker interviews, and a child interview. According to Strub and Black (1993), the clinical history may include a description of present illness, relevant organic behavioral symptoms, and psychiatric symptoms as well as birth, developmental, academic, and family histories. Additionally, a thorough developmental history should provide a review of pregnancy, labor, and delivery; acquisition of developmental milestones in language, motor, behavioral, and emotional domains; illnesses, accidents, drug and alcohol or toxin exposure; and, hospitalizations that may be relevant to present levels of functioning.

Despite the informal nature of the clinical interview, this process is susceptible to the same cultural concerns raised by more formal measures. Families in some cultures may have a greater or lesser degree of involvement with the interview process. Individuals from certain cultures may be more or less hesitant about discussing personal or family problems with non-family members (Sattler, 2001). Newly immigrated families may be preoccupied with pressing issues such as seeking housing and employment. For many CLD groups, extended family members should be involved in the interview process, as they play a significant role in child-rearing (Gopaul-McNicol & Armour-Thomas, 2002). Issues of loyalty and respect for elders may impact upon the CLD child's willingness to discuss negative feelings about parents to a stranger (Gopaul-McNicol & Armour-Thomas). Variations in cultural norms regarding eye contact, facial expressions, body posture, and interpersonal space may also be a source of misinterpretation of nonverbal cues when assessing CLD individuals (Sattler). These nonverbal cues may be more important indicators than spoken words when working with many CLD children and their families (Marlowe, 2000).

The examiner may identify additional data of particular importance to the understanding of presenting concerns. For example, the interview may highlight the political climate of the CLD child's country of origin, factors that influenced family emigration, trauma incurred, family values and customs, and acculturation history (Gopaul-McNicol & Armour-Thomas, 2002). The examiner should also be aware of differences in acculturation levels between parents and children, which may impact the reason for referral and interview. Additionally, determining a family's attitude toward mental health services and providers may facilitate the interview and assessment processes.

Direct observation is another method of data collection that provides an opportunity to examine an individual's behavior as well as the environmental context of the behavior (Merrell, 2003). Observations of a child also allows the examiner to assess gross motor functioning, including gait and balance, and fine motor functioning, including grasping ability and left-right discrimination (Riccio & Wolfe, 2003). The examiner should compare the identified child's behaviors with those of children of similar backgrounds as well as children who are in the majority group (Merrell). Home visits and direct observation are often the most effective manner of gathering information about the functioning of a CLD preschool child and her or his family background (Marlowe, 2000). Home visits, however, may be considered intrusive in some cultures.

Given their significance, examiners must take appropriate steps to maximize the effectiveness of the direct observation and interview processes. Effort on the part of the examiner to communicate warmth as well as to provide information about the duration and scope of the interview may alleviate the anxiety of the individual and family (Nell, 2000). Asking direct questions may be more or less effective than allowing for an open-ended conversation, depending on the cultural background of interview participants (Marlowe). Additionally, learning about the CLD child's culture and language, considering culturally-relevant factors when attempting to establish rapport, avoiding technical jargon, and making an attempt at understanding the cultural perspectives of the child and the family may improve the effectiveness of interviews with CLD children (Sattler, 1998; as cited in Merrell, 2003). Understanding the communication style of the family and the perception of a disability may also facilitate the assessment (Cohen & Spenciner, 1998). The examiner should also make an effort to fully inform the family of the assessment process and the reason for the detailed nature of the interview (Marlowe, 2000). When a family member fully understands the nature of the examination and interview, it is likely that she or he will participate more fully in the process.

Attention, concentration, and orientation.   Assessment of attention, concentration, and orientation are basic components of a neuropsychological evaluation. Problems within these domains are often the impetus for a child coming to the attention of a mental health professional. Issues with attention and concentration are symptoms frequently associated with referral for a neuropsychological evaluation (Riccio & Wolfe, 2003). The construct of attention consists of "several different capacities or processes that are related aspects of how the organism becomes receptive to stimuli and how it may begin processing incoming or attended-to excitation" (Lezak, 1995, p. 39). Attention is a prerequisite skill for higher-level cognitive functions. Concentration, a highly related construct, refers to vigilance or the ability to sustain attention over a period of time (Strub & Black, 1993). Before assessing complex functions such as memory, attention and concentration must be evaluated. Orientation refers to an awareness of self in relation to surroundings (Lezak). Relevant areas to assess may include orientation to person, place, and time.

Referral for a neuropsychological evaluation is often made by the school system. A CLD child unfamiliar with the educational system may not speak the mainstream language and may appear to have a deficit in the areas of attention, concentration, or orientation. The CLD child may also process directions in a second language and can appear to exhibit deficits in attention, concentration and orientation. The deficits may be more accurately defined as a period of acculturation to the new environment as well as lack dominant language skills. Anxiety experienced by the child can impact these domains. A CLD child may also have difficulty with orientation because of a lack of familiarity with her or his adoptive country.

It is important, therefore, to consider carefully culturally-relevant factors when a CLD child presents with deficits in attention, concentration, or orientation. While a number of rating scales exist for the assessment of attention, Barkley (1998) indicates that the best measure of attentional functioning is direct observation. A continuous performance task (CPT) is often used to measure attention (Riccio & Wolfe, 2003). Current CPT's are predominantly administered on a personal computer and may pose an unfair challenge to a CLD child unfamiliar with such devices. Additionally, unforeseen language demands may make it difficult for the CLD child to interpret directions for a CPT. Riccio and Wolfe also note that the most effective assessments of attention, concentration, and orientation involve multi-modal measures including tests presented in visual and auditory domains.

Intelligence. The neuropsychological domain of intelligence and the assessment tools traditionally utilized have been a source of intense social controversy since the early 1900s (Reynolds, 2000). The actual construct of intelligence and the factors of which it is comprised, the predictive utility of intelligence tools, as well as the social implications of intelligence testing such as labeling effects remain discussions ever present in the field. While intelligence will be briefly described in this chapter, a more detailed description of the cognitive assessment of CLD children is provided within this text.

Discussion of the relevance of intellectual assessment with CLD children may engender vehement opposition based on the premise that this population has not been exposed to cultural circumstances similar to those of the white middle class (Reynolds & Kaiser, 2003). According to Nell (2000), formal schooling and familiarity with classroom skills (such as paying attention and following directions) impact significantly upon test performance. Additional issues that have been raised with regard to the assessment of CLD children include the few tests developed for such populations (Cohen & Spenciner, 1998), the possibility that students from CLD backgrounds may have had less exposure to formal testing than other students (Cohen & Spenciner; Nell, 1999, 2000), and the relative important of speed, a component important in many assessment measures, across cultures (Nell, 1999; Sattler, 1988).

Sattler (1988, 2001) proposed arguments that support intelligence testing with children who are ethic minorities. These arguments included the usefulness of current levels of ability, access to special programs and services, program evaluation, and identification of unequal opportunities available to different groups. Furthermore, regarding the issue of test bias, it has been suggested "that the hypothesis of cultural bias on tests is not a particularly strong one at present" (Reynolds & Kaiser, 2003, p. 555).

It is recommended that more than one measure be used to assess the intellectual abilities of CLD children (Ochoa, 2003). Additionally, it is cautioned that assessing the intelligence of CLD children in English may not provide valid results. Alternatives to traditional assessment batteries include nonverbal tests that measure "essentially the same construct" as general intelligence tests with verbal and nonverbal content (Bracken & Naglieri, 2003, p. 247). Examiners using nonverbal measures of intelligence are cautioned to review the standardization procedures to determine the instrument's appropriateness for the CLD child. When interpreting the results of cognitive assessments with CLD children, it is important that the examiner acknowledge the relevant limitations of the test (Ochoa).

Visuoconstructive skills.   Visuoconstructive skills "combine perceptual skill with motor response in the context of a spatial task" (Lacks, 2000, p. 401). The measurement of these skills is an important component of a neuropsychological evaluation, as visuospatial skills involve many brain functions. Measures involved in the assessment of visuoconstructive skills involve timed and untimed tasks that require a child to assemble parts of puzzles, determine the gestalt of figures, and copy designs in a structured or freehand format (Lacks). These skills are most frequently compromised by damage to the brain (Lezak, 1995).

The existence of ethnic differences in visuoconstructive performance has been documented (Mayes, Jahoda, & Neilson, 1988). Rather than being a reflection of neurological deficits, variation in performance may be explained by a difference in subjects' familiarity with these tasks and cultural differences in the interpretation of visual stimuli (Gopaul-McNicol & Armour-Thomas, 2002). In addition, the limited time provided for visual spatial measures is often insufficient for CLD children who may not have an internalized appreciation for working quickly (Gopaul-McNicol & Armour-Thomas; Nell, 2000).

In assessing CLD children's visuoconstructive skills, it is necessary to modify traditional administration procedures, combining a quantitative approach with one that is more qualitative (Gopaul-McNicol & Armour-Thomas, 2002; Nell, 2000). It is important to observe a child's behavior and approach to the visuoconstructive task in order to gain a more comprehensive understanding of CLD children's strategies. Testing limits is especially important when assessing the visuoconstructive functioning of CLD children. Adding time may allow an examiner working with a CLD child to determine whether errors are clinical or cultural in origin (Gopaul-McNicol & Armour-Thomas).

Processing speed.   Processing speed is a measure of how quickly simple perceptual or mental operations can be performed (Hedden et al., 2002). Processing speed is sensitive to brain damage, is related to a variety of cognitive skills, and requires children to maintain focused attention and concentration. Studies have found that CLD individuals perform significantly poorer on measures of processing speed than European Americans (Nabors, Evans, & Strickland, 2000; Puente & Ardila, 2000). However, these differences may not be due to neuropsychological differences but may be influenced by cultural factors. Some CLD children may favor thoughtful deliberation over speed, thus negatively affecting their processing speed performance (Nell, 2000; Puente & Ardila, 2000). Lack of experience with performing tasks accurately under a time constraint may also affect the performance of a CLD child.

When assessing the processing speed of a CLD child, it is important to give children a thorough explanation of what is expected of them for processing speed tasks. The examiner should clarify that the child must work as quickly and accurately as possible. Practice with processing speed tasks may also benefit CLD children if they will be evaluated with traditional measures.

Memory. Memory refers to the encoding, storage, and retrieval of information (Parkin, 2001). Much research in the area of memory focuses on declarative memory, or the learning and recalling of information, objects, and events (Lezak, 1995). Procedural memory refers to the memory of actions such as walking, talking, dressing, and eating (Lezak, 1995). There are several distinct types of memory that have been investigated including short-term memory, working memory, and long-term storage and retrieval skills. Short-term memory involves the apprehension and immediate use of information (Woodcock, 1993). Working memory refers to the process "involved in the temporary maintenance and manipulation of information" (Baddeley, 2002, p. 85). Long-term storage and retrieval consists of the ability to store information in long-term memory and then to retrieve it later through associations (McGrew & Flanagan, 1998; Woodcock, 1993). Distinctions also exist between verbal memory and nonverbal memory. Learning represents a complex array of memory-related tasks. As children experience events in academic and social environments, they rely on all aspects of memory functioning. Neurological disorders may affect a child's ability to encode, store, and retrieve information needed for learning (Riccio & Wolfe, 2003).

There are specific issues that the examiner needs to consider when assessing a CLD child's memory functioning and these issues may differ as a function of the specific culture. For example, in the United States, individuals are accustomed to repeating a seven-digit sequence when using the telephone whereas Spanish-speakers tend to cluster numbers by two and three numbers (Ardila et al., 2000). Additional consideration needs to be given to familiarity with the content of specific instruments. For example, list learning tasks often used to assess memory function tend to include culture-specific words. Factors such as lack of familiarity with the testing situation may also impact upon memory functioning in that reduced comfort can be expected to heighten anxiety and potentially decrease the child's performance.

Research on CLD individuals and working memory suggests that when assessment tasks involve digits (e.g., traditional digit span tests), even with Arabic numbers, which are familiar to many cultures other than mainstream American culture, cultural differences emerge (Trey et al., 2002). Cultural differences on these digit tasks have been suggested to be related to linguistic differences between spoken languages (e.g., length of time it takes to articulate the numeral). Visual spatial measures of working memory have been found to not be as significantly influenced by culture (Trey et al.). Luer et al. (1998) further caution that nonverbal or visual memory span tasks are culturally fair only if the stimuli are difficult or impossible to verbalize or memorize verbally. This again corresponds to the concept that linguistic differences impact time to encode information, which in turn impacts memory span.

Memory is a complex process comprised of numerous subskills that can be assessed by a wide array of tasks. Tests of memory include digit repetition, visual design reproductions, and list learning tasks. Lezak (1995) recommends that an assessment of memory include tasks that measure immediate retention span; short-term retention with interference; learning capacity and retention of newly learned material; and, efficiency of retrieval of recently learned and long-stored information. When assessing children in academic settings, it is more useful that an assessment of memory "includes tasks more similar to everyday tasks and list learning, so that a learning slope can be determined" (Riccio & Wolfe, 2003, p. 311).

Examiners assessing the memory functions of a CLD child must remain aware of the impact of culture and language and take necessary precautions to maximize the utility of their assessments, such as use multiple measures to assess the multiple memory subskills and consider potential limitations when interpreting the results.

Executive functioning.   The measurement of executive functioning typically involves a review of higher-order processes, including organization, planning, and problem solving skills (Riccio & Wolfe, 2003). With regard to the assessment of children, Riccio and Wolfe warn that most measures intended for the assessment of children's executive functioning are downward extensions of their adult counterparts. As executive functioning is rooted in areas of the brain that continue to develop throughout adolescence, it is difficult to assess. Riccio and Wolfe suggest that the measurement of executive functioning in children be completed with tasks that "have sufficient items across the continuum of difficulty level in order to measure the developmental trajectory" (p. 311).

Beyond second-language concerns, a child who is unfamiliar with her or his adoptive country's culture may misinterpret a number of tasks that are indicative of higher-level functioning. The CLD child may exhibit culturally-related deficits when expected to demonstrate abstract reasoning skills and interpret proverbs, humor, or other, subtle communication devices. The CLD child may also present organization strategies that differ from what may be expected from native children. As executive functioning represents a developing area of neurological functioning, the CLD child is more likely to exhibit delays unrelated to her or his true functioning in this domain than for neurological functions associated with more stable brain structures.

As the measurement of executive functioning for all children appears to present a number of concerns, the use of the same measures with CLD children is further cautioned. Sbordone (2000) notes that informal assessments of executive functioning can be completed during the interview process by using specific open-ended questions that may reveal deficits in planning, organization, and problem solving. For example, an examiner may ask, "How would you go about putting on a birthday party for a close friend?" to highlight potential concerns with the analysis of the question, the organization of a response, and the evaluation of the outcome (Sbordone, p. 439). In general, an examiner who shares the same background and language with the CLD child is strongly suggested when assessing executive functioning. A more functional evaluation of the CLD child's higher order reasoning abilities is also suggested. This can be accomplished through an informal and more qualitative assessment of how the CLD child problem-solves and uses her or his planning skills in real, day-to-day situations, rather than of structured tests.

Social-emotional functioning and assessment of behavior and personality.
Behavioral or social-emotional problems in children may result from a myriad of factors. In neuropsychological referrals, these problems may result from hormonal, neurological, or other physiological disturbances, environmental issues, or an interaction between the physical and environmental factors. Additionally, it is not uncommon for neurological conditions to co-exist with behavioral and social-emotional issues. A comprehensive assessment of behavioral functioning includes the integration of multiple assessment methods gathered from multiple sources and across multiple settings (Merrell, 2003; Reid, 1995). Methods can include direct observation, behavior rating scales, and interviews; sources can include the child, family, teachers, and peer group; and, settings can include the home, school, and community (Merrell).

Behavior rating scales are the most common approach to assessing social-emotional and behavioral functioning (Riccio & Wolfe, 2003). These scales can be used to gather information from parents, teachers, and children. According to Reid (1995), the validity of behavior rating scales with CLD children is questionable if the domains assessed are interpreted differently across cultures. Concerns with the use of behavior rating scales with CLD children include the potential for meaning or content changes in translation, the acceptability of behavior in different cultures, and the variability in the interpretation of Likert scales by individuals of different cultural backgrounds. Comparisons of rating scale results for CLD children to the norm group may be misleading due to differences in the interpretation of scale items and behaviors by CLD raters (Reid).

Examiners should carefully assess the manuals of behavior rating scales before deciding to use them with children of diverse backgrounds, as scales may not be normed for use with CLD children or children with neuropsychological conditions (Merrell, 2003). Behavior rating scales, if deemed appropriate, should not replace direct interviews of family members and teachers where relevant.

Within the realm of behavioral and social-emotional difficulties, issues confronted by CLD children require special consideration for their potential role in the reason for referral. According to Sattler (2001), CLD children may be confronted with racism, poverty, concerns related to acculturation (e.g., leaving friends in their country of origin, difficulty with the English language), and other issues. Immigrant families may have had to flee from their country of origin, and the CLD child's reaction to these stressors may lead an examiner to consider an adjustment disorder when appropriate (Gopaul-McNicol & Armour-Thomas, 2002). When evaluating and diagnosing CLD children with problems within the affective or behavioral domain, the examiner must proceed with extreme caution so as to accurately and fairly determine the presence and nature of cultural influences.

IMPLICATIONS FOR FUTURE RESEARCH AND PRACTICE

Specific recommendations have been provided in each domain of functioning to guide the examiner working in a school setting so that she or he will be able to provide a thorough, psychometrically accurate, and ethically sound neuropsychological assessment of a CLD child. Each neuropsychological domain presents with its own particular challenges, but a few general points apply to the assessment process as a whole. The examiner conducting a neuropsychological evaluation of a CLD child is encouraged to be flexible in her or his approach to testing and engage in multimethod, multisource assessments across multiple settings. It is important to examine all neuropsychological assessment manuals to determine whether there is any information regarding the instrument's use with CLD children and to adhere to the exclusionary criteria (Ochoa, Powell, & Robles-Pina, 1996). The development of proper norming methods for CLD children is essential. To obtain valid results, examiners should become familiar with the culture of the CLD child and make an effort to build rapport with the child and her or his family. As with any client, the examiner needs to consult with other professionals, especially when the issue of language is involved. The failure to address CLD children's specific linguistic and cultural backgrounds may result in the underutilization of services, the inaccurate diagnosis of neurological conditions, and the application of inappropriate interventions (Fisher, 2003). Despite advances in the neuropsychological assessment of CLD children, most neuropsychological tests still omit specific data on ethnic minorities and fail to account for the effects of cultural and educational variables (Baron, 2004). The examiner completing a neuropsychological assessment with a CLD child cannot simply note ethnic or cultural differences. She or he "must define, measure, and adjust for racial/cultural group rather than merely assigning an individual to a race/ethnicity group and making a judgment without consideration of other relevant and more pertinent factors" (Baron, p. 23).

Multiple challenges exist in the neuropsychological evaluation of the CLD child. Much of the information that is garnered from the neuropsychological assessment of children is based on medically-oriented models. More research in the area of educationally relevant intervention planning based on neuropsychological information is needed (Riccio & Wolfe, 2003). It is clear that the application of neuropsychological principles in a school setting necessitates not only a great deal of specific training and clinical expertise, but also an awareness of developmental issues (Hale & Fiorello, 2004). When performing a neuropsychological evaluation on a CLD child, cultural and linguistic variables are as critical as developmental issues, especially when the assessment method will be guiding subsequent recommendations and interventions. As Marlowe (2000) notes, "the opportunity to study the interaction of culture and behavior is greater and more critical than ever" (p. 158). The examiner working with the CLD child should strive to engage in best practices when working with this multidimensional, underserved population.

BIBLIOGRAPHY

Fletcher-Janzen, E., Strickland, T. L., & Reynolds, C. R. (Eds.). (2000). *Handbook of cross-cultural neuropsychology.* New York: Kluwer Academic/Plenum.

Hale, J. B., & Fiorello, C. A. (2004). *School neuropsychology: A practitioner's handbook.* New York: Guilford Press.

Hebben, N., & Milberg, W. (2002). *Essentials of neuropsychological assessment.* New York: John Wiley & Sons.

Kolb, B., & Whishaw, I. Q. (2003). *Fundamentals of human neuropsychology* (5th ed.). New York: Worth Publishers.

Nell, V. (2000). *Cross-cultural neuropsychological assessment theory and practice.* Mahwah, NJ: Erlbaum.

Reynolds, C. R., & Fletcher-Janzen, E. (1997). *Handbook of clinical child neuropsychology* (2nd ed.). New York: Plenum Press.

Reynolds, C. R., & Kamphaus, R. W. (Eds.). (2003). *Handbook of psychological & educational assessment of children. Intelligence, aptitude, and achievement* (2nd ed.). New York: Guildford Press.

Yeates, K. O., Ris, M. D., & Taylor, H. G. (2000). *Pediatric neuropsychology: Research, theory, and practice.* New York: Guildford Press.

RESOURCES

American Academy of Clinical Neuropsychology:
    http://www.theacn.org
American Board of Clinical Neuropsychology:
    http://www.theabcn.org
American Board of Professional Neuropsychology:
    http://www.abpn.net
Division 40 of the American Psychological Association:
    http://www.div40.org/
National Association of School Psychologists:
    http://www.nasponline.org

REFERENCES

American Psychological Association. (1989). Definition of a clinical neuropsychologist. *The Clinical Neuropsychologist, 3,* 22.

Ardila, A., Rosselli, M., Ostrosky-Solis, F., Marcos, J., Granda, G., & Soto, M. (2002). Synatictic comprehension, verbal memory, and calculation abilities in Spanish English bilinguals. *Applied neuropsychology, 7,* 3–16.

Ardila, A., Rosselli, M., & Puente, A. E. (1994). Introduction: Neuropsychological assessment in different cultural contexts. In A. Ardila, M. Rosselli, & A. E. Puente (Eds.), *Neuropsychological evaluation of the Spanish speaker* (pp. 1–6). New York: Plenum Press.

Baddeley, A. D. (2002). Is working memory still working? *European Psychologist, 7,* 85–97.

Barkley, R. A. (1998). *Attention-deficit hyperactivity disorder: A handbook for diagnosis and treatment* (2nd ed.). New York: Guilford Press.

Baron, I. S. (2004). *Neuropsychological Evaluation of the Child.* New York: Oxford.

Batchelor, E. S., Jr. (1996). Neuropsychological assessment of children. In. E. S. Batchelor, Jr. & R. S. Dean (Eds.), *Pediatric neuropsychology: Interfacing assessment and treatment for rehabilitation* (pp. 9–26). Boston: Allyn & Bacon.

Berry, J. W. (1980). Acculturation as varieties of adaptation. In A. M. Padilla (Ed.), *Acculturation: Theory, models, and some new findings* (pp. 9–25). Boulder, CO: Westview.

Berry, J. W., Trimble, J. E., & Olmeda, E. L. (1986). Assessment of acculturation. In W. J. Lonner & J. W. Berry (Eds.), *Field methods in cross-cultural research* (pp. 291–324). Beverly Hills, CA: Sage.

Bornstein, R. A. (1990). Neuropsychological test batteries in neuropsychological assessment. In A. A. Boulton, G. B. Baker, & M. Hiscock (Eds.), *Neuromethods: Neuropsychology* (pp. 281-310). Clifton, New Jersey: Humana Press.

Bracken, B. A., & Naglieri, J. A. (2003). Assessing diverse populations with nonverbal tests of general intelligence. In C. R. Reynolds & R. W. Kamphaus (Eds.), *Handbook of psychological and educational assessment of children: Intelligence aptitude, and achievement* (2nd ed., pp. 243–274). New York: Guilford Press.

Canino, I. A., & Spurlock, J. (2000) . *Culturally diverse children and adolescents: Assessment, diagnosis, and treatment* (2nd ed.). New York: Guilford Press.

Centeno, J. G., & Obler, L. K. (2001). Principles of bilingualism. In M. O. Ponton & J. Leon-Carrion (Eds.), *Neuropsychology and the Hispanic patient: A clinical handbook* (pp. 75–86). Mahwah, NJ: Erlbaum.

Cohen, L. C., & Spenciner, L. J. (1998). *Assessment of children and youth.* New York: Longman.

Cummins, J. (1984). *Bilingualism and special education: Issues in assessment and pedagogy.* San Diego, CA: College-Hill.

Echemendía, R. J., & Julian, L. (2002). Neuropsychological assessment of Latino children. In F. R. Ferraro (Ed.), *Minority and cross-cultural aspects of neuropsychological assessment* (pp. 181–203). Exton, PA: Swets & Zeitlinger.

Fisher, C. B. (2003). *Decoding the ethics code: A practical guide for psychologists.* Thousand Oaks, CA: Sage.

Fletcher, J. M., & Taylor, H. G. (1984). Neurological assessment of children: A developmental approach. *Texas Psychologist, 36,* 14–20.

Fradd, S. H., Barona, A., & Santos De Barona, M. (1989). Implementing change and monitoring progress. In S. H. Fradd & M. J. Weismantel (Eds.), *Meeting the needs of culturally and linguistically different students: A handbook for educators* (pp. 63–105). Boston: College Hill.

Friedman, C. A., & Clayton, R. J. (1996). Multiculturalism and neuropsychological assessment. In L. A. Suzuki, P. J. Meller, & J. G. Ponterotto (Eds.), *Handbook of multicultural assessment: Clinical, psychological, and educational applications* (pp. 291–318). San Francisco: Jossey-Bass.

Gopaul-McNicol, S., & Armour-Thomas, E. (2002). *Assessment and culture: Psychological tests with minority populations.* San Diego, CA: Academic Press.

Groth-Marnat, G. (2000). *Neuropsychological assessment in clinical practice: A guide to test interpretation and integration.* New York: John Wiley & Sons.

Guarnaccia, P. J., & Rodriguez, O. (1996). Concepts of culture and their role in the development of culturally competent mental health services. *Hispanic Journal of Behavioral Sciences, 18,* 419–443.

Hale, J. B., & Fiorello, C. A. (2004). *School neuropsychology: A practitioner's handbook.* New York: Guilford Press.

Harris, J. G., Echemendía, R., Ardila, A., & Rosselli, M. (2001). Cross-cultural cognitive and neuropsychological assessment. In J. J. W. Andrews, D. H. Saklofske, & H. L. Janzen (Eds.), *Handbook of psychoeducational assessment: Ability, achievement, and behavior in children* (pp. 391–414). San Diego, CA: Academic Press.

Hedden, T., Park, D. C., Nisbett, R., Ji, L., Jing, Q., & Jiao, S. (2002). Cultural variation in verbal versus spatial neuropsychological function across the lifespan. *Neuropsychology, 16*, 65–73.

Holmes-Bernstein, J., & Waber, D. P. (1990). Developmental neuropsychological assessment: The systemic approach. In A. A. Boulton, G. B. Baker, & M. Hiscock (Eds.), *Neuromethods: Neuropsychology* (pp. 311–371). Clifton, New Jersey: Humana Press.

Horton, A. M., Jr., Carrington, C. H., & Lewis-Jack, O. (2001). Neuropsychological assessment in a multicultural context. In. L. A. Suzuki, J. J. Ponterotto, & P. J. Meller (Eds.), *Handbook of multicultural assessment: Clinical, psychological, and educational applications* (2nd ed., pp.433–460). San Francisco: Jossey Bass.

Kolb, B., & Fantie, B. (Eds.). (1997). Development of the child's brain and behavior. In C. R. Reynolds & E. Fletcher-Janzen, *Handbook of clinical child neuropsychology* (2nd ed.). New York: Plenum Press.

Kolb, B., & Whishaw, I. Q. (2003). *Fundamentals of human neuropsychology* (5th ed.). New York: Worth Publishers.

Lacks, P. (2000). Visuoconstructive abilities. In G. Groth-Marnat (Ed.), *Neuropsychological assessment in clinical practice: A guide to test interpretation and integration* (pp. 401–436). New York: Wiley.

Lamberty, G. J. (2002). Traditions and trends in neuropsychological assessment. In F. R. Ferraro (Ed.), *Minority and cross-cultural aspects of neuropsychological assessment* (pp. 3–15). Exton, PA: Swets & Zeitlinger.

Lezak, M. D. (1995). *Neuropsychological assessment.* (3rd ed). New York: Oxford University Press.

Luer, G., Becker, D., Lass, U., Fang, Y., Guopeng, C., & Zhongming, W. (1998). Memory span in German and Chinese: Evidence for the phonological loop. *European Psychologist, 3*, 102–112.

Marin, G. (1992). Issues in the measurement of acculturation among Hispanics. In K. F. Geisinger (Ed.), *Psychological testing of Hispanics* (pp. 235–251). Washington, DC: American Psychological Association.

Marlowe, W. B., (2000). Multicultural perspectives on the neuropsychological assessment of children and adolescents. In E. Fletcher-Janzen, T. L. Strickland, & C. R. Reynolds (Eds.), *Handbook of cross-cultural neuropsychology* (pp. 145–165). New York: Kluwer Academic/Plenum.

Mayes, J. T., Jahoda, G., & Neilson, I. (1988). Patterns of visual-spatial performance and 'spatial ability': Dissociation of ethnic and sex differences. *British Journal of Psychology, 79*, 105–119.

McGrew, K. S., & Flanagan, D. P. (1998). *The intelligence test desk reference (ITDR): Gf-Gc cross-battery assessment.* Needham Heights, MA: Allyn & Bacon.

Merrell, K. W. (2003). *Behavioral, social, and emotional assessment of children and adolescents* (2nd ed.). Mahwah, NJ: Erlbaum.

Nabors, N. A., Evans, J. D., & Strickland, T. L. (2000). Neuropsychological assessment and intervention with African Americans. In E. Fletcher-Janzen, T.L. Strickland, & C. R.

Reynolds (Eds.), *Handbook of cross-cultural neuropsychology* (pp. 31–42). New York: Kluwer Academic/Plenum.

National Association of School Psychologists. (2000). *Standards for training and field placement programs in school psychology.* Retrieved from http://www.nasponline.org

Nell, V. (1999). Standardising the WAIS-III and the WMS-III for South Africa: Legislative, psychometric, and policy issues. *South African Journal of Psychology, 29,* 128–139.

Nell, V. (2000). *Cross-cultural neuropsychological assessment theory and practice.* Mahwah, NJ: Erlbaum.

Ochoa, S. H. (2003). Assessment of culturally and linguistically diverse children. In C. R. Reynolds & R. W. Kamphaus (Eds.), *Handbook of Psychological and educational assessment of children: Intelligence aptitude, and achievement* (2nd ed.). New York: Guilford.

Ochoa, S. H., Powel, M. P., & Robles-Pina, R. (1996). School psychologists' assessment practices with bilingual and limited-English-proficient students. *The Journal of Psychoeducational Assessment, 14,* 250–275.

Organista, P. B., Chun, K. M., & Marin, G. (1998). *Readings in ethnic psychology.* New York: Routledge.

Parkin, A. J. (2001). The structure and mechanisms of memory. In B. Rapp (Ed.), *The handbook of cognitive neuropsychology: What deficits reveal about the human mind.* Philadelphia: Psychology Press.

Puente, A. E., & Ardila, A. (2000). Neuropsychological assessment of Hispanics. In E. Fletcher-Janzen, T. L. Strickland, & C. R. Reynolds (Eds.), *Handbook of cross cultural neuropsychology.* New York: Kluwer Academic/Plenum.

Puente, A. E., Mora, M. S., & Munoz-Cespedes, J. M. (1997). Neuropsychological assessment of Spanish-speaking children and youth. In C. R. Reynolds & E. Fletcher-Janzen (Eds.), *Handbook of clinical child neuropsychology* (2nd ed.). New York: Plenum Press.

Reid, R. (1995). Assessment of ADHD with culturally different groups: The use of behavioral rating scales. *School Psychology Review, 24,* 537–560.

Reynolds, C. R. (2000). Methods for detecting and evaluating cultural bias in neuropsychological tests. In E. Fletcher-Janzen, T. L. Strickland, & C. R. Reynolds (Eds.), *Handbook of cross-cultural neuropsychology* (pp. 249–285). New York: Kluwer Academic/Plenum.

Reynolds, C. R., & Fletcher-Janzen, E. (1997). *Handbook of clinical child Neuropsychology* (2nd ed.). New York: Plenum Press.

Reynolds, C. R., & Kaiser, S. M. (2003). Bias in assessment of aptitude. In C. R. Reynolds & R. W. Kamphaus (Eds.), *Handbook of psychological and educational assessment of children: Intelligence aptitude, and achievement* (2nd ed., pp. 519–562). New York: Guilford Press.

Rhodes, R. L., Kayser, H., & Hess, R. S. (2000). Neuropsychological differential diagnosis of Spanish-speaking preschool children. In E. Fletcher-Janzen, T. L. Strickland, & C. R. Reynolds (Eds.), *Handbook of cross-cultural neuropsychology* (pp. 317–333). New York: Kluwer Academic/Plenum.

Riccio, C. A., & Wolfe, M. E. (2003). Neuropsychological perspectives on the assessment of children. In C. R. Reynolds & R. W. Kamphaus (Eds.), *Handbook of psychological and educational assessment of children: Intelligence aptitude, and achievement* (2nd ed., pp. 305–324). New York: Guilford Press.

Rogers, M. R. (1998). Psychoeducational assessment of culturally and linguistically diverse children and youth. In H. B. Vance (Ed.), *Psychological assessment of children: Best practices for school and clinical settings* (2nd ed., pp. 355–384) New York: John Wiley & Sons.

Sattler, J. M. (2001). *Assessment of children: Cognitive applications* (4th ed.). San Diego, CA: Author.

Sattler, J. M. (1988). *Assessment of children* (3rd ed.). San Diego, CA: Author.

Sbordone, R. J. (2000). The executive functions of the brain. In G. Groth-Marnat (Ed.), *Neuropsychological assessment in clinical practice: A guide to test interpretation and integration* (pp. 437–456). New York: Wiley.

Spreen, O., & Strauss, E. (1998). *A compendium of neuropsychogical tests: Administration, norms, and commentary* (2nd ed.). New York: Oxford University Press.

Strub, R. L., & Black, F. W. (1993). *The mental status examination in neurology* (3rd ed.). Philadelphia: F. A. Davis.

Sue, D. W., & Sue, D. (1990). *Counseling the culturally different.* New York: Wiley.

Szapocznik, J., Scopetta, M. A., Kurtines, W., & de los Angeles-Aranalde, M. (1978). Theory and measurement of acculturation. *Interamerican Journal of Psychology, 12,* 113–130.

Trey, H., Park, D. C., Nisbett, R., Ji, L., Jing, Q., & Jiao, S. (2002). Cultural variation in verbal versus spatial neuropsychological function across the life span. *Neuropsychology, 16,* 65–73.

Walker, N. W., Boling, M. S., & Cobb, H. (1999). The pediatric neuropsychologist: Training of school psychologists in neuropsychology and brain injury: Results of a national survey of training programs. *Child Neuropsychology, 5,* 137–142.

Woodcock, R. W. (1993). An information processing view of Gf-Gc theory. In B. A. Bracken & S. R. McCallum (Eds.), *Woodcock-Johnson Psycho-Educational Battery-Revised. Journal of Psychoeducational Assessment Monograph Series: Advances in psychoeducational assessment* (pp. 80–102). Brandon, VT: Clinical Psychology Publishing.

16

MULTICULTURAL VOCATIONAL ASSESSMENT IN SCHOOLS: UNEXPLORED BARRIERS AND UNTAPPED RESOURCES

Margo A. Jackson, Jaclyn Mendelsohn Kacanski,
and Mariana Rotenberg
Fordham University

Vocational or career development is a specific aspect of general human development (Tolbert, 1980) and has been defined as a lifelong learning process by which individuals form and integrate their work values and identities (Peterson & Gonzalez, 2000). Beginning in elementary school, "self-awareness provides the foundation for processing career information" (Niles & Harris-Bowlsbey, 2002, p. 257). Throughout their school years, youths engage in the processes of developing self-awareness, learning how to set and evaluate goals, and making educational decisions with significant relevance for their future work and life roles (National Occupational Information Coordinating Committee [NOICC], 1992). The degree to which individuals learn to effectively negotiate vocational development processes has been linked to educational and occupational achievement outcomes (Arbona, 2000; Lapan, Gysbers, & Petroski, 2001; Whiston, Sexton, & Lasoff, 1998). Facilitating these processes through career counseling and psychoeducational interventions can benefit all students and, in particular, culturally and linguistically diverse (CLD) youths who may be at risk for low academic achievement.

School counselors and psychologists need accurate and useful assessment information on which to base their intervention recommendations and plans in order to help students develop academic and vocational competencies. Culturally appropriate assessment is the basis for ethical and effective interventions (Fouad, 1993; Gainor, 2001; Padilla, 2001; Ridley, Hill, & Wiese, 2001). There is ample evidence that CLD youths—particularly those in low-income, urban schools—do not have equal access to education and career opportunities (Education Trust, 2000; Kozol, 1991; National Center for Education Statistics [NCES], 2001a; U.S. Equal Employment Opportunity Commission [EEOC], 2000). Because of the pervasive and controversial nature of the issue of systemic inequality (McIntosh, 1998), counseling professionals may have difficulty recognizing and constructively addressing the possible influences of discrimination (Ridley, 1995) when gathering vocational assessment information with CLD youths (Jackson & Nutini, 2002). Thus, well-meaning and otherwise culturally aware counselors may unintentionally conduct incomplete or inaccurate vocational assessments with CLD youths, resulting in potentially unhelpful intervention recommendations (Jackson & Nutini, 2002).

This chapter will provide a discussion of unexplored barriers and untapped resources for middle and high school counselors and psychologists for using culturally relevant vocational assessment to facilitate academic achievement motivation with CLD adolescents. Although, as noted above, vocational development at the elementary school level is foundational, space limits our focus here to middle and high school levels. Also, the general term of "counselors" will be used to refer to both school counselors and school psychologists, except when discussing their roles separately. Social workers and other helping professionals and educators working in schools may find this information useful, as well, in their roles. Moreover, a rationale will be given for this topic, grounded in theoretical perspectives in social learning career and multicultural counseling and therapy. Examples will be offered of practical applications from the authors' experience and related research with CLD youths in public schools in low-income, urban, culturally diverse communities (predominantly African American, Afro-Caribbean, and Puerto Rican). This is the population with whom the third author has served as a school psychologist and the first 2 authors (in counseling psychology) have served as counselors, counselor educators, and consultants to school counselors. Finally, the chapter will conclude with a discussion of implications for future research and practice then suggest relevant useful resources.

THEORETICAL AND RESEARCH BASE

Several authors (e.g., Gonzalez, Brusca-Vega, & Yawkey, 1997; Gopaul-McNicol & Thomas-Presswood, 1998) have noted that the U.S. public school system has historically focused on serving so-called mainstream students (especially males) who are monolingual, English-speaking, heterosexual Caucasians; with no apparent physical or cognitive impairments to learning; and offspring of U.S.-born middle-class parents. A growing proportion of the school-age population that has been poorly served includes students of color, those who speak a language other than English, students with learning difficulties, and those from low-income homes. Despite the U.S. creed espousing equal rights, equal opportunity, and liberty and justice for all, our public education system has excluded CLD students from resources for academic achievement.

> The segregation of students of color by states and school districts, the denial of educational services to students with disabilities, the tracking of certain ethnic and cultural

groups into non-college-bound curricula [and girls into non-science and non-math options], the lack of services to students learning English as a second language, inequitable state funding patterns for education, and curriculum written without regard to cultural diversity are all ways in which students outside the mainstream have been poorly served by American schools. (Gonzalez et al., 1997, p. 4).

In particular, youths in low-income, urban public schools with large concentrations of African Americans and Latino/as are at risk for low educational attainment, limited future career options, and severely reduced earnings potential (Education Trust, 2000; Kozol, 1991; NCES, 1999, 2001a, 2001b; U.S. EEOC, 2000). Educational and career achievement gaps that disadvantage girls and women also persist (Hansen, 2003; Sadker, 2002; Sanders, 2002; Yoder, 2000).

Systemically, therefore, CLD students are at risk for low academic achievement and, consequently, limited access to a range of career choices (Arbona, 1996; Betz, 1994). Elementary and middle school children may foreclose on considering career aspirations with high prestige based on expectations of limits by gender, social class, and race/ethnicity (Gottfredson, 1981, 1996; Tracey & Ward, 1998). High school students from various ethnic and socioeconomic groups understand that a good education leads to good jobs (Steinberg, Dornbusch, & Brown, 1992). However, faced with limited access to educational attainment and occupational choice, many low-income African American and Hispanic students develop compensatory beliefs about the value of academic effort and performance; they believe that academic effort and achievement will *not* pay off *for them* (Graham, Taylor, & Hudley, 1998; Mickelson, 1990; Steinberg et al., 1992). They develop alternative beliefs about getting ahead. For example, Ogbu (1992), Fordham and Ogbu (1986), and Steele (1997) found evidence that African American students maintain their self-esteem in the face of persistent educational and economic systemic barriers by *disidentifying* with academic achievement. Other researchers (e.g., Major, Spencer, Schmader, Wolfe, & Crocker, 1998) have found evidence that one strategy African American students use to cope with negative stereotypes about their intellectual performance is to *psychologically disengage* their self-esteem from their performance in school.

Therefore, compensatory beliefs about the value of academic effort and performance—although likely a self-esteem protective coping strategy in the face of racial, ethnic, gender, and class discrimination and objective disadvantage in U.S. school and work settings—may further constrain (beyond the systemic barriers that do exist) the education and career achievement of students from low-income, ethnic minority, and immigrant groups. We propose that school counselors and psychologists who understand this dilemma could incorporate culturally and developmentally appropriate vocational assessment and interventions in their work with CLD youths, not only as a means to advocate for needed sources of support for their learning needs but also as a means to challenge their unhelpful beliefs and learn more constructive strategies to develop academic and vocational competencies. For example, multiculturally competent school counselors could use cultural and career assessment information as a foundation for helping CLD youths learn about their career interests and educational requirements in relation to their individual, family, and cultural values. Then, based on this information, counselors could help CLD youths learn strategies to develop and achieve career and education goals that include negotiating barriers (both environmental and psychological) and accessing vital resources and support.

As an extension of his social learning theory of career decision making (Krumboltz, 1979; Mitchell & Krumboltz, 1990), Krumboltz proposed a learning theory of career choice and counseling (LTCC; Krumboltz, 1996; Mitchell & Krumboltz, 1996) that described the goal of career counseling as learning and the role of career counselors as facilitating learning. Krumboltz and Jackson (1993) viewed vocational assessment as a learning tool, not only to summarize individuals' past learning experiences and match these with congruent education or occupational environments, but also as a basis for helping individuals explore or create new learning opportunities that could be relevant to potential career goals. From an LTCC perspective, environmental contexts (e.g., school contexts) as well as the expectations and beliefs that individuals learn in these contexts can either facilitate or impede their progress in developing career and learning potentials. Krumboltz and colleagues (Krumboltz, 1991; Krumboltz & Jackson, 1993; Levin, Krumboltz, & Krumboltz, 1995) have developed career assessment tools and methods to use in the process of career counseling to affirm individuals' facilitative beliefs and challenge their unhelpful beliefs. As an extension of the LTCC for adolescents vulnerable to discrimination, Jackson and Nutini (2002) proposed a career assessment framework for considering potentially unrecognized resources and barriers (both contextual and psychological) for helping these youths expand their learning opportunities, aspirations, and achievement in academic and career development.

Foundational to this career assessment framework are the underlying assumptions and propositions presented by Sue, Ivey, and Pedersen (1996) in their theory of multicultural counseling and therapy (MCT theory, a full discussion of which is beyond the scope of this chapter; we recommend this source to readers). In particular, training and practice implications of MCT theory for school counselors striving to effectively use career assessment information to design culturally appropriate interventions for CLD youths include the following goals for school counselor attitudes/beliefs, knowledge, and skills (Sue et al., 1998). In career assessment and counseling in schools, multiculturally competent counselors should work to: (a) become more culturally aware of their own values, biases, stereotypes, and assumptions about how CLD youths' behavior and beliefs facilitate or impede their academic achievement and career development; (b) acquire knowledge and understanding of the worldview and learning experiences of CLD youths; and (c) develop skills to critically evaluate and appropriately adapt assessment tools to inform ethical and culturally appropriate intervention strategies.

IMPLICATIONS FOR PRACTICE

Counselors and psychologists in middle and high schools could use developmentally and culturally appropriate vocational assessment instruments and methods to expand CLD students' self-awareness and learning about potential career and educational interests, abilities, and values as well as develop constructive beliefs and success strategies. Several barriers as well as resources exist for counselors to implement effective multicultural vocational assessment toward these goals, particularly in low-income, culturally diverse, urban middle and high schools. Some of these barriers and resources are more easily recognized and others are more hidden or unexplored.

Whose Role Is it to Facilitate CLD Students' Career/Educational Development?

Role of school counselor. One relatively apparent barrier is that despite school counselors' specialized training in career development, in practice various other responsibilities often take precedence. Fundamental components of training programs designed to prepare school counselors to facilitate students' development in the interrelated domains of academic, personal, social, and career development typically include learning about theories of career development, vocational assessment, and career counseling practice (Campbell & Dahir, 1997). "Throughout its history... the school counseling profession has been closely associated with vocational guidance and career development ...In reality, however, most school counselors are charged with a wide range of responsibilities [in addition to] career counseling" (Herring, 1998, p. 271). It has been far too common that school counselors are assigned so many ancillary-support service or administrative-clerical duties (e.g., discipline tasks of a principal or assistant principal, lunch room supervision, service as a substitute teacher, or social activities committee work) that they have little time remaining for vital counseling functions (Gysbers, 2001; Gysbers & Henderson, 2001). Few, if any, schools have an adequate ratio of school counselors-to-students to provide career assessment and counseling on an individual basis (school counselor caseloads in U.S. schools tend to range from 300 to 500 students; Sciarra, 2001). Moreover, in poorly supported urban public schools with ongoing safety concerns, the school counselor's role in remedial crisis intervention may frequently take precedence over preventative/developmental career assessment and vocational counseling functions (Freeman, 1996). As these schools typically have higher proportions of CLD youths (Gonzalez et al., 1997), such youths may be further limited in their access to school counselor assistance via career/educational assessment to learn about their potential interests, abilities, and goals as well as career/educational counseling to develop constructive beliefs and success strategies.

One promising potential resource for more effectively tapping school counselors' specialized training in career development in order to better serve all students is the growing empirical support for establishing and fully implementing in school districts comprehensive guidance and counseling programs (e.g., Gysbers, 2001; Gysbers & Henderson, 2000; Lapan et al., 2001). Such programs incorporate content (facilitating student competencies in career, academic, personal, and social domains), an organizational framework (that includes integration with K–12 school curriculum, school wide activities, and ongoing system support) and resources (e.g., human, financial, and political; Gysbers & Henderson, 2001). Moreover, a fundamental component of comprehensive guidance and counseling programs is the use of appraisal—including vocational assessment—whereby counselors help students to learn about their abilities, interests, and achievements to develop short- and long-range plans to realize personal, educational, and career goals.

Role of school psychologist. One untapped potential resource for facilitating CLD youths' academic achievement and career development may be for school psychologists to incorporate multicultural vocational assessment information in their educational evaluations. School psychologists commonly focus on assessing a student's academic, cognitive, affective, social, and behavioral functioning in developing psychoeducational evaluation reports and recommendations (Fagan, 2002; Jacob-Timm & Hartshorne, 1998; National Association of School Psychologists, 2000). In some cases, they may refer students (e.g., those with certain developmental disabilities) to vocational rehabilitation specialists for assessment and placement. However, for CLD students who are performing below academic standards and/or manifesting behavioral problems, school psychologists might gain additional helpful insights for their educational evaluations from the results of culturally appropriate vocational assessment.

For example, Jackson and Nutini (2002) proposed a conceptual model for career assessment with adolescents vulnerable to discrimination (e.g., CLD youths) that identifies barriers to career/educational learning (e.g., unsafe environment, negative role models, and low self-efficacy for academic achievement) and resources for career/educational learning (e.g., positive role models, social support, and coping strategies). With such vocational assessment results, school psychologists might use specific information about the sources of a CLD student's low academic self-efficacy as well as particular resources for social support to better inform their educational evaluations and recommendations. Furthermore, school psychologists might incorporate career assessment information about a student's vocational interests, extracurricular abilities, and cultural values in order to generate new strategies to develop the student's academic achievement motivation. School psychologists could obtain such potentially helpful results from multicultural vocational assessment through referral to and consultation with school counselors who are trained in selecting, administering, and interpreting developmentally and culturally appropriate career assessment instruments and methods.

In summary, one potential resource might be for school psychologists and school counselors to work collaboratively to use multicultural vocational assessment to facilitate CLD students' learning and development in the interrelated domains of career, personal, social, and academic goals and achievement. Yet, one unexplored barrier in career/educational assessment and counseling with CLD students concerns hidden counselor biases or blind spots that may unintentionally function to limit our effectiveness in promoting these students' career/educational development.

Hidden Counselor Biases

When you, the reader, perused the introduction to this chapter regarding the systemic inequities that exclude CLD students from resources for academic and career achievement, what were your reactions? Were you surprised, angry, dismissive, concerned, defensive, or thinking about whom to blame? We submit that any or all of these reactions are likely because, at least in part, our biases relevant to CLD issues tend to be ingrained and unexplored (Abreu, 2001; Sue, 2003). Several authors have offered explanations for why it may be difficult for us counselors to recognize, acknowledge, and deal constructively with our own part in prejudice and discrimination that may affect our CLD clients. For example, on some level most counselors are unlikely to accept responsibility for such an unjust public school system because we take for granted the myth of meritocracy and deny personal prejudice and privilege. Counselors—regardless of their membership in dominant or marginalized groups in U.S. society—are acculturated to some extent to the beliefs, values, and behaviors of White Americans by virtue of their extended academic experience and their professional training in psychology (Carter, 1995; Sue & Sue, 2003). Therefore, we counselors are likely to believe in the myth of meritocracy, that democratic choice and opportunity are equally available to all, and thus be surprised at or discount evidence to the contrary (McIntosh, 1998; Sue, 2003; Tatum, 1992). We would like to think that our own educational and professional success can be attributed solely to our own efforts and ability, while failing to recognize the uneven playing field of advantages that some of us may take for granted—e.g., embedded systemic privileges afforded by gender, race, ethnicity, or socioeconomic class. Implications for our career assessment and counseling with CLD students is that we may fail to recognize potential barriers for them, both in their environments and in their psychological responses to prejudice and discrimination (Jackson & Nutini, 2002). These blind spots may leave important gaps in vocational assessment data that could limit our effectiveness in promoting career/educational development with our CLD students.

Potentially more harmful are the negative stereotypes and prejudiced attitudes and beliefs that we may subtly, automatically, and unintentionally harbor toward CLD students such as attributing their academic and behavioral difficulties to their own (or their parents') laziness, apathy, or lack of intellect. In contrast to the overt bigotry and hate crimes of others that many of us associate with prejudice and discrimination, it is our own personal lack of awareness of how social biases affect our own judgments and behavior toward marginalized group members that is most insidious and harmful (Sue, 2003). Social scientists have established that even though most people (including counselors) embrace egalitarian values toward racial diversity, they harbor toward racial minority people negative perceptual biases that are automatic, unconscious, and normative (Dovidio, Evans, & Tyler, 1986; Fiske, 1998; Greenwald, McGhee, & Schwartz, 1998). Abreu (2001) noted that multicultural counseling trainees in the process of confronting such socially and ethically undesirable hidden biases may understandably become defensive about exploring, acknowledging, and ameliorating their personal attitudes and beliefs toward CLD clients. In order to promote the process of exploring hidden biases and develop more multiculturally competent counseling approaches, Abreu argued that counselors need to learn about the theory and research on stereotypes and perceptual bias (for which he has provided an excellent didactic resource that we highly recommend).

Although counselors' multicultural blind spots may be unintentional, they nevertheless can harm our CLD clients (Ridley, 1995). Counselors' lack of attention to or awareness of systemic career/education barriers and the influence of our own hidden biases may leave important gaps in our assessments that may further disadvantage our CLD clients (Jackson & Nutini, 2002). Therefore, in order to adhere to the ethical principle of counselors and psychologists that we do no harm (American Psychological Association, 2002), it is imperative that we become more culturally aware of our own values, biases, stereotypes, and assumptions in conducting career/educational assessments with CLD students.

IMPLEMENTATION AND APPROACHES

Selecting Career Assessments

In addition to continually monitoring and working to ameliorate our own hidden biases, multiculturally competent counselors and psychologists in schools must develop skills to critically evaluate and appropriately adapt assessment tools that will help inform ethical and culturally appropriate intervention strategies with CLD students. First, we will outline definitions and general guidelines for selecting and using career assessment tools. Then, we will discuss barriers and resources for how to address cultural biases in career assessment with CLD students.

In general, Niles and Harris-Bowlsbey (2002) define assessment as "the use of any formal or informal technique or instrument to collect data about a client" (p. 153). They distinguish *formal* assessments used in career counseling as standardized instruments and offer examples of *informal* assessments as card sorts, checklists, fantasy exercises, forced-choice activities, and structured (or semi-structured) interviews. Ponterotto, Gretchen, and Chauhan (2001) categorized assessments as *nomothetic*, i.e., standardized to allow comparison of individual client responses with a larger normative data set, versus *idiographic*, i.e., personalized to gather "a descriptive and comprehensive understanding of an individual client without regard to comparative normative data" (p. 68). We agree with Ponterotto and his colleagues that both quantitative (or *formal*) and qualitative (or *informal*) assessment tools can be useful in understanding and helping our multicultural clients. Moreover, we suggest that counselors in schools may need to develop methods to use nomothetic vocational assessment data in both culturally relevant and idiographic ways in order to facilitate CLD students' academic and career development.

To date, most of the literature on how to select and use career assessments refers to quantitative pencil-and-paper inventories; two recommended resources are *A Counselor's Guide to Career Assessment Instruments* (Kapes & Whitfield, 2002) and the *Standards of Educational and Psychological Testing* developed by the Joint Committee on Testing Practices (American Educational Research Association, American Psychological Association, & National Council on Measurement in Education, 1999). Other examples of quantitative tools are computer applications in career assessment, such as computer-assisted career guidance systems and Internet-based tools; resources for counselors to evaluate the benefits and limitations of these career assessments are reviewed by Sampson, Lumsden, and Carr (2002).

Two examples of qualitative tools for multicultural career assessment are semi-structured intake protocols—the Career-in-Culture Interview (Ponterotto, Rivera, & Sueyoshi, 2000) and interview guide questions to assess resources, barriers, and possible discrimination influences in CLD youths' career learning (Jackson & Nutini, 2002). Another potentially useful qualitative tool for career assessment with CLD youths is the family genogram (Sueyoshi, Rivera, & Ponterotto, 2001). Although developed for ethnic minority women, the Career Counseling Checklist (Ward & Bingham, 1993) could be adapted for culture-specific career assessment with CLD students.

Addressing Cultural Biases of Career Assessment Inventories and Methods

Some barriers as well as resources exist regarding the use of vocational assessment tools to facilitate CLD youths' academic achievement and career development in schools. To summarize the literature on how counselors might address cultural biases of vocational assessment with CLD students, we will discuss two types of potential barriers—underlying theories/assumptions and instrument content—and recommend counselor methods. While much of this literature refers to standardized pencil-and-paper inventories and methods of vocational assessment, many of the recommendations may apply to other quantitative and qualitative approaches to multicultural career assessment. As a resource, several scholars (e.g., Betz & Fitzgerald, 1995; Fouad, 1993; Gainor, 2001; Herring, 1998) have outlined important aspects for evaluating the reliability and validity of vocational assessment inventories for use with individuals from culturally diverse groups as well as recommended methods for counselors to conduct career assessments and make meaning of the results. Spokane (1991) noted that an advantage of using career inventories is that it may afford practitioners an efficient way to assess respondents' interests and potential success and satisfaction in educational and career pursuits. In order to use vocational assessments ethically and effectively with CLD youths, however, it is imperative that counselors develop skills for identifying potential cultural biases in the content of vocational instruments and in their own counseling conceptualizations and methods.

Underlying theories and assumptions. Racial, gender, class, and other cultural biases that are pervasive in the U.S. public education system are also pervasive in the content of most vocational inventories, the underlying theories from which these assessment tools were developed, and the ways in which they are used by many counselors with members of CLD groups. Most vocational assessment instruments were constructed based on theories of career development and choice from Eurocentric (or European American), Caucasian, English-speaking, middle-class, heterosexual male perspectives that may differ or conflict with the values of other cultural groups (Fitzgerald & Betz, 1994; Leong & Gim-Chung, 1995). For example, underlying career development theories that may influence counselors' interpretations of career assessment results tend to idealize such Eurocentric values over culturally different values as individualism over collectivism, materialism over spirituality, and competition over cooperation (Sue & Sue, 2003). Thus, a counselor might inappropriately conclude from career assessment results that a CLD student has a maladaptive and dependent decision-making style instead of an adaptive collectivist orientation, i.e., an approach consistent with that individual's cultural values to consider as a priority the views and needs of one's family and community in decision-making. In order for counselors to avoid unconsciously and mistakenly assuming that all individuals share Eurocentric values, they need to recognize that alternative belief systems exist and strive to understand the cultural values most relevant to the CLD youths with whom they work.

Furthermore, counselors need to recognize that most vocational assessment inventories are based on career development theories that neither reflect the experiences of CLD group members with historical and current discrimination (Gainor, 2001) nor the influence of discrimination in limiting education and career opportunities for CLD adolescents (Jackson & Nutini, 2002). Because CLD students may have high career aspirations but low expectations of their accessibility (Arbona, 1996; Graham et al., 1998), it may be important to assess both barriers relevant to discrimination and potential resources for negotiating these challenges (Jackson & Nutini, 2002; Lent, Hackett, & Brown, 1999). In addition, relevant to multicultural vocational assessment, counselors should explore with CLD youths their cultural orientation (e.g., acculturation; Dana, 1998) and identity development statuses (e.g., cultural identity; Hartung et al., 1998), racial identity (Helms & Piper, 1994), ethnic identity (Phinney, 1992), or multidimensional identity (Reynolds & Pope, 1991).

Instrument content.   Likewise, in order for counselors to ethically and effectively use vocational assessment tools to facilitate CLD youths' academic achievement and career development in schools, they need to be aware of the potential biases and limitations of the inventories. The state of our current knowledge about career assessment with members of culturally diverse groups is inadequate, particularly regarding relevant norms and evidence for reliability and validity (Gainor, 2001). Insufficient representation of CLD youths in the normative samples for many career assessment instruments threatens the validity of these tools by violating the principle of generalizability, thus limiting statistical support for interpretations of results for CLD youths. Alternatively, counselors might interpret the meaning of career assessment results with CLD youths in ways that include possible explanations of how the comparison (norm) group may differ from their own.

Most career assessment inventories were developed for individuals whose primary language is English (Gainor, 2001). Assessments used cross-culturally should be validly translated and have conceptual and linguistic equivalence (Fouad, 1993). Lonner (1985) outlined 4 levels of conceptual and linguistic equivalence relevant to evaluating the reliability and validity of vocational assessment inventories for use with CLD youths. First, the inventory should have functional equivalence regarding the role that assessed behaviors play across cultures; e.g., functional equivalence may be limited if inventory items do not reflect that the role of work in people's lives may vary in different cultures (Richardson, 1993). Second, an inventory translated into English should have conceptual equivalence for the meanings assigned to behaviors or concepts. An example cited by Fouad (1993) of a term that would not have conceptual equivalence when translated from Spanish to English was that of a *church worker*; in Mexico this term would refer to an elderly widow who no longer fully resides at home, whereas in the U.S. this term would refer to a church volunteer. Third, Lonner (1985) suggested that an inventory used cross-culturally should have metric equivalence such that it measures the same constructs in different cultures. Fourth, inventories translated from English should have linguistic equivalence; e.g., Fouad (1993) recommended the following steps for valid translation—literal translation, back-translation, committee consensus, and bilingual field testing. Therefore, counselors should evaluate the CLD student's proficiency in English, then determine whether a version in the student's native language of a vocational inventory would be more appropriate. If a translation exists, counselors need to consult the manual of the instrument they are considering adopting, as well as relevant literature on its development and validation in order to determine if and how they might use the tool with a CLD student in a culturally relevant way.

Expanding Career Related Learning With CLD Students

Multiculturally competent counselors in schools need to expand their exploration with CLD students to help them learn more about career and educational areas from which they have been excluded. As Gainor (2001, p. 170) noted:

> Vocational assessment in its most ethical and democratic form should broaden the career options available to people and increase their chances of satisfaction and success. Therefore, each counseling professional engaged in vocational assessment with any client has a choice: either use it to perpetuate an oppressive system that denies equal access to occupational opportunities to all, or use it to increase access for those who have been previously denied access. The former happens more easily than one might think. Even the well-meaning, culturally aware counseling profession[al] can unintentionally behave in ways that maintain the status quo. (Ridley, 1995)

For example, research has shown that with many African Americans and girls who score high in social interests on vocational assessment measures, counselors may limit their consideration to social occupations. Counselors may fail to explore with African Americans or girls how they might learn about and potentially develop new interests in math and science occupations; i.e., higher-paying and higher-status occupations in which they have been discriminated against historically and persistent negative stereotypes continue to discourage access (Gainor, 2001; Hackett & Byars, 1996). Alternatively, school counselors and psychologists could help CLD students explore vocational options for integrating social and math/science interests with their cultural values. For example, one CLD youth who participated in a vocational assessment study with these authors was an altruistic Black Puerto Rican girl interested in biology who explored an aspiration to establish a bilingual medical practice in her community.

Hispanic children in U.S. schools tend to have high vocational aspirations but low educational achievement, particularly in math and science, thus as adults they are disproportionately represented in unskilled and semi-skilled occupations (Fouad, 1995). Relevant to vocational assessment with CLD students, Fouad cautioned counselors to avoid tracking these students into non-college preparatory classes, particularly in math and science courses that serve as *gatekeepers*, or prerequisites for a wide range of college majors. Alternatively, counselors may need to facilitate CLD students' access to multiple academic resources for performing well in math and science.

Also, counselors could help CLD students develop self-efficacy beliefs in and realistic strategies for promoting academic effort and achievement that *will* more likely pay off *for them* in expanded educational and career opportunities (i.e., constructively challenging their compensatory beliefs to the contrary in the face of educational/vocational discrimination, as noted by Ogbu, 1992, and others). For example, Jackson and Nutini (2002) proposed that one untapped area of career assessment is that of helping CLD youths to recognize and develop their current and potential resources by learning about their transferable skills. As they explained:

> The concept of functional/transferable skills, derived from Bolles (2002), is that one naturally learns skills from all aspects of one's life—such as teaching, organizing, persuading, assembling, supervising, computing, researching, analyzing, deciding, operating, designing, or repairing—that might transfer or be applied in other areas, such as in academic or career settings. For example, a Latino middle school child may benefit from learning to label some of the skills that he has enjoyed developing while completing a social studies project, such as researching, analyzing, and organizing information, as well as how he might use these skills in other academic domains (e.g., science) or apply these skills to a wide variety of careers. (Jackson & Nutini, 2002, p. 72)

IMPLICATIONS FOR FUTURE RESEARCH AND PRACTICE

Counselors and psychologists in schools could use culturally relevant vocational assessment to inform interventions that promote greater social justice by expanding CLD students' educational and career development. Future research studies—particularly multidisciplinary efforts (Byars & McCubbin, 2001) that include school practitioners and university researchers (Whiston, 1996)—could examine several unexplored barriers and untapped resources for effective multicultural career assessment with CLD middle and high school students at risk for low academic and career achievement. Such collaborative efforts among practitioners, researchers, and trainers might facilitate more informed practice, theory, and research in this area as well as expand shared access to practical resources (such time, funding, and service providers). Moreover, as noted by Sciarra (2001), school practitioners can enhance their effectiveness by consulting with parents, teachers, and other school staff, and by networking with community resources, including religious leaders.

There is some empirical evidence that systematic career guidance programs in schools that incorporate vocational assessment can be effective in facilitating students' educational and career development (e.g., Lapan et al., 2001). Furthermore, over the past decade, the focus of school psychoeducational service delivery has shifted from a problem-solving approach to one of problem prevention (Short, 1997; Natassi, 2000). Particularly for CLD youths who are at risk for low educational and career achievement, school psychologists and counselors could coordinate prevention programs using career assessment for expanding students' vocational learning (e.g., learning about their transferable skills and cultural resources).

However, a considerable gap in the research literature concerns which vocational assessment tools and methods may be most helpful for which CLD students, particularly for those in low-income, urban middle and high schools with limited access and expectations regarding educational/career achievement (Arbona, 1996; Hansen, 2003; Pope, 2003). We will discuss several possible reasons for this gap in the literature as well as recommendations for future research.

In a survey of practicing high school counselors who were members of the American School Counselor Association, Freeman (1996) found that, despite the high value placed on students' career development by the association and by parents, counselors reported relatively low rates of using computer and paper-and-pencil career assessment tools. Freeman suggested several hypotheses to explain these results that future research might address. For example, the current roles of counselors in many schools may be too fragmented to allow for systemic career development activities. School practitioners (and administrators) may perceive career assessment activities to be a lower priority than crisis intervention and academic remediation, thus shortchanging time devoted to career assessment that could be used to support academic achievement motivation. School counselors may have low self-efficacy and inadequate or outdated training on how to effectively use career assessment tools with their students. As recently as 2001, Bingham and Krantz in their biannual review of vocational assessment research literature found no articles on career assessment training in graduate school programs. Also relevant to Freeman's findings, "it might be hypothesized that the field is developing more instruments rather than defining the effectiveness of a [core array of instruments that might be] used and perceived as highly effective by school counselors and assessment researchers alike" (p. 193).

Savickas (2003) observed, "For example, hundreds of studies on the predictive validity of interest inventories have improved the inventories but not helped counselors use these inventories more effectively" (p. 90). His and others' recommendations are to focus future research on the process (in addition to the outcome) of career assessment and counseling, then to more effectively share empirically based information that supports the judgment of career counselors in practice. In particular, Savickas recalled Williamson and Bordin's (1941) call for research to address the question: "What counseling techniques (and conditions) will produce what types of results with what types of students?" (p. 8).

A substantial body of literature supports the effectiveness of career assessment and counseling outcomes for adolescents, particularly for Caucasians but also for ethnic minority students, of middle-class and at least average academic achievement (Arbona, 1996; Brown & Krane, 2000; Swanson, 1995; Whiston et al., 1998). Nevertheless, Arbona (1996) suggested that for academically successful, middle-class CLD youths—compared to their Caucasian counterparts—"achieving is an identity issue [and] developing a sense of ethnic identity is an additional developmental task" (p. 50). The meanings of academic and career achievement for proving negative stereotypes wrong, on the one hand, but possibly distancing themselves from their cultural group, on the other hand, have implications in the process of defining who they are and coming to terms with negative stereotypes about their cultural group. Thus, particularly relevant for CLD youths, Arbona and others (e.g., Hartung et al., 1998; Helms & Piper, 1994; Leong & Gim-Chung, 1995) have argued that future research needs to explore how racial/ethnic and cultural identity formation relates to educational and career development. Furthermore, we need to know more about how acculturation issues for immigrant CLD youths affect their motivation for and access to academic and career achievement (Dana, 1998; Gainor, 2001).

For academically unsuccessful, low-income CLD students who might especially benefit from culturally relevant and effective vocational assessment, there is currently a dearth of empirical literature to guide school counselors and psychologists.

Low educational attainment severely limits access to occupational options, therefore it is imperative that we learn more about how to effectively promote beliefs, values, and strategies that help these students succeed academically and vocationally (Arbona, 2000). Toward that aim, we recommend two additional areas of future research. Building on previous research on academic disidentification as a compensatory strategy for racial/ethnic minority students (e.g., Ogbu, 1992; Steele, 1997; Steinberg et al., 1992), future studies might investigate how to assess the beliefs of CLD youths about whether academic effort and persistence will pay off *for them* in career options and opportunities. These assessment results might then be used to design and empirically evaluate the effectiveness of interventions to constructively challenge CLD students' negative beliefs and support positive beliefs for promoting academic achievement and vocational development outcomes.

Another area we recommend for future research is to investigate strategies to identify and ameliorate counselors' hidden biases that may impair their multicultural assessments with CLD youths. Despite considerable evidence that CLD youths do not have equal access to education and career opportunities (e.g., Education Trust, 2000), many counseling professionals fail to attend to such cultural factors in their assessments (Ramirez, Wassef, Paniagua, & Linsky, 1996; Ridley, 1995). Fundamental to ethical and effective vocational assessment with CLD students, counselors and counselor educators must demonstrate and continually develop their competencies in multicultural counseling (Arrendondo et al., 1996; Sue et al., 1998) and career counseling (National Career Development Association Professional Standards Committee, 1997). Madonna Constantine has continued to contribute an important line of research that examines the attitudes and beliefs of school counselors and trainees that facilitate or impede their multicultural counseling competence (Constantine, 2001, 2002; Constantine, Arorash, Barakett, Blackmon, Donnelly, & Edles, 2001; Constantine & Gushue, 2003; Constantine & Yeh, 2001). As suggested by Jackson and Nutini (2002) in their analysis of vocational assessment interviews with adolescents vulnerable to discrimination, one hypothesis that future research might examine is that hidden counselor biases may operate to limit their attention to the possible discrimination influences in their CLD students' perceptions and experiences relevant to education and career goals.

The normative, unconscious, automatic, and unintentional nature of negative counselor biases in their perceptions of multicultural clients may have harmful effects (e.g., Ridley, 1995; Sue, 2003). With CLD students, hidden counselor biases may distort vocational assessments and impede effective interventions. Therefore, it is imperative that future studies investigate the effectiveness of various multicultural training approaches to help counselors overcome likely defensiveness and constructively challenge their hidden biases and stereotyped perceptions. Abreu (2001) offered several useful recommendations for such research. Future studies might also empirically evaluate the effectiveness of various methods for dealing with resistance to multicultural training suggested by others (e.g., Carter, 1995; Jackson, 1999; Kiselica, 1999; Mio & Awakuni, 2000; Ponterotto & Pedersen, 1993; Sue, 2003).

In this chapter, a discussion was presented of unexplored barriers and untapped resources for middle and high school counselors and psychologists using culturally relevant vocational assessment to promote access and motivation for academic and career achievement with marginalized CLD students. It is hoped that by becoming more culturally aware of our own values, biases, stereotypes, and assumptions in conducting career/educational assessments with CLD students, we can learn how to more effectively promote beliefs, values, and strategies that help these students succeed academically and vocationally.

ANNOTATED BIBLIOGRAPHY

Jackson, M. A., & Nutini, C. D. (September 2002). Hidden resources and barriers in career learning: Assessment with adolescents vulnerable to discrimination. *Career Development Quarterly*, 51(1), 56–77.

This article addresses the contextual barriers and resources affecting career-related choices amongst multicultural middle school students.

Kapes, J. T. & Whitfield, E. A. (2001). *A counselor's guide to career assessment instruments* (4th ed.). Columbus, OH: National Career Development Association.

The book reviews some of the researched instruments designed to measure career beliefs, career thoughts, career maturity, interests, skills, aptitudes, abilities, personality traits, values, and other internal variables.

RESOURCES

Career Development Quarterly.

The journal of the National Career Development Association. The journal is published four times each year and reports the latest in career development research and practice.

Journal of Career Assessment.

Published by Sage; focuses on all those means developed and used to assess and evaluate individuals and environments in the field of career counseling and development.

Professional School Counseling, spring 2003.

Websites

ASVAB Career Exploration Program:
http://www.asvabprogram.com/

The ASVAB Program recently was re-designed to provide information to virtually all students, whether they are planning on immediate employment after high school in civilian or military occupations, or if they plan to pursue further education at a university, community college, or vocational institution.

Association of Computer-Based Systems for Career Information:
http://www.acsci.org/

ACSCI is a professional association, formed for the advancement of career information and its delivery.

National Career Development Association (NCDA):
http://www.ncda.org/

A division of the American Counseling Association (ACA). The mission of NCDA is to promote the career development of all individuals.

Society for Vocational Psychology:
http://www.div17.org/vocpsych/

The Society for Vocational Psychology is a Section in the Counseling Psychology Division (17) of the American Psychological Association. Its purpose is to encourage, promote, and facilitate contributions to research, teaching, practice, and public interest in vocational psychology and career interventions.

REFERENCES

Abreu, J. M. (2001). Theory and research on stereotypes and perceptual bias: A didactic resource for multicultural counseling trainers. Counseling Psychologist, 29, 487–512.

American Educational Research Association, American Psychological Association, & National Council on Measurement in Education. (1999). Standards for educational and psychological testing. Washington, DC: American Educational Research Association.

American Psychological Association. (2002). Ethical principles of psychologists and code of conduct. American Psychologist, 57, 1060–1073.

Arbona, C. (1996). Career theory and practice in a multicultural context. In M. L. Savickas & W. B. Walsh (Eds.), *Handbook of career counseling theory and practice* (pp. 45–54). Palo Alto, CA: Davies-Black.

Arbona, C. (2000). The development of academic achievement in school-aged children: precursors to career development. In S. D. Brown & R. W. Lent (Eds.), *Handbook of counseling psychology* (3rd ed., pp. 270–309). New York: Wiley.

Arrendondo, P., Toporek, R., Brown, S., Jones, J., Locke, D. C., Sanchez, J., et al. (1996). Operationalization of the multicultural counseling competencies. *Journal of Multicultural Counseling and Development, 24,* 42–78.

Betz, N. E. (1994). *Basic issues and concepts in career counseling for women.* In W.B. Walsh & S. H. Osipow (Eds.), Career counseling for women (pp. 1–41). Hillsdale, NJ: Erlbaum.

Betz, N. E., & Fitzgerald, L. S. (1995). Career assessment and intervention with racial and ethnic minorities. In F. T. L. Leong (Ed.), *Career development and vocational behavior of racial and ethnic minorities* (pp. 263–279). Mahwah, NJ: Erlbaum.

Bingham, R. P., & Krantz, J. (2001). Career and vocational assessment 1997–1998: A biennial review. *Journal of Career Assessment, 9,* 1–24.

Bolles, R. N. (2002). *What color is your parachute?* Berkeley, CA: Ten Speed Press.

Brown, S. D., & Krane, N. E. R. (2000). Four (or five) sessions and a cloud of dust: Old assumptions and new observations about career counseling. In S. D. Brown & R. W. Lent (Eds.), *Handbook of counseling psychology* (3rd ed., pp. 740–766). New York: Wiley.

Byars, A. M., & McCubbin, L. D. (2001). Trends in career development research with racial/ethnic minorities. In L. A. Suzuki, J. G. Ponterotto, & P. J. Meller (Eds.), *Handbook of multi-*

cultural assessment: Clinical psychological, and educational applications (2nd ed., pp. 633–654). San Francisco, CA: Jossey-Bass.

Campbell, C. A., & Dahir, C. A. (1997). *The national standards for school counseling programs*. Alexandria, VA: American School Counselor Association.

Carter, R. T. (1995). *The influence of race and racial identity in psychotherapy: Toward a racially inclusive model*. New York: Wiley.

Constantine, M. G. (2001). Theoretical orientation, empathy, and multicultural counseling competence in school counselor trainees. *Professional School Counseling, 4,* 342–348.

Constantine, M. G. (2002). Racism attitudes, white racial identity attitudes, and multicultural counseling competence in school counselor trainees. *Counselor Education and Supervision, 41,* 162–174.

Constantine, M. G., Arorash, T. J., Barakett, M. D., Blackmon, S. M., Donnelly, P. C., & Edles, P. A. (2001). School counselors' universal-diverse orientation and aspects of their multicultural counseling competence. *Professional School Counseling, 5,* 13–18.

Constantine, M. G., & Gushue, G. V. (2003). School counselors' ethnic tolerance attitudes and racism attitudes as predictors of their multicultural case conceptualization of an immigrant student. *Journal of Counseling and Development, 81,* 185–191.

Constantine, M. G., & Yeh, C. J. (2001). Multicultural training, self-construals, and multicultural competence of school counselors. *Professional School Counseling, 4,* 202–207.

Dana, R. H. (1998). Understanding cultural identity in intervention and assessment. Thousand Oaks, CA: Sage.

Dovidio, J. F., Evans, N. E., & Tyler, R. B. (1986). Racial stereotypes: The contents of their cognitive representations. *Journal of Experimental Psychology, 22,* 22–37.

Education Trust. (2000, April). *Achievement in America: GEAR UP*. Washington, DC: Author.

Fagan, T. K. (2002). Trends in the history of school psychology in the United States. In A. Thomas, & J. Grimes (Eds.), *Best practices in school psychology IV* (pp. 202–221). Washington, DC: National Association of School Psychologists.

Fiske, S. T. (1998). Stereotyping, prejudice, and discrimination. In D. T. Gilbert, S. T. Fiske, & G. Lindzey (Eds.), *The handbook of social psychology* (4th ed., Vol. 2, pp. 357–411). Boston: McGraw-Hill.

Fitzgerald, L. F., & Betz, N. E. (1994). Career development in cultural context: The role of gender, race, class, and sexual orientation. In M. L. Savickas & R. W. Lent (Eds.), *Convergence in career development theories: Implications for science and practice* (pp. 103–117). Palo Alto, CA: Consulting Psychologists Press.

Fordham, S., & Ogbu, J. (1986). Black students' school success: Coping with the "burden of 'acting White.'" *Urban Review, 18,* 176–206.

Fouad, N. A. (1993). Cross-cultural vocational assessment. *Career Development Quarterly, 42,* 4–12.

Fouad, N. A. (1995). Career behavior of Hispanics: Assessment and career intervention. In F. T. L. Leong (Ed.), *Career development and vocational behavior of racial and ethnic minorities* (pp. 165–191). Hillsdale, NJ: Erlbaum.

Freeman, B. (1996). The use and perceived effectiveness of career assessment tools: A survey of high school counselors. *Journal of Career Development, 22,* 185–196.

Gainor, K. A. (2001). Vocational assessment with culturally diverse populations. In L. A. Suzuki, J. G. Ponterotto, & P. J. Meller (Eds.), *Handbook of multicultural assessment: Clinical, psychological, and educational applications* (2nd ed., pp. 169–189). San Francisco, CA: Jossey-Bass.

Gonzalez, V., Brusca-Vega, R., & Yawkey, T. (1997). *Assessment and instruction of culturally and linguistically diverse students with or at-risk of learning problems*. Needham Heights, MA: Allyn & Bacon.

Gopaul-McNicol, S., & Thomas-Presswood, T. (1998). *Working with linguistically and cultur-ally different children: Innovative clinical and educational approaches.* Needham Heights, MA: Allyn & Bacon.

Gottfredson, L. S. (1981). Circumscription and compromise: A developmental theory of oc-cupational aspirations. *Journal of Counseling Psychology, 28,* 545–579.

Gottfredson, L. S. (1996). Gottfreson's theory of circumscription and compromise. In D. Brown & L. Brooks (Eds.), *Career choice and development* (3rd ed., pp. 179–232). San Fran-cisco: Jossey-Bass.

Graham, S., Taylor, A. Z., & Hudley, C. (1998). Exploring achievement values among eth-nic minority early adolescents. *Journal of Educational Psychology, 90,* 606–620.

Greenwald, A. G., McGhee, D. E., & Schwartz, L. K. (1998). Measuring individual differ-ences in implicit cognition: The implicit association test. *Journal of Personality and Social Psychology, 74,* 1464–1480.

Gysbers, N. C. (2001). School guidance and counseling in the 21st century: Remember the past into the future. *Professional School Counseling, 5,* 96–106.

Gysbers, N. C., & Henderson, P. (2000). *Developing and managing your school guidance pro-gram* (3rd ed.). Alexandria, VA: American Counseling Association.

Gysbers, N. C., & Henderson, P. (2001). Comprehensive guidance and counseling pro-grams: A rich history and a bright future. *Professional School Counseling, 4,* 246–257.

Hackett, G., & Byars, A. M. (1996). Social cognitive theory and the career development of African American women. *Career Development Quarterly, 44,* 322–340.

Hansen, S. S. (2003). Career counselors as advocates and change agents for equality. *Career Development Quarterly, 52,* 43–53.

Hartung, P. J., Vandiver, B. J., Leong, F. T. L., Pope, M., Niles, S. G., & Farrow, B. (1998). Appraising cultural identity in career-development assessment and counseling. *Career Development Quarterly, 46,* 276–293.

Helms, J. E., & Piper, R. E. (1994). Implications of racial identity theory for vocational psy-chology. *Journal of Vocational Behavior, 44,* 124–138.

Herring, R. D. (1998). *Career counseling in the schools: Multicultural and developmental perspec-tives.* Alexandria, VA: American Counseling Association.

Jackson, M. A. (1999). Stereotype reversal and triad methods of counselor training: Ex-panding perspective taking in conceptualizing presenting problems of racial/ethnic minority clients (Doctoral dissertation, Stanford University, 1999). *Dissertation Abstracts International, 60–08A.* (Accession No. AAG9943672).

Jackson, M. A., & Nutini,C. D. (2002). Hidden resources and barriers in career learning as-sessment with adolescents vulnerable to discrimination. *Career Development Quarterly, 51,* 56–77.

Jacob-Timm, S., & Hartshorne, T. S. (1998). *Ethics and law for school psychologists* (3rd ed.). New York: Wiley.

Kapes, J. T., & Whitfield, E. A. (Eds.). (2002). *A counselor's guide to career assessment instru-ments* (4th ed.). Tulsa, OK: National Career Development Association.

Kiselica, M. S. (Ed.). (1999). *Confronting prejudice and racism during multicultural training.* Alexandria, VA: American Counseling Association.

Kozol, J. (1991). *Savage inequalities: Children in America's schools.* New York: Crown.

Krumboltz, J. D. (1979). A social learning theory of career choice. In A. M. Mitchell, G. B. Jones, & J. D. Krumboltz (Eds.), *Social learning theory and career decision making* (pp. 194–199). Cranson, RI: Carroll Press.

Krumboltz, J. D. (1991). *A manual for the Career Beliefs Inventory.* Palo Alto, CA: Consulting Psychologists Press.

Krumboltz, J. D. (1996). A learning theory of career counseling. In M. L. Savickas & W. B. Walsh (Eds.), *Handbook of career counseling theory and practice* (pp. 55–80). Palo Alto, CA: Davies-Black.

Krumboltz, J. D., & Jackson, M. A. (1993). Career assessment as a learning tool. *Journal of Career Assessment, 1,* 398–409.

Lapan, R. T., Gysbers, N. C., & Petroski, G. F. (2001). Helping seventh graders be safe and successful: A statewide study of the impact of comprehensive guidance and counseling programs. *Journal of Counseling and Development, 79,* 320–341.

Leong, F. T. L., & Gim-Chung, R. H. (1995). Career assessment and intervention with Asian Americans. In F. T. L. Leong (Ed.), *Career development and vocational behavior of racial and ethnic minorities* (pp. 193–226). Hillsdale, NJ: Erlbaum.

Lent, R. W., Hackett, G., & Brown, S. D. (1999). A social cognitive view of school-to-work transition. *Career Development Quarterly, 47,* 297–311.

Levin, A. S., Krumboltz, J. D., & Krumboltz, B. L. (1995). *Exploring your career beliefs: A workbook for the Career Beliefs Inventory with techniques for integrating your Strong and MBTI results.* Palo Alto, CA: Consulting Psychologists Press.

Lonner, W. J. (1985). Issues in testing and assessment in cross-cultural counseling. *Counseling Psychologist, 13,* 599–614.

Major, B., Spencer, S., Schmader, T., Wolfe, C., & Crocker, J. (1998). Coping with negative stereotypes about intellectual performance: The role of psychological disengagement. *Personality and Social Psychology Bulletin, 24,* 34–50.

McIntosh, P. (1998). Unpacking the invisible knapsack. In M. McGoldrick (Ed.), *Revisioning family therapy: Race, culture, and gender in clinical practice* (pp. 147–152). New York: Guildford Press.

Mio, J. S., & Awakuni, G. I. (2000). *Resistance to multiculturalism: Issues and interventions.* Philadelphia: Brunner/Mazel.

Mickelson, R. A. (1990). The attitude-achievement paradox among Black adolescents. *Sociology of Education, 63,* 44–61.

Mitchell, L. K., & Krumboltz, J. D. (1990). Social learning approach to career decision making: Krumboltz's theory. In D. Brown, L. Brooks, & Associates (Eds.), *Career choice and development: Applying contemporary theories to practice* (2nd ed., pp. 197–261). San Francisco: Jossey-Bass.

Mitchell, L. K., & Krumboltz, J. D. (1996). Krumboltz's learning theory of career choice and counseling. In D. Brown, L. Brooks, & Associates (Eds.), *Career choice and development: Applying contemporary theories to practice* (3rd ed., pp. 233–280). San Francisco: Jossey-Bass.

Natassi, B. K. (2000). School psychologists as health-care providers in the 21st century: Conceptual framework, professional identity, and professional practice. *School Psychology Review, 29,* 540–554.

National Association of School Psychologists. (2000). *Standards for training and field placement programs in school psychology.* Washington, DC: Author.

National Career Development Association Professional Standards Committee. (1997). *Career counseling competencies.* Alexandria, VA: National Career Development Association.

National Center for Education Statistics. (1999). *The condition of education.* Washington, DC: U.S. Department of Education.

National Center for Education Statistics. (2001a). *The condition of education.* Washington, DC: U.S. Department of Education.

National Center for Education Statistics. (2001b). *The nation's report card..* Washington, DC: U.S. Department of Education.

National Occupational Information Coordinating Committee (NOICC). (1992). *The national career development guidelines project.* Washington, DC: U.S. Government Printing Office.

Niles, S. G., & Harris-Bowlsbey, J. (2002). *Career development interventions in the 21st century.* Upper Saddle River, NJ: Merrill Prentice Hall.

Ogbu, J. U. (1992). Understanding cultural diversity and learning. *Educational Research, 21,* 5–14.

Padilla, A. M. (2001). Issues in culturally appropriate assessment. In L. A. Suzuki, J. G. Ponterotto, & P. J. Meller (Eds.), *Handbook of multicultural assessment: Clinical, psychological, and educational applications* (2nd ed., pp. 5–28). San Francisco, CA: Jossey-Bass.

Peterson, N., & Gonzalez, R. C. (2000). *The role of work in people's lives: Applied career counseling and vocational psychology.* Belmont, CA: Brooks/Cole.

Phinney, J. S. (1992). The Multigroup Ethnic Identity Measure: A new scale for use with diverse groups. *Journal of Adolescent Research, 7,* 156–176.

Ponterotto, J. G., Gretchen, D., & Chauhan, R. V. (2001). Cultural identity and multicultural assessment: Quantitative and qualitative tools for clinicians. In L. A. Suzuki, J. G. Ponterotto, & P. J. Meller (Eds.), *Handbook of multicultural assessment: Clinical psychological, and educational applications* (2nd ed., pp. 67–99). San Francisco, CA: Jossey-Bass.

Ponterotto, J. G., & Pedersen, P. B. (1993). *Preventing prejudice: A guide for counselors and educators.* Newbury, CA: Sage.

Ponterotto, J. G., Rivera, L., & Sueyoshi, L. A. (2000). The Career-in-Culture Interview: A semi-structured protocol for the cross-cultural intake interview. *Career Development Quarterly, 49,* 85–96.

Pope, M. (2003). Career counseling in the twenty-first century: Beyond cultural encapsulation. *Career Development Quarterly, 52,* 54–60.

Ramirez, S. Z., Wassef, A., Paniagua, F. A., & Linsky, A. O. (1996). Mental health providers' perceptions of cultural variables in evaluating ethnically diverse clients. *Professional Psychology: Research and Practice, 27,* 284–288.

Reynolds, A. L., & Pope, R. L. (1991). The complexities of diversity: Exploring multiple oppressions. *Journal of Counseling and Development, 70,* 174–180.

Richardson, M. S. (1993). Work in people's lives: A location for counseling psychologists. *Journal of Counseling Psychology, 40,* 425–433.

Ridley, C. R. (1995). *Overcoming unintentional racism in counseling and therapy.* Thousand Oaks, CA: Sage.

Ridley, C. R., Hill, C. L., & Wiese, D. L. (2001). Ethics in multicultural assessment: A model of reasoned application. In L. A. Suzuki, J. G. Ponterotto, & P. J. Meller (Eds.), *Handbook of multicultural assessment: Clinical, psychological, and educational applications* (2nd ed., pp. 29–48). San Francisco, CA: Jossey-Bass.

Sadker, D. (2002, November). An educator's primer on the gender war. *Phi Delta Kappan,* 235–240, 244.

Sanders, J. (2002, November). Something is missing from teacher education: Attention to two genders. *Phi Delta Kappan,* 241–244.

Sampson, J. P., Jr., Lumsden, J. A., & Carr, D. L. (2002). Computer-assisted career assessment. In J. T. Kapes & E. A. Whitfield, (Eds.), *A counselor's guide to career assessment instruments* (4th ed., pp. 47–63). Tulsa, OK: National Career Development Association.

Savickas, M. L. (2003). Advancing the career counseling profession: Objectives and strategies for the next decade. *Career Development Quarterly, 52,* 87–96.

Sciarra, D. T. (2001). School counseling in a multicultural society. In J. G. Ponterotto, J. M. Casas, L. A. Suzuki, & C. M. Alexander (Eds.), *Handbook of multicultural counseling* (2nd ed., pp. 701–728). Thousand Oaks, CA: Sage.

Short, R. J. (1997). Rethinking psychology and the schools: Implications of recent national/policy. *American Psychologist, 52,* 234–240.

Spokane, A. R. (1991). *Career intervention.* Englewood Cliffs, NJ: Prentice-Hall.

Steele, C. M. (1997). A threat in the air: How stereotypes shape the intellectual identity and performance. *American Psychologist, 52,* 613–629.

Steinberg, L., Dornbusch, S. M., & Brown, B. B. (1992). Ethnic differences in adolescent achievement: An ecological perspective. *American Psychologist, 47,* 723–729.

Sue, D. W. (2003). *Overcoming our racism: The journey to liberation.* San Francisco, CA: Jossey-Bass.

Sue, D. W., Carter, R. T., Casas, J. M., Fouad, N. A., Ivey, A. E., Jensen, M., et al. (1998). *Multicultural counseling competencies: Individual and organizational development.* Thousand Oaks, CA: Sage.

Sue, D. W., Ivey, A. E., & Pedersen, P. B. (1996). *A theory of multicultural counseling and therapy.* Pacific Grove, CA: Brooks/Cole.

Sue, D. W., & Sue, D. (2003). *Counseling the culturally different: Theory and practice.* (4th ed.). New York: Wiley.

Sueyoshi, L. A., Rivera, L., & Ponterotto, J. G. (2001). The family genogram as a tool in multicultural career counseling. In J. G. Ponterotto, J. M. Casas, L. A. Suzuki, & C. M. Alexander (Eds.), *Handbook of multicultural counseling* (2nd ed., pp. 655–671). Thousand Oaks, CA: Sage.

Swanson, J. L. (1995). The process and outcome of career counseling. In W. B. Walsh & S. H. Osipow (Eds.), *Handbook of vocational psychology* (2nd ed., pp. 217–259). Mahwah, NJ: Erlbaum.

Tatum, B. D. (1992). Talking about race, learning about racism: The application of racial identity development theory in the classroom. *Harvard Educational Review, 62,* 1–24.

Tolbert, E. L. (1980). *Counseling for career development* (2nd ed.). Boston: Houghton Mifflin.

Tracey, T. J., & Ward, C. C. (1998). The structure of children's interests and competence perceptions. *Journal of Counseling Psychology, 45,* 290–303.

U.S. Equal Employment Opportunity Commission. (2000). Washington, DC: U.S. Government Printing Office.

Ward, C. M., & Bingham, R. P. (1993). Career assessment of ethnic minority women. *Journal of Career Assessment, 1,* 246–257.

Whiston, S. C. (1996). Accountability through action research: Research methods for practitioners. *Journal of Counseling and Development, 74,* 616–623.

Whiston, S. C., Sexton, T. L., & Lasoff, D. L. (1998). Career-intervention outcome: A replication and extension of Oliver and Spokane (1988). *Journal of Counseling Psychology, 45,* 150–165.

Williamson, E. G., & Bordin, E. S. (1941). The evaluation of vocational and educational counseling: A critique of the methodology of experiments. *Educational and Psychological Measurement, 1,* 5–24.

Yoder, J. D. (2000). Women and work. In M. Biaggio & M. Hersen (Eds.), *Issues in the psychology of women* (pp. 71–91). New York: Kluwer/Plenum.

17

ASSESSMENT OF ACCULTURATION

Catherine Collier
Cross-Cultural Developmental Education Services

Alejandro E. Brice
University of Central Florida

Geraldine V. Oades-Sese
Fordham University

It is evident from a review of previous research that the interrelationship of cultural and educational characteristics is central to answering questions about appropriate identification and instruction of culturally and linguistically diverse (CLD) exceptional children. It is also evident from a review of these studies that the results of acculturation research have not been considered in this interrelationship. Indeed, acculturation plays a major role in gaining a better understanding of the education of CLD students (Rogler, Cortés, & Malgady, 1991).

There is ample evidence that cultural, linguistic, and psychological changes occur among populations undergoing acculturation (Berry, 1980, 1994). The usefulness for education personnel of acculturation theory and the measurement of acculturation has been well established (Atkinson, Morten, & Sue, 1998). This is of particular concern for educators because the effects of acculturation are similar to and may be confused with some of the behaviors for which children are referred to special education. Knowledge of the characteristics and needs of the CLD population is incomplete without knowledge of the effects of acculturation upon this population and how acculturation factors relate to exceptionality.

EXPLORATION OF ACCULTURATION THEORY AND RESEARCH

The common concept of acculturation or culture change is that of the melting pot, the complete assimilation of one group into another. However, assimilation is just one of the possible results of the complex process of culture change known as acculturation. Acculturation has been defined and redefined many times during the last seven decades. For example, Redfield, Linton, and Herskovits (1936) define it thus: "Acculturation comprises those phenomena which result when groups of individuals sharing different cultures come into continuous first-hand contact, with subsequent changes in the original culture patterns of either or both groups" (p. 149). Four decades later, Szapocznik, Scopetta, and Kurtines (1978) proposed that acculturation involved changes in two dimensions: behaviors and values. According to Szapocznik and Kurtines (1980), the behavioral dimension of acculturation includes language use and participation in other cultural activities, and the values dimension reflects relational style, person–nature relationships, beliefs about human nature, and time orientation. Padilla (1995) further expanded this understanding of acculturation by suggesting that this process also included cultural awareness and ethnic loyalty. Recently, Cuellar, Arnold, and Maldonado (1995) defined acculturation in terms of changes at three levels of functioning: behavioral, affective, and cognitive, which encompass language, cultural mores and expressions, and emotions that have cultural connections.

Most social scientists would agree with Spicer (1962) that every contact between cultures involves some degree of social and cultural integration. However, there are several ways to look at what happens during this contact and integration process. Before one can understand the dynamic process of culture change, one must consider first what is changing, that is, culture. Culture is a very broad and complex term usually viewed as the shared concept of reality or patterns of interaction, communication, and socialization held in common by a particular group of people.

Education professionals express interest in other people's cultures while regretting that they do not have "a culture" of their own. They must first understand the impact of culture on their own lives. All human beings are raised within a cultural context, and their language and cognitive development occurs within this cultural context. The process of learning this context is called *enculturation*. Enculturation occurs through the child-rearing practices of a group of people (Redfield et al., 1936).

Another aspect of culture is that a group of people, in addition to sharing behavioral patterns and values, also share a common sense of identity. There is an identifiable boundary between members and nonmembers in the particular culture. This self and external identity becomes especially meaningful in the establishment and longevity of ethnic groups.

Many cultural elements or indicators are shared by different cultures, especially those that occur at similar times or in geographic proximity to one another. This sharing is frequently a result of the process of culture change, a dynamic source of some elements within a particular culture at a particular point in time. Culture itself is dynamic, and no two individual members of the cultural group share exactly the same system of cultural knowledge. Social scientists all have a slightly different view of culture, depending on their peculiar perspective. As used in this chapter, culture is a cognitive construct: Culture is whatever it is one has to know or believe in order to operate in a manner acceptable to members of a group. Culture is not a material phenomenon; it does not consist of things, behavior, or emotions. Rather, it is an organization of these things. It is the form of things that people have in mind and their models of perceiving, relating, and otherwise interpreting them.

As used here, culture change, or acculturation, is an adaptation to the presence of two (or more) cultures in the environment. Just as goods and services may be exchanged by the two cultures, so may values, languages, and behavior patterns. Padilla (1980) proposes that there are three stages of culture change: contact, conflict, and adaptation. He posits that any measurement of culture change must consider each of these three stages at both group and individual levels. The purpose of the contact must also be considered. The history, persistence, duration, purpose, and permanence of the contact; the nature of conflict and adaptations to this contact; as well as the individual's exposure to the second culture, interpersonal conflicts, and personal adaptations must all be considered. This includes examining the different adaptation patterns of "voluntary" and "involuntary" minorities (Ogbu & Simons, 1998). For example, less culture change may be expected when the purpose of the contact is mutually desired trade, as in the 19th century between the Tlingits and the British in southeast Alaska, as opposed to the forced exchange between the Russians and Yup'ik in southwest Alaska during the same time period. Voluntary minorities such as Chinese immigrants to America considered education to be an important route to succeeding in society and were less concerned with prejudice and discrimination, as opposed to involuntary minorities such as African Americans (Ogbu & Simons, 1998).

Where there is deliberate extermination of beliefs over a long period of time we find even greater culture change. For example, the Moravian missionaries in Alaska engaged in a systematic destruction of Yup'ik culture (Trennert, 1975). There is almost always some degree of resistance to change, as most cultural groups do not give up valued practices lightly, whether economic, religious, or communicative. This conflict may be manifested in many ways, especially as psychological stress or physical aggression, but will always lead to some form of adaptation. Adaptation is in this sense a reduction of conflict and may take several forms, to be discussed later in the chapter.

Another effect of culture change, of key importance to educators, is *acculturative stress*. This stress is common though not inevitable during culture change (Berry, 1970). Berry (1997) stated that acculturative stress is characterized by deviant behavior, psychosomatic symptoms, and feelings of marginality. As well, Berry (1998) found that variations in stress and culture change patterns were dependent to some extent on the cultural and psychological characteristics of the culture group and the degree and nature of previous contact with culturally diverse groups. This type of stress has particular implications for educators, as the side effects look a lot like the indications of learning disabilities commonly noted for placement of children in special education classes.

Ogbu and Matute-Bianchi (1986) have suggested several other survival strategies as means of coping with cultural change patterns and stress. These have included (a) *passing*, that is, passing as someone else. This may be done by claiming a different descent (i.e., Spanish vs. Mexican American), change of ethnic identification (i.e., Spanish white vs. Hispanic of Indian origin), and personal name changes; (b) *clientship*, that is, developing a patron–client relationship with the dominant culture (e.g., the relationship between laborers and their employers); (c) *caste-leakage*, that is, moving to a larger area where the status of immigration is not so strongly influenced; (d) *collective struggle*, that is, forming a group of organized individuals lobbying together, for example, the League of United Latin American Citizens (LULAC); and (e) *deviant behavior*, that is, forming a group or series of behaviors that are in direct opposition to the dominant group's expectations (e.g., gangs).

In one study of Hispanic culture change, Szapocznik and Kurtines (1980) found that stress from the culture change process could result in emotional and substance abuse problems. This was shown to be a continuing issue in a 1996 study by Short and Porro-Salinas. Stress occurred when family members adjusting to life in mainstream American culture did not integrate their home culture and language with that of the mainstream community. Although living in a community with two languages and cultures, parents and teenagers in the study rejected one culture and tried to identify exclusively with only the other incumbent culture. These families were compared with families where parents and teenagers were bilingual and developed cross-cultural methods of adapting to their new communities. The bilingual and cross-cultural families had fewer incidents of substance abuse and dysfunctional interactions than the "monocultural" families.

Acculturation is a type of culture change that occurs when an enculturated individual comes into the proximity of one or more new or different cultures or subcultures. This may occur by moving into a new environment or location populated by people raised with a different language or culture. It may occur by going to a new school or moving to a new region of the country. It may also occur through exposure to movies, television, and books. The dynamics of acculturation include selective adoption of the new value system and the integration and differentiation processes of that adoption. It refers to the process by which members of one culture or subculture adapt to the presence of another. This adaptation may take varied forms. The process of acculturation may be accompanied by some degree of shock depending on how different the new situation is from that to which the individual is enculturated. This can be very deeply disturbing or only mildly uncomfortable, but it is a normal part of our adaptation to things that are new to us. On the extreme end, refugees can experience several different degrees of this psychological process when surviving and escaping imprisonment, adjusting to life in a refugee camp, and then immigrating to a new country unable to speak that country's language. On the milder end, all children who move frequently will experience this "culture shock" whenever they must leave a school where they have made friends and know the teachers to attend a new school in a new community. There is a recognized pattern of response to acculturation, and those going through this culture shock may go through it in a recurring cyclical manner. Educators who work with CLD students who have learning and behavior problems must address the effects of acculturation in order to give these students appropriate assistance.

Both enculturation and acculturation influence the diverse student's cultural identity. The common concept of acculturation is the "melting pot," that is, the assimilation of one cultural group into another. However, assimilation is only one element of the complex process of acculturation.

Acculturation is the process of adaptation to a new cultural environment. *Assimilation* occurs when the native culture is essentially eliminated from the person's cognitive behavior as the second culture takes its place. This particular acculturative response is actually rather rare; instead, a person more frequently integrates new cultural patterns into the cognitive and behavioral framework of the first culture. For example, a newcomer might assimilate in the sense that he or she learns and uses English in most communications, retaining, however, the habits and speech patterns that reflect the heritage language(s) and how he or she was raised. This more common response to the acculturative process, *integration*, usually results in better mental health. Other examples include where children feel societal pressure to speak English. This is illustrated in the following quote from a teenage student: "I didn't like feel comfortable because everybody knew English, and they would talk to me, and I really didn't understand it." Another example illustrates this point: "I remember once when I was little, and I was playing on the monkey bars, and somebody called me a slow poke. I didn't know what a slow poke was, and everybody started laughing. I remember thinking that it must have been something really horrible because everybody was just looking at me laughing, and I just felt really, really bad." As a consequence of the pressure to learn English, many students may lose their ability to communicate with family and community members in their native language. The various types of acculturative response are discussed in more detail later in this chapter.

There have been several studies done on the impact of integrative acculturation upon the mental health of immigrant families (Bornstein & Cote, 2004; Szapocznik & Kurtines, 1980) and the subsequent cognitive development of children in these families, as examined, for example, by Gonzales and Roll (1985). These studies provide insight into the nature of parenting cognitions generally and those of immigrant mothers specifically, and thus into the parenting climate in which immigrant children are reared.

Of special concern to education professionals are the psychological responses to the acculturation experience that are very similar to indicators of disabling conditions. These experiences may be exacerbated by an inability to communicate associated with normal second language difficulties. Table 17–1 provides commonalities in behaviors seen in second language learning, acculturation, and learning disabilities.

The side effects of acculturation include heightened anxiety, confusion in locus of control, code-switching, silence or withdrawal, distractibility, response fatigue, and other indications of stress response (Collier, 1989; Padilla, 1980; Schnell, 1996; Short & Porro-Salinas, 1996). Another effect of acculturation, previously mentioned, is acculturative stress. Berry (1976) found that some Native American groups experience high stress when the traditional culture is less similar to the second or mainstream culture. Groups experience lower stress when their culture is more similar to the second culture and has greater contact with other cultural groups.

TABLE 17–1

Second Language Learning, Acculturation, and Learning Disabilities: Some Commonalities

Behavior	Second Language Difference	Language Learning Disability	Characteristics of the Disability/Disorder
Inattention	Difficulty processing and understanding spoken and written language.	Attention deficit hyperactivity disorder	Inconsistent with the child's developmental level. The behaviors must persist for at least six months. The behaviors are maladaptive. The behaviors were present in the first language.
Impulsivity	Difficulty processing and understanding spoken and written language. Boredom; frustration. Fatigue with processing a second language.	Attention deficit hyperactivity disorder	The behaviors begin before 7 years of age and were present in the first language. The symptoms are present in at least two environments (e.g., home, school, social settings).
Poor expressive language skills	Limited social interaction with proficient speakers of the target second language. Limited need to communicate. Limited support and feedback from others. Limited second language vocabulary. Difficulty with selection of appropriate vocabulary (e.g., L2 vocabulary interference). Difficulty with second language syntax (e.g., L2 syntactic interference). Silent period or inner-directed learning strategy.	Expressive language disorder	May manifest itself by marked limited vocabulary in both L1 and L2. Making tense errors in L1 and L2. Difficulty recalling words or producing words in both L1 and L2. Sentences may be incomplete of very short according to developmental levels in both L1 and L2. The disorder may interfere with communication at home and school and also interfere with school success.

Source: American Psychiatric Association (2000); Brice (2002); Swain (1985); Wong-Fillmore (1992).

Because students who consistently demonstrate heightened anxiety or stress, confused locus of control, or lack of response are often referred for special services, it is imperative that teachers working with diverse students who are experiencing acculturation consider the psychological "side effects" of acculturation in assessment and programming. Appropriate placement for these students may be in cross-cultural counseling or acculturation assistance programs rather than in a special education program.

Studying other possible effects of acculturation and academic performance, Gonzales and Roll (1985) examined the relationship between acculturation, cognitive style, and intelligence. Findings of this study suggest that cognitive style does not play a particularly important role in an individual's performance on intelligence tests. However, it should be noted that a relationship does seem to exist (i.e., in either the strong or weak versions of the Sapir-Whorf hypotheses). According to Whorf (1956), there is a systematic relationship between semantics and syntax that a person speaks and how that person understands and interacts with the world.

In their 1983 study, Elliott and Argulewicz looked at the influence of student ethnicity on teachers' behavior ratings of normal and learning disabled children using the Devereux Elementary School Behavior Rating scale (DESB; Swift, 1982). Sixty-four learning disabled (LD) or non-LD Anglo and Mexican American second through sixth graders were analyzed to explore the influence of ethnicity and diagnostic label on behavior ratings by Anglo teachers and the relationship between the behavior ratings of a sample of Mexican American children and the normative sample of the DESB. Significant multivariate factors were observed for the main effects of ethnicity and diagnostic label. Univariate analyses of ethnicity revealed that Mexican American and Anglo students were rated as being significantly different on three factors: (a) comprehension, (b) creative initiative, and (c) closeness to the teacher. The LD and non-LD students differed significantly on DESB factors such as Classroom Disturbance, Inattentive-Withdrawn, and Slow Worker. Similar findings occurred in a study 16 years later (Masten, Plata, Wenglar, & Thedford, 1999) where differences between teacher ratings of 87 Anglo-American and 63 Hispanic fifth grade students were compared. Anglo-American students were rated higher on characteristics relating to learning, motivation, creativity, and leadership. Highly acculturated Hispanic students received higher ratings than did less acculturated Hispanics.

The above studies contrast with Collier's (1989) study which looked at 95 Hispanic Limited English Proficient (LEP) elementary students enrolled in bilingual/English as a Second Language (ESL) programs. Of these 95 students, 51 had never been referred to special education, 27 had been referred but not placed, and 17 had been referred and placed in special education within the past two years. Students were compared on 15 acculturation and education variables, acculturation variables that focused on the effect of numerous cultural and linguistic factors on the successful acculturation of CLD students (Adler, 1975; Juffer, 1983; Padilla, 1980), and education variables regularly considered in the referral and placement of any child in special education (Knoff, 1983; Ysseldyke & Algozzine, 1981). Padilla (1980) indicated that there should be only slight individual differences in acculturation variables within a population of the same age, socioeconomic status, and ethnic background. However, Collier (1989) showed that, while CLD children

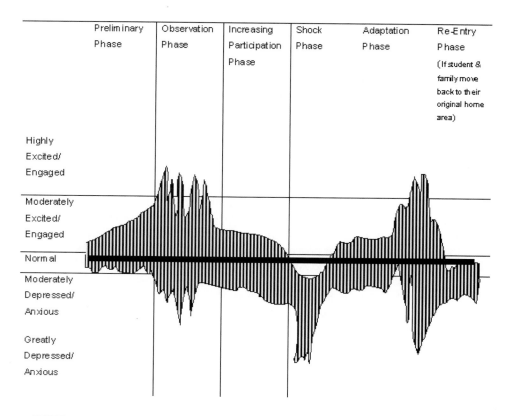

FIGURE 17–1   The pattern of culture shock.

referred to special education did not differ at a statistically significant level on their education profiles, they did differ significantly in acculturation characteristics. Students actually placed appeared to be even more highly acculturated, more bilingual, and more English proficient than either nonreferred or referred/not placed students. Referred but not placed students appeared to be the least acculturated, were the least proficient in English, and had the lowest achievement scores.

IMPLICATION FOR PRACTICE

Studies of the effect of acculturation upon individuals have looked at the various phases involved and the degree of culture shock experienced (Adler, 1975; Juffer, 1983; Schnell, 1996). The experience of acculturating is as varied as the individual students and their families who undergo it and the settings in which it occurs. It is nevertheless informed by a coherent pattern that sets it apart from other kinds of school experience. Figure 17–1 illustrates the ebb and flow of this experience over the course of the individual's adaptation to the new school environment. The figure is a modification of Gullahorn and Gullahorn's W-curve (1963) and Kohls's (1984) research into the psychological process of culture shock for individuals interacting outside of their familiar culture and society.

Each phase delineated by Figure 17–1 is marked by a number of characteristic features, one of which is usually predominant for the individual student in the school setting. The first, or *Preliminary Phase*, includes the initial awareness of the future school environment and school culture, the decision to leave home, preparations for attending school, farewell activities and ceremonies if any, and the effects of the trip from the home to school. This phase is generally marked by a rising sense of anticipation tempered by, or alternating with, regret at leaving home. This phase is also referred to as the Fascination Stage where the newcomer or beginner finds the new environment or situation interesting and exciting. The newcomer puts a lot of energy into listening to the new sounds, intonations, and rhythms of the new language. They may try doing and saying things in the new culture, situation, and language that are interesting to them. They may try out new activities, words, and attitudes with a lot of enthusiasm.

The second phase is usually referred to as the *Observation Phase* and begins with the student's arrival in the new school and ends when the early experiences there begin to decrease. Arrival is usually accompanied by a rising tide of emotions, among which the student may experience seemingly erratic mood swings. Initial impressions, which at first express a sense of the monumentality of the experience, later tend to focus inward at an increasingly unmanageable rate and to devolve at times into barely distinguishable blurs. Throughout this stage the student can be characterized as a largely passive, but alert, observer and listener. This stage can also be accompanied by what is a "silent" speaking phase, wherein the student's verbal output drops dramatically (Krupa-Kwiatkowski, 1998). The Observation Phase usually comes to an end when it becomes no longer feasible to maintain the passive stance toward school culture and when the intensity of the new impressions subsides. The more the newcomer learns about the new situation and tries to speak and act like others in the new environment, the more apparent differences between the new and the previous will become. This may lead to what is termed disenchantment, and sometimes the latter part of the observation phase is called the *Disenchantment Stage* of acculturation. This stage occurs as the newcomer encounters problems with being accepted and with participating in the new environment. At first these problems will be focused on getting basic needs met; later, more complex problems will emerge. There are likely to be problems due to misunderstandings related to language, customs, and mannerisms.

During the third phase, the *Increasing Participation Phase*, the student, sometimes willingly or sometimes unwillingly, begins to take a more active role in the new setting. He or she is now more a participant than an observer. At first, this new role may produce frustration because of the difficulty of coping with even the most elementary aspects of everyday school life and learning. But once a student begins to accept the difficulties inherent in the cross-cultural learning situation, it becomes possible to devote attention to making sense of them, to venture forth and engage oneself, even if only tentatively, in those areas of the school and learning environment that hold at least limited appeal to the student. There comes a point in this phase when the difficulties the student initially encounters may become challenges to accept rather than unpleasant situations to avoid. And, as the number of challenges and accomplishments accumulate, the earlier discouragement often gives way to a growing sense of self-esteem, satisfaction, and self-confidence. Conversely, it is in the increasing participation phase that the cross-cultural learning experience varies the greatest from person to person. Characteristically it involves a clash of cultures, a conflict between one's own culture-based learning behaviors and values and those of the school environment and education personnel. It may result in extreme resistance to adaptation and a more or less straight-line descent into the most serious conditions of culture shock. The disenchantment common at the end of the observation phase often leads to a sense of isolation during the Increasing Participation Phase. This is sometimes referred to as the *Mental Isolation Stage* of acculturation. At this stage, newcomers experience a kind of homesickness. They miss their "home" culture and feel more like an outsider in the new one. They may limit or avoid all contact with the new culture. They may spend more or all of their time with their own culture or language group. This progress of gradual adaptation, fascination, disenchantment, and mental isolation may continue in a repeating cycle for some time without full adjustment. This is especially true with students or young people whose families are moving them in and out of school situations, for example, migrant and seasonal agricultural workers.

For the more flexible student, this cycle may mean a series of small adjustments as problems are overcome one by one. Others experience a series of highs and lows as they surmount barriers to communication and interaction only to discover significant differences in values and perceptions. For those students who are more successful, the phase of increasing participation constitutes an acceptance of, and tentative involvement with, the external manifestations of the school culture. But as the student develops a greater ability to tolerate and cope with the external cultural patterns of the school, little by little they become internalized, relegated to areas of the subconscious. Eventually the individual student acquires alternative ways of learning, behaving, feeling, and responding to others, all of which seem equally valid: one has been instilled by the processes of enculturation at home; the other has been acquired through interaction with schoolmates and school personnel.

At some point during this process, however, that culture shock frequently occurs. This is a kind of crisis of personality, or identity, a period when the individual feels balanced precariously between home and school. It is as though the student's awareness of the ability to function well in the school culture has triggered an awareness of the completeness of his or her separation from the home culture. It is at this *Shock Phase* that learners' efforts can seem artificial and pointless to them. There is a deep sense of the ambiguity of one's position: on the one hand, the newly acquired cultural learning identity opens significantly new vistas of experience, knowledge, and opportunity; yet on the other hand, those vistas are gained through an emerging awareness that all experience is culturally determined. The student at this stage may become concerned that values are fundamentally a fabrication, an illusion, a kind of grand pretense supported by the vast majority of people. Thus the Shock Phase strikes those who achieve some success in their first efforts at adaptation, as well as those who do not. Most individuals who pass through this phase of the experience of acculturation do not recognize it in precisely these terms if, indeed, they recognize it at all.

Usually a student who has been getting along in the school quite well for a good length of time will find him or herself, for no immediately identifiable reason, sunk into a lethargy or depression, indifferent both to classmates and to neighborhood friends and peers. This state can persist and develop to crisis proportions, with the student manifesting a number of symptoms similar to severe psychological disorder. The Shock Phase represents a kind of existential confrontation with the sense of meaninglessness that separates the two cultures the individual has internalized. Once the effects of facing this gulf have abated, subsequent experience usually leads to a more thorough adaptation to school.

Adaptation is the endpoint of the acculturation experience, the point at which the sense of being an alien no longer exists. In learning a second language, the equivalent to adaptation is not so much the achievement of native proficiency as it is surmounting the need to think through what one is going to say before saying it. Now thinking and speaking become simultaneous activities of the mind, the one being merely the internalized aspect of the other. Some theorists refer to this as the *Adjustment* or *Recovery Stage* of acculturation. At this stage, basic needs are met and a routine has been established. There is a noticeable improvement in transition language skills and cross-cultural interactions. Transitions language skills may correspond to formulaic language satisfying immediate and predictable needs, that is, a zero or one on a five-point Likert scale on the International Second Language Proficiency Ratings (Wylie & Ingram, 1999). The newcomer experiences more positive experiences with the new culture and feels more comfortable communicating in the new language or dialect. As those raised in highly mobile families know, over time, adaptation strategies—ways to adjust to and deal with all the changes that help make the next change a little less traumatic—are learned.

For some students and their families there may be an additional phase of acculturation, usually referred to as the *Reentry Phase*. This stage of adaptation may occur if the student or his or her family or both return to their place of origin as is common with the families of international students attending American schools for several years. The student may experience some stress when interacting within their home or heritage culture. The adaptation cycle may be repeated as they reenter their heritage community. This happens frequently with foreign exchange families and students. Refugees experience this when returning to visit surviving family after a change in regime. It is important to remember that this cycle has no end per se. Any event that is new, strange, or unusual can retrigger the process for even the most accomplished participant in cross-cultural interactions.

The graph in Figure 17–1 and the previous description of the pattern of acculturation and its accompanying culture shock should be regarded more as an approximation than as a scientifically accurate and predictive representation of what will happen to a person who undertakes to live and learn in another culture. Just as personalities and situations differ, so is each individual's sense of his or her experience likely to differ from the general pattern. For some students the

Assimilation Home/heritage replaced by school/new culture/ language	**Integration** Home/heritage blended with school/new culture/ language
Deculturation (Marginalization) Acceptance of neither home/heritage nor school/new culture/language	**Rejection** Intentional rejection of home/heritage for school/new culture/ language OR intentional rejection of school/new culture/language for home/heritage

FIGURE 17–2   Acculturation matrix.

initial period of excitement or fascination may be missing or greatly reduced; for others the period of mental isolation or shock may be only barely noticeable or the memory of it may be suppressed; and for still others, there may be no emergence from the frustration and disappointment usually experienced at the outset of the disenchantment occasioned by the increasing participation phase. Still, despite the differences in individual instances, the pattern generally seems to hold for a majority of cases.

Major variables that affect acculturation include the amount of time spent in the process, the quantity and quality of interaction, ethnicity or nation of origin, and particular language proficiency. Wong-Fillmore (1992) has identified several attributes for successful second language learning: (a) a need to communicate; (b) access to speakers from that language (e.g., English); (c) interaction, support, and feedback from speakers of that language; and (d) sufficient time to practice and speak the language. These acculturation variables are especially relevant to assessment for placement in special education. A review of the literature shows several critical factors identified as relating to success in acculturation:

1. Presence of bilingual and ESL programs (Collier, 1989; Finn, 1982).
2. Strength in English language skills (Juffer, 1983).
3. Strength in one or both first and second language skills (Cummins, 1984; Knoff, 1983; Szapocznik & Kurtines, 1980).
4. Length of time in school (Juffer, 1983).

    5. Amount of interaction with mainstream American students (Argulewicz & Elliott 1981; Collier, 1989; Juffer, 1983).

It must be noted that it is extremely important to identify how children are acculturating to the mainstream school environment. A simple grid is discussed here that will assist educators in identifying at a very preliminary level how particular students are handling the acculturation experience. More thorough tools available to the educator and counselor are discussed later in this chapter. The Acculturation Matrix in Figure 17–2 may be used as a type of triage device for school personnel needing a quick estimate of where an individual student is in the acculturation process.

The Acculturation Matrix has quadrants illustrating four types of adaptation to the acculturative experience. It is a modification of the fourfold framework developed by Berry and his colleagues (Berry, Kim, Power, Young, & Bajaki, 1989; Berry, Trimble, & Olmeda, 1986) to organize the acculturation constructs into four generic types, depending on the relative importance of the first culture (F) and the contact culture (C). Berry's four generic types are commonly shown as (a) the contact culture is favored (–F +C), (b) the first culture is favored (+F –C), (c) both are favored (+F +C), or (d) both are disfavored (–F –C). Rather than use the F and C identification, the Acculturation Matrix uses C1 for first culture and L1 for first language and C2 for the contact culture and L2 for the language of the contact culture.

This is illustrated in the Matrix by the four quadrants. To use the Matrix, the education professional should think about a student of concern in relation to the fourfold framework. Matrix users list all the things observed concerning their student related to each of the four acculturation aspects.

In the upper left quadrant is *Assimilation*. This corresponds somewhat to Berry's –F +C. As discussed earlier, assimilation occurs when the home or heritage culture and language are completely replaced by the second or new language and culture. An example of this is the student who stops wearing traditional garb and adopts the clothing of his mainstream peers or who stops attending church with his family and converts wholly to the religion of some new group and regards that replacement as a positive aspect of his or her life. Matrix users will list all the things observed concerning their student where he or she has completely substituted aspects of the mainstream for those in his or her home/heritage, for example, behaviors, words, clothing, manners, or other characteristic patterns.

In the upper right quadrant is *Integration*. This corresponds to Berry's +F +C. In this box, Matrix users will list all of the ways the student of concern has integrated language, behavior, clothing, food, religion, and other characteristic patterns from both the mainstream and his or her home/heritage. An example would be a student who is learning to speak English and uses it appropriately in responses while still speaking his or her heritage language with family members and other members of the speech community, who dresses in American style for school functions but wears appropriate garb for his or her family religious activities, or who eats a hamburger with fries and special ethnic dishes with equal pleasure.

The two quadrants representing Assimilation and Integration on the top half of Figure 17–2 are the positive adaptation responses to acculturation. The two quadrants on the bottom half are negative, destructive responses to acculturation. It is important to identify ways in which a student has positive versus negative elements so that appropriate interventions may be instituted.

The lower right quadrant is *Rejection*, which is similar to assimilation in its being an essentially monocultural response to acculturation, but differs in its intent and impact. Berry's –F +C and +F –C aspects are the flip sides of rejection. Rejection is when a person intentionally, and by deliberate choice and action, chooses to adhere to only one pattern of behavior and language, either their first language/culture or the second language/culture. On the one hand, the person may reject the new culture and language situation and while living in this environment keep using only his or her home or heritage language, practicing only the traditional way of life, food, clothing, shelter, and so forth, with absolutely no attempt at integration. On the flip side of this, the person may intentionally cut himself or herself off from all contact with the home and heritage and reject all use of that language and culture, trying to assimilate to the new environment forcibly by rejecting and denying anything that is not part of the new situation or language. This has been the case as a survival tactic for many refugees whose homelands were destroyed, particularly those traveling to a new world alone and with no hope of ever returning to their past situation. An example is a new arrival temporarily cutting all ties with non-Americans and becoming very negative about "ethnic" activities. There can be a serious long-term psychological price to pay for such rejection, as indicated in Padilla's 1980 research cited earlier. Rejection can be temporary, changing as the newcomer becomes more comfortable with being safe in the adopted country, but identifying and addressing it is critical for education professionals.

An even more serious long-term impact on an individual is posed by *Deculturation* or *Marginalization*. This quadrant corresponds to Berry's –F –C aspect of acculturation. Deculturation is the loss of connection to the traditional, home, or heritage culture and language while not making the transition to the new culture or language. This can result from marginalization. Marginalization represents the attitude of an individual with no interest in maintaining or acquiring proficiency in any culture, native, or host. As a result, the person may lose their ability to speak in any language with proficiency and as a consequence become semi-lingual, a linguistic marginalization (Skutnabb-Kangas, 1981). Deculturation or marginalization can result from not responding with effective interventions to rejection behaviors, but can also occur when children, students, or families are cut off from supportive community interactions within their home or heritage community and are not given assistance to transition into effective participation in the new language, culture, or community situation. An example of this is the gang affiliation and criminal behavior among Mexican American teenagers noted in the research by Szapocznik and Kurtines (1980) cited earlier.

The user should study a student of concern and make note of indications of either deculturation or rejection in his or her behavior and list these in the two lower quadrants in the diagram. These are the priority areas for intervention and are indications of learning and behavior needs that must be addressed to reduce the degree of risk for the student.

Acculturation Screening Tools: An Overview

Early acculturation studies conceptualized acculturation as a process taking place along a single or unilinear continuum (Szapocznik et al., 1978). "According to the unilinear model, acculturation occurs when a person moves from one end of a continuum, reflecting involvement in the culture of origin, to the other end of the same continuum, reflecting involvement in the host culture" (Kim & Abreu, 2001, p. 397). Many of the current instruments used to measure acculturation are dual-cultural unilinear measurements based on a single continuum, with one end reflecting high adherence to the indigenous culture and the other indicating high adherence to the dominant culture. Szapocznik, Kurtines, and Fernandez (1980) developed the first bilinear measurement model of acculturation in which one continuum represented either cultural involvement or marginality, while the other continuum reflected either monoculturalism or biculturalism. There have been several formal and informal screening tools developed to measure and monitor the level and rate of acculturation. In the United States these tools have been primarily developed to study the adaptation of Spanish-speaking students from Mexico, Cuba, and Puerto Rico. There are also specific tools to assess the acculturation of Asian American, African American, and Native American backgrounds. Table 17–2 compares the most recent of these tools by language focus, age range, and other factors.

Acculturation of Diverse Populations

There are a number of instruments specifically designed to examine the acculturation of multiple groups of diverse learners and a few that can be used for intergroup acculturation measurement. The *Acculturation, Habits, and Interests Multicultural Scale for Adolescents* (AHIMSA; Unger, Gallaher, & Shakib, 2002) acculturation scale was developed for examining acculturation of adolescents from diverse backgrounds. Previous research had shown that few acculturation scales are appropriate for adolescent surveys because they are too long, are not applicable to differing ethnic groups, or are language based only. The AHIMSA was developed in Los Angeles and measures U.S. orientation (Assimilation), other country orientation (Separation), both countries orientation (Integration), and neither country orientation (Marginalization).

The *Minority–Majority Relations Scale* (Sodowsky, Lai, & Plake, 1991) examined the effects of sociocultural variables on acculturation attitudes of Asian and Hispanic students. Among the subjects, 82% saw a relationship between their culture and their identity. Asian Americans perceived racial discrimination significantly more than did the Hispanics. On the three subscales, respondents who were first-generation immigrants perceived more prejudice, were less acculturated, and used less English than did those who were second, third, and fourth generation. Political refugees perceived more prejudice, were more closely affiliated with their cultural groups, and used English less than did voluntary immigrants. Those who observed Eastern religions were the least acculturated, and Protestants the most. Statistics reported include tests of internal consistency, confirmatory factor analy-

TABLE 17-2
Comparison of Acculturation Measurement

Title/Author	Source	Range	Purpose	Ethnic Focus	Language Focus	Results	Research Example
Acculturation, Habits, and Interests Multicultural Scale for Adolescents (AHIMSA; Unger et al., 2002).	2002 Journal of Early Adolescence	Grade 6	Measures acculturation associated with adolescent health-risk behaviors.	Multicultural	English	Measures orientation to U.S., orientation to home country, integration, and marginalization.	n/a
Acculturation Quick Screen (AQS; Collier, 2000).	1987/2002 NABE Theory Research and Application	6–20 years old, grades 1–12	Measures level and rate of acculturation to public schools in U.S. and Canada.	All indigenous, immigrant, refugee, and migrant groups in U.S. and Canada.	English and all languages and dialects	Five levels of acculturation with specific recommendations for strategies to facilitate integration.	Compared differences among Hispanic students who were or might be referred and placed in special education.
Acculturation Scale for Vietnamese Adolescents (ASVA; Nguyen, Meesé & Stollack, 1999)	1999/2002 International Journal of Behavioral Development	10–23 years old	Measures the bi-dimensional acculturation of Vietnamese adolescents.	Vietnamese	Vietnamese English	Involvement in U.S. culture predicted positive functioning in personal, interpersonal, and achievement domains.	Used to study the adaptation of Vietnamese middle and high school students in Michigan.

Instrument	Year	Source	Population	Description	Ethnicity	Language	Results	Usage
Brief Acculturation Scale for Hispanics (Norris, Ford, & Bova, 1996)	1996	Hispanic Journal of Behavioral Sciences	Adolescents, young adults	Measures acculturation of adolescents living in urban, low-income households.	Puerto Rican Mexican Americans	English	Results support the use of this measure of acculturation as a simple, inexpensive measure that involves minimal respondent burden	n/a
Children's Hispanic Background Scale (Martinez, Norman, & Delany, 1984)	1984	Hispanic Journal of Behavioral Sciences	Elementary school	Measures acculturation of Hispanic children after attending U.S. schools.	Hispanic Chicano	English/Spanish	Focused on Spanish usage, food preference, and general cultural exposure.	Used to study Chicano fourth graders.
Latino Youth Acculturation Scale (LYAS; Pillen & Hoewing-Roberson, 1992)	1992	Chicago Public Schools	Grades 5–8	Measures level of acculturation for Latino youth.	Puerto Rican/Mexican/Latino	Spanish/English	Four key factors appear to drive acculturation: family identity, self/peer identity, customs, and food.	Used to compare with high-risk behavior rate.
Mexican American Acculturation Scale (Montgomery, 1992)	1992	Hispanic Journal of Behavioral Sciences	Secondary	Measures variation in cultural adaptation within school.	Mexican American	English	Looked at extent of cultural orientation and comfort with ethnic identity.	Compared three student populations in Texas.

Table 17–2 (continued)

369

TABLE 17–2
(continued)

Title/Author	Source	Range	Purpose	Ethnic Focus	Language Focus	Results	Research Example
Orthogonal Cultural Identification Scale (OCIS; Oetting & Beauvais, 1991)	1985 Psychological Reports	All	Measures identification with a traditional culture vs. identification with other cultures.	All ethnic groups	English	Has been validated for: Native American youth & adult Mission Indians, as well as other populations.	Compared ethnic identification of Asian American university students vs. acculturation using the Suinn-Lew Scale (1987); compared Native American and Anglo American adolescents.
Short Acculturation Scale for Hispanic Youth (SASH-Y; Barona & Miller, 1994)	1994 Hispanic Journal of Behavioral Sciences	Grades 5–8	Modification of an existing acculturation scale for Hispanic adults	Hispanic youth	Spanish/English (assumed)	Analysis indicated relevance of extrafamilial and familial language use, and ethnic social relations.	n/a
Societal, Attitudinal, Familial, & Environmental Acculturative Stress Scale – Rev./ D. (SAFE; Chavez, 1997) Original author A. Padilla	1997/1985 Hispanic Journal of Behavioral Sciences	8–10 years-old	Measures level of acculturative stress	Latino	Spanish/English (assumed)	U.S.-born Latinos experienced significantly more acculturative stress than mainstream peers	Compared U.S.-born Latino and Euro-American children ages 8–10; has also been specifically adapted for Korean American adolescents.

Suinn-Lew Asian Self-Identity Acculturation Scale (SL-ASIA; Suinn, Rickard-Figueroa, Lew, & Virgil, 1987)	1992/1987 Educational & Psychological Measurement	Students	Modeled after a successful Hispanic scale to apply to Asian subjects	Asian	English	Reliability and validity data reported for two samples of Asian subjects	Revalidated with Chinese- and Filipino-Americans; 18 years and older

sis, and coefficients of factor congruence across two samples, indicating high levels of reliability and content validity.

Phinney (1992) developed a questionnaire called the *Multigroup Ethnic Identity Measure* based on the elements of ethnic identity that are common across groups so that it can be used with all ethnic groups. The questionnaire was administered to Asian American, African American, Hispanic, White, Native American, and mixed background college and high school students.

The *Acculturation Quick Screen* (AQS; Collier, 2000) was developed to assess the level and rate of acculturation of students from diverse cultural and linguistic backgrounds attending public schools in the United States and Canada. It has been used successfully with students at all grade levels, K–12, and from such diverse language and cultural backgrounds as African American, Russian, Somali, Guatemalan, Vietnamese, Spanish, Chinese, Bosnian, Navajo, Ukrainian, Laotian, Hmong, Mexican, Slovak, Tongan, Japanese, and indigenous populations from North, Central, and South America.

The Acculturation Quick Screen (AQS)

The AQS is discussed in depth here because it is not specific to any one language or ethnic group and is used to measure the relative level and rate of acculturation of students to public school culture throughout the United States and Canada. It is a specific tool for school psychologists and general education personnel, which measures adaptation to academic instructional settings. The AQS is based on research (cited earlier) on the factors that predict the degree of successful integration for those who are experiencing culture shock.

Because students acculturate to new environments at different rates it is often difficult to tell who is still experiencing difficulty and who is not. The AQS measures this acculturation and leads directly to strategies to address culture shock. The AQS can also be used to monitor the rate of acculturation of diverse students. Most diverse students will acculturate gradually over several years and at a steady rate relative to the elements measured on the AQS. Those who do not show change year to year may have some unidentified difficulty or may be having some other destabilizing stressful experience. Thus the AQS can be used to separate difference from disability concerns when diverse learners exhibit learning and behavior problems. It can also be used to monitor the adaptation progress being made by migrant, immigrant, and refugee students and provide an early warning system for education personnel when something is not working correctly or most effectively for these students within the school or district.

The AQS measures the student's approximate level and rate of acculturation to mainstream American school culture. It is not intended for use in isolation or as a predictive tool, but provides a useful piece of supplemental assessment information when students from diverse cultural and linguistic backgrounds enroll in a school district. It should be part of the screening routinely done to determine eligibility for newcomers or other special language or culture assistance services. In addition, it is recommended for use as part of the information gathered to make instructional decisions during the pre-referral intervention period or for prevention/intervention instructional activities. It may be used to plan the selection of specific intensive learning and behavior interventions for culturally/linguistically diverse students rather than referring them to an evaluation and staffing. The AQS is also useful for substantiating decisions to modify testing evaluation and assessment procedures. In general, students scoring at the lower acculturation levels should not be assessed with standardized assessment instruments without case-specific modification of administration and interpretation. The AQS provides documentation and guidance to school psychologists and other evaluation specialists working with CLD students.

The AQS should be administered at least four weeks after students have entered the school. This will allow the user to assess their language abilities and to obtain previous school records. This first AQS will be the baseline from which to measure rate and level of acculturation. Students should be assessed every year at the same time to obtain an ongoing record and documentation of their rate of adaptation to the school system. The results map against a range from less acculturated to more acculturated on a 48-point scale. The AQS measures five levels of acculturation: (a) significantly less acculturated, (b) less acculturated, (c) in transition, (d) more acculturated, and (e) significantly more acculturated. The average rate of acculturation is between 10% and 12% each school year, depending on type of program offered to students. Students from diverse cultural and linguistic backgrounds will vary in their rate and level of acculturation to public school culture, but all are affected by various factors. These include individual characteristics of the students and their school.

Although any student may be assessed with the AQS, it is most useful for students who come from a cultural or linguistic background that differs significantly from the mainstream of their particular public school. For example, the AQS will be useful with an American student from an ethnically, linguistically, or racially diverse background who may be demonstrating learning or behavior difficulties. It also provides a significant profile for placement of refugee or immigrant students.

This chapter has focused primarily on the nature and measurement of acculturation as a critical element in the education of diverse learners. But testing is merely an interesting exercise unless it results in instructionally meaningful information that is used to improve student learning and achievement. Almost all of the instruments mentioned can be used to profile various aspects of the acculturation of diverse learners; however, profiles are not helpful unless they inform and guide instruction and services.

The questions of great practical significance for school professionals are (a) to what degree can the student's pattern of culture shock be remedied, (b) what are the most effective strategies for maintaining a normal rate of acculturation, and (c) what are the most effective strategies to facilitate the student's adaptation and success? With children experiencing acculturation, strategies should be as diversified as their responses to culture shock.

Effective Strategies

Strategy selection and implementation must be based on data delineating the student's rate and level of acculturation. This data can be elicited from many of the acculturation measurement tools cited earlier. For example, based on the current student sample (from western states), the average minimal rate of acculturation on the AQS is 11% per annum. Students scored annually who do not achieve or maintain this rate need immediate intervention, as they may not be receiving appropriate instructional support or intervention or may have some other contributing factor. Most LEP immigrants receiving substantial assistance through either bilingual or ESL programs make more than a 12% gain on the AQS per annum. By monitoring the students' rate of acculturation annually, school personnel can identify when students are not receiving appropriate or effective instruction support. By measuring their level of acculturation, school personnel can make instructional implementation decisions consistent with best practice. Following are recommended strategies found to be effective for students at various levels of acculturation.

Significantly less acculturated.   This student is at the beginning stage of adjustment to the school environment and is probably experiencing severe culture shock and several symptoms of acculturative stress such as distractibility, response fatigue, withdrawal, silence or not responding, code-switching, and confusion in locus of control. This student should be receiving assistance with the acculturation process via culturally and linguistically appropriate instruction, ESL instruction, and bilingual instruction in content areas. This student should not be tested with standardized assessment and diagnostic tools without cross-cultural and bilingual modifications in all aspects of the evaluation process and interpretation. Interventions appropriate for significantly less acculturated students include translation, interpretation, and modification of normed instruments; assistance with acculturation process; bilingual assistance and bilingual materials; cross-cultural communication strategies and first language instruction in content areas; school survival and adaptation assistance; and sheltered instruction. Other techniques and strategies appropriate for and effective with significantly less acculturated students include relaxation techniques, Total Physical Response (TPR), and survival strategies.

Less acculturated.   The student scoring as less acculturated is at a critical phase in his or her cross-cultural adaptation and may exhibit high levels of anxiety followed by periods of depression due to the intensity of the adjustment he or she is facing. Care should be used at this stage because this phase can be accompanied by a variety of unexpected emotional reactions. The emotional reactions can be accompanied by signs of culture shock and symptoms of acculturative stress such as distractibility, response fatigue, withdrawal, silence or not responding, code-switching, and confusion in locus of control. This student should be receiving assistance not only with the acculturation process but also with stress reduction and positive coping methods. Instructional adaptations should include culturally and linguistically appropriate instruction, ESL instruction, and bilingual instruction in content areas.

This student should not be tested with standardized assessment and diagnostic tools without cross-cultural and bilingual modifications in all aspects of the evaluation process and interpretation. Interventions appropriate for less acculturated students include (a) translation, interpretation, and modification of normed instruments; (b) assistance with acculturation process; (c) bilingual assistance and bilingual materials; (d) cross-cultural communication strategies and first language instruction in content areas; (e) school survival and adaptation assistance; and (f) sheltered instruction. Also appropriate for and effective with less acculturated students are language transition instruction, mediated stimuli in the classroom, role playing, self-monitoring, sheltered instruction, and others.

More acculturated. Although students at this stage are fairly well acculturated, they will still have some cross-cultural education needs. They may be as well acculturated as many of their classmates. Their cross-cultural education needs can be met with conventional mainstream instruction, assessment, and diagnostic procedures with sheltered instruction and minor adjustment for differences in cognitive learning style. They may need encouragement to participate in diverse community activities to strengthen and maintain their connection to ethnic heritage. Interventions appropriate for more acculturated students include (a) cultural adaptation of content, (b) access to translation as needed, (c) training in cross-cultural communication, and (d) cross-cultural cognitive learning strategies. Other techniques and strategies appropriate for and effective with more acculturated students include cognitive learning strategies, self-monitoring, conflict resolution techniques, and others.

Highly acculturated. The highly acculturated student may have some cross-cultural education needs, but conventional mainstream instruction, assessment, and diagnostic procedures should be possible without adaptation. Differences in cognitive learning style should be addressed. These students may need assistance in remaining connected to their ethnic community and encouraged to enhance and maintain their high level of bilingual proficiency. They may need assistance with strengthening their cross-cultural competence. Interventions appropriate for highly acculturated students include (a) access to translation as needed, (b) opportunities to assist as peer tutors, (c) training in cross-cultural communication, (d) opportunities to participate in ethnic community activities, and (e) cross-cultural cognitive learning strategies. These and other strategies specifically effective for families of students may be found in textbooks and on the Internet.[1]

SUMMARY AND IMPLICATIONS FOR FUTURE RESEARCH

The key purpose of this chapter is to raise awareness of the fact that students who are in the process of adapting to a new culture/social environment may behave in a manner that is similar to a learning disability or other inhibiting factor. Examples and preliminary strategies are provided. The evaluation of diverse students for eligibility in special education programs must include the assessment and consideration of these observable consequences of culture shock that may be confused with the commonly used criteria for learning or emotional disabilities. Where students are significantly less acculturated as measured by any of the various tools described in this chapter, assessment and evaluation personnel must modify their evaluation procedures and choice of assessment tools to reflect the level of acculturation. The interpretation of evaluation findings must also include discussion of

---

[1]Specifically, *Separating Difference from Disability* by C. Collier (2004) and http://www.crosscultured.com

the impact of the students' level and rate of acculturation as a factor contributing to all evaluation findings. Furthermore, research on the relationship of acculturation levels and learning, acculturation, and biculturalism and their effects on adjustment are important to help optimize the allocation of limited resources within the school and the district, while providing each student with the most appropriate assistance. Continued research comparing acculturation across immigrant groups and additional studies developing and validating more measures of acculturation is clearly needed. This research would contribute significantly to a better understanding of the cultural enablers and the contextual factors that are essential to the development and academic advancement of culturally and linguistically diverse students.

Further directions for research include examination of the impact on acculturation of burgeoning electronic communications and computer-based media, as students are bombarded with American images and culture. This may prove to be offset to some degree by the ubiquity of the Internet as it facilitates maintained and increased contact with home cultures left behind; however, the presence of the World Wide Web demands the revalidation of many of the studies, benchmarks, and tenets used in acculturation evaluation today.

RESOURCES

Chun, K. M., Balls-Organista, P., & Marin, G. (Eds.). (2002). *Acculturation: Advances in theory, measurement, and applied research.* Washington, DC: American Psychological Association.

Collier, C. (2004). *Separating difference from disability: Assessing diverse learners.* Ferndale, WA: CrossCultural Developmental Education Services.

Harper, F. D., & McFadden, J. (Eds.). (2003). *Culture and counseling: New approaches.* Boston: Allyn & Bacon.

Ruiz-de-Velasco, J., & Fix, M. (2000). *Overlooked and underserved: Immigrant students in U.S. secondary schools.* Washington, DC: Urban Institute.

Witkin, H. A., & Berry, J. W. (1975). Psychological differentiation in cross cultural perspective. *Journal of Cross Cultural Psychology, 6,* 4–87.

Ysseldyke, J. E., & Algozzine, B. (1981). Special education services for normal children: Better safe than sorry? *Exceptional Children, 48,* 238–243.

Acculturation Measures of Children, Adolescents, and Families

Abe-Kim, J., Okazaki, S., & Goto, S. G. (2001). Unidimensional versus multidimensional approaches to the assessment of acculturation for Asian American populations. *Cultural Diversity and Ethnic Minority Psychology, 7,* 232–246.

Cabassa, L. J. (2003). Measuring acculturation: Where we are and where we need to go. *Hispanic Journal of Behavioral Sciences, 25,* 127–146.

Dana, R. H. (1996). Assessment of acculturation in Hispanic populations. *Hispanic Journal of Behavioral Sciences, 18,* 317–328.

Eshel, Y., & Rosenthal-Sokolov, M. (2000). Acculturation attitudes and sociocultural adjustment of sojourner youth in Israel. *Journal of Social Psychology, 140,* 677–691.

Mendoza-Newman, M. C., Greene R. L., & Velasquez, R. J. (2000). Acculturation, SES, and the MMPI-A performance of Hispanic adolescents. (ERIC Document Reproduction Service No. ED450295).

Montgomery, G. T. (1992). Comfort with acculturation status among students from south Texas. *Hispanic Journal of Behavioral Sciences, 14*, 201–223.

Negy, C., & Woods, D. J. (1991). Mexican- and Anglo-American differences on the Psychological Screening Inventory. (ERIC Document Reproduction Service No. ED333296).

Norris, A. E., Ford, K., & Bova, C. A. (1996). Psychometrics of a Brief Acculturation Scale for Hispanics in a probability sample of urban Hispanic adolescents and young adults. *Hispanic Journal of Behavioral Sciences, 18*, 29–38.

Ponterotto, J. G., Baluch, S., & Carielli, D. (1998). The Suinn-Lew Asian Self-Identity Acculturation Scale (SL-ASIA): Critique and research recommendations. *Measurement and Evaluation in Counseling and Development, 31*, 109–124.

Ratzlaff, C., LeRoux, J., Nishinohara, H., Vogt, A. L., Kim, C., & Matsumoto, D. (1998). ICAPS: A New Scale of Intercultural Adjustment II. (ERIC Document Reproduction Service No. ED430171).

Serrano, E. & Anderson, J. (2003). Assessment of a refined short acculturation scale for Latino preteens in rural Colorado. *Hispanic Journal of Behavioral Sciences, 25*, 240–253.

Unger, J. B., Gallahen, P., Shakib, S., Ritt-Olson, A., Palmer, P. H., & Johnson, C. A. (2002). The AHIMSA acculturation scale: A new measure of acculturation for adolescents in a multicultural society. *Journal of Early Adolescence, 22*, 225–251.

Whitney, J. M. (2002). Using the MMPI/MMPI–2 with the Hispanic/Latino population. (ERIC Document Reproduction Service No. ED469602).

Wolfe, M. M., Yang, P. H., Wong, E. C., & Atkinson, D. R. (2001). Design and development of the European American Values Scale for Asian Americans. *Cultural Diversity and Ethnic Minority Psychology, 7*, 274–283.

Zea, M. C., Asner-Self, K. K, Birman, D., & Buki, L. P. (2003). The abbreviated multidimensional acculturation scale: Empirical validation with two Latino/Latina samples. *Cultural Diversity and Ethnic Minority Psychology, 9*, 107–126.

REFERENCES

Adler, P. S. (1975). The transitional experience: An alternative view of culture shock. *Journal of Humanistic Psychology, 151*, 13–23.

American Psychiatric Association. (2000). *Diagnostic and statistical manual of mental disorders* (4th ed.). Washington, DC: Author.

Argulewicz, E. D., & Elliott, S. N. (1981). *Validity of the SRBCSS for Hispanic and gifted students*. Paper presented at the meeting of the American Psychological Association, Los Angeles, CA.

Atkinson, D. R., Morten, G., & Sue, D. W. (1998). *Counseling American minorities* (5th ed.). Boston: McGraw-Hill.

Barona, A., & Miller, J. A. (1994). Short Acculturation Scale for Hispanic Youth (SASH-Y): A preliminary report. *Hispanic Journal of Behavioral Sciences, 16*, 155–162.

Berry, J. W. (1970). Marginality, stress and ethnic identification in an acculturated aboriginal community. *Journal of Cross Culture Psychology, 1*, 239–252.

Berry, J. W. (1976). *Human ecology and cognitive style: Comparative studies in cultural psychological adaptation.* New York: Sage/Halstead.

Berry, J. W. (1980). Acculturation as varieties of adaptation. In A. Padilla (Ed.), *Acculturation: Theory, models and some new findings* (pp. 9–27). Boulder, CO: Westview.

Berry, J. W. (1994). Acculturation and psychological adaptation: An overview. In A. Bouvy, F. J. R. van de Vijver, P. Boski, & P. Schmitz (Eds.), *Journeys into cross-cultural psychology* (pp. 129–141). Amsterdam: Swets & Zeitlinger.

Berry, J. W. (1997). Immigration, acculturation and adaptation. *Applied Psychology: An International Review, 46,* 5–68.

Berry, J. W. (1998). Acculturation and health: Theory and research. In S. S. Kazarian & D. R. Evans (Eds.), *Cultural clinical psychology: Theory, research and practice* (pp. 39–57). New York: Oxford University Press.

Berry, J. W., Kim, U., Power, S., Young, M., & Bajaki, M. (1989). Acculturation attitudes in plural societies. *Applied Psychology: An International Review, 38,* 185–206.

Berry, J. W., Trimble, J. E., & Olmeda, E. L. (1986). Assessment of acculturation. In W. J. Lonner & J. W. Berry (Eds.), *Field methods in cross-cultural research* (pp. 291–324). Newbury Park, CA: Sage.

Bornstein, M. H., & Cote, L. R. (2004). Mothers' parenting cognitions in cultures of origin, acculturating cultures, and cultures of destination. *Child Development, 75,* 221–235.

Brice, A. (2002). *The Hispanic child: Speech, language, culture and education.* Boston: Allyn & Bacon.

Chavez, D. V. (1997). Acculturative stress in children: A modification of the SAFE Scale. *Hispanic Journal of Behavioral Sciences, 19,* 34–44.

Collier, C. (1989). Comparison of acculturation and education characteristics of referred and non-referred culturally and linguistically different children. In L. M. Malave (Ed.), *NABE theory, research and application: Selected papers.* Buffalo, NY: State University of New York.

Collier, C. (2000). *Acculturation Quick Screen.* Ferndale, WA: CrossCultural Developmental Education Services.

Collier, C., & Pennington, L. (1997). Annual performance report for Eleanor Roosevelt Bilingual Literacy Project. (Report to Department of Education, Title VII).

Cuellar, I., Arnold, B., & Maldonado, R. (1995). Acculturation Rating Scale for Mexican Americans II: A revision of the original ARSMA scale. *Hispanic Journal of Behavioral Science, 17,* 275–304.

Cummins, J. (1984). *Bilingualism and special education: Issues in assessment and pedagogy.* Avon, England: Multilingual Matters.

Elliott, S., & Argulewicz, E. (1983). The influence of student ethnicity on teachers' behavior ratings of normal and learning disabled children. *Hispanic Journal of Behavioral Sciences, 5,* 337–345.

Finn, J. D. (1982). Patterns in special education placement as revealed by the OCR surveys. In K. A. Heller, W. H. Holtzmann, & S. Messich (Eds.), *Placing children in special education: A strategy for equity.* Washington, DC: National Academy Press.

Gonzales, R. R., & Roll, S. (1985) Relationship between acculturation, cognitive style, and intelligence: A cross-sectional study. *Journal of Cross-Cultural Psychology, 16,* 190–205.

Gullahorn, J. T., & Gullahorn, J. E. (1963). An extension of the U-curve hypothesis. *Journal of Social Issues, 19,* 33–47.

Juffer, K. A. (1983). Initial development and validation of an instrument to access degree of culture adaptation. In R. J. Bransford (Ed.), *Monograph series 4.* Boulder, CO: BUENO Center for Multicultural Education.

Kim, B. S. K., & Abreu, J. M. (2001). Acculturation measurement: Theory, current instruments, and future directions. In J. G. Ponterotto, J. M. Casas, L. A. Suzuki, & C. M. Alexander (Eds.), *Handbook of multicultural counseling* (2nd ed., pp. 394–424). Thousand Oaks, CA: Sage.

Knoff, H. M. (1983). Effect of diagnostic information on special education placement decisions. *Exceptional Children, 49*, 440–444.

Kohls, L. R. (1984). *Survival kit for overseas living.* Yarmouth, ME: Intercultural.

Krupa-Kwiatkowski, M. (1998). "You shouldn't have brought me here!": Interaction strategies in the silent period on an inner-directed second language learner. *Research on Language and Social Interaction, 31*, 133–175.

Martinez, R., Norman, R. D., & Delany, H. D. (1984) A children's Hispanic background scale. *Hispanic Journal of Behavioral Sciences, 6*, 103–112.

Masten, W., Plata, M., Wenglar, K., & Thedford, J. (1999) Acculturation and teacher ratings of Hispanic and Anglo-American students. *Roeper Review, 22*, 64–65.

Montgomery, G. T. (1992). Comfort with acculturation status among students from South Texas. *Hispanic Journal of Behavioral Sciences, 14*, 201–223.

Nguyen, H. H., Messé, L. A., & Stollak, G. E. (1999). Toward a more complex understanding of acculturation and adjustment: Cultural involvements and psychosocial functioning in Vietnamese youth. *Journal of Cross-Cultural Psychology, 30*, 5–31.

Norris, A. E., Ford, K., & Bova, C. A. (1996). Psychometrics of a Brief Acculturation Scale for Hispanics in a probability sample of urban Hispanic adolescents and young adults. *Hispanic Journal of Behavioral Sciences, 18*, 29–38.

Oetting, E. R., & Beauvais, F. (1991). Orthogonal cultural identification theory: The cultural identification of minority adolescents. *International Journal of Addictions, 25*, 655–685.

Ogbu, J., & Matute-Bianchi, M. E. (1986). Understanding sociocultural factors: Knowledge, identity and school adjustment. In California State Department of Education (Ed.), *Beyond language: Social and cultural factors in schooling language minority students* (pp. 73–142). Los Angeles: Evaluation Dissemination and Assessment Center, California State University.

Ogbu, J., & Simons, H. D. (1998). Voluntary and involuntary minorities: A cultural-ecological theory of school performance with some implications for education. *Anthropology and Education Quarterly, 29*, 155–188.

Padilla, A. (Ed.). (1980). Acculturation: Theory, models, and some new findings. *American Association for the Advancement of Science, Symposium Series 39*. Boulder, CO: Westview.

Padilla, A. (Ed.). (1995). *Hispanic psychology.* Thousand Oaks, CA: Sage.

Phinney, J. S. (1992). The Multigroup Ethnic Identity Measure: A new scale for use with diverse groups. *Journal of Adolescent Research, 7*, 156–176.

Pillen, M. B., & Hoewing-Roberson, R. C. (1992). *Development of an acculturation measure for Latino youth.* Unpublished paper. Chicago: Chicago Public Schools. (ERIC Document Reproduction Service No. ED 352 411).

Redfield, R., Linton, R., & Herskovits, M. J. (1936). Memorandum on the study of acculturation. *American Psychologist, 38*, 149–152.

Rogler, L. H., Cortés, D. E., & Malgady, R. G. (1991). Acculturation and mental health status among Hispanics: Convergence and new directions for research. *American Psychologist, 46*, 585–597.

Schnell, J. (1996). *Understanding the shock in culture shock.* Unpublished paper. (ERIC Document Reproduction Service No. ED 398 616).

Short, J. L., & Porro-Salinas, P. M. (1996*). Acculturation, coping and psychological adjustment of Central American immigrants.* Paper presented at annual meeting of the American Psychological Association, Toronto, Canada.

Skutnabb-Kangas, T. (1981). *Bilingualism or not: The education of minorities.* Clevedon, England: Multilingual Matters.

Sodowsky, G. R., Lai, E. W. M., & Plake, B. S. (1991). Moderating effects of sociocultural variables on acculturation attitudes of Hispanics and Asian Americans. *Journal of Counseling & Development, 70,* 194–204.

Spicer, E. (1962). *Cycles of conquest: The impact of Spain, Mexico, and the United States on the Indians of the southwest, 1533–1960.* Tucson: University of Arizona Press.

Suinn, R. M., Rickard-Figueroa, K., Lew, S., & Vigil, P. (1987). The Suinn-Lew Asian Self-Identity Acculturation Scale: An initial report. *Educational and Psychological Measurement, 47,* 401–407.

Swain, M. (1985). Communicative competence: Some roles of comprehensible input and comprehensible output in its development. In S. Gass & C. Madden (Eds.), *Input in second language acquisition* (pp. 235–256). Rowley, MA: Newbury House.

Swift, M. (1982). *Devereux Elementary School Behavior Rating scale II (DESB-II).* Villanova, PA: Devereux Foundation.

Szapocznik, J., & Kurtines, W. (1980). Acculturation, biculturalism and adjustment among Cuban Americans. In A. Padilla (Ed.), *Acculturation: Theory, modes, and some new findings. American Association for the Advancement of Science, Symposium Series 39* (pp. 139–159). Boulder, CO: Westview.

Szapocznik, J., Kurtines, W. M., & Fernandez, T. (1980). Bicultural involvement and adjustment in Hispanic-American youths. *International Journal of Intercultural Relations, 4,* 353–365.

Szapocznik, J., Scopetta, M. A., & Kurtines, W. (1978). Theory and measurement of acculturation. *Interamerican Journal of Psychology, 12,* 113–120.

Trennert, R. A. (1975) *Alternative to extinction: Federal Indian policy and the beginnings of the reservation system, 1846–51.* Philadelphia: Temple University Press.

Unger, J. B., Gallaher, P., Shakib, S. (2002). The AHIMSA Acculturation Scale: A new measure of acculturation for adolescents in a multicultural society. *Journal of Early Adolescence, 22,* 225–251.

Whorf, B. L. (1956). *Language, thought and reality.* Cambridge: Massachusetts Institute of Technology.

Wong-Fillmore, L. W. (1992). *When does 1 + 1 = < 2?* Paper presented at Bilingualism/Bilingüismo: A Clinical Forum, Miami, FL.

Wylie, E., & Ingram, D. (1999). *International second language proficiency ratings.* Brisbane, Australia: Griffith University.

Ysseldyke, J. E., & Algozzine, B. (1981). Diagnostic classification decision as a function of referral information. *Journal of Special Education, 15,* 429–435.

18

ACADEMIC ASSESSMENT OF BILINGUAL AND ENGLISH LANGUAGE LEARNING STUDENTS

Danielle Martines and Ofelia Rodriquez-Srednicki
Montclair State University

This chapter focuses on the academic assessment of students who are bilingual students and English language learners (ELLs), a subgroup of culturally and linguistically diverse (CLD) students who are at varying stages of second language acquisition and bilingual proficiency. Curriculum-Based Assessment (CBA) procedures are emphasized as useful in assessing the academic functioning of these students when applied in the context of cultural and language factors. Issues related to culture, bilingualism, and second language development are highlighted in view of their importance to academic performance and academic assessment methods.

BILINGUAL AND ELL STUDENTS

According to the U.S. Department of Education (2005) there were more than 4 million Limited English Proficient (LEP) or ELL students in U.S. schools during the 2003–2004 school year. Since No Child Left Behind (NCLB, 2005) was enacted, all 50 states have Title III sub-grantees that use at least one type of English as a second language (ESL) instructional program, and 40 states use both ESL and bilingual instructional programs to instruct ELL and bilingual students.

Approximately 73% of ELL students are native Spanish speakers, while other ELL groups speak a variety of Asian (e.g., Vietnamese or Hmong), Middle Eastern, and European languages (American Federation of Teachers, 2002). According to these data, Latino ELLs and bilingual students therefore represent the single largest group of school-age children. A significant number of Latino students are underachieving or not performing well academically. For example, the National Assessment of Educational Progress (NAEP) reports that only 14% of Latino fourth graders reached proficient or advanced reading levels and that 57% did not attain basic levels of proficiency (Education Trust, 2003). Concerns are similar in math, because only 9% of Latino eighth graders reached or scored above proficient levels. Moreover, 60% perform below basic levels in math. Although the Biennial Evaluation Report indicates some improvement since the NCLB implementation, concerns remain, given that out of the 42 states that provided targets and performance data, only 33 reported meeting their expected targets for students making progress in learning English, and 41 met a few of the student attainment targets in English language proficiency (U.S. Department of Education, 2005).

In 2002, the American Federation of Teachers (AFT) reported, "A disturbingly large percentage of ELL students receive low grades, score below their classmates on standardized reading and mathematics tests, and drop out of school" (p. 6). The situation appears largely unchanged in those states in which the majority of ELLs and bilingual students live, including California, Texas, and New York (Echevarria, Short, & Powers, 2005). For example, in the 2002–2003 school year, the Texas Education Authority reported that 31.8% of fifth grade students classified as LEP or ELL met Texas State requirements in English on all tests, in comparison to 80.1% of White students, and 65.9% of all students. In Grade 9, 16.9% of ELL students met the state's requirements in comparison to 61.7% of all students (Texas Education Authority, 2003).

Many factors are discussed as contributing to the low performance profiles of ELL and bilingual students, including poverty and parental low educational levels (Baker & Good, 1995; Echevarria et al., 2005; Genesee, Lindholm-Leary, Saunders, & Christian, 2005). Factors such as a lack of access to quality education programs and well-trained teachers are also cited as contributors. An additional concern is the current nature of academic assessment and testing, which focuses on normed assessment tools that are not tied to the curriculum of ELL and bilingual students and may not be appropriate for those students. Assessing ELL and bilingual students requires attention to multiple cultural and language factors. Ignoring these variables can result in biased assessment practices and misidentification of academic difficulties (Echevarria et al., 2005; Kramer, Robertson, & Rodriguez, 2005; Montes, 2002)

ACADEMIC ASSESSMENT

Rhodes, Ochoa, and Ortiz (2005) provide a list of factors that impact the assessment of ELL students, which include language proficiency, culture, and educational history. The academic assessment process is straightforward for monolingual students and is based on determining the levels of proficiency in various subjects, including reading and writing, taking into account any apparent learning difficulties. However, for ELL and bilingual students, the language(s) used in testing, the tools used in the process, and how the tests are presented, including format, can mean the difference between culturally sensitive assessment or an assessment process that is misleading because it fails to establish if genuine academic difficulties exist.

The essential language proficiency issues to review prior to the assessment are the student's level of oral and written proficiency in English (L2) and the student's primary language (L1). A review of the student's levels of language proficiency will help assessors to determine the appropriate language(s) of assessment and instruction. For example, language proficiency assessment should distinguish between levels of language proficiency involving basic interpersonal communicative skills (BICS), the ability to use language in context-embedded situations and cognitive academic language skills (CALPS), or the ability to use language in academic and context-reduced situations (Cummins, 1994).

A number of school-related factors should also be examined within the context of current and prior instruction. For example, obtaining a history of the language(s) of instruction and instructional practices is helpful for assessors in understanding the students' learning difficulties as well as the instructional strategies that were successful. The instructional or schooling history encompasses the amount of formal elementary and secondary schooling in the students' home country and in U.S. schools. Obtaining a thorough history of schooling is important because academic assessment needs to determine if the observed learning difficulties are present in a student's native language as well as in English. Rhodes et al. (2005) emphasize other factors that are also important to explore in the academic assessment process including the types of educational programs students experienced and their educational outcomes.

The main cultural issues that need to be considered in the assessment process are background experiences, such as family practices that might impact academic performance (e.g., how homework is managed and monitored) and family value systems in relation to schooling and socialization. Acculturation issues should also be considered. Acculturation is defined as the process by which "individuals, who have developed in one cultural context, manage to adapt to new contexts that impinge on them as a result of migration, colonization, or other forms of intercultural encounters" (Berry & Sam, 1997, p. 293). Children and adults acculturate at different rates and in different ways. For example, some individuals assimilate into the mainstream culture, whereas others integrate values of the mainstream culture with values from their native culture. Acculturation influences children's attitudes, beliefs, and behaviors and can therefore influence achievement (e.g., children who are more acculturated into the mainstream culture have more access to knowledge valued by the mainstream culture) and second language development (e.g., children who are more acculturated or have more access to the mainstream culture will have more opportunities to learn the language of the mainstream culture). Rhodes et al. (2005) recommend incorporating acculturation in the list of variables that need to be explored when assessing bilingual and ELL students. Among the tools recommended to examine children's acculturation issues are interviews, observations, and questionnaires. Acculturation scales are also available, and readers should refer to the chapter in this handbook discussing acculturation for additional information.

Academic functioning may be assessed using a variety of methods. Normed instruments are one alternative that is frequently used to assess students' academic skills. CBA methods are other alternatives that are strongly recommended in this chapter to assess the academic skills of bilingual and ELL students.

NORMED INSTRUMENTS

Normed instruments are frequently used to assess students' academic skills. Ochoa, Powell, and Robles-Pina (1996) surveyed school psychologists and reported that 40 English and 22 Spanish achievement tests were used to assess Hispanic bilingual and LEP students. The main advantage of using normed tests is that these provide scores that help assessors to establish how individual students compare to their peers. However, normed instruments have several pitfalls. For example, test items in published norm-referenced instruments are not necessarily representative of the instructional content covered in the curriculum (Bell, Lentz, & Graden, 1992; Good & Salvia, 1988). According to Lentz and Shapiro (1986), measures used for academic assessments should be concrete, specific (idiographic), and capable of indicating the academic progress made by individual students over long periods of time. However, norm-referenced tests contradict these criteria because those measures are often nomothetic (i.e., they deal with abstract, general, or universal statements) and are employed to make cross-student comparisons at a single point in time (Shapiro & Elliott, 1999).

Commercial, wide-scale content assessments (i.e., standardized tests) are available and intended for students who are native speakers of English, or at least highly proficient English speakers (Butler & Stevens, 2001). The assumption therefore is that such tests are entirely comprehensible to all test takers. However, few, if any, ELL students are actually included in the norming samples of the most widely used academic standardized tests, and because of the English language limitations of ELLs and bilingual students, these tools would most likely be inappropriate (Davidson, 1994; Stevens, Butler, & Castellon-Wellington, 2000). Standardized testing is heavily reliant on a knowledge of English, and while more advanced ELL students may demonstrate sufficient English language skills to respond to tasks, the majority of ELL students struggle with standardized tests because the tests require high levels of language proficiency and communicative competence (e.g., they require not only understanding a statement or question but also responding appropriately and communicating effectively through oral and written means; Barootchi & Keshavarz, 2002).

Due to budget shortfalls and deficiencies of skilled teachers and bilingual education programs, ELL students typically spend 3 years in English for Speakers of Other Languages (ESOL) programs (also referred to as ESL programs), where they receive instruction in English designed to increase their language proficiency skills. After 3 years, most of those students are exited from ESOL programs and are classified as English language proficient, at which point they are academically assessed together with their native English-speaking peers (Abella, Urrutia, & Shneyderman, 2005). However, recent studies indicate that academic language proficiency or the language skills needed to master academic vocabulary and content in specific subjects can take 7 to 10 years to acquire (Hakuta, Butler, & Witt, 2000; Thomas & Collier, 1997). The implications are that ELL students who are exited from ESOL programs after 3 years of instruction may still need support in English because they have not acquired sufficient academic language skills to succeed in general education settings (Abella et al., 2005). Even ELLs classified as English language proficient are often unable to exhibit their content-area knowledge and skills on English language achievement tests because of the academic language issue. In this context, "academic" means the ability to comprehend and interpret the academic questions typical of standardized tests as well as the ability to use vocabulary and language that is academic in nature (e.g., using technical vocabulary in science, writing academic essays).

Attempts by education authorities to remedy such problems with standardized tests by translating tests available in English to other languages for ELL students have not always been successful and miss the point. In Texas, for example, the Texas Assessment of Knowledge Skills (Kramer et al., 2005) assessments were not designed for native Spanish speakers but were translated or "transadapted" to Spanish from tests designed in English. As a result, according to Kramer et al. (2005), "the reading level of the transadapted tests is above the English reading level of the grade being assessed, creating a testing bias against LEP classified students" (p. 7).

Given the need for students to demonstrate high levels of English language proficiency to perform adequately in academic normed tests, ELL students' scores may reflect a lack of language proficiency rather than real academic insufficiency or inadequacy of education in the country from which the student emigrated. Furthermore, other equally important issues must be considered, such as cultural-specific test content, differences in school curricula between the home country of the ELL and bilingual students and the United States, students' lack of background knowledge and experiences in certain topics (e.g., social and political history of the United States), and differences in teaching methods (e.g., in Asian and Latino countries students are encouraged to memorize information and to work individually, whereas classrooms in the United States may emphasize group approaches and problem solving; Ovando, Collier, & Combs, 2003).

CURRICULUM-BASED ASSESSMENT

Given the inherent problems encountered when administering normed tests to ELL and bilingual students, it is clear that alternative forms of assessment are needed. Shapiro and Elliott (1999) argue that curriculum-based criterion-referenced assessments are superior to published norm-referenced tests (PNRTs) for several reasons: (a) CBAs assess students directly on the materials that they are expected to learn; (b) the outcomes of CBAs are linked directly to instruction; (c) CBAs have been shown to provide reliable and valid measures of students' performance in reading, spelling, and writing; (d) CBAs are highly sensitive to short- and long-term changes in students' performance; and (e) CBAs can be used both on an idiographic basis (i.e., for evaluating the progress of individual students) and on a nomothetic basis (i.e., in accordance with program-based evaluation efforts).

The application of CBA can be particularly useful for bilingual and ELL students for several reasons. First, if language proficiency is taken into consideration when assessing students, CBA materials can be adapted to the students' individual levels of language proficiency. Second, CBA can be conducted bilingually if needed. Third, CBA can incorporate multicultural materials that can be used to determine if those materials motivate students to learn and help them to learn by accessing their background knowledge. Fourth, CBA can also be used to assess bilingual and ELL students' functioning within the context of the actual curricula used in programs designed for those students (e.g., ESOL and bilingual education programs). In a nutshell, CBA has multiple advantages for ELL and bilingual populations and can be used as a means of examining academic progress within the context of language proficiency. The obtained assessment data can also be used to plan for ESL instruction and for language and academic instruction in the classroom.

RESEARCH AND THEORETICAL BASIS OF CURRICULUM-BASED ASSESSMENT

The goal of CBA is to "assess the student's entry skills in order to design instruction and learning tasks that move the student forward relative to his or her performance in the assigned curriculum" (Gravois & Gickling, 2002, p. 886). Salvia and Ysseldyke (2004) argue that CBA requires both reliability and validity data to verify its theoretical soundness. In a review of the theoretical basis underpinning CBA in consultation, Burns (2004) noted that the reliability of CBA is adequate for instructional decision making in reading but is lacking in domains outside of reading and absent for children with learning disabilities. The content validity of CBA is assured because of the match between assessment and the curriculum (i.e., the curriculum is used for the assessment). However, Peverly and Kitzen (1998) warn that the validity of any CBA tool is partly related to the alignment between the curriculum and the underlying constructs of the curriculum because the "defining feature of CBA" is the relationship between the assessment and the curriculum itself (p. 30). Evidence of construct validity is available for the establishment of instructional levels, acquisition rates of learning, and expected developmental changes (see Burns, 2004, for review).

In a survey of school psychologist assessment practices with bilingual and LEP students, Ochoa et al. (1996) found that two thirds of the respondents reported using CBA. The researchers also noted that CBA methods were one of the most frequently used tools with bilingual and LEP students. In general, the survey results suggested that school psychologists are using CBA methods when conducting bilingual evaluations with bilingual and LEP students.

Curriculum-Based Assessment Methods

Rhodes et al. (2005) define CBA assessment as "the process of determining a student's instructional needs within a curriculum by directly assessing specific curriculum skills. CBA is generally considered a type of criterion-referenced measurement in which a standard or criterion is designated within a set of items to indicate mastery of instructional content" (p. 211). In more specific terms, it is a general label representing a collection of methods that differ in their underlying assumptions regarding the link between assessment data and instruction, test formats, types of student responses required, foci of material for monitoring student progress, and level of technical adequacy (Shinn, Rosenfield, & Knutson, 1989). CBA methods can include Curriculum-Based Measurement (CBM), portfolio assessment, structured observations, error analyses, and informal reading inventories (Rhodes et al., 2005). Each of these will be briefly described, but the focus primarily concerns the first three (i.e., CBM, portfolio assessment, and structured observations), because research with bilinguals and ELLs has mostly been restricted to those methods.

Curriculum-based measurement.   CBM is defined as "a set of standardized and validated short duration tests that are used … for the purpose of evaluating the effects of … instructional programs" in reading, spelling, math, and written language (Shinn, 2002, p. 671). CBM may be used to determine an ELL student's progress in an intervention, particularly when a plateau might have been reached, signifying that the intervention needs reevaluation or modification. CBM uses short-duration testing involving frequent and repeated measures with product responses, such as 1-minute short passages of reading, 2 minutes of spelling from dictation, 2 minutes of math computations, and 3 minutes of writing a story (Burns, 2004; Deno 1987, 2003). CBM emphasizes standardization, short assessment intervals, and the students' ability to demonstrate accuracy and speed (Shinn, 2002). It places the focus on short-term objectives of instructional interventions and provides a specific and evidence-based set of criteria to make instructional decisions. Fewster and MacMillan (2002) found that CBM scores are able to reliably predict student performance and differentiate between various proficiency levels. The available research indicates that CBM has the potential to discriminate between special education students and those who are ineligible for special education (Shapiro & Elliott, 1999; Shinn, 1998; Shinn, Collins, & Gallagher, 1998). In addition, research shows that CBM data can be utilized to monitor the effectiveness of ongoing interventions (Burns, MacQuarrie, & Campbell, 1999).

The use of CBM by school psychologists to assess students who speak English as a second language appears to have increased. In a recent survey, McCloskey and Athanasiou (2000) found that over half of their school psychologist respondents used CBM when assessing second language learners. Baker and Good (1995) examined the reliability and validity of CBM through reading in English with bilingual Hispanic students. The researchers found that "CBM reading in English was as reliable and valid for bilingual students as for English-only students" (p. 561). Moreover, CBM showed major utility as a measure of English reading proficiency using both convergent (i.e., via correlations with criterion reading measures) and discriminant construct (i.e., via correlation with criterion measures of English language) validity evidence.

Despite these promising results, Bentz and Pavri (2000) caution that there is much that we do not yet know about the use of CBM with bilingual students. For example, they point out that the relationship between reading fluency and reading proficiency is not well understood because "the sequence of skill acquisition may be different" for students learning to read English as a second language (p. 243). They argue that bilingual students learning to read and understand text in English use a variety of different skills (e.g., translating words from English to their first language) that may influence the construct validity of CBM reading as a measure of reading proficiency. As such, a global measure of English CBM reading proficiency could be influenced by language proficiency factors. Bilingual students learning English as a second language may also demonstrate reading patterns in CBM measures that are unique to their bilingual experience, as in the case of bilingual students who read languages that are very different from English syntactically and alphabetically (e.g., Mandarin).

Portfolio assessment.   Portfolio assessment is another method by which a student's academic growth can be recorded over time through compilation of the student's work in one or more subjects. Student's academic growth is determined by matching the portfolio's contents to specific learning goals and objectives and by developing criteria to determine academic progress (Dettmer, Thurston, & Dyck, 2002). School psychologists report using portfolio assessments in the process of evaluating second language learners (McCloskey & Athanasiou, 2000). In portfolio assessment, bilingual and ELL students can take an active part in selecting the methods for evaluating their progress, as well as choosing which content items to include. Academic items may include progress charts, completed learning packets, artwork, student-made books, lists of mastered vocabulary or spelling words, research reports, creative writing samples, autobiographies, classroom tests, records of scores, teacher observations, audio or videotapes products, solutions to problems, checklists of portfolio contents, and descriptions of good deeds and helpful behaviors.

Barootchi and Keshavarz (2002) investigated the relationship between portfolio assessment scores and those of teacher-made tests with a group of Iranian high school female sophomores. The students were divided into control and experimental groups. The experimental group was assessed with both the teacher-made tests and the portfolio. The experimental group's portfolio assessment score correlated highly with the teacher-made tests. The portfolios also increased the students' awareness of their progress and increased the teachers' opportunities to "identify students' needs, interests, abilities and potentials" (p. 285).

Observations.   Structured observations systems are designed to investigate environmental variables such as the classroom environment, the teachers' teaching styles, and the students' learning styles. The intent is to determine whether the students are learning what is being taught and the effectiveness of the various teaching and learning strategies. Little research has been published on the specific subject of ELL and bilingual students and structured observation systems. Some studies do include such groups in broader investigations (see, e.g., Arreaga-Mayer, Utley, Perdomo-Rivera, & Greenwood, 2000; Wallace, Anderson, Bartholomay, & Hupp, 2002). There is increasing evidence that state and local education authorities are taking structured observation systems seriously in regard to assessing ELL and bilingual populations (see, e.g., Williamson County School District, 2005). However, in part because there are so many different systems, and because no systematic comparison research has been conducted in the context of bilingual and ELL populations, it is difficult to recommend one system over another.

Waxman, Tharp, and Soleste Hilberg (2004) describe elements that are frequently a part of observational systems: "(a) a purpose of the observation, (b) operational definitions of all the observed behaviors, (c) training procedures for observers, (d) a specific observational focus, (e) a setting, (f) a unit of time, (g) an observation schedule, (h) a method to record the data, and (i) methods to process and analyze the data" (p. 2). Within the research, systemic classroom observations have been used to describe instruction, examine "instructional inequities for different groups of students" (p. 3), use the data to improve instructional programs, and provide feedback to teachers to improve classroom instruction (see Waxman et al., 2004, for discussion of literature).

Error analysis.   Research shows that achievement in English reading for ELL and bilingual students depends on depth of vocabulary in English and an underlying comprehension of story structure and meaning (Genesee et al., 2005). Phonological awareness in English is also highly correlated to English reading skills (McKoon, 2003). In error analysis, assessors attempt to identify missing skills by analyzing students' errors in oral and written literacy measures. Peverly and Kitzen (1998) stress that error analysis must include determining the causes of errors, otherwise the identified deficiencies will not be helpful. Once this is accomplished, assessors can work directly with students and teachers to modify the instruction.

Studies suggest that children who are learning how to read in a second language lack basic skills such as auditory discrimination of phonemes, an understanding of phonemic rules, an extensive vocabulary, and effective sentence processing skills (i.e., poor proficiency means poor ability to retain strings of words in short-term memory). All these factors influence the types of errors made in decoding and reading comprehension in the second language (Chiappe & Siegel, 1999; Verhoeven, 1990). The research on cross-language transfer also indicates that children transfer the reading skills they have in the first language (e.g., phonological skills, comprehension skills and strategies) to reading in the second language in such areas as phonology, vocabulary knowledge, and reading comprehension (Durgunolu, Nagy, & Hancin-Bhatt, 1993; Ordoñez, Carlo, Snow, & McLaughlin, 2002; Royer & Carlo, 1991). A knowledge base of those transfer skills can help assessors to determine if the errors being made by bilingual and ELL students are a function of students transferring their knowledge base of the first language to the second language (e.g., student may be decoding words in English by using phonic sounds in the first language).

Informal reading inventories.   Informal reading inventories (IRI) are published nonstandardized assessment tools consisting of narrative or expository reading passages of gradually increasing difficulty, usually ranging from preprimer through sixth grade level or beyond (e.g., Burns & Roe, 2001; Johns, 2005; Leslie & Caldwell, 2006). Most IRIs are designed to help assessors identify students' decoding and reading comprehension proficiency levels, processing strategies, background knowledge, topic interest levels, and specific areas of strengths and needs that may be applied to instructional interventions. Basic administration procedures consist of asking the student to sequentially read each of the graded passages and to respond to a set of factual, comprehension, and probing questions following each passage. The process ends when the student reaches a ceiling level of difficulty (Peregoy & Boyle, 2004).

The assessment can be tape recorded during the administration process to facilitate subsequent coding and analysis of skill areas, such as oral reading errors (e.g., dialectical, pronunciation, suffix or prefix omissions), patterns of miscues (e.g., word substitutions, altered sequencing), processing strategies employed (e.g., use of contextual cues, self-correction), and grade levels of reading attained. The assessor is also able to gauge the student's independent, instructional, and frustration levels of reading. Interpretation of yielded data may be used to target areas and determine instructional approaches to help students progress to the next level of reading and to select reading materials that might be appropriate for their development. Benchmarks for further assessment and instruction are created in a cyclical and progressive manner (Peregoy & Boyle, 2004). This reciprocal link between assessment and instruction lends itself to ascertaining students' responsiveness to interventions (RTI), consistent with current models of outcome effectiveness.

Several studies have provided evidence for the utility of IRIs in assessing ELL students. For example, Blachowicz (1999) described a case study in which informal reading inventories were used to assess a seventh grade Hispanic student's reading proficiency and comprehension in English. The assessment results indicated that the student demonstrated significant difficulties in reading fluency and comprehension as a result of poor vocabulary knowledge in English and a lack of background information to understand the passages. An intervention plan was developed based on the assessment to focus on building "important concepts, background knowledge, and ... a conceptual network of new vocabulary" (p. 230). Neal and Kelly (1999) examined the effectiveness of the Reading Recovery and Descubriendo la Lectura reading programs, which were designed to teach reading literacy skills to ELL students. The researchers used two reading surveys with IRI components, the Observation Survey of Early Literacy Achievement (Clay, 2002) and the Instrumento de Observacion de los Logros de la Lecto-Escritura Inicial (Escamilla & Clay, 1996), in conjunction with normed achievement tests. The IRIs were useful to the researchers in identifying students who had not developed specific literacy skills or who were taking longer to develop those skills and who needed referrals to longer term interventions.

Similarly, Peregoy and Boyle (2004) illustrate the effective use of the Qualitative Reading Inventory-II (QRI-II; Leslie, Caldwell, & Leslie, 1995) through a case study of a 13-year-old Chinese bilingual student in the eighth grade. The student had only been in the United States for 4 years and had achieved an intermediate level of English language proficiency. The informal reading assessment suggested that the student was reading in English at an independent level in fourth-grade narrative passages and at an instructional level in fourth-grade unfamiliar expository passages. He showed strengths in sight vocabulary, decoding simple unfamiliar words, and reading for meaning. Oral pronunciation miscues were attributed to second language learning interference and deemed nonsignificant in affecting reading comprehension. Decoding errors in suffixes were found to be related to lack of knowledge of compound words in English. The analysis of these patterns of errors and strengths were used to determine the level and targets for instruction in the context of second language learning.

Overall, there is limited empirical research on the reliability and validity of IRIs, particularly when applied to ELL students (e.g., Flood, Lapp, Squire, & Jensen,

2003; Kamil, Mosenthal, Pearson, & Barr, 2000). Given the semistructured and informal nature of the inventories, their utility as an educational tool is enhanced when used as part of a comprehensive portfolio or multimethod assessment process (Gredler & Johnson, 2004; Harp, 2006). A specific advantage of IRIs lies in the interactive manner in which the assessment is conducted (Brozo, 1990). For example, the Burke Reading Inventories (Goodman, Watson, & Burke, 1987), a qualitative measure, yielded more positive results than standardized measures in assessing metacognitive reading strategies of bilingual Spanish dominant students in the context of Spanish reading (Muñiz-Swicegood, 1994). The authors suggested that the informal interviews in Spanish were less structured and provided for a more enhanced interpersonal testing environment.

Another positive element of IRIs is their use in bilingual reading assessments and their benefits when adapted to bilingual or multicultural classroom settings (Coelho, 1998). Although bilingual IRIs are limited to Spanish-English versions (Flynt & Cooter, 1999, 2004), English speaking versions may be systematically modified to another language when assessing reading performance in that language. It is also possible to develop inventories using curriculum materials or reading program graded materials because IRIs are easily adaptable to any type of text and alternate procedures (Goodman, Watson, & Burke, 1996). A salient example is the Informal Reading Thinking Inventory (IR-TI), which allows for extensive probing of second language learners in assessing higher order thinking skills in the reading process (Manzo, Manzo, & McKenna, 1995).

IMPLICATIONS FOR PRACTICE

General Assessment Practices and CBA

The use of CBA methods is highly recommended when conducting instructional consultation with teachers (Rosenfield, 1987). In the instructional consultation model, the consultant and the teacher must decide on the child's instructional level based on the aptitude of the child in learning a new skill and determine the variables that influence learning. The model explores the "instructional mismatch" between the learner's capabilities and the curriculum. Burns (2002) highlights this mismatch by referring to Gickling's CBA model (Gickling & Havertape, 1981; Kovaleski, Tucker, & Duffy, 1995). Gickling suggested that students who are appropriately challenged with academic work that is at their instructional level performed optimally, and other researchers have since confirmed this premise (Roberts & Shapiro, 1996; Shapiro, 1992).

Within the consultation model, consultants and consultees explore instructional mismatches (Rosenfield, 1987). Exploring instructional mismatches means that the school psychologist works collaboratively with the teacher to collect data and identify the possible mismatch between the student's ability level and the level of the instructional materials. In this model, the student is viewed as a "vulnerable learner" confronted with the effects of inadequate instruction. The exploration of the student and the classroom environment is accomplished via several methods that include classroom systematic and unstructured observations, a task analysis of the student's instructional tasks, a process analysis of the lessons' content and the student's manner of processing the information imparted, and an analysis of the student's errors when completing the academic tasks. The assessment phase is followed by the introduction of interventions designed to target the student's academic weaknesses and to modify the instructional environment.

A nontraditional assessment method developed from CBA, which has come to be referred to as "brief experimental analysis," combines the data sampling of curriculum-based approaches with the experimental aspects of functional assessment (Chafouleas, Riley-Tillman, & Eckert, 2003). As student progress is systematically sampled, the acquired data are used to select two or more possible academic interventions. In essence, a baseline measure of performance in the specified academic domain is compared to performance levels during implementation of each of the chosen interventions. Performance levels dictate the utility of each chosen intervention and the degree to which the selected intervention should be modified for maximum student support. This process is consistent with the facilitative and emerging role of the school psychologist as a collaborative teacher consultant (Noell, Freeland, Witt, & Gansle, 2001). It is also consistent with the current practice to evaluate the RTI to assess learning disabilities (Brown-Chidsey, 2005).

Another area in which CBA can play a role with regard to ELL and bilingual students is determining if these students are receiving adequate opportunities to learn or the "necessary content instruction" to perform adequately in classroom tasks and tests (Butler & Stevens, 2001, p. 420). Butler and Stevens cite several studies in which the opportunity to learn (OTL) significantly influenced students' poor performances in tests. CBA can be useful in determining if OTL is a factor with bilingual and ELL students, as in cases where students perform poorly because the classroom instruction has not prepared those students adequately to understand the vocabulary and content within the lessons. In the case of ELL students who are exited from ESOL programs but who are still in need of further developing their academic language skills in English, CBA can be used to ascertain if the curriculum in the general education program is appropriate for these students. The CBA data can also be used to decide the types of ESOL supports that the students need to succeed in the general education program.

Despite the applicability of CBA techniques for ELL and bilingual children and youth, they should always be supplemented by ethnographic assessment methods (Laing & Kamhi, 2003). Ethnographic assessment involves the observation of a child in a variety of contexts and is used to examine the child's language abilities in naturalistic situations. It can include such tools as language sampling and ethnographic interviews. Language samples involve observing the child's functional level of language and literacy in a variety of different settings and with different communication partners. Ethnographic interviews are used to elicit pertinent information from key individuals in the child's life, as well as to build rapport with parents, gain understanding of cultural differences, and facilitate the planning and implementation of effective interventions.

Using CBA Methods

There are some disadvantages in using CBA methods to assess the academic functioning of ELL and bilingual students. Rhodes et al. (2005) provide a discussion of some of the disadvantages of using CBA: (a) teacher-constructed criterion-referenced measures may vary from teacher to teacher, (b) student mobility may "affect utility of measures," (c) comparison of a student's performance across settings is difficult (e.g., class to class or district to district), (d) the use of "scope-and-sequence charts from a published curriculum" may not match the student's actual classroom instruction and educational experiences, (e) the reliance of CBM on "visual inspection of the data" introduces sources of error, (f) teachers may "teach to the test" based on the sample of curricular content selected for assessment, and (g) informal measures alone do not provide sufficient information for determining services in most states (p. 213).

When analyzing the results of CBA methods with ELL and bilingual populations, assessors need to take into account students' education curriculum histories, levels of proficiency in the first and second languages, as well as the amount of educational instruction in both languages. In addition, assessors will need to consider if the CBA procedures incorporate content that is culturally appropriate for the students being assessed (Bentz & Pavri, 2000). Part of the assessment and intervention phases can entail helping classroom teachers to incorporate multicultural materials into the curriculum to access students' background knowledge and to increase students' levels of motivation.

Using CBA methods with ELL and bilingual students implies that CBA methods must be adapted to fit the needs of these students. The following sections review some of the CBA methods recommended by Dettmer et al. (2002) and provide a discussion of potential adaptations for ELL and bilingual students.

Portfolio Assessment

Portfolio assessment methods suitable for bilingual or ELL populations are available and published in vehicles such as *The Learning Record* (Barr, Craig, Fisette, & Syverson, 1998), a three-part system that guides the collection of data relating to the student's literacy throughout the course of the academic year:

1. Part A, Documenting Prior Experience, is completed early in the year, and contains data on the student's language background, parents' or caregivers' descriptions of the student as a learner, and the student's own description of his or her accomplishments and goals.
2. Part B, Documenting Student Learning, takes place throughout the year. Teachers and students use standardized data collection forms to record evidence about what and how the student is learning. These data are tied to content standards and performance criteria congruent with those set by the district and the state. Near the end of the third quarter, the teacher prepares

a summary of the student's achievements accumulated in the data collection forms.

3. Part C, Reflecting on the Year's Work, takes place at the end of the year. Parents and students review the record of achievement described in Parts A and B, and add comments to complete the portfolio. The teacher updates the record and recommends the next steps to be taken.

The principles on which this method of portfolio assessment is based include (a) thoughtfulness over rote learning, (b) performance capabilities rather than deficits, (c) fostering individual development within a framework of grade level expectations, and (d) emphases on bilingualism and the value of understanding cultures beyond one's own, which might involve work that utilizes more than one language or material that is multicultural. While time-consuming for teachers, and requiring planning and storage space for materials, the process of developing portfolio assessment is an excellent opportunity for school psychologists to form joint relationships with teachers and assist in the organizational development of the portfolio. In addition, school psychologists can simultaneously aid in enhancing the teachers' cultural awareness, knowledge, and skills, as well as suggesting culturally appropriate portfolio contents and suitable measures of grading for ELL and bilingual children.

As a result of criticisms aimed at standardized tests, portfolio assessment has become a popular alternative to standardized testing. Moya and O'Malley (1994) argue that students' portfolios allow examiners to better monitor student learning and evaluate the effectiveness of instructional programs. According to Gomez (1999), portfolio assessment is an advantageous method of informal assessment because it can be used with all students, and particularly with ELL students, to provide valid and reliable data and improve accountability. Furthermore, the technique can be designed to involve all stakeholders—teachers, administrators, parents, and students—which results in a shared vision, and with sufficient teacher training, can lead to a more learner-centered model. Both Baker and Good (1995) and McCloskey and Athanasiou (2000) also emphasize the method's ability to keep track of ELL and bilingual students as they progress through different grades and schools. It can also be used to augment other data compiled for determining individual interventions. In addition, the method is well suited to document progress in different types of classrooms and programs, including ESL and bilingual education programs.

One of the major limitations of using portfolio assessment is that scoring criteria may lack validity and reliability. Portfolios do not generate traditional scores and are typically scored via criterion reference methods, and thus it is often difficult to compare portfolio ratings to other assessment scores, for example, standard scores from normed tests (Gomez, 1999). However, interrater reliability can be addressed, provided raters are well trained and the measurement criteria clearly stated (McCloskey & Athanasiou, 2000). State legislatures also have concerns about the validity of portfolios because portfolios lack standardized procedures for administration, which means that variability exists in terms of the amount of support students receive from teachers or other sources (e.g., parents, tutors) and the amount of time that students are allowed to work on portfolios (Gomez, 1999). Gomez argues that standardized testing conditions can be incorporated within specific sections of the portfolio assessment to control for such variable administration conditions.

Curriculum-Based Measurement

Although ready-made CBM inventories exist, Dettmer et al. (2002) caution users of market-ready CBM prepared packages because they most likely will not comprise adequate measures of the curriculum in a specific school. The alternative is to produce CBM probes and materials that are taken directly from the class curriculum (Fuchs, Fuchs, & Hamlet, 1990).

Any procedures that employ standardized measures and that incorporate "probes" must be carefully examined to determine its appropriateness for ELL and bilingual populations. CBM scoring procedures and scores must also be examined within the context of the ELL students' cultural backgrounds, English language proficiency skills, and history of educational programs (e.g., length of time receiving bilingual and/or ESL services). A key study conducted by Baker and Good (1995) suggests that CBM is an effective means to monitor Spanish/English bilingual students' progress in learning to read English. The researchers suggest that CBM is useful to screen bilinguals for reading problems and to plan for their instructional needs.

Structured Systematic Observational Systems

Structured observation systems are recommended to help school psychologists to conduct systematic classroom observations within an instructional consultation framework (Rosenfield, 1987). Several observation systems have been designed and validated with culturally and linguistically diverse students, and with emphases on principles from ESOL and bilingual education theory and research (Waxman et al., 2004). For example, Echevarria and Short (2004) developed an observation system, the Sheltered Instruction Observation Protocol (SIOP), designed to collect observation data regarding the effectiveness of Sheltered Instruction (SI). SI is an ESOL approach to teach content (e.g., science, social studies) to ELL students in ways that make the content more comprehensible. The Classroom Observation Schedule (COS) is designed to collected observation data about students' interactions with teachers and students, the classroom setting and activities, the materials used for instruction, and the languages used in the classroom (Waxman & Padron, 2004). The COS has been found to be useful in providing teachers with feedback about instructional strategies and students' classroom behaviors.

The Functional Assessment of Academic Behavior: Creating Successful Learning Environments (FAAB; Ysseldyke & Christensen, 2002) is a system designed to evaluate aspects of the classroom environment, with a follow-up student–psychologist interview after the classroom observation to determine if the student learned what was taught. The rationale for conducting classroom observations is to determine the student's level of comprehension and learning style in addition to the teacher's teaching style. The critical question becomes is there a "mismatch" between the teacher's teaching style and the student's learning style? The

FAAB system does not focus on the students' deficiencies but on aspects of the learning environment, including both home and school settings, so that learning can be optimized. This aspect of the FAAB is particularly applicable to ELL students who have the potential of being erroneously labeled or identified as learning impaired due to their lack of background experiences with academic content or culturally different styles in the classroom.

The Code for Instructional Structure and Student Academic Response (CISSAR) originated by Stanley and Greenwood (1981) is another systematic observation approach that assesses the efficacy of instruction and interventions in the school milieu. It comprises five categories of teacher-oriented factors (i.e., activity, task, teaching structure, teaching position, and teaching behavior) and three categories of observable student responses (i.e., academic responding, task management, and competing behavior). Activities can include observations of reading, mathematics, spelling, language, social studies, and science. The teacher behavior module also notes if the instructor was approving or disapproving and lists other modes of teacher feedback to students. The CISSAR system is used with computer software to facilitate data graphing and collection. It gauges the student's academic performance from a systemic, not a solitary, point of view, taking into consideration all areas of the environment—teacher, classroom, method of instruction, and student academic responses.

Technology-based approaches greatly facilitate the utilization of such systems. For example, the Ecobehavioral Assessment Systems Software (EBASS) is a computer-assisted, standard classroom observational system used by school psychologists and educational professionals. It comprises three instruments broadly employed for special education research and was designed for exceptional children (see Greenwood, Carta, Kamps, Terry, & Delquadri, 1994). Structured systems of observation have also been developed for preschoolers. The Ecobehavioral System for Complex Analyses of Preschool Environments (ESCAPE; Carta, Greenwood, & Atwater, 1985) is designed for 3- to 5-year-old children.

Special care should be taken prior to selecting any systematic observation system to use with ELL and bilingual students, and educators must be aware that these observation system have not been adequately validated with bilingual and ELL students. It is possible that as a result of cultural differences, ELL or bilingual students could engage in behaviors that are different from the norm. The school psychologist must apply a culturally responsive approach when conducting the observations and when interpreting the culturally diverse students' behaviors (see National Association of School Psychologists, 2003).

IMPLEMENTATION AND APPROACHES

This section briefly focuses on describing the Cognitive Academic Language Learning Approach (CALLA), an instructional program for bilingual and ELL students (Chamot & O'Malley, 1994). CALLA was chosen because of its strong theoretical and research bases and because it is an example of an instructional program that incorporates a variety of CBA assessment methods for bilingual and ELL students.

The Cognitive Academic Language Learning Approach (CALLA)

The CALLA program was developed by Chamot and O'Malley (1994) and was designed to increase the achievement of students learning English as a second language. The model integrates research conducted by Cummins (1994) and Collier (1989) on second language acquisition (Thomas & Collier, 1997). CALLA emphasizes the development of academic language skills and native language instruction to develop content knowledge in English (Grabe, 1991; McLaughlin, 1990; McLeod & McLaughlin, 1986).

Another important component of the CALLA model is its emphasis on incorporating language and content for ESL instruction. Traditional ESL curriculums tended to emphasize linguistic and grammatical knowledge, whereas more recent models, such as CALLA, emphasize the integration of language development and content knowledge within ESL instruction (DeAvila & Ducan, 1984; Genesee, 1987; Mohan, 1986).

The research focused on the learning strategies of effective learners also influenced the CALLA model. According to Chamot and O'Malley (1996), "Effective language learners are more adept at selecting and deploying appropriate strategies for a language-learning task than are less effective students" (p. 261). The model emphasizes teaching students three learning strategies: metacognitive, cognitive, and social/affective strategies. Metacognitive strategies help ELL students to plan, monitor, and evaluate their own learning activities. Cognitive strategies are techniques to help students link information to previous or new knowledge. Social/affective strategies are used in learning and communication tasks and may entail asking questions for clarification or working collaboratively with others. Available studies suggest that the CALLA model is effective in teaching ELL students to use these various learning strategies within academic contexts (e.g., Cardelle-Elawar and Náñez, 1992; Chamot, Dale, O'Malley, & Spanos, 1992).

Assessment in the CALLA Model

Teachers implementing CALLA programs are required to choose assessment methods and tools that match the knowledge and skills that are being taught and measured in the curricula. The CALLA model encourages teachers to adapt assessment methods to the ELL student's instructional needs. Moreover, this approach is in keeping with CBA assessment practices that are described in this chapter as linking assessment and intervention by using assessment tools and content that are directly linked to the curriculum.

Within CALLA programs, standardized tests alone are not considered adequate to assess students' skills because they do not monitor student interim progress within the instructional program. Furthermore, Chamot and O'Malley (1996) argue that standardized tools are not sufficient because they only assess content knowledge and do not measure functioning in the three areas in which objectives are designed within the program: language development, content knowledge, and learning strategies. Another crucial factor the CALLA originators emphasize is assessing the language functions that are essential to the academic language (i.e., CALPS) being used in the curriculum (O'Malley, 1989).

The CALLA model emphasizes functional academic assessment through a variety of methods and tools. For example, teachers use "think-aloud" interviews in which students are prompted to describe their thinking processes as they attempt to solve mathematics problems. The think-aloud protocol is immediately followed by a retrospective interview in which the students are asked questions about their specific approaches to solving problems (Chamot, Dale, O'Malley, & Spanos, 1992). Formal and standardized assessment tools are also used in conjunction with CBA approaches such as reading inventories and teacher constructed tests. Other types of assessments recommended by Chamot (1995) include student diaries, teacher structured interviews, teacher and student questionnaires, and classroom observations.

IMPLICATIONS FOR FUTURE RESEARCH AND PRACTICE

One of the most valuable functions a school psychologist can perform is to assist teachers with the identification and assessment of ELL and bilingual students who need academic support. Factors such as language and cultural diversity have a significant impact on the education of bilingual and ELL students, and school psychologists must be proactive in adequately identifying the learning needs of these students and developing well-designed and effective instructional interventions.

Cromey and Hanson (2000) suggested that striving toward a more efficient use of assessment methods in the school system is crucial for the successful implementation of assessment systems. Training assessors to use various alternative assessment tools and methods is important so that time is not wasted in administering tests that yield little additional and useful information. Adequate training with a wider range of methods, such as those described in this chapter, will allow practitioners to select and administer only the most appropriate assessments. Matching the assessment tool to the curriculum is also a salient task. The continued implementation of the curriculum-aligned methods described in this chapter will require more training for school psychologists as well as teachers to address the instructional needs of bilingual and ELL students.

To date, research on CBA applications with ELL and bilingual populations has been minimal. CBA be validated not only for these populations but also for the various curricula used with these students in bilingual and ESOL programs. In order to better tailor interventions for these students, the instructional issues facing these children need to be better understood and the most appropriate assessment tools selected. Ochoa et al. (1996) argue that "researchers should examine the psychometric properties and the differential item functioning of the more commonly used instruments .... Additionally, test authors and publishers should consider the need to develop more psychometrically sound tests for assessing LEP students" (p. 272). Many questions need to be explored that will help educators to better understand how to assess the academic skills of ELL and bilingual students. For example, how valid are the CBA techniques when applied to bilingual and ELL students? Because the research to date has been conducted exclusively with Hispanics, does the validity change when different languages and cultures are involved? Do the techniques have equal utility in other areas of the curriculum, for example, mathematics or science? Do these techniques have to be modified when applied to bilinguals and ELLs in different educational programs (e.g., ESOL or bilingual programs)? Last, can CBA effectively differentiate between problems involving second language proficiency and genuine learning difficulties?

In general, future directions for training and practice lie in the development of multicultural competencies. Programs preparing school psychologists and educators need to incorporate the development of multicultural assessment and intervention competencies in the curriculum. Increasing professional understanding of the critical multicultural educational and assessment issues will imbue the next generation of school psychology students and practitioners with a much improved acceptance of cultural diversity and multicultural expertise in addressing the instructional needs of ELL and bilingual children in the schools.

ANNOTATED BIBLIOGRAPHY

Lozardo, A., & Notari-Syverson, A. (2001). *Alternative approaches to assessing young children.* Baltimore, MD: Paul H. Brookes.

> This book examines six alternative assessment methods: naturalistic, focused, performance, portfolio, dynamic, and curriculum-based language. Each chapter of the book provides the reader with a detailed description of the approach, a summary of advantages and limitations, specific guidelines for implementation, suggestions for working in inclusive environments, and samples of data collection forms.

Rhodes, R. L., Ochoa, S. H., & Ortiz, S. O. (2005). *Assessing culturally and linguistically diverse students: A practical guide.* New York: Guilford.

> A comprehensive and practice resource for any school professional involved in assessing children and youth from culturally and linguistically diverse backgrounds. The book covers a wide variety of methods procedures, tools, and issues. An excellent resource for practitioners and trainers.

Waxman, H. C, Tharp, R. G., & Hilberg, S. R. (Eds.). (2004) *Observational research in U.S. classrooms: New approaches for understanding cultural and linguistic diversity.* Cambridge, England: Cambridge University Press.

> The authors offer theoretical frameworks and substantive research findings on a variety of classroom observation systems. The observation systems were developed through research on effective teaching practices for culturally and linguistically diverse students.

RESOURCES

Ehlers-Zavala, F. (2005). *Assessment of the English language learner: An ESL training module.* Chicago: Chicago Public Schools, Office of Language and Culture: http://www.olce.org/fileBroker.php/62/Assessment Module-done.pdf

> This is one of the most comprehensive guides to assessing ESLs written from a state education authority's perspective, and primarily intended for teachers.

ERIC Clearinghouse on Disabilities and Gifted Education. (2003). Identifying learning disabilities (LD) in culturally diverse students: http://ericec.org/faq/ld-esl.html

An excellent resource for articles and links to Web sites for both teachers and school psychologists. The resources focus on assessing ELLs, particularly those who may have learning problems or disabilities.

Kramer, B., Roberston, S., & Rodriguez, A. (2005). Analysis of the problem: The Texas accountability system fails our English language learners. University of Texas: http://www.ebd.utexas.edu/faculty/valenzuela/analysis.pdf

In states that host large populations of ELLs, such as Texas, intensive debates over state-mandated testing are taking place, and this report articulates many the issues that have surfaced as a result.

NASP. (2003). Culturally competent practice: http://www.nasponline.org/culturalcompetence/

The section English Language Learners on this Web page contains links to access several downloadable pdf files that teachers, educators, and school psychologists will find useful to learn about issues involving assessment of ELLs.

REFERENCES

Abella, R., Urrutia, J., & Shneyderman, A. (2005). An examination of the validity of English-language achievement test scores in an English language learner population. *Bilingual Research Journal, 29,* 127–144.

American Federation of Teachers. (2002). Teaching English-language learners: What does the research say? *Educational Issues Policy Brief, 14,* 1–8. Retrieved July 17, 2005, from www.aft.org/pubs-reports/downloads/teachers/policy14.pdf

Arreaga-Mayer, C., Utley, C. A., Perdomo-Rivera, C., & Greenwood, C. R. (2000). Ecobehavioral assessment of instructional contexts in bilingual special education programs for English language learners at risk for developmental disabilities. *Focus on Autism and Other Developmental Studies, 18,* 28–40.

Baker, S. K., & Good, R. (1995). Curriculum-based measurement of English reading with bilingual Hispanic students: A validation study with second grade students. *School Psychology Review, 24,* 561–578.

Barootchi, N., & Keschavarz, M. H. (2002). Assessment of achievement through portfolios and teacher-made tests. *Educational Research, 44,* 279–288.

Barr, M. B., Craig, D. A., Fisette, D., & Syverson, M. A. (1998). *Assessing literacy with the learning record: A handbook for teachers, grades K–6.* Portsmouth, NH: Heinemann.

Bell, P. F., Lentz, F. E., & Graden, J. L. (1992). Effects of curriculum-test overlap on standardized test scores: Identifying systematic confounds in educational decision-making. *School Psychology Review, 21,* 644–655.

Bentz, J., & Pavri, S. (2000). Curriculum-based measurement in assessing bilingual students: A promising new direction. *Diagnostique, 25*(3), 229–248.

Berry, J. W., & Sam, D. L. (1997). Acculturation and adaptation. In J. W. Berry, M. H. Segall, & C. Kagitcibasi (Eds.), *Handbook of cross-cultural psychology: Vol. 4. Social behavior and applications* (2nd ed., pp. 291–326). Boston: Allyn & Bacon.

Blachowicz, C. L. Z. (1999). Vocabulary in dynamic reading assessment. *Reading Psychology, 20,* 213–236.

Brown-Chidsey, R. (2005). The role of published norm-referenced tests in problem-solving-based assessment. In R. Brown-Chidsey (Ed.), *Assessment for intervention: A problem solving approach* (pp. 247–264). New York: Guilford.

Brozo, W. G. (1990). Learning how at-risk readers learn best: A case for interactive assessment. *Journal of Reading, 5,* 522–527.

Burns, M. K. (2002). Comprehensive system of assessment to intervention using curriculum-based assessments. *Intervention in School and Clinic, 38*, 8–13.

Burns, M. K. (2004). Using curriculum-based assessment in the consultative process: A useful innovation or an educational fad. *Journal of Educational and Psychological Consultation, 14*, 63–78.

Burns, M. K., MacQuarrie, L. I., & Campbell, D. T. (1999). The difference between instructional assessment (curriculum based assessment) and achievement measurements: A focus on purpose and result. *Communiqué, 27*, 18–19.

Burns, P. C., & Roe, B. D. (2001). *Informal reading inventory: Preprimer to twelfth grade* (6th ed.). Boston: Houghton Mifflin.

Butler, F. A., & Stevens, R. (2001). Standardized assessment of the content knowledge of English language learners K–12: Current trends and old dilemmas. *Language Testing, 18*(4), 409–427.

Cardelle-Elawar, M., & Náñez, J. E., Sr. (1992). A metacognitive approach to teaching bilingual students. In R. V. Padilla & A. H. Benavides (Eds.), *Critical perspectives on bilingual education research* (pp. 221–241). Tempe, AZ: Bilingual Press/Editorial Bilingue.

Carta, J. J., Greenwood, C. R., & Atwater, J. (1985). *Ecobehavioral system for complex assessments of preschool environments (ESCAPE)*. Kansas City: Juniper Gardens Children's Project, Bureau of Child Research, University of Kansas.

Chafouleas, S. M., Riley-Tillman, T. C., & Eckert, T. L. (2003). A comparison of school psychologists' acceptability, training, and use of norm-referenced, curriculum-based, and brief experimental analysis methods to assess reading. *School Psychology Review, 32*, 272–281.

Chamot, A. U. (1995). Learning strategies and listening comprehension. In D. J. Mendelsohn & J. Rubin (Eds.), *A guide for the teaching of second language listening*. San Diego, CA: Dominie.

Chamot, A. U., Dale, M., O'Malley, J. M., & Spanos, G. A. (1992). Learning and problem solving strategies of ESL students. *Bilingual Research Journal, 16*, 1–34.

Chamot, A. U., & O'Malley, J. M. (1994). *The CALLA handbook: Implementing the cognitive academic language learning approach*. Reading, MA: Addison-Wesley.

Chamot, A. U., & O'Malley, J. M. (1996). The cognitive academic language learning approach: A model for linguistically diverse classrooms. *The Elementary School Journal, 96*, 259–273.

Chiappe, P., & Siegel, L. S. (1999). Phonological awareness and reading acquisition in English and Punjabi-speaking Canadian children. *Journal of Educational Psychology, 91*, 20–28.

Clay, M. M. (2002). *An observation survey of early literacy achievement*. Portsmouth, NH: Heinemann.

Coelho, E. (1998). *Teaching and learning in multicultural schools: An integrated approach*. PA: Multilingual Matters.

Collier, V. P. (1989). How Long? A synthesis of research on academic achievement in a second language. *TESOL Quarterly, 13*, 171–182.

Cromey, A., & Hanson, M. (2000). An exploratory analysis of school-based student assessment systems. Retrieved July 27, 2005, from http://www.ncrel.org/policy/pubs/html/data/

Cummins, J. (1994). The acquisition of English as a second language. In K. Spangenberg-Urbschat & I. Pritchard (Eds.), *Kids come in all languages: Reading instruction for ESL students* (pp. 36–62). Newark, DE: International Reading Association.

Davidson, F. (1994). Norms appropriacy of achievement tests: Spanish speaking children and English children's norms. *Language Testing, 11*, 83–95.

DeAvila, E. A., & Ducan, S. E. (1984). *Finding Out/Descubrimiento: Training manual*. San Rafael, CA: Linguametrics Group.

Deno, S. L. (1987). Curriculum-based measurement. *Teaching Exceptional Children, 20,* 41–47.

Deno, S. L. (2003). Developments in curriculum-based measurement. *Journal of Special Education, 37,* 184–192.

Dettmer, P., Thurston, L. P., & Dyck, N. (2002). *Consultation, collaboration, and teamwork: For students with special needs.* Boston: Allyn & Bacon.

Durgunolu, A. Y., Nagy, W. E., & Hancin-Bhatt, B. J. (1993). Cross-language transfer of phonological awareness. *Journal of Educational Psychology, 85,* 453–465.

Echevarria, J., & Short, D. J. (2004). Using multiple perspectives in observations of diverse classrooms: The Sheltered Instruction Observation Protocol. In H. C. Waxman, R. G. Tharp, & R. Soleste Hilberg (Eds.), *Observational research in U.S. classrooms: New approaches for understanding cultural and linguistic diversity* (pp. 21–47). Cambridge, England: Cambridge University Press.

Echevarria, J., Short, D., & Powers, K. (2005). School reform and standards-based education: How do teachers help English language learners? *Journal of Educational Research,* in press.

Education Trust. (2003). Latino achievement in America. Washington, DC: Author. Retrieved July 14, 2005, from http://www2.edtrust.org/NR/rdonlyres/7DC36C7E-EBBE–43BB–8392-CDC618E1F762/0/LatAchievEnglish.pdf

Escamilla, K. C., & Clay, M. M. (1996). *Instrumento de observacion de los logros de la lecto-escritura inicial: A bilingual text.* Portsmouth, NH: Heinemann.

Fewster, S., & MacMillan, P. (2002). School based evidence for the validity of curriculum based assessment measurement of reading and writing. *Remedial & Special Education, 23,* 149.

Flood, J., Lapp, D., Squire, J. R., & Jensen, J. L. (2003). *Handbook of research on teaching the English language arts* (2nd ed.). Mahwah, NJ: Erlbaum.

Flynt, S. E., & Cooter, R. B. (1999). *English-Español reading inventory for the classroom.* Upper Saddle River, NJ: Prentice Hall.

Flynt, S. E., & Cooter, R. B. (2004). *Flynt-Cooter reading inventory for the classroom* (5th ed.). Upper Saddle River, NJ: Merrill.

Fuchs, L. S., Fuchs, D., & Hamlet, C. L. (1990). Curriculum-based measurement: A standardized, long-term goal approach to monitoring student progress. *Academic Therapy, 25,* 615–632.

Genesee, F. (1987). *Learning through two languages: Studies of immersion and bilingual education.* Rowley, MA: Newbury House.

Genesee, F., Lindholm-Leary, K., Saunders, W., & Christian, D. (2005). English language learners in U.S. schools: An overview of research findings. *Journal of Education for Students Placed at Risk, 10,* 363–385.

Gickling, E. F., & Havertape, S. (1981). *Curriculum-based assessment.* Minneapolis, MN: School Psychology In-service Training Network.

Gomez, E. (1999, March). Creating large-scale assessment portfolios that include English language learners. In *Perspectives on policy and practice.* Providence, RI: Northeast and Islands Regional Educational Laboratory. Retrieved on July 2, 2005, from http://www.alliance.brown.edu/pubs/PolPerELL.pdf

Good, R. H., & Salvia, J. (1988). Curriculum bias in published, norm-referenced reading tests: Demonstrable effects. *School Psychology Review, 17,* 51–60.

Goodman, Y. M., Watson, D. J., & Burke, C. L. (1987). *Reading miscue inventory.* New York: Richard C. Owen.

Goodman, Y. M., Watson, D. J., & Burke, C. L. (1996). *Reading strategies: Focus on comprehension.* Katonah, NY: R. C. Owen.

Grabe, W. (1991). Current development in second language reading research. *TESOL Quarterly, 25,* 375–406.

Gravois, T. A., & Gickling, E. E. (2002). Best practices in curriculum-based assessment. In A. Thomas & J. Grimes (Eds.), *Best practices in school psychology IV* (Vol. 1; pp. 885–898). Bethesda, MD: National Association of School Psychologists.

Gredler, M. E., & Johnson, R. L. (2004). *Assessment in the literacy classroom.* Boston: Allyn & Bacon.

Greenwood, C. R., Carta, J. J., Kamps, D., Terry, B., & Delquadri, J. (1994). Development and validation of standard classroom observation systems for school practitioners: Ecobehavioral assessment systems software (EBASS). (Special technology-based assessment within special education). *Exceptional Children, 61,* 197–211.

Hakuta, K., Butler, Y. G., & Witt, D. (2000). *How long does it take English language learners to attain proficiency?* The University of California Linguistic Minority Research Institute, Policy Report, 2000–2001.

Harp, B. (2006). *The handbook of literary assessment and evaluation* (3rd ed.). Norwood, MA: Christopher Gordon.

Johns, J. (2005). *Basic reading inventory: Pre-primer through grade twelve and early literacy assessments.* Kendall/Hunt.

Kamil, M. L., Mosenthal, P. B., Pearson, P. D., & Barr, R. (Eds.). (2000). *Handbook of reading research* (Vol. 3). Mahwah, NJ: Erlbaum.

Kovaleski, J. F., Tucker, J. A., & Duffy, D. J. (1995). School reform through instructional support: The Pennsylvania Initiative (Part 1). *Communiqué, 23,* 8.

Kramer, B., Roberston, S., & Rodriguez, A. (2005). Analysis of the problem: The Texas accountability system fails our English language learners. University of Texas. Retrieved July 15, 2005, from http://www.ebd.utexas.edu/faculty/valenzuela/analysis.pdf

Laing, S., & Kamhi, A. (2003). Alternative assessment of language and literacy in culturally and linguistically diverse populations. *Language, Speech, and Hearing in Schools, 34,* 44–55.

Lentz, F. E., & Shapiro, E. S. (1986). Functional assessment of academic environments. *School Psychology Review, 15,* 346–357.

Leslie, L., & Caldwell, J. (2006). *Qualitative reading inventory–4* (4th ed.). Boston: Allyn & Bacon.

Leslie, L., Caldwell, J. A., & Leslie, L. (1995). *Qualitative reading inventory II.* New York: HarperCollins.

Manzo, A. V., Manzo, U. C., & McKenna, M. C. (1995). *Informal reading inventory.* Orlando, FL: Harcourt Brace.

McCloskey, D., & Athanasiou, M. S. (2000). Assessment and intervention practices with second-language learners among practicing school psychologists. *Psychology in the Schools, 37,* 209–225.

McKoon, G. (2003). Assessment of English proficiency for children learning English as a second language. In *National symposium on learning disabilities in English language learners* (pp. 4–6). Washington, DC.

McLaughlin, B. (1990). Restructuring. *Applied Linguistics, 11,* 113–128.

McLeod, B., & McLaughlin, B. (1986). Restructuring or automatization? Reading in a second language. *Language Learning, 36,* 109–126.

Mohan, B. A. (1986). *Language and content.* Reading, MA: Addison-Wesley.

Montes, F. (2002). Enhancing content areas through a cognitive academic language learning based collaborative in South Texas. *Bilingual Research Journal, 26,* 697–716.

Moya, S. S., & O'Malley, J. M. (1994). A portfolio assessment model for ESL. *The Journal of Educational Issues of Language Minority Students, 13,* 13–36.

Muñiz-Swicegood, M. (1994). The effects of metacognitive reading strategy training on the reading performance and student reading analysis strategies of third grade bilingual students. *Bilingual Research Journal, 18,* 83–97.

National Association of School Psychologists. (2003). *Portraits of children: Culturally competent assessment.* Video and CD-ROM Training Package. ASPIRE/IDEA.

Neal, J. C., & Kelly, P. R. (1999). The success of Reading Recovery for English language learners and Descubriendo La Lectura for bilingual students in California. *Literacy Teaching and Learning, 4,* 81–108.

No Child Left Behind. (2005). Overview-Introduction: No Child Left Behind Act. Retrieved July 27, 2005, from http://www.ed.gov/nclb/overview/intro/edpicks.jhtml

Noell, G. H., Freeland, J. T., Witt, J. C., & Gansle, K. A. (2001). Using brief assessments to identify effective interventions for individual students. *Journal of School Psychology, 39,* 335–355.

Ochoa, S. H., Powell, M. P., & Robles-Pina, R. (1996). School psychologists' assessment practices with bilingual and limited-English-proficient students. *Journal of Psychoeducational Assessment, 14,* 250–275.

O'Malley, J. M. (1989). Language proficiency testing with limited English proficient students. In J. E. Alatis (Ed.), *Georgetown University roundtable on language and linguistics* (pp. 235–244). Washington, DC: Georgetown University.

Ordoñez, C. L., Carlo, M. S., Snow, C. E., & McLaughlin, B. (2002). Depth and breadth of vocabulary in two languages: Which vocabulary skills transfer? *Journal of Educational Psychology, 94,* 719–728.

Ovando, C. J., Collier, V. P., & Combs, M. C. (2003). *Bilingual and ESL classrooms: Teaching in multicultural contexts* (3rd ed.). Boston: McGraw-Hill.

Peregoy, S. F., & Boyle, O. F. (2004). *Reading, writing, and learning in ESL: A resource book for K–12 teachers* (4th ed.), Boston: Allyn & Bacon.

Peverly, S. T., & Kitzen, K. R. (1998). Curriculum-based assessment of reading skills: Consideration and caveats for school psychologists. *Psychology in the Schools, 35,* 29–47.

Rhodes, R. L., Ochoa, S. H., & Ortiz, S. O. (2005). *Assessing culturally and linguistically diverse students: A practical guide.* New York: Guilford.

Roberts, M. L., & Shapiro, E. S. (1996). Effects of instructional ratios on students' reading performance in a regular education program. *Journal of School Psychology, 34,* 73–91.

Rosenfield, S. (1987). *Instructional consultation.* Hillside, NJ: Erlbaum.

Royer, J. M., & Carlo, M. S. (1991). Transfer of comprehension skills from native to second language. *Journal of Reading, 34,* 450–455.

Salvia, J., & Ysseldyke, J. (2004). *Assessment* (9th ed.). Boston: Houghton Mifflin.

Shapiro, E. S. (1992). Use of Gickling's model of curriculum-based assessment to improve reading in elementary age students. *School Psychology Review, 21,* 168–176.

Shapiro, E. S., & Elliott, S. N. (1999). Curriculum-based assessment and other performance-based assessment strategies. In C. R. Reynold & T. B. Gutkin (Eds.), *The handbook of school psychology.* New York: John Wiley & Sons.

Shinn, M. (1998). Curriculum-based measurement: Assessing special children. In M. R. Shinn (Ed.), *Advanced applications of curriculum-based measurement* (pp. 214–256). New York: Guilford.

Shinn, M., Collins, V. L., & Gallagher, S. (1998). Curriculum-based measurement and its use in a problem-solving model with students from minority backgrounds. In M. R. Shinn (Ed.), *Advanced applications of curriculum-based measurement* (pp. 143–174). New York: Guilford.

Shinn, M., Rosenfield, S., & Knutson, N. (1989). Curriculum-based assessment: A comparison of models. *School Psychology Review, 18,* 299–316.

Shinn, M. R. (2002). Best practices in using curriculum-based measurement in a problem-solving model. In A. Thomas & J. Grimes (Eds.), *Best practices in school psychology IV* (Vol. 1, pp. 671–698). Bethesda, MD: National Association of School Psychologists.

Stanley, S. O., & Greenwood, C. R. (1981). *Code for instructional structure and student academic response: CISSAR.* Kansas City: Juniper Gardens Children's Project, Bureau of Child Research, University of Kansas.

Stevens, R. A., Butler, F. A, & Castellon-Wellington, M. (2000). *Academic language and content assessment: Measuring the progress of English language learners.* CSE Technical Report No. 552. Los Angeles: University of California, National Center for Research on Evaluation, Standards, and Student Testing.

Texas Education Authority. (2003). Academic excellence indicator system: 2002–2003 state performance report. Retrieved July 15, 2004, from http://www.tea.state.tx.us/perfreport/aeis/2003/state.html

Thomas, W. P., & Collier, V. (1997). *School effectiveness for language minority students.* Washington, DC: National Clearinghouse for Bilingual Education.

U.S. Department of Education. (2005). Biennial evaluation report to Congress on the implementation of Title III, Part A of the ESEA: Executive Summary (pp. i–vi). Retrieved July 14, 2005, from http://www.ed.gov/about/offices/list/oela/index.html?src = oc

Verhoeven, L. T. (1990). Acquisition of reading in a second language. *Reading Research Quarterly, 25,* 90–114.

Wallace, T., Anderson, A. R., Bartholomay, T., & Hupp, S. (2002). An ecobehavioral examination of high school classrooms that include students with disabilities. *Exceptional Children, 68,* 345–359.

Waxman, H. C., & Padron, Y. N. (2004). The uses of the Classroom Observation Schedule to improve classroom instruction. In H. C. Waxman, R. G. Tharp, & R. Soleste Hilberg (Eds.), *Observational research in U.S. classrooms: New approaches for understanding cultural and linguistic diversity* (pp. 72–96). Cambridge, England: Cambridge University Press.

Waxman, H. C., Tharp, R. G., & Soleste Hilberg, R. (Eds.). (2004). *Observational research in U.S. classrooms: New approaches for understanding cultural and linguistic diversity.* Cambridge, England: Cambridge University Press.

Williamson County School District, Franklin, TN. (2005). *Chapter 5: Initial evaluation.* Retrieved July 19, 2005, from http://www.wcs.edu/Staff/ProcedManual/Chapter 20PDFS/Chapter 05.pdf

Ysseldyke, J. E., & Christensen, S. (2002). *Functional assessment of academic behavior: Creating successful learning environments.* Longmont, CO: Sopris West.

V

MULTICULTURAL THERAPEUTIC INTERVENTIONS

19

COUNSELING CULTURALLY AND LINGUISTICALLY DIVERSE CHILDREN AND YOUTH: A SELF-REGULATORY APPROACH

Jairo N. Fuertes, Vincent C. Alfonso, and Janet T. Schultz
Fordham University

U.S. Census Bureau statistics indicate that in 2000 almost 30% of the U.S. population consisted of ethnic minority individuals. It is also estimated that by 2050 minority groups will encompass over 50% of the U.S. population (Bernal & Scharron-Del-Rio, 2001). Schools in the United States now house approximately 30% culturally and linguistically diverse children, and this percentage is estimated to rise dramatically in the next 50 years (National Center of Educational Statistics [NCES], 2000). The significant demographic changes in the United States are due to higher birth rates among ethnic minority groups, particularly Hispanics, and the migration of 3,000 immigrants a day to the United States (the great majority of whom come from Mexico, Central and South America, and Asia). Current NCES reports suggest that almost 5% of school-age children in the United States speak a language other than English at home, and these same reports suggest that cultural and linguistic diversity will continue to rise in schools due to demographic changes in the general population.

As will become evident in this chapter, the increasing cultural and linguistic diversity in the U.S. educational system presents challenges and opportunities for school psychologists, counselors, and other professionals working to promote the academic, social, and emotional development of culturally and linguistically diverse children and youth in schools. The challenges include the significantly lower academic performance of ethnic minority and immigrant students in school that culminates in high dropout rates (with the exception of some Asian American subgroups), in comparison with White American students (NCES, 2000). In addition, ethnic minority and immigrant students experience disproportionably higher rates of psychosocial difficulties (e.g., teen pregnancy, gang membership, drug use) as they acculturate and live in the United States.

This chapter summarizes relevant literature on the challenges and social-emotional difficulties that immigrant children face in U.S. educational settings. These challenges are discussed in terms of three areas: acculturation, discrimination, and second language acquisition. The groups addressed are defined as follows: (a) immigrants are persons born outside of the United States and who now reside in this country, (b) children and youth refer to school-age individuals between 7 and 18 years of age, and (c) cultural and linguistic diversity refers to immigrants whose first language is not English and whose worldviews, values, and/or socialization experiences may be objectively or subjectively considered distinct from those experienced by U.S.-born citizens. The focus is on immigrant populations, primarily because, with these groups, issues of acculturation, poverty, discrimination, and language use are so deeply prevalent (Bernal & Scharron-Del-Rio, 2001). However, the discussion is also relevant to U.S.-born culturally and linguistically diverse children and youth, particularly to those who (a) are visible ethnic group members and who have parents who were born outside the United States, (b) do not speak English, and (c) are not fully acculturated to the U.S. ways of life.

The specific content covered includes the literature on the process of psychosocial and academic self-regulation and presents a model of adjustment that is anchored on self-regulation processes. Interventions are proposed that may promote the adjustment and development of culturally and linguistically diverse children and youth (hereafter CLD children and youth) in three broad contexts: family relationships, peer groups, and school performance.

THEORETICAL AND RESEARCH BASIS OF SOCIAL-EMOTIONAL STRESSORS

Acculturation

Acculturation is a process of learning and development that can be stimulating. However, this process is also confusing, stressful, and developmentally disruptive. Williams and Berry (1991) described acculturation as a process of change that individuals experience when they come into contact with another culture. These changes can be evident in behavior, thought patterns, values, and social activities that occur as a result of contact with a new culture (Gordon, 1964). According to Mirsky and Kaushinsky (1989), the acculturation process may take, on average, 3 to 4 years for most immigrants and represents a complex phenomenon that incorporates three different modes of social-psychological functioning—cognitive, behavioral, and affective.

Factors that exacerbate the level of acculturative stress experienced by the individual include the reason for acculturation, socioeconomic status, acceptance or prestige of one's group, opportunity for contact with other cultural groups, and prior knowledge of the new culture (Fuertes & Westbrook, 1996; Williams & Berry, 1991). Acculturative stress can manifest itself in psychological difficulties such as anxiety, depression, feelings of marginality and isolation, elevated psychosomatic symptoms, and identity confusion (Williams & Berry, 1991).

There is evidence that the process of migration and acculturation can lead to conflicts within the family (Rogers et al., 1999). These conflicts often center on the expected role of parents, the family, and children; preferences in language use at home; preferences in values and customs, such as type of dress/fashion and social activity; and vocational preferences (Baruth & Manning, 1991). Family difficulties have a negative influence on school performance, and *acculturative gaps* between parents and children exacerbate these problems by limiting the contact and communication between children and parents and parents and school professionals. These gaps lead to alienation for the child and have the potential to create the insidious effect of inducing the child to seek support and advice from negative external sources (e.g., gangs or others similarly alienated). Family difficulties are also associated with increased problem behavior susceptibility in areas such as conduct disorder, depression, and other behavioral problems (Birman & Trickett, 2001; Dinh, Roosa, Tein, & Lopez, 2002; Dumka, Roosa, & Jackson, 1997).

A child's peers impact academic achievement and may even represent a stronger factor than parents in influencing overall academic performance (Steinberg, 1996). Researchers have identified a significant relationship between peer relations and school adjustment. For example, Diehl, Lemerise, Caverly, Ramsay, and Roberts (1998) investigated the role that peer acceptance, friendship, social status, and age contributed to school adjustment in mixed-age classrooms. Their results demonstrated that the greatest risk factor for poor school performance is rejection by appropriate peers, whereas the presence of at least one friend serves as an asset for school performance. In addition, they found that peer acceptance and friendship positively influence school achievement. These results are consistent with results from previous research suggesting that children's social competence and social supports, such as peers, function as predictors of children's early school adjustment (Ladd 1989, 1990; Piaget, 1965). Leondari (2001) investigated peer acceptance among immigrant and nonimmigrant (host) children and found that peer interactions were affected by a child's immigrant status, especially for boys. However, immigrant children did not differ from host children in regard to their feelings of loneliness, self-perceptions, and social competence (Leondari, 2001). Thus counselors should consider differences in acculturation levels and how these relate to the manifestation of immigrant students' presenting problems.

CLD children and youth experience significant difficulties in school performance. For example, the dropout rate among Puerto Rican youth in New York City ranges from 42% to 80%, in comparison to general dropout rates in the United States of about 5% to 20%. Native American students (50%) and African American urban students (40% to 60%) also exhibit higher rates of dropout than Whites or Asian Americans. While the process of acculturation may be implicated in school performance, clearly poverty, the role of the family unit, and the quality of education are factors that may explain underperformance by CLD students. For example, the Forum on Child and Family Statistics (1999) discovered that in families with children from ages 6 to 17, the poverty rate was 35% for African Americans and Hispanics, compared with 14% for Whites (Meece & Kurtz-Costes, 2001). Economic difficulties impact the quality of education that immigrant children receive by limiting resources and allowing for less rigorously trained teachers.

Discrimination

Studies have shown that children's racial attitudes are shaped and internalized according to the ones that adult role models have displayed (Pacino, Stanford, & Yamamoto, 2001). For example, Phinney, Madden, and Santos (1998) investigated the psychological variables that predicted perceived ethnic discrimination among 164 adolescent immigrant children (Mexican American, Armenian, and Vietnamese). The findings demonstrated that lower intergroup competence, higher depression, and anxiety scores are associated with perceived discrimination. This suggests that immigrant children who feel incompetent interacting with other cultural groups or who experience internalizing symptoms also experience elevated levels of perceived discrimination. Porter (2000) writes that when negative stereotypes or images are internalized, the result may be restricted identity exploration and the emergence of negative identity that is characterized by ineffective, even destructive, out-of-control behavior. This phenomenon is particularly deleterious when teachers, counselors, and even parents or siblings convey, even if it is done unconsciously or indirectly, these negative beliefs and stereotypes about the child.

Second Language Acquisition

Another factor that strongly impacts the adjustment of immigrant children in schools is the challenge of learning a new language. Learning a second language is often a frightening task for immigrant children. Many times this fear may paralyze students in a group activity and even result in "elective mutism" among bilingual students (Esquivel & Keitel, 1990). Cummins (1982) found that there is a difference between Basic Interpersonal Communication Skills (BICS) that are related to social conversation and Cognitive Academic Language Proficiency Skills (CALPS) that are related to cognitive and academic functioning. Cummins proposed that CLD children may take up to 5 years to master the CALPS and that they often score lower than monolingual students in reading and language arts. Esquivel and Keitel (1990) recommend investigating the quality and quantity of former schooling, literacy level in the native language, native language mastery, and how different the target language differs from the native language when assessing a child's level of acculturation. If a child is unable to participate and interact with peers, he or she may experience failure, frustration, lowered self-esteem, and academic difficulties (Esquivel & Keitel, 1990). The stressors increase for children who were not exposed to formal learning experiences in their native country (Cummins, 1982). Sources of stress include fear of rejection by peers and teachers, exposure to negative views of the minority group that others may promulgate, and the need to learn and master a new language and to fit in with a new culture.

Previous Models of Intervention for Counseling CLD Children

The literature abounds with articles, chapters, and books on the topic of multicultural counseling, although there seem to be fewer sources that are empirical in nature or that focus specifically on the topic of counseling CLD children and youth. There are also many research articles that promote counseling approaches for specific ethnic minority groups. However, the validity of such approaches has yet to be empirically validated, including factors such as within-group differences among groups and possible effects in promoting stereotypic thinking and behavior on the part of school professionals. In general, these approaches also tend to de-emphasize the uniqueness of the individual, including the set of circumstances, assets, and deficits that children and youth bring to the counseling situation (e.g., family history and structure, level of cognitive functioning, learning disabilities, motivation). Another limitation of many of the research articles on counseling minority populations is that they do not provide empirically based interventions (EBI). That is, these research articles tend to be based on conceptualizations of culture that are often undefined and thus fail to provide specific interventions for specific problems.

However, despite the limitations noted, a discussion is presented on several research articles and models that make contributions to the literature on counseling CLD children and youth. Porter (2000) discusses the sociocultural factors that affect ethnic minority youth, including poverty, language issues, and stereotypes and also discusses psychological issues that are prevalent in these populations, including identity conflicts, substance abuse, and teen pregnancy. She presents a model of individual therapy that emphasizes the use of problem-solving skills, time-limited interventions, and the strengthening of coping skills. The primary emphasis in her model is the therapeutic relationship, especially for adolescents, who may be apathetic or hostile to the therapist. Porter also discusses the importance of family therapy, particularly to address communication and altered structures that come from acculturation and stressful events. Porter further reviews a model proposed by Ho (1992), which emphasizes group treatment for specific issues, including exploring ethnic awareness and identity, strengthening bicultural skills, and decreasing feelings of isolation and loneliness.

Gopaul-McNicol and Thomas-Presswood (1998) adapted a model for treating CLD children and youth. The model is comprehensive and allows the counselor or therapist flexibility to draw from various theories and approaches to develop and implement a treatment plan. The model is composed of four phases, and the authors note that the phases may recur as the treatment unfolds. The structure of the model includes (a) the assessment process that comprises various substages such as assessment, establishing trust, and determining acculturation level; (b) an educational treatment process; (c) a psychological treatment process; and (d) an empowerment treatment process. The comprehensive nature of this model is impressive, although there is a need for specificity and clarity of description presented for each of the phases. The model is particularly lacking in detail in the psychological treatment phase, and thus it is unclear to the reader as to how counselors actually intervene. Gopaul-McNicol and Thomas-Presswood (1998) note that Lazarus's multimodal approach, Minuchin's structural therapy, and Bowen's family treatment approach are most helpful in helping CLD children and families, but do not explain why these approaches are effective or selected, how these approaches are used, how they relate to the other phases of the model, or for which specific problems these approaches are intended. Despite these limitations, the authors provide a framework for intervening with CLD children that is structured and attends to educational and psychological issues for CLD children.

Cartledge and Loe (2001) and Kopala and Esquivel (1994) provided some excellent guidelines for working with CLD ethnic minority and immigrant children. Cartledge and Loe focus on classroom interventions and the role that teachers may play in socializing and educating minority children, whereas Kopala and Esquivel provide useful interventions that are more consistent with the traditional role of counselors. Cartledge and Loe focus on establishing cultural competence in schools by suggesting a multicultural curriculum and culturally sensitive disciplinary policies. They also argue for teacher sensitivity in their perceptions of, communication with, and evaluations of ethnic minority students. They present interventions for classroom management that promote affirming and supportive environments and suggestions for understanding and redirecting ethnic minority students who may display disruptive or socially inappropriate behaviors. Kopala and Esquivel focus on the theme of stress, migration, and acculturation. They present outreach interventions that are intended to increase the amount of external support to immigrant students and their families and that facilitate students' social interactions through skill training in areas such as communication, decision making, and relaxation training. They also place emphasis on involving parents in school activities, which promotes parent–child interaction and behavior monitoring as well as school–parent collaboration. These latter suggestions are consistent with those offered by Zayas and Solari (1994) that emphasize parenting skill programs to increase parent involvement and mediation between children and schools. Last, we note a contribution by Esquivel (1998), which focuses on group interventions with culturally and linguistically diverse students. Esquivel notes that group strategies may be very appropriate for collectivistic or group-oriented students and also describes school- and community-based interventions that may be effective in a group-counseling modality. The intervention strategies described include cuento therapy (Costantino, Malgady, & Rogler, 1986), hero-heroine modeling, and Unitas, all of which have been empirically validated. Esquivel also provides a discussion of other culturally sensitive issues in group work with CLD children, such as assessment of acculturation level of group members, the cultural competence of the group facilitator, and underlying cultural dynamics of group interactions.

The aforementioned models make useful contributions to the literature on counseling CLD children and youth (and their families). Despite the value of these sources, however, it is evident that there is need for a model that connects salient issues in the process of acculturation and adaptation and that provides a conceptual framework for intervention. A model of self-regulation will be proposed that may accomplish such purpose. First, the literature on the topic of psychological self-regulation is presented as a basis for this model.

Self-Regulation

Self-regulation, or self-control, is a basic yet complex developmental task for all children; it has been shown to be associated with school performance and psychological and interpersonal competence. A fundamental premise in this chapter is that self-regulation, not to mention optimal functioning, is severely strained by migration and the challenging tasks that come with it: acculturation, learning a new language, making new friends, reestablishing social contacts with the expatriate community, finding support, and so on. For children, migration also complicates, at least temporarily, age-appropriate tasks of emotional and psychological development, including identity formation, cognitive development, and social skills learning. Promoting, or "boosting," self-control strategies for CLD children and youth in schools may result in children successfully navigating the challenges of migration and may increase their adjustment and performance in three important areas: family relations, peer interactions, and school performance.

In the past 10 to 15 years the construct of self-regulation has been studied and written about extensively in the research and practice literature (e.g., Baumeister & Vohs, 2004; Kochanska, Coy, & Murray, 2001). It has been the topic of inquiry in multiple disciplines including psychology and education and their related fields such as neuropsychology, cognitive psychology, early childhood, and learning disabilities. Perhaps the primary reason for the high and ever-increasing interest this construct has received is its relationship to a highly valued outcome in our society: academic achievement. There is little argument that self-regulation is positively related to academic success for most individuals regardless of age, gender, race/ethnicity, or intellectual level (Blair, 2002; Gottfried, 1990; Zimmerman & Risemberg, 1997). Given the significant academic challenges that CLD children and youth face in the United States, the more relevant and possibly applicable this knowledge is may help these populations.

Zimmerman and Risemberg (1997) note that high achievers demonstrate the following adaptive and valued self-regulatory processes: (a) manage study time well, (b) set higher specific and proximal goals, (c) monitor their behavior and progress more frequently and accurately, (d) set a higher standard for satisfaction, (e) are more self-efficacious, and (f) persist despite obstacles. Those individuals who do not achieve or have extreme difficulties achieving do not evidence these self-regulatory processes and in fact exhibit the opposite characteristics. That is, they tend to be more impulsive, set lower academic goals, are less accurate in assessing their skills and competencies, are more critical of themselves, and persevere less at academic tasks (Borkowski & Thorpe, 1994; Zimmerman & Risemberg, 1997). Moreover, it appears that the accumulated effect of poor self-regulatory processes interferes not only with academic achievement but also with interpersonal relationships including parents, teachers, and peers who in distinct ways can be facilitators of academic and social success.

A definition of self-regulation is found in Schunk (1994). He states, "Self-regulation refers to the process whereby students activate and sustain cognitions, behaviors, and affects that are systematically oriented toward the attainment of goals"

(Schunk, 1994, p. 75). Barkley's (1998) definition is probably the most succinct and understandable way of characterizing self-regulation, that is, self-control. Most people do not have difficulty understanding what is meant by self-control or the consequences of those who exhibit limited or marked self-control in academic and/or social settings. However, for our purposes a synthesized definition of self-regulation is the ability of an individual, given his or her developmental level, to engage in adaptive, socially acceptable relationships and to employ strategies in academic settings that enable the person to learn effectively (Blair, 2002). With respect to CLD populations, the individual's ability to use internal and external resources to regulate the difficulties associated with migration is essential (e.g., acculturation, second language acquisition).

Interpersonal Regulation

Research has shown that preschoolers, school-aged children, and adolescents who have a hard time controlling their behavior also have many interpersonal difficulties (e.g., Birch & Ladd, 1998; VanDerHeyden, Witt, & Gatti, 2001). As early as three years of age, those children who exhibit externalizing behavior problems such as hitting others, destroying property, and being disruptive in social settings soon realize that friends are difficult to find and keep (Eisenberg, Smith, Sadovsky, & Spinrad, 2004; Papatheodorou, 2000). In addition, these children may not be well liked by adults such as family members, preschool teachers, and day care personnel (Rimm-Kaufman, Pianta, & Cox, 2000). Although some may think that young children who evidence these behaviors will "grow out" of them, the research literature clearly demonstrates that this may not be the case. For example, these children may be on a negative trajectory toward more severe behavior problems including possible diagnoses such as Oppositional Defiant Disorder and Conduct Disorder (Barkley, 1998; Miller, 1994; Webster-Stratton, 1993).

Even children who manifest less intense externalizing behavior problems such as inattention, impulsivity, and hyperactivity or internalizing behavior difficulties such as withdrawal, somatization, and depression may often find themselves disliked by many authority figures who would otherwise be helpful to them (Barkley, 1998). Indeed, these children are often characterized as having attention deficit hyperactivity disorder (ADHD), the most frequently diagnosed childhood behavior disorder rendered today, or disorders of adjustment, anxiety, and depression. Although persons diagnosed with ADHD manifest different behaviors over the course of development, they continue to encounter interpersonal and eventually occupational difficulties (Barkley, 1998). Thus the inability of individuals to control their behavior, respond in socially appropriate ways in academic and social settings, and alter their negative behavioral trajectory is a large problem with severe consequences. These individuals tend to alienate others, encounter academic difficulties because they are not behaviorally prepared to learn, and fail or drop out of school. They are not high achievers when it comes to school and other educational settings (Borkowski & Thorpe, 1994).

Another aspect of interpersonal self-regulation pertains to emotional reactivity or the ways in which individuals react affectively (i.e., emotionally) and behaviorally to certain stimuli in their environment. For example, children who react too much or too little to stimuli (e.g., parents, peers, teachers) because of externalizing or internalizing behavior problems respectively tend to encounter interpersonal difficulties and eventually academic problems as well. This is evident very early in life and is usually associated with infants' temperament. It is clear that young children's temperament is a good predictor of later temperament, emotional reactivity, self-regulation skills, and self-regulated learning (Blair, 2002; Martin, Drew, Gaddis, & Moseley, 1988). It is also generally accepted that infants and toddlers who evidence high or low negative reactivity require especially skilled parents in order to develop any type of high-quality self-regulatory skills. In fact, Blair (2002) writes, "self-regulation ability emerges gradually over time, that basic cognitive abilities in infancy, such as attention, support self-regulation behavior, and that emotionality and the interaction of emotionality with rearing experience are likely to be central to a full understanding of self-regulation and its development" (p. 113).

Teachers also tend to report that they would prefer to work with children who are emotionally "stable" rather than with those who are academically strong, but emotionally and behaviorally difficult (i.e., externalizing or internalizing behavior problems; Lewitt & Baker, 1995). This is probably the case because it is very difficult to instruct children while managing their behavior and controlling their emotional reactions to the environment. Thus teachers may believe that they are not doing their job if academic instruction has been replaced with behavior management. This situation can occur as early as the preschool level, which may be the time for teachers and other adult figures to assist in the development of self-regulatory skills because it is unlikely that these skills will develop without early intervention. With respect to CLD children and youth, the literature cited earlier and inferences drawn from theory and clinical experience suggest that it is precisely those children with propensities to have problems with self-regulation, even prior to migration, that have the most difficulty adjusting academically and interpersonally to the United States. Thus a direct and fundamental intervention in helping these children entails teaching and rehearsing self-regulatory strategies that promote adjustment.

Adapted Model of Self-Regulation and Adjustment

Children have a strong adaptive system that serves as an internal regulator in helping them overcome significant stressors in their lives (Masten & Coatsworth, 1998). A child's overall resiliency can be strengthened through targeting parent–child relationships, cognitive development, and self-regulation of attention, emotion, and behavior. Resiliency is present when an individual overcomes a significant obstacle of high-risk status (i.e., poverty, domestic violence, single parenthood) or has been exposed to a threat such as violence, war, death, or abuse (Masten & Coatsworth, 1998). Masten (2001) proposed an indirect model of risk and resilience in which risks and assets are mediated by critical adaptive systems, such as parenting, which are associated with resilience. In this chapter, Masten's (2001) model has been adapted and a "new" model proposed that focuses on self-regulation strategies to reduce risk and promote resilience in the adaptive processes of CLD children and youth (see Figure 19–1).

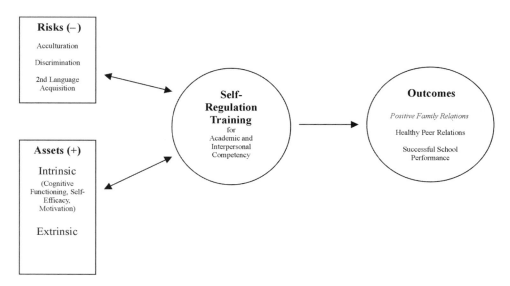

FIGURE 19–1   A model of adjustment based on self-regulation for CLD children and youth.

This model includes risks and assets as two broad categories that have a potentially adverse impact on behavioral, interpersonal, and academic self-regulation. There are two factors that need to be considered when attempting to achieve positive outcomes and goals, risks and assets. In the present model, the risks are major stressors that CLD children and youth experience, such as having to learn a new language or having to face poverty or discrimination. Conversely, assets comprise a positive mechanism associated with resilience in children. Intrinsic assets are inherent qualities that, for the most part, stem from within the individual, such as level of cognitive functioning, self-efficacy, and motivation. Extrinsic assets include external influences on children that may include family members, school personnel, and caretakers and/or peers. These external assets function as supportive buffers that help children adapt and adjust to their new environment. These factors in isolation are not sole contributors to an immigrant child's adaptation and adjustment in school; rather, self-regulation is seen as moderating behavior and performance. The outcome of proficient self-regulation is healthy adaptation to the environment, and in the present model this is reflected in positive family relations, healthy intercultural peer relations, culturally adaptive responses, and successful school performance.

IMPLICATIONS FOR PRACTICE AND IMPLEMENTATION AND APPROACHES

The American Psychological Association (APA) published a set of nine guidelines for providers of psychological services to CLD populations (APA, 1993). These include the need for psychologists to inform clients regarding goals, expectations, and scope of service in both oral and written forms; learn about relevant research and practice issues such as the limits of expertise and validity of instruments and procedures; and recognize the impact of ethnicity and culture on psychological processes. In addition, the Office of Ethnic Minority Affairs of the APA recommends respecting family roles, values, and cultural and religious beliefs and utilizing the language preferred by the client or referring to a mental health professional competent in the language or a certified translator. Finally, cultural factors such as the reason for immigration, English fluency, type of family involvement, community resources, prior educational level, relationships with individuals from other cultures, change in social status, and acculturative stress level should be investigated during assessment.

These are all important recommendations and to the extent that they are followed may limit the harm and maximize the benefit that interventions may have for CLD populations. However, as discussed earlier, the primary limitation of the literature on counseling CLD children and youth is the lack of models that explain behavioral outcomes and ways that counselors may be able to intervene psychologically or psychosocially to help students. The model presented here advances the state of the literature by presenting a process for understanding risk, adaptation, and performance in CLD children and youth. One way of applying the model is presented in the following section, and it is intended to help CLD children and youth regulate their behavior more optimally.

Self-Regulatory Training

It is clear that important persons in the environment can assist individuals in becoming better self-regulators that will, in turn, lead to greater academic and interpersonal success. For example, several authors have investigated the positive role that parents can play in the academic achievement of their children (e.g., Carlton & Winsler, 1999; Gottfried, Fleming, & Gottfried, 1994; Grolnick & Ryan, 1989; Grolnick & Slowiaczek, 1994). Other authors have focused on peers and peer circles of motivational and academic influence (e.g., Berndt & Keefe, 1995; Ladd, Birch, & Buhs, 1999; Ryan, 2000; Schunk & Zimmerman, 1998). Finally, there is an extensive body of research on the roles that teachers can play in fostering academic self-regulation as well as specific strategies they can use in various educational settings (e.g., Phye, 1997; Schunk & Zimmerman, 1994).

Despite the increasing attention given to self-regulation, there is a scarcity of research that has examined self-regulatory training as a counseling intervention. Thus the goals in this section are to borrow and parallel interventions in the academic achievement literature and to propose self-regulatory strategies that may be implemented by school counselors and psychologists. Self-regulatory training can take shape in various formats and be implemented by various adults in a child's life, including counselors, teachers, and invested parents. Counselors can intervene despite their theoretical or technical perspectives (e.g., cognitive or behavioral interventions, reality therapy, rational emotive behavior treatment, applied behavioral analysis) as long as the counselor proposes to deliver interventions that are practical, targeted, and easy for the child to implement and as long as the progress is measurable.

Self-regulatory training as part of counseling interventions to help CLD children and adolescents adjust requires multicultural competencies and must involve the following: (a) despite the cognitive-behavioral flavor of self-regulatory training, the quality of the relationship between the child and the counselor is essential to gaining client participation and collaboration with this training (an understanding of the child's affective and communication style is important in establishing this relationship); (b) it is necessary to conduct a culturally based assessment of the nature and severity of the difficulties the child is having in the targeted outcome areas: family life, peer relationships, and school performance; (c) a counselor who is competent and comfortable in being direct in devising specific goals of outcome behavior yet one who can also be flexible in adapting the approach in a way that is consistent with the child's cultural experiences; (d) a counselor who will seek the collaboration of parents/family and other school personnel and engage them in a process in a way that is congruent with their cultural values and expectations. This collaboration is important for legal and ethical reasons based on due process and parental rights but also from the practical perspective that parents and teachers spend a significant amount of time and have influence over children's ability to implement, practice, evaluate, and correct their behavior; and (e) while the modality for intervention is assumed to be individual counseling, there may be situations when self-regulatory training might include group or family counseling. These therapeutic modalities may be particularly important when family issues are significant or when the child has poor peer relations. The choice of a group or family modality needs to be based on an understanding of cultural group and family values and the process conducted with cultural sensitivity and skill (Esquivel, 1998; Fong, 2004; McGoldrick, Giordano, & Garcia-Prieto, 2005).

School performance issues that may be targeted as specific goals include (a) the manner, speed, and quality of the child's second language acquisition, particularly in reading and writing; (b) the amount of time the child is studying, including a review of academic subjects that the child is avoiding or having difficulty with, a review of study strategies used by the child, and/or the amount of time spent with parents studying; (c) classroom behaviors, including compliance with teacher assignments and directives and appropriate peer interactions; and (d) an evaluation of the mechanisms by which the child identifies when and where to seek help and reinforcement for his or her efforts. *Family issues* that may be covered under self-regulatory training may include (a) improving the quality of communication with parents and increasing parental involvement and support directly with the child and in school; (b) increasing parent–child collaboration regarding expectations and rules at home, including home tasks; and (c) helping the child understand differences in cultures between the school and the family. Issues related to *peer relations* that may be included in self-regulatory training include (a) teaching of social skills, including communication and assertiveness; (b) promoting health behaviors, decreasing risky behaviors, and managing peer influence; (c) promoting participation in sports and other school activities; and (d) coping with racism and discrimination.

Zimmerman's (1998) self-regulated learning cycle model provides the basis for the proposed self-regulatory counseling intervention with CLD children. The three cycle phases include *forethought*, *performance control*, and *self-reflection*

(Zimmerman, 1998). Interestingly, these three phases parallel the three broad stages that seem to underlie many counseling interventions, as discussed by Hill and O'Brien (1999): *exploration*, *insight*, and *action*. These two models complement each other and provide a more complete perspective for intervention in a counseling context. According to Zimmerman, *forethought* refers to an assessment and preparatory phase that reviews processes and beliefs that precede learning and includes goal setting (i.e., desired outcomes), strategic planning (i.e., strategies and methods for achieving the desired outcomes), self-efficacy beliefs (fostering "I can" attitudes), goal orientation (i.e., a progress vs. performance outcome orientation), and promoting intrinsic interest (i.e., persistence despite rewards). Hill and O'Brien provide an additional and important component to this first phase. They note that the primary tasks of the counselor during the *exploration* stage involves establishing rapport, learning the client's perspective, and encouraging the client to explore thoughts and feeling and to express them to the counselor.

In Zimmerman's second phase, *performance control* refers to processes that occur during the learning period, as the child begins to implement new behaviors and strategies. These processes help the child focus on the tasks and maximize performance. Performance control strategies include attention focusing, self-instruction/imagery, and self-monitoring. Similarly, Hill and O'Brien suggest that the primary tasks of the counselor during the *insight* stage involve helping clients make connections and gain understanding of options and objectives; helping clients explore their role in handling thoughts, feelings, and behaviors; and dealing with issues in the counseling relationship, such as attachment issues, trust, and apathy.

In Zimmerman's model, the third self-regulatory phase is *self-reflection* and involves "processes that occur after learning efforts and influences a learner's reactions to that experience. These reflections, in turn, influence forethought regarding subsequent learning efforts, thus completing the self-regulatory cycle" (Zimmerman, 1998, p. 2). Tasks associated with self-reflection include self-evaluation, an analysis of attributions made by the child about his or her success/failure or progress on his or her behavior, and an analysis of self-reactions. Hill and O'Brien describe the *action* stage as one where counselors help clients decide on actions, develop skills for action, provide feedback on attempted changes, and help clients to evaluate changes and modify action plans.

Self-regulation training is likely to result in increased motivation and behavioral/emotional self-control. The child learns to evaluate and choose behavior options and develops confidence to manage more complex and developmentally appropriate tasks. Increased motivation and social-emotional self-control contribute to the development of self-efficacy, which improves performance, coping, and persistence. As mentioned earlier, beyond school performance, self-regulatory training may also help children find appropriate options for play and diversion and to cope effectively with conflicts and demands that may arise at home during the process of acculturation (e.g., helping parents with language issues, aiding parents with home tasks, value conflicts with parents due to different levels of acculturation or role expectancies). Depending on the level of apathy or hostility of the child, parents and school personnel will need to devote a significant amount of time learning about the child and considerable energy in communicating warmth, empathy, and care to foster trust and motivation. In fact, self-regulation has at its core an intra–inter-personal dimension: a trusting and supportive relationship with an authority figure is essential to a child's success in school and interpersonal relationships.

IMPLICATIONS FOR RESEARCH AND TRAINING

The literature on self-regulation has grown dramatically in the last decade. However, this literature has thus far been directed primarily at solving school performance problems. Self-regulation may be an effective strategy for helping CLD children and youth cope with many social and interpersonal difficulties associated with migration to the United States. Given the extensive empirical literature on self-regulatory processes, it seems timely to examine empirically the applicability of self-regulatory training to socioemotional and personal problems with CLD children and youth. Obviously, future researchers need to evaluate the depth and breadth of this proposed model and put to the test the value of self-regulatory training as a counseling intervention. Researchers may also examine the effectiveness of teaching self-regulation to aid second language acquisition and school progress, for example, in bilingual education programs versus monolingual education. Researchers may also examine the effectiveness of teaching parents self-regulation, so that they may become more involved in helping their children in their education and cultural adjustment. Evidence of self-regulatory training helping CLD children and youth adjust along our three general targeted areas will have implications for training school counselors and psychologists, as well as other school personnel.

SUMMARY

This chapter presented information regarding the problems that CLD children and youth encounter in U.S. schools and the society as a whole. A review of various models of intervention for counseling CLD children and youth was presented, with the conclusion drawn that many of the models currently in the literature need to be more specific and/or based on empirical evidence to support them. A brief, yet concentrated discussion on the construct of self-regulation was presented, using the existing database on this construct and the Hill and O'Brien (1999) counseling model to adapt an intervention for CLD children and youth. An ongoing program of research is needed to explore the clinical utility of and empirically validate self-regulatory training in helping CLD children and youth cope and surpass the unique socioemotional difficulties they exhibit.

ANNOTATED BIBLIOGRAPHY

Lynch, E. W., & Hanson, M. J. (Eds.). (1998). *Developing cross cultural competence: A guide for working with children and their families* (2nd ed.). Baltimore, MD: Paul H. Brookes.

   Provides information and practical advice for professionals working with children and families from diverse cultural and linguistic backgrounds.

Saldaña, D. (2001). Cultural competency: A practical guide for mental health service providers. Hogg Foundation for Mental Health, University of Texas at Austin.

Defines cultural competency and provides concrete strategies to help develop this skill. Author is a clinical psychologist who discusses culturally related syndromes, tests appropriate for diverse groups, methods of conducting culturally sensitive assessments, and engages in outreach with culturally and linguistically diverse populations. Retrieved September 18, 2005, from http://www.hogg.utexas.edu/PDF/Saldana.pdf

Vernon, R. F. (2004). A brief history of resilience: From early beginnings to current constructions. In C. S. Clauss-Ehlers & M. D. Weist (Eds.), *Community planning to foster resiliency in children*. New York: Kluwer Academic.

This chapter provides an informative and concise historical overview of the construct of resilience and directions for future research.

RESOURCES

Immigrant Students and Mental Health On-Line Clearinghouse:
http://smhp.psych.ucla.edu/qf/immigrantkids.htm

This clearinghouse provides a vast array of publications, documents, agencies, and Web sites that focus on immigrant children in the United States. One can find information on immigration law, cultural concerns in addressing barriers to learning, and related articles discussing the health and well-being of children in immigrant families. Resources are pertinent to mental health professionals, teachers, and parents interested in providing transition support for immigrant students, becoming familiar with facts and findings on educational attainment, and obtaining practical information relating to accessing health care and college education.

National Association of School Psychologists. (n.d.). *Promoting cultural diversity and cultural competency: Self-assessment checklist for personnel providing services and supports to children and their families:*
http://www.nasponline.org/culturalcompetence/checklist.html

This checklist serves as a reflective tool to assess one's cultural competency and provides examples of values and practices to foster a positive counseling environment for culturally and linguistically diverse children and their families.

Responding to linguistic and cultural diversity recommendations for effective early childhood education: A position statement of the National Association for the Education of Young Children. (1995):
http://www.naeyc.org/about/positions/pdf/PSDIV98.PDF

This resource provides information and strategies for early childhood educators striving to create a responsive learning environment by facilitating second language acquisition. Retrieved September 18, 2005, from

REFERENCES

APA Office of Ethnic Minority Affairs. (1993). Guidelines for providers of psychological services to ethnic, linguistic, and culturally diverse populations. *American Psychologist, 48,* 45–48.

Barkley, R. A. (1998). *Attention deficit hyperactivity disorder: A handbook for diagnosis and treatment* (2nd ed.). New York: Guilford.

Baruth, L. G., & Manning, M. L. (1991). *Multicultural counseling and psychotherapy: A lifespan perspective.* New York: Merrill Macmillan.

Baumeister, R. F., & Vohs, K. D. (Eds.). (2004). *Handbook of self-regulation: Research, theory, and applications.* New York: Guilford.

Bernal, G., & Scharron-Del-Rio, M. R. (2001). Are empirically supported treatments valid for ethnic minorities? Toward an alternative approach for treatment research. *Cultural Diversity and Ethnic Minority Psychology, 7,* 328–342.

Berndt, T. J., & Keefe, K. (1995). Friends' influence on adolescents' adjustment to school. *Child Development, 66,* 1312–1329.

Birch, S. H., & Ladd, G. W. (1998). Children's interpersonal behaviors and the teacher-child relationship. *Developmental Psychology, 34,* 934–946.

Birman, D., & Trickett, E. J. (2001). Cultural transitions in first-generation immigrants: Acculturation of Soviet Jewish refugee adolescents and parents. *Journal of Cross-Cultural Psychology, 32,* 456–477.

Blair, C. (2002). School readiness: Integrating cognition and emotion in a neurobiological conceptualization of children's functioning at school entry. *American Psychologist, 57,* 111–127.

Borkowski, J. G., & Thorpe, P. K. (1994). Self-regulation and motivation: A life-span perspective on underachievement. In D. S. Schunk & B. J. Zimmerman (Eds.), *Self-regulation of learning and performance: Issues and educational applications* (pp. 45–74). Hillsdale, NJ: Erlbaum.

Carlton, M. P., & Winsler, A. (1999). School readiness: The need for a paradigm shift. *School Psychology Review, 28,* 338–352.

Cartledge, G., & Loe, S. A. (2001). Cultural diversity and social skill instruction. *Exceptionality, 9,* 33–46.

Costantino, G., Malgady, R. G., & Rogler, L. H. (1986). Cuento therapy: A culturally sensitive modality for Puerto Rican children. *Journal of Consulting and Clinical Psychology, 54,* 639–645.

Cummins, J. (1982). Test achievement and bilingual students. *Focus, 9,* 1–7.

Diehl, D. S., Lemerise, E. A., Caverly, S. L., Ramsay, S. & Roberts, J. (1998). Peer relations and school adjustment in ungraded primary children. *Journal of Educational Psychology, 90,* 506–515.

Dinh, K. T., Roosa, M. W., Tein, J., & Lopez, V. A. (2002). The relationship between acculturation and problem proneness in a Hispanic youth sample: A longitudinal mediational model. *Journal of Abnormal Child Psychology, 30,* 295–309.

Dumka, L. E., Roosa, M. W., & Jackson, K. M. (1997). Risk, conflict, mothers' parenting and children's adjustment in low-income, Mexican immigrant, and Mexican American families. *Journal of Marriage & The Family, 59,* 309–323.

Eisenberg, N., Smith, C. L., Sadovsky, A., & Spinrad, T. L. (2004). Effort control: Relations with emotion regulation, adjustment, and socialization in childhood. In R. F. Baumeister & K. D. Vohs (Eds.), *Handbook of self-regulation: Research, theory, and applications* (pp. 259–282). New York: Guilford.

Esquivel, G. B. (1998). Group interventions with culturally and linguistically diverse students. In K. C. Stoiber & T. R. Kratochwill (Eds.), *Handbook of group intervention for children and families* (pp. 252–267). Boston: Allyn & Bacon.

Esquivel, G. B., & Keitel, M. A. (1990). Counseling immigrant children in the schools. *Elementary School Guidance & Counseling, 23,* 213–221.

Fong. R. (Ed.). (2004). *Culturally competent practice with immigrant and refugee children and families* (3rd ed.). New York: Guilford.

Fuertes, J. N., & Westbrook, F. D. (1996). Using the S.A.F.E. Acculturation Stress Scale to assess the adjustment needs of Hispanic college students. *Measurement and Evaluation in Counseling and Development, 29,* 67–76.

Gopaul-McNicol, S., & Thomas-Presswood, T. (1998). *Working with linguistically and culturally different children: Innovative clinical and educational approaches.* Boston: Allyn & Bacon.

Gordon, M. M. (1964). *Assimilation in American life.* New York: Oxford University Press.

Gottfried, A. E. (1990). Academic intrinsic motivation in young elementary school children. *Journal of Educational Psychology, 82,* 525–538.

Gottfried, A. E., Fleming, J. S., & Gottried, A. W. (1994). Role of parental motivational practices in children's academic intrinsic motivation and achievement. *Journal of Educational Psychology, 86,* 104–113.

Grolnick, W. S., & Ryan, R. M. (1989). Parent styles associated with children's self-regulation and competence in school. *Journal of Educational Psychology, 81,* 143–154.

Grolnick, W. S., & Slowiaczek, M. L. (1994). Parents' involvement in children's schooling: A multidimensional conceptualization and motivational model. *Child Development, 65,* 237–252.

Hill, C. E., & O'Brien, K. M. (1999). *Helping skills: Facilitating exploration, insight, and action.* Washington, DC: American Psychological Association.

Ho, M. K. (1992). *Minority children and adolescents in therapy.* Newbury Park, CA: Sage.

Kochanska, G., Coy, K. C., & Murray, K. T. (2001). The development of self-regulations in the first four years of life. *Child Development, 72,* 1091–1111.

Kopala, M., & Esquivel, G. (1994) Counseling approaches for immigrant children: Facilitating the acculturative process. *School Counselor, 41,* 352–359.

Ladd, G. W. (1989). Children's social competence and social supports: Precursors of early school adjustment? In B. H. Schnieder, G. Attili, J. Nadel, & R. Weissberg (Eds.), *Social competence in developmental perspective* (pp. 1373–1400). Amsterdam: Kluwer.

Ladd, G. W. (1990). Having friends, keeping friends, making friends, and being liked by peers in the classroom: Predictors of children's early school adjustment? *Child Development, 67,* 1081–1118.

Ladd, G. W., Birch, S. H., & Buhs, E. S. (1999). Children's social and scholastic lives in kindergarten: Related spheres of influence. *Child Development, 70,* 1373–1400.

Leondari, A. (2001). The impact of acculturation on immigrant children's self-perceptions, feelings of loneliness, and social status. *Educational & Child Psychology, 18,* 35–46.

Lewitt, E. M., & Baker, L. S. (1995). School readiness. *Critical Issues for Children and Youths, 5,* 128–139.

Martin, R. P., Drew, D., Gaddis, L. R., & Moseley, M. (1988). Prediction of elementary school achievement from preschool temperament: Three studies. *School Psychology Review, 17,* 125–137.

Masten, A. S. (2001). Ordinary magic-resilience processes in development. *American Psychologist, 56,* 227–238.

Masten, A. S., & Coatsworth, J. D. (1998). The development of competence in favorable and unfavorable environments: Lessons from research on successful children. *American Psychologist, 53,* 205–220.

McGoldrick, J., Giordano, J. & Garcia-Preto, N. (Eds.). (2005). *Ethnicity and family therapy* (3rd ed.). New York: Guilford.

Meece, J. L., & Kurtz-Costes, B. (2001). Introduction: The schooling of ethnic minority children and youth. *Educational Psychologist, 36,* 1–7.

Miller, L. S. (1994). Primary prevention of conduct disorder. *Psychiatric Quarterly, 65,* 273–285.

Mirsky, J., & Kaushinsky, F. (1989). Migration and growth: Separation-individuation processes in immigrant students in Israel. *Adolescence, 24,* 225–240.

National Center of Educational Statistics. (2000). *The condition of education.* Washington, DC: U.S. Department of Education, Office of Educational Research and Improvement.

Pacino, M. A. (2001). Differing cultures and the morality of schooling. In B. H. Stanford & K. Yamamoto (Eds.), *Children and stress: Understanding and helping* (pp. 43–54). Olney, MD: Association for Childhood Education International.

Papatheodorou, T. (2000). Management approaches employed by teachers to deal with children's behavior problems in nursery classes. *School Psychology International, 21,* 415–440.

Phinney, J. S., Madden, T., & Santos, L. J. (1998). Psychological variables as predictors of perceived ethnic discrimination among minority and immigrant adolescents. *Journal of Applied Social Psychology, 28,* 937–953.

Phye, G. D. (Ed.). (1997). *Handbook of academic learning: Construction of knowledge.* New York: Academic.

Piaget, J. (1965). *The moral judgment of the child.* New York: Free Press.

Porter, R. Y. (2000). Understanding and treating ethnic minority youth. In J. F. Aponte & J. Wohl (Eds.), *Psychological intervention and cultural diversity* (pp. 167–182). Boston: Allyn & Bacon.

Rimm-Kaufman, S. E., Pianta, R. C., & Cox, M. J. (2000). Teachers' judgments of problems in the transition to kindergarten. *Early Childhood Research Quarterly, 15,* 147–166.

Rogers, M. R., Ingraham, C. L., Bursztyn, A., Cajigas-Segredo, N., Esquivel, G., Hess, R., et al. (1999). Providing psychological services to racially, ethnically, culturally, and linguistically diverse individuals in the schools. *School Psychology International, 20,* 243–264.

Ryan, A. M. (2000). Peer groups as a context for socialization of adolescents' motivation, engagement, and achievement in school. *Educational Psychologist, 35,* 101–112.

Schunk, D. H. (1994). Self-regulation of self-efficacy and attributions in academic settings. In D. S. Schunk & B. J. Zimmerman (Eds.), *Self-regulation of learning and performance: Issues and educational applications* (pp. 75–100). Hillsdale, NJ: Erlbaum.

Schunk, D. H., & Zimmerman, B. J. (Eds.). (1994). *Self-regulation of learning and performance: Issues and educational applications.* Hillsdale, NJ: Erlbaum.

Schunk, D. H., & Zimmerman, B. J. (Eds.). (1998). *Self-regulated learning: From teaching to self-reflective practice.* New York: Guilford.

Steinberg, L. (1996). *Beyond the classroom: Why school reform has failed and what parents need to do.* New York: Simon & Schuster.

VanDerHeyden, A. M., Witt, J. C., & Gatti, S. (2001). Research into practice: Descriptive assessment method to reduce overall disruptive behavior in a preschool classroom. *School Psychology Review, 30*(4), 548–567.

Webster-Stratton, C. (1993). Strategies for helping early school-aged children with oppositional defiant and conduct disorders: The importance of home–school partnerships. *School Psychology Review, 22,* 437–457.

Williams, C. L., & Berry, J. W. (1991). Primary prevention of acculturative stress among refugees: Application of psychological theory and practice. *American Psychologist, 46,* 632–641.

Zayas, L. H., & Solari, F. (1994). Early childhood socialization in Hispanic families: Context, culture, and practice implications. *Professional Psychology: Research and Practice, 25,* 200–206.

Zimmerman, B. J. (1998). Developing self-fulfilling cycles of academic regulation: An analysis of exemplary instructional models. In D. S. Schunk & B. J. Zimmerman (Eds.),

Self-regulated learning: From teaching to self-reflective practice (pp. 1–19). New York: Guilford.

Zimmerman, B. J., & Risemberg, R. (1997). Self-regulatory dimensions of academic learning and motivation. In G. D. Phye (Ed.), *Handbook of academic learning: Construction of knowledge* (pp. 106–127). New York: Academic.

20

MULTICULTURAL VOCATIONAL INTERVENTIONS WITH DIVERSE ADOLESCENTS IN LOW-INCOME URBAN SCHOOLS

Margo A. Jackson, Jonathan P. Rust,
and Natasha DeFio Santiago

Fordham University

Youth in low-income, culturally diverse, inner-city schools are at risk for low educational attainment, limited future career options, and severely reduced earnings potential (Education Trust, 2000; Hotchkiss & Borow, 1996; National Center for Education Statistics, 2001, 2004; U.S. Department of Education, 1996; U.S. Equal Employment Opportunity Commission, 2000). Yet evidence suggests that students who learn to effectively negotiate vocational development processes (e.g., identifying, exploring, and gaining knowledge about their occupational and educational interests, abilities, values, beliefs, options, and goals) also develop more positive academic motivation and skills for educational and occupational planning and achievement (Baker & Taylor, 1998; Evans & Burck, 1992; Lapan, Gysbers, & Petroski, 2001; Lapan, Gysbers, & Sun, 1997; Nelson & Gardner, 1998; Smith, 2000; Whiston & Sexton, 1998). Thus one approach to helping all students succeed—and in particular, reducing the educational and occupational achievement gap for culturally and linguistically diverse (CLD) youth in low-income urban schools—may be for counselors to facilitate effective career interventions in these schools.

Vocational or career development has been defined as the continuous process by which an individual learns about and develops a vocational identity and work values and how one integrates these concepts into one's overall life and identity (Peterson & Gonzalez, 2005). Career development is closely associated with how and why one makes educational and occupational choices. Although this is a lifelong process, and career development interventions may be especially critical at the elementary school level (Arbona, 2000), in this chapter we focus primarily on CLD adolescents in schools. Raskin (1994) has noted that a critical developmental task for adolescents is the formation of a vocational identity as part of an overall process including social, religious, gender, and ethnic identity formation. One important context in which this process takes place is in school. Other contexts for the process of vocational identity formation include the culture and society, family, peers, and work. According to Raskin (1994), the task of adolescent vocational development is to explore occupational and educational options and make tentative choices. In the course of vocational identity development, adolescents learn about their interests, abilities, and values and how these relate to different occupations, educational requirements, work environments, and working relationships with others. The more successful adolescents are in this stage of vocational identity development, the more likely they will be successful in choosing and acquiring knowledge, skills, and attitudes for attaining satisfying and rewarding careers as adults who contribute meaningfully to society (Hoyt, 1977; National Occupational Information Coordinating Committee [NOICC], 1992; Raskin, 1994).

Niles and Harris-Bowlsbey (2002) offered the following definition of career development interventions:

> Career development interventions, defined broadly, involve any activities that empower people to cope effectively with career development tasks (Spokane, 1991). For example, activities that help people develop self-awareness, develop occupational awareness, learn decision-making skills, acquire job search skills, adjust to occupational choices after they have been implemented, and cope with job stress can each be labeled as career development interventions. Specifically, these activities include individual and group career counseling, career development programs, career education, computer-assisted career development programs, and computer information delivery systems, as well as other forms of delivering career information to clients. (p. 7)

Any or all of the career development activities listed previously may be relevant for CLD adolescents for their impending transition from school to work (Blustein, Juntunen, & Worthington, 2000) or to postsecondary education (Education Trust, 2000; Jackson & Nutini, 2002) and for CLD youth who may also need to work part-time during their school years to help support their families (Newman, 1999).

In this chapter, the discussion first focuses on what we know to date from theory and research about effective career development interventions for low-income CLD adolescents in inner-city middle and high schools. Next, practice implications are reviewed and then highlighted through four examples of multicultural vocational interventions with low-income urban CLD youth that were based in theory and research and developed in collaboration with college and school counseling professionals, educators, administrators, and community members. Finally, recommendations for future research, advocacy efforts, and relevant useful resources are presented.

THEORETICAL AND RESEARCH BASE

What do we know so far about effective career interventions for low-income CLD youth in urban schools? To date, the professional literature offers few empirical studies to directly address this question. However, relevant meta-analyses and theoretical developments may inform this line of inquiry. Reviewers of the career counseling and intervention literature have consistently concluded that career interventions are effective (e.g., Oliver & Spokane, 1988; Swanson, 1995; Whiston, Sexton, & Lasoff, 1998). However, most reviewers have also noted that we know too little about how, why, and for whom career interventions are effective (Brown & Krane, 2000). In particular, we do not know if, how, and why career interventions may be effective for CLD youth. For example, in Ryan's (1999) meta-analysis of 62 studies, only 21% of the studies identified participants by race and ethnicity. Furthermore, as reviewers have noted (Brown & Krane, 2000; Whiston et al., 1998), few studies have examined Aptitude x Treatment interactions among the characteristics of client/student, vocational problem, and treatment that might moderate the effects of the career intervention. In addition to relevant multicultural and psychological characteristics of individuals, more research is needed on contextual factors in effective career intervention with CLD youth in low-income urban settings (e.g., environmental safety, social support, discrimination influences, quality of instruction, and access to educational and occupational resources).

Despite significant limitations in our current knowledge about how career interventions may be effective, specifically for at-risk CLD youth in schools, several meta-analyses of relevant literature provide a basis for further investigation. Whiston and Sexton (1998) conducted a review of school counseling outcome research and found tentative support for the positive effects of school counseling activities in career planning. In another meta-analytic review of the research literature, Baker and Taylor (1998) found positive effects of career education interventions for students in kindergarten through Grade 12. A meta-analysis by Evans and Burck (1992) found positive effects of career education interventions on student academic achievement in Grades 1–12. In summary, evidence from these meta-analyses suggests that career development interventions in schools may be effective in facilitating adolescents in their vocational identity development, academic achievement, and educational/vocational planning. Yet most of the research reviewed to date has used predominantly middle-class White students. Therefore we need further research to investigate if the essential aspects of effective career interventions in schools suggested by these meta-analyses have cultural validity with CLD youth and if other culturally specific aspects are needed. (We further discuss this issue in the section Implications for Future Research and Practice).

In order for school counselors and psychologists to practice ethically as well as determine and disseminate what we learn about what works for whom and why, we must design and evaluate career development interventions for CLD adolescents that are soundly based on culturally appropriate vocational assessment (see Jackson, Mendelsohn, & Rotenberg, this volume) and explicitly grounded in culturally relevant theories and conceptual models (Betz & Fitzgerald, 1995; Kiselica,

Changizi, Cureton, & Gridley, 1995; Strong, 1991; Swanson & Fouad, 1999). Harris-Bowlsbey (2003) noted that the "career counseling profession has a rich theoretical base" (p. 18), and she reviewed the contributions of several theorists to our understanding of career choice and development. However, she also noted (as have many other authors) that mainstream theories of career development have focused disproportionately on White, middle-class young men. In response to a call to the profession to address these limitations to our understanding of multicultural career development (e.g., Leong & Brown, 1995), one trend in recent research has been to examine the cultural validity of mainstream career theories and constructs (Byars & McCubbin, 2001). For example, Hackett and Byars (1996) examined applications of social cognitive career theory (Lent, Brown, & Hackett, 1994) to the educational and occupational self-efficacy beliefs and outcome expectations of African American girls and women.

Another evolving line of research has examined culturally specific variables such as racial/ethnic identity, acculturation, and perceived discrimination (Byars & McCubbin, 2001). For example, Jackson and Nutini (2002) examined discrimination influences on resources and barriers for career learning with low-income, urban CLD middle school students. Yet another area of inquiry relevant to individuals with constrained access to educational and career opportunities, such as working-class adults and urban CLD youth, are studies that have examined such individuals' conceptions of work primarily as a means to make money and earn a living to support themselves and their families (Blustein et al., 2002; Chaves et al. 2004) and as one among other important cultural and community roles and priorities (Hansen, 2001). These conceptualizations of work contrast with the middle-class, male, and culturally encapsulated Western assumptions underlying mainstream career development theories that the role of work is central in people's lives (as opposed to family, community, spiritual, and recreational roles, for example) and that work serves primarily as a means for individual self-expression or satisfaction (Blustein, 2001; Richardson, 1993).

The issue of how to integrate mainstream theories of career development and practice continues to be debated (e.g., Leong & Serafica, 2001; Savickas & Walsh, 1996). Subich and Simonson (2001) noted that in response to the limitations of adapting mainstream theories of career development to practice, three emergent models of career counseling show promise for more effective and culturally relevant theory-to-practice integration—Fouad and Bingham's (1995) culturally appropriate career counseling model, Krumboltz's (1996) learning theory of career counseling (LTCC), and Chartrand's (1996) sociocognitive interactional model of career counseling. Subich and Simonson defined emergent theories as "those that present a potentially nonlinear process of career counseling and develop and recognize the importance of environmental/social/emotional counseling process and client empowerment" (p. 258). Among the three emergent models, Krumboltz's LTCC has been used to inform the design of a career development intervention study with low-income urban CLD high school students (Jackson, Mendelsohn, Rust, Beck, & Lambert, 2004).

An evolving conceptual framework proposed for counseling practice and research in schools is developmental-contextualism and its emphasis on "how human development (a) is affected by context, (b) involves bio-psycho-social levels,

(c) occurs during the lifespan, and (d) includes strengths and deficits" (Walsh, Galassi, Murphy, & Park-Taylor, 2002, p. 682). Applications of a developmental-contextualism framework to career development interventions with low-income urban CLD youth include Achieving Success Identity Pathways and Tools for Tomorrow (Solberg, Howard, Blustein, & Close, 2002). (We describe these two interventions later in the chapter under Implementation and Approaches.)

IMPLICATIONS FOR PRACTICE

According to the learning theory of career counseling, the role of career counselors is to help clients expand their learning and clarify beliefs that facilitate and hinder their career development (Krumboltz, 1996). From this perspective, school counselors and psychologists could use culturally and developmentally appropriate vocational interventions to expand CLD students' learning about potential career and educational interests, abilities, and beliefs, as well as develop constructive beliefs and success strategies. From a developmental-contextualism framework, some promising collaborative efforts of counseling psychologists with middle and high schools are addressing the educational/occupational achievement gap for CLD students by promoting connections between educational and career development and building students' psychological resources to prepare for more positive future educational and vocational transitions (Blustein, 2003; Solberg et al., 2002). Foundational to facilitating the career development of CLD youth, Arbona (1996, 2000) has argued that throughout the school years counselors need to focus on building these youth's cognitive and academic competencies while providing support and advocacy for their social, emotional, and cultural needs.

School counselors are trained to facilitate students' development in the interrelated domains of academic, personal, social, and career development (Campbell & Dahir, 1997). In schools, it is school counselors who typically assume primary responsibility for promoting students' career development (Campbell & Dahir, 1997). School psychologists might collaborate with school counselors in promoting students' career development by expanding their educational evaluation recommendations to include culturally appropriate vocational intervention plans.

A discussion of two models designed for school counselors to facilitate students' development in academic, career, and personal/social domains throughout their school years follow. One model is presented in the career development guidelines of the National Occupational Information Coordinating Committee (NOICC, 1992). Designed to help counselors identify developmentally appropriate career development goals and interventions across the life span, the NOICC guidelines include outlines of specific career development competencies for students at the elementary, middle/junior high, and high school levels. These career development competencies are organized under three categories—self-knowledge, educational and occupational exploration, and career planning. These three categories build on Parson's (1909) foundational approach to career development interventions advocating a three-step process of gaining knowledge of self, obtaining knowledge of the world of work, and applying decision-making skills to making occupational choices.

However, from the perspective of Krumboltz's (1996) learning theory of career counseling, such an approach might be considered a necessary but insufficient component of effective career development interventions in the schools. Krumboltz noted that trait-and-factor Parsonian approaches are commonly used by career counselors to suggest how people might match their *current* interests, abilities, and values with related educational and occupational environments. Beyond this step, Krumboltz argued, counselors must design interventions to help individuals to expand their learning experiences and develop *new* interests, abilities, and values in order to prepare for and cope with the changing demands of a contemporary work world. For example, Krumboltz explained that instead of interpreting ability assessments as aptitudes that are unchangeable, career counselors might use such assessments to target new learning goals for how to improve one's performance. Such an approach might constructively challenge low ability expectations and enhance motivation with CLD students at risk for low academic and career achievement.

Another model for integrating academic, career, and personal/social development in the schools has been proposed by Gysbers and Henderson (2000). For example, in addition to incorporating career counseling in individual sessions with students, in some school districts school counselors have engaged in systematic and coordinated planning with their school communities and university researchers to implement and evaluate career development programs as part of the curriculum throughout elementary and secondary levels. Along with the benefits of systemic coordination, strengths of such comprehensive career education programs include how the interventions were theoretically grounded and informed by assessment. While empirical evidence has supported the effectiveness of more fully implemented comprehensive career guidance programs (Lapan et al., 1997, 2001; Nelson & Gardner, 1998), the student participants in this research were predominantly White of middle-class socioeconomic status. Less is known to date about if or how these models might apply with CLD youths in low-income urban schools (Turner & Lapan, 2003). Furthermore, in most school districts (particularly in low-income, urban, culturally diverse settings), school counselors have been charged with a wide variety of responsibilities and minimal time and support for incorporating systematic career development programs (Herring, 1998).

Gysbers and Henderson's (2000) model for designing and managing comprehensive career guidance programs and the NOICC (1992) career development guidelines provide resources that counselors and psychologists can use to work collaboratively in schools and incorporate developmentally appropriate career interventions to facilitate all students' academic, career, and personal/social growth. We submit, however, that these models fall short of addressing cultural factors that may be critical for effective career development interventions with CLD adolescents in low-income urban schools. For example, McWhirter, Hackett, and Bandalos (1998) found that among Hispanic individuals, level of acculturation was an important influence on educational and occupational expectations. Also, CLD adolescents have additional identity development tasks to negotiate regarding racial, ethnic, and/or cultural identity development (e.g., negotiating to what degree and in what contexts they will adopt the attitudes, feelings, and behaviors of their cultural identity group or mainstream/dominant cultural groups; Markstrom-Adams & Spencer, 1994; Rotheran-Borus & Wyche, 1994). Therefore relevant cultural factors such as acculturation status and racial/ethnic/cultural identity development likely need to be incorporated in career development interventions with CLD adolescents in schools.

Perhaps the most critical cultural factor that needs to be addressed in multicultural vocational interventions is discrimination. Despite U.S. democratic ideals, discrimination continues to operate on systemic and individual levels so that compared to middle-class White youth, low-income and CLD youth do not have equal access to good-quality educational resources and a broad range of career options (Blustein, 2001; Education Trust, 2000; Kozol, 1991; Lee & Dean, 2004; Richardson, 1993; Sue, 2003). As Arbona (1996) pointed out, vocational interventions based on existing theories of career development and choice have little to offer to low-income CLD youth with thwarted access to educational resources and career options. Nevertheless, we submit that school counselors and psychologists can work at both systemic and individual levels to constructively address these influences of discrimination and design more effective multicultural vocational interventions.

For example, at the systemic level, counselors, psychologists, and other members of our school and broader communities need to continue to advocate for more equitable and sustained funding that includes support for effective multicultural vocational interventions in the schools. Several educational reform initiatives in the 1980s lead to the passage of the School-to-Work Opportunities Act (STWOA; U.S. Congress, 1994). STWOA funded many new programs to provide non–college-bound or work-bound youth (a group disproportionately represented by low-income CLD youth) with competitive skills and competencies to make successful transitions from high school graduation to the workforce and earning livable wages (Blustein et al., 2000). STWOA and, more recently, the U.S. Department of Education GEAR UP (Gaining Early Awareness and Readiness for Undergraduate Programs), have provided funding for school-university-community partnerships that include vocational interventions for low-income and urban CLD youth (e.g., Jackson et al., 2004; Lapan, Osana, Tucker, & Kosciulek, 2002; Mobley & Berkel, 2004). Lapan et al. suggested, "Now would be an opportune time for career development theorists and practitioners to form partnerships that could both shape and develop new state and federal workforce education/development policies" (2002, p. 188). Such alliances could advocate for systemic change for effective interventions in school settings (Walsh et al., 2002) and ameliorate discrimination influences that limit CLD youth's educational and career achievement.

At a more individual level, there are several key ways that school counselors and psychologists can work to constructively address these influences of discrimination and design more effective multicultural vocational interventions. For one, school counselors and psychologists need to become more culturally aware of their own values, biases, stereotypes, and assumptions regarding CLD youth. Regardless of good intentions, all counselors are prone to unintentional biases with multicultural clients that can limit the effectiveness of their interventions, or worse, do harm (Ridley, 1995; Sue, 2003; see the discussion on Hidden Counselor Biases in Jackson et al., this volume). For example, school counselors and psychologists may subtly, automatically, and unintentionally harbor negative stereo-types toward CLD students such as attributing their academic and behavioral difficulties to their own (or their parents') laziness, apathy, or lack of intellect. Counselors' lack of attention to or awareness of systemic discrimination factors or education/career barriers and the influence of their own hidden biases may leave important gaps in their assessments, misinform their intervention designs, and further disadvantage CLD students (Jackson & Nutini, 2002). Despite consid-erable evidence that CLD youth do not have equal access to education and career opportunities (e.g., Education Trust, 2000), many counseling professionals fail to attend to such cultural factors in their assessments and interventions (Ramirez, Wassef, Paniagua, & Linsky, 1996; Ridley, 1995). Fundamental to ethical and ef-fective career development intervention with CLD students, school counselors and psychologists must learn to increase their awareness of discrimination influ-ences (Abreu, 2001; Constantine, 2002) and continually develop their competen-cies in multicultural counseling (Arrendondo et al., 1996; Constantine & Yeh, 2001; Sue et al., 1998) as well as career counseling (National Career Development Association Professional Standards Committee, 1997).

For effective multicultural vocational intervention, school counselors and psy-chologists need to address the psychological effects of discrimination on CLD youth's educational and career development, such as academic disidentification and school disengagement. Ogbu (1990, 1992) noted that schools are institutions that prepare students for their future adult roles, and in U.S. schools there is a psychological caste system where different racial/cultural groups have internal-ized messages about their group status or power. These internalized messages af-fect individuals' thoughts, attitudes, feelings, and behaviors about what mem-bers of their group are entitled to or can do. Ogbu suggested that African Americans are at the lower end of this caste system and that this leads to both real and perceived limits to their educational options. As a consequence, African American and other minority students may disengage from goals to be success-ful in school because they do not believe that their efforts will be rewarded (Ogbu, 2003). Likewise, Steele (1997) suggested that many racial minority stu-dents may disidentify with academic achievement and school performance as a defensive mechanism to protect their self-esteem against negative stereotypes. Murdock (1999) found evidence of the effects of discrimination by race and social class on indicators of students' disengagement from school (e.g., disciplinary problems and perceptions of the future limited economic value of education); low-income African American youth were more disengaged from school than higher income White youth. Therefore culturally appropriate and sound career development interventions are needed to counter the effects of school disengage-ment for low-income CLD youth and connect the relevance of school to future achievable career options (e.g., Blustein et al., 2001).

IMPLEMENTATIONS AND APPROACHES

In terms of implementation, four examples of multicultural vocational interven-tions with low-income urban CLD adolescents that were grounded in theory and research are discussed in the following sections. Three of these interventions were conducted in schools. One was conducted as an intensive summer program at a college campus.

Career Linking

Fouad (1995) noted that (a) African Americans, Hispanics, and women are underrepresented among math and science college majors and careers; (b) math and science preparation is not only important for success in many professions but also reaps higher advancement and financial rewards than the occupations where women and minority group members are segregated; and (c) employers are thus missing large numbers of potentially qualified workers. She reviewed literature on how minority and female students avoid math and science because of poor academic preparation, lack of educational/career planning, few helpful role models, and low self-efficacy in math and science skills. She argued that school counselors need to intervene with CLD youth before critical high school course selections are made in order to facilitate the development of their self-efficacy and educational/career planning to include math and science access and options.

Fouad (1995) described a one-year intervention designed to promote math and science career awareness among 118 eighth grade CLD students at an inner-city middle school (the majority of participants were female and African American or Hispanic American). Titled Career Linking, several 6-week intensive and interdisciplinary career awareness models were infused into the eighth grade curricula in math, science, English, and history. "A 6-week model was developed around a career field that included an introduction to the career field, field trips, speakers, shadowing experiences, and evaluation exercises. Each 6-week period focused on a different field (e.g., health careers, robotics, natural sciences)" (p. 528). (Readers can refer to the article by Fouad for an overview of the week-by-week organization of the career units.) Methods included educational/career counseling, parent participation, and real-world experiences. The teachers of each subject worked together with the school counselor, a graduate student in counseling, and university faculty in a partnership with the University of Wisconsin—Milwaukee. Before beginning the units on various career fields, several joint school-university activities were conducted to introduce students to the program and encourage them to identify with the Career Linking goals. During the last week of each career unit, students and teachers evaluated the unit and made revision suggestions.

Results of Fouad's (1995) study showed that the Career Linking intervention effectively increased students' career knowledge and informed high school choices. The intervention was moderately successful for participants compared to a control group for increasing self-esteem and selecting high school math and science courses. Less support was found for the hypothesis that participants would show increased effort and achievement in math and science over the course of the one-year intervention.

Fouad offered the following recommendations to counselors for implementing this multicultural vocational intervention: (a) work closely with teachers to promote the integration of the career units into their curricula, (b) develop a library of printed and audiovisual materials as career unit curricular resources available to teachers as they need them, (c) solicit teachers' input in planning tours and speakers, (d) assign graduate student interns or practicum students to help with the time-consuming tasks of organizing and coordinating tours and speakers, and (e) augment the intervention focus on career awareness activities with career exploration and decision-making activities to help CLD students relate career information to their own interests and abilities.

Career Horizons Program

O'Brien, Dukstein, Jackson, Tomlinson, and Kamatuka (1999) described the Career Horizons Program for adolescents in at-risk environments (e.g., due to socioeconomic status, gender, or ethnicity) for academic/vocational underachievement. To provide these students with experiences to raise their career self-efficacy and expand their educational and occupational opportunities, the program was developed by a collaborative team comprised of a university faculty member and practitioners from Educational Talent Search, an initiative sponsored by the U.S. Department of Education, to encourage participants to pursue higher education. During the summer before entering the seventh grade, 57 low-income CLD students (the majority was comprised of racial/ethnic minority individuals, mostly African Americans) participated in the program on a midwestern university campus free of charge. They met in classes of approximately nine students taught by an assistant professor and doctoral student in counseling psychology for six hours a day for one week. Each group of students also had a trained staff mentor who supervised and encouraged their active participation. After completing the summer program, participants attended follow-up activities four and nine months later.

Consistent with NOICC career development guidelines for middle school competencies and based on the Missouri Comprehensive Guidance System (Starr & Gysbers, 1992), the Career Horizons Program provided classes in three areas—career exploration, career self-awareness, and math and science careers. The program included a health and physical education session and recreational activities in order to foster a sense of connectedness, relieve stress, and get physical exercise. Incorporated throughout the program were self-efficacy building opportunities designed to facilitate performance accomplishments, positive vicarious learning and verbal persuasion, and emotional regulation for effective learning (i.e., based on the four sources of self-efficacy hypothesized by Bandura, 1977). Activities highlighting the importance of culture in career aspirations were infused into the curriculum, and the instructors and staff members generated discussions with students about the influences of their culture and U.S. society on career decision making and vocational achievement.

O'Brien et al. (1999) found that the students who completed the Career Horizons Program showed increases in career planning and exploration efficacy, educational and vocational development efficacy, number of careers considered, and congruence between their interests and career choices. Consistent with self-efficacy theory, they interpreted these students' heightened efficacy as likely to enhance their ability to initiate action to constructively manage career development tasks, persist in the face of obstacles, and eventually succeed. They cautioned, however, "that overall increases in confidence should never be a focus of an efficacy intervention because attempts at tasks that are too difficult might result in failure and subsequent loss of desired levels of efficacy" (p. 225). Instead, interventions should be designed to increase efficacy at developmental levels where students possess the skills needed to accomplish the given tasks.

One recommendation offered by O'Brien et al. (1999) was to extend the length of the Career Horizons Program to provide interactive career experiences and support at intervals throughout the year in order to maintain optimum efficacy in educational/occupational development for students at risk of academic/vocational underachievement. Although not specified by O'Brien et al., we expect that such an extension of a university-based multicultural vocational intervention throughout the school year might be coordinated with and enhanced by counselors and psychologists at the students' schools.

Despite participants' gains from the Career Horizons Program, O'Brien et al. (1999) noted that the students' frequent references to adverse environmental stressors during the intervention might be expected to impede their focus on sustaining educational/vocational development. Specifically, these low-income CLD students "shared concerns about gang violence, teen pregnancy, alcohol and drug use, and unsafe neighborhoods. Given their concern about these issues, students may regard self-knowledge and career exploration as secondary concerns at best" (p. 225). Jackson and Nutini (2002) in their vocational assessment interviews with low-income urban CLD middle school students found similar concerns regarding environmental risk factors likely to impede students' career-related learning. These findings highlight not only the importance of vocational interventions for at-risk CLD adolescents but also the need to incorporate, or at least connect with, supports for helping these students constructively negotiate environmental barriers.

Achieving Success Identity Pathways

Solberg et al. (2002) described an ongoing psycho-educational program designed to promote successful school-to-work-to life transitions among CLD (predominantly Latino American) ninth and tenth graders in a low-income urban high school in Milwaukee, Wisconsin. Called Achieving Success Identity Pathways (ASIP), formerly the Adaptive Success Identity Plan (Solberg, 2001; Solberg, Close, & Metz, 2001), the ASIP program is a series of structured classroom/group curricula focused on empowering youth to define for themselves the specific challenges they face in making successful school transitions; to build vocational, academic, social, emotional, and physical skills; and to establish stronger relational connections with teachers and peers. Solberg et al. explained that the ASIP program strives to help students develop a sense of personal agency and a success identity whereby they believe that "they possess the skills to adapt effectively to changing life circumstances and perceive potentially threatening situations as challenges to be overcome rather than barriers to be avoided" (2002, p. 712).

In a variety of subject areas throughout the ninth and tenth grade years, four classroom/group curricula are cofacilitated by an ASIP staff member and the school counseling staff and/or trained classroom teacher. First, the ASIP *Navigator* curriculum provides a workbook to students to explore their personal academic and career goals with information from an individualized bar graph of their levels of academic and social efficacy, persistence intentions, stress, emotional and physical well-being, family support, connections with teachers and peers, and a comparison of their personal rating to the average rating of school peers making successful academic progress by grades and attendance. The second ASIP curriculum, *Hear My Story*, encourages students to write about their life experiences (including challenges with daily environmental stressors such as discrimination, poverty, and exposure to violence) and share these experiences with their teachers. Third, the *Action Theater* curriculum uses the support of adult facilitators to have students role-play interpersonal conflicts, include additional students to role-play alternative success scenarios, and explore with the class the reciprocal effects of the players' behaviors. The final ASIP curriculum is implemented in the tenth grade and consists of vocational development activities to help students explore their interests, values, and other personal characteristics in relation to seeking and obtaining career and postsecondary options.

Evaluation findings reported by Solberg et al. (2002) with more than 1,500 low-income CLD youth in the previous four years at this urban high school indicated that higher levels of exposure to the ASIP curricula contributed to increases in grades, credits earned, percentage of classes passed, and attendance rate. As an educational/vocational reform movement seeking to transform the interactions between youth and their educational context to facilitate successful school-to-work-to-life transitions, Solberg et al. noted that efforts were underway to disseminate the ASIP program to adapt to other middle and high schools by training professionals at community-based organizations or other federally funded programs to implement the ASIP curricula.

Tools for Tomorrow

Another ongoing psycho-educational intervention called Tools for Tomorrow (Blustein et al., 2001; Solberg et al., 2002) is designed to help low-income urban CLD high school students internalize the connections between school, work, and life. Participants in the program include more than 600 ninth graders (predominantly Black Caribbean, African American, and Hispanic/Latino/a) in two urban high schools in Boston, Massachusetts (Solberg et al., 2002). The program fosters interprofessional collaboration in its planning and curriculum development teams, and the intervention staff consists of Boston public school teachers, counselors, and administrators working in equal partnership with Boston College staff members. Weekly group sessions are cofacilitated by a trained counselor and teacher through three interrelated modules, titled (a) Who Am I? (b) Connecting School to Career, and (c) Identifying Resources and Barriers. The goals of the Tools for Tomorrow program are to "enhance self-knowledge, clarify career and educational goals, develop adult mentors, affirmatively integrate ethnic and racial identity factors, and deal effectively with family issues" (Solberg et al., 2002, p. 717). Ongoing formative and summative evaluation data is being collected, including indicators of school engagement (e.g., attendance rate and homework completion), academic attitudes, and career development.

In summary, these are four examples of multicultural vocational interventions with low-income urban CLD adolescents that were based in theory and research and developed in collaboration with college and school counseling professionals, educators, administrators, and community members. Reports to date on these career intervention approaches have contributed useful recommendations for and promising evidence of the potential to help all students, including at-risk CLD youth, access and achieve academic and career success.

IMPLICATIONS FOR FUTURE RESEARCH AND PRACTICE

In a special issue of the *Career Development Quarterly* on the future of the career counseling profession, Savickas (2003) included in his review and integration of authors' analyses the recommendation to "advance theory that is more holistic, contextual, and multicultural" (p. 89). Progress could be made toward this recommendation in further research that examines practice applications of theory-based vocational interventions for low-income urban CLD middle and high school students. In this chapter we highlighted examples of vocational interventions in schools that were informed by more holistic, contextual, and multicultural theories. Two interventions, Tools for Tomorrow and Achieving Success Identity Pathways, were grounded in a developmental-contextualism theoretical framework (Solberg et al., 2002). Among the surge in research during the past decade investigating applications of the social cognitive career theory (Lent et al., 1994; Lent, Brown, & Hackett, 2000), the Career Linking project (Fouad, 1995) and Career Horizons Program (O'Brien et al., 1999) are examples of interventions with low-income urban CLD middle school students that used social cognitive constructs and measures.

Among emergent models of career counseling that are more nonlinear and attend to environmental, social, and emotional factors in the process of empowering client/student vocational development (Subich & Simonson, 2001), Krumboltz's (1996) learning theory of career counseling has been used to inform the design of a career development intervention study with low-income urban CLD high school students involved in a school-university-community partnership project (Jackson et al., 2004). While one strength of these vocational interventions is that their designs were informed by more holistic, contextual, and multicultural theories, future research is needed to investigate which theoretical applications have both cultural validity and appropriate cultural specificity (Leong & Brown, 1995) for low-income urban CLD middle and high school students.

Likewise, we need further research to investigate if the essential aspects of effective career interventions in schools suggested by meta-analytic reviews have cultural validity with low-income urban CLD youth and if additional culturally specific aspects are needed. In their meta-analysis, Evans and Burck (1992) found that the positive effects of career education interventions on academic achievement were greatest when implemented in math and English classes with elementary students of average academic ability. Arbona (2000) has argued that early intervention to facilitate academic achievement (i.e., before middle and high school), particularly in math and English, is imperative for low-income CLD youth in order to develop prerequisite foundational skills to overcome barriers and improve their access to later educational and career opportunities. Future research, including longitudinal studies, might examine the reciprocal effectiveness of academic and career interventions in urban schools at elementary as well as secondary levels for low-income CLD youth.

Whiston and Sexton (1998) found in their review of research on school counseling outcomes that individual planning interventions had a positive impact on the career plans of students, including CLD youth, with academic ability levels ranging from learning disabled to gifted. This finding affirms the expertise of school counselors to effectively adapt vocational interventions to students of varying academic ability levels. Yet a question remains about whether individual or group interventions are more efficacious. On the one hand, group interventions may appeal more to the group-oriented cultural norms of African American and other racial/ethnic minority students (Bowman, 1995). In school settings, group counseling is often used to provide students with opportunities for peer feedback, role modeling, and bonding with students experiencing common issues (Holcomb-McCoy, 2003). Group interventions can also offer students opportunities to share resources and ideas with other group members and thus facilitate learning new strategies for negotiating their career concerns (Kivlighan, 1990). In schools where counselors have very high caseloads, which is especially common in low-income urban schools (Herring, 1998), group career counseling may be the most efficient mode of service delivery that maximizes the counselor's time (Niles & Harris-Bowlsbey, 2002). On the other hand, in their meta-analytic review of career intervention outcome research, Whiston et al. (1998) found that individual counseling was the most effective treatment modality, producing the greatest client gain per hour or session. This replicated a similar finding by Oliver and Spokane (1988).

In addition, Brown and Krane (2000) reported the results of meta-analyses indicating that one of five critical components of effective career interventions was *individualized interpretations* and *feedback* involving one-to-one dialogue between the counselor and client. "Interventions that were coded in this category frequently involved the provision of test interpretation information, whether in a group or individual counseling context, that was individually tailored and provided to each participant" (p. 746). Thus future research should investigate if school counselors might deliver career development interventions that are as effective through group modalities as through individual counseling so long as they provide students with direct and individually focused feedback on their vocational planning and decision-making strategies. Furthermore, we need empirical evidence of what types and components of vocational interventions are most effective for low-income urban CLD students.

Such research should also examine variations in the degree of structure and length of group interventions. More structured groups tend to focus on specific career development topics, use didactic approaches to impart information such as through career guidance activities, and meet for three to seven sessions (Niles & Harris-Bowlsbey, 2002), whereas less structured groups tend to focus on intrapersonal and interpersonal issues experienced by group members in their career development, use process- and affect-oriented approaches, and meet over a longer time period than more structured groups (Niles & Harris-Bowlsbey, 2002). Brown and Krane (2000) reported evidence that brief career interventions (specifically four to five sessions) produced the greatest effect sizes. Alternatively, Evans and Burck (1992) suggested that lesser gains in academic achievement during the second year of 2-year-long career education interventions might reflect efforts at maintaining the larger gains of the first year.

Drawing from the designs of several current career intervention projects in low-income urban schools with CLD ninth and tenth graders (Blustein et al., 2001; Jackson et al., 2004; Mobley & Berkel, 2004; Solberg et al., 2002), it appears that a combination of structure and length may be warranted. For example, more brief and structured group interventions (such as Mobley & Berkel's, 2004) may be most effective for relaying didactic information to students regarding how their interests, abilities, values, and goals relate to occupations and educational requirements. In addition, less-structured or semistructured interventions may be most effective for exploring with CLD students their personal cultural identity issues and identifying specific resources and barriers for their own vocational development (such as those incorporated in the briefer workshop structure of that of Jackson et al., 2004, or in the 1- to 2-year structures of Blustein et al., 2001, and Solberg et al., 2002). Research is needed to address these hypotheses.

In addition to providing career counseling clients with individualized interpretations and feedback, Brown and Krane (2000) found four other critical components of effective interventions: (a) allowing clients to clarify their career and life goals in writing, (b) imparting up-to-date information on the requirements and probable consequences of considered career plans, (c) exposing clients to models who demonstrate effective educational/vocational planning and coping strategies, and (d) helping clients build support networks that will facilitate their capacities to pursue their vocational aspirations. Future research is needed to empirically verify the individual and collective effects of these components for effective vocational interventions with low-income urban CLD youth in schools.

In other words, school counselors and psychologists need more evidence-based practice knowledge about what vocational intervention designs work best for facilitating educational and career development for all students, including low-income urban CLD youth. There has been a growing trend toward more evidence-based practice in education (Evensen & Hmelo, 2000; National Reading Panel, 2000), counseling and psychotherapy (Wampold, Lichtenberg, & Waehler, 2002), and school psychology (Reschly, 2000). Nevertheless, Lapan et al. (2002) observed that

> Despite a significant amount of research that has consistently found positive relationships between increased academic achievement and time spent by students on relevant career development activities (e.g., see for reviews Baker & Taylor, 1998; Evans & Burck, 1992), many administrators and teachers believe that time spent on such activities will actually hurt students' academic performance (Hershey et al., 1999; Hoyt, 1997). (pp. 186–187)

Therefore school counselors and psychologists need to better document and more effectively communicate to administrators, teachers, and governmental policymakers the growing research support for the value of psycho-educational vocational development interventions for increasing academic achievement and career attainment (Lapan et al., 2002; Whiston, 2002).

Another area recommended for future research (and discussed further in Jackson et al., this volume) is to investigate strategies to identify and ameliorate school counselors' and psychologists' hidden biases (e.g., automatic and unintentional negative stereotypes and failure to attend to relevant cultural and discrimination factors) that likely limit their effectiveness in designing and implementing vocational interventions with low-income CLD youth. It is imperative that future studies investigate the effectiveness of various multicultural training approaches to help school counseling professionals (e.g., Constantine, 2002) to overcome normative defensiveness, constructively challenge their hidden biases, and continually develop their multicultural competencies for ethical and effective practice with low-income CLD youth.

Considerable evidence exists that low-income urban CLD youth do not have equal access to education and career opportunities (e.g., Education Trust, 2000). One promising approach to reducing the educational/career achievement gap for CLD youth and helping all students succeed may be for counselors to facilitate effective multicultural career development interventions in the schools. Hansen (2003) contends that career counselors can serve not only as change agents for individuals' optimum development but also as advocates for social justice in fostering progress toward democratic ideals. In Coleman and Baskin's (2003) words:

> At the core of the multiculturally competent school counselor's success is his or her ability to facilitate in each child a sense of belongingness in the school community that will stimulate that child's motivation to set and accomplish pro-social goals such as academic achievement and career attainment...[thus] we will achieve, in the aggregate, true social change. (p. 112)

ANNOTATED BIBLIOGRAPHY

Gysbers, N. C., & Henderson, P. (2000). *Developing and managing your school guidance program* (3rd ed.). Alexandria, VA: American Counseling Association.

"This book presents the authors' K–12 model for planning, designing, implementing, evaluating, and enhancing content-based guidance programs" (from the cover).

Herring, R. D. (1998). Career counseling in the schools: Multicultural and developmental perspectives. Alexandria, VA: American Counseling Association.

Multicultural career counseling in schools.

Peterson, N., & Gonzalez, R. C. (2000). *Career counseling models for diverse populations: Hands-on applications by practitioners.* Belmont, CA: Wadsworth/Thomson Learning.

Written by vocational practitioners and experts with their respective client groups and vocational issues, 22 chapters describe specific vocational counseling models and are ordered by age or developmental stage, beginning with preschoolers and ending with adults in retirement. The programs described include a range of populations and career counseling approaches and techniques implemented in schools, community colleges and universities, prisons, employment organizations, and residential settings (women's shelters, children's homes for at-risk youth, and community-based programs for chronically mentally ill individuals).

Sue, D. W., & Sue, D. (2003). *Counseling the culturally diverse: Theory and practice* (4th ed.). New York: Wiley.

Multicultural counseling theory and practice.

RESOURCES

Practice Guidelines

Arrendondo, P., Toporek, R., Brown, S., Jones, J., Locke, D. C., Sanchez, J., et al. (1996). Operationalization of the multicultural counseling competencies. *Journal of Multicultural Counseling and Development, 24,* 42–78.

National Career Development Association Professional Standards Committee. (1997). *Career counseling competencies.* Alexandria, VA: National Career Development Association.

National Occupational Information Coordinating Committee. (1992). *The national career development guidelines, local handbook.* Washington, DC: Author.

Secretary's Commission for Achieving Necessary Skills. (1992). *Learning a living: A blueprint for high performance.* Washington, DC: U.S. Department of Labor.

This report outlines five competencies (effective work-based characteristics and behaviors transferable across occupations) and three foundational academic skill areas deemed necessary for successful performance in the contemporary world of work.

Research

Career Development Quarterly

Annual reviews of career counseling research

Journal of Career Development

Focuses on the impact of career development theory and research on practice

Journal of Vocational Behavior

Theoretical and empirical research on vocational behavior and career development

Professional School Counseling, spring 2003

Special issue on career development in school counseling

Web Sites

American School Counselor Association:
http://www.schoolcounselor.org
Association of Computer-Based Systems for Career Information:
http://www.acsci.org
ASVAB Career Exploration Program:
http://www.asvabprogram.com
Gaining Early Awareness and Readiness for Undergraduate Programs (GEAR UP):
http://www.ed.gov/programs/gearup/index.html
National Association of School Psychologists:
http://www.naspweb.org
National Career Development Association:
http://www.ncda.org
Society for Vocational Psychology:
http://www.div17.org/vocpsych/

REFERENCES

Abreu, J. M. (2001). Theory and research on stereotypes and perceptual bias: A didactic resource for multicultural counseling trainers. *Counseling Psychologist, 29,* 487–512.

Arbona, C. (1996). Career theory and practice in a multicultural context. In M. L. Savickas & W. B. Walsh (Eds.), *Handbook of career counseling theory and practice* (pp. 45–54). Palo Alto, CA: Davies-Black.

Arbona, C. (2000). The development of academic achievement in school aged children: Precursors to career development. In S. D. Brown & R. W. Lent (Eds.), *Handbook of counseling psychology* (3rd ed., pp. 270–309). New York: Wiley.

Arrendondo, P., Toporek, R., Brown, S., Jones, J., Locke, D. C., Sanchez, J., et al. (1996). Operationalization of the multicultural counseling competencies. *Journal of Multicultural Counseling and Development, 24,* 42–78.

Baker, S. B., & Taylor, J. G. (1998). Effects of career education interventions: A meta-analysis. *Career Development Quarterly, 46,* 376–385.

Bandura, A. (1977). Self-efficacy: Toward a unifying theory of behavior change. *Psychological Review, 84,* 191–215.

Betz, N. E., & Fitzgerald, L. S. (1995). Career assessment and intervention with racial and ethnic minorities. In F. T. L. Leong (Ed.), *Career development and vocational behavior of racial and ethnic minorities* (pp. 263–279). Mahwah, NJ: Erlbaum.

Blustein, D. L. (2001). Extending the reach of vocational psychology: Toward an inclusive and integrative psychology of working. *Journal of Vocational Behavior, 59,* 171–182.

Blustein, D. L. (2003, Summer). School and work: Contexts and transitions sixth bi-annual conference of the Society for Vocational Psychology. *Vocational Psychology News, 14,* 1–8.

Blustein, D. L., Chaves, A. P., Diemer, M. A., Gallagher, L. A., Marshall, K. G., Sirin, S., et al. (2002). Voices of the forgotten half: The role of social class in the school-to-work transition. *Journal of Counseling Psychology, 49,* 311–323.

Blustein, D. L., Jackson, J., Kenny, M. E., Sparks, E., Chaves, A., Diemer, M. A., et al. (2001, March). *Social action within an urban context: The Tools for Tomorrow project.* Paper presented at the Fourth National Counseling Psychology conference, Houston, TX.

Blustein, D. L., Juntunen, C. L., & Worthington, R. L. (2000). The school-to-work transition: Adjustment challenges of the forgotten half. In S. D. Brown & R. W. Lent (Eds.), *Handbook of counseling psychology* (3rd ed., pp. 435–470). New York: Wiley.

Bowman, S. L. (1995). Career intervention strategies and assessment issues for African Americans. In F. T. L. Leong (Ed.), *Career development and vocational behavior of racial and ethnic minorities* (pp. 137–164). Mahwah, NJ: Erlbaum.

Brown, S. D., & Krane, N. E. R. (2000). Four (or five) sessions and a cloud of dust: Old assumptions and new observations about career counseling. In S. D. Brown & R. W. Lent (Eds.), *Handbook of counseling psychology* (3rd ed., pp. 740–766). New York: Wiley.

Byars, A. M., & McCubbin, L. D. (2001). Trends in career development research with racial/ethnic minorities. In J. G. Ponterotto, J. M. Casas, L. A. Suzuki, & C. M. Alexander (Eds.), *Handbook of multicultural counseling* (2nd ed., pp. 633–654). Thousand Oaks, CA: Sage.

Campbell, C. A., & Dahir, C. A. (1997). *The national standards for school counseling programs.* Alexandria, VA: American School Counselor Association.

Chartrand, J. M. (1996). Linking theory with practice: A sociocognitive interactional model for career counseling. In M. L. Savickas & W. B. Walsh (Eds.), *Handbook of career counseling theory and practice* (pp. 121–134). Palo Alto, CA: Davies-Black.

Chaves, A. P., Diemer, M. A., Blustein, D. L., Gallagher, L. A., DeVoy, J. E., Casares, M. T., et al. (2004). Conceptions of work: The view from urban youth. *Journal of Counseling Psychology, 51,* 275–286.

Coleman, H. L. K., & Baskin, T. (2003). Multiculturally competent school counseling. In D. B. Pope-Davis, H. L. K. Coleman, W. M. Liu, & R. L. Toporek (Eds.), *Handbook of multicultural competencies in counseling & psychology* (pp. 103–113). Thousand Oaks, CA: Sage.

Constantine, M. G. (2002). Racism attitudes, white racial identity attitudes, and multicultural counseling competence in school counselor trainees. *Counselor Education and Supervision, 41,* 162–174.

Constantine, M. G., & Yeh, C. J. (2001). Multicultural training, self-construals, and multicultural competence of school counselors. *Professional School Counseling, 4,* 202–207.

Education Trust. (2000, April). *Achievement in America: GEAR UP.* Washington, DC: Author.

Evans, J. H., & Burck, H. D. (1992). The effects of career education interventions on academic achievement: A meta-analysis. *Journal of Counseling & Development, 71,* 63–68.

Evensen, D. H., & Hmelo, C. E. (2000). *Problem-based learning: A research perspective on learning interactions.* Mahwah, NJ: Erlbaum.

Fouad, N. A. (1995). Career behavior of Hispanics: Assessment and career intervention. In F. T. L. Leong (Ed.), *Career development and vocational behavior of racial and ethnic minorities* (pp. 165–191). Hillsdale, NJ: Erlbaum.

Fouad, N. A., & Bingham, R. P. (1995). Career counseling with racial and ethnic minorities. In W. B. Walsh & S. H. Osipow (Eds.), *Handbook of vocational psychology: Theory, research, and practice* (2nd ed., pp. 331–365). Mahwah, NJ: Erlbaum.

Gysbers, N. C., & Henderson, P. (2000). *Developing and managing your school guidance program* (3rd ed.). Alexandria, VA: American Counseling Association.

Hackett, G., & Byars, A. M. (1996). Social cognitive theory and the career development of African American women. *Career Development Quarterly, 44,* 322–340.

Hansen, L. S. (2001). Integrating work, family, and community through holistic life planning. *Career Development Quarterly, 49,* 261–274.

Hansen, S. S. (2003). Career counselors as advocates and change agents for equality. *Career Development Quarterly, 52,* 43–53.

Harris-Bowlsbey, J. (2003). A rich past and a future vision. *Career Development Quarterly, 52,* 18–25.

Herring, R. D. (1998). *Career counseling in the schools: Multicultural and developmental perspectives.* Alexandria, VA: American Counseling Association.

Holcomb-McCoy, C. C. (2003). Multicultural competence in school settings. In D. B. Pope-Davis, H. L. K. Coleman, W. M. Liu, & R. L. Toporek (Eds.), *Handbook of multicultural competencies in counseling & psychology* (pp. 406–419). Thousand Oaks, CA: Sage.

Hotchkiss, L., & Borow, H. (1996). Sociological perspective on work and career development. In D. Brown & L. Brooks (Eds.), *Career choice and development* (3rd ed., pp. 281–336). San Francisco: Jossey-Bass.

Hoyt, K. B. (1977). *A primer for career education.* Washington, DC: Superintendent of Documents, U.S. Printing Office.

Jackson, M. A., Mendelsohn, J. W., & Rotenberg, M. (this volume). Multicultural vocational assessment in schools: Unexplored barriers and untapped resources. In G. B. Esquivel, E. Lopez, & S. Nahari (Eds.), *Handbook of multicultural school psychology.* Mahwah, NJ: Erlbaum.

Jackson, M. A., Mendelsohn, J. W., Rust, J. P., Beck, S. E., & Lambert, J. E. (2004, July). Constructively challenging diverse inner-city youth's beliefs about educational/career barriers/supports. Paper presented at the 112th annual American Psychological Association Convention, Honolulu, HI.

Jackson, M. A., & Nutini, C. D. (2002). Hidden resources and barriers in career learning assessment with adolescents vulnerable to discrimination. *Career Development Quarterly, 51,* 56–77.

Kiselica, M. S., Changizi, J. C., Cureton, V. L., & Gridley, B. E. (1995). Counseling children and adolescents in schools: Salient multicultural issues. In J. G. Ponterotto, J. M. Casas, L. A. Suzuki, & C. M. Alexander (Eds.), *Handbook of multicultural counseling* (pp. 516–532). Thousand Oaks, CA: Sage.

Kivlighan, D. M. (1990). Career group therapy. *The Counseling Psychologist, 18,* 64–80.

Kozol, J. (1991). *Savage inequalities: Children in America's schools.* New York: Crown.

Krumboltz, J. D. (1996). A learning theory of career counseling. In M. L. Savickas & W. B. Walsh (Eds.), *Handbook of career counseling theory and practice* (pp. 55–80). Palo Alto, CA: Davies-Black.

Lapan, R. T., Gysbers, N. C., & Petroski, G. F. (2001). Helping seventh graders be safe and successful: A statewide study of the impact of comprehensive guidance and counseling programs. *Journal of Counseling and Development, 79,* 320–341.

Lapan, R. T., Gysbers, N. C., & Sun, Y. (1997). The impact of more fully implemented guidance programs on the school experiences of high school students: A statewide evaluation study. *Journal of Counseling and Development, 75,* 292–302.

Lapan, R. T., Osana, H. P., Tucker, B., & Kosciulek, J. F. (2002). Challenges for creating community career partnerships: Perspectives from practitioners. *Career Development Quarterly, 51,* 172–190.

Lee, R. M., & Dean, B. L. (2004). Middle-class mythology in an age of immigration and segmented assimilation: Implication for counseling psychology. *Journal of Counseling Psychology, 51,* 19–24.

Lent, R. W., Brown, S. D., & Hackett, G. (1994). Toward a unifying social cognitive theory of career and academic interest, choice, and performance. [Monograph]. *Journal of Vocational Behavior, 45,* 79–122.

Lent, R. W., Brown, S. D., & Hackett, G. (2000). Context supports and barriers to career choice: A social cognitive analysis. *Journal of Counseling Psychology, 47,* 36–49.

Leong, F. T. L., & Brown, M. T. (1995). Theoretical issues in cross-cultural career development: Cultural validity and cultural specificity. In W. B. Walsh & S. H. Osipow (Eds.), *Handbook of vocational psychology: Theory, research, and practice* (2nd ed., pp. 143–180). Mahwah, NJ: Erlbaum.

Leong, F. T. L., & Serafica, F. C. (2001). Cross-cultural perspective on Super's career development theory: Career maturity and cultural accommodation. In F. T. L. Leong & A. Barak (Eds.), *Contemporary models in vocational psychology: A volume in honor of Samuel H. Osipow* (pp. 167–206). Mahwah, NJ: Erlbaum.

Markstrom-Adams, C., & Spencer, M. B. (1994). A model for identity intervention with minority adolescents. In S. L. Archer (Ed.), *Interventions for adolescent identity development* (pp. 84–101). Thousand Oaks, CA: Sage.

McWhirter, E. H., Hackett, G., & Bandalos, D. L. (1998). A causal model of the educational plans and career expectations of Mexican American high school girls. *Journal of Counseling Psychology, 45,* 166–181.

Mobley, M., & Berkel, L. A. (2004, July). Career exploration journey: A career intervention program for African American urban students. Paper presented at the 112th annual American Psychological Association Convention, Honolulu, HI.

Murdock, T. B. (1999). The social context of risk: Status and motivational predictors of alienation in middle school. *Journal of Educational Psychology, 91,* 62–75.

National Career Development Association Professional Standards Committee. (1997). *Career counseling competencies.* Alexandria, VA: National Career Development Association.

National Center for Education Statistics. (2001). *The condition of education.* Washington, DC: U.S. Department of Education.

National Center for Education Statistics. (2004). *Indicators of school crime and safety.* Washington, DC: U.S. Department of Education.

National Occupational Information Coordinating Committee (NOICC). (1992). *The national career development guidelines, local handbook.* Washington, DC: Author.

National Reading Panel. (2000). *Report of the Reading Panel: Teaching children to read: An evidence-based assessment of the scientific research literature on reading and its implications for reading instruction.* Washington, DC: National Institute of Child Health and Development.

Nelsen, D. E., & Gardner, J. L. (1998). *An evaluation of the comprehensive guidance program in Utah public schools.* Salt Lake City: Utah State Office of Education.

Newman, K. S. (1999). *No shame in my game.* New York: Vintage.

Niles, S. G., & Harris-Bowlsbey, J. (2002). *Career development interventions in the 21st century.* Upper Saddle River, NJ: Merrill Prentice Hall.

O'Brien, K. M., Dukstein, R. D., Jackson, S. L., Tomlinson, M. J., & Kamatuka, N. A. (1999). Broadening career horizons for students in at-risk environments. *Career Development Quarterly, 47,* 215–229.

Ogbu, J. U. (1990). Minority education in comparative perspective. *Journal of Negro Education, 59,* 45–57.

Ogbu, J. U. (1992). Understanding cultural diversity and learning. *Educational Research, 21,* 5–14.

Ogbu, J. U. (2003). *Black American students in an affluent suburb: A study of academic disengagement.* Mahwah, NJ: Erlbaum.

Oliver, L. W., & Spokane, A. R. (1988). Career-intervention outcome: What contributes to client gain? *Journal of Counseling Psychology, 35,* 447–462.

Parsons, F. (1909). *Choosing a vocation.* Boston: Houghton Mifflin.

Peterson, N., & Gonzalez, R. C. (2005). *The role of work in people's lives: Applied career counseling and vocational psychology* (2nd ed.). Belmont, CA: Brooks/Cole.

Ramirez, S. Z., Wassef, A., Paniagua, F. A., & Linsky, A. O. (1996). Mental health providers' perceptions of cultural variables in evaluating ethnically diverse clients. *Professional Psychology: Research and Practice, 27,* 284–288.

Raskin, P. M. (1994). Identity and the career counseling of adolescents: The development of vocational identity. In S. L. Archer (Ed.), *Interventions for adolescent identity development* (pp. 155–173). Thousand Oaks, CA: Sage.

Reschly, D. J. (2000). The present and future status of school psychology in the United States. *School Psychology Review, 29,* 507–523.

Richardson, M. S. (1993). Work in people's lives: A location for counseling psychologists. *Journal of Counseling Psychology, 40,* 425–433.

Ridley, C. R. (1995). *Overcoming unintentional racism in counseling and therapy.* Thousand Oaks, CA: Sage.

Rotheram-Borus, M. J. & Wyche, K. F. (1994). Ethnic differences in identity development in the United States. In S. L. Archer (Ed.), *Interventions for adolescent identity development* (pp. 62–83). Thousand Oaks, CA: Sage.

Ryan, N. E. (1999). *Career counseling and career choice goal attainment: A meta-analytically derived model for career counseling practice.* Unpublished doctoral dissertation, Loyola University, Chicago.

Savickas, M. L. (2003). Advancing the career counseling profession: Objectives and strategies for the next decade. *Career Development Quarterly, 52,* 87–96.

Savickas, M. L., & Walsh, W. B. (Eds.). (1996). *Handbook of career counseling theory and practice.* Palo Alto, CA: Davies-Black.

Smith, A. E. (2000, Summer). Middle school career exploration: The role of teachers and principals. *Education, 120,* 626–631.

Solberg, V. S. (2001). *ASIP evaluation report.* Milwaukee, WI: Author.

Solberg, V. S., Close, W., & Metz, A. J. (2001). Promoting success pathways for middle and high school students: Introducing the Adaptive Success Identity Plan for school counselors: "It's about making school successful for all students." In C. Juntunen & D. Atkinson (Eds.), *Counseling strategies* (pp. 135–157). Thousand Oaks, CA: Sage.

Solberg, V. S., Howard, K. A., Blustein, D. L., & Close, W. (2002). Career development in the schools: Connecting school-to-work-to-life. *The Counseling Psychologist, 30,* 705–725.

Starr, M., & Gysbers, N. C. (1992). *Missouri comprehensive guidance: A model for program development, implementation, and evaluation.* Jefferson City: Missouri Department of Elementary and Secondary Education.

Steele, C. M. (1997). A threat in the air: How stereotypes shape intellectual identity and performance. *American Psychologist, 52,* 613–629.

Strong, S. R. (1991). Theory-driven science and naïve empiricism in counseling psychology. *Journal of Counseling Psychology, 38,* 204–207.

Subich, L. M., & Simonson, K. (2001). Career counseling: The evolution of theory. In F. T. L. Leong & A. Barak (Eds.), *Contemporary models of vocational psychology: A volume in honor of Samuel H. Osipow* (pp. 257–278). Mahwah, NJ: Erlbaum.

Sue, D. W. (2003). *Overcoming our racism: The journey to liberation.* San Francisco, CA: Jossey-Bass.

Sue, D. W., Carter, R. T., Casas, J. M., Fouad, N. A., Ivey, A. E., Jensen, M., et al. (1998). *Multicultural counseling competencies: Individual and organizational development.* Thousand Oaks, CA: Sage.

Swanson, J. L. (1995). The process and outcome of career counseling. In W. B. Walsh & S. H. Osipow (Eds.), *Handbook of vocational psychology* (2nd ed., pp. 217–259). Mahwah, NJ: Erlbaum.

Swanson, J. L., & Fouad, N. A. (1999). *Career theory and practice: Learning through case studies.* Thousand Oaks, CA: Sage.

Turner, S. L., & Lapan, R. T. (2003). The measurement of career interests among at-risk inner-city and middle-class suburban adolescents. *Journal of Career Assessment, 11,* 405–420.

U.S. Congress. (1994). *School to Work Opportunities Act of 1994* (P.L. No. 103–239). Washington, DC: Author.

U.S. Department of Education. (1996). *Urban schools: The challenge of location and poverty* (NCES Publication No. 96–184r). Washington, DC: U.S. Government Printing Office.

U.S. Equal Employment Opportunity Commission. (2000). Washington, DC: U.S. Government Printing Office.

Walsh, M. E., Galassi, J. P., Murphy, J. A., & Park-Taylor, J. (2002). A conceptual framework for counseling psychologists in schools. *The Counseling Psychologist, 30,* 682–725.

Wampold, B. E., Lichtenberg, J. W., & Waehler, C. A. (2002). Principles of empirically supported interventions in counseling psychology. *The Counseling Psychologist, 30,* 197–217.

Whiston, S. C. (2002). Response to the past, present, and future of school counseling: Raising some issues. *Professional School Counseling, 5,* 148–157.

Whiston, S. C., & Sexton, T. L. (1998). A review of school counseling outcome research: Implications for practice. *Journal of Counseling & Development, 76,* 412–426.

Whiston, S. C., Sexton, T. L., & Lasoff, D. L. (1998). Career-intervention outcome: A replication and extension of Oliver and Spokane (1988). *Journal of Counseling Psychology, 45,* 150–165.

VI

SPECIAL POPULATIONS

21

IDENTIFYING GIFTED AND TALENTED CULTURALLY AND LINGUISTICALLY DIVERSE CHILDREN AND ADOLESCENTS

Geraldine V. Oades-Sese, Giselle B. Esquivel, and Cecilia Añon

Fordham University

The United States' commitment to gifted education, and the relative importance the government has placed on it, has fluctuated throughout its compulsory education history. The presiding political and societal beliefs of the times have been reflected in how the construct of "giftedness" was defined and how this definition influenced both the identification process and the specialized education for gifted children and adolescents (Colangelo & Davis, 1997; Ross, 1997). The U.S. population is becoming increasingly diverse and is projected to increase by 50% among culturally and linguistically diverse groups in the year 2050 (U.S. Census Bureau, 1996). Therefore it is imperative to advance our understanding of giftedness and culture to develop procedures that will facilitate the identification of special gifts and talents among culturally and linguistically diverse (CLD) children and adolescents.

The goal of this chapter is to provide a comprehensive review of identification methods used with gifted and talented CLD children and adolescents. A historical background is provided to illustrate the evolution of the definition of giftedness from one that was unitary in nature toward a multidimensional construct based on theory and research, as well as the challenges faced when identifying CLD children and adolescents. This is followed by a review of culturally sensitive approaches and alternative assessment procedures and their implications on the interdisciplinary practices of school psychologists, teachers, and parents. Finally, the authors provide suggestions for a comprehensive multicultural identification model of giftedness and its implications for future research and practice.

THEORETICAL AND RESEARCH BASE

Historical Background

A unidimensional conceptualization of giftedness may be traced to Sir Francis Galton (1869) who believed that superior intellectual ability was possessed by a few genetically endowed individuals. Galton set the precedent for defining giftedness in terms of intelligence and heredity and influenced the work of Lewis Terman. Since Lewis Terman first used the term *gifted* in the 1920s, a narrow conceptualization has guided identification procedures and resulted in the exclusion of a significant number of children with outstanding abilities and unrecognized potentials. Terman defined the "gifted" as the top 1% level in general intellectual ability (IQ ≥ 140) as measured by the Stanford-Binet Intelligence scales or comparable normed instruments. However, even during Terman's time, not all educators and researchers fully embraced his conceptualization of giftedness. Among the advocates for definitions of giftedness that went beyond high intellectual and academic ability was Leta Hollingworth (1926), who, like Terman, defined gifted children as those who were in the top 1% of general intelligence, but she also believed that children's potential for giftedness manifested in a variety of different talents (e.g., music, art, mechanical aptitude, abstract intelligence, and literacy).

Since the 1930s, educators recognized the limitations of relying exclusively on standardized test scores of intelligence, aptitude, and achievement for the identification of gifted children and adolescents. Many argued that intelligence tests could not provide information on students with potential for unique creativity and talents (Frasier & Passow, 1994; Sternberg & Grigorenko, 2000–2001). Thurstone (1938) facilitated the gradual theoretical shift away from psychometric constructs of giftedness toward one that was more multidimensional and psychological in nature by positing 20 specific talents, including those of verbal reasoning, word fluency, number facility, memory, spatial relations, and perceptual speed.

As an extension to Thurstone's theory, J. P. Guilford (1967) theorized a three-dimensional Structure of Intellect (SOI) that organized 120 specific high-level talents categorized by mental operations utilized, the content of the thinking process, and the resulting product. He played a significant role in altering the conceptualization of intelligence as a unitary trait and expanding it to include creativity, which influenced the view of giftedness. His model for creativity emphasized the importance of flexibility, fluency, originality, and elaboration in divergent thinking. As an application of Guilford's model, a number of tests were developed and used in identifying gifted students, such as the SOI Learning Abilities Test and SOI Gifted Screening Form (Meeker & Meeker, 1975) and the Torrance Test of Creative Thinking (Torrance, 1974).

Similarly, Torrance (1960, 1965) maintained that creativity should be an additional criterion for identifying gifted and talented students. Because sociocultural factors influence how creativity is defined, expressed, and rewarded, Torrance (1984) recommended careful selection of assessment procedures used with culturally diverse children to reflect the gifts and talents valued by the culture to which they belong. In addition to creativity, other researchers have recognized other areas such as social competence (Strang, 1958), motivation, and persistence (Taylor, 1968) as aspects of giftedness. As the multidimensional definition of giftedness evolved, a distinction between high intellectual ability, talents, and creativity began to emerge as essential expressive forms of "giftedness."

As theories evolved to reflect the multidimensional nature of giftedness, federal definitions used to identify gifted and talented children also reflected these changes. One of the first federal definitions of gifted and talented students found in the 1969 Education Amendments stated that gifted and talented children were those with outstanding intellectual ability or creative talent (Stephens & Karnes, 2000). The concept of giftedness began to include disadvantaged and CLD children. In 1972, the Marland report enhanced the definition to include children with demonstrated or "potential" ability in one or more of the following areas: (a) general intellectual ability, (b) specific academic aptitude, (c) creative or productive thinking, (d) leadership ability, (e) ability in the visual or performing arts, and/or (f) psychomotor ability. This definition urged educators to identify children with a broader spectrum of talent potential (Frasier & Passow, 1994; Stephens & Karnes, 2000). The 1972 definition was modified in 1978 to include preschool, elementary, and secondary level children and adolescents possessing demonstrated and/or potential abilities. However, psychomotor ability was removed from the 1978 definition.

The federal definition was also modified by the 1988 Jacob K. Javits Gifted and Talented Students Education Act removing the inclusion of the performing arts. Furthermore, the 1994 federal definition reflects the knowledge and thinking to date (National Excellence, 1993). This definition acknowledged that "outstanding talents are present in children and adolescents from all cultural groups, across all economic strata, and in all areas of human endeavor" (p. 38). The term *gifted* was excluded from this definition because it suggested a developed ability rather than one that needed development. By emphasizing the need to identify potential rather than actualized giftedness, a broader net was cast with which to catch students that may not be demonstrating their full potential due to environmental influences (Frasier, 1997a).

Landmark studies emerged around this time period investigating giftedness in children from diverse cultural backgrounds. A seminal study conducted by Ernesto Bernal (1974) investigated Mexican American "barrios" in metropolitan areas of Texas and found that Mexican Americans conceptualized giftedness in terms of behavioral attributes rather than the traditional, mainstream view measured by standardized tests. Bernal and Reyna (1974) identified several gifted characteristics among Mexican American children (see Table 21–1). In a study among disadvantaged African American children, Torrance (1969) found qualities such as the ability to express emotions and demonstrate kinesthetic movements as gifted characteristics (see Table 21–1 for details). Among Asian American children, Chen and Goon (1976) identified gifted characteristics as possessing the ability to work diligently, demonstrating social competence with adults, and excelling in math. Specific and shared gifted characteristics of CLD children and adolescents are presented in Table 21–1. It is important to recognize that these are general characteristics and that differences within an ethnic group are greater than between group differences. An increased understanding of and sensitivity to cultural and environmental differences are essential to the recognition and interpretation of gifted behaviors (Csikszentmihalyi & Robinson, 1986; Passow & Frasier, 1996).

Researchers have also offered their own broad and multidimensional definitions of giftedness that led to the development of identification procedures tailored to meet their definitions. Renzulli's (1978) Three-Ring Conception of Giftedness emphasized the interaction among above-average ability (top 15% to 20% of performance), task commitment, and creativity in any areas valued by society or a particular culture. Renzulli's conception of giftedness led to the development of identification procedures, using a type of dynamic assessment called the Triad/Revolving Door system (see Renzulli, 1984) and the scales for rating the behavioral characteristics of superior students (Renzulli, Smith, White, Callahan, & Hartman, 1976) by teachers to nominate students.

In addition to characteristics inherent in gifted children and adolescents, Tannenbaum (1983) expanded the conceptualization of giftedness to include environmental influences required to actualize giftedness. He suggested that giftedness embodies five psychosocial factors of general intelligence, special ability, nonintellectual factors (personality traits), environmental factors, and chance factors. A pluralistic view of intelligence was posited by Gardner's (1983) theory of multiple intelligences (i.e., linguistic, logical-mathematical, musical, interpersonal, intrapersonal, spatial, bodily-kinesthetic, naturalistic, and emotional intelligences). Gardner helped advance the view that talent can exist in many areas and fields other than those that are academically related and emphasized that specific intelligences are stimulated and developed by activities valued within the individual's culture (Gardner, 1993). Gardner's theory led to the development of a performance-based assessment identification model called DISCOVER (see Maker, Nielson, & Rogers, 1994).

Another theory and corresponding identification approach was developed by Sternberg's (1985) triarchic theory of intelligence, which distinguished between three types of intelligence: analytic, creative, and practical. Furthermore, his pentagonal implicit theory of giftedness (Zhang & Sternberg, 1998) proposed five criteria necessary for the identification of giftedness: excellence, rarity of attribute, productivity, demonstrability via the use of valid measures, and sociocultural valued factors. The inclusion of talent development that expanded the view of giftedness was put forth by Feldhusen (1986), who proposed an integration of general intellectual ability, special talents, a positive self-concept, and achievement motivation to his concept of giftedness. Gagne (1990) viewed gifted children and adolescents as those possessing gifts or abilities that develop into academic, technical, artistic, interpersonal, and/or athletic talents. Identification models that included talent in their conceptualization of giftedness include the Talent Identification and Development Model (TIDE; Feldhusen, 1995) that emphasized the recognition of high precocious academic, artistic, vocational/technical, and interpersonal/social talents. Similarly, Piirto (1999) created the pyramid of talent development that suggested that certain personality attributes, a minimum IQ threshold, and a particular talent were necessary for the realization of superior talent (Piirto, 1999).

Most recently, a neurological perspective was put forth by Barbara Clark's (1997) brain-mind theory of giftedness, which indicated that giftedness involved an advanced and accelerated development of brain functions expressed in cognition, academic aptitude, leadership, or creative behaviors through visual or performing arts. These high abilities are the result of the interaction of inherited potentials and experiences acquired from the environment.

This brief history outlines the evolution toward what current educators agree is the most appropriate conceptualization of giftedness, one that is multidimensional and inclusive, and one that takes into account the interaction of inherent abilities and environmental/sociocultural factors. Despite this broadened perspective of giftedness, there are many challenges that prevail in the identification of children and adolescents for gifted programs, especially those from culturally and linguistically diverse backgrounds.

Challenges to Identification

Frasier (1997a) suggested that perhaps the most serious and prevailing obstacle to proportionate representation of CLD students in gifted programs was inadequate funding of education and gifted programs. Faced with decisions as to how to allocate funds, gifted programs often lose out in the erroneous belief that children with special gifts will succeed despite the system's shortcomings (Bernal, 1994). Evidence seems to indicate that gifted students will not develop their gifts and talents without special services to nurture their potential (Bernal, 1994; Colangelo & Davis, 1997). The underrepresentation of CLD students by at least 50% (Ford & Harris, 1996; Frasier, Garcia, & Passow, 1995; Konstantopoulos, Modi, & Hedges, 2001; Maker, 1996; National Excellence, 1993; Passow & Frasier, 1996) can, however, be attributed to a variety of philosophical sociopolitical, theoretical, psychological, and procedural factors (Frasier et al., 1995; Kloosterman, 1998). These underlying factors include the overreliance of IQ scores in identification procedures, issues of language proficiency, gender role issues, multicultural competence, teachers' expectations, and lack of parent involvement.

Although most gifted programs espouse broader identification criteria that "throw a wider net" with which to identify gifted children, they nevertheless continue to place primary weight on high IQ scores (Frasier & Passow, 1994). Reliance on IQ may be misleading and can be a poor indicator of the abilities of gifted CLD students (Kogan, 2001). Clark (2002) stated that any test that utilizes "rational-linear thinking processes" as in intelligence tests must be viewed as limited because it fails to encompass other forms of thinking, processes, and exceptional abilities.

Biases in standardized testing have been repeatedly cited as a major cause for underrepresentation of CLD students. CLD populations' mean group IQ and achievement performance continues to be lower than those of mainstream populations even they have great potential for giftedness (Bernal, 1994; Maker, 1996). Researchers argue that tests are unfair to ethnic minorities, the economically disadvantaged, and individuals whose first language is not English (Frasier et al., 1995). Attempts to construct "culture-fair" tests have been unsuccessful primarily because the construction and development of these tests are intrinsically culture bound (Borland & Wright, 1994; Sattler, 2001). Others argue that test construction, norms, and translated versions of tests work against CLD students (Borland, 1986; Kogan, 2001; Maker, 1996), whose cognitive and learning styles and cultural and experiential backgrounds differ from the mainstream. Although these issues remain controversial and are continually debated, there is little doubt that exclusive reliance on standardized tests contributes to the underrepresentation of CLD children and adolescents (Frasier et al., 1995).

Moreover, uninformed perspectives on limited English proficiency (LEP) or second language learning significantly contributes to CLD children's underrepresentation (Barkan & Bernal, 1991; Brice & Brice, 2004; Kitano & Espinosa, 1995). Although controversy exists about best practices for children entering school with primary languages other than English, the system's goal, in general, is to assimilate children into monolingual English instruction as quickly as possible (Kloosterman, 1998). Given a lack of understanding about CLD students, the potentially gifted are typically referred and identified, if at all, only after they have mastered English and have been moved to a monolingual, English classroom (Barkan & Bernal, 1991).

Bilingualism has been traditionally considered a cause of lower intelligence and academic achievement (Díaz, 2002). Labeled a "language handicap," bilingualism has been thought to promote bilingual confusion and emotional and educational maladjustment. Barkan and Bernal (1991) maintained that one does not have to speak English to be gifted. Much research has been conducted since the 1960s pointing to the positive influence of bilingualism on the cognitive development of children (González, 2002). Furthermore, the identification of linguistically diverse students is complicated by several factors including broad range of students' cultural customs and traditions, individual and family acculturation levels, and levels of basic interpersonal communication skills (BICS) versus cognitive academic linguistic proficiency skills (CALPS) in each language (Cummins, 1980; Kogan, 2001).

Gender role issues also account for underrepresentation of the gifted and talented (Powell & Siegle, 2000). Gender specific behaviors and characteristics differ between and within cultural and linguistic groups. Masculine characteristics have traditionally been associated with high achievement, whereas low achievement has been related to more feminine characteristics. Males are considered to excel in physical and technical skills, while females are seen as more able in artistic and socioaffective domains (Gagne, 1993). Without stepping outside of the traditional gender expectations, educators run the risk of overlooking gifted and talented CLD children and adolescents who do not fit into these stereotypes (Frasier & Passow, 1994).

Educators' limited awareness and understanding of gifted behaviors in CLD students are a further impediment to the identification of the gifted and talented (Bermudez & Rakow, 1990; Bernal, 2002; Frasier, 1997a; Kogan, 2001). Educators may have negative stereotypes of CLD children's values, beliefs, and characteristics (Frasier et al., 1995; Maker, 1996; Woods & Achey, 1990) that affect their instructional practices, performance expectations, and the rates at which they consider students for gifted programs. For example, what traditional educators may interpret as slowness may be a reflection of cultural values that encourage listening and contemplation before speaking. In addition, CLD parents' limited knowledge of and involvement with the educational system and gifted organizations and groups may contribute to the problem (Frasier et al., 1995). Scott, Perou, Urbano, Hogan, and Gold (1992) found that fewer African American and Hispanic parents refer their children to gifted programs than White parents. Education in identifying giftedness as well as extending the types of referrals to include community members, parents, self, and peers would increase the number of CLD children considered for gifted programs.

Given these challenges in the identification of CLD children and adolescents, identification procedures that embody the fundamental principles of defensibility, advocacy, equity, pluralism, comprehensiveness, and pragmatism are greatly warranted (Richert, Alvino, & McDonnel, 1982). These principles promote identification procedures that prevent exclusion of the CLD students, as well as underachieving, handicapped, or economically disadvantaged students, and guard against stigmatizing labels and "implicit hierarchies" that limit potential. Identification procedures that mirror the multidimensional nature of giftedness and are comprehensive, research-based, and expert-recommended are critical for students whose abilities are difficult to measure using traditional assessment methods. Subsequently, identification procedures that use a multiple criteria approach fulfill the fundamental principles of identification and move toward realization of potentials among children and adolescents from culturally and linguistically diverse backgrounds.

IMPLEMENTATION AND APPROACHES

Alternative Assessment

Contrary to traditional models, multiple criteria approaches enhance the identification of gifted CLD children and adolescents (Frasier & Passow, 1994; Plucker, Callahan, & Tomchin, 1996). It is a comprehensive approach that includes informal and formal measures such as dynamic, nonverbal, bilingual, and performance-based assessments and student portfolios (Castellano & Díaz, 2001; Frasier, 1997b). Alternative assessment procedures benefit all students from diverse backgrounds and recognize that gifted traits and behaviors manifest differently within cultures (Hunsaker, 1994). Frasier (1994) illustrated this concept with the following formula: diverse population = diverse expression = diverse procedures. The Frasier Talent Assessment Profile (F-TAP) was designed to facilitate the collection, display, and interpretation of data using a multiple criteria approach and to avoid relying on test scores as a primary criterion. Research studies support the effectiveness of the F-TAP for CLD and economically disadvantaged students (Cowan & Gollmar, 1994).

Like any assessment procedure, there are a number of advantages and limitations in using a multiple criteria approach. Advantages of multiple criteria include accountability, access, and program development (Castellano, 2001; Frasier, 1997b). Achievement of accountability is based on a variety of criteria that provide the information needed to make "positive pedagogical decisions" and facilitates inclusion of children who are from culturally and linguistically diverse backgrounds, economically disadvantaged, and whose gifted potentials cannot be assessed by traditional standardized tests. The data collected from the multiple criteria approach link the identification process to instructional and program development (Frasier, 1997b). The cost and time required for this approach, especially when serving a large population, and the vulnerability to teacher or evaluator subjectivity, however, are cited limitations to the multiple criteria approach (Frasier, 1997b; Plucker et al., 1996).

Dynamic Assessment

Dynamic assessment, as a component of a multiple criteria approach, is useful in identifying gifted CLD, economically disadvantaged, and learning and/or physically disabled students because it focuses on learning potential (Bolig & Day, 1993; Losardo & Notari-Syverson, 2001). Dynamic assessment originates from a Vygotskian (1962) concept of the "the zone of proximal development" or "potential" using a test-teach-retest model that considers how a child independently performs a task using previously acquired knowledge and metacognitive skills, and then guides the student to the discovery of the solution by scaffolding instruction (Kirschenbaum, 1998). This is particularly salient to CLD children and adolescents who are unable to meet the high test score criterion, focusing instead on students' improved performances after mediated instruction. Furthermore, changes in teachers' expectations and preconceived notions regarding a student's ability have been a positive outcome to this approach. Dynamic assessment is enhanced by the inclusion of portfolio and performance-based assessments. This approach, however, is time-consuming and requires trained and experienced practitioners in child development and cross-cultural assessment (Losardo & Notari-Syverson, 2001). Identification models that use dynamic assessment include the Revolving Door Identification Model (see Renzulli, Reis, & Smith, 1981) and the Eureka Model (see Zorman, 1997).

Nonverbal Assessment

Nonverbal assessment methods are purported to minimize "culturally-based linguistic differences" on tests results (Harris, Reynolds, & Koegel, 1996) and increase the identification of gifted and talented CLD students. Practitioners have used the following most current nonverbal tests commercially available: (a) Leiter International Performance Scale—Revised (Roid & Miller, 1997), (b) Test of Nonverbal Intelligence–3 (Brown, Sherbenou, & Johnsen, 1997), (c) Naglieri Nonverbal Ability Tests (Naglieri, 1997), and (d) the Universal Nonverbal Intelligence Test (Bracken & McCallum, 1998). Naglieri and Ford (2003, 2005) found that the Naglieri Nonverbal Ability Test (NNAT) resulted in similar percentages of White (5.6%), Black (5.1%), and Hispanic (4.4%) children earning a standard score of 125 (95th percentile rank), which suggests that the NNAT may be a useful instrument to identify CLD children. Lohman (2005), however, argues that using nonverbal tests should be used as a "last resort."

Overall, the results regarding the effectiveness of nonverbal assessment tools are mixed (Frasier & Passow, 1994) and are not necessarily "culture-free" (Harris et al., 1996; Lohman, 2005). This is because "most nonverbal tests measure verbally mediated cognitive processes" (Lohman, 2005, p. 111). Lohman states that pictorial items and stimuli regarding common objects in these tests are culture-bound, for example, vegetables used at home. Furthermore, these paper and pencil tests assume prior exposure to printed test materials and left-to-right visual reading conventions.

Bilingual Assessment

Because children and adolescents developing second language proficiency express different behaviors as they progress through various stages of language acquisition (Robisheaux, 2002), educators should be aware that children may code switch or switch between two languages in various ways. Code-switching may reflect a high level proficiency in one or more languages, advanced-level vocabulary, or an accelerated rate of language acquisition, all of which may suggest gifted potential (Granada, 2002).

A multisetting, multi-informant, and multimethod approach to bilingual assessment takes into account students' specific cultural customs and traditions, individual and family acculturation levels, and levels of BICS and CALPS in each language (Cummins, 1980). Prior baseline data on language acquisition and usage (Granada, 2002) guides the development and planning of the gifted and talented (GT) program curriculum mode. Although psychometrically sound measures of language proficiency are still very limited, one possibility is using the Woodcock-Muñoz Language Survey—Revised (Woodcock & Muñoz-Sandoval, 2004). Other measures include the Hispanic Bilingual Gifted Screening Instrument (Irby & Lara-Alecio, 1999), which was designed to account for gifted Hispanic children's familial, social, and linguistic characteristics, and the Bilingual Talent Portfolio, a strength-based assessment approach that evaluates students' interests, abilities, expression-style preferences, and potential talents in their primary language (Kloosterman, 2002).

Performance-Based Assessment

Performance-based assessment aims to provide students with opportunities to demonstrate and apply knowledge. Curiosity, concentration, persistence, creativity, motivation, problem solving, and reasoning can be observed and usually assessed in the child's dominant language (Sarouphim, 2001). Gifted CLD students may respond more favorably to opportunities to demonstrate their potential, especially when tasks coincide more with their interests, knowledge, or experiences (VanTassel-Baska, Johnson, & Avery, 2002).

Van Tassel-Baska, Johnson, and Avery (2002) recommended criteria for developing verbal and nonverbal tasks to assess varied skills. First, they emphasized thinking and problem-solving tasks that evaluate fluid cognitive abilities rather than acquired knowledge, which may be confounded by past educational experience. Second, they stressed that open-ended formats encourage creative responses and thinking. Accordingly, performance-based models should utilize rubrics that delineate scores obtained for different ranges of responses on a given task. Students receiving 80% or more of the total possible score within a given domain should be judged high-ability learners.

Major advantages for using performance-based assessment include (a) the approach is strength based; (b) the context is meaningful and provides qualitative information on complex behaviors that are difficult to quantify by traditional testing; (c) it promotes collaboration and communication between family members, teachers, specialists, and paraprofessionals; and (d) it is nonintrusive because tasks tend to be part of the everyday life experience (Losardo & Notari-Syverson, 2001). This approach is valuable with linguistically diverse children and adolescents because language and literacy skills are not necessary requirements.

Performance-based assessments also have several limitations (Losardo & Notari-Syverson, 2001; Sarouphim, 2001; VanTassel-Baska et al., 2002). Because students' high abilities are identified in specific domains, rather than on a measure of general intellectual ability, it is especially important to modify and match GT program curriculums to particular skills or talents that need nurturance. For example, students who show gifted abilities in the arts will not thrive in a program intended to develop math skills. Although the flexibility of this approach is one of its advantages, performance-based assessments are time-consuming, costly, and lack standardized evaluation criteria.

Perhaps the most well-known performance-based assessment program is the Discovering Intellectual Strengths and Capabilities through Observation while allowing for Varied Ethnic Responses (DISCOVER; Maker et al., 1994), which is grounded in Gardner's (1983) multiple intelligence theory, and Maker's (1993) definition of giftedness (i.e., the ability to solve complex problems in the most efficient, effective, and economical ways). Different activities are designed to measure spatial, logical-mathematical, and linguistic intelligences, among others. Performance is classified into four rating categories of "Unknown," "Maybe," "Probably," and "Definitely" gifted, which are guided by flexible checklists. Several studies have evaluated the psychometric validity and reliability properties of DISCOVER favorably (Sarouphim, 1999, 2001, 2002).

Portfolio Assessment

A portfolio is a "collection of a student's work that can be used to document a child's efforts, progress and achievement over time" (Losardo & Notari-Syverson, 2001, p. 100; Piirto, 1999; Wright & Borland, 1993). Depending on the educational goals and purposes of the portfolio it can include a variety of the student's work samples as well as documentation of behaviors from teachers' and parents' observations. Products can include photographs of projects, writing samples, picture journals, audiotaped conversations, songs, Lego constructions, as well as products produced from dynamic, nonverbal, bilingual, and performance-based assessments. It is important to collect materials across the students' many environments, especially for children from CLD backgrounds. Researchers have promoted the use of portfolios as the best comprehensive method with which to assess advanced products and performance of gifted bilingual/bicultural students (Granada, 2002; Robisheaux, 2002).

Portfolios can include assessment tools designed for identification of specific gifted and talented children. These alternative measures include the American Indian Gifted and Talented Assessment Model (AIGTAM; Tonemah & Brittan, 1985), the Gifted Attitudes Inventory for Navahos (Abbott, 1983), and the SOI-Learning Abilities Test (Meeker & Meeker, 1985).

The criteria for selecting and evaluating the content of the portfolio must be clear and, as with all alternative identification models, reflect the goals of the target gifted program's curriculum. This should ideally provide incentives for modification and/or creation of gifted programs to nurture the varied potential gifts and talents children exhibit. In addition, student participation in creating a portfolio encourages children's interests and motivates them to develop their unique abilities. The portfolio is also a reflection of a student's own linguistic and cultural backgrounds and experiences, thus validating each student's unique background.

Student portfolios have a number of advantages. Teachers have stated that using portfolios promotes viewing their students as individuals, allowing them to look more carefully at individual students, their strengths and development, and serves in increasing a student's self-esteem (Wright & Borland, 1993). Culturally sensitive portfolio models are flexible in the selection of content and the evaluation criteria. Creative factors such as flexibility, fluency, elaboration, and originality are possible ways to evaluate portfolios and provide a rich body of information. Because of the model's flexibility and comprehensiveness, this approach has the potential to increase identification of traditionally underrepresented children and youth.

Limitations include time and labor intensiveness (Wright & Borland, 1993). Furthermore, portfolios may not meet high standards of reliability, given that evaluation criteria tend to be more flexible in nature. Clear and specific guidelines and procedures for evaluation are needed on an individual basis so as to avoid bias (Wright & Borland, 1993). Data from two cohorts of Project Synergy at Columbia University suggested that the identification process, of which an early childhood developmental portfolio is a part, has predictive validity for future placement in a school for the gifted (Johnson & Ryser; 1996).

IMPLICATIONS FOR PRACTICE

Role of the School Psychologist

Best practices highlight the importance of bridging between home and school when identifying gifted CLD students. Whenever possible, school psychologists should be proficient in the student's primary language. If necessary, a trained interpreter should be used in the assessment process. Assessment methods should be conducted in the student's primary language as determined by an initial language proficiency evaluation and should coincide with specific goals of the targeted program (Sattler, 2001).

Since expectations, attitudes, and experiences influence the identification process, Castellano and Díaz (2002) suggest that an important role of school psychologists should be to make time to establish rapport with CLD or economically disadvantaged students. Observing students in their classroom provides initial information on performance ability, especially when they are involved in cooperative group activities that require problem solving and critical thinking. In addition, school psychologists should prepare students and their families for the assessment process (Castellano & Díaz, 2002). Parents should be informed of how giftedness is conceptualized. In addition, Castellano and Díaz recommend the practice of re-norming test scores to factor out any bias inherent in standardized tests. For a more extensive discussion on the process of re-norming test scores, the reader is referred to their text.

When selecting measurement instruments, educational history, acculturation levels, socioeconomic status, and cultural background are factors to consider. The psychometric integrity and limitations of these tests should also be carefully reviewed. Testing of the limits in which task demonstrations, time extensions, and changes in presentation modes are utilized has been recommended by Sattler (2001). When standardized tests are used, tests should be adapted to the target population, appropriately translated, and demonstrate that the constructs measured by these tests are relevant across cultures (APA, 2003).

Use of observation scales, checklists, inventories, language samples, performance-based assessments, interviews, portfolios, biographical data, and case studies have all been recommended to explore talents and creative abilities. Lopez (2000) suggests that these flexible assessment methods be combined with cognitive tests. Flexible and broad measures of talents, skills, and creativity are encouraged despite expressed dissatisfaction of school personnel with cost- and time-intensiveness (Hunsaker, 1994).

Essentially, the previous recommendations rely on the school psychologists' multicultural competence. Multicultural competence is defined "as the ability to understand and constructively relate to the uniqueness of each client in light of diverse cultures that influence each person's perspectives" (Stuart, 2004, p. 6). Recommendations have been offered to facilitate multicultural competence (see Stuart, 2004, and APA, 2003), particularly when evaluating cross-cultural research and applying it to practice. These suggestions are particularly salient when identifying CLD children and adolescents for GT programs, taking into account sociocultural factors that influence gifted behaviors. The following are Stuart's twelve suggestions that facilitate multicultural competence:

1. Develop skill in discovering each person's unique cultural outlook.
2. Acknowledge and control personal biases by articulating your worldview and evaluating its sources and validity.
3. Develop sensitivity to cultural differences without overemphasizing them.
4. Uncouple theory from culture.
5. Develop a sufficiently complex set of cultural categories.
6. Critically evaluate the methods used to collect culturally relevant data before applying the findings in psychological services.
7. Develop a means of determining a person's acceptance of relevant cultural themes.
8. Develop a means of determining the salience of ethnic identity for each client.
9. Match any psychological tests to client characteristics.
10. Contextualize all assessments.
11. Consider clients' ethnic and world views in selecting...intervention goals, and methods.
12. Respect clients' beliefs, but attempt to... [expand] them when necessary.

Teacher and Staff Development

A child may be viewed as gifted by some teachers and not by others. This phenomenon occurs because of what Zhang and Sternberg (1998) call implicit theories. Implicit theories of giftedness "are conceptions of giftedness that reside in the minds of theorists, who can either be experts or lay persons" (p. 149). These theories differ from explicit theories developed by researchers that been discussed earlier (e.g., Three-Ring Conception of Giftedness) in that implicit theories are subjective perceptions that guide how a teacher perceives or discriminates between gifted and nongifted students or how educators influence criteria used for identification processes. Because of inherent implicit theories that lie among teachers, school psychologists, and other school personnel, training and staff development are key to developing effective and multiculturally sound identification procedures.

Training and competency in cross-cultural assessment is important for educators responsible for identifying potentially gifted CLD students. Professionals should be knowledgeable and comfortable with traditional customs and communication styles of Hispanics Americans, African Americans, Asian Americans, Native Americans, and other cultural groups. Padilla and Medina (1996) recommend that evaluators incorporate the nonmainstream community in the identification process and selection of instruments to be implemented in schools because it increases trust among the minority community on test practices and results in more appropriate assessment and decision-making processes.

Teacher and staff development should be an ongoing process rather than a "one-shot" training workshop. Training should highlight the importance of identification of cognitive strengths rather than weaknesses (Lopez, 2000); multiple types of intelligence (Gardner, 1983); task commitment and creativity (Renzulli, 1978); and special talents in art, music, sports, and other performance areas (Richert, 1985; Torrance, 1977). The potential influence of different cultural, linguistic, socioeconomic, and language backgrounds must be emphasized (Cline & Schwartz, 1999; Melesky, 1984; Torrance, 1984). Gifted characteristics generally exhibited by some, but not all, CLD gifted children and adolescents are shown in Table 21–1. These gifted characteristics presented in Table 21–1 are a compilation of some of the findings in the research literature that add to the knowledge base of teachers and school personnel. This information should not be interpreted as "set" assumptions placed on a particular ethnic group, but rather as useful guidelines for teachers to generate a list of hypotheses during the identification process.

Teachers should be encouraged to understand different students' learning styles (see Irvine & York, 1995) and how their own learning styles and biases may affect their perception of gifted students' learning. Although research on learning styles fails to support that a given ethnic group exhibits a distinctive style, learning styles should be used in the development of effective instruction and programs because they enhance achievement for CLD students (Irvine & York, 1995; Sandler & Esquivel, 2000; Stuart, 2004). Also, assessing a student's creative style provides additional information regarding the student's approach during the creative process (Houtz et al., 2003). Furthermore, educators should be encouraged to stay up-to-date on trends in the field and current issues that affect education of gifted CLD students.

Parental Involvement

Parental involvement leads to better student attendance, improved achievement, higher high school graduation rates and college enrollment, increased teacher morale, and improved school quality (Castellano, 2003). Parents are excellent referral sources for CLD gifted children because they are able to assess talents and abilities that are culturally specific. They are experts on their child's behavior and have critical insights in the home setting and other situations (Kogan, 2001; Lopez, 2000). Interviewing parents is an asset in gathering information about special talents and skills (Melesky, 1984). For example, using the teacher-administered Let-Me-Tell-You-About-My-Child cards requires parents to list their child's special abilities and interests observed in the home (Borland & Wright, 1994).

The success of parental involvement is predicated on establishing good communication between the student's home and school. Considerations of cultural factors and attitudes toward the role of educators are also important. For example, parents from culturally and linguistically diverse backgrounds may not believe that they have anything of worth to contribute to the education of their children because they view teachers as experts in the area. Language barriers are also an obstacle to the process, for which trained interpreters may be useful. Melesky (1984) suggests that improving the communication with the community increases parent involvement in identification. Communication between home and school should be a two-way process that can be facilitated through newsletters, assignment books, and parent-teacher meetings.

Partnership Between Bilingual Education and Gifted and Talented Programs

Many educators and researchers have emphasized the importance of building on the assets children bring to school (Barkan & Bernal, 1991). For potentially gifted CLD children and adolescents, this means reinforcing and developing students' primary and secondary languages (Castellano, 2001). Many researchers stress that the potentially gifted, both monolingual and bilingual, are a population that could easily benefit from the rewards of additive bilingualism (Barkan & Bernal, 1991; Bernal, 2002; Kloosterman, 2002). Promoting partnerships between bilingual education and GT programs serves to include traditionally underrepresented CLD students and to broaden the educational experience for all students (Castellano, 2001; Gonzalez, Bauerle, & Felix-Holt, 1996).

Bernal (2002) stresses the importance of recruiting CLD teachers in GT programs to expose mainstream students to the "perspectives that minority instructors bring to the classroom" (Bernal, 2002, p. 86). Students' CLD expressions of giftedness are validated in such environments. Kloosterman (2002) suggests that diverse students will be "more motivated to learn a second language if the enrichment learning and teaching process is configured in a positive and challenging atmosphere in which students' cultural backgrounds as well as personal characteristics are protected and valued" (p. 195).

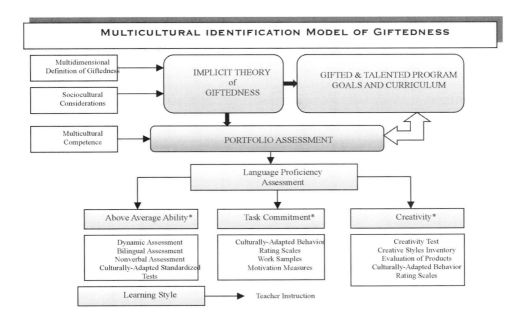

FIGURE 21–1. Multicultural identification model of giftedness.
*Categories of Above Average Ability, Task Commitment, and Creativity were adapted from the Three-Ring Conception of Giftedness in Renzulli (1978). Adapted with permission.

Systemic Schoolwide Identification and Enrichment Efforts

The Schoolwide Enrichment Model (SEM) was created in the 1970s by Joseph S. Renzulli. It is an educational model intended primarily for gifted and talented students, which has evolved into a plan for total school improvement for all students (Kloosterman, 2002). It aims to develop the potentials of all children and adolescents by providing enrichment opportunities, resources, and services to develop their talent, strengths, and creativity. It highlights the importance of curriculum differentiation to nurture the unique interests and skills of all children. The SEM proposes continual assessment, rather than isolated cases of identification, where the detrimental effect of traditional identification methods is acknowledged. Assessment, programming, and evaluation should be interrelated. The diverse cognitive, linguistic, and socioemotional characteristics of CLD students should be carefully incorporated in the identification procedures, primarily by promoting flexible criteria and modes of data collection. All students, including mainstream children who may not fit the traditional characteristics of gifted children, benefit from this approach.

TABLE 21–1
Research-Based General and Culture-Specific Characteristics of Gifted Behaviors

Hispanic American	African American	Native American
Bernal & Reyna (1974)	*Torrance (1969)*	*Maker & Schiever (1989)*
Rapid acquisition of the English language	Ability to express feelings and emotions	Good mediator
Exhibits leadership abilities in both dynamic-expressive and quiet but influential ways	Improvises with commonplace materials	Values traditions, heritage, and cultural beliefs
Socializes with older peers and easily engages adults in conversation	Uses creative movement and dance	Has personal and religious integrity
Enjoys intelligent and risk-taking behaviors, often accompanied by a sense of drama	Uses rich imagery in language	Communicates effectively the collective idea of the tribe
Can preoccupy self with imaginative games and ingenious application	Utilizes figural fluency and flexibility, problem solving	Recalls old legends and reproduces designs and symbols
Takes on the responsibilities of older children at home	Uses humor	Creates stories and poems
"Streetwise" and is recognized by peers as having the ability to "make it" in the White world	Demonstrates originality in ideas and problem solving	Creative, generates original ideas and solutions
Maker & Schiever (1989)	Problem-centered	Leadership ability
Communicates fluently with peers and community	Ability in visual arts	Excellent memory
Requires touching, eye contact, feeling of support to achieve maximum academic productivity	Articulateness in role-playing and storytelling	Unusual sensitivity to expectations and feelings of others
Personal initiative, independent thought, and verbal aggressiveness, often inhibited in females	Expressiveness of gestures and body language	Encourages others to explore and develop abilities while developing own abilities

Family (nuclear and extended) closeness is highly valued   Music ability   High language development

Functions successfully between two cultures   Expressive speech   Sense of justice and advanced moral development

Works better in a group   Idealistic

Aguirre & Hernandez (1999)

Eagerly shares native culture with others; has strong desire to teach native language to others; has strong sense of pride in cultural heritage and ethnic background; eagerly translates to peers and adults; balances appropriate behaviors of both cultures; possesses advanced knowledge of idioms and native dialects with the ability to translate and explain meanings in English; understands jokes and puns related to cultural differences; reads in native language two grades above grade level; has language proficiency levels above nongifted peers who are LEP; code-switches; possesses cross-cultural flexibility; has a sense of global community; learns languages at an accelerated pace; excels in math tests; demonstrates strength in creative areas of fluency, elaboration, originality, and flexibility; and demonstrates leadership abilities outside of the school setting.

469

IMPLICATIONS FOR FUTURE RESEARCH

Although theories of intelligence and definitions of giftedness have evolved to re-flect the diverse and multifaceted construct of giftedness, the identification process for gifted programs still greatly emphasizes standardized test scores as a major cri-terion (Artilles & Zamora-Duran, 1997; Renzulli, 2002). As a result, many gifted and talented CLD children remain underrepresented in gifted programs. The au-thors have integrated the information offered in this chapter and created a cultur-ally sensitive approach to the identification of gifted CLD children and adolescents called the "Multicultural Identification Model of Giftedness." This approach is based on Renzulli's Three-Ring Conception of Giftedness as a theoretical frame-work. Although the general components of the model offered are not original, and have been offered by others in one form or another, the authors have integrated re-search-based assessment procedures appropriate for the identification of gifted CLD children to better include children with potential talents that may have been overlooked by current identification methods.

The Multicultural Identification Model of Giftedness (see Figure 21–1) includes the following:

1. Implicit Theory of Giftedness. An implicit theory of giftedness refers to an evaluator's perception of giftedness (see Zhang & Sternberg, 1998), which influences whether a student is identified as gifted. The implicit theory of giftedness must espouse a *multidimensional definition of giftedness*, while tak-ing into account *sociocultural considerations* such as those presented in Table 21–1. The implicit theory of giftedness influences two components in the model: the criteria and assessment methods used in the Portfolio Assess-ment, and the goals and curriculum of a gifted program.

2. Portfolio Assessment. The portfolio assessment must match the goals and curriculum of the GT program for which a student is being considered. As-sessment is guided by the *multicultural competence* of school psychologists and educators. Assessment begins with a language proficiency test (Lan-guage Proficiency Assessment) to determine the student's dominant lan-guage and to ensure that the student's dominant language is used through-out the assessment process. Students are assessed in the following areas conceptualized by Renzulli: *Above Average Ability, Task Commitment*, and *Creativity*.

3. Assessment of Above Average Ability. Abilities in the above average range can be assessed through dynamic, bilingual, nonverbal, and other alterna-tive assessment methods. If standardized tests are used, the test must be adapted to and normed on the target population and translated in the stu-dent's dominant language.

4. Assessment of Task Commitment. Task commitment can be demonstrated by culturally adapted behavior rating scales, observation, measures of moti-vation, and inclusion of products such as writing samples, artwork, photo-graphs, audiotapes, videotapes, and so on.

5. Assessment of Creativity. Creativity can be demonstrated by using verbal and nonverbal creativity tests, creative styles inventory, product evaluation

rating scales (e.g., Appraisal Rating Scale of Artwork and Talent in the Arts; Khatena, 1997), and culturally adapted behavior rating scales, and so on.

6. Explanation of Students' Learning Style. Learning style is also determined by using learning style measures such as the Learning Style Inventory (Dunn, Dunn, & Price, 1985) to inform instruction in the GT program and maximize student's learning.

School administrators, psychologists, and teachers can utilize the Multicultural Identification Model of Giftedness by choosing two or more criteria under each component of the student's above average ability, creativity, and task commitment. The main purpose of a portfolio is to gather evidence to validate decisions made in the identification process. The authors believe that this identification process reflects the principles delineated by the National Report on Identification of Defensibility, Advocacy, Equity, Pluralism, Comprehensiveness, and Pragmaticism (Richert et al., 1982). Future research should examine the rubrics for evaluating each component's and the model's effectiveness, reliability, and validity in "casting a wider net" to include culturally and linguistically diverse children in GT programs.

ANNOTATED BIBLIOGRAPHY

Baldwin, A. Y. (2004). *Culturally diverse and underserved populations of gifted students: Vol. 6. Essential readings in gifted education*. Thousand Oaks, CA: Corwin.

> A compilation of must-read research articles published in the *Gifted Child Quarterly* on various authentic assessments and performance-based identification procedures applicable for economically disadvantaged, twice-exceptional, or culturally diverse students.

Castellano, J. A., & Díaz, E. (2001). *Reaching new horizon: Gifted and talented education for culturally and linguistically diverse students*. New York: Allyn & Bacon.

> A comprehensive text on the interface between bilingual education and gifted education. Chapter 5 offers recommended practices for identification and assessment of Hispanic gifted students.

Esquivel, G. B., & Houtz, J. C. (Eds.). (2000). *Creativity and giftedness in culturally diverse students*. Cresskill, NJ: Hampton.

> A comprehensive perspective for understanding creativity and giftedness in culturally and linguistically diverse children and adolescents. This book addresses multicultural issues in assessment and identification/selection procedures.

Kogan, E. (2001). *Gifted bilingual students: A paradox?* New York: Peter Lang.

> A review of definitions and conceptions of giftedness and recommended practices for the identification and assessment of bilingual students. Illustrative case studies are also offered.

Smutny, J. F. (Ed.). (2003). *Underserved gifted population: Responding to their needs and abilities*. Cresskill, NJ: Hampton.

> This volume covers environmental and cultural factors that challenge the identification of underserved gifted populations and offers creative solutions that embrace the strengths of culturally diverse students.

RESOURCES

Council of Exceptional Children: ERIC Information Center on Disabilities and Gifted Education:
  http://www.ericec.org
National Association for Gifted Children:
  www.nagc.org
National Research Center for the Gifted and Talented:
  www.gifted.uconn.edu

REFERENCES

Abbott, J. (1983). *The gifted attitudes inventory for Navajos: Directions for administering and scoring the gain, and technical supplement.* Farmington, NM: Bi'olta Research Institute.

American Psychological Association. (2003). Guidelines on multicultural education, training, research, practice, and organizational change for psychologists. *American Psychologist, 58,* 377–402.

Artilles, A. J., & Zamora-Duran, G. (1997). *Reducing disproportionate representation of culturally diverse students in special and gifted education.* Reston, VA: Council for Exceptional Children.

Barkan, J. H., & Bernal, E. M. (1991). Gifted education for bilingual and limited English proficient students. *Gifted Child Quarterly, 35,* 144–147.

Bermudez, A. B., & Rakow, S. J. (1990). Analyzing teachers' perceptions of identification procedures for the gifted and talented Hispanic limited English-proficient students at risk. *Educational Issues of Language Minority Students, 7,* 21–34.

Bernal, E. M. (1974). Gifted Mexican American children: An ethno-scientific perspective. *California Journal of Educational Research, 25,* 261–273.

Bernal, E. M. (1994) *Finding and cultivating minority gifted/talented students.* Paper presented at the National Conference on Alternative Teacher Certification. Washington, DC (ERIC Document Reproduction Service No. ED390345).

Bernal, E. M. (2002). Three ways to achieve a more equitable representation of culturally and linguistically different students in GT programs. *Roeper Review, 24,* 82–88.

Bernal, E. M., & Reyna, J. (1974). *Analysis of giftedness in Mexican American children and design of a prototype identification instrument.* Austin, TX: Southwest Educational Development Laboratory (ERIC Document Reproduction Service No. ED090743).

Bolig, S., & Day, J. (1993). Dynamic assessment of giftedness: The promise of assessing training responsiveness. *Roeper Review, 16,* 110–113.

Borland, J. H. (1986). I.Q. test: Throwing out the bathwater, saving the baby. *Roeper Review, 8,* 163–167.

Borland, J. H., & Wright, L. (1994). Identifying young, potentially gifted, economically disadvantaged students. *Gifted Child Quarterly, 38,* 164–171.

Bracken, B. A., & McCallum, R. S. (1998). *The universal nonverbal intelligence test.* Itasca, IL: Riverside.

Brice, A., & Brice, R. (2004). Identifying Hispanic gifted children: A screening. *Rural Special Education Quarterly, 23,* 8–15.

Brown, L., Sherbenou, R. J., & Johnsen, S. K. (1997). *Test of Nonverbal Intelligence–3.* Austin, TX: Pro-Ed.

Castellano, J. A. (2001). Renavigating the waters: The identification and assessment of culturally and linguistically diverse students for gifted and talented education. In J. A.

Castellano & E. I. Díaz (Eds.), *Reaching new horizons: Gifted and talented education for culturally and linguistically diverse students* (pp. 94–116). Boston: Allyn & Bacon.

Castellano, J. A. (2003). *Special education in gifted education: Working with diverse gifted learners.* New York: Allyn & Bacon.

Castellano, J. A., & Díaz, E. I. (2001). *Reaching new horizons: Gifted and talented education for culturally and linguistically diverse students.* Boston: Allyn & Bacon.

Chen, J., & Goon, S. (1976). Recognition of the gifted among the disadvantaged Asian American. *Gifted Child Quarterly, 20,* 157–164.

Csikszentmihalyi, M., & Robinson, R. E. (1986). Culture, time, and the development of talent. In R. J. Sternberg & J. E. Davidson (Eds.), *Conceptions of giftedness* (pp. 264–284). Cambridge: Cambridge University Press.

Clark, B. (1997). *Growing up gifted* (5th ed.). Columbus, OH: Merrill/Prentice Hall.

Clark, B. (2002). *Growing up gifted* (6th ed.). Columbus, OH: Merrill/Prentice Hall.

Cline, S., & Schwartz, D. (1999). *Diverse populations of gifted children: Meeting their needs in the regular classroom and beyond.* Upper Saddle River, NJ: Merrill.

Colangelo, N., & Davis, G. A. (1997). Introduction and overview. In N. Colangelo & G. A. Davis (Eds.), *Handbook of gifted education* (2nd ed., pp. 3–9). Boston: Allyn & Bacon.

Cowan, R. S., & Gollmar, S. M. (1994). *Breaking traditional barriers: A new paradigm for gifted programs* (Interim Report No. 1). Lawrenceville, GA: Gwinnett County Public Schools.

Cummins, J. (1980). The cross-lingual dimensions of language proficiency: Implications for bilingual education and the optimal age issue. *TESOL Quarterly, 14,* 175–187.

Díaz, E. I. (2002). Framing an historical context for the education of culturally and linguistically diverse students with gifted potential: 1850s to 1980s. In J. A. Castellano & E. I. Díaz (Eds.), *Reaching new horizons: Gifted and talented education for culturally and linguistically diverse students* (pp. 1–28). Boston: Allyn & Bacon.

Dunn, R., Dunn, K., & Price, G. (1985). *Learning style inventory.* Lawrence, KS: Price Systems.

Feldhusen, J. F. (1986). A conception of giftedness. In R. J. Sternberg & J. E. Davidson (Eds.), *Conceptions of giftedness* (pp. 112–127). Cambridge: Cambridge University Press.

Feldhusen, J. F. (1995). Identiacion y dessarralo del talento en la educacion (TIDE). *Ideacion, 4,* 12–19.

Ford, D. Y., & Harris, J. J. (1996). Recruiting and retaining diverse students in gifted education: Pitfalls and promises. *Tempo, 16* (1), 8–12.

Frasier, M. M. (1994). *A manual for implementing the Frasier Talent Assessment Profile (F-TAP): A multiple criteria model for the identification and education of gifted students.* Athens: Georgia Southern Press.

Frasier, M. M. (1997a). Gifted minority students: Reframing approaches to their identification and education. In N. Colangelo & G. A. Davis (Eds.), *Handbook of gifted education* (2nd ed., pp. 498–515). Boston: Allyn & Bacon.

Frasier, M. M. (1997b). Multiple criteria: The mandate and the challenge. *Roeper Review, 20,* A4–A6.

Frasier, M. M., Garcia, J. H., & Passow, A. H. (1995). *A review of assessment issues in gifted education and their implications for identifying gifted minority students.* Storrs, CT: National Research Center on the Gifted and Talented (ERIC Document Reproduction Service No. ED388024).

Frasier, M. M., & Passow, A. H. (1994). *Towards a new paradigm for identifying talent potential. Research monogram 94112* (ERIC Document Reproduction Service No. ED388020)

Gagne, E. (1990). Toward a differentiated model of giftedness and talent. In N. Colangelo & G. Davis (Eds.), *Handbook of gifted education* (pp. 61–81). Needham Heights, MA: Allyn & Bacon.

Gagne, E. (1993). Differences in the aptitude and talents of children as judged by peers and teachers. *Gifted Child Quarterly, 37,* 69–77.

Galton, F. (1869). *Hereditary genius.* London: Macmillan.

Gardner, H. (1983). *Frames of mind: The theory of multiple intelligences.* New York: Basic Books.

Gardner, H. (1993). Multiple intelligence: The theory in practice. New York: Basic Books.

González, V. (2002). Advanced cognitive development and bilingualism: Methodological flaws and suggestions for measuring first- and second-language proficiency, language dominance, and intelligence in minority children. In J. A. Castellano & E. I. Díaz (Eds.), *Reaching new horizons: Gifted and talented education for culturally and linguistically diverse students* (pp. 47–75). Boston: Allyn & Bacon.

González, V., Bauerle, P., & Felix-Holt, M. (1996). Theoretical and practical implications of assessing cognitive and language development in bilingual children with qualitative methods. *The Bilingual Research Journal, 20,* 93–131.

Granada, A. J. (2002). Addressing the curriculum, instruction, and assessment needs of the gifted bilingual/bicultural student. In J. A. Castellano & E. I. Díaz (Eds.), *Reaching new horizons: Gifted and talented education for culturally and linguistically diverse Students* (pp. 133–153). Boston: Allyn & Bacon.

Guilford, J. P. (1967). *The nature of human intelligence.* New York: McGraw-Hill.

Harris, A. M., Reynolds, M. A., & Koegel, H. M. (1996). Nonverbal assessment: Multicultural perspectives. In L. A. Suzuki, P. J. Meller, & J. G. Ponterotto (Eds.), *Handbook of multicultural assessment: Clinical, psychological, and educational applications* (pp. 223–252). San Francisco: Jossey-Bass.

Hollingworth, L. (1926). *Gifted children, their nature and nurture.* New York: Macmillan.

Houtz, J. C., Selby, E., Esquivel, G. B., Okoye, R. A., Peters, K. M., & Treffinger, D. J. (2003). Creative styles and personal type. *Creativity Research Journal, 15,* 321–330.

Hunsaker, S. L. (1994). Adjustments to traditional procedures for identifying underserved students: Successes and failures. *Exceptional Children, 61,* 72–76.

Irby, B. J., & Lara-Alecio, R. (1999). *Hispanic Bilingual Gifted Screening Instrument.* Retrieved from http://www.teachbilingual.com

Irvine, J. J., & York, D. E. (1995). Learning styles and culturally diverse students: A literature review. In J. A. Banks & C. A. M. Banks (Eds.), *Handbook of research on cultural education* (pp. 484–497). New York: Macmillan.

Johnson, S. K., & Ryser, G. R. (1996). An overview of effective practices with gifted students in general education. *Journal for the Education of the Gifted, 19,* 379–404.

Khatena, J. (1997). *Appraisal rating scales for art work.* Mississippi University. Unpublished manuscript.

Kirschenbaum, R. J. (1998). Dynamic assessment and its use with underserved gifted and talented populations. *Gifted Child Quarterly, 42,* 140–147.

Kitano, M. K., & Espinosa, R. (1995). Language diversity and giftedness: Working with gifted English language learners. *Journal for the Education of the Gifted, 18,* 234–254.

Kloosterman, V. (1998). *Building a bridge: A combined effort between gifted and bilingual education.* Storrs, CT: National Research Center on the Gifted and Talented (ERIC Document Reproduction Service No. ED424712).

Kloosterman, V. I. (2002). The Schoolwide Enrichment Model: Promoting diversity and excellence in gifted education. In J. A. Castellano & E. I. Díaz (Eds.), *Reaching new horizons: Gifted and talented education for culturally and linguistically diverse students* (pp. 175–199). Boston: Allyn & Bacon.

Kogan, E. (2001). *Gifted bilingual students: A paradox?* New York: Peter Lang.

Konstantopoulos, S., Modi, M., & Hedges, L. V. (2001). Who are America's gifted? *American Journal of Education, 109,* 344–382.

Lohman, D. F. (2005). The role of nonverbal ability tests in identifying academically gifted students: An aptitude perspective. *Gifted Child Quarterly, 49,* 111–138.

Lopez, E. C. (2000). Identifying gifted and creative linguistically and culturally diverse children. In G. B. Esquivel & J. C. Houtz (Eds.), *Creativity and giftedness in culturally diverse students* (pp. 125–145). Cresskill, NJ: Hampton.

Losardo, A., & Notari-Syverson, A. (2001). *Alternative approaches to assessing young children.* Baltimore, MD: Paul H. Brookes.

Maker, C. J. (1993). Creativity, intelligence, problem-solving: A definition and design for cross-cultural research and measurement related to giftedness. *Gifted Educational International, 9,* 68–77.

Maker, C. J. (1996). Identification of gifted minority students: A national problem, needed changes and a promising solution. *Gifted Child Quarterly, 40,* 41–50.

Maker, C. J., Nielson, A. B., & Rogers, J. A. (1994). Giftedness, diversity, and problem solving. *Teaching Exceptional Children, 27,* 4–19.

Meeker, M. N., & Meeker, R. J. (1975). *SOI screening test for gifted.* Vida, OR: SOI Systems.

Meeker, M. N., & Meeker, R. J. (1985). *SOI assessment test.* Vida, OR: SOI Systems.

Melesky, T. J. (1984). Identifying and providing for the gifted child. *NABE, 9,* 43–57.

Naglieri, J. A. (1997). *Naglieri Nonverbal Ability Test.* San Antonio, TX: Psychological Corporation.

Naglieri, J. A., & Ford, D. Y. (2003). Addressing underrepresentation of gifted minority children using the Naglieri Nonverbal Ability Test (NNAT). *Gifted Child Quarterly, 47,* 155–169.

Naglieri, J. A., & Ford, D. Y. (2005). Increasing minority children's participation in gifted classes using the NNAT: A response to Lohman. *Gifted Child Quarterly, 49,* 29–36.

National Excellence. (1993) *National excellence: A case for developing America's talent.* Washington, DC: U.S. Government Printing Office.

Padilla, A. M., & Medina, A. (1996). Cross-cultural sensitivity in assessment: Using tests in culturally appropriate ways. In L. A. Suzuki, P. J. Meller, & J. G. Ponterotto (Eds.), *Handbook of multicultural assessment: Clinical, psychological, and educational applications* (pp. 3–28). San Francisco: Jossey-Bass.

Passow, A. H., & Frasier, M. M. (1996). Toward improving identification of talent potential among minority and disadvantaged students. *Roeper Review, 18,* 198–202.

Piirto, J. (1999). *Talented children and adults: Their development and education.* Upper Saddle River, NJ: Prentice Hall.

Powell, T., & Siegle, D. (2000, Spring). Teacher bias in identifying gifted and talented students. *National Research Center on Gifted and Talented Newsletter,* 13–15.

Plucker, J. A., Callahan, C. M., & Tomchin, E. M. (1996). Wherefore art thou, multiple intelligences? Alternative assessments for the identifying talent in ethnically diverse and low income students. *Gifted Child Quarterly, 40,* 81–92.

Renzulli, J. S. (1978). What makes giftedness? Reexamining a definition. *Phi Delta Kappan, 60,* 180–184.

Renzulli, J. S. (1984). The Triad/Revolving Door System: A research based approach to identification and programming for the gifted and talented. *Gifted Child Quarterly, 28,* 163–171.

Renzulli, J. S. (2002). Emerging conceptions of giftedness: Building a new bridge to the new century. *Exceptionality, 10,* 67–75.

Renzulli, J. S., Reis, S. M., & Smith, L. H. (1981). *The resolving door identifying model.* Mansfield Center, CT: Creative Learning.

Renzulli, J. S., Smith, L. H., White, A. J., Callahan, C. M., & Hartman, R. K. (1976). *Scales for rating the behavioral characteristics of superior students.* Mansfield Center, CT: Creative Learning.

Richert, E. S. (1985). Identification of gifted students: An update. *Roeper Review, 8,* 68–72.

Richert, E. S., Alvino, J., & McDonnel, R. (1982). *The national report on identification: Assessment and recommendations for comprehensive identification of gifted and talented youth.* Sewell, NJ: U.S. Department of Education.

Robisheaux, J. A. (2002). The intersection of language, high potential, and culture in gifted English as a second language students. In J. A. Castellano & E. I. Díaz (Eds.), *Reaching new horizons: Gifted and talented education for culturally and linguistically diverse students* (pp. 154–174). Boston: Allyn & Bacon.

Roid, G. H., & Miller, L. J. (1997). *Leiter International Performance Scale—Revised.* Lutz, FL: Psychological Assessment Resources.

Ross, P. O. (1997). Federal policy on gifted and talented education. In N. Colangelo & G. A. Davis (Eds.), *Handbook of gifted education* (2nd ed., pp. 553–559). Needham Heights, MA: Allyn & Bacon.

Sandler, F., & Esquivel, G. B. (2000). Learning styles and creativity in culturally diverse children. In G. B. Esquivel & J. C. Houtz (Eds.), *Creativity and giftedness in culturally diverse students* (pp. 47–60). Cresskill, NJ: Hampton.

Sattler, J. M. (2001). *Assessment of children: Cognitive applications.* La Mesa, CA: Jerome M. Sattler.

Sarouphim, K. M. (1999). Discovering multiple intelligences through a performance-based assessment: Consistency with independent ratings. *Exceptional Children, 65,* 151–161.

Sarouphim, K. M. (2001). DISCOVER: Concurrent validity, gender differences, and identification of minority students. *Gifted Child Quarterly, 45,* 130–138.

Sarouphim, K. M. (2002). DISCOVER in high school: Identifying gifted Hispanic and Native American students. *The Journal of Secondary Gifted Education, 14*(1), 30–38.

Scott, M. S., Perou, R., Urbano, R., Hogan, A., & Gold, S. (1992). The identification of giftedness: A comparison of white, Hispanic, and black families. *Gifted Child Quarterly, 36,* 131–139.

Stephens, K. R., & Karnes, F. A. (2000). State definitions for the gifted and talented revisited. *Exceptional Children, 66,* 219–238.

Sternberg, R. J. (1985). *Beyond IQ: A triarchic theory of human intelligence.* New York: Cambridge University Press.

Sternberg, R. J., & Grigorenko, E. L. (2000–2001). Guilford's structure of the intellect model and model of creativity: Contributions and limitations. *Creativity Research Journal, 13,* 309–316.

Strang, R. (1958). The nature of giftedness. In N. B. Henry (Ed.), *Education for the gifted: Fifty-seventh yearbook of the National Society for the Study of Education* (Pt. II, pp. 64–86). Chicago: University of Chicago.

Stuart, R. B. (2004). Twelve practical suggestions for achieving multicultural competence. *Professional Psychology: Research and Practice, 35,* 3–9.

Tannenbaum, A. J. (1983). *Gifted children: Psychological and educational perspectives.* New York: Macmillan.

Taylor, C. W. (1968). Cultivating new talents: A way to reach the educationally deprived. *Journal of Creative Behavior, 2,* 83–90.

Thurstone, L. L. (1938). *Primary mental abilities.* Chicago: University of Chicago Press.

Tonemah, S. A., & Brittan, M. A. (1985). *American Indian gifted and talented assessment model.* Norman, OK: American Indian Research and Development.

Torrance, E. P. (1960). Explorations in creative thinking. *Education, 81,* 216–220.

Torrance, E. P. (1965). *Rewarding creative behavior: Experiments in classroom creativity.* Englewood Cliffs, NJ: Prentice Hall.

Torrance, E. P. (1969). Creative positives of disadvantaged children and youth. *Gifted Child Quarterly, 13,* 71–81.

Torrance, E. P. (1974). *Torrance test of creative thinking.* Lexington, MA: Personnel.

Torrance, E. P. (1977). *Creativity in the classroom.* Washington, DC: National Education Association.

Torrance, E. P. (1984). The role of creativity in identification of gifted and talented. *Gifted Child Quarterly, 28,* 153–156.

U.S. Census Bureau. (1996). *Population projections of the United States by age, sex, race, and Hispanic origin: 1995 to 2050: Current population reports.* Washington, DC: Author.

VanTassel-Baska, J., Johnson, D., & Avery, L. D. (2002). Using performance tasks in the identification of economically disadvantaged and minority gifted learners: Findings from Project STAR. *Gifted Child Quarterly, 46,* 110–123.

Vygotsky, L. S. (1962). *Thought and language.* Cambridge, MA: MIT Press.

Woodcock, R. W., & Muñoz-Sandoval, A. F. (2004). *Woodcock-Muñoz Language Survey—Revised comprehensive manual.* Chicago, IL: Riverside.

Woods, S. B., & Achey, V. H. (1990). Successful identification of gifted racial/ethnic group students without changing classification requirements. *Roeper Review, 13,* 21–26.

Wright, L., & Borland J. H. (1993). Using early childhood developmental portfolios in the identification of young, economically disadvantaged, potentially gifted students. *Roeper Review, 15,* 205–210.

Zhang, L. F., & Sternberg, R. J. (1998). The pentagonal implicit theory of giftedness revisited: A cross-validation in Hong Kong. *Roeper Review, 21,* 149–153.

Zorman, R. (1997). Eureka: The cross-cultural model for identification of hidden talent through enrichment. *Roeper Review, 20,* 54–61.

22

EDUCATING CULTURALLY AND LINGUISTICALLY DIVERSE GIFTED AND TALENTED STUDENTS THROUGH A DUAL-LANGUAGE, MULTICULTURAL CURRICULUM

Ernesto M. Bernal

San Antonio Gifted Education Foundation

SIGNIFICANT PROBLEMS UNIQUELY ENCOUNTERED BY CLD CHILDREN

One of the general problems that culturally and linguistically diverse (CLD) children encounter is that the curriculum to which they are exposed basically attempts to *deracinate* them, making it difficult to validate who they are or their sense of identity (Dana, 1993; Padilla, 2001). These programs rarely incorporate ethnic social issues into their social studies curriculum, have little minority representation—particularly *American* minority—in the literature they read, rarely or never bring other American cultures' music to the high school concert stage or the elementary school recital, or seek other countries' perspectives on historical events. In short, CLD gifted and talented (GT) students rarely see realistic images of themselves in the curriculum (García, 2001; Tafolla & Bernal, 1989).

The aforementioned omissions indicate the presence of what critics have called a *deficit ideology*, which is the belief that minorities are somehow "behind" and "need to be fixed" or helped to "catch up." How do standard educational practices reflect an *assimilationist belief system*—that nondominant cultural groups need to be brought into conformity with the dominant group's values and behaviors—in our schools? (See Lee, 2003, for a clear discussion of the deficit ideology and its roots in behaviorist educational psychology.) In truth, most GT programs often send mixed messages to different socioeconomic status (SES) and gender groups, not just to ethnic groups (Ford, 1996). Students who are poor or working class clearly do not hold intellectual status in the curriculum, students whose cultures are not sufficiently "competitive" are discounted (Baker, 1996), females find few professional role models in nontraditional fields, Black males are especially vulnerable to stereotypes (Graybill, 1997), and CLD students have no authentic or current reflections of themselves in topics, texts, or lessons, not to mention dialect or home language.[1]

This lack not only disrespects local cultures, but is also part of the general disregard of the intellect in American education generally and quite often in GT education as well (C. B. Howley, A. Howley, & Pendarvis, 1995). The making of meaning, in short, is limited to "safe" topics, and students are not permitted to strike out very far on their own, where they must go to learn responsibility and independence of thought. The canon in literature and social studies—even in science—teaches students more what to think, and less how to think, precisely because it is designed to be culturally restrictive. How many GT children—regardless of ethnicity—are really taught to discover or to ask basic, critical questions? (See Bruner, 1961; Taba, 1962, for early insights; see Bowers & Flinders, 1990, for a later point of view.) Critical theory views these limiting practices as maintaining the status quo (Bourdieu, 1984; McLaren & Muñoz, 2000; Nieto, 2000).

One of the realizations that all educators need to reach is that CLD GT children will not be able to effect changes in the development of a healthy identity and actualization of their potential alone; they will need the expressed cooperation of the dominant ethnic group. Educators, for example, must be willing to consider the meaning and implications of being White as members of a dominant group and in relation to members of nondominant ethnic groups (McLaren & Muñoz, 2000).

THEORETICAL AND RESEARCH BASES

Current teaching practices, in traditional systems, are not based on educational theories that emphasize the development of the whole person. Rather, they are narrowly focused on the mere acquisition of knowledge, and the knowledge that is acquired is "practical" and job related, not valuable for its own sake. Teaching and learning here do not serve intellect (Howley et al., 1995), nor do they serve the needs of an evolving democratic society to promote greater debate, involvement, social equity, and enhanced opportunities for deeper personal fulfillment (Bourdieu, 1984; Freire, 1970). In this fashion, schooling maintains pressures to acculturate on CLD students and upward mobility on economically disadvantaged students, with subsequent risks to the mental health of these children (Padilla, 2001; Ramírez, 1973; Taba, 1962). Consumerism is taught to all, however subtly, by the society in general as well as by the schools. The important point is that there is very limited reflection and critical thought about any of the familiar, everyday assumptions that surround us.

---

[1]Even modern language teachers often make local students, who are native speakers of the tongue, feel as if they speak an inferior version of the language.

THEORETICAL FOUNDATIONS FOR A DUAL-LANGUAGE, MULTICULTURAL, GT CURRICULUM

This chapter is founded on four sociopolitical educational premises: (a) that societal inequalities are inherently divisive, (b) that social institutions perpetuate the power of social elites over nondominant groups in subtle and self-justifying ways (Bourdieu, 1984) that often compromise the integrity of gifted and other individuals from the nondominant groups (Dana, 1993), (c) that gifted adults should take a more active role in resolving these social issues, and (d) that schools—GT programs, in particular—should impart the knowledge and cognitive skills necessary for students from all ethnic backgrounds to explore these social issues and learn the skills of leadership necessary to formulate new social policy in the near future. Thus, creating a dual-language, multicultural curriculum for GT students of all ethnic backgrounds should promote a modern version of a classical education (especially the acquisition of one or more modern languages) combined with a new level of awareness and empowerment. If GT students are to reach their full civic potential as adults, then they must contribute an informed creativity to the solution of social problems even as they pursue their careers.

The incongruence between the theoretical premises for a dual-language multicultural curriculum and actual teaching practices implies that gifted children have actually been "mis-serviced" by public education. They have subtly been denied the full opportunity to cultivate their minds. When it comes to CLD GT students, the disempowerment is more evident, because these children are kept out, pushed out, and frequently deracinated as the natural result of the monolingual-monocultural GT curriculum to which they are exposed. As Philips reported (1976), the presence of CLD students in the school resulted in educators' creation not of new and effective ways to educate these students, but of elaborate rationalizations for their poor performance. Terms such as "culturally deprived" were introduced into the educational literature of the 1960s and 1970s, and "compensatory education" was coined during this era as well. There was no way these groups would be treated equitably by the public schools, for example, by finding and honoring their cultural and intellectual traditions, and so Padilla's (2001) notion of *local rationality* applies to the curriculum that educators have designed without deep reflection and the beliefs (or institutional culture) they have perpetuated.

Local rationality could also serve to explain some of the schools' seeming inability to adapt. Local rationality refers to student and educator behaviors and (often) tacit beliefs that promote dropout behaviors—that rationalize them, if you would—but are not viewed negatively by these actors. For example, getting a high school diploma is, for students from nondominant ethnic groups at least, most often associated with getting a job; and, in a sense, both the teachers and the minority students expect this kind of thinking and valuing. They rarely question why getting a high school diploma is not promoted as a way of getting into a 4-year college or university. Similarly, few GT students, GT teachers, or even GT coordinators actively pursue the matter of underrepresentation of CLD students in the GT program, or naively believe that the problem lies purely with the matter of qualifying the students for admission through traditional channels, even though these are sometimes invalid (see Bernal, 2003, for three instances of invalid identification-selection based on IQ tests that were simply presumed valid; and Bernal, 2000a, for the importance of evaluating the very processes of identification).

Local rationality might also help explain the "acting White" attitude among some Black (Gregory, 1992) and other CLD students toward their peers who have been admitted into the GT program. These students "know their place," as it were, and find it uncomfortable when one of their own breaks the line. If more of them were part of the GT program, and if the program had a reputation of responding to children from nondominant ethnic groups in a positive manner, then the "acting White" phenomenon could become a reaction of the past. It is clear, however, that CLD students want to be successful on their own terms (see Gregory, 1992).

IMPLICATIONS FOR PRACTICE: MULTICULTURAL EDUCATION IN PROGRAMS FOR THE GIFTED AND TALENTED

What Is Multicultural Education?

Multicultural education is the type of education that a GT program, which believes that all children are equal in human value, would undertake. Multicultural education is not a token nod to various cultures. It is much more than setting up a Black History Month display in the school library or teaching a 30-minute period of Spanish every day. Studying facts about different cultures is, after all, just an infusion of largely unrelated cultural elements. "Multicultural education ... values cultural pluralism" (Ford, 1996, p. 145). "The assimilationist advocates Anglo-centric conformity ... , whereas the cultural pluralist advocates ethnic pride and cultural diversity" (Exum & Colangelo, 1981, p. 15). Multicultural education is designed to make this happen.

Programs that have the notion that students who come from ethnic groups that are not in the social mainstream need somehow to be compensated for their deficiencies—as seen from the dominant ethnic group's point of view—are the ones that are not keen about changing what they believe is already working very well, that is, a monocultural curriculum and a monocultural GT program with its exclusionary, traditional practices.

Multicultural education, on the other hand, "is about nurturing a fuller understanding of society" (Bigelow, 1999); it is the incorporation of different cultures' intellectual, philosophical, and ethical traditions into all areas of the core curriculum and the legitimation of cultural diversity (Nieto, 2000). Local cultures ordinarily are emphasized. It is, therefore, a personal and cultural enrichment that could easily complement a rigorous GT program. Historical points of view are legitimate, but to be dynamic—as intended—multicultural education deals with current issues and leaders as well. It uses the differences among groups to explore the underlying realities that are at the core of the problem, and to investigate what is constructed (Lee, 2003), what is natural, and how we come to understand such realities (epistemology) as cognition, logic, affect, protocols of communication, time orientation, space, social organization, ethics and morality, and notions of causality and environmental control (Burger, 1971).

A multicultural GT program must also be willing to deal with several sensitive matters having to do with counseling and related activities. Beyond the usual questions of multipotentiality and the need for optimizing career choice and decision-making skills (Greene, 2002), which all GT students must face, CLD GT students must also treat issues of socioeconomic mobility, acculturation, "mixed" dating and marriage, and maintaining cultural ties or developing a bicultural lifestyle. Broaching these topics in ethnically integrated groups may help resolve these issues for some, but clearly many GT children will prefer individual counseling (Strop, 2002), and culturally sensitive counselors must be available for these students. Many Mexican American gifted secondary students, for example, trust their school counselors for advice on academically and career-related questions, as well as college choice, but not with the profound personal questions that each must answer (Goertz, Rodríguez, & Bernal, 1997). Counseling with these students' parents and finding scholarship opportunities can also loom large (Kelly & Cobb, 1991). Helping to arrange for summer work opportunities in needy students' fields of interest could provide them with professional career experiences and badly needed income in some cases, as well as a certain form of mentoring. Getting closer to these students is important if counselors are to have much impact on their personal lives.

Multicultural education would reform the current educational system in public and private schools in order to change the future of our society by promoting social understanding among the many cultural sectors that compose our society and contribute to its well-being. Multicultural education, however, is not compensatory education in any sense (Bernal et al., 1986). Some GT programs wrestle with the questions of equity versus quality, affirmative action versus offering special courses to "prepare" children from nondominant ethnic groups to enter GT programs or compete for GT schools with limited admissions—all to little or no avail. (For a prime example of such compensatory measures, which never question the ascendancy of the White monocultural canon of education, see Gewertz, 2002.) Multicultural education shows the futility of such meanderings simply by bringing what persons from different cultures consider their intellectual best to the GT program, including their philosophical and artistic traditions. Latinos, for example, do not believe that the mark of an educated individual is not how "objectively" or dispassionately that person discusses important questions, but rather how rational and flexible the person can be about matters that are deeply felt and personally consequential. Such a matter can be useful to start a discussion on which point of view is "correct" or whether both can be amalgamated.

Multicultural education is hard to do well. It requires not only that all educators learn new attitudes, new pedagogy, and new content, but also that they integrate these into their everyday work with all students, not just with "the ethnic minorities." Multicultural education helps White students discover whiteness (McLaren & Muñoz, 2000); examines White privilege and domination of economic, political, and educational institutions in the United States (Harris, 1993); honors diverse cultural traditions and moral values; reflects the artistic, literary, philosophical, and scientific accomplishments of the different groups; utilizes pedagogy that capitalizes on the previous learning and learning styles of each group (Ramírez, 1973); and purchases educational materials that reflect their diversities and social realities. No one, of course, can cover each and every group, but local cultures should become the bases for comparative studies.

Multicultural education makes learning interesting and engaging for all students by raising to the level of consciousness the dynamics of personal identity and enculturation, intercultural contact, cultural conflict, and cultural confluence. It also legitimizes individual choice, so that "majority" and "minority" students alike can acculturate without shame, maintain their cultural identities and native languages if they choose, or even become biculturally or bilingually competent. Multicultural education moves beyond the traditional educational position of tolerance (Dabney, 1991; Glazer, 1977; Hébert, 1996; Smith & Pérez, 1992) to one of inquiry and respect for differences.

Examples of Multicultural Content for GT Programs

A topic like nonviolent resistance can be studied historically through its early religious roots, through Gandhi in India, to Martin Luther King and modern community-based organizational theory (e.g., that of Saul Alinski) right here in the United States. A unit on astronomy might incorporate not only the traditional Western star patterns, such as Taurus, but also introduce the star patterns seen by the Mayas, then launch into an understanding of how such patterns help the scientist divine the structure of the heavens, despite the differences in the patterns themselves. GT students studying geometry in seventh or eighth grade may benefit from considering the Pythagorean Theorem from different cultural points of view, such as the Babylonian, Chinese, and Indian explanations (Tafolla & Bernal, 1989). High school students can examine critically the issue of so-called racial differences in IQ from biological, sociological, and political or economic points of view, and perhaps learn something of critical theory while they are at it—the questioning of basic assumptions about social processes (e.g., "The poor will always be with us;" "America is a melting pot") to see if any hidden agendas are possibly operating in these "explanations," finding who is advantaged by the results (McLaren & Muñoz, 2000), and testing proposals that could ameliorate conditions through surveys to see who agrees, who objects, and why they feel the way they do (Bernal, 2002b).

Specialized vocabulary—culture, enculturation, acculturation, assimilation, deracination, marginality, anomie, ethnicity, dominant and nondominant ethnic groups, social elites, and biculturation—would also be introduced. Important social theories, such as social identity theory, would be explored to see how ingroups and outgroups form. And cooperative educational opportunities across ethnic groups would be used to foster greater interethnic understanding and appreciation (August & Hakuta, 1997). What is more, the underlying motive for engaging these activities is to empower students to act responsibly (Dubos, 1969), exert greater control over their own destinies, and make a difference in society as well (Freire, 1970; Jairrels & Wortham, 1997; Lee, 2003).

Middle school GT students could read different literary accounts of slavery and compare them, then discuss the differences between historical and literary accounts. Elementary school GT students could capture the folk stories of their fore-bears, write them down, and share them with the class during their reading period (a Foxfire approach). One might even present all or part of a report in a language other than English (Bernal, 1998; Nieto, 2000).

A Dual-Language GT Program

Modern programs for the gifted reflect a multicultural America and a broadened lin-guistic environment. Private schools for the gifted, for example, frequently offer modern languages at the elementary and secondary levels. There is no good reason not to offer selected modern languages to the brightest children in public schools and to do so in a way that complements the linguistic strengths of some nondominant ethnic groups in the same schools (see Bernal, 2000b; Barkan & Bernal, 1991; Smith & Perez, 1992). Very specifically, Bernal has proposed that GT and bilingual and mod-ern language programs get together to provide a two-way bilingual option for aca-demically gifted students (Bernal, 1998), an option that offers intensive modern lan-guage instruction to native speakers of English while the English-language learners, who are native speakers of that same modern language, begin their gifted program bilingually; immediate or eventual integration of both groups would occur in a cur-riculum where core subject content would be taught bilingually, producing highly fluent, literate bilinguals over the long run (Bernal, 1998).

The situation is quite different for language minority children who are learn-ing the language of the dominant ethnic group. In the United States, English must be introduced carefully, not to damage the children's continuing develop-ment of their first language, because of the potential cognitive and sociocultural losses to children, as well as the risks to their mental health. "English for the Children" (anti-bilingual education) and other forms of "subtractive bilingual-ism" actually occur in many bilingual and ESL programs throughout the country (Hakuta, 1986). CLD children will learn some English, but often at the cost of fail-ing to master other subject matter and, tragically, even losing the skills they have in their native tongue as well (García, 1995; Wong-Fillmore, 1995), out of a very complicated, double sense of shame (for losing their L1 and for being ashamed of who they are, ethnically). This insidious process is complemented by the "subtractive" general nature of schooling once the transition to an English mono-lingual curriculum has occurred, which further restricts CLD students to the "regular" education track or less (Valenzuela, 1999) and negatively affects their life chances of being placed in a GT program.

One way to achieve the cognitive advancement of English-language learners (ELL) is to provide these students with a bilingual program that does not force them to "transition into English" prematurely or that deracinates them. Indeed, one of the best ways to find GT students among the ELLs is to set up a talent pool, usually K–2, during which time there is ample time to attempt differenti-ated instruction—controlling the pacing, depth, and complexity of instruction—in order to observe how the different students take to these opportunities to move ahead and to learn more (Bernal, 2000b).

Language proficiency—limited English proficiency (LEP) or fluent English pro-ficiency (FEP)—is determined at the very start of the talent pool process, and placement in either a linguistically integrated GT classroom or bilingual GT talent pool setting occurs, depending on the linguistic makeup of the student body. The talent pool model allows the child to be watched closely and assessed informally (Bernal, 2002d), as discussed earlier. This model presupposes that qualified bilingual teachers have been taught to teach GT students in the early elementary grades.

Placement in the GT talent pool is flexible, subject to revision, depending on periodic decisions about the child's success in the enriched, accelerated setting. Both formal and informal assessments—including authentic (or alternative) assessments of academic skills, creativity, and critical thinking—can be used during this 3-year window to make the determination of the student's qualification for the GT program.[2] Indeed, the length of time involved in the assessment further reduces the unreliability of the professional judgments necessary to admit the qualified youngsters into the GT program.

One of the principal advantages of selecting students through the talent pool is that the students who stand out in this setting and take to the accelerated instruction are selected not so much on the basis of IQ as on their demonstrated abilities. What is more, low English-language proficiency will not keep a bright ELL student out of the GT program. Finally, it is important when the time to "exit" officially from the ELL status to the fluent English status (because the child can now handle academic content in English) comes along that the now proficiently bilingual GT student remain in the dual-language GT curriculum or at least a multicultural GT program and not be mistakenly assigned to either the regular (non-GT) curriculum or to the all-English, monocultural GT program, as has happened on more than a few occasions (Bernal, 2002c). [3] Many schools and school districts, of course, do not utilize the talent pool model, and so have to construct new, dual-language, multicultural versions of GT programs in order to integrate culturally diverse and dominant group GT students and accommodate their instructional and emotional needs.

There is a plethora of research showing that the most successful dual-language programs continue to develop their students' L1 (be this English or another modern language, e.g., Spanish) while doing content instruction at least half the time in the students' L2 (August & Hakuta, 1997; Chamot & O'Malley, 1986; Crawford, 1997). In such mixed settings, the ELLs and the, say, second language learners (SLLs) serve as one another's "language buddies" to help each other negotiate meaning in the content areas when they are being taught in their "other" language (Cummins, 1981; García, 1995; Hakuta, 1986). This type of cooperative learning among GT peers is not to be confused with mixed ability groups, where the bright students often do more than their share of the work (Robinson, 1998).

A few school districts now offer dual-language gifted and talented programs in some of their elementary schools. At present, there is only one program that currently extends this model to the middle school and high school, the Connecting

---

[2]In equity, all students, regardless of their ethnicity, IQ, or the status of their parents, should demonstrate their fitness for the work of a GT program. The talent pool model provides just such an opportunity.

[3]Some school systems—or at least some schools within school systems—do not identify GT students after the elementary grades, as this author's experience working with GT coordinators has uncovered. This practice contributes to the underrepresentation of CLD students in the ranks of the GT.

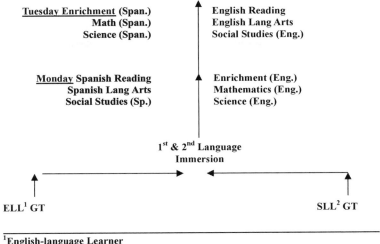

FIGURE 22–1.   Two-way (50:50) bilingual immersion, language-integrated model for full-time GT classrooms.

Worlds/Mundos Unidos (CW/MU) Project of the El Paso Independent School District. Interest in these programs is growing, however, because they bring together the brightest children early in their school careers in a bicultural or multicultural setting and avoid the personal stigma and political controversies that often attend segregated, transitional bilingual programs (Bernal, 2002b). This model integrates students who are Spanish-language learners with English-language learners (see Figure 22–1). There are, of course, variations on this simple illustration, but the basic notion is that the teachers teach all the core content areas in both languages without translation or repetition in the other tongue. The next section presents an example of how this model works.

How This Model Works: Connecting Worlds/Mundos Unidos

The dual-language GT program at Mesita Elementary School and Wiggs Middle School in El Paso, Texas, began in fall 1997 with three classrooms, for grades 1, 2, and 3. Teachers and parents approached the principal and asked if their program could incorporate Spanish as a differentiating factor for the curriculum, so that the students might become bilingually proficient in reading, writing, and speaking. The Connecting Worlds/Mundos Unidos program has been growing at one grade level per year, and at the time of this publication was installed in grades 1 through 11.

The CW/MU program uses three established techniques (see Chamot, 1981; Chamot & O'Malley, 1986; Crandall, 1987; Crawford, 1997). First, a 50–50 model of instruction ensures that all core academic subjects are taught in both languages, half the day in English and half in Spanish. Second, lessons are taught without translation, but the latest second language methods are used to ensure comprehension. Finally, native speakers of English are paired with native speakers of Spanish—language buddies who help one another understand the instruction and help the second language learner formulate responses to teachers' questions. The gifted children have done very well on standardized tests, although native speakers of English still do better on achievement tests in English, whereas native speakers of Spanish have higher average scores on tests in Spanish (Bernal, 2004). The economically disadvantaged GT students have also done quite well; in the spring 2002 testing, no more than six NCE points separated them from their nondisadvantaged peers on three Terra Nova tests: reading, language, and mathematics (Bernal, 2002a).

The CW/MU experience makes two important points. First, the process of selecting language minority students for the GT program should not be postponed until they have learned enough academic English to be tested in it. It is a form of discrimination that occurs far too often, but especially where GT programs have recruited few or no minority teachers. Programs should use alternative assessments, if necessary, to select these children early, including evidence of actual performance and creativity in either the first or the second language. Second, a multicultural ambience should be provided that honors social and individual differences and incorporates highly personalized contact among students and between students and teachers, because all GT students respond well to such schooling.

Dual-language programs provide culturally and linguistically diverse GT students with the benefits of a classical education and also achieve a substantial measure of equity among them. Highly proficient bilingual students generally enjoy certain cognitive advantages, especially in creativity, problem definition, and problem solving (Latham, 1998). They also may gain an edge in the economic future of this country. Dual-language programs will provide academic and social advantages over English monolingual programs to the participating GT students who can meet the challenge.

SUMMARY: WHAT IS REQUIRED TO IMPLEMENT MULTICULTURAL OR DUAL-LANGUAGE MULTICULTURAL EDUCATION IN GT PROGRAMS?

It is important to bring together the various recommendations for action, the measures that can be implemented to bring about a multicultural or dual-language multicultural program:

1. Recruit more teachers of color—individuals who are politically and socially active members of nondominant ethnic groups—into the ranks of GT teachers (Banks, 1973; Bernal, 2002d ; Tafolla & Bernal, 1989).
2. Place more GT teachers from nondominant ethnic groups into schools with GT programs where members of the dominant ethnic group predominate (Bernal, 2002d).
3. Conduct extensive staff development (Banks, 1977, 1993; Burger, 1971) with an emphasis on teacher sensitivities about race, gender, competition versus cooperation (and other ethnic differences that impact classroom behavior), and the notion that children from nondominant ethnic groups are just as valuable as children from the Anglo upper middle class and need to be

treated with the same respect and deference. Discuss or introduce topics for the teachers themselves to learn about as necessary, topics that can be handled at the appropriate grade levels, including slavery, African American art, intelligence theories, farm workers, current leaders from nondominant ethnic groups, and so on (see Exum & Colangelo, 1979, for other topics).

4. Recruit bilingual teachers and train them in the ways of gifted education (Bernal, 2002c).

5. Cooperative curriculum development among GT teachers from different ethnic groups. Emphasis should be placed on the knowledge base, educational materials, second language methods, and multicultural-cognitive methodology.

6. Greater involvement of minority parents in the planning and operation of the GT program. Parents are natural resources for multiculturalism.

"In order to bring this curriculum to fruition the classroom must be reality oriented and experiential as well as symbolic. It must be the kind of community in which the culture of every child is honored and its strengths revealed and where children educate each other, as well as the adults" (Dabney, 1991, p. 4).

FUTURE DIRECTIONS IN RESEARCH AND PRACTICE: DOCUMENTING AND EVALUATING THE CONSEQUENCES TO THE GT PROGRAM OF A BILINGUAL MULTICULTURAL MODEL

Moving an established GT program to a multicultural mode is not without risks. Among the potential issues that future research and evaluation efforts need to examine as GT bilingual multicultural programs spring up are the following:

1. Are different groups of parents and policymakers becoming more supportive of GT education, or does the multicultural/dual-language aspect of the curriculum appear to impede this support?

2. Does the GT program's academic reputation becomes compromised as proportionately more students from nondominant ethnic groups are admitted?

3. Has there been any resistance by school administrators, who might, for example, feel that direct instruction of basic skills should be the sole focus of classroom instruction, so that students may pass state-mandated tests (Bigelow, 1999)?

4. Are there any noticeable enrollment trends and retention in the program by gender and ethnic group?

5. Are the gaps in achievement among students of varying socioeconomic status changing, becoming less marked?

6. Is there evidence of enhanced critical thinking and creativity on the part of students because of the various cultural perspectives acquired? Tests of critical thinking, some of which are embedded in achievement test batteries, may test this dimension.

7. Have the teachers noticed an increase in student self-understanding and social awareness, coupled with empowering explanations or theories (explicit knowledge)?

8. Is there any evidence of reduced personal prejudices among the students? Sociometric questionnaires that are coded by ethnicity of responder and the person chosen could help here.

9. Has there been a growing realization among professional GT educators—as evidenced in the curriculum and in their classroom behaviors—that GT students from nondominant ethnic groups do not have to be "compensated" for their differences?

10. Do classroom observations evidence the utilization of a broader range of teaching methodologies in GT classrooms? Do teachers and students alike show growth in multidisciplinary ways of thinking?

11. Has there been a greater representation of nondominant students in the GT program? Has there been a subsequent reduction in the charge of elitism?

12. Do follow-up studies reveal that former GT students become informed citizens whose contributions to their communities and to the solution of pressing and complex social problems can be documented?

13. Are more minority students getting academic scholarships to universities, and more attending top universities?

This move to multiculturalism requires committed leadership that keeps everyone focused on the goal, which is to provide effective GT services to all gifted students. One of the best ways to introduce major educational change is to have the practitioners themselves evaluate it. Action research (also called practice-sensitive research) would be introduced at the same time that teachers and administrators are asked to make the change from a monocultural curriculum to a multicultural curriculum. In that way, perhaps greater understanding (Maxwell, 1992) and focused buy-in (Schmuck, 1997) may be achieved at every level from teaching to administration.

Practitioners need to ask the tough questions: Is the GT program drawing more students from nondominant ethnic groups? Are these students having greater success in the program than before? What is happening to the achievement scores of the students (disaggregated, of course, by ethnicity and gender)? Are White students suffering from the introduction of multicultural education in any way? What is happening to interethnic student dynamics? These questions can all be broken down into researchable projects that use everything from achievement tests to sociometric techniques to surveys to find the answers, and qualitative as well as quantitative procedures for gathering data can be employed.

Involving a resource person—such as an evaluator from the district's research and evaluation office—to help train the teachers to gather and analyze the data they need, to evaluate the effects of what they themselves are doing (see Viadero, 2002), would also be a good idea, because it provides expertise and establishes contact with an important policy group. Among the topics of the training would be small sample techniques, qualitative documentation, and dealing with contradictory findings by different teachers. One important issue is the matter of unanticipated effects, both positive and negative, which if left unexplored could vitiate the results of an otherwise good small study.

This method allows local professionals to take the lead in certain topics, modeling the practices one wants to disseminate within the school system. These results can also be used to disseminate the results to the larger profession through confer-ence presentations and professional publications. This is a crucial difference be-tween a case story and a case study, and although some politicians prefer case sto-ries that are easily digested by the media, professionals expect to examine case studies.

Moreover, involving the persons who are leading the change to a multicultural curriculum in the evaluation of their efforts will avoid the problems of a top-down decision by allowing the process to be custom fitted, as it were, to the local cam-puses. There are few things in the teaching profession that are more satisfying than examining the effects that one creates among the students, because this implies that one is also empowered to improve on these measures.

CONCLUSIONS

The United States has always been multicultural, although the power elite has pre-ferred to promote the image of the melting pot through the educational system (Fishkin, 1995). Ethnographic research has shown that minority students who re-sist acculturation and assimilation are often the ones who have the greatest aca-demic success (Schiller, 1986; Valenzuela, 1999). This should also obtain for the gifted among them.

The motivation to engage a multicultural curriculum could begin with the real-ization that the GT programs that bring out the highest achievement and creativity in their students are those that can accommodate the inherent diversity of giftedness (Strop, 2002). Thus, it would be appropriate for GT programs to be among the first to embrace the multicultural model, adding thereby not only an-other dimension to individual diversity, but also a new dimension to the instruc-tion that the GT students receive. A multicultural curriculum would add immea-surably to the combinatorial possibilities of the GT program's instructional units, because almost every topic could be examined from a cultural perspective in addi-tion to those the teacher already provides.

There is no such thing as a culturally neutral model of education. If the educa-tion that children receive is not explicitly multicultural, then it perforce will be monocultural.

ANNOTATED BIBLIOGRAPHY

Castellano, J. A. (Ed.). (2003). *Special populations in gifted education: Working with diverse gifted learners*. Boston: Allyn & Bacon.

This volume contains chapters that make the dual-language connection with gifted education, special curricular issues, multicultural GT education, and working effec-tively with special populations of GT students. The final chapter on evaluating prog-ress toward numerical goals is very apropos to the purpose of increasing the participa-tion of CLD students and ensuring their continued involvement in the GT program.

Esquivel, G. B., & Houtz, J. C. (Eds.). (2000). *Creativity and giftedness in culturally diverse stu-dents*. Cresskill, NJ: Hampton.

This book sets out to familiarize the reader with the basic rationale for blending GT and minority students together. Practical, as well as theoretical, topics are discussed by various authors, which include such notables as Sternberg and Bernal, as well as the editors themselves. Unlike most books on teaching the gifted, creativity is high-lighted.

Howley, C. B., Howley, A., & Pendarvis, E. D. (1995). *Out of our minds: Anti-intellectualism and talent development in American schooling*. New York: Teachers College Press.

The authors present a disturbing picture of intelligence and schooling in support of industrial greed in the United States, and the subsequent love–hate relationship that our society has with intellectuals and intellectualism. This is critical theory focused on giftedness and gifted education at its best.

Padilla, R. V. (2001). *Pedagogy of engagement: Mapping possibilities for educational improvement* [CD]. Boerne, TX: Author.

This unusual conceptualization of multicultural education and the social dynamics of intercultural contact in school settings is a must. It is a bit of a mind bender, but it ex-emplifies dramatically some of the cognitive benefits of multicultural ways of think-ing and the social benefits of including culturally diverse individuals in the educa-tional dialog. The resistance to change the schools on the part of educators is also explicated in ways that suggest solutions to the persistent problem of failing to engage all students in empowering ways, so that they may make equality among one another.

Smutny, J. F. (Ed.). (2003). *Underserved gifted populations: Responding to their needs and abilities*. Cresskill, NJ: Hampton.

This is one of the most comprehensive tomes devoted to the topic of special popula-tions generally. Very importantly, a chapter by Bernal (pp. 141–156) presents models of dual-language, GT education.

RESOURCES

National Association for Gifted Children (NAGC):
   http://www.nagc.org
Padilla, R. V. (2001). *Pedagogy of engagement: Mapping possibilities for educational improvement* [CD]. Boerne, TX: Author.
   http://hyperqual@ev1.net
San Antonio Gifted Education Foundation:
   http://www.Camino.ManilaSites.com/
Supporting the Emotional Needs of the Gifted (SENG):
   http://www. sengifted@sbcglobal.net
The Association for the Gifted (TAG), which is a division of the Council for Exceptional Children:
   http://www.cectag.org

REFERENCES

August, D., & Hakuta, K. (Eds.). (1997). *Improving schooling for language-minority children: A research agenda* (National Research Council). Washington, DC: National Academy.

Baker, R. (1996). Sociological field research with junior high school teachers: The discounting of Mexican American students. *Journal of Educational Issues of Language Minority Students, 18*, 49–66.

Banks, J. A. (1973). Teaching Black studies for social change. In J. Banks (Ed.), *Teaching ethnic studies: Concepts and strategies*. Washington, DC: National Council for the Social Studies.

Banks, J. A. (1977). The implications of multicultural education for teacher education. In F. Klassen & D. Gollnich (Eds.), *Pluralism and the American teacher: Issues and case studies*. Washington, DC: American Association of Colleges for Teacher Education, Ethnic Heritage Center for Teacher Education.

Banks, J. A. (1993). Multicultural education: Development, dimensions, and challenges. *Phi Delta Kappan, 75*, 22–28.

Barkan, J. H., & Bernal, E. M. (1991). Gifted education for bilingual and limited English proficient students. *Gifted Child Quarterly, 35*, 144–147.

Bernal, E. M. (1998). Could gifted English-language learners save gifted and talented programs in an age of reform and inclusion? *TAGT Tempo, 18*, 11–14.

Bernal, E. M. (2000a). As state performance standards for GT programs increase, so does the need for program evaluation. *TAGT Tempo, 20*, 4–5, 15–17.

Bernal, E. M. (2000b). The quintessential features of gifted education as seen from a multicultural perspective. In G. B. Esquivel & J. C. Houtz (Eds.), *Creativity and giftedness in culturally diverse students* (pp. 159–191). Cresskill, NJ: Hampton.

Bernal, E. M. (2002a). *Annual report, 2002: Connecting Worlds/Mundos Unidos*. Evaluation report. San Antonio, TX: Author.

Bernal, E. M. (2002b, Summer). Dual-language education for gifted children. *Duke Gifted Letter, 2*(4), 7.

Bernal, E. M. (2002c). Social-emotional needs of culturally diverse gifted students. In E. Bernal (Chair), *Social-emotional needs of diverse gifted populations: Cultural, ADHD, LD, Asperger's, and gay/lesbian*. Panel presentation at the meeting of Supporting Emotional Needs of the Gifted (SENG), Minneapolis, MN.

Bernal, E. M. (2002d). Three ways to achieve a more equitable representation of culturally and linguistically different students in GT programs. *Roeper Review, 24*, 82–88.

Bernal, E. M. (2003). An empirical method for selecting tests for the identification of gifted and talented CLD students. *Tempo, 23*, 8–11.

Bernal, E. M. (2004, September). *Evaluation report: Connecting worlds/Mundos Unidos, 2004* (Javits Project, El Paso ISD). San Antonio, TX: Author.

Bernal, E. M., Cleary, M., Connelly, M. J., Gerard, M. L., Kryspin, J., & Nicodemus, E. (1986). A taxonomy of the knowledge base for professional studies. In D. W. Jones (Ed.), *Knowledge base for teacher education* (pp. 20–44). Muncie, IN: Ball State University, North Central Association Teacher Education Project.

Bigelow, B. (1999). Why standardized tests threaten multiculturalism. *Educational Leadership, 56*, 37–40.

Bourdieu, P. (1984). *Distinction: A social critique of the judgment of taste*. Cambridge, MA: Harvard University Press.

Bowers, C. A., & Flinders, D. J. (1990). *Responsive teaching: An econolgical approach to classroom patterns of language, culture, and thought*. New York: Teachers College Press.

Bruner, J. S. (1961). The act of discovery. *Harvard Educational Review, 31*, 124–135.

Burger, H. G. (1971). *"Ethno-pedagogy": A manual in cultural sensitivity, with techniques for improving cross-cultural teaching by fitting ethnic patterns*. Albuquerque, NM: Southwestern Cooperative Educational Laboratory.

Chamot, A. U. (1981, September). *Applications of second language acquisition research to the bilingual classroom* (Focus Paper on Bilingual Education No. 8). Rosslyn, VA: National Clearinghouse on Bilingual Education.

Chamot, A. U., & O'Malley, J. M. (1986). *A cognitive academic language learning approach: An ESL content-based curriculum*. Wheaton, MD: National Clearinghouse for Bilingual Education.

Crandall, J. A. (1987). *ESL through content-area instruction: Mathematics, science, social studies*. Englewood Cliffs, NJ: Prentice-Hall Regents/Center for Applied Linguistics.

Crawford, J. (1997). *Best evidence: Research foundations of the Bilingual Education Act*. Washington, DC: National Clearinghouse for Bilingual Education.

Cummins, J. (1981). Four misconceptions about language proficiency in bilingual education. *NABE Journal, 5*, 31–45.

Dabney, M. (1991, May). Creating humanities curricula with a multicultural focus. In J. L. Baytops (Ed.), *Project Mandala concept papers* (pp. 1–5). Williamsburg, VA: College of William & Mary, School of Education, Project Mandala.

Dana, R. H. (1993). *Multicultural assessment perspectives for professional psychology*. Boston: Allyn & Bacon.

Dubos, R. (1969, Spring). Biological individuality. *Columbia Forum*, 5–9.

Exum, H. A., & Colangelo, N. (1979). Enhancing self-concept with gifted Black students. *Roeper Review, 1*, 5–6.

Exum, H. A., & Colangelo, N. (1981). Culturally diverse gifted: The need for ethnic identity. *Roeper Review, 3*, 15–17.

Fishkin, S. F. (1995, March 10). The multiculturalism of "traditional" culture. *Chronicle of Higher Education*, p. A48.

Ford, D. Y. (1996). *Reversing underachievement among gifted Black students: Promising practices and programs*. New York: Teachers College Press.

Freire, P. (1970). *Cultural action for freedom*. Cambridge, MA: Harvard Educational Review and the Center for the Study of Development and Social Change.

García, E. E. (1995). *Meeting the challenge of linguistic and cultural diversity in early childhood education*. New York: Teachers College Press.

García, E. E. (2001). *Hispanic education in the United States: Raíces y alas*. New York: Rowman & Littlefield.

Gewertz, C. (2002, February 6). Affirmative re-action. *Education Week, 21*, 26–32.

Glazer, N. (1977). Public education and American pluralism. In J. Coleman et al. (Eds.), *Parents, teachers and children: Prospects for choices in American Education*. San Francisco: Institute for Contemporary Studies.

Goertz, J., Rodríguez, A. M., & Bernal, E. M. (1997). Mexican American secondary students' perceptions of counselors. *National Association for Gifted Children's Research Briefs, 11*, 90–99.

Graybill, S. W. (1997). Questions of race and culture: How they relate to the classroom for African American students. *Clearing House, 70*(6), 311–318.

Greene, M. J. (2002). Career counseling for gifted and talented students. In M. Niehart, S. Reis, N. Robinson, & S. Moon (Eds.), *The social and emotional development of gifted children* (pp. 223–235). Washington, DC: National Association for Gifted Children.

Gregory, S. S. (1992, March 16). The hidden hurdle. *Time*, 44–46.

Hakuta, K. (1986). *Mirror of language: The debate on bilingualism*. New York: Basic Books.

Harris, C. I. (1993). Whiteness as property. *Harvard Law Review, 106*, 1709–1791.

Hébert, T. P. (1996). Portraits of resilience: The urban life experience of gifted Latino young men. *Roeper Review, 19*, 82–90.

Howley, C. B., Howley, A., & Pendarvis, E. D. (1995). *Out of our minds: Anti-intellectualism and talent development in American schooling*. New York: Teachers College Press.

Jairrels, V., & Wortham, J. F. (1997, Spring/Summer). A generic framework for teaching in a multicultural society. *Baylor Educator, 22*, 18–23.

Kelly, K. R., & Cobb, S. J. (1991). A profile of the career development characteristics of young gifted adolescents: Examining gender and intercultural differences. *Roeper Review, 13*, 202–206.

Latham, A. S. (1998). The advantages of bilingualism. *Educational Leadership, 56*, 79–80.

Lee, J. O. (2003). Implementing high standards in urban schools: Problems and solutions. *Phi Delta Kappan, 84*, 449–455.

Maxwell, J. A. (1992). Understanding and validity in qualitative research. *Harvard Educational Review, 62*(3), 279–300.

McLaren, P., & Muñoz, J. S. (2000). Contesting whiteness: Critical perspectives in the struggle for social justice. In C. Ovando & P. McLaren (Eds.), *The politics of multiculturalism and bilingual education* (pp. 23–49). New York: McGraw-Hill Higher Education.

Nieto, S. (2000). *Affirming diversity* (3rd ed.). New York: Longman.

Padilla, R. V. (2001). *Pedagogy of engagement: Mapping possibilities for educational improvement* [CD]. Boerne, TX: Author.

Philips, S. U. (1976). Commentary: Access to power and maintenance of ethnic identity as goals of multi-cultural education. *Anthropology and Education Quarterly, 7*, 30–32.

Ramírez, M., III. (1973). Cognitive styles and cultural democracy in education. *Social Science Quarterly, 53*, 897–905.

Robinson, A. (1998). Cooperative learning, curriculum access, and the challenge of acceleration. *Tempo, 18*, 1, 6–7.

Schiller, P. (1986, September). *Biculturalism and psychosocial adjustment among Native American university students.* Paper presented at the fourth CSWE/BPD Conference, San Antonio, TX.

Schmuck, R. A. (1997). *Practical action research for change.* Arlington Heights, IL: IRI/Skylight.

Smith, E., & Pérez, R. (1992). Cultural diversity in gifted education: A better chance at succeeding. *Journal of the California Association for the Gifted, 22*, 1, 42–43.

Strop, J. (2002). Meeting the emotional needs of gifted adolescents: A personal and contextual journey. *Understanding Our Gifted, 14*, 7–11.

Taba, H. (1962). *Curriculum development: Theory and practice.* New York: Harcourt, Brace, & World.

Tafolla, C., & Bernal, E. M. (1989, June). *Institutional options in denying, accommodating, or engaging cultural pluralism.* Paper presented at the second National Conference on Ethnic and Race Relations in American Higher Education.

Valenzuela, A. (1999). *Subtractive schooling: U.S.-Mexican youth and the politics of caring.* Albany, NY: State University of New York Press.

Viadero, D. (2002, June 12). Holding up a mirror: Teacher-researchers use their own classrooms to investigate questions. *Education Week, 21*, 32–35.

Wong-Fillmore, L. (1995). When learning a second language means losing the first. In G. González & L. Maez (Eds.), *Compendium of research on bilingual education* (pp. 19–36). Washington, DC: George Washington University, National Clearinghouse for Bilingual Education.

23

CULTURALLY AND LINGUISTICALLY DIVERSE PRESCHOOL CHILDREN

Graciela Elizalde-Utnick

Brooklyn College, City University of New York

Over the last several decades, there has been increased awareness of the difficulties encountered by culturally and linguistically diverse (CLD) children entering the school system (Fong, 2004; Gopaul-McNicol & Thomas-Presswood, 1998; Tabors, 1997). These children are often referred to as English-language learners (ELLs) or bilingual students. One of the major problems faced by these students is their overreferral and overrepresentation in special education (Artiles, Rueda, Salazar, & Higareda, 2005; Grossman, 1995; New York State Education Department, n.d.).

The literature cites various reasons for the inappropriate placement of CLD students in special education (Ortiz, 1997). There are a number of variables that need to be considered prior to a referral in order to determine the appropriateness of the referral itself. First, the criteria and process for referrals are based on limited understanding of cultural and linguistic issues. School psychologists and other school personnel are often unaware of the factors (e.g., sociocultural, linguistic, acculturative) that affect learning and the social-emotional functioning of young immigrant children from low socioeconomic backgrounds (McLoyd, 1998). A second reason has to do with the appropriateness of the evaluation process. Evaluators are often unaware of the limitations of many instruments when assessing these children (Gopaul-McNicol & Thomas-Presswood, 1998; Lopez, 1995, 1997). A third, important reason is the interpretation of assessment results. Potential or ongoing problems related to limited English proficiency, as well as normative processes in second language acquisition, must be differentiated from either language disorders or learning difficulties to avoid misclassifying CLD students as disabled (Lenski, Daniel, Ehlers-Savala, & Alvayero, 2004). This is particularly true for young children who generally show lags or variations in speech and language development.

School psychologists and other personnel who work with preschoolers understand the importance of collaborating with parents; this is especially true given the dependence and strong connection between young children and their families. Furthermore, legal mandates (Individuals With Disabilities Act, IDEA, Public Law 102–119, reauthorized in 1997 as Public Law 105–17) require that school personnel involve families, the assessment of preschoolers be conducted in a nondiscriminatory fashion, and children be evaluated in their native language. These mandates can be difficult to fulfill due to the shortages of qualified bilingual personnel (Elizalde-Utnick, 2002; Paredes Scribner, 2002) and the fact that most assessment instruments are not developed for use with CLD preschool children. Furthermore, a conceptual framework for understanding CLD children's ecological context, including cultural family values (e.g., the role of the extended family), has not been established to adequately guide practice.

In sum, the extent and complexity of issues to consider in the assessment of CLD preschool children and in planning developmentally appropriate interventions for them, calls for an understanding of these issues from a broader perspective. Thus, the purpose of this chapter is to present an ecological model for conceptualizing CLD preschool children and their families, discuss implications of this model for practice (e.g., development of cross-cultural competence, establishment of family–professional collaboration, culturally sensitive assessment and intervention planning), and recommend directions for future research and practice.

THEORETICAL AND RESEARCH BASIS

Ecological Context of the CLD Preschooler

Many scholars emphasize an ecological approach to working with children and their families (Bronfenbrenner, 1977, 1979; Christenson & Sheridan, 2001; Nuttall, Nuttall-Vazquez, & Hampel, 1999). An ecological perspective views the child as an active participant in a system that is connected at all levels. Bronfenbrenner (1977, 1979) described these levels as nesting of ecological systems that are interrelated and influence children's learning and social-emotional development over time. Based on this perspective, Nuttall et al. (1999) suggested the use of an ecological model for CLD preschoolers and their families. Such a model views the CLD preschooler as being nested within the family and home. In turn, the family and home system is nested within the community, and the community is nested within the larger system of values and culture. Elizalde-Utnick (2001a) expanded this model to include the relationship between the child's present ecosystem (child–family–home–community) and the ecosystem that exists in the country of origin (see Figure 23–1). The latter is particularly important to consider with CLD children who travel to and from their native land.

School psychologists working with CLD preschoolers need to assess children directly and also within each level of the ecosystem. The immediate level of assessment (or innermost system, as shown in Figure 23–1) is that of the individual child. This level focuses on the child's functioning within a number of skill domains: lan-

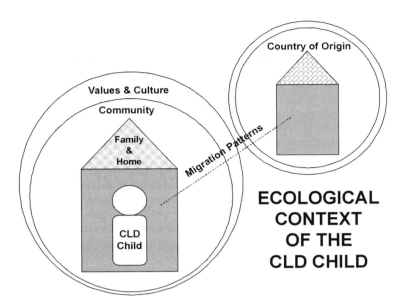

FIGURE 23–1.   The CLD child develops within an ecological context, which consists of the individual child, the family and home, the community, and values and culture, that provides a framework for the children and their family. It is important to also consider the child's country of origin, as there are CLD children who travel back and forth.

guage development (first language, second language, etc.), cognitive development, motor skills (fine and gross motor skills), social-emotional development (e.g., self-concept, interpersonal skills, play behaviors), adaptive daily living skills, and academic readiness.

The next level focuses on the family and home environment, which includes immediate and extended family members, as well as caretakers. The next focus is the community, which encompasses neighbors and friends (family friends, neighborhood friends, school friends), as well as preschools, center-based programs, home-based programs, religious institutions, and other community organizations.

The outermost level, or system, deals with values and culture. Nuttall et al. (1999) note that "preschool children are more purely products of their particular culture than children who have been socialized for several years into American culture by the schools" (p. 7). This level encompasses the child's ethnic, racial, and religious background and social class. It also includes cultural beliefs systems, as well as child–family interaction patterns (including communication styles) and childrearing patterns.

Multidimensional Approach

Consistent with an ecological perspective on CLD preschoolers is the use of a multidimensional approach. A multidimensional approach requires gathering and integrating data from multiple sources and settings and with multiple methods (Elizalde-Utnick, 2001b; Knoff, 2002; Knoff, Stollar, Johnson, & Chenneville, 1999). Thus, CLD preschoolers should be observed and assessed in a variety of contexts (i.e., informal settings, such as home, playground; formal settings, such as the classroom), using multiple methods (i.e., formal and informal assessment techniques; alternative assessment procedures) and drawing from multiple sources (i.e., child, parents, and other family members and/or caretakers; service providers, such as teacher, speech therapist, etc.). This approach will be elaborated on later in the chapter.

IMPLICATIONS FOR PRACTICE

Cross-Cultural Competence

School psychologists, now more than ever, are likely to be working in culturally diverse settings and experiencing cross-cultural encounters. Furthermore, effective school psychology practice entails an understanding of the impact of culture on the psychological and social functioning of CLD children and families (Elizalde-Utnick, 2002; Paredes Scribner, 2002). The overreferral and overrepresentation of ethnic minority children in special education classes (Artiles et al., 2005) underscore the need for school psychologists to become culturally competent. Paniagua (1998) points out that the assessment and treatment of CLD individuals without cultural understanding might be considered a violation of ethical principles.

The development of cross-cultural competence is an arduous, multifaceted process that requires individuals to "take risks, lower their defenses, and set aside their own beliefs in an attempt to adopt another's viewpoint" (Flanagan & Miranda, 1995, p.1054). The development of cross-cultural competence has a number of components, including cultural self-awareness, awareness and understanding of other cultures, understanding of the immigrant experience, and awareness of communication patterns.

Cultural Self-Awareness

Cultural self-awareness is the first step in developing cross-cultural competence (Lynch & Hanson, 1998; Miranda, 2002). It is important to understand one's own culture, including subgroup cultural values and migration history, as a premise for learning about the cultural values of others. There are different strategies that may be employed in order to gain greater cultural self-awareness, but talking with older family members is generally very helpful. The author's own experience with training graduate students in bilingual school psychology and counseling has been that the students begin to engage in rich dialogues over migration history with elder extended family members. This intergenerational dialogue serves to highlight the oral or narrative transmission and culture specificity of value systems. It is also critical to be aware of how one's own cultural values influence daily practice. Similarly, it is important to analyze mainstream or host cultural values, including the emphasis given to individuality and autonomy. By becoming aware of the degree to which one identifies with mainstream values, one can come to understand its impact on work with CLD children and families.

Culture-Specific Awareness and Understanding

An understanding of one's own cultural values and awareness of how these values impact working with others facilitates the ability to learn about other cultures (Lynch, 1998; Miranda, 2002). The process of learning about other cultures may occur in a variety of ways. Knowledge may be gained through reading books; watching films that depict life in another culture or the immigrant experience; talking and interacting with individuals from other cultures, including knowledgeable colleagues (clients can also be used as a resource to explain characteristic values and social patterns); attending cultural events (e.g., religious ceremonies); and learning the language of clients with whom we work. Part of intercultural understanding entails learning how one's own values might be consistent with, as well as differ from, those of individuals from other cultures.

Observing CLD preschoolers and their families within a multidimensional perspective (including community and cultural and linguistic issues) enables school psychologists to have a better understanding of diverse populations (Miranda, 2002). When applying such a perspective with this young population, it is important to consider the nuclear and extended family cultural belief systems, interaction patterns, childrearing patterns, and children's play behavior across cultures.

Cultural belief systems. An understanding of children's development and the interpretation of their daily experiences needs to be based on knowledge of the culture-specific developmental expectations and values held by parents (Greenfield, 1994; Harkness & Super, 1996). Understanding parents' cultural belief systems can provide valuable insights into culturally constructed parental practices and their consequences for children's development and behavior. Harkness and Super (1996) point out:

Parents' understanding about the nature of children, the structure of development, and the meaning of behavior are to a large extent shared by members of a cultural group or subgroup. These understandings are developed in the context of life in a particular cultural place and time, and they are related to understandings about other aspects of life as experienced by parents, including most immediately the nature and meaning of parenthood, the family, and the self in society. (p. 2)

Cultural belief systems relate directly to how parents raise their children, including parent–child interaction styles and discipline strategies. Learning about parental cultural belief systems requires an understanding of *culture*. Culture has been defined as a framework that guides behaviors in daily life (Anderson & Fenichel, 1989). Rather than viewing culture as a rigid prescription of specific behaviors to follow, culture can be viewed as a framework or context that allows individuals to mediate their behavior. However, one must recognize that although individuals within a particular culture share similar characteristics and tendencies, they do not necessarily behave in the same way. Although it is critical to be sensitive to cultural differences, it is tantamount not to generalize (or essentially stereotype) a given behavior to all members of a particular culture.

Individualism–Collectivism Continuum.

Cultures differ in many ways. One way to understand cultures is to place them along the individualism–collectivism (or alternatively, the independence–interdependence) continuum (Greenfield, 1994; Triandis, 1995). Individualism, or independence, which is valued typically by Western cultures (e.g., the United States and Western Europe), is characterized by individual initiative and emotional independence (Triandis, 1995). In contrast, collectivism, or interdependence, which is held by about 70% of the world's population (including Latin America, Asia, Africa, Eastern Europe), is characterized by strong cohesive groups, collective identity, group decisions, and emotional dependence (Greenfield, 1994; Triandis, 1995).

Most people grow up in a collective network by way of their attachments with their families, but with time become detached or independent from their families to varying degrees. The detachment process in collectivist cultures can be minimal because people in these cultures think of themselves as part of the collective group. In individualistic cultures, the detachment may be more pronounced (Triandis, 1995). An example of this dichotomy in practice may surface when the school psychologist or teacher assesses a CLD preschooler's adaptive behavior functioning. One aspect of adaptive behavior is the child's "ability to function independently to a developmentally appropriate degree" (Knoff et al., 1999, p. 155). In this context, such a skill domain can be culturally loaded, because collectivist cultures typically do not foster independence in young children (Lynch, 1998). For example, in traditional Korean families, young children are perceived as incapable of taking care of themselves (Kim & Choi, 1994). Korean children often are not encouraged to eat by themselves until age 3 and, even then, they are not pressured to do so if they refuse (Kim & Choi, 1994). Similarly, Latino preschoolers may be dressed by their parents and allowed to continue to drink milk from a baby bottle (Zuniga, 1998). The priority given to such interdependence is compounded by the presence of a disability in a collectivist family. Zuniga (1998) notes that when a young child has a disability, parents and/or extended family members might not impose demands on the child. Due to these cultural differences, CLD preschoolers may score "delayed" in adaptive behavior scales when the scales use U.S. cultural norms (i.e., independence is valued); therefore, evaluators must keep in mind that such levels of functioning might be consistent with the family's cultural values (therefore, culturally appropriate), particularly if interdependence is valued.

It should also be noted that in addition to intercultural differences, there are also intracultural differences (e.g., Latino cultures can differ from each other), as well as differing levels of acculturation. This is further complicated by the fact that there are diverse (collectivist) cultures that do foster some level of self-reliance in their children. For instance, Yoruba parents expect children to become self-reliant from a young age (Zeitlin, 1996). By age 2, Yoruba children help with chores and wash and dry their faces; and by age 5 they are expected to have mastered many self-help skills as well as run errands for their parents. By age 7, Yoruba children are considered essentially full members of society in that they are responsible for their own care and that of younger siblings. Thus, exploring a diverse family's cultural background is key because it pertains to adaptive behavior functioning.

Beliefs about cognitive development. In addition to influencing adaptive behavior, family cultural values affect young children's cognitive development (Gaskins, 1996; Greenfield & Cocking, 1994; Palacios & Moreno, 1996). Parents possess culturally based paradigms about how children learn. In the United States, there is an emphasis on children's cognitive development, with a priority given to providing a language-rich environment (New & Richman, 1996). However, not all cultures place a similar emphasis on the development of verbal abilities in children. For instance, Yoruba parents place a priority on motor skills development in their very young children (Zeitlin, 1996). That is not to say that these parents do not value verbal communication. The difference is that a priority is not given to actively fostering verbal skills. Rabain-Jamin (1994) studied the interaction of African mothers with their preverbal children and noted that with respect to children's verbalizations, the emphasis is on social relatedness. That is, the mothers consistently responded to their children when they engaged in social communication (e.g., smiling, laughing, vocalizing), but not when the children's communication revolved around an object (e.g., a toy).

Similar attitudinal differences regarding language development are found in other cultures. For instance, within the Chinese culture, less reinforcement of language development has been found when compared with Euro-American children (Ho, 1994). Furthermore, in the Chinese culture, exploratory behavior tends to be thwarted during infancy and early childhood. These are behaviors that are consistent with cultural expectations for adult behavior: Both physical aggression and verbal assertiveness have to be restrained.

Parents also possess notions regarding their children's ability to reason (Delgado-Gaitan, 1994; Gaskins, 1996). Gaskins (1996) studied the Mayan Indians of Yucatan, Mexico. Between ages 2 and 4, children are thought to be "beginning-to-start-to-understand-children." It is at the age when children can consistently follow verbal directives that they are no longer considered infants. Furthermore, between ages 4 and 6, they are observed as performing some tasks well, "although they cannot be expected to show much judgment or reasoning ability" (Gaskins, 1996, p. 353). Therefore, tasks such as household chores need to be assigned to them. Interestingly, Gaskins found that the Mayans view development as an innate and automatic process, and not under the control of children or their parents. Therefore, there is rarely concern over monitoring children's development in terms of norms (as in the United States) or age, and children are not generally compared. The following anecdotal example illustrates this finding: During an interview that the author conducted with a Mexican mother of a preschooler being evaluated for possible speech and language delays, the mother turned to the author and noted that the questions (e.g., regarding verbal ability, adaptive behavior, and play behavior) she was being asked about her son would never be asked back in Mexico. In fact, she added, no one would be concerned that her son was not talking yet—eventually he would. If it were not for the recommendation of her son's pediatrician, then this mother would not have sought help for her son.

Delgado-Gaitan (1994) found that the notion of critical thinking, which is fostered in the United States, often collides with the Mexican value of respect. Any opinion provided by a child toward an adult is considered disrespectful, especially if it differs from that of an adult. In other words, it is viewed as arguing/and or questioning an authority figure. In Delgado-Gaitan's study, recent Mexican immigrants were followed-up over a 2-year period. Initially, children's critical thinking behaviors were perceived by their parents as rebelliousness. However, 2 years later, parental perceptions had changed. The parents' reactions became contextualized depending on the activity. Specifically, if the child offered an opinion during the context of daily routines, such behavior was viewed as disrespectful. However, if the child was discussing school-related matters, then such verbal interaction was accepted and encouraged. Delgado-Gaitan interpreted this change as a function of the parents' realization that such behavior was necessary for educational progress in the United States.

Attitudes toward disability.   In order for school psychologists to work effectively with CLD families, it is important for them to understand how cultures attach meaning to the presence of a disability. Parents' views regarding a disability and its cause range from those that focus on the role of fate to those that place the burden of responsibility on the children or their family (Hanson, Lynch, & Wayman, 1990). Studies on the relationship between culture and attitudes toward disabilities have found that there are generally four ways of interpreting major disabilities: retribution for sins of either parents or ancestors, possession by evil spirits, the result of specific behaviors of the mother during pregnancy, and the imbalance of physiological functions (Chan, 1998; Hanson et al., 1990; Harry, 1992; Sharifzadeh, 1998). A common explanation provided to the author (Elizalde-Utnick) by Latino parents, especially Mexican parents, is that the mother experienced a frightening event during the first several months of pregnancy, and this event is viewed as a possible cause of the disability or developmental delay. Furthermore, in the author's experience, these parents' theories are substantiated by family members, friends, and/or neighbors who ask about the mother's behavior and experiences during the pregnancy.

The strong sense of familialism, with its traditional view of the individual as a reflection of the family, makes acceptance of severe disabilities very difficult for Latino parents (Harry, 1992). As is the case with many Latino families, major disabilities (e.g., mental retardation, sensory or physical disabilities) carry considerable stigma in Asian cultures (Chan, 1998). This is due to the cultural belief that a child's acts contribute either to the pride or shame of the family (i.e., the disability is thought to reflect on the family's behavior, past or present). Asian parents might respond with resignation and with tolerance of atypical behavior in young children, and as a result, resist seeking help. With less severe forms of disability, Asian parents might have different attitudes, often believing that such difficulties exist due to the child being lazy or oppositional (Chan, 1998). As previously emphasized, such cultural differences, although established in the literature, should not be generalized to all members of a given group due to inter- and intragroup differences and variations in levels of acculturation.

Interaction Patterns

In addition to examining parents' beliefs about cognitive development, it is also helpful to examine interaction patterns, childrearing styles, and play behavior across cultures. In terms of child–family interaction patterns, Gaskins (1996) found that Mayan parents believe that children learn on their own:

> Caregivers define their caregiving role in terms of insuring the safety and well-being of the child and in keeping the child content by responding to its needs and desires, not in terms of stimulation and interaction. They believe young children develop and learn largely independently of caregivers' behavior toward them. (Gaskins, 1996, p. 361)

Therefore, with the exception of impending danger, Mayan parents provide little input to their young children about the environment, including toys and objects.

Parents are not the only members of the family who are responsible for socializing their young children. Often, siblings play an important role. Furthermore, socialization through observation and modeling is often the case in diverse families (Greenfield, 1994). This is the case with Hawaiians, who value observational learning over given explicit verbal instructions (Tharp, 1994). In this cultural group, child care is shared by parents and older siblings. By age 2 or 3, children turn to older siblings, rather than parents, for routine needs. In this manner, children learn appropriate behavior by imitating older siblings.

There is also an emphasis on the use of siblings for the socialization process among the Nso children of Cameroon (Nsamenang & Lamb, 1994). In Cameroon, infant care is conducted in sibling groups (multigender, multiage) ranging from 20 months to 7 years of age, who are under the guidance of one or two children (usually girls), from age 8 to 10. In this culture, where social intelligence is very important, young children undergo a "hands-on" socialization process under the mentorship of older siblings and peers—more so than with parents or other adults. This child-to-child socialization process teaches self-care, appropriate affect, and cognitive skills.

Gender roles and behaviors are typically taught from a very young age (McAdoo, 1999). For example, Muslim girls, as in other cultures, are typically encouraged to be shy and modest (Sherif, 1999). In contrast, boys across the world are expected to exhibit "toughness" (Tharp, 1994). Among West African cultures, children learn gender-appropriate behavior by working alongside an adult of the same gender. That is, adults are assisted in tasks by children of the same gender (Nsamenang & Lamb, 1994).

Mexican children are also reared differently, depending on gender (Sanchez, 1997). Boys are traditionally overindulged and given a higher status than females. Martinez (1999) notes that with Mexican American families, there is variability in the extent to which they adhere to traditional parenting practices, but acknowledges that such gender differences might be accurate for some contemporary Mexican American families.

The interaction patterns of CLD families can also be examined within the context of communication styles. Communication can be both verbal (using words, thereby explicit) and nonverbal (using gestures and/or facial expressions, thereby open to interpretation), and cultures differ in the extent to which information is communicated directly or indirectly (Lynch, 1998). Whereas some cultures value the direct transmission of information with strong emphasis on spoken/written language (e.g., United States, England, Scandinavia), other cultures are not so explicit, leaving much unsaid, thereby leaving much to context (i.e., the relationship between speakers, dynamics of role, age, physical cues, the situation) (Hall, 1976). Many cultures also value body contact between mother and child as a means of communication (Lebra, 1994).

Childrearing Patterns

There are great differences in childrearing patterns across families and cultures. Families differ in daily routine practices (e.g., feeding, sleeping, dressing) as well as discipline strategies.

Daily routines. Families differ, within and across cultures, with respect to daily routine practices, and diverse families' practices can differ from mainstream U.S. practices and expectations (Lynch, 1998). One such area is feeding practices: The meal may or may not be highly structured. In a study that compared New England and Italian families, New and Richman (1996) found that the New England youngsters were allowed to regulate their own feeding, whereas the Italian children were not given such freedom to regulate their own feeding. As described previously, collectivist cultures typically do not foster independence in their young children; consequently, some CLD preschoolers might not be encouraged to eat by themselves.

Sleep practices also vary widely within and across cultures. In the United States, experts typically recommend that young children sleep in their own bed (Wolf, Lozoff, Latz, & Paludetto, 1996). However, co-sleeping is common in many cultures. Wolf et al. (1996) note that co-sleeping is not simply due to economic considerations, such as room availability; rather, it fosters interpersonal relatedness. For instance, in Japan, children co-sleep because it is considered important for the parent–child relationship (Lebra, 1994). That is, parent and child sleeping in the same bed allows for bodily contact, which is viewed as an important source of communication in Japan. Japanese youngsters also bathe with their parents because it allows for bodily contact, which is believed to foster nonverbal communication between parents and children.

In terms of sleeping practices in the United States, it should be noted that co-sleeping does, in fact, exist. For example, Medansky and Edelbrock (1990) and Wolf et al. (1996) found that many African American children co-sleep. Abbott (1992) found that within the Appalachian community, 71% of children age 2 and younger co-sleep and 47% of children between ages 2 and 4 co-sleep. New and Richman (1996) compared the sleeping practices of New England and Italian babies and found that New England babies were sleeping in their own beds by 4 months of age. Furthermore, bedtime routines were established in infancy. In contrast, Italian mothers did not establish any sleep routine with their infants, and the infants often shared the same room with their parents until about their second birthday. Wolf et al. (1996) also report frequent co-sleeping among Italian families, and suggest that the higher incidence of co-sleeping in Japanese, Italian, and African American families, when compared to White families in the United States, might be related to the greater number of elders present in these families. The mothers in the families that co-sleep might rely more on the advice of elder family members than on outside advice (e.g., the advice of pediatricians in the United States, who are often opposed to co-sleeping). These authors also suggest that the demand for living space provided to the elder family members limits the available space for the rest of the family, thereby increasing the likelihood of co-sleeping.

Similar to feeding and sleeping practices, families differ in the degree to which preschoolers are expected to dress and undress themselves (Lynch, 1998). Latino and Asian families often do not foster independence in young children, and often dress their children in order to facilitate the dressing process (Chan, 1998; Zuniga, 1998). That does not mean that Latino and Asian preschoolers do not acquire self-help skills; it is just not encouraged as early as in American culture. In contrast, other diverse cultural groups, such as African and Native Americans, do encourage self-reliance from a young age (Joe & Malach, 1998; Nsamenang & Lamb, 1994).

Discipline. Discipline strategies and what practices a culture considers normal vary greatly, ranging from overindulgence all the way to corporal punishment (Gopaul-McNicol & Thomas-Presswood, 1998). Part of the interview process should entail asking parents about their discipline styles and cultural expectations regarding disciplining children.

Many cultures, especially collectivist cultures, value the importance of showing respect to elders. Rabain-Jamin (1994) found that once African children begin speaking, their parents expect their children to behave respectfully toward them (i.e., understand hierarchical rules—respect toward elders, especially toward parents). However, there is more latitude allowed with grandparents, as the relationship between grandparents and grandchildren is often described as "joking" (Rabain-Jamin, 1994, p.162). Similarly, Muslim children are taught not to question authority (Sherif, 1999).

Many cultures utilize corporal punishment whenever a child behaves in a disrespectful manner. Corporal punishment is the norm within the Yoruba culture (Zeitlin, 1996). A parent generally tells a child once what to do, and if the child does not comply, then physical punishment is the consequence. Like many cultures around the world, proverbs often reveal much about cultural practice. This is the case with the methods used by Yoruba parents in disciplining their children.

Yoruba views regarding the necessity of physical punishment are expressed in two proverbs (Babatunde, 1992): (a)"When the child behaves foolishly, one prays that he may not die; what kills more quickly than foolishness?" This expresses the understanding that punishment is an act of kindness. (b)"When we use the right hand to flog him, we use the left hand to draw him back to ourselves." This expresses the inseparability of the punishment from the need to comfort the child for the pain experienced during the punishment (Zeitlin, 1996, p. 416). Thus, whereas some individuals in the United States might view these practices as harsh, they are not viewed that way in cultures that believe in the use of such punishment. Although school psychologists need to respect cultural differences, in the case of corporal punishment it is critical to explain to CLD parents about child abuse mandates in the United States and how such laws could impact them.

Some cultures do not emphasize discipline with young children. For instance, Kim and Choi (1994) describe Korean parents as not being discipline oriented. Similarly, Ho (1994) notes that Chinese parents do not consider young children to be capable of great understanding. As a result, young children are not held responsible for their actions (Ho, 1994). Like in Korea and China, there is the belief in Japan that young children should be allowed to be children, and that childlike behavior needs to be accepted. Furthermore, any attempts at changing a young child's behavior are viewed as unnatural (Lebra, 1994).

Permissive parental attitudes toward playful behavior or mischief in Asian children do not imply lack of discipline. In Japan, for example, children are disciplined by the mother appealing to feelings. That is, the child should follow the mother's directive because it would otherwise "hurt" her feelings. Such a strategy is thought to foster empathy, as well as the very important cultural value of not shaming the mother by doing what one is told.

Another technique used in some cultures for fostering appropriate behaviors in children is through the use of proverbs and folktales. Many cultures, especially those with strong oral traditions, utilize proverbs and folktales in order to transmit culturally appropriate practices (Burciaga, 1997). Among Mexican American families, *dichos*, or proverbs, are used (especially by grandparents) to socialize young children (Chahin, Villarruel, & Viramontez, 1999). According to Martinez (1999), "the use of *dichos* among [Mexican adults] and their children allows parents to keep their feet in two cultural worlds" (p. 161).

It should be noted that across Spanish-speaking countries there are dialectical differences; the surface meaning might be different, but the underlying message is the same. One proverb that the author (whose parents are from Argentina) grew up with is "De piolas esta lleno el mundo." Whereas the surface meaning is not understood by the author's colleagues from other Spanish-speaking countries, Argentines understand the proverb's meaning: The world is full of people who may take advantage of you. Another common proverb is "Quien mal anda mal acaba" (He who has a bad behavior has a bad ending).

Play Behavior Across Cultures

Children play all over the world, however parents' beliefs about such activities differ and come to impact on their children's play behaviors (Greenfield, 1994). It is therefore important to consider cultural values and practices when assessing a CLD preschooler's play. For instance, Mayan parents provide little or no encouragement for children to play or give directions as to how to play (Gaskins, 1996). They think that play is merely a childhood activity that children enjoy, but with little worth. Mayan adults often prefer that their children engage in some productive activity, such as household chores, rather than play. The actual toys children play with can differ as well. For instance, it is not a West African tradition to give children commercial toys. Instead, they are encouraged to create their own play things (Nsamenang & Lamb, 1994).

Understanding the Immigrant Experience

In addition to cultural self-awareness and awareness and understanding of other cultures, cross-cultural competence entails understanding the immigrant experience. Often when working with CLD preschoolers, the child's parents (and perhaps the child) might have immigrated recently to the United States. Gaining understanding about the experiences that immigrants undergo and how they impact on the young child is crucial. The areas relevant for the school psychologist are the acculturation process, second language acquisition, and parents' beliefs about the education system.

Acculturation process.   Acculturation is described as a process by which the behaviors of a person from a given culture are modified due to contact with a new culture (Gopaul-McNicol & Thomas-Presswood, 1998). Berry (2003) describes the acculturation process as stressful and proposes that there are different modes of acculturation, which include *assimilation*, *integration*, and *separation*. When assimilating, individuals give up their cultural identity and take on the beliefs, attitudes, and behaviors of the majority culture. Individuals integrate when they continue to hold on to their cultural identity, but also become integral members of the majority culture. Separation involves the individual withdrawing from the majority culture. When interpreting data during the assessment process, it is critical to assess a family's level of acculturation. It should be noted that individual members of a family acculturate at different rates, and children often acculturate faster than adults (Berry, 2003).

Second language acquisition.   Preschool ELLs are in the process of learning two languages. It is critical that school psychologists understand the process of second language learning. Second language (L2) acquisition is very much like first language (L1) acquisition in many ways. The rate and pattern of language development are the same regardless of whether a child acquires only one language and becomes monolingual or acquires two languages and becomes bilingual (Grosjean, 1982). Psychosocial factors (e.g., language usage in the home or in school) affect when, to what extent, and for how long a child will be bilingual. For example, a child might decide to stop speaking L1 at home because peers at school are only speaking English.

There are two main types of bilingualism: (a) *simultaneous*, or *childhood*, bilingualism; and (b) *sequential* bilingualism. McLaughlin (1978) utilizes an age criterion to differentiate between the two types of language acquisition. A child who acquires two languages prior to age 3 does so simultaneously; and a child who acquires one language in infancy and then another after age 3 does so sequentially.

The degree of bilingualism attained is not related to whether languages are attained simultaneously or sequentially (Grosjean, 1982).

Studies of childhood bilingualism suggest that the simultaneous acquisition of two languages does not differ significantly from the acquisition of a single language (Swain, 1972). Following an initial period of confusion, the rules of each code begin to be differentiated by the learner. An interesting phenomenon of childhood bilingualism is the person–language bond. Young children often attach a particular language to a person. If that person addresses the child in the other language, then it may cause some distress and the child might pretend to not understand what is being said (Fantini, 1978). Such reactions may be due to the fact that the child is in the process of differentiating the two languages. One strategy for differentiation is to first determine which language is being spoken with a person and then to use the identified language when speaking to that person.

Another phenomenon that is common when children are learning a second a language is *passive* bilingualism. Passive bilingualism occurs when a child understands L1 but prefers to speak L2. For example, parents speak to the child in Spanish, and the child responds in English. This is very common and is to be expected, especially if the parents comprehend English (Elizalde-Utnick, Lopez, & Nahari, 2003).

There is a consistent developmental sequence exhibited by preschool ELLs in a monolingual English classroom (Tabors, 1997):

1. There may be a period of time when the young child continues to use L1 in the classroom (L2 is the language of instruction).
2. The child enters a silent period (i.e., nonverbal period) when the child discovers that L1 is ineffective in the classroom. During the silent period, which lasts approximately 4 to 5 months, the child focuses on listening and trying to comprehend. It should be noted that in a bilingual classroom, the silent period is characterized by the child attempting to talk only with those who speak L1 and avoiding verbal interactions with speakers of L2.
3. As children's receptive language skills in L2 grow, they begin to speak in one- to two-word utterances in L2.
4. The child begins to engage in conversations with others in L2.

The silent period is a normal process of second language acquisition. However, there are instances in which the silent period continues well beyond this 4- to 5-month period, and it becomes necessary to differentiate between the silent period and selective mutism (Elizalde-Utnick, 2003).

Beliefs about the education system.   Parents' experiences and expectations regarding the education of their young CLD children might differ from that of school professionals in the United States. The customs and beliefs of diverse immigrants often conflict with those of the U.S. education system (Elizalde-Utnick, 1998). As exemplified previously in the discussion on cultural belief systems, parents might have different beliefs regarding their role in the education of their children. For instance, among Spanish-speaking cultures, the roles of the school and family are generally clearly specified. Whereas the family is responsible for socializing the child (e.g., teaching appropriate behavior), the school is responsible for providing formal knowledge (Elizalde-Utnick, 1998). Furthermore, close-knit families that prefer to resolve difficulties within the confines of the family would view professionals as outsiders (Kalyanpur & Harry, 1999).

Cross-cultural Communication

As previously discussed, cross-cultural competence is multifaceted and entails cultural self-awareness, understanding and knowledge of other cultures, and understanding the immigrant experience. The fourth component of cross-cultural competence is understanding cross-cultural communication patterns. Clashes in cross-cultural communication are often due to a variety of "stumbling blocks" that include language, assumptions and stereotypes, and emotions (i.e., high anxiety and tension experienced during cross-cultural encounters; Barna, 1983). Language often serves as a barrier between linguistically diverse parents and schools (U.S. Department of Education, 1998). Therefore, it is critical that information be provided in the parents' native language. It is equally important to consider preconceived notions that one might have about a given cultural group. Although it is important to be sensitive about cultural differences, it is also crucial that members of a given cultural group not be stereotyped. Strategies for effective communication with families will be discussed later in this chapter.

Thus far in this section of the chapter, the development of cross-cultural competence has been discussed as an implication for school psychology practice. Another implication for practice is the establishment of family–professional collaboration. In order to work effectively with CLD preschoolers, one must establish collaborative relationships with their families.

ESTABLISHMENT OF FAMILY–PROFESSIONAL COLLABORATION

The benefits of home–school collaboration are undisputed (Elizalde-Utnick, 2002). In order to plan and implement effective and appropriate interventions, school psychologists and other professionals need to work together with families. It is not always easy to involve parents in school activities, and the task becomes daunting when one tries to collaborate with diverse families who do not necessarily share a philosophy of active participation in schools (Elizalde-Utnick, 1998, 2002). For instance, in the Yoruba culture, people believe that weaknesses in children may be corrected by prayer and sacrifice (Zeitlin, 1996). Thus, CLD parents might not consider approaching an outsider for help. Working collaboratively with parents, now more than ever, hinges on the school professional understanding the interaction between school and cultural contexts.

ASSESSMENT AND INTERVENTION PLANNING

Assessment and intervention planning requires that the school psychologist and family work together. Lynch and Hanson (1998) describe this process as involving three steps: (a) establishing a collaborative relationship and planning the assessment, (b) data gathering and assessment, and (c) developing an intervention plan. It is critical that the assessment should be based on the family's concerns and priorities, and the approaches utilized take into account linguistic and cultural variables. Strategies for effective assessment and intervention planning are described in the next section.

IMPLEMENTATION AND APPROACHES

Perspective Taking: Posture of Cultural Reciprocity

Providing culturally responsive services to CLD preschoolers and their families requires school psychologists to bridge or establish connections between the cultures of these families and the culture of the school (Harry, Kalyanpur, & Day, 1999). To accomplish this goal, school psychologists should initiate a two-way process of understanding and information sharing. As consultants, school psychologists already engage in this kind of two-way communication (Elizalde-Utnick, 2002).

Kalyanpur and Harry (1999) describe such a reciprocal process of perspective taking that they refer to as the *posture of cultural reciprocity*. This approach entails families and school psychologists engaging in a multistep sharing of perspectives—a process that includes listening to and respecting multiple perspectives. Kalyanpur and Harry note that this process is helpful because it avoids stereotyping, goes beyond awareness of differences to self-awareness, and ensures that both families and professionals are empowered. Harry et al. (1999) outline the following four steps for developing a posture of cultural reciprocity:

1. School psychologists identify the cultural values embedded in their professional practices. A school psychologist can ask: What cultural values are embedded in my interpretations of a child's difficulties or in the development of an intervention? Example: The school psychologist might value independence and individuality both personally and professionally.
2. The school psychologist finds out if the family recognizes and values these assumptions and, if not, how their view differs from that of the school psychologist. Example: The family values interdependence.
3. School psychologists recognize and respect any cultural differences identified, and fully explain the cultural basis of their assumptions. For instance, when the school psychologist explains to the family that a recommendation is rooted in the cultural value of independence, the psychologist is offering information about mainstream cultural values. In addition, by asking the family for its perspective, school psychologists are demonstrating an understanding that their own cultural beliefs are not the only way to view the world.
4. Through two-way communication and collaboration, school psychologists determine the most effective way to adapt their professional interpretation or recommendations to the family's cultural value system.

Case Example

Mrs. Hernandez approached the school psychologist because she is having difficulty managing her 3-year-old daughter's behavior during mealtime. Mrs. Hernandez and her husband immigrated to the United States from Mexico 5 years ago, shortly after getting married. Mrs. Hernandez stays home caring for her daughter, Maria, while her husband works longs hours as a truck loader. The meeting was also attended by her daughter's speech therapist. For the last 8 months, Mrs. Hernandez has found herself battling with her daughter during meals. She reported that her daughter often refuses to eat, and so she runs after her daughter with a filled spoon in her hand. She also gives in to her daughter's demands in an effort to facilitate the feeding process. Although Maria is able to feed herself (and she does so in school), Mrs. Hernandez typically feeds her daughter in order to ensure that Maria has eaten a sufficient amount of food. She added that the variety of foods that her daughter will eat is very limited. Furthermore, every night when Mr. Hernandez comes home from work, he criticizes his wife because Maria seems too thin (in actuality, Maria's weight is within normal limits) and accuses her of not being a good mother. At this point in the meeting, Mrs. Hernandez begins to cry. How should the school psychologist and speech therapist respond? What are the issues involved in this scenario?

The school psychologist and speech therapist might interpret this situation on a behavioral level. After all, Mrs. Hernandez reinforces Maria's behaviors by attending to her running away from the table. Furthermore, by engaging in a battle, she is empowering Maria. The speech therapist, who is experienced with oral-motor difficulties, might consider that Maria's oral-motor weaknesses are at play and/or that there may be sensory issues (i.e., her limited diet might be a function of a sensitivity to certain textures of foods).

Putting these interpretations aside, along with any concerns regarding Mr. and Mrs. Hernandez's marital relationship, this case can be analyzed from a cultural value perspective. Applying the posture of cultural reciprocity, the school psychologist and speech therapist should look at each member's cultural points of view, including their own. Mrs. Hernandez's manner of interacting with her daughter reflects her cultural background. In Latino families, children are highly regarded, and young children are nurtured and often overindulged (Zuniga, 1998). In the author's (Elizalde-Utnick) experience with Mexican families, there is often a value placed on a well-fed child; that is, a good parent makes sure a child is well-fed. Furthermore, plump children are often viewed as cute and cared for. Such a value was shared by both Mr. and Mrs. Hernandez. Maria, on the other hand, is learning other cultural values from school. She is attending a center-based early childhood program where she receives special education and speech therapy. Maria's classroom teacher is fostering Maria's autonomy, which is consistent with the mainstream U.S. value of individualism. In the classroom, Maria is given a choice of foods during snack time and she eats how much she wants.

By looking at each person's cultural perspective, each value is understood to be adaptive within its social context. What about the school psychologist's and speech therapist's perspectives? Would it make a difference? The answer is "yes." The school psychologist and speech therapist might believe that Mr. and Mrs. Hernandez should let Maria be—that Maria is asserting her sense of autonomy. But doesn't this reflect the American value of individualism? It is critical that school psychologists and other school professionals be sensitive to different worldviews and understand behaviors within their cultural context.

It would be helpful, in this case, for the school psychologist to discuss each individual's perspective in terms of cultural values. In other words, Mrs. Hernandez's parenting style can be validated within the context of her culture. She can also come to understand that Maria is acculturating to U.S. mainstream values as she attends school. Once this is understood, then the school psychologist and speech therapist, together with Mrs. Hernandez, can develop a behavioral intervention plan to be implemented in the home, a plan that makes sense to all parties involved.

DATA GATHERING APPROACHES: RESPONSIVE ASSESSMENT

An ecological approach is needed when assessing CLD preschoolers (Nuttall et al., 1999). This entails assessing the child across a variety of contexts, gathering information from multiple sources, and interpreting the information in a culturally responsive manner. A culturally responsive approach entails interpreting gathering data via multiple observations, direct assessment, communication sampling, and discussions with caregivers and service providers. A culturally responsive approach also entails interpreting those data within the context of cultural and language differences. Potential or ongoing problems related to limited English proficiency must be separated from either language disorders or learning difficulties.

Interviews With Caregivers and Service Providers

A child's success as a learner depends on parents as well as teachers and other service providers (e.g., speech therapist, special educator). Therefore, caregivers and service providers need to be interviewed regarding the child's performance across skill domains. When interviewing parents, Sigel and Kim (1996) provide a word of caution in utilizing a standardized interview protocol (e.g., an adaptive behavior scale or checklist):

High standardized questioning reflect[s] a unidirectional communication, thereby not providing an opportunity for true discourse. In effect, our findings confirm Mishler's (1986) critique of the stimulus–response model. His critique is important, not only for us but also for any of the ethnographic interviews done in anthropology and developmental or clinical psychology. Elaborating on his thesis that interviews in effect are speech events, which he describes as a thematic progression involving turn taking and following conversational rules, Mishler (1986) writes: "Defining interviews, as I do, marks a fundamental contrast between the standard anti-linguistic, stimulus response model and an alternative approach to interviews as discourse between speakers." (p. 77, in Sigel & Kim, 1996, pp. 113–114)

When interviewing caregivers about the family's level of acculturation, the following should be ascertained: length of time in the United States, reasons for immigration, contact with homeland (migration patterns), family attitudes, languages spoken at home, languages of peers and community, languages in school, languages in an afterschool setting, and languages used in leisure time (e.g., television, play) (Elizalde-Utnick, et al. 2003.). The parent interview should also include a discussion of parental beliefs and attitudes, the child's history of first and second language acquisition, literacy experiences in the home (including languages of interaction), and parents' degree of bilingualism. Assessors should also consider the language in which the services are provided to the child, becuase the languages used influence how well a child learns a particular language. It is the author's experience with speech- and language-delayed CLD toddlers that such a variable (i.e., the language of intervention) is critical when interpreting assessment data. For instance, a toddler who is dominant in L1 (e.g., Spanish), whose family speaks only L1 (e.g., Spanish) at home, and who is receiving speech therapy and special instruction in English (L2), is not necessarily developing L1 skills as well as, for example, a speech-delayed youngster receiving services in the child's primary language.

Multiple Observations in Different Contexts

Observation data should be gathered in different settings, both formal (during evaluation, classroom) and informal (playground, home). Observing students interacting with different individuals (i.e., parent, siblings, peers, service providers) also provides important information, because young children can behave differently with different individuals. The author evaluated a young Latino child who had not had experience playing with an adult; his play experiences were exclusively with other children. As a result, the author initially interpreted the child's seemingly limited play behaviors as possibly reflecting cognitive delays. However, during a subsequent parent interview in the child's presence, the child was observed playing with his brother. The child's symbolic play with his brother was much more elaborate, making it clear that the author had misinterpreted the child's earlier play behaviors. Only with multiple observations of a child in different contexts does a more complete picture of the child emerge.

Play-Based Assessment

Play-based assessment is a natural, functional approach to assessment and intervention (Linder, Holm, & Walsh, 1999). This approach is less intimidating for the child and results in meaningful information. It also provides information regarding the child's skills in cognitive, speech and language, visual-motor, and social-emotional development. Play-based assessment provides flexibility in testing, unlike standardized tests that follow a prescribed set of tasks in a standardized manner and can be conducted individually or in teams (arena style). Because the traditional standardized instruments have not been developed for use with CLD children, alternative procedures are necessary in order to obtain a holistic picture of the child's abilities. Some alternative procedures include (a) naturalistic observations; (b) observational instruments that assess child's play with a parent, child–child (with peers) play, and isolated play; (c) arena (i.e., a team of evaluators assess a child together at the same time) assessments; and (d) parent interviews and rating scales (Linder et al., 1999).

Direct Assessment: Formal and Informal Approaches

Direct assessment entails assessment of cognitive functioning, pre-readiness skills, social-emotional functioning, and adaptive behavior functioning (Elizalde-Utnick, 2001b; Romero, 1999). It is important to consider cultural and linguistic variables when assessing these areas. Standardized measures are often inadequate for use with CLD children due to poor norms (i.e., lack of validity and reliability).

There are concerns that cognitive tests typically fail to measure the cognitive functioning of bilingual children and instead assess these children's language abilities (Lopez, 1995; Padilla, 2001). Alternative procedures include nonverbal tests; however, caution should be taken in interpreting test results because nonverbal tests, particularly unidimensional measures (based on a few types of tasks), measure a narrow set of cognitive skills (Bracken & McCallum, 2001). Dynamic assessment procedures (i.e., pretest–intervention–posttest; Lidz, 2001), such as Lidz's (1991) preschool learning assessment device, provide other alternatives.

Communication Sampling

Communication sampling involves the assessment of language proficiency, which includes collecting language samples focusing on receptive and expressive language, as well as pragmatics (i.e., discourse, or the ability to communicate effectively with others). Few language proficiency tests are available for bilingual children, and they are generally considered inappropriate due to a lack of validity and reliability (Lopez, 1995). Informal procedures can be quite helpful. Interviewing the parent and service providers is critical in order to explore language development and language usage. Informal language samples (in both first and second languages) need to be obtained across different contexts (e.g., home, playground, classroom) and with different individuals communicating with the child (e.g., parents, siblings, peers, other adults).

INTERVENTION STRATEGIES

Effective interventions require collaboration between the school psychologist, the family, and other school personnel. Lopez (1995) notes that there needs to be ongoing monitoring of interventions in order to determine their effectiveness and need for any modifications.

Language(s) of Intervention

In selecting the language of intervention for the CLD preschooler, a number of factors need to be considered: the child's proficiency in the first and second languages, the parent's preference and the child's comfort level in each language, the nature of the child's disability, and the availability of programs and bilingual personnel. It should be noted that a bilingual class provides a special, nurturing environment for young children (Hirschler, 1994; Tabors, 1997). But, if it is unavailable, then a language-rich environment is a helpful alternative as it provides incentives for children to learn and values the culture CLD students bring to the classroom (Bunce, 1995; Tabors; 1997).

Classroom Interventions

Communication strategies.   A variety of strategies can be used to foster CLD preschoolers' learning in the classroom. When working with ELLs, it is critical to use communication to support second language learning (McLaughlin, 1995). ELLs need a great deal of time to become familiar with the classroom and a new cultural and linguistic setting before being approached with questions and directives in English. When speaking to the young child in the second language, Tabors (1997) emphasizes the notion of buttressing communication, reiteration, and repetition. Buttressing communication involves using words in conjunction with some type of gesture, action, or directed gaze. Reiteration involves the teacher restating a message in a form that is more understandable. With repetition, teachers repeat their statements in order to foster comprehension in young ELLs. For instance, teachers can use strategies such as re-reading and re-telling of certain stories, as well as repetition of language units (Morrow, 2001).

Brice (2002) recommends that bilingual students be allowed to code switch (switching or alternating between languages or codes) with bilingual peers in the classroom because it "will allow students to practice speaking and transition into using English at their readiness level" (p.139). This is based on research by Brice and colleagues, who investigated code switching in English as a second language (ESL) classrooms (Brice, 2000; Brice, Mastin, & Perkins, 1997). They found that 100% of the utterances were correct and therefore not indicative of language confusion or of a language disorder. It should be noted that a common myth regarding second language learners is that code switching is indicative of a language difficulty (Brice, 2002). In fact, research indicated quite the opposite: Code switching may reflect high level skills in both L1 and L2 (Brice, 2000; Brice et al., 1997).

Organization of the classroom.   There should be "safe havens" in the classroom; that is, there should be activities (e.g., manipulatives such as puzzles, legos, clocks, play dough) available that allow ELLs to pursue an activity without asking for help from anyone else or having to negotiate play with other children. In this manner, ELLs move into the rest of the classroom activities when they are ready.

Classroom routines should be implemented in ways that are sensitive to the ELL's needs. For example, a consistent set of routines (daily schedule of arrival, free play, clean-up, circle time, snack time, gym time) and a visual display of the schedule with pictures are very helpful. The routines allow the ELLs to pick up cues as to what to do. When implementing small-group activities, ELLs can be grouped with other ELLs and English speakers (Kagan & McGroarty, 1993). Pairing ELLs with English-speaking "buddies" helps to reduce their isolation and fosters the development of English as a second language (Ovando, Collier, & Combs, 2003).

Using the Curriculum With ELLs

ELLs benefit from experiences that include hands-on activities, literacy activities, circle time, and playground/gym (Tabors, 1997). Children gain vocabulary and conceptual knowledge, as well as engage in social interaction, with hands-on activities. Although many such activities can be child directed, there are numerous opportunities to implement teacher-directed activities. Through the latter, teachers can provide a "running commentary," which entails explaining their actions and the actions of others as an activity occurs (Tabors, 1997).

Consultation With Families and School Personnel

School psychologists are in the position to bridge between the cultures of diverse families and the culture of schools. This connection may be accomplished when school psychologists engage in a two-way process of information sharing and understanding. As consultants, school psychologists already engage in this two-way communication process (Elizalde-Utnick, 2002). Consulting with families can be helpful in addressing family concerns as well as "exploring with the family the appropriateness of the recommended interventions from a cultural perspective" (Lopez, 1995, p. 1119).

In addition to consulting with families, school psychologists can consult with school personnel working with CLD preschoolers. The result could be helping school professionals address the difficulties CLD students encounter in the classroom, as well as maximize the learning potential of a given environment (e.g., classroom, speech therapy session).

IMPLICATIONS FOR FUTURE RESEARCH AND PRACTICE

This chapter has provided a theoretical and practical framework for working with CLD preschoolers and their families. Nevertheless, there are many barriers to effective practice. In order to truly reduce the bias inherently present in current assessment practices when applied to CLD children, a number of system changes are necessary. First, the development and implementation of high-quality services that are culturally and linguistically appropriate and effective is a must. To accomplish those goals, we have to be committed to changing discriminatory practices. Furthermore, training programs must recruit CLD individuals to encourage them to enter school-related professions like school psychology and education. Staff development focusing on increasing the cross-cultural competencies of school professionals is crucial. The latter entails going beyond offering workshops that school personnel sign up for on a voluntary basis. It is the author's experience that those individuals who attend such workshops are already committed to making a difference. The point is to achieve systemic change, and this requires mandating schoolwide training.

Another systemic recommended change is the creation of a culturally and linguistically responsive assessment and intervention process. First and foremost, this entails integrating family–professional collaboration into the culture of the school. Although consulting with school personnel and families is a critical role of the school psychologist in the 21st century, there are many school psychologists who spend more time assessing students for special education than engaging in pre-referral interventions (Curtis & Stoller, 2002; Curtis & Van Wagener, 1988). If the overreferral and overrepresentation of CLD students in special education is going to decrease, then school cultures will have to change so that family–professional collaboration is the norm. In addition to collaboration, there needs to be systemwide use of best practices for data gathering and intervention planning. This is not just important for evaluators integrating best practices, but it is also imperative for administrators who make placement decisions for CLD students. Finally, there needs to be monitoring and evaluation of assessment and intervention processes.

There are a number of avenues for future research. Much of the research on child development is based on Euro-American children and Western cultures. Furthermore, what is known about the cross-cultural roots of the developing CLD child is based primarily on studies conducted in a variety of cultures outside of the United States. Research needs to focus on CLD children growing up in the United States in families that may or may not be acculturating to mainstream U.S. values. For instance, does the Yoruba parent's view of child development and parenting change as a function of acculturation? Delgado-Gaitan's (1994) work with Mexican American families suggests that exposure to Western values does impact on families' worldviews. More work is needed in this area. Another area for future research is examining the variables involved in facilitating collaborative relationships with parents of CLD preschoolers. The key to the school psychologist's work with CLD preschoolers is to make connections with their families. After all, the child is just one piece of the ecosystem—just one piece of the whole puzzle.

ANNOTATED BIBLIOGRAPHY

Kalyanpur, M., & Harry, B. (1999). *Culture in special education: Building reciprocal family–professional relationships*. Baltimore: Paul H. Brookes.

This is an excellent resource that describes the potential impact of embedded and often unrecognized cultural assumptions influencing interactions between families and school professionals. It includes case examples, theoretical discussions, and personal anecdotes.

Lynch, E. W., & Hanson, M. J. (Eds.). (2004). *Developing cross-cultural competence: A guide for working with children and their families* (3rd ed.). Baltimore: Paul H. Brookes.

This is a frequently cited book that should be in every school psychologist's professional library. Its focus is on working with young children and their families. It is filled with case examples and helpful appendices.

Vazquez Nuttall, E., Romero, I., & Kalesnik, J. (Eds.). (1999). *Assessing and screening preschoolers: Psychological and educational dimensions* (2nd ed.). Boston: Allyn & Bacon.

This is a comprehensive text with practical guidelines and an emphasis on multiculturalism.

Tabors, P. O. (1997). *One child, two languages: A guide for preschool educators of children learning English as a second language.* Baltimore: Paul H. Brookes.

This is a helpful guide for creating supportive classroom environments for ELLs.

RESOURCES

Carroll, S. A., Romero, I., & Lopez, R. (Eds.). (2001). *Helping children at home and school: Handouts from your school psychologist—Spanish edition.* Washington, DC: National Association of School Psychologists.

This book includes reproducible handouts for parents, educators, child advocates, and teens on a wide range of issues affecting learning and behavior.

Early Childhood Resource Library:
http://www.healthcare.uiowa.edu/cdd/multiple/drl/EarlyChildhoodRL.htm

This resource library is located at the Center for Disabilities and Development (CDD) at the University of Iowa and serves as a resource for healthcare, training, research, and information for people with disabilities.

Raising Children Bilingually (CAL resource guide online):
http://www.cal.org/resources/faqs/rgos/bilingual_children.html

This resource is from the Center for Applied Linguistics on the World Wide Web (CAL). CAL carries out a wide range of activities including research, teacher education, analysis and dissemination of information, design and development of instructional materials, technical assistance, conference planning, program evaluation, and policy analysis.

The Center for the Improvement of Child Caring (CICC):
http://www.ciccparenting.org

The center creates, evaluates, delivers, and disseminates a variety of parenting skill-building programs that are taught in communities in the form of parenting classes, seminars, and workshops. (800) 325–2422

REFERENCES

Abbott, S. (1992). Holding on and pushing away: Comparative perspectives on an Eastern Kentucky child-rearing practice. *Ethos, 20,* 33–65.

Anderson, P. P., & Fenichel, E. S. (1989). *Serving culturally diverse families of infants and toddlers with disabilities.* Washington, DC: National Center for Clinical Infant Programs.

Artiles, A. J., Rueda, R., Salazar, J. J., & Higareda, I. (2005). Within-group diversity in minority disproportionate representation: English language learners in urban school districts. *Exceptional Children, 71,* 283–300.

Babatunde, E. D. (1992). *Culture, religion and the self: A critical study of Bini and Yoruba value systems in change.* Lewiston, NY: Edwin Mellen Press.

Barna, L. M. (1983). The stress factor in intercultural relations. In D. Landis & R. W. Brislin (Eds.), *Handbook of intercultural training* (Vol. 2, pp. 95–102). New York: Pergamon.

Berry, J. W. (2003). Conceptual approaches to acculturation. In K. M. Chun, P. B. Organista, & G. Marin (Eds.), *Acculturation: Advances in theory, measurement, and applied research* (pp. 17–37). Washington, DC: American Psychological Association.

Bracken, B. A., & McCallum, R. S. (2001). Assessing intelligence in a population that speaks more than two hundred languages: A nonverbal solution. In L. A. Suzuki, J. G. Ponterotto, & P. J. Meller (Eds.), *Handbook of multicultural assessment: Clinical, psychological, and educational applications* (2nd ed., pp. 405–431). San Francisco: Jossey-Bass.

Brice, A. E. (2000). Code switching and code mixing in the ESL classroom: A study of pragmatic and syntactic features. *Advances in Speech Language Pathology. Journal of the Speech Pathology Association of Australia, 20*(1), 19–28.

Brice, A. E. (2002). *The Hispanic child: Speech, language, culture and education.* Boston: Allyn & Bacon.

Brice, A. E., Mastin, M., & Perkins, C. (1997). English, Spanish, and code switching use in the ESL classroom: An ethnographic study. *Journal of Children's Communication Development, 19*(2), 11–20.

Bronfenbrenner, U. (1977). Toward an experimental ecology of human development. *American Psychologist, 32,* 513–531.

Bronfenbrenner, U. (1979). *The ecology of human development.* Cambridge, MA: Harvard University Press.

Bunce, B. H. (1995). *Building a language-focused curriculum for the preschool classroom: Vol. II. A planning guide.* Baltimore: Paul H. Brookes.

Burciaga, J. A. (1997). *In few words/En pocas palabras: A compendium of Latino folk, wit, and wisdom.* San Francisco: Mercury House.

Chahin, J., Villarruel, F. A., & Viramontez, R. A. (1999). *Dichos y refranes: The transmission of cultural values and beliefs.* In H. P. McAdoo (Ed.), *Family ethnicity: Strength in diversity* (2nd ed., pp. 153–170). Thousand Oakes, CA: Sage.

Chan, S. (1998). Families with Asian roots. In E. W. Lynch & M. J. Hanson (Eds.), *Developing cross-cultural competence: A guide for working with children and their families* (2nd ed., pp. 251–354). Baltimore: Paul H. Brookes.

Christenson, S. L., & Sheridan, S. M. (2001). *Schools and families: Essential support linkages for student performance.* New York: Guilford.

Curtis, M. J., & Stoller, S.A. (2002). Best practices in system-level change. In A. Thomas & J. Grimes (Eds.), *Best practices in school psychology IV* (pp. 223–234). Washington, DC: National Association of School Psychologists.

Curtis, M. J., & Van Wagener, E. (1988, April). *An analysis of failed consultation.* Paper presented at the annual meeting of the National Association of School Psychologists, Chicago.

Delgado-Gaitan, C. (1994). Socializing young children in Mexican-American families: An intergenerational perspective. In P. M. Greenfield & R. R. Cocking (Eds.), *Cross-cultural roots of minority child development* (pp. 55–86). Hillsdale, NJ: Lawrence Erlbaum Associates.

Elizalde-Utnick, G. (1998). Parents as partners: Working with culturally and linguistically diverse families. *The School Psychologist, 52,* 50–51, 63.

Elizalde-Utnick, G. (2001a, April). *Building partnerships with culturally and linguistically diverse families.* Paper presented at the meeting of the National Association of School Psychologists 2001 annual convention, Washington, DC.

Elizalde-Utnick, G. (2001b, April). *Reducing bias in the assessment of bilingual preschoolers.* Paper presented at the meeting of the National Association of School Psychologists, Washington, DC.

Elizalde-Utnick, G. (2002). Best practices in building partnerships with families. In A. Thomas & J. Grimes (Eds.), *Best practices in school psychology IV* (pp. 413–429). Washington, DC: National Association of School Psychologists.

Elizalde-Utnick, G. (2003, April). *Selective mutism and English language learners.* Paper presented at the meeting of the Long Island ESOL conference, Rockville Centre, New York.

Elizalde-Utnick, G., Lopez, E., & Nahari, S. (2003). *Language proficiency assessment: Assessing limited English proficient, learners of English as a second language, and bilingual students.* NYS Education Department (VESID).

Fantini, A. (1978). Bilingual behavior and social cues: Case studies of two bilingual children. In M. Paradis (Ed.), *Aspects of bilingualism* (pp. 283–301). Columbus, SC: Hornbeam Press.

Flanagan, D. P., & Miranda, A. H. (1995). Best practices in working with culturally different families. In A. Thomas & J. Grimes (Eds.), *Best practices in school psychology III* (pp. 1049–1060). Washington, DC: National Association of School Psychologists.

Fong, R. (2004). Overview of immigrant and refugee children and families. In R. Fong (Ed.), *Culturally competent practice with immigrant and refugee children and families* (pp. 1–18). New York: Guilford.

Gaskins, S. (1996). How Mayan parental theories come into play. In S. Harkness & C. M. Super (Eds.), *Parents' cultural belief systems: Their origins, expressions, and consequences* (pp. 345–363). New York: Guilford.

Gopaul-McNicol, S., & Thomas-Presswood, T. (1998). *Working with linguistically and culturally different children: Innovative clinical and educational approaches.* Boston: Allyn & Bacon.

Greenfield, P. (1994). Independence and interdependence as developmental scripts: Implications for theory, research, and practice. In P. M. Greenfield & R. R. Cocking (Eds.), *Cross-cultural roots of minority child development* (pp. 1–40). Hillsdale, NJ: Erlbaum.

Greenfield, P. M., & Cocking, R. R. (Eds.). (1994). *Cross-cultural roots of minority child development.* Hillsdale, NJ: Erlbaum.

Grosjean, F. (1982). *Life with two languages: An introduction to bilingualism.* Cambridge, MA: Harvard University Press.

Grossman, H. (1995). *Special education in a diverse society.* Boston: Allyn & Bacon.

Hall, E. T. (1976). *Beyond culture.* New York: Anchor.

Hanson, M. J., Lynch, E. W., & Wayman, K. I. (1990). Honoring the cultural diversity of families when gathering data. *Topics in Early Childhood Special Education, 10,* 112–131.

Harkness, S., & Super, C. M. (Eds.). (1996). *Parents' cultural belief systems: Their origins, expressions, and consequences.* New York: Guilford.

Harry, B. (1992). *Cultural diversity, families, and the special education system: Communication and empowerment.* New York: Teachers College Press.

Harry, B., Kalyanpur, M., & Day, M. (1999). *Building cultural reciprocity with families: Case studies in special education.* Baltimore: Paul H. Brookes.

Hirschler, J. (1994, Winter). Preschool children's help to second language learners. *Journal of Educational Issues of Language Minority Students, 14,* 227–240.

Ho, D. Y. F. (1994). Cognitive socialization in Confucian heritage cultures. In P. M. Greenfield & R. R. Cocking (Eds.), *Cross-cultural roots of minority child development* (pp. 285–314). Hillsdale, NJ: Erlbaum.

Joe, J. R., & Malach, R. S. (1998). Families with Native-American roots. In E. W. Lynch & M. J. Hanson (Eds.), *Developing cross-cultural competence: A guide for working with children and their families* (2nd ed., pp. 127–164). Baltimore: Paul H. Brookes.

Kagan, S., & McGroarty, M. (1993). Principles of cooperative learning for language and content gains. In D. D. Holt (Ed.), *Cooperative learning: A response to linguistic and cultural diversity* (pp. 47–66). McHenry, IL: Delta Systems.

Kalyanpur, M., & Harry, B. (1999). *Culture in special education: Building reciprocal family–professional relationships.* Baltimore: Paul H. Brookes.

Kim, U., & Choi, S. (1994). Individualism, collectivism, and child development: A Korean perspective. In P. M. Greenfield & R. R. Cocking (Eds.), *Cross-cultural roots of minority child development* (pp. 227–258). Hillsdale, NJ: Erlbaum.

Knoff, H. M. (2002). Best practices in personality assessment. In A. Thomas & J. Grimes (Eds.), *Best practices in school psychology IV* (Vol. 2, pp. 1281–1302). Washington, DC: National Association of School Psychologists.

Knoff, H. M., Stoller, S. A., Johnson, J. J., & Chenneville, T. A. (1999). Assessment of social-emotional functioning and adaptive behavior. In E. Vazquez-Nuttall, I. Romero, & J. Kalesnik (Eds.), *Assessing and screening preschoolers: Psychological and educational dimensions* (2nd ed., pp. 126–160). Boston: Allyn & Bacon.

Lebra, T. S. (1994). Mother and child in Japanese socialization: A Japan–U.S. comparison. In P. M. Greenfield & R. R. Cocking (Eds.), *Cross-cultural roots of minority child development* (pp. 259–274). Hillsdale, NJ: Erlbaum.

Lenski, D., Daniel, M., Ehlers-Zavala, F., & Alvayero, M. (2004). Assessing struggling English language learners. *Illinois Reading Council Journal, 32,* 21–30.

Lidz, C. S. (1991). *Practitioner's guide to dynamic assessment.* New York: Guilford.

Lidz, C. S. (2001). Multicultural issues and dynamic assessment. In L. A. Suzuki, J. G. Ponterotto, & P. J. Meller (Eds.), *Handbook of multicultural assessment: Clinical, psychological, and educational applications* (2nd ed., pp. 523–540). San Francisco: Jossey-Bass.

Linder, T. W., Holm, C. B., & Walsh, K. A. (1999). Transdisciplinary play-based assessment. In E. Vazquez-Nuttall, I. Romero, & J. Kalesnik (Eds.), *Assessing and screening preschoolers: Psychological and educational dimensions* (2nd ed., pp. 161–185). Boston: Allyn & Bacon.

Lopez, E. C. (1995). Best practices in working with bilingual children. In A. Thomas & J. Grimes (Eds.), *Best practices in school psychology III* (pp. 1111–1121). Washington, DC: National Association of School Psychologists.

Lopez, E. C. (1997). The cognitive assessment of limited English proficient and bilingual children. In D. P. Flanagan, J. L. Genshaft, & P. L. Harrison (Eds.), *Contemporary intellectual assessment: Theories, tests, and issues* (pp. 503–516). New York: Guilford.

Lynch, E. W. (1998). Developing cross-cultural competence. In E. W. Lynch & M. J. Hanson (Eds.), *Developing cross-cultural competence: A guide for working with children and their families* (2nd ed., pp. 47–89). Baltimore: Paul H. Brookes.

Lynch, E. W., & Hanson, M. J. (Eds.) (1998). *Developing cross-cultural competence: A guide for working with children and their families* (2nd ed.). Baltimore: Paul H. Brookes.

Martinez, E. A. (1999). Mexican American/Chicano families: Parenting as diverse as the families themselves. In H. P. McAdoo (Ed.), *Family ethnicity: Strength in diversity* (2nd ed., pp. 121–134). Thousand Oakes, CA: Sage.

McAdoo, H.P. (1999). Families of color: Strengths that come from diversity. In H. P. McAdoo (Ed.) *Family ethnicity: Strength in diversity* (2nd ed., pp. 3–14). Thousand Oaks, CA: Sage.

McLaughlin, B. (1978). *Second language acquisition in childhood.* Hillsdale, NJ: Erlbaum.

McLaughlin, B. (1995). *Fostering second language learning in young children.* (Educational Practice Report No. 14). Washington, DC: National Center for Research on Cultural Diversity and Second Language Learning.

McLoyd, V. C. (1998). Socioeconomic disadvantage and child development. *American Psychologist, 52,* 447–458.

Medansky, D., & Edelbrock, C. (1990). Cosleeping in a community sample of 2- and 3-year olds. *Pediatrics, 86,* 197–203.

Miranda, A. H. (2002). Best practices in increasing cross-cultural competence. In A. Thomas & J. Grimes (Eds.), *Best practices in school psychology IV* (Vol. 2, pp. 353–362). Washington, DC: National Association of School Psychologists.

Mishler, E. G. (1986). *Research interviewing: Context or narrative.* Cambridge, MA: Harvard University Press.

Morrow, L.M. (2001). *Literacy development in the early years: Helping children read and write* (4th ed.). Boston: Allyn & Bacon.

New, R. S., & Richman, A. L. (1996). Maternal beliefs and infant care practices in Italy and the United States. In S. Harkness & C. M. Super (Eds.), *Parents' cultural belief systems: Their origins, expressions, and consequences* (pp. 385–406). New York: Guilford.

New York State Education Department. (n.d.). *Report on the implementation of Chapter 405 of the Laws of 1999.* Retrieved March 7, 2002, from http://www.web.nysed.gov/vesid/sped/policy/chapter405.htm

Nuttall, E. V., Nuttall-Vazquez, K., & Hampel, A. (1999). Introduction. In E. Vazquez-Nuttall, I. Romero, & J. Kalesnik (Eds.), *Assessing and screening preschoolers: Psychological and educational dimensions* (2nd ed., pp. 1–8). Boston: Allyn & Bacon.

Nsamenang, A. B., & Lamb, M. E. (1994). Socialization of Nso children in the Bamenda Grassfields of Northwest Cameroon. In P. M. Greenfield & R. R. Cocking (Eds.), *Cross-cultural roots of minority child development* (pp. 133–146). Hillsdale, NJ: Erlbaum.

Ortiz, A. A. (1997) Learning disabilities occurring concomitantly with linguistic differences. *Journal of Learning Disabilities, 30,* 321–332.

Ovando, C. J., Collier, V. P., & Combs, M. C. (2003). *Bilingual and ESL classrooms: Teaching in multicultural contexts* (3rd ed.). Boston: McGraw-Hill.

Padilla, A. M. (2001). Issues in culturally appropriate assessment. In L. A. Suzuki, J. G. Ponterotto, & P. J. Meller (Eds.), *Handbook of multicultural assessment: Clinical, psychological, and educational applications* (2nd ed., pp. 5–28). San Francisco: Jossey-Bass.

Palacios, J., & Moreno, M. C. (1996). Parents' and adolescents' ideas on children: Origins and transmission of intracultural diversity. In S. Harkness & C. M. Super (Eds.), *Parents' cultural belief systems: Their origins, expressions, and consequences* (pp. 215–253). New York: Guilford.

Paniagua, F. A. (1998). *Assessing and treating culturally diverse clients: A practical guide* (2nd ed.). Thousand Oakes, CA: Sage.

Paredes Scribner, A. (2002). Best assessment and intervention practices with second language learners. In A. Thomas & J. Grimes (Eds.), *Best practices in school psychology IV* (pp. 1485–1499). Washington, DC: National Association of School Psychologists.

Rabain-Jamin, J. (1994). Language and socialization of the child in African families living in France. In P. M. Greenfield & R. R. Cocking (Eds.), *Cross-cultural roots of minority child development* (pp. 147–166). Hillsdale, NJ: Erlbaum.

Romero, I. (1999). Individual assessment procedures with preschool children. In E. Vazquez-Nuttall, I. Romero, & J. Kalesnik (Eds.), *Assessing and screening preschoolers: Psychological and educational dimensions* (2nd ed., pp.59–71). Boston: Allyn & Bacon.

Sanchez, Y. M. (1997). Families of Mexican origin. In M. K. DeGenova (Ed.), *Families in cultural context* (pp. 61–81). San Francisco: Mayfield.

Sharifzadeh, V. (1998). Families with Middle Eastern roots. In E. W. Lynch & M. J. Hanson (Eds.), *Developing cross-cultural competence: A guide for working with children and their families* (2nd ed., pp. 441–482). Baltimore: Paul H. Brookes.

Sherif, B. (1999). Islamic family ideals and their relevance to American families. In H. P. McAdoo (Ed.), *Family ethnicity: Strength in diversity* (2nd ed., pp. 203–212). Thousand Oakes, CA: Sage.

Sigel, I. E., & Kim, M. (1996). The answer depends on the question: A conceptual and methodological analysis of a parent belief-behavior interview regarding children's learning. In S. Harkness & C. M. Super (Eds.), *Parents' cultural belief systems: Their origins, expressions, and consequences* (pp. 83–122). New York: Guilford.

Swain, M. (1972). *Bilingualism as a first language.* Unpublished doctoral dissertation, University of California at Irvine.

Tabors, P. O. (1997). *One child, two languages: A guide for preschool educators of children learning English as a second language.* Baltimore: Paul H. Brookes.

Tharp, R. G. (1994). Intergroup differences among Native Americans in socialization and child cognition: An ethnogenetic analysis. In P. M. Greenfield & R. R. Cocking (Eds.), *Cross-cultural roots of minority child development* (pp. 87–106). Hillsdale, NJ: Erlbaum.

Triandis, H. C. (1995). *Individualism and collectivism.* Boulder, CO: Westview.

U.S. Department of Education (1998). Partnership for family involvement in education. In *Community Update.* Washington, DC: Office of Intergovernmental and Interagency Affairs.

Wolf, A. W., Lozoff, B., Latz, S., & Paludetto, R. (1996). Parental theories in the management of young children's sleep in Japan, Italy, and the United States. In S. Harkness & C. M. Super (Eds.), *Parents' cultural belief systems: Their origins, expressions, and consequences* (pp. 364–384). New York: Guilford.

Zeitlin, M. (1996). My child is my crown: Yoruba parental theories and practices in early childhood. In S. Harkness & C. M. Super (Eds.), *Parents' cultural belief systems: Their origins, expressions, and consequences* (pp. 407–427). New York: Guilford.

Zuniga, M. E. (1998). Families with Latino roots. In E. W. Lynch & M. J. Hanson (Eds.), *Developing cross-cultural competence: A guide for working with children and their families* (2nd ed., pp. 441–482). Baltimore: Paul H. Brookes.

24

CULTURALLY AND LINGUISTICALLY DIVERSE CHILDREN AND YOUTH WITH LOW INCIDENCE DISABILITIES

Craig A. Michaels and Sara G. Nahari

Queens College, City University of New York

The number of students from culturally and linguistically diverse (CLD) backgrounds attending schools in the United States is increasing rapidly, with census data indicating that, in 2000, approximately 39% of public school students were considered to be part of a minority group (National Center of Education Statistics, 2004). In fact, in almost every major city what was once the minority is now the majority, with conservative estimates suggesting that approximately 10 million students come from homes where a language other than English is spoken (Yates & Ortiz, 2004).

With these changing demographics, many of the original inequities in meeting the needs of CLD students become more pronounced (Salend, Whittaker, Duhaney, & Smith, 2003; Smith-Davis, 2000). In other words, the high levels of retention and school dropout, the disproportionate representation in special education, and the overall lack of academic success have also intensified with national performance data on CLD students indicating "that they are achieving below their potential and at a level that is not commensurate with their white peers" (Salend et al., 2003, p. 315). Diversity data reported to Congress on the implementation of the Individuals With Disabilities Education Act, documents a 53% increase for Hispanic Americans, a 13.2% increase for African Americans, and a 107.8% increase for Asian Americans among students receiving special education services and supports in public schools across the United States over the last 10 years (U.S. Department of Education, 1998). Among children receiving preschool services under IDEA from 1999 to 2000, the proportion of Hispanic preschoolers served grew by 1.7%, while the proportion of white preschoolers served declined by 1.6%. African American students with disabilities exceeded their representation among the resident population with the most noticeable disparities in those classified as children with mental retardation and developmental delays. This report to Congress proposed that CLD preschool children may be adversely disadvantaged in the assessment and evaluation process (U.S. Department of Education, 2001).

An increase in CLD students represents a major challenge to special education as "referral to special education of culturally and linguistically diverse students experiencing achievement difficulties is a frequent response of the general education system to achievement difficulties of such students" (Yates & Ortiz, 2004, p. 40). Special education professionals, however, are typically not any better prepared than their general education colleagues to address the learning and support needs of CLD students (Yates & Ortiz, 2004). Illustrative of this fact, "until the Supreme Court abolished capital punishment of people with a label of mental retardation, 30 of the 44 individuals labeled with mental retardation executed between 1976 and 2000 were men and women of color" (Edwards, 2004, p. 4).

This chapter focuses on those issues and inequities associated with CLD students with low incidence disabilities and offers specific recommendations for school psychologists when working with CLD families and students with low incidence disabilities. It advocates that school psychologists and other school professionals can and must play a central role in promoting the inclusion and support of CLD students with low incidence disabilities within schools and community, and building a more tolerant and pluralistic society. The "convergence of race, language, culture, socioeconomic status, and disability" (Sorrells, Webb-Johnson, & Townsend, 2004, pp. 75–76) necessitates a renewed focus on inclusion and culturally responsive pedagogy, especially within the urban context. "The discrimination and bias that exists in the larger society is also found in the human services system (e.g., special education and adult services for people with disabilities)" (Edwards, 2004, p. 3) and, as Brown and Michaels (2003) point out, "within urban public education, race and ethnic diversity, when combined with disability, may have multiple (or perhaps exponential) exclusionary effects" (p. 235).

THEORETICAL AND RESEARCH BASIS

Low Incidence Disabilities Defined

The term *low incidence disabilities* refers to those disabilities described by the Individuals With Disabilities Education Act (IDEA, 1997) as "severe disabilities" and "multiple disabilities." They are frequently referred to as low incidence disabilities based on their low prevalence rates within the general population. In 2001, for example, the U.S. Department of Education reported that the number of students with multiple disabilities served through special education programs represents less than .2% of the total special education population (translating roughly into about 112,993 students between ages 6 and 21).

The IDEA definition of *multiple disabilities* states that:

> Multiple disabilities means concomitant impairments (such as mental retardation-blindness, mental retardation-orthopedic impairment, etc.), the combination of which causes such severe educational problems that they cannot be accommodated in special education programs solely for one of the impairments. The term does not include deaf-blindness. (34 C.F.R., sec. 300 [b] [6])

Students with severe disabilities are not tracked separately by the U.S. Department of Education, so IDEA implementation data on the prevalence of students within this group is not available. In some instances (e.g., intelligence), "*severe*" simply represents a statistical variation on a given trait based on the normal curve distribution that is equal to or greater than a z score of -4 (i.e., four standard deviation units below the population mean).

The IDEA definition of *severe disabilities* states that:

> The term "children with severe disabilities" refers to children with disabilities who, because of the intensity of their physical, mental, or emotional problems, need highly specialized education, social, psychological, and medical services in order to maximize their potential for useful and meaningful participation in society and for self-fulfillment. The term includes those children … who have two or more serious disabilities such as deaf-blindness, mental retardation and blindness, and cerebral palsy and deafness. (34 C.F.R., sec. 315.4 [d])

Characteristics of Students With Multiple and Severe Disabilities

R. Turnbull, A. Turnbull, Shank, and Smith (2004) suggest that two overarching characteristics are common to both students with multiple disabilities and students with severe disabilities: "The extent of support required by students across all adaptive skill areas is usually extensive or pervasive, and two or more disabilities typically occur simultaneously" (p. 256). *Support* refers to the services, resources, and assistance required to function, learn, and live, and *adaptive skills* refers to the self-care, daily living, and age-appropriate practical and social competencies required for functioning in the community. Acknowledging that among individuals with multiple and severe disabilities, the heterogeneity is probably equal to or greater than the heterogeneity within the general population, five common characteristics or functional domains used in conceptualizing students with multiple and severe disabilities are intellectual functioning, adaptive skills, motor development, sensory impairments, and communication (R. Turnbull et al., 2004):

1. *Intellectual functioning*—most students with multiple and severe disabilities have significant impairment in intellectual functioning.
2. *Adaptive skills*—students with multiple and severe disabilities typically have significant adaptive skill deficits.

3. *Motor development*—students with multiple and severe disabilities often have delays in fine and gross motor development related to areas like motor planning, muscle tone, and motor movements.
4. *Sensory impairments*—many students with multiple and severe disabilities (approximately 2 out of 5) have vision and hearing impairments as well.
5. *Communication*—challenges within the area of communication are common to all students with multiple and severe disabilities. Obviously, communication challenges are compounded for CLD students with multiple and severe disabilities.

Cultural and Linguistic Diversity and Students With Low Incidence Disabilities

Park and Lian (2001) issued a challenge to both the field of multicultural education and the field of severe disabilities to infuse culture into education for students with the most severe disabilities. This partnership would seem to make sense as "the education of students with severe disabilities draws upon, reflects, and echoes the same concerns as in multicultural education—equity, justice, and quality of life and full participation in a pluralistic and democratic society" (p. 135). Unfortunately, the focus on cultural and linguistic diversity and students with multiple and severe disabilities seems conspicuously absent within the professional literature (Park & Lian, 2001; Pugach, 2001; Sorrells et al., 2004). According to Pugach (2001), school professionals and the research community continue to "lose a significant opportunity for taking full account of how special education research and practice is positioned with respect to issues of race, culture, and language. As a result, [we may unwittingly] delimit the stories of diversity that are told by special education scholars, opting instead for stories of disability alone" (p. 448).

Disproportionate Representation of CLD Students in Special Education

Whereas the overrepresentation of CLD students in special education is well documented, the majority of this research has focused on students with mild disabilities with little clear evidence of known biological etiology (i.e., those classified as students with learning disabilities, emotional disturbance, or mild mental retardation). Much research on overrepresentation cites distorted or inaccurate judgments of school professionals "about the capabilities of such students [that] may be biased by cultural, linguistic, or social class assumptions. For students with moderate to severe disabilities, on the other hand, these matters have received little attention" (Harry et al., 1995, p. 100). Perhaps when school professionals begin focusing on the extensive support needs of students with multiple and severe disabilities they may mistakenly assume that culture does not really matter all that much. Lack of research in the overrepresentation of CLD students with low incidence disabilities may also be due in part to the assumption that assessment of developmental deficits is based on objective criteria and therefore less likely to be influenced by bias (Harry et al., 1995).

The overrepresentation of minorities in special education during the 1970s and 1980s, especially in classes for students with mental retardation, and the lack of appropriate services encouraged a series of court cases such as *Lau v. Nichols* (1974) and *Jose P. v. Ambach* (1983). The results of these cases raised concerns about the validity of using a variety of psychological assessment tools with CLD students. IDEA's current nondiscriminatory evaluation procedural safeguards for CLD students and families ensure that:

1. No single procedure or test may be used as the sole basis of evaluation.
2. There should be a documented measure of the extent to which a child who has limited English proficiency has a disability and needs special education rather than just English-language skills.
3. Assessment procedures that are selected and instruments that are administered should not be discriminatory on a racial or cultural basis.
4. Assessments should be administered in a student's native language or other mode of communication.
5. Parental notice, consent, and full participation is an essential component of the assessment process and interpreter services needs to be provided if necessary. (Turnbull et al., 2004)

Historically, culturally and linguistically diverse students with low incidence disabilities were not included either on research conducted on the area of overrepresentation, or on aspects of non-biased assessment and provision of appropriate supports. In 2003, the National Center on Low Incidence Disabilities (NCLID, 2004) began to collect statewide assessment data on the performance of students with low incidence disabilities. Their findings indicate that (a) few states disaggregate their results by type of disability; (b) sometimes no students were tested in a category, or no results were reported, and sometimes the numbers of students taking the test were not reported; (c) data does not exist for all disability groups for all grade levels or for all subjects; and (d) no information is available on CLD students.

School psychologists and other school professionals should be concerned about the disproportionate representation of CLD students in special education for three primary reasons (Burnette, 1998). Some CLD students may be underserved or receiving services that do not meet their needs. Others may be misclassified or inappropriately classified. More insidious is the possibility that placement of CLD students into special education may represent an overt form of discrimination.

The Individuals With Disabilities Act

The part B regulations of the Individuals With Disabilities Education Act (IDEA, 1997) establish and clarify the legal requirements concerning services to CLD students, which IDEA refers to as limited English proficient (LEP) students:

1. A LEP child with a disability may require special education and related services for those aspects of the educational program that address the develop-

ment of English-language skills and other aspects of the child's educational program.

2. For a LEP child with a disability, the Individualized Educational Plan (IEP) must address whether the special education and related services that the child needs will be provided in a language other than English.

IDEA stipulates that family concerns need to be considered in the development and review of the IEP [IDEA Regulations, 1997, 300.343(c)(iii), 300.346(a)(1)(i), 300.346(b)]. In practice, however, many IEP goals are set in isolation by individual disciplines with little collaboration of parents. In fact, rather than encouraging collaboration, school professionals may actually engage in actions that are disempowering to parents and students and that overtly endorse their expert power (A. Turnbull & R. Turnbull, 2001). This may be particularly detrimental to CLD families leading to a "'we–they' posture" in planning and goal setting (R. Turnbull et al., 2004, p. 82), which makes shared collaboration difficult. Blue-Banning, A. P. Turnbull, and Pereira (2000), for example, conducted focus groups with Latino families and professionals and report that power and authority differences seem to be a major barrier to successful partnering, collaboration, and shared decision making.

A. Turnbull and R. Turnbull (2001) propose that the full participation within the referral, classification, and IEP development process as guaranteed by IDEA may be compromised by language and cultural barriers for many CLD families. Turnbull et al. (2004) suggest that many CLD families require both the use of skilled translators, who will work on facilitating communication through written materials, and interpreters, who will focus on oral communication in order to minimize these language and cultural barriers (R. Turnbull et al., 2004). Unfortunately, translators and interpreters are rarely part of the planning process. Smith and Ryan, for example, report that in the cases of 59 Chinese families, 58 of whom spoke Chinese as their primary language, no school professionals involved in the diagnosis of their child were able to speak to them in Chinese. As a result, the parents reported being confused and feeling alone and helpless (as cited in R. Turnbull et al., 2004)

The findings of Bermúdez and Márquez (1996) indicate that CLD families remain alienated from the school system due to a variety of circumstances. Among these are "(a) insufficient English language skills, (b) lack of understanding of the home–school partnership, (c) difficulty in understanding the school system, (d) lack of confidence, (e) work interference, (f) negative past experiences with schools, and (g) insensitivity and hostility on the part of school personnel" (p. 3). In addition, "despite specific differences among cultures, a common theme in the growing body of information on parent school interaction is a striking pattern of cross-cultural dissonance that results in inadequate understanding by parents of the educational system in the United States" (Harry, 1992, p. xvi). Table 24–1 indicates that the dominant cultural view of disability may not be embraced by all families. These different views on disability may have significant ramifications for how families cope with their sons and daughters, as well as the relationships they form with service providers and the educational system.

TABLE 24–1
Variety of Cultural Assumptions About Disability

Dominant Cultural View of Disability	*Alternative Cultural View of Disability*
• Disability is a physical phenomenon.	• Disability is a spiritual phenomenon.
• Disability is an individual phenomenon.	• Disability is a group phenomenon.
• Disability is a chronic illness.	• Disability is a time-limited phenomenon.
• Disability requires remediation or fixing.	• Disability must be accepted.

Note. Adapted from *Cultural Reciprocity Aids Collaboration With Families* (ERIC/OSEP Digest No. E614), by C. Wargner, 2001. Arlington, VA: ERIC Clearinghouse on Disabilities and Gifted Education.

Bilingual Special Education

Currently, in the United States, the methods used in bilingual special education are focused on the second language of the student. It is the common belief among educators that students will need to survive in environments where English is the dominant language. In fact, the question of whether students with low incidence disabilities should be taught in bilingual settings tends to be neglected or overlooked altogether (Gerstein & Woodward, 1994). Baca and Cervantes (1998) suggest that instruction in the native language is very often not recommended by school teams because of the lack of personnel available in the districts to provide this type of service, even when mandated. Baca and Cervantes (1998) proposed a common boundary between special education and bilingual education whereby the needs of bilingual students who where eligible for special education services could receive an appropriate education. Similar to bilingual education programs, bilingual special education programs feature a wide range of interventions using two languages, one of the languages being English. The model most frequently implemented in the United States is the transitional model, which relies on both a student's native language and English for instruction until competence in English is achieved. When English competence is achieved, students are placed in monolingual programs (Winzer & Mazurk, 1998).

Mandates and regulations notwithstanding, there is still considerable discussion concerning the provision of bilingual special education programs. These questions are an extension of the ongoing inquiry in the field of bilingual education where there is still no agreement as to which programs provide the best type of services, bearing in mind the heterogeneity of the population, the exit and entry criteria, and the equal protection of the law. Furthermore, the transition of a special bilingual student to a monolingual program is seen as a way to help to improve their problem, based on a general belief among the educators that the additional pressures of bilingualism are just an added burden for students in special education (Arreaga-Mayer, 1993; Baca & de Valenzuela, 1998; Baker, 2001). Of particular concern is the scant body of research on bilingual education for students with more significant disabilities. This lack of research compels educators to make decisions for instruction and language intervention for CLD students with low incidence disabilities based solely on findings from general bilingual education.

IMPLICATIONS FOR PRACTICE

Focusing on Support Needs Rather Than Limitations

Again acknowledging the heterogeneity among CLD students with low incidence disabilities, a more useful and functional approach when considering, defining, and conceptualizing shared characteristics associated with these students may be to focus on the levels and intensity of support needs across various activities and environments (American Association on Mental Retardation, 2002; Kennedy & Horn, 2004; Luckasson & Reeves, 2001; R. Turnbull et al., 2004). Rather than focusing on the inherent limitations of CLD students with multiple and severe disabilities, shifting the focus to support needs allows school professionals to work more collaboratively with families in identifying the levels and types of support or assistance students require to achieve mutually defined goals.

Focusing on supports is perceived to be more productive and aligned with the values of inclusion (Luckasson & Reeves, 2001). Focusing on support is also useful in conceptualizing and defining the unique needs of those students with multiple and severe disabilities who also are from culturally and linguistically diverse families, because this approach naturally brings in the context of family, the community, and cultural values as support components (Harry et al., 1995; Pugach, 2001; A. Turnbull & R. Turnbull, 2001). "Current terminology focuses on how much assistance a person requires from others to lead as normal a life as possible … people typically talk about a student's support needs, rather than the extent of their disability" (Kennedy & Horn, 2004, pp. 7–8). From the support perspective, CLD students with multiple and severe disabilities are considered capable of being included and achieving many of the same things as there peers. They will, however, require the systematic support of others to do so.

In 2002, the American Association on Mental Retardation (AAMR) defined supports as services, resources, and assistance to improve the ways that an individual functions, learns, and lives. The AAMR described four levels of support—intermittent, limited, extensive, and pervasive. *Intermittent supports* are episodic in nature and tend to be provided as needed. *Limited supports* tend to be more intense and provided in a more consistent way, but on a time-limited basis. *Extensive supports* are characterized by a level of regularly (i.e., long term) and consistency within at least certain environments. *Pervasive supports* are characterized by their consistency, intensity (often involving multiple disciplines), and their provision across multiple environments. Table 24–2 highlights this approach, addressing implications for supporting the inclusion of students with severe and multiple disabilities in the areas of communication, adaptive behavior, problem behavior, systematic instruction, family-centered practices, social relationships, sensory and motor needs, and collaboration.

TABLE 24–2
What Professionals Should Consider When Developing Support Plans for Students With Low Incidence Disabilities

Support Domain and Associated Issues	*Support Challenges*
Communication	
• Communication may be inconsistent and in a variety of forms • Students may use a variety of spoken word, gesture, sign, facial expression, augmentative or alternative communication device, and behavior	• Learning to understand what is being communicated and helping student communicate that to others
Adaptive Behavior	
• Adaptive behavior may need to be addressed to promote independence in functional and age-appropriate ways • Students may need to develop skills related to reading sight words, eating lunch in the cafeteria, or getting around the school building	• Increasing adaptive behavior within the context of the general curriculum and the general education classroom
Problem Behavior	
• Problem behaviors may manifest in part due to communication and adaptive behavior difficulties • Students may engage in behaviors that are self-injurious (e.g., hand biting), aggressive (e.g., hitting others), or related to destroying property (e.g., breaking windows)	• Identifying the function of problem behaviors and developing interventions to reduce these responses while increasing access to the general education curriculum and classroom
Systematic Instruction	
• Systematic instruction takes into account that students will take longer to learn skills than peers and need specific instruction to transfer and generalize • Systematic instruction often uses task analysis to breaks down the learning process into its elemental parts and behavioral strategies to teach skills systematically and monitor progress on instructional goals and objectives	• Designing instructional strategies that are systematic and powerful enough to facilitate skill acquisition and mastery of age-appropriate routines

Note. Adapted from *Including Students With Severe Disabilities*, by C. H. Kennedy and E. M. Horn, 2004, Boston: Allyn & Bacon.

Language and Assessment

All states, local education agencies, and schools in the United States must have and implement legally acceptable means of identifying limited English proficient (LEP) students. Various federal laws upheld by the Office of Civil Rights enforce this obligation. In addition, Section 7501 of the Bilingual Education Act, reauthorized in 1994 under ESEA, identifies the LEP student as a student who was not born in the United States or whose native language is a language other than English and comes from an environment where a language other than English is dominant; or is a Native American or Alaska Native or who is a native resident of the outlying areas and comes from an environment where a language other than English has had a significant impact on such an individual's level of English language proficiency; or is migratory and whose native language is other than English and comes from an environment where a language other than English is dominant.

Although the determination of language dominance and language proficiency may be legally required, professionals frequently fail to consider two critical factors: There are different domains of language usage, and these constructs vary according to the conversational context. In other words, a student may be dominant in English in terms of academic skills and native language dominant when usage of language revolves around home and community (Baca & Cervantes, 1998). Additionally, when considering CLD students with low incidence disabilities, it becomes increasing more important to focus on the evaluation of receptive language in their native language. These students may also appear to be nonverbal, having virtually no expressive verbal language. Typically, these same students, based on the severity of their support needs, have full-time caregivers from their extended family who speak to them in their native language (e.g., a grandmother) and have greater receptive language skills within this native language than many school professionals anticipate.

Alternative and Ecological Assessments

The 1997 amendments to IDEA and the No Child Left Behind Act (2002) were intended to better align special education programs and policies with the larger national school improvement effort focusing on higher content standards, use of assessment to measure how schools and students are meeting the standards, and an emphasis on holding educators and students accountable. Thus, national and state standards have increasingly emphasized high-stakes testing and greater accountability for all students (Walpole, Justice, & Invernizzi, 2004). To meet these requirements, states are creating alternate performance indicators for students with severe disabilities that require alternate and often individualized assessment formats as determined by each student's individualized education program (VESID, 2004). Alternative assessment is an ongoing process of evaluation that typically involves students and the assessor in the attainment of information to determine a student's academic progress using nonconventional strategies and requires teachers to consider the ecological domains in which students are functioning (Snell & Brown, 2000).

Other approaches to assessment that are appropriate for use with CLD students with low incidence disabilities include the use of nonstandardized and standardized methods, dynamic assessment, nonverbal measures of ability, multiple informants, and multiple methods (Goupal-McNicol & Thomas-Presswood, 1998). Best practices in assessing CLD students include testing in both the native and second language and making sure that students meet the criteria for disability classification both in their first language and in English (Overton, Fielding, & Simonsson, 2004; Rogers et al., 1999). For students with low levels of communication, an ecological assessment of communication needs in the natural environment can be particularly important. Such an assessment will assist school professionals when making decisions regarding language, and will allow professionals to incorporate information related to what family members believe is important for their sons and daughters to learn in their native tongue (Harry et al., 1995; Westling & Fox, 1995).

The validity and reliability of many of the more traditional psychological assessment instruments for CLD students with low incidence disabilities is questionable. These instruments include content that may not be applicable or appropriate and language bias. Furthermore, most norms are not representative of the CLD population. This suggests that school psychologists will need to be creative and make use of a number of alternative techniques and strategies to gather meaningful information and make accurate clinical judgments.

Parents as co-assessors. The ability to understand and value each family's uniqueness is crucial in developing culturally relevant and sensitive intervention plans (Fox, Vaughn, Llanes, Wyatte, & Dunlap, 2002). Of equal importance is developing new systems of functional assessment that address needs across home and the school environments. For school psychologists, then, parents must be viewed as collaborative partners and co-assessors, rather than only as sources of information about developmental histories.

Alternative assessments typically include information collected over a period of time across instructional environments, which is used to document achievement, called a *data folio*. The data folio typically includes a parent survey, which systematically gathers essential information about a family's perception of student performance. School psychologists should work collaboratively with families to gather information regarding background information, socioeconomic status, family history, and cultural and sociolinguistic background as they relate to the evaluation or students' learning and behavior. The role of CLD parents in the assessment process of students with low incidence disabilities requires an understanding of the family's cultural interpretation of disability and childrearing traditions. Parent desired long-term outcomes for students, behavior states, physical/medical needs, communication needs, home language, and cultural considerations are all essential considerations for school professionals to gather information about students' strengths and support needs as part of a comprehensive assessment process for CLD students with low incidence disabilities.

Person-centered planning. Person-centered planning has emerged as one of the most promising planning and assessment practices for creating and sustaining full citizenship for students with multiple and severe disabilities. Person-centered planning holds tremendous promise when conducting with CLD students with

TABLE 24–3
**What Professionals Should Consider When Developing Culturally Inclusive
Services for Students With Low Incidence Disabilities**

Building Relationships With Families

• *Do not make assumptions about home language.* Often the family members attending school meetings are the most fluent English speakers. Frequently, however, extended family members are the primary caregivers of students.

• *Ground goals in culturally appropriate developmental norms.* Independence, traditionally one of the highest ideals for students with severe disabilities, may be interpreted very differently in other cultures.

• *Meaning or cultural interpretation of disability may promote different views of treatment.* Saving face, stoicism and self-sacrifice, an emphasis on a mind-body continuum, the view that disability is an act of God to be accepted rather than changed all are interpretations of disability that are culturally rooted.

• *Concept of family may be culturally defined and influence attitudes toward disabilities.* Cultures that embrace more extended family structures tend to define the health of an individual in relation to the family as a whole.

• *Culture can influence the perception and acceptance of alternative and augmentative communication strategies.* Whereas the dominant culture tends to highly technological, parents of CLD children may resist the use of augmentative communication systems or perceive such systems and unnatural and highly stigmatizing.

• *Cultural values may influence childrearing practices and participation in the assessment and special education planning process.* Cultures that value authoritarian and hierarchical social patterns may not believe in providing students with the decision-making power or equality assumed by IDEA and so many school professionals.

Placement and Instruction Considerations

• *Inclusion in neighborhood schools may be particularly important for CLD students with severe disabilities.* Neighborhood school placements often represent communities of like cultures and may minimize cultural and linguistic dissonance for students with severe disabilities

• *Community-based instruction can facilitate culturally congruent relationships.* Students with severe disabilities are often isolated from their communities. Community-based instruction can increase the number and variety of community places students know and promote access to the social network of community and the development of personal relationships and friendships, which in turn promotes cultural access for CLD students.

• *Just because CLD students may be non-verbal, do not overlook the importance of native language instruction.* Frequently, these students have significantly stronger receptive language skills that may go untapped when instruction is not within students' native language. Augmentative communication devices should also be bilingually programmed or in students' native language.

disabilities as person-centered planning is grounded in building and sustaining inclusive communities. Person-centered approaches to planning grew out of the concept of normalization (Wolfensberger, Nirje, Olshansky, Perske, & Roos, 1972), which focused on creating ways to serve people with more severe disabilities that were as culturally normative as possible, both in terms of process and outcomes. Person-centered approaches grew out of the search for new ways to involve people with different perspectives in creating community memberships for people with disabilities who had historically been marginalized and excluded from community participation. Person-centered planning honors diversity and multicultural approaches to community building by bringing together both formal (paid professionals) and informal (friends, relatives, and family members) supports to create community memberships for people with disabilities. In this way, culturally and linguistically appropriate strategies can be generated that result in the building of connections, valued roles, competencies, and relationships for both CLD students and their families (C. L. O'Brien, J. O'Brien, & Mount, 1997).

Cross-Cultural Competencies

"Working effectively with families from cultures that differ from one's own requires an understanding of one's beliefs and values as well as recognition that one's language, culture and ethnicity influence interaction" (Lynch, 1992, p. 37). Lynch describes cross-cultural competence as "the ability to think, feel, and act in ways that acknowledge, respect, and build upon ethnic, cultural, and linguistic diversity" (p. 50). Cross-cultural competence, cultural sensitivity, and the ability to collaborate with others, such as bilingual personnel, families, and teachers are essential requirements for staff working with CLD students (de Valenzuela & Cervantes, 1998).

In 1995, Harry et al. coined the term "cultural inclusion" to center attention and discussion on how the principles of multicultural education, cultural competence, and inclusion might share common characteristics. These authors concluded that "in the process of cultural inclusion, professionals would address cultural features as they plan for including individuals with severe disabilities in the mainstream of society and schools. … For too long, [school professionals have] expected families from culturally diverse backgrounds to do all the adapting" (p. 101). Table 24–3 focuses on two critical aspects of developing and supporting cultural competence related to CLD students with low incidence disabilities: building relationships with CLD families and placing and supporting CLD students in age-appropriate, inclusive classrooms. According to Sailor, Gee, and Karasoff (2000), inclusion efforts with CLD students with severe disabilities will be most successful when creative, culturally sensitive, and relevant strategies are used for embedding instruction within the general education curriculum, "where the natural cues and opportunities exist" (p. 20).

Instruction

Developing appropriate instructional interventions and individualized education programs (IEPs) for CLD students with multiple and severe disabilities requires that school teams work collaboratively with families to consider a variety of student factors, language/communication needs, and curriculum-related issues. Figure 24–1 graphically illustrates some of these considerations for building meaningful and culturally relevant educational experiences for CLD students with low incidences disabilities.

Although there is limited research literature that addresses the specific instructional needs of bilingual students in special education with multiple and severe

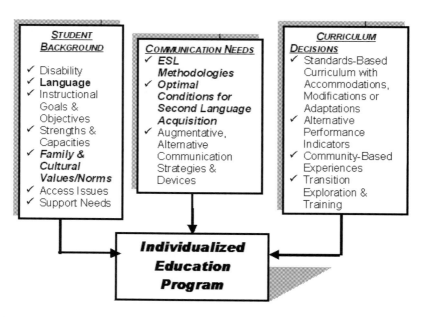

FIGURE 24–1.   Factors for school teams to consider when planning for CLD students with multiple and severe disabilities.

disabilities, the following interventions are adapted from the general theoretical perspectives of researchers in the field of bilingual instruction (Baker, 2001; Cloud 2002; Gonzalez, Brusca-Vega, & Yawkey, 1997; Krashen, 1981). Special education instructional techniques should be developed with consideration of the family's language and culture (Baca & de Valenzuela, 1998), should incorporate materials that are culturally familiar, and should be grounded in the students' strengths.

CLD students with multiple and severe disabilities may appear to have no consistent communication skills in any language and have discrepancies between expressive and receptive language. Flexible instruction in a variety of modes of communication (Krashen, 1981), including alternative and augmentative forms of communication, need to be available to CLD students with low incidence disabilities throughout the day and at home, including use of the native language, graphic symbols, gestures/manual signs. Thurlow, Albus, Shyyan, Liu, and Barrera (2004) suggest strategies for teaching CLD students with disabilities, especially those students with ESL needs. For reading, they suggest pre-, during-, and postreading strategies, and fluency building and direct teaching of vocabulary through listening, seeing, reading, and writing in short time segments. For mathematics, they suggest the use of tactile, concrete experiences of mathematics, daily re-looping of previously learned material, and problem-solving instruction and task analysis strategies. For science, they suggest the use of hands-on active participation, using visuals and pictures to demonstrate steps (Thurlow et al., 2004).

Transition and Community Integration

The transition from school to adult life of students with multiple and severe disabilities has been described as a developmental process deeply rooted in the physiological, social, and emotional life changes and adjustments associated with moving from childhood through adolescence into adulthood (Halpern, 1994; Michaels, 1997; Wehman, 2001). Major life changes or transitions during this time can include movement from residing at home with family to living independently in the community (O'Connor & Racino, 1993; Parent, Unger, Gibson, & Clements, 1994; Racino & Taylor, 1993); attending secondary school to postsecondary education, vocational training, or employment (Adelman & Vogel, 1992; DuChoissois & Michaels, 1994; Fairweather & Shaver, 1991); and being a part of one family to establishing new intimate relationships and one's own nuclear family (Hayes, Bain, & Batshaw, 1997; Racino & Taylor, 1993).

According to IDEA, transition is a coordinated set of activities for a student, which promotes movement from school to postschool activities, including postsecondary education, vocational training, integrated employment (including supported employment), continuing and adult education, adult services, independent living or community participation. Transition plans and goals should be based on the individual student's needs, taking into account the student's preferences and interests. This includes instruction, related services, community experiences, the development of employment and other postschool adult living objectives, and, when appropriate, acquisition of daily living skills and functional vocational evaluation.

Cultural perspectives on independence, employment, and adulthood must be explored and addressed as part of the planning process for the transition from school to adult life for CLD students with low incidence disabilities. Even with the best collaboration among school professionals, transition achievements are likely to be limited if families and students are not co-collaborators. When transition goals reflect what professionals think are best for students rather than what is preferred by students and families, it is likely that these goals or outcomes will not be achieved (Wehman, Moon, Everson, Wood, & Barcus, 1988). Among diverse cultures, independence and remunerated employment, so valued by Western cultures, are not always understood by CLD families (Harry et al., 1995). Another key aspect of the transition from school to adulthood that may be viewed differently many CLD families is the focus in the dominant culture on "self-determination." Self-determination refers to the ability of learners to advocate, evaluate, and make their own choices in their lives (Grigal, Neubert, Moon, & Graham, 2003). Self-determination is grounded in the accepted cultural norm or belief that it is appropriate for an individual to act as "the primary causal agent in one's life … making choices and decisions regarding one's qualify of life free from undue external influence or interference" (Wehmeyer & Lawrence, 1995, p. 74). School professionals need to be cognizant of the fact that there may also be significant gender differences associated with perceptions of independence, paid employment, and self-determination existing in CLD families, not as prevalent within the dominant culture.

Several studies on cultural views of independent living describe some of these differences. Clay (1992), for example, reports that Native American culture is centered on the family as a unit. The needs of the family unit play an important role in guiding the individual so that independent living services or transitional services must consider the family (Clay, 1992). Blue-Banning, A. P. Turnbull, and Pereira (2002) examined the perspectives of Hispanic parents of youth and young adults with disabilities regarding their hopes and expectations for their children. These researchers report that many parents did not expect that their sons or daughters would ever live outside of the family home. They also did not envision employment as an achievable outcome for their children.

Assistive Technology

A considerable body of literature within the field of special education documents the potential importance of assistive technology to the academic success and inclusion of students with disabilities in elementary and secondary school programs (e.g., Blackhurst & MacArthur, 1986; Inge & Shepherd, 1995; Smith, 2000). In fact, the appropriate application of assistive technology may be one of the greatest equalizing forces in the education and meaningful inclusion of students with disabilities both in terms of promoting access to the general curriculum and in facilitating the ability of students to demonstrate mastery of that knowledge (Bryant, Erin, Lock, Allan, & Resta, 1998; Michaels, 2000; Michaels, Prezant, Morabito, & Jackson, 2002). Assistive technology can promote fuller participation and inclusion within school, home, and community environments and improve the overall quality of life for individuals with disabilities (Bryant et al., 1998; U.S. Department of Education, 2000).

Assistive technology (AT) refers to both *AT devices* and *AT services*, as described in the 1994 Reauthorization of the Technology-Related Assistance Act for Individuals Act and the Individuals With Disabilities Education Act (IDEA). According to IDEA (1997), an AT device refers to "any item, piece of equipment, or product system, whether acquired commercially off the shelf, modified, or customized, that is used to increase, maintain, or improve the functional capacity of individuals with disabilities" (20 U.S.C. 1401[25]). IDEA 1997 describes an AT service as "any service that directly assists an individual with a disability in the selection, acquisition, or use of an assistive technology device" (20 U.S.C. 1401[25]). IDEA stresses the importance of the integration of AT into curriculum and instruction and of meeting the technology needs of every student who receives special education services (Edyburn & Gardner, 1999; IDEA, 1997; Research Connections, 1998).

Professionals working with CLD students with low incidence disabilities especially must feel confident that both the AT technology and the implementation strategies that they suggest will match students' needs and provide students with opportunities to participate in the general curriculum in meaningful ways. Although families must also be actively involved in all AT decisions, this is particularly critical for CLD families (Parette & McMahan, 2002). School professionals must develop competencies to assist CLD families in making informed decisions regarding the use and acquisition of AT in ways that acknowledge the family values and that are culturally respectful (Parette & McMahan, 2002; Parette, VanBiervliet, & Hourcade, 2000). When working with CLD families, it is equally important that school professionals understand any potential cultural or familial barriers to the implementation of AT solutions and potential resources or strategies to assist CLD families in obtaining funding for AT supports (Beyerbach, Walsh, & Vannatta, 2001; Lovingfoss, Molloy, Harris, & Graham, 2001; National Association of State Directors of Special Education, 2002).

IMPLICATIONS FOR FUTURE RESEARCH AND PRACTICE

This chapter reviewed some of the critical issues affecting CLD students with multiple and severe disabilities. Perhaps most salient is the fact that special education services for this population have typically been designed and delivered without consideration to cultural and linguistic variables. These findings support the need for more inclusive educational practices that focus on creating family and community partnerships that are culturally sensitive and address the diverse support/instructional needs of CLD students with low incidence disabilities across a variety of school, home, and community environments. Creating professionals and services that are culturally sensitive requires that preparation courses include coursework that helps future practitioners understand and value cultural diversity and work collaboratively with CLD families and communities. Additionally, school psychologists must receive training in creating inclusive school communities where all learners are valued and supported. Focusing on the support needs of CLD students with low incidence disabilities and the hopes and dreams of their families, rather than their deficits, will allow professionals to work in new and creative ways to promote inclusion. These efforts to promote schoolwide inclusion may have major implications for CLD families and students with and without disabilities. In helping to shift school culture to become more inclusive, school psychologists should engage in serious reflection on three questions:

1. Is diversity valued in the school?
2. Are we a community? [and]
3. Do we expect excellence and equity for all students? (Janney & Snell, 2004, p. 11)

ACKNOWLEDGMENTS

The authors wish to thank Gila Rivera and Pedro Ruiz for sharing their expertise in instructional interventions and Nilofer Naqvi for her research work.

ANNOTATED BIBLIOGRAPHY

Artiles, J. A., & Ortiz, A. A. (Eds.). (2002). *English language learners with special education needs: Identification, placement, and instruction* (2nd ed.). Washington DC: Center for Applied Linguistics.

> Compiles research and best practice from the practice from the past 30 years into concise guide for determining appropriate referrals to special education and reviews applicable assessment and classroom interventions for English-language learners.

Baca, L., & Cervantes, H. T. (Eds.). (2004). *The bilingual special education interface* (3rd ed.). Upper Saddle River, NJ: Prentice-Hall.

> Resources for school professionals who are interested in classroom teaching strategies, current legislation, and how bilingual education practices dovetail with the principles of instruction in special education.

Snell, M., & Brown, F. (2005). *Instruction of students with severe disabilities* (6th ed.). Upper Saddle River, NJ: Pearson Publishers.

> Explains best practices, time-proven techniques, theory, and research on a full range of topics related to educating individuals with severe disabilities.

RESOURCES

Council for Exceptional Children (CEC):
> http://www.cec.sped.org

> > Supports professionals working on behalf of individuals with disabilities, providing professional development, resources, and advocacy.

TASH:
> http://www.tash.org

> > Works to promote the full inclusion and participation of persons with severe disabilities in all aspects of life.

The National Center for Culturally Responsive Educational Systems (NCCRESt):
> http://www.NCCRESt.org

> > Provides technical assistance and professional development to close the achievement gap between students from culturally and linguistically diverse backgrounds and their peers, and reduce inappropriate referrals to special education.

REFERENCES

Adelman, P., & Vogel, S. (1992). The success of college students with learning disabilities: Factors related to educational attainment. *Journal of Learning Disabilities, 25,* 430–441.

American Association on Mental Retardation (2002). *Mental retardation: Definition, classification, and systems of support* (10th ed.). Washington, DC: Author.

Arreaga-Mayer, C. (1993) Ecobehavioral assessment of exceptional culturally and linguistically diverse students: Evaluating effective bilingual special education programs. In *Proceedings of the third national research symposium on limited English proficient student is-*

sues: Focus on middle and high school issues. Washington, DC: U.S. Department of Education Office of Bilingual Education and Minority Languages Affairs.

Baca, L. A., & Cervantes, H. T. (Eds.). (1998). *The bilingual special education interface* (3rd ed.). Upper Saddle River, NJ: Merrill.

Baca, L. M., & de Valenzuela, J. S. (1998). Development of the bilingual special education interface. In L. M. Baca & H. T. Cervantes (Eds.), *The bilingual special education interface* (3rd ed., pp. 2–22). Upper Saddle River, NJ: Merrill.

Baker, C. (2001). *Foundations of bilingual education and bilingualism* (3rd ed.). Cleveland, England: Multilingual Matters.

Bermúdez, A. B., & Márquez, J. A. (1996). An examination of a four-way collaborative to increase parent involvement in the schools. *Journal of Educational Issues of Language Minority Students, 16,* 1–16.

Beyerbach, B., Walsh, C., & Vannatta, R. (2001). From teaching technology to using technology to enhance student learning: Pre-service teachers changing perception of technology infusion. *Journal of Technology and Teacher Education, 9,* 105–127.

Blackhurst, E. A., & McArthur, C. (1986). Microcomputer use in special education personnel preparation programs. *Teacher Education and Special Education, 7*(3), 27–36.

Blue-Banning, M. J., Turnbull, A. P., & Pereira, L. (2000). Group action planning as a support strategy for Hispanic families: Parent and professional perspectives. *Mental Retardation, 38,* 262–275.

Blue-Bannning, M. J., Turnbull, A. P., & Pereira, L. (2002). Hispanic youth/young adults with disabilities: Parents' visions for the future. *Research and Practice for Persons With Severe Disabilities, 3,* 204–219.

Brown, F., & Michaels, C. A. (2003). The shaping of inclusion: Efforts in Detroit and other urban settings. In D. Fisher (Ed.), *Inclusive urban schools* (pp. 231–243). Baltimore: Paul H. Brookes.

Bryant, D. P., Erin, J., Lock, R., Allan, J. M., & Resta, P. E. (1998). Infusing a teacher preparation program in learning disabilities with assistive technology. *Journal of Learning Disabilities, 31,* 55–66. .

Burnette, J. (1998). Reducing the disproportionate representation of minority students in special education. (ERIC/OSEP Digest No. E566). Arlington, VA: ERIC Clearinghouse on Disabilities and Gifted Education.

Cloud, N. (2002). Culturally and linguistically responsive instructional planning. In A. J. Artiles & A. A. Ortiz (Eds.), *English language learners with special education needs: Identification, assessment, and instruction* (pp. 107–132). Washington, DC: ERIC Clearinghouse on Languages and Linguistics, Center for Applied Linguistics.

Clay, J. A. (1992). Native American independent living. *Rural Special Education Quarterly, 11*(1), 41–50.

de Valenzuela, J. S., & Cervantes, H. (1998). Procedures and techniques for assessing the bilingual exceptional child. In L. Baca & H. Cervantes (Eds.), *The bilingual special education interface* (3rd ed., pp. 170–186). Upper Saddle River, NJ: Merrill.

Duchossois, G., & Michaels, C. A. (1994). Postsecondary education. In C. A. Michaels (Ed.), *Transition strategies for persons with learning disabilities* (pp. 79–118). San Diego, CA: Singular Publishing Group.

Edwards, R. (2004). Ethnicity and disability. *TASH Connections, 30*(11/12), 3–4.

Edyburn, D. L., & Gardner, J. E. (1999). Integrating technology into special education teacher preparation programs: Creating shared visions. *Journal of Technology Special Education, 14*(2), 3–20.

Fairweather, J. S., & Shaver, D. M. (1991). Making the transition to postsecondary education and training. *Exceptional Children, 57,* 264–270.

Fox, L., Vaughn, B. J., Llanes, W., & Dunlop, J. (2002). "We can't expect other people to understand": Family perspectives on problem behavior. *Exceptional Children, 68,* 437–450.

Gerstein, R., & Woodward, J. (1994). The language minority student and special education: Issues, trends and paradoxes. *Exceptional Children, 60,* 310–322.

Gonzalez, V., Brusca-Vega, R., & Yawkey, T. D. (1997). *Assessment of culturally and linguistically different students with or at-risk of learning problems: From research to practice.* Needham Heights, MA: Allyn & Bacon.

Goupal-McNicol, S., & Thomas-Presswood, T. (1998). *Working with linguistically and culturally different children: Innovative, clinical and educational approaches.* Boston: Allyn & Bacon.

Grigal, M., Neubert, D. A., Moon, M. S., & Graham, S. (2003). Self-determination for students with disabilities: Views of parents and teachers. *Exceptional Children, 70,* 97–112.

Halpern, A. S. (1994). The transition of youth with disabilities to adult life: A position statement of the Division on Career Development and Transition, the Council for Exceptional Children. *Career Development for Exceptional Individuals, 17,* 115–124.

Harry, B. (1992). Making sense of disability: Low-income Puerto Rican parents' theories of the problem. *Exceptional Children, 59,* 27–40.

Harry, B., Grenot-Scheyer, M., Smith-Lewis, M., Park, H. S., Xin, F., & Schwartz, I. (1995). Developing culturally inclusive services for individuals with severe disabilities. *Journal of the Association for Persons With Severe Handicaps, 20,* 99–109.

Hayes, A., Bain, L. J., & Batshaw, M. L. (1997). Adulthood: What the future holds. In M. L. Batshaw (Ed.), *Children with disabilities* (4th ed., pp. 757–772). Baltimore: Paul H. Brookes.

Individuals With Disabilities Education Act, 20 U.S.C. § 1400 *et seq.* (1997).

Inge, K. J., & Shepherd, J. (1995). Assistive technology applications and strategies for school system personnel. In K. F. Flippo, K. J. Inge, & J. M. Bacus (Eds.), *Assistive technology: A resource for school, work, and community* (pp. 133–166). Baltimore: Paul H. Brookes.

Janney, R., & Snell, M. E. (2004). *Modifying schoolwork* (2nd ed.). Baltimore: Paul H. Brookes.

Jose, P. v. Ambach (1983). 557 F. Supp. 11230 (E.D.N.Y.).

Kennedy, C. H., & Horn, E. M. (2004). *Including students with severe disabilities.* Boston: Allyn & Bacon.

Krashen, S. (1981). *Principles and practice in second language acquisition.* Oxford, England: Pergamon.

Lau v. Nichols (1974). 414 US. 563.

Lovingfoss, D., Molloy, D. E., Harris, K. R., & Graham, S. (2001). Preparation, practice, and program reform: Crafting the University of Maryland's five-year, multicategorical undergraduate program in special education. *Journal of Special Education, 35,* 105–14.

Luckasson, R., & Reeves, A. (2001). Naming, defining, and classifying in mental retardation. *Mental Retardation, 39,* 47–52.

Lynn, E. W. (1992). From culture shock to cultural learning. In E. W. Lynch & M. J. Hanson (Eds.), *Developing cross-cultural competence: A guide for working with young children and their families* (pp. 19–33). Baltimore: Paul H Brookes.

Michaels, C. A. (1997). Preparation for employment: Counseling practices for promoting personal competency. In P. J. Gerber & D. S. Brown (Eds.), *Learning disabilities and employment* (pp. 187–214). Austin, TX: Pro-Ed.

Michaels, C. A. (2000). Technical assistance to staff, students, and families. In *Promising practices in technology: Supporting access to, and progress in, the general curriculum* (pp. 38–45). Washington, DC: U.S. Office of Special Education Programs.

Michaels, C. A., Prezant, F. P., Morabito, S. P., & Jackson, K. (2002). Assistive and instructional technology for college students with disabilities: A national snapshot of postsecondary service providers. *Journal of Special Education Technology, 17,* 5–14.

National Association of State Directors of Special Education (2002). Research institute for assistive and training technologies. Retrieved May 17, 2002, from http://www.nasdse.org/riatt.htm

National Center for Education Statistics (2004). Washington, DC: U.S. Department of Education. Retrieved October 29, 2004, from http://nces.ed.gov//programs/coe/2004/section1/indicator05.asp

National Center on Low Incidence Disabilities (2004). Retrieved October 22, 2004, from http://nclid.unco.edu/newnclid/toolboxmaterial.php

No Child Left Behind Act of 2001. (2002). Pub. L. No. 107–110, 115, Stat. 1425, codified in 20 U.S.C. § 6301 et seq.

O'Brien, C. L., O'Brien, J., & Mount, B. (1997). Person-centered planning has arrived … or has it?. Reprinted in 1999 in J. O'Brien & C. L O'Brien (Eds.), *A little book about person-centered planning* (pp. 19–26). Toronto: Inclusion Press.

O'Connor, S., & Racino, J. A. (1993). "A home of my own": Community housing options and strategies. In J. A. Racino, P. Walker, S. O'Connor, & S. J. Taylor (Eds.), *Housing, support, and community: Choices and strategies for adults with disabilities* (pp. 137–160). Baltimore: Paul H. Brookes.

Overton, T., Fielding, C., & Simonsson, M. (2004). Decision making in determining eligibility of culturally and linguistically diverse learners: Reasons given by assessment personnel. *Journal of Learning Disabilities, 37*, 319–331.

Park, H., & Lian, G. J. (2001). Series editors' comments: Introduction to special series on culturally and linguistically diverse learners with severe disabilities. *Journal of the Association for the Persons With Severe Handicaps, 26*, 33.

Parent, W., Unger, D., Gibson, K., & Clements, C. (1994). The role of job coach: Orchestrating community and workplace supports. *American Rehabilitation, 20*(3), 2–11.

Parette, P., & McMahan, G. A. (2002). What should we expect of assistive technology? Being sensitive to family goals. *Exceptional Children, 35*, 56–61.

Parette, P., VanBiervliet, A., & Hourcade, J. J. (2002). Family-centered decision making in assistive technology. *Journal of Special Education Technology, 15*, 45–55.

Pugach, M. C. (2001). The stories we choose to tell: Fulfilling the promise of qualitative research in special education. *Exceptional Children, 67*, 439–453.

Racino, J. A., & Taylor, S. J. (1993). "People first": Approaches to housing and support. In J. A. Racino, P. Walker, S. O'Conner, & S. J. Taylor (Eds.), *Housing, support, and community: Choices and strategies for adults with disabilities* (pp. 33–56). Baltimore: Paul H. Brookes.

Research Connections. (1998). Integrating technology: Promising practices. Retrieved April 23, 2001, from http://www.cec.sped.org/osep/section2.html

Rogers, M. R., Ingraham, C. L., Bursztyn, A., Cajigas-Segredo, N., Esquivel, G., Hess, R. S., Nahari, S. G., & Lopez, E. C. (1999). Best practices in providing psychological services to racially, ethnically, culturally, and linguistically diverse individuals in the schools. *School Psychology International, 20*, 243–264.

Salend, S. J., Whittaker, C. R., Duhaney, L. M. G., & Smith, R. M. (2003). Diversifying teacher education programs to recruit and graduate culturally and linguistically diverse teachers. *Teacher Education and Special Education, 26*, 315–327.

Sailor, W., Gee, K., & Karasoff, P. (2000). Inclusion and school restructuring. In M. E. Snell (Ed.), *Instruction of students with severe disabilities* (5th ed., pp. 1–30). Upper Saddle River, NJ: Merrill.

Smith, S. (2000). Teacher education—associate editor's column. *Journal of Special Education Technology, 15*, 59–62.

Smith-Davis, J. (2000). *Issues arising from insufficient diversity among educational personnel.* Nashville: Peabody College/Vanderbilt University Alliance Project.

Snell, M. E., & Brown, F. (Eds.). (2000). *Instruction of students with severe disabilities* (5th ed.).Upper Saddle River, NJ: Merrill.

Sorrells, A. M., Webb-Johnson, G., & Townsend, B. L. (2004). Multicultural perspectives in special education: A call for responsibility in research, practice, and teacher preparation. In A. M. Sorrells, H. J. Rieth, & P. T. Sindelar (Eds.), *Critical issues in special education: Access, diversity, and accountability* (pp. 73–91). Boston: Allyn & Bacon.

Thurlow, M., Albus, D., Shyyan, V., Liu, K., & Barrera, M. (2004). *Educator perceptions of instructional strategies for standards-based education of English language learners with disabilities* (ELLs With Disabilities Report No. 7). Minneapolis, MN: University of Minnesota, National Center on Educational Outcomes.

Turnbull, A., & Turnbull, R. (2001). *Families, professionals, and exceptionalities: Collaborating for empowerment* (4th ed.) Upper Saddle River, NJ: Merrill.

Turnbull, R., Turnbull, A., Shank, M., & Smith, S. J. (2004). *Exceptional lives: Special education in today's schools* (4th ed.). Upper Saddle River, NJ: Merrill.

U.S. Department of Education (1998). *To assure the free appropriate public education of all children with disabilities: Twentieth annual report to Congress on the Implementation of the Individuals With Disabilities Education Act.* Washington, DC: Author.

U.S. Department of Education (2000). Promising practices in technology: Supporting access to and progress in the general curriculum. Available at http://www.air.org/techideas

U.S. Department of Education (2001). *To assure the free appropriate public education of all children with disabilities: Twenty-third annual report to Congress on the Implementation of the Individuals with Disabilities Education Act.* Washington, DC: Author.

Vocational Educational Services for Individuals With Disabilities (VESID) (2004). The New York State Alternate Assessment for Students With Severe Disabilities. Retrieved November 22, 2004, from http://www.vesid.nysed.gov/specialed/publications/policy/broch.htm

Walpole, S., Justice, L. M., & Invernizzi, M. A. (2004). Closing the gap between research and practice: Case study of school-wide literacy reform. *Reading and Writing Quarterly, 20,* 261–283.

Wehman, P. (Ed.). (2001). *Life beyond the classroom: Transition strategies for young people with disabilities* (3rd ed.). Baltimore: Paul H. Brookes.

Wehman, P., Moon, M. S., Everson, J. M., Wood, W., & Barcus, J. M. (1988). *Transition from school to work.* Baltimore: Paul H. Brookes.

Wehmeyer, M. L., & Lawrence, M. (1995). Whose future is it anyway? Promoting student involvement in transition planning. *Career Development for Exceptional Individuals, 18,* 69–83.

Westling, D. L., & Fox, L. (1995). *Teaching students with severe disabilities.* Englewood Cliffs, NJ: Merrill.

Winzer, M. A. & Mazurk, K. (1998). *Special education in multicultural contexts.* Upper Saddle River, NJ: Prentice-Hall.

Wolfensberger, W., Nirje, B., Olshansky, S., Perske, R., & Roos, P. (1972). *The principle of normalization in human services.* Toronto, Canada: National Institute on Mental Retardation.

Yates, J. R., & Ortiz, A. A. (2004). Classification issues in special education for English Language Learners. In A. M. Sorrells, H. J. Rieth, & P. T. Sindelar (Eds.), *Critical issues in special education: Access, diversity, and accountability* (pp. 38–56). Boston: Pearson Education.

25

WORKING WITH MIGRANT CHILDREN AND THEIR FAMILIES

Mary M. Clare and Georgina García
Lewis & Clark College

Gracias a la vida.

—Mercedes Sosa

A gritos y a sombrerasos salimos.
(We got through it, but not without some yelling and sombrero tossing.)

—Mexican dicho

There are people who do the work that no one else in our country wants to do. They labor in the fields tending and harvesting the food we eat. As the U.S. Department of Labor (2000) reports:

> U.S. agriculture is benefiting economically from increased access to global markets but agricultural workers are not sharing in the benefits of the expanding agricultural economy. Production of fruits and vegetables has increased and global demand for American produce continues to grow, but agricultural worker earnings and working conditions are either stagnant or in decline. (p. 2)

Most agricultural workers come to the United States from Mexico (Ruiz-de-Velasco & Fix, 2000). Many choose this work out of desperation when the poverty they encounter in their own country calls for extreme measures. For example, Javier and Manuel were cousins who left their family in Oaxaca, aware of the extreme poverty faced at that time by their siblings, parents, and grandparents. They, like many fathers and uncles before them, ventured out at 14 and 13 years of age, respectively, to enter the migrant stream as undocumented workers. They hoped to be able to provide some relief to their family. They began their work in southern California and moved north with the season and the ripening of fruits and vegetables. When Mary Clare met these young men, it was summer[1] and they were attending evening classes in English and other academic areas after spending all day in the fields harvesting raspberries in Oregon. They spoke from behind smiles of great courage; their fatigue came not only from rising before the sun to spend the day bent over prickly vines, but also from learning the ways of migrancy in the United States. They were young, intimidated by working alongside older Mexican men, but determined to do their parts to support their family in Oaxaca. Neither young man indicated a wish to live in the United States. Both saw their time here as serving to meet their family's needs in crisis and both wished to return to Oaxaca for their adult lives.

Due to shifts in immigration policy making documentation as a visiting worker increasingly difficult to secure, Javier and Manuel would now represent approximately 50% of migrant workers (U.S. Department of Labor, 2000). Only 10 years ago, over 80% of migrant farm laborers were documented as U.S. citizens or as legally recognized visiting workers (Fix & Passel, 1994). The median age of migrant farm laborers is 30, and 67% of those workers are under 35 (U.S. Department of Labor, 2000). Women make up only 20% of this workforce and most migrant farm laborers have children (Mines, Gabbard, & Boccalandro, 1991; Ruiz-de-Velasco & Fix, 2000).

Migrant families follow the same seasonal shifts as all migrant farm laborers. The "migrant stream" is the flow of seasonal laborers responding to the temporary increased need for farm workers at peak harvesting times. The stream of laborers moves from southern California or Florida for citrus harvests, gradually north through the eastern or western coastal states for seasonal harvesting through early autumn. Figure 25–1 illustrates the movement of the 29,000 school-age migrant children (ages 0–21) through the state of Oregon during the academic year 2000–2001 (Oregon Migrant Education Service Center, 2001).

By birth and by nature, Mexican and Latino migrant children are as capable as any children to learn and develop skills for participating in the wide range of careers and activities (civic and domestic) of the adult world. However, these children are among the learners placed most at risk for receiving inadequate educations due to issues of access linked with their migrancy, their language, their poverty, and the institutionalized bias systems that persist in relation to Latinos in general and migrant laborers specifically (C. Suarez-Orozco & M. Suarez-Orozco, 1995; Valenzuela, 1999). In this chapter and in the context of school psychology, where the experiences of these learners has hardly been considered (Henning-Stout, 1996), we explore and offer some possible ways school psychologists and other school professionals can respond to the needs and interests of children and youth who live on the migrant stream.

---

[1]During the academic year 1993–1994 and in the summer 1995, Mary Clare (formerly Henning-Stout) conducted numerous interviews with people on the migrant stream. Unless otherwise noted, the stories presented herein are excerpted or paraphrased from those interviews.

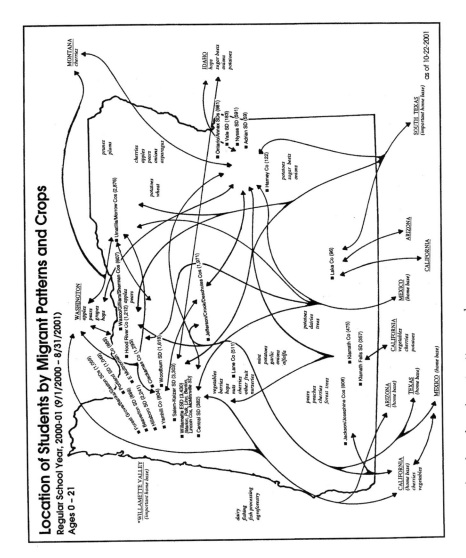

FIGURE 25–1   Location of students by migrant patterns and crops.

THE CIRCUMSTANCES OF MIGRANT LEARNERS:
THEORETICAL AND RESEARCH BASES

The theory and research related to the experiences of migrant people involved with the educational and mental health systems of this country do not form a unified knowledge base, but instead are both scant and scattered among the literatures of psychology, education, sociology, anthropology, and reports generated by the federal government regarding census, population trends, and particular evaluations of civic needs and services. Of equal relevance to the scholarly understandings of migrant experience are the reports of migrant people themselves. All of these sources are represented in the summary presented here.

Children of migrant farmworking families and farmworkers themselves who are 21 or younger compose a group of children and youth eligible for full access to public education. This group also represents a subcategory of people recognized under the federal demographic designation Hispanic, which is the demographic group now holding the majority among school-age children in the United States (National Public Radio, 2002). Of all children in the United States, those whose parents are from Mexico are least likely to graduate from high school and are also least likely to enter and complete undergraduate programs (García, 2001; Gibson & Bejinez, 2002; Gutierrez, Baquedano-Lopez, & Alvarez, 2000; Ruiz-de-Velasco & Fix, 2000). For the children within this demographic group who live with their families on the migrant stream, the numbers are far lower (Darder, 1991; Valenzuela, 1999).

Because of the particular challenges faced by school-age migrant children, the Migrant Education Program (MEP) was established by the federal government in 1966. According to Merced Flores, Associate Superintendent for the Oregon Department of Education and Director of Migrant Education in Oregon, the funds from this federal program are allotted to the states with the instruction for the states to develop their own systems for ensuring migrant students have equal access to public education (personal communication, December 9, 2002). This access includes having every opportunity any mainstream student has relative to relevant and effective curriculum, quality instruction, support services, and educational and extracurricular activities.

The contemporary mission and delivery of MEP services are grounded firmly in federal law established with *Pyler v. Doe* in 1982, which holds that no educational services may be denied or curtailed based on any suspected or confirmed civil status associated with a learner. According to this law, the only justification for refusal of educational access to any learner (age 0–21) is immunization records that are not up to date. We mention this here to make clear the fundamental right to education migrant children share with all school-age children. As with all rights, there are immediate implications for the responsibilities and related services necessary from governmental agencies like schools. Migrant students have particular needs associated with their transience, the challenges of learning a new language and culture, and the stresses of poverty and other forms of oppression.

Migration and Education

Early in the establishment of MEP, the federal government, in a collaboration between departments of health and education, supported the establishment of a national database known as the Migrant Student Record Transfer System (MSRTS). From 1969 to 1994, the MSRTS was used to identify and serve migrant students as they moved within and between states. The database contained information on each student's school and immunization history. The MSRTS also included a mechanism for ensuring the transfer of health and educational documents from students' birth countries.

One of the primary hindrances to the success of migrant students in the education system has resulted from gaps in the records documenting their educational participation and progress (M. Flores, personal communication, December 9, 2002). Many learners and their families make great and consistent efforts to be enrolled in school, but the records of their engagement have not always been available. Without records, students find themselves repeating grades they have already completed. The time and energy required with such unnecessary redundancy was often linked with students' decisions to leave the educational system—that is, to drop out (Fine, 1995; Gandara, 1995).

During its existence, the MSRTS served drastically to reduce problems associated with record keeping. However, when the federal government, in the 1996 reauthorization of MEP, determined that states would work independently to provide MEP services, the funding for MSRTS was eliminated and the communication among states was essentially lost. In the meantime, each state developed its own tracking system, but the consistency and linkage between states has remained weak (M. Flores, personal communication, December 9, 2002).

Language, Culture, and Education

When Mexican and Latino migrant children enter schools in the United States, they are, like all children, met with curricular and instructional environments structured to support learning. These environments are, of necessity, products of the dominant culture of this country and, in the vast majority of schools, based only in the English language. Such circumstances have required most migrant children to engage with academic material simultaneously acquiring a new language and navigating a new set of cultural rules, expectations, and ways of understanding and interpreting life experience and social interaction (Cummins, 1999; Quezada, 2001; Wortham, Murillo, & Hamann, 2001). The enormity of these tasks is unimaginable for most adults in the educational system who, in their own educational experiences, matched better with the culture of schooling.

Cuando recién llegamos a Oregon y mi hijo entro a middle school tuvo muchos problemas porque en ese tiempo no había casi nadie que hablara Español en la escuela. Se las vió bien difícil y el no sabía nada de Inglés. Solamente el maestro de ESL que le ayudaba pero solamente en su clase en las demás ya no. Mi hijo lloró varios días y no quería ir a la escuela. Como decen a gritos y a sombrerazos salimos y ahora ya sabe Inglés.

[When we first arrived to Oregon my son was in middle school and he had lots of problems because in those days there was hardly anyone who spoke Spanish in the school. It was a very difficult time for him and he did not know any English. Only the ESL teacher helped him but only during that class time. The rest of the time there was none. My son cried for days and he did not want to go to school. Like the saying says, *"A gritos y sombrerazos."* We did it and now he knows English.] (Maria Moreida)

Considerable bodies of research, along with legal requirements, support the importance of bilingual education for learners, who like migrant children, enter public schools as English-language learners (Green, 1998; Mora, 2002). Repeatedly, the academic success of English-language learners has been shown to be far greater when those learners build their basic skills in their first language as they are learning and gradually transitioning to receiving instruction in English (see Cloud, chap.10 in this volume). Although interpreted in various ways, the legal requirements of *Lau v. Nichols* (1974), a U.S. Supreme Court decision, supports the use of bilingual instruction by indicating that school districts must provide language-minority students with equal access to core curriculum and must remove language barriers so that all students may have "parity of participation" in the academic and social aspects of schooling.

Mi hijo se perdió tantas oportunidades desde la middle school simplemente por no enterarse de lo que estaba pasando en la escuela. Hay otra cosa también que piensan que los Hispanos porque no hablan bien Inglés no van a participar. Yo creo que los muchachos deben de participar en todo. Yo he visto que las porristas son todas Norte Americanas. ¿Por qué no hay ninguna Hispana? Hay muchas que tienen esa energía. ¿Por qué no los dejan participar en todos las actividades y los deportes?

[My son missed out on so many opportunities since middle school simply because he was not informed of what was going on in school. Also, there is the idea that Hispanos will not participate because they do not speak English well. I think that our youth should participate in everything. I have seen the cheerleaders and they are all North American. Why is there not a Hispanic? There are lots of girls with that energy. Why don't they let them participate in school activities and sports?] (Maria Morieda)

Poverty and Education

In addition to the challenges of learning a new language and culture, while also making the frequent moves required of migrancy, most migrant families live in poverty (Fix & Passel, 1994; U.S. Department of Labor, 2000). The condition of economic poverty has been demonstrated to have the greatest consistently negative impact on students' educational progress (Rumberger & Larson, 1998). In 1998, 22.8% of U.S. citizens identifying themselves as Hispanic lived in poverty (U.S. Census Bureau, 2001). The numbers for Mexican and Latino families are far larger (Ruiz-de-Velasco & Fix, 2000). Merced Flores, Associate Superintendent of Education and Director of Migrant Education for Oregon, was raised on the migrant stream and refers to the migrant life as "poverty with a view" (personal communication, December 9, 2002). Describing current conditions faced by migrant farm laborers, the U.S. Department of Labor reports:

In 1997–1998 (compared to 1989–1990) there was a modest increase in the number of farm workers who reported having access in the fields to toilets, as well as to potable water for drinking and washing. But by most measures, farm workers were worse off in 1998 than they were in 1988. In 1997–1998, farm workers found fewer weeks of employment, earned less per hour in real terms, continued to have poverty level earnings, and were less likely to utilize public assistance/programs designed to help ameliorate the effects of poverty on the working poor. (p. 10)

Consistent with the realities facing families in poverty and particular to the experiences of farmworkers and their families, migrant children are affected by lack of child care, exposure to pesticides, and overcrowded and unsafe living conditions. In many cases, family poverty forces all able family members to work. Because labor laws set the age of 12 as the legal lower limit for farmwork employees and allow exemptions for children as young as 10 or 11, many children help to support their families by joining their parents in the fields. The economic and health situations of Mexican migrant farmworkers and their children are severe (National Advisory Council on Migrant Health, 2001; Ruiz-de-Velasco & Fix, 2000), yet employment is still available and migration continues to be substantial (Fix & Passel, 1994; U.S. Department of Labor, 2000). The desperate circumstances of these families are illustrated by their continuing to work in and subject their children to these conditions.

Public Policy Barriers

Strong legal decisions support the rights all children have to public education. As mentioned earlier, these rights are further guaranteed to migrant children with the *Pyler v. Doe* (1982) decision, which prevents denial of access to education based on civil status. According to this decision, questions of immigrant status may not legally be asked in public schools. In addition, public law dictates that language barriers must be overcome to ensure equal access to learning for all students (*Lau v. Nichols*, 1974). Nonetheless, the conversation continues in the public arena through the mechanisms of legislation and popular vote regarding the characteristics of education for particular groups of people.

In states where migrant labor is most needed and sustained, the attempts to limit the access of migrant students to education have been most common. California, the state enrolling 45% of the nation's immigrant population, seems consistently to set precedent for the articulation and implementation of laws affecting this population; other states with growing migrant populations (e.g., Arizona, Colorado, Georgia, Massachusetts, New York, Oregon, Texas, and Utah) tend to follow suit (Mora, 2002; Reyes, 2003). Two recent California laws illustrate the way this public discussion erects institutional barriers to learning specifically for second language learners like most migrant children. In 1998, California legislation virtually eliminated bilingual education (i.e., California Proposition 227, which became EC 300–340 of the California Education Code, 1998). That same year, the state passed into law a "Pupil Promotion and Retention" policy requiring that students be retained in grade who cannot perform on tests said to measure grade-level accomplishment (Mora, 2002).

Proposition 227 requires that all second language learners be served in structured English immersion (SEI) classes for 1 year, followed by full matriculation in mainstream classrooms. The rationale for this decision is confusing in light of the decades of empirical research and practical experience with educational programming that has revealed effective principles and practices supporting learning for second language learners (Greene, 1998; Mora, 2002). Research has clearly indicated that building on first language skill as a new language is introduced is most effective in supporting learning progress (Cummins, 2001). In addition, the acquisition of English as a new language sufficient to support academic functioning has been shown to require 4–7 years in bilingual instruction and 7–10 years in English immersion situations (Thomas & Collier, 1997).

By requiring English immersion, Proposition 227 shifted the responsibility for education of language minority students from those most qualified to untrained teachers with the expectation that they do in 1 year what took 3–5 years with highly specialized bilingual teachers (Mora, 2002). The result has been that increasing numbers of English-language learners—migrant students, in particular—are being retained in grades when they have not been given the opportunity to progress academically; they have not been given the opportunity to learn in their first languages as they develop linguistic skills in English.

THE STRENGTHS OF MIGRANT LEARNERS: IMPLICATIONS FOR PRACTICE

In the context of migration, language and cultural difference, poverty, and political controversy, children and youth of Mexican and Latino migrant families continue to enter schools to gain education. The breakdown of the educational process is the riddle that looms large in discussions of migrant learners. As illustrated up to now in this chapter, there are large and persistent conditions that pose great challenges to migrant learners. The tendency among academicians and practitioners is to focus on what is considered problematic, for example, a systemic inadequacy or some learner-centered pathology.

To address the realities of families, children and youth who live as migrant farm laborers, a different focus may be most useful. Close consideration of the strengths, assets, and desires of migrant people provides school psychologists with the opportunity to base service on listening to and honoring the wisdom closest to the concerns at hand—the wisdom of the migrant people themselves. In speaking about their lives, people who have lived on the migrant stream relay insights into the strength of their culture as it is expressed through devotion to family, hard work, education for their children, and spiritual practice.

> *¿Quiere usted que sus hijos mantengan el Español?* [Do you want your children to retain Spanish?]
> *Si, es muy importante.* [Yes, it is very important]
> *¿Es importante la cultura?* [Is culture important?]

Si, que mantengan su cultura y que aprendan la de aquí. Que mantengan nuestra cultura siempre. [Yes, that they maintain their culture and learn the culture here. That they maintain our culture always]. (Irma Santiago)

Family

Migrant families provide a wealth of emotional resources to their children. Mexican and Latino family structures include relatives of both sides of the family that live nearby or visit for extended periods of time (Lopez, Scribner, & Mahitivanichcha, 2001; Valdes, 1996; Valenzuela, 1999). Whether a migrant worker is temporarily working away from family or a family as a unit has come to work on the migrant stream, the larger family remains a strong support system visited as often as possible.

Migrant children and youth live in the constancy of family, experiencing and witnessing every decision filtered through consideration of the family's best interest (Valdes, 1996; Valenzuela, 1999). Mexican and Latino parents teach their children to grant respect to and earn respect from others (Y. G. Martinez & Velaquez, 2001; Valdes, 1996). Children are taught to honor elders and the role they occupy as relatives who have lived long and learned much. Children also come to see that not all older people are considered elders. By observing the models set forth in their families, children learn that respect is earned by acting responsibly to fulfill one's role in the family. In the case of many migrant workers, that role may include leaving the family for a time to find work in the fields of a foreign land.

Georgina Garcia recalls that her father would share the stories of his experience as a "bracero," [2] the injustices he endured, and the endless hours of hard work and unsanitary living conditions. In the end, he would always say, "I don't want my children to suffer like I did. I want them to get and education. To have the opportunity I never had." This story and wish of Garcia's father for his children is consistent with the responsibility Latino parents feel and demonstrate for teaching their children how to live. Among Mexican and Latino families, this practice is known as giving *consejos*, or the bits of wisdom that parents share with their children through stories about life experiences (Atkin, 1993; Delgado-Gaitan, 1993; Valdes, 1996).

The centrality of family in migrant life is illustrated by the influence family responsibility and connection have on the way migrant laborers separated from their families and migrant families separated from extended family continue both to consider those left behind in decision making and to take every opportunity for returning for extended visits (Valdes, 1996; Valenzuela, 1999). For families with children in schools, it is common for such visits to occur at religious holiday times like Christmas and Easter. Particularly during the winter season, when farm work is less available, extended visits are likely and may interfere with school attendance (Lopez et al., 2001).

---

[2]The bracero program was initiated in the 1940s when, during the war years, there was a shortage of laborers, particularly for farm work (Gamboa, 1990). Although Mexican nationals had pursued work in the United States for years prior, this program was the first U.S.-sponsored recruitment of Mexican workers for farm labor.

Work

The strong and unquestioned work ethic demonstrated by Mexican and Latino migrant farm laborers is evident in their perseverance even in the face of challenging working situations and persistent poverty. The consistent application of this high value on work to all areas of life reflects its centrality within migrant culture (Y. G. Martinez & Velaquez, 2001). Georgina Garcia recalls, "A phrase that plays like a broken record in my mind is, 'Nada es gratis, todo cuesta (Nothing is free, everything has a price).' That price, my parents taught us, is always hard work and determination. I remember this when I'm struggling to do school work. It reminds me to persevere."

Consistent with this strong work ethic, migrant parents teach the value of education by exposing their children to hard work. Children are given the choice to work hard in the fields or work hard at school (Lopez et al., 2001). Garcia continues:

> When we were children my parents would take us out to work with them. Our job would be to cut the stems off the avocados. My brother and I had competitions to see who could finish a pile first. By the end of the day what started out as fun turned into hard work. As we headed home at sunset my brother and I complained about how hard we had worked. That is when my father would say, "I want you to get an education so that you don't have to work like me, breaking my back; but, you never have to be ashamed of honest work." His words made me feel proud to be able to do my part as a family member but I also learned that I did not want to work in the field.

Education

Frequent in the wisdom passed on by migrant parents is emphasis on the importance of education (Delgado-Gaitan, 1993; Lopez et al., 2001; Villenas & Deyhle, 1999). Consistent in the culture of Mexican Americans has been demonstration of these values in activism, specifically in historic struggles for equal educational opportunity (San Miguel & Valencia, 1998). Despite the historic and contemporary presence of parent activism and the considerable documentation of parental involvement in the literature of education and psychology, educators continue to apply deficit thinking to all groups associated with Mexican Americans, including Mexican and Latino farmworkers (Delgado-Gaitan, 1993). In a case study of transgenerational support for education, Valencia and Black (2002) offer illustration of the value Mexican American parents of low-income families have on education. Interviews with four grandparents and six parents revealed subtle ways attitudes and behaviors related to education are consistently apparent in homelife. These authors conclude, "Such actions as telling family stories about school experiences and making sure children arrive at school on time each day are examples of parents' involvement with school *internally*; that is, through private, family behaviors within the home" (p. 97, original emphasis).

In interviews with Valencia and Black (2002), one grandmother told this story: "I cried and cried for days when I had to quit school. I didn't want to quit, but it was a matter of some of us not having enough to eat if I didn't. … Reading was my favorite subject. I went to a spelling bee once on the radio … but I didn't win. I loved going to school" (p. 98). Another grandmother spoke of scolding her daughter who wanted to skip a day of school: "Do you want to be like me and know nothing? The only job I could get is in the laundry or the kitchen. No money. Do you want that?" (p. 98).

Spirituality

Faith gives migrant families strength to continue. Although many Mexican and Latino people affiliate with the Catholic religion, contemporary religious practices in Mexico and the Central American countries continue to be profoundly affected by indigenous cosmology and symbols (Castillo, 2000). Specifically, the central importance retained by the Native American goddess Tonantzin Coatlalopeuh, whose temple remains in Mexico City, but whose name has been changed to Our Lady of Guadalupe and is associated through colonization with Catholicism and Saint Mary (Gallegos, 2002). The vitality of regard for and trust in this goddess is evident in the daily lives of many migrant workers. Georgina Garcia recalls being raised with devotion to the belief reflected in the consejo, "Our Lady of Guadalupe promises to defend the smallest of children." The personal refuge found in Our Lady of Guadalupe generalizes to public realms as when the United Farmworkers Union, under the leadership of Cesar Chávez, organized a boycott against an abusive landowner. During their demonstrations, workers marched behind the image of Our Lady of Guadalupe. Their faith in her promise fueled their courage and hope for a better future (United Farm Workers, 1998).

The spirituality of migrant families is often a central anchor for their well-being. Cervantes and Ramirez (1992) refer to this amalgam of European cosmology brought to the Americas by the Spanish with indigenous cosmologies as *mestizo* spirituality. This spirituality carries stories and beliefs explaining good and bad fortune and may be central to a family's conceptualizations of psychological or educational problems.

REAL SUPPORT FOR MIGRANT LEARNERS: IMPLEMENTATION AND APPROACHES

Drawing together the interests of migrant families and the motivation to service on the part of educators and psychologists raises questions about what to do. Continuing in the spirit of responsiveness and respect (Henning-Stout, 1994), we offer the following thoughts on ways to meet migrant children, youth, and families in their strength so that relevant service may be realized. The essential finding from our investigation of research, theory, and the reported experiences of migrant people is that, in general, these people are not broken or sick. They are situated in lives and circumstances that mediate what and how learning and other activities nurturing of community may best take place. We offer this view as the most fundamental, and likely most effective, antidote to the barriers migrant people have historically faced when seeking education for their children and other social services for their families.

In addition, stemming from this view are four general suggestions for what have come to be known as best practices. We suggest that school psychologists make an effort to understand the social context of migrant learners, support and facilitate parent involvement, identify and implement relevant instruction and assessment, and become informed of and address oppression consistently and directly.

Understand the Social Context of Migrant Learners

All learning takes place in social context. The more comfortable the learners are in their educational setting and the closer the match between the learners' culture and sense of the world and the culture of the school, the more successful their learning experience (Noddings, 1992; Ogbu & Simons, 1998). Educators can serve children and youth from migrant families by coming more deeply to understand the circumstances these learners must navigate as they engage in schooling. In their recent book on immigrant children, C. Suarez-Orozco and M. Suarez-Orozco (2001) suggest that among the most powerful mediators of these children's educational and socioemotional well-being is what they term *social mirroring*. In all encounters with the culture they are entering, immigrant and migrant children are consistently vigilant to how they are being perceived by others. Recognizing the power of our responses, verbal and nonverbal, is a vital first step in coming to understand the daily reality of these learners' lives.

Belonging and Expectations

> *Yo escuché un comentario de una muchacha que estuvo en otra escuela. Dijo que allá era diferente. "Aquí solamente les dan sus trabajos pero nadie se preocupa por ellos. Se encuentran con los maestros en los corredores de la escuela y no los saludan. En la otra escuela dice que los maestros los saludaban y les preguntaban cómo estaban. Aquí no se preocupan por nosotros y siento muy feo."*
>
> [I heard a comment from a young girl about another school she had attended. She said things were different over there. "Here they give us our work but nobody cares about us. We run into the teachers in the hall and they don't bother to greet us. At the other school the teachers would greet us and ask how we were doing. Here they don't care about us and that makes me feel awful."] (Maria Morieda)

González and Padilla (1997) found students' sense of belonging was the only significant predictor of academic resilience and achievement in a study of 2,169 Mexican American high school students. In an investigation of a Migrant Education Program (MEP), Gibson and Bejinez (2002) identified variables influencing this sense of belonging among migrant students. When education is working well for migrant learners, they possess social capital and connection with key institutional agents like teachers and other educators. Gibson and Bejinez define social capital as "students' access to the social relationships that enable them to obtain the resources needed to be successful in school" (p. 157). This access is mediated by the presence of unequal power relations and the distribution of resources like curricula and instructional approaches that are linguistically and culturally meaningful.

Schools are either facilitators of or impediments to the availability of social capital and positive contact with educators. For migrant students, personal contact that provides social mirroring of acceptance and respect sets the stage for academic success. For school psychologists, understanding and providing of social capital is key to supporting learning. One immediate way of enhancing the social capital of migrant students involves exposing and raising expectations. A common experience of Latino learners is to be faced with low teacher expectations (M. D. Martinez, 2003). These expectations are expressed not only in lack of encouragement for students considered less capable because of their poverty or ethnic status, but also more overtly in comments regarding these students' qualifications for academic programs (Darder, 1991). In one of a series of extensive interviews reported by M. D. Martinez (2003), a college-bound student named Javier described his recent experiences of low expectations: "My guidance counselor, for example, felt very strongly that I should not attend any 4-year institution. … [Another time] I asked a teacher if I could go to the library to complete a scholarship application and he indicated that it was a waste of my time" (p. 17).

In everyday practice, the presence or absence of acceptance resides in personal encounters in classrooms, school buildings, and other community settings. Offering responsive service becomes more challenging when the values of the schools or community agencies themselves, often derived from the dominant culture, recognize or allow alternative approaches that support the sense of belonging for migrant students. For example, Wortham and Contreras (2002) relate the experience of the second author, an English as a second language (ESL) teacher, who worked to make her classroom consistent with the culture of her Mexican and Latino students. As part of her effort, she made home visits to become acquainted with her students' families and home lives. When her efforts became known, the teacher was criticized by colleagues and administration for the blurring of home–school boundaries and for unprofessional behavior in schools that necessarily represent dominant cultural values (Wortham & Contreras, 2002).

Spatiotemporal fluidity. Cultural influence occurs at every level of human experience with many of these influences far less apparent than what may generally be considered by educators and psychologists. For example, the cultural relevance of instruction, assessment, or counseling can be significantly affected by the structure of activity in space and time (Azmita, Cooper, Garcia, & Dunbar, 1996; Velez-Ibanez, 1996). The home and community settings of White people tend to be characterized by relatively firm spatial and temporal boundaries. Activities happen in particular areas at particular times; for example, homework is often completed in one sitting and in a particular place with few distractions, and TVs are usually located in a common room and turned off during meals. In contrast, the spatial and temporal boundaries between activities are more fluid among many rural, labor-class Latinos, where the simultaneous presence of academic (e.g., homework), leisure (e.g., TV or conversation), and domestic (e.g., cooking) activity is common, even as attention to particular activities are easily and successfully maintained (Wortham & Contreras, 2002).

The subtlety of this variation in culture can be profoundly relevant in a learning setting. Again, however, systemic values may not support the efforts service providers make to provide learning environments that are more familiar and thereby more supportive of learning for migrant children and youth. When the ESL teacher mentioned previously, a White woman, included more fluid spatiotemporal boundaries for learning activities in her classroom, many of her White colleagues found the setting overwhelming. "With a few exceptions most school staff interpreted the multiple activities and fluid boundaries in Margaret's room as evidence of sloppiness. As they conceived it, Margaret might be doing successful 'mentoring,' and perhaps occasional 'tutoring,' but she did *not* do 'instruction'" (Wortham & Contreras, 2002, p. 140, emphasis in original).

Daily realities of migrancy.   The children of migrant families face particular challenges that can be understood, at least, and accommodated, at best, by public service agencies like schools. Merced Flores, Associate Superintendent for the Oregon Department of Education and Director of Migrant Education in Oregon, makes two concrete observations. According to Flores, free and reduced breakfast and lunch programs are vital to the health and educational progress of these learners. In addition, efforts to support any state and national systems for placing the educational records of migrant students in an easily accessible database can ease the necessity of frequent moves between schools (personal communication, December 9, 2002).

Very often, the accommodations that could make supportive differences in the lives of migrant learners do not require unusual effort on the part of school psychologists. A concrete example of the need for this kind of flexibility comes from a young woman who had enrolled and been successful in advanced placement classes in her high school, but was refused the opportunity to complete final examinations early when the migrant camp closed and her family was required to move several weeks prior to the end of the school year (M. D. Martinez, 2003).

Support and Facilitate Parent Involvement

> *Cuando hay una junta en la escuela no nos toman en cuenta para mandarnos en Español el aviso y si uno llega a la junta todo es en Inglés. No entiende uno todo lo que están diciendo. Quisiera uno que alguien pudiera ayudarnos en eso. Que a todas las familias nos mandaran a llamar y que todas participaran.*
>
> [When there is a meeting at school they don't acknowledge us by sending a notice in Spanish, and if one does attend the meeting it is all in English. I do not understand everything that is being said. I wish there was someone who could help us with this. All of the families should be notified so that all may participate.] (Maria Morieda)

In addition to the low expectations placed on migrant learners (Darder, 1991), educational professionals also tend to have negative expectations concerning the interest of migrant parents in the education of their children (Lopez et al., 2001; M. D. Martinez, 2003; Valencia & Black, 2002). As described earlier, the experiences of migrant children themselves, as well as the history of activism on the part of Mexican American parents, indicate quite another reality. Texts of comments by migrant learners are scant to nonexistent, however, M. D. Martinez (2003) relates the stories of several Latino learners from low income families who comment on their parents' educational values. "The basic idea inculcated was the notion that education was the key to success and necessary to avoid blue-collar work. It was made clear that more than a high school education was required" (Javier, p. 16). "My parents always thought a college education was necessary to live well" (Angel, p. 17). "[My mother] always says, 'Si you tuviera tu edad y estuviera soltera, you estudiaria todo lo posible…'" (If I were your age and single, I would study everything possible … ; Lynnette, p. 17).

Enacting responsive service and respect requires that school psychologists and other educational and psychological service providers become familiar with the culture and language of the migrant children and their families. Consistent with the circumstances best suited to learning, personal contact is imperative to engaging migrant parents fully in the learning lives of their children. The values are there. The barrier is in the failure of schools to establish culturally recognizable pathways for the involvement of migrant parents beyond the messages and values they pass on at home (Gibson & Bejinez, 2002; Noddings, 1984). Developing such pathways may require school personnel to make visits to families when the learners are home (Wortham & Contrereas, 2002). In addition, close and ongoing attention to what is unsaid and current in the lives of migrant students is helpful, because substantive understanding of the lives and families of these learners cannot be reduced to any formula (Noddings, 1992).

Finally, specific strategies for involving migrant parents in classrooms are beginning to be available (Lopez et al., 2001). For example, some articles summarize successful techniques for engaging parent support for the development of reading skills (Arzubiaga, Rueda, & Monzo, 2002) and for the establishment of mathematical reasoning (Anhalt, Allexsaht-Snider, & Civil, 2002). In a correlational study, Arzubiaga et al. (2002) found three factors of family life significantly related to children's success with reading. Children were more likely to succeed with reading when their families spend time together and promote values and identity. Reading was stronger for children whose families involve them in literacy related to religious activity. Finally, children's success with reading was inversely related to the family's domestic workload, a variable that increases with poverty and requires contribution of children to family survival. Each of these factors points to school-based interventions to support family time, encourage religious literacy activities, and collaborate with social service agencies that can help reduce family's domestic workloads.

A second example of classroom strategy comes from Anhalt et al.'s (2002) initial evaluation of a mathematical reasoning program. Their findings indicate that Latino parents are best able to support their children's success with mathematics when they have the opportunity to observe instruction. Linking this finding with those of Arzubiaga and her colleagues (2002) indicates the necessity of attending to the domestic context of migrant families and their children so that barriers to their engagement and success with schooling may be overcome.

Identify and Implement Relevant Instruction and Assessment

Language and culture mediate the expression of cognitive ability (Rogoff & Chavajay, 1995). Learners of great cognitive ability are likely overlooked when their ways of demonstrating knowledge do not match with those recognized by the culture of the school. In addition, learners who are becoming bilingual and bicultural frequently lose some proficiency in their first language as they gain fluency in their second language (Schiff-Myers, Djukic, McGovern-Lawler, & Perez, 1993). The availability of bilingual education and culturally relevant assessment and intervention for learning difficulties is of particular importance for migrant students who, due to their transience, will gain most from educational interactions that meet them where their learning is most likely to occur.

Bilingual education.   The two primary principles of bilingual instruction upheld by the considerable literature of that practice involve building on the literacy learners already have in their first languages as the new language is being introduced, and attending to and strengthening students' cultural awareness and identity (Cummins, 2001; Gibson & Bejinez, 2002; Greene, 1998; Mora, 2001). As a specific example, practice has indicated the isolation of literacy instruction to English phonics is particularly ineffective with migrant learners who do best with bilingual teachers who can support the strength of literacy in the original language as facility with a new language emerges (Quezada, 2001; Zuniga-Hill & Yopp, 1996). (For a more detailed discussion of bilingual education please see Cloud, chap. 10 in this volume.)

Assessment.   Involving students and their family in the assessment and intervention planning and implementation processes is most supportive of learning for migrant children (Henning-Stout, 1994). In addition, recognizing and adjusting for the cultural ignorance of test instruments (Flanagan & Ortiz, 2000) and the limited interpretive understandings afforded by most school psychology training programs (Ochoa, Rivera, & Ford, 1997) is vital to making assessment a service to the learner. The consistent practice of identifying the purpose of assessment (e.g., to support the learning of this migrant student) and anchoring all practice in service to that purpose will afford the greatest integrity of effort and the most respect and support to the learner (Henning-Stout, 1994). (For additional consideration of assessment, please see part IV of this volume: Multicultural and Bilingual Assessment.)

Intervention

> *Mi hijo estuvo atrasado en sus trabajos por el idioma. Y hubo un maestro (ESL) que le pusieron después de clases. Ese maestro le ayudó bastante, le agradezco mucho.*
> [My son was behind on his work because of the language barrier. There was an ESL teacher that was assigned to help him after school. That teacher helped him plenty. I'm very grateful to him.] (Maria Morieda)

Migrant children are perhaps more influenced by their families than many dominant culture children. For learning success to be most soundly supported, intervention planning and implementation must involve family members (M. D. Martinez, 2003; Valencia & Black, 2002; Wortham & Contreras, 2002). The availability of tutoring and social support from programs that employ bilingual and bicultural educators can also be central to the success of any intervention for improving educational progress for migrant learners (e.g., the MEP program described by Gibson & Bejinez, 2002; the TRIO program described by M. D. Martinez, 2003). (Please also see part III of this volume: Instructional and Classroom Interventions.)

Become Informed of and Address Oppression Directly

The attitude of dominant culture U.S. citizens toward migrant farm laborers is reflected in the policy initiatives of communities, states, and the federal government. In the 1940s, when World War II engaged large numbers of workers in its effort, the federal government initiated the bracero program, which formally invited and sponsored Mexican migrant laborers (Davis, 1990). There have been myriad examples of formal and informal activity aimed at either ignoring border crossing or heavily enforcing border patrol depending on the economic needs of the United States (Graham, 1996). The realities of poverty (and, in some cases, homeland oppression) that force Mexican and Latino people to seek work in the United States continue, as does the need for farm labor (Fix & Passel, 1994; U.S. Department of Labor, 2000).

In the mid 1990's, the discussion became elevated once more with the passage of Proposition 187 in California, a publicly supported law centered on the denial of health care, education, and welfare to non-citizens. This law was ruled unconstitutional and never put in force, but it set a tone for subsequent measures limiting bilingual education and otherwise restricting the rights of migrant people (e.g., Proposition 227 described earlier; Mora, 2002; Petronicolos & New, 2000). The larger social context created by such policies and public sentiments has direct impact on the experiences of migrant people and likely affects the educational experiences of migrant children.

Evidence of the affects on learners is plentiful. Investigations of school experiences have revealed migrant learners' discomfort in personal relationships with their teachers (Gibson & Bejinez, 2002; Sheets, 2002), concern with limitations in the relevance and responsiveness of instruction to their lives (Gutierrez, Asato, & Baquedano-Lopez, 2000; Valdes, 1996), awareness of teachers' lower expectations and the bias in educators' responses to students (M. D. Martinez, 2003), and tendency to dropout—a trend numerous scholars link with the hostile learning environment created both by public policy and personal interactions (Fine, 1995; Ogbu & Simons, 1998).

Georgina Garcia, one of the authors of this chapter, shares the following memory:

> My high school advisor called me into her office my junior year. She told me I should drop my college prep classes because I was not applying to a university and I was taking up valuable space for another student. She never bothered to inform me of the application procedures or help me. I'm glad I didn't listen to her because I would not be where I am today, in graduate school.

School psychologists and other educational specialists who become informed of these pressures may respond by taking personal interest in migrant students as individual learners (Gibson & Bejinez, 2002). Through inservice and other methods of sharing information, school psychologists may increase the knowledge and understanding of their educational colleagues so that school-building personnel may work together to identify and provide curriculum and instruction that taps in to what is culturally and linguistically familiar to migrant children and youth (e.g., Wortham & Contreras, 2002). One area of system-level intervention was illustrated in Sheets' (2002) ethnographic investigation of clashing worldviews regarding school discipline. Sheets' inquiry revealed great differences in attitudes, values, and beliefs between teachers and Chicano students. One student Sheets interviewed said of a disciplinary situation, "You try to explain why you're late and teachers trip. Next thing you know we're yelling at each other. Then you get kicked out and then you don't ever go back. It's just too embarrassing" (p. 113). Sheets quotes another student as saying, "The teacher was so caught up in that we were wrong that she wouldn't listen. Nobody would listen. We could have worked something out" (p. 112).

In all areas of their educational experience, migrant learners are affected by systems of cultural bias, particularly as those forces remain invisible to educational professionals like school psychologists. Two antidotes seem vital: (a) making systems of oppression visible, and (b) bringing school practices in line with the consistent research findings that academic engagement and success increases (and inoculation to systems of oppression is greater) when learning is linked with Mexican and Latino students' home languages, experiences, and culture (Cummins 2001; Gandara, 1995; Gibson & Bejinez, 2002; Mora, 2001; Rumberger & Larson, 1998).

SUGGESTIONS FOR FUTURE RESEARCH AND PRACTICE

There is relatively little in the literature of psychology and education about migrant populations. This situation makes expanding that knowledge base more urgent even as it leaves vast options for scholarly and practical contribution. We argue the research and practice related to migrant children and their families will be of greatest service when it is based directly in the experiences of the people (Henning-Stout & Meyers, 2000). The expectation that migrant learners should fit within the dominant culture's notion of what a student looks like is remarkably ineffective. School psychologists are uniquely situated to support the establishment of programs that represent, respect, and build on the cultural, social, economic, and political realities of migrant life.

With the experiences and wisdom of migrant people as guides, consider four general areas of research investigation and expansion of school psychology practice:

1. Efforts will be useful that build on the knowledge base of Latino studies with particular emphasis on the psychological and educational experiences of migrant children and families. Two sources of initial work in these areas are the *Journal of Latinos and Education* and the National Association of State Directors of Migrant Education, which annually sponsors the National Migrant Education Conference.

2. Related to extension of the knowledge base is identification of programs that work (Mora, 2001; Slavin & Calderon, 2001). This contribution to the understanding and support of education for migrant children will include the careful evaluation of both programs (Gibson & Bejinez, 2002; M. D. Martinez, 2003) and public policy (Mora, 2002; Petronicholos & New, 2000).

3. Perhaps the most powerful action that could be taken by school psychologists individually and by the profession's organizations and training pro-

grams would be systematic encouragement for the educational mobility and advancement of migrant people through active mentoring and financial support. The presence of people with migrant experience in educational roles improves services to this population and provides successful models. As a staff member of the MEP program said, "[Students] know we come from the same background, that our parents work in the field, [that] we worked in the field. We live in the same neighborhood. We eat what they eat. We listen to what they listen to and it's just, kids just feel that and they know that this [getting an education and a good job] is what they can do. That it's not impossible" (Gibson & Bejinez, 2002, p. 167).

4. Finally, it is time for school psychologists and all of education to engage the hardest questions of what defines culturally relevant education and mental health service (Valdes, 1996). Education happens everywhere and is acquired differently depending on the cultural, sociopolitical, and economic realities of learners. The current offerings of schools may not be relevant to the lives of many who are enrolled in school programs. It is time to identify and implement novel ways of supporting learning outside conventional practices, with the guidance and involvement of those people least successful in current structures. The presence of migrant children, youth, and their families in our schools provides an urgent and immediate opportunity for this long overdue revision of the ways school, home, and community collaborate.

CONCLUSIONS

Mora (2002) has warned of "a mentality toward non-English-speaking immigrants where they are considered 'domestic foreigners.' Such populations as migrant workers and low-wage laborers are not viewed as part of the larger society. Out of this perspective [grows] the philosophy that coercive policies are necessary to isolate and remove them, or to assimilate them into the dominant Anglo-American culture" (p. 35). The subtle, yet relentless, harm done to migrant learners with the persistence of this kind of thinking is worth our concern. Perhaps most insidious is the invisibility of the harm inherent in these dominant ideas and practices. Regardless of our ethnic or socioeconomic background, those of us who work as school psychologists in education and mental health settings must take full advantage of our orientations toward service to see and challenge the subtle barriers erected by dominant culture thinking. We must dignify the learners and families themselves by listening to and learning from them, thereby engaging them as active and primary agents in the processes developed for supporting their learning and psychosocial well-being. In the case of children, youth, and adults from the migrant farmworking families, the simplest instruction for us is in the guidance offered by the Cesar E. Chávez, "The end of all education must be service to others."[3]

---

[3]As quoted in the Education, Arts, and Culture page of the Cesar Chávez Foundation Web site. Available at http://www.cesarechavez.org/pdf/EducationArtsCulture.pdf

ACKNOWLEDGMENTS

In preparing this chapter, we have attempted to let the voices of migrant people speak. Georgina Garcia contributed her skill with library research and translation, but perhaps more crucial to this chapter has been her experience as a Mexican American woman raised by parents who were farm laborers working both as migrants and as resident employees. Hers, of course, is the experience of one person and cannot reflect the experiences of a group. However, as we suggest in the conclusion of this chapter, the perspectives and experiences of the people affected by membership in a marginalized group are vital to the exposure and reparation of the destructive effects of that marginalization. In service to this reparation, Mary Clare's contribution involved placing in narrative structure and disciplinary context the experiences, concerns, and interests of migrant children and families as reflected in the stories of Ms. Garcia and the other people whose words appear in this chapter.

ANNOTATED BIBLIOGRAPHY

Atkin, S. B. (2000). *Voices from the fields: Children of migrant farmworkers tell their stories*. Boston: Little, Brown.

This author combines photography with the narratives of children who live on the migrant stream. These stories give profound illustration and contour to the lives of migrant children in school, in their families, in their communities, and in the field.

Green, P. E. (2003). The undocumented: Educating the children of migrant workers in America. *Bilingual Research Journal, 27*, 51–71.

The author reviews the literature related to migrant children within the contexts of immigration issues, migration patterns, the impact of poverty and mobility on educational achievement, and migrant education.

Valenzuela, A. (1999). *Subtractive schooling: U.S.–Mexican youth and the politics of caring*. Albany, NY: State University of New York Press.

Applying her expertise in both education and ethnography, Angela Valenzuela presents the daily school lives of U.S.–Mexican youth. Her rendition and interpretation provide insights and suggestions of immediate relevance to supporting the learning of migrant youth. She provides ways of identifying and addressing educational circumstances that subtract form the natural learning capacity of these youth.

RESOURCES

Journal of Latinos and Education. Mahwah, NJ: Lawrence Erlbaum Associates.

A young journal, in its third year of publication, *JLE* is already a powerful voice for Latino concerns and interests in education. The journal draws directly from Latino experience with research, theoretical, and practical articles immediately relevant to all professionals in education, and other public service venues.

National Association of State Directors of Migrant Education. http://www.nasdme.org

NASDME is the professional organization that serves to connect state officials charged with the administrative responsibilities of using federal funds to help migrant children succeed in school. NASDME provides its members with notice of professional events and activities, and offers training, guidance, and counsel. The organization generates publications to inform educators, policymakers, and the public about migrant education and represents migrant learners, their families, and communities in continuing dialogues with the federal government.

REFERENCES

Anhalt, C. O., Allexsaht-Snider, M., & Civil, M. (2002). Middle school mathematics classrooms: A place for Latina parents' involvement. *Journal of Latinos and Education, 1,* 255–262.

Arzubiaga, A., Rueda, R., & Monzo, L. (2002). Family matters related to the reading engagement of Latino children. *Journal of Latinos and Education, 1,* 231–243.

Atkin, S. B. (1993). *Voices from the fields: Children of migrant farmworkers tell their stories.* Boston: Little, Brown.

Azumita, M., Cooper, C., Garcia, E., & Dunbar, N. (1996). The ecology of family guidance in low-income Mexican-American and European-American families. *Social Development, 5,* 1–23.

Castillo, A. (2000). *La diosa de las Americas* [Goddess of the Americas]. New York: Vintage.

Cervantes, J. M., & Ramírez, O. (1992). Spirituality and family dynamics in psychotherapy with Latino children. In L. A. Vargas & J. D. Koss-Chioino (Eds.), *Working with culture: Psychotherapeutic interventions with ethnic minority children and adolescents* (pp. 103–128). San Francisco: Jossey-Bass.

Cummins, J. (1999). Alternative paradigms in bilingual education research: Does theory have a place. *Educational Researcher, 28,* 26–34.

Cummins, J. (2001) Empowering minority students: A framework for intervention. *Harvard Educational Review, 71,* 656–675.

Darder, A. (1991). *Culture and power in the classroom.* Westport, CT: Bergin & Garvey.

Davis, M. P. (1990). *Mexican voices/American dreams.* New York: Henry Holt.

Delgado-Gaitan, C. (1993). Parenting in two generations of Mexican American families. *International Journal of Behavioral Development, 16,* 409–27.

Fine, M. (1995). The politics of who is "at risk." In B. B. Swadener & S. Lubeck (Eds.), *Children and families "at promise": Deconstructing the discourse of risk* (pp. 76–94). Albany, NY: State University of New York Press.

Fix, M., & Passel, J. S. (1994). *Immigration and immigrants: Setting the record straight.* Washington, DC: The Urban Institute.

Flanagan, D. P., & Ortiz, S. O. (2000). *Essentials of cross-battery assessment.* New York: Wiley.

Gallegos, B. P. (2002). Whose Lady of Guadalupe? Indigenous performances, Latina/o identities, and the postcolonial project. *Journal of Latinos and Education, 1,* 177–191.

Gamboa, E. (1990). *Mexican labor and World War II: Bracerso in the Pacific Northwest.* Austin, TX: University of Texas Press.

Gandara, P. (1995). *Over the ivy walls: The educational mobility of low-income Chicanos.* New York: State University of New York Press.

García, E. E. (2001). *Hispanic education in the United States: Raices y alas.* Lanham, MD: Rowman & Littlefield.

Gibson, M. A., & Bejinez, L. F. (2002). Dropout prevention: How migrant education supports Mexican youth. *Journal of Latinos and Education, 1,* 155–175.

González, R., & Padilla, A. M. (1997). The academic resilience of Mexican American high school students. *Hispanic Journal of Behavioral Sciences, 19,* 301–317.

Graham, W. (1996, July). Masters of the game: How the U.S. protects the trafic in cheap Mexican labor. *Harpers Magazine*, 35–50.

Green, J. (1998). *A meta-analysis of the effectiveness of bilingual education*. Claremont, CA: Thomas Rivera Policy Institute.

Gutierrez, K., Baquedano-Lopez, P., & Alvarez, H. H. (2000). The crisis in Latino education. In C. Tejada, C. Martinez, & Z. Leonardo (Eds.), *Charting new terrains of Chicana(o)/Latina(o) education* (pp. 213–232). Creskill, NJ: Hampton.

Gutierrez, K. D., Asato, J., & Baquedano-Lopez, P. (2000). "English for the children": The new literacy of the old world order, language policy and educational reform. *Bilingual Research Journal*, 24, 87–112.

Henning-Stout, M. (1994). *Responsive assessment: A new way of thinking about learning*. San Francisco: Jossey-Bass.

Henning-Stout, M. (1996). Que podemos hacer?: Roles for school psychologists with Mexican and Latino migrant children and families. *School Psychology Review*, 25, 152–164.

Henning-Stout, M., & Meyers, J. (2000). Consultation and human diversity: First things first. *School Psychology Review, 29*, 419–425.

Lau v. Nichols. (1974). 414 U.S. 563.

Lopez, G. R., Scribner, J. D., & Mahitivanichcha, K. (2001). Redefining parental involvement: Lessons from high-performing migrant-impacted schools. *American Educational Research Journal*, 38, 253–288.

Martinez, M. D. (2003). Missing in action: Reconstructing hope and possibility among Latino students placed at risk. *Journal of Latinos and Education, 2*, 13–21.

Martinez, Y. G., & Velazquez, J. (2001). *Involving migrant families in education*. Charleston, WV: Clearinghouse on Rural Education & Small Schools. (ERIC Document Reproduction Service No. ED 1.331/2:EDO-RC–00–4)

Mora, J. K. (2001). Effective instructional practices and assessment for literacy and biliteracy development. In S. R. Hurley & J. V. Tinajero (Eds.), *Literacy assessment of second language learners* (pp. 149–166). Boston: Allyn & Bacon.

Mora, J. K. (2002). Caught in a policy web: The impact of education reform on Latino education. *Journal of Latinos and Education, 1*, 29–44.

Mines, R., Gabbard, S., & Boccalandro, B. (1991, July). *Findings from the agricultural workers survey (NAWS) 1990: A demographic and employment profile of perishable crop farm workers*. Washington, DC: U.S. Department of Labor, Office of Program Economics.

National Advisory Council on Migrant Health. (2001). *Migrant health issues: Monograph series*. Buda, TX: National Center for Framworker Health. Retrieved January 14, 2004, from http://www.ncfh.org

National Public Radio. (2002). Educating Latinos: An NPR special report. *NPR Programming*. Retrieved December 19, 2002, from http://www.npr.org/programs/atc/features/2002/nov/educating_latinos/index.html

Noddings, N. (1984). *Caring: A feminine approach to ethics and moral education*. Berkeley: University of California Press.

Noddings, N. (1992). *The challenge to care in schools: An alternative approach to education*. New York: Teachers College Press.

Ochoa, S. H., Rivera, B. D., & Ford, L. (1997). An investigation of school psychology training pertaining to bilingual psycho-educational assessment of primarily Hispanic students: Twenty-five years after *Diana v. California. Journal of School Psychology*, 35, 329–349.

Ogbu, J. U., & Simons, H. D. (1998). Voluntary and involuntary minorities: A cultural- ecological theory of school performance with some implications for education. *Anthropology and Education Quarterly*, 29, 155–188.

Oregon Migrant Education Center. (2001). *Oregon migrant education program 2001– 2002 directory*. Salem, OR: Author.

Petronicolos, L., & New, W. S. (2000). Anti-immigrant legislation, social justice, and the right to equal educational opportunity. *American Educational Research Journal, 36,* 373–408.

Pyler v. Doe. (1982). 457 U.S. 202, 102 S. Ct. 2382.

Quezada, M. S. (2001). Is sounding out words enough? *The Multilingual Educator, 2,* 12–15.

Reyes, L. O. (2003). Surviving the "perfect storm": Bilingual education policymaking in New York City. *Journal of Latinos and Education, 2,* 23–30.

Rogoff, B., & Chavajay, P. (1995). What's become of research on the cultural basis of cognitive development? *American Psychologist, 50,* 859–877.

Ruiz-de-Velasco, J., & Fix, M. (2000). *Overlooked and underserved: Immigrant students in U.S. secondary schools.* Washington, DC: The Urban Institute.

Rumberger, R. W., & Larson, K. A. (1998). Toward explaining differences in educational achievement among Mexican American language minority students. *Sociology of Education, 71,* 69–93.

San Miguel, G, Jr., & Valencia, R. R. (1998). From the Treaty of Guadalupe Hidalgo to Hopwood: The educational plight and struggle of Mexican Americans in the Southwest. *Harvard Educational Review, 68,* 353–412.

Schiff-Myers, N. B., Djukic, J., McGovern-Lawler, J., & Perez, D. (1993). Assessment considerations in the evaluation of L2 learners: A case study. *Exceptional Children, 60,* 237–249.

Sheets, R. H. (2002). "You're just a kid that's there"—Chicano perception of disciplinary events. *Journal of Latinos and Education, 1,* 105–122.

Slavin, R. E., & Calderón, M. (Eds.). (2001). *Effective programs for Latino students.* Mahwah, NJ: Erlbaum.

Suarez-Orozco, C., & Suarez-Orozco, M. (1995). *Transformations: Migrant family life and achievement motivation among Latino adolescents.* Stanford, CA: Stanford University Press.

Suarez-Orozco, C., & Suarez-Orozco, M. (2001). *Children of immigration.* Cambridge, MA: Harvard University Press.

Thomas, W. P., & Collier, V. (1997). *School effectiveness for language minority students* (NCBE Resource Collection Series, No. 9). Washington, DC: National Clearinghouse for Bilingual Education [On-line]. Available from http://www.ncbe.gwu.edu/ncbepubs/resource/effectiveness/

United Farm Workers. (1998). The story of Cesar Chávez. Retrieved January 14, 2004, from http://www.ufw.org/cecstory.htm

U.S. Census Bureau. (2001). *Poverty in the United States: 2000.* Washington, DC: Author.

U.S. Department of labor. (2000, December). *The agricultural labor market: Status and recommendations.* Washington, DC: Author. Available from http://migration.ucdavis.edu/rmn/labor_resources/dec_2000_labor.htm

Valdes, G. (1996). *Con respeto: Bridging the distance between culturally diverse families and schools. An ethnographic portrait.* New York: Teachers College Press.

Valencia, R. R., & Black, M. S. (2002). "Mexican Americans don't value education!"—On the basis of the myth, mythmaking, and debunking. *Journal of Latinos and Education, 1,* 81–103.

Valenzuela, A. (1999). *Subtractive schooling: U.S.–Mexican youth and the politics of caring.* Albany, NY: State University of New York Press.

Velez-Ibanez, C. (1996). *Border visions.* Tucson, AZ: University of Arizona Press.

Villenas, S., & Deyhle, D. (1999). Critical race theory and ethnographies challenging the stereotypes: Latino families, schooling, resilience, and resistance. *Curriculum Inquiry, 29,* 413–445.

Wortham, S., & Contreras, M. (2002). Struggling toward culturally relevant pedagogy in the Latino diaspora. *Journal of Latinos and Education, 1,* 133–144.

Wortham, S., Murillo, E., & Hamann, E. (Eds.). (2001). *Education, policy, and the politics of identity in the new Latino diaspora*. Westport, CT: Ablex.

Zuniga-Hill, C., & Yopp, R. H. (1996). Practices of exemplary elementary school teachers of second language learners. *Teacher Education Quarterly, 23*, 83–97.

26

CULTURALLY AND LINGUISTICALLY DIVERSE CHILDREN AND YOUTH WITH LEARNING DISABILITIES

Joan Silverstein

Clark County School District, Las Vegas

Chun Zhang

Fordham University

The over- and underrepresentation of students from culturally and linguistically diverse (CLD) backgrounds in special education have been persistent concerns for more than three decades (Artiles & Zamora-Duran, 1997; Coutinho, Oswald, & Best, 2002; Dunn, 1968). For example, during the 1998–1999 school year, African American youth accounted for 14.8% of the general population, with 18.3% of the population identified with learning disabilities (LD). Hispanic American youth accounted for 14.2% of the general population, with 15.8% of the population identified with a learning disability. Learning disability continues to be the most prevalent eligibility category for all students, representing more than one half of the students with disabilities served under the Individuals With Disabilities Education Act (IDEA; U.S. Department of Education, 2001). U.S. Department of Education data analyses indicate overrepresentation of Native American students in classes for learning disabilities, underrepresentation of Hispanic and Asian Pacific Islander students in the LD category, and overrepresentation of African American students in the mentally retarded and emotionally disturbed categories. CLD students, particularly African American and Hispanic American students, are underrepresented in gifted education programs (National Alliance of Black School Educators, NABSE, & IDEA Local Implementation by Local Administrators, ILIAD, Project, 2002).

According to the National Association of School Psychologists (NASP, 2003a), problems with inappropriate referrals and identification are not unique to CLD students, but are exacerbated for this population of students. Both over- and underidentification of culturally diverse students with LD may result from a limited understanding of cultural and linguistic differences, leading to misunderstandings and misinterpretations of students' behaviors, patterns, social interactions, and learning styles (NASBE & ILIAD Project, 2002). School districts may also discourage and delay referrals of English-language learners (ELLs), attributing their learning difficulties to acculturation and second language acquisition issues rather than learning disabilities. Both the over- and underreferrals of CLD students to special education cause serious concerns in educational settings. A NASP/National Coalition of Advocates for Students (NCAS) position statement noted that it is not a benign action to erroneously label children as having a disability, even when this is done to provide students with services unavailable in general education (NASP/NCAS, 2002). Ramifications of the misidentification and misplacement of CLD students in special education may include deprivation of the right to a free and appropriate public education (Individuals With Disabilities Education Act of 1997, 20 .U.S.C. §1400 .et seq.); lowered teacher and parental expectations; denial of access to the general education curriculum, with possible exposure to inappropriate instructional methods; and possible feelings of alienation resulting from stigmatization (Cloud, 2002). In addition, if the learning problems are considered to be caused by a disability internal to the students, there is the risk of a self-fulfilling prophecy because school professionals and parents may abdicate responsibility for changing or enriching the school and home environments (e.g., NABSE & ILIAD Project). Conversely, students with unidentified and untreated learning disabilities who are misidentified as only having second language acquisition issues may struggle and fail in general education classrooms when they truly need special education services.

This chapter focuses on issues related to identifying, assessing, and intervening with CLD students with learning disabilities, including methods for differentiating learning disabilities from such factors as cultural differences and second language acquisition processes. The chapter begins with a definition of learning disabilities and an overview of issues related to identification. Theoretical and research bases, including relevant learning theories, are addressed, followed by a discussion of implications for practice. A model is presented for identifying and assessing CLD students with potential learning disabilities, and for developing and implementing interventions. Finally, recommendations for practice and directions for future research are explored.

DEFINITIONS OF LEARNING DISABILITIES

IDEA '97 Final Regulations (§300.7) (1999) defined a specific learning disability as a basic psychological processes disorder that affects reading, written expression, mathematics, listening comprehension, and oral expression. Learning problems due to other disabilities, or that are the result of cultural, environmental, or economic factors, were excluded. In order to be considered eligible as a student with a specific learning disability, the student had to demonstrate a significant discrepancy between ability as measured by an intelligence test, and achievement as measured by an achievement test (Telzrow & Tankersley, 2000). The reauthorization of IDEA was signed into law as the Individuals With Disabilities Education Improvement Act (Public Law No: 108–446). Building on the No Child Left Behind Act, the IDEA reauthorization focuses on such areas as: (a) increasing the focus on academic achievement for students with disabilities;(b) allowing local education agencies (LEA) to use the response to intervention model as an acceptable option to replace the IQ–achievement discrepancy formula within evaluation procedures (i.e., when intelligence tests are used, it is recommended that the results are placed "within the larger context of the child's individual abilities"; House Report as cited in Klotz & Nealis, 2005, p. 2); (c) strengthening early intervention programs and strategies by using a portion of federal funds and other funding sources for professional development for teachers and other school staff in such areas as "scientifically-based academic and behavioral interventions," and "educational and behavioral evaluations, services, and supports, including scientifically-based literacy instruction" (House Report, as cited in Klotz & Nealis, p. 2); (d) mandating school districts with significant overidentification of minority students to provide early intervention programs to prevent overreferral and overidentification for special education; (e) expanding parental rights and services, including providing parent training and supports that focus on parents of students with disabilities who are low income, LEP, and CLD; and (f) providing and administering evaluations in the "language and form" that will provide the most accurate information about the students' functioning in academic, developmental, and functional areas, where this is feasible (Council for Exceptional Children, November 2004, p. 14). Other relevant aspects of the Act include providing supports to teachers and schools, such as training teachers and school personnel in positive behavioral supports and strategies to prevent misidentification of students with disabilities; modifying discipline provisions; reducing litigation and paperwork; and reforming special education funding streams (Council for Exceptional Children; Klotz & Nealis, 2005; Urban Special Education Leadership Collaborative, 2004).

IDENTIFYING CLD STUDENTS WITH LEARNING DISABILITIES

The dramatic increase in the rate of identifying students with LD over the last 25 years, including those from CLD backgrounds, has raised concern about the use of discrepancy models to identify students eligible for special education. L. S. Fuchs, D. Fuchs, and Speece, (2002) indicated that discrepancy models are problematic for many reasons, including poor reliability of difference scores and confounding factors that may affect the validity of the scores or mask a discrepancy between ability and achievement due to such factors as giftedness or profound learning disability. Further questions have been raised about the reliance on discrepancy scores to operationally define a learning disability among CLD populations (Garcia & Fong, 2000). For example, many CLD students are still in the process of acquiring English proficiency and may demonstrate characteristics similar to those of students with LD, including delays in decoding skills, reading comprehension, written expression, and language processing (Lock & Layton, 2002). It also may be difficult to distinguish between extrinsic factors (e.g., lack of adequate instruction, poverty) and intrinsic factors (e.g., processing deficits), particularly with English-language learners (Coutinho et al., 2002; Lock & Layton, 2002). Theoretical and research bases pertaining to identifying, assessing, and intervening with CLD children who exhibit LD are discussed in the following section.

THEORETICAL AND RESEARCH BASIS

From an ecological perspective, a number of interacting environmental factors affect the identification, assessment, diagnosis, and education of CLD students with learning difficulties (Bronfenbrenner, 1979). At the societal level, forces such as power differences, racism, poverty, national and state laws, and regulations affect the quality of, and access to, educational opportunities for CLD students. At the school and classroom level, such factors as school and classroom climate, curriculum and instructional methods, teacher–student relationships, family–school relationships, power hierarchies, and school professionals' beliefs and values influence students' educational outcomes. At the home and community level, factors such as community attitudes toward students' language, culture, and ethnicity; peer group values and practices; family worldviews, levels of acculturation, education, and socioeconomic status; and family stressors directly impact students' functioning in school (Cummins, 1986; Grossman, 1995; Ortiz & Yates, 2002).

Contemporary cognitive and learning theories increasingly emphasize the impact of culture, context, and social interaction on learning and assessment (Poplin & Phillips, 1993; Rueda, 1997). When assessing and educating CLD students, it is important to consider the interaction of learning, language development, second language acquisition, dialectical differences, and social/emotional development within the sociocultural contexts of the student's home, school, and community (Lopez, 1995).

Over the last two decades, much has been written about second language acquisition theories for bilingual students. Research suggests that a solid grounding in the student's primary language increases the likelihood that the child will acquire concepts and strategies to enhance second language acquisition (Cummins, 1984). Cummins noted that language proficiency in basic interpersonal communication skills (BICS) takes up to 2 years to develop under ideal circumstances. However, the acquisition of cognitive academic language proficiency (CALP), which is necessary for such learning tasks as cognitive and academic development, takes between 5 and 10 years to develop to the fluency level of native speakers (Collier, 1992).

The second language acquisition process can be conceptualized in terms of five interrelated factors (Ellis, as cited in Vaughn, Bos, & Schumm, 2003): *Situational factors* are the contexts or environments (e.g., home, school, friends) in which formal and informal second language learning takes place. *Linguistic input* includes the level of comprehensible input provided when one listens to or reads a second language (Krashen, 1985). *Learners' characteristics* include age, self-confidence, intention, motivation, and facility for second language acquisition, grounding in the primary language, and knowledge of learning strategies to assist in language acquisition (Cummins, 1991; Vaughn et al., 2003). The *learning and developmental processes* involving the development of BICS and CALP vary widely depending on the situational factors, linguistic input, and learners' characteristics already described. For example, students may understand a language for listening and reading, but may not be proficient in producing the language through speaking and writing. Because receptive language skills typically develop before expressive language skills, second language learners often experience a silent or nonverbal period during which they are absorbing information and language but do not yet feel comfortable speaking or writing (Roseberry-McKibbin, 2002). The integration of all these factors affects students' *second language output*. Opportunities for students to develop comprehensible output in a variety of environments are important for the acquisition of a second language (Swain, 1985).

Several characteristics common in normal second language acquisition may be misinterpreted as indicating a learning disability. For example, if students demonstrate proficiency in conversational situations (BICS), then teachers may assume that LEP students are also able to succeed at such academic tasks as comprehending textbooks, understanding lectures, or understanding the linguistic demands of formal and classroom assessments. However, in many academic learning contexts, the level of proficiency in CALP required takes much longer to develop (Cummins, 1984). Consequently, students may be misdiagnosed as having a learning disability when the issue is actually lack of sufficient development of CALP to meet the task demands (Roseberry-McKibbin, 2002).

Currently, a paradigm shift is taking place in conceptualizing the process of assessing CLD students, moving from a standardized, psychometric, medical model of assessment that focuses on identifying pathology within the student (e.g., a learning disability) to other assessment paradigms that emphasize multidimensional, holistic approaches such as authentic, ethnographic, and dynamic assessment methods (e.g., Figueroa, 2002; Ortiz & Yates, 2002; S. Ortiz, 2002; Roseberry-McKibbin, 2002). One goal of these multidimensional assessment approaches is to reduce bias that contributes to the rate of inappropriate referrals in order to increase the provision of appropriate services and interventions. Scant empirical research exists in the areas of assessment and interventions for learning disabilities occurring concurrently with linguistic and cultural differences (A. A. Ortiz, 1997). However, there seems to be a conceptual consensus toward the use of an ecological framework for assessing and providing interventions to CLD students with LD (e.g., S. Ortiz, 2002; Roseberry-McKibbin, 2002).

The paradigm shift includes a change from the use of standardized assessment instruments to the assessment of students' progress when they are exposed to research-based interventions implemented as designed (e.g., Upah & Tilly, 2002). L. S. Fuchs et al. (2002) proposed a treatment validity approach based on two criteria: significantly low underachievement and insufficient response to intervention. These criteria are found in many recommendations for special education identification and eligibility reform (e.g., NASP, 2003a; Reschley & Ysseldyke, 2002). For example, L. S. Fuchs et al. recommended that the assessment system document that: (a) the regular classroom is producing acceptable growth for many students, (b) discrepancies for performance level and growth rate exist when comparing a target child with classroom peers, (c) inadequate individual learning occurs even with general education adaptations, and (d) improved growth can be found with the provision of special education. NASP recommended that the ability–achievement discrepancy requirement be replaced with a multitiered model based on two criteria: "significantly low underachievement" and "insufficient response to intervention" (p. 2). Before evaluation for special education by a multidisciplinary team is considered, two tiers of supports within the general education classroom would be required. Tier 1 is the provision of research-based quality interventions for all students within the general education setting. Tier 2 supports include intensive interventions targeted toward students who are not progressing at a rate commensurate with their grades and settings despite Tier 1 interventions. Students who continue to demonstrate low achievement with insufficient response to research-based interventions at the Tier 2 level would be referred to Tier 3 for a multidisciplinary team comprehensive evaluation to determine whether they need special education services.

A paradigm shift is also occurring in the conceptualization of special education services. Special education is no longer viewed as a place. Rather, it is "a set of services to support the needs of children with disabilities to succeed in the curriculum" (NABSE & ILIAD Project, 2002, p. 13) with the site of services determined by the student's needs.

IMPLICATIONS FOR PRACTICE

Both over- and underidentification of learning disabilities prevent CLD students from receiving the appropriate education they need in order to succeed academically. Therefore, it is crucial that school psychologists and other professionals correctly distinguish between cultural/linguistic differences and disabilities. Case law and federal regulations emphasize the use of culturally and linguistically appropriate assessment practices when assessing students from CLD backgrounds. Cases including *Diana v. State Board of Education* (1970) and *Larry P. v. Riles* (1972) dealt with such major assessment issues as requiring the use of the child's primary language during assessment, and the use of multiple measures of performance rather than relying solely on an IQ test score to determine eligibility. IDEA Amendments (1997), IDEA Final Regulations (1999), and the Individuals With Disabilities Education Improvement Act of 2004 (Cernosia, 2005) all specify the use of a variety of assessment methods and materials that are not racially or culturally discriminatory; utilize the student's primary language or other primary means of communication; draw on a variety of sources, including parents' and students' participation in the general education classroom curriculum; and demonstrate that second language acquisition and lack of English proficiency are not the primary causes of the learning disability (§300.532).

The American Psychological Association (APA) and NASP ethical codes and guidelines also stress the use of culturally and linguistically appropriate assessment practices, including respecting cultural and ethnic differences, choosing culturally appropriate assessment techniques and treatment methods that have established validity for the population bring evaluated, and working sensitively with people from a variety of backgrounds (APA, 2002; NASP Principles for Professional Ethics cited in Thomas & Grimes, 2002). It is also important to rule out bias in the evaluator or in the assessment process (e.g., S. Ortiz, 2002). The following section explores assessment approaches to assist in limiting bias when assessing and intervening with CLD students.

IMPLEMENTATION AND APPROACHES

A number of authors and organizations recommend a multiphase process to help differentiate between a learning/language difference and a disability, and to plan interventions (e.g., Marston, Carter, Lau, & Muyskens, 2002; NASP, 2003a; A. A. Ortiz, 2002; S. Ortiz, 2002). A multiphase process has the potential to reduce bias and prevent inappropriate special education referrals and placement for CLD students. The model presented in this chapter and in Figure 26–1 incorporates concepts and frameworks proposed by L. S. Fuchs et al. (2002), Marston et al. (2002), M. Hauret (personal communications, May 13, 2003, September 22, 2004, December 13, 2004); NASBE and ILIAD Project (2002), NASP (2003a, 2003b), A. A. Ortiz (2002), Ortiz and Garcia (1988), S. Ortiz (2002), R. Shaw (personal communications, September 7, 2004, September 13, 2004, December 7, 2004), Reschley (2004a, 2004b), and Upah and Tilly (2002). In addition, the first author drew on her experience as a participant in a pilot program studying Response to Intervention in the Clark County School District in Nevada. This three-phase process is based on two assumptions:

1. Students in the general education classroom demonstrate a satisfactory overall level and rate of academic progress in the classroom. If the majority of students are not making satisfactory progress, then the focus of the intervention should shift from the referred student to the classroom, the school, and the district.
2. Despite the provision of research-based instructional interventions and remedial interventions at the individual and group level in the general education classroom (Phase I), the referred student is still achieving significantly below the performance of classmates and demonstrating lack of satisfactory response to intervention.

Phase I assumes that all students are receiving high levels of quality instruction, including group and individual instruction and behavioral interventions within the general education classroom (NASP, 2003a). During Phase I, teachers utilize support personnel such as school psychologists, literacy specialists, English as a second language (ESL) teachers, and bilingual teachers to assist in planning and implementing classroom and small group interventions. They also consult with other teachers to assist in implementing targeted small group instruction. If students are not succeeding in Phase I, then they are referred for further individualized interventions in Phase II.

Phase II utilizes a problem-solving process to identify and analyze the problems, plan and implement interventions, and evaluate the program. One example of a useful problem- solving process that can be utilized for interventions in all phases was developed by Upah and Tilly (2002), who drew on a number of problem-solving processes (e.g., Bergan & Kratochwill, 1990; Reschley, Tilly, & Grimes, 1999). Their problem-solving process includes the following stages and components: "(a) problem identification (behavioral definition, baseline data, problem validation); (b) problem analysis (problem analysis steps); (c) implementation plan (goal setting, intervention plan development, measurement strategy, decision-making

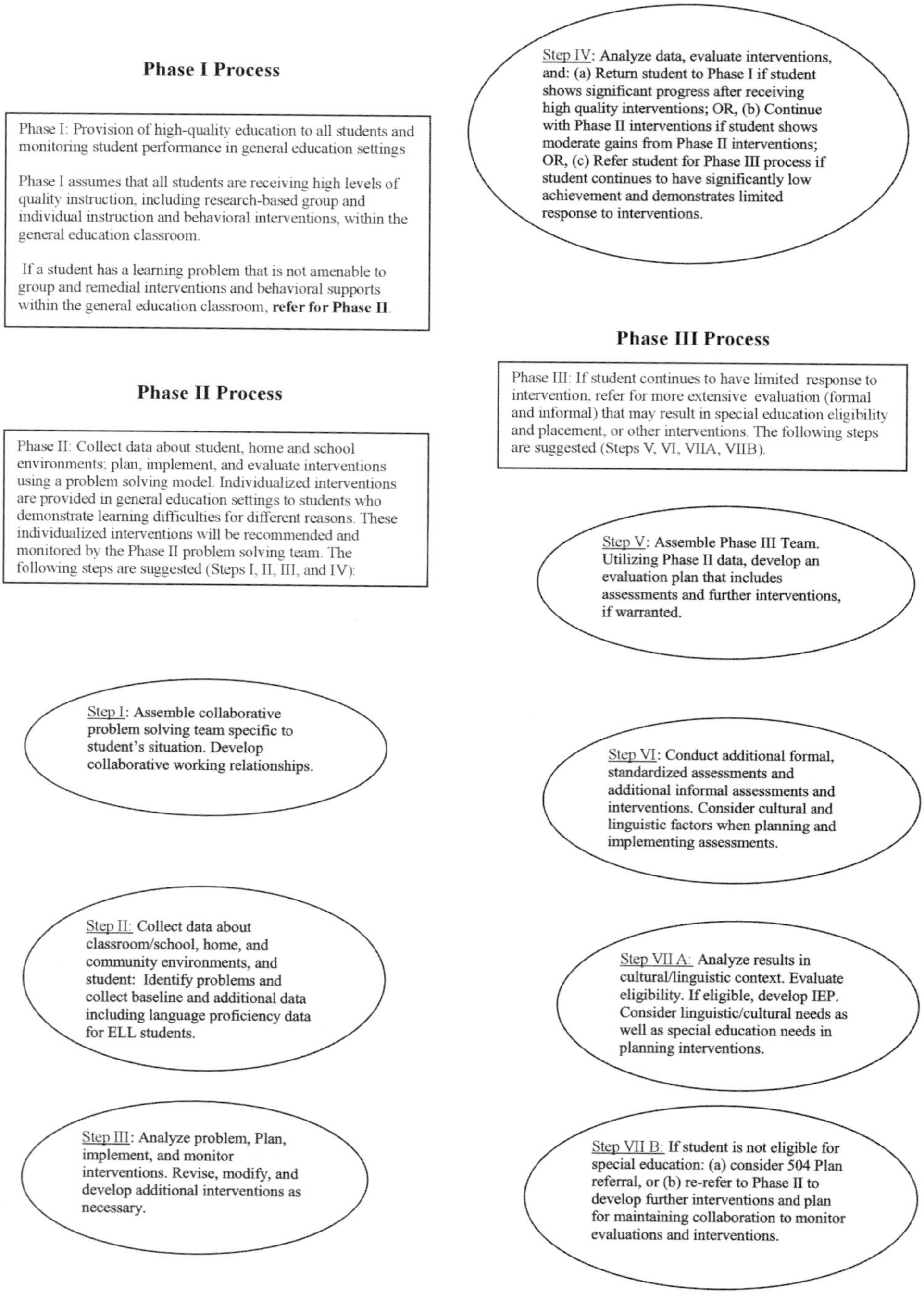

Phase I Process

Phase I: Provision of high-quality education to all students and monitoring student performance in general education settings

Phase I assumes that all students are receiving high levels of quality instruction, including research-based group and individual instruction and behavioral interventions, within the general education classroom.

If a student has a learning problem that is not amenable to group and remedial interventions and behavioral supports within the general education classroom, **refer for Phase II**.

Phase II Process

Phase II: Collect data about student, home and school environments; plan, implement, and evaluate interventions using a problem solving model. Individualized interventions are provided in general education settings to students who demonstrate learning difficulties for different reasons. These individualized interventions will be recommended and monitored by the Phase II problem solving team. The following steps are suggested (Steps I, II, III, and IV):

Step I: Assemble collaborative problem solving team specific to student's situation. Develop collaborative working relationships.

Step II: Collect data about classroom/school, home, and community environments, and student: Identify problems and collect baseline and additional data including language proficiency data for ELL students.

Step III: Analyze problem, Plan, implement, and monitor interventions. Revise, modify, and develop additional interventions as necessary.

Step IV: Analyze data, evaluate interventions, and: (a) Return student to Phase I if student shows significant progress after receiving high quality interventions; OR, (b) Continue with Phase II interventions if student shows moderate gains from Phase II interventions; OR, (c) Refer student for Phase III process if student continues to have significantly low achievement and demonstrates limited response to interventions.

Phase III Process

Phase III: If student continues to have limited response to intervention, refer for more extensive evaluation (formal and informal) that may result in special education eligibility and placement, or other interventions. The following steps are suggested (Steps V, VI, VIIA, VIIB).

Step V: Assemble Phase III Team. Utilizing Phase II data, develop an evaluation plan that includes assessments and further interventions, if warranted.

Step VI: Conduct additional formal, standardized assessments and additional informal assessments and interventions. Consider cultural and linguistic factors when planning and implementing assessments.

Step VII A: Analyze results in cultural/linguistic context. Evaluate eligibility. If eligible, develop IEP. Consider linguistic/cultural needs as well as special education needs in planning interventions.

Step VII B: If student is not eligible for special education: (a) consider 504 Plan referral, or (b) re-refer to Phase II to develop further interventions and plan for maintaining collaboration to monitor evaluations and interventions.

FIGURE 26–1.   The three-phase process to reduce bias in the assessment of CLD students suspected of having specific learning disabilities.

plan); and (d) program evaluation (progress monitoring, formative evaluation, treatment integrity, and summative evaluation)" (Upah & Tilly, 2002, p. 485).

The nature and extent of the Phase II process should be based on the unique needs of each student. Not all students being considered in Phase II need to go through the entire extensive data collection, hypotheses generation, assessment, and intervention processes outlined in Figure 26–1 and Table 26–1. For example, if information regarding the student's cultural, ethnic, and linguistic backgrounds or other environmental factors is already available, then there is no need to collect it again. However, it is important that school professionals consider all the factors listed here and in Table 26–1 so that the sources of the student's difficulties are not automatically attributed to a single factor, such as bilingualism or a disability, when multiple interacting factors may be responsible.

Phase II is necessary before any student is considered for referral to Phase III, which involves the formal process of evaluation to determine whether the student is eligible for special education (e.g., Marston et al., 2002; NASP, 2003a; Ortiz & Yates, 2002; S. Ortiz, 2002). Even when the nature of the disability appears evident, Phase II data collection and interventions should be implemented concurrently with the Phase III evaluations and interventions. Some guiding questions to consider during Phases II and III appear in Table 26–1.

Phase II of the process involves a series of interacting data collection and intervention stages that begin when a student is initially identified by parents or teachers as having learning difficulties. Phase II interventions utilize a collaborative problem-solving team (the Phase II team) to: (a) determine the existence, nature, and extent of the problems, including the collection of baseline data; (b) analyze and operationalize the problems and develop specific hypotheses and target goals, including conducting informal and short-term assessments that assist in identifying patterns of strengths and weaknesses in the environment and within the student; (c) plan and implement interventions, including setting goals, identifying and providing resources and supports for interventions, and developing and implementing monitoring strategies and plans to deal with decision making; and (d) evaluate the individualized interventions both during and following the program to determine whether the program is succeeding and the interventions are being implemented as intended. Individualized interventions should include validated, research-based interventions where progress can be documented. When considering the student's problems and progress, the student should be compared with other students of the same age or grade with similar cultural and linguistic backgrounds and similar migration and acculturation experiences (Ortiz & Yates, 2002; s. Ortiz, 2002; Upah & Tilly, 2002).

The primary objective of Phase II is to develop methods to maintain students in general education. Once the sources of difficulties are identified and appropriate interventions are implemented, most students in the Phase II process should be able to improve their functioning enough to remain in the general education curriculum. It is possible that some students will receive support from the Phase II process throughout much or all of their educational career (Reschley, 2004b). If the student makes insufficient progress during the initial interventions, then the Phase II team should review the data to determine whether to implement additional interventions. It is important that the interventions be implemented for a sufficient pe-

TABLE 26–1
Questions to Examine During Phases II and III

1. What classroom, school, and community factors are influencing student functioning and learning? These include:

   - instructional characteristics (e.g., traditional lecture style, use of a variety of active teaching to engage students, use of modifications to address needs of individual students)

   - teacher characteristics (e.g., expectations, knowledge of students' cultures, attitudes, training, and experience)

   - classroom and school characteristics (e.g., types of programs available for students, instructional resources; classroom, school climate issues, and parental involvement)

   - environmental and community factors (e.g., the community's attitude toward diversity and toward the students' languages and cultures, support for and opportunities to utilize the students' primary languages, expression of cultural practices and beliefs within the community, the availability of community agencies for support for the student and family— including referral if appropriate—and influence of youth groups and gangs)

   - the student's and family's environmental, cultural, and linguistic backgrounds (e.g., current languages of the home; students' primary language, informal and formal experiences with and fluency in L1 and L2; family members' levels of acculturation, education, and socioeconomic status; migration and acculturation experiences, transience; family disruptions and stressors; educational and employment history; health and medical history

2. What individual student factors are influencing student functioning and learning? These include:

   - the student's attributes that affect learning (e.g., number of schools attended, transience, absences, and lateness; student's background knowledge; exposure to the curriculum; mastery of basic skills, higher cognitive skills, and meta-cognitive strategies; learning style(s); locus of control/locus of attribution; rate of learning and response to intervention)

   - the student's health, sensory, medical, and motor functioning and developmental histories

   - social/emotional or behavioral factors that influence the student's learning

   - the student's strengths and interests that can be fostered during interventions

3. What factors influence ELL students' learning and language development? These include:

   - language development, proficiency, and dominance in the primary language

   - match between the student's primary language and languages of instruction

   - number of years of instruction in the primary and secondary languages

   - quality of instruction in all languages

   - language(s) used to teach each academic skill

   - degree of socialization with peers, and language(s) spoken by peers

   - the student's progress with second language acquisition and development in comparison to typical peers with similar backgrounds and experiences

4. What was the nature and quality of the Phase II and Phase III interventions?

   - Were the majority of the interventions research-based?

   - Were the interventions implemented as they were designed and intended?

   - Were methods to monitor and evaluate progress determined in advance?

   - Were guidelines for acceptable rates of progress based on developmental and curriculum standards developed in advance to determine whether the rate of progress is acceptable given the standards?

TABLE 26–1 (continued)

- What was the quality and rate of progress exhibited by the student when given appropriate instruction during interventions implemented in the classroom during Phases II and III?
- What amounts and types of individualized attention and structure were required for the student to acquire new skills?
- Is the student making steady progress at an acceptable rate even if the student is behind his/her age/grade level?
- Did the student continue to have difficulty despite intensive, effective interventions? What was the intensity of instruction necessary to achieve progress?
- What are the patterns of the difficulties, and are they similar to those seen in students with learning disabilities?

5. Did any factors affect the assessment process, such as student's degree of familiarity and comfort with the assessment process (e.g., methods and tasks utilized during evaluations) and degree of student's comfort with the examiner?

6. Are the student's learning difficulties better explained by issues of bias in the referral, intervention, or assessment stages rather than by the validity of the test results?

7. Do the results of the assessments and interventions correspond with the student's functioning at home, in the community, and in school?

riod of time to provide opportunities for the student to experience success. If the youngster continues to struggle despite valid interventions implemented as designed, then the team may consider referring the student for a Phase III evaluation to assess possible eligibility for special education.

Another function of the Phase II team is to analyze and synthesize the information obtained from multiple interventions in order to recommend interventions to improve achievement at the classroom and school levels. Areas of focus might include student supports, modifications in instructional methods, modifications in classroom and schoolwide discipline methods, and professional development activities (NABSE & ILIAD Project, 2002).

The composition of the Phase II team should reflect the referred child's specific situation and incorporate family members, teachers, and other appropriate school personnel, the student (where appropriate), as well as other persons familiar with the student. In addition to the general education teachers, other school personnel to consider at Phase II are: ESL and bilingual teachers, reading and math specialists, related service providers, and administrators. Resource people familiar with the student's and family's culture and situation should be consulted as needed. Administrative participation and support is crucial to the success of the team in order to provide authoritative support, identify and provide resources, and provide time for the team to carry out its functions (NABSE & ILIAD Project, 2002).

All Phase II team members should work collaboratively during the problem-solving process to prevent teachers, parents, and other team members from feeling blamed during the examination of external factors contributing to the student's learning difficulties. Table 26–1 provides a list of questions to examine during the Phase II process. The order and extent to which each question is examined depends on the student's specific circumstances as determined by the Phase II team.

Methods to gather information about the questions outlined in Table 26–1 include interviews with the student, family members, teachers, and others who are familiar with the student's learning; record reviews; surveys; observations in multiple settings, including school, home, and the community; reviews of the student's work samples; and observations of clinical teaching. In addition, health, sensory, medical, and motor functioning and developmental histories need to be reviewed to determine whether any of these factors affect learning. It also is important to identify any social/emotional or behavioral difficulties that might be affecting the student's learning.

For ELL students, language development, proficiency, and dominance in the primary and second languages should be determined, including dialects. An evaluation should be conducted that incorporates formal and informal assessment methods such as language samples, interviews, observations, and tests that tap language skills in the student's primary language and any other language(s) utilized in the student's learning tasks (Roseberry-McKibbin, 2002; Salend & Salinas, 2003). Members of the bilingual assessment team should be, whenever possible, bilingual and proficient in the students' native language. If necessary, as a less preferable option, trained interpreters might assist school professionals (e.g., Ortiz & Yates, 2002).

An accurate history of learning and language development in the primary language and any other languages is helpful when interpreting the results. Determining the student's language proficiency will also help to establish the language(s) to be used for assessment. There are very few valid formal assessment instruments available to evaluate proficiency in most languages other than Spanish and dialects other than Standard American English (SAE) (Lopez, 1995; Roseberry-McKibbin, 2002). In addition, few English proficiency tests evaluate CALP (Roseberry-McKibbin, 2002). When the student's level of CALP in English is unknown, it is not possible to interpret tests standardized only on English-speaking monolingual students. Furthermore, when the student's level of CALP is unknown in the primary language, it is not possible to draw valid inferences about learning or language disabilities from tests administered and standardized in English. It is important to utilize a wide range of assessment tools to evaluate language development and proficiency, tapping a variety of settings and tasks, including the evaluation of "communication competence" (Roseberry-McKibbin, p. 238), the effectiveness of functional and pragmatic skills in all social domains, as well as oral and written proficiency levels in all languages (e.g., Grossman, 1995; S. Ortiz, 2002; Roseberry-McKibbin, 2002).

After information about the student, family, classroom, community, and other environments has been collected and analyzed to gain understanding about the sources of the student's strengths, weaknesses, and learning difficulties, the next step is to use a problem-solving model to develop, implement, and monitor interventions that are targeted to the student's needs (e.g., Upah & Tilly, 2002). School psychologists should play an influential role in developing, monitoring, and evaluating these interventions. Table 26–1 lists issues to consider regarding the development, implementation, and monitoring of these interventions.

When collecting baseline data, informal and brief assessments such as curriculum-based assessment (CBA) (e.g., Gravois & Gickling, 2002) and curriculum-based measurement (CBM) (e.g., Shinn, 2002) provide valuable information for assessing the student's learning styles, instructional needs, and progress based on materials utilized in the classroom. The data are also helpful in developing educational interventions and modifications tailored to the student's unique strengths and needs. Repeated measures aid in tracking changes in progress and provide information to modify instructional methods in the classroom (e.g., L. S. Fuchs et al., 2002). Performance can be compared between assessments conducted in the student's primary and second languages to help determine whether difficulties are due to second language acquisition or to a disability (Ortiz & Yates, 2002). Portfolio assessments provide a development perspective in specific areas, including cognitive, academic, and language development over time (e.g., Gonzales et al., 1997). It is important to include observations in a variety of natural settings in order to obtain information about the student's overall communication, behavior, problem solving, and social skills at school and home. Results can be summarized using such methods as graphs, frequency charts, or descriptive reports (e.g., Upah & Tilly, 2002). Although the focus is on monitoring academic and behavioral progress in response to interventions, brief cognitive or academic assessments sometimes may assist in answering targeted questions and providing baseline data. However, during Phase II, the student's level of cognitive functioning generally is inferred from the response to interventions, rather than from direct assessment (Marston et al., 2002).

The extensive interventions conducted during Phase II need to be documented and evaluated for efficacy to determine whether or not they have resolved the learning difficulties. To do this, it is essential to analyze the multiple sources of data collected such as background information and the results of research-based, validated interventions implemented as designed to test and revise hypotheses and develop further interventions to meet any unmet needs (Upah & Tilly, 2002). All data must be evaluated in light of knowledge of the student's cultural, experiential, educational, familial, and linguistic contexts (S. Ortiz, 2002). The student's responsiveness to interventions during Phase II is evaluated periodically (approximately every 6–8 weeks) to determine whether there is an adequate rate of progress and to determine whether the current interventions can be maintained or need modification (NASP, 2003a). Examples of culturally responsive interventions are in Table 26–2 and in part III, Instructional and Classroom Interventions, of this volume.

If the student's difficulties persist, or if the rate of progress is inadequate within a reasonable period of time (approximately 6–8 weeks) following effective interventions that are implemented as designed, then it is important to analyze the sources of difficulties and look for other supports available in the classroom, school, and community (Ortiz & Garcia, 1998; S. Ortiz, 2002; Upah & Tilly, 2002). Based on the source(s) of the student's difficulties, the Phase II team determines whether to modify the current interventions or implement additional interventions.

TABLE 26–2
Recommended Instructional and Environmental Strategies for CLD Students

- Creating a learning community in the classroom and the school
- Fostering collaborative school and community relationships
- Incorporating students' culture and language into curriculum materials, classroom, and school environments in a meaningful way
- Using language that is comprehensible to students
- Making learning relevant by building on students' experiences, culture, and language
- Developing literacy and language skills in all aspects of the curriculum
- Adapting language content and levels to students' language proficiency level
- Modifying instructional methods to accommodate a variety of learning, relationship, communicational, and motivational styles
- Using a multisensory approach to learning and presenting information in multiple ways
- Using a variety of learning structures including large and small groups; dyads; individual configurations; student-directed and teacher-directed formats; and cooperative, individualistic, and competitive structures
- Teaching students to become responsible for their own learning
- Reinforcing independent learning by providing students with cognitive and metacognitive strategies that help them develop organization, self-regulation, and self-monitoring skills
- Providing frequent opportunities for practice, feedback, and generalization of learning
- Breaking down assignments and tasks into smaller components
- Providing multiple ways for students to demonstrate learning and knowledge
- Using learning tools such as computers and tape recorders
- Providing conceptual organizers, including mapping, story webs, advance organizers, vocabulary lists, and study guides to pre-teach and teach concepts and content
- Providing frequent opportunities to review information, practice new skills, and apply concepts

Note. Strategies recommended in the following sources: Cummins (1986); Cloud (2000); Figueroa (2002); Gersten & Baker (2000); Gersten, Baker & Marks (1998); Grossman (1995); NABSE & ILIAD Project (2002(; Roseberry-McKibbin (2002); Santamaria, Fletcher, & Bos (2002); Sileo & Prater (1998(; Vaughn et al. (1997).

If the difficulties persist despite the extensive interventions conducted during Phase II and a need for more intensive individualized instruction is indicated, then a referral for a Phase III assessment is appropriate to explore the need for special education services (NASP, 2003a; S. Ortiz, 2002). A Phase III team is then formed that includes members of the Phase II team with new members added if they have information or resources to assist with the Phase III problem- solving process. As is the case in Phase II, the goal of any Phase III assessments is to determine interventions to help the student succeed in school. Additional interventions may also be conducted at this time to provide new information about the student's responsiveness to specific interventions. During Phase III, team members conduct assessments to determine whether the student has a disability, and whether the student is eligible for special education services or for a referral for a

504 Plan that provides accommodations in the general education classroom. A third option is referring the student for more Phase II interventions if the student is not found eligible for special education or a 504 Plan. If the student is found eligible for special education, then Phase III assessments will result in the development and implementation of interventions, such as an individualized education program (IEP) and methods to monitor student progress.

Members of the Phase III team begin by utilizing the data collected during Phase II to devise a plan to guide the Phase III assessment and intervention process, including planning assessments, assuring that necessary information is collected for intervention planning, and developing and monitoring additional interventions. As part of the plan, the members of the team, such as the school psychologist, special education teachers, and speech/language specialists, need to determine the appropriate assessment methods/instruments necessary to conduct a nondiscriminatory assessment that minimizes bias.

Phase III assessment instruments include formal, standardized norm-referenced procedures, as well as measures like CBM, CBA, observations, and portfolio assessments that tap such areas as cognition, achievement, and behavioral/social-emotional functioning. Dynamic assessment is a useful method to gather information about the student's ability to learn in response to instruction and mediation (e.g., Feuerstein, 1979). Formal assessments can include standardized cognitive and achievement assessments. Assessment theory and practical applications for CLD students in the areas of cognitive, language, academic, neuropsychological, vocational, and personality and behavioral assessments are discussed in detail in part IV of this volume.

The results of interventions conducted during the assessment process play a crucial role in determining the source of learning difficulties (Figueroa, 2002). When interpreting assessment data, the results of informal measures should be compared with the results of standardized assessments. Low or uneven levels of performance on standardized and informal measures, combined with similar unevenness in the student's language, cognitive, and adaptive functioning in the home setting, may suggest the presence of a learning disability (Ortiz & Yates, 2002; Roseberry-McKibbin, 2002).

When there are problems with validity in assessment instruments, such as when test administration instructions are modified or when norms are not valid for the student's group, scores derived from these tests should not be used for such purposes as computing discrepancy formulas and for determining special education eligibility. Instead, the data should be described and used diagnostically to determine patterns of strengths and weaknesses and to identify areas of focus for planning interventions (Ortiz & Yates, 2002). Determination of eligibility should never be based solely on test results. Instead, data from Phase I, II, and III interventions, observations, and interviews should be integrated with formal and informal assessment results to determine whether there is significantly low underachievement and insufficient response to interventions (A. A. Ortiz & Yates, 2002; Roseberry-McKibbin, 2002). The results should also be examined in light of the student's cultural/linguistic background to place the information within a broader context when determining validity. As part of this Phase III review, it is important to explore the family's cultural and personal beliefs and attitudes toward disability in order to help them explore the impact of the young-ster's potential disability on the child and the family (Cloud, 2002).

Eligibility for special education services should be considered only when there is a determination that the learning difficulties are a result of a disability rather than due to such factors as limited exposure to curriculum; linguistic or cultural differ-ences; and problems that are primarily the result of visual, hearing, motor disabili-ties, mental retardation, emotional disturbance, environmental, cultural, or eco-nomic disadvantages (IDEA, 1997), including traumas, other upheavals, or family stressors. Only when these exclusionary factors are ruled out as the primary causes of the learning difficulty, and need is demonstrated by the student's lack of ade-quate responsiveness to Phase II and Phase III interventions, should the youngster be considered to have a learning disability (e.g., NASP, 2003a).

Whether or not a student is found eligible for special education, it is important that the assessment results be utilized to plan for continuing interventions in school, home, and community settings as appropriate. In all cases, an important outcome of Phase III is that the team develops methods to continue the communi-cation and collaboration among home, school, and community, and to continue to monitor and evaluate student progress.

Interventions should evolve from the team's problem-solving process and should be both "culturally and linguistically responsive" when developing the in-dividualized education program's (IEP) goals and objectives (Cloud, 2002, p. 107). Interventions may take place in the classroom, school, and community, as appro-priate. Table 26–2 describes instructional and environmental intervention strate-gies that have been found helpful for CLD students and students with learning dif-ficulties, and therefore are likely to be helpful for CLD students with learning disabilities.

When placement is made in special education for CLD students who are ELL, consideration must also be given to the nature and severity of both the second lan-guage needs and the disability (Roseberry-McKibbin, 2002). As is the case for all students placed in special education, the primary program placement options uti-lized in special education for CLD students include full inclusion in the general ed-ucation, bilingual education, or sheltered English classrooms with consultative and collaborative instruction provided by special education and speech-language per-sonnel within the classroom. Other options include inclusion in general education, or in a bilingual education or sheltered English classroom with pullout resource and speech-language services. More restrictive classrooms should be used with ex-treme caution, and substantial inclusion with appropriate supports should be pro-vided.

RECOMMENDATIONS FOR FUTURE PRACTICE AND RESEARCH

Broadening the role of school psychologists.   Working with CLD students provides exciting opportunities for school psychologists to enhance their roles in the schools. Recent changes occurring in the larger context of education (e.g., educational reform movement, No Child Left Behind Act, and the reauthorization of IDEA) stimulated questions and heated debate about the nature and role of assessment, and the implications for school psychologists, both in special education and general education (e.g., Gresham et al., 2003; Hyman et al., 2003; Rueda, 1997). It is important that the conceptual basis for assessment be broadened beyond narrow psychoeducational considerations to take into account children's entire learning environments, including school, home, and community (Cummins, 1989; Marston et al., 2002). Therefore, it becomes even more crucial to actively involve families and community resource members as key participants in problem-solving teams at all stages of the process, rather than paying lip service to the concept of family/parental involvement (Silverstein, Springer, & Russo, 1992). Rather than viewing the initial identification process as inevitably ending with admission to special education, we can choose to view the process as the impetus for a collaborative problem-solving process among school, family, and student, to provide interventions and develop student potential.

School psychologists should take a leadership role in this process by consulting with school, home, and community problem-solving team members to develop interventions to identify and change the underlying systemic forces that prevent change from occurring and to enhance the forces that support positive change (Canter, 2003; Sarason, 1996). Through such activities, school psychologists and other professionals can serve as advocates for students who have not always been well served by the current educational system.

Interdisciplinary collaboration. To best serve all students—including CLD students—school personnel, family members, and community members must work collaboratively to support students' development and learning in all school, home, and community contexts. It is important to develop a comprehensive procedure that utilizes the talents and expertise of professionals from multiple disciplines, administrative support and participation, and the talents and expertise of family and community members (e.g., Garcia, 2002; NABSE & ILIAD Project, 2002).

The problem-solving team approach requires systematic data collection and analysis, particularly when combined with district, state, and national data, in order to determine the adequacy of services and instruction provided to and received by all students (NASP, 2003a). It is important that the team determine methods for data collection, measurement and analysis, and how the data will be used (Upah & Tilly, 2002). The collaborative problem-solving team can assist in the collection and analysis of data to determine possible sources of bias that may be present in the classroom and in the Phase I, II, and III processes (S. Ortiz, 2002). The results may lead to recommendations for system change and professional development activities. School psychologists, with their unique combination of training and skills, should play a leadership role in the change process.

Systemic improvement of assessment, instruction, and structure. A focus solely on the assessment process cannot solve the complex problems of misidentification, misdiagnosis, and misplacement of CLD students. This narrow focus ignores the link between assessment and intervention, including instructional interventions targeted at students' specific needs and the underlying structures that reinforce power relationships that mitigate against effective change. Important components in improving the quality of educational services for all children include: (a) combining effective, research-based, instructional practices with systematic improvement at all phases of the educational decision-making process and all phases of the teaching–learning structures, and (b) assuring that appropriate and adequate resources are allocated to implement the interventions (NABSE & ILIAD Project, 2002; NASP, 2003a).

The overrepresentation of CLD students in special education and the high drop-out rates among CLD students indicate that a large number of these students are falling through the cracks, and often do not appear to receive adequate instructional assistance targeted to their cultural and linguistic needs (Gersten & Woodward, 1994). The NASBE and ILIAD Project (2002) members noted that overrepresentation of these students in special education generally is not an issue in schools where all school personnel and parents believe that all children can learn, have high expectations for students' learning, positively reinforce student participation and achievement, and work collaboratively to help students succeed. In contrast, in many school districts, only a limited number of support services and programs are available for CLD students who are experiencing academic difficulties. Programs available to CLD students often are fragmented, with little or no collaboration among the pullout special education programs, language assistance programs, remedial programs, and general education (Garcia & Fong, 2000). Without collaboration, integrated services and supports will not be available to meet the multifaceted needs of CLD students. School psychologists and other school professionals can play an important role in advocating and developing integrated services and supports.

Professional development and support for school personnel.   In   addition to teaching academic, cognitive, language, and social skills, effective teachers and other professionals incorporate students' cultures and languages in the teaching–learning process, incorporate respect for students' diverse backgrounds, and reinforce students' cultural identities to maximize their potential (A. A. Ortiz, 1997). Until these topics are effectively incorporated into preservice training programs, school personnel will likely need training at the inservice level in such areas as the interaction and influence of culture, language, communication, motivation, learning and relationship styles on the development and learning of CLD students, as well as training in methods and strategies that facilitate learning. In addition, the Phase II and Phase III collaborative problem-solving team members will likely need training and consultation in methods of problem solving and collaboration, as well as training in culturally and linguistically responsive assessments and interventions, including interventions to change the underlying regularities in schools (Cummins, 1986; Sarason, 1996). School psychologists should play an important role in advocating for and developing training programs, as well as serving as trainers and consultants where appropriate.

Recommendations for Research

Despite the large number of students from diverse cultures in the schools, there is a lack of empirically derived data to effectively explain the cognitive, psycholinguistic, emotional, and social development of CLD students, as well as the interaction of these developmental processes. For example, the rate and/or process of development in such areas as language and learning styles for students from bilingual and bicultural backgrounds may differ from that of monolingual students and may differ depending on the students' level of second language acquisition (Figueroa, 2002). Research is needed in these areas to guide the development of assessment instruments with appropriate norms for these groups, as well as to provide data-based theory for assessment and intervention. The deficit exists to some extent for all linguistic groups, but is most glaring for students who speak languages other than Spanish. The lack of comprehensive theoretical frameworks and the limited empirical data is even more glaring for CLD students with learning disabilities. Research to understand the nature of learning and language disabilities occurring concomitantly with linguistic and cultural differences, and research on assessing and intervening with CLD students with learning disabilities and language disorders is relatively scarce, given the extent of the problem and the needs of the increasing student population (Coutinho et al., 2002). Currently, much of the information in the literature regarding procedures to assess and intervene with CLD students with learning disabilities is experiential and anecdotal and has not been validated through empirical research, thus rendering a weak theoretical and research basis for developing interventions for change (Gonzalez et al., 1997; Roseberry-McKibbin, 2002). The three-phase model described in this chapter needs to be validated for its utility and effectiveness.

Current literature calls attention to issues that need to be investigated, including the disproportional representation of minority students in special education, appropriate instruments and procedures for assessing CLD students, effective instructional and intervention strategies to work with CLD students and their families, and the need for preservice and inservice training programs to ensure that educators have competencies to meet the needs of CLD students in both general and special education (e.g., Yates & Ortiz, 1991). Researchers from such disciplines as school and educational psychology, general education, special education, speech/language pathology, and bilingual and ESL education need to work collaboratively to examine these and other research issues related to CLD students with LD and to establish a stronger theoretical and research basis in this area (A. A. Ortiz, 1997).

The analysis of the factors and causes for both the disproportionate representation of CLD students in special education and the large number of CLD students who struggle in general education without being provided with appropriate instruction and services indicate an urgent need for the educational community to transcend the focus on technical aspects and expand to include sociocultural, sociohistorical, and political perspectives in practice and research. Research regarding misidentification and misplacement of CLD students needs to encompass issues such as equity and social justice in education (Mithaug, 1996), an advocacy approach for CLD students (Cummins, 1989), differentiation between disability and difference (Peters, 1993), and a sociocultural perspective in the teaching and learning process (Artiles & Zamora-Duran, 1997).

ANNOTATED BIBLIOGRAPHY

Artiles, A. J., & Ortiz, A. A. (2002). *English language learners with special education needs: Identification, assessment, and instruction.* Washington, DC: Center for Applied Linguistics.

This book describes the challenges involved in identifying, assessing, placing, and teaching English-language learners with special education needs. It describes program models and approaches, and assessment methods for guiding parent–school collaboration, and native and dual-language instruction.

Roseberry-McKibbin, C. (2002). *Multicultural students with special language needs: Practical strategies for assessment and intervention* (2nd ed.). Oceanside, CA: Academic Communication Associates.

This book, written by a speech-language pathologist, provides valuable, practical information for school professionals in such areas as cultural and linguistic factors that affect service delivery and the assessment of CLD students, and interventions for CLD students with special needs.

McCardle, P., Mele-McCarthy, J., Cutting, L., & Leos, K. (2005). Learning disabilities in English language learners: Identifying the issues [Special issue]. *Learning Disabilities: Research and Practice, 20,* 1–78.

A special issue that reviews recent developments in the field of learning disabilities relevant to English-language learners.

Thomas, A., & Grimes, J. (Eds.). (2002). *Best practices in school psychology—IV.* Bethesda, MD: National Association of School Psychologists.

This two-volume reference is the latest in a series that deals with such important topics as prevention, intervention, assessment, collaboration, consultation, problem solving, legal and ethical issues, training, and professional standards. The chapters present valuable suggestions for working with CLD children and youth, their families, and school personnel.

Vaughn, S., Bos, C., & Schumm, J. (2003). *Teaching exceptional, diverse, and at-risk students in the general education classroom* (3rd ed.). Boston: Pearson Allyn & Bacon.

This text provides practical strategies for working with students with disabilities, culturally diverse students, students with limited English proficiency, economically disadvantaged students, and other students at risk. This book suggests numerous learning activities, sample lessons, and curriculum adaptations addressing both elementary and secondary classrooms for teaching reading, writing, mathematics, and content areas.

RESOURCES

National Association of School Psychologists:
http://www.nasponline.org

The website contains information about the organization, position statements, publications, and links and resources for working with students and families and for advocacy with legislators.

Council for Exceptional Children:
http://www.cec-sped.org

The website contains information about organizations, publication catalogs, and resources for working with children with disabilities from a wide range of linguistic and cultural backgrounds.

Culturally and Linguistically Appropriate Services Institute from the University of Illinois at Urbana-Champaign:
http://www.clas.uiuc.edu

The website is a resource and clearinghouse designed specifically for CLD young children with disabilities and their families.

REFERENCES

American Psychological Association. (2002). Ethical principles of psychologists and code of conduct. *American Psychologist, 57*, 1060–1073.

Artiles, A. J., & Zamora-Duran, G. (1997). Disproportionate representation: A continuous and unsolved predicament. In A. J. Artiles & G. Zamora-Duran (Eds.), *Reducing disproportion representation of culturally diverse students in special and gifted education* (pp.1–6). Reston, VA: Council for Exceptional Children.

Bergan, J. E., & Kratochwill, T. R. (1990). *Behavioral consultation and therapy*. New York: Plenum.

Bronfenbrenner, U. (1979). *The ecology of human development: Experiments by nature and design.* Cambridge, MA: Harvard University Press.

Canter, A. (2003, May). Recommendations regarding LD identification: Fear versus data. *Communique, 31*(7), 9.

Cernosia, A. (2005, June). *The reauthorization IDEA and new case law.* Workshop conducted in the County School District, Las Vegas, NV.

Cloud, N. (2002). Culturally and linguistically responsive instructional planning. In A. J. Artiles & A. A. Ortiz (Eds.), *English language learners with special education needs: Identification, assessment, and instruction* (pp. 107–132). McHenry, IL: Center for Applied Linguistics & Delta Systems.

Collier, V. P. (1992). A synthesis of studies examining long-term language minority student data on academic achievement. *Bilingual Research Journal, 23*, 509–531.

Council for Exceptional Children. (2004, November). *The New IDEA: CEC's summary of significant issues.* Retrieved January 9, 2005, from http://www.cec-sped.org

Coutinho, M. J., Oswald, D. P., & Best, A. M. (2002). The influence of sociodemographics and gender on the disproportionate identification of minority students as having learning disabilities. *Remedial and Special Education, 23*, 49–59.

Cummins, J. (1984). *Bilingualism and special education: Issues in assessment and pedagogy.* San Diego, CA: College-Hill.

Cummins, J. (1986). Empowering minority students: A framework for intervention. In C. Baker & N. Hornberger (Eds.), *Introductory reader to the writings of Jim Cummins* (pp. 175–199). Clevedon, England: Multilingual Matters.

Cummins, J. (1989). A theoretical framework for bilingual special education. *Exceptional Children, 56*, 111–119.

Cummins, J. (1991). Interdependence of first and second language proficiency in bilingual children. In E. Bialystok (Ed.), *Language processing in bilingual children* (pp. 70–89). Cambridge, England: Cambridge University Press.

Damico, J. S. (1991). Descriptive assessment of communicative ability in limited English proficient students. In E. V. Hamayan & J. S. Damico (Eds.), *Limiting bias in the assessment of bilingual students* (pp. 157–217). Austin, TX: Pro-Ed.

Diana v. State Board of Education. No. C–70–37 (N.D. CA 1970).

Dunn, L. M. (1968). Special education for the mildly retarded: Is much of it justifiable? *Exceptional Children, 23*, 5–21.

Feuerstein, R. (1979). *Dynamic assessment of retarded performers: The learning potential assessment device, theory, instruments, and techniques.* Baltimore: University Park Press.

Figueroa, R. A. (2002). Toward a new model of assessment. In A. J. Artiles & A. A. Ortiz (Eds.), *English language learners with special education needs: Identification, assessment, and instruction* (pp. 51–64). McHenry, IL: Center for Applied Linguistics & Delta Systems.

Fuchs, L. S., Fuchs, D., & Speece, D. L. (2002). Treatment validity as a unifying construct for identifying learning disabilities. *Learning Disability Quarterly, 25*, 33–45.

Garcia, P., & Fong, K. (2000). Profiles of Asian American students with LD at initial referral, assessment, and placement in special education. *Journal of Learning Disabilities, 33*, 61–72.

Garcia, S. B. (2002). Parent-professional collaboration in culturally sensitive assessment. In A. J. Artiles & A. A. Ortiz (Eds.), *English language learners with special education needs: Identification, assessment, and instruction* (pp. 87–103). McHenry, IL: Center for Applied Linguistics & Delta Systems.

Gersten, R., & Baker, S. (2000). What we know about effective instructional practices for English language learners. *Exceptional Children, 66*, 454–470.

Gersten, R., Baker, S. K., & Marks, S. U. (1998). *Teaching English-language learners with leaning difficulties. Guiding principles and examples from research-based practice.* Reston, VA: Council for Exceptional Children, ERIC Clearinghouse on Disabilities and Gifted Education. (ERIC Document Reproduction Service No. ED 427 448)

Gersten, R., & Woodward, J. (1994). The language-minority student and special education: Issues, trends, and paradoxes. *Exceptional Children, 60*, 310–322.

Gonzales, V., Brusca-Vega, R., & Yawkey, T. (1997). *Assessment and instruction of culturally and linguistically diverse students with or at-risk of learning problems: From research to practice.* Boston: Allyn & Bacon.

Gravois, T., & Gickling, E. (2002). *Best practices in curriculum-based assessment.* In A. Thomas & J. Grimes (Eds.), *Best practices in school psychology IV* (pp. 885–898). Bethesda, MD: National Association of School Psychologists.

Gresham, F., Vanderwood, M., McCurdy, M., Watson, T. S., Noell, G., & Witt, J. (2003). Identification and intervention with learning disabilities: An empirical perspective. *Communique, 31*(8), 6–13.

Grossman, H. (1995). *Special education in a diverse society.* Boston: Allyn & Bacon.

Hyman, I., Fiorello, C., Blue, L., Kalberer, S., Quann, R., & Mattie, D. (2003). Diagnosing and intervening with learning disabilities: "Déjà vu all over again." *Communique, 31*(6), 10–14.

Individuals With Disabilities Education Act (IDEA). (1997). 20 U.S.C. Ch 33. Sec 1400.

Individuals With Disabilities Education Act (IDEA). (1999). Regulations, 4 C.F.R. Part 300.

Klotz, M. B., & Nealis, L. (2005). *The new IDEA: A summary of significant reforms.* Retrieved January 9, 2005, from http://www.nasponline.org

Krashen, S. D. (1985). *The input hypothesis: Issues and implications.* London: Longman.

Larry P. v. Riles. 343 F. Supp. 1306 (N.D. CA. 1972), affr 502 F.2d 963 (9th Cir. 1974), 495 f. Supp 926 (N.D. CA. 1979).

Lock, R. H., & Layton, C. A. (2002). Isolating intrinsic processing disorders from second language acquisition. *Bilingual Research Journal, 26*, 383–394.

Lopez, E. C. (1995). Best practices in working with bilingual children. In A. Thomas & J. Grimes (Eds.), *Best practices in school psychology III* (pp. 1111–1121). Washington, DC: National Association of School Psychologists.

Marston, D., Canter, A., Lau, M., & Muyskens, P. (2002). *NASP Communique, 30*(8), 15–16.

Mattes, L. J., & Omark, D. R. (1991). *Speech and language assessement for the bilingual handicapped* (2nd ed.). Oceanside, CA: Academic Communication Associates.

Mithaug, D. E. (1996). *Equal opportunity theory.* Thousand Oaks, CA: Sage.

National Alliance of Black School Educators & IDEA Local Implementation by Local Administrators Project. (2002). *Addressing over-representation of African American students in special education: The prereferral intervention process—An administrator's guide.* Arlington, VA: Council for Exceptional Children, and Washington, DC: National Alliance of Black School Educators.

National Association of School Psychologists. (2003a). NASP recommendations: LD eligibility and identification for IDEA reauthorization. Position statement. *Communique, 31*(8), 1–6.

National Association of School Psychologists. (2003b). *Portraits of the children: Culturally competent assessment* [Videotape and CD-ROM]. Bethesda, MD: Author.

National Association of School Psychologists/National Coalition of Advocates for Students (2002). NASP position statement advocating for appropriate educational services for all children. In A. Thomas & J. Grimes (Eds.), *Best practices in school psychology IV* (pp. 1683–1685). Bethesda, MD: Author.

Ortiz, A. A. (1997). Learning disabilities occurring concomitantly with linguistic differences. *Journal of Learning Disabilities, 30*, 321–332.

Ortiz, A. A. (2002). Prevention of school failure and early intervention for English language learners. In A. J. Artiles & A. A. Ortiz (Eds.), *English language learners with special education needs: Identification, assessment, and instruction* (pp. 31–48). McHenry, IL: Center for Applied Linguistics & Delta Systems.

Ortiz, A. A., & Garcia, S. B. (1988). A prereferral process for preventing inappropriate referrals of Hispanic students to special education. In A. A. Ortiz & B. A. Ramirez (Eds.), *Schools and the culturally diverse exceptional student: Promising practices and future directions* (pp. 6–18). Reston, VA: Council for Exceptional Children.

Ortiz, A. A., & Yates, J. R. (2002). Considerations in the assessment of English language learners referred to special education. In A. J. Artiles, & A. A. Ortiz (Eds.), *English language learners with special education needs: Identification, assessment, and instruction* (pp. 65–85). McHenry, IL: Center for Applied Linguistics & Delta Systems.

Ortiz, S. (2002). Best practices in nondiscriminatory assessment. In A. Thomas & J. Grimes (Eds.), *Best practices in school psychology IV* (pp. 1321–1336). Bethesda, MD: National Association of School Psychologists.

Peters, S. J. (1993). An ideological-cultural framework for the study of disability. In S. J. Peters (Ed.), *Education and disability in cross-cultural perspective* (pp. 19–37). New York: Garland.

Poplin, M., & Phillips, L. (1993). Sociocultural aspects of language and literacy: Issues facing educators of students with learning disabilities. *Learning Disability Quarterly, 16*, 245–255.

Reschley, D. J. (2004a, March). *Disproportionate minority representation: New solutions to old problems.* Workshop conducted at the Visions Conference, Clark County School District, Las Vegas, NV.

Reschley, D. J. (2004b, March). *Special education reform: School psychology "I told you so."* Keynote address conducted at the Visions Conference, Clark County School District, Las Vegas, NV.

Reschley, D., Tilly, W. D., III., & Grimes, J. (Eds.). (1999). *Special education in transition: Functional assessment and non-categorical programming.* Longmont, CD: Sopris West.

Reschley, D., & Ysseldyke, J. (2002). Paradigm shift: The past is not the future. In A. Thomas & J. Grimes (Eds.), *Best practices in school psychology IV* (pp. 3–20). Bethesda, MD: National Association of School Psychologists.

Riles, L. P. (1972). C–71–2270 USC, 343 F. Supplement 120 (N.D. Cal. 1972).

Roseberry-McKibbin, C. (2002). *Multicultural students with special language needs: Practical strategies for assessment and intervention* (2nd ed.). Oceanside, CA: Academic Communication Associates.

Rueda, R. (1997). Changing the context of assessment: The move to portfolios and authentic assessment. In A. J. Artiles & G. Zamora-Duran (Eds.), *Reducing disproportion representation of culturally diverse students in special and gifted education* (pp. 7–25). Reston, VA: Council for Exceptional Children.

Salend, S. J., & Salinas, A. (2003). Language differences or learning difficulties: The work of the multidisciplinary team. *Teaching Exceptional Children, 35*(4), 36–43.

Santamaria, L. J., Fletcher, T. V., & Bos, C. S. (2002). Effective pedagogy for English language learners in inclusive classrooms. In A. J. Artiles & A. A. Ortiz (Eds.), *English language learners with special education needs: Identification, assessment, and instruction* (pp. 133–157). McHenry, IL: Center for Applied Linguistics & Delta Systems.

Sarason, S. B. (1996). *Revisiting "The culture of the school and the problem of change."* New York: Teachers College Press.

Shinn, M. R. (2002). Best practices in using curriculum-based measurement in a problem-solving model. In A. Thomas & J. Grimes (Eds.), *Best practices in school psychology IV* (pp. 671–698). Bethesda, MD: National Association of School Psychologists.

Sileo, T., & Prater, M. A. (1998). Creating classroom environments that address the linguistic and cultural backgrounds of students with disabilities: An Asian Pacific American perspective. *Remedial and Special Education, 19*, 323–357.

Silverstein, J., Springer, J., & Russo, N. (1992). Involving parents in the special education process. In S. L. Christenson & J. C. Conoley (Eds.), *Home–school collaboration: Enhancing children's academic and social competence* (pp. 383–407). Silver Spring, MD: National Association of School Psychologists.

Swain, M. (1985). Communicative competence: Some roles of comprehensible input and comprehensible output in its development. In S. M. Gass & C. G. Madden (Eds.), *Input in second language acquistion* (pp. 235–253). Rowley, MA: Newbury House.

Telzrow, C., & Tankersley, M. (2000). *IDEA amendments of 1997: Practice guidelines for school based teams.* Bethesda, MD: National Association of School Psychologists.

Thomas, A., & Grimes, J. (Eds.). (2002). *Best practices in school psychology—IV* (pp. 1615–1636). Bethesda, MD: National Association of School Psychologists.

U.S. Department of Education. (2001). The 23rd annual report to Congress on the implementation of the Individuals With Disabilities Education Act. Retrieved June 20, 2005, from http://www.ed.gov/about/reports/annual/osep/2000/execsumm.html

Upah, K., & Tilly, W. D. (2002). Best practices in designing, implementing, and evaluating quality interventions. In A. Thomas & J. Grimes (Eds.), *Best practices in school psychology IV* (pp. 483–501). Bethesda, MD: National Association of School Psychologists.

Urban Special Education Leadership Collaborative. (2004, November 19). IDEA reauthorization: Congress passes special education bill. *CollabNews, 7, Special IDEA Report.* Retrieved January 9, 2005, from http://www. Urbancollaborative.org

Vaughn, S., Bos, C., & Schumm, J. (2003). *Teaching mainstreamed, diverse, and at-risk students in the general education classroom* (3rd ed.). Boston: Allyn & Bacon.

Yates, J. R., & Ortiz, A. A. (1991). Professional development needs of teachers who serve exceptional language minorities in today's schools. *Teacher Education and Special Education, 14*, 11–18.

27

CULTURALLY AND LINGUISTICALLY DIVERSE COLLEGE-AGE STUDENTS

Judith Kaufman and Jonell Sanchez

Fairleigh Dickinson University

"The University is simply the canary in the coalmine. It is the most sensitive barometer of social change."

—James Perkins

"Prejudice is a burden which confuses the past, threatens the future and renders the present inaccessible."

—Maya Angelou

"What sets the world in motion is the interplay of differences, their attractions and repulsions. Life is plurality, death uniformity. By suppressing differences and peculiarities, by eliminating different civilizations and cultures, progress weakens life and favors death."

—Octavio Paz (1967)

The nature of the college campus has changed significantly in the past 25 years. Campuses that saw predominately White middle-class men are now populated by both men and women of all classes, with a least 25% non-White students attending college. In addition, college campuses not only welcome, but also actively recruit, international students from all over the world, and have become increasingly global in orientation and outlook. The United States hosts the largest number of international students of any country in the world, with over 40% of the international students coming from Asia (Zikopoulous, 1990).

Although the change in the overall complexion of universities provides exciting educational, cultural, and social opportunities, there are significant concerns about facilitating positive adjustment of the culturally and linguistically different student, as well as the international student. If the acculturation process is not successfully negotiated and supported, there can be a significant impact on self-esteem and challenges to the transition to productive adulthood (Lee, 1987).

Research targeting the culturally and linguistically diverse (CLD) and the international student is limited, although a body of literature does exist that focuses on the meaning of college to students in general. Further, there is a limited amount of research focusing on second-language learning for the college student population and even less evidenced-based research clarifying the mental health needs of CLD, immigrant, and international students.

The remainder of the chapter identifies the particular needs for the three identified groups, focusing on the campus environment as well as individual and interpersonal issues. Although less than 8% of colleges and universities employ school psychologists (Tuite & Kaufman, 1998), the potential role of the school psychologist in program development, direct service, and consultation is addressed. Suggestions for prevention, early intervention, and treatment, as well as the importance of developing an environment of cultural pluralism and training individuals who are culturally competent, are addressed.

THEORETICAL AND RESEARCH BASIS

The acceptance and celebration of diversity are included in many university mission statements. How these statements are translated into campus climate, programming, and support services varies considerably. Levine (1989) discussed the "changing demographic landscape" (p. 5) in American higher education, reflected by a radical shift to include new populations attending college. There are, of course, regional differences, and all areas of the country have not been affected in the same way.

Admissions decisions not only impact on the individual attending college, but on the entire social context of the institution (Orfield, 2001). In some institutions, demographic change became a social and political imperative (Traub, 2003), recruiting diverse students with little change in orientation, philosophy, services, or pedagogical delivery systems. Thus, the institution can meet the goal of affirmative action that is quantitative, rather than "affirmative diversity," which is substantive and qualitative, with a focused attempt to discover ways in which the diversity of humanity contributes to resiliency and strength. Orfield (2001) indicates that schools with rich diversity offer a more expanded education and intellectually richer campus life because students who are exposed to diverse experiences learn to think about more complex issues.

In 1978, the U.S Supreme Court ruled (referred to as the Bakke decision) that universities could consider race as a "plus factor" in admissions polices, but could not impose quotas (Ball, 2000). The rationale was to ensure a diversity of viewpoints. Recently challenged by the actions of the University of Michigan, the Supreme Court's June 2003 ruling upheld the use of race-awareness admissions policies' certain stipulations to "obtain educational benefits that flow from a diverse student body" (Lane, 2003; Kersting & Dittmann, 2003).

Although the intent of the law may be positive, significant issues must be addressed, particularly that of the impact of poor elementary and secondary education in poor and minority communities. Thus, the "plus factor" individuals may potentially be handicapped in competing in the more traditional academic arenas (Traub, 2003). Merely admitting a diversity of students does not guarantee that the climate, faculty, flexibility, and content will change, nor that they will succeed.

Current attrition rates attest to higher education's failure to meet the needs of CLD students. Although postsecondary enrollment of CLD students has increased significantly—from 17.4% minority in 1975 to 26.4% in 1999 (NCES, 2002)—the numbers lag behind that of the White population. African Americans and Hispanics together constitute 26% of the American population, yet hey represent only 16% of the students enrolled in 4-year colleges and universities (NCES, 2002). Similarly, college completion rates for these same students lag far behind that of White students, with a recent significant decrease in retention rates for Hispanic students specifically and for minority males in general. Asian American students demonstrate the highest retention rates among the CLD population (U.S. Department of Education, 2002).

Although it is well substantiated that institutions of higher education actively recruit international students, no data are available reflecting degree completion rates for international students.

At least three separate groups contribute to the cultural and linguistic diversity of our campuses: the American-born CLD, the immigrant/exile/refugee population or those who come from other countries during their childhood years and make the United States their home, and the international student population who come to the United States for educational reasons and expect to return to their mother country. Although institutions of higher education are meeting their social responsibility and admitting CLD students, it becomes clear that at many levels these same institutions are not meeting the academic, linguistic, and mental health needs of these populations. Our colleges and universities may not, in fact, be aware of the needs of the populations, as demonstrated by the paucity of research in the area, nor do they have the resources to provide the necessary services.

Although there is a certain artificiality in categorizing these three groups, the focus of the chapter is to highlight both the similarity and differences in the needs of these groups, as well as consider primarily the traditional college-age student.

What Happens to Students in College?

The meaning/purpose of college continues to be debated and ranges from the cynical, "Four more years to support and avoid the world of work" to the attribution of a transformational experience, cognitively, socially, and academically (Astin, 1993; Pascarella & Terenzini, 1991). The understanding of what college means to students can provide insight into the issues and concerns that arise during these critical years. With the foundation of examining what college means in general, it is then possible to examine the unique challenges college brings for the CLD student.

Obviously growth and development continue regardless of whether a student has attended college. However, the issue becomes: What is the value added through college attendance? The answer to this complex question derives from examining the interaction of the college characteristics—size, type, location, and campus culture—in combination with student characteristics to examine students' affective and cognitive characteristics subsequent to exposure or college involvement (Astin, 1993). Over 50% of students do not graduate from the institution at which they started; this suggests that finding a good match is a difficult task.

The most influential theorist on the study of college student development is Chickering (1969), who focuses on the seven vectors of student development, all of which only evolve if the environment stimulates the growth. With a primary focus on identity, not dissimilar to Erikson (1978), the vectors or directions include: (a) achieving competence in social and interpersonal relations as well as intellectual areas, with an emphasis on sense of competence or one's ability to cope; (b) managing emotions, particularly those dealing with sex and aggression, without parental supervision and developing an increasing capacity for passion and commitment through intelligent behavior; (c) developing autonomy with independence and maturity that is both emotional and instrumental; (d) establishing identity, which includes a solid sense of self; (e) freeing interpersonal relationships with an increased tolerance and respect for those of different backgrounds and lifestyles; (f) developing a purpose or focus with an integration of priorities; and (g) developing integrity in the evolution of a personal set of beliefs.

The transition into adult roles or emerging adulthood that extends from the late teens to mid-20s, coinciding with the typical college years, is characterized by self-focused exploration of possibilities of love, work, and worldviews and preparation for participation in an adult society (Arnett, 2002). Obviously the environment plays a critical role in developmental change and adjustment, and thus changes during the college years cannot take place without a context.

Some of the characteristics that point to satisfaction with college include: living on campus, a student-oriented culture as opposed to a research institution, faculty satisfaction with the institution, and satisfaction with a peer group, even at this level of education. In fact, peer group involvement emerges as the most important variable impacting on cognitive, affective, psychological, and behavioral change leading to student satisfaction. If college is successful, changes are seen in the further development of positive self-image, establishing a greater sense of interpersonal and intellectual competency, and the development of altruism and a sense of social justice. Conversely, if the campus culture and the peer group relationships are a poor match, the individual's sense of well-being can significantly decline and contribute to significant mental health problems.

It should be noted that where students evaluated the impact of incorporating diversity, positive gains were demonstrated in an increase in college satisfaction, a decrease in materialistic values, an increase in political awareness, and an increase in the ability to deal with complex problem solving. According to Light (2001), students report that racial and ethnic diversity enhance learning experiences in the classroom and beyond.

College has been viewed as the transition from childhood to adulthood, and the 4 years of college have been likened to an abbreviated developmental life span (Koplewicz, 2002). Although college experiences vary, adulthood has been defined in a relatively homogeneous way, with minimal consideration of ethnic and cultural variation (Erikson, 1978). It is interesting to note that American culture, through the law, uses the term *adulthood* merely to differentiate from *childhood*, which ends legally at age 18 in most situations, and does not set forth standards of ethical and moral behavior except for those minimal standards that are in keeping with the law.

The cultural and ethnic variations, along with the developmental expectations, impact on what college means and, ultimately, on the philosophical and actual campus climate. It has been well established that climate can impact on perceptions and behavior and ultimately on the mental health of the college student. In addressing the concept of ecological validity, Brofenbrenner (1977) discusses whether the environment experienced by the participants has the properties it is supposed to or presumed to have by those creating the environment. Thus, if the college landscape does not incorporate the diverse perceptions, values, and interpretations of its participants, there clearly can be a significant dissonance that can directly impact on the psychological well-being of the student population and the professionals who support them.

LINGUISTIC AND MENTAL HEALTH ISSUES AND CHALLENGES

The college years present a unique developmental challenge incorporating all of the challenges of adolescence without, in many cases, parental awareness of or presence in the day-to-day life events. During freshman year, the student deals with issues of separation, forms new social relationships, develops a future orientation through choice of major and potential career, develops personal ethics, separates from parents with both freedom and responsibility, reconciles fantasy with reality (particularly the fantasy of reinventing oneself), and experiences sleep deprivation and the challenges of peer pressure, sex, drugs, and alcohol, as well as the challenge of dealing with increasingly complex information and concepts. During sophomore and junior years, challenges include: academics, career choices and goals, finding the right major, relationships (both romantic and in friendship), issues surrounding sexual orientation, clarification of a value system, and emerging as being potentially different from one's family of origin. During senior year, confronting of the end of a significant phase of life, facing reality, and renegotiating relationships with the shift to the independent adult world are significant challenges (Koplewicz, 2002).

College can be a challenging road to negotiate for all students. What happens in college may have long-term consequences for the individual. Many students have encountered multiple stressors prior to entering college, coupled with the typical stressors, such as leaving home, choosing a major, keeping up grades, creating and maintaining friendships, and negotiating intimate relationships.

IMPLICATIONS FOR PRACTICE

There are, of course, unique challenges for CLD and international students. Without taking into account culture and its impact on adjustment to the college experience, we stand to either over- or underidentify mental health concerns. There is a critical balance between the consideration of cultural issues and variables and the contemporary context and acceptability of the behaviors.

Cultural Diversity and Mental Health Challenges

All too often the burden of adjustment to the mainstream campus culture is placed on the student, rather than the institution in meeting the student halfway. Along with the normatively occurring developmental stressors, the CLD student needs to become aware of: (a) the college's learning demands, (b) negotiating an unfamiliar cultural milieu, (c) adapting to different/new expectations without cultural/familial support, (d) feeling different, (e) different normative cultures and expectations, and (f) dealing with issues of marginalization.

These risk factors may exaggerate the adjustment variables present for all college students. It is debatable whether all CLD students are faced with similar stressors and mental health challenges or whether there are issues and solutions particular to a specific cultural group independent of individual differences. However, it should be noted that a cultural context, such as a college campus, can be a major stressor by confronting individuals with demands that may exceed their ability and resources to cope (Marsella, 1998). Yoder (1995) suggests that there are cultural differences in the definition of selfhood and personhood when coming from a collectivistic versus individualistic culture and whether the emergence of symptomatology will be in the somatic or interpersonal domains. Although there is limited data-based evidence, the speculation warrants serious consideration.

Marsella (1998) highlights the cultural limitations and ethnocentrism in *Diagnostic and Statistical Manual of Mental Disorders* (4th ed. [*DSM–IV*]; American Psychiatric Association, 1994) as it decontextualizes behavior and does not account for cultural expectations. He raises a series of defining questions that are critical to keep in mind:

1. What role do cultural variables play in the etiology of mental disorders?
2. Are there cultural variations in standards of normality/abnormality?
3. Are there cultural variations in the classification and diagnosis of psychopathology?
4. Are there cultural variations in the expression, course, and outcome of psychopathology?

A survey conducted by the American College Health Association (cited in Koplewicz, 2002) reported that a significant percentage of American college students feel very bad a good deal of the time, with a majority of those individuals reporting intense hopelessness at least some of the time. At least 3 million adolescents have been reported to have symptoms of depression (Wingert & Kantrowitz, 2002), and among college students, reports of depressive symptoms have almost doubled. There is a reported increase in college counseling services over the past 10 years, with more complex issues and problems documented (Benton et al., 2003; O'Connor, 2001). To further complicate the issue, there are few professionals who are bilingual and/or ethnically diverse in proportion to the number of students in need.

An additional layer of complexity is the management of the mental health needs of the international students who are appearing on our campuses in increased numbers (Mori, 2000; Oropeza, Fitzgibbon, & Baron, 1991). Depression and anxiety have proved to be the two great mental health concerns (Roberts, Roberts, & Chen, 1997; Weinberg & Emslie, 1987), along with a sense of helplessness, social withdrawal, loneliness, homesickness, paranoia, and Obsessive–Compulsive Disorder (OCD). The intensity of these symptoms may vary with ethnicity and have been exacerbated for students from the Middle East since 9/11 (Coates, et al., 2003). To highlight specific cultural issues, findings from culturally specific research are cited. Cheng's research (1997) points to the different coping styles between Chinese and American late adolescents. The Elizabeth Shinn case at MIT painfully highlights the ways in which different cultures deal with stress. Elizabeth was identified by her peers as being seriously depressed. However, she did not seek any support services and ultimately committed suicide in her residence hall room (Sontag, 2002). It has been well documented that individuals who are of an Asian background have a significant tendency to somatize depression. Roberts et al. (1997) highlights the high rate of depression among Mexican Americans, with females demonstrating the highest rates. Fatalism appears to be a prevailing outlook, with feelings of lack of control leading to impaired coping and, ultimately, psychological distress (Weinberg & Emslie, 1987).

One of the primary considerations in understanding the international student is the nature of culture shock. Culture shock may impact those entering college from a significantly different background and has been identified as a psychological change in the cultural environment. Symptoms include depression (Willie, 1988), hopelessness (Brislin, 1981), a negative reaction to the new surroundings, homesickness, loneliness and withdrawal, and the quest for a more familiar environment (Parr, Bradley, & Bingi, 1992). Research has indicated that the acute point is between the 3rd and 12th months of stay (Oropeza et al., 1991). The degree of culture shock is dependent on the degree of cultural difference, the level of maturity of the student and tolerance for ambiguity, and the degree of satisfaction with the mother culture, with a high degree of satisfaction relating to a better adjustment of the new culture and the preparation for adjustment.

Linguistic Diversity and the College Student

Language usage is a critical factor in all human interactions. Language competence contributes significantly to overall adjustment and cultural participation (Ying, 1995). Taiwanese international students who only associated with other Chinese peers reported lower depression levels (Ying & Liese, 1994) because they were protected from cultural differences and misunderstandings. However, those who ventured forth and tolerated the discomfort formed significant friendships with non-Chinese and reported better adjustment overall.

Individuals who are not understood by the larger community in which they live may be labeled more quickly as pathological and emotionally withdrawn or withholding (Bemack & Chung, 2000; Berry & Kim, 1988). There is a limited amount of research addressing the language needs of the college student whose first language is not English. For individuals who are citizens of the United States or enter college with the United States as their home country, there is no screening, aside from state-mandated basic skills testing. Students who attend college from other countries (including English-speaking countries) are typically given the Test of English as a Foreign Language (TOEFL), which is intended to measure proficiency in English in an academic setting (Pederson, 1991). Although assuring a baseline understanding of English for all students, there is a pronounced gap in the actual reading, comprehension, writing skills, and communication in the classroom and in the campus milieu (Jamison et al., 2000). Therefore, although the international student may score in the passing range, his or her ability to keep up in the classroom may be limited, as well as the ability to communicate with classmates and roommates. All too often international students socialize with individuals of their own linguistic background. Further, should an international student seek mental health services, the expression of thoughts and feelings might be extremely difficult in a language other than the mother tongue (Oropeza, Fitzgibbon, & Baron, 1991).

Second-language proficiency is a daunting and frustrating experience (McLaughlin, 1992). What is less apparent are the linguistic difficulties American-born and immigrant students of different linguistic backgrounds may be experiencing and their struggle to compete with the native-English-speaking student. Even for those individuals who can communicate fluently in English, some may not have mastered the more disembedded and decontextualized aspects of the language, referred to as the "Linguistic façade" (Cummins, 1980).

IMPLEMENTATION AND APPROACHES

Transition Programs

The development of and participation in quality transition programs is essential to CLD and international students' adjustment to the college environment. If, indeed, culture shock is a critical variable and brings with it the negative consequences as discussed by Oropeza et al. (1996), anticipating the issues and need of our populations can serve as a primary prevention.

Mentoring

What role can good mentoring play in supporting the transition to college and throughout the college years for CLD students? Although Liang et al. (2002) focus on women in particular, looking at quality and nature of relations rather than quantity, their findings may have broader implications. Connections (Liang ,et al. 2002; Sullivan, 1996) are at the forefront of development. In mutually self-disclosing relationships, which have empathic qualities, emotional resilience is fostered. Most mentoring programs, unfortunately, have offered limited training, with few guidelines as to the content and outcomes expected, and have yielded results less than expected. However, with training and an emphasis on engagement, authenticity, and empowerment, mentoring models can have an important impact on the adjustment of CLD individuals on college campuses.

Training for Cultural Competency

At all levels of education, psychologists must develop cultural competence, which is a constant learning process (Lopez & Rogers, 2001; Sleek, 1998), and be in a position to facilitate that growth in others. This is particularly important on our college campuses, where individuals other than student affairs staff are deeply involved in their own academic discipline and/or job responsibility and there is a lack of awareness and understanding of the evolving college landscape. Among the core competencies associated with becoming culturally literate are awareness, counseling competence, knowledge of legal and ethical issues, assessment, and knowledge of cross-cultural research (Lopez & Rogers, 2001).

Leadership Training for Students

With the demonstrated effectiveness of mentorship programs, it is important to consider the role that students can play in creating a campus embracing affirmative diversity. An approach that has received attention includes developing student leaders who can become stewards and teaching people to care about and respect one another and to care about community building within the university. Under the direction of the psychologist, identified students can be trained to develop those skills to manage conflict and develop empathic understanding. Students define the campus climate and can promote values for a future society including those of inclusiveness, empathic communication, and one that honors and respects diversity (Jones & Thorne, 1987).

Changes in Pedagogical Strategies

It may be surprising to think about a psychologist's involvement in facilitating changes in pedagogical strategies on the postsecondary level. In reality, few faculty members have training beyond their specialty area and, as such, may not be at all aware of the changing cognitive styles and learning needs of their students. Content may be their primary focus, with responsibility for learning solely on the student. Thus, there may be a clear role for the school psychologist in helping faculty to educate the CLD and international student. Research points to strategies that might be effective. Hurtado (1990) suggests equal status interactions, with well-designed group work incorporating active learning. Female faculty members are more likely to engage in group projects and field-based studies. It has been demonstrated that when all students, and particularly CLD students, are involved in classrooms using such methods, they are able to engage in more complex thinking and problem solving.

Over 700 studies in the past 90 years have compared the effectiveness of cooperative, competitive, and individualistic learning (Johnson, Johnson, & Smith, 1991). Following Astin's compelling studies, whereby interaction among students and interaction among students and faculty carried the greatest weight in college success, the incorporation of cooperative learning can contribute to these factors. Further, for the student who feels different or has anxiety about the ability to communicate, cooperative learning provides a strategy for involvement and interaction that otherwise may not be possible (Smith, 1994). The psychologist may be in a position to coordinate workshops on the effectiveness of strategies and techniques for the incorporation of cooperative education that would benefit all students.

English as a Second Language (ESL)

It would be legitimate to question whether the university has the responsibility of ESL education after a student has received a passing grade on a test such as the TOEFL. It may be possible that the test is insufficiently sensitive to relate to practical application or there is a disparity among the components of linguistic skills (Bongaerts, van Summeren, Planken, & Schils, 1997; Cummins, 1980; Schachter, 1998). The psychologist on the college campus can facilitate the integration of services for those ESL students who might require extra training or resources, such as more specialized or intensive tutorial services, or develop situations that provide opportunities for ESL students to informally communicate with native English speakers. Programs such as Conversation Partners—where native English speakers are paired with individuals whose mother tongue is different for informal and social conversation—has proved to be effective. The more opportunities for training and practice, the less marginal ESL students feel, whether they are CLD or from another country.

Facilitating Changes in Campus Climate

> If the United States is a melting pot, the cultural stew still has a lot of lumps.
> —Galanti (1991, p. 1)

How can a mentally healthy campus be created? How can a campus philosophy be generated that is inclusive and incorporates the perceptions, interpretations, and expectations of its participants? Sue (1984) proposed the notion of *cultural pluralism*, which has relevance to and impact on today's college campuses. Defined as valuing differences and the plurality of cultures, as opposed to a mass or monoculturalism, the approach generates important questions: (a) What constitutes a cultural difference?, (b) How do I view myself as a member of a special culture?, and (c) Can I tolerate the right of others to be different?

In adopting a pluralistic attitude, one is compelled to examine and reexamine values with respect to norm setting, quality of life judgments, and what issues *really* require intervention. In a pluralistic environment, sufficient freedom should exist to permit individuals to define lifestyles and goals consistent with their cultural backgrounds. This is not to say that there aren't common standards that generate more global or universal standards. However, an effective system permits the understanding of cultures, social practices, and social problems and their impact on psychological frame of reference. Institutional pluralism needs (Schofield & Eurich-Fulcer, 2001) consistent support from those in power, cooperation among members of diverse groups to help foster academic achievement, and social skills and equal status for all members of the community. The psychologist can play a significant role in consultation, mediation, and education in order to create and sustain such an environment. Psychologists as educators need to assume the role of helping individuals negotiate multiple cultural landscapes as individuals become socialized in multiple cultural contexts (Carnevale, 1999).

Providing Opportunities for Community Outreach

Not every college campus has the resources to completely provide for campus diversity. The psychologist, in a facilitator role, can begin to network with community resources, local churches, community groups, town councils, and mayor and selectman offices to generate a pool of potential community host families. Community relation initiatives build and strengthen alliances with culturally diverse communities and ethnocultural organizations, where they exist. When resources are limited, the community can supplement the needs of the university as well as provide opportunities for the community to be comfortable with the college population. The enhancement of town/gown relationships can be a key role for the psychologist.

Developing Proactive Approaches in Counseling Outreach

Individuals from diverse backgrounds are reluctant to seek mental health services on their own (Sandu, 1995). It becomes crucial for psychologists at the postsecondary level to increase the visibility and accessibility of services. Working closely with the office for international students and those individuals who may be more familiar with the population, along with faculty and student organizations, is essential for generating referrals. Because many international students have a propensity to somatize their distress, working closely with student health services is crucial. The psychologist needs to be visible at campus events and orientation sessions so that he or she becomes a familiar, supportive individual and can be seen as having a genuine interest and concern about the welfare of the student (Sue, 1994). Training in cultural competence becomes critically important to the mental health professionals. Although one is not able to learn about all cultural issues, it is important for the therapist to inquire about the patient's cultural identity to determine the cultural reference group and language abilities as potential cultural expectations of the distress or illness and what the cultural elements might be in the patient–therapist relationship (Surgeon General's Report, 2000).

In conclusion, the roles and functions of the school psychologist, at both the elementary and secondary levels, can be translated to functioning on the higher education level. When focusing on mental health on college campuses and the school psychologist's role, a tripartite approach is essential: What can be done on the macrolevel (consultation)? What can be done on the group level (early intervention)? What is the role on the individual level (treatment and crisis intervention)?

IMPLICATIONS FOR FUTURE RESEARCH AND PRACTICE

Research in the area of CLD college students, with the inclusion of immigrants and international students, is a void in our literature. The paucity of research addressing the postsecondary population in general and the CLD in particular provides a wealth of target areas. The limited amount of evidenced-based studies indicates the gap between theory and practice. Although student affairs professionals and psychologists provide programming and services to this population 24/7, there is little available to provide guidance as to the best mental health practices on campuses, how to facilitate institutional change to support changing demographics, what kinds of training work to enhance cultural competence, and how to enhance retention for the marginalized student.

Areas that should be targeted for research and practice include:

1. What environments encourage cultural purism? How do we effectively evaluate systems on the postsecondary level (Sarason, 2003)?
2. How do we train for cultural awareness and cultural competence?
3. When is the best time to introduce supports, consultation, and training?
4. How do we develop coordinated services on college campuses without just waiting for problems to emerge?
5. How do we include a larger number of school psychology services on college campuses?
6. What are the best practices in providing training, consultation, and intervention to the CLD and international student communities?

SUMMARY

The complexity of ethnicity, race, culture, and linguistic proficiency and their interaction need to be carefully considered; further, this dynamic interaction needs to be considered in light of the context or the host environment–the university. A restricted environment does nothing to challenge cultural identity exploration and may bring about premature identity foreclosure or unfocused acting out, which interferes with positive or adaptive growth. An environment without focus and guidelines can easily induce confusion or marginality. However, an environment that offers a range of choices, mentorship, and anticipatory guidance with a commitment for training for cultural competence and a philosophy of cultural pluralism can facilitate and support growth opportunities that enhance the educational opportunities for all students—what the ideal college experiences should be.

There is a long and challenging road ahead for mental health providers on college campuses, particularly in understanding and addressing the needs of CLD students, not the least of which is to include school psychological services at the postsecondary level. School psychologists and other mental health practitioners can have an enormous impact on creating and supporting a positive campus climate through the provision of direct services, consultation, and training of student affairs personnel and faculty and administration and through systems-based service in the areas of training and educational support.

ANNOTATED BIBLIOGRAPHY

Carney, C. M. (1999). *Native American higher education in the United States*. New Brunswick, NJ: Transaction.

> This manuscript surveys the historical development of higher education for Native Americans from the Colonial Period to the late 20th century. It is a major resource on the history and background of Native American education.

Kraemer, B. (1997). The academic and social integration of Hispanic students into college. *The Review of Higher Education, 20,* 163–179.

> Academic and social integration were found to be significantly related to the persistence of Hispanic students in a 2-year college population, although the operational definition of these constructs was different for this cultural group. The need for appropriately defining academic and social integration was highlighted when discussing attrition and persistence decisions for Hispanic students in university settings.

Jones, L. (Ed.). (2001). *Retaining African Americans in higher education: Challenging paradigms for students, faculty, and administrators*. Sterling, VA: Stylus.

> This book contains essays by 16 authors who offer practical recommendations along with research reviews. Recommendations are made to students, faculty, and administrators working or studying with African American college students, graduate students, and faculty members to improve the institutional climate for African American students in traditionally White institutions.

Misra, R. (2004). Academic stress among college students: Comparison of American and international students. *International Journal of Stress Management, 11*(2), 132–148.

> This study compared the academic stressors (e.g., conflicts, pressures) and reactions (i.e., physiological, emotional, cognitive, behavioral) between American and international students from two midwestern universities. The findings emphasize the need to recognize cultural differences in stress management. The author discusses implications for mental health providers.

Poyrazli, S., Kavanaugh, P. R., Baker, A., & Al-Timimi, N. (2004). Social support and demographic correlates of acculturative stress in international students. *Journal of College Counseling, 7*(1), 73–82.

> This study examined the social support and demographics correlated with acculturative stress among international students in the United States. Social support and English proficiency were found to uniquely contribute to the variance in students' acculturative stress. Additionally, students from Asian countries experienced more acculturative stress compared with other subgroups.

Tseng, V. (2004). Family interdependence and academic adjustment in college youth from immigrant and U.S.-born families. *Child Development, 75*(3), 966–983.

> This study examined the ethnic and generational differences in family interdependence and its implications for academic adjustment among late adolescents and young adults in college. Available at http://www.ala.org/ala/acrlbucket/is/publicationsarl/diversebib.htm.

RESOURCES

Web Resources

The Association for Institutional Research (AIR):
http://www.airweb.org

A professional association of institutional researchers, planners, and decision makers from higher education institutions around the world. AIR's mission is to help advance research that will improve the understanding, planning, and operation of higher education institutions.

The Higher Education Research Institute (HERI):
http://www.gseis.UCLA.edu/heri/heir.html

UCLA serves as an interdisciplinary center for research, evaluation, information, policy studies, and research training in postsecondary education. HERI's research program covers a variety of topics, including the outcomes of postsecondary education, leadership development, faculty performance, federal and state policy, and educational equity.

Test Resource

Goodenow, C. (1993). The psychological sense of school membership among adolescents: Scale development and educational correlates. *Psychology in the Schools, 30*(1), 79–90.

The Psychological Sense of School Membership (PSM) is an 18 item Likert-type measure of adolescent students' perceptions of belonging in the educational environment. It has shown good internal consistency reliability with urban and suburban students and in both English and Spanish versions. PSM was found to be correlated with self-reported school motivation and to a lesser degree with grades and teacher-rated effort.

REFERENCES

American Psychiatric Association. (1994). *Diagnostic and Statistical Manual of Mental Disorders* (4th ed.). Washington, DC: Author.

Arnett, J. J. (2002).The psychology of globalization. *American Psychologist, 57,* 774–783.

Astin, A. W. (1993). *What matters in college: Four critical years revisited.* San Francisco: Jossey-Bass.

Ball, H. (2000). *The Bakke case: Race, education, and affirmative action.* Topeka: University Press of Kansas.

Bemack, F. P., & Chung, R. C. (2000). Psychological intervention with immigrants and refugees. In J. F. Aponte & J. Wohl (Eds.), *Psychological intervention and cultural diversity* (2nd ed., pp. 200–213). Boston: Allyn & Bacon.

Benton, S. A., Robertson, J. M., Tseng, W. C., Newton, F. B., & Benton, S. L. (2003). Changes in counseling center client problems across 13 years. *Professional Psychology: Research and Practice, 34,* 66–72.

Berry, J., & Kim, U. (1988). Acculturation and mental health. In P. Dasen , J. W. Berry, & J. W. Berry (Eds.), *Health and cross cultural psychology: Towards application* (pp. 207–236). London: Sage.

Bongaerts, T., van Summeren, C., Planken, B., & Schils, E. (1997). Age and ultimate attainment in the pronunciation of a foreign language. *Studies in Second Language Acquisition, 19,* 447–465.

Brislin, R. W. (1981). *Cross cultural encounters: Face to face interaction.* London, Eng.: Ingram.

Brofenbrenner, U. (1977). Toward an experimental ecology of human development. *American Psychologist, 32,* 513–531.

Carnevale, D. (1999, November 12). How to proctor from a distance. *The Chronicle of Higher Education.*

Cheng, C. (1997). Assessment of major life events for Hong Kong adolescents: The Chinese adolescent life event scale. *American Journal of Community Psychology, 25,* 17–32.

Chickering, A. W. (1969). *Education and identity.* San Francisco: Jossey-Bass.

Coates, S., Rosenthal, M., & Schecter, D. (2003). *September 11th: Trauma and human bonds. Relation Perspectives Book Series* (Vol. 23). Lawrence, KS: Analytic.

Cummins, J. (1980). The cross-lingual dimensions of language proficiency: Implications for bilingual education and the optimal age issue. *TESOL Quarterly, 14*(2), 175–187.

Erikson, E. (1978). *Adulthood.* New York: W. W. Norton.

Galante, G. A. (1991). *Caring for patients from different cultures.* Philadelphia: University of Pennsylvania Press.

Hurtado, S. (1990). *Campus racial climates and educational outcomes.* Unpublished doctoral dissertation. Los Angeles: University of California Press.

Jamieson, D., & O'Mara, J. (1991). *Managing workforce, 2000.* San Francisco: Jossey-Bass.

Jamieson, J., Jones, S., Kirsch, I., Mosenthal, P., & Taylor, C. (2000). *TOEFL 2000 framework: A working paper.* (TOEFL Monograph Series Report No. 16). Princeton, NJ: Educational Testing Service.

Johnson, D. W., Johnson, R., & Smith, K. A. (1991). *Active learning: Cooperation in the college classroom.* Edina, MN: Interaction Book Company.

Jones, E. E., & Thorne, A. (1987). Rediscovery of the subject: Intercultural approaches to clinical assessment. *Journal of Consulting and Clinical Psychology, 55,* 488–495.

Jones, J. (1990). Who's training our ethnic minority psychologists and are they doing it right? In G. Stricker (Ed.), *Toward ethnic diversity in psychology education and training* (pp. 17–34). Washington, DC: American Psychological Association.

Jones, J. (1994). Our similarities are different: Toward a psychology of affirmative diversity. In E. J. Trickett, J. Watts, & D. Birman (Eds.), *Human diversity: Perspectives on people in context* (pp. 27–45). San Francisco: Jossey-Bass.

Kersting, K., & Dittman, M. (2003). Supreme court rules on cases that drew APA interest and input. *Monitor on Psychology, 34,* 48–49.

Koplewicz, H. S. (2002). *More than moody: Recognizing and treating adolescent depression.* New York: G. P. Putnam & Sons.

Lane, C. (2003, February 11). University of Michigan gets broad support using race. *Washington Post,* p. A1.

Lee. E. (1989). Assessment and treatment of Chinese American immigrant families. *Journal of Psychotherapy and the Family, 61,* 99–122.

Levine, A., & Associates. (1989). *Shaping higher education's future.* San Francisco: Jossey-Bass.

Light, R. J. (2001). *Making the most of college: Students speak out.* Cambridge, MA: Harvard University Press.

Liang, B., Tracy, A. J., Taylor, C. A., & Williams, L. M. (2002). Mentoring college-age women: A relational approach. *American Journal of Community Psychology, 30,* 271–288.

Lopez, E. C., & Rogers, M. R. (2001). Conceptualizing cross-cultural school psychology competencies. *School Psychology Quarterly, 16,* 270–302.

Marsella, A. J. (1998). Urbanization, mental health, and social deviancy: A review of issues and research. American Psychologist, 53, 624–634.

McLaughlin, B. (1992). *Myths and misconceptions about second language learning: What every teacher needs to unlearn. Educational Practice Report: 5.* Washington, DC: National Center for Research on Cultural Diversity and Second Language Learning.

Mori, S. (2000). Addressing the mental health concerns of international students. *Journal of Counseling and Development, 178,* 137–145.

National Center for Educational Statistics. (1997). *Digest of educational statistics* (NCES No. 98–015). Washington, DC: U.S. Government Printing Office.

National Center for Educational Statistics. (2002). *Digest of educational statistics* (NCES No. 2003060). Washington, DC: U.S. Government Printing Office.

Norfles, N. S. (2003, November). *Revisiting Tinto's community of learning.* Presentation at the American Association for Higher Education, Washington, DC.

O'Connor, E. M. (2001, September). Student mental health: Secondary education no more. *Monitor on Psychology,* 44–47.

Orfield, G. (2001). *Diversity challenged: Evidence on the impact of affirmative action.* Cambridge, MA: Harvard University Press.

Oropeza, B. A., Fitzgibbon, M., & Baron, A., Jr. (1991). Managing mental crises of foreign college students. *Journal of Counseling and Development, 69,* 280–283.

Parr, G., Bradley, L., & Bingi, R. (1992). Concerns and feelings of international students. *Journal of College Student Development, 33,* 20-25.

Pascarella, E. T., & Terenzini, P. T. (1991). *How college affects students.* San Francisco: Jossey-Bass.

Paz, O. (1967). *The labyrinth of solitude.* London: Penguin.

Pederson, P. B. (1991). Counseling international students. *Counseling Psychologist, 19,* 10–58.

Roberts, R. E., Roberts, C. R., & Chen, Y. R. (1997). Ethnocultural differences in prevalence of adolescent depression. *American Journal of Community Psychology 25,* 95–110.

Sandu, D. S. (1995). An examination of the psychological needs of the international students: Implication for counseling and psychotherapy. *International Journal for the Advancement of Counseling, 17,* 229–239.

Sarason, S. B. (2003). *And what do you mean by learning?* Portsmouth, NH: Heinemann.

Schachter, J. (1998). Recent research in language learning studies: Promises and problems. *Language Learning, 48,* 557–583.

Schofield, J. W., & Eurich-Fulcer, R. (2001). When and how school desegregation improves intergroup relations. In R. Brown & S. Gaertner (Eds.), *Blackwell handbook of social psychology: Intergroup processes* (Vol. 4, pp. 475–494). New York: Blackwell.

Sleek, S. (1998, December). Psychology's cultural competence, once "simplistic" now broadening. *APA Monitor, 29,* 1.

Smith, K. A. (1987). Educational engineering: Heuristics for improving learning effectiveness and efficiency. *Engineering Education, 77,* 274–279.

Sontag, D. (2002, April 28). Who was responsible for Elizabeth Shin? *New York Times,* p. 67.

Sue, S. (1994). Mental health. In N. W. Zane, D. T. Takeuchi, & K. N. J. Young (Eds.), *Confronting critical health issues of Asian and Pacific Islander Americans* (pp. 266–288). Thousand Oaks, CA: Sage.

Sullivan, A. M. (1996). From mentor to muse: Recasting the role of women in relationship with urban adolescent girls. In B. J. Ross Leadbeater & N. Way (Eds.), *Urban girls: Resisting stereotypes, creating identities* (pp. 226–254). New York: New York University Press.

Surgeon General's Report. (2000). *Mental health: Culture, race, ethnicity.* Washington, DC: U.S. Department of Health and Human Services.

Traub, J. (2003, February 2). Forget diversity. *New York Times Magazine,* pp. 15–16.

Tuite, M., & Kaufman, J. (1998). *School psychologists in university settings.* Unpublished manuscript.

U.S. Department of Education, National Center for Education Statistics. (2002). *Status and trends in the education of Hispanics* (NCES 2003–08). Washington, DC: U.S. Government Printing Office.

Weinberg, W. A., & Emslie, G. J. (1987). Depression and suicide in adolescents. *International Pediatrics, 2*, 154–159.

Willie, C. (1984). Mental health and ethnicity. In S. Sue, T. Moore, I. Iscoe, & D. K. Nogata (Eds.), *The pluralistic society* (pp. 33–46). New York: Human Sciences Press.

Wingert, P., & Kantrowitz, B. (2002, October 7). Young and depressed. *Newsweek, 140,* 52–61.

Ying, Y. W. (1995). Cultural orientation and psychological well-being in Chinese Americans. *American Journal of Community Psychology, 23*, 893–911.

Ying, Y. W., & Liese, L. (1994). Initial adjustment of Taiwan students to the United States: The impact of post arrival variables. *Journal of Cross-Cultural Psychology, 25*, 466–477.

Yoder, P. S. (1995). Ethnomedical knowledge of diarrhea disorders in Lumbumbashi Swahili. *Medical Anthropology, 16*, 211–247.

Zikopoulous, M. (1990). *Open doors: 1989/90 report on international educational exchange.* New York: Institute of International Education.

28

BRIDGING CULTURES® IN PARENT CONFERENCES: IMPLICATIONS FOR SCHOOL PSYCHOLOGY

Elise Trumbull
California State University, Northridge

Patricia M. Greenfield
University of California, Los Angeles

Carrie Rothstein-Fisch
California State University, Northridge

Blanca Quiroz
Texas A&M University

In this chapter, we discuss how one of the most common forms of parent involvement in children's schooling—the parent conference—is an opportunity to examine the role of culture in home–school relationships. We draw on sociocultural theory, teacher research, and the collaborative action research of the Bridging Cultures® Project[1] to show how conferences between school staff and families can

---

[1]The Bridging Cultures® Project, a collaboration among four professional researchers and seven teacher-researchers, explored the applicability of cultureal theory and research to the education of immigrant Latino students.

be more effective when school professionals have a deeper understanding of both
the culture of school and the cultures of the families they serve.

SCHOOL PSYCHOLOGISTS, PARENT CONFERENCES, AND CULTURAL COMPETENCE

School psychologists often meet with parents to talk about assessment results, intervention plans, intervention results, and other matters. Indeed, by federal law,
school psychologists must meet with parents before formulating an Individual Education Plan (IEP; Fagan & Wise, 1994). Given the increasing diversity in the United
States, a great many school psychologists are likely to find themselves working
with families from communities with which they have had little experience (National Association of School Psychologists, 2004).

Students of school psychology may learn about cultural diversity in some of
their courses; however, they are unlikely to get the adequate instruction, direct supervision, and field experience to support the development of cultural
competence[2] (Ortiz & Flanagan, 2002). Nor are they likely to learn about alternative
problem-solving strategies in the educational setting that are based on cultural understanding (W. Laija-Rodriguez, personal communication, September 5, 2003).
Thus, many school psychologists enter the field underprepared to serve the diverse
families whose children attend the schools in which they practice (Ortiz &
Flanagan, 2002). We hope our chapter can serve as one resource to address this gap.

THE TRADITION OF PARENT CONFERENCES

Parent conferences are a ubiquitous feature in U.S. schools (Carey, Lewis, & Farris,
1998; Raffaele & Knoff, 1999). They are widely accepted as an opportunity for parents and school personnel to exchange perceptions about students' school adjustment and performance. Although the parent conference is often used to emphasize
parents' role in the development and education of their children, the ways that conferences are carried out can effectively minimize the role of minority[3] parents
(Harry, Allen, & McLaughlin, 1995). Harry et al. note, "The main vehicle for parental advocacy in special education is formal conferences held at prespecified periods. …Yet the data [of our study] showed the inadequacy of this structure as a vehicle for communication or advocacy" (p. 370). One reason that communication and
advocacy fail, we contend, is likely to be culture-based differences in assumptions
about goals for children and about the roles that parents, teachers, school psychologists, and other school personnel should take.

---

[2]The National Association of School Psychologists (NASP; 2004) defines *cultural competence* as "a set
of congruent behaviors, attitudes, and policies that come together in a system, agency, or among professionals and enables that system, agency, or those professionals to work effectively in cross-cultural situations" (p. 1).

[3]The term *minority* is offensive to some, suggesting less than or even being inaccurate in settings
where people from nondominant cultures are in the majority. We use it sparingly—either when citing
others' work or when a lengthy qualifying phrase would be awkward. Using the specific labels people
choose for themselves is, of course, preferable, and we do so whenever possible.

Why Focus on Parent Conferences?

Although the parent conference is just one strategy that schools use to engage parents, it is a pivotal exchange that deserves careful attention for several reasons. First, as mentioned, it is a virtually ubiquitous means for home–school communication. Second, the parent conference is almost a mini-laboratory for discovering how differences in values shape different understandings of children's development and create problems in home–school communication. Third, we have first-hand data on cross-cultural parent conferences, along with a simple method for analyzing parent communication that others can use to monitor the success of the conference (Greenfield, Quiroz, & Raeff, 2000).

When Is a Conference Cross-Cultural?

One thinks of a cross-cultural conference as one in which the parents are from one cultural background and the school professional(s) from another, but it is far more useful to think in terms of whether people are communicating across different value systems than across ethnicities. In this view, the cross-cultural parent conference is one in which the school psychologist or other service provider has internalized and operates from the perspective of the individualistic values of the school system, whereas the parents have internalized and operate from a contrasting sets of cultural values that are explored further in this chapter. The school professional's cultural values generate one set of educational priorities, whereas the parents' cultural values generate another. In this kind of situation, school professionals may interpret behaviors that serve parents' goals as evidence of deficiencies rather than differences (Lott, 2003).

Research supports the view that parents and teachers from the same ethnic group can find themselves having a cross-cultural conference (Raeff, Greenfield, & Quiroz, 2000). This can happen because the educational process that psychologists and educators go through tends to inculcate mainstream cultural values (Delpit, 1995; Nelson-Barber & Mitchell, 1992). These values, which have their origins in western Europe, are independence, autonomy, individual achievement, interpersonal competition, self-reliance, and the rights of the individual (cf. Kalyanpur & Harry, 1999; Ortiz & Flanagan, 2002).

SOURCES OF MISCOMMUNICATION IN THE PARENT CONFERENCE

Miscommunication may have numerous causes, of course, but some can be avoided through understanding potential cultural differences. The consequences of miscommunication are not *neutral*. In fact, parents and school personnel alike have observed that it is a highly *negative* experience for both (Greenfield, Quiroz, & Raeff, 2000; cf. Valdés, 1996).

Different Expectations

Parents' expectations of their children, and of the school, guide how they interpret what the school psychologist says and vice versa. When there is miscommunication, it is often not the spoken words that cause the problem, but the (usually unconscious) expectations underlying the words that present stumbling blocks (cf., Lopez, 2002). When parents and school psychologists share common values, they are likely to share assumptions about the goals of child development and education. Such underlying agreement leads to a similar set of expectations for the child. When the participants do not share the same values, there is a real risk of misunderstanding. For instance, parents who have taught their children to show respect by listening rather than talking may be uncomfortable with the expectation that children speak out in class and express personal opinions. School personnel may interpret parents' discomfort as not valuing education or not being interested in the welfare of their own children.

Power Differences

Power is not equally distributed throughout the larger society. Those from dominant groups (e.g., native-born, White, Euro-American, native-English-speaking, male, heterosexual) benefit from privileged status regardless of whether they recognize it (Lindsey, Nuri Robins, & Terrell, 2003). Because of power differences between minority parents and school personnel, the latter often prevail in decisions about students (Harry et al., 1995). The use of psycho-educational jargon by specialists may also contribute to the power differential by widening the gulf between parents and specialists (cf. Harry et al., 1995).

A common criticism of Latino immigrant families is that parents fail to show up for conferences related to the diagnosis of and educational planning for their special needs child (W. Laija-Rodriguez, personal communication, September 5, 2003). Perhaps many of them anticipate that their words will not be heard. One study of Mexican American mothers in the southwestern United States showed that the way school professionals communicated with them at their children's IEP conferences left them feeling alienated and disrespected (Salas, 2004). "[A]lthough these women wanted to be involved in the decision-making process regarding their children, they were silenced by overt or covert messages that told them their voices were not valued" (p. 181). We have found that our Bridging Cultures paradigm has the power to shift dynamics such as these.

THEORETICAL AND RESEARCH FOUNDATIONS OF THE BRIDGING CULTURES PROJECT

A Perspective on Culture

Culture has many definitions, perhaps the simplest being, "the total way of life of a people" (Kroeber & Kluckhohn, 1954, p. 24). We take a "cognitive" (Fetterman, 1989, p. 27) approach to culture, focusing on its ideational or symbolic aspects: a group's ideas, beliefs, values, knowledge, and ways of acquiring knowledge and passing it on. It is these elements that are most germane to understanding where parents and schools may diverge.

Not only do individuals and groups have cultures, but institutions do as well. Schools have cultures, and school culture tends to look the same throughout districts across the country (Hollins, 1996). For instance, in most cases, children are segregated by age and grade, an individual teacher is responsible for instruction in the elementary grades, individual grades are periodically assigned on report cards, and students move into separate content area classes in middle school. The list could go on. In fact, the norms of schools are nearly always based on the values of the larger society. In the case of many of the practices cited earlier, the underlying values of mainstream culture's individualism are apparent. In this respect, the school could be described as an important acculturating agent (Ortiz & Flanagan, 2002).

Research on Cross-Cultural Parent Conferences

Greenfield et al. (2000) videotaped nine parent conferences between immigrant parents from Mexico and El Salvador and their children's Euro-American teacher. The classroom was a combination of third and fourth grades. The conferences were naturally occurring, not specially scheduled for the study. The cross-cultural miscommunication issues revealed in the videotapes are equally likely to occur in the conferences that school psychologists have with Latino immigrant or other parents from less individualistic cultures, particularly those with little opportunity for formal education.

The parent–teacher meetings in the video study showed instances of both harmonious and discordant communication. However, there was considerably more discord than harmony in the social construction of children by teachers and parents (i.e., the ways each envisioned an ideal child in the classroom or family). Analysis of the communication patterns of the nine conferences revealed that far more often than not parent and teacher disagreed on goals for children. For example, teachers were more interested in discussing cognitive skills, whereas parents were more interested in talking about social behavior. The latter reflects an interdependent or collectivistic value orientation, whereas the former is representative of an independent or individualistic one.

Individualism and Collectivism: Framing Constructs for the Bridging Cultures Project[4]

The continuum of individualism–collectivism represents the degree to which a culture emphasizes individual fulfillment and choice versus interdependent relations, social responsibility, and the well-being of the group. Individualism makes the former a priority, collectivism the latter. Although the dominant U.S. culture is extremely individualistic, many immigrant cultures are strongly collectivistic, as are Native American and Alaska Native cultures (Greenfield & Cocking, 1994) and African American culture in certain ways (Blake, 1994).

About 70% of the world's cultures could be described as collectivistic (Triandis, 1989). The fundamental difference between individualism and collectivism is the degree of emphasis on the individual versus the group. It could be characterized as

---

[4]The Bridging Cultures Project is described in Trumbull et al. (2001), as well as in Trumbull et al. (2003).

the difference between standing out and fitting in. In collectivistic cultures, people are more likely to identify their own personal goals with those of the group—extended family, religion, or other valued group (Brislin, 1993). When asked to complete the statement, "I am….," collectivists are more likely to respond with reference to an organization, family, or religion. Individualists tend to list trait labels, referring to aspects of their personalities, such as hard-working, intelligent, or athletic (Triandis, Brislin, & Hui, 1988).

The Utility of the Bridging Cultures Framework

A framework based on individualism and collectivism is both *economical* and *generative*. It is economical because it incorporates and explains the relationship among many elements that have previously been regarded as separate, such as conceptions of schooling and education, attitudes toward family, expectations for role maintenance or flexibility (including sex roles), duties toward elders, authority structures, attitudes toward discipline, ways of dealing with property, and many aspects of communication. The framework is generative because it suggests interpretations of and explanations for an endless set of interactions among students in a classroom, between school professionals and student(s), between school professionals and parents, and between a school and the communities it serves.

Cautions Regarding Use of the Framework

Variation within a cultural group.   A framework of individualism and collectivism is useful for understanding some of the most basic differences between cultures—differences with wide-ranging implications (Hofstede, 1983; Markus & Kitayama, 1991). Yet we caution that characterizations of cultures are fraught with the potential for overgeneralization and stereotyping. Observable patterns of thought and behavior among cultural groups cannot be translated as predictors of individual behavior. Rather, they can point to meaningful differences whose understanding can improve cross-cultural relations within schools and other social institutions (Rogoff, 2003).

Cultural complexity and change.   It must be emphasized that there are elements of both individualism and collectivism in any society, and that cultures change particularly when they come in contact with each other. As Goldenberg and Gallimore (1995) observe, "Both continuity and discontinuity across generations are part of the process of cultural evolution, a complex dynamic that contributes to change and variability within cultures" (p. 188). One example is how parents' views about what counts as appropriate education for girls have changed between the current and previous generation of Mexican American parents (cf. Valdés, 1996). In contrast to their parents, they may tend to believe that girls should have the opportunity to go to college.

Differences in acculturation.   The process of becoming proficient in the ways of a culture is called *acculturation*. Acculturating to a new environment is different from person to person; it is influenced by the age at which one is faced with the need to function in a new culture, along with many other factors. Not only do one's personal experiences influence the process, but the historical and social relationships between the old and new cultures also come into play (Ortiz & Flanagan, 2002; Trumbull, Greenfield, & Quiroz, 2003). For immigrant Latino families, for instance, values and practices vary based on the length of time they have been in the United States, the level of education they attained in their countries of origin, the length of time in an urban setting, and numerous other factors. In addition, cultures change over time on the basis of changes in their circumstances. There is strong evidence to suggest that, as they become more economically advanced and have greater access to formal education, cultures become more individualistic (Tapia Uribe, LeVine, & LeVine, 1994).

MOVING BEYOND A SINGLE MODEL FOR CHILD DEVELOPMENT

The United States has a highly diverse population, representing peoples with many different cultural histories. Among them are recent immigrants from many countries, descendants of involuntary immigrants brought to the North American continent as slaves from Africa, descendants of colonized Mexicans, and indigenous peoples. Their historical roots continue to influence their childrearing, norms of social behavior and communication, as well as approaches to learning (Greenfield, 1994). Yet school psychologists' understanding about how children develop, learn, and communicate is shaped primarily by a Euro-American model that represents what is normal for only one segment of the students they serve. Based on our research with teachers, this is likely to be true even for school psychologists who come from collectivistic cultures, but who have been schooled in a Euro-American-style educational system (cf. Raeff, Greenfield, & Quiroz, 2000). School psychologists who have studied the usual developmental theories tend to value independence, autonomy, and individual achievement in young children and may not understand why some parents place more emphasis on cooperation and social development (Ortiz & Flanagan, 2002).

Inadvertent Alienation of Students and Parents

Divergent cultural expectations can lead students to feel as if they do not belong in the school, affecting their engagement in learning and, consequently, their achievement (Osterman, 2000). Likewise, parents can come to feel at home or alienated in their children's schools, on the basis of the ways in which the school and its personnel interact with them (McCaleb, 1997). A study of African American parents whose children needed special services concluded that, "the way parental participation was structured tended to delegitimize parental perspectives and that parents often withdrew from participation in confusion or resentment" (Harry et al., 1995, p. 365).

Many parents are offended by schools' assumptions that they need to be taught how to parent their own children (Onikama, Hammond, & Koki, 1998). Criticism of parents' childrearing practices is often implied (or stated) by school personnel, who believe they are acting in a student's best interests, but are ignorant of families' cultural values (Greenfield et al., 2000). If schools are to engender and sustain real parental involvement, they need to interrogate these kinds of practices and look to frameworks for understanding cultural differences that can suggest alternative approaches.

DIAGNOSING AND REPAIRING COMMUNICATION PROBLEMS DURING PARENT CONFERENCES[5]

As suggested, often the most serious communication problems are actually below the conversational level, in the kinds of assumptions each person is making about what is most important—for example, the individual child or the family unit, the child's social development, or the child's academic development. School personnel can employ some relatively simple strategies to shape communication that works for the needs of everyone: school psychologist, teacher, parent, and, ultimately, the child. To recognize cross-cultural value conflicts, school psychologists and other school personnel must go beyond conversational content to look at their interactions with parents. The school psychologist can monitor the success of the conversation by considering the following questions (based on the study by Greenfield et al., 2000):

1. Does the parent ratify (validate/acknowledge) a topic you have brought up by verbal or nonverbal means?
2. Does the parent verbally elaborate on the same topic you have introduced?
3. Does the parent confirm a specific comment or observation you have made?

Ratification, elaboration, and confirmation are all signs that the parent is in agreement with the school professional about the importance of what he or she is saying and that the parent agrees with the professional's interpretation of the facts (Greenfield et al., 2000). In such cooperative conversations, parent and professional are on the same wavelength. Of course, communication is a reciprocal process: Both professional and parent should be introducing topics and responding to the other's comments. Consequently, a school psychologist might want to reverse the roles in the prior questions and ask:

1. Do I ratify (validate) a topic the parent has brought up by verbal or nonverbal means?
2. Do I elaborate on the same topic the parent has introduced (verbally)?
3. Do I confirm a specific comment or observation the parent has made (verbally or nonverbally)?

Table 28–1 presents excerpts from actual parent conferences. The excerpts illustrate the applications of each of these questions.

---

[5]The text in this section is a close adaptation of material that in Trumbull, Rothstein-Fisch, Greenfield, and Quiroz (2001, pp. 59–69). Table 28–1 is adapted from material that appeared in Greenfield, Quiroz, and Raeff (2000) originally.

TABLE 28–1
Discourse Samples From Actual Conferences

A. Parent ratification of a topic introduced by teacher

---

1. *Teacher:* Also I hope that she has, has time to read orally.

2. *Mother:* (Nodding and smiling) Ahhuh.

3. *Teacher:* And also silent every night.

4: *Mother:* Ahhuh.

B. Parent elaboration of a topic introduced by teacher

(Continuation of conversation above)

5. *Teacher:* With you orally and with her silent in the bed for a book which she has an interest

6. *Mother:* Ahhuh. She took out from the library. How many? Seven?

C. Parents' confirmation of teacher's comment

---

1. *Teacher:* (Pointing to report card): Takes pride in her work. Most of the time her work is neat, but I'd like her to work a li: :ttle bit harder on trying to make sure that just - not perfect, but [t as] =

2. *Father:* Yeah.

3. *Teacher:* As neat as possible.

4. *Mother:* Yeah, a little bit.

5. *Teacher:* Yeah, a little neater.

6. *Mother:* A little bit neater.

7. *Teacher:* Yeah, work on your handwriting a little bit.

8. *Mother:* Yeah, she could improve it.

D. Lack of parent ratification of a topic introduced by teacher

---

1. *Teacher:* She's doing great. She's doing beautifully in English and in reading. *And* in writing, *and* in speaking.

2. *Father:* Looks down at lap.

E. Changing of teacher's topic by parent

(Continuation of conversation above)

3. *Teacher:* It's wonderful.

4. *Father:* (Turning to point to younger son)

The same, this guy, h[e]

5. *Teacher:* (Interrupting, with shrill tone) [G]o: :d!

6. *Father:* [He can] write =

7. *Teacher:* (Cutting him off) He can write in English?

8. *Father:* = Well, his name.

Notes.   Examples A, B, and C are from one conference. Examples D and E are from another.

Samples are from Greenfield, Quiroz, and Raeff, (2000), as adapted in Trumbull, Rothstein-Fisch, Greenfield, and Quiroz (2001).

Key to linguistic notations: : : symbolizes lengthening of a syllable; […] when brackets are lined up vertically, the material in both sets of brackets was said simultaneously; = signs link parts of an utterance that was interrupted by another speaker

Instances of Conversational Harmony (Cooperative Discourse)

Examples A and B in Table 28–1 show teacher and parent in apparent agreement that reading orally and silently are important activities for the child. They may not have the same reasons for believing so, but there is no conversational discord at this point. In Example C (taken from the same parent–teacher conference), one can see apparent agreement on a learning goal: the improvement of the child's handwriting. Note how harmonious the conversation is when the teacher makes a criticism about the child's handwriting and says it could be neater. This is because, in the value system of collectivism, criticism is valued as a way to help a child conform to group norms; collectivists worry about praise because it may develop conceit in a child (Greenfield et al., 2000; Lipka & Yanez, 1998). In contrast, in the value system of individualism, praise is valued as a way to help the child develop self-esteem; individualists worry about criticism because it may injure self-esteem. It is significant that such conversational harmony was found only in one conference, this one, in which the parents had been to high school in the United States and so had received considerable acculturation to individualism at a relatively young age (Greenfield et al., 2000).

Instances of Conversational Discord (Noncooperative Discourse)

If a parent does not acknowledge what a school professional has said, becomes silent, or actually changes the topic, he or she probably either does not agree with what has been said or does not think the topic is important. Such conversation could be characterized as *noncooperative*. The examples labeled D and E in Table 28–1 show a striking failure in communication. The father does not pick up on the teacher's desire to talk about the child's academic success, and the teacher seems uncomfortable discussing the academic merits of another family member. The researchers explain:

The father shows discomfort when the teacher recognizes his daughter as outstanding, as she does in Turn 1; he responds by looking down at his lap in Turn 2. According to our analysis, her recognition may threaten the collectivistic goal of integrating each child as an equal contributing part of the family group. Hence when the teacher symbolically constructs his daughter as an outstanding individual learner, the father implicitly *reconstructs* her as a normative part of the family group by equating her academic skills to those of her younger brother. (Greenfield et al., 2000, p. 101)

Another videotaped parent–teacher conference reveals cross-cultural conflict around the issue of the student's verbal expression. The teacher has been talking about how well the child is using language to express herself and ask questions. When she asks the father toward the end of the conference whether he has any questions, he asks, "How is she doing? She don't talk too much?" (Greenfield et al., 2000, p. 102). By encouraging the child to talk more in class, the teacher is promoting behavior that is positively valued in school, but negatively valued in the child's home community, where respectful silence is the desired norm. This creates a conflict for both parent and child, and this type of conflict has the potential to alienate children from their parents (or from the school). By the same token, it could alienate parents from their children or from their children's school (Greenfield et al., 2000).

Monitoring the Communication

When the parent ratifies what the school professional is saying, elaborates on his or her comments, or confirms them, the communication is going well. Likewise, school professionals should note whether they are responding to parents' topics adequately. Awareness of the collectivistic perspective and possible points of conflict may enable professionals to repair communication breakdown. For example, perhaps the teacher in Table 28–1 could have started the conference by acknowledging the younger son and the family as a whole.

It is not worthwhile for school professionals to pursue a topic they have initiated when the parent has become disconnected from the dialogue. Yet this situation can be difficult for professionals. For example, it can be highly frustrating for school professionals who define their mission as the academic accomplishment of students to communicate with parents who value social comportment more highly and believe it to be the foundation for academic success (cf. Ortiz & Flanagan, 2002). Yet this latter value is a basic component of the collectivistic perspective. What can be done in such cases? Because the difference is one of priorities more than an either/or choice, one pragmatic strategy is for the professional to simply change the order of topics and deal with the parents' priority first. Once parents are reassured that the child is behaving correctly in class, they may be more open to hearing about academic or cognitive matters. The goal should be to find common ground, not to reform parents' notions of education or childrearing.

Other Cultural Contexts

Although the conversational examples used here pertain to immigrant Latino parents and a Euro-American teacher, the strategies for monitoring a conversation can be used with other cultural combinations. Of course, to understand why conversational problems occur, it is necessary to know something about the backgrounds of both parents. The Bridging Cultures paradigm provides one important lens for analyzing conversational breakdown.

Using Cultural Knowledge to Enhance Communication in the Conference

A school psychologist can become an ethnographer—one who learns directly from his or her students and parents about their cultures. Teacher aides, or paraprofessionals, who often are from the same background as the children are also an important source of cultural knowledge (Monzó & Rueda, 2001) and can serve as cultural brokers (Lewis, 2004). In many schools, they are the only adults who understand the cultures and speak the languages of students from groups that have recently emigrated. Even when the language of students is widely spoken, a paraprofessional who comes from the particular background of students and their families can bring critical cultural understanding into the realm of school. Other community members and professional colleagues from students' backgrounds—

as well as community-based organizations—are also invaluable resources for understanding students' lives and cultures (Collignon, Men, & Tan, 2001).

The suggestions outlined in Table 28–2 come from the perspective of a cultural insider, Blanca Quiroz. They parallel those found in the literature on cross-cultural communication (e.g., Lustig & Koester, 1999; Scollon & Scollon, 1995). As a parent who emigrated from Mexico in adulthood and later became a teacher and researcher, the author of these suggestions has been able to reflect on her own first-hand experience through the theoretical lens of individualism and collectivism. She draws on her cultural knowledge, as well as her experience on both sides of the parent conference. Again, although our context is working with immigrant Latino parents, this approach may well be helpful in many contexts, particularly with parents from other collectivistic cultures.

We do not mean to suggest that school personnel should memorize a set of rules for conversing with immigrant Latino parents or anyone from a collectivistic culture. Rather, we want to encourage them to learn enough about a collectivistic orientation to acquire a sense of how a parent from such a background might think and feel, and to come to understand the expectations such a parent might have of the school. Understanding the potential differences between a collectivistic culture at home and the mainstream culture at school can engender empathy, something that is far more helpful than prescriptions about question-asking or pronoun usage. But, then, empathy with the ways of the culture would naturally lead to respectful pronoun usage of the sort discussed in Table 28–2.

Knowledge of how individualism and collectivism operate also helps school personnel to adapt their interaction style to parents' styles. For example, Latino parents with more years of formal schooling, or who have been to school in the United States, may be more comfortable with a conference that focuses on academic achievement. Some students and families will have acculturated more than others, and this fact must be considered in approaching parents and in planning for a student's needs (Goldenberg & Gallimore, 1995; Helms, 1997; Ortiz & Flanagan, 2002). The key is to open the door to understanding differences and shape conferences accordingly.

It is clear that one conference style does not fit all. Participating in a parent conference in the ways schools expect may be alien to the parent whose home culture implicitly encourages the parent to listen respectfully to school personnel (Mapp, 2003; Pollock, Coffman, & Lopez, 2002). Hesitation to communicate in a parent conference should not be taken to mean lack of interest (Pollock et al., 2002). Rather, silence must be evaluated to determine whether it conveys respect, misunderstanding, or conflict.

APPROACH FOR IMPROVING PARENT CONFERENCES: EXAMPLES FROM THE BRIDGING CULTURES PROJECT

Time Allotment for Conferences

In the Bridging Cultures Project, we found that teachers were struggling with the logistics of parent conferences. One problem was that conferences were usually too short. In fact, 15 to 20 minutes per child is often all that is allocated within the

TABLE 28–2
Fostering Communication With Immigrant Latino Families

- Begin the conversation with a personal exchange, not with formal discussion of a student's progress or needs.

- Maintain a personal connection throughout the conference. Parents may want to intersperse academic talk with informal talk.

- If using Spanish, maintain use of the polite second-person pronoun (you) *usted*, rather than the familiar *tu*.

- Show respect (*respeto*) by focusing on the family, not just the child who is being discussed or only on bureaucratic procedures and the purpose of the conference as the school sees it (see also Sosa, 1997).

- Use indirect questions and be patient if it takes several attempts to gather information from the parents. For example, rather than ask if the student has a designated time and space for doing homework, the school professional may make an observation such as, "Sometimes parents say it's hard to seat their children at a specific place to do homework or study, because some of us live in small places and have other people around us all the time."

- Recognize that the notion of "private space" is an individualistic one and may not be a natural concept for collectivistic families.

- Recognize that establishing goals for children is a personal matter, and avoid approaching that process like the development of a business plan.

- Refer to the experiences of other parents as a source of suggestions for solutions to problems rather than offering direct prescriptions. This approach acknowledges other parents' problem-solving strategies and helps parents without embarrassing them. It also situates the parent as part of a group of parents rather than as an individual.

- Because modesty is valued by many immigrant Latino families, discuss students' achievements in the context of the classroom or peer group and emphasize how such achievements contribute to the well-being of the group.

- Recognize that many immigrant Latino parents feel especially comfortable in hearing about areas where additional effort is needed for the child to come up to group norms and less comfortable with public praise (Greenfield, Quiroz, & Raeff, 2000).

- Do explain the expectations and goals of the school, but be aware that parents' goals may conflict with some of them. Work with parents to find common ground.

- Create a sense of common purpose and communicate a message of caring through the use of the pronoun we rather than the pronouns I and you. This also communicates that parents and school personnel are a team.

---

school schedule for parent–teacher conferences. Similarly, school psychologists and other members of the team who meet with parents to plan interventions or individualized educational plans (IEPs) for students may each be expected to cover specific issues in the space of a few minutes (Harry et al., 1995). However, if the conference is to be used to forge cross-cultural understanding when parents and teachers do not start off with the same assumptions about schooling and learning, even more time than usual is required. The Bridging Cultures teachers have continued to experiment with strategies for getting more time with parents. The results of this experimentation can be directly applied by school psychologists in IEP conferences with parents, for instance.

Student-Led Conferences

It is not always evident to school professionals which innovations are culturally appropriate and which are not. For instance, having children who have become proficient in English translate for their parents who have not seems practical on the surface. However, according to some, "[p]lacing children in a position of equal status with adults creates dysfunction within the family hierarchy" for Latino parents (Finders & Lewis, 1994, p. 52).

A related problem was recognized by the teachers in the Bridging Cultures Project when they had a chance to discuss student-led conferences together in one of the whole-group meetings. At the time, student-led conferences were a highly recommended innovation. However, teachers came to realize, as a result of the Bridging Cultures workshops, that having students actually lead the conferences would violate role norms, but agreed that it would probably be acceptable for them to show their parents around the room and point out examples of their work to them. The professional should be taking the lead in discussing the child's progress, and then she or he and the parent(s) should jointly discuss what the child's needs are. Many districts have become enamored with student-led conferences, touting them as one way to promote student self-evaluation (e.g., Countryman & Schroeder, 1996). However, before student-led conferences become more widely institutionalized, questions should be raised about their appropriateness for families holding respect for elders as a cultural value.

Group Conferences

Four teachers from the Bridging Cultures Project explored an alternative conference format that *is* culturally appropriate for their settings. It is possible that school psychologists could use this format when working with parents from more collectivistic cultures. The project teachers have found small-group conferences to be successful with immigrant Latino parents. A kindergarten teacher brought parents together on the basis of their children's ability groups. Grouping parents in that manner resulted in considerable verbal interaction among parents. In each group, at least one parent was willing to talk, and that seemed to make other parents comfortable to participate as well. A second-grade teacher had long met with parents in small groups, along with her two partner teachers—an arrangement she describes as reflecting the family approach she and her colleagues take. A third-grade teacher also found small groups to work better than individual conferences. She reflected on the first time she tried groups:

The parents shared so much, and it was heartfelt. They were thankful for the opportunity to get to know each other....Here they were, engaged in conversation—looking at common problems or goals, possibilities. They felt and expressed that it was different, and they were very thankful for it.

An upper elementary teacher did group conferences for the first time in the fall of 1998. A full account of her experience appears in Trumbull, Rothstein-Fisch, Greenfield, and Quiroz (2001). Here we quote briefly from her assessment of the method:

Parents seemed very pleased with the new approach to conferencing. A friendly, comfortable, and warm feeling came across during the conferencing. Many parents had questions that benefitted the other parents. Parents' conferencing together lent a source of mutual support, like family members all supporting each other.

The new group format organized by the teacher appears to be well liked, efficient, and culturally congruent for immigrant Latino parents. As teachers from the Bridging Cultures Project observe, such parents may feel more comfortable speaking in a group, with one parent's ideas stimulating another parent to comment or ask a question. A Bridging Cultures kindergarten teacher remarked that with group conferences the interaction is much more give and take, and she finds that she therefore does much less talking. As for teachers, group conferences mean that they get less burned out explaining the same thing over and over and can be more genuinely present to the experience. Perhaps most important, parents gain a sense of empowerment from the opportunity to participate as part of a group. This innovation might also have value for mainstream parents and help them develop a greater sense of community along with a concern for the development and accomplishments of other people's children.

It is important to find out from parents what they prefer, however. The group conference is an option, but it should not be automatically imposed on any set of parents any more than individual conferences or student-led conferences should be imposed without consideration for the particular cultural context. In fact, those teachers in the project who conduct group conferences always retain individual conferencing as an option for any parent.

Issues of Interpretation and Translation in Parent Conferences

When school psychologists do not have a language in common with the parents in a conference, interpreters may be necessary. An important aspect of respect for the parents is to have an interpreter who is familiar with the concepts and terms that will be discussed in the parent conference (Lopez, 2002). For instance, if discussion focuses on special education placement, the interpreter needs to be familiar with appropriate terminology related to that topic. As Lopez (2002) notes, "For interpreters, it is particularly important to have a repertoire of vocabulary in the target language" (p. 1424) that accurately communicates diagnostic categories and psychological concepts in ways families will understand.

Another aspect of respect is to allow time for the interpreter to interpret before going on, as well as to give space and explicit permission for the interpreter to ask the psychologist if he or she does not understand something (W. Laija-Rodriguez, personal communication, September 5, 2003; Lopez, 2002). More generally, it is important to take into account the educational level of the parents and make communication less technical for those with a lower level of formal education. One of the teachers in the Bridging Cultures Project commented that the approach used by psychologists at the IEP parent meetings sometimes did not support parents' understanding of the implications of their child's assessment. When school personnel ask, "Do you *really* need a copy translated?" a respectful parent may feel obligated to decline asking for a translation, when in fact he or she truly does need a translation in order to have a meaningful record of the plan for the child. However, a translation may in fact *not* be useful because it will be too technical to be understood by someone with the parent's level of formal education.

IMPLICATIONS FOR FUTURE DIRECTIONS IN SCHOOL PSYCHOLOGY

School psychologists, as a professional group, have been increasingly cognizant of the importance of culturally competent consultation with parents. As the National Association of School Psychologists (NASP) Web site states, "Given the growing diversity of the U.S. population, it is imperative that school psychologists and other educational professionals engage in culturally competent practices" (National Association of School Psychologists, 2004, p. 5). Involving parents in their children's schooling is widely recommended (Henderson & Mapp, 2002) and legally required for students with an IEP; and studies show that minority parents *want* to be involved in their children's schooling (Chavkin & Williams, 1993; Goldenberg & Gallimore, 1995; Lott, 2001), but schools have often been unsuccessful in engaging them in the ways they would like (Chavkin & Williams; Lott, 2003). Part of the reason is that many minority families are under economic stress (Lott, 2003). Another reason is that schools tend to approach parents from a set of culture-based expectations that may not be comprehensible or attractive to them (Lopez, Scribner, & Mahitivanichcha, 2001; Trumbull et al., 2001).

School psychologists, as part of evaluation and intervention teams, can help engage parents meaningfully in framing plans for their own children if they are able to show understanding of and respect for parents' perspectives (Ortiz & Flanagan, 2002). Furthermore, when school psychologists understand potential cultural sources of difference in test performance or differences in the predictive validity of tests (depending on a student's background and experience), they can help parents and educators make the best sense of test outcomes (Helms, 1997).

The suggestions we offer are compatible with the philosophy of NASP, which has emphasized partnerships and collaborative goal setting between parents and school psychologists. According to Raffaele and Knoff (1999), "Effective home-school collaboration engenders parental empowerment through positive, meaningful two-way communication...based upon mutual respect and trust" (p. 452). Trust is, certainly, built to some degree on mutual understanding; and understanding requires some knowledge of the cultural values and personal histories that underlie surface behavior (Espinosa, 1995; Trumbull et al., 2001).

At this point, we would like to recommend three interrelated steps that could be taken to advance the agenda of cultural competence for school psychologists.

First, school psychologists should consider how cultural frameworks like the one used for Bridging Cultures could be uniquely applied to the work of school psychologists. Based on our work with teachers, we believe that the Bridging Cultures training is one promising resource to school psychologists, both for those in preparation and those currently in practice. The framework could be woven into graduate coursework with an assignment of observing conferences with parents for conflict along the dimensions of individualism and collectivism. For established practitioners, professional development akin to that of the Bridging Cultures longitudinal collaborative action research project could reveal new ways that school psychologists could learn to examine and increase cultural competence.[6]

The teachers in the Bridging Cultures Project had some ideas for applying Bridging Cultures to school psychology as a result of their work with school psychologists in the IEP planning process. Some of their comments point to the need to reach all school personnel with theoretically based and tested approaches to cross-cultural home–school collaboration. One teacher believed that knowledge of the Bridging Cultures framework definitely influenced his work with families of children with special needs:

> I have always had good parent conferences. Now I know why I do what I do based on the Bridging Cultures framework. I believe that more culturally-sensitive teachers reach parents better. In the IEPs, parents are physically isolated from the rest of the group. In utilizing the framework, I always try to seat myself by the parents and discuss home issues so that parents feel they are contributing.

Another teacher noted:

> It would be nice to see the parents a little more involved in the [IEP] process than I presently see. I believe that the Bridging Cultures framework helps foster collaborative relationships, which will enhance involvement of parents in the IEP. When I find success in using Bridging Cultures, I see the reaction more intensely from parents with children of special needs.

Second, empirical research should be conducted in order to learn more about what constitutes culturally competent (or perhaps incompetent) consultation with parents. A variety of methods from videotaping, to observation, interviews, and journaling could be used to identify more and less successful strategies for conducting cross-cultural parent conferences involving school psychologists and other school personnel. These investigations should address a range of contexts related to schools and the nature of the communities they serve. They should also be longitudinal: Building relationships with and learning from families takes time, and changes in practice are not likely to occur all at once. Moreover, permanent or long-term relationships are the ones most valued in a collectivistic cultural framework.

The *Bridging Cultures Teacher Education Module* (Rothstein-Fisch, 2003) could be piloted with small groups of school psychology candidates and in-service professionals, and then participants could be followed to determine the impact of such training on their attitudes, knowledge, and skills with families and students from diverse backgrounds. It is our experience that the framework stimulates immediate self-questioning and exploration. Teachers in the project found that they quickly experienced different attitudes toward families and soon thereafter engaged in new practices that had positive payoff for relationships with them (Trumbull et al., 2001; Trumbull, Rothstein-Fisch, & Hernandez, 2003).

Third, building on a strong Internet Web site, NASP members should establish and cultivate a site for school psychologists to share their experiences in exploring

---

[6]Our Bridging Cultures team is available for professional development; please contact Dr. Carrie Rothstein-Fisch at carrie.rothstein-fisch@csun.edu. West Ed, which supported the original Bridging Culutres Project, also offers workshops (see www.wested.org)

culturally competent practices. For example, a school psychologist might want to try a group meeting with families who have children experiencing similar learning challenges. This experiment could be documented and shared with others.

CONCLUSION

It is in the best interests of students' optimal development and learning to have school professionals who understand and engage parents in ways that respect and build on the strengths of the family as well as the resources of the school. Because of their skills in working with families, school psychologists can take a strong role in promoting good family–school connections (Epstein, 1992), in part as liaisons between parents and teachers (Christenson, Hurley, Sheridan, & Fenstermacher, 1997). When cultural competence is integrated into their repertoire of professional skills, school psychologists stand to have a crucial role in improving schools' responsiveness to families—a role that reflects the professional mission of those who serve children and families in the educational system. In such a role, school psychologists are in a unique position to continuously develop, emulate, and model cultural competence.

ACKNOWLEDGMENTS

Portions of this chapter appeared in Trumbull, Rothstein-Fisch, Greenfield, and Quiroz (2001)—specifically, the examples of parent–teacher discourse in parent conferences and strategies for improving communication with parents on pages 11–17. We would like to thank our seven teacher collaborators and WestEd, the regional laboratory based in San Francisco, for their support. We also thank Anna M. Pena and members of the California State University, Northridge faculty who helped us understand school psychology better.

ANNOTATED BIBLIOGRAPHY

Trumbull, E., Rothstein-Fisch, C., Greenfield, P. M., & Quiroz, B. (2001). *Bridging cultures between home and school: A guide for teachers.* Mahwah, NJ: Lawrence Erlbaum Associates.

    Although this book is titled *A Guide for Teachers,* it is useful to school psychologists because of the in-depth treatment of the topic of how to work cross-culturally with families. The book examines standard practices and suggests alternatives that are more appropriate for families who are not from mainstream cultures. Although the examples pertain to immigrant Latino families, many of the principles apply to families from any other culture that is more collectivistic than the dominant U.S. culture.

Rothstein-Fisch, C. (Ed.). (2003). *Readings for bridging cultures.* Mahwah, NJ: Lawrence Elbaum Associates.

    As an adjunct to the *Guide,* this compendium of six articles ranges from a 12-page introduction to the Bridging Cultures Project to two articles about the empirical research on which the project is based. The first three articles are ideal for introductory professional development presentations.

Boethel, M. (2003). *Diversity: School, family, & community connections* (Annual Synthesis 2003). Austin, TX: National Center for Family & Community Connections with Schools, Southwest Educational Development Laboratory.

This review of 64 recent key research studies on "diversity as it relates to student achievement and school, family, and community connections" (p. v) is an excellent resource for school professionals. By scanning through the studies that are summarized, one begins to appreciate the importance of schools', communities', and families' working together. The final chapter summarizes 12 specific strategies to strengthen home–school connections, all based on the research presented.

RESOURCES

Center for Research on Education, Diversity, and Excellence (CREDE): http://crede.berkeley.edu

The Center has publications and summaries of research that can be downloaded. A subsection of the CREDE Web site (http://www.crede.org/links/diversity.html) has links to dozens of organizations concerned with diversity in education.

Family Involvement Network of Educators (FINE): http://www.gse.harvard.edu/hfrp/projects/fine.html.

FINE is a service of the Harvard Family Research Project. It is a network of over 4,000 educators who are interested in fostering partnerships among schools, families, and communities. Many useful publications can be downloaded from this site.

National Center for Family and Community Connections with Schools: www.sedl.org/connections/

This Web site is dedicated to linking research and practice in the area of home–school–community connections.

REFERENCES

Blake, I. K. (1994). Language development and socialization in young African-American children. In P. M. Greenfield & R. R. Cocking (Eds.), *Cross-cultural roots of minority child development* (pp. 167–195). Hillsdale, NJ: Erlbaum.

Brislin, R. (1993). *Understanding culture's influence on behavior*. Fort Worth, TX: Harcourt Brace College.

Carey, N., Lewis, L., & Farris, E. (1998). *Parent involvement in children's education: Efforts by public elementary schools*. Washington, DC: National Center for Education Statistics, U.S. Department of Education, Office of Educational Research and Improvement.

Chavkin, N. F., & Williams, D. L. (1993). Minority parents and the elementary school: Attitudes and practices. In N. F. Chavkin (Ed.), *Families and schools in a pluralistic society* (pp. 73–83). New York: State University of New York Press.

Christenson, S. L., Hurley, C. M., Sheridan, S. M., & Fenstermacher, K. (1997). Parents' and school psychologists' perspectives on parent involvement activities. *School Psychology Review, 26,* 111–130.

Collignon, F. F., Men, M., & Tan, S. (2001). Finding ways in: Community-based perspectives on Southeast Asian family involvement with schools in a New England state. *Journal of Education for Students Placed at Risk, 6* (1&2), 27–44.

Countryman, L. L., & Schroeder, M. (1996). When students lead parent–teacher confer-
    ences. *Educational Leadership, 53*(7), 64–68.

Delpit, L. (1995). *Other people's children.* New York: The New Press.

Epstein, J. L. (1992). School and family partnerships: Leadership roles for school psycholo-
    gists. In S. L. Christenson & J. C. Conoley (Eds.), *Home–school collaboration: Enhancing
    children's academic and social competence* (pp. 499–515). Silver Spring, MD: National Asso-
    ciation of School Psychologists.

Espinosa, L. M. (1995). *Hispanic parent involvement in early childhood programs* (Report No.
    EDO-PS–95–3). Urbana, IL: ERIC Clearinghouse on Elementary and Early Childhood
    Education. (ERIC Document Reproduction Service No. ED382412)

Fagan, T. K., & Wise, P. S. (1994). *School psychology: Past, present, and future.* New York:
    Longman.

Fetterman, D. M. (1989). *Ethnography step by step. Applied Social Research Methods Series: Vol.
    17.* Newbury Park, CA: Sage.

Finders, M., & Lewis, C. (1994). Why some parents don't come to school. *Educational Lead-
    ership, 51*(8), 50–54.

Goldenberg, C., & Gallimore, R. (1995). Immigrant Latino parents' values and beliefs
    about their children's education: Continuities and discontinuities across cultures and
    generations. In P. Pintrich & M. Maehr (Eds.), *Advances in achievement motivation: Vol. 9*
    (pp. 183–228). Greenwich, CT: JAI.

Greenfield, P. (1994). Independence and interdependence as developmental scripts: Impli-
    cations for theory, research, and practice. In P. M. Greenfield & R. R. Cocking (Eds.),
    Cross-cultural roots of minority child development (pp. 1–37). Hillsdale, NJ: Erlbaum.

Greenfield, P. M., & Cocking, R. R. (Eds.). (1994). *Cross-cultural roots of minority child devel-
    opment.* Hillsdale, NJ: Erlbaum.

Greenfield, P. M., Quiroz, B., & Raeff, C. (2000). Cross-cultural conflict and harmony in the
    social construction of the child. In S. Harkness, C. Raeff, & C. M. Super (Eds.), *Variabil-
    ity in the social construction of the child* (pp. 93–108). *New Directions for Child and Adoles-
    cent Development, No. 87.* San Francisco: Jossey-Bass.

Harry, B., Allen, N., & McLaughlin, M. (1995). Communication versus compliance: Afri-
    can-American parents' involvement in special education. *Exceptional Children, 61,*
    364–377.

Helms, J. E. (1997). The triple quandary of race, culture, and social class in standardized
    cognitive ability testing. In D. P. Flanagan, J. L. Genshaft, & P. L. Harrison (Eds.), *Con-
    temporary intellectual assessment: Theories, tests, and issues* (pp. 517–532). New York:
    Guilford.

Henderson, A. T., & Mapp, K. L. (2002). *A new wave of evidence: The impact of school, family,
    and community connections on student achievement* (Annual Synthesis 2002). Austin, TX:
    National Center for Family & Community Connections with Schools.

Hofstede, G. (1983). National cultures revisited. *Behavior Science Revisited, 18,* 285–305.

Hollins, E. R. (1996). *Culture in school learning.* Mahwah, NJ: Erlbaum.

Kalyanpur, M., & Harry, B. (1999). *Culture in special education: Building reciprocal family rela-
    tionships.* Baltimore: Brookes.

Kroeber, A., & Kluckhohn, C. (1954). *Culture: A critical review of concepts and definitions.*
    Cambridge, MA: Vintage Books.

Lewis, K. C. (2004). Instructional aides: Colleagues or cultural brokers? *The School Commu-
    nity Journal, 14*(1), 91–111.

Lindsey, R. B., Nuri Robins, K., & Terrell, R. D. (2003). *Cultural proficiency, a manual for
    school leaders* (2nd ed.). Thousand Oaks, CA: Corwin.

Lipka, J., & Yanez, E. (1998). Identifying and understanding cultural differences: Toward a
    culturally based pedagogy. In J. Lipka, G. V. Mohatt, & the Ciulistet Group (Eds.), *Trans-*

forming the culture of schools: Yup'ik Eskimo examples (pp. 111–137). Mahwah, NJ: Lawrence Erlbaum Associates.

Lopez, E. C. (2002). Best practices in working with school interpreters to deliver psychological services to children and families. In A. Thomas & J. Grimes (Eds.), *Best practices in school psychology IV* (Vol. 2, pp. 1419–1432). Bethesda, MD: National Association of School Psychologists.

Lopez, G. R., Scribner, J. D., & Mahitivanichcha, K. (2001). Redefining parental involvement: Lessons from high-performing migrant-impacted schools. *American Educational Research Journal, 38,* 253–288.

Lott, B. (2001). Low-income parents and the public schools. *Journal of Social Issues, 57,* 247–260.

Lott, B. (2003). Recognizing and welcoming the standpoint of low-income parents in the public schools. *Journal of Educational and Psychological Consultation, 14,* 91–104.

Lustig, M. W., & Koester, J. (1999). *Intercultural competence: Interpersonal communication across cultures.* New York: HarperCollins College.

Mapp, K. L. (2003). Having their say: Parents describe why and how they are engaged in their children's learning. *School Community Journal, 13*(1), 35–64.

Markus, H., & Kitayama, S. (1991). Culture and the self: Implications for cognition, emotion, and motivation. *Psychological Review, 98,* 224–253.

McCaleb, S. P. (1997). *Building a community of learners: A collaboration among teachers, students, families, and community.* Mahwah, NJ: Erlbaum.

Monzó, L. D., & Rueda, R. (2001). *Sociocultural factors in social relationships: Examining Latino teachers' and paraeducators' interactions with Latino students* (Research Report No. 9). Santa Cruz, CA: Center for Research on Education, Diversity, and Excellence.

National Association of School Psychologists. (2004). *Culturally competent practice.* Retrieved November 23, 2004, from http://www.nasponline.org/culturalcompetence

Nelson-Barber, S., & Mitchell, J. (1992). Restructuring for diversity: Five regional portraits. In M. E. Dilworth (Ed.), *Diversity in teacher education* (pp. 229–262). San Francisco: Jossey-Bass.

Onikama, D. L., Hammond, O. W., & Koki, S. (1998). *Family involvement in education: A synthesis of research for Pacific educators.* Honolulu: Pacific Resources for Education and Learning.

Ortiz, S. O., & Flanagan, D. P. (2002). Best practices in working with culturally diverse children and families. In A. Thomas & J. Grimes (Eds.), *Best practices in school psychology IV* (Vol. 1, pp. 337–351). Bethesda, MD: National Association of School Psychologists.

Osterman, K. (2000). Students' need for belonging in the school community. *Review of Educational Research, 70,* 323–367.

Pollock, A., Coffman, J., & Lopez, M. E. (2002). Using behavior change theory to communicate effectively: The case of Latino parent involvement. *The Evaluation Exchange, 8*(3), 1–5. Retrieved March 19, 2003, from www.gse.harvard.edu/hfrp/eval/issue20/theory.html

Raeff, C., Greenfield, P. M., & Quiroz, B. (2000). Conceptualizing interpersonal relationships in the cultural contexts of individualism and collectivism. In S. Harkness, C. Raeff, & C. Super (Eds.), *The social construction of the child: Nature and sources of variability. New directions in child development* (pp. 59–74). San Francisco: Jossey-Bass.

Raffaele, L. M., & Knoff, H. M. (1999). Improving home–school collaboration with disadvantaged families: Organizational principles, perspectives, and approaches. *School Psychology Review, 28,* 448–466.

Rogoff, B. (2003). *The cultural nature of human development.* Oxford: Oxford University Press.

Rothstein-Fisch, C. (2003). *Bridging cultures teacher education module.* Mahwah, NJ: Erlbaum..

Salas, L. (2004). Individualized educational plan (IEP) meetings and Mexican American parents: Let's talk about it. *Journal of Latinos and Education, 3*(3), 181–192.

Scollon, R., & Scollon, S. W. (1995). *Intercultural communication.* Cambridge, MA: Blackwell.

Sosa, A. S. (1997). Involving Hispanic parents in educational activities through collaborative relationships. *Bilingual Research Journal, 21*(2&3), 1–8. Retrieved January 17, 2003, from brj.asu.edu/archives/23v21/articles/art9.html

Tapia Uribe, F. M., LeVine, R. A., & LeVine, S. E. (1994). Maternal behavior in a Mexican community: The changing environments of children. In P. M. Greenfield & R. R. Cocking (Eds.), *Cross-cultural roots of minority child development* (pp. 41–54). Hillsdale, NJ: Erlbaum.

Triandis, H. (1989). Cross-cultural studies of individualism and collectivism. *Nebraska Symposium on Motivation, 37,* 43–133.

Triandis, H., Brislin, R., & Hui, C. H. (1988). Cross-cultural training across the individualism–collective divide. *International Journal of Intercultural Relations, 12,* 269–289.

Trumbull, E., Greenfield, P. M., & Quiroz, B. (2003). Cultural values in learning and education. In B. Williams (Ed.), *Closing the achievement gap: A vision for changing beliefs and practices* (2nd ed., pp. 67–98). Alexandria, VA: Association for Supervision and Curriculum Development.

Trumbull, E., Rothstein-Fisch, C., Greenfield, P. M., & Quiroz, B. (2001). *Bridging cultures between home and school: A guide for teachers.* Mahwah, NJ: Erlbaum.

Trumbull, E., Rothstein-Fisch, C., & Hernandez, E. (2003). Parent involvement—according to whose values? *School Community Journal, 13*(2), 45–72.

Valdés, G. (1996). *Con respeto [With respect].* New York: Teachers College.

VII

FUTURE PERSPECTIVES

29

DIRECTIONS FOR FUTURE RESEARCH: A RESEARCH AGENDA FOR MULTICULTURAL ISSUES IN EDUCATION, ASSESSMENT, AND INTERVENTION

Alberto M. Bursztyn
Brooklyn College, City University of New York

Cultural and linguistic diversity issues have steadily gained attention within the field of school psychology. As this volume and numerous other scholarly publications attest, multiculturalism is no longer a marginal topic taken up by a few isolated researchers and practitioners (Canino & Spurlock, 1994; Geisinger, 1992; Rogers et al., 1999). Yet concerns about and understanding of human diversity issues continue to be poorly integrated in training, research, and practice in school psychology. As a rule, major texts in the field continue to address multicultural populations in separate chapters, if at all; and training programs address diversity through designated, but separate, courses. An obstacle to integrating cultural and linguistic differences more fully in the discipline is rooted in the implicit, but persistent, dichotomy whereby children are classified as members of exclusive categories: mainstream or minority cultures. Although clearly articulated understandings of these categories have not emerged, only cultural minority categories are routinely studied for their presumed influences on child behavior and performance. A reader of school psychology literature may be led to believe that there are two co-existing models of practice: one for minority populations and one for nonminority (*regular*) students.

Advances in multicultural research are mainly in the area of increased awareness, but studies that take diversity issues tend to remain a special case bounded by notions of departure from mainstream populations. To arrive at an integrated approach to all populations, we must explore more fully basic questions and assumptions that affect all research projects, such as: How is knowledge about mainstream and diverse cultural and linguistic groups generated in school psychology? What assumptions underlie school psychology research? Are contemporary methods of research in psychology compatible with the study of diverse populations? Who frames research questions and for what purposes? How are research results interpreted and disseminated? In this chapter, I explore these questions and their implications for future research.

Historically, school psychology has focused attention on student functioning and individual differences (Lubinski, 2000; Ross, Powell, & Elias, 2002) and less often on systems and systemic change (Conoley & Gutkin, 1995; Curtis & Stollar, 2002). School psychology's research agenda has sought to investigate most aspects of child adjustment to school, including the development and dissemination of treatment modalities and focused intervention strategies (Kratochwill & Shernoff, 2003). In applied settings, the discipline has assisted educators in curricular matters and has provided powerful tools for decision making about individual students (Fagan & Wise, 2000). The focus on individual student learning and adjustment has yielded valuable knowledge and positioned school psychologists ubiquitously, although not always securely, in school organizations (Reschly, 2000; Ross et al., 2002).

Despite the disciplinary gains, traditional models of research have not adequately accounted for the contribution of contextual variables to outcomes (Sheridan & Gutkin, 2000) and have not been particularly effective in addressing the more intractable problems in education that are found in multicultural, urban, and poor schools (Burnette, 1998; Gersten & Woodward, 1994; Harry, 1994; Robertson, Kushner, Starks, & Drescher, 1994). In fact, it may be argued that school psychology's slow progress in integrating multicultural issues is a manifestation of the limitation of present models of research and practice, which fail to deal appropriately with ecological and other variables (Hughes, 2000).

In the present national context, the study of culturally and linguistically diverse (CLD) children has acquired new urgency because of persistent gaps in their academic performance, incidences of poor adjustment to school, and dropout rates (Artiles & Zamora-Duran, 1997). The large proportion of CLD children who fail to make adequate academic progress, the stubbornly high rate of referrals, and the large proportion of placements in special education affecting these students continue to dog school psychology (Bursztyn, 2002; Figueroa, 1989) and present a serious challenge and potential vulnerability to school psychology within the larger discourse in public education (Markowitz, 1996).

Psychological testing of CLD students has been singled out as a source of bias and potentially unfair professional practice (Barrera, 1995; Cummins, 1986; Mercer, 1973), and behavioral interventions have been critiqued as a form of oppression (Kincheloe, Steinberg, & Villaverde, 1999). These chronic problems have yet to be adequately addressed by school psychologists (Ingraham & Bursztyn, 1999). Dismissing our critics without examining the potential validity of their concerns can only isolate and weaken the profession (Bursztyn, 1997, 2002). Therefore, efforts to develop cultural competence among practitioners must be identified as a high priority (Grossman, 1998). Addressing the persistent educational outcome gaps among categories of students requires a thorough review of existing research and a candid evaluation of the appropriateness of that research to answer those questions.

The emergence of multicultural research presents a particular set of challenges to the established theoretical models and traditional empirical approaches in school psychology. Traditional empiricism approaches may not serve us well in multicultural research. This chapter seeks to clarify how and when traditional science applied to multicultural populations will yield results of questionable validity. It also presents models of research that are gaining prominence in other areas of psychology and related social sciences; these alternative frameworks offer promising avenues for expanding our knowledge of diverse populations and for improving services and practices. In this respect, the chapter advances the premise that a multicultural research agenda must encompass a wide range of research approaches, beyond those historically endorsed by the profession.

CULTURE AS A RESEARCHABLE CONSTRUCT
AND/OR EXPLANATORY VARIABLE

School psychology, following established and traditional research approaches in psychology, has not explored the cultural ecologies from within, as would be more typically done in anthropology or sociology. Instead, it has sought to understand cultural effects on a wide array of outcomes (e.g., school achievement). Generally speaking, school psychologists studying CLD students fall into a fallacy known as the hypothesis of cultural specificity. Typically, researchers seek to understand the effect of cultural membership by studying how culture interacts with treatment. Wampold (2002) succinctly questioned the assumptions underlying this premise. First, he argued, the approach assumes that it is the specific ingredients in the intervention that will affect some cultures differently than others, and that those ingredients are responsible for the benefits. Those conclusions might not necessarily correct because they overlook other potentially meaningful intervening and confounding variables (Betancourt & Lopez, 1993). Second, he suggested that, in that model of research, the provider of the intervention is unimportant—an assumption that has also been empirically and convincingly challenged in sister disciplines, particularly in counseling psychology (Ponterotto, Casas, Suzuki, & Alexander, 1995).

Further, Wampold pointed out that persons can be classified on constructs relevant to their response to treatments, but those classifications may not match the participants' self-identification. When a research study examines the relative efficacy of treatments across racial groups (e.g., African Americans, Asian Americans, Hispanic Americans, Euro-Americans), then the construct of *race*, as defined in the research, is elevated in importance vis-à-vis treatments. However, racial groups are confounded with other variables, including socioeconomic status (SES), levels of education, acculturation, motivation, and identity, to name a few.

Perhaps more troublesome is the seldom explored within-group differences, which tend to be pronounced among diverse populations. For example, Hispanics rarely identify themselves as such, preferring group identifications as Cuban,

Puerto Rican, or Mexican. The category Hispanic does not, by definition, represent a racial group; in fact, Hispanics are racially diverse; beyond race, their within-group variability includes substantial differences in cultural, religious, and linguistic practices.

Although the construct of race or culture may be used expediently in research, most investigators in school psychology do not adequately define these constructs empirically or theoretically. Moreover, researchers that attempt to study person characteristics by treatment interaction are pragmatically limited by the multiple variables that are necessary to take into account. Consequently, grouping participants arbitrarily by ethnic identification raises multiple internal and external validity concerns. Cultural membership is only one of a wide array of possible variables, including gender, education, SES, motivation, values, and religion (Betancourt & Lopez, 1993; Wampold, 2002). Although the cultural specificity hypothesis may be appealing for its simplicity and face validity, conclusions drawn from culture by treatment interactions are subject to the previous confounds and therefore potentially incorrect. Given the potential pitfalls described earlier, studies that seek to investigate cultural variables must take a broader account of contextual variables and recognize the limitations of subject groupings.

RESEARCH METHODS: EPISTEMOLOGICAL PERSPECTIVES

Research methods in the social sciences have been the subject of much debate over the past two decades, as researchers have questioned the prevailing positivistic inquiry models adopted early in the past century. Some have characterized this reexamination of research as a profound crisis because it has led some to question the foundations of their disciplinary knowledge (Woolgar, 1996). Scholars in school psychology have remained relatively unengaged in this discourse and have sought to strengthen empirical science as evidenced in the nature of the recommendations of the task force on evidence-based methods (EBM; Kratochwill & Shernoff, 2003; Kratochwill & Stoiber, 2000).

This is not to imply that school psychologists have failed to question the scope of research methods and engaged in projects to focus the discipline on the needs of children and schools. Notably, Conoley and Gutkin (1995) argued a decade ago for a research agenda in school psychology that would be ecologically informed. They stated,

School psychology does not suffer from a lack of good science. It suffers from a science that is devoted almost exclusively to answer the wrong set of questions. It is a science that is preoccupied with the problems of individuals rather than the ecologies in which people function. (p. 210)

Although these authors' critique of the field seemed to hit its target, the relative lack of progress along their recommendations suggests that the focus and methodology of research needs to change (Sheridan & Gutkin, 2000). In fact, to study human ecologies, we need to reconsider and perhaps redefine our research paradigms. As it stands now, school psychology science is best suited for understanding individuals, particularly those who can be treated in highly structured contexts, such as Applied Behavior Analysis (ABA). School psychology science suffers from predictable weaknesses when it attempts to study complex systems, exemplified in schools populated by diverse groups of individuals interacting, with varying roles, motivations, and identities. In essence, empiricist science serves us well for studying individuals under well-structured conditions, but it encounters challenges when exploring the complex human ecologies that multicultural school environments now represent. To move the discourse on school psychology's disciplinary knowledge forward, we must ask, how do we come to know what we know? What ways of knowing have been sanctioned? Are there viable alternatives? Could we tolerate or perhaps embrace a model of research that encompasses multiple methodological paradigms?

THEORETICAL PERSPECTIVES: WHAT IS EPISTEMOLOGY?

Epistemology is concerned with the implicit theories about knowledge that underpin research methods. In regard to school psychology, it is appropriate to ask what model supports school psychology science and what assumptions are embedded in our research practices. School psychologists in the United States have been trained almost invariably within a positivistic framework of research. A positivistic model seeks to predict and explain social events by searching for regularities and establishing causal relationships. A corollary of this epistemological framework is that knowledge grows in an orderly and cumulative fashion as new validated information is added and faulty hypotheses are discarded (Bernstein, 1983; Skrtic, 1991, 1995).

Another central aspect of research in school psychology is to ensure objectivity of results by ruling out the influence of subjectivity, particularly that of the researcher (Stoppard, 2002). Given the rather uniform nature of training in school psychology research, assumptions that underlie the positivistic paradigm tend to be rendered invisible; research is understood exclusively within the positivistic frame. In effect, models of inquiry that depart from conventional empiricist science are typically deemed as lacking rigor or not meeting objective criteria. Yet before alternative research paradigms are dismissed, it is important to learn about them and consider how other ways of knowing may challenge accepted, but unexplored, assumptions in our field.

There is a lively debate now taking place within social science research about the limitations of the positivistic paradigm, which is rooted in the natural sciences (Hacking, 1999). Some researchers contend that positivistic science is poorly suited as the main tool for understanding social interactions and human behavior (Trueba, 1993). This debate is particularly relevant to multicultural issues because it has profoundly influenced modern cultural anthropology (Gibson & Ogbu, 1991). In education, including special education, and to a lesser degree in other fields of psychology, new attention to qualitative research methods points to a need for alternative ways of understanding and interpreting human behavior (Woolgar, 1996).

LIMITATIONS OF POSITIVISM IN SOCIAL SCIENCE RESEARCH

Objectivity is a pillar of positivism; therefore, subjective influences on this type of research are seen as antithetical to the enterprise. The potential subjective perspectives of researchers are understood as particularly detrimental and are targeted for elimination. In ideal research conditions, researchers are unaware of whether the subjects studied are members of a treatment or control group. Investigators' use of randomization strategies, rating scales, standardized administration procedures, uniform training of raters, anonymous response forms, and other common procedures are also aimed at reducing subjectivity and, in turn, increasing objectivity. Critics of the positivistic model claim that, despite these conscious efforts to eliminate subjective bias, researchers' judgments remain an unexplored and ever-present source of error (Tolman & Brydon-Miller, 2001).

Positivistic science, emphasizing neutrality, objectivity, and rationality, does not address basic questions, such as researchers' motivation and its effect on choice of research topics, methods of investigation, and analysis and interpretation of results (Woolgar, 1996). In other words, the subjective dimension of the research enterprise remains in the shadow. Striving for objectivity, researchers assume the role of experts who generate knowledge in a process they view as unbiased and value-free. In contrast, research subjects are seen simply as sources of data and are inherently in a disempowered position in relation to the investigator.

Stoppard (2002) argued that the fundamental problem with positivistic epistemology in psychology is not only the spurious objectivity, but also its avoidance of these questions: Who is this research for? Whom does it benefit? These questions have great potency among groups who perceive that psychological research and practices have contributed to oppressive or marginalizing school policies (Cummins, 1986, 1989; Freire, 1995; Kincheloe, Steinberg, & Villaverde, 1999).

Since Kuhn's influential analysis of scientific processes in the late 1960s and early 1970s, there has been much discussion about paradigms in science and paradigm shifts. Kuhn's notions of paradigms have been widely applied in multiple settings to the point that it is often unclear what the concept may represent within various disciplines. Kuhn's work focused on the physical sciences and served to dispel pivotal unquestioned notions and misunderstandings about scientific inquiry. Rather than the expected rational, objective, orderly, and linear growth in scientific knowledge, Kuhn found that science, as practiced by natural scientists, is a nonrational cultural and subjective activity. He stated that science progresses slowly through the phases of normal science, and these relatively quiet periods are preludes to revolutionary science. It is in the periods of revolutionary science that existing theories fail to account for new data. What ensues may be described as a crisis; the unpredictable process of change that culminates in a new paradigm that has greater explanatory power. A paradigm shift takes places only when the scientific community shifts allegiances and accepts the premises that extend from the new paradigm. A period of normal science then follows as evidence supporting the new paradigm continues to be generated and organized.

Kuhn's work transformed the accepted views of science because he described the central roles of culture, tradition, and convention in scientific pursuits. The scientific view of the physical world, informed by Kuhn and his followers, is not the product of objective and rational-technical, dispassionate scientists. Rather, it reflects culturally derived constructions and conventions within a scientific community. Scientific knowledge about the world may be better understood as historically situated knowledge, or as knowledge that has temporary validity and utility. In effect, scientists are better described as engaged in constructing knowledge, rather than discovering unalterable facts that are free from time and context (Hacking, 1999; Krohn, 1981). By emphasizing the subjective, Kuhn did not intend to critique the scientific method per se. Rather, he sought to demystify the view of science as an objective orderly and rational enterprise. Science, like most human activity, is based on tradition and cultural conventions and is fraught with irrationality.

Although Kuhn's work addressed only the physical sciences, his observations are relevant to all scientific enterprise because it elucidates the contributions of culture and subjectivity in the construction of all human knowledge. This model of scientific revolutions he described, however, does not resonate with the work in the social sciences. In psychology, multiple paradigms coexist, often offering contradictory views of the same phenomenon. It seems as if when the empiricist paradigm is applied to the social sciences, researchers either fail to discard false hypotheses or continue to generate alternative viable explanations for the same phenomena. More troublesome is the weak predictive power of social science research. Using the terminology of constructivism, different branches or disciplines within the social sciences develop versions of the social world that are consistent with their respective research paradigms. The multiple concurrent and often contradictory approaches to define and treat learning disabilities is a case in point (Sleeter, 1986).

The study of subjectivity intrigued pioneers of psychology, but ironically in contemporary school psychology the issues related to subjectivity have been largely neglected. Instead, school psychology science typically insists on a contrived objectivity, presuming that researchers have no personal investment in the area of study and are capable of being neutral about the results of their investigations. In school psychology, the conventional tools of research—performance on tests, questionnaires, behavior checklists, and other validated instruments—cannot adequately inform researchers about the subjective experience of participants, their ways of making meaning, or how they explain and understand their own behavior. Not only are the researchers opaque and unknowable, but the subjects of their investigation are also poorly described. Participants' understanding of their own performance generally remains unknown (Korn, 2004).

To explore human experiences, and particularly when those experiences are informed by cultures and contexts unfamiliar to us, the subjective perspectives of participants in research are more than a curiosity. Those subjectivities must be acknowledged, addressed, and studied in order to access information relevant to the meaning of participants' behaviors. It may be argued that the ideological bases of the positivistic research paradigm unwittingly become an obstacle to comprehend the complexity of human experience. By insisting on the necessity to minimize contextual influences, homogenize treatments, and investigate only key significant variables, researchers reduce experience to a narrow focus. Consequently, researchers are drawn to conclusions that may reflect their worldviews, but neglect or remain uninformed about others'> (subjects') perspectives on reality.

Multicultural research, to be valid, must seek to clarify how different cultures, statuses, contexts, and roles inform the subjective experience of subjects. Although this does not imply a challenge to the notion that there is a reality outside human experience independent of human perception, any knowledge we have of that reality is mediated by history, culture, and personal experience. In other words, we cannot pretend to understand human experience without taking into account the sociopolitical contextual nature of that experience (Bhaskar, 1989).

The idea that individuals construct their version of reality is generally alien to a research paradigm that discounts context and equates subjectivity with bias. Instead, a positivistic research approach aims to create predictive models by isolating variables and evaluating their contribution to behavioral outcomes. As a result of following this model, school psychology researchers have gravitated toward investigating phenomena that are amenable to this approach. Studies of behavioral intervention are more typical of our field than identity formation, for example.

The argument being made here is that the demands of reducing behavior to measurable components lead to an impoverished understanding of subjects' motives. A naive reader of our literature may be surprised by school psychology's remarkable silence on such topics as the lived experience of immigrant children, the palpable incidence of racism in particular schools, the internal dynamics of clicks in specific middle schools, or the choices adolescents make by joining gangs and gravitating toward drug use. These are just a few examples of students' experiences that are highly contextualized and difficult to explore with our current methods. Rather than obtaining information directly from the students (i.e., tapping their sense of reality), we position ourselves as objective observers and seek to infer the meaning of their actions. Predictably, the greater our distance from the lived experience of those we study, the more likely we are to draw the wrong conclusions about their behavior. Contextualized observations, to be valid, hinge on the observers' intimate familiarity with both subjects and the environment.

The high incidence of dropout and drug use among urban youths, for example, has been extensively studied. Yet school psychology science has only described the contours of those problems perhaps because we, as researchers, may have little personal experience with these problems. Clearly, if we seek to understand participants' experiences and consciousness, we must expand our research modalities to include qualitative approaches because those methods are more suitable to uncover the meanings of human behaviors (Stoppard, 2002).

IMPLICATIONS FOR PRACTICE

The problems worthy of research in multicultural school psychology do not lend themselves well to experimentation. Beyond the difficulties associated with randomization of subjects and assignment to conditions, it is virtually impossible to isolate and manipulate variables as proxies for linguistic and cultural factors. Therefore, research about multicultural populations is best conducted in natural settings. The following section describes a number of research modalities that may

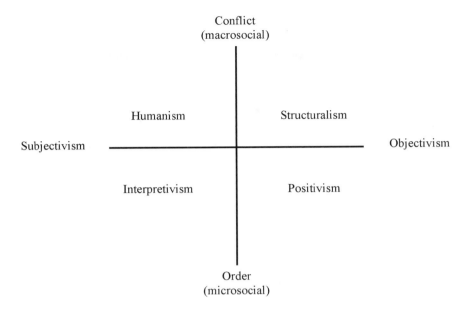

FIGURE 29–1. Adapted for Burrell, G., & Morgan, G. (1979). *Sociological paradigms and organizational analysis*. London: Heinemann.

complement and expand existing approaches to knowledge generation in multicultural school psychology.

Complementary Approaches

Expanding the field's research options requires that we review approaches that have taken root in related disciplines. Burrell and Morgan (1979) developed a framework that represents a schematic overview of social science research and may be useful for explaining the relationship among various research paradigms. Notably, Skrtic (1991, 1995) and Danford and Taff (2004) elaborated their thinking by relating the implications of this framework to special education. They outlined four basic paradigms encompassing the major philosophical underpinnings of modern social thought. These paradigms describe bedrock assumptions that undergird belief systems about the social world; emerging research methodologies spring from and are consistent with these belief systems (Danford & Taff, 2004). Sktric (1995) suggested that beliefs about the social world, and specifically about special education practices, may be displayed graphically, as in Figure 29–1.

The vertical axis in the diagram represents the continuum regarding beliefs about society and education. Locating school psychology research within this framework provides a valuable perspective on the field. School psychologists, inferring from our research literature, tend to be found toward the order end of this dimension, embracing the belief that society and schools are primarily orderly and predictable. They hold that most people agree on central values and desire similar lifestyles. The underlying assumption is that current arrangements in society, including the distribution of resources and wealth, are generally just and should be maintained. Change, to the extent that is needed, should be gradual, incremental, and rational. The role of the profession, seen from the perspective of order, is to help individuals fit in–to adjust to the demands of schools and society.

At the other end of this continuum, society is viewed as composed of many competing groups and agendas. The conflicting interests of social classes and racial, ethnic, and religious groups fragment society and schools; access to power and privilege are not equitable. From this vantage point, people understand that struggles are not limited to access to resources, but they also entail assertion of human rights, attaining social status and preserving dignity. Committed individuals who challenge the status quo and expose the injustices created by societal arrangements bring about change in society. Reformers confront the disparities between the rhetoric of democracy and the realities of disempowerment. Change is necessary and messy; it requires advocacy and personal investment. If school psychology were to reflect beliefs at the conflict end of the continuum, it would strive to bring about changes in schools consistent with agendas for social reform and equity. School would become instruments for social change.

The graph's horizontal axis stands for beliefs about knowledge and knowledge generation. Essentially, this refers to what type of knowledge people view as most trustworthy and useful. Objectivism, at the right end of the continuum, represents the belief that knowledge generated following standard scientific procedures is most valuable and desirable; this is consistent with the principles of positivism derived from the natural (hard) sciences. The researcher maintaining a neutral, rational, and objective stance in relation to the object of study characterizes this approach. Objectivism calls for the identification and quantification of variables, allowing for a dispassionate, unbiased analysis of data that logically serves to support or reject hypotheses. These procedures reflect the detached and value-free stance of the researcher. Also, knowledge is seen as cumulative, convergent, and objective—it presumes to bring us closer to the discovery of a stable truth that is free from time and context.

Recent efforts in school psychology to promote evidence-based interventions (EBI) reflect a commitment to objectivism (positivism). Proponents postulate that the best path to generate knowledge in school psychology is through the principles of modern objectivist science. Although the task force on EBI defines *empiricism* broadly, to include qualitative research, within categories of EBI, it privileges well-controlled quantitative experimental studies. Other forms of evidence are accepted where such studies do not exist or are not feasible (Kratochwill & Shernoff, 2003).

Subjectivists, in contrast, propose that detachment and neutrality may in fact be obstacles to understanding human beings and social interaction. Proponents of this view argue that what one knows best is related to one's personal experience. We know by interacting and gaining intimate knowledge of our objects of study. All people, including researchers, are understood to be emotional, subjective, biased, ideological, and idiosyncratic. Anti-objectivists reject any possibility of a neutral, rational, and objective vantage point to understand human activities (Bernstein, 1983). At the extreme end of subjectivism, there is no single, uncontested, and authoritative truth in the social realm; instead, we are characteristically championing our own versions of truth that have emerged from our limited and value-laden experiences (Danford & Taff, 2004).

School psychology has historically been closely associated with the objectivist and order dimensions outlined earlier. Professional training and research has been closely tied to rules of evidence derived from positivistic methods; as a consequence, the traditional arrangements in the profession may be described as follows. Researchers are at the pinnacle because their role is to add to the professional knowledge base. Trainers translate that knowledge into interventions (engineering) and incorporate them into the preservice curriculum; practitioners are then prepared at a training program to carry out and implement validated practices. Once working in the field, practitioners become consumers of research. They are expected to review and assimilate findings reported in professional journals in order to update their skills (Skrtic, 1995).

This hierarchical model of knowledge production in school psychology reflects the structure found in most modern professions. Like other human service professions based on traditional social science research (i.e., psychiatry, counseling psychology, social work, special education), school psychology must respond to the challenge of subjectivism and its implied critique of conventional research methodology. The stakes in this discourse are substantial, if theoretical knowledge is subject to doubt; the entire professional training enterprise would be compromised (Schon, 1983). Possibly because of the magnitude of this challenge, which would require a major re-assessment of our identity and professional practices, the discipline has yet to engage in a sustained discussion on the value of different research paradigms. Nevertheless, a recent NASP (2005) position statement and other officially sanctioned publications, such as the EBI Task Force of Division 16 (APA), include qualitative research, case study, and ethnography as potentially valuable inquiry methods (Kratochwill & Shernoff, 2004).

IMPLEMENTATION AND APPROACHES

In this segment, illustrations are offered on how different research approaches may be adopted and adapted to inquiry in school psychology. Although research studies may incorporate different methodologies to answer a particular research question or explore specific school ecologies (Tashakkori & Teddlie, 2003), researchers must be aware of the inherent difficulties associated with integrating data gathered through different and potentially conflicting approaches. This may be the case when the researcher is attempting to be an ethnographic participant observer while trying to minimize researcher effect on a controlled intervention at the site of the investigation. The following four approaches to research reflect polar positions quadrants derived from Figure 29–1.

Interpretivism

Interpretivism suggests a way of knowing that springs from personal experience and maintains a relatively narrow, locally situated focus (micro). Individual narratives provide the best examples of the interpretivist approach. In this vein, Bruner (1996) suggested that we learn from our encounters with the world, and that through these transactions we develop a sense of selfhood that gives meaning to our existence. The philosophical roots of interpretivism are in phenomenology, which may be described as the study of individual experience as well as ways of deriving meaning from those experiences.

Positivistic trained researchers are typically uncomfortable with the idea that findings that emerge from interpretivist (qualitative) studies lack standardization and generalizability. However, one needs to bear in mind that these studies are not intended to yield the capacity to predict behavior, control outcomes, or arrive at indisputable facts. Instead, interpretivist narratives seek to focus on and yield understanding (Danford & Taff, 2004). One may ask, given an array of options: Which intervention is better? From another perspective, one may ask: What happens when a particular intervention is implemented? The positivistic derived method offers ways to assess outcomes, appropriate for the first question. An interpretivist informed approach would be better suited for gaining insight into the second question (Edelsky, 1990).

There are multiple implications for multicultural research in embracing an interpretivist approach. First, it allows for the exploration of individual experiences that may lie beyond the cultural mainstream, without falling into the predictable stereotypes of contrived federal census categories. Second, the idea that our sense of reality is a cultural construction permits and encourages researchers to consider that participants in the study understand the world differently. Third, those different perspectives and ways of making meaning of experience are worthy of exploration. Finally, it focuses attention on the idiosyncratic nature of social arrangements, leaving open the possibility of increasing mutual understanding and collaboration toward a common good.

Attention to interpretivism has been scant in school psychology (Korn, 1997). Green and Gredler (2002) offered an informative article on constructivism that is relevant to this discussion. Constructivism is central to interpretivism because it posits that individuals construct a sense of self through experience, and that learning occurs in socially constructed contexts that support it. While recognizing that constructivism is an emerging and powerful set of constructs that are influencing the literature on learning and school reform, these authors emphasized in their article that constructivism has "no strong supporting research base." They later elaborated on their reasons for addressing the implications of constructivism to the field, "... not to recommend that school psychologists adopt constructivist approaches, but to highlight current school psychology practices that may be useful when school psychologists encounter the constructivist perspective" (p. 62). The authors lamented that the application of constructivist concepts to classroom practices has not been adequately investigated, although they observe that they are becoming widely accepted. In fact, constructivism has taken root in many schools as teachers and administrators are increasingly exposed to those constructs in pre- and in-service training (Mintrop, 2001).

Yet the claim that constructivism lacks research validity may be unfounded; the theories of human learning and cognition of such notable constructivists as Piaget and Vygotsky have been amply studied and validated by multiple research methods. Perhaps the theorists' focus on intrapsychic structures are anathema to some empirical researchers—such as radical behaviorists—who would accept only behavioral outcomes as valid evidence. Other empiricists are likely to question the value of constructivist theories in classroom practice because they are not enacted as a standardized set of lessons or practices subject to comparison with other competing approaches. Despite a lack of unequivocal endorsement by science, constructivism has captured the imagination of many teachers and teacher educators, influencing their approaches to pedagogical practice (Fischetti, Dittmer, & Kyle, 1996).

Constructivism, as a topic of inquiry, could be explored in different ways. Adopting an interpretivist stance, multicultural school psychology researchers would not limit themselves to validating constructivism's instructional effectiveness; they would study how this ideology shapes school culture and informs teacher practice. Another related agenda could explore more deeply *how* children learn when taught using these approaches. Interpretivist, qualitative methods of research applied in school contexts could be useful for understanding the processes involved, beyond their measurable outcomes. This example illustrates how constructivists might frame research questions differently from quantitative researchers; their focus is primarily on understanding processes and experiences, rather than on validating efficiency or effectiveness of treatments.

Humanism

According to Burrell and Morgan (1979), humanists share assumptions of subjectivity and social construction, akin to interpretivists, but their focus is on a macroscale because they are interested in social change. Their perspective on social organization emphasizes the presence of conflict in society. Integral to the humanist stance is the effort to expose injustices and limitation created by ideological systems embedded in values and cultures. Societal structures and traditions are seen as inhibiting human potential, which may be promoted by making the oppressive aspects of culture transparent and accessible to consciousness (Bernstein, 1983; Hacking, 1999; Skrtic, 1995). Research that emanates from this paradigm seeks to elucidate contradictions in our perceptions and beliefs about society, and how it really is. It seeks to dispel myths, ideologies, and traditions in order to promote human growth, dignity, and freedom.

The relevance of this paradigm to multicultural school psychology is obvious. Multicultural concerns have historically been associated not only with difference, but also with minority status. The humanist approach would serve school psychology to engage in progressive research agendas. For example, school psychology has not engaged in meaningful research on racism, sexism, or discrimination on the bases of disability, sexual orientation, or class status. Although these have been some of the central social concerns in the past decades, our disciplinary research project has skirted them. Clearly these social issues impact on children, teachers, and school communities, yet our journals step cautiously, if at all, into those waters. Why? Perhaps, it may be argued, because it is difficult to explore such areas of study employing traditional positivistic models. More likely it is due to the contrived objective stance required of researchers and the reluctance to appear to take sides on ideologically charged issues. Research questions such as how prejudice impacts on children's mental health or how immigrant children experience the challenges of acculturation are worthy of study and are possibly more appropriately understood when investigators adopt a humanist approach. Most qualitative research methods are consistent with humanistic beliefs.

Structuralism

This paradigm shares with the objectivists the premise of an objective social reality, but its focus is on macrostructures within cultures and the inevitable inequalities found across social groups—present even in liberal democracies. It emphasizes the conflicts and struggles within the social world and seeks to promote change by addressing the asymmetrical power relationships among groups. Rather than attending to subjective consciousness, as would be typical of humanists, structuralists are more likely to analyze social organization along distinct and concrete grouping (i.e., gender, class, race, ethnicity, and disability status). Seeking to promote a more egalitarian society, structuralists are concerned with the distribution of power in institutions, economies, and governments (Danford & Taff, 2004). In school settings, objectivists may describe students' behaviors as noncompliant or deviant; structuralists are likely to interpret those same behaviors as natural responses to coercion or oppression.

Applying this paradigm to multicultural school psychology requires a greater awareness of how schools may inadvertently perpetuate unjust structures and differentiated access to privilege (Bursztyn, 2004). An example of thinking within this paradigm would be a research agenda that seeks to understand the dynamics of school practices that lead to disproportionate rates of referral of African American children to special education. Another area of structuralists' concern is the degree of racial and class segregation in American schools. These issues have been present in traditional school psychology research, but given the self-imposed limitation of neutrality and distance, school psychology has not interpreted the research as a call for major social reform. Instead, our literature describes the trends and makes modest recommendations to address these problems.

Working toward school change is part of school psychology's professional culture. Challenging power structures and promoting social change are not. One may argue that a consequence of not working toward social change is the strengthening of the status quo. This is clear, for example, when studying the academic performance of urban children. Researchers rarely report on the higher incidence of poverty, discrimination, acculturation processes, or other life stresses affecting their lives and their families. Also, they often neglect to state the qualifications of teachers in those schools and their attrition rates. Similarly, funding and resources tend to be scarce in poor urban schools, but our literature pays little attention to those contextual complexities. Consequently, studies that report only on urban students' relatively lower scores on standardized tests may serve as instruments in ideologically charged arguments. That was illustrated in the controversial and misinformed debate spurred by The Bell Curve in the mid-1990s (Herrnstein & Murray, 1994). Structuralists would tell us that a multicultural research agenda that is not focused on social justice is likely to be used to perpetuate social injustice.

As we consider various research paradigms, it becomes clear that research is not a neutral activity. Problem conceptualization and research design priorities impact the nature of data collection and interpretation of results. Heightening awareness of these inherent difficulties in multicultural studies may serve us well as we move toward a more comprehensive approach to research and a more thoughtful response to public policies (Dawson et al., 2004).

IMPLICATIONS FOR FUTURE RESEARCH

Research methodologies that support theory building, increase professional knowledge, and inform applied practices tend to be linked to a single social science paradigm. Historically, this has been true in school psychology. Yet the emerging and urgent need to increase the professional knowledge base to work effectively cross-culturally present a unique and timely set of challenges. Limiting the profession to a single paradigm may hinder efforts to develop the necessary competencies for work in diverse and cross-cultural contexts. Therefore, a future research agenda in our field must go beyond identifying areas in need of research. It must: (a) include an expanded repertoire of research methodologies, (b) develop awareness of how school psychology science shapes the profession, and (c) explore how our science affects the diverse individuals and populations we seek to help.

An agenda for future research in multicultural school psychology should not be defined by a single method, nor should one method be deemed most valid, thus relegating all other approaches to categories of deficiency. Instead, we should adopt a pragmatist approach, as advocated early in the 20th century by the pioneering psychologists William James and John Dewey. Such an approach is less committed to a specific philosophy than to solving a real-life problem. Action research in social science reflects this approach, and as Kurt Lewin demonstrated, it is further strengthened by involving stakeholders in the inquiry process. Defining a real-world problem worthy of research is the key conceptual step that informs action researchers on potential paths to inquiry. When this is accomplished as part of a collaborative process, involving researchers and stakeholders, it leads to greater potential impact and openness to change (McNiff, 2002).

An action research paradigm is eclectic and flexible. It may focus primarily on a need for understanding, such as why immigrant students continue to drop out of high school despite efforts to retain them; or it may fall in a more traditional domain of inquiry, such as what method of mathematics instruction is more promising. In the first case, an ethnographic or case study approach may be advisable, but it should be complemented by an accurate assessment of the rate and nature of dropout in the target school. In the second example, learning that a particular method yielded higher scores may not be sufficient to declare it superior. Understanding what cognitive processes are engaged in student learning, accessed through qualitative methods, would answer questions that otherwise would be left to speculation. Qualitative data may also be useful for theorizing, and therefore eliciting the next set of questions to be researched.

While offering the previous examples as illustrations of the advantages of a mixed method design, we might ask rhetorically, what study in a natural setting would not benefit from an array of inquiry approaches? If we begin the premise that research is a way of enriching our understanding of human nature, then a wide array of methods of investigation is more likely to provide a more nuanced and complete depiction of the human condition under study.

To embrace an action research paradigm that includes a range of methodologies tailored for problem solving, school psychologist researchers must become familiar and competent in deploying diverse methodologies, recognize the limitations of various approaches, and be capable of identifying compatible and complementary strategies. Implications for training are self-evident. School psychology programs would not only need to reexamine the way that future researchers are prepared, but they must also be open to consider a wider range of research evidence—beyond that available in positivistic professional journals.

Considering the significant demographic shifts in the United States and the cultural and technological developments that are transforming that ways people interact, school psychology practices must adapt and respond to remain viable. Our science must do the same. Questions about knowledge production, dissemination, and use are brought into sharper focus by the increasing diversity of the populations we serve. In response to this challenge, it has been argued through this presentation that school psychology should adopt a more decentralized and context-driven approach to research—one that seeks to solve local problems by deploying a variety of inquiry methods. This approach may serve to integrate questions associated with human diversity into the mainstream (instead of compartmentalized knowledge of minority populations), and thus improve the profession's standing and promote its viability as a discipline that serves the common good.

ANNOTATED REFERENCES

Danforth, D., & Taff, S. D. (2004). *Crucial readings in special education.* Upper Saddle River, NJ: Pearson/Merrill Prentice-Hall.

This volume is a compilation of previously published controversial and thought-provoking articles in special education. It includes chapters on research and evaluation methods in special education and provides critical insights into the limitations of current models and practices.

Ponterotto, J. G., Casas, J. M., Suzuki, L. A., & Alexander, C. M. (Eds.). (2001). *Handbook of multicultural counseling.* Thousand Oaks, CA: Sage.

This text's second edition features an expanded section on research and evaluation. Traditional research methods are deployed in an effort to answer questions about the legitimacy of multicultural counseling.

Richardson, J. (1996). *The handbook for qualitative research methods for psychology and the social sciences.* Leicester, UK: British Psychological Society Books.

This volume presents a diverse array of qualitative methodologies and their applications to psychological problems. It is an excellent introductory text, drawing on the perspectives and scholarship of prominent qualitative researches.

Kratochwill, T. R., & Stoiber, K. C. (2002, Winter). Evidence-based interventions in school psychology: The state of the art and future directions [Special Issue]. *School Psychology Quarterly.*

This issue of the SPQ presents the conceptual, philosophical, and methodological basis for the *Procedural and Coding Manual for Review of Evidence-Based Interventions*. It introduces the concept of a coding system to be implemented by practitioners to develop a knowledge base on what works in practice to help bridge the gap between research and practice. This volume is a good example of traditional approaches to research in school psychology.

RESOURCES

http://www.groundedtheory.com/

The Grounded Theory Institute is a nonprofit organization that promotes the use of Grounded Theory as formulated by Barney G. Glaser, PhD. The Institute also publishes a journal: *The Grounded Theory Review.*

http://www.nova.edu/ssss/QR/

The Qualitative Report, accessed through the Nova University website, is an online journal of qualitative research in the social sciences. The site also offers resources and links of interest to qualitative researchers.

http://www.vanguard.edu/faculty/ddegelman/amoebaweb/index

This website, maintained by Douglas Degelman, PhD, Professor of Psychology at Vanguard University of Southern California, posts a wide array of resources and articles to assist graduate students conducting research in psychology.

http://www.sosig.ac.uk/roads/subject-listing/World-cat/meth.html

The Social Science Information Gateway site is managed by Exeter University, England. It lists Internet resources that can support social research across the disciplines. The Research Tools and Methods section offers access to those resources. The target audience is researchers and students interested in social science research.

REFERENCES

Artiles, A., & Zamora-Duran, G. (1997). *Reducing the disproportionate representation of culturally diverse students in special and gifted education.* Reston, VA: Council for Exceptional Children.

Barrera, I. (1995). To refer or not to refer: Untangling the web of diversity, "deficit" and disability in preschool children from culturally diverse populations. *NYSABE Journal, 10,* 54–66.

Bernstein, R. J. (1983). *Beyond objectivism and relativism: Science, hermeneutics and praxis.* Philadelphia: University of Pennsylvania Press.

Betancourt, H., & Lopez, S. R. (1993). The study of culture, ethnicity, and race in American psychology. *American Psychologist, 48*(6), 629–637.

Bhaskar, R. (1989). *Reclaiming reality: A critical introduction to contemporary philosophy*. London: Verso.

Bruner, J. (1996). *The culture of education*. Cambridge, MA: Harvard University Press.

Burnette, J. (1998). Reducing the disproportionate representation of minority students in special education (ERIC-OSEP Digest No. E566).

Burrell, G., & Morgan, G. (1979). *Sociological paradigms and organizational analysis*. London: Heinemann.

Bursztyn, A. M. (1997, Spring). Multicultural dialogue in school psychology. *The School Psychologist, 51,* 40–41.

Bursztyn, A. M. (2002). The path to academic disability: Javier's school experience. In C. Korn & A. Bursztyn (Eds.), *Rethinking multicultural education: Case studies in cultural transition* (pp. 160–183). New Haven, CT: Bergin & Garvey.

Bursztyn, A. M. (2004). Special education, urban schools and the uncertain path to social justice. In J. L. Kincheloe, A. Bursztyn, & S. R. Steinberg (Eds.), *Teaching teachers: Building a quality school of urban education* (pp.135–166). New York: Peter Lang.

Canino, I. A., & Spurlock, J. S. (1994). *Culturally diverse children and adolescents. Assessment, diagnosis and treatment*. New York: Guilford.

Conoley, J. C., & Gutkin, T. B. (1995). Why didn't—why doesn't—school psychology realize its promise? *Journal of School Psychology, 33,* 209–217.

Cummins, J. (1986). Psychological assessment of minority students: Out of context, out of control? *Journal of Reading, Writing and Learning Disabilities International, 2,* 1–8.

Cummins, J. (1989). *Empowering minority students*. Sacramento, CA: California Association of Bilingual Education.

Curtis, M. J., & Stollar, S. A. (2002). Best practices in systems level change. In A. Thomas & J. Grimes (Eds.), *Best practices in school psychology IV* (pp. 223–234). Bethesda, MD: National Association of School Psychologists.

Danford, D., & Taff, S. D. (2004). *Crucial readings in special education*. Upper Saddle River, NJ: Pearson/Merrill Prentice-Hall.

Dawson, M., Cummings, J. A., Harrison, P. L., Short, R. J., Gorin, S., & Palomares, R. (2004). The 2002 multisite Conference on the Future of School Psychology: Next steps. *School Psychology Review, 33,* 115–125.

Edelsky, C. (1990). Whose agenda is this anyway? A response to McKenna, Robinson, & Miller. *Educational Researcher, 19,* 7–13.

Fagan, T. K., & Wise, P. S. (2000). *School psychology: Past, present and future*. Bethesda, MD: National Association of School Psychologists.

Figueroa, R. A. (1989). Psychological testing of linguistic minority students: Knowledge gaps and regulations. *Exceptional Children, 56,* 111–119.

Fischetti, J., Dittmer, A., & Kyle, D. W. (1996). Shifting paradigms: Emerging issues for educational policy and practice. *Teacher Educator, 3,* 189–201.

Freire, P. (1995). *Pedagogy of hope: Reliving pedagogy of the oppressed*. New York: Continuum.

Geisinger, F. (1992). *Psychological testing of Hispanics*. Washington, DC: American Psychological Association.

Gersten, R., & Woodward, J. (1994). The language minority student and special education: Issues, trends, and paradoxes. *Exceptional Children, 60,* 310–322.

Gibson, M. A., & Ogbu, J. U. (1991). *Minority status and schooling: A comparative study of immigrant and involuntary minorities*. New York: Garland.

Green, S. K., & Gredler, M. E. (2002). A review and analysis of constructivism for school-based practice. *School Psychology Review, 31*, 53–70.

Grossman, H. (1998). *Ending discrimination in special education.* Springfield, IL: Charles C. Thomas.

Hacking, I. (1999). *The social construction of what?* Cambridge, MA: Harvard University Press.

Harry, B. (1994). *The disproportionate representation of minority students in special education: Theories and recommendations* (Project FORUM, Final Report). (ERIC Document Reproduction Service No. ED374637)

Herrnstein, R. J., & Murray, C. (1994). *The bell curve: Intelligence and class structure in American life.* New York: The Free Press.

Hughes, J. N. (2000). The role of theory in the science of treating children: Beyond empirically supported treatments. *Journal of School Psychology, 38*, 301–330.

Ingraham, C. L., & Bursztyn, A. (1999, August). Systems interventions: Psychologists' roles in shaping school culture, educational policy, and institutional advocacy. In M. Rogers (Chair), *Cross-cultural school psychology: Advances in the field.* Washington, DC: American Psychological Association.

Kincheloe J. L., Steinberg S. R., & Villaverde, L. (1999). *Rethinking intelligence: Confronting psychological assumptions about teaching and learning.* New York: Routledge.

Korn, C. (1997). Applying a narrative frame to the assessment of children. *Canadian Journal of School Psychology, 13*, 28–37.

Korn, C. (2004). Run Jane run: Researching teacher practice frame by frame. In J. L. Kincheloe, A. Bursztyn, & S. R. Steinberg (Eds.), *Teaching teachers: Building a quality school of urban education* (pp. 157–178). New York: Peter Lang.

Kratochwill, T. R., & Shernoff, E. S. (2003). Evidenced-based practice: Promoting evidence-based interventions in school psychology. *School Psychology Quarterly, 18*, 389–408.

Kratochwill, T. R., & Shernoff, E. S. (2004). Evidenced-based practice: Promoting evidence-based interventions in school psychology. *School Psychology Review, 33*(1), 34–48.

Kratochwill, T. R., & Stoiber, K. C. (2000). Uncovering critical research agendas for school psychology: Conceptual dimensions and future directions. *School Psychology Review, 29*, 591–603.

Krohn, R. (1981). Introduction: Toward the empirical study of scientific practice. In K. D. Korr, R. Krohn, & R. Whitley (Eds.), *The social process of scientific investigation* (pp. 7–25). Boston: D. Reidel.

Lubinski, D. (2000). Scientific and social significance of assessing individual differences: "Sinking shafts at a few critical points." *Annual Review of Psychology, 51*, 405–444.

Markowitz, J. (1996). *Disproportionate representation: A critique of state and local strategies* (Policy Forum, Final Report). Washington, DC. (ERIC Document Reproduction Service No. ED392195)

McNiff, J., with Whitehead, J. (2002). *Action research: Principles and practice* (2nd ed.). London: Routledge

Mercer, J. R. (1973). *Labeling the mentally retarded.* Berkeley, CA: University of California Press.

Mintrop, H. (2001). Educating students to teach in a constructivist way—Can it all be done? *Teachers-College-Record, 103*(2), 207–239.

National Association of School Psychologists. (2005). *Position statement on prevention and intervention research in the schools.* Bethesda, MD: NASP Publications.

Ponterotto, J. G., Casas, J. M., Suzuki, L. A., & Alexander, C. M. (Eds.). (1995). *Handbook of multicultural counseling.* Thousand Oaks, CA: Sage.

Reschly, D. J. (2000). The present and future status of school psychology in the United States. *School Psychology Review, 29*, 507–522.

Robertson, P., Kushner, M., Starks, J., & Drescher, C. (1994). An update of participation of culturally and linguistically diverse students in special education: The need for a research and policy agenda. *The Bilingual Special Education Perspective, 14*, 3–9.

Rogers, M., Ingraham, C., Bursztyn, A. M., Cajigas-Segredo, N., Esquivel, G., Hess, R., Lopez, E., & Nahari, S. (1999). Providing psychological services to racially, ethnically, culturally, and linguistically diverse individuals in the schools. *School Psychology International, 20*, 243–264.

Ross, M. R., Powell, S. R., & Elias, M. J. (2002). New roles for school psychologists: Addressing the social and emotional needs of students. *School Psychology Review, 31*, 43–52.

Schon, D. A. (1983). *The reflective practitioner: How professional think in action.* New York: Basic Books.

Sheridan, S. M., & Gutkin, T. B. (2000). The ecology of school psychology: Examining and changing our paradigm for the 21st century. *School Psychology Review, 29*, 485–502.

Skrtic, T. M. (1991). Students with special educational needs: Artifacts of the traditional curriculum . In M. Aincow (Ed.), *Effective schools for all* (pp. 20–42). London: David Fulton.

Skrtic, T. M. (1995). *Disability and democracy: Reconstructing (special) education for postmodernity.* New York: Teachers College Press.

Sleeter, C. E. (1986). Learning disabilities: The social construction of a special education category. *Exceptional Children, 53*, 46–54.

Stoppard, J. M. (2002). Navigating the hazards of orthodoxy: Introducing a graduate course on qualitative methods into the psychology curriculum. *Canadian Psychology, 43*, 143–153.

Tashakkori, A., & Teddlie, C. (2003). *Handbook of mixed methods in social and behavioral research.* Thousand Oaks, CA: Sage.

Tolman, D. L., & Brydon-Miller, M. (2001). *From subjects to subjectivities: A handbook of interpretive and participatory methods.* New York: New York University Press.

Trueba, H. T. (1993). Cultural diversity and conflict: The role of educational anthropology in healing multicultural America. In P. Phelan & A. L. Davidson (Eds.), *Renegotiating cultural diversity in American schools* (pp. 195–215). New York: Teachers College Press.

Wampold, B. E. (2002). An examination of the bases of evidence-based interventions. *School Psychology Quarterly, 17*, 500–507.

Woolgar, S. (1996). Psychology, qualitative methods and the ideas of science. In J. T. E. Richardson (Ed.), *Handbook of qualitative research for psychology and the social sciences* (pp. 11–24). Leicester, UK: British Psychological Society Books.

30

FUTURE DIRECTIONS FOR PRACTITIONERS, TRAINERS, AND RESEARCHERS: INTERDISCIPLINARY PERSPECTIVES

Various disciplines within psychology and education have accumulated an impressive array of literature and research in the area of multiculturalism. School psychologists and other school professionals have much to learn from the body of multicultural knowledge generated by these disciplines. The last chapter in this handbook takes a unique approach by presenting five commentaries written by experts in the fields of bilingual special education, counseling psychology clinical psychology, social psychology, and organizational psychology. The authors of these commentaries were asked to reflect on the applicability and implications of the multicultural knowledge base within their individual disciplines to future practice, research, and training in school psychology. Their commentaries provide important insights about current practices and future directions.

COMMENTARY 1

The Education of English Language Learners With Special Needs: The Challenge for School Psychologists

Leonard Baca
BUENO Center for Multicultural Education, Boulder

English Language Learners (ELL) is the term currently used to refer to students from non-English language backgrounds in our schools (Baca & Cervantes, 2004). These children may also be referred to as bilingual students and students with limited English proficiency (LEP). School psychologists will have an increasing number of these bilingual students on their caseloads in the future. It is clear from the U.S. Census data that this group of students continues to grow at a rapid pace (Klingner & Artiles, 2003). The U.S. Department of Education (2003) estimates that more than 3.5 million students in U.S. schools are LEP. Approximately 75% of these students are Hispanic. Hispanics are the fastest-growing ethnic group in U.S. schools, surpassing African Americans as the largest minority group in the country (U.S. Census Bureau, 2003).

When one examines the achievement levels of ELL students, it is clear that there is a significant achievement gap between them and mainstream students. The high school dropout rate for these students is also much higher than the dropout rate for mainstream students. In 1998, for example, only 63% of 18- to 24-year-old Hispanics finished high school, compared with 85% of the total population (U.S. Department of Education, 2003). It is interesting to note that this achievement gap has existed for many years (Abedi & Dietel, 2004). Lee (2002) observed that the achievement between minority and nonminority students narrowed in the 1970s and 1980s, it widened in the late 1980s and 1990s, and it remains large today.

Over the years, there have been several policy-related efforts to address this achievement gap. In 1968, the federal government passed the Bilingual Education Act in an effort to provide bilingual programs for all students. This same legislation also provided English as a Second Language (ESL) programs for many of these students. In 1974, the U.S. Supreme Court ruled in *Lau v. Nichols* that these students should be given special help to make their education more effective. Research on the effectiveness of bilingual and ESL programs has shown them to be effective in improving the educational achievement of ELL students (Baca & Cervantes, 2004). Although there has been some debate as to whether ESL or bilingual programs are more effective, the literature has generally found bilingual programs to be more effective (Thomas & Collier, 2001; Ramirez, Yuen, Ramey, & Pasta, 1991). In a recent article in *Education Week*, Zehr (2004) states: "Bilingual approaches are more effective than English-only methods in teaching children who speak other languages to read in English, concludes a review of 30 yeas of studies on programs for English-language learners" (p. 1).

Because these students are in the process of learning English, they are more likely to be identified as possibly needing special education services. Prior to the advent of bilingual education, ELL students were overrepresented in special education and still are in some states and school districts (Donovan & Cross, 2002). When bilingual programs became more available, schools and teachers tended to place them in bilingual and ESL programs, rather than in special education. Nonetheless, the problem of misplacement still remains. In a recent report of the National Research Council, Donovan and Cross (2002) state:

The nationally aggregated data have been interpreted to suggest no overrepresentation of Hispanic students in Learning Disabilities. But state-level data tell a more complex story. For Hispanic students, the risk index ranges from 2.43 in Georgia to 8.93 in Delaware. Clearly, there is overrepresentation for Hispanics in the LD category in some states. (p. 67)

Because disabilities are found in all racial and ethnic groups, they are also found among ELL students. The process of valid identification and effective education of ELL students with disabilities remains a difficult challenge for our schools. The goal of this commentary is to explore various aspects of this challenge and report on the progress being made to meet the needs of ELL students with special needs in our schools in the areas of prereferral interventions, identification and assessment, and Individualized Education Plan (IEP) development.

PREREFERRAL INTERVENTIONS

Prereferral interventions for students who are experiencing academic failure are fairly common in most schools today. The research on the effectiveness of prereferral intervention is mixed (Baca, Baca, & de Valenzuela, 2004). For prereferral interventions to be effective, the following important conditions must be met: (a) there must be strong administrative support for the program, (b) planning time must be provided for the teachers involved, and (c) ongoing professional development must be provided to all the teachers involved. Because these conditions are not always in place, one can predict that prereferral intervention efforts are not always going to be effective. Additional conditions must be considered when ELL students are the focus of prereferral interventions (Baca, Baca, & de Valenzuela): high-quality native language instruction, effective ESL curriculum, meaningful and effective collaboration between teachers, and parental involvement. Because not all of these conditions and resources are available in every school, the needs of some ELL students often go unmet. Many learning problems can be prevented if early intervention services are offered. One approach to prereferral intervention is the Teacher Assistance Team (TAT). These teams can help teachers resolve the problems they encounter when instructing ELL students in the regular classroom (Chalfant & Psysh, 1981). These teams should include bilingual and second-language specialists who can help identify students' problems and suggest effective intervention strategies. They can also help the teacher implement the plan and provide follow-up services. Research suggests that special education referrals tend to decrease after implementing effective prereferral consultation teams (e.g., Fuchs, Fuchs, Harris, & Roberts, 1996).

IDENTIFICATION AND ASSESSMENT

When it is clear that prereferral interventions are inadequate to meet the needs of an ELL student, the student should be referred for special education assessment. The district should have a bilingual assessment team available that is experienced and trained to work with ELL students. As recommended in various chapters in this handbook, the assessment plan should focus on assessing students in the areas of (a) language and cultural background, (b) experiential background of the student, (c) the stage and pattern of acculturation of the student, (d) sociolinguistic development and language transfer of the student, and (e) cognitive and learning style of the student.

The entire assessment should be conducted bilingually. If a bilingual examiner is not available, a trained interpreter should be used. Because standardized tests are generally inappropriate for ELL students, the assessment team should utilize informal measures, including classroom observations, and parent and teacher interviews. A recent article by Brown (2004) suggests that a new term be adopted for culturally and linguistically different students who perform poorly on English language tasks. She proposes that the field use the term *Second- Language Acquisition-Associated Phenomenon* (SLAAP). This label would alert educators to the high probability that the SLAPP student is an ELL student struggling to acquire English, rather than a student with a language or learning disability. She goes on to suggest that this would help educators more carefully differentiate between SLAAP and true language disabilities, and thus help reduce the overrepresentations of ELL students in special education.

IEP DEVELOPMENT

If after a comprehensive bilingual assessment it is determined that the ELL student does indeed have a disability that requires special education services, then the special education team must develop an appropriate IEP. The first issue to be considered is language of instruction. If the student is more proficient in the native language, then the native language should be used as the language of instruction. ESL should also be written into the IEP. In addition, the disability should be taken into account in terms of curricular adaptation. A parental involvement component should also be included. Above all, meaningful collaboration between the special education and the bilingual ESL teachers should be planned to maximize students' learning.

CURRENT TRENDS AND ISSUES IN THE FIELD

The education of ELL students with disabilities is the primary responsibility of special education. However, the Individuals With Disabilities Education Act (IDEA; 1997) requires that special education students be educated in the least restrictive environment. It is important that there be a strong partnership between special education and general education, including bilingual and ESL education staff. For inclusion to be effective, a strong culture of collaboration is necessary. Although this appears to be an easy element, it is actually a difficult challenge for many schools. The prevailing culture in most schools fosters the independence of each classroom and each teacher. The prevailing factory paradigm of most school organizational models emphasizes loosely coupled and independent classroom units. Collaboration has not been a requirement or cultural value in our schools in the past. However, making collaboration a regular part of our school culture and an expectation of all teachers and other school professionals, such as school psychologists, has proved to be a difficult challenge and one that will demand ongoing attention and staff development if ELL students with disabilities are going to benefit from special education.

There is also a serious shortage of special education teachers and an even more serious shortage of other school personnel, such as school psychologists, who are specially trained to work with ELL students. A recent study by Development Associates (2003) reported that there were 729,603 teachers working with special education LEP students in 2002. Of this number, 11% had ESL certification and only 2% had bilingual certification. What this has meant in practice is that a growing number of ELL students with disabilities are being educated entirely in English. This teacher shortage is compounded by the rapidly growing number of ELL students in our schools and the relatively few programs at the university level that provide bilingual and/or ESL special education training (Baca & Cervantes, 2004).

Another factor that is having a negative impact on the provision of educational service to ELL students is the English-only political climate. With the passage of Proposition 227 in California, for example, recent studies show that ELL special education students are receiving more and more of their instruction in English (Baca, Almanza De Schonewise, & Vanchu-Orosco, 2004; Singer, 2004). In a recent study, Baca and his colleagues found that many special education teachers in California think that Proposition 227 does not allow them to teach in the native language. Actually, federal law always supersedes state law, and thus these ELL students with special needs in California can and should be educated in their native language.

What the future holds for bilingual/ESL special education remains to be seen. Baca and Baca (2004) suggest the following:

1. The number of LEP children with disabilities will more than likely increase at a greater rate than the rest of the student population. This increase will be due to a larger number of foreign students coming into the United States. The probable lower socioeconomic background of these students will also be a contributing factor.
2. Psychological and diagnostic assessment procedures for LEP students with disabilities will continue to improve as research and training efforts improve and as more bilingual professionals become available.
3. There will be an increasing trend to classify LEP children with disabilities by their educational needs, rather than by the current medical model. This change in classification will come about because of the trend away from categorical funding and the increasing concern over the negative stigma attached to the current classification system.
4. IEPs for LEP students with disabilities will increasingly reflect the language and cultural needs of these students. This change will occur because of improved pre- and in-service training and because of continued litigation.
5. Bilingual special education instruction in self-contained classes will be kept to a minimum. Bilingual special education resource rooms will continue to be used to a limited extent. The majority of LEP children with disabilities will be educated in regular classrooms, with a variety of support services uniquely designed and based on the resources of each individual school.
6. There will be an increased emphasis on early intervention with LEP children with disabilities. This emphasis will be based on demonstrated educational and cost benefits of early childhood education.

7. The use of educational technology with LEP students with disabilities will become important as the appropriate hardware and software become more readily available.

As mentioned earlier, the future of bilingual special education rests primarily on the future of general education. The American educational system is in need of reform. The public schools must develop the capacity to respond to an ever-increasing range of individual differences. All students in our schools should be treated as unique individuals. IEPs should be developed for every child in our schools. School psychologists can help in this effort. When these conditions exist, the future of bilingual special education will be the present.

COMMENTARY 2

Counseling Strategies to Embrace Diversity and Eliminate Racism in Schools

Charles R. Ridley
Indiana University

Shannon M. Kelly
YWCA of Metropolitan Chicago

We would like to think of schools as safe havens for our children, insulated from the troubles of the world. Unfortunately, schools often are the stages on which society's ills are enacted. The nation's struggles with violent crime eventually pierced the walls of Columbine High School, for example, and its battle against sexism surfaces each time a girl must fight to draw her teacher's attention away from her male classmates. Neither are our schools immune to *racism*, which Ridley (1995) defines as "any behavior or pattern of behavior that tends to systematically deny access to opportunities or privileges to members of one racial group while perpetuating access to opportunities and privileges to members of another racial group" (p. 28). Indeed, the history of this country's education system is marked by segregationist mandates barring African American children from White schools— policies that were punctuated by the slurs and rocks thrown at students like Ruby Bridges, a 6-year-old girl who became the first African American child to desegregate an elementary school (Hall, 2000).

Although the United States now has laws banning hate crimes and protecting the civil rights of all people, racism persists in schools. Studies have shown, for instance, that teachers' interactions with African American students often are strictly task-oriented, whereas their interactions with White students are both task- and person-oriented (Holcomb-McCoy, 2004). Such discrepancies extend directly to the domain of school psychologists and counselors, as African American students are more likely than White students to be labeled *emotionally handicapped* and placed in special education or vocational tracks (Ridley, 1995).

Given the rapidly growing diversity of the student population, eliminating racism in schools is an increasingly urgent task. Currently, more than one third of U.S. public school students represent racial minority groups, and by 2020, the majority of school-age children will hail from racial, ethnic, linguistic, and cultural minority backgrounds (Holcomb-McCoy, 2004; Yeh, 2004). Students differing from the majority White culture already are facing barriers stemming from their minority status, including culture shock, stereotyping, and stress from balancing their native cultures with those of predominately White schools (Baruth & Manning, 2000; Yeh, 2004). These extra difficulties may contribute to many minority students' decisions to drop out of high school; in 2000, 6.9% of White students ages 16 to 24 dropped out, whereas 13.1% of African American students and 27.8% of Hispanic students in this age group dropped out (National Center for Educational Statistics, 2001).

School psychologists and counselors are in prime positions to help minority students cope with their unique struggles in school. According to the American School Counselor Association (ASCA; 1997), "Comprehensive school counseling programs help ensure equal opportunities for all students to participate fully in the educational process." The American School Counselor Association (1999) also states, "School counselors take action to ensure students of culturally diverse backgrounds have access to appropriate services and opportunities promoting the individual's maximum development." To fulfill these obligations, school psychologists and counselors must develop their competence in serving diverse students, a task that involves recognizing unintentional racism and combating it individually and institutionally (American School Counselor Association, 1997, 1999; Holcomb-McCoy, 2004; National Association of School Psychologists, 2000a, 2000b; Romano & Kachgal, 2004). As outlined next, numerous strategies from the field of counseling psychology can contribute to the pursuit of these goals.

RECOGNIZING UNINTENTIONAL RACISM

Most school counselors and psychologists enter their profession with the admirable intention of helping students. Ultimately, however, "good intentions are not good enough" (Ridley, 1995, p. 10): Even if executed with the best of intentions, an intervention can still inflict harm. Indeed, many counselors would be surprised to learn that they unintentionally perpetuate racism through the models they draw from, the judgments they make, and the dynamics of their sessions with students.

Models of Mental Health

The assumptions underlying popular models of mental health can lead school psychologists and counselors to perpetuate the racism they are obligated to combat. Counselors adhering to the overtly racist deficit model, which considers minorities as inherently flawed, may uphold minority students to particularly low standards (e.g., by discouraging them from applying to competitive colleges) or to particularly high standards (e.g., by requiring minorities to earn higher grades than White students to enter honors classes; Ridley, 1995). Some counselors, in contrast, may adhere to a medical model, which emphasizes intrapsychic illness; this focus can lead counselors to ignore social influences on minority students' behavior and to overpathologize them. Other counselors may compare minority students' behavior to that of all students, labeling low-frequency patterns as *abnormal* and high-frequency patterns as *normal*. This confirmatory model can lead to racism, however, because it imposes the norms of majority students onto minority students. Thus, minority students must measure up to White standards to be deemed normal even if the norms of their culture run contrary to majority norms. Finally, some counselors may follow the biopsychosocial model, treating students holistically by considering physical, psychological, and social influences on their health. This model does not have underlying racist assumptions. In fact, failure to use this model can lead to unintentional racism, as counselors neglecting this perspective would overlook social and biological contributions to students' health.

Judgmental Errors

School psychologists and counselors also may be unintentionally racist by committing common judgmental errors (Ridley, 1995). A White counselor may hear from a principal, for example, that an African American student has been arguing with his teachers, annoying his classmates, blaming others for his misbehavior, and acting generally touchy. The counselor suspects oppositional defiant disorder (ODD) and meets with the student. The student hesitates to speak, and the counselor erroneously assumes that his lack of self-disclosure signals paranoia without considering that minority students can be culturally conditioned to mistrust White counselors, as trusting Whites can leave them vulnerable to racism. Next, the counselor exhibits confirmatory bias by asking the student for information confirming her initial hypothesis of ODD, rather than considering other explanations for the student's behavior. Finally, the counselor commits the Fundamental Attribution Error when the student mentions that White classmates have been teasing him; she asks the student how he has been provoking his classmates, blaming the issue on his disposition, rather than other students' racism. Herring (1998) notes that school counselors are especially prone to this error because they often ignore the sociopolitical contexts of students' presenting issues, opting to focus instead on students. Clearly, by attributing paranoia to students, showing confirmatory bias, and committing the Fundamental Attribution Error, counselors can be unintentionally racist by ignoring the role that outside factors, including racism, can play in students' circumstances.

In-Session Dynamics

School psychologists and counselors also can perpetuate racism through the defenses they bring to their work with minority students (Ridley, 1995). Some counselors may adhere to the notion of color-blindness, assuming that we're all the same and that minority students are no different from the majority. By overlooking students' cultures and measuring them against majority norms, counselors adhering to this approach easily can misdiagnose and overpathologize minority children. Counselors who are too color-conscious also may mistreat students, however, as they assume that the problems of minorities always stem from color-related issues, thereby overlooking individual contributions to various problems and perhaps underestimating the severity of a disorder. Finally, overidentifying with students also can lead to mis- or underdiagnosis, as counselors who have encountered racism in their own lives may be so predisposed to attributing minority students' problems to racism that they deny organic and intrapsychic factors.

OVERCOMING RACISM

School psychologists and counselors may wonder how they ever could find time to combat racism in addition to their other duties. After all, they often carry much heavier caseloads than counseling psychologists (ASCA recommends a realistic counselor:student ratio as 1:250), and they spend approximately one third of their time buried in paperwork and other tasks (American School Counselor Association, 1997). According to Ridley (1995), however, "Failing to combat racism is racism. ... Certainly, mental health professionals face a great challenge. But if they do not at least try to stop racism, they actually behave in a racist manner by allowing it to continue" (pp. 22–23). Thus, unless school psychologists and counselors find time to curtail racism, they will contribute to the problem. Fortunately, racism can be curbed at the individual and institutional levels.

STRATEGIES FOR OVERCOMING RACISM WITH INDIVIDUAL STUDENTS

Counsel Idiographically

School psychologists and counselors can combat racism by adopting an idiographic approach, honoring each student as an individual with a unique blend of qualities, experiences, roles, and identities (Ridley, 1995; Yeh, 2004). Counselors must avoid stereotyping minority students and recognize that, despite what they may have read about a certain group, they should be open to learning about each student as a unique person who may or may not fit group stereotypes. Once counselors understand students as individuals, they must determine students' major cultural roles and incorporate this information into their work. Effective integration of cultural considerations requires flexibility, however, as many counseling theories and interventions are Eurocentric, promoting values like individualism and independence that characterize White, Western culture (Romano & Kachgal, 2004). Thus, although a Eurocentric intervention may be effective with a highly acculturated Mexican American student, it likely will not be so effective with a recently immigrated Asian student.

Therefore, to ensure that each student receives the most appropriate intervention, counselors must not only learn about students' individual cultures, but also examine the underlying biases of their approaches and make necessary adjustments. Furthermore, school psychologists and counselors should explore their own cultures and biases, perhaps through personal counseling, to guard against imposing their values and assumptions on students. As Ridley (1995) asserts, "Unless counselors take a good hard look at themselves and examine their personal agendas, they are likely to ignore, distort, or underemphasize a client's idiographic experience" (p. 88).

Manage Resistance

The ability to manage resistance also is essential to working effectively with minority students. Resistance, or countertherapeutic behavior intended to avoid the pain that accompanies change, can surface through actions like missing appointments and evading questions (Ridley, 1995). Both Baruth and Manning (2000) and Ridley (1995) note that resistance can reflect on a client's cultural norms. Clients adhering to traditional Asian values, for example, may hesitate to self-disclose to a school counselor, believing that such disclosure will shame their families. Counselors can competently manage resistance through strategies like empathizing with and validating clients' fears about disclosing, recognizing the anxiety-reducing function of resistance, and respectfully confronting resistance when necessary. Counselors also should anticipate resistance to prepare themselves to respond competently. If counselors do not employ these strategies, they risk reacting defensively toward minority clients through behaviors like avoiding discussions about racial issues, talking excessively about racial issues, or making their expectations of minority students particularly lax or stringent.

Culturally Competent Assessment

As Holcomb-McCoy (2004) notes, school psychologists and counselors often are responsible for administering assessments to students, many of which strongly influence students' academic careers. In selecting and administering both formal and informal assessments, school psychologists and counselors must remember that the purpose of assessments is to help form a comprehensive picture of a student, not to generate a label or category (Ridley, Li, & Hill, 1998). Because culture permeates peoples' lives, assessments of any portion of a student's abilities, knowledge, or experiences must account for cultural background. Thus, according to Ridley et al. (1998), "The question for the clinician is never, 'Is culture relevant to this particular client?' A better question is this: 'How is culture relevant to understanding this client?'" (p. 857). Failure to consider students' culture in the selection, administration, and interpretation of assessments can result in misdiagnosis, mistreatment, and perpetuated racism.

Counselors can begin incorporating students' culture into their use of assessments by asking themselves whether a particular assessment is right for a particular student for a particular purpose. Particularizing assessments to each child involves understanding a student's cultural background and determining whether a given assessment is appropriate for someone of that background (Ridley, 1995). A counselor should ascertain whether a student's racial group is represented in an assessment's norming sample, for example, as well as whether an assessment in a student's native language has been properly validated.

Counselors also should be willing to use multiple, nonstandard methods of assessment (Ridley, 1995; Ridley et al., 1998). When multiple assessments are employed, the advantages of one can compensate for the disadvantages of another. After administering a standardized aptitude test, for example, a counselor might conduct a postassessment narrative, asking students about their experiences with and reactions to the test. This method would provide valuable insight into possible influences on students' test results, including cultural values and language barriers.

This example speaks to another strategy for competently using assessments: contextualize the results and consider alternative interpretations. As Ridley (1995) warns, "Test results indicate how well individuals perform at the time of testing, but they do not indicate why they perform as they do" (p. 123). If, for example, a student immigrated to New York City from an isolated, rural Russian town, he or she likely would not perform well on a math placement test requiring students to calculate the arrival times of subway trains. Unlike children who had ridden subways, an immigrant who had never seen a subway before would have difficulty visualizing and solving these problems. Thus, although a counselor may initially assume that the immigrant student's low test score reflects low math ability, contextualizing the score would yield an alternative explanation: The student simply could not understand or relate to certain items.

STRATEGIES FOR OVERCOMING INSTITUTIONAL RACISM

Although the techniques outlined previously may increase school counselors' and psychologists' competence in working with multicultural student bodies and combating racism, they may not be enough. As Yeh (2004) points out, many students do not seek out school counselors because of cultural stigmas attached to counseling, mistrust of counselors, and language barriers. Furthermore, school counselors and psychologists have the duty not only to improve individual students' lives, but also to serve as agents of systemic change who "use a variety of strategies to increase sensitivity of students and parents to cultural diversity and to enhance the total school and community climate" (Romano & Kachgal, 2004, p. 196; see also American School Counselor Association, 1999). School counselors and psychologists, therefore, are obligated to extend their fight against racism beyond their offices. A few methods for combating racism on the school and community level are described next.

Curriculum Committees

Romano and Kachgal (2004) suggest that school psychologists and counselors serve on curriculum committees to ensure that classroom lessons and materials adequately accommodate students of diverse backgrounds. Counselors alert to the dynamics of racism might object to textbooks that gloss over the atrocities of slavery, for example (Loewen, 1996). They also could provide input regarding schoolwide assessments, taking into account issues like language and sampling bias that administrators might overlook.

Promote a Dialogue

School psychologists and counselors also could enhance educational climates by encouraging students and teachers to engage in a continuing dialogue about race and culture. Unlike the lectures about these issues that students may receive on Martin Luther King, Jr., Day and other isolated celebrations, however, the goal of these dialogues should be behavior change rather than simple awareness-raising (Ridley, 1995). To truly effect change, counselors must teach students, faculty, and staff how to recognize racist behavior and how to act in nonracist ways (Ridley, 1995). Counselors also should develop networks of social reinforcement for nonracist behaviors to encourage children and adults to persist in their efforts to embrace diversity.

Get Involved in the Community

Ultimately, school psychologists and counselors must recognize that children live in the context of a community. As mentioned earlier, the problems of society, including violence and racism, have permeated school walls through shootings, segregation, and selective mistreatment of minority students. To truly eliminate such harsh realities from students' lives, school psychologists and counselors must cross school walls, teaching members of the community how to fight racism and advocating for laws that decrease disparities between majority and minority populations (Holcomb-McCoy, 2004; National Association of School Psychologists, 2000a, 2000b). By embracing the strategies outlined throughout this commentary and struggling for social justice, school psychologists can join counseling psychologists in a commitment to diversity, equality, and tolerance.

COMMENTARY 3

Multicultural Lessons Learned From Clinical Psychology and Implications for School Psychology

Stanley Sue
University of California, Davis

As in all fields, clinical psychology has been grappling with multicultural issues. Two developments have been particularly challenging to the field—namely, the adoption by the American Psychological Association (2002) of *Guidelines on Multicultural Education, Training, Research, Practice, and Organizational Change for Psychologists* and the U.S. Surgeon General's (2001) *Mental Health: Culture, Race, and Ethnicity report*. Both documents indicate the importance of ethnicity and culture in areas pertinent to clinical psychology, such as psychopathology, treatment, and research.

Let me briefly comment on the developments and their relevance to school psychology.

PSYCHOPATHOLOGY AND DEVIANCE

There is a growing awareness that the distribution and correlates of disorders appear to vary as a function of race and ethnicity (Sue & Chu, 2003). For example, compared to other Americans, African Americans appear to have low rates, American Indians and Alaska Natives have high rates, and Mexican Americans, Asian Americans, and Pacific Islanders show slightly lower or similar rates of mental disorders as non-Hispanic Whites. Asian Americans also seem to have high rates of neurasthenia (involving fatigue and somatic complaints). Why do groups vary in the prevalence of disorders? One view supported by the U.S. Surgeon General (2001) is that disparities in disorders are attributable to differences in the quality and effectiveness of mental health services provided to different groups. Another view is that prevalence rates may vary because of cultural or ethnic differences in stress and coping and family or community resources (Sue & Chu, 2003). Still another dilemma is to explain why, with increased acculturation and time in the United States, Mexican Americans have an increased prevalence of mental disorders. It is unclear why acculturation is negatively related to disorders among Mexican Americans. Moreover, in addition to differences in the rate and distribution of disorders, different cultural groups may show variations in the way symptoms are manifested.

The implications for school psychology and family functioning are clear. Are children from different ethnic or racial groups likely to exhibit differences in disorders or behavioral problems in schools? It is often observed that African American children are more likely to show externalizing (acting out) behaviors and less likely to exhibit internalizing behaviors than Asian American children. Why do these differences occur? What conditions in the home, community, or society influence these behaviors? In what ways are ethnic minority children likely to encounter greater stress? For many children, cultural conflicts, acculturation issues, and English language proficiency are important in affecting the prevalence of disorders and symptoms. Minority group status (e.g., experiences with prejudice and discrimination) may also affect one's identity, stress levels, and functioning.

In clinical psychology, other issues related to psychopathology have been raised. How does one evaluate the behaviors of persons from different cultures? A universalistic position would maintain that behaviors are deviant or psychopathological if they occur or reach a certain threshold. A relativistic position is that psychopathology cannot be evaluated simply by the presence or absence of predefined behaviors. In this view, the cultural context of behaviors helps determine how the behaviors are to be interpreted. This issue in clinical psychology is, of course, recognizable in school psychology. How do we know whether certain behaviors of school children are indicative of psychopathology of cultural upbringing? Is it possible for stereotyping and bias to enter into the psychological, intellectual, and diagnostic evaluations of children? In the mental health field, various strategies have been used to understand the meaning of behaviors and symptoms and to reduce cultural bias in evaluations. These include the use of cultural experts to assist in the interpretation of behaviors exhibited by members of various ethnic groups, steps to recognize how culture can impact evaluations, and means to control biases in assessment tasks (U.S. Surgeon General, 2001).

TREATMENT AND INTERVENTION

One lesson learned in clinical psychology is that disparities exist in the access and quality of mental health care accorded to members of ethnic minority groups. The President's New Freedom Commission on Mental Health (2003) noted that the mental health system has neglected to incorporate an understanding of the histories, traditions, beliefs, languages, and value systems of culturally diverse groups. Consequently, ethnic minority group clients may be less likely to receive quality care and benefit from treatment. As a result, there have been increased calls for cultural competency in treatment. Cultural competency has been defined in many different ways. Perhaps the most important feature is the strategy of recognizing, appreciating, and using the cultural values and patterns of members of ethnic minority groups to become more effective as therapists.

Although cultural competency has gained strength, there is also resistance to it. Earlier it was mentioned that different perspectives are taken by those adopting a universalistic versus a relativistic stance. Universalistic and relativistic differences are also apparent in modes of intervention or prevention, with the former position more likely to adopt a single strategy and the latter advocating for interventions that vary according to the individual's cultural background. For example, some persons believe that traditional forms of psychotherapy can be applied to individuals regardless of culture. Others champion cultural competency and attempt to modify existing treatments to consider the culture of the client. Fortunately, the field is increasingly cognizant of the disparities that exist in treatment outcome on the basis of ethnicity, and the cultural competency movement is intended to improve the value of treatment for ethnic minority group clients.

The training and use of bilingual and/or bicultural therapists and education and training programs to increase skills in working with culturally diverse populations have been employed. Another important awareness is that interventions must be embedded in a context. Cultural competency strategies also include the incorporation of family, community, and cultural resources in alleviating the problems of individuals. Culturally appropriate psychological applications are based on awareness and knowledge about one's worldview as a cultural being and as a professional psychologist, and the worldview of others particularly as influenced by ethnic/racial heritage (American Psychological Association, 2002). It is not necessary to develop an entirely new repertoire of psychological skills in order to be effective. Rather, it is helpful for psychologists to realize that there will likely be situations where culturally competent adaptations in interventions and practices will be more effective.

Differential outcomes for various cultural groups are also evident in our educational system. Children from different ethnic groups vary in educational accomplishments, adaptation and adjustment, acculturation, English language proficiency, and so on. Why do these differences occur? What can be done? For example, what are the best instructional strategies to use with children from different cultural groups? Is bilingual education versus English immersion for language minority children more effective? How can children with externalizing or internalizing problems be best helped? As indicated by the many outstanding contributors to this book, we also see attempts to devise culturally competent interventions ranging from teaching to treatment of behavior disorders, classroom management, work with students with disabilities, and so on. Obviously, the same issues are confronting our school systems and mental health systems.

RESEARCH

Compared to mainstream Americans, research on ethnic minority populations has been sparse (U.S. Surgeon General, 2001). One major reason for this state of affairs is that research on these populations is difficult and complex. To devise valid research designs, a multitude of cultural issues must be considered. These issues are involved in all phases of research. For example, Sue and Sue (2003) indicated how the following phases of research must deal with cultural issues.

Planning for Research

The first phase begins with the research question that is asked. Goodwin (1996) identified three steps: generation of the research question, suitability of the research question, and piloting the research question. They are all embedded in the researcher's cultural milieu. One problem in this preliminary stage is that there is often a smaller knowledge base on which to guide the research because there is often a paucity of research findings on ethnic minority populations. Furthermore, because theories and measures used in previous research are largely based on Anglo populations, it is unclear whether they are applicable to various ethnic minority groups. Although theories and measures may have cross-cultural validity, one does not know this a priori. Thus, even in this preliminary stage of research, complexities confront researchers.

Definition of Variables

Contrary to popular beliefs, defining of variables and identifying explanatory variables are often difficult tasks. For example, in studying racial differences, the definition has been controversial. The definition of *race* usually involves reference to genetically determined, physical characteristics that characterize one group from another (Jones, 1997). Yet the mapping of the human genome reveals that physical characteristics (hair, skin color, facial features, etc.) cannot be used to distinctly separate groups into races—that differences in physical characteristics are largely quantitative rather than qualitative in nature. Scientists primarily use self-designation (one's self-reported race), not biological markers, to divide people. Furthermore, race is often used as a proxy variable that is mediated by, or correlated with, other variables (Walsh, Smith, Morales, & Sechrest, 2000). These other variables may be of greater explanatory value. For example, Asian Americans may be more reluctant than members of other ethnic groups to use mental health services. Yet being Asian American fails to explain this reluctance. Rather, characteristics such as shame and stigma may be the ultimate reasons for the avoidance of services.

Selecting Measures and Establishing Cross-cultural Language Equivalency

When studying members of ethnic minority groups, especially in the case of recent immigrants who have limited English proficiency, what assessment instruments or measures should be employed? This is a significant question because psychologists must ensure that the instruments measure meaningful psychological concepts in a valid fashion for individuals from different cultures. Brislin (1993) maintained that, in studying ethnic minority populations with instruments primarily constructed for non-Hispanic White or mainstream populations, establishing several types of equivalence is necessary: (a) translation or language equivalence (when the descriptors and measures of psychological concepts can be translated accurately across languages), (b) conceptual equivalence (whether the construct being measured exists in the target culture and is understood in the same way), and (c) metric equivalence (whether the scale of the measure can be directly compared for different cultural groups; e.g., whether an IQ score of 100 on an English intelligence scale may be truly equivalent to a score of 100 on the translated version of the same intelligence scale). Thus, researchers interested in the study of ethnic minority populations cannot simply use existing psychological measures and tools without first considering the equivalence of the measures. They must confront the difficult task of finding or devising measures that provide equivalence across cultures.

Selection and Sampling of the Population

Scientific principles of selection and sampling of the population are no different for a cross-cultural or ethnic population as for the general population. However, complications arise because of the relative sizes of many ethnic minority populations and possible differences in responding. Given the sizes of ethnic minority populations, it is often difficult to find representative samples and adequate samples. Because of their cultural background, some respondents may find participation in research to be invasive or foreign because of unfamiliarity with the research process and anxiety over how the collected information can be used. Refugees may fear that their responses can somehow be used against them. Because of the problems in finding a representative and cooperatives, ethnic minority research is costly and difficult to initiate.

The difficulties in finding adequate samples of certain ethnic minority populations have sometimes led researchers to rely on convenience samples from quite different sources. For example, researchers may select names from lists of ethnic organizations, names suggested by other respondents (the snowballing technique), and students from universities rather than communities at large. Another strategy is to combine groups so that an adequate sample size is reached. Instead of studying a specific sample of Puerto Rican Americans, a researcher may broaden the base by including all Hispanics. Although these strategies can increase sample sizes, they obviously run the risk of subject self-selection, lack of representation of the population, and increased heterogeneity.

Research Design and Strategies

The field of clinical psychology is scientific as well as professional. Knowledge is primarily acquired by observations and experiments. Many cultural investigators have emphasized qualitative methodologies that are more holistic in order to understand the meanings, patterns, rules, and behaviors that exist in ethnic minority communities. Qualitative methodologies are often used with phenomena that are difficult to quantify or measure using existing instruments. A number of qualitative strategies can be found, such as ethnographic research (the study of the practices and beliefs of cultures and communities), case study, phenomenological research, participative inquiry, and focus groups (Mertens, 1998). Most of the training in psychology is based on quantitative and experimental methodology. Although the learning of such methodology is essential, training in qualitative approaches has typically been neglected. Thus, many investigators who want to study ethnicity find themselves ill trained for qualitative methods.

Interpretation of Findings/Validity

Cultural issues also arise in the interpretation or evaluation of research findings. Comparisons are made between various ethnic minority groups. However, differences between the groups cannot be assumed to simply reflect desirable or undesirable characteristics. The value assigned to the characteristics may be simply a reflection of one's own norms. (This should not be construed as adopting an absolute relativism in which there are no standards that cross all groups. Rather, researchers must always consider whether their conclusions are biased in the direction of ethnic stereotypes and misunderstandings.) Investigators must also be sensitive to how characterizations are viewed by members of the ethnic group. The interpretation of findings should always take into account the perspectives of insiders and outsiders to the ethnic group being investigated.

All of these research issues that confront clinical psychology can also be found in school psychology. Conducting valid assessments of performance and adjustment, determining the effectiveness of teaching and counseling strategies, and so on require culturally competent research plans, designs, methods, and interpretations.

FINAL COMMENTS

In this commentary, I have tried to indicate the many multicultural issues that the field of clinical psychology has encountered. The intent was not to imply that clinical psychology has found solutions to the issues or that the field is more advanced than other fields of psychology. The real purpose was to reflect on multicultural issues and note the similar problems that are encountered in clinical as well as school psychology.

In many ways, we live in an exciting time. Given the fact that our society is among the most culturally diverse in the world and our collective goal is to provide fair and effective educational and psychological services to all, we have an enormous challenge. This challenge requires innovation and creativity in establishing culturally competent services and research. It also requires a change from some past notions that support culturally encapsulated views and practices. Although my discussion has primarily focused on clinical and school psychology, we see this happening in all fields of psychology.

COMMENTARY 4

Social Psychology in the Multicultural Classroom

Harold Takooshian
Fordham University

Tresmaine R. Grimes
Iona College

Demographic data for the United States show a rise in multicultural classrooms at every turn in U.S. cities, nonurban areas, and Americans studying overseas. If *social psychology* (SP) is defined as the science of interpersonal relations, what can SP research in the past 50 years advise us about multicultural classrooms? This review examines three applications of SP to the multicultural classroom: (a) effective integration of cultural groups, (b) violence reduction, and (c) expectancy effects impacting individual achievement. The findings of SP research certainly can help in facing the challenges and promises of multicultural education.

MUTICULTURAL CLASSROOMS

Like never before in world history, today's multicultural classroom is clearly the classroom of the future at several turns. First, across U.S. cities, classrooms are increasing sharply in ethnic diversity. For example, one U.S. Congressional District alone—South Central Los Angeles/Hollywood—has schoolchildren speaking 129 languages/dialects. Its U.S. Representative, Dr. Diane Watson, estimates these children are about one third African American, one third Hispanic, and one third from other ethnic backgrounds (including thousands of Greeks, Armenians, and Koreans), all rubbing shoulders in the same classroom. Cities have become such magnets for ethnic diversity that it is hard to imagine a more heterogeneous cauldron of cultural groups. As of 2005, the number of foreign-born people in the United States totaled 33.5 million, which "now exceeds the entire population of Canada" (World Almanac, 2005, p. 619).

Second, outside of cities as well, U.S. suburban and rural schools are experiencing unprecedented ethnic diversity. In suburban New Jersey, for example, "an annual survey by the school district listed 65 languages other than English spoken in the homes of students" (Ratish, 2003, p. A–1), with over half of the 10,000 schoolchildren coming from a multilingual home. Since 1990, close to half of the 12 million immigrants into the United States have settled in nonurban areas, and this influx continues unabated, even after the convulsive 9–11 terrorist attack (Wright, 2003). A post–9–11 U.S. census found 600,000 international students on visas studying in U.S. colleges.

Third, there is a quiet growth of U.S. students in classrooms outside the United States. As of 2003, there is a hidden but growing network of 900 U.S.-curriculum international schools educating tens of thousands of U.S. youngsters in 190 nations (Beaman, 2002). These demographic increases are compounded by legal developments that further contribute to increased diversity in the classroom: compulsory education, elimination of tracking in schools, improved methods of testing, and Public Law 94–142 to mainstream handicapped youngsters (Esquivel, Warren, & Littman, chap. 1, this volume).

SOCIAL PSYCHOLOGY: THE RISE OF CULTURAL SOCIAL PSYCHOLOGY

SP has long been defined as the scientific study of interpersonal behavior (Allport, 1954). From its origins in 1884, SP is based on two premises: (a) All of our interpersonal behavior is governed by invisible yet potent rules, and (b) these invisible rules can be made visible by use of scientific methods (Kerlinger, 1984). Just as the physicist can study unseen yet potent gravity, so SP can use experiments, surveys, and other techniques to probe the invisible rules that govern interpersonal behavior in our families, classrooms, offices, and elsewhere.

Today SP is the hybrid overlap of the fields of psychology (of the individual, or PSP) and sociology (of the group, or SSP). SP studies the dynamics of individual behavior in groups on topics such as attitudes, gender, pro/antisocial behavior, nonverbal communication, and social influence (Richard, Bond, & Stokes-Zoota, 2003). Compared to other specialties like clinical psychology (Sue, chap. 30, this volume) and school psychology (Esquivel, Warren, & Littman, chap. 1, this volume), SP has long studied cultural topics such as interethnic relations (Ross, 1908) and prejudice (Bogardus, 1925) in order to identify universal principles of social behavior that transcend culture. Sadly, until the 1970s, too much past SP research was based on nondiverse samples, including White college sophomores (Graham, 1992; Sears, 1986). But just as there has been more international and cross-cultural work in other specialties like school psychology (Saigh & Oakland, 1989), clinical (Sue, chap. 30, this volume), and counseling psychology (Ponterotto, Casas, Suzuki, & Alexander, 2001), so has SP become increasingly cross cultural in its methods since the 1990s— to the point where cultural social psychology (CSP) is now emerging as an alternative to universal social psychology (USP; Moghaddam, 1998; Peplau & Taylor, 1997; Takooshian, Mrinal, & Mrinal, 2001). A clear example of CSP is the work of Harry Triandis (1994), who finds that individualist (Western) versus collectivist

(Eastern) cultures are dramatically different in shaping individuals' social behavior.

There are three bodies of SP research that help inform our view of today's multicultural classroom: integrating frictions, violence reduction, and expectancy effects. Each body of research is briefly reviewed next.

Intergroup Frictions: Beyond Integration

Certainly the single greatest impact of SP in the classroom occurred a half century ago, in the famous footnote 11 of the U.S. Supreme Court's decision to end racial segregation in U.S. public schools in *Brown v. Topeka Board of Education* (Zirkel & Cantor, 2004). Here the nation's highest court boldly cited the doll studies of social psychologists Mamie and Kenneth Clark, using behavioral research to document how the racial segregation widespread in U.S. southern and northern schools had a detrimental impact on children. Segregation created children's unequal status, lower self-concept, lower aspirations, self-denigration, and feelings ranging from doubt to inferiority (Pickren, 2002, 2004; Takooshian, 2003). Change was actually slow after 1954, until Congress enacted the 1964 U.S. Civil Rights Act to accelerate compliance, and the rate of African American children in segregated schools in the south dropped from 99% in 1964 to 56% in 1972. More recent follow-ups find that the way racial integration is implemented determines its success; it is typically more swift and successful when mandatory (externally court ordered) rather than voluntary (designed by parents and school boards). When done successfully, desegregation has salutary effects on both African American and White children, as well as the interactions between them (Oskamp & Schultz, 1998).

At the same time, SP has long recognized that simply bringing different groups into physical proximity is insufficient to increase intergroup harmony and may even decrease it (Sherif, 1956). The experimental work by Muzafer Sherif confirmed what inner-city school teachers already know—that gangs and other social groups may become more or less hostile when put into the same space depending on the way this is done. Sherif's 30 years of work here advocated two helpful ideas:

1. Teachers can easily construct a sociogram survey, using lines and arrows to visually chart how children relate to one another—the stars, outcasts, and clusters within the classroom. These sociograms can be used to design and monitor interventions.
2. Teachers should give their class what he termed a *superordinate goal* to have children work on some common project that requires intergroup cooperation to achieve success.

This notion was further refined by the jigsaw classroom technique first developed by Aronson and colleagues (1978). This is based on three premises: (a) equal-status contact between groups, (b) aimed at a common goal, and (c) supported by authority. In this jigsaw technique, students are divided into problem-solving groups of about six. Each child is given a different part of the material to solve the problem. In this way, children are forced into interdependence to study the material, solve the problem, and earn a high grade for themselves. Documented dividends of the jigsaw technique include students' greater liking for schoolwork, higher self-esteem, replacement of intergroup competition with cooperation, and increased achievement. Such cooperative learning holds special promise in ethnically diverse classrooms. One publisher, Scarecrow Press, publishes a helpful series of resources for the multicultural classroom, such as Landsman's (2002) *Diversity Days*, which offers a calendar of ethnic holidays and projects for use in the classroom.

Violence Reduction

Even before the Columbine shootings, another problem especially facing multicultural schools was the rise of youth violence. Some schools have become battle zones rife with bullying, assaults, harassment, and children who bring weapons to school to protect themselves from others. By 1990, homicide was the second cause of death among youth ages 15 to 24, first among minority youths (Eron, Gentry, & Schlegel, 1994).

The SP approach to violence reduction is competence training. This is based on the view that violent behavior is simply a breakdown in more healthy forms of communication and dispute resolution and may be reduced by a few types of skills training: (a) role playing, where students are put into hypothetical conflict situations to practice nonviolent responses while others watch and evaluate these responses; (b) monitoring, where students are sensitized to previolent interactions such as teasing or harassment so they can properly avoid these situations; (c) conflict resolution, where students are taught specific techniques to de-escalate conflict situations; and (d) peer mediation, where some student leaders are trained to be rapid-response resource people for other students in need of intervention (Johnson & Johnson, 1995). In one unusually creative program in New York City's public schools, some experienced teens developed their own step-by-step intervention program to teach the teachers how to avert classroom violence (Guardian Angels, 2003).

Expectancy Effects

SP has long documented how children's self-concept and actual achievement can be subtly yet profoundly shaped by the expectations of their teachers and others. Starting in 1968, with a series of controversial and now classic experiments, Rosenthal and his colleagues documented the power of what he terms *Pygmalion in the classroom*. This Pygmalion effect is one type of self-fulfilling prophecy, named for the mythical Roman sculptor who loved his statue of Galatea so intensely that his expectation actually brought her statue to life. (Pygmalion was also the basis for George Bernard Shaw's play, *My Fair Lady*, where the gentleman's expectations transform a charwoman into a lady.) In the 1970s, Rosenthal's initial findings of large IQ shifts based purely on teacher expectations were so dramatic that scientists openly challenged his team's results until independent investigators also verified the Pygmalion effect.

Through careful observational research on nonverbal communication between teachers and students, Rosenthal (1998) has gone on to identify the four subtle classroom processes that mediate teachers' expectations and students' increased achievement: (a) climate or teachers' affective behaviors, such as warmth, smiling, eye contact, and support; (b) input or greater difficulty or amount of material presented to students; (c) output or greater opportunities for students to respond, such as homework or in-class questions; and (d) feedback or more comments on work submitted by students, whether praise or criticism. Of course the reverse of these four can cause even able students to wither in their performance, if they feel teachers to be cold, disinterested in their work, giving little input, and demanding little output. To the extent that ethnic biases can be deeply unconscious, this places a greater onus on multicultural classroom teachers' nonverbal communications with ethnic students. One meta-analysis found that teachers expect more from Anglo Americans than African Americans (Dusek & Joseph, 1983). Based on Rosenthal's 30 years of findings, it is the wise teachers who occasionally videotape and review a sample class to monitor any trends in their nonverbal communication with students—when and how they ask questions, respond to answers, and interact with their students.

One pernicious type of expectancy effect is the stereotype threat, first identified by Steele and Aronson (1995): When a group stereotype indicts one's intellectual ability, the threat of confirming the stereotype or being judged by it can be disruptive enough to degrade intellectual performance in one's tests and grades.

In marking the 15th anniversary of the 1954 *Brown* decision, social psychologists Zirkel and Cantor (2004) recently noted that "*Brown v Board of Education* (1954) opened the door to widespread social change that is, perhaps only now, 50 years later, beginning to reach its true fruition" (p. 11). Indeed, the current consensus among social psychologists is that multiethnic education today, when properly implemented, is a win–win situation in which children may thrive socially as well as academically in their schools.

COMMENTARY 5

Reorganizing Student Support to Enhance Equity

Howard S. Adelman and Linda Taylor
University of California, Los Angeles

School systems are not responsible for meeting every need of their students. But when the need directly affects learning, the school must meet the challenge.

—Carnegie Task Force on Education of Young Adolescents (1989, p. 61)

For society, *No Child Left Behind* (No Child Left Behind Act, 2001) must be a commitment to equity. For education, the commitment must be to enable every student to have an equal opportunity for success at school. This requires good schools and good teaching.

Good schools are ones where the staff works cohesively not only to teach effectively, but also to address barriers to student learning. They are designed to prevent learning, behavior, and emotional problems and to address problems quickly and effectively when they do arise. They do all this in ways that promote positive socioemotional development and create an atmosphere that encourages mutual support, caring, and a sense of community. Schools whose improvement plans do not assign these matters a high priority are unlikely to address diversity as an instructional consideration or incorporate a multicultural focus into the classroom curriculum and the school-wide context. Such schools must rethink school improvement policies and practices. The focus on improving instruction must be accompanied by a fundamental reorganization of every school's approach to enabling student learning.

TOO MANY STUDENTS ARE NOT DOING WELL

Ask Any Teacher

Most days, how many of your students come to class motivationally ready and able to learn what you have planned to teach them? We have asked that question across the country. The consistency of response is surprising and disturbing. In urban and rural schools serving economically disadvantaged families, teachers tell us they are lucky if 10% to 15% of their students fall into this group. In suburbia, teachers usually say 75% fit that profile. Reports on student achievement continue to show a significant gap between those who have traditionally done well in the nation's public schools and those who come from culturally and linguistically diverse (CLD) backgrounds (National Center for Education Statistics, 2003). Although reliable data do not exist, some sources suggest that at least 30% of public school students in the United States are not doing well academically and could be described as having learning and related behavior problems (Hodgkinson, 1989). It is not surprising, therefore, that teachers continuously ask for help.

Talk With Students

Students report experiencing many barriers to learning, most of which stem from unaccommodating and often hostile environments. For example, student surveys consistently indicate that bullying and harassment at school are widespread problems (National Center for Education Statistics, 2001). More generally, students across the country suggest that many who drop out are really *pushed out* by systems that do not accommodate difference, diversity, and disability (Center for Mental Health in Schools, 2002; Dryfoos, 1990) (Ironically, many young teachers who seem to burn out quickly could also be described as *pushouts*.)

We all treasure the fact that some individuals manifest the type of resiliency that enables them to succeed despite experiencing adverse conditions. The reality in poor urban and rural neighborhoods, however, is that many children suffer from restricted opportunities associated with poverty and low income, difficult and diverse family circumstances, high transience rates, lack of English language skills, violent neighborhoods, problems related to substance abuse, inadequate health care, and lack of enrichment opportunities (Cohen & Lotan, 2003; Dryfoos, 1990; Hodgkinson, 1989). Some youngsters, of course, also have intrinsic conditions that make some facets of learning and performing at school difficult. Most schools in these neighborhoods are not designed to address the complexities that result from such factors. As a result, teachers at every grade level encounter students who are not ready and able to learn what curricula standards and high-stakes testing demand of them.

Youngsters' problems are exacerbated as they internalize the frustrations of confronting so many barriers and the debilitating effects of performing poorly at school. In some locales, over 50% of students manifest problems in behavior, learning, and emotional problems as they move into the upper elementary grades and beyond (Kauffman, Alt, & Chapman, 2001). In most schools in these neighborhoods, teachers are ill prepared to address the problems of students from cultural and linguistically diverse backgrounds. Thus, when students are not doing well, the trend increasingly is to refer them directly for counseling or assessment in hopes of referral for special help—perhaps even special education assignment. Stemming the tide of unnecessary referrals requires enhancing the competence of teachers, support staff, and administrators with respect to differentially assessing the source of student problems and designing programs that are personalized to match student motivation and capabilities (Quintana, Castillo, & Zamarripa, 2000; Taylor & Adelman, 1999).

The number of referrals can be dramatic and often overrepresent minority students (Lorsen & Orfield, 2002). Where special teams have been established to review teacher requests for help, the list grows as the year proceeds. The longer the list, the longer the lag time for review—to the point that, by the end of the school year, such teams have only been able to review a small percentage on the list. No matter how many are reviewed, there are always more referrals than can be served.

One solution might be to fund more services. However, even if the policy climate favored expanding public services, an overemphasis on health and social services ignores the need to address the many external factors interfering with students having an equal opportunity to succeed at school. Certainly, more services to treat student problems are needed. But so are prevention and early-after-onset programs that can reduce the number of students who end up being referred for special assistance. Schools must be designed to prevent and, when necessary, respond appropriately each day to external and internal barriers to learning and teaching. Those that aren't so designed promote inequities and collude with practices that tend to blame the victims (Ryan, 1971).

SCHOOLS AREN'T ORGANIZED WELL FOR ADDRESSING
BARRIERS TO LEARNING

Most teachers have a clear picture of the external and internal factors that interfere with effective learning and teaching at their school. They aren't making excuses; they are stating facts. Moreover, schools are aware of the need to help address such barriers. With passage of the No Child Left Behind Act, the federal government set in motion events that require even more attention to providing supplemental services.

As a result, a considerable expenditure of resources goes for student support programs and the growing number of initiatives to enhance school–community collaboration (Adelman & Taylor, 2002a). Most districts offer a wide range of programs and services oriented to student needs and problems. Some are provided throughout a school district, whereas others are carried out at or linked to targeted schools. Some are owned and operated by schools; some are from community agencies. The interventions may be for all students in a school, for those in specified grades, for those identified as at risk, for those in need of compensatory or special education, and/or for those new to the country.

Student and teacher supports are provided by various divisions in a district, each with a specialized focus such as curriculum and instruction (e.g., bilingual education programs), student support services, compensatory education, special education, language acquisition (e.g., English as a second language [ESL] programs), parent involvement, intergroup relations, and adult and career education. Such divisions commonly are organized and operate as relatively independent entities. For example, many school-owned and operated services are offered as part of what are called pupil personnel or support services. Federal and state mandates tend to determine how many pupil services professionals are employed, and states regulate compliance with mandates.

Governance of their daily practice usually is centralized at the school district level. In large districts, psychologists, counselors, social workers, and other specialists may be organized into separate units. Such units overlap regular, special, and compensatory education.

At the school level, analyses of the current state of affairs find a tendency for student support staff to function in relative isolation of each other and other stakeholders, with a great deal of the work oriented to discrete problems and with an overreliance on specialized services for individuals and small groups. The implications for CLD students are that, in some schools, students identified as English language learners (ELL) and as having learning difficulties receive services from multiple programs (e.g., bilingual education, special education, ESL) that operate independently of each other and may not work together to plan instruction and learning support. Such fragmentation is not only costly, but it works against developing cohesiveness and effectiveness, and the limited focus on services works against developing more comprehensive, multifaceted approaches to prevent problems and improve student achievement (Adelman & Taylor, 1997).

In short, a variety of divisions and support staff are dealing with the same common barriers to learning (e.g., instruction that inadequately accounts for diversity and disability, inadequate support for student transitions, hostile school environments, difficult home conditions). In doing so, however, they tend to respond with service-oriented strategies, little or no coordination, and sparse attention to developing comprehensive, multifaceted, and integrated efforts. Furthermore, in every aspect of a school district's operations, an unproductive separation usually is manifested between those focused directly on instruction and those concerned with student support. It is not surprising, then, that efforts to address barriers to learning and teaching are planned, implemented, and evaluated in a narrow, fragmented, and piecemeal manner. This can compound the problems of CLD students.

Moreover, despite the variety of activities across a school district, it is common knowledge that few schools come close to having enough resources to respond when confronted with a large number of students experiencing barriers to learning. Many schools offer only bare essentials. Too many schools do not even meet basic needs. Thus, it comes as no surprise to those who work in schools that teachers usually do not have the supports they need to effectively accommodate the wide range of diversity in their classrooms and address problems when they arise. The limited, dwindling, and inequitable distribution of resources to most schools serving students raised in poverty and/or coming from culturally and linguistically diverse backgrounds makes it especially difficult to provide the supports that are essential for meeting instructional needs.

Clearly, school improvement and capacity-building efforts (including pre- and in-service staff development and consultation practices) have yet to deal effectively with the fundamental enterprise of providing supports for a broad and diverse range of students and teachers. The simple psychometric reality is that, in schools where a large proportion of students encounter major barriers to learning, achievement levels are unlikely to increase adequately until such supports are rethought and redesigned. Schools that do not take steps to do so will remain ill equipped to meet their mission.

RETHINKING STUDENT AND TEACHER SUPPORTS

Policymakers have come to appreciate the relationship between limited intervention efficacy and the widespread tendency for programs to operate in isolation. Concern has focused on the plethora of piecemeal, categorically funded approaches, such as those created to compensate for restricted opportunities associated with poverty, account for disabilities, accommodate language and cultural differences, and reduce substance abuse, violence, dropouts, delinquency, and pregnancy. Some major initiatives have been designed to reduce the fragmentation. For examples of how such fragmentation can be reduced, readers are encouraged to review such efforts as the transition programs for immigrant students (Cardenas, Taylor, & Adelman, 1993) and other programs designed to create inclusive schools to accommodate diversity (Riehl, 2000). Policymakers, however, have failed to deal with the overriding issue—namely, that addressing barriers to development and learning remains a marginalized aspect of school policy and practice. The whole enterprise is treated as supplementary (often referred to as auxiliary services).

The degree to which marginalization is the case is seen in the lack of attention given to addressing barriers to learning and teaching in consolidated school improvement plans and certification reviews. It is also seen in the lack of attention to mapping, analyzing, and rethinking how the resources used to address barriers are organized and allocated. For example, educational reformers virtually have ignored the need to reframe the work of pupil services professionals and other student support staff and, in doing so, enhancing competence for addressing the many forms of human diversity. All this seriously hampers efforts to provide the caring help teachers and their CLD students so desperately need.

Needed: A Policy Shift

Clearly, current policies designed to enhance support for teachers and students are seriously flawed. It is unlikely that an agenda for enhancing equity of opportunity in schools can succeed in the absence of concerted attention to ending the marginalized status of efforts to address barriers to learning and teaching (Adelman & Taylor, 2000a, 2002b).

Increasing awareness of the policy deficiencies has stimulated analyses that indicate current policy is dominated by a two-component model of school improvement. That is, the primary thrust is on improving instruction and school management. Although these two facets obviously are necessary, effectively addressing barriers requires establishing a third component—a component to enable students to learn and teachers to teach. Such an enabling component provides both a basis for combating marginalization and a focal point for developing a comprehensive framework to guide policy and practice. To be effective, however, it must be established as essential and fully integrated with the other two components in policy and practice.

Various states and localities are moving in the direction of a three-component approach for school improvement. In doing so, they are adopting different labels for their enabling component. For example, the California Department of Education and districts such as the Los Angeles Unified School District call it a Learning Supports component. This is also the terminology used by the New American Schools' Urban Learning Center comprehensive school reform model. Some states use the term Supportive Learning Environment. The Hawaii Department of Education calls it a Comprehensive Student Support System (CSSS). In each case, policy shifts have recognized that schools must do much more to enable *all* students to learn and *all* teachers to teach effectively. In effect, such shifts recognize that, over time, good schools play a major role in establishing a continuum of interventions ranging from a broad-based emphasis on promoting healthy development and preventing problems, through approaches for responding to problems early after onset and extending on to narrowly focused treatments for severe problems.

REFRAMING HOW SCHOOLS ADDRESS BARRIERS TO LEARNING

School-wide approaches to address barriers to learning are especially important where large numbers of students are not doing well and at any school not yet paying adequate attention to considerations related to equity and diversity. Leaving no child behind means addressing the problems of the many who are not benefiting from instructional reforms.

Because of the complexity of ensuring that all students have an equal opportunity to succeed at school, policymakers and practitioners need an operational framework to guide development of a comprehensive, multifaceted, and cohesive enabling/learning supports component. Pioneering efforts have operationalized such a component into six programmatic arenas. Based on this work, the intervention arenas are conceived as (a) enhancing regular classroom strategies to enable learning (i.e., ensuring teachers can accommodate student diversity, and improving instruction for students who have become disengaged from learning at school and for those with mild to moderate learning and behavior problems); (b) supporting transitions (e.g., supporting newcomers, especially immigrant populations; assisting students and families as they negotiate school and grade changes and many other transitions); (c) increasing home and school connections and doing so in ways that specifically address the needs of families from culturally and linguistically diverse backgrounds; (d) responding to, and where feasible, preventing crises; (e) increasing community involvement and support (outreach to develop greater community involvement and support, including enhanced use of volunteers from diverse backgrounds); and (f) facilitating student and family access as needed to effective services and special assistance that are sensitive to diversity. As a whole, this six-area framework provides a unifying umbrella to guide the reframing and restructuring of the daily work of all staff who provide learning supports at a school. Extensive work has been done in delineating each of these arenas for intervention. A brief overview is provided in various published works (e.g., Adelman, Taylor, & Schnieder, 1999). (For surveys covering each arena, see Center for Mental Health in Schools, 1997).

Redesigning Infrastructure

Infrastructure redesign is essential if schools are to enhance their capacity for addressing barriers to learning and promoting healthy development (Adelman & Taylor, 1997, 2000b; Center for Mental Health in Schools, 1999). Such redesign must ensure there are effective and interconnected organizational and operational mechanisms to provide oversight, leadership, resource development, and ongoing support at a school, for a family of schools, and system-wide. More specifically, the mechanisms must provide ways to (a) arrive at decisions about resource allocation; (b) maximize systematic and integrated planning, implementation, maintenance, and evaluation of innovations; (c) outreach to create formal working relationships with community resources to bring some to a school and establish special linkages with others; and (d) upgrade and modernize all activity to reflect the best intervention thinking and use of technology. At each system level, accomplishing such tasks requires that staff adopt some new roles and functions, and that parents, students, and other representatives from the community enhance their involvement. Cost-effectiveness also calls for redeployment of existing resources.

From a school's perspective, few programs or services have relevance if they don't play out effectively at the school site or in the local community. It is a good idea, therefore, to conceive systemic change from the school outward. That is, the first focus is on mechanisms at the school–neighborhood level. Then, based on analyses of what is needed to facilitate and enhance efforts at a locality, mechanisms are conceived that enable several schools and localities to work together to increase efficiency and effectiveness and achieve economies of scale. Then, system-wide mechanisms can be (re)designed to provide support for what each school and its surrounding neighborhood are trying to develop. A brief discussion of mechanisms at each level follows.

Site-Based Resource-Oriented Team

From a school's perspective, there are four overlapping challenges in moving from piecemeal approaches to an integrated approach for addressing barriers to learning and promoting healthy development. One involves weaving existing activity together to enhance cohesiveness and minimize redundancy. A second entails adopting a unifying framework for evolving existing activity into a comprehensive, multifaceted continuum of interventions to enhance effectiveness. The third encompasses reorganizing to develop such a unified, comprehensive approach. The fourth challenge is to reach out to others in ways that fill gaps and expand resources. Outreach encompasses forming collaborations with other schools, establishing formal linkages with community resources, and attracting more volunteers, professionals in training, and the resources of the business community to work at the school site.

Meeting these challenges requires development of well-conceived mechanisms that are appropriately sanctioned and endowed by governance bodies (Adelman, 1993; Adelman & Taylor, 2002a; Center for Mental Health in Schools, 1999, 2001; Rosenblum, DiCecco, Taylor, & Adelman, 1995). A good starting place is to establish a school-based resource-oriented team (e.g., a resource coordinating team). Properly constituted, a resource team leads and nurtures efforts to maintain and improve a multifaceted and integrated approach. Such a team reduces fragmentation and enhances cost-efficacy by analyzing, planning, coordinating, integrating, monitoring, evaluating, and strengthening ongoing school and community efforts. In a school with families from diverse backgrounds, this provides a valuable forum for their concerns to be heard and addressed.

Because most schools are unable to establish many new program areas simultaneously, they must establish priorities and plans for how to develop and phase in new programs. The initial emphasis, of course, should be on weaving together existing resources and developing work groups designed to meet the school's most pressing needs, such as enhancing programs to provide student and family assistance, crisis assistance and prevention, and ways to enhance how classrooms accommodate difference, diversity, and disability.

Another key infrastructure concern is administrative leadership. Most schools do not have an administrator whose job definition outlines a leadership role and functions related to activities that are not primarily focused on academics, and this is not a role for which most principals have time. Thus, it is imperative to establish a policy and restructure jobs to ensure there is a site administrative leader who is accountable for moving the school from piecemeal activity to an integrated approach for addressing barriers to learning and promoting healthy development. This leader must be part of the resource-oriented team and represent and advocate for the team's recommendations at the administrative and governing body tables, and wherever else decisions are made regarding programs and operations—especially decisions about use of space, time, budget, and personnel.

Paralleling the administrative lead is the position of a staff lead. This individual can be identified from the cadre of line staff who have expertise with respect to addressing barriers to student learning and promoting healthy development, such as support service personnel. If a site has a center facility, such as a Family or Parent Resource Center or a Health Center, the center coordinator might fill this role. This individual also must sit on the resource team and advocate at key times for the team's recommendations at the administrative and governance body tables.

Besides facilitating the development of a potent approach for enhancing equity of student opportunity, both the administrative and staff leads play key operational roles related to daily implementation, monitoring, and problem solving. Obviously, if they are to have the time to carry out these special functions, their job descriptions must be rewritten to delineate their new responsibilities and associated accountabilities (see Center for Mental Health in Schools, 1999). It is this daily focus that provides the type of monitoring that ensures appropriate accommodation and support for diverse populations.

At the Feeder Pattern and Neighborhood Level

Neighboring schools have common concerns and may have programmatic activity that can use the same resources. By sharing, they can eliminate redundancy and reduce costs. Some school districts already pull together clusters of schools to combine and integrate personnel and programs. These are sometimes called complexes or families of schools. A multilocality resource-oriented council provides a mechanism to help ensure cohesive and equitable deployment of resources and also can enhance the pooling of resources to reduce costs. Such councils can be particularly useful for pulling together the overlapping work of high schools and their feeder middle and elementary schools and integrating neighborhood efforts. Connecting the work of feeder schools is particularly important because they often encompass families with youngsters attending several levels of schooling at the same time.

To create a council, one to two representatives from each school's resource team can be chosen to meet at least once a month and more frequently as necessary. The functions of such a mechanism include (a) coordinating and integrating programs serving multiple schools and neighborhoods, (b) identifying and meeting common needs with respect to guidelines and staff development, and (c) creating linkages and collaborations among schools and agencies. More generally, the council provides a useful mechanism for leadership, communication, maintenance, quality improvement, and ongoing development of a comprehensive continuum of programs and services. Natural starting points for councils are the sharing of needs assessment, resource mapping, analyses, and recommendations for reform and restructuring to better address barriers to learning and development. Specific areas of initial focus may be on such matters as addressing community–school partnerships to support CLD students and their families.

System-wide

Matters related to enhancing equity of student opportunity appear regularly on the agenda of school district administrators and local school boards. Too often each matter is handled in an ad hoc manner, without sufficient attention to the big picture. One result is that the administrative structure in the school district is not organized in ways that coalesce its various interventions. The piecemeal structure reflects the marginalized status of such functions and both creates and maintains the fragmented policies and practices that characterize efforts to address barriers to learning, development, and teaching.

To correct the problem, several system-wide mechanisms have been identified to ensure coherent oversight and leadership in developing, maintaining, and enhancing the component for addressing barriers to learning, development, and teaching. One is a system-wide leader (e.g., an assistant superintendent) with the responsibility and accountability for system-wide vision and strategic planning related to an enabling component. Large districts require additional organizational and administrative mechanisms to provide a critical mass of system-wide leaders, coordinate resources, and develop and integrate programs that accommodate and support diverse populations.

CONCLUDING COMMENTS

Good schools enable learning by playing a major role in addressing factors that interfere with students having an equal opportunity to succeed at school. The programs that emerge from a well-designed and developed enabling component are fundamental to enhancing a context for learning that embraces diversity as an instructional consideration and embeds a multicultural focus into the classroom and school-wide. The climate that emerges is supportive and caring and generates a psychological sense of community. The implications for student and staff morale, for learning, and for the future of all concerned are more than evident.

Ultimately, of course, enhancing equity must be approached from a societal perspective and requires fundamental systemic reforms that play out every day in every neighborhood and school. To do less is to maintain a status quo that not only is inequitable, but is self-defeating.

REFERENCES

Abedi, J., & Dietel, R. (2004, Winter). Challenges in the No Child Left Behind Act for English language learners. *CREST Policy Brief, 1.*

Adelman, H. S. (1993). School-linked mental health interventions: Toward mechanisms for service coordination and integration. *Journal of Community Psychology, 21,* 309–319.

Adelman, H. S., & Taylor, L. (1997). Addressing barriers to learning: Beyond school-linked services and full service schools. *American Journal of Orthopsychiatry, 67,* 408–421.

Adelman, H. S., & Taylor, L. (2002a). Creating school and community partnerships for substance abuse prevention programs. *The Journal of Primary Prevention, 23,* 329–369.

Adelman, H. S., & Taylor, L. (2002b). Building comprehensive, multifaceted, and integrated approaches to address barriers to student learning. *Childhood Education, 78,* 261–268.

Adelman, H. S., & Taylor, L. (2000a). Looking at school health and school reform policy through the lens of addressing barriers to learning. *Children's Services: Social Policy, Research, and Practice, 3,* 117–132.

Adelman, H. S., & Taylor, L. (2000b). Moving prevention from the fringes into the fabric of school improvement. *Journal of Educational and Psychological Consultation, 11,* 7–36.

Adelman, H. S., Taylor, L., & Schnieder, M. V. (1999). A school-wide component to address barriers to learning. *Reading & Writing Quarterly, 15,* 277–302.

Allport, G. W. (1954). The historical background of modern social psychology. In G. Lindzey & E. Aronson (Eds.), *The handbook of social psychology* (Vol. 1, pp. 1–50). Reading, MA: Addison Wesley.

American Psychological Association. (2002). *Guidelines on multicultural education, training, research, practice, and organizational change for psychologists.* Washington, DC: Author.

American School Counselor Association. (1997). *Position statement: Comprehensive programs.* Retrieved May 9, 2004, from http://www.schoolcounselor.org/content.cfm?L1 = 1000&L2 = 9

American School Counselor Association. (1999). *Position statement: Multicultural counseling.* Retrieved May 9, 2004, from http://www.schoolcounselor.org/content.cfm?L1 = 1000&L2 = 26

Aronson, E., Blaney, N., Stephan, C., Sikes, J., & Snapp, M. (1978). *The jigsaw classroom.* Beverly Hills, CA: Sage.

Baca, L., Almanza De Schonewise, E., & Vanchu-Orosco, M. (2004). Teaching English language learners with disabilities in an English-only environment: A pilot study. *NABE News, 27,* 16.

Baca, L., & Baca, E. (2004). Issues in policy development and implementation. In L. Baca & H. Cervantes (Eds.), *The bilingual special education interface* (pp. 382–423). Upper Saddle River, NJ: Merrill.

Baca, L., Baca, E., & de Valenzuela, J. S. (2004). Background and rationale for bilingual special education. In L. M. Baca & H. T. Cervantes (Eds.), *The bilingual special education interface* (4th ed., pp. 1–20). Upper Saddle River: NJ: Merrill.

Baca, L., & Cervantes, H. (2004). *The bilingual special education interface.* Upper Saddle River, NJ: Merrill.

Baruth, L. G., & Manning, M. L. (2000). A call for multicultural counseling in middle schools. *Clearing House, 73,* 243–246.

Beaman, A. L. (2002, Winter). The hidden world of international education. *International Psychology Reporter, 6,* 11–12.

Bogardus, E. (1925). Social distance and its origins. *Journal of Applied Sociology, 9,* 216–226.

Brislin, R. W. (1993). *Understanding culture's influence on behavior.* New York: Harcourt Brace College.

Brown, C. L. (2004). Reducing the over-referral of culturally and linguistically diverse students (CLD) for language disabilities. *NABE Journal of Research and Practice, 2,* 226.

Cárdenas, J., Taylor, L., & Adelman, H. S. (1993). Transition support for immigrant students. *Journal of Multicultural Counseling and Development, 21,* 203–210.

Center for Mental Health in Schools. (1997). *Addressing barriers to learning: A set of surveys to map what a school has and what it needs.* Los Angeles, CA: Author. Available from http://smhp.psych.ucla.edu/pdfdocs/Surveys/Set1.pdf

Center for Mental Health in Schools. (1999). *New directions in enhancing educational results: Policymaker' guide to restructuring student support resources to address barriers to learning.* Los Angeles, CA: Author. Available from http://smhp.psych.ucla.edu/pdfdocs/policymakers/restrucguide.pdf

Center for Mental Health in Schools. (2001). *Resource-oriented teams: Key infrastructure mechanisms for enhancing education supports.* Los Angeles, CA: Author. Available from http://smhp.psych.ucla.edu/qf/infrastructure_tt/makingthecase.pdf

Center for Mental Health in Schools. (2002). *Bullying prevention.* Los Angeles, CA: Author. Available from http://smhp.psych.ucla.edu/qf/bully_qt/bully_programs.pdf

Chaflant, J. C., & Psysh, M. V. D. (1981). Teacher assistance teams: A model for within-building problem solving. *Counterpoint,* pp. 16–21.

Cohen, E. G., & Lotan, R. A. (2003). Equity in heterogeneous classrooms. In J. A. Banks & C. A. M. Banks (Eds.), *Handbook of research on multicultural education* (2nd ed, pp. 736–750). San Francisco: Jossey-Bass.

Development Associates. (2003). Descriptive study of services to LEP students and LEP students with disabilities. *Development, 26,* 2–12.

Donovan, M. S., & Cross, C. T. (2002). *Minority students in special and gifted education.* Washington, DC: National Research Council.

Dryfoos, J. (1990). *Adolescents at risk: Prevalence and prevention.* London: Oxford University Press.

Dusek, J. B., & Joseph, G. (1983). The bases of teacher expectation: A meta-analysis. *Journal of Educational Psychology, 75,* 327–346.

Eron, L. D., Gentry, J. H., & Schlegel, P. (Eds.). (1994). *Reason to hope: A psychosocial perspective on violence and youth.* Washington DC: American Psychological Association.

Fuchs, D., Fuchs, L. S., Harris, A. H., & Roberts, P. H. (1996). Bridging the research-to-practice gap with mainstream assistance teams: A cautionary tale. *School Psychology Quarterly, 11,* 244–266.

Goodwin, R. (1996). A brief guide to cross-cultural psychological research. In J. Haworth (Ed.), *Psychological research: Innovative methods and strategies* (pp. 78–91). Thousand Oaks, CA: Sage.

Graham, S. (1992). Most of the students were white and middle class: Trends in published research on African Americans in selected APA journals, 1970–1989. *American Psychologist, 47,* 629–639.

Guardian Angels. (2003). *Role models for real life.* New York: Author.

Hall, R. B. (2000). *The education of Ruby Nell.* Retrieved May 9, 2004, from http://www.rubybridges.org/story.htm

Herring, R. D. (1998). The future direction of multicultural counseling: An assessment of preservice school counselors' thoughts. *Journal of Multicultural Counseling and Development, 26,* 2–12.

Hodgkinson, H. L. (1989). *The same client: The demographics of education and service delivery systems.* Washington, DC: Institute of Educational Leadership, Inc./Center for Demographic Policy.

Holcomb-McCoy, C. (2004). Assessing the multicultural competence of school counselors: A checklist. *Professional School Counseling, 7,* 178–183.

Individuals with Disabilities Education Act (1997). 20 U.S.C. 1400 et seq.

Johnson, D. W., & Johnson, R. T. (1995). Social interdependence: Cooperative learning in education. In B. B. Bunker & J. Z. Rubin (Eds.), *Conflict, cooperation, and justice* (pp. 205–251). San Francisco: Jossey-Bass.

Jones, J. M. (1997). *Prejudice and racism.* San Francisco: McGraw-Hill.

Kauffman, P., Alt, M. N., & Chapman, C. (2001). *Dropout rates in the United States: 2000.* Washington DC: National Center for Educational Statistics.

Kerlinger, F. (1984). *Foundations of behavioral research* (3rd ed.). New York: Holt Rinehart.

Klingner, J., & Artiles, A. (2003). When should bilingual students be in special education? *Educational Leadership, 61,* 66–71.

Landsman, J. (2002). *Diversity days: A teacher's calendar of ideas.* Lanham, MD: Scarecrow.

Lau v. Nichols, 414 U.S. 563 (1974).

Lee, J. (2002). Racial and ethnic achievement gap trends: Reversing the progress toward equity. *Educational Researcher, 31,* 3–12.

Loewen, J. W. (1996). *Lies my teacher told me: Everything your American history textbook got wrong.* New York: Simon & Schuster.

Lorsen, D., & Orfield, G. (2002). *Racial inequity in special education.* Cambridge, MA: Harvard Education Publishing Group.

Mertens, D. M. (1998). *Research methods in education and psychology.* Thousand Oaks, CA: Sage.

Moghaddam, F. M. (1998). *Social psychology: Exploring universals across cultures.* New York: W. H. Freeman.

National Association of School Psychologists. (2000a). *The provision of culturally competent services in the school setting.* Retrieved May 9, 2004, from http://www.nasponline.org/culturalcompetence/provision_cultcompsvcs.html

National Association of School Psychologists. (2000b). *Six domains of culturally competent service delivery.* Retrieved May 9, 2004, from http://www.nasponline.org/culturalcompetence/sixdomains.html

National Center for Education Statistics. (2001a). *Dropout rates in the United States: 2000.* Retrieved May 10, 2004, from http://nces.ed.gov/pubs2002/droppub_2001/

National Center for Education Statistics. (2001b). *Indicators of school crime.* Washington, DC: Author.

National Center for Education Statistics. (2003). *The nation's report card.* Washington, DC: Author.

No Child Left Behind Act (2001). 20 U.S.C. 6301. Retrieved November 29, 2003, from http://www.ed.gov/legislation/ESEA02/index.html

Oskamp, S., & Schultz, P. W. (1998). *Applied social psychology* (2nd ed.). Upper Saddle River, NJ: Prentice-Hall.

Peplau, L. A., & Taylor, S .E. (Eds.). (1997). *Sociocultural perspectives in social psychology.* Upper Saddle River, NJ: Prentice-Hall.

Pickren, W. E. (2002). The contributions of Kenneth B. and Mamie Phipps Clark. *American Psychologist, 57,* 1–8.

Pickren, W. E. (Ed.). (2004). Brown v Board of Education and American psychology, 1954–2004. *American Psychologist, 59,* 493–556.

Ponterotto, J. G., Casas, J. M., Suzuki, L. A., & Alexander, C. M. (Eds.). (2001). *Handbook of multicultural counseling* (2nd ed.). Thousand Oaks CA: Sage.

President's New Freedom Commission on Mental Health. (2003). *Achieving the promise: Transforming mental health care in America.* Rockville, MD: Author.

Quintana, S. M., Castillo, E. M., & Zamarripa, M. X. (2000). Assessment of ethnic and linguistic minority children. In E. S. Shapiro, T. R. Kratochwill, et al. (Eds.), *Behavioral assessment in schools: Theory, research, and clinical foundations* (2nd ed., pp. 435–463). New York: Guilford.

Ramirez, D. J., Yuen, S. D., Ramey, D. R., & Pasta, D. J. (1991). *Longitudinal study of structured English immersion strategy, early-exit, and late-exit transitional bilingual education programs for language minority children.* San Mateo, CA: Aguirre International.

Ratish, R. (2003, January 3). City of the world: Clifton. *The Record*, pp. A1, A7.

Richard, F. D., Bond, C. F., & Stokes-Zoota, J. J. (2003). One hundred years of social psychology quantitatively described. *Review of General Psychology, 7,* 331–363.

Ridley, C. R. (1995). *Overcoming unintentional racism in counseling and therapy: A practitione's guide to intentional intervention.* Thousand Oaks, CA: Sage.

Ridley, C. R., Li, L. C., & Hill, C. L. (1998). Multicultural assessment: Reexamination, reconceptualization, and practical application. *The Counseling Psychologist, 26,* 827–910.

Riehl, C. J. (2000). The principal's role in creating inclusive schools for diverse students: A review of normative, empirical, and critical literature on the practice of educational administration. *Review of Educational Research, 70,* 55–81.

Romano, J. L., & Kachgal, M. M. (2004). Counseling psychology and school counseling: An underutilized partnership. *The Counseling Psychologist, 32,* 184–215.

Rosenblum, L., DiCecco, M. B., Taylor, L., & Adelman, H. S. (1995). Upgrading school support programs through collaboration: Resource Coordinating Teams. *Social Work in Education, 17,* 117–124.

Rosenthal, R. (1998, Fall). Covert communication in classrooms, clinics, and courtrooms. *Eye on Psi Chi, 2,* 18–22.

Rosenthal, R., & Jacobsen, L. (1968). *Pygmalion in the classroom.* New York: Holt, Rinehart, & Winston.

Ross, E. A. (1908). *Social psychology: An outline and sourcebook.* New York: Macmillan.

Ryan, W. (1971). *Blaming the victim.* New York: Random House.

Saigh, P. A., & Oakland, T. (1989). *International perspectives on school psychology.* Hillsdale, NJ: Erlbaum.

Sears, D. O. (1986). College sophomores in the laboratory: Influences of a narrow data base on psychology's view of human nature. *Journal of Personality and Social Psychology, 51,* 515–530.

Sherif, M. (1956). Experiments in group conflict. *Scientific American, 195,* 1–7.

Singer, J. H. S. (2004). Who decides the language of instruction for English learners with severe disabilities in the public schools? *Linguistic Minority Research Institute Newsletter, 13,* 1.

Steele, C. M., & Aronson, J. (1995). Stereotype threat and the intellectual test performance of African Americans. *Journal of Personality and Social Psychology, 69,* 797–811.

Sue, S., & Chu, J. (2003). The mental health of ethnic minority groups: Challenges posed by the U.S. Surgeon General. *Culture, Medicine and Psychiatry, 27,* 433–442.

Sue, S., & Sue, L. (2003). Ethnic research is good science. In G. Bernal, J. E. Trimble, A. K. Burlew, & F. T. L. Leong (Eds.), *Handbook of racial and ethnic minority psychology.* Thousand Oaks, CA: Sage.

Takooshian, H. (2003). Kenneth Bancroft Clark. In W. L. O'Neill (Ed.), *The Scribner Encyclopedia of American lives: The sixties* (pp. 178–180). New York: Charles Scribner's Sons.

Takooshian, H., Mrinal, N. R., & Mrinal, U.S. (2001). Research methods for studies in the field. In L. L. Adler & U. P. Gielen (Eds.), *Cross-cultural topics in psychology* (2nd ed., pp. 29–46).). Westport CT: Praeger.

Taylor, L., & Adelman, H. S. (1999). Personalizing classroom instruction to account for motivational and developmental differences. *Reading and Writing Quarterly, 15,* 255–276.

Thomas, W., & Collier, V. (2001). *A national study of school effectiveness for language minority students' long-term academic achievement.* Santa Cruz, CA: Center for Research on Education, Diversity & Excellence, University of California.

Triandis, H. C. (1994). *Culture and social behavior.* New York: McGraw-Hill.

U.S. Census Bureau. (2003). *Census bureau, population division.* Retrieved February 25, 2003, from http://www.ed.gov/population/www/cen2000/phc-t20.html

U.S. Department of Education. (2003). *Key indicators of Hispanic student achievement: National goals and benchmarks for the next decade.* Retrieved June 14, 2003, from http://www.ed.gov/pub/hispanicindicators

U.S. Surgeon General. (2001). *Mental health: Culture, race, and ethnicity: A supplement to mental health. A report of the Surgeon General.* Rockville, MD: U.S. Department of Health and Human Services.

Walsh, M., Smith, R., Morales, A., & Sechrest, L. (2000). *Ethnocultural research: A mental health researcher's guide to the study of race, ethnicity, and culture.* Cambridge, MA: Health Services Research Institute

World Almanac. (2005). *World alamanac.* New York: WRC Media.

Wright, J. W. (Ed.). (2003). *The New York Times almanac.* New York: Penguin.

Yeh, C. J. (2004). Multicultural and contextual research and practice in school counseling. *The Counseling Psychologist, 32,* 278–285.

Zehr, M. A. (2004). Study gives advantage to bilingual education over focus on English. *Education Week, 23,* 10.

Zirkel, S., & Cantor, N. (2004). 50 years after Brown v Board of Education: The promise and challenge of multicultural education. *Journal of Social Issues, 60,* 1–15.

AUTHOR INDEX

SUBJECT INDEX

A

ABIC, 14

Academia and training programs, 47–62. *See also* Professional development
  in cognitive assessment, 282–283
  in cultural competency, 605
  diversity and, 47–48
  in ethical standards and guidelines, 40–41
  in multicultural competencies, 57–60
  multicultural curriculum, 49–52
  multiculturalism in, 15–16, 17, 22–23
  in neuropsychological assessment, 313
  in personality and behavioral assessment, 302
  in systemic change competencies, 151
  training centers, 57–58

Academic achievement. *See* School performance

Academic assessment of bilingual and ELL students, 381–399
  academic assessment, 382–383
  bilingual and ELL students, 381–382
  curriculum-based assessment, 385–393
  curriculum-based measurement, 395
  implementation, 396–398
  implications for practice, 391–396
  normed instruments, 384–385
  portfolio assessment, 393–395
  research agenda, 398–399
  structured systematic observational systems, 395–396

Academic content standards, language proficiency standards and, 259

Academic discourse, 225, 226

Academic expectations, belonging and, 560–562

Academic success, language use and, 85–86

Accountability, language assessment and, 252, 254–255, 258

Acculturation, 354–360. *See also* Acculturation assessment
  academic assessment and, 383
  cognitive assessment and, 266–272
  defined, 123, 314, 354, 355
  differences in, 620–621
  of diverse population, 367–372
  factors related to success in, 364
  of immigrants, 509
  instructional strategies for various levels of, 373–375
  language proficiency and, 274–275, 315
  learning disabilities and, 358
  levels of, 373–375
  multicultural vocational interventions and, 435
  neuropsychological assessment and level of, 314–315
  parent consultation and, 123–124
  personality and behavioral assessment and level of, 293
  psychological responses to, 357–358
  second language learning, learning disabilities, and, 358
  as social-emotional stressor, 410–412
  stages of, 355, 361–363

Acculturation, Habits, and Interests Multicultural Scale for Adolescents (AHIMSA), 367, 368

Acculturation assessment, 353–376
  acculturation of diverse populations, 367–372

Acculturation Quick Screen, 367, 368, 372–373
  acculturation theory, 354–360
  effective strategies, 373–375
  implication for practice, 360–375
  research agenda, 375–376
  screening tools, 366–367

Acculturation matrix, 364, 365